J. W. Mitchell H.S
2323 Little Rd.
New Port Richey, FL 34655
727-774-9200

Physics

Florida

Serway • Faughn

AUTHORS

Raymond A. Serway, Ph.D.
Professor Emeritus
James Madison University

Jerry S. Faughn, Ph.D.
Professor Emeritus
Eastern Kentucky University

On the cover: A soap bubble sprays droplets as it bursts.

Cover Photo Credits: *Bubble* ©Don Farrall/Photodisc/Getty Images; *luger* ©Rolf Kosecki/Corbis

2019 Edition
Copyright © by Houghton Mifflin Harcourt Publishing Company
Copyright © 2019 by Raymond A. Serway

Florida Standards courtesy of the Florida Department of Education.

Printed in the U.S.A.

ISBN 978-1-328-79292-1

3 4 5 6 7 8 9 10   0868   26 25 24 23 22 21 20 19 18

4500709497   A B C D E F G

ACKNOWLEDGMENTS

Lab Reviewers

Christopher Barnett
Richard DeCoster
Elizabeth Ramsayer
Joseph Serpico
Niles West High School
Niles, Illinois

Mary L. Brake, Ph.D.
Physics Teacher
Mercy High School
Farmington Hills, Michigan

Gregory Puskar
Laboratory Manager
Physics Department
West Virginia University
Morgantown, West Virginia

Richard Sorensen
Vernier Software & Technology
Beaverton, Oregon

Martin Taylor
Sargent-Welch/VWR
Buffalo Grove, Illinois

Academic Reviewers

Mary L. Brake, Ph.D.
Physics Teacher
Mercy High School
Farmington Hills, Michigan

James C. Brown, Jr., Ph.D.
Adjunct Assistant Professor of Physics
Austin Community College
Austin, Texas

Anil R Chourasia, Ph.D.
Associate Professor
Department of Physics
Texas A&M University–Commerce
Commerce, Texas

David S. Coco, Ph.D.
Senior Research Physicist
Applied Research Laboratories
The University of Texas at Austin
Austin, Texas

Thomas Joseph Connolly, Ph.D.
Assistant Professor
Department of Mechanical Engineering
and Biomechanics
The University of Texas at San Antonio
San Antonio, Texas

Bill Deutschmann, Ph.D.
President
Oregon Laser Consultants
Klamath Falls, Oregon

Brad de Young
Professor
Department of Physics and Physical
Oceanography
Memorial University
St. John's, Newfoundland, Canada

Arthur A. Few
*Professor of Space Physics and
Environmental Science*
Rice University
Houston, Texas

Scott Fricke, Ph.D.
Schlumberger Oilfield Services
Sugarland, Texas

Simonetta Fritelli
Associate Professor of Physics
Duquesne University
Pittsburgh, Pennsylvania

David S. Hall, Ph.D.
Assistant Professor of Physics
Amherst College
Amherst, Massachusetts

Roy W. Hann, Jr., Ph.D.
Professor of Civil Engineering
Texas A&M University
College Station, Texas

Sally Hicks, Ph.D.
Professor
Department of Physics
University of Dallas
Irving, Texas

William Ingham, Ph.D.
Professor of Physics
James Madison University
Harrisonburg, Virginia

Karen B. Kwitter, Ph.D.
Professor of Astronomy
Williams College
Williamstown, Massachusetts

Phillip LaRoe
Professor of Physics
Helena College of Technology
Helena, Montana

Joseph A. McClure, Ph.D.
Associate Professor Emeritus
Department of Physics
Georgetown University
Washington, D.C.

Ralph McGrew
Associate Professor
Engineering Science Department
Broome Community College
Binghamton, New York

Clement J. Moses, Ph.D.
Associate Professor of Physics
Utica College
Utica, New York

Alvin M. Saperstein, Ph.D.
*Professor of Physics; Fellow of Center for
Peace and Conflict Studies*
Department of Physics and Astronomy
Wayne State University
Detroit, Michigan

Donald E. Simanek, Ph.D.
Emeritus Professor of Physics
Lock Haven University
Lock Haven, Pennsylvania

H. Michael Sommermann, Ph.D.
Professor of Physics
Westmont College
Santa Barbara, California

Jack B. Swift, Ph.D.
Professor
Department of Physics
The University of Texas at Austin
Austin, Texas

Thomas H. Troland, Ph.D.
Physics Department
University of Kentucky
Lexington, Kentucky

Mary L. White
Coastal Ecology Institute
Louisiana State University
Baton Rouge, Louisiana

Jerome Williams, M.S.
Professor Emeritus
Oceanography Department
U.S. Naval Academy
Annapolis, Maryland

Carol J. Zimmerman, Ph.D.
Exxon Exploration Company
Houston, Texas

ACKNOWLEDGMENTS, continued

Teacher Reviewers

John Adamowski
Chairperson of Science Department
Fenton High School
Bensenville, Illinois

John Ahlquist, M.S.
Anoka High School
Anoka, Minnesota

Maurice Belanger
Science Department Head
Nashua High School
Nashua, New Hampshire

Larry G. Brown
Morgan Park Academy
Chicago, Illinois

William K. Conway, Ph.D.
Lake Forest High School
Lake Forest, Illinois

Jack Cooper
Ennis High School
Ennis, Texas

William D. Ellis
Chairman of Science Department
Butler Senior High School
Butler, Pennsylvania

Diego Enciso
Troy, Michigan

Ron Esman
Plano Senior High School
Plano, Texas

Bruce Esser
Marian High School
Omaha, Nebraska

Curtis Goehring
Palm Springs High School
Palm Springs, California

Lyle Goines
West Brook High School
Beaumont, Texas

Herbert H. Gottlieb
Science Education Department
City College of New York
New York City, New York

David J. Hamilton, Ed.D.
Benjamin Franklin High School
Portland, Oregon

J. Philip Holden, Ph.D.
Physics Education Consultant
Michigan Dept. of Education
Lansing, Michigan

Joseph Hutchinson
Wichita High School East
Wichita, Kansas

Douglas C. Jenkins
Chairman, Science Department
Warren Central High School
Bowling Green, Kentucky

David S. Jones
Miami Sunset Senior High School
Miami, Florida

Roger Kassebaum
Millard North High School
Omaha, Nebraska

Mervin W. Koehlinger, M.S.
Concordia Lutheran High School
Fort Wayne, Indiana

Phillip LaRoe
Central Community College
Grand Island, Nebraska

William Lash
Westwood High School
Round Rock, Texas

Norman A. Mankins
Science Curriculum Specialist
Canton City Schools
Canton, Ohio

Renee Martinez, M.S. C&I
Tegeler Career Center
Pasadena, Texas

John McGehee
Palos Verdes Peninsula High School
Rolling Hills Estates, California

Debra Schell
Austintown Fitch High School
Austintown, Ohio

Edward Schweber
Solomon Schechter Day School
West Orange, New Jersey

Larry Stookey, P.E. Science
Antigo High School
Antigo, Wisconsin

Joseph A. Taylor
Middletown Area High School
Middletown, Pennsylvania

Leonard L. Thompson
North Allegheny Senior High School
Wexford, Pennsylvania

Keith C. Tipton
Lubbock, Texas

John T. Vieira
Science Department Head
B.M.C. Durfee High School
Fall River, Massachusetts

Andrew D. Werner, M.Ed.
Socorro Independent School District
El Paso, Texas

David White, M.ChE.
Pearland High School
Pearland, Texas

Virginia Wood
Richmond High School
Richmond, Michigan

Tim Wright
Stevens Point Area Senior High School,
Stevens Point, Wisconsin

Mary R. Yeomans
Hopewell Valley Central High School
Pennington, New Jersey

G. Patrick Zober
Science Curriculum Coordinator
Yough Senior High School
Herminie, Pennsylvania

Patricia J. Zober
Ringgold High School
Monongahela, Pennsylvania

HMH ⊙ PHYSICS

Yes, it's educational.
No, it's not boring.

Student Edition
Explore the world around you with pages of colorful photos, helpful illustrations, and activities using everyday materials. This book is built to help you succeed in physics, with content chunked into Main Ideas, relevant and motivating features, and in-depth skills support.

Interactive Online Edition
The new Interactive Online Edition provides 24/7 point-of-use access to all program resources. In addition to a complete eBook version of your textbook, the Online Edition includes alternative explanations and experiences through a wealth of multimedia activities, including animations, virtual labs, and exciting review games.

New Focus on Engineering
Added resources help you concentrate on STEM (Science, Technology, Engineering, and Math) skills—and introduce you to the 21st-century careers that use those skills.

Interactive Online Edition

GO ONLINE
Animated Physics
HMHScience.com

Bring physics concepts and principles to life with animations and simulations.

NEW

Google Expeditions

Take virtual-reality field trips into the unknown with Google Expeditions!

ONLINE
Interactive Demo
HMHScience.com

ee problem-solving
echniques in action,
nd get extra practice.

ONLINE
WebLinks
HMHScience.com

xtend and enrich
ach chapter's content
ith hand-selected
esource links.

GO ONLINE
SOLUTION TUTOR
HMHScience.com

Get hints and personalized feedback as the Solution Tutor walks you through key problems step by step.

Labs Online ⟶ HMHScience.com

Standard Labs

Focus on experimental skills and the application of chapter concepts through the use of scientific methods.

QuickLabs

Encounter key concepts in your classroom with QuickLabs. They're right in your book!

Open Inquiry Labs

Drive the lab activity—you make decisions about what to research and how to do it.

Core Skill Labs

Practice hands-on skills and techniques.

STEM Labs

Explore the engineering design process through hands-on inquiry projects.

Probeware Labs

Integrate data-collection technology into your labs.

Forensics Labs

Investigate practical applications of science, such as crime-scene analysis.

Virtual Labs

Conduct meaningful experiments with tools, instruments, and techniques that take you beyond your classroom.

VIRTUAL Lab

CONTENTS

(tl) ©Philippe Psaila/Photo Researchers, Inc.; (bl) ©Wendell Metzen/Index Stock Imagery/Photolibrary; (cl) ©Robert Harding World Imagery/Alamy Photos

(br) ©Mike Powell/Getty Images; (tr) ©Nicholas Pinturas/Getty Images; (cr) ©Houghton Mifflin Harcourt

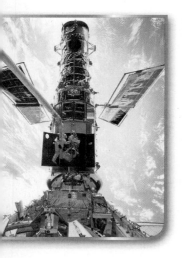

HMHScience.com

Go online for the full complement of labs.

HMHScience.com

Go online for the full complement of labs.

HMHScience.com

Go online for the full complement of labs.

(tl) ©NASA Johnson Space Center; (c) ©David Madison/Getty Images; (bl) ©Lena Johansson/Getty Images

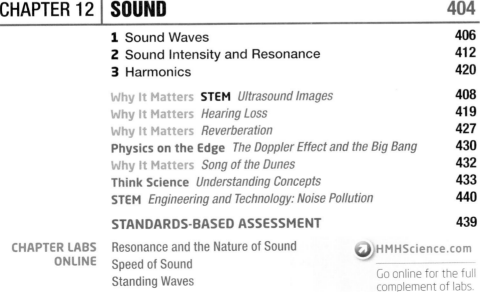

(cr) ©Comstock/Getty Images; (tr) ©Cindy Yamanaka/National Geographic Society; (br) ©Jeff Rotman/naturepl.com

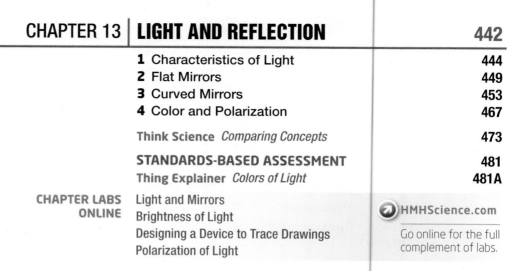

(cr) ©Steve Murray/Alamy; (tr) ©Andrew Sacks/Getty Images; (br) ©Comstock/Getty Images

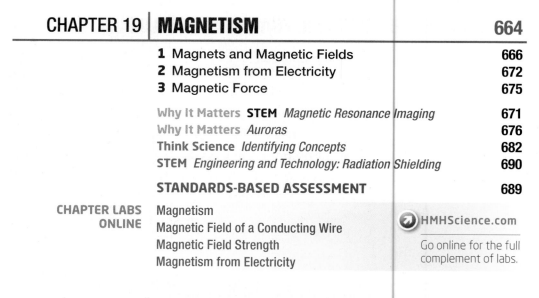

HMHScience.com

Go online for the full complement of labs.

HMHScience.com

Go online for the full complement of labs.

HMHScience.com

Go online for the full complement of labs.

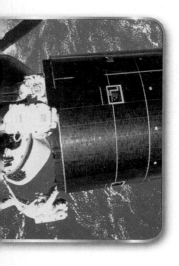

(cl) ©Aaron Jones Studio/Getty Images; (bl) ©Karrapavan/Shutterstock; (tl) ©StockTrek/PhotoSpin, Inc./Alamy Images

HMHScience.com

Go online for the full complement of labs.

REFERENCE

FEATURES

STRATEGIES FOR ENGLISH LANGUAGE LEARNERS

Are you learning English? You can learn science and English at the same time. You already know a lot about science from the world around you. You can also learn English from the world around you. Your teacher will help you. Other students will be happy to help. But there are things you can do too.

Below are some ideas that will help you get ready to learn English. Other ideas will help you learn better in class and while you read. There are also some ideas to help you remember and use what you learn.

GET READY TO LEARN

You can do these things before you go to science class.

GET READY TO LEARN STRATEGIES	
Visit Your Classroom and Teacher	Go with other students if you can. Look carefully around the room. What things are there? • Ask your teacher to tell you the names of things you do not know. You can ask, "What is this?" or "Will we use this in class?" or "What does it do?" • Learn how to say and read the names of things you will use to learn science. • Are there signs on the wall? What do they say? If you do not know, ask your teacher or other students, "What does this sign say? What does it mean?" • Remember the words on signs. Signs in many places can have the same words.
Learn Some Science Words	You will learn a lot of new words in your science class. It is easier to learn them if you already know a few science words. • Ask your teacher to say and write some words you need to know. • Ask what the words mean. Then learn the words very well. • Learn how to say and read the words. Learn what they mean.
Ask Your Teacher for Help with Reading	Your teacher can help you read your science book. He or she can help you learn new words that you need to know before you read. • Your teacher might give you a list of the important words or ideas you will read or a list of questions to answer when you read. • He or she might give you a graphic organizer to help you understand what you read. A graphic organizer is a drawing that helps you learn and remember.
Read Before Class	Your teacher tells you what he or she will talk about tomorrow. If part of your book tells about the same thing, read the book today. When you are done reading, you already know some of what the teacher will say. Then it is easier for you to understand when the teacher talks.

GET READY TO LEARN STRATEGIES	
Look at Pictures Before You Read	You need to read some pages in your science book. • What should you do first? Look at the pictures. Use what you already know. • If there are words with the pictures, read the words. Try to figure out what the pictures show. • It will be easier to read the pages if you already know a little bit from looking at the pictures.
Get Ready to Ask Questions	You might have a question about what you read before class. • First, write down your question. If you are worried about how to say the question, practice it. • Bring your question to class. Listen carefully when the teacher talks about the same thing as your question. Maybe the teacher will answer the question. • If you still do not have an answer, raise your hand. Ask the question you wrote and practiced. • Listen carefully to the answer.
Start Taking Notes Before Class	Taking notes means writing something to help you remember what you read or hear. • You do not write all the words you read or hear. Write just a few important words or make drawings. • It can be hard to take notes when you listen. It is easier if you start your notes before class, when you read your book. Write down important words that you read. Write your own words or draw something to help you remember important ideas. Leave lots of space on your paper. • Then, take your notes to class. Use the same paper to take notes when you listen in class. Write more notes in the space you left.
Get Ready to Answer Questions	Science teachers ask a lot of questions. Learn these question words: *what*, *where*, *when*, *who*, *why*, *how much*, *is it*, *will it*. Learn how to answer questions that use each word. • *What:* Tell the name of a thing. • *What will happen, what happened, what happens when we:* Tell how something changes or stays the same. • *Where:* Tell a place. • *When:* Tell a time (you can also say *before* or *after* something). • *Who:* Tell a person. Your teacher might ask, "Who can tell me . . .?" That means, "Do you know the answer?" If you do, raise your hand. • *How much:* Tell an amount. • *Why:* Tell what made something happen or explain a reason. • *Is it or Will it:* Answer yes or no. You can also give a reason for your answer.

WHILE YOU LEARN

You can do these things in your science class.

WHILE YOU LEARN STRATEGIES	
Use What You Know	When you hear or read about something new, think about what you already know.
	If a new word sounds like a word you already know, maybe the two words mean close to the same thing. Maybe you already know something about a new idea.
	Use what you know to help you understand the new word or idea.
Get Help If You Do Not Understand	If you don't understand something, get help.
	• Ask your teacher or another student. Raise your hand and ask in class or wait until the teacher is done talking.
	• If you do not understand a word, try to say the word. Then ask, "What does that word mean?"
	• If you do not know how to do something, you can ask, "How do I do this?"
	• If you do not understand an idea or picture, tell what you do know. Then ask about the part you do not understand.
Understand Instructions	Instructions tell you how to do something. They are sometimes called directions.
	You need to follow instructions many times in science class. Sometimes your teacher says the instructions. Sometimes you need to read the instructions.
	Most instructions have many parts, called steps. Sometimes the teacher or book will use numbers (1, 2, 3 . . .) to tell you when to do each step.
	Other times, instructions use words. Learn the words that tell you when to do things:
	• *first*
	• *then*
	• *next*
	• *before*
	• *after*
	• *while*
	• *last*
	Listen and look for these words in instructions. Use them to help you know when to do things.
	You can also use these words to give other people instructions. You can use them when you write or tell about something you did.

WHILE YOU LEARN STRATEGIES	
Answer Questions	When your teacher asks you a question, you need to answer. Here are some things that can help you: • Listen carefully to the question. If you do not understand the words, you can ask, "Could you repeat the question?" or "Can you say that more slowly?" • Listen for the question word. It tells you what kind of answer to give. • Look to see if the teacher is pointing at something. The question is probably about that thing. You can talk about that thing in your answer. • Remember what the teacher said before the question. The question might be about what the teacher said. Maybe you can use some of the teacher's words in your answer. • If you do not know an answer, tell the teacher you do not know. You can say, "I don't know" or "I did not understand that very well" or "I don't remember that."
Talk in Groups	In science class, you often work with other students. You need to understand what your group should do. • Read instructions if you have them. You can ask, "Can I have some more time to read?" • If you do not understand the instructions, you can ask, "Do you understand Step 4?" or "Can you help me understand this step?" • Talk about the instructions after you read. You can ask, "Who should . . .?" or "What should we do first?" • Tell what you can do. Ask the other students what they will do. • As you work, you can ask your partner for help. You can say, "Can you hold this?" or "What do we do next?" • Be sure to help your partner. You can say, "Do you need me to pour that?" • If you have an idea, you can say, "I think we should do this" or "What if we do it this way?" or "I have an idea."

REMEMBER AND USE WHAT YOU LEARN

You can do these things to help you learn important science words and ideas. Do them before class, in class, or after class.

REMEMBER AND USE WHAT YOU LEARN STRATEGIES	
Say It Again (and Again and Again)	One way to learn new words is to repeat them, or say them many times. • First, make sure that you can say the word correctly. • Be sure you know what it means too. Ask a friend or your teacher. Have the person tell you if you need to say the word differently or if you do not have the right meaning. • When you can say the word correctly and know what it means, say the word several times. This is more fun with a partner. Take turns saying the word and telling each other the meaning. • You will remember better if you say the meaning in your own words. You will remember even better if you say your own sentence that uses the word. Try to say a different sentence each time you repeat.
Use Flash Cards	Flash cards help you learn new words. • To make flash cards, use some pieces of paper that are all the same size. Get the words you need to learn. • Write one word on a piece of paper. Turn the paper over. Write the meaning of the word. • Use your own words or draw pictures to help you remember. • Write the other words on other pieces of paper. Write the meaning of each word on the back of the paper. To use flash cards, look at a word. Say what you think it means. Check the back of the paper. • If you got the meaning right, do not look at that card again. Do this with all your words. • If you get some wrong, look at them again and again. You can use flash cards alone or with a partner.
Tell Somebody	Ask a friend or a person in your family to help you learn. Have the person ask you a question. If you need to learn some science words, have him or her ask you what the words mean. If you need to remember how something in science works, have the person ask you. Then use your own words to tell what you know from your book or class. Tell the person what the words mean or how something works. Answer all the person's questions. Helping that person understand helps you understand and remember too.

Make a Picture

Sometimes a picture can help you remember better than words can.

You can draw pictures when you take notes. Draw your own picture or use a graphic organizer.

A graphic organizer is a drawing that helps you learn and remember. There are many different graphic organizers.

A concept map shows how information is connected. Write one word or idea in the large circle. Write and draw lines to other words to show how they explain or are like the thing in the large circle.

Use a Venn diagram to show how two things are the same and how they are different. Write how they are different in the two circles. Write how they are the same where the two circles come together.

Use a drawing like this to show a main idea and some important details to remember about the idea.

Summarize

When you use your own words to tell the most important parts of something, you summarize it.

- You can summarize what your teacher says in class.
- You can summarize what you read.

Write or say in your own words what you learned in class or from your reading. Do not tell everything. Tell only the most important parts.

Summarizing can help you understand and remember better.

SAFETY SYMBOLS

Remember that the safety symbols shown here apply to a specific activity, but the numbered rules on the following pages apply to all laboratory work.

 ## EYE PROTECTION

- Wear safety goggles when working around chemicals, acids, bases, flames, or heating devices. Contents under pressure may become projectiles and cause serious injury.
- Never look directly at the sun through any optical device or use direct sunlight to illuminate a microscope.

 ## CLOTHING PROTECTION

- Secure loose clothing and remove dangling jewelry. Do not wear open-toed shoes or sandals in the lab.
- Wear an apron or lab coat to protect your clothing when you are working with chemicals.

 ## CHEMICAL SAFETY

- Always wear appropriate protective equipment. Always wear eye goggles, gloves, and a lab apron or lab coat when you are working with any chemical or chemical solution.
- Never taste, touch, or smell chemicals unless your instructor directs you to do so.
- Do not allow radioactive materials to come into contact with your skin, hair, clothing, or personal belongings. Although the materials used in this lab are not hazardous when used properly, radioactive materials can cause serious illness and may have permanent effects.

 ## ELECTRICAL SAFETY

- Do not place electrical cords in walking areas or let cords hang over a table edge in a way that could cause equipment to fall if the cord is accidentally pulled.
- Do not use equipment that has frayed electrical cords or loose plugs.
- Be sure that equipment is in the "off" position before you plug it in.
- Never use an electrical appliance around water or with wet hands or clothing.
- Be sure to turn off and unplug electrical equipment when you are finished using it.
- Never close a circuit until it has been approved by your teacher. Never rewire or adjust any element of a closed circuit.
- If the pointer on any kind of meter moves off scale, open the circuit immediately by opening the switch.
- Do not work with any batteries, electrical devices, or magnets other than those provided by your teacher.

 ## HEATING SAFETY

- Avoid wearing hair spray or hair gel on lab days.
- Whenever possible, use an electric hot plate instead of an open flame as a heat source.
- When heating materials in a test tube, always angle the test tube away from yourself and others.
- Glass containers used for heating should be made of heat-resistant glass.

 ## SHARP OBJECT SAFETY

- Use knives and other sharp instruments with extreme care.

 ## HAND SAFETY

- Perform this experiment in a clear area. Attach masses securely. Falling, dropped, or swinging objects can cause serious injury.
- Use a hot mitt to handle resistors, light sources, and other equipment that may be hot. Allow all equipment to cool before storing it.
- To avoid burns, wear heat-resistant gloves whenever instructed to do so.
- Always wear protective gloves when working with an open flame, chemicals, solutions, or wild or unknown plants.
- If you do not know whether an object is hot, do not touch it.
- Use tongs when heating test tubes. Never hold a test tube in your hand to heat the test tube.

 ## GLASSWARE SAFETY

- Check the condition of glassware before and after using it. Inform your teacher of any broken, chipped, or cracked glassware, because it should not be used.
- Do not pick up broken glass with your bare hands. Place broken glass in a specially designated disposal container.

 ## WASTE DISPOSAL

- Clean and decontaminate all work surfaces and personal protective equipment as directed by your instructor.
- Dispose of all broken glass, contaminated sharp objects, and other contaminated materials (biological and chemical) in special containers as directed by your instructor.

SAFETY IN THE PHYSICS LABORATORY

Systematic, careful lab work is an essential part of any science program, because lab work is the key to progress in science. In this class, you will practice some of the same fundamental laboratory procedures and techniques that experimental physicists use to pursue new knowledge.

The equipment and apparatus you will use involve various safety hazards, just as they do for working physicists. You must be aware of these hazards. Your teacher will guide you in properly using the equipment and carrying out the experiments, but you must also take responsibility for your part in this process. With the active involvement of you and your teacher, these risks can be minimized so that working in the physics laboratory can be a safe, enjoyable process of discovery.

THESE SAFETY RULES ALWAYS APPLY IN THE LAB:

1. **Always wear a lab apron and safety goggles.** Wear these safety devices whenever you are in the lab, not just when you are working on an experiment.

2. **No contact lenses in the lab.** Contact lenses should not be worn during any investigations using chemicals (even if you are wearing goggles). In the event of an accident, chemicals can get behind contact lenses and cause serious damage before the lenses can be removed. If your doctor requires that you wear contact lenses instead of glasses, you should wear eye-cup safety goggles in the lab. Ask your doctor or your teacher how to use this very important and special eye protection.

3. **Personal apparel should be appropriate for laboratory work.** On lab days, avoid wearing long necklaces, dangling bracelets, bulky jewelry, and bulky or loose-fitting clothing. Loose, flopping, or dangling items may get caught in moving parts, accidentally contact electrical connections, or interfere with the investigation in some potentially hazardous manner. In addition, chemical fumes may react with some jewelry, such as pearl jewelry, and ruin them. Cotton clothing is preferable to clothes made of wool, nylon, or polyester.

Tie back long hair. Wear shoes that will protect your feet from chemical spills and falling objects. Do not wear open-toed shoes or sandals or shoes with woven leather straps.

4. **NEVER work alone in the laboratory.** Work in the lab only while under the supervision of your teacher. Do not leave equipment unattended while it is in operation.

5. **Only books and notebooks needed for the experiment should be in the lab.** Only the lab notebook and perhaps the textbook should be in the lab. Keep other books, backpacks, purses, and similar items in your desk, locker, or designated storage area.

6. **Read the entire experiment before entering the lab.** Your teacher will review any applicable safety precautions before the lab. If you are not sure of something, ask your teacher.

7. **Heed all safety symbols and cautions written in the experimental investigations and handouts, posted in the room, and given verbally by your teacher.** They are provided for a reason: YOUR SAFETY.

8. **Know the proper fire-drill procedures and the locations of fire exits and emergency equipment.** Make sure you know the procedures to follow in case of a fire or emergency.

9. **If your clothing catches on fire, do not run; WALK to the safety shower, stand under it, and turn it on.** Call to your teacher while you do this.

10. **Report all accidents to the teacher immediately, no matter how minor.** In addition, if you get a headache, feel sick to your stomach, or feel dizzy, tell your teacher immediately.

11. **Report all spills to your teacher immediately.** Call your teacher rather than trying to clean a spill yourself. Your teacher will tell you if it is safe for you to clean up the spill; if not, your teacher will know how the spill should be cleaned up safely.

12. **Student-designed inquiry investigations, such as Open Inquiry labs, must be approved by the teacher before being attempted by the student.**

13. **DO NOT perform unauthorized experiments or use equipment and apparatus in a manner for which they are not intended.** Use only materials and equipment listed in the activity equipment list or authorized by your teacher. Steps in a procedure should only be performed as described in the book or lab manual or as approved by your teacher.

14. **Stay alert in the lab, and proceed with caution.** Be aware of others near you or your equipment when you are about to do something in the lab. If you are not sure of how to proceed, ask your teacher.

15. **Fooling around in the lab is very dangerous.** Laboratory equipment and apparatus are not toys; never play in the lab or use lab time or equipment for anything other than their intended purpose.

16. **Food, beverages, chewing gum, and tobacco products are NEVER permitted in the laboratory.**

17. **NEVER taste chemicals. Do not touch chemicals or allow them to contact areas of bare skin.**

18. **Use extreme CAUTION when working with hot plates or other heating devices.** Keep your head, hands, hair, and clothing away from the flame or heating area, and turn the devices off when they are not in use. Remember that metal surfaces connected to the heated area will become hot by conduction. Gas burners should only be lit with a spark lighter. Make sure all heating devices and gas valves are turned off before leaving the laboratory. Never leave a hot plate or other heating device unattended when it is in use. Remember that many metal, ceramic, and glass items do not always look hot when they are hot. Allow all items to cool before storing.

19. **Exercise caution when working with electrical equipment.** Do not use electrical equipment with frayed or twisted wires. Be sure your hands are dry before using electrical equipment. Do not let electrical cords dangle from work stations; dangling cords can cause tripping or electrical shocks.

20. **Keep work areas and apparatus clean and neat.** Always clean up any clutter made during the course of lab work, rearrange apparatus in an orderly manner, and report any damaged or missing items.

21. **Always thoroughly wash your hands with soap and water at the conclusion of each investigation.**

NEXT GENERATION SUNSHINE STATE STANDARDS: PHYSICS

The *HMH Physics* program provides a full year of interactive experiences that address the Next Generation Sunshine State Standards: Physics. As you read, experiment, and interact with print and digital content, you will be learning what you need to know and be able to do to complete this course. The Florida standards explain the content, concept, and principles of major themes in Physics. The standards are listed here for your convenience. You will also see them referenced throughout this book.

Nature of Science
SC.912.N.1: The Practice of Science

SC.912.N.1.1 Define a problem based on a specific body of knowledge, for example: biology, chemistry, physics, and earth/space science, and do the following:

1. pose questions about the natural world,
2. conduct systematic observations,
3. examine books and other sources of information to see what is already known,
4. review what is known in light of empirical evidence,
5. plan investigations,
6. use tools to gather, analyze, and interpret data (this includes the use of measurement in metric and other systems, and also the generation and interpretation of graphical representations of data, including data tables and graphs),
7. pose answers, explanations, or descriptions of events,
8. generate explanations that explicate or describe natural phenomena (inferences),
9. use appropriate evidence and reasoning to justify these explanations to others,
10. communicate results of scientific investigations, and
11. evaluate the merits of the explanations produced by others.

SC.912.N.1.2 Describe and explain what characterizes science and its methods.

SC.912.N.1.5 Describe and provide examples of how similar investigations conducted in many parts of the world result in the same outcome.

SC.912.N.1.6 Describe how scientific inferences are drawn from scientific observations and provide examples from the content being studied.

SC.912.N.1.7 Recognize the role of creativity in constructing scientific questions, methods and explanations.

SC.912.N.2: The Characteristics of Scientific Knowledge

SC.912.N.2.2 Identify which questions can be answered through science and which questions are outside the boundaries of scientific investigation, such as questions addressed by other ways of knowing, such as art, philosophy, and religion.

SC.912.N.2.4 Explain that scientific knowledge is both durable and robust and open to change. Scientific knowledge can change because it is often examined and re-examined by new investigations and scientific argumentation. Because of these frequent examinations, scientific knowledge becomes stronger, leading to its durability.

SC.912.N.2.5 Describe instances in which scientists' varied backgrounds, talents, interests, and goals influence the inferences and thus the explanations that they make about observations of natural phenomena and describe that competing interpretations (explanations) of scientists are a strength of science as they are a source of new, testable ideas that have the potential to add new evidence to support one or another of the explanations.

SC.912.N.3: The Role of Theories, Laws, Hypotheses, and Model

SC.912.N.3.2 Describe the role consensus plays in the historical development of a theory in any one of the disciplines of science.

SC.912.N.3.3 Explain that scientific laws are descriptions of specific relationships under given conditions in nature, but do not offer explanations for those relationships.

SC.912.N.3.4: Recognize that theories do not become laws, nor do laws become theories; theories are well supported explanations and laws are well supported descriptions.

SC.912.N.3.5 Describe the function of models in science, and identify the wide range of models used in science.

SC.912.N.4: Science and Society

SC.912.N.4.1 Explain how scientific knowledge and reasoning provide an empirically-based perspective to inform society's decision making.

Earth and Space Science
SC.912.E.5: Earth in Space and Time

SC.912.E.5.2: Identify patterns in the organization and distribution of matter in the universe and the forces that determine them.

SC.912.E.5.6: Develop logical connections through physical principles, including Kepler's and Newton's Laws about the relationships and the effects of Earth, Moon, and Sun on each other.

Physical Science
SC.912.P.8: Matter

SC.912.P.8.1 Differentiate among the four states of matter.

SC.912.P.8.3 Explore the scientific theory of atoms (also known as atomic theory) by describing changes in the atomic model over time and why those changes were necessitated by experimental evidence.

NEXT GENERATION SUNSHINE STATE STANDARDS: PHYSICS (CONTINUED)

SC.912.P.10: Energy

SC.912.P.10.1 Differentiate among the various forms of energy and recognize that they can be transformed from one form to others.

SC.912.P.10.2: Explore the Law of Conservation of Energy by differentiating among open, closed, and isolated systems and explain that the total energy in an isolated system is a conserved quantity.

SC.912.P.10.3: Compare and contrast work and power qualitatively and quantitatively.

SC.912.P.10.4: Describe heat as the energy transferred by convection, conduction, and radiation, and explain the connection of heat to change in temperature or states of matter.

SC.912.P.10.5 Relate temperature to the average molecular kinetic energy.

SC.912.P.10.10: Compare the magnitude and range of the four fundamental forces (gravitational, electromagnetic, weak nuclear, strong nuclear).

SC.912.P.10.13: Relate the configuration of static charges to the electric field, electric force, electric potential, and electric potential energy.

SC.912.P.10.14: Differentiate among conductors, semiconductors, and insulators.

SC.912.P.10.15: Investigate and explain the relationships among current, voltage, resistance, and power.

SC.912.P.10.18 Explore the theory of electromagnetism by comparing and contrasting the different parts of the electromagnetic spectrum in terms of wavelength, frequency, and energy, and relate them to phenomena and applications.

SC.912.P.10.20: Describe the measurable properties of waves and explain the relationships among them and how these properties change when the wave moves from one medium to another.

SC.912.P.10.21: Qualitatively describe the shift in frequency in sound or electromagnetic waves due to the relative motion of a source or a receiver.

SC.912.P.10.22: Construct ray diagrams and use thin lens and mirror equations to locate the images formed by lenses and mirrors.

SC.912.P.12: Motion

SC.912.P.12.1: Distinguish between scalar and vector quantities and assess which should be used to describe an event.

SC.912.P.12.2: Analyze the motion of an object in terms of its position, velocity, and acceleration (with respect to a frame of reference) as functions of time.

SC.912.P.12.3: Interpret and apply Newton's three laws of motion.

SC.912.P.12.4: Describe how the gravitational force between two objects depends on their masses and the distance between them.

SC.912.P.12.5: Apply the law of conservation of linear momentum to interactions, such as collisions between objects.

SC.912.P.12.7: Recognize that nothing travels faster than the speed of light in vacuum which is the same for all observers no matter how they or the light source are moving.

SC.912.P.12.9: Recognize that time, length, and energy depend on the frame of reference.

Language Arts Florida Standards: Reading in Science and Technical Subjects

LAFS.1112.RST.1.1 Cite specific textual evidence to support analysis of science and technical texts, attending to important distinctions the author makes and to any gaps or inconsistencies in the account.

LAFS.1112.RST.1.2 Determine the central ideas or conclusions of a text; summarize complex concepts, processes, or information presented in a text by paraphrasing them in simpler but still accurate terms.

LAFS.1112.RST.1.3 Follow precisely a complex multistep procedure when carrying out experiments, taking measurements, or performing technical tasks; analyze the specific results based on explanations in the text.

LAFS.1112.RST.2.4 Determine the meaning of symbols, key terms, and other domain-specific words and phrases as they are used in a specific scientific or technical context relevant to grades 11–12 texts and topics.

LAFS.1112.RST.2.5 Analyze how the text structures information or ideas into categories or hierarchies, demonstrating understanding of the information or ideas.

LAFS.1112.RST.2.6: Analyze the author's purpose in providing an explanation, describing a procedure, or discussing an experiment in a text, identifying important issues that remain unresolved.

LAFS.1112.RST.3.7: Integrate and evaluate multiple sources of information presented in diverse formats and media (e.g., quantitative data, video, multimedia) in order to address a question or solve a problem.

LAFS.1112.RST.3.8: Evaluate the hypotheses, data, analysis, and conclusions in a science or technical text, verifying the data when possible and corroborating or challenging conclusions with other sources of information.

LAFS.1112.RST.3.9: Synthesize information from a range of sources (e.g., texts, experiments, simulations) into a coherent understanding of a process, phenomenon, or concept, resolving conflicting information when possible.

LAFS.1112.RST.4.10: By the end of grade 12, read and comprehend science/technical texts in the grades 11–12 text complexity band independently and proficiently.

NEXT GENERATION SUNSHINE STATE STANDARDS: PHYSICS (CONTINUED)

Language Arts Florida Standards: Speaking and Listening

LAFS.1112.SL.1.1: Initiate and participate effectively in a range of collaborative discussions (one-on-one, in groups, and teacher-led) with diverse partners on grades 11–12 topics, texts, and issues, building on others' ideas and expressing their own clearly and persuasively.

a. Come to discussions prepared, having read and researched material under study; explicitly draw on that preparation by referring to evidence from texts and other research on the topic or issue to stimulate a thoughtful, well-reasoned exchange of ideas.

b. Work with peers to promote civil, democratic discussions and decision-making, set clear goals and deadlines, and establish individual roles as needed.

c. Propel conversations by posing and responding to questions that probe reasoning and evidence; ensure a hearing for a full range of positions on a topic or issue; clarify, verify, or challenge ideas and conclusions; and promote divergent and creative perspectives.

d. Respond thoughtfully to diverse perspectives; synthesize comments, claims, and evidence made on all sides of an issue; resolve contradictions when possible; and determine what additional information or research is required to deepen the investigation or complete the task.

LAFS.1112.SL.1.2 Integrate multiple sources of information presented in diverse formats and media (e.g., visually, quantitatively, orally) in order to make informed decisions and solve problems, evaluating the credibility and accuracy of each source and noting any discrepancies among the data.

LAFS.1112.SL.1.3 Evaluate a speaker's point of view, reasoning, and use of evidence and rhetoric, assessing the stance, premises, links among ideas, word choice, points of emphasis, and tone used.

LAFS.1112.SL.2.4 Present information, findings, and supporting evidence, conveying a clear and distinct perspective, such that listeners can follow the line of reasoning, alternative or opposing perspectives are addressed, and the organization, development, substance, and style are appropriate to purpose, audience, and a range of formal and informal tasks.

LAFS.1112.SL.2.5 Make strategic use of digital media (e.g., textual, graphical, audio, visual, and interactive elements) in presentations to enhance understanding of findings, reasoning, and evidence and to add interest.

Language Arts Florida Standards: Writing in Science and Technical Subjects

LAFS.1112.WHST.1.1 Write arguments focused on discipline-specific content.

a. Introduce precise, knowledgeable claim(s), establish the significance of the claim(s), distinguish the claim(s) from alternate or opposing claims, and create an organization that logically sequences the claim(s), counterclaims, reasons, and evidence.

b. Develop claim(s) and counterclaims fairly and thoroughly, supplying the most relevant data and evidence for each while pointing out the strengths and limitations of both claim(s) and counterclaims in a discipline-appropriate form that anticipates the audience's knowledge level, concerns, values, and possible biases.

c. Use words, phrases, and clauses as well as varied syntax to link the major sections of the text, create cohesion, and clarify the relationships between claim(s) and reasons, between reasons and evidence, and between claim(s) and counterclaims.

d. Establish and maintain a formal style and objective tone while attending to the norms and conventions of the discipline in which they are writing.

e. Provide a concluding statement or section that follows from or supports the argument presented.

LAFS.1112.WHST.1.2 Write informative/explanatory texts, including the narration of historical events, scientific procedures/ experiments, or technical processes.

a. Introduce a topic and organize complex ideas, concepts, and information so that each new element builds on that which precedes it to create a unified whole; include formatting (e.g., headings), graphics (e.g., figures, tables), and multimedia when useful to aiding comprehension.

b. Develop the topic thoroughly by selecting the most significant and relevant facts, extended definitions, concrete details, quotations, or other information and examples appropriate to the audience's knowledge of the topic.

c. Use varied transitions and sentence structures to link the major sections of the text, create cohesion, and clarify the relationships among complex ideas and concepts.

d. Use precise language, domain-specific vocabulary and techniques such as metaphor, simile, and analogy to manage the complexity of the topic; convey a knowledgeable stance in a style that responds to the discipline and context as well as to the expertise of likely readers.

e. Provide a concluding statement or section that follows from and supports the information or explanation provided (e.g., articulating implications or the significance of the topic).

LAFS.1112.WHST.2.4 Produce clear and coherent writing in which the development, organization, and style are appropriate to task, purpose, and audience.

LAFS.1112.WHST.2.5 Develop and strengthen writing as needed by planning, revising, editing, rewriting, or trying a new approach, focusing on addressing what is most significant for a specific purpose and audience.

LAFS.1112.WHST.2.6 Use technology, including the Internet, to produce, publish, and update individual or shared writing products in response to ongoing feedback, including new arguments or information.

LAFS.1112.WHST.3.7 Conduct short as well as more sustained research projects to answer a question (including a self-generated question) or solve a problem; narrow or broaden the inquiry when appropriate; synthesize multiple sources on the subject, demonstrating understanding of the subject under investigation.

LAFS.1112.WHST.3.8 Gather relevant information from multiple authoritative print and digital sources, using advanced searches effectively; assess the strengths and limitations of each source in terms of the specific task, purpose, and audience; integrate information into the text selectively to maintain the flow of ideas, avoiding plagiarism and overreliance on any one source and following a standard format for citation.

NEXT GENERATION SUNSHINE STATE STANDARDS: PHYSICS (CONTINUED)

LAFS.1112.WHST.3.9 Draw evidence from informational texts to support analysis, reflection, and research.

LAFS.1112.WHST.4.10 Write routinely over extended time frames (time for reflection and revision) and shorter time frames (a single sitting or a day or two) for a range of discipline-specific tasks, purposes, and audiences.

Mathematics Florida Standards

MAFS.912.F-IF.2.4 For a function that models a relationship between two quantities, interpret key features of graphs and tables in terms of the quantities, and sketch graphs showing key features given a verbal description of the relationship. *Key features include: intercepts; intervals where the function is increasing, decreasing, positive, or negative; relative maximums and minimums; symmetries; end behavior; and periodicity.*

MAFS.912.F-IF.3.7 Graph functions expressed symbolically and show key features of the graph, by hand in simple cases and using technology for more complicated cases. ★

   a. Graph linear and quadratic functions and show intercepts, maxima, and minima.

   b. Graph square root, cube root, and piecewise-defined functions, including step functions and absolute value functions.

   c. Graph polynomial functions, identifying zeros when suitable factorizations are available, and showing end behavior.

   d. Graph rational functions, identifying zeros and asymptotes when suitable factorizations are available, and showing end behavior.

   e. Graph exponential and logarithmic functions, showing intercepts and end behavior, and trigonometric functions, showing period, midline, and amplitude, and using phase shift.

MAFS.912.G-MG.1.2: Apply concepts of density based on area and volume in modeling situations (e.g., persons per square mile, BTUs per cubic foot). ★

MAFS.912.N-Q.1.1 Use units as a way to understand problems and to guide the solution of multi-step problems; choose and interpret units consistently in formulas; choose and interpret the scale and the origin in graphs and data displays. ★

MAFS.912.N-Q.1.3 Choose a level of accuracy appropriate to limitations on measurement when reporting quantities. ★

MAFS.912.N-VM.1.3: Solve problems involving velocity and other quantities that can be represented by vectors.

MAFS.912.S-ID.1.1 Represent data with plots on the real number line (dot plots, histograms, and box plots). ★

MAFS.912.S-ID.1.2 Use statistics appropriate to the shape of the data distribution to compare center (median, mean) and spread (interquartile range, standard deviation) of two or more different data sets. ★

MAFS.912.S-ID.1.3 Interpret differences in shape, center, and spread in the context of the data sets, accounting for possible effects of extreme data points (outliers). ★

MAFS.912.S-ID.1.4 Use the mean and standard deviation of a data set to fit it to a normal distribution and to estimate population percentages. Recognize that there are data sets for which such a procedure is not appropriate. Use calculators, spreadsheets, and tables to estimate areas under the normal curve. ★

MAFS.912.S-ID.2.5 Summarize categorical data for two categories in two-way frequency tables. Interpret relative frequencies in the context of the data (including joint, marginal, and conditional relative frequencies). Recognize possible associations and trends in the data. ★

MAFS.K12.MP.1.1 Make sense of problems and persevere in solving them.

MAFS.K12.MP.2.1 Reason abstractly and quantitatively.

MAFS.K12.MP.3.1 Construct viable arguments and critique the reasoning of others.

MAFS.K12.MP.4.1 Model with mathematics.

MAFS.K12.MP.5.1 Use appropriate tools strategically.

MAFS.K12.MP.6.1 Attend to precision.

MAFS.K12.MP.7.1 Look for and make use of structure.

MAFS.K12.MP.8.1 Look for and express regularity in repeated reasoning.

English Language Development Standards

ELD.K12.ELL.SC.1 English language learners communicate information, ideas and concepts necessary for academic success in the content area of Science.

ELD.K12.ELL.SI.1 English language learners communicate for social and instructional purposes within the school setting.

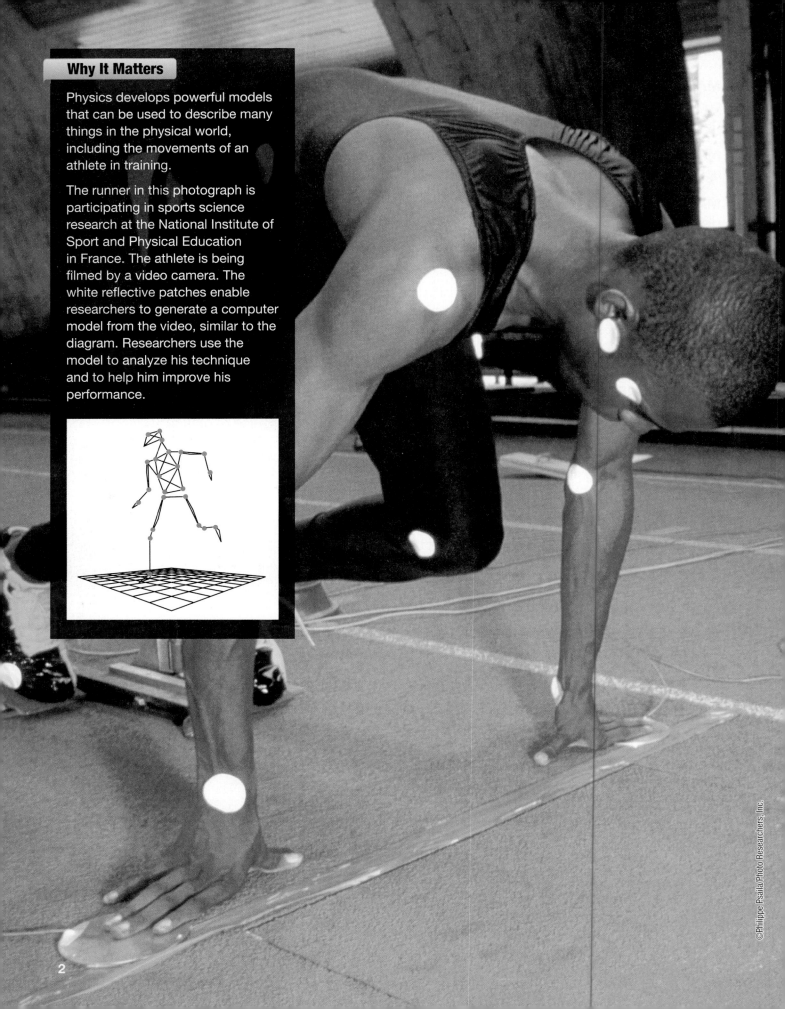

Why It Matters

Physics develops powerful models that can be used to describe many things in the physical world, including the movements of an athlete in training.

The runner in this photograph is participating in sports science research at the National Institute of Sport and Physical Education in France. The athlete is being filmed by a video camera. The white reflective patches enable researchers to generate a computer model from the video, similar to the diagram. Researchers use the model to analyze his technique and to help him improve his performance.

2

CHAPTER 1
The Science of Physics

BIG IDEA

Physics is the science of matter, energy, and forces. Physicists form hypotheses, design and perform experiments, and create models to help understand the world.

ONLINE Physics
HMHScience.com

ONLINE LABS
- The Circumference-Diameter Ratio of a Circle
- Physics and Measurement
- S.T.E.M. Lab Bubble Solutions

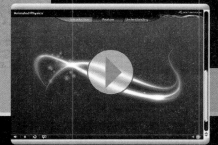

GO ONLINE **Animated Physics**
HMHScience.com

Scientific Models

3

SC.912.N.1.1.5, SC.912.N.1.2,
SC.912.N.3.3, SC.912.N.3.5

Objectives

▶ Identify activities and fields that involve the major areas within physics.

▶ Describe the processes of the scientific method.

▶ Describe the role of models and diagrams in physics.

SC.912.N.1.1.5 Plan investigations.
SC.912.N.1.2 Describe and explain what characterizes science and its methods.
SC.912.N.3.3 Explain that scientific laws are descriptions of specific relationships under given conditions in nature, but do not offer explanations for those relationships.
SC.912.N.3.5 Describe the function of models in science, and identify the wide range of models used in science.

FIGURE 1.1

The Physics of Cars Without knowledge of many of the areas of physics, making cars would be impossible.

What Is Physics?

Key Terms

model   hypothesis
system   controlled experiment

The Topics of Physics

Many people consider physics to be a difficult science that is far removed from their lives. This may be because many of the world's most famous physicists study topics such as the structure of the universe or the incredibly small particles within an atom, often using complicated tools to observe and measure what they are studying.

But everything around you can be described by using the tools of physics. The goal of physics is to use a small number of basic concepts, equations, and assumptions to describe the physical world. These physics principles can then be used to make predictions about a broad range of phenomena. For example, the same physics principles that are used to describe the interaction between two planets can be used to describe the motion of a soccer ball moving toward a goal.

Many physicists study the laws of nature simply to satisfy their curiosity about the world we live in. Learning the laws of physics can be rewarding just for its own sake. Also, many of the inventions, appliances, tools, and buildings we live with today are made possible by the application of physics principles. Physics discoveries often turn out to have unexpected practical applications, and advances in technology can in turn lead to new physics discoveries. **Figure 1.1** indicates how the areas of physics apply to building and operating a car.

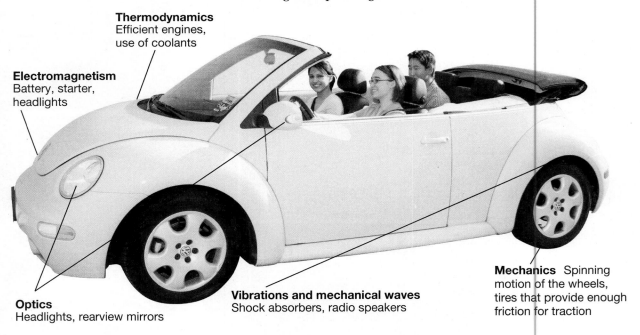

Thermodynamics Efficient engines, use of coolants

Electromagnetism Battery, starter, headlights

Optics Headlights, rearview mirrors

Vibrations and mechanical waves Shock absorbers, radio speakers

Mechanics Spinning motion of the wheels, tires that provide enough friction for traction

Physics is everywhere.

We are surrounded by principles of physics in our everyday lives. In fact, most people know much more about physics than they realize. For example, when you buy a carton of ice cream at the store and put it in the freezer at home, you do so because from past experience you know enough about the laws of physics to know that the ice cream will melt if you leave it on the counter.

People who design, build, and operate sailboats, such as the ones shown in **Figure 1.2,** need a working knowledge of the principles of physics. Designers figure out the best shape for the boat's hull so that it remains stable and floating yet quick-moving and maneuverable. This design requires knowledge of the physics of fluids. Determining the most efficient shapes for the sails and how to arrange them requires an understanding of the science of motion and its causes. Balancing loads in the construction of a sailboat requires knowledge of mechanics. Some of the same physics principles can also explain how the keel keeps the boat moving in one direction even when the wind is from a slightly different direction.

Any problem that deals with temperature, size, motion, position, shape, or color involves physics. Physicists categorize the topics they study in a number of different ways. **Figure 1.3** shows some of the major areas of physics that will be described in this book.

FIGURE 1.2

The Physics of Sailboats
Sailboat designers rely on knowledge from many branches of physics.

FIGURE 1.3

AREAS WITHIN PHYSICS		
Name	**Subjects**	**Examples**
mechanics	motion and its causes, interactions between objects	falling objects, friction, weight, spinning objects
thermodynamics	heat and temperature	melting and freezing processes, engines, refrigerators
vibrations and wave phenomena	specific types of repetitive motions	springs, pendulums, sound
optics	light	mirrors, lenses, color, astronomy
electromagnetism	electricity, magnetism, and light	electrical charge, circuitry, permanent magnets, electromagnets
relativity	particles moving at any speed, including very high speeds	particle collisions, particle accelerators, nuclear energy
quantum mechanics	behavior of submicroscopic particles	the atom and its parts

The Scientific Method

When scientists look at the world, they see a network of rules and relationships that determine what will happen in a given situation. Everything you will study in this course was learned because someone looked out at the world and asked questions about how things work.

There is no single procedure that scientists follow in their work. However, there are certain steps common to all good scientific investigations. These steps, called the *scientific method*, are summarized in **Figure 1.4.** This simple chart is easy to understand, but in reality, most scientific work is not so easily separated. Sometimes, exploratory experiments are performed as a part of the first step in order to generate observations that can lead to a focused question. A revised hypothesis may require more experiments.

Physics uses models that describe phenomena.

Although the physical world is very complex, physicists often use **models** to explain the most fundamental features of various phenomena. Physics has developed powerful models that have been very successful in describing nature. Many of the models currently used in physics are mathematical models. Simple models are usually developed first. It is often easier to study and model parts of a system or phenomenon one at a time. These simple models can then be synthesized into more-comprehensive models.

When developing a model, physicists must decide which parts of the phenomenon are relevant and which parts can be disregarded. For example, let's say you wish to study the motion of the ball shown in **Figure 1.5.** Many observations can be made about the situation,

FIGURE 1.4

The Scientific Method
Physics, like all other sciences, is based on the scientific method.

Make observations and collect data that lead to a question.

⬇

Formulate and objectively test hypotheses by experiments.

⬇

Interpret results, and revise the hypothesis if necessary.

⬇

State conclusions in a form that can be evaluated by others.

model a pattern, plan, representation, or description designed to show the structure or workings of an object, system, or concept

FIGURE 1.5

Analyzing Basketball Motion This basketball game involves great complexity.

including the ball's surroundings, size, spin, weight, color, time in the air, speed, and sound when hitting the ground. The first step toward simplifying this complicated situation is to decide what to study, that is, to define the **system.** Typically, a single object and the items that immediately affect it are the focus of attention. For instance, suppose you decide to study the ball's motion in the air (before it potentially reaches any of the other players), as shown in **Figure 1.6.** To study this situation, you can eliminate everything except information that affects the ball's motion.

system a set of particles or interacting components considered to be a distinct physical entity for the purpose of study

FIGURE 1.6

Motion of a Basketball To analyze the basketball's motion, isolate the objects that will affect its motion.

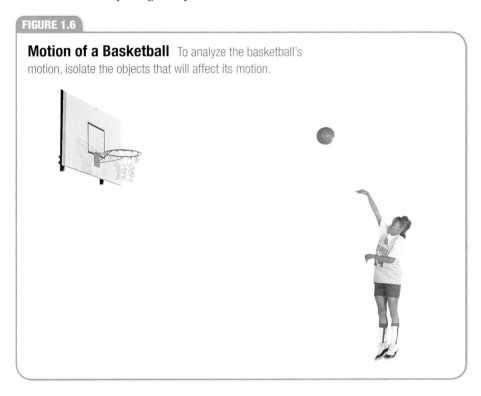

You can disregard characteristics of the ball that have little or no effect on its motion, such as the ball's color. In some studies of motion, even the ball's spin and size are disregarded, and the change in the position of the ball will be the only quantity investigated.

In effect, the physicist studies the motion of a ball by first creating a simple model of the ball and its motion. Unlike the real ball, the model object is isolated; it has no color, spin, or size, and it makes no noise on impact. Frequently, a model can be summarized with a diagram. Another way to summarize these models is to build a computer simulation or small-scale replica of the situation.

Without models to simplify matters, situations such as building a car or sailing a boat would be too complex to study. For instance, analyzing the motion of a sailboat is simplified by imagining that the push on the boat from the wind is steady and consistent. The boat is also treated as an object with a certain mass being pushed through the water. In other words, the color of the boat, the model of the boat, and the details of its shape are left out of the analysis. Furthermore, the water the boat moves through is treated as if it were a perfectly smooth-flowing liquid with no internal friction. In spite of these simplifications, the analysis can still make useful predictions of how the sailboat will move.

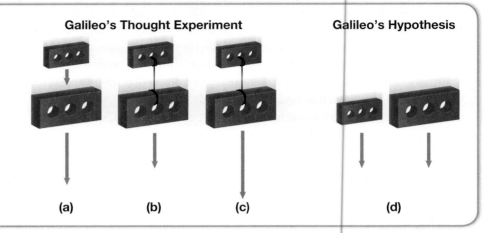

FIGURE 1.7

Galileo's Thought Experiment If heavier objects fell faster than slower ones, would two bricks of different masses tied together fall slower **(b)** or faster **(c)** than the heavy brick alone **(a)**? Because of this contradiction, Galileo hypothesized instead that all objects fall at the same rate, as in **(d)**.

Galileo's Thought Experiment

Galileo's Hypothesis

(a)   **(b)**   **(c)**   **(d)**

hypothesis an explanation that is based on prior scientific research or observations—one that can be tested

Models can help build hypotheses.

A scientific **hypothesis** is a reasonable explanation for observations—one that can be tested with additional experiments. The process of simplifying and modeling a situation can help you determine the relevant variables and identify a hypothesis for testing.

Consider the example of Galileo's "thought experiment," in which he modeled the behavior of falling objects in order to develop a hypothesis about how objects fell. At the time Galileo published his work on falling objects, in 1638, scientists believed that a heavy object would fall faster than a lighter object.

Galileo imagined two objects of different masses tied together and released at the same time from the same height, such as the two bricks of different masses shown in **Figure 1.7.** Suppose that the heavier brick falls faster than the lighter brick when they are separate, as in **(a)**. When tied together, the heavier brick will speed up the fall of the lighter brick somewhat, and the lighter brick will slow the fall of the heavier brick somewhat. Thus, the tied bricks should fall at a rate *in between* that of either brick alone, as in **(b)**.

However, the two bricks together have a greater mass than the heavier brick alone. For this reason, the tied bricks should fall *faster* than the heavier brick, as in **(c)**. Galileo used this logical contradiction to refute the idea that different masses fall at different rates. He hypothesized instead that all objects fall at the same rate in the absence of air resistance, as in **(d)**.

Models help guide experimental design.

Galileo performed many experiments to test his hypothesis. To be certain he was observing differences due to weight, he kept all other variables the same: the objects he tested had the same size (but different weights) and were measured falling from the same point.

The measuring devices at that time were not precise enough to measure the motion of objects falling in air. So Galileo used the motion of a ball rolling down a ramp as a model of the motion of a falling ball.

The steeper the ramp, the closer the model came to representing a falling object. These ramp experiments provided data that matched the predictions Galileo made in his hypothesis.

Like Galileo's hypothesis, any hypothesis must be tested in a **controlled experiment.** In an experiment to test a hypothesis, you must change one variable at a time to determine what influences the phenomenon you are observing. Galileo performed a series of experiments using balls of different weights on one ramp before determining the time they took to roll down a steeper ramp.

controlled experiment an experiment that tests only one factor at a time by comparing a control group with an experimental group

The best physics models can make predictions in new situations.

Until the invention of the air pump, it was not possible to perform direct tests of Galileo's model by observing objects falling in the absence of air resistance. But even though it was not completely testable, Galileo's model was used to make reasonably accurate predictions about the motion of many objects, from raindrops to boulders (even though they all experience air resistance).

Even if some experiments produce results that support a certain model, at any time another experiment may produce results that do not support the model. When this occurs, scientists repeat the experiment until they are sure that the results are not in error. If the unexpected results are confirmed, the model must be abandoned or revised. That is why the last step of the scientific method is so important. A conclusion is valid only if it can be verified by other people.

Did YOU Know?

In addition to conducting experiments to test their hypotheses, scientists also research the work of other scientists. The steps of this type of research include
- identifying reliable sources
- searching the sources to find references
- checking for opposing views
- documenting sources
- presenting findings to other scientists for review and discussion

✓ SECTION 1 **FORMATIVE ASSESSMENT**

1. Name the major areas of physics.

2. Identify the area of physics that is most relevant to each of the following situations. Explain your reasoning.
   a. a high school football game
   b. food preparation for the prom
   c. playing in the school band
   d. lightning in a thunderstorm
   e. wearing a pair of sunglasses outside in the sun

3. What are the activities involved in the scientific method?

4. Give two examples of ways that physicists model the physical world.

✓ Critical Thinking

5. Identify the area of physics involved in each of the following tests of a lightweight metal alloy proposed for use in sailboat hulls:
   a. testing the effects of a collision on the alloy
   b. testing the effects of extreme heat and cold on the alloy
   c. testing whether the alloy can affect a magnetic compass needle

SECTION 2

SC.912.N.1.1.6, MAFS.912.N-Q.1.1,
MAFS.912.N-Q.1.3, MAFS.912.S-ID.1.1,
MAFS.912.S-ID.1.2, MAFS.912.S-ID.1.3,
MAFS.912.S-ID.1.4, MAFS.K12.MP.1.6

Measurements in Experiments

Objectives

▶ List basic SI units and the quantities they describe.

▶ Convert measurements into scientific notation.

▶ Distinguish between *accuracy* and *precision*.

▶ Use significant figures in measurements and calculations.

Key Terms
accuracy
precision
significant figures

Numbers as Measurements

Physicists perform experiments to test hypotheses about how changing one variable in a situation affects another variable. An accurate analysis of such experiments requires numerical measurements.

Numerical measurements are different than the numbers used in a mathematics class. In mathematics, a number like 7 can stand alone and be used in equations. In science, measurements are more than just a number. For example, a measurement reported as 7 leads to several questions. What physical quantity is being measured—length, mass, time, or something else? If it is length that is being measured, what units were used for the measurement—meters, feet, inches, miles, or light-years?

The description of *what kind* of physical quantity is represented by a certain measurement is called *dimension*. You are probably already familiar with three basic dimensions: length, mass, and time. Many other measurements can be expressed in terms of these three dimensions. For example, physical quantities such as force, velocity, energy, volume, and acceleration can all be described as combinations of length, mass, and time. When we learn about heat and electricity, we will need to add two other dimensions to our list, one for temperature and one for electric current.

The description of *how much* of a physical quantity is represented by a certain numerical measurement and by the *unit* with which the quantity is measured. Although each dimension is unique, a dimension can be measured using different units. For example, the dimension of time can be measured in seconds, hours, or years.

SI is the standard measurement system for science.

When scientists do research, they must communicate the results of their experiments with each other and agree on a system of units for their measurements. In 1960, an international committee agreed on a system of standards, such as the standard shown in **Figure 2.1**. They also agreed on designations for the fundamental quantities needed for measurements. This system of units is called the *Système International d'Unités* (SI). In SI, there are only seven base units. Each base unit describes a single dimension, such as length, mass, or time.

FIGURE 2.1

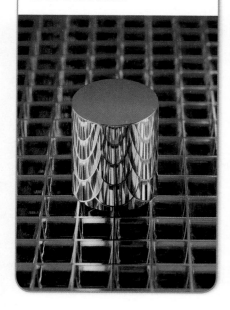

Standard Kilogram The kilogram is currently the only SI unit that is defined by a material object. The platinum-iridium cylinder shown here is the primary kilogram standard for the United States.

FIGURE 2.2

SI STANDARDS

Unit	Original standard	Current standard
meter (length)	$\frac{1}{10\ 000\ 000}$ distance from equator to North Pole	the distance traveled by light in a vacuum in $3.33564095 \times 10^{-9}$ s
kilogram (mass)	mass of 0.001 cubic meters of water	the mass of a specific platinum-iridium alloy cylinder
second (time)	$\left(\frac{1}{60}\right)\left(\frac{1}{60}\right)\left(\frac{1}{24}\right) =$ 0.000 011 574 average solar days	9 192 631 770 times the period of a radio wave emitted from a cesium-133 atom

The base units of length, mass, and time are the meter, kilogram, and second, respectively. In most measurements, these units will be abbreviated as m, kg, and s, respectively.

These units are defined by the standards described in **Figure 2.2** and are reproduced so that every meterstick, kilogram mass, and clock in the world is calibrated to give consistent results. We will use SI units throughout this book because they are almost universally accepted in science and industry.

Not every observation can be described using one of these units, but the units can be combined to form derived units. Derived units are formed by combining the seven base units with multiplication or division. For example, speeds are typically expressed in units of meters per second (m/s).

In other cases, it may appear that a new unit that is not one of the base units is being introduced, but often these new units merely serve as shorthand ways to refer to combinations of units. For example, forces and weights are typically measured in units of newtons (N), but a newton is defined as being exactly equivalent to one kilogram multiplied by meters per second squared (1 kg•m/s^2). Derived units, such as newtons, will be explained throughout this book as they are introduced.

SI uses prefixes to accommodate extremes.

Physics is a science that describes a broad range of topics and requires a wide range of measurements, from very large to very small. For example, distance measurements can range from the distances between stars (about 100 000 000 000 000 000 m) to the distances between atoms in a solid (0.000 000 001 m). Because these numbers can be extremely difficult to read and write, they are often expressed in powers of 10, such as 1×10^{17} m or 1×10^{-9} m.

Another approach commonly used in SI is to combine the units with prefixes that symbolize certain powers of 10, as illustrated in **Figure 2.3**.

Did YOU Know?

NIST-F1, an atomic clock at the National Institute of Standards and Technology in Colorado, is one of the most accurate timing devices in the world. NIST-F1 is so accurate that it will not gain or lose a second in more than 100 million years. As a public service, the institute broadcasts the time given by NIST-F1 through the Internet, radio stations WWV and WWVB, and satellite signals.

FIGURE 2.3

Units with Prefixes The mass of this mosquito can be expressed several different ways: 1×10^{-5} kg, 0.01 g, or 10 mg.

MATERIALS

- balance (0.01 g precision or better)
- 50 sheets of loose-leaf paper

METRIC PREFIXES

Record the following measurements (with appropriate units and metric prefixes):

- the mass of a single sheet of paper
- the mass of exactly 10 sheets of paper
- the mass of exactly 50 sheets of paper

Use each of these measurements to determine the mass of a single sheet of paper. How many different ways can you express each of these measurements? Use your results to estimate the mass of one ream (500 sheets) of paper. How many ways can you express this mass? Which is the most practical approach? Give reasons for your answer.

FIGURE 2.4

SOME PREFIXES FOR POWERS OF 10 USED WITH METRIC UNITS

Power	Prefix	Abbreviation	Power	Prefix	Abbreviation
10^{-18}	atto-	a	10^{1}	deka-	da
10^{-15}	femto-	f	10^{3}	kilo-	k
10^{-12}	pico-	p	10^{6}	mega-	M
10^{-9}	nano-	n	10^{9}	giga-	G
10^{-6}	micro-	μ (Greek letter *mu*)	10^{12}	tera-	T
10^{-3}	milli-	m	10^{15}	peta-	P
10^{-2}	centi-	c	10^{18}	exa-	E
10^{-1}	deci-	d			

The most common prefixes and their symbols are shown in **Figure 2.4.** For example, the length of a housefly, 5×10^{-3} m, is equivalent to 5 millimeters (mm), and the distance of a satellite 8.25×10^{5} m from Earth's surface can be expressed as 825 kilometers (km). A year, which is about 3.2×10^{7} s, can also be expressed as 32 megaseconds (Ms).

Converting a measurement from its prefix form is easy to do. You can build conversion factors from any equivalent relationship, including those in **Figure 2.4.** Just put the quantity on one side of the equation in the numerator and the quantity on the other side in the denominator, as shown below for the case of the conversion 1 mm $= 1 \times 10^{-3}$ m. Because these two quantities are equal, the following equations are also true:

$$\frac{1 \text{ mm}}{10^{-3} \text{ m}} = 1 \quad \text{and} \quad \frac{10^{-3} \text{ m}}{1 \text{ mm}} = 1$$

Thus, any measurement multiplied by either one of these fractions will be multiplied by 1. The number and the unit will change, but the quantity described by the measurement will stay the same.

To convert measurements, use the conversion factor that will cancel with the units you are given to provide the units you need, as shown in the example below. Typically, the units to which you are converting should be placed in the numerator. It is useful to cross out units that cancel to help keep track of them. If you have arranged your terms correctly, the units you are converting from will cancel, leaving you with the unit that you want. If you use the wrong conversion, you will get units that don't cancel.

$$\text{Units } don't \text{ cancel: } 37.2 \text{ mm} \times \frac{1 \text{ mm}}{10^{-3} \text{ m}} = 3.72 \times 10^{4} \frac{\text{mm}^2}{\text{m}}$$

$$\text{Units } do \text{ cancel: } 37.2 \text{ mm} \times \frac{10^{-3} \text{ m}}{1 \text{ mm}} = 3.72 \times 10^{-2} \text{ m}$$

The *Mars Climate Orbiter* Mission

The *Mars Climate Orbiter* was a NASA spacecraft designed to take pictures of the Martian surface, generate daily weather maps, and analyze the Martian atmosphere from an orbit about 80 km (50 mi) above Mars. It was also supposed to relay signals from its companion, the *Mars Polar Lander,* which was scheduled to land near the edge of the southern polar cap of Mars shortly after the orbiter arrived.

The orbiter was launched from Cape Canaveral, Florida, on December 11, 1998. Its thrusters were fired several times along the way to direct it along its path. The orbiter reached Mars nine and a half months later, on September 23, 1999. A signal was sent to the orbiter to fire the thrusters a final time in order to push the spacecraft into orbit around the planet. However, the orbiter did not respond to this final signal. NASA soon determined that the orbiter had passed closer to the planet than intended, as close as 60 km (36 mi). The orbiter most likely overheated because of friction in the Martian atmosphere and then passed beyond the planet into space, fatally damaged.

The *Mars Climate Orbiter* was built by Lockheed Martin in Denver, Colorado, while the mission was run by a NASA flight control team at Jet Propulsion Laboratory in Pasadena, California. Review of the failed mission revealed that engineers at Lockheed Martin sent thrust specifications to the flight control team in English units of pounds of force, while the flight control team assumed that the thrust specifications were in newtons, the SI unit for force. Such a problem normally would be caught by others checking and double-checking specifications, but somehow the error escaped notice until it was too late.

Unfortunately, communication with the *Mars Polar Lander* was also lost as the lander entered the Martian atmosphere on December 3, 1999. The failure of these and other space exploration missions reveals the inherent difficulty in sending complex technology into the distant, harsh, and often unknown conditions in space and on other planets. However, NASA has had many more successes than

The $125 million Mars Orbiter mission failed because of a miscommunication about units of measurement.

failures. A later Mars mission, the Exploration Rover mission, successfully placed two rovers named *Spirit* and *Opportunity* on the surface of Mars, where they collected a wide range of data. Among other things, the rovers found convincing evidence that liquid water once flowed on the surface of Mars. Thus, it is possible that Mars supported life sometime in the past.

The Spirit *and* Opportunity *rovers have explored the surface of Mars with a variety of scientific instruments, including cameras, spectrometers, magnets, and a rock-grinding tool.*

FIGURE 2.5

Choosing Units When determining area by multiplying measurements of length and width, be sure the measurements are expressed in the same units.

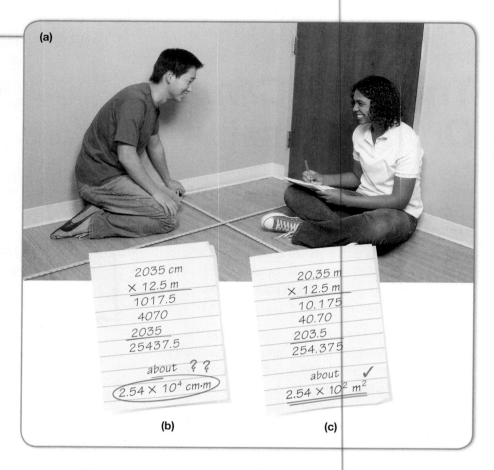

(a)

2035 cm
× 12.5 m
1017.5
4070
2035
25437.5

about ? ?
2.54 × 10⁴ cm·m

(b)

20.35 m
× 12.5 m
10.175
40.70
203.5
254.375

about ✓
2.54 × 10² m²

(c)

Both dimension and units must agree.

Measurements of physical quantities must be expressed in units that match the dimensions of that quantity. For example, measurements of length cannot be expressed in units of kilograms, because units of kilograms describe the dimension of mass. It is very important to be certain that a measurement is expressed in units that refer to the correct dimension. One good technique for avoiding errors in physics is to check the units in an answer to be certain they are appropriate for the dimension of the physical quantity that is being sought in a problem or calculation.

In addition to having the correct dimension, measurements used in calculations should also have the same units. As an example, consider **Figure 2.5(a),** which shows two people measuring a room to determine the room's area. Suppose one person measures the length in meters and the other person measures the width in centimeters. When the numbers are multiplied to find the area, they will give a difficult-to-interpret answer in units of cm•m, as shown in **Figure 2.5(b).** On the other hand, if both measurements are made using the same units, the calculated area is much easier to interpret because it is expressed in units of m², as shown in **Figure 2.5(c).** Even if the measurements were made in different units, as in the example above, one unit can be easily converted to the other because centimeters and meters are both units of length. It is also necessary to convert one unit to another when working with units from two different systems, such as meters and feet. In order to avoid confusion, it is better to make the conversion to the same units before doing any more arithmetic.

Metric Prefixes

Sample Problem A A scanning tunneling microscope (STM) has a magnifying ability of 100 million and can distinguish between two objects that are separated by only 3.0×10^{-10} m, or about one-hundredth the diameter of an atom. Express 3.0×10^{-10} m in

    a. nanometers.

    b. picometers

① ANALYZE

Given: distance $= 3.0 \times 10^{-10}$ m

Unknown: distance $= ?$ nm   distance $= ?$ pm

② SOLVE

Build conversion factors from the relationships given in **Figure 2.4.** Two possibilities are shown below.

$$\frac{1 \text{ nm}}{1 \times 10^{-9} \text{ m}}$$

$$\frac{1 \text{ pm}}{1 \times 10^{-12} \text{ m}}$$

Convert from meters to nanometers by multiplying the distance by the first conversion factor.

$$\text{distance} = 3.0 \times 10^{-10} \text{ m} \times \frac{1 \text{ nm}}{1 \times 10^{-9} \text{ m}} = 3.0 \times 10^{-1} \text{ nm} = \boxed{0.30 \text{ nm}}$$

Convert from meters to picometers by multiplying the distance by the second conversion factor.

$$\text{distance} = 3.0 \times 10^{-10} \text{ m} \times \frac{1 \text{ pm}}{1 \times 10^{-12} \text{ m}} = \boxed{3.0 \times 10^2 \text{ pm}}$$

Practice

1. A human hair is approximately 50 μm in diameter. Express this diameter in meters.

2. If a radio wave has a period of 1 μs, what is the wave's period in seconds?

3. It is estimated that the sun will exhaust all of its energy in about ten billion years. By that time, it will have radiated about 1.2×10^{44} J (joules) of energy. Express this amount of energy in kilojoules.

4. The distance between the sun and Earth is about 1.5×10^{11} m. Express this distance with an SI prefix and in kilometers.

5. The Pacific Ocean has a surface area of about 166 241 700 km² and an average depth of 3940 m. Estimate the volume of the Pacific Ocean in cubic centimeters.

Accuracy and Precision

Because theories are based on observation and experiment, careful measurements are very important in physics. But no measurement is perfect. In describing the imperfection of a measurement, one must consider both the **accuracy,** which describes how close the measurement is to the correct value, and the **precision,** which describes how exact the measurement is. Although these terms are often used interchangeably in everyday speech, they have specific meanings in a scientific discussion. A numeric measure of confidence in a measurement or result is known as *uncertainty*. A lower uncertainty indicates greater confidence. Uncertainties are usually expressed by using statistical methods.

accuracy a description of how close a measurement is to the correct or accepted value of the quantity measured

precision the degree of exactness of a measurement

Error in experiments must be minimized.

Experimental work is never free of error, but it is important to minimize error in order to obtain accurate results. An error can occur, for example, if a mistake is made in reading an instrument or recording the results. One way to minimize error from human oversight or carelessness is to take repeated measurements to be certain they are consistent.

If some measurements are taken using one method and some are taken using a different method, a type of error called *method error* will result. Method error can be greatly reduced by standardizing the method of taking measurements. For example, when measuring a length with a meterstick, choose a line of sight directly over what is being measured, as shown in **Figure 2.6(a).** If you are too far to one side, you are likely to overestimate or underestimate the measurement, as shown in **Figure 2.6(b)** and **Figure 2.6(c).**

Another type of error is *instrument error*. If a meterstick or balance is not in good working order, this will introduce error into any measurements made with the device. For this reason, it is important to be careful with lab equipment. Rough handling can damage balances. If a wooden meterstick gets wet, it can warp, making accurate measurements difficult.

FIGURE 2.6

Line of Sight Affects Measurements If you measure this window by keeping your line of sight directly over the measurement **(a)**, you will find that it is 165.2 cm long. If you do not keep your eye directly above the mark, as in **(b)** and **(c)**, you may report a measurement with significant error.

(a)

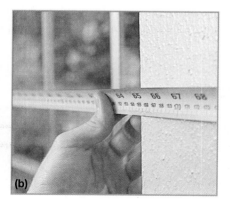
(b)

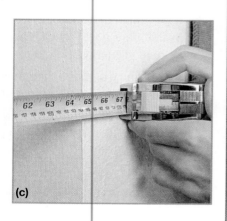
(c)

Because the ends of a meterstick can be easily damaged or worn, it is best to minimize instrument error by making measurements with a portion of the scale that is in the middle of the meterstick. Instead of measuring from the end (0 cm), try measuring from the 10 cm line.

Precision describes the limitations of the measuring instrument.

Poor accuracy involves errors that can often be corrected. On the other hand, precision describes how exact a measurement can possibly be. For example, a measurement of 1.325 m is more precise than a measurement of 1.3 m. A lack of precision is typically due to limitations of the measuring instrument and is not the result of human error or lack of calibration. For example, if a meterstick is divided only into centimeters, it will be difficult to measure something only a few millimeters thick with it.

In many situations, you can improve the precision of a measurement. This can be done by making a reasonable estimation of where the mark on the instrument would have been. Suppose that in a laboratory experiment you are asked to measure the length of a pencil with a meterstick marked in centimeters, as shown in **Figure 2.7**. The end of the pencil lies somewhere between 18 cm and 18.5 cm. The length you have actually measured is slightly more than 18 cm. You can make a reasonable estimation of how far between the two marks the end of the pencil is and add a digit to the end of the actual measurement. In this case, the end of the pencil seems to be less than halfway between the two marks, so you would report the measurement as 18.2 cm.

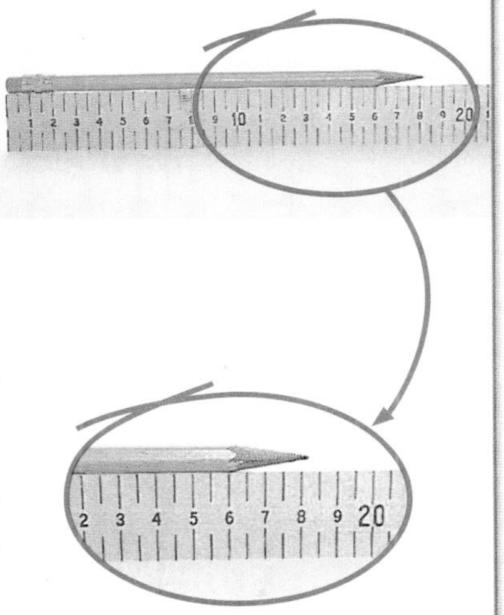

Significant figures help keep track of imprecision.

It is important to record the precision of your measurements so that other people can understand and interpret your results. A common convention used in science to indicate precision is known as **significant figures.** The figures that are significant are the ones that are known for certain, as well as the first digit that is uncertain.

In the case of the measurement of the pencil as about 18.2 cm, the measurement has three significant figures. The significant figures of a measurement include all the digits that are actually measured (18 cm), plus one *estimated* digit. Note that the number of significant figures is determined by the precision of the markings on the measuring scale.

The last digit is reported as a 0.2 (for the estimated 0.2 cm past the 18 cm mark). Because this digit is an estimate, the true value for the measurement is actually somewhere between 18.15 cm and 18.25 cm.

When the last digit in a recorded measurement is a zero, it is difficult to tell whether the zero is there as a placeholder or as a significant digit. For example, if a length is recorded as 230 mm, it is impossible to tell whether this number has two or three significant digits. In other words, it can be difficult to know whether the measurement of 230 mm means the measurement is known to be between 225 mm and 235 mm or is known more precisely to be between 229.5 mm and 230.5 mm.

FIGURE 2.7

Estimation in Measurement
Even though this ruler is marked in only centimeters and half-centimeters, if you estimate, you can use it to report measurements to a precision of a millimeter.

significant figures those digits in a measurement that are known with certainty plus the first digit that is uncertain

FIGURE 2.8

Precision If a mountain's height is known with an uncertainty of 5 m, the addition of 0.20 m of rocks will not appreciably change the height.

One way to solve such problems is to report all values using scientific notation. In scientific notation, the measurement is recorded to a power of 10, and all of the figures given are significant. For example, if the length of 230 cm has two significant figures, it would be recorded in scientific notation as 2.3×10^2 cm. If it has three significant figures, it would be recorded as 2.30×10^2 cm.

Scientific notation is also helpful when the zero in a recorded measurement appears in front of the measured digits. For example, a measurement such as 0.000 15 cm should be expressed in scientific notation as 1.5×10^{-4} cm if it has two significant figures. The three zeros between the decimal point and the digit 1 are not counted as significant figures because they are present only to locate the decimal point and to indicate the order of magnitude. The rules for determining how many significant figures are in a measurement that includes zeros are shown in **Figure 2.9.**

Significant figures in calculations require special rules.

In calculations, the number of significant figures in your result depends on the number of significant figures in each measurement. For example, if someone reports that the height of a mountaintop, like the one shown in **Figure 2.8,** is 1710 m, that implies that its actual height is between 1705 and 1715 m. If another person builds a pile of rocks 0.20 m high on top of the mountain, that would not suddenly make the mountain's new height known accurately enough to be measured as 1710.20 m. The final reported height cannot be more precise than the least-precise measurement used to find the answer. Therefore, the reported height should be rounded off to 1710 m even if the pile of rocks is included.

FIGURE 2.9

RULES FOR DETERMINING WHETHER ZEROS ARE SIGNIFICANT FIGURES

Rule	Examples
1. Zeros between other nonzero digits are significant.	**a.** 50.3 m has three significant figures. **b.** 3.0025 s has five significant figures.
2. Zeros in front of nonzero digits are not significant.	**a.** 0.892 kg has three significant figures. **b.** 0.0008 ms has one significant figure.
3. Zeros that are at the end of a number and also to the right of the decimal are significant.	**a.** 57.00 g has four significant figures. **b.** 2.000 000 kg has seven significant figures.
4. Zeros at the end of a number but to the left of a decimal are significant if they have been measured or are the first estimated digit; otherwise, they are *not* significant. In this book, they will be treated as *not* significant. (Some books place a bar over a zero at the end of a number to indicate that it is significant. This textbook will use scientific notation for these cases instead.)	**a.** 1000 m may contain from one to four significant figures, depending on the precision of the measurement, but in this book it will be assumed that measurements like this have one significant figure. **b.** 20 m may contain one or two significant figures, but in this book it will be assumed to have one significant figure.

Similar rules apply to multiplication. Suppose that you calculate the area of a room by multiplying the width and length. If the room's dimensions are 4.6 m by 6.7 m, the product of these values would be 30.82 m². However, this answer contains four significant figures, which implies that it is more precise than the measurements of the length and width. Because the room could be as small as 4.55 m by 6.65 m or as large as 4.65 m by 6.75 m, the area of the room is known only to be between 30.26 m² and 31.39 m². The area of the room can have only two significant figures because each measurement has only two. So the area must be rounded off to 31 m². **Figure 2.10** summarizes the two basic rules for determining significant figures when you are performing calculations.

FIGURE 2.10

RULES FOR CALCULATING WITH SIGNIFICANT FIGURES

Type of calculation	Rule	Examples
addition or subtraction	Given that addition and subtraction take place in columns, round the final answer to the *first column from the left containing an estimated digit.*	97.3 + 5.85 ——— 103.15 —round off→ 103.2
multiplication or division	The final answer has the same number of significant figures as the measurement having the *smallest* number of *significant figures.*	123 × 5.35 ——— 658.05 —round off→ 658

Calculators do not pay attention to significant figures.

When you use a calculator to analyze problems or measurements, you may be able to save time because the calculator can compute faster than you can. However, the calculator does not keep track of significant figures.

Calculators often exaggerate the precision of your final results by returning answers with as many digits as the display can show. To reinforce the correct approach, the answers to the sample problems in this book will always show only the number of significant figures that the measurements justify.

Providing answers with the correct number of significant figures often requires rounding the results of a calculation. The rules listed in **Figure 2.11** on the next page will be used in this book for rounding, and the results of a calculation will be rounded after each type of mathematical operation. For example, the result of a series of multiplications should be rounded using the multiplication/division rule before it is added to another number. Similarly, the sum of several numbers should be rounded according to the addition/subtraction rule before the sum is multiplied by another number. Multiple roundings can increase the error in a calculation, but with this method there is no ambiguity about which rule to apply. You should consult your teacher to find out whether to round this way or to delay rounding until the end of all calculations.

FIGURE 2.11

RULES FOR ROUNDING IN CALCULATIONS

What to do	When to do it	Examples
round down	• whenever the digit following the last significant figure is a 0, 1, 2, 3, or 4	30.24 becomes 30.2
	• if the last significant figure is an even number and the next digit is a 5, with no other nonzero digits	32.25 becomes 32.2 32.650 00 becomes 32.6
round up	• whenever the digit following the last significant figure is a 6, 7, 8, or 9	22.49 becomes 22.5
	• if the digit following the last significant figure is a 5 followed by a nonzero digit	54.7511 becomes 54.8
	• if the last significant figure is an odd number and the next digit is a 5, with no other nonzero digits	54.75 becomes 54.8 79.3500 becomes 79.4

Error Analysis

As you have learned, gathering results and carefully making measurements, including the use of appropriate equipment, units, and number-rounding techniques, are extremely important for collecting quality data. However, analyzing those data, including identifying and quantifying errors, is a necessary step toward completing a successful investigation.

Multiple trials can minimize the effects of experimental errors.

Performing an experiment multiple times is important. Performing a sufficient number of trials allows you to be more confident that your results are correct, and it helps you distinguish between real results and those that resulted from errors. Suppose a class wants to measure the time it takes a toy car to travel a given distance. In this experiment, detailed in **Figure 2.12**, the class is going to accomplish multiple trials by having 10 individual students make 10 measurements at the same time, rather than performing the same experiment multiple times.

FIGURE 2.12

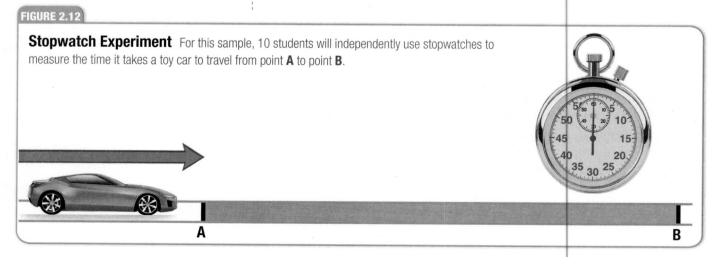

Stopwatch Experiment For this sample, 10 students will independently use stopwatches to measure the time it takes a toy car to travel from point **A** to point **B**.

A   B

Mean, median, and mode describe experimental data.

Mean, median, and *mode* describe the tendency of data sets to group around central values. Mean is calculated by adding the values in the data set and dividing by the number of data points. Median is the value of the middle data point when the numbers are arranged in ascending order. Mode is the number that appears most often in the data set. **Figure 2.13** lists the mean, median, and mode of the data collected in the stopwatch experiment.

FIGURE 2.13

SAMPLE STOPWATCH EXPERIMENT RESULTS

Student	1	2	3	4	5	6	7	8	9	10
Time (seconds)	9.7	9.9	10.2	10.0	10.5	10.0	9.9	10.1	10.1	9.9
Mean (seconds)	10.0									
Median (seconds)	10.0									
Mode (seconds)	9.9									

Mean Value for a Sample

$$\text{Mean} = \frac{\text{sum of the values}}{\text{number of values}}$$

Standard deviation can indicate the quality of experimental data.

If enough trials are performed for an experiment, graphing the data points and calculating the *standard deviation* can provide an indication of the quality of the data set, as well as helping to identify any errors.

Figure 2.14(a) is a visual representation of how the data from the stopwatch experiment were distributed, including the mean value for the data set. The standard deviation represents how much the data vary, compared with the mean. The yellow region in **Figure 2.14(b)** indicates the boundaries of the standard deviation. This data set appears as an approximately *normal distribution,* which results in a roughly bell-shaped curve, with most of the data points falling within one or two standard deviations of the mean. Notice that one of the data points is far away from the mean and is not within the standard-deviation zones. This data point is an *outlier* and likely indicates an error in measurement.

FIGURE 2.14

Distribution of Data Calculation of the standard deviation and visualization of data show how data are distributed and help identify data points that are likely to reflect errors in measurement.

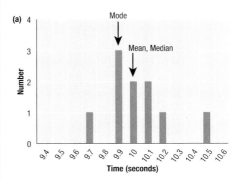

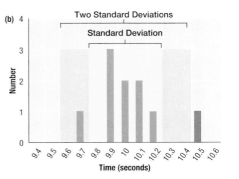

Percentage error compares experimental results with an accepted value.

For some types of data, the accuracy of an individual value or of an average experimental value can be compared quantitatively with the correct, or accepted, value by calculating the *percentage error*. For example, if you conduct an experiment to find the acceleration due to gravity at your location, you can compare your value to the accepted value by calculating the percentage error, as follows:

Percentage Error

$$\text{Percentage error} = \frac{\text{Value}_{\text{experimental}} - \text{Value}_{\text{accepted}}}{\text{Value}_{\text{accepted}}} \times 100$$

Percentage error has a negative value if the accepted value is greater than the experimental value. It has a positive value if the accepted value is less than the experimental value. Percentage error is also known as relative error. More information about relative error is available in Appendix A.

SECTION 2 FORMATIVE ASSESSMENT

▶ Reviewing Main Ideas

1. Which SI units would you use for the following measurements?
   a. the length of a swimming pool
   b. the mass of the water in the pool
   c. the time it takes a swimmer to swim a lap
2. Express the following measurements as indicated.
   a. 6.20 mg in kilograms
   b. 3×10^{-9} s in milliseconds
   c. 88.0 km in meters
3. Perform these calculations, following the rules for significant figures.
   a. $26 \times 0.025\,84 = ?$
   b. $15.3 \div 1.1 = ?$
   c. $782.45 - 3.5328 = ?$
   d. $63.258 + 734.2 = ?$

✔ Critical Thinking

4. The following students measure the density of a piece of lead three times. The density of lead is actually 11.34 g/cm^3. Considering all of the results, which person's results were accurate? Which were precise? Were any both accurate and precise?
   a. Rachel: 11.32 g/cm^3, 11.35 g/cm^3, 11.33 g/cm^3
   b. Daniel: 11.43 g/cm^3, 11.44 g/cm^3, 11.42 g/cm^3
   c. Leah: 11.55 g/cm^3, 11.34 g/cm^3, 11.04 g/cm^3
5. How might error analysis help scientists identify and quantify the causes and effects of uncertainties in measured data? Why is it important to perform multiple trials in an experiment?

The Language of Physics

Objectives

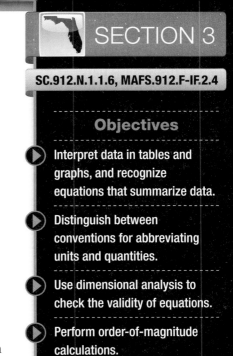

▶ Interpret data in tables and graphs, and recognize equations that summarize data.

▶ Distinguish between conventions for abbreviating units and quantities.

▶ Use dimensional analysis to check the validity of equations.

▶ Perform order-of-magnitude calculations.

Mathematics and Physics

Just as physicists create simplified models to better understand the real world, they use the tools of mathematics to analyze and summarize their observations. Then they can use the mathematical relationships among physical quantities to help predict what will happen in new situations.

Tables, graphs, and equations can make data easier to understand.

There are many ways to organize data. Consider the experiment shown in **Figure 3.1**, which tests Galileo's hypothesis that all objects fall at the same rate in the absence of air resistance. In this experiment, a table-tennis ball and a golf ball are dropped in a vacuum. The results are recorded as a set of numbers corresponding to the times of the fall and the distance each ball falls. A convenient way to organize the data is to form a table like **Figure 3.2**.

SC.912.N.1.1.6 Use tools to gather, analyze, and interpret data (this includes the use of measurement in metric and other systems, and also the generation and interpretation of graphical representations of data, including data tables and graphs).

FIGURE 3.2

DATA FROM DROPPED-BALL EXPERIMENT		
Time (s)	Distance golf ball falls (cm)	Distance table-tennis ball falls (cm)
0.067	2.20	2.20
0.133	8.67	8.67
0.200	19.60	19.59
0.267	34.93	34.92
0.333	54.34	54.33
0.400	78.40	78.39

FIGURE 3.1

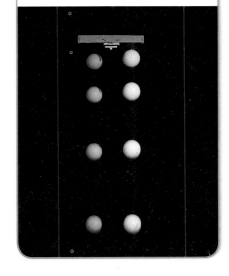

Two Balls Falling in a Vacuum This experiment tests Galileo's hypothesis by having two balls with different masses dropped simultaneously in a vacuum.

One method for analyzing the data in **Figure 3.2** is to construct a graph of the distance the balls have fallen versus the elapsed time since they were released. This graph is shown in **Figure 3.3** on the next page. Because the graph shows an obvious pattern, we can draw a smooth curve through the data points to make estimations for times when we have no data. The shape of the graph also provides information about the relationship between time and distance.

FIGURE 3.3

Graph of Dropped-Ball Data

The graph of these data provides a convenient way to summarize the data and indicate the relationship between the time an object has been falling and the distance it has fallen.

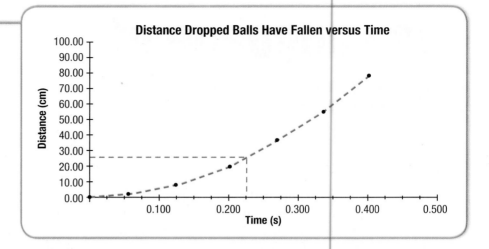

Distance Dropped Balls Have Fallen versus Time

We can also use the following equation to describe the relationship between the variables in the experiment:

(change in position in meters) = 4.9 × (time of fall in seconds)²

This equation allows you to reproduce the graph and make predictions about the change in position for any arbitrary time during the fall.

Physics equations describe relationships.

While mathematicians use equations to describe relationships between variables, physicists use the tools of mathematics to describe measured or predicted relationships between physical quantities in a situation. For example, one or more variables may affect the outcome of an experiment. In the case of a prediction, the physical equation is a compact statement based on a model of the situation. It shows how two or more variables are related. Many of the equations in physics represent a simple description of the relationship between physical quantities.

To make expressions as simple as possible, physicists often use letters to describe specific quantities in an equation. For example, the letter v is used to denote speed. Sometimes, Greek letters are used to describe mathematical operations. For example, the Greek letter Δ (delta) is often used to mean "difference or change in," and the Greek letter Σ (sigma) is used to mean "sum" or "total."

With these conventions, the word equation above can be written as follows:

$$\Delta y = 4.9(\Delta t)^2$$

The abbreviation Δy indicates the vertical change in a ball's position from its starting point, and Δt indicates the time elapsed.

The units in which these quantities are measured are also often abbreviated with symbols consisting of a letter or two. Most physics books provide some clues to help you keep track of which letters refer to quantities and variables and which letters are used to indicate units. Typically, variables and other specific quantities are abbreviated with letters that are **boldfaced** or *italicized*. (The difference between the two is described in the chapter "Two-Dimensional Motion and Vectors.") Units are abbreviated with regular letters (sometimes called roman letters). Some examples of variable symbols and the abbreviations for the units that measure them are shown in **Figure 3.4.**

As you continue to study physics, note the introduction of new variable quantities and recognize which units go with them. The tables provided in Appendices C–E can help you keep track of these abbreviations.

Variables with proportional relationships have predictable effects on each other.

In many physics equations, a change in one variable will cause another variable to change as well. Sometimes two variables will be *directly proportional*, meaning that if one variable is changed by a particular factor, the other variable will change by the same factor. In the chapter "Forces and the Laws of Motion," you will examine the relationship between force, mass, and acceleration, expressed as follows:

$$\text{Force} = \text{mass} \times \text{acceleration}$$

As this equation shows, doubling the force will double the acceleration for a given mass, because force and acceleration have a directly proportional relationship.

In an *inversely proportional* relationship, a change in one variable will be accompanied by an inverse change of the same factor in the other variable. Using the same equation as above, consider the relationship between mass and acceleration. If the force remains constant, doubling the mass will reduce the acceleration by half. When solving physics problems, identifying proportional relationships among variables can allow for an easy prediction of how a change in one variable will affect other variables within an equation.

Evaluating Physics Equations

Although an experiment is the ultimate way to check the validity of a physics equation, several techniques can be used to evaluate whether an equation or result can possibly be valid.

Dimensional analysis can weed out invalid equations.

Suppose a car, such as the one in **Figure 3.5,** is moving at a speed of 88 km/h and you want to know how much time it will take it to travel 725 km. How can you decide a good way to solve the problem?

You can use a powerful procedure called *dimensional analysis.* Dimensional analysis makes use of the fact that *dimensions can be treated as algebraic quantities.* For example, quantities can be added or subtracted only if they have the same dimensions, and the two sides of any given equation must have the same dimensions.

FIGURE 3.4

ABBREVIATIONS FOR VARIABLES AND UNITS

Quantity	Symbol	Units	Unit abbreviations
change in vertical position	Δy	meters	m
time interval	Δt	seconds	s
mass	m	kilograms	kg

FIGURE 3.5

Dimensional Analysis in Speed Calculations

Dimensional analysis can be a useful check for many types of problems, including those involving how much time it would take for this car to travel 725 km if it moves with a speed of 88 km/h.

Let us apply this technique to the problem of the car moving at a speed of 88 km/h. This measurement is given in dimensions of length over time. The total distance traveled has the dimension of length. Multiplying these numbers together gives the following dimensions:

$$\frac{\text{length}}{\text{time}} \times \text{length} = \frac{\text{length}^2}{\text{time}}$$

Clearly, the result of this calculation does not have the dimensions of time, which is what you are calculating. This equation is not a valid one for this situation.

To calculate an answer that will have the dimension of time, you should take the distance and divide it by the speed of the car, as follows:

$$\frac{\text{length}}{\text{length/time}} = \frac{\text{length} \times \text{time}}{\text{length}} = \text{time} \qquad \frac{725 \text{ km} \times 1.0 \text{ h}}{88 \text{ km}} = 8.2 \text{ h}$$

Did YOU Know?

The physicist Enrico Fermi made the first nuclear reactor at the University of Chicago in 1942. Fermi was also well known for his ability to make quick order-of-magnitude calculations, such as estimating the number of piano tuners in New York City.

In a simple example like this one, you might be able to identify the valid equation without dimensional analysis. But with more complicated problems, it is a good idea to check your final equation with dimensional analysis before calculating your answer. This step will prevent you from wasting time computing an invalid equation.

Order-of-magnitude estimations check answers.

Because the scope of physics is so wide and the numbers may be astronomically large or subatomically small, it is often useful to estimate an answer to a problem before trying to solve the problem exactly. This kind of estimate is called an *order-of-magnitude* calculation, which means determining the power of 10 that is closest to the actual numerical value of the quantity. Once you have done this, you will be in a position to judge whether the answer you get from a more exact procedure is correct.

For example, consider the car trip described in the discussion of dimensional analysis. We must divide the distance by the speed to find the time. The distance, 725 km, is closer to 10^3 km (or 1000 km) than to 10^2 km (or 100 km), so we use 10^3 km. The speed, 88 km/h, is about 10^2 km/h (or 100 km/h).

$$\frac{10^3 \text{ km}}{10^2 \text{ km/h}} = 10 \text{ h}$$

This estimate indicates that the answer should be closer to 10 than to 1 or to 100 (or 10^2). The correct answer (8.2 h) certainly fits this range.

Order-of-magnitude estimates can also be used to estimate numbers in situations in which little information is given. For example, how could you estimate how many gallons of gasoline are used annually by all of the cars in the United States?

To find an estimate, you will need to make some assumptions about the average household size, the number of cars per household, the distance traveled, and the average gas mileage.

First, consider that the United States has about 300 million people. Assuming that each family of about five people has two cars, an estimate of the number of cars in the country is 120 million.

Next, decide the order of magnitude of the average distance each car travels every year. Some cars travel as few as 1000 mi per year, while others travel more than 100 000 mi per year. The appropriate order of magnitude to include in the estimate is 10 000 mi, or 10^4 mi, per year.

If we assume that cars average 20 mi for every gallon of gas, each car needs about 500 gal per year.

$$\left(\frac{10\ 000\ \cancel{mi}}{1\ year}\right)\left(\frac{1\ gal}{20\ \cancel{mi}}\right) = 500\ gal/year\ for\ each\ car$$

Multiplying this by the estimate of the total number of cars in the United States gives an annual consumption of 6×10^{10} gal.

$$(12 \times 10^7\ \cancel{cars})\left(\frac{500\ gal}{1\ \cancel{car}}\right) = 6 \times 10^{10}\ gal$$

✓ SECTION 3 FORMATIVE ASSESSMENT

▶ Reviewing Main Ideas

1. Indicate which of the following physics symbols denote units and which denote variables or quantities.
 a. C   **b.** c   **c.** C   **d.** t   **e.** T   **f.** T

2. Determine the units of the quantity described by each of the following combinations of units:
 a. kg (m/s) (1/s)   **b.** (kg/s) (m/s^2)
 c. (kg/s) (m/s)^2 **d.** (kg/s) (m/s)

3. Which of the following is the best order-of-magnitude estimate in meters of the height of a mountain?
 a. 1 m   **b.** 10 m   **c.** 100 m   **d.** 1000 m

Interpreting Graphics

4. Which graph in **Figure 3.6** best matches the data?

Volume of air (m³)	Mass of air (kg)
0.50	0.644
1.50	1.936
2.25	2.899
4.00	5.159
5.50	7.096

✓ Critical Thinking

5. Which of the following equations best matches the data from item 4?
 a. (mass)^2 = 1.29 (volume)   **b.** (mass)(volume) = 1.29
 c. mass = 1.29 (volume)   **d.** mass = 1.29 (volume)^2

FIGURE 3.6

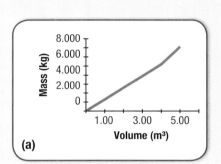

(a)

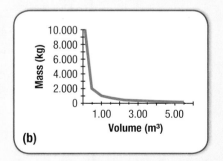

(b)

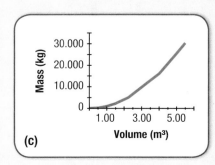

(c)

The Engineering Design Process

When scientists set out to understand phenomena, they usually follow certain steps called the scientific method. These steps involve making observations and collecting data, experimenting, interpreting results, and communicating their findings. When engineers begin a project, they often follow steps that are similar to the scientific method. These steps are referred to as the engineering design process. Some of these steps are the same as you might use when you design a solution to a problem in your daily life.

There are three phases of the engineering design process.

1. Engineers begin by defining a problem, such as How will a bridge be built to cross a certain chasm? In this first phase, they describe the criteria needed for the project to be a success and list the limitations of the project.

2. In the second phase, engineers research the problem and propose a number of possible solutions, such as several different types of bridges and what kind of materials each should be made of. In this phase, it is important to consider as many ideas as possible. Engineers usually don't settle on just one idea until after they look at many possibilities.

3. Finally, engineers test and refine solutions. To do this, they build prototypes, which are full-scale working models of the final product. A prototype might be made with cheaper materials than those used for the final product, or materials that are easier to work with. As they begin, engineers often make several simple prototypes to represent systems within the project. For example, one prototype can be a type of suspension bridge; another can be the kind of road surface that will be used on the bridge. Using the prototypes, engineers test their designs to see what works and what doesn't. They troubleshoot the designs and reflect on the lessons they learned with each try. When one method doesn't work, engineers can try other ideas that they had listed in the second phase.

Usually, engineers work with a deadline that marks the point when no more major changes can be made to the planned design. Before that deadline passes, the design can be changed with some flexibility.

Engineers communicate what they find out. They make drawings of their designs. In the drawings, they show how each system is connected to the others and explain how different parts represent critical design decisions.

- Think about how the scientific method and the engineering design process are similar. Which steps are the same? Which steps are different?

- Why is it important for engineers to consider even "wild dream" ideas for a design?

- Why would an engineer spend time building prototypes before making a final design?

CHAPTER 1 Summary

SECTION 1 What Is Physics?

- Physics is the study of the physical world, from motion and energy to light and electricity.
- Physics uses the scientific method to discover general laws that can be used to make predictions about a variety of situations.
- A common technique in physics for analyzing a complex situation is to disregard irrelevant factors and create a model that describes the essence of a system or situation.

KEY TERMS

model
system
hypothesis
controlled experiment

SECTION 2 Measurements in Experiments

- Physics measurements are typically made and expressed in SI, a system that uses a set of base units and prefixes to describe measurements of physical quantities.
- *Accuracy* describes how close a measurement is to reality. *Precision* results from the limitations of the measuring device used.
- The significant figures of a measurement include all of the digits that are actually measured plus one estimated digit.
- Significant-figure rules provide a means to ensure that calculations do not report results that are more precise than the data used to make them.

KEY TERMS

accuracy
precision
significant figures

SECTION 3 The Language of Physics

- Physicists make their work easier by summarizing data in tables and graphs and by abbreviating quantities in equations.
- Dimensional analysis can help identify whether a physics equation is invalid.
- Order-of-magnitude calculations provide a quick way to evaluate the appropriateness of an answer.

VARIABLE SYMBOLS			
Quantities		**Units**	
Δy	change in vertical position	m	meters
Δt	time interval	s	seconds
m	mass	kg	kilograms

Problem Solving

If you need more problem-solving practice, see **Appendix I: Additional Problems.**

The Science of Physics

▶ REVIEWING MAIN IDEAS

1. Refer to **Figure 1.3** of this chapter to identify at least two areas of physics involved in the following:
   a. building a louder stereo system in your car
   b. bungee jumping
   c. judging how hot an electric stove burner is by looking at it
   d. cooling off on a hot day by diving into a swimming pool

2. Which of the following scenarios fit the approach of the scientific method?
   a. An auto mechanic listens to how a car runs and comes up with an idea of what might be wrong. The mechanic tests the idea by adjusting the idle speed. Then the mechanic decides his idea was wrong based on this evidence. Finally, the mechanic decides the only other problem could be the fuel pump, and he consults with the shop's other mechanics about his conclusion.
   b. Because of a difference of opinions about where to take the class trip, the class president holds an election. The majority of the students decide to go to the amusement park instead of to the shore.
   c. Your school's basketball team has advanced to the regional playoffs. A friend from another school says their team will win because their players want to win more than your school's team does.
   d. A water fountain does not squirt high enough. The handle on the fountain seems loose, so you try to push the handle in as you turn it. When you do this, the water squirts high enough that you can get a drink. You make sure to tell all your friends how you did it.

3. You have decided to select a new car by using the scientific method. How might you proceed?

4. Consider the phrase "The quick brown fox jumps over the lazy dog." Which details of this situation would a physicist who is modeling the path of a fox ignore?

SI Units

▶ REVIEWING MAIN IDEAS

5. List an appropriate SI base unit (with a prefix as needed) for measuring the following:
   a. the time it takes to play a CD in your stereo
   b. the mass of a sports car
   c. the length of a soccer field
   d. the diameter of a large pizza
   e. the mass of a single slice of pepperoni
   f. a semester at your school
   g. the distance from your home to your school
   h. your mass
   i. the length of your physics lab room
   j. your height

6. If you square the speed expressed in meters per second, in what units will the answer be expressed?

7. If you divide a force measured in newtons (1 newton = 1 kg·m/s^2) by a speed expressed in meters per second, in what units will the answer be expressed?

CONCEPTUAL QUESTIONS

8. The height of a horse is sometimes given in units of "hands." Why was this a poor standard of length before it was redefined to refer to exactly 4 in.?

9. Explain the advantages in having the meter officially defined in terms of the distance light travels in a given time rather than as the length of a specific metal bar.

10. Einstein's famous equation indicates that $E = mc^2$, where c is the speed of light and m is the object's mass. Given this, what is the SI unit for E?

PRACTICE PROBLEMS

For problems 11–14, see Sample Problem A.

11. Express each of the following as indicated:
    a. 2 dm expressed in millimeters
    b. 2 h 10 min expressed in seconds
    c. 16 g expressed in micrograms
    d. 0.75 km expressed in centimeters
    e. 0.675 mg expressed in grams
    f. 462 μm expressed in centimeters
    g. 35 km/h expressed in meters per second

12. Use the SI prefixes in **Figure 2.4** of this chapter to convert these *hypothetical* units of measure into appropriate quantities:
    a. 10 rations
    b. 2000 mockingbirds
    c. 10^{-6} phones
    d. 10^{-9} goats
    e. 10^{18} miners

13. Use the fact that the speed of light in a vacuum is about 3.00×10^8 m/s to determine how many kilometers a pulse from a laser beam travels in exactly one hour.

14. If a metric ton is 1.000×10^3 kg, how many 85 kg people can safely occupy an elevator that can hold a maximum mass of exactly 1 metric ton?

Accuracy, Precision, and Significant Figures

▶ REVIEWING MAIN IDEAS

15. Can a set of measurements be precise but not accurate? Explain.

16. How many significant figures are in the following measurements?
    a. 300 000 000 m/s
    b. 3.00×10^8 m/s
    c. 25.030°C
    d. 0.006 070°C
    e. 1.004 J
    f. 1.305 20 MHz

17. The photographs below show unit conversions on the labels of some grocery-store items. Check the accuracy of these conversions. Are the manufacturers using significant figures correctly?

(a)

(b)

(c)

(d)

18. The value of the speed of light is now known to be $2.997\ 924\ 58 \times 10^8$ m/s. Express the speed of light in the following ways:
    a. with three significant figures
    b. with five significant figures
    c. with seven significant figures

19. How many significant figures are there in the following measurements?
    a. 78.9 ± 0.2 m
    b. 3.788×10^9 s
    c. 2.46×10^6 kg
    d. 0.0032 mm

20. Carry out the following arithmetic operations:
    a. Find the sum of the measurements 756 g, 37.2 g, 0.83 g, and 2.5 g.
    b. Find the quotient of 3.2 m/3.563 s.
    c. Find the product of 5.67 mm × π.
    d. Find the difference of 27.54 s and 3.8 s.

21. A fisherman catches two sturgeons. The smaller of the two has a measured length of 93.46 cm (two decimal places and four significant figures), and the larger fish has a measured length of 135.3 cm (one decimal place and four significant figures). What is the total length of the two fish?

22. A farmer measures the distance around a rectangular field. The length of each long side of the rectangle is found to be 38.44 m, and the length of each short side is found to be 19.5 m. What is the total distance around the field?

Dimensional Analysis and Order-of-Magnitude Estimates

Note: In developing answers to order-of-magnitude calculations, you should state your important assumptions, including the numerical values assigned to parameters used in the solution. Since only order-of-magnitude results are expected, do not be surprised if your results differ from those of other students.

▶ REVIEWING MAIN IDEAS

23. Suppose that two quantities, *A* and *B*, have different dimensions. Which of the following arithmetic operations *could* be physically meaningful?
   a. $A + B$
   b. A/B
   c. $A \times B$
   d. $A - B$

24. Estimate the order of magnitude of the length in meters of each of the following:
   a. a ladybug
   b. your leg
   c. your school building
   d. a giraffe
   e. a city block

25. If an equation is dimensionally correct, does this mean that the equation is true?

26. The radius of a circle inscribed in any triangle whose sides are *a*, *b*, and *c* is given by the following equation, in which *s* is an abbreviation for $(a + b + c) \div 2$. Check this formula for dimensional consistency.

$$r = \sqrt{\frac{(s-a)(s-b)(s-c)}{s}}$$

27. The period of a simple pendulum, defined as the time necessary for one complete oscillation, is measured in time units and is given by the equation

$$T = 2\pi \sqrt{\frac{L}{a_g}}$$

   where *L* is the length of the pendulum and a_g is the acceleration due to gravity, which has units of length divided by time squared. Check this equation for dimensional consistency.

CONCEPTUAL QUESTIONS

28. In a desperate attempt to come up with an equation to solve a problem during an examination, a student tries the following: (velocity in m/s)^2 = (acceleration in m/s^2) × (time in s). Use dimensional analysis to determine whether this equation might be valid.

29. Estimate the number of breaths taken by a person during 70 years.

30. Estimate the number of times your heart beats in an average day.

31. Estimate the magnitude of your age, as measured in units of seconds.

32. An automobile tire is rated to last for 50 000 mi. Estimate the number of revolutions the tire will make in its lifetime.

33. Imagine that you are the equipment manager of a professional baseball team. One of your jobs is to keep a supply of baseballs for games in your home ballpark. Balls are sometimes lost when players hit them into the stands as either home runs or foul balls. Estimate how many baseballs you have to buy per season in order to make up for such losses. Assume your team plays an 81-game home schedule in a season.

34. A chain of hamburger restaurants advertises that it has sold more than 50 billion hamburgers over the years. Estimate how many pounds of hamburger meat must have been used by the restaurant chain to make 50 billion hamburgers and how many head of cattle were required to furnish the meat for these hamburgers.

35. Estimate the number of piano tuners living in New York City. (The population of New York City is approximately 8 million.) This problem was first proposed by the physicist Enrico Fermi, who was well known for his ability to quickly make order-of-magnitude calculations.

36. Estimate the number of table-tennis balls that would fit (without being crushed) into a room that is 4 m long, 4 m wide, and 3 m high. Assume that the diameter of a ball is 3.8 cm.

Mixed Review

37. Calculate the circumference and area for the following circles. (Use the following formulas: circumference $= 2\pi r$ and area $= \pi r^2$.)
  a. a circle of radius 3.5 cm
  b. a circle of radius 4.65 cm

38. A billionaire offers to give you (1) $5 billion if you will count out the amount in $1 bills or (2) a lump sum of $5000. Which offer should you accept? Explain your answer. (Assume that you can count at an average rate of one bill per second, and be sure to allow for the fact that you need about 10 hours a day for sleeping and eating. Your answer does not need to be limited to one significant figure.)

39. Exactly 1 quart of ice cream is to be made in the form of a cube. What should be the length of one side in meters for the container to have the appropriate volume? (Use the following conversion: 4 qt $= 3.786 \times 10^{-3}$ m^3.)

40. You can obtain a rough estimate of the size of a molecule with the following simple experiment: Let a droplet of oil spread out on a fairly large but smooth water surface. The resulting "oil slick" that forms on the surface of the water will be approximately one molecule thick. Given an oil droplet with a mass of 9.00×10^{-7} kg and a density of 918 kg/m^3 that spreads out to form a circle with a radius of 41.8 cm on the water surface, what is the approximate diameter of an oil molecule?

GRAPHING CALCULATOR PRACTICE

Mass versus Length

What is the relationship between the mass and length of three wires, each of which is made of a different substance? All three wires have the same diameter. Because the wires have the same diameter, their cross-sectional areas are the same. The cross-sectional area of any circle is equal to πr^2. Consider a wire with a diameter of 0.50 cm and a density of 8.96 g/cm^3. The following equation describes the mass of the wire as a function of the length:

$$Y_1 = 8.96X \times \pi(0.25)^2$$

In this equation, Y_1 represents the mass of the wire in grams, and X represents the length of the wire in centimeters. Each of the three wires is made of a different substance, so each wire has a different density and a different relationship between its mass and length.

In this graphing calculator activity, you will
- use dimensional analysis
- observe the relationship between a mathematical function and a graph
- determine values from a graph
- gain a better conceptual understanding of density

Go online to HMHScience.com to find the skillsheet and program for this graphing calculator activity.

41. An ancient unit of length called the cubit was equal to approximately 50 centimeters, which is, of course, approximately 0.50 meters. It has been said that Noah's ark was 300 cubits long, 50 cubits wide, and 30 cubits high. Estimate the volume of the ark in cubic meters. Also estimate the volume of a typical home, and compare it with the ark's volume.

42. If one micrometeorite (a sphere with a diameter of 1.0×10^{-6} m) struck each square meter of the moon each second, it would take many years to cover the moon with micrometeorites to a depth of 1.0 m. Consider a cubic box, 1.0 m on a side, on the moon. Estimate how long it would take to completely fill the box with micrometeorites.

43. One cubic centimeter (1.0 cm^3) of water has a mass of 1.0×10^{-3} kg at 25°C. Determine the mass of 1.0 m^3 of water at 25°C.

44. Assuming biological substances are 90 percent water and the density of water is $1.0 \times 10^3 \text{ kg/m}^3$, estimate the masses (density multiplied by volume) of the following:

   a. a spherical cell with a diameter of 1.0 μm (volume $= \frac{4}{3}\pi r^3$)

   b. a fly, which can be approximated by a cylinder 4.0 mm long and 2.0 mm in diameter (volume $= l\pi r^2$)

45. The radius of the planet Saturn is 6.03×10^7 m, and its mass is 5.68×10^{26} kg.

   a. Find the density of Saturn (its mass divided by its volume) in grams per cubic centimeter. (The volume of a sphere is given by $\frac{4}{3}\pi r^3$.)

   b. Find the surface area of Saturn in square meters. (The surface area of a sphere is given by $4\pi r^2$.)

ALTERNATIVE ASSESSMENT

1. Imagine that you are a member of your state's highway board. In order to comply with a bill passed in the state legislature, all of your state's highway signs must show distances in miles and kilometers. Two plans are before you. One plan suggests adding metric equivalents to all highway signs as follows: Dallas 300 mi (483 km). Proponents of the other plan say that the first plan makes the metric system seem more cumbersome, so they propose replacing the old signs with new signs every 50 km as follows: Dallas 300 km (186 mi). Participate in a class debate about which plan should be followed.

2. Can you measure the mass of a five-cent coin with a bathroom scale? Record the mass in grams displayed by your scale as you place coins on the scale, one at a time. Then, divide each measurement by the number of coins to determine the approximate mass of a single five-cent coin, but remember to follow the rules for significant figures in calculations. Which estimate do you think is the most accurate? Which is the most precise?

3. Find out who were the Nobel laureates for physics last year, and research their work. Alternatively, explore the history of the Nobel Prizes. Who founded the awards? Why? Who delivers the award? Where? Document your sources, and present your findings in a brochure, poster, or presentation.

4. You have a clock with a second hand, a ruler marked in millimeters, a graduated cylinder marked in milliliters, and balances sensitive to 1 mg. How would you measure the mass of a drop of water? How would you measure the period of a swing? How would you measure the volume of a paper clip? How can you improve the accuracy of your measurements? Write the procedures clearly so that a partner can follow them and obtain reasonable results.

5. Create a poster or other presentation depicting the possible ranges of measurement for a dimension, such as distance, time, temperature, speed, or mass. Depict examples ranging from the very large to the very small. Include several examples that are typical of your own experiences.

Standards-Based Assessment

Record your answers on a separate piece of paper.

MULTIPLE CHOICE

1 A teacher arrives at school and flips on the light switch upon entering the classroom. The lights do not come on. The custodian's hypothesis is that a circuit breaker is open. However, the custodian finds that the classroom's breaker is not open. What is the next best step to solve the problem?

A Make sure the lights are plugged in.

B Check whether other breakers are open.

C Notify the school administrators.

D Develop a new hypothesis for why the lights don't turn on.

2 A student is measuring the mass of a standard brass mass labeled "50.0 g." When she measures the mass on a triple-beam balance, the balance reads 50.9 g, 51.0 g, 50.8 g, and 50.9 g in four successive measurements. The equipment and the brass mass have recently been calibrated by a professional. What is the most likely reason that her measurements don't agree with the label?

A The standard mass is damaged and no longer has the same value.

B The student is accidentally pressing on the scale.

C The student forgot to zero the balance before starting the measurements.

D They do agree with the standard, within experimental error.

3 A student plans to calculate the density of a solid brass square. When she measures the mass on a triple-beam balance, she gets 32.8 g, 32.0 g, 31.5 g and 33.1 g in four successive measurements. The label states that the mass is 33.4 g. Since her mass measurements are different from the label, how will this affect her density calculation?

A It won't have any effect since her weight measurement will differ also.

B It won't have any effect since her volume measurement will differ also.

C Her density measurement will be a bit lower than if she used the label.

D Her density measurement will be a bit higher than if she used the label.

4 The graph below shows the relationship between time and distance for a ball dropped vertically from rest.

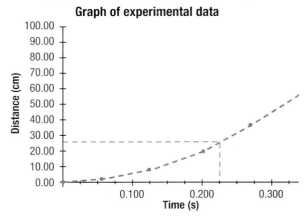

Graph of experimental data

About how far has the ball fallen after 0.200 s?

A 5.00 cm

C 20.00 cm

B 10.00 cm

D 30.00 cm

5 A physics student arrives home from a movie and turns on a lamp upon entering the house. The lights do not come on. His hypothesis is that the light bulb has burned out. Is that a valid hypothesis?

A yes, because that's almost always the problem when the light doesn't come on

B yes, because it can be tested by replacing the bulb

C no, because it is not scientific enough

D no, because it is probably just not plugged in

6 A student measures the volume of a copper cylinder by displacing water in a graduated cylinder. In successive measurements, the student gets results of 32.1 mL, 32.4 mL, 31.8 mL, and 31.9 mL. What is the best way to record the resulting volume of the cylinder?

A 32.1 mL

C 32.05 mL ±0.25 mL

B 32.05 mL

D 32.1 mL ±0.3 mL

GRIDDED RESPONSE

7 Calculate the following sum, and express the answer in meters. Follow the rules for significant figures.

$$(25.873 \text{ km}) + (1024 \text{ m}) + (3.0 \text{ cm})$$

Why It Matters

High-speed passenger trains such as the one shown here are used in many countries, including Japan, France, England, Germany, and South Korea. These trains have operational speeds from 200 to 300 km/h. A train moving along a straight track is an example of one-dimensional motion. The train in the diagram is covering greater distances in equal time intervals— in other words, it is accelerating.

Velocity and acceleration are involved in many aspects of everyday life, from riding a bicycle to driving a car to traveling on a high-speed train. The definitions and equations you will study in this chapter allow you to make predictions about these aspects of motion, given certain initial conditions.

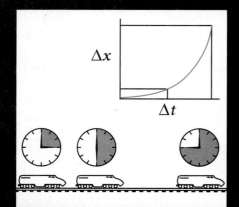

CHAPTER 2
Motion in One Dimension

BIG IDEA

The motion of an obje[ct]
can be described and
predicted using know[n]
relationships betwee[n]
the following variables[:]
displacement, velocity[,]
acceleration, and time[.]

ONLINE Physics
HMHScience.com

ONLINE LABS
- Motion
- Free-Fall Acceleration
- S.T.E.M. Lab Race-Car
  Construction

GO ONLINE **Animated**
Physics
HMHScience.com

Acceleration in One Dimension

SC.912.P.12.2, SC.912.P.12.9, MAFS.912.N-VM.1.3

Objectives

▶ Describe motion in terms of frame of reference, displacement, time, and velocity.

▶ Calculate the displacement of an object traveling at a known velocity for a specific time interval.

▶ Construct and interpret graphs of position versus time.

SC.912.P.12.2 Analyze the motion of an object in terms of its position, velocity, and acceleration (with respect to a frame of reference) as functions of time.
SC.912.P.12.9 Recognize that nothing travels faster than the speed of light in vacuum which is the same for all observers no matter how they or the light source are moving.
MAFS.912.N-VM.1.3 Solve problems involving velocity and other quantities that can be represented by vectors.

frame of reference a system for specifying the precise location of objects in space and time

Displacement and Velocity

Key Terms

frame of reference
displacement

average velocity
instantaneous velocity

Motion

Motion happens all around us. Every day, we see objects such as cars, people, and soccer balls move in different directions with different speeds. In this chapter, we will discover how to analyze motion as a physicist does.

One-dimensional motion is the simplest form of motion.

One way to simplify the concept of motion is to consider only the kinds of motion that take place in one direction. An example of this one-dimensional motion is the motion of a commuter train on a straight track, as in **Figure 1.1**.

In this one-dimensional motion, the train can move either forward or backward along the tracks. It cannot move left and right or up and down. This chapter deals only with one-dimensional motion. In later chapters, you will learn how to describe more complicated motions such as the motion of thrown baseballs and other projectiles.

Motion takes place over time and depends upon the frame of reference.

It seems simple to describe the motion of the train. As the train in **Figure 1.1** begins its route, it is at the first station. Later, it will be at another station farther down the tracks. But Earth is spinning on its axis, so the train, the stations, and the tracks are also moving around the axis. At the same time, Earth is moving around the sun. The sun and the rest of the solar system are moving through our galaxy. This galaxy is traveling through space as well.

When faced with a complex situation like this, physicists break it down into simpler parts. One key approach is to choose a **frame of reference** against which you can measure changes in position. In the case of the train, any of the stations along its route could serve as a convenient frame of reference. When you select a reference frame, note that it remains fixed for the problem in question and has an origin, or starting point, from which the motion is measured.

FIGURE 1.1

Frames of Reference The motion of a commuter train traveling along a straight route is an example of one-dimensional motion. Each train can move only forward and backward along the tracks.

If an object is at rest (not moving), its position does not change with respect to a fixed frame of reference. For example, the benches on the platform of one subway station never move down the tracks to another station.

In physics, any frame of reference can be chosen as long as it is used consistently. If you are consistent, you will get the same results, no matter which frame of reference you choose. But some frames of reference can make explaining things easier than other frames of reference.

For example, when considering the motion of the gecko in **Figure 1.2**, it is useful to imagine a stick marked in centimeters placed under the gecko's feet to define the frame of reference. The measuring stick serves as an x-axis. You can use it to identify the gecko's initial position and its final position.

Displacement

As any object moves from one position to another, the length of the straight line drawn from its initial position to the object's final position is called the **displacement** of the object.

Displacement is a change in position.

The gecko in **Figure 1.2** moves from left to right along the x-axis from an initial position, x_i, to a final position, x_f. The gecko's displacement is the difference between its final and initial coordinates, or $x_f - x_i$. In this case, the displacement is about 61 cm (85 cm − 24 cm). The Greek letter *delta* (Δ) before the x denotes a change in the position of an object.

Displacement

$$\Delta x = x_f - x_i$$

displacement = change in position = final position − initial position

FIGURE 1.2

Measuring Displacement

A gecko moving along the x-axis from x_i to x_f undergoes a displacement of $\Delta x = x_f - x_i$.

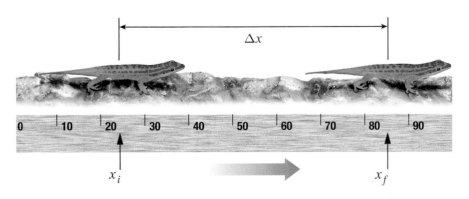

Space Shuttle A space shuttle took off from Florida and circled Earth several times, finally landing in California. While the shuttle was in flight, a photographer flew from the launch point in Florida to the landing point in California to take pictures of the astronauts as they stepped off the shuttle. Who underwent the greater displacement, the photographer or the astronauts?

Roundtrip What is the difference between the displacement of the photographer flying from Florida to California and the displacement of the astronauts flying from California to Florida?

displacement the change in position of an object

Tips and Tricks

A change in any quantity, indicated by the Greek letter delta (Δ), is equal to the final value minus the initial value. When calculating displacement, always be sure to subtract the initial position from the final position so that your answer has the correct sign.

FIGURE 1.3

Comparing Displacement and Distance

When the gecko is climbing a tree, the displacement is measured on the *y*-axis. Again, the gecko's position is determined by the position of the same point on its body.

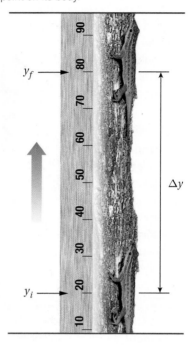

Now suppose the gecko runs up a tree, as shown in **Figure 1.3**. In this case, we place the measuring stick parallel to the tree. The measuring stick can serve as the *y*-axis of our coordinate system. The gecko's initial and final positions are indicated by y_i and y_f, respectively, and the gecko's displacement is denoted as Δy.

Displacement is not always equal to the distance traveled.

Displacement does not always tell you the distance an object has moved. For example, what if the gecko in **Figure 1.3** runs up the tree from the 20 cm marker (its initial position) to the 80 cm marker. After that, it retreats down the tree to the 50 cm marker (its final position). It has traveled a total distance of 90 cm. However, its displacement is only 30 cm ($y_f - y_i = 50$ cm $- 20$ cm $= 30$ cm). If the gecko were to return to its starting point, its displacement would be zero because its initial position and final position would be the same.

Displacement can be positive or negative.

Displacement also includes a description of the direction of motion. In one-dimensional motion, there are only two directions in which an object can move, and these directions can be described as positive or negative.

In this book, unless otherwise stated, the right (or east) will be considered the positive direction, and the left (or west) will be considered the negative direction. Similarly, upward (or north) will be considered positive, and downward (or south) will be considered negative. **Figure 1.4** gives examples of determining displacements for a variety of situations.

FIGURE 1.4

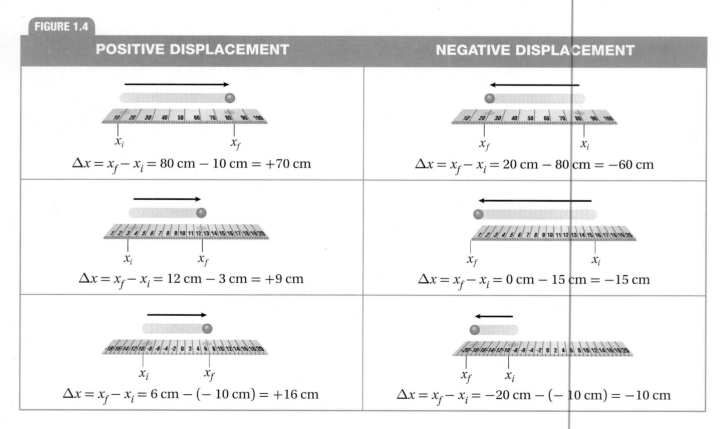

POSITIVE DISPLACEMENT	NEGATIVE DISPLACEMENT
$\Delta x = x_f - x_i = 80$ cm $- 10$ cm $= +70$ cm	$\Delta x = x_f - x_i = 20$ cm $- 80$ cm $= -60$ cm
$\Delta x = x_f - x_i = 12$ cm $- 3$ cm $= +9$ cm	$\Delta x = x_f - x_i = 0$ cm $- 15$ cm $= -15$ cm
$\Delta x = x_f - x_i = 6$ cm $- (-10$ cm$) = +16$ cm	$\Delta x = x_f - x_i = -20$ cm $- (-10$ cm$) = -10$ cm

Velocity

Where an object started and where it stopped does not completely describe the motion of the object. For example, the ground that you're standing on may move 8.0 cm to the left. This motion could take several years and be a sign of the normal slow movement of Earth's tectonic plates. If this motion takes place in just a second, however, you may be experiencing an earthquake or a landslide. Knowing the speed is important when evaluating motion.

Average velocity is displacement divided by the time interval.

Consider the car in **Figure 1.5**. The car is moving along a highway in a straight line (the x-axis). Suppose that the positions of the car are x_i at time t_i and x_f at time t_f. In the time interval $\Delta t = t_f - t_i$, the displacement of the car is $\Delta x = x_f - x_i$. The **average velocity,** v_{avg}, is defined as the displacement divided by the time interval during which the displacement occurred. In SI, the unit of velocity is meters per second, abbreviated as m/s.

average velocity the total displacement divided by the time interval during which the displacement occurred

Average Velocity

$$v_{avg} = \frac{\Delta x}{\Delta t} = \frac{x_f - x_i}{t_f - t_i}$$

$$\text{average velocity} = \frac{\text{change in position}}{\text{change in time}} = \frac{\text{displacement}}{\text{time interval}}$$

Tips and Tricks

Average velocity is not always equal to the average of the initial and final velocities. For instance, if you drive first at 40 km/h west and later at 60 km/h west, your average velocity is not necessarily 50 km/h west.

The average velocity of an object can be positive or negative, depending on the sign of the displacement. (The time interval is always positive.) As an example, consider a car trip to a friend's house 370 km to the west (the negative direction) along a straight highway. If you left your house at 10 A.M. and arrived at your friend's house at 3 P.M., your average velocity would be as follows:

$$v_{avg} = \frac{\Delta x}{\Delta t} = \frac{-370 \text{ km}}{5.0 \text{ h}} = -74 \text{ km/h} = 74 \text{ km/h west}$$

This value is an average. You probably did not travel exactly 74 km/h at every moment. You may have stopped to buy gas or have lunch. At other times, you may have traveled more slowly as a result of heavy traffic. To make up for such delays, when you were traveling slower than 74 km/h, there must also have been other times when you traveled faster than 74 km/h.

The average velocity is equal to the constant velocity needed to cover the given displacement in a given time interval. In the example above, if you left your house and maintained a velocity of 74 km/h to the west at every moment, it would take you 5.0 h to travel 370 km.

FIGURE 1.5

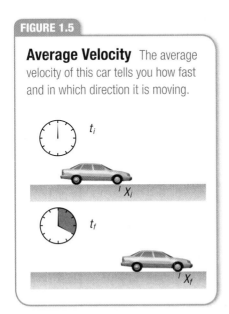

Average Velocity The average velocity of this car tells you how fast and in which direction it is moving.

Average Velocity and Displacement

Sample Problem A During a race on level ground, Andrea runs with an average velocity of 6.02 m/s to the east. What is Andrea's displacement after 137 s?

① ANALYZE

Given: $v_{avg} = 6.02 \text{ m/s}$

$\Delta t = 137 \text{ s}$

Unknown: $\Delta x = ?$

Tips and Tricks

The calculator answer is 824.74 m, but both the values for velocity and time have three significant figures, so the displacement must be reported as 825 m.

② SOLVE

Rearrange the average velocity equation to solve for displacement.

$$v_{avg} = \frac{\Delta x}{\Delta t}$$

$$\Delta x = v_{avg} \Delta t$$

$$\Delta x = v_{avg} \Delta t = (6.02 \text{ m/s})(137 \text{ s}) = \boxed{825 \text{ m to the east}}$$

Practice

1. Heather and Matthew walk with an average velocity of 0.98 m/s eastward. If it takes them 34 min to walk to the store, what is their displacement?

2. If Joe rides his bicycle in a straight line for 15 min with an average velocity of 12.5 km/h south, how far has he ridden?

3. It takes you 9.5 min to walk with an average velocity of 1.2 m/s to the north from the bus stop to the museum entrance. What is your displacement?

4. Simpson drives his car with an average velocity of 48.0 km/h to the east. How long will it take him to drive 144 km on a straight highway?

5. Look back at item 4. How much time would Simpson save by increasing his average velocity to 56.0 km/h to the east?

6. A bus travels 280 km south along a straight path with an average velocity of 88 km/h to the south. The bus stops for 24 min. Then, it travels 210 km south with an average velocity of 75 km/h to the south.

   a. How long does the total trip last?

   b. What is the average velocity for the total trip?

Velocity is not the same as speed.

In everyday language, the terms *speed* and *velocity* are used interchangeably. In physics, however, there is an important distinction between these two terms. As we have seen, velocity describes motion with both a direction and a numerical value (a magnitude) indicating how fast something moves. However, speed has no direction, only magnitude. An object's average speed is equal to the distance traveled divided by the time interval for the motion.

$$\text{average speed} = \frac{\text{distance traveled}}{\text{time of travel}}$$

Velocity can be interpreted graphically.

The velocity of an object can be determined if the object's position is known at specific times along its path. One way to determine this is to make a graph of the motion. **Figure 1.6** represents such a graph. Notice that time is plotted on the horizontal axis and position is plotted on the vertical axis.

The object moves 4.0 m in the time interval between $t = 0$ s and $t = 4.0$ s. Likewise, the object moves an additional 4.0 m in the time interval between $t = 4.0$ s and $t = 8.0$ s. From these data, we see that the average velocity for each of these time intervals is $+1.0$ m/s (because $v_{avg} = \Delta x / \Delta t = 4.0$ m/4.0 s). Because the average velocity does not change, the object is moving with a constant velocity of $+1.0$ m/s, and its motion is represented by a straight line on the position-time graph.

For any position-time graph, we can also determine the average velocity by drawing a straight line between any two points on the graph. The slope of this line indicates the average velocity between the positions and times represented by these points. To better understand this concept, compare the equation for the slope of the line with the equation for the average velocity.

Slope of a Line

$$\text{slope} = \frac{\text{rise}}{\text{run}} = \frac{\text{change in vertical coordinates}}{\text{change in horizontal coordinates}}$$

Average Velocity

$$v_{avg} = \frac{\Delta x}{\Delta t} = \frac{x_f - x_i}{t_f - t_i}$$

FIGURE 1.6

Position-Time Graph The motion of an object moving with constant velocity will provide a straight-line graph of position versus time. The slope of this graph indicates the velocity.

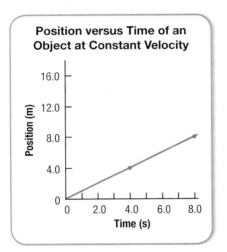

Position versus Time of an Object at Constant Velocity

Conceptual Challenge

Book on a Table A book is moved once around the edge of a tabletop with dimensions 1.75 m × 2.25 m. If the book ends up at its initial position, what is its displacement? If it completes its motion in 23 s, what is its average velocity? What is its average speed?

Travel Car A travels from New York to Miami at a speed of 25 m/s. Car B travels from New York to Chicago, also at a speed of 25 m/s. Are the velocities of the cars equal? Explain.

FIGURE 1.7

Position-Time Graphs
These position-versus-time graphs show that Object 1 moves with a constant positive velocity. Object 2 is at rest. Object 3 moves with a constant negative velocity.

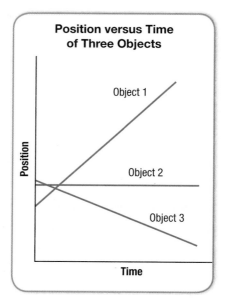

Position versus Time of Three Objects

instantaneous velocity the velocity of an object at some instant or at a specific point in the object's path

Figure 1.7 represents straight-line graphs of position versus time for three different objects. Object 1 has a constant positive velocity because its position increases uniformly with time. Thus, the slope of this line is positive. Object 2 has zero velocity because its position does not change (the object is at rest). Hence, the slope of this line is zero. Object 3 has a constant negative velocity because its position decreases with time. As a result, the slope of this line is negative.

Instantaneous velocity may not be the same as average velocity.

Now consider an object whose position-versus-time graph is not a straight line but a curve, as in **Figure 1.8**. The object moves through larger and larger displacements as each second passes. Thus, its velocity increases with time.

For example, between $t = 0$ s and $t = 2.0$ s, the object moves 8.0 m, and its average velocity in this time interval is 4.0 m/s (because $v_{avg} = 8.0$ m/2.0 s). However, between $t = 0$ s and $t = 4.0$ s, it moves 32 m, so its average velocity in this time interval is 8.0 m/s (because $v_{avg} = 32$ m/4.0 s). We obtain different average velocities, depending on the time interval we choose. But how can we find the velocity at an instant of time?

To determine the velocity at some instant, such as $t = 3.0$ s, we study a small time interval near that instant. As the intervals become smaller and smaller, the average velocity over that interval approaches the exact velocity at $t = 3.0$ s. This is called the **instantaneous velocity.** One way to determine the instantaneous velocity is to construct a straight line that is *tangent* to the position-versus-time graph at that instant. The slope of this tangent line is equal to the value of the instantaneous velocity at that point. For example, the instantaneous velocity of the object in **Figure 1.8** at $t = 3.0$ s is 12 m/s. The table lists the instantaneous velocities of the object described by the graph in **Figure 1.8**. You can verify some of these values by measuring the slope of the curve.

FIGURE 1.8

Finding Instantaneous Velocity
The instantaneous velocity at a given time can be determined by measuring the slope of the line that is tangent to that point on the position-versus-time graph.

VELOCITY-TIME DATA	
t (s)	*v* (m/s)
0.0	0.0
1.0	4.0
2.0	8.0
3.0	12.0
4.0	16.0

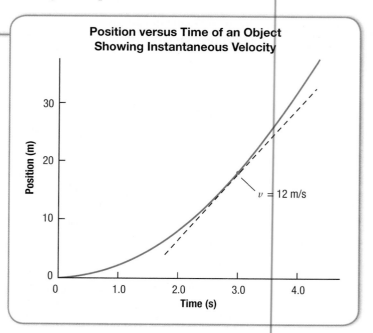

Position versus Time of an Object Showing Instantaneous Velocity

$v = 12$ m/s

▶ **Reviewing Main Ideas**

1. What is the shortest possible time in which a bacterium could travel a distance of 8.4 cm across a Petri dish at a constant speed of 3.5 mm/s?

2. A child is pushing a shopping cart at a speed of 1.5 m/s. How long will it take this child to push the cart down an aisle with a length of 9.3 m?

3. An athlete swims from the north end to the south end of a 50.0 m pool in 20.0 s and makes the return trip to the starting position in 22.0 s.
   a. What is the average velocity for the first half of the swim?
   b. What is the average velocity for the second half of the swim?
   c. What is the average velocity for the roundtrip?

4. Two students walk in the same direction along a straight path at a constant speed—one at 0.90 m/s and the other at 1.90 m/s.
   a. Assuming that they start at the same point and the same time, how much sooner does the faster student arrive at a destination 780 m away?
   b. How far would the students have to walk so that the faster student arrives 5.50 min before the slower student?

✔ **Critical Thinking**

5. Does knowing the distance between two objects give you enough information to locate the objects? Explain.

Interpreting Graphics

6. **Figure 1.9** shows position-time graphs of the straight-line movement of two brown bears in a wildlife preserve. Which bear has the greater average velocity over the entire period? Which bear has the greater velocity at $t = 8.0$ min? Is the velocity of bear A always positive? Is the velocity of bear B ever negative?

FIGURE 1.9

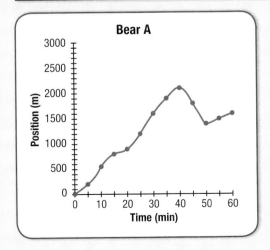

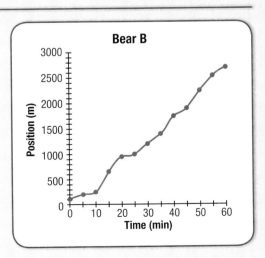

Acceleration

Objectives

▶ Describe motion in terms changing velocity.

▶ Compare graphical representations of accelerated and nonaccelerated motions.

▶ Apply kinematic equations to calculate distance, time, or velocity under conditions of constant acceleration.

SC.912.P.12.2 Analyze the motion of an object in terms of its position, velocity, and acceleration (with respect to a frame of reference) as functions of time.
MAFS.912.N-VM.1.3 Solve problems involving velocity and other quantities that can be represented by vectors.

acceleration the rate at which velocity changes over time; an object accelerates if its speed, its direction, or both change

Key Term
acceleration

Changes in Velocity

Many bullet trains have a top speed of about 300 km/h. Because a train stops to load and unload passengers, it does not always travel at that top speed. For some of the time the train is in motion, its velocity is either increasing or decreasing. It loses speed as it slows down to stop and gains speed as it pulls away and heads for the next station.

Acceleration is the rate of change of velocity with respect to time.

When a shuttle bus approaches a stop, the driver begins to apply the brakes to slow down 5.0 s before actually reaching the stop. The speed changes from 9.0 m/s to 0 m/s over a time interval of 5.0 s. Sometimes, however, the shuttle stops much more quickly. For example, if the driver slams on the brakes to avoid hitting a dog, the bus slows from 9.0 m/s to 0 m/s in just 1.5 s.

Clearly, these two stops are very different, even though the shuttle's velocity changes by the same amount in both cases. What is different in these two examples is the time interval during which the change in velocity occurs. As you can imagine, this difference has a great effect on the motion of the bus, as well as on the comfort and safety of the passengers. A sudden change in velocity feels very different from a slow, gradual change.

The rate of change of velocity is called **acceleration.** The magnitude of the average acceleration is calculated by dividing the total change in an object's velocity by the time interval in which the change occurs.

Average Acceleration

$$a_{avg} = \frac{\Delta v}{\Delta t} = \frac{v_f - v_i}{t_f - t_i}$$

$$\text{average acceleration} = \frac{\text{change in velocity}}{\text{time required for change}}$$

Acceleration has dimensions of length divided by time squared. The units of acceleration in SI are meters per second per second, which is written as meters per second squared, as shown below. When measured in these units, acceleration describes how much the velocity changes in each second.

$$\frac{(m/s)}{s} = \frac{m}{s} \times \frac{1}{s} = \frac{m}{s^2}$$

Average Acceleration

GO ONLINE

Interactive Demo
HMHScience.com

SOLUTION
TUTOR

HMHScience.com

Sample Problem B A shuttle bus slows down with an average acceleration of $-1.8\ \text{m/s}^2$. How long does it take the bus to slow from 9.0 m/s to a complete stop?

① ANALYZE

Given:

$$v_i = 9.0\ \text{m/s}$$

$$v_f = 0\ \text{m/s}$$

$$a_{avg} = -1.8\ \text{m/s}^2$$

Unknown: $\Delta t = ?$

② SOLVE

Rearrange the average acceleration equation to solve for the time interval.

$$a_{avg} = \frac{\Delta v}{\Delta t}$$

$$\Delta t = \frac{\Delta v}{a_{avg}} = \frac{v_f - v_i}{a_{avg}} = \frac{0\ \text{m/s} - 9.0\ \text{m/s}}{-1.8\ \text{m/s}^2}$$

$$\boxed{\Delta t = 5.0\ \text{m/s}}$$

Practice

1. As the shuttle bus comes to a sudden stop to avoid hitting a dog, it accelerates uniformly at $-4.1\ \text{m/s}^2$ as it slows from 9.0 m/s to 0.0 m/s. Find the time interval of acceleration for the bus.

2. A car traveling at 7.0 m/s accelerates uniformly at $2.5\ \text{m/s}^2$ to reach a speed of 12.0 m/s. How long does it take for this acceleration to occur?

3. With an average acceleration of $-1.2\ \text{m/s}^2$, how long will it take a cyclist to bring a bicycle with an initial speed of 6.5 m/s to a complete stop?

4. Turner's treadmill runs with a velocity of $-1.2\ \text{m/s}$ and speeds up at regular intervals during a half-hour workout. After 25 min, the treadmill has a velocity of $-6.5\ \text{m/s}$. What is the average acceleration of the treadmill during this period?

5. Suppose a treadmill has an average acceleration of $4.7 \times 10^{-3}\ \text{m/s}^2$.
   a. How much does its speed change after 5.0 min?
   b. If the treadmill's initial speed is 1.7 m/s, what will its final speed be?

FIGURE 2.1

High-Speed Train High-speed trains such as this one can travel at speeds of about 300 km/h (186 mi/h).

Fly Ball If a baseball has zero velocity at some instant, is the acceleration of the baseball necessarily zero at that instant? Explain, and give examples.

Runaway Train If a passenger train is traveling on a straight track with a negative velocity and a positive acceleration, is it speeding up or slowing down?

Hike-and-Bike Trail When Jennifer is out for a ride, she slows down on her bike as she approaches a group of hikers on a trail. Explain how her acceleration can be positive even though her speed is decreasing.

Acceleration has direction and magnitude.

Figure 2.1 shows a high-speed train leaving a station. Imagine that the train is moving to the right so that the displacement and the velocity are positive. The velocity increases in magnitude as the train picks up speed. Therefore, the final velocity will be greater than the initial velocity, and Δv will be positive. When Δv is positive, the acceleration is positive.

On long trips with no stops, the train may travel for a while at a constant velocity. In this situation, because the velocity is not changing, $\Delta v = 0$ m/s. When the velocity is constant, the acceleration is equal to zero.

Imagine that the train, still traveling in the positive direction, slows down as it approaches the next station. In this case, the velocity is still positive, but the initial velocity is larger than the final velocity, so Δv will be negative. When Δv is negative, the acceleration is negative.

The slope and shape of the graph describe the object's motion.

As with all motion graphs, the slope and shape of the velocity-time graph in **Figure 2.2** allow a detailed analysis of the train's motion over time. When the train leaves the station, its speed is increasing over time. The line on the graph plotting this motion slopes up and to the right, as at point **A** on the graph.

When the train moves with a constant velocity, the line on the graph continues to the right, but it is horizontal, with a slope equal to zero. This indicates that the train's velocity is constant, as at point **B** on the graph.

Finally, as the train approaches the station, its velocity decreases over time. The graph segment representing this motion slopes down to the right, as at point **C** on the graph. This downward slope indicates that the velocity is decreasing over time.

Acceleration can be positive or negative.

A negative value for the acceleration does not always indicate a decrease in speed. For example, if the train were moving in the negative direction, the acceleration would be negative when the train gained speed to leave a station and positive when the train lost speed to enter a station.

FIGURE 2.2

Velocity-Time Graphs When the velocity in the positive direction is increasing, the acceleration is positive, as at point **A**. When the velocity is constant, there is no acceleration, as at point **B**. When the velocity in the positive direction is decreasing, the acceleration is negative, as at point **C**.

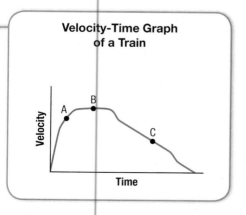

Velocity-Time Graph of a Train

Figure 2.3 shows how the signs of the velocity and acceleration can be combined to give a description of an object's motion. From this table, you can see that a negative acceleration can describe an object that is speeding up (when the velocity is negative) or an object that is slowing down (when the velocity is positive). Use this table to check your answers to problems involving acceleration.

For example, in **Figure 2.2,** the initial velocity v_i of the train is positive. At point **A** on the graph, the train's velocity is still increasing, so its acceleration is positive as well. The first entry in **Figure 2.3** shows that in this situation, the train is speeding up. At point **C**, the velocity is still positive, but it is decreasing, so the train's acceleration is negative. **Figure 2.3** tells you that in this case, the train is slowing down.

Decreases in speed are sometimes called decelerations. Despite the sound of the name, decelerations are really a special case of acceleration in which the magnitude of the velocity—and thus the speed—decreases with time.

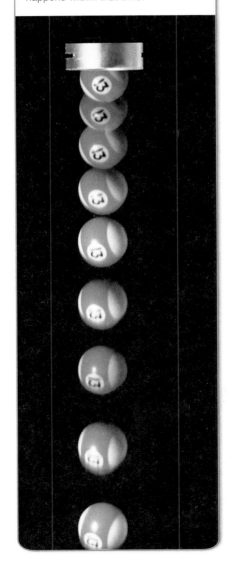

FIGURE 2.4

Motion of a Falling Ball

The motion in this picture took place in about 1.00 s. In this short time interval, your eyes could only detect a blur. This photo shows what really happens within that time.

FIGURE 2.3

SIGNS OF VELOCITY AND ACCELERATION

v_i	a	Motion
+	+	speeding up
−	−	speeding up
+	−	slowing down
−	+	slowing down
− or +	0	constant velocity
0	− or +	speeding up from rest
0	0	remaining at rest

Acceleration can be constant.

Figure 2.4 is a strobe photograph of a ball moving in a straight line with constant acceleration. While the ball was moving, its image was captured ten times in one second, so the time interval between successive images is 0.10 s. As the ball's velocity increases, the ball travels a greater distance during each time interval. In this example, the velocity increases by exactly the same amount during each time interval. Thus, the acceleration is constant. Because the velocity increases for each time interval, the successive change in displacement for each time interval increases. You can see this in the photograph by noting that the distance between images increases while the time interval between images remains constant. The relationships between displacement, velocity, and constant acceleration are expressed by equations that apply to any object moving with constant acceleration.

FIGURE 2.5

Constant Acceleration and Average Velocity If a ball moved for the same time with a constant velocity equal to v_{avg}, it would have the same displacement as the ball in **Figure 2.4** moving with constant acceleration.

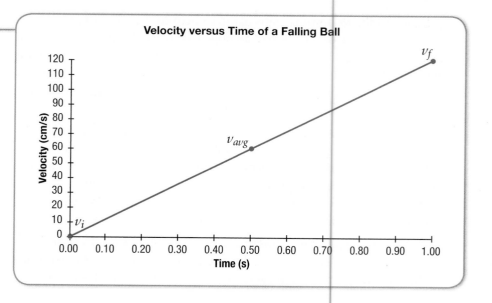

Displacement depends on acceleration, initial velocity, and time.

Figure 2.5 is a graph of the ball's velocity plotted against time. The initial, final, and average velocities are marked on the graph. We know that the average velocity is equal to displacement divided by the time interval.

$$v_{avg} = \frac{\Delta x}{\Delta t}$$

For an object moving with constant acceleration, the average velocity is equal to the average of the initial velocity and the final velocity.

$$v_{avg} = \frac{v_i + v_f}{2} \qquad \text{average velocity} = \frac{\text{initial velocity} + \text{final velocity}}{2}$$

To find an expression for the displacement in terms of the initial and final velocity, we can set the expressions for average velocity equal to each other.

$$\frac{\Delta x}{\Delta t} = v_{avg} = \frac{v_i + v_f}{2}$$

$$\frac{\text{displacement}}{\text{time interval}} = \frac{\text{initial velocity} + \text{final velocity}}{2}$$

Multiplying both sides of the equation by Δt gives us an expression for the displacement as a function of time. This equation can be used to find the displacement of any object moving with constant acceleration.

Displacement with Constant Acceleration

$$\Delta x = \tfrac{1}{2}(v_i + v_f)\Delta t$$

displacement = $\tfrac{1}{2}$(initial velocity + final velocity)(time interval)

Displacement with Constant Acceleration

 GO ONLINE

Interactive Demo
HMHScience.com

Sample Problem C A racing car reaches a speed of 42 m/s. It then begins a uniform negative acceleration, using its parachute and braking system, and comes to rest 5.5 s later. Find the distance that the car travels during braking.

1 ANALYZE

Given:

$$v_i = 42 \text{ m/s}$$

$$v_f = 0 \text{ m/s}$$

$$\Delta t = 5.5 \text{ s}$$

Unknown: $\Delta x = ?$

2 SOLVE

Use the equation that relates displacement, initial and final velocities, and the time interval.

$$\Delta x = \frac{1}{2}(v_i + v_f)\Delta t$$

$$\Delta x = \frac{1}{2}(42 \text{ m/s} + 0 \text{ m/s})(5.5 \text{ s})$$

$$\boxed{\Delta x = 120 \text{ m}}$$

Tips and Tricks

Remember that this equation applies only when acceleration is constant. In this problem, you know that acceleration is constant by the phrase "uniform negative acceleration." All of the kinematic equations introduced in this chapter are valid only for constant acceleration.

Calculator Solution

The calculator answer is 115.5. However, the initial velocity and time values have only two significant figures each, so the answer is reported as 120 m.

Practice

1. A car accelerates uniformly from rest to a speed of 6.6 m/s in 6.5 s. Find the distance the car travels during this time.

2. When Maggie applies the brakes of her car, the car slows uniformly from 15.0 m/s to 0.0 m/s in 2.50 s. How many meters before a stop sign must she apply her brakes in order to stop at the sign?

3. A driver in a car traveling at a speed of 21.8 m/s sees a cat 101 m away on the road. How long will it take for the car to accelerate uniformly to a stop in exactly 99 m?

4. A car enters the freeway with a speed of 6.4 m/s and accelerates uniformly for 3.2 km in 3.5 min. How fast (in m/s) is the car moving after this time?

Final velocity depends on initial velocity, acceleration, and time.

What if the final velocity of the ball is not known but we still want to calculate the displacement? If we know the initial velocity, the acceleration, and the elapsed time, we can find the final velocity. We can then use this value for the final velocity to find the total displacement of the ball.

By rearranging the equation for acceleration, we can find a value for the final velocity.

$$a = \frac{\Delta v}{\Delta t} = \frac{v_f - v_i}{\Delta t}$$

$$a\Delta t = v_f - v_i$$

By adding the initial velocity to both sides of the equation, we get an equation for the final velocity of the ball.

$$a\Delta t + v_i = v_f$$

Velocity with Constant Acceleration

$$v_f = v_i + a\Delta t$$

final velocity = initial velocity + (acceleration × time interval)

You can use this equation to find the final velocity of an object after it has accelerated at a constant rate for any time interval.

If you want to know the displacement of an object moving with constant acceleration over some certain time interval, you can obtain another useful expression for displacement by substituting the expression for v_f into the expression for Δx.

$$\Delta x = \tfrac{1}{2}(v_i + v_f)\Delta t$$

$$\Delta x = \tfrac{1}{2}(v_i + v_i + a\Delta t)\Delta t$$

$$\Delta x = \tfrac{1}{2}[2v_i\Delta t + a(\Delta t)^2]$$

Displacement with Constant Acceleration

$$\Delta x = v_i\Delta t + \tfrac{1}{2}a(\Delta t)^2$$

displacement = (initial velocity × time interval) + $\tfrac{1}{2}$ acceleration × (time interval)²

This equation is useful not only for finding the displacement of an object moving with constant acceleration but also for finding the displacement required for an object to reach a certain speed or to come to a stop. For the latter situation, you need to use both this equation and the equation given above.

Velocity and Displacement with Constant Acceleration

GO ONLINE

Interactive Demo
HMHScience.com

Sample Problem D A barge moving with a speed of 1.00 m/s increases speed uniformly, so that in 30.0 s it has traveled 60.2 m. What is the magnitude of the barge's acceleration?

❶ ANALYZE

Given: $v_i = 1.00$ m/s

$\Delta t = 30.0$ s

$\Delta x = 60.2$ m

Unknown: $a = ?$

❷ SOLVE

Use the equation for displacement with constant uniform acceleration.

$$\Delta x = v_i \Delta t + \frac{1}{2} a \Delta t^2$$

Rearrange the equation to solve for a.

$$\frac{1}{2} a \Delta t^2 = \Delta x - v_i \Delta t$$

$$a = \frac{2(\Delta x - v_i \Delta t)}{\Delta t^2}$$

$$a = \frac{(2)[60.2 \text{ m} - (1.00 \text{ m/s})(30.0 \text{ s})]}{(30.0 \text{ s})^2}$$

$$a = \frac{(2)(60.2 \text{ m} - 30.0 \text{ m})}{9.00 \times 10^2 \text{ s}^2}$$

$$a = \frac{(2)(30.2 \text{ m})}{9.00 \times 10^2 \text{ s}^2}$$

$$\boxed{a = 6.71 \times 10^{-2} \text{ m/s}^2}$$

Practice

1. In 1986, the first flight around the globe without a single refueling was completed. The aircraft's average speed was 186 km/h. If the airplane landed at this speed and accelerated at -1.5 m/s^2, how long did it take for the airplane to stop?

2. An automobile with an initial speed of 4.30 m/s accelerates uniformly at the rate of 3.00 m/s^2. Find the final speed and the displacement after 5.00 s.

3. A car starts from rest and travels for 5.0 s with a constant acceleration of -1.5 m/s^2. What is the final velocity of the car? How far does the car travel in this time interval?

4. In 1991, four English teenagers built an electric car that could attain a speed 30.0 m/s. Suppose it takes 8.0 s for this car to accelerate from 18.0 m/s to 30.0 m/s. What is the magnitude of the car's acceleration?

Final velocity depends on initial velocity, acceleration, and displacement.

So far, all of the equations for motion under uniform acceleration have required knowing the time interval. We can also obtain an expression that relates displacement, velocity, and acceleration without using the time interval. This method involves rearranging one equation to solve for Δt and substituting that expression in another equation, making it possible to find the final velocity of a uniformly accelerated object without knowing how long it has been accelerating. Start with the following equation for displacement:

$$\Delta x = \frac{1}{2}(v_i + v_f)\Delta t \qquad \text{Now multiply both sides by 2.}$$

$$2\Delta x = (v_i + v_f)\Delta t \qquad \text{Next, divide both sides by } (v_i + v_f) \text{ to solve for } \Delta t.$$

$$\left(\frac{2\Delta x}{v_i + v_f}\right) = \Delta t$$

Now that we have an expression for Δt, we can substitute this expression into the equation for the final velocity.

$$v_f = v_i + a(\Delta t)$$

$$v_f = v_i + a\left(\frac{2\Delta x}{v_i + v_f}\right)$$

In its present form, this equation is not very helpful because v_f appears on both sides. To solve for v_f, first subtract v_i from both sides of the equation.

$$v_f - v_i = a\left(\frac{2\Delta x}{v_i + v_f}\right)$$

Next, multiply both sides by $(v_i + v_f)$ to get all the velocities on the same side of the equation.

$$(v_f - v_i)(v_f + v_i) = 2a\Delta x = v_f^2 - v_i^2$$

Add v_i^2 to both sides to solve for v_f^2.

> ### Final Velocity After Any Displacement
>
> $$v_f^2 = v_i^2 + 2a\Delta x$$
>
> **(final velocity)^2 = (initial velocity)^2 + 2(acceleration)(displacement)**

When using this equation, you must take the square root of the right side of the equation to find the final velocity. Remember that the square root may be either positive or negative. If you have been consistent in your use of the sign convention, you will be able to determine which value is the right answer by reasoning based on the direction of the motion.

Final Velocity After Any Displacement

GO ONLINE

SOLUTION TUTOR

HMHScience.com

Sample Problem E A person pushing a stroller starts from rest, uniformly accelerating at a rate of 0.500 m/s². What is the velocity of the stroller after it has traveled 4.75 m?

1 ANALYZE

Given:

$$v_i = 0 \text{ m/s}$$
$$a = 0.500 \text{ m/s}^2$$
$$\Delta x = 4.75 \text{ m}$$

Unknown: $v_f = ?$

Diagram:

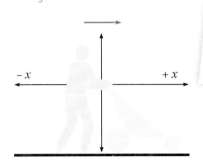

Choose a coordinate system. The most convenient one has an origin at the initial location of the stroller. The positive direction is to the right.

2 PLAN

Choose an equation or situation:
Because the initial velocity, acceleration, and displacement are known, the final velocity can be found by using the following equation:

$$v_f^2 = v_i^2 + 2a\Delta x$$

Rearrange the equation to isolate the unknown:
Take the square root of both sides to isolate v_f.

$$v_f = \pm\sqrt{(v_i)^2 + 2a\Delta x}$$

Tips and Tricks

Think about the physical situation to determine whether to keep the positive or negative answer from the square root. In this case, the stroller is speeding up because it starts from rest and ends with a speed of 2.18 m/s. An object that is speeding up and has a positive acceleration must have a positive velocity, as shown in **Figure 2.3**. So the final velocity must be positive.

3 SOLVE

Substitute the values into the equation and solve:

$$v_f = \pm\sqrt{(0 \text{ m/s})^2 + 2(0.500 \text{ m/s}^2)(4.75 \text{ m})}$$

$$\boxed{v_f = +2.18 \text{ m/s}}$$

4 CHECK YOUR WORK

The stroller's velocity after accelerating for 4.75 m is 2.18 m/s to the right.

Continued

Final Velocity After Any Displacement (continued)

Practice

1. Find the velocity after the stroller in Sample Problem E has traveled 6.32 m.

2. A car traveling initially at +7.0 m/s accelerates uniformly at the rate of +0.80 m/s² for a distance of 245 m.

   a. What is its velocity at the end of the acceleration?

   b. What is its velocity after it accelerates for 125 m?

   c. What is its velocity after it accelerates for 67 m?

3. A car accelerates uniformly in a straight line from rest at the rate of 2.3 m/s².

   a. What is the speed of the car after it has traveled 55 m?

   b. How long does it take the car to travel 55 m?

4. A motorboat accelerates uniformly from a velocity of 6.5 m/s to the west to a velocity of 1.5 m/s to the west. If its acceleration was 2.7 m/s² to the east, how far did it travel during the acceleration?

5. An aircraft has a liftoff speed of 33 m/s. What minimum constant acceleration does this require if the aircraft is to be airborne after a takeoff run of 240 m?

6. A certain car is capable of accelerating at a uniform rate of 0.85 m/s². What is the magnitude of the car's displacement as it accelerates uniformly from a speed of 83 km/h to one of 94 km/h?

With the four equations presented in this section, it is possible to solve any problem involving one-dimensional motion with uniform acceleration. For your convenience, the equations that are used most often are listed in **Figure 2.6.** The first column of the table gives the equations in their standard form. For an object initially at rest, $v_i = 0$. Using this value for v_i in the equations in the first column will result in the equations in the second column. It is not necessary to memorize the equations in the second column. If $v_i = 0$ in any problem, you will naturally derive this form of the equation. Referring back to the sample problems in this chapter will guide you through using these equations to solve many problems.

FIGURE 2.6

EQUATIONS FOR CONSTANTLY ACCELERATED STRAIGHT-LINE MOTION

Form to use when accelerating object has an initial velocity	Form to use when object accelerating starts from rest
$\Delta x = \frac{1}{2}(v_i + v_f)\Delta t$	$\Delta x = \frac{1}{2}v_f\Delta t$
$v_f = v_i + a\Delta t$	$v_f = a\Delta t$
$\Delta x = v_i\Delta t + \frac{1}{2}a(\Delta t)^2$	$\Delta x = \frac{1}{2}a(\Delta t)^2$
$v_f^2 = v_i^2 + 2a\Delta x$	$v_f^2 = 2a\Delta x$

SECTION 2 **FORMATIVE ASSESSMENT**

▶ Reviewing Main Ideas

1. Marissa's car accelerates uniformly at a rate of $+2.60$ m/s². How long does it take for Marissa's car to accelerate from a speed of 24.6 m/s to a speed of 26.8 m/s?

2. A bowling ball with a negative initial velocity slows down as it rolls down the lane toward the pins. Is the bowling ball's acceleration positive or negative as it rolls toward the pins?

3. Nathan accelerates his skateboard uniformly along a straight path from rest to 12.5 m/s in 2.5 s.
   a. What is Nathan's acceleration?
   b. What is Nathan's displacement during this time interval?
   c. What is Nathan's average velocity during this time interval?

✔ Critical Thinking

4. Two cars are moving in the same direction in parallel lanes along a highway. At some instant, the instantaneous velocity of car A exceeds the instantaneous velocity of car B. Does this mean that car A's acceleration is greater than car B's? Explain, and use examples.

Interpreting Graphics

5. The velocity-versus-time graph for a shuttle bus moving along a straight path is shown in **Figure 2.7**.
   a. Identify the time intervals during which the velocity of the shuttle bus is constant.
   b. Identify the time intervals during which the acceleration of the shuttle bus is constant.
   c. Find the value for the average velocity of the shuttle bus during each time interval identified in **b**.
   d. Find the acceleration of the shuttle bus during each time interval identified in **b**.
   e. Identify the times at which the instantaneous velocity of the shuttle bus is zero.
   f. Identify the times at which the acceleration of the shuttle bus is zero.
   g. Explain what the slope of the graph reveals about the acceleration in each time interval.

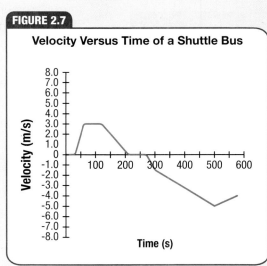

FIGURE 2.7

Velocity Versus Time of a Shuttle Bus

6. Is the shuttle bus in item 5 always moving in the same direction? Explain, and refer to the time intervals shown on the graph.

Objectives

▶ Relate the motion of a freely falling body to motion with constant acceleration.

▶ Calculate displacement, velocity, and time during the motion of a freely falling object.

SC.912.P.12.2 Analyze the motion of an object in terms of its position, velocity, and acceleration (with respect to a frame of reference) as functions of time.

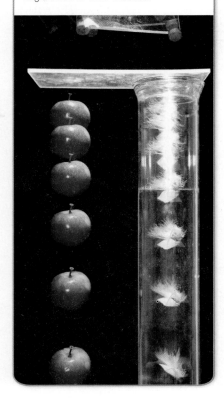

FIGURE 3.1

Free Fall in a Vacuum When there is no air resistance, all objects fall with the same acceleration regardless of their masses.

free fall the motion of a body when only the force due to gravity is acting on the body

Falling Objects

Key Term

free fall

Free Fall

On August 2, 1971, a demonstration was conducted on the moon by astronaut David Scott. He simultaneously released a hammer and a feather from the same height above the moon's surface. The hammer and the feather both fell straight down and landed on the lunar surface at exactly the same moment. Although the hammer is more massive than the feather, both objects fell at the same rate. That is, they traveled the same displacement in the same amount of time.

Freely falling bodies undergo constant acceleration.

In **Figure 3.1,** a feather and an apple are released from rest in a vacuum chamber. The two objects fell at exactly the same rate, as indicated by the horizontal alignment of the multiple images.

The amount of time that passed between each successive image is the same. However, as shown in the picture, the displacement in each time interval did not remain constant. Therefore, the velocity was not constant. The apple and the feather were accelerating.

Compare the displacement between the first and second images to the displacement between the second and third images. As you can see, within each time interval, the displacement of the feather increased by the same amount as the displacement of the apple. Because the time intervals are the same, we know that the velocity of each object is increasing by the same amount in each time interval. In other words, the apple and the feather are falling with the same constant acceleration.

If air resistance is disregarded, all objects dropped near the surface of a planet fall with the same constant acceleration. This acceleration is due to gravitational force, and the motion is referred to as **free fall.** The acceleration due to gravity is denoted with the symbols a_g (generally) or g (on Earth's surface). The magnitude of g is about 9.81 m/s^2, or 32 ft/s^2. Unless stated otherwise, this book will use the value 9.81 m/s^2 for calculations. This acceleration is directed downward, toward the center of Earth. In our usual choice of coordinates, the downward direction is negative. Thus, the acceleration of objects in free fall near the surface of Earth is $a_g = -g = -9.81$ m/s^2. Because an object in free fall is acted on only by gravity, a_g is also known as free-fall acceleration.

Acceleration is constant during upward and downward motion.

Figure 3.2 is a strobe photograph of a ball thrown up into the air with an initial upward velocity of +10.5 m/s. The photo on the left shows the ball moving up from its release toward the top of its path, and the photo on the right shows the ball falling back down. Everyday experience shows that when we throw an object up in the air, it will continue to move upward for some time, stop momentarily at the peak, and then change direction and begin to fall. Because the object changes direction, it may seem that the velocity and acceleration are both changing. Actually, objects thrown into the air have a downward acceleration as soon as they are released.

In the photograph on the left, the upward displacement of the ball between each successive image is smaller and smaller until the ball stops and finally begins to move with an increasing downward velocity, as shown on the right. As soon as the ball is released with an initial upward velocity of +10.5 m/s, it has an acceleration of −9.81 m/s^2. After 1.0 s ($\Delta t = 1.0$ s), the ball's velocity will change by −9.81 m/s to 0.69 m/s upward. After 2.0 s ($\Delta t = 2.0$ s), the ball's velocity will again change by −9.81 m/s, to −9.12 m/s.

The graph in **Figure 3.3** shows the velocity of the ball plotted against time. As you can see, there is an instant when the velocity of the ball is equal to 0 m/s. This happens at the instant when the ball reaches the peak of its upward motion and is about to begin moving downward. Although the velocity is zero at the instant the ball reaches the peak, the acceleration is equal to −9.81 m/s^2 at every instant regardless of the magnitude or direction of the velocity. It is important to note that the acceleration is −9.81 m/s^2 even at the peak where the velocity is zero. The straight-line slope of the graph indicates that the acceleration is constant at every moment.

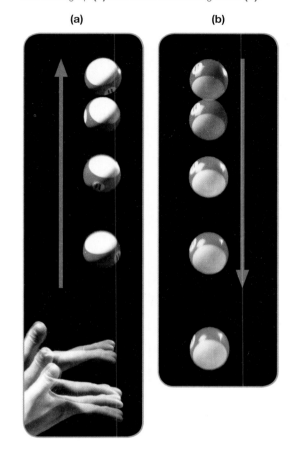

FIGURE 3.2

Motion of a Tossed Ball At the very top of its path, the ball's velocity is zero, but the ball's acceleration is −9.81 m/s^2 at every point—both when it is moving up **(a)** and when it is moving down **(b)**.

(a)   (b)

FIGURE 3.3

Slope of a Velocity-Time Graph

On this velocity-time graph, the slope of the line, which is equal to the ball's acceleration, is constant from the moment the ball is released ($t = 0.00$ s) and throughout its motion.

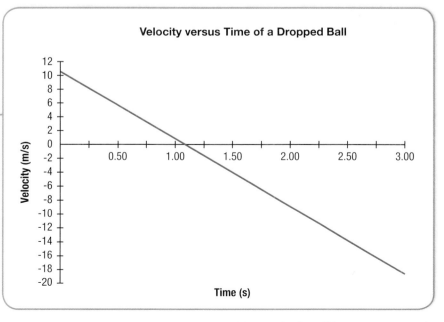

Velocity versus Time of a Dropped Ball

Velocity (m/s)

Time (s)

Freely falling objects always have the same downward acceleration.

It may seem a little confusing to think of something that is moving upward, like the ball in the example, as having a downward acceleration. Thinking of this motion as motion with a positive velocity and a negative acceleration may help. The downward acceleration is the same when an object is moving up, when it is at rest at the top of its path, and when it is moving down. The only things changing are the position and the magnitude and direction of the velocity.

When an object is thrown up in the air, it has a positive velocity and a negative acceleration. From **Figure 2.3,** we see that this means the object is slowing down as it rises in the air. From the example of the ball and from everyday experience, we know that this makes sense. The object continues to move upward but with a smaller and smaller speed. In the photograph of the ball, this decrease in speed is shown by the smaller and smaller displacements as the ball moves up to the top of its path.

At the top of its path, the object's velocity has decreased until it is zero. Although it is impossible to see this because it happens so quickly, the object is actually at rest at the instant it reaches its peak position. Even though the velocity is zero at this instant, the acceleration is still -9.81 m/s^2.

When the object begins moving down, it has a negative velocity, and its acceleration is still negative. From **Figure 2.3,** we see that a negative acceleration and a negative velocity indicate an object that is speeding up. In fact, this is what happens when objects undergo free-fall acceleration. Objects that are falling toward Earth move faster and faster as they fall. In the photograph of the ball in **Figure 3.2** (on the previous page), this increase in speed is shown by the greater and greater displacements between the images as the ball falls.

Knowing the free-fall acceleration makes it easy to calculate the velocity, time, and displacement of many different motions using the equations for constantly accelerated motion. Because the acceleration is the same throughout the entire motion, you can analyze the motion of a freely falling object during any time interval.

QuickLAB · TIME INTERVAL OF FREE FALL

Your reaction time affects your performance in all kinds of activities—from sports to driving to catching something that you drop. Your reaction time is the time interval between an event and your response to it.

Determine your reaction time by having a friend hold a meterstick vertically between the thumb and index finger of your open hand. The meterstick should be held

so that the zero mark is between your fingers with the 1 cm mark above it.

You should not be touching the meterstick, and your catching hand must be resting on a table. Without warning you, your friend should release the meterstick so that it falls between your thumb and your finger. Catch the meterstick as quickly as you can. You can calculate your reaction time

from the free-fall acceleration and the distance the meterstick has fallen through your grasp.

MATERIALS
- meterstick or ruler

SAFETY

Avoid eye injury; do not swing metersticks.

Falling Object

Sample Problem F The famous Gateway to the West Arch in St. Louis, Missouri, is about 192 m tall at its highest point. Suppose Sally, a stuntwoman, jumps off the top of the arch. If it takes Sally 6.4 s to land on the safety pad at the base of the arch, what is her average acceleration? What is her final velocity?

 ANALYZE

Given: $v_i = 0 \text{ m/s}$

$\Delta y = -192 \text{ m}$

$\Delta t = 6.4 \text{ s}$

Unknown: $a = ?$

$v_f = ?$

 PLAN

Choose an equation or situation:
Both the acceleration and the final speed are unknown. Therefore, first solve for the acceleration during the fall using the equation that requires only the known variables.

$$\Delta y = v_i \Delta t + \frac{1}{2} a \Delta t^2$$

Then the equation for v_f that involves acceleration can be used to solve for v_f.

$$v_f = v_i + a \Delta t$$

Rearrange the equation to isolate the unknowns:

$$a = \frac{2(\Delta y - v_i \Delta t)}{\Delta t^2}$$

$$v_f = v_i + a \Delta t$$

 CALCULATE

Substitute the values into the equation and solve:

$$a = \frac{(2) \left[(-192 \text{ m}) - (0 \frac{\text{m}}{\text{s}})(6.4 \text{ s}) \right]}{(6.4 \text{ s})^2} = -9.4 \frac{\text{m}}{\text{s}^2}$$

$$v_f = 0 \frac{\text{m}}{\text{s}} + \left(-9.4 \frac{\text{m}}{\text{s}^2} \right)(6.4 \text{ s}) = -6.0 \times 10^1 \frac{\text{m}}{\text{s}}$$

 CHECK YOUR WORK

Sally's downward acceleration is less than the free-fall acceleration at Earth's surface (9.81 m/s²). This indicates that air resistance reduces her downward acceleration by 0.4 m/s². Sally's final speed, 60 m/s, is such that if she could fall at this speed at the beginning of her jump with no acceleration, she would travel a distance equal to the arch's height in just a little more than 3 s.

Continued

1. A robot probe drops a camera off the rim of a 239 m high cliff on Mars, where the free-fall acceleration is -3.7 m/s^2.

   a. Find the velocity with which the camera hits the ground.

   b. Find the time required for it to hit the ground.

2. A flowerpot falls from a windowsill 25.0 m above the sidewalk.

   a. How fast is the flowerpot moving when it strikes the ground?

   b. How much time does a passerby on the sidewalk below have to move out of the way before the flowerpot hits the ground?

3. A tennis ball is thrown vertically upward with an initial velocity of $+8.0 \text{ m/s}$.

   a. What will the ball's speed be when it returns to its starting point?

   b. How long will the ball take to reach its starting point?

4. A volleyball is hit upward with an initial velocity of 6.0 m/s. Calculate the displacement of the volleyball when its final velocity is 1.1 m/s upward.

WHY IT MATTERS

Skydiving

When these skydivers jump from an airplane, they plummet toward the ground. If Earth had no atmosphere, the skydivers would accelerate with the free-fall acceleration, a_g, equal to -9.81 m/s^2. They would not slow down even after opening their parachutes.

Fortunately, Earth does have an atmosphere, and the acceleration of the skydivers does not remain constant. Instead, because of air resistance, the acceleration decreases as they fall. After a few seconds, the acceleration drops to zero, and the speed becomes constant. The constant speed an object reaches when falling through a resisting medium is called *terminal velocity*.

The terminal velocity of an object depends on the object's mass, shape, and size. When a skydiver is spread out horizontally to the ground, the skydiver's terminal velocity is typically about 55 m/s (123 mi/h). If the skydiver curls into a ball, the terminal velocity may increase to close to 90 m/s (200 mi/h). In 2015 the world record for the fastest terminal velocity was 148 m/s (331 mi/h). When the skydiver opens the parachute, air resistance increases, and the skydiver decelerates to a new, slower terminal velocity. For a skydiver with an open parachute, the terminal velocity is typically about 5 m/s (11 mi/h).

▶ **Reviewing Main Ideas**

1. A coin is tossed vertically upward.
   a. What happens to its velocity while it is in the air?
   b. Does its acceleration increase, decrease, or remain constant while it is in the air?

2. A pebble is dropped down a well and hits the water 1.5 s later. Using the equations for motion with constant acceleration, determine the distance from the edge of the well to the water's surface.

3. A ball is thrown vertically upward. What are its velocity and acceleration when it reaches its maximum altitude? What is its acceleration just before it hits the ground?

4. Two children are bouncing rubber balls. One child simply drops a ball. At the same time, the other child throws a ball downward with an initial speed of 10 m/s. What is the acceleration of each ball while in motion?

✔ **Critical Thinking**

5. A gymnast practices two dismounts from the high bar on the uneven parallel bars. During one dismount, she swings up off the bar with an initial upward velocity of +4.0 m/s. In the second, she releases from the same height but with an initial downward velocity of −3.0 m/s. What is her acceleration in each case? How does the first final instantaneous velocity as the gymnast reaches the ground differ from the second final instantaneous velocity?

Interpreting Graphics

6. **Figure 3.4** is a position-time graph of the motion of a basketball thrown straight up. Use the graph to sketch the path of the basketball and to sketch a velocity-time graph of the basketball's motion.

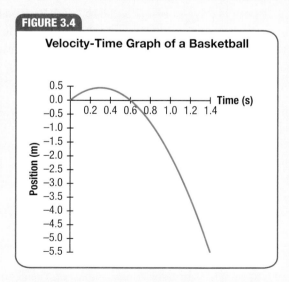

FIGURE 3.4

Velocity-Time Graph of a Basketball

   a. Is the velocity of the basketball constant?
   b. Is the acceleration of the basketball constant?
   c. What is the initial velocity of the basketball?

Angular Kinematics

FIGURE 1

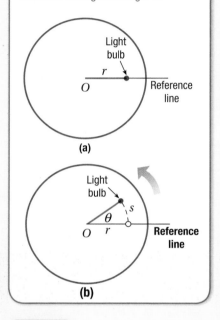

Circular Motion A light bulb on a rotating Ferris wheel **(a)** begins at a point along a reference line and **(b)** moves through an arc length s and therefore through the angle θ.

A point on an object that rotates about a fixed axis undergoes circular motion around that axis. The linear quantities introduced previously cannot be used for circular motion because we are considering the rotational motion of an extended object rather than the linear motion of a particle. For this reason, circular motion is described in terms of the change in angular position. All points on a rigid rotating object, except the points on the axis, move through the same angle during any time interval.

Measuring Angles with Radians

Many of the equations that describe circular motion require that angles be measured in **radians** (rad) rather than in degrees. To see how radians are measured, consider **Figure 1,** which illustrates a light bulb on a rotating Ferris wheel. At $t = 0$, the bulb is on a fixed reference line, as shown in **Figure 1(a).** After a time interval Δt, the bulb advances to a new position, as shown in **Figure 1(b).** In this time interval, the line from the center to the bulb (depicted with a red line in both diagrams) moved through the angle θ with respect to the reference line. Likewise, the bulb moved a distance s, measured along the circumference of the circle; s is the *arc length*.

In general, any angle θ measured in radians is defined by the following equation:

$$\theta = \frac{\text{arc length}}{\text{radius}} = \frac{s}{r}$$

FIGURE 2

Angular Motion Angular motion is measured in units of radians. Because there are 2π radians in a full circle, radians are often expressed as a multiple of π.

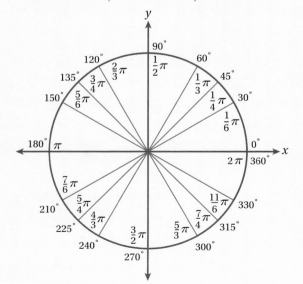

Note that if the arc length, s, is equal to the length of the radius, r, the angle θ swept by r is equal to 1 rad. Because θ is the ratio of an arc length (a distance) to the length of the radius (also a distance), the units cancel, and the abbreviation *rad* is substituted in their place. In other words, the radian is a pure number, with no dimensions.

When the bulb on the Ferris wheel moves through an angle of 360° (one revolution of the wheel), the arc length s is equal to the circumference of the circle, or $2\pi r$. Substituting this value for s into the equation above gives the corresponding angle in radians.

$$\theta = \frac{s}{r} = \frac{2\pi r}{r} = 2\pi \text{ rad}$$

Thus, 360° equals 2π rad, or one complete revolution. In other words, one revolution corresponds to an angle of approximately $2(3.14) = 6.28$ rad. **Figure 2** on the previous page depicts a circle marked with both radians and degrees.

It follows that any angle in degrees can be converted to an angle in radians by multiplying the angle measured in degrees by $2\pi/360°$. In this way, the degrees cancel out, and the measurement is left in radians. The conversion relationship can be simplified as follows:

$$\theta\,(\text{rad}) = \frac{\pi}{180°}\,\theta\,(\text{deg})$$

Angular Displacement

Just as an angle in radians is the ratio of the arc length to the radius, the **angular displacement** traveled by the bulb on the Ferris wheel is the change in the arc length, Δs, divided by the distance of the bulb from the axis of rotation. This relationship is depicted in **Figure 3**.

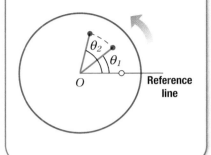

FIGURE 3

Angular Displacement

A light bulb on a rotating Ferris wheel rotates through an angular displacement of $\Delta\theta = \theta_2 - \theta_1$.

Angular Displacement

$$\Delta\theta = \frac{\Delta s}{r}$$

$$\text{angular displacement (in radians)} = \frac{\text{change in arc length}}{\text{distance from axis}}$$

This equation is similar to the equation for linear displacement in that this equation denotes a change in position. The difference is that this equation gives a change in *angular* position rather than a change in *linear* position.

For the purposes of this textbook, when a rotating object is viewed from above, the arc length, s, is considered positive when the point rotates counterclockwise and negative when it rotates clockwise. In other words, $\Delta\theta$ is positive when the object rotates counterclockwise and negative when the object rotates clockwise.

*Quick*LAB   RADIANS AND ARC LENGTH

Use the compass to draw a circle on a sheet of paper, and mark the center point of the circle. Measure the radius of the circle, and cut several pieces of wire equal to the length of this radius. Bend the pieces of wire, and lay them along the circle you drew with your compass. Approximately how many pieces of wire do you use to go all the way around the circle? Draw lines from the center of the circle to each end of one of the wires. Note that the angle between these two lines equals 1 rad.

How many of these angles are there in this circle? Repeat the experiment with a larger circle, and compare the results of each trial.

MATERIALS
- drawing compass
- paper
- thin wire
- wire cutters or scissors

SAFETY

 Cut ends of wire are sharp. Cut and handle wire carefully.

Angular Velocity

Angular velocity is defined in a manner similar to that for linear velocity. The average angular velocity of a rotating rigid object is the ratio of the angular displacement, $\Delta\theta$, to the corresponding time interval, Δt. Thus, angular velocity describes how quickly the rotation occurs. Angular velocity is abbreviated as ω_{avg} (ω is the Greek letter *omega*).

Angular Velocity

$$\omega_{avg} = \frac{\Delta\theta}{\Delta t}$$

$$\text{average angular velocity} = \frac{\text{angular displacement}}{\text{time interval}}$$

Angular velocity is given in units of radians per second (rad/s). Sometimes, angular velocities are given in revolutions per unit time. Recall that 1 rev = 2π rad. The magnitude of angular velocity is called *angular speed*.

Angular Acceleration

Figure 4 shows a bicycle turned upside down so that a repairperson can work on the rear wheel. The bicycle pedals are turned so that at time t_1 the wheel has angular velocity ω_1, as shown in **Figure 4(a).** At a later time, t_2, it has angular velocity ω_2, as shown in **Figure 4(b).** Because the angular velocity is changing, there is an **angular acceleration.** The average angular acceleration, α_{avg} (α is the Greek letter *alpha*), of an object is given by the relationship shown below. Angular acceleration has the units radians per second per second (rad/s²).

Angular Acceleration

$$\alpha_{avg} = \frac{\omega_2 - \omega_1}{t_2 - t_1} = \frac{\Delta\omega}{\Delta t}$$

$$\text{average angular acceleration} = \frac{\text{change in angular velocity}}{\text{time interval}}$$

The relationships between the signs of angular displacement, angular velocity, and angular acceleration are similar to those of the related linear quantities. As discussed earlier, by convention, angular displacement is positive when an object rotates counterclockwise and negative when an object rotates clockwise. Thus, by definition, angular velocity is also positive when an object rotates counterclockwise and negative when an object rotates clockwise. Angular acceleration has the same sign as the angular velocity when it increases the magnitude of the angular velocity and the opposite sign when it decreases the magnitude.

FIGURE 4

Angular Acceleration

An accelerating bicycle wheel rotates with **(a)** an angular velocity ω_1 at time t_1 and **(b)** an angular velocity ω_2 at time t_2. Thus, the wheel has an angular acceleration.

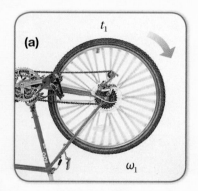

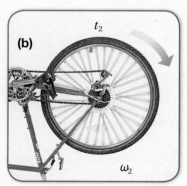

If a point on the rim of a bicycle wheel had an angular velocity greater than a point nearer the center, the shape of the wheel would be changing. Thus, for a rotating object to remain rigid, as does a bicycle wheel or a Ferris wheel, every portion of the object must have the same angular velocity and the same angular acceleration. This fact is precisely what makes angular velocity and angular acceleration so useful for describing rotational motion.

Kinematic Equations for Constant Angular Acceleration

All of the equations for rotational motion defined thus far are analogous to the linear quantities defined in the chapter "Motion in One Dimension." For example, consider the following two equations:

$$\omega_{avg} = \frac{\theta_f - \theta_i}{t_f - t_i} = \frac{\Delta\theta}{\Delta t} \qquad v_{avg} = \frac{x_f - x_i}{t_f - t_i} = \frac{\Delta x}{\Delta t}$$

The equations are similar, with θ replacing x and ω replacing v. The correlations between angular and linear variables are shown in **Figure 5**.

In light of the similarities between variables in linear motion and those in rotational motion, it should be no surprise that the kinematic equations of rotational motion are similar to the linear kinematic equations. The equations of rotational kinematics under constant angular acceleration are summarized in **Figure 6,** along with the corresponding equations for linear motion under constant acceleration. The rotational motion equations apply only for objects rotating about a fixed axis with constant angular acceleration.

FIGURE 5

ANGULAR SUBSTITUTES FOR LINEAR QUANTITIES

Angular	Linear
θ	x
ω	v
α	a

FIGURE 6

ROTATIONAL AND LINEAR KINEMATIC EQUATIONS

Rotational motion with constant angular acceleration	Linear motion with constant acceleration
$\omega_f = \omega_i + \alpha\Delta t$	$v_f = v_i + a\Delta t$
$\Delta\theta = \omega_i\Delta t + \frac{1}{2}\alpha(\Delta t)^2$	$\Delta x = v_i\Delta t + \frac{1}{2}a(\Delta t)^2$
$\omega_f^2 = \omega_i^2 + 2\alpha\Delta\theta$	$v_f^2 = v_i^2 + 2a\Delta x$
$\Delta\theta = \frac{1}{2}(\omega_i + \omega_f)\Delta t$	$\Delta x = \frac{1}{2}(v_i + v_f)\Delta t$

The quantity ω in these equations represents the *instantaneous angular velocity* of the rotating object rather than the average angular velocity.

Special Relativity and Time Dilation

While learning about kinematics, you worked with equations that describe motion in terms of a time interval (Δt). Before Einstein developed the special theory of relativity, everyone assumed that Δt must be the same for any observer, whether that observer is at rest or in motion with respect to the event being measured. This idea is often expressed by the statement that time is *absolute*.

The Relativity of Time

In 1905, Einstein challenged the assumption that time is absolute in a paper titled "The Electrodynamics of Moving Bodies," which contained his special theory of relativity. The special theory of relativity applies to observers and events that are moving with constant velocity (in uniform motion) with respect to one another. One of the consequences of this theory is that Δt *does* depend on the observer's motion.

Consider a passenger in a train that is moving uniformly with respect to an observer standing beside the track, as shown in **Figure 1.** The passenger on the train shines a pulse of light toward a mirror directly above him and measures the amount of time it takes for the pulse to return. Because the passenger is moving along with the train, he sees the pulse of light travel directly up and then directly back down, as in **Figure 1(a).** The observer beside the track, however, sees the pulse hit the mirror at an angle, as in **Figure 1(b),** because the train is moving with respect to the track. Thus, the distance the light travels according to the observer is *greater* than the distance the light travels from the perspective of the passenger.

One of the postulates of Einstein's theory of relativity, which follows from James Clerk Maxwell's equations about light waves, is that the speed of light is the same for *any* observer, even when there is motion between the source of light and the observer. Light is different from all other phenomena in this respect. Although this postulate seems counterintuitive, it was strongly supported by an experiment performed in 1851 by Armand Fizeau. But if the speed of light is the same for both the passenger on the train and the

Measurement of Time Depends on Perspective of Observer

Mirror

Passenger's Perspective

(a) A passenger on a train sends a pulse of light toward a mirror directly above.

Observer's Perspective

(b) Relative to a stationary observer beside the track, the distance the light travels is greater than that measured by the passenger.

observer beside the track while the distances traveled are different, the time intervals observed by each person must also be different. Thus, the observer beside the track measures a longer time interval than the passenger does. This effect is known as *time dilation*.

Calculating Time Dilation

Time dilation is given by the following equation, where $\Delta t'$ represents the time interval measured by the person beside the track and Δt represents the time interval measured by the person on the train:

$$\Delta t' = \frac{\Delta t}{\sqrt{1 - \frac{v^2}{c^2}}}$$

In this equation, v represents the speed of the train relative to the person beside the track, and c is the speed of light in a vacuum, 3.00×10^8 m/s. At speeds with which we are familiar, where v is much smaller than c, the term $\frac{v^2}{c^2}$ is such a small fraction that $\Delta t'$ is essentially equal to Δt. For this reason, we do not observe the effects of time dilation in our typical experiences. But when speeds are closer to the speed of light, time dilation becomes more noticeable. As seen by this equation, time dilation becomes infinite as v approaches the speed of light.

According to Einstein, the motion between the train and the track is *relative*; that is, either system can be considered to be in motion with respect to the other. For the passenger, the train is stationary, and the observer beside the track is in motion. If the light experiment is repeated by the observer beside the track, then the passenger would see the light travel a greater distance than the observer would. So according to the passenger, it is the observer beside the track whose clock runs more slowly. Observers see their clocks running as if they were not moving. Any clocks in motion relative to the observers will seem to the observers to run slowly. Similarly, by comparing the differences between the time intervals of their own clocks and clocks moving relative to theirs, observers can determine how fast the other clocks are moving with respect to their own.

Experimental Verification

The effects we have been considering hold true for all physical processes, including chemical and biological reactions. Scientists have demonstrated time dilation by comparing the lifetime of muons (a type of unstable elementary particle) traveling at $0.9994c$ with the lifetime of stationary muons. In another experiment, atomic clocks on jet planes flying around the world were compared with identical clocks at the U.S. Naval Observatory. In both cases, time dilations were observed that matched the predictions of Einstein's theory of special relativity within the limits of experimental error.

Science Writer

Science writers explain science to their readers in a clear and entertaining way. To learn more about science writing as a career, read the interview with Marcia Bartusiak, author of numerous books and articles on physics and astronomy and professor of science writing at the Massachusetts Institute of Technology.

What do you do as a science writer? What do you write about?

I specialize in writing about physics and astronomy for popular books and magazines. When starting out in my career, I primarily reported on new discoveries or novel experimental techniques—on the existence of cosmic dark matter or the capture of neutrinos from the sun, for example. I spend most of my time doing research and interviewing scientists. If I'm writing a longer story, such as for a magazine, I often get to travel to a site. This allows me to set the scene for my readers, to let people get a peek at a laboratory or observatory that they wouldn't otherwise have a chance to see.

What made you decide to become a science writer?

When you talk to science writers, you find that we come from many different backgrounds, but we all have something in common: we all have an interest in both science *and* writing. In college I majored in journalism and then worked as a reporter for four years. But I then realized that I wanted to specialize in writing about science, so I returned to school and got a master's degree in physics, the subject I loved best for its insights on the workings of nature.

What advice do you have to students interested in writing about science?

Students don't necessarily need to major in science in college. Although having a strong background in science helps, it's not necessary. For example, I can read papers from scientific journals and directly recognize when an important discovery is unfolding. My advice would be for

Bartusiak has visited the world's largest astronomical observatory, located on Mauna Kea, Big Island, Hawaii.

students to maintain a curiosity about the world and to write, write, write. Find every opportunity to write, whether it's for your high-school newspaper, college newspaper, or on a blog. These are ways to start flexing your writing muscles. Science writing is all about translating complex scientific ideas into everyday language and then telling a story—in this case, the story of science. The more you do it, the better you get at it.

What is the favorite part about your job?

I love the traveling. I have visited every major observatory in the Northern Hemisphere. Now I'm trying for the Southern Hemisphere. It's exhilarating to watch astronomers carrying out their observations, then contacting them afterwards and seeing how a new universe is being fashioned before their eyes. These are some of the best moments of my life. I get to escape from my computer and become acquainted with some of the world's top physicists and astronomers.

Marcia Bartusiak

Theories in Motion

For millennia, scientists have studied the motion of objects. They have observed natural physical phenomena and suggested hypotheses to explain their observations. A hypothesis is a tentative, testable explanation that can be supported by evidence. Scientists test hypotheses by making observations and performing experiments. When a hypothesis is found to be reliable across a wide range of conditions, scientists combine that hypothesis with related hypotheses to form theories.

Falling Objects

Aristotle's theories of motion, developed in the fourth century BCE, provided qualitative explanations of motion. Aristotle suggested that a falling object has a natural motion and that the speed at which an object falls is directly related to its mass. Although we now know this to be wrong, the idea was incredibly durable and was accepted by scientists for nearly 2000 years.

In the fourteenth century, developments in scientific thinking led to new quantitative analyses of motion, which challenged Aristotle's views. By approximately 1600, Galileo, among many other scientists, had developed substantially different ideas about motion. In particular, he theorized that objects fell at the same speed, independent of mass. In contrast to Aristotle, Galileo collected experimental and observational evidence to support his explanations. Over the next century, testing by independent scientists and the development of Newton's theory of gravitation supported and clarified Galileo's assertion, fully displacing Aristotle's explanation of falling objects.

- How is a theory distinct from a hypothesis?
- How can hypotheses contribute to theories?
- Why must a well-developed theory be capable of being tested by multiple independent researchers?
- Aristotle's theories of motion are described as *qualitative*. How is this distinct from Galileo's approach to explaining motion?

Conceptual Challenge

The ability to make assumptions and generate rough estimates is a valuable skill to scientists. Quick estimates allow scientists to narrow the range of possibilities and focus on the most reasonable hypotheses.

Estimating Distance How far does a basketball player move during a basketball game?

You can begin examining the scenario by asking questions such as the following:

- What are reasonable approximations of a player's speeds when walking and running?
- How quickly, on average, does a player move?
- How long does a basketball game last?
- For how much of the game is the player moving?
- For what percentage of the game is the player moving?

SECTION 1 **Displacement and Velocity**

KEY TERMS

- Displacement is a change of position in a certain direction, not the total distance traveled.
- The average velocity of an object during some time interval is equal to the displacement of the object divided by the time interval. Like displacement, velocity has both a magnitude (called speed) and a direction.
- The average velocity is equal to the slope of the straight line connecting the initial and final points on a graph of the position of the object versus time.

frame of reference

displacement

average velocity

instantaneous velocity

SECTION 2 **Acceleration**

KEY TERM

- The average acceleration of an object during a certain time interval is equal to the change in the object's velocity divided by the time interval. Acceleration has both magnitude and direction.
- The direction of the acceleration is not always the same as the direction of the velocity. The direction of the acceleration depends on the direction of the motion and on whether the velocity is increasing or decreasing.
- The average acceleration is equal to the slope of the straight line connecting the initial and final points on the graph of the velocity of the object versus time.
- The equations in **Figure 2.6** are valid whenever acceleration is constant.

acceleration

SECTION 3 **Falling Objects**

KEY TERM

- An object thrown or dropped in the presence of Earth's gravity experiences a constant acceleration directed toward the center of Earth. This acceleration is called the free-fall acceleration, or the acceleration due to gravity.
- Free-fall acceleration is the same for all objects, regardless of mass.
- The value for free-fall acceleration on Earth's surface used in this book is $a_g = -g = -9.81$ m/s^2. The direction of the free-fall acceleration is considered to be negative because the object accelerates toward Earth.

free fall

VARIABLE SYMBOLS			
Quantities		**Units**	
x	position	m	meters
Δx	displacement	m	meters
y	position	m	meters
Δy	displacement	m	meters
v	velocity	m/s	meters per second
a	acceleration	m/s^2	meters per second^2

Problem Solving

See **Appendix D: Equations** for a summary of the equations introduced in this chapter. If you need more problem-solving practice, see **Appendix I: Additional Problems.**

Displacement and Velocity

▶ **REVIEWING MAIN IDEAS**

1. On the graph below, what is the total distance traveled during the recorded time interval? What is the displacement?

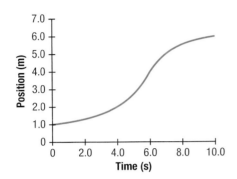

2. On a position-time graph such as the one above, what represents the instantaneous velocity?

3. The position-time graph for a bug crawling along a line is shown in item 4 below. Determine whether the velocity is positive, negative, or zero at each of the times marked on the graph.

4. Use the position-time graph below to answer the following questions:
   a. During which time interval(s) is the velocity negative?
   b. During which time interval(s) is the velocity positive?

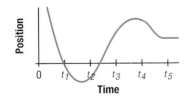

CONCEPTUAL QUESTIONS

5. If the average velocity of a duck is zero in a given time interval, how do you describe the displacement of the duck for that interval?

6. Velocity can be either positive or negative or zero, depending on displacement. The time interval, Δt, is always positive. Why?

PRACTICE PROBLEMS

For problems 7–11, see Sample Problem A.

7. A school bus takes 0.530 h to reach the school from your house. If the average velocity of the bus is 19.0 km/h to the east, what is the displacement?

8. An Olympic runner completes a marathon in 2.00 h, 9.00 min, 21.0 s. If the average speed of this runner is 5.436 m/s, what is the marathon distance?

9. Two cars are traveling on a desert road, as shown below. After 5.0 s, they are side by side at the next telephone pole. The distance between the poles is 70.0 m. Identify the following quantities:
   a. the displacement of car A after 5.0 s
   b. the displacement of car B after 5.0 s
   c. the average velocity of car A during 5.0 s
   d. the average velocity of car B during 5.0 s

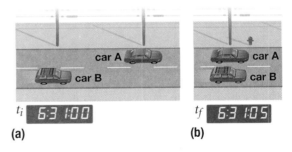

10. Sally travels by car from one city to another. She drives for 30.0 min at 80.0 km/h, 12.0 min at 105 km/h, and 45.0 min at 40.0 km/h, and she spends 15.0 min eating lunch and buying gas.
  a. Determine the average speed for the trip.
  b. Determine the total distance traveled.

11. Runner A is initially 6.0 km west of a flagpole and is running with a constant velocity of 9.0 km/h due east. Runner B is initially 5.0 km east of the flagpole and is running with a constant velocity of 8.0 km/h due west. What will be the distance of the two runners from the flagpole when their paths cross? (It is not necessary to convert your answer from kilometers to meters for this problem. You may leave it in kilometers.)

Acceleration

▶ REVIEWING MAIN IDEAS

12. What would be the acceleration of a turtle that is moving with a constant velocity of 0.25 m/s to the right?

13. Sketch the velocity-time graphs for the following motions.
  a. a city bus that is moving with a constant velocity
  b. a wheelbarrow that is speeding up at a uniform rate of acceleration while moving in the positive direction
  c. a tiger that is speeding up at a uniform rate of acceleration while moving in the negative direction
  d. an iguana that is slowing down at a uniform rate of acceleration while moving in the positive direction
  e. a camel that is slowing down at a uniform rate of acceleration while moving in the negative direction

CONCEPTUAL QUESTIONS

14. If a car is traveling eastward, can its acceleration be westward? Communicate your answer, and use an example in your explanation.

15. The diagrams below show a disk moving from left to right under different conditions. The time interval between images is constant. Assuming that the direction to the right is positive, identify the following types of motion in each photograph. (Some may have more than one type of motion.)
  a. the acceleration is positive
  b. the acceleration is negative
  c. the velocity is constant

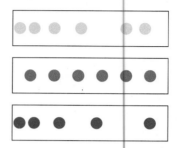

PRACTICE PROBLEMS

For problems 16–17, see Sample Problem B.

16. A car traveling in a straight line has a velocity of +5.0 m/s. After an acceleration of 0.75 m/s², the car's velocity is +8.0 m/s. In what time interval did the acceleration occur?

17. The velocity-time graph for an object moving along a straight path is shown below. Find the average accelerations during the time intervals 0.0 s to 5.0 s, 5.0 s to 15.0 s, and 0.0 s to 20.0 s.

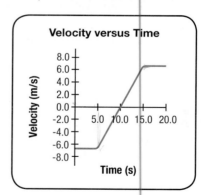

For problems 18–19, see Sample Problem C.

18. A bus slows down uniformly from 75.0 km/h (21 m/s) to 0 km/h in 21 s. How far does it travel before stopping?

19. A car accelerates uniformly from rest to a speed of 65 km/h (18 m/s) in 12 s. Find the distance the car travels during this time.

For problems 20–23, see Sample Problem D.

20. A car traveling at $+7.0$ m/s accelerates at the rate of $+0.80$ m/s^2 for an interval of 2.0 s. Find v_f.

21. A car accelerates from rest at -3.00 m/s^2.
  a. What is the velocity at the end of 5.0 s?
  b. What is the displacement after 5.0 s?

22. A car starts from rest and travels for 5.0 s with a uniform acceleration of $+1.5$ m/s^2. The driver then applies the brakes, causing a uniform acceleration of -2.0 m/s^2. If the brakes are applied for 3.0 s, how fast is the car going at the end of the braking period, and how far has it gone from its start?

23. A boy sledding down a hill accelerates at 1.40 m/s^2. If he started from rest, in what distance would he reach a speed of 7.00 m/s?

For problems 24–25, see Sample Problem E.

24. A sailboat starts from rest and accelerates at a rate of 0.21 m/s^2 over a distance of 280 m.
  a. Find the magnitude of the boat's final velocity.
  b. Find the time it takes the boat to travel this distance.

25. An elevator is moving upward at 1.20 m/s when it experiences an acceleration of 0.31 m/s^2 downward, over a distance of 0.75 m. What will be its final velocity?

Falling Objects

▶ REVIEWING MAIN IDEAS

26. A ball is thrown vertically upward.
  a. What happens to the ball's velocity while the ball is in the air?
  b. What is its velocity when it reaches its maximum altitude?
  c. What is its acceleration when it reaches its maximum altitude?
  d. What is its acceleration just before it hits the ground?
  e. Does its acceleration increase, decrease, or remain constant?

27. The image at right is a strobe photograph of two falling balls released simultaneously. (This motion does not take place in a vacuum.) The time intervals between successive photographs are equal. The ball on the left side is solid, and the ball on the right side is a hollow table-tennis ball. Analyze the motion of both balls in terms of velocity and acceleration.

28. A juggler throws a bowling pin into the air with an initial velocity v_i. Another juggler drops a pin at the same instant. Compare the accelerations of the two pins while they are in the air.

29. A bouquet is thrown upward.
  a. Will the value for the bouquet's displacement be the same no matter where you place the origin of the coordinate system?
  b. Will the value for the bouquet's velocity be the same?
  c. Will the value for the bouquet's acceleration be the same?

PRACTICE PROBLEMS

For problems 30–32, see Sample Problem F.

30. A worker drops a wrench from the top of a tower 80.0 m tall. What is the velocity when the wrench strikes the ground?

31. A peregrine falcon dives at a pigeon. The falcon starts downward from rest with free-fall acceleration. If the pigeon is 76.0 m below the initial position of the falcon, how long does the falcon take to reach the pigeon? Assume that the pigeon remains at rest.

32. A ball is thrown upward from the ground with an initial speed of 25 m/s; at the same instant, a ball is dropped from rest from a building 15 m high. After how long will the balls be at the same height?

Mixed Review

▶ REVIEWING MAIN IDEAS

33. If the average speed of an orbiting space shuttle is 27 800 km/h, determine the time required for it to circle Earth. Assume that the shuttle is orbiting about 320.0 km above Earth's surface and that Earth's radius is 6380 km.

34. A ball is thrown directly upward into the air. The graph below shows the vertical position of the ball with respect to time.

 a. How much time does the ball take to reach its maximum height?

 b. How much time does the ball take to reach one-half its maximum height?

 c. Estimate the slope $\Delta y/\Delta t$ at $t = 0.05$ s, $t = 0.10$ s, $t = 0.15$ s, and $t = 0.20$ s. On your paper, draw a coordinate system with velocity (v) on the y-axis and time (t) on the x-axis. Plot your velocity estimates against time.

 d. From your graph, determine what the acceleration on the ball is.

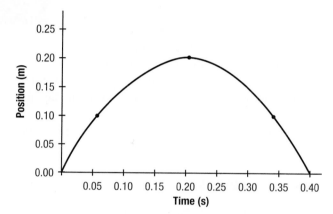

35. A train travels between stations 1 and 2, as shown below. The engineer of the train is instructed to start from rest at station 1 and accelerate uniformly between points A and B, then coast with a uniform velocity between points B and C, and finally accelerate uniformly between points C and D until the train stops at station 2. The distances AB, BC, and CD are all equal, and it takes 5.00 min to travel between the two stations. Assume that the uniform accelerations have the same magnitude, even when they are opposite in direction.

 a. How much of this 5.00 min period does the train spend between points A and B?

 b. How much of this 5.00 min period does the train spend between points B and C?

 c. How much of this 5.00 min period does the train spend between points C and D?

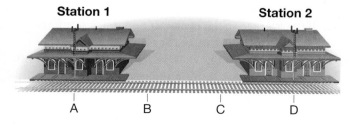

36. Two students are on a balcony 19.6 m above the street. One student throws a ball vertically downward at 14.7 m/s. At the same instant, the other student throws a ball vertically upward at the same speed. The second ball just misses the balcony on the way down.

 a. What is the difference in the time the balls spend in the air?

 b. What is the velocity of each ball as it strikes the ground?

 c. How far apart are the balls 0.800 s after they are thrown?

37. A rocket moves upward, starting from rest, with an acceleration of $+29.4$ m/s^2 for 3.98 s. It runs out of fuel at the end of the 3.98 s but does not stop. How high does it rise above the ground?

38. Two cars travel westward along a straight highway, one at a constant velocity of 85 km/h and the other at a constant velocity of 115 km/h.

 a. Assuming that both cars start at the same point, how much sooner does the faster car arrive at a destination 16 km away?

 b. How far must the cars travel for the faster car to arrive 15 min before the slower car?

39. A small first-aid kit is dropped by a rock climber who is descending steadily at 1.3 m/s. After 2.5 s, what is the velocity of the first-aid kit, and how far is the kit below the climber?

40. A small fish is dropped by a pelican that is rising steadily at 0.50 m/s.

 a. After 2.5 s, what is the velocity of the fish?

 b. How far below the pelican is the fish after 2.5 s?

41. A ranger in a national park is driving at 56 km/h when a deer jumps onto the road 65 m ahead of the vehicle. After a reaction time of t s, the ranger applies the brakes to produce an acceleration of -3.0 m/s^2. What is the maximum reaction time allowed if the ranger is to avoid hitting the deer?

42. A speeder passes a parked police car at 30.0 m/s. The police car starts from rest with a uniform acceleration of 2.44 m/s^2. (Assume that the police car starts at the exact moment the car passes by.)
   a. How much time passes before the speeder is overtaken by the police car?
   b. How far does the speeder get before being overtaken by the police car?

43. An ice sled powered by a rocket engine starts from rest on a large frozen lake and accelerates at +13.0 m/s^2. At t_1 the rocket engine is shut down and the sled moves with constant velocity v until t_2. The total distance traveled by the sled is 5.30×10^3 m, and the total time is 90.0 s. Find t_1, t_2, and v.

44. At the 5800 m mark, the sled in the previous question begins to accelerate at -7.0 m/s^2. Use your answers from item 43 to answer the following questions.
   a. What is the final position of the sled when it comes to rest?
   b. How long does it take for the sled to come to rest?

45. A tennis ball with a velocity of $+10.0$ m/s to the right is thrown perpendicularly at a wall. After striking the wall, the ball rebounds in the opposite direction with a velocity of -8.0 m/s to the left. If the ball is in contact with the wall for 0.012 s, what is the average acceleration of the ball while it is in contact with the wall?

46. A parachutist descending at a speed of 10.0 m/s loses a shoe at an altitude of 50.0 m.
   a. When does the shoe reach the ground?
   b. What is the velocity of the shoe just before it hits the ground?

47. A mountain climber stands at the top of a 50.0 m cliff hanging over a calm pool of water. The climber throws two stones vertically 1.0 s apart and observes that they cause a single splash when they hit the water. The first stone has an initial velocity of $+2.0$ m/s.
   a. How long after release of the first stone will the two stones hit the water?
   b. What is the initial velocity of the second stone when it is thrown?
   c. What will the velocity of each stone be at the instant both stones hit the water?

48. A model rocket is launched straight upward with an initial speed of 50.0 m/s. It accelerates with a constant upward acceleration of 2.00 m/s^2 until its engines stop at an altitude of 150 m.
   a. What is the maximum height reached by the rocket?
   b. When does the rocket reach maximum height?
   c. How long is the rocket in the air?

49. A professional racecar driver buys a car that can accelerate at $+5.9$ m/s^2. The racer decides to race against another driver in a souped-up stock car. Both start from rest, but the stock-car driver leaves 1.0 s before the driver of the racecar. The stock car moves with a constant acceleration of $+3.6$ m/s^2.
   a. Find the time it takes the racecar driver to overtake the stock-car driver.
   b. Find the distance the two drivers travel before they are side by side.
   c. Find the velocities of both cars at the instant they are side by side.

50. Two cars are traveling along a straight line in the same direction, the lead car at 25 m/s and the other car at 35 m/s. At the moment the cars are 45 m apart, the lead driver applies the brakes, causing the car to have an acceleration of -2.0 m/s^2.
   a. How long does it take for the lead car to stop?
   b. Assume that the driver of the chasing car applies the brakes at the same time as the driver of the lead car. What must the chasing car's minimum negative acceleration be to avoid hitting the lead car?
   c. How long does it take the chasing car to stop?

51. One swimmer in a relay race has a 0.50 s lead and is swimming at a constant speed of 4.00 m/s. The swimmer has 20.0 m to swim before reaching the end of the pool. A second swimmer moves in the same direction as the leader. What constant speed must the second swimmer have in order to catch up to the leader at the end of the pool?

ALTERNATIVE ASSESSMENT

1. Can a boat moving eastward accelerate to the west? What happens to the boat's velocity? Name other examples of objects accelerating in the direction opposite their motion, including one with numerical values. Create diagrams and graphs.

2. Two stones are thrown from a cliff at the same time with the same speed, one upward and one downward. Which stone, if either, hits the ground first? Which, if either, hits with the higher speed? In a group discussion, make your best argument for each possible prediction. Set up numerical examples, and solve them to test your prediction.

3. Research typical values for velocities and acceleration of various objects. Include many examples, such as different animals, means of transportation, sports, continental drift, light, subatomic particles, and planets. Organize your findings for display on a poster or some other form.

4. The study of various motions in nature requires devices for measuring periods of time. Prepare a presentation on a specific type of clock, such as water clocks, sand clocks, pendulum clocks, wind-up clocks, atomic clocks, or biological clocks. Who invented or discovered the clock? What scale of time does it measure? What are the principles or phenomena behind each clock? Can they be calibrated?

5. Research Galileo's work on falling bodies. What did he want to demonstrate? What opinions or theories was he trying to refute? What arguments did he use to persuade others that he was right? Did he depend on experiments, logic, findings of other scientists, or other approaches?

GRAPHING CALCULATOR PRACTICE

Motion in One Dimension

At what speed does a falling hailstone travel? Does the speed depend on the distance that the hailstone falls?

In this graphing calculator activity, you will have the opportunity to answer these questions. Your calculator will display two graphs: one for displacement (distance fallen) versus time and the other for speed versus time. These two graphs correspond to the following two equations:

$$Y_1 = 4.9X^2$$
$$Y_2 = 9.8X$$

You should be able to use the table below to correlate these equations with those for an accelerating object that starts from rest.

Motion Equations for an Object with Constant Acceleration That Started from Rest
$\Delta x = \frac{1}{2} v_f \Delta t$
$v_f = a \Delta t$
$\Delta x = \frac{1}{2} a (\Delta t)^2$
$v_f^2 = 2a\Delta x$

Go online to HMHScience.com to find the skillsheet and program for this graphing calculator activity.

Standards-Based Assessment

Record your answers on a separate piece of paper.

MULTIPLE CHOICE

Use the graphs below to answer questions 1-3.

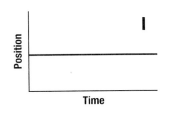
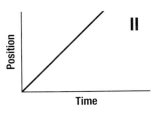

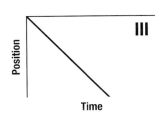
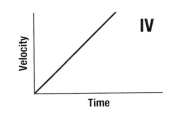

1 Which graph represents an object moving with a constant positive velocity?

  A I
  B II
  C III
  D IV

2 Which graph represents an object at rest?

  A I
  B II
  C III
  D IV

3 Which graph represents an object moving with constant positive acceleration?

  A I
  B II
  C III
  D IV

4 A bus travels from El Paso, Texas, to Chihuahua, Mexico, in 5.2 h with an average velocity of 73 km/h to the south. What is the bus's displacement?

  A 73 km to the south
  B 370 km to the south
  C 380 km to the south
  D 14 km/h to the south

5 A ball initially at rest rolls down a hill and has an acceleration of 3.3 m/s². If it accelerates for 7.5 s, how far will it move during this time?

  A 12 m
  B 93 m
  C 120 m
  D 190 m

6 Which of the following is true for a ball thrown vertically upward? The ball has —

  A a negative acceleration on the way up and a positive acceleration on the way down.
  B a positive acceleration on the way up and a negative acceleration on the way down.
  C zero acceleration on the way up and a positive acceleration on the way down.
  D a constant acceleration throughout its flight.

7 The graph below shows the position of a runner at different times during a run. Use the graph to determine the runner's displacement and average velocity for $t = 20.0$ min to $t = 30.0$ min.

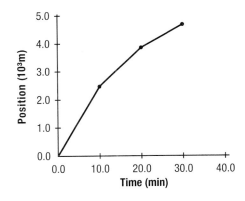

  A $\Delta x = +2400$ m; $v = +4.0$ m/s
  B $\Delta x = +1500$ m; $v = +2.5$ m/s
  C $\Delta x = +900$ m; $v = +2$ m/s
  D $\Delta x = +4800$ m; $v = +2.7$ m/s

GRIDDED RESPONSE

8 A car moving due east increases its speed uniformly from 16 m/s to 32 m/s in 10.0 s. How far, in meters, did the car travel while accelerating?

LIFTING ROOM
Boxes that carry people up and down

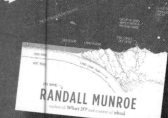

You've learned about both horizontal and vertical one-dimensional motion. A classic example of vertical one-dimensional motion is an elevator. Here's an explanation of how elevators work—and why they are a safe way to travel up and down.

RANDALL MUNROE
XKCD.COM

THE STORY OF LIFTING ROOMS

A LIFTING ROOM IS A BOX THAT CARRIES PEOPLE UP AND DOWN IN A BUILDING.

TODAY'S CITIES WOULDN'T MAKE SENSE WITHOUT LIFTING ROOMS. IF WE HAD TALL BUILDINGS WITHOUT THEM, EVERYONE WOULD WANT TO STAY ON THEIR OWN FLOOR, BECAUSE GOING UP OR DOWN WOULD TAKE A LOT MORE WORK THAN GOING THE SAME DISTANCE TO THE SIDE.

TALL BUILDINGS MIGHT HAVE TO JOIN UP WITH EACH OTHER, AND PEOPLE WOULD MOSTLY MOVE BETWEEN THEM WHILE STAYING ON THEIR OWN FLOORS.

MOST LIFTING ROOMS GO STRAIGHT UP AND DOWN.

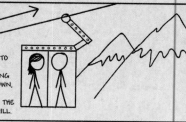

A FEW GO TO THE SIDE WHILE GOING UP AND DOWN, TO TAKE PEOPLE TO THE TOP OF A HILL.

THERE ARE ALSO LIFTING ROOMS THAT ONLY MOVE SIDE TO SIDE; THOSE ARE CALLED TRAINS.

LIFTING ROOMS ARE SAFE; THERE'S ALMOST NO WAY THEY CAN FALL. THERE ARE A LOT OF DIFFERENT PARTS THAT HELP LIFT THEM, AND EACH PART IS MADE TO STOP THE ROOM —INSTEAD OF LETTING IT GO— IF SOMETHING GOES WRONG.

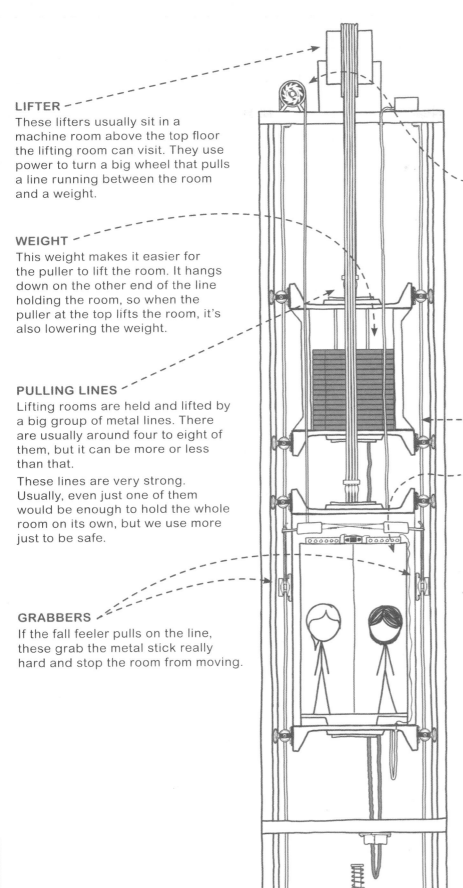

LIFTER

These lifters usually sit in a machine room above the top floor the lifting room can visit. They use power to turn a big wheel that pulls a line running between the room and a weight.

WEIGHT

This weight makes it easier for the puller to lift the room. It hangs down on the other end of the line holding the room, so when the puller at the top lifts the room, it's also lowering the weight.

PULLING LINES

Lifting rooms are held and lifted by a big group of metal lines. There are usually around four to eight of them, but it can be more or less than that.

These lines are very strong. Usually, even just one of them would be enough to hold the whole room on its own, but we use more just to be safe.

GRABBERS

If the fall feeler pulls on the line, these grab the metal stick really hard and stop the room from moving.

FALL FEELER

This wheel is joined to the room's stopping grabbers by a line. As the room moves up and down, the wheel turns.

If the room starts going down fast, the wheel starts spinning fast, and the little arms in the middle of the wheel swing out and catch onto the teeth around them. This makes the wheel stop turning, which makes the room suddenly pull on the line—setting off the room's stopping grabbers.

METAL STICK

LIFTING ROOM

PRETEND CONTROLS

There are controls on the inside of a lifting room that you use to tell it where you want to go. Some of these controls, like the one marked "DOOR CLOSE," don't always seem to do anything.

Some people say that those controls don't even go anywhere, because the lifting room's computer knows when to open and close the door better than you do.

This is half true. On some new lifting rooms, the DOOR CLOSE control might not normally do anything. This is different in different buildings; it's up to the person who owns the building to decide whether to make these controls work.

But the DOOR OPEN control *is* always joined to the lifting room's systems, in case fire fighters need to take full control of the lifters—by putting a special key into the control place—to use them while fighting a fire.

LIFTING ROOM

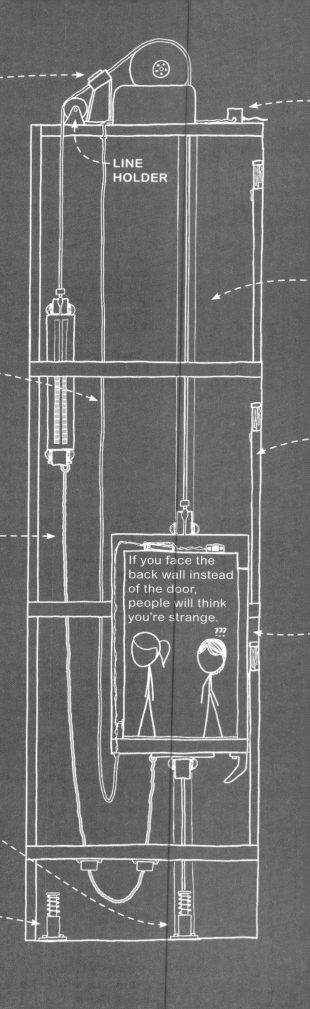

LINE STOPPER

This thing listens to the different parts of the machines, sometimes with the help of a computer, and grabs the line if anything goes wrong.

The line stopper also grabs the line when the room stops at a floor to make sure it doesn't move while people get on and off. It's made so it will keep holding on if the power goes out.

POWER LINE

This line brings power for the lights and controls in the lifting room. It sometimes runs to the top of the hallway, where the pulling machines are, or sometimes to the side of the wall part of the way up the hallway.

WEIGHT LINE

This line is used in the lifting rooms in tall buildings to help keep the weight on the puller even.

When a room is all the way at the top or bottom, the lines holding it add to the weight on one side. When that happens, most of the weight of this line hangs on the other side, which keeps things even.

CATCHER

If a lifting room does fall, these catchers hit a metal plate on the bottom of the room and make the landing a little softer.

There's a second catcher for the weight.

LINE HOLDER

If you face the back wall instead of the door, people will think you're strange.

???

POWER FROM BUILDING
Lifting rooms use a lot of power, but the lights and air systems in the building use even more.

TALL HALLWAY
The lifting room sits inside a long hallway that goes up and down instead of to the side. It can be longer than any of the normal hallways in the building, but most people never see it.

DOORS
These doors line up with the doors on the room. When the lifting room stops, both doors open together.

EMPTY ROOM
Lifting rooms are usually empty. People don't put chairs or tables in them except to move those things to other floors. If you tried to use one of these rooms as an office, someone would probably yell at you.

POWER FROM BUILDING

LIFTER

LINE HOLDER

PULLING LINES

DING!

HI, CAN I HELP YOU?

Why It Matters

Without air resistance, any object that is thrown or launched into the air and that is subject to gravitational force—such as the water droplets in this fountain—will follow a parabolic path. The velocity of any object in two-dimensional motion can be separated into horizontal and vertical components.

For example, the diagram shows the horizontal and vertical components of a water droplet from the fountain. In this chapter, you will use vectors and vector components such as these to analyze two-dimensional motion and to solve problems in which objects are projected into the air.

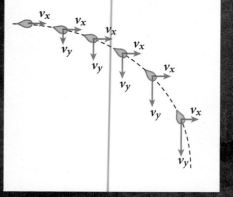

CHAPTER 3

Two-Dimensional Motion and Vectors

SECTION 1
Introduction to Vectors

SECTION 2
Vector Operations

SECTION 3
Projectile Motion

SECTION 4
Relative Motion

BIG IDEA

Vectors can be used to represent and predict the two-dimensional motion of an object.

ONLINE Physics
HMHScience.com

ONLINE LABS
- Vector Treasure Hunt
- Velocity of a Projectile
- S.T.E.M. Lab Parabolic Path
- S.T.E.M. Lab The Path of a Human Cannonball

GO ONLINE **Animated**
Physics
HMHScience.com

Projectile Motion

SC.912.P.12.1 Distinguish between scalar and vector quantities and assess which should be used to describe an event.
SC.912.P.12.2 Analyze the motion of an object in terms of its position, velocity, and acceleration (with respect to a frame of reference) as functions of time.
MAFS.912.N-VM.1.3 Solve problems involving velocity and other quantities that can be represented by vectors.

scalar a physical quantity that has magnitude but no direction

vector a physical quantity that has both magnitude and direction

Introduction to Vectors

Key Terms

scalar   vector   resultant

Scalars and Vectors

In the chapter "Motion in One Dimension," our discussion of motion was limited to two directions, forward and backward. Mathematically, we described these directions of motion with a positive or negative sign. That method works only for motion in a straight line. This chapter explains a method of describing the motion of objects that do not travel along a straight line.

Vectors indicate direction; scalars do not.

Each of the physical quantities encountered in this book can be categorized as either a scalar quantity or a vector quantity. A **scalar** is a quantity that has magnitude but no direction. Examples of scalar quantities are speed, volume, and the number of pages in this textbook. A **vector** is a physical quantity that has both direction and magnitude.

Displacement is an example of a vector quantity. An airline pilot planning a trip must know exactly how far and which way to fly. Velocity is also a vector quantity. If we wish to describe the velocity of a bird, we must specify both its speed (say, 3.5 m/s) and the direction in which the bird is flying (say, northeast). Another example of a vector quantity is acceleration.

Vectors are represented by boldface symbols.

In physics, quantities are often represented by symbols, such as t for time. To help you keep track of which symbols represent vector quantities and which are used to indicate scalar quantities, this book will use **boldface** type to indicate vector quantities. Scalar quantities will be in *italics*. For example, the speed of a bird is written as $v = 3.5$ m/s. But a velocity, which includes a direction, is written as **v** $= 3.5$ m/s to the northeast. When writing a vector on your paper, you can distinguish it from a scalar by drawing an arrow above the abbreviation for a quantity, such as $\vec{v} = 3.5$ m/s to the northeast.

One way to keep track of vectors and their directions is to use diagrams. In diagrams, vectors are shown as arrows that point in the direction of the vector. The length of a vector arrow in a diagram is proportional to the vector's magnitude. For example, in **Figure 1.1**, the arrows represent the velocities of the two soccer players running toward the soccer ball.

FIGURE 1.1

Length of Vector Arrows

The lengths of the vector arrows represent the magnitudes of these two soccer players' velocities.

A resultant vector represents the sum of two or more vectors.

When adding vectors, you must make certain that they have the same units and describe similar quantities. For example, it would be meaningless to add a velocity vector to a displacement vector because they describe different physical quantities. Similarly, it would be meaningless, as well as incorrect, to add two displacement vectors that are not expressed in the same units. For example, you cannot add meters and feet together.

The chapter "Motion in One Dimension" covered vector addition and subtraction in one dimension. Think back to the example of the gecko that ran up a tree from a 20 cm marker to an 80 cm marker. Then the gecko reversed direction and ran back to the 50 cm marker. Because the two parts of this displacement are each vectors, they can be added together to give a total displacement of 30 cm. The answer found by adding two vectors in this way is called the **resultant.**

Vectors can be added graphically.

Consider a student walking 1600 m to a friend's house and then 1600 m to school, as shown in **Figure 1.2**. The student's total displacement during his walk to school is in a direction from his house to the school, as shown by the dotted line. This direct path is the *vector sum* of the student's displacement from his house to his friend's house and his displacement from the friend's house to school. How can this resultant displacement be found?

One way to predict the magnitude and direction of the student's total displacement is to draw the situation to scale on paper. Use a reasonable scale, such as 50 m on land equals 1 cm on paper. First draw the vector representing the student's displacement from his house to his friend's house, giving the proper direction and scaled magnitude. Then draw the vector representing his walk to the school, starting with the tail at the head of the first vector. Again give its scaled magnitude and the right direction.

The magnitude of the resultant vector can then be determined by using a ruler. Measure the length of the vector pointing from the tail of the first vector to the head of the second vector. The length of that vector can then be multiplied by 50 (or whatever scale you have chosen) to get the actual magnitude of the student's total displacement in meters.

The direction of the resultant vector may be determined by using a protractor to measure the angle between the resultant and the first vector or between the resultant and any chosen reference line.

FIGURE 1.2

Graphical Method of Vector Addition A student walks from his house to his friend's house **(a)** and then from his friend's house to the school **(b)**. The student's resultant displacement **(c)** can be found by using a ruler and a protractor.

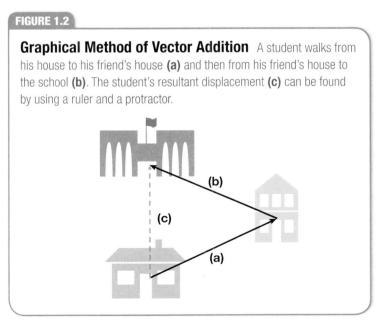

Properties of Vectors

Now consider a case in which two or more vectors act at the same point. When this occurs, it is possible to find a resultant vector that has the same net effect as the combination of the individual vectors. Imagine looking down from the second level of an airport at a toy car moving at 0.80 m/s across a walkway that moves at 1.5 m/s. How can you determine what the car's resultant velocity will look like from your viewpoint?

Vectors can be moved parallel to themselves in a diagram.

Note that the car's resultant velocity while moving from one side of the walkway to the other will be the combination of two independent motions. Thus, the moving car can be thought of as traveling first at 0.80 m/s across the walkway and then at 1.5 m/s down the walkway. In this way, we can draw a given vector anywhere in the diagram as long as the vector is parallel to its previous alignment (so that it still points in the same direction).

Thus, you can draw one vector with its tail starting at the tip of the other as long as the size and direction of each vector do not change. This process is illustrated in **Figure 1.3**. Although both vectors act on the car at the same point, the horizontal vector has been moved up so that its tail begins at the tip of the vertical vector. The resultant vector can then be drawn from the tail of the first vector to the tip of the last vector. This method is known as the *triangle* (or *polygon*) *method of addition*.

Again, the magnitude of the resultant vector can be measured using a ruler, and the angle can be measured with a protractor. In the next section, we will develop a technique for adding vectors that is less time-consuming because it involves a calculator instead of a ruler and protractor.

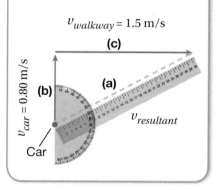
Vectors can be added in any order.

When two or more vectors are added, the sum is independent of the order of the addition. This idea is demonstrated by a runner practicing for a marathon along city streets, as represented in **Figure 1.4**. The runner executes the same four displacements in each case, but the order is different. Regardless of which path the runner takes, the runner will have the same total displacement, expressed as **d**. Similarly, the vector sum of two or more vectors is the same regardless of the order in which the vectors are added, provided that the magnitude and direction of each vector remain the same.

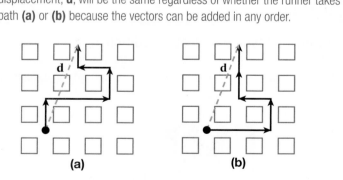

FIGURE 1.4

Commutative Property of Vectors A marathon runner's displacement, **d**, will be the same regardless of whether the runner takes path **(a)** or **(b)** because the vectors can be added in any order.

(a)   (b)

To subtract a vector, add its opposite.

Vector subtraction makes use of the definition of the negative of a vector. The negative of a vector is defined as a vector with the same magnitude as the original vector but opposite in direction. For instance, the negative of the velocity of a car traveling 30 m/s to the west is −30 m/s to the west.

This is equivalent to +30 m/s to the east. Thus, adding a vector to its negative vector gives zero. When subtracting vectors in two dimensions, first draw the negative of the vector to be subtracted. Then add that negative vector to the other vector by using the triangle method of addition.

Multiplying or dividing vectors by scalars results in vectors.

There are mathematical operations in which vectors can multiply other vectors, but they are not needed in this book. This book does, however, make use of vectors multiplied by scalars, with a vector as the result. For example, if a cab driver obeys a customer who tells him to go twice as fast, that cab's original velocity vector, $\mathbf{v}_{cab}$, is multiplied by the scalar number 2. The result, written $2\mathbf{v}_{cab}$, is a vector with a magnitude twice that of the original vector and pointing in the same direction.

On the other hand, if another cab driver is told to go twice as fast in the opposite direction, this is the same as multiplying by the scalar number -2. The result is a vector with a magnitude two times the initial velocity but pointing in the opposite direction, written as $-2\mathbf{v}_{cab}$.

 SECTION 1 **FORMATIVE ASSESSMENT**

▶ Reviewing Main Ideas

1. Which of the following quantities are scalars, and which are vectors?
   a. the acceleration of a plane as it takes off
   b. the number of passengers on the plane
   c. the duration of the flight
   d. the displacement of the flight
   e. the amount of fuel required for the flight

2. A roller coaster moves 85 m horizontally and then travels 45 m at an angle of 30.0° above the horizontal. Use graphical techniques to predict its displacement from its starting point.

3. A novice pilot sets a plane's controls, thinking the plane will fly at 2.50×10^2 km/h to the north. If the wind blows at 75 km/h toward the southeast, what is the plane's resultant velocity? Use graphical techniques.

4. While flying over the Grand Canyon, the pilot slows the plane down to one-half the velocity in item 3. If the wind's velocity is still 75 km/h toward the southeast, predict the plane's new resultant velocity. Use graphical techniques.

✓ Critical Thinking

5. The water used in many sprinkler systems is recycled. For instance, a single water particle in a sprinkler system travels 85 m and then returns to the same point. What is the displacement of this water particle during one cycle?

Vector Operations

Objectives

▶ Identify appropriate coordinate systems for solving problems with vectors.

▶ Apply the Pythagorean theorem and tangent function to calculate the magnitude and direction of a resultant vector.

▶ Resolve vectors into components using the sine and cosine functions.

Key Term

components of a vector

Coordinate Systems in Two Dimensions

In the chapter "Motion in One Dimension," the motion of a gecko climbing a tree was described as motion along the y-axis. The direction of the displacement of the gecko was denoted by a positive or negative sign. The displacement of the gecko can now be described by an arrow pointing along the y-axis, as shown in **Figure 2.1**. A more versatile system for diagramming the motion of an object, however, employs vectors and the use of both the x- and y-axes simultaneously.

The addition of another axis helps describe motion in two dimensions and simplifies analysis of motion in one dimension. For example, two methods can be used to describe the motion of a jet moving at 300 m/s to the northeast. In one approach, the coordinate system can be turned so that the plane is depicted as moving along the y-axis, as in **Figure 2.2(a)**. The jet's motion also can be depicted on a two-dimensional coordinate system whose axes point north and east, as shown in **Figure 2.2(b)**.

One problem with the first method is that the axis must be turned again if the direction of the plane changes. Another problem is that the first method provides no way to deal with a second airplane that is not traveling in the same direction as the first airplane. Thus, axes are often designated using fixed directions. For example, in **Figure 2.2(b)**, the positive y-axis points north, and the positive x-axis points east. Similarly, when you analyze the motion of objects thrown into the air, orienting the y-axis parallel to the vertical direction simplifies problem solving.

FIGURE 2.1

Using a Coordinate System
A gecko's displacement while climbing a tree can be represented by an arrow pointing along the y-axis.

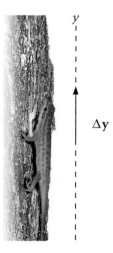

$\Delta \mathbf{y}$

> **Tips and Tricks**
>
> There are no firm rules for applying coordinate systems to situations involving vectors. As long as you are consistent, the final answer will be correct regardless of the system you choose. Perhaps your best choice for orienting axes is the approach that makes solving the problem easiest for you.

FIGURE 2.2

Two Different Coordinate Systems A plane traveling northeast at a velocity of 300 m/s can be represented as either **(a)** moving along a y-axis chosen to point to the northeast or **(b)** moving at an angle of 45° to both the x- and y-axes, which line up with west-east and south-north, respectively.

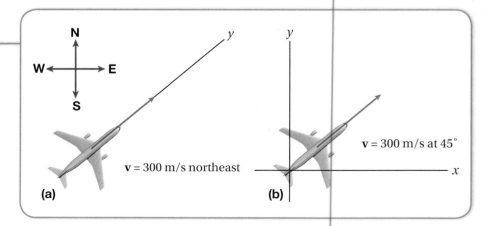

(a) $\mathbf{v} = 300$ m/s northeast

(b) $\mathbf{v} = 300$ m/s at 45°

Determining Resultant Magnitude and Direction

Earlier, we found the magnitude and direction of a resultant graphically. However, this approach is time-consuming, and the accuracy of the answer depends on how carefully the diagram is drawn and measured. A simpler method uses the Pythagorean theorem and the tangent function.

Use the Pythagorean theorem to find the magnitude of the resultant.

Imagine a tourist climbing a pyramid in Egypt. The tourist knows the height and width of the pyramid and would like to know the distance covered in a climb from the bottom to the top of the pyramid. Assume that the tourist climbs directly up the middle of one face.

As can be seen in **Figure 2.3**, the magnitude of the tourist's vertical displacement, Δy, is the height of the pyramid. The magnitude of the horizontal displacement, Δx, equals the distance from one edge of the pyramid to the middle, or half the pyramid's width. Notice that these two vectors are perpendicular and form a right triangle with the displacement, **d**.

As shown in **Figure 2.4(a)**, the Pythagorean theorem states that for any right triangle, the square of the hypotenuse—the side opposite the right angle—equals the sum of the squares of the other two sides, or legs.

FIGURE 2.3

A Triangle Inside of a Pyramid
Because the base and height of a pyramid are perpendicular, we can find a tourist's total displacement, **d**, if we know the height, Δy, and width, $2\Delta x$, of the pyramid.

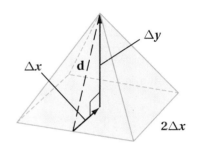

Pythagorean Theorem for Right Triangles
$$c^2 = a^2 + b^2$$

(length of hypotenuse)^2 = (length of one leg)^2 + (length of other leg)^2

In **Figure 2.4(b)**, the Pythagorean theorem is applied to find the tourist's displacement. The square of the magnitude of the displacement is equal to the sum of the square of the horizontal displacement and the square of the vertical displacement. In this way, you can find out the magnitude of the displacement, d.

FIGURE 2.4

Using the Pythagorean Theorem
(a) The Pythagorean theorem can be applied to any right triangle.
(b) It can also be applied to find the magnitude of a resultant displacement.

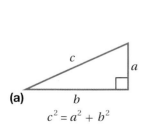

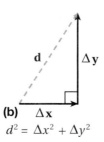

(a)
$$c^2 = a^2 + b^2$$

(b)
$$d^2 = \Delta x^2 + \Delta y^2$$

FIGURE 2.5

Using the Tangent Function

(a) The tangent function can be applied to any right triangle, and (b) it can also be used to find the direction of a resultant displacement.

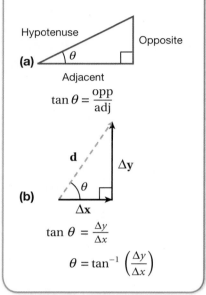

(a)
$$\tan \theta = \frac{\text{opp}}{\text{adj}}$$

(b)
$$\tan \theta = \frac{\Delta y}{\Delta x}$$
$$\theta = \tan^{-1} \left(\frac{\Delta y}{\Delta x} \right)$$

Use the tangent function to find the direction of the resultant.

In order to completely describe the tourist's displacement, you must also know the direction of the tourist's motion. Because Δx, Δy, and $\mathbf{d}$ form a right triangle, as shown in **Figure 2.5(b)**, the inverse tangent function can be used to find the angle θ, which denotes the direction of the tourist's displacement.

For any right triangle, the tangent of an angle is defined as the ratio of the opposite and adjacent legs with respect to a specified acute angle of a right triangle, as shown in **Figure 2.5(a)**.

As shown below, the magnitude of the opposite leg divided by the magnitude of the adjacent leg equals the tangent of the angle.

> ### Definition of the Tangent Function for Right Triangles
>
> $$\tan \theta = \frac{\text{opp}}{\text{adj}} \qquad \text{tangent of angle} = \frac{\text{opposite leg}}{\text{adjacent leg}}$$

The inverse of the tangent function, which is shown below, gives the angle.

$$\theta = \tan^{-1} \left(\frac{\text{opp}}{\text{adj}} \right)$$

Finding Resultant Magnitude and Direction

Sample Problem A An archaeologist climbs the Great Pyramid in Giza, Egypt. The pyramid's height is 136 m, and its width is 2.30×10^2 m. What is the magnitude and the direction of the displacement of the archaeologist after she has climbed from the bottom of the pyramid to the top?

1 ANALYZE

Given: $\Delta y = 136$ m $\qquad \Delta x = \frac{1}{2}(\text{width}) = 115$ m

Unknown: $d = ?$ $\qquad \theta = ?$

Diagram: Choose the archaeologist's starting position as the origin of the coordinate system.

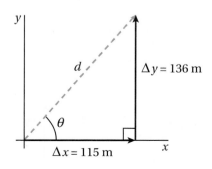

Continued

Finding Resultant Magnitude and Direction (continued)

② PLAN

Choose an equation or situation:
The Pythagorean theorem can be used to find the magnitude of the archaeologist's displacement. The direction of the displacement can be found by using the tangent function.

$$d^2 = \Delta x^2 + \Delta y^2$$
$$\tan \theta = \frac{\Delta y}{\Delta x}$$

Tips and Tricks
Be sure your calculator is set to calculate angles measured in degrees. Some calculators have a button labeled "DRG" that, when pressed, toggles between degrees, radians, and grads.

Rearrange the equations to isolate the unknowns:

$$d = \sqrt{\Delta x^2 + \Delta y^2}$$
$$\theta = \tan^{-1}\left(\frac{\Delta y}{\Delta x}\right)$$

③ SOLVE

Substitute the values into the equations and solve:

$$d = \sqrt{(115 \text{ m})^2 + (136 \text{ m})^2}$$

$$\boxed{d = 178 \text{ m}}$$

$$\theta = \tan^{-1}\left(\frac{136 \text{ m}}{115 \text{ m}}\right)$$

$$\boxed{\theta = 49.8°}$$

④ CHECK YOUR WORK

Because d is the hypotenuse, the archaeologist's displacement should be less than the sum of the height and half of the width. The angle is expected to be more than 45° because the height is greater than half of the width.

Practice

1. A truck driver is attempting to deliver some furniture. First, he travels 8 km east, and then he turns around and travels 3 km west. Finally, he turns again and travels 12 km east to his destination.

   a. What distance has the driver traveled?

   b. What is the driver's total displacement?

2. While following the directions on a treasure map, a pirate walks 45.0 m north and then turns and walks 7.5 m east. What single straight-line displacement could the pirate have taken to reach the treasure?

3. Emily passes a soccer ball 6.0 m directly across the field to Kara. Kara then kicks the ball 14.5 m directly down the field to Luisa. What is the total displacement of the ball as it travels between Emily and Luisa?

4. A hummingbird, 3.4 m above the ground, flies 1.2 m along a straight path. Upon spotting a flower below, the hummingbird drops directly downward 1.4 m to hover in front of the flower. What is the hummingbird's total displacement?

Resolving Vectors into Components

In the pyramid example, the horizontal and vertical parts that add up to give the tourist's actual displacement are called **components.** The *x*-component is parallel to the *x*-axis. The *y*-component is parallel to the *y*-axis. Any vector can be completely described by a set of perpendicular components.

In this textbook, components of vectors are shown as outlined, open arrows. Components have arrowheads to indicate their direction. Components are scalars (numbers), but they are signed numbers. The direction is important to determine their sign in a coordinate system.

You can often describe an object's motion more conveniently by breaking a single vector into two components, or *resolving* the vector. Resolving a vector allows you to analyze the motion in each direction.

This point is illustrated by examining a scene on the set of an action movie. For this scene, a plane travels at 95 km/h at an angle of 20° relative to the ground. Filming the plane from below, a camera team travels in a truck directly beneath the plane at all times, as shown in **Figure 2.6.**

To find the velocity that the truck must maintain to stay beneath the plane, we must know the horizontal component of the plane's velocity. Once more, the key to solving the problem is to recognize that a right triangle can be drawn using the plane's velocity and its *x*- and *y*-components. The situation can then be analyzed using trigonometry.

The sine and cosine functions are defined in terms of the lengths of the sides of such right triangles. The sine of an angle is the ratio of the leg opposite that angle to the hypotenuse.

> **Definition of the Sine Function for Right Triangles**
>
> $$\sin \theta = \frac{\text{opp}}{\text{hyp}} \qquad \text{sine of an angle} = \frac{\text{opposite leg}}{\text{hypotenuse}}$$

In **Figure 2.7**, the leg opposite the 20° angle represents the *y*-component, v_y, which describes the vertical speed of the airplane. The hypotenuse, $\mathbf{v}_{\text{plane}}$, is the resultant vector that describes the airplane's total velocity.

The cosine of an angle is the ratio between the leg adjacent to that angle and the hypotenuse.

> **Definition of the Cosine Function for Right Triangles**
>
> $$\cos \theta = \frac{\text{adj}}{\text{hyp}} \qquad \text{cosine of an angle} = \frac{\text{adjacent leg}}{\text{hypotenuse}}$$

In **Figure 2.7**, the adjacent leg represents the *x*-component, v_x, which describes the airplane's horizontal speed. This *x*-component equals the speed required of the truck to remain beneath the plane. Thus, the truck must maintain a speed of $v_x = (\cos 20°)(95 \text{ km/h}) = 90 \text{ km/h}$.

components of a vector the projections of a vector along the axes of a coordinate system

FIGURE 2.6

Diagramming a Movie Scene

A truck carrying a film crew must be driven at the correct velocity to enable the crew to film the underside of a plane. The plane flies at 95 km/h at an angle of 20° relative to the ground.

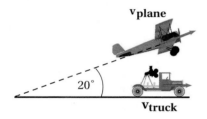

FIGURE 2.7

Using Vector Components

To stay beneath the biplane, the truck must be driven with a velocity equal to the *x*-component (v_x) of the biplane's velocity.

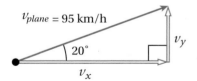

GO ONLINE

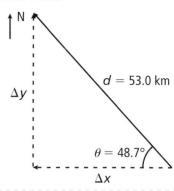

Interactive Demo
HMHScience.com

Sample Problem B The straight stretch of Interstate Highway 5 from Mettler, California, to a point near Buttonwillow, California, is 53.0 km long and makes an angle of 48.7° north of west. What are the northern and western components of this highway segment?

① ANALYZE

Given: $d = 53.0$ km $\quad \theta = 48.7°$ north of west

Unknown: $\Delta x = ?$ $\quad \Delta y = ?$

Diagram:

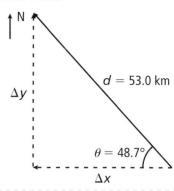

$d = 53.0$ km
Δy
$\theta = 48.7°$
Δx

② PLAN

Choose an equation or situation:
Because the axes are perpendicular, the sine and cosine functions can be used to find the components.

$$\sin \theta = \frac{\Delta y}{d}$$

$$\cos \theta = \frac{\Delta x}{d}$$

Rearrange the equations to isolate the unknowns:

$$\Delta x = d \, (\cos \theta)$$

$$\Delta y = d \, (\sin \theta)$$

Tips and Tricks

Don't assume that the cosine function can always be used for the x-component and the sine function can always be used for the y-component. The correct choice of function depends on where the given angle is located. Instead, always check to see which component is adjacent and which component is opposite to the given angle.

③ SOLVE

Substitute the values into the equations and solve:

$$\Delta x = (53.0 \text{ km}) \, (\cos 48.7°)$$

$$\boxed{\Delta x = 35.0 \text{ km, west}}$$

$$\Delta y = (53.0 \text{ km}) \, (\sin 48.7°)$$

$$\boxed{\Delta y = 39.8 \text{ km, north}}$$

④ CHECK YOUR ANSWER

Using the Pythagorean theorem to check the answers confirms the magnitudes of the components.

$$d^2 = \Delta x^2 + \Delta y^2$$

$$(53.0 \text{ km})^2 = (35.0 \text{ km})^2 + (39.8 \text{ km})^2$$

$$2.80 \times 10^3 \text{ km}^2 = 1.22 \times 10^3 \text{ km}^2 + 1.58 \times 10^3 \text{ km}^2$$

$$2.80 \times 10^3 \text{ km}^2 = 2.80 \times 10^3 \text{ km}^2$$

Resolving Vectors (continued)

Practice

1. How fast must a truck travel to stay beneath an airplane that is moving 105 km/h at an angle of 25° to the ground?

2. What is the magnitude of the vertical component of the velocity of the plane in item 1?

3. A skyrocket travels 113 m at an angle of 82.4° with respect to the ground and toward the south. What is the rocket's horizontal displacement?

4. A tiger leaps with an initial velocity of 55.0 km/h at an angle of 13.0° with respect to the horizontal. What are the components of the tiger's velocity?

Adding Vectors That Are Not Perpendicular

Until this point, the vector-addition problems concerned vectors that are perpendicular to one another. However, many objects move in one direction and then turn at an angle before continuing their motion.

Suppose that a plane initially travels 5 km at an angle of 35° to the ground, then climbs at only 10° relative to the ground for 22 km. How can you determine the magnitude and direction for the vector denoting the total displacement of the plane?

Because the original displacement vectors do not form a right triangle, you cannot apply the tangent function or the Pythagorean theorem when adding the original two vectors.

Determining the magnitude and the direction of the resultant can be achieved by resolving each of the plane's displacement vectors into its x- and y-components. Then the components along each axis can be added together. As shown in **Figure 2.8**, these sums will be the two perpendicular components of the resultant, **d**. The resultant's magnitude can then be found by using the Pythagorean theorem, and its direction can be found by using the inverse tangent function.

FIGURE 2.8

Adding Vectors That Are Not Perpendicular Add the components of the original displacement vectors to find two components that form a right triangle with the resultant vector.

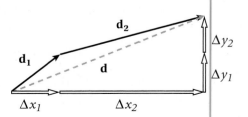

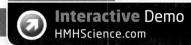
Adding Vectors Algebraically

Sample Problem C A hiker walks 27.0 km from her base camp at 35° south of east. The next day, she walks 41.0 km in a direction 65° north of east and discovers a forest ranger's tower. Find the magnitude and direction of her resultant displacement between the base camp and the tower.

1 ANALYZE

Select a coordinate system. Then sketch and label each vector.

Given: $d_1 = 27.0 \text{ km}$ $\theta_1 = -35°$

$d_2 = 41.0 \text{ km}$ $\theta_2 = 65°$

Unknown: $d = ?$ $\theta = ?$

Tips and Tricks

θ_1 is negative, because clockwise angles from the positive *x*-axis are conventionally considered to be negative.

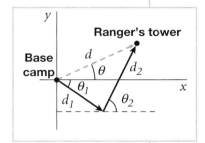

2 PLAN

Find the *x*- and *y*-components of all vectors.
Make a separate sketch of the displacements for each day. Use the cosine and sine functions to find the displacement components.

$$\cos \theta = \frac{\Delta x}{d} \qquad \sin \theta = \frac{\Delta y}{d}$$

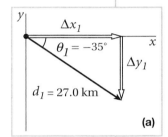

(a)

(a) For day 1:

$$\Delta x_1 = d_1 \cos \theta_1 = (27.0 \text{ km}) [\cos (-35°)] = 22 \text{ km}$$

$$\Delta y_1 = d_1 \sin \theta_1 = (27.0 \text{ km}) [\sin (-35°)] = -15 \text{ km}$$

(b) For day 2:

$$\Delta x_2 = d_2 \cos \theta_2 = (41.0 \text{ km}) (\cos 65°) = 17 \text{ km}$$

$$\Delta y_2 = d_2 \sin \theta_2 = (41.0 \text{ km}) (\sin 65°) = 37 \text{ km}$$

Find the *x*- and *y*-components of the total displacement.

$$\Delta x_{tot} = \Delta x_1 + \Delta x_2 = 22 \text{ km} + 17 \text{ km} = 39 \text{ km}$$

$$\Delta y_{tot} = \Delta y_1 + \Delta y_2 = -15 \text{ km} + 37 \text{ km} = 22 \text{ km}$$

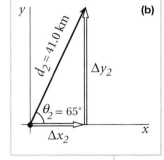

(b)

3 SOLVE

Use the Pythagorean theorem to find the magnitude of the resultant vector.

$$d^2 = (\Delta x_{tot})^2 + (\Delta y_{tot})^2$$

$$d = \sqrt{(\Delta x_{tot})^2 + (\Delta y_{tot})^2} = \sqrt{(39 \text{ km})^2 + (22 \text{ km})^2} = \boxed{45 \text{ km}}$$

Use a suitable trigonometric function to find the angle.

$$\theta = \tan^{-1}\left(\frac{\Delta y_{tot}}{\Delta x_{tot}}\right) = \tan^{-1}\left(\frac{22 \text{ km}}{39 \text{ km}}\right) = \boxed{29° \text{ north of east}}$$

Adding Vectors Algebraically (continued)

Practice

1 A football player runs directly down the field for 35 m before turning to the right at an angle of 25° from his original direction and running an additional 15 m before getting tackled. What is the magnitude and direction of the runner's total displacement?

2. A plane travels 2.5 km at an angle of 35° to the ground and then changes direction and travels 5.2 km at an angle of 22° to the ground. What is the magnitude and direction of the plane's total displacement?

3. During a rodeo, a clown runs 8.0 m north, turns 55° north of east, and runs 3.5 m. Then, after waiting for the bull to come near, the clown turns due east and runs 5.0 m to exit the arena. What is the clown's total displacement?

4. An airplane flying parallel to the ground undergoes two consecutive displacements. The first is 75 km 30.0° west of north, and the second is 155 km 60.0° east of north. What is the total displacement of the airplane?

 SECTION 2 FORMATIVE ASSESSMENT

▶ Reviewing Main Ideas

1. Identify a convenient coordinate system for analyzing each of the following situations:
   a. a dog walking along a sidewalk
   b. an acrobat walking along a high wire
   c. a submarine submerging at an angle of 30° to the horizontal

2. Find the magnitude and direction of the resultant velocity vector for the following perpendicular velocities:
   a. a fish swimming at 3.0 m/s relative to the water across a river that moves at 5.0 m/s
   b. a surfer traveling at 1.0 m/s relative to the water across a wave that is traveling at 6.0 m/s

3. Find the vector components along the directions noted in parentheses.
   a. a car displaced 45° north of east by 10.0 km (north and east)
   b. a duck accelerating away from a hunter at 2.0 m/s² at an angle of 35° to the ground (horizontal and vertical)

✔ Critical Thinking

4. Why do nonperpendicular vectors need to be resolved into components before you can add the vectors together?

Projectile Motion

Key Term

projectile motion

Two-Dimensional Motion

Previously, we showed how quantities such as displacement and velocity were vectors that could be resolved into components. In this section, these components will be used to understand and predict the motion of objects thrown into the air.

Use of components avoids vector multiplication.

How can you know the displacement, velocity, and acceleration of a ball at any point in time during its flight? All of the kinematic equations could be rewritten in terms of vector quantities. However, when an object is propelled into the air in a direction other than straight up or down, the velocity, acceleration, and displacement of the object do not all point in the same direction. This makes the vector forms of the equations difficult to solve.

One way to deal with these situations is to avoid using the complicated vector forms of the equations altogether. Instead, apply the technique of resolving vectors into components. Then you can apply the simpler one-dimensional forms of the equations for each component. Finally, you can recombine the components to determine the resultant.

Components simplify projectile motion.

When a long jumper approaches his jump, he runs along a straight line, which can be called the *x*-axis. When he jumps, as shown in **Figure 3.1**, his velocity has both horizontal and vertical components. Movement in this plane can be depicted by using both the *x*- and *y*-axes.

Note that in **Figure 3.2(b)**, a jumper's velocity vector is resolved into its two vector components. This way, the jumper's motion can be analyzed using the kinematic equations applied to one direction at a time.

SECTION 3

Objectives

▶ Recognize examples of projectile motion.

▶ Describe the path of a projectile as a parabola.

▶ Resolve vectors into components and apply kinematic equations to solve problems involving projectile motion.

FIGURE 3.1

Motion of a Long Jumper

When the long jumper is in the air, his velocity has both a horizontal and a vertical component.

FIGURE 3.2

Components of a Long Jumper's Velocity

(a) A long jumper's velocity while sprinting along the runway can be represented by a horizontal vector.
(b) Once the jumper is airborne, the jumper's velocity at any instant can be described by the components of the velocity.

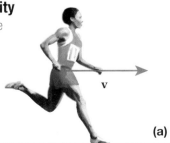

$\mathbf{v}$

(a)

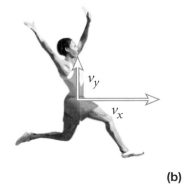

v_y

v_x

(b)

©Michael Wong/Corbis

FIGURE 3.3

Air Resistance Affects Projectile Motion (a) Without air resistance, the soccer ball would travel along a parabola. (b) With air resistance, the soccer ball would travel along a shorter path.

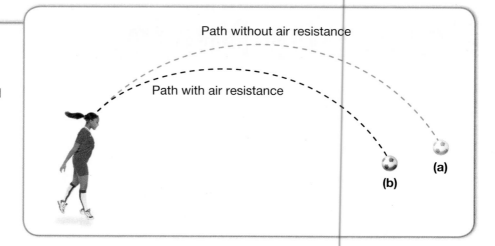

Path without air resistance

Path with air resistance

(a)

(b)

projectile motion the motion that an object exhibits when thrown, launched, or otherwise projected near the surface of Earth

In this section, we will focus on the form of two-dimensional motion called **projectile motion.** Objects that are thrown or launched into the air and are subject to gravity are called *projectiles.* Some examples of projectiles are softballs, footballs, and arrows when they are projected through the air. Even a long jumper can be considered a projectile.

Projectiles follow parabolic trajectories.

The path of a projectile is a curve called a *parabola,* as shown in **Figure 3.3(a).** Many people mistakenly think that projectiles eventually fall straight down in much the same way that a cartoon character does after running off a cliff. But if an object has an initial horizontal velocity, there will be horizontal motion throughout the flight of the projectile. *Note that for the purposes of samples and exercises in this book, the horizontal velocity of projectiles will be considered constant.* This velocity would not be constant if we accounted for air resistance. With air resistance, projectiles slow down as they collide with air particles, as shown in **Figure 3.3(b).**

Projectile motion is free fall with an initial horizontal velocity.

To understand the motion a projectile undergoes, first examine **Figure 3.4** on the following page. The red ball was dropped at the same instant the yellow ball was launched horizontally. If air resistance is disregarded, both balls hit the ground at the same time. By examining each ball's position in relation to the horizontal lines and to one another, we see that the two balls fall at the same rate. This may seem impossible because one is given an initial velocity and the other begins from rest. But if the motion is analyzed one component at a time, it makes sense.

First, consider the red ball that falls straight down. It has no motion in the horizontal direction. In the vertical direction, it starts from rest ($v_{y,i} = 0$ m/s) and proceeds in free fall. Thus, the kinematic equations from the chapter "Motion in One Dimension" can be applied to analyze the vertical motion of the falling ball, as shown on the next page. Note that on Earth's surface, the acceleration (a_y) will equal $-g$ (-9.81 m/s^2) because the only vertical component of acceleration is free-fall acceleration. Note also that Δy is negative.

Did YOU Know?

The greatest distance a regulation-size baseball has ever been thrown is 135.9 m, by Glen Gorbous in 1957.

Vertical Motion of a Projectile That Falls from Rest

$$v_{y,f} = a_y \Delta t$$
$$v_{y,f}^2 = 2a_y \Delta y$$
$$\Delta y = \frac{1}{2}a_y(\Delta t)^2$$

Now consider the components of motion of the yellow ball that is launched in **Figure 3.4**. This ball undergoes the same horizontal displacement during each time interval. This means that the ball's horizontal velocity remains constant (if air resistance is assumed to be negligible). Thus, when the kinematic equations are used to analyze the horizontal motion of a projectile, the initial horizontal velocity is equal to the horizontal velocity throughout the projectile's flight. A projectile's horizontal motion is described by the following equation.

Horizontal Motion of a Projectile

$$v_x = v_{x,i} = \text{constant}$$
$$\Delta x = v_x \Delta t$$

Next consider the initial motion of the launched yellow ball in **Figure 3.4**. Despite having an initial horizontal velocity, the launched ball has no initial velocity in the vertical direction. Just like the red ball that falls straight down, the launched yellow ball is in free fall. The vertical motion of the launched yellow ball is described by the same free-fall equations. In any time interval, the launched ball undergoes the same vertical displacement as the ball that falls straight down. For this reason, both balls reach the ground at the same time.

To find the velocity of a projectile at any point during its flight, find the vector that has the known components. Specifically, use the Pythagorean theorem to find the magnitude of the velocity, and use the tangent function to find the direction of the velocity.

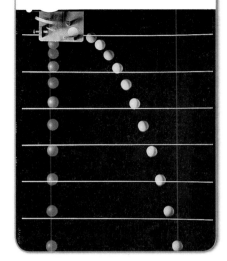

FIGURE 3.4

Vertical Motion of a Projectile This is a strobe photograph of two table-tennis balls released at the same time. Even though the yellow ball is given an initial horizontal velocity and the red ball is simply dropped, both balls fall at the same rate.

QuickLAB — PROJECTILE MOTION

Roll a ball off a table. At the instant the rolling ball leaves the table, drop a second ball from the same height above the floor. Do the two balls hit the floor at the same time?

Try varying the speed at which you roll the first ball off the table. Does varying the speed affect whether the two balls strike the ground at the same time? Next roll one of the balls down a slope. Drop the other ball from the base of the slope at the instant the first ball leaves the slope. Which of the balls hits the ground first in this situation?

MATERIALS
- 2 identical balls
- slope or ramp

SAFETY

Perform this experiment away from walls and furniture that can be damaged.

Projectiles Launched Horizontally

GO ONLINE

Interactive Demo
HMHScience.com

Sample Problem D The Royal Gorge Bridge in Colorado rises 321 m above the Arkansas River. Suppose you kick a rock horizontally off the bridge. The magnitude of the rock's horizontal displacement is 45.0 m. Find the speed at which the rock was kicked.

① ANALYZE

Given: $\Delta y = -321$ m $\Delta x = 45.0$ m $a_y = -g = -9.81$ m/s^2

Unknown: $v_i = v_x = ?$

Diagram: The initial velocity vector of the rock has only a horizontal component. Choose the coordinate system oriented so that the positive y direction points upward and the positive x direction points to the right.

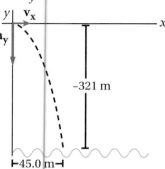

② PLAN

Choose an equation or situation:
Because air resistance can be neglected, the rock's horizontal velocity remains constant.

$$\Delta x = v_x \Delta t$$

Because there is no initial vertical velocity, the following equation applies.

$$\Delta y = \frac{1}{2}a_y(\Delta t)^2$$

Rearrange the equations to isolate the unknowns:
Note that the time interval is the same for the vertical and horizontal displacements, so the second equation can be rearranged to solve for Δt.

> **Tips and Tricks**
> The value for v_x can be either positive or negative because of the square root. Because the object is moving in what has been selected as the positive direction, you choose the positive answer.

$$\Delta t = \sqrt{\frac{2\Delta y}{a_y}}$$

Next rearrange the first equation for v_x, and substitute the above value of Δt into the new equation.

$$v_x = \frac{\Delta x}{\Delta t} = \left(\sqrt{\frac{a_y}{2\Delta y}}\right)\Delta x$$

③ SOLVE

Substitute the values into the equation and solve:

$$v_x = \sqrt{\frac{-9.81 \text{ m/s}^2}{(2)(-321 \text{ m})}}(45.0 \text{ m}) = \boxed{5.56 \text{ m/s}}$$

④ CHECK YOUR ANSWER

To check your work, estimate the value of the time interval for Δx and solve for Δy. If v_x is about 5.5 m/s and $\Delta x = 45$ m, $\Delta t \approx 8$ s. If you use an approximate value of 10 m/s^2 for g, $\Delta y \approx -320$ m, almost identical to the given value.

Continued

Projectiles Launched Horizontally (continued)

Practice

1. A baseball rolls off a 0.70 m high desk and strikes the floor 0.25 m away from the base of the desk. How fast was the ball rolling?

2. A cat chases a mouse across a 1.0 m high table. The mouse steps out of the way, and the cat slides off the table and strikes the floor 2.2 m from the edge of the table. When the cat slid off the table, what was its speed?

3. A pelican flying along a horizontal path drops a fish from a height of 5.4 m. The fish travels 8.0 m horizontally before it hits the water below. What is the pelican's speed?

4. If the pelican in item 3 was traveling at the same speed but was only 2.7 m above the water, how far would the fish travel horizontally before hitting the water below?

Use components to analyze objects launched at an angle.

Let us examine a case in which a projectile is launched at an angle to the horizontal, as shown in **Figure 3.5**. The projectile has an initial vertical component of velocity as well as a horizontal component of velocity.

Suppose the initial velocity vector makes an angle θ with the horizontal. Again, to analyze the motion of such a projectile, you must resolve the initial velocity vector into its components. The sine and cosine functions can be used to find the horizontal and vertical components of the initial velocity.

$$v_{x,i} = v_i \cos \theta \quad \text{and} \quad v_{y,i} = v_i \sin \theta$$

We can substitute these values for $v_{x,i}$ and $v_{y,i}$ into the kinematic equations to obtain a set of equations that can be used to analyze the motion of a projectile launched at an angle.

Projectiles Launched at an Angle

$$v_x = v_{x,i} = v_i \cos \theta = \text{constant}$$
$$\Delta x = (v_i \cos \theta)\Delta t$$
$$v_{y,f} = v_i \sin \theta + a_y \Delta t$$
$$v_{y,f}^2 = v_i^2 (\sin \theta)^2 + 2a_y \Delta y$$
$$\Delta y = (v_i \sin \theta)\Delta t + \frac{1}{2}a_y(\Delta t)^2$$

As we have seen, the velocity of a projectile launched at an angle to the ground has both horizontal and vertical components. The vertical motion is similar to that of an object that is thrown straight up with an initial velocity.

FIGURE 3.5

Components of Initial Velocity

An object is projected with an initial velocity, $\mathbf{v_i}$, at an angle of θ. Resolve the initial velocity into its x- and y-components. Then, the kinematic equations can be applied to describe the motion of the projectile throughout its flight.

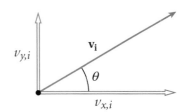

Projectiles Launched at an Angle

Sample Problem E Seil Sound in Scotland is a narrow strait that lies between the mainland and the island of Seil. The strait is only about 6.0 m wide. Suppose an athlete wanting to jump "over the sea" leaps at an angle of 35° with respect to the horizontal. What is the minimum initial speed that would allow the athlete to complete the jump? Neglect air resistance.

① ANALYZE

Given:

$$\Delta x = 6.0 \text{ m}$$

$$\theta = 35° \text{ m}$$

$$a_y = -g = -9.81 \text{ m/s}^2$$

Unknown: $v_i = ?$

② PLAN

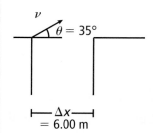

$\theta = 35°$

$\vdash \!\!\!-\Delta x-\!\!\!\dashv$
$= 6.00 \text{ m}$

Choose an equation or situation: The horizontal component of the athlete's velocity, v_x, is equal to the initial speed multiplied by the cosine of the angle, θ, which is equal to the magnitude of the horizontal displacement, Δx, divided by the time interval required for the complete jump.

$$v_x = v_i \cos \theta = \frac{\Delta x}{\Delta t}$$

At the midpoint of the jump, the vertical component of the athlete's velocity, v_y, equals zero. The time required for this to occur is half the time necessary for the total jump.

$$v_y = v_i \sin \theta + a_y \left(\frac{\Delta t}{2} \right) = 0$$

$$v_i \sin \theta = \frac{-a_y \Delta t}{2}$$

Rearrange the equations to isolate the unknowns: Express Δt in the second equation in terms of the displacement and velocity component in the first equation.

$$v_i \sin \theta = \frac{-a_y}{2} \left(\frac{\Delta x}{v_i \cos \theta} \right)$$

$$v_i^2 = \frac{-a_y \Delta x}{2 \sin \theta \cos \theta}$$

$$v_i = \sqrt{\frac{-a_y \Delta x}{2 \sin \theta \cos \theta}}$$

③ SOLVE

Substitute the values into the equations and solve: Select the positive root for v_i.

$$v_i = \sqrt{\frac{-(-9.81 \text{ m/s}^2)(6.0 \text{ m})}{(2)(\sin 35°)(\cos 35°)}}$$

$$\boxed{v_i = 7.9 \text{ m/s}}$$

① CHECK YOUR WORK

By substituting the value for v_i into the original equations, you can determine the time for the jump to be completed, which is 0.92 s. From this, the height of the jump is found to equal 1.0 m.

Continued

Projectiles Launched at an Angle (continued)

Practice

1. Measurements made in 1910 indicate that the common flea is an impressive jumper, given its size. Assume that a flea's initial speed is 2.2 m/s, and that it leaps at an angle of 21° with respect to the horizontal. If the jump lasts 0.16 s, what is the magnitude of the flea's horizontal displacement? How high does the flea jump?

2. A scared kangaroo cleared a fence by jumping with a speed of 8.42 m/s at an angle of 55.2° with respect to the ground. If the jump lasted 1.40 s, how high was the fence? What was the kangaroo's horizontal displacement?

3. A baseball is thrown at an angle of 25° relative to the ground at a speed of 23.0 m/s. If the ball is caught 42.0 m from the thrower, how long was it in the air? How high above the thrower did the ball travel?

4. Salmon often jump waterfalls to reach their breeding grounds. One salmon starts 2.00 m from a waterfall that is 0.55 m tall and jumps at an angle of 32.0°. What must be the salmon's minimum speed to reach the waterfall?

 ## SECTION 3 FORMATIVE ASSESSMENT

▶ Reviewing Main Ideas

1. Which of the following exhibit parabolic motion?
   a. a flat rock skipping across the surface of a lake
   b. a three-point shot in basketball
   c. a space shuttle while orbiting Earth
   d. a ball bouncing across a room
   e. a life preserver dropped from a stationary helicopter

2. During a thunderstorm, a tornado lifts a car to a height of 125 m above the ground. Increasing in strength, the tornado flings the car horizontally with a speed of 90.0 m/s. How long does the car take to reach the ground? How far horizontally does the car travel before hitting the ground?

Interpreting Graphics

3. An Alaskan rescue plane drops a package of emergency rations to a stranded party of explorers, as illustrated in **Figure 3.6**. The plane is traveling horizontally at 30.0 m/s at a height of 200.0 m above the ground.
   a. What horizontal distance does the package fall before landing?
   b. Find the velocity of the package just before it hits the ground.

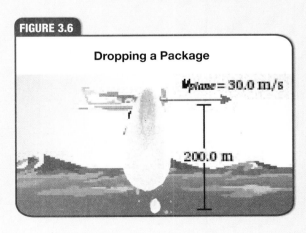

FIGURE 3.6

Dropping a Package

$v_{plane} = 30.0$ m/s

200.0 m

Relative Motion

Frames of Reference

If you are moving at 80 km/h north and a car passes you going 90 km/h
north, to you the faster car seems to be moving north at 10 km/h.
Someone standing on the side of the road would measure the velocity of
the faster car as 90 km/h north. This simple example demonstrates that
velocity measurements depend on the frame of reference of the observer.

Velocity measurements differ in different frames of reference.

Observers using different frames of reference may measure different
displacements or velocities for an object in motion. That is, two observers
moving with respect to each other would generally not agree on some
features of the motion.

Consider a stunt dummy that is dropped from an airplane flying
horizontally over Earth with a constant velocity. As shown in **Figure 4.1(a)**,
a passenger on the airplane would describe the motion of the dummy as
a straight line toward Earth. An observer on the ground would view the
trajectory of the dummy as that of a projectile, as shown in **Figure 4.1(b)**.
Relative to the ground, the dummy would have a vertical component of
velocity (resulting from free-fall acceleration and equal to the velocity
measured by the observer in the airplane) *and* a horizontal component of
velocity given to it by the airplane's motion. If the airplane continued to
move horizontally with the same velocity, the dummy would enter the
swimming pool directly beneath the airplane (assuming negligible air
resistance).

FIGURE 4.1

Frames of Reference When
viewed from the plane **(a),** the stunt
dummy (represented by the maroon dot)
falls straight down. When viewed from a
stationary position on the ground **(b),**
the stunt dummy follows a parabolic
projectile path.

(a)

(b)

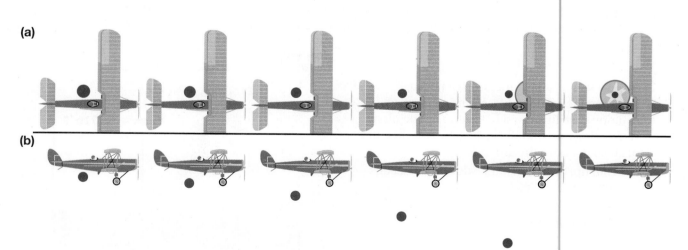

Relative Velocity

The case of the faster car overtaking your car was easy to solve with a minimum of thought and effort, but you will encounter many situations in which a more systematic method of solving such problems is beneficial. To develop this method, write down all the information that is given and that you want to know in the form of velocities with subscripts appended.

$\mathbf{v_{se}}$ = +80 km/h north (Here the subscript *se* means the velocity of the *slower* car with respect to *Earth*.)

$\mathbf{v_{fe}}$ = +90 km/h north (The subscript *fe* means the velocity of the *fast* car with respect to *Earth*.)

We want to know $\mathbf{v_{fs}}$, which is the velocity of the fast car with respect to the slower car. To find this, we write an equation for $\mathbf{v_{fs}}$ in terms of the other velocities, so on the right side of the equation the subscripts start with *f* and eventually end with *s*. Also, each velocity subscript starts with the letter that ended the preceding velocity subscript.

$$\mathbf{v_{fs}} = \mathbf{v_{fe}} + \mathbf{v_{es}}$$

The boldface notation indicates that velocity is a vector quantity. This approach to adding and monitoring subscripts is similar to vector addition, in which vector arrows are placed head to tail to find a resultant.

We know that $\mathbf{v_{es}} = -\mathbf{v_{se}}$ because an observer in the slow car perceives Earth as moving south at a velocity of 80 km/h while a stationary observer on the ground (Earth) views the car as moving north at a velocity of 80 km/h. Thus, this problem can be solved as follows:

$$\mathbf{v_{fs}} = \mathbf{v_{fe}} + \mathbf{v_{es}} = \mathbf{v_{fe}} - \mathbf{v_{se}}$$

$$\mathbf{v_{fs}} = (+90 \text{ km/h north}) - (+80 \text{ km/h north}) = +10 \text{ km/h north}$$

When solving relative velocity problems, follow the above technique for writing subscripts. The particular subscripts will vary depending on the problem, but the method for ordering the subscripts does not change. A general form of the relative velocity equation is $\mathbf{v_{ac}} = \mathbf{v_{ab}} + \mathbf{v_{bc}}$. This general form may help you remember the technique for writing subscripts.

Conceptual Challenge

1. Elevator Acceleration A boy bounces a rubber ball in an elevator that is going down. If the boy drops the ball as the elevator is slowing down, is the magnitude of the ball's acceleration relative to the elevator less than or greater than the magnitude of its acceleration relative to the ground?

2. Aircraft Carrier Is the velocity of a plane relative to an aircraft carrier slower when it approaches from the stern (rear) or from the bow (front)?

Relative Velocity

Sample Problem F The world's fastest current is in Slingsby Channel, Canada, where the speed of the water reaches 30.0 km/h. Suppose a motorboat crosses the channel perpendicular to the bank at a speed of 18.0 km/h relative to the bank. Find the velocity of the motorboat relative to the water.

❶ ANALYZE

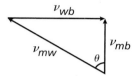

Given: $v_{wb} = 30.0$ km/h along the channel
(velocity of the *water, w*, with respect to the bank, *b*)

$v_{mb} = 18.0$ km/h perpendicular to the channel
(velocity of the *motorboat, m*, with respect to the bank, *b*)

Unknown: $v_{mw} = ?$ $\theta = ?$

Diagram: See the diagram on the left.

To proceed straight across the channel, the motorboat must be angled sharply upstream. The result of this diagonal motion and the current is that the horizontal components cancel, leaving v_{mb}.

❷ PLAN

Choose an equation: Use the Pythagorean theorem to calculate the magnitude of the hypotenuse, and use the tangent function to find the direction.

$$v_{mw}^2 = v_{mb}^2 + v_{wb}^2$$

$$\tan \theta = \frac{v_{mb}}{v_{mb}}$$

Rearrange the equations to isolate the unknowns:

$$v_{mw} = \sqrt{(v_{mb})^2 + (v_{wb})^2}$$

$$\theta = \tan^{-1}\left(\frac{v_{wb}}{v_{mb}}\right)$$

❸ SOLVE

Substitute the values into the equations and solve: Choose the positive root for v_{mw}.

$$v_{mw} = \sqrt{\left(18.0\,\frac{km}{h}\right)^2 + \left(30.0\,\frac{km}{h}\right)^2}$$

$$\boxed{v_{mw} = 35.0\,\frac{km}{h}}$$

The angle between v_{mb} and v_{mw} is as follows:

$$\theta = \tan^{-1}\left(\frac{30.0\,\frac{km}{h}}{18.0\,\frac{km}{h}}\right) = 59.0° \text{ away from the oncoming current}$$

❹ CHECK YOUR WORK

The motorboat must move in a direction 59° with respect to v_{mb} and against the current, and with a speed of 35.0 km/h in order to move 18.0 km/h perpendicular to the bank.

Continued ▶

Relative Velocity (continued)

Practice

1. George V Coast in Antarctica is the windiest place on Earth. Wind speeds there can reach 3.00×10^2 km/h. If a research plane flies against the wind with a speed of 4.50×10^2 km/h relative to the wind, how long does it take the plane to fly between two research stations that are 250 km apart?

2. A spy runs from the front to the back of an aircraft carrier at a velocity of 3.5 m/s. If the aircraft carrier is moving forward at 18.0 m/s, how fast does the spy appear to be running when viewed by an observer on a nearby stationary submarine?

3. California sea lions can swim as fast as 40.0 km/h. Suppose a sea lion begins to chase a fish at this speed when the fish is 60.0 m away. The fish, of course, does not wait, and swims away at a speed of 16.0 km/h. How long would it take the sea lion to catch the fish?

4. A pet-store supply truck moves at 25.0 m/s north along a highway. Inside, a dog moves at 1.75 m/s at an angle of 35.0° east of north. What is the velocity of the dog relative to the road?

 ## SECTION 4 FORMATIVE ASSESSMENT

▶ Reviewing Main Ideas

1. A woman on a ten-speed bicycle travels at 9 m/s relative to the ground as she passes a little boy on a tricycle going in the opposite direction. If the boy is traveling at 1 m/s relative to the ground, how fast does the boy appear to be moving relative to the woman?

2. A girl at an airport rolls a ball north on a moving walkway that moves east. If the ball's speed with respect to the walkway is 0.15 m/s and the walkway moves at a speed of 1.50 m/s, what is the velocity of the ball relative to the ground?

✔ Critical Thinking

3. Describe the motion of the following objects if they are observed from the stated frames of reference:
   a. a person standing on a platform viewed from a train traveling north
   b. a train traveling north viewed by a person standing on a platform
   c. a ball dropped by a boy walking at a speed of 1 m/s viewed by the boy
   d. a ball dropped by a boy walking 1 m/s as seen by a nearby viewer who is stationary

Special Relativity and Velocities

In the chapter "Two-Dimensional Motion and Vectors," you learned that velocity measurements are not absolute; every velocity measurement depends on the frame of reference of the observer with respect to the moving object. For example, imagine that someone riding a bike toward you at 25 m/s (v) throws a softball toward you. If the bicyclist measures the softball's speed (u') to be 15 m/s, you would perceive the ball to be moving toward you at 40 m/s (u) because you have a different frame of reference than the bicyclist does. This is expressed mathematically by the equation $u = v + u'$, which is also known as the classical addition of velocities.

The Speed of Light

As stated in the feature "Special Relativity and Time Dilation," according to Einstein's special theory of relativity, the speed of light is absolute, or independent of all frames of reference. If, instead of a softball, the bicyclist were to shine a beam of light toward you, both you and the bicyclist would measure the light's speed as 3.0×10^8 m/s. This would remain true even if the bicyclist were moving toward you at 99 percent of the speed of light. Thus, Einstein's theory requires a different approach to the addition of velocities. Einstein's modification of the classical formula, which he derived in his 1905 paper on special relativity, covers both the case of the softball and the case of the light beam.

$$u = \frac{v + u'}{1 + (vu'/c^2)}$$

In the equation, u is the velocity of an object in a reference frame, u' is the velocity of the same object in another reference frame, v is the velocity of one reference frame relative to another, and c is the speed of light.

The Universality of Einstein's Equation

How does Einstein's equation cover both cases? First we shall consider the bicyclist throwing a softball. Because c^2 is such a large number, the vu'/c^2 term in the denominator is very small for velocities typical of our everyday experience. As a result, the denominator of the equation is essentially equal to 1. Hence, for speeds that are small compared with c, the two theories give nearly the same result, $u = v + u'$, and the classical addition of velocities can be used.

However, when speeds approach the speed of light, vu'/c^2 increases, and the denominator becomes greater than 1 but never more than 2.

FIGURE 1

Nothing Can Travel Faster Than the Speed of Light

According to Einstein's relativistic equation for the addition of velocities, material particles can never reach the speed of light.

When this occurs, the difference between the two theories becomes significant. For example, if a bicyclist moving toward you at 80 percent of the speed of light were to throw a ball to you at 70 percent of the speed of light, you would observe the ball moving toward you at about 96 percent of the speed of light rather than the 150 percent of the speed of light predicted by classical theory. In this case, the difference between the velocities predicted by each theory cannot be ignored, and the relativistic addition of velocities must be used.

In this last example, it is significant that classical addition predicts a speed greater than the speed of light ($1.5c$), while the relativistic addition predicts a speed less than the speed of light ($0.96c$). In fact, no matter how close the speeds involved are to the speed of light, the relativistic equation yields a result less than the speed of light, as seen in **Figure 2**.

How does Einstein's equation cover the second case, in which the bicyclist shines a beam of light toward you? Einstein's equation predicts that any object traveling at the speed of light ($u' = c$) will appear to travel at the speed of light ($u = c$) for an observer in any reference frame:

$$u = \frac{v + u'}{1 + (vu'/c^2)} = \frac{v + c}{1 + (vc/c^2)} = \frac{v + c}{1 + (v/c)} = \frac{v + c}{(c + v)/c} = c$$

This corresponds with our earlier statement that the bicyclist measures the beam of light traveling at the same speed that you do, 3.0×10^8 m/s, even though you have a different reference frame than the bicyclist does. This occurs regardless of how fast the bicycle is moving because v (the bicycle's speed) cancels from the equation. Thus, Einstein's relativistic equation successfully covers both cases. So Einstein's equation is a more general case of the classical equation, which is simply the limiting case.

FIGURE 2

CLASSICAL AND RELATIVISTIC ADDITION OF VELOCITIES

$c = 299\ 792\ 458$ m/s		Classical addition	Relativistic addition
Speed between frames (v)	Speed measured in A (u')	Speed measured in B (u)	Speed measured in B (u)
25 m/s	15 m/s	40 m/s	40 m/s
100 000 m/s	100 000 m/s	200 000 m/s	200 000 m/s
50% of c	50% of c	299 792 458 m/s	239 833 966 m/s
90% of c	90% of c	539 626 424 m/s	298 136 146 m/s
99.99% of c	99.99% of c	599 524 958 m/s	299 792 457 m/s

Kinesiologist

Lisa Griffin applies an electrical stimulus to a nerve in a patient's wrist. This experiment tested the best patterns of stimulation to recreate movement in paralyzed hands.

How does the body move? This question is just one of the many that kinesiology continually asks. To learn more about kinesiology as a career, read the interview with Lisa Griffin, who teaches in the Department of Kinesiology and Health Education at the University of Texas at Austin.

What training did you receive in order to become a kinesiologist?

I received a B.Sc. degree in human kinetics with a minor in biochemistry and M.Sc. and Ph.D. degrees in neuroscience. Kinesiology typically covers motor control, biomechanics, and exercise physiology. People who work in these branches are known as neuroscientists, biomechanists, and physiologists, respectively.

What makes kinesiology interesting to you?

The field of kinesiology allows me to explore how the central nervous system (CNS) controls human movement. Thus we work with people, and the findings of our work can be used to help others.

What is the nature of your research?

We record force output and single motor unit firing patterns from the muscles of human participants during fatigue and training. We then use these frequency patterns to stimulate their hands artificially with electrical stimulation. We are working toward developing an electrical stimulation system that people with paralysis could use to generate limb movement. This could help many who have spinal cord injuries from accidents or brain damage from stroke.

How does your work address two-dimensional motion and vectors?

I investigate motor unit firing frequencies required to generate force output from muscle over time. Thus we record muscle contraction with strain gauge force transducers, bridge amplifiers, an analog-to-digital converter, and a computer data acquisition and analysis program. For example, the muscles of the thumb produce force in both x and y directions. We record the x and y forces on two different channels, and then we calculate the resultant force online so that we can view the net output during contraction.

What are your most and least favorite things about your work?

My favorite thing is coming up with new ideas and working with students who are excited about their work. The thing I would most like to change is the amount of time it takes to get the results of the experiments after you think of the ideas.

What advice would you offer to students who are interested in this field?

Do not underestimate the depth of the questions that can be addressed with human participants.

Lisa Griffin

Hypothesis or Theory?

As scientists make observations and carry out investigations, they generate, analyze, and compare data. Their observations, analyses, and comparisons can lead to the formation of hypotheses and theories. Both hypotheses and theories are tools used by scientists, but they are very different from one another.

Hypotheses are testable statements that must be able to be supported or not supported by observational evidence. A hypothesis usually serves as a basis for a single experiment and, therefore, relates only to a limited amount of data. Even if a hypothesis is supported by the data from one experiment, many more experiments would have to be performed and much more data collected in support of the hypothesis before the hypothesis could be used to predict results of other experiments and explain observations.

Theories, on the other hand, are explanations that are based on vast amounts of data accumulated over long periods of time. Theories usually incorporate the observations, data, and explanations of many scientists. Theories are broad generalizations that can explain a body of information and observations. Although scientific theories are occasionally modified as the result of new scientific information, they have been repeatedly verified by many individuals, and are highly reliable explanations for natural phenomena. Scientific theories are the basis for developing hypotheses and making predictions that can be tested through investigations.

Theory of Special Relativity

Einstein's theory of special relativity describes how the measurement of time varies depending on the perspective of the observer, and that the speed of light is the same for all observers. Einstein's proposals represented major revelations when introduced in 1905, but over the years, many scientists have tested and observed the phenomena, such as time dilation, predicted by Einstein's theory.

- One experiment that was performed to observe the time dilation predicted by special relativity involved flying an atomic clock around the world. The clock's time was compared to the time of an identical clock that was kept stationary. Briefly research this experiment, and propose a hypothesis that the scientists might have generated before performing the experiment. How is this hypothesis distinct from Einstein's theory of special relativity?

Conceptual Challenge

The ability to make assumptions and generate rough estimates is a valuable skill to scientists. Quick estimates allow scientists to narrow the range of possibilities and focus on the most reasonable hypotheses.

Speed of Light How long would it take a traveller to go around Earth in a typical passenger jet? How long would it take if the traveller was moving at the speed of light?

You can begin examining the scenario by asking questions such as the following:

- How far is the distance around Earth?

- How fast does a passenger jet travel?

- What is the speed of light?

BIG IDEA Vectors can be used to represent and predict the two-dimensional motion of an object.

SECTION 1 **Introduction to Vectors**

KEY TERMS

- A scalar is a quantity completely specified by only a number with appropriate units, whereas a vector is a quantity that has magnitude and direction.
- Vectors can be added graphically using the triangle method of addition, in which the tail of one vector is placed at the head of the other. The resultant is the vector drawn from the tail of the first vector to the head of the last vector.

scalar
vector
resultant

SECTION 2 **Vector Operations**

KEY TERM

- The Pythagorean theorem and the inverse tangent function can be used to find the magnitude and direction of a resultant vector.
- Any vector can be resolved into its component vectors by using the sine and cosine functions.

components of a vector

SECTION 3 **Projectile Motion**

KEY TERM

- Neglecting air resistance, a projectile has a constant horizontal velocity and a constant downward free-fall acceleration.
- In the absence of air resistance, projectiles follow a parabolic path.

projectile motion

SECTION 4 **Relative Motion**

- If the frame of reference is denoted with subscripts ($\mathbf{v}_{ab}$ is the velocity of object or frame a with respect to object or frame b), then the velocity of an object with respect to a different frame of reference can be found by adding the known velocities so that the subscript starts with the letter that ends the preceding velocity subscript: $\mathbf{v}_{ac} = \mathbf{v}_{ab} + \mathbf{v}_{bc}$.
- If the order of the subscripts is reversed, there is a change in sign; for example, $\mathbf{v}_{cd} = -\mathbf{v}_{dc}$.

VARIABLE SYMBOLS			
Quantities		**Units**	
d (vector)	displacement	m	meters
v (vector)	velocity	m/s	meters/second
a (vector)	acceleration	m/s^2	meters/second^2
Δx (scalar)	horizontal component	m	meters
Δy (scalar)	vertical component	m	meters

DIAGRAM SYMBOLS	
$\longrightarrow$	displacement vector
$\longrightarrow$	velocity vector
$\longrightarrow$	acceleration vector
$----\rightarrow$	resultant vector
$\Longrightarrow$	component

Problem Solving

See **Appendix D : Equations** for a summary of the equations introduced in this chapter. If you need more problem-solving practice, see **Appendix I: Additional Problems.**

Vectors and the Graphical Method

▶ **REVIEWING MAIN IDEAS**

1. The magnitude of a vector is a scalar. Explain this statement.

2. If two vectors have unequal magnitudes, can their sum be zero? Explain.

3. What is the relationship between instantaneous speed and instantaneous velocity?

4. What is another way of saying −30 m/s west?

5. Is it possible to add a vector quantity to a scalar quantity? Explain.

6. Vector **A** is 3.00 units in length and points along the positive *x*-axis. Vector **B** is 4.00 units in length and points along the negative *y*-axis. Use graphical methods to find the magnitude and direction of the following vectors:
   a. **A** + **B**
   b. **A** − **B**
   c. **A** + 2**B**
   d. **B** − **A**

7. Each of the displacement vectors **A** and **B** shown in the figure below has a magnitude of 3.00 m. Graphically find the following:
   a. **A** + **B**
   b. **A** − **B**
   c. **B** − **A**
   d. **A** − 2**B**

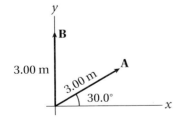

8. A dog searching for a bone walks 3.50 m south, then 8.20 m at an angle of 30.0° north of east, and finally 15.0 m west. Use graphical techniques to find the dog's resultant displacement vector.

9. A man lost in a maze makes three consecutive displacements so that at the end of the walk he is back where he started, as shown below. The first displacement is 8.00 m westward, and the second is 13.0 m northward. Use the graphical method to find the third displacement.

CONCEPTUAL QUESTIONS

10. If **B** is added to **A,** under what conditions does the resultant have the magnitude equal to *A* + *B*?

11. Give an example of a moving object that has a velocity vector and an acceleration vector in the same direction and an example of one that has velocity and acceleration vectors in opposite directions.

12. A student accurately uses the method for combining vectors. The two vectors she combines have magnitudes of 55 and 25 units. The answer that she gets is either 85, 20, or 55. Pick the correct answer, and explain why it is the only one of the three that can be correct.

13. If a set of vectors laid head to tail forms a closed polygon, the resultant is zero. Is this statement true? Explain your reasoning.

Vector Operations

 REVIEWING MAIN IDEAS

14. Can a vector have a component equal to zero and still have a nonzero magnitude?

15. Can a vector have a component greater than its magnitude?

16. Explain the difference between vector addition and vector resolution.

17. How would you add two vectors that are not perpendicular or parallel?

CONCEPTUAL QUESTIONS

18. If **A** + **B** equals 0, what can you say about the components of the two vectors?

19. Under what circumstances would a vector have components that are equal in magnitude?

20. The vector sum of three vectors gives a resultant equal to zero. What can you say about the vectors?

PRACTICE PROBLEMS

For problems 21–23, see Sample Problem A.

21. A girl delivering newspapers travels three blocks west, four blocks north, and then six blocks east.
   a. What is her resultant displacement?
   b. What is the total distance she travels?

22. A quarterback takes the ball from the line of scrimmage, runs backward for 10.0 yards, and then runs sideways parallel to the line of scrimmage for 15.0 yards. At this point, he throws a 50.0-yard forward pass straight down the field. What is the magnitude of the football's resultant displacement?

23. A shopper pushes a cart 40.0 m south down one aisle and then turns 90.0° and moves 15.0 m. He then makes another 90.0° turn and moves 20.0 m. Find the shopper's total displacement. (There could be more than one correct answer.)

For problems 24–25, see Sample Problem B.

24. A submarine dives 110.0 m at an angle of 10.0° below the horizontal. What are the two components?

25. A person walks 25.0° north of east for 3.10 km. How far would another person walk due north and due east to arrive at the same location?

For problem 26, see Sample Problem C.

26. A person walks the path shown below. The total trip consists of four straight-line paths. At the end of the walk, what is the person's resultant displacement measured from the starting point?

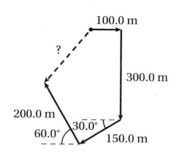

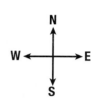

Projectile Motion

 **REVIEWING MAIN IDEAS**

27. A dart is fired horizontally from a dart gun, and another dart is dropped simultaneously from the same height. If air resistance can be neglected, which dart hits the ground first?

28. If a rock is dropped from the top of a sailboat's mast, will it hit the deck at the same point whether the boat is at rest or in motion at constant velocity?

29. Does a ball dropped out of the window of a moving car take longer to reach the ground than one dropped at the same height from a car at rest?

30. A rock is dropped at the same instant that a ball at the same elevation is thrown horizontally. Which will have the greater speed when it reaches ground level?

PRACTICE PROBLEMS

For problems 31–33, see Sample Problem D.

31. In 1974, Nolan Ryan broke the existing record for the fastest pitch thrown in Major League Baseball. If this pitch were thrown horizontally, the ball would fall 0.809 m (2.65 ft) by the time it reached home plate, 18.3 m (60 ft) away. How fast was Ryan's pitch?

32. A person standing at the edge of a seaside cliff kicks a stone over the edge with a speed of 18 m/s. The cliff is 52 m above the water's surface, as shown at right. How long does it take for the stone to fall to the water? With what speed does it strike the water?

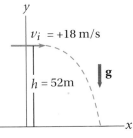

33. A spy in a speed boat is being chased down a river by government officials in a faster craft. Just as the officials' boat pulls up next to the spy's boat, both boats reach the edge of a 5.0 m waterfall. If the spy's speed is 15 m/s and the officials' speed is 26 m/s, how far apart will the two vessels be when they land below the waterfall?

For problems 34–37, see Sample Problem E.

34. A shell is fired from the ground with an initial speed of 1.70×10^3 m/s (approximately five times the speed of sound) at an initial angle of 55.0° to the horizontal. Neglecting air resistance, find
 a. the shell's horizontal range
 b. the amount of time the shell is in motion

35. A place kicker must kick a football from a point 36.0 m (about 40.0 yd) from the goal. As a result of the kick, the ball must clear the crossbar, which is 3.05 m high. When kicked, the ball leaves the ground with a speed of 20.0 m/s at an angle of 53° to the horizontal.
 a. By how much does the ball clear or fall short of clearing the crossbar?
 b. Does the ball approach the crossbar while still rising or while falling?

36. When a water gun is fired while being held horizontally at a height of 1.00 m above ground level, the water travels a horizontal distance of 5.00 m. A child, who is holding the same gun in a horizontal position, is also sliding down a 45.0° incline at a constant speed of 2.00 m/s. If the child fires the gun when it is 1.00 m above the ground and the water takes 0.329 s to reach the ground, how far will the water travel horizontally?

37. A ship maneuvers to within 2.50×10^3 m of an island's 1.80×10^3 m high mountain peak and fires a projectile at an enemy ship 6.10×10^2 m on the other side of the peak, as illustrated below. If the ship shoots the projectile with an initial velocity of 2.50×10^2 m/s at an angle of 75.0°, how close to the enemy ship does the projectile land? How close (vertically) does the projectile come to the peak?

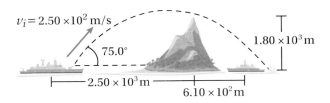

Relative Motion

▶ **REVIEWING MAIN IDEAS**

38. Explain the statement "All motion is relative."

39. What is a frame of reference?

40. When we describe motion, what is a common frame of reference?

41. A small airplane is flying at 50 m/s toward the east. A wind of 20 m/s toward the east suddenly begins to blow and gives the plane a velocity of 70 m/s east.
 a. Which vector is the resultant vector?
 b. What is the magnitude of the wind velocity?

42. A ball is thrown upward in the air by a passenger on a train that is moving with constant velocity.
 a. Describe the path of the ball as seen by the passenger. Describe the path as seen by a stationary observer outside the train.
 b. How would these observations change if the train were accelerating along the track?

PRACTICE PROBLEMS

For problems 43–46, see Sample Problem F.

43. A river flows due east at 1.50 m/s. A boat crosses the river from the south shore to the north shore by maintaining a constant velocity of 10.0 m/s due north relative to the water.
 a. What is the velocity of the boat as viewed by an observer on shore?
 b. If the river is 325 m wide, how far downstream is the boat when it reaches the north shore?

44. The pilot of an aircraft wishes to fly due west in a 50.0 km/h wind blowing toward the south. The speed of the aircraft in the absence of a wind is 205 km/h.
  a. In what direction should the aircraft head?
  b. What should its speed relative to the ground be?

45. A hunter wishes to cross a river that is 1.5 km wide and that flows with a speed of 5.0 km/h. The hunter uses a small powerboat that moves at a maximum speed of 12 km/h with respect to the water. What is the minimum time necessary for crossing?

46. A swimmer can swim in still water at a speed of 9.50 m/s. He intends to swim directly across a river that has a downstream current of 3.75 m/s.
  a. What must the swimmer's direction be?
  b. What is his velocity relative to the bank?

Mixed Review

47. A ballplayer hits a home run, and the baseball just clears a wall 21.0 m high located 130.0 m from home plate. The ball is hit at an angle of 35.0° to the horizontal, and air resistance is negligible. Assume the ball is hit at a height of 1.0 m above the ground.
  a. What is the initial speed of the ball?
  b. How much time does it take for the ball to reach the wall?
  c. Find the components of the velocity and the speed of the ball when it reaches the wall.

48. A daredevil jumps a canyon 12 m wide. To do so, he drives a car up a 15° incline.
  a. What minimum speed must he achieve to clear the canyon?
  b. If the daredevil jumps at this minimum speed, what will his speed be when he reaches the other side?

49. A 2.00 m tall basketball player attempts a goal 10.00 m from the basket (3.05 m high). If he shoots the ball at a 45.0° angle, at what initial speed must he throw the basketball so that it goes through the hoop without striking the backboard?

50. An escalator is 20.0 m long. If a person stands on the escalator, it takes 50.0 s to ride to the top.
  a. If a person walks up the moving escalator with a speed of 0.500 m/s relative to the escalator, how long does it take the person to get to the top?
  b. If a person walks down the "up" escalator with the same relative speed as in item (a), how long does it take to reach the bottom?

51. A ball is projected horizontally from the edge of a table that is 1.00 m high, and it strikes the floor at a point 1.20 m from the base of the table.
  a. What is the initial speed of the ball?
  b. How high is the ball above the floor when its velocity vector makes a 45.0° angle with the horizontal?

52. How long does it take an automobile traveling 60.0 km/h to become even with a car that is traveling in another lane at 40.0 km/h if the cars' front bumpers are initially 125 m apart?

53. The eye of a hurricane passes over Grand Bahama Island. It is moving in a direction 60.0° north of west with a speed of 41.0 km/h. Exactly three hours later, the course of the hurricane shifts due north, and its speed slows to 25.0 km/h, as shown below. How far from Grand Bahama is the hurricane 4.50 h after it passes over the island?

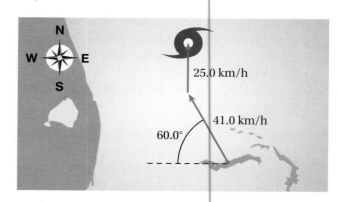

54. A boat moves through a river at 7.5 m/s relative to the water, regardless of the boat's direction. If the water in the river is flowing at 1.5 m/s, how long does it take the boat to make a roundtrip consisting of a 250 m displacement downstream followed by a 250 m displacement upstream?

55. A car is parked on a cliff overlooking the ocean on an incline that makes an angle of 24.0° below the horizontal. The negligent driver leaves the car in neutral, and the emergency brakes are defective. The car rolls from rest down the incline with a constant acceleration of 4.00 m/s² and travels 50.0 m to the edge of the cliff. The cliff is 30.0 m above the ocean.
   a. What is the car's position relative to the base of the cliff when the car lands in the ocean?
   b. How long is the car in the air?

56. A golf ball with an initial angle of 34° lands exactly 240 m down the range on a level course.
   a. Neglecting air friction, what initial speed would achieve this result?
   b. Using the speed determined in item (a), find the maximum height reached by the ball.

57. A car travels due east with a speed of 50.0 km/h. Rain is falling vertically with respect to Earth. The traces of the rain on the side windows of the car make an angle of 60.0° with the vertical. Find the velocity of the rain with respect to the following:
   a. the car
   b. Earth

58. A shopper in a department store can walk up a stationary escalator in 30.0 s. If the escalator can carry the standing shopper to the next floor in 20.0 s when it is moving, how long would it take the shopper to walk up the moving escalator? Assume the same walking effort for the shopper whether the escalator is stopped or moving.

59. If a person can jump a horizontal distance of 3.0 m on Earth, how far could the person jump on the moon, where the free-fall acceleration is $g/6$ and $g = 9.81$ m/s²? How far could the person jump on Mars, where the acceleration due to gravity is $0.38g$?

60. A science student riding on a flatcar of a train moving at a constant speed of 10.0 m/s throws a ball toward the caboose along a path that the student judges as making an initial angle of 60.0° with the horizontal. The teacher, who is standing on the ground nearby, observes the ball rising vertically. How high does the ball rise?

61. A football is thrown directly toward a receiver with an initial speed of 18.0 m/s at an angle of 35.0° above the horizontal. At that instant, the receiver is 18.0 m from the quarterback. In what direction and with what constant speed should the receiver run to catch the football at the level at which it was thrown?

62. A rocket is launched at an angle of 53° above the horizontal with an initial speed of 75 m/s, as shown below. It moves for 25 s along its initial line of motion with an acceleration of 25 m/s². At this time, its engines fail, and the rocket proceeds to move as a free body.
   a. What is the rocket's maximum altitude?
   b. What is the rocket's total time of flight?
   c. What is the rocket's horizontal range?

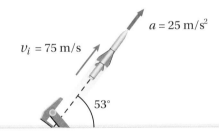

ALTERNATIVE ASSESSMENT

1. Work in cooperative groups to analyze a game of chess in terms of displacement vectors. Make a model chessboard, and draw arrows showing all the possible moves for each piece as vectors made of horizontal and vertical components. Then have two members of your group play the game while the others keep track of each piece's moves. Be prepared to demonstrate how vector addition can be used to explain where a piece would be after several moves.

2. Use a garden hose to investigate the laws of projectile motion. Design experiments to investigate how the angle of the hose affects the range of the water stream. (Assume that the initial speed of water is constant and is determined by the pressure indicated by the faucet's setting.) What quantities will you measure, and how will you measure them? What variables do you need to control? What is the shape of the water stream? How can you reach the maximum range? How can you reach the highest point? Present your results to the rest of the class and discuss the conclusions.

3. You are helping NASA engineers design a basketball court for a colony on the moon. How do you anticipate the ball's motion compared with its motion on Earth? What changes will there be for the players—how they move and how they throw the ball? What changes would you recommend for the size of the court, the basket height, and other regulations in order to adapt the sport to the moon's low gravity? Create a presentation or a report presenting your suggestions, and include the physics concepts behind your recommendations.

4. There is conflicting testimony in a court case. A police officer claims that his radar monitor indicated that a car was traveling at 176 km/h (110 mi/h). The driver argues that the radar must have recorded the relative velocity because he was only going 88 km/h (55 mi/h). Is it possible that both are telling the truth? Could one be lying? Prepare scripts for expert witnesses, for both the prosecution and the defense, that use physics to justify their positions before the jury. Create visual aids to be used as evidence to support the different arguments.

GRAPHING CALCULATOR PRACTICE

Two-Dimensional Motion

Recall the following equation from your studies of projectiles launched at an angle.

$$\Delta y = (v_i \sin \theta)\Delta t + \frac{1}{2}a_y(\Delta t)^2$$

Consider a baseball that is thrown straight up in the air. The equation for projectile motion can be entered as Y_1 on a graphing calculator.

$$Y_1 = VX - 4.9X^2$$

Given the initial velocity (V), your graphing calculator can calculate the height (Y_1) of the baseball versus the time interval (X) that the ball remains in the air. Why is the factor $\sin \theta$ missing from the equation for Y_1?

In this activity, you will determine the maximum height and flight time of a baseball thrown vertically at various initial velocities.

Go online to HMHScience.com to find the skillsheet and program for this graphing calculator activity.

Standards-Based Assessment

Record your answers on a separate piece of paper.

MULTIPLE CHOICE

1 Vector **A** has a magnitude of 30 units. Vector **B** is perpendicular to vector **A** and has a magnitude of 40 units. What would the magnitude of the resultant vector **A** + **B** be?

A 10 units
B 50 units
C 70 units
D zero

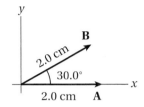

2 Based on the diagram above, what is the direction of the resultant vector **A** − **B**?

A 15° above the x-axis
B 75° above the x-axis
C 15° below the x-axis
D 75° below the x-axis

3 What term represents the magnitude of a velocity vector?

A acceleration
B momentum
C speed
D velocity

4 A motorboat heads due east at 5.0 m/s across a river that flows toward the south at a speed of 5.0 m/s. What is the resultant velocity relative to an observer on the shore?

A 3.2 m/s to the southeast
B 5.0 m/s to the southeast
C 7.1 m/s to the southeast
D 10.0 m/s to the southeast

5 The pilot of a plane measures an air velocity of 165 km/h south relative to the plane. An observer on the ground sees the plane pass overhead at a velocity of 145 km/h toward the north. What is the velocity of the wind that is affecting the plane relative to the observer?

A 20 km/h to the north
B 20 km/h to the south
C 165 km/h to the north
D 310 km/h to the south

6 A golfer takes two putts to sink his ball in the hole once he is on the green. The first putt displaces the ball 6.00 m east, and the second putt displaces the ball 5.40 m south. What displacement would put the ball in the hole in one putt?

A 11.40 m southeast
B 8.07 m at 48.0° south of east
C 3.32 m at 42.0° south of east
D 8.07 m at 42.0° south of east

7 A girl riding a bicycle at 2.0 m/s throws a tennis ball horizontally forward at a speed of 1.0 m/s from a height of 1.5 m. At the same moment, a boy standing on the sidewalk drops a tennis ball straight down from a height of 1.5 m.

If air resistance is disregarded, which ball will have a greater speed (relative to the ground) when it hits the ground?

A the boy's ball
B the girl's ball
C neither
D The answer cannot be determined from the given information.

GRIDDED RESPONSE

8 A ball is thrown straight upward and returns to the thrower's hand after 3.00 s in the air. A second ball is thrown at an angle of 30.0° with the horizontal. At what speed, in meters per second, must the second ball be thrown to reach the same height as the one thrown vertically?

Why It Matters

Technicians study the accelerations and forces involved in car crashes in order to design safer cars and more-effective restraint systems. For example, at General Motors' Milford Proving Grounds in Michigan, technicians place a crash-test dummy behind the steering wheel of a new car, as shown in the photograph.

When the car crashes, the dummy continues moving forward and hits the dashboard. The dashboard then exerts a force on the dummy that accelerates the dummy backward, as shown in the illustration. Sensors in the dummy record the forces and accelerations involved in the collision.

CHAPTER 4

Forces and the Laws of Motion

BIG IDEA

Newton's laws describe the predictable ways in which forces interact to change the motion of objects. Free-body diagrams help depict the multiple forces that are acting on an object.

ONLINE Physics
HMHScience.com

ONLINE LABS
- Discovering Newton's Laws
- S.T.E.M. Lab Parachute
- S.T.E.M. Lab Friction: Testing Materials

GO ONLINE **Animated Physics**
HMHScience.com

Force

(br) ©Jupiter Images/Getty Images

SC.912.P.10.10 Compare the magnitude and range of the four fundamental forces (gravitational, electromagnetic, weak nuclear, strong nuclear).

force an action exerted on an object that may change the object's state of rest or motion

Changes in Motion

Key Term
force

Force

You exert a **force** on a ball when you throw or kick the ball, and you exert a force on a chair when you sit in the chair. Forces describe the interactions between an object and its environment.

Forces can cause accelerations.

In many situations, a force exerted on an object can change the object's velocity with respect to time. Some examples of these situations are shown in **Figure 1.1**. A force can cause a stationary object to move, as when you throw a ball. Force also causes moving objects to stop, as when you catch a ball. A force can also cause a moving object to change direction, such as when a baseball collides with a bat and flies off in another direction. Notice that in each of these cases, the force is responsible for a change in velocity with respect to time—an acceleration.

FIGURE 1.1

Three Ways That Forces Change Motion Force can cause objects to **(a)** start moving, **(b)** stop moving, and/or **(c)** change direction.

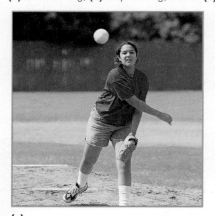

(a)

(b)

(c)

The SI unit of force is the newton.

The SI unit of force is the newton, named after Sir Isaac Newton (1642–1727), whose work contributed much to the modern understanding of force and motion. The newton (N) is defined as the amount of force that, when acting on a 1 kg mass, produces an acceleration of 1 m/s². Therefore, $1\text{ N} = 1\text{ kg} \times 1\text{ m/s}^2$.

The weight of an object is a measure of the magnitude of the gravitational force exerted on the object. It is the result of the interaction of an

FIGURE 1.2

UNITS OF MASS, ACCELERATION, AND FORCE			
System	Mass	Acceleration	Force
SI	kg	m/s^2	$N = kg{\bullet}m/s^2$
cgs	g	cm/s^2	$dyne = g{\bullet}cm/s^2$
Avoirdupois	slug	ft/s^2	$lb = slug{\bullet}ft/s^2$

Did YOU Know?

The symbol for the pound, lb, comes from *libra*, the Latin word for "pound," a unit of measure that has been used since medieval times to measure weight.

object's mass with the gravitational field of another object, such as Earth. As shown in **Figure 1.2**, many of the terms and units you use every day to talk about weight are really units of force that can be converted to newtons. For example, a $\frac{1}{4}$ lb stick of margarine has a weight equivalent to a force of about 1 N, as shown in the following conversions:

$$1\ lb = 4.448\ N$$
$$1\ N = 0.225\ lb$$

Forces can act through contact or at a distance.

If you pull on a spring, the spring stretches. If you pull on a wagon, the wagon moves. When a football is caught, its motion is stopped. These pushes and pulls are examples of *contact forces*, which are so named because they result from physical contact between two objects. Contact forces are usually easy to identify when you analyze a situation.

Another class of forces—called *field forces*—does not involve physical contact between two objects. One example of this kind of force is gravitational force. Whenever an object falls to Earth, the object is accelerated by Earth's gravity. In other words, Earth exerts a force on the object even when Earth is not in immediate physical contact with the object.

Another common example of a field force is the attraction or repulsion between electric charges. You can observe this force by rubbing a balloon against your hair and then observing how little pieces of paper appear to jump up and cling to the balloon's surface, as shown in **Figure 1.3**. The paper is pulled by the balloon's electric field. This type of field force is discussed in detail in the chapter "Electric Forces and Fields."

The theory of fields was developed as a tool to explain how objects could exert force on each other without touching. According to this theory, masses create gravitational fields in the space around them. An object falls to Earth because of the interaction between the object's mass and Earth's gravitational field. Similarly, charged objects create electromagnetic fields.

The distinction between contact forces and field forces is useful when dealing with forces that we observe at the macroscopic level. (*Macroscopic* refers to the realm of phenomena that are visible to the naked eye.) As we will see later, all macroscopic contact forces are actually due to microscopic field forces. For instance, contact forces in a collision are due to electric fields between atoms and molecules. In fact, every force can be categorized as one of four fundamental field forces.

FIGURE 1.3

Electric Force The electric field around the rubbed balloon exerts an attractive electric force on the pieces of paper.

Force Diagrams

When you push a toy car, it accelerates. If you push the car harder, the acceleration will be greater. In other words, the acceleration of the car depends on the force's *magnitude*. The direction in which the car moves depends on the *direction* of the force. For example, if you push the toy car from the front, the car will move in a different direction than if you push it from behind.

Force is a vector.

Because the effect of a force depends on both magnitude and direction, force is a vector quantity. Diagrams that show force vectors as arrows, such as **Figure 1.4(a)**, are called *force diagrams*. In this book, the arrows used to represent forces are blue. The tail of an arrow is attached to the object on which the force is acting. A force vector points in the direction of the force, and its length is proportional to the magnitude of the force.

In this chapter, we will disregard the size and shape of objects and assume that all forces act at the center of an object. Therefore, all forces are drawn as if they act at that point, no matter where the force is applied.

A free-body diagram helps analyze a situation.

After engineers analyzing a test-car crash have identified all of the forces involved, they isolate the car from the other objects in its environment. One of their goals is to determine which forces affect the car and its passengers. **Figure 1.4(b)** is a free-body diagram. This diagram represents the same collision that the force diagram **(a)** does but shows only the car and the forces acting on the car. The forces exerted *by* the car on other objects are not included in the free-body diagram because they do not affect the motion of the car.

A free-body diagram is used to analyze only the forces affecting the motion of a single object. Free-body diagrams are constructed and analyzed just like other vector diagrams. In Sample Problem A, you will learn to draw free-body diagrams for some situations described in this book. Later, you will learn to use free-body diagrams to find component and resultant forces.

Quick **LAB**

MATERIALS
- 1 toy car
- 1 book

FORCE AND CHANGES IN MOTION

Use a toy car and a book to model a car colliding with a brick wall. Observe the motion of the car before and after the crash. Identify as many changes in its motion as you can, such as changes in speed or direction. Make a list of all of the changes, and try to identify the forces that caused them. Make a force diagram of the collision.

FIGURE 1.4

Force Diagrams Versus Free-body Diagrams **(a)** In a force diagram, vector arrows represent all the forces acting in a situation. **(b)** A free-body diagram shows only the forces acting on the object of interest—in this case, the car.

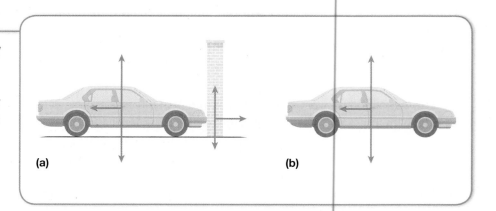

(a)   (b)

Drawing Free-Body Diagrams

Sample Problem A In the early morning, a park ranger in a canoe is observing wildlife on the nearby shore. Earth's gravitational force on the ranger is 760 N downward, and its gravitational force on the boat is 190 N downward. The water keeps the canoe afloat by exerting a 950 N force upward on it. Draw a free-body diagram of the canoe.

① ANALYZE

Identify the forces acting on the object and the directions of the forces.
- Earth exerts a force of 190 N downward on the canoe.
- The park ranger exerts a force of 760 N downward on the canoe.
- The water exerts an upward force of 950 N on the canoe.

> **Tips and Tricks**
> In a free-body diagram, only include forces acting on the object. Do not include forces that the object exerts on other objects. In this problem, the forces are given, but later in the chapter, you will need to identify the forces when drawing a free-body diagram.

(a)

② PLAN

Draw a diagram to represent the isolated object.
The canoe can be represented by a simple outline, as shown in **(a)**.

③ SOLVE

Draw and label vector arrows for all external forces acting on the object.
A free-body diagram of the canoe will show all the forces acting on the canoe as if the forces are acting on the center of the canoe. First, draw and label the gravitational force acting on the canoe, which is directed toward the center of Earth, as shown in **(b)**. Be sure that the length of the arrow approximately represents the magnitude of the force.

> **Tips and Tricks**
> When you draw an arrow representing a force, it is important to label the arrow with either the magnitude of the force or a name that will distinguish it from the other forces acting on the object. Also, be sure that the length of the arrow approximately represents the magnitude of the force.

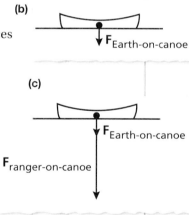

Next, draw and label the downward force that is exerted on the boat by Earth's gravitational attraction on the ranger, as shown in **(c)**. Finally, draw and label the upward force exerted by the water on the canoe as shown in **(d)**. Diagram **(d)** is the completed free-body diagram of the floating canoe.

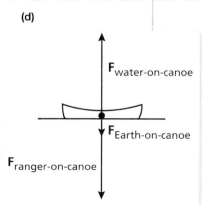

Continued ▶

Drawing Free-Body Diagrams (continued)

Practice

1. After a skydiver jumps from a plane, the only force initially acting on the diver is Earth's gravitational attraction. After about ten seconds of falling, air resistance on the diver will have increased so that its magnitude on the diver is now equal in magnitude to Earth's gravitational force on the diver. At this time, a diver in a belly-down position will be falling at a constant speed of about 190 km/h.

   a. Draw a free-body diagram of the skydiver when the diver initially leaves the plane.

   b. Draw a free-body diagram of the skydiver at the tenth second of the falling.

2. A physics book is at rest on a desk. Gravitational force pulls the book down. The desk exerts an upward force on the book that is equal in magnitude to the gravitational force. Draw a free-body diagram of the book.

SECTION 1 FORMATIVE ASSESSMENT

▶ Reviewing Main Ideas

1. List three examples of each of the following:
   a. a force causing an object to start moving
   b. a force causing an object to stop moving
   c. a force causing an object to change its direction of motion

2. Give two examples of field forces described in this section and two examples of contact forces you observe in everyday life. Explain why you think that these are forces.

3. What is the SI unit of force? What is this unit equivalent to in terms of fundamental units?

4. Why is force a vector quantity?

5. Draw a free-body diagram of a football being kicked. Assume that the only forces acting on the ball are the force due to gravity and the force exerted by the kicker.

Interpreting Graphics

6. Study the force diagram on the right. Redraw the diagram, and label each vector arrow with a description of the force. In each description, include the object exerting the force and the object on which the force is acting.

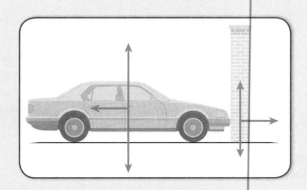

Newton's First Law

Key Terms
inertia
net force
equilibrium

Objectives

▶ Explain the relationship between the motion of an object and the net external force acting on the object.

▶ Determine the net external force on an object.

SC.912.P.12.3 Interpret and apply Newton's three laws of motion.

Inertia

A hovercraft, such as the one in **Figure 2.1**, glides along the surface of the water on a cushion of air. A common misconception is that an object on which no force is acting will always be at rest. This situation is not always the case. If the hovercraft shown in **Figure 2.1** is moving at a constant velocity, then there is no net force acting on it. To see why this is the case, consider how a block will slide on different surfaces.

First, imagine a block on a deep, thick carpet. If you apply a force by pushing the block, the block will begin sliding, but soon after you remove the force, the block will come to rest. Next, imagine pushing the same block across a smooth, waxed floor. When you push with the same force, the block will slide much farther before coming to rest. In fact, a block sliding on a perfectly smooth, horizontal surface would slide forever in the absence of an applied force.

In the 1630s, Galileo concluded correctly that it is an object's nature to *maintain its state of motion or rest*. Note that an object on which no force is acting is not necessarily at rest; the object could also be moving with a constant velocity. This concept was further developed by Newton in 1687 and has come to be known as **Newton's first law of motion**.

FIGURE 2.1

Hovercraft on Air A hovercraft floats on a cushion of air above the water. Air provides less resistance to motion than water does.

Newton's First Law

An object at rest remains at rest, and an object in motion continues in motion with constant velocity (that is, constant speed in a straight line) unless the object experiences a net external force.

Inertia is the tendency of an object not to accelerate. Newton's first law is often referred to as the *law of inertia* because it states that in the absence of a net force, a body will preserve its state of motion. In other words, Newton's first law says that *when the net external force on an object is zero, the object's acceleration (or the change in the object's velocity) is zero*.

inertia the tendency of an object to resist being moved or, if the object is moving, to resist a change in speed or direction

FIGURE 2.2

Net Force Although several forces are acting on this car, the vector sum of the forces is zero, so the car moves at a constant velocity.

$$F_{ground-on-car}$$

$$F_{resistance}$$

$$F_{forward}$$

$$F_{gravity}$$

net force a single force whose external effects on a rigid body are the same as the effects of several actual forces acting on the body

The sum of forces acting on an object is the net force.

Consider a car traveling at a constant velocity. Newton's first law tells us that the net external force on the car must be equal to zero. However, **Figure 2.2** shows that many forces act on a car in motion. The vector $F_{forward}$ represents the forward force of the road on the tires. The vector $F_{resistance}$, which acts in the opposite direction, is due partly to friction between the road surface and tires and is due partly to air resistance. The vector $F_{gravity}$ represents the downward gravitational force on the car, and the vector $F_{ground-on-car}$ represents the upward force that the road exerts on the car.

To understand how a car under the influence of so many forces can maintain a constant velocity, you must understand the distinction between external force and net external force. An *external force* is a single force that acts on an object as a result of the interaction between the object and its environment. All four forces in **Figure 2.2** are external forces acting on the car. The **net force** is the vector sum of all forces acting on an object.

When many forces act on an object, it may move in a particular direction with a particular velocity and acceleration. The net force is the force that, when acting alone, produces exactly the same change in motion. When all external forces acting on an object are known, the net force can be found by using the methods for finding resultant vectors. Although four forces are acting on the car in **Figure 2.2**, the car will maintain a constant velocity if the vector sum of these forces is equal to zero.

Mass is a measure of inertia.

Imagine a basketball and a bowling ball at rest side by side on the ground. Newton's first law states that both balls remain at rest as long as no net external force acts on them. Now, imagine supplying a net force by pushing each ball. If the two are pushed with equal force, the basketball will accelerate more than the bowling ball. The bowling ball experiences a smaller acceleration because it has more inertia than the basketball.

As the example of the bowling ball and the basketball shows, the inertia of an object is proportional to the object's mass. The greater the mass of a body, the less the body accelerates under an applied force. Similarly, a light object undergoes a larger acceleration than does a heavy object under the same force. Therefore, *mass,* which is a measure of the amount of matter in an object, is also a measure of the inertia of an object.

QuickLAB INERTIA

Place a small ball on the rear end of a skateboard or cart. Push the skateboard across the floor and into a wall. You may need to either hold the ball in place while pushing the skateboard up to speed or accelerate the skateboard slowly so that friction holds the ball in place. Observe what happens to the ball when the skateboard hits the wall. Can you explain your observation in terms of inertia? Repeat the procedure using balls with different masses, and compare the results.

MATERIALS
- skateboard or cart
- toy balls with various masses

SAFETY

Perform this experiment away from walls and furniture that can be damaged.

Sample Problem B The muscle responsible for closing the mouth is the strongest muscle in the human body. It may be able to exert a force great enough to lift a mass of 400 kg. The force of biting has been recorded at 4.33×10^3 N. If each force shown in the diagram below has a magnitude equal to the force of the bite, determine the net force.

① ANALYZE

Define the problem, and identify the variables.

Given:
$F_1 = -4.33 \times 10^3$ N
$F_2 = 4.33 \times 10^3$ N
$F_3 = 4.33 \times 10^3$ N

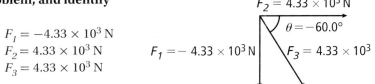

Unknown: $F_{net} = ?$ $\qquad$ $\theta_{net} = ?$

Diagram: See the diagram on the right.

Tips and Tricks
To simplify the problem, always choose the coordinate system in which as many forces as possible lie on the x- and y-axes.

② PLAN

Select a coordinate system, and apply it to the free-body diagram:
Let F_1 lie along the negative y-axis and F_2 lie along the positive x-axis. Now F_3 must be resolved into x- and y-components.

③ SOLVE

Find the x- and y-components of all vectors:
Because the angle between F_2 and F_3 is in the quadrant bounded by the positive x-axis and negative y-axis, it has a negative value.
$$F_{3,x} = F_3 (\cos \theta) = (4.33 \times 10^3 \text{ N}) [\cos (-60.0°)] = 2.16 \times 10^3 \text{ N}$$
$$F_{3,y} = F_3 (\sin \theta) = (4.33 \times 10^3 \text{ N}) [\sin (-60.0°)] = -3.75 \times 10^3 \text{ N}$$

Find the net external force in both the x and y directions.
For the x direction: $\Sigma F_x = F_2 + F_{3,x} = F_{x,net}$
$$\Sigma F_x = 4.33 \times 10^3 \text{ N} + 2.16 \times 10^3 \text{ N} = 6.49 \times 10^3 \text{ N}$$
For the y direction: $\Sigma F_y = F_1 + F_{3,y} = F_{y,net}$
$$\Sigma F_y = (-4.33 \times 10^3 \text{ N}) + (-3.75 \times 10^3 \text{ N}) = -8.08 \times 10^3 \text{ N}$$

Find the net external force.
Use the Pythagorean theorem to calculate F_{net}. Use $\theta_{net} = \tan^{-1}\left(\dfrac{F_y, net}{F_x, net}\right)$ to find the angle between the net force and the x-axis.

$$F_{net} = \sqrt{(F_{x,net})^2 + (F_{y,net})^2}$$

$$F_{net} = \sqrt{(6.49 \times 10^3 \text{N})^2 + (-8.08 \times 10^3 \text{N})^2} = \sqrt{10.74 \times 10^7 \text{N}^2}$$

$$F_{net} = \boxed{1.036 \times 10^4 \text{N}}$$

$$\theta_{net} = \tan^{-1}\left(\frac{-8.08 \times 10^3 \text{N}}{6.49 \times 10^3 \text{N}}\right) = \boxed{-51.2°}$$

④ CHECK YOUR WORK

The net force is larger than the individual forces, but it is not quite three times as large as any one force, which would be the case if all three forces were acting in one direction only. The angle is negative to indicate that it is in the quadrant below the positive x-axis. The net force is 1.036×10^4 N at an angle of 51.2° below the positive x-axis.

Practice

> **Tips and Tricks**
> If there is a net force in both the x- and y-directions, use vector addition to find the total net force.

1. A man is pulling on his dog with a force of 70.0 N directed at an angle of $+30.0°$ to the horizontal. Find the x- and y-components of this force.

2. A gust of wind blows an apple from a tree. As the apple falls, the gravitational force on the apple is 2.25 N downward, and the force of the wind on the apple is 1.05 N to the right. Find the magnitude and direction of the net force on the apple.

3. Two tugboats pull a barge across the harbor. One boat exerts a force of 7.5×10^4 N north, while the second boat exerts a force of 9.5×10^4 N at 15.0° north of west. Precisely, in what direction does the barge move?

WHY IT MATTERS

Astronaut Workouts

Gravity helps to keep bones strong. Loss of bone density is a serious outcome of time spent in space. Astronauts routinely exercise on treadmills to counteract the effects of microgravity on their skeletal systems. But is it possible to increase the value of their workouts by increasing their mass? And does it matter if they run or walk?

A team of scientists recruited runners to help find out. The runners used treadmills that measured the net force on their legs, or ground reaction force, while they ran and walked. The runners' inertia was changed by adding masses to a weighted vest. A spring system supported them as they exercised. Although the spring system did not simulate weightless conditions, it kept their weight the same even as their inertia was changed by the added mass. This mimicked the situation in Earth's orbit, where a change in mass does not result in a change in weight.

The scientists were surprised to discover that ground reaction force did not increase with mass while the subjects were running. Ground reaction force did increase with mass while the subjects were walking. But overall, ground reaction force for running was still greater. So astronauts still need to run, not walk—and they can't shorten their workouts by carrying more mass.

Equilibrium

Objects that are either at rest or moving with constant velocity are said to be in **equilibrium.** Newton's first law describes objects in equilibrium, whether they are at rest or moving with a constant velocity. Newton's first law states one condition that must be true for equilibrium: the net force acting on a body in equilibrium must be equal to zero.

equilibrium the state in which the net force on an object is zero

The net force on the fishing bob in **Figure 2.3(a)** is equal to zero because the bob is at rest. Imagine that a fish bites the bait, as shown in **Figure 2.3(b)**. Because a net force is acting on the line, the bob accelerates toward the hooked fish.

Now, consider a different scenario. Suppose that at the instant the fish begins pulling on the line, the person reacts by applying a force to the bob that is equal and opposite to the force exerted by the fish. In this case, the net force on the bob remains zero, as shown in **Figure 2.3(c)**, and the bob remains at rest. In this example, the bob is at rest while in equilibrium, but an object can also be in equilibrium while moving at a constant velocity.

An object is in equilibrium when the vector sum of the forces acting on the object is equal to zero. To determine whether a body is in equilibrium, find the net force, as shown in Sample Problem B. If the net force is zero, the body is in equilibrium. If there is a net force, a second force equal and opposite to this net force will put the body in equilibrium.

FIGURE 2.3

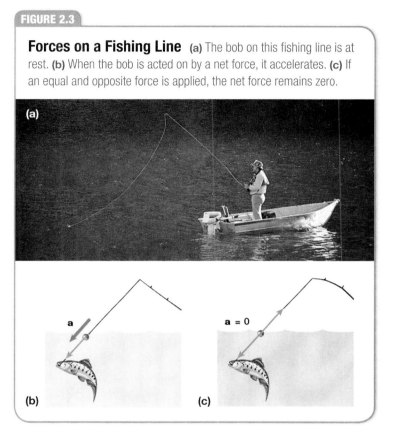

Forces on a Fishing Line (a) The bob on this fishing line is at rest. (b) When the bob is acted on by a net force, it accelerates. (c) If an equal and opposite force is applied, the net force remains zero.

(a)

a

(b)

a = 0

(c)

✔ SECTION 2 FORMATIVE ASSESSMENT

▶ Reviewing Main Ideas

1. If a car is traveling with a constant velocity of 20 m/s westward, what is the net force acting on the car?

2. If a car is accelerating downhill under a net force of 3674 N, what additional force would cause the car to have a constant velocity?

3. The sensor in the torso of a crash-test dummy records the magnitude and direction of the net force acting on the dummy. If the dummy is thrown forward with a force of 130.0 N while simultaneously being hit from the side with a force of 4500.0 N, what force will the sensor report?

4. What force will the seat belt have to exert on the dummy in item 3 to hold the dummy in the seat?

✔ Critical Thinking

5. Can an object be in equilibrium if only one force acts on the object?

Objectives

▶ Describe an object's acceleration in terms of its mass and the net force acting on it.

▶ Predict the direction and magnitude of the acceleration caused by a known net force.

▶ Identify action-reaction pairs.

SC.912.P.12.3 Interpret and apply Newton's three laws of motion.

Newton's Second and Third Laws

Newton's Second Law

From Newton's first law, we know that an object with no net force acting on it is in a state of equilibrium. We also know that an object experiencing a net force undergoes a change in its velocity. But exactly how much does a known force affect the motion of an object?

Force is proportional to mass and acceleration.

Imagine pushing a stalled car through a level intersection, as shown in **Figure 3.1**. Because a net force causes an object to accelerate, the speed of the car will increase. When you push the car by yourself, however, the acceleration will be so small that it will take a long time for you to notice an increase in the car's speed. If you get several friends to help you, the net force on the car is much greater, and the car will soon be moving so fast that you will have to run to keep up with it. This change happens because the acceleration of an object is directly proportional to the net force acting on the object. (Note that this is an idealized example that disregards any friction forces that would hinder the motion. In reality, the car accelerates when the push is greater than the frictional force. However, when the force exerted by the pushers equals the frictional force, the net force becomes zero, and the car moves at a constant velocity.)

Experience reveals that the mass of an object also affects the object's acceleration. A lightweight car accelerates more than a heavy truck if the same force is applied to both. Thus, it requires less force to accelerate a low-mass object than it does to accelerate a high-mass object at the same rate.

FIGURE 3.1

Relationship Between Force and Acceleration **(a)** A small force on an object causes a small acceleration, but **(b)** a larger force causes a larger acceleration.

(a)

(b)

Newton's second law relates force, mass, and acceleration.

The relationships between mass, force, and acceleration are quantified in **Newton's second law**.

> ### Newton's Second Law
>
> **The acceleration of an object is directly proportional to the net force acting on the object and inversely proportional to the object's mass.**

According to Newton's second law, if equal forces are applied to two objects of different masses, the object with greater mass will experience a smaller acceleration, and the object with less mass will experience a greater acceleration.

In equation form, we can state Newton's law as follows:

> ### Newton's Second Law
> $$\Sigma\mathbf{F} = m\mathbf{a}$$
> net force = mass × acceleration

In this equation, **a** is the acceleration of the object, and m is the object's mass. Note that Σ is the Greek capital letter *sigma*, which represents the sum of the quantities that come after it. In this case, $\Sigma\mathbf{F}$ represents the *vector sum of all external forces acting on the object*, or the net force.

Newton's Second Law

GO ONLINE

Interactive Demo
HMHScience.com

SOLUTION TUTOR

HMHScience.com

Sample Problem C Roberto and Laura are studying across from each other at a wide table. Laura slides a 2.2 kg book toward Roberto. If the net force acting on the book is 1.6 N to the right, what is the book's acceleration?

1 ANALYZE

Given: $m = 2.2 \text{ kg}$

$\mathbf{F}_{\text{net}} = \Sigma\mathbf{F} = 1.6 \text{ N to the right}$

Unknown: $\mathbf{a} = ?$

2 SOLVE

Use Newton's second law, and solve for **a**.

$$\Sigma\mathbf{F} = m\mathbf{a}, \text{ so } \mathbf{a} = \frac{\Sigma\mathbf{F}}{m}$$

$$\mathbf{a} = \frac{1.6 \text{ N}}{2.2 \text{ kg}} = 0.73 \text{ m/s}^2$$

$$\boxed{\mathbf{a} = 0.73 \text{ m/s}^2 \text{ to the right}}$$

Tips and Tricks

If more than one force is acting on an object, you must find the net force as shown in Sample Problem B before applying Newton's second law. The acceleration will be in the direction of the net force.

Continued

Newton's Second Law (continued)

Practice

> **Tips and Tricks**
>
> For some problems, it may be easier to use the equation for Newton's second law twice: once for all of the forces acting in the *x*-direction ($\Sigma F_x = ma_x$) and once for all of the forces acting in the *y*-direction ($\Sigma F_y = ma_y$). If the net force in both directions is zero, then **a** = 0, which corresponds to the equilibrium situation in which **v** is either constant or zero.

1. The net force on the propeller of a 3.2 kg model airplane is 7.0 N forward. What is the acceleration of the airplane?

2. The net force on a golf cart is 390 N north. If the cart has a total mass of 270 kg, what are the magnitude and direction of the cart's acceleration?

3. A car has a mass of 1.50×10^3 kg. If the force acting on the car is 6.75×10^3 N to the east, what is the car's acceleration?

4. A soccer ball kicked with a force of 13.5 N accelerates at 6.5 m/s^2 to the right. What is the mass of the ball?

5. A 2.0 kg otter starts from rest at the top of a muddy incline 85 cm long and slides down to the bottom in 0.50 s. What net force acts on the otter along the incline?

Newton's Third Law

A force is exerted on an object when that object interacts with another object in its environment. Consider a moving car colliding with a concrete barrier. The car exerts a force on the barrier at the moment of collision. Furthermore, the barrier exerts a force on the car so that the car rapidly slows down after coming into contact with the barrier. Similarly, when your hand applies a force to a door to push it open, the door simultaneously exerts a force back on your hand.

Forces always exist in pairs.

From examples like those discussed in the previous paragraph, Newton recognized that a single isolated force cannot exist. Instead, *forces always exist in pairs*. The car exerts a force on the barrier, and at the same time, the barrier exerts a force on the car. Newton described this type of situation with his **third law of motion**.

Conceptual Challenge

1. Gravity and Rocks The force due to gravity is twice as great on a 2 kg rock as it is on a 1 kg rock. Why doesn't the 2 kg rock have a greater free-fall acceleration?

2. Leaking Truck A truck loaded with sand accelerates at 0.5 m/s^2 on the highway. If the driving force on the truck remains constant, what happens to the truck's acceleration if sand leaks at a constant rate from a hole in the truck bed?

Newton's Third Law

If two objects interact, the magnitude of the force exerted on object 1 by object 2 is equal to the magnitude of the force simultaneously exerted on object 2 by object 1, and these two forces are opposite in direction.

An alternative statement of this law is that *for every action, there is an equal and opposite reaction.* When two objects interact with one another, the forces that the objects exert on each other are called an *action-reaction pair*. The force that object 1 exerts on object 2 is sometimes called the *action force*, while the force that object 2 exerts on object 1 is called the *reaction force*. The action force is equal in magnitude and opposite in direction to the reaction force. The terms *action* and *reaction* sometimes cause confusion because they are used a little differently in physics than they are in everyday speech. In everyday speech, the word *reaction* is used to refer to something that happens *after* and *in response to* an event. In physics, however, the reaction force occurs at exactly the same time as the action force.

Because the action and reaction forces coexist, either force can be called the action or the reaction. For example, you could call the force that the car exerts on the barrier the action and the force that the barrier exerts on the car the reaction. Likewise, you could choose to call the force that the barrier exerts on the car the action and the force that the car exerts on the barrier the reaction.

Action and reaction forces each act on different objects.

One important thing to remember about action-reaction pairs is that each force acts on a different object. Consider the task of driving a nail into wood, as illustrated in **Figure 3.2.** To accelerate the nail and drive it into the wood, the hammer exerts a force on the nail. According to Newton's third law, the nail exerts a force on the hammer that is equal to the magnitude of the force that the hammer exerts on the nail.

The concept of action-reaction pairs is a common source of confusion because some people assume incorrectly that the equal and opposite forces balance one another and make any change in the state of motion impossible. If the force that the nail exerts on the hammer is equal to the force the hammer exerts on the nail, why doesn't the nail remain at rest?

The motion of the nail is affected only by the forces acting on the nail. To determine whether the nail will accelerate, draw a free-body diagram to isolate the forces acting on the nail, as shown in **Figure 3.3.** The force of the nail on the hammer is not included in the diagram because it does not act on the nail. According to the diagram, the nail will be driven into the wood because there is a net force acting on the nail. Thus, action-reaction pairs do not imply that the net force on either object is zero. The action-reaction forces are equal and opposite, but either object may still have a net force acting on it.

FIGURE 3.2

Forces on a Hammer and Nail The force that the nail exerts on the hammer is equal and opposite to the force that the hammer exerts on the nail.

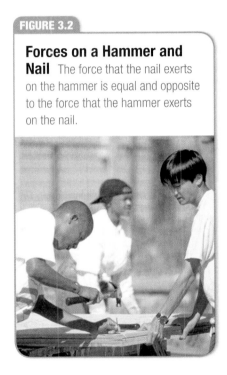

FIGURE 3.3

Net Force on a Nail The net force acting on the nail drives the nail into the wood.

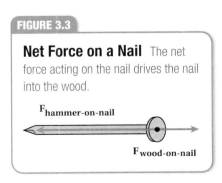

$F_{\text{hammer-on-nail}}$

$F_{\text{wood-on-nail}}$

Field forces also exist in pairs.

Newton's third law also applies to field forces. For example, consider the gravitational force exerted by Earth on an object. During calibration at the crash-test site, engineers calibrate the sensors in the heads of crash-test dummies by removing the heads and dropping them from a known height.

The force that Earth exerts on a dummy's head is $\mathbf{F_g}$. Let's call this force the action. What is the reaction? Because $\mathbf{F_g}$ is the force exerted on the falling head by Earth, the reaction to $\mathbf{F_g}$ is the force exerted on Earth by the falling head.

According to Newton's third law, the force of the dummy on Earth is equal to the force of Earth on the dummy. Thus, as a falling object accelerates toward Earth, Earth also accelerates toward the object.

The thought that Earth accelerates toward the dummy's head may seem to contradict our experience. One way to make sense of this idea is to refer to Newton's second law. The mass of Earth is much greater than that of the dummy's head. Therefore, while the dummy's head undergoes a large acceleration due to the force of Earth, the acceleration of Earth due to this reaction force is negligibly small because of Earth's enormous mass.

✔ SECTION 3 FORMATIVE ASSESSMENT

▶ Reviewing Main Ideas

1. A 6.0 kg object undergoes an acceleration of magnitude 2.0 m/s^2.
   a. What is the magnitude of the net force acting on the object?
   b. If this same force is applied to a 4.0 kg object, what acceleration is produced?

2. A child causes a wagon to accelerate by pulling it with a horizontal force. Newton's third law says that the wagon exerts an equal and opposite force on the child. How can the wagon accelerate? (Hint: Draw a free-body diagram for each object.)

3. Identify the action-reaction pairs in the following situations:
   a. A person takes a step.
   b. A snowball hits someone in the back.
   c. A baseball player catches a ball.
   d. A gust of wind strikes a window.

4. The forces acting on a sailboat are 390 N north and 180 N east. If the boat (including crew) has a mass of 270 kg, what are the magnitude and direction of the boat's acceleration?

✔ Critical Thinking

5. A small sports car collides head-on with a massive truck. Use proportional reasoning and Newton's second law to predict which vehicle experiences the greater impact force, and which vehicle experiences the greater acceleration. Use equations to express your reasoning.

Everyday Forces

Key Terms

weight
normal force

static friction
kinetic friction

coefficient of friction

Objectives

- Explain the difference between mass and weight.
- Find the direction and magnitude of normal forces.
- Describe air resistance as a form of friction.
- Use coefficients of friction to calculate frictional force.

Weight

How do you know that a bowling ball weighs more than a tennis ball? If you imagine holding one ball in each hand, you can imagine the downward forces acting on your hands. Because the bowling ball has more mass than the tennis ball does, gravitational force pulls more strongly on the bowling ball. Thus, the bowling ball pushes your hand down with more force than the tennis ball does.

The gravitational force exerted on the ball by Earth, $\mathbf{F_g}$, is a vector quantity, directed toward the center of Earth. The magnitude of this force, F_g, is a scalar quantity called **weight.** The weight of an object can be calculated using the equation $F_g = ma_g$, where a_g is the magnitude of the acceleration due to gravity, or free-fall acceleration. On the surface of Earth, $a_g = g$, and $F_g = mg$. In this book, $g = 9.81$ m/s^2 unless otherwise specified.

Weight, unlike mass, is not an inherent property of an object. Because it is equal to the magnitude of the force due to gravity, weight depends on location. For example, if the astronaut in **Figure 4.1** weighs 800 N (180 lb) on Earth, he would weigh only about 130 N (30 lb) on the moon. The value of a_g on the surface of a planet depends on the planet's mass and radius. On the moon, a_g is about 1.6 m/s^2—much smaller than 9.81 m/s^2.

Even on Earth, an object's weight may vary with location. Objects weigh less at higher altitudes than they do at sea level because the value of a_g decreases as distance from the surface of Earth increases. The value of a_g also varies slightly with changes in latitude.

SC.912.P.10.10 Compare the magnitude and range of the four fundamental forces (gravitational, electromagnetic, weak nuclear, strong nuclear).

FIGURE 4.1

Weight on the Moon On the moon, astronauts weigh much less than they do on Earth.

The Normal Force

Imagine a television set at rest on a table. We know that the gravitational force is acting on the television. How can we use Newton's laws to explain why the television does not continue to fall toward the center of Earth?

An analysis of the forces acting on the television will reveal the forces that are in equilibrium. First, we know that the gravitational force of Earth, $\mathbf{F_g}$, is acting downward. Because the television is in equilibrium, we know that another force, equal in magnitude to $\mathbf{F_g}$ but in the opposite direction, must be acting on it. This force is the force exerted on the television by the table. This force is called the **normal force, $\mathbf{F_n}$.**

weight a measure of the gravitational force exerted on an object; its value can change with the location of the object in the universe

normal force a force that acts on an object lying on a surface, acting in a direction perpendicular to the surface

Forces and the Laws of Motion **135**

©Photo Researchers, Inc.

FIGURE 4.2

Normal Force

In this example, the normal force, **F_n**, is equal and opposite to the force due to gravity, **F_g**.

The word *normal* is used because the direction of the contact force is perpendicular to the table surface and one meaning of the word *normal* is "perpendicular." **Figure 4.2** shows the forces acting on the television.

The normal force is always perpendicular to the contact surface but is not always opposite in direction to the force due to gravity. **Figure 4.3** shows a free-body diagram of a refrigerator on a loading ramp. The normal force is perpendicular to the ramp, not directly opposite the force due to gravity. In the absence of other forces, the normal force, **F_n**, is equal and opposite to the component of **F_g** that is perpendicular to the contact surface. The magnitude of the normal force can be calculated as $F_n = mg \cos \theta$. The angle θ is the angle between the normal force and a vertical line and is also the angle between the contact surface and a horizontal line.

FIGURE 4.3

Normal Force When an Object Is on a Ramp

The normal force is not always opposite the force due to gravity, as shown by this example of a refrigerator on a loading ramp.

The Force of Friction

Consider a jug of juice at rest (in equilibrium) on a table, as in **Figure 4.4(a)**. We know from Newton's first law that the net force acting on the jug is zero. Newton's second law tells us that any additional unbalanced force applied to the jug will cause the jug to accelerate and to remain in motion unless acted on by another force. But experience tells us that the jug will not move at all if we apply a very small horizontal force. Even when we apply a force large enough to move the jug, the jug will stop moving almost as soon as we remove this applied force.

Friction opposes the applied force.

When the jug is at rest, the only forces acting on it are the force due to gravity and the normal force exerted by the table. These forces are equal and opposite, so the jug is in equilibrium. When you push the jug with a small horizontal force **F**, as shown in **Figure 4.4(b)**, the table exerts an equal force in the opposite direction. As a result, the jug remains in equilibrium and therefore also remains at rest. The resistive force that keeps the jug from moving is called the force of **static friction,** abbreviated as **F_s** .

static friction the force that resists the initiation of sliding motion between two surfaces that are in contact and at rest

FIGURE 4.4

Overcoming the Force of Friction

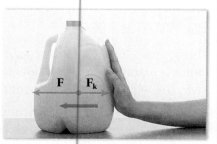

(a) Because this jug of juice is in equilibrium, any unbalanced horizontal force applied to it will cause the jug to accelerate.

(b) When a small force is applied, the jug remains in equilibrium because the static-friction force is equal but opposite to the applied force.

(c) The jug begins to accelerate as soon as the applied force exceeds the opposing friction force.

As long as the jug does not move, the force of static friction is always equal to and opposite in direction to the component of the applied force that is parallel to the surface ($F_s = -F_{applied}$). As the applied force increases, the force of static friction also increases; if the applied force decreases, the force of static friction also decreases. When the applied force is as great as it can be without causing the jug to move, the force of static friction reaches its maximum value, $\mathbf{F_{s,max}}$.

Kinetic friction is less than static friction.

When the applied force on the jug exceeds $\mathbf{F_{s,max}}$, the jug begins to move with an acceleration to the left, as shown in **Figure 4.4(c)**. A frictional force is still acting on the jug as the jug moves, but that force is actually less than $\mathbf{F_{s,max}}$. The retarding frictional force on an object in motion is called the force of **kinetic friction ($\mathbf{F_k}$)**. The magnitude of the net force acting on the object is equal to the difference between the applied force and the force of kinetic friction ($F_{applied} - F_k$).

At the microscopic level, frictional forces arise from complex interactions between contacting surfaces. Most surfaces, even those that seem very smooth to the touch, are actually quite rough at the microscopic level, as illustrated in **Figure 4.5**. Notice that the surfaces are in contact at only a few points. When two surfaces are stationary with respect to each other, the surfaces stick together somewhat at the contact points. This *adhesion* is caused by electrostatic forces between molecules of the two surfaces.

kinetic friction the force that opposes the movement of two surfaces that are in contact and are sliding over each other

> **Tips and Tricks**
>
> In free-body diagrams, the force of friction is always parallel to the surface of contact. The force of kinetic friction is always opposite the direction of motion. To determine the direction of the force of static friction, use the principle of equilibrium. For an object in equilibrium, the frictional force must point in the direction that results in a net force of zero.

The force of friction is proportional to the normal force.

It is easier to push a chair across the floor at a constant speed than to push a heavy desk across the floor at the same speed. Experimental observations show that the magnitude of the force of friction is approximately proportional to the magnitude of the normal force that a surface exerts on an object. Because the desk is heavier than the chair, the desk also experiences a greater normal force and therefore greater friction.

Friction can be calculated approximately.

Keep in mind that the force of friction is really a macroscopic effect caused by a complex combination of forces at a microscopic level. However, we can approximately calculate the force of friction with certain assumptions. The relationship between normal force and the force of friction is one factor that affects friction. For instance, it is easier to slide a light textbook across a desk than it is to slide a heavier textbook. The relationship between the normal force and the force of friction provides a good approximation for the friction between dry, flat surfaces that are at rest or sliding past one another.

FIGURE 4.5

Microscopic View of Surfaces in Contact On the microscopic level, even very smooth surfaces make contact at only a few points.

coefficient of friction the ratio of the magnitude of the force of friction between two objects in contact to the magnitude of the normal force with which the objects press against each other

The force of friction also depends on the composition and qualities of the surfaces in contact. For example, it is easier to push a desk across a tile floor than across a floor covered with carpet. Although the normal force on the desk is the same in both cases, the force of friction between the desk and the carpet is higher than the force of friction between the desk and the tile. The quantity that expresses the dependence of frictional forces on the particular surfaces in contact is called the **coefficient of friction.** The coefficient of friction between a waxed snowboard and the snow will affect the acceleration of the snowboarder shown in **Figure 4.6**. The coefficient of friction is represented by the symbol μ, the lowercase Greek letter *mu*.

The coefficient of friction is a ratio of forces.

The coefficient of friction is defined as the ratio of the force of friction to the normal force between two surfaces. The *coefficient of kinetic friction* is the ratio of the force of kinetic friction to the normal force.

$$\mu_k = \frac{F_k}{F_n}$$

The *coefficient of static friction* is the ratio of the maximum value of the force of static friction to the normal force.

$$\mu_s = \frac{F_{s,max}}{F_n}$$

If the value of μ and the normal force on the object are known, then the magnitude of the force of friction can be calculated directly.

$$F_f = \mu F_n$$

Figure 4.7 shows some experimental values of μ_s and μ_k for different materials. Because kinetic friction is less than or equal to the maximum static friction, the coefficient of kinetic friction is always less than or equal to the coefficient of static friction.

FIGURE 4.6

Minimizing Friction

Snowboarders wax their boards to minimize the coefficient of friction between the boards and the snow.

FIGURE 4.7

COEFFICIENTS OF FRICTION (APPROXIMATE VALUES)

	μ_s	μ_k		μ_s	μ_k
steel on steel	0.74	0.57	waxed wood on wet snow	0.14	0.1
aluminum on steel	0.61	0.47	waxed wood on dry snow	–	0.04
rubber on dry concrete	1.0	0.8	metal on metal (lubricated)	0.15	0.06
rubber on wet concrete	–	0.5	ice on ice	0.1	0.03
wood on wood	0.4	0.2	Teflon on Teflon	0.04	0.04
glass on glass	0.9	0.4	synovial joints in humans	0.01	0.003

Coefficients of Friction

Sample Problem D A 20.0 kg trunk is pushed across the floor of a moving van by a horizontal force. If the coefficient of kinetic friction between the trunk and the floor is 0.255, what is the magnitude of the frictional force opposing the applied force?

① ANALYZE

Given: $m = 20.0$ kg
$\mu_k = 0.255$
$g = 9.81$ m/s^2

Unknown: $F_k = ?$

② SOLVE

Use the equation for frictional force, substituting mg for the normal force F_n.

$$F_k = \mu_k F_n = \mu_k mg$$
$$F_k = (0.255)(20.0 \text{ kg})(9.81 \text{ m/s}^2)$$

$$\boxed{F_k = 50.0 \text{ N}}$$

Practice

1. A man lifted a 281.5 kg load off the ground using his teeth. Suppose he can hold just three times that mass on a 30.0° slope using the same force. What is the coefficient of static friction between the load and the slope?

2. A 25 kg chair initially at rest on a horizontal floor requires a 165 N horizontal force to set it in motion. Once the chair is in motion, a 127 N horizontal force keeps it moving at a constant velocity.
   a. Find the coefficient of static friction between the chair and the floor.
   b. Find the coefficient of kinetic friction between the chair and the floor.

3. A museum curator moves artifacts into place on various different display surfaces. Use the values in **Figure 4.7** to find $F_{s,max}$ and F_k for the following situations:
   a. moving a 145 kg aluminum sculpture across a horizontal steel platform
   b. pulling a 15 kg steel sword across a horizontal steel shield
   c. pushing a 250 kg wood bed on a horizontal wood floor
   d. sliding a 0.55 kg glass amulet on a horizontal glass display case

Overcoming Friction

Sample Problem E A student attaches a rope to a 20.0 kg box of books. He pulls with a force of 90.0 N at an angle of 30.0° with the horizontal. The coefficient of kinetic friction between the box and the sidewalk is 0.500. Find the acceleration of the box.

①　ANALYZE

Given:　　$m = 20.0 \text{ kg} \quad \mu_k = 0.500$

$\mathbf{F}_{applied} = 90.0 \text{ N at } \theta = 30.0°$

Unknown:　$\mathbf{a} = ?$

Diagram:

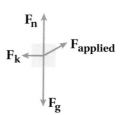

②　PLAN

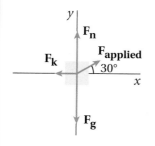

Choose a convenient coordinate system, and find the x- and y-components of all forces.

The diagram at left shows the most convenient coordinate system, because the only force to resolve into components is $\mathbf{F}_{applied}$.

$$F_{applied,y} = (90.0 \text{ N})(\sin 30.0°) = 45.0 \text{ N (upward)}$$

$$F_{applied,x} = (90.0 \text{ N})(\cos 30.0°) = 77.9 \text{ N (to the right)}$$

Choose an equation or situation:

A. Find the normal force, F_n, by applying the condition of equilibrium in the vertical direction: $\Sigma F_y = 0$.

B. Calculate the force of kinetic friction on the box:
$F_k = \mu_k F_n$.

C. Apply Newton's second law along the horizontal direction to find the acceleration of the box:
$\Sigma F_x = ma_x$.

③　SOLVE

Substitute the values into the equations and solve:

A. To apply the condition of equilibrium in the vertical direction, you need to account for all of the forces in the y-direction: F_g, F_n, and $F_{applied,y}$. You know $F_{applied,y}$ and can use the box's mass to find F_g.

$$F_{applied,y} = 45.0 \text{ N}$$

$$F_g = (20.0 \text{ kg})(9.81 \text{ m/s}^2) = 196 \text{ N}$$

Continued ▶

Overcoming Friction (continued)

Next, apply the equilibrium condition, $\Sigma F_y = 0$, and solve for F_n.

Tips and Tricks

Remember to pay attention to the direction of forces. Here, F_g is subtracted from F_n and $F_{applied,\ y}$ because F_g is directed downward.

$$\Sigma F_y = F_n + F_{applied,\ y} - F_g = 0$$

$$F_n + 45.0\ \text{N} - 196\ \text{N} = 0$$

$$F_n = -45.0\ \text{N} + 196\ \text{N} = 151\ \text{N}$$

B. Use the normal force to find the force of kinetic friction.

$$F_k = \mu_k F_n = (0.500)(151\ \text{N}) = 75.5\ \text{N}$$

C. Use Newton's second law to determine the horizontal acceleration.

$$\Sigma F_x = F_{applied,\ x} - F_k = ma_x$$

Tips and Tricks

F_k is directed toward the left, opposite the direction of $F_{applied,\ x}$. As a result, when you find the sum of the forces in the x-direction, you need to subtract F_k from $F_{applied,\ x}$.

$$a_x = \frac{F_{applied,\ x} - F_k}{m} = \frac{77.9\ \text{N} - 75.5\ \text{N}}{20.0\ \text{kg}} = \frac{2.4\ \text{N}}{20.0\ \text{kg}}$$

$$= \frac{2.4\ \text{kg} \cdot \text{m/s}^2}{20.0\ \text{kg}}$$

$$\boxed{\mathbf{a} = 0.12\ \text{m/s}^2 \text{ to the right}}$$

❹ CHECK YOUR WORK

In this example, the normal force is not equal in magnitude to the weight because the y-component of the student's pull on the rope helps support the box.

Practice

1. A student pulls on a rope attached to a box of books and moves the box down the hall. The student pulls with a force of 185 N at an angle of 25.0° above the horizontal. The box has a mass of 35.0 kg, and μ_k between the box and the floor is 0.27. Find the acceleration of the box.

2. The student in item 1 moves the box up a ramp inclined at 12° with the horizontal. If the box starts from rest at the bottom of the ramp and is pulled at an angle of 25.0° with respect to the incline and with the same 185 N force, what is the acceleration up the ramp? Assume that $\mu_k = 0.27$.

3. A 75 kg box slides down a 25.0° ramp with an acceleration of 3.60 m/s².

   a. Find μ_k between the box and the ramp.

   b. What acceleration would a 175 kg box have on this ramp?

4. A box of books weighing 325 N moves at a constant velocity across the floor when the box is pushed with a force of 425 N exerted downward at an angle of 35.2° below the horizontal. Find μ_k between the box and the floor.

Air resistance is a form of friction.

Another type of friction, the retarding force produced by air resistance, is important in the analysis of motion. Whenever an object moves through a fluid medium, such as air or water, the fluid provides a resistance to the object's motion.

For example, the force of air resistance, $\mathbf{F_R}$, on a moving car acts in the direction opposite the direction of the car's motion. At low speeds, the magnitude of $\mathbf{F_R}$ is roughly proportional to the car's speed. At higher speeds, $\mathbf{F_R}$ is roughly proportional to the square of the car's speed. When the magnitude of $\mathbf{F_R}$ equals the magnitude of the force moving the car forward, the net force is zero, and the car moves at a constant speed.

A similar situation occurs when an object falls through air. As a free-falling body accelerates, its velocity increases. As the velocity increases, the resistance of the air to the object's motion also constantly increases. When the upward force of air resistance balances the downward gravitational force, the net force on the object is zero, and the object continues to move downward with a constant maximum speed, called the *terminal speed*.

Driving and Friction

Accelerating a car seems simple to the driver. It is just a matter of pressing on a pedal or turning a wheel. But what are the forces involved?

A car moves because as its wheels turn, they push back against the road. It is actually the reaction force of the road pushing on the car that causes the car to accelerate. Without the friction between the tires and the road, the wheels would not be able to exert this force and the car would not experience a reaction force. Thus, acceleration requires this friction. Water and snow provide less friction and therefore reduce the amount of control the driver has over the direction and speed of the car.

As a car moves slowly over an area of water on the road, the water is squeezed out from under the tires. If the car moves too quickly, there is not enough time for the weight of the car to squeeze the water out from under the tires. The water trapped between the tires and the road will lift the tires and car off the road, a phenomenon called *hydroplaning*. When this situation occurs, there is very little friction between the tires and the water, and the car becomes difficult to control. To prevent hydroplaning, rain tires, such as the one shown above, keep water from accumulating between the tire and the road. Deep channels down the center of the tire provide a place for the water to accumulate, and curved grooves in the tread channel the water outward.

Because snow moves even less easily than water, snow tires have several deep grooves in their tread, enabling the tire to cut through the snow and make contact with the pavement. These deep grooves push against the snow and, like the paddle blades of a riverboat, use the snow's inertia to provide resistance.

There are four fundamental forces.

At the microscopic level, friction results from interactions between the protons and electrons in atoms and molecules. Magnetic force also results from atomic phenomena. These forces are classified as *electromagnetic forces*. The electromagnetic force is one of four fundamental forces in nature. The other three fundamental forces are gravitational force, the strong nuclear force, and the weak nuclear force. All four fundamental forces are field forces. The forces are described in greater detail in the chapter "Atomic Physics."

The strong and weak nuclear forces have very small ranges, so their effects are not directly observable. The electromagnetic and gravitational forces act over long ranges. Thus, any force you can observe at the macroscopic level is either due to gravitational or electromagnetic forces.

The strong nuclear force is the strongest of all four fundamental forces. Gravity is the weakest. Although the force due to gravity holds the planets, stars, and galaxies together, its effect on subatomic particles is negligible. This explains why electric and magnetic effects can easily overcome gravity. For example, a bar magnet has the ability to lift another magnet off a desk.

SECTION 4 FORMATIVE ASSESSMENT

▶ Reviewing Main Ideas

1. Draw a free-body diagram for each of the following objects:
   a. a projectile accelerating downward in the presence of air resistance
   b. a crate being pushed across a flat surface at a constant speed

2. A bag of sugar has a mass of 2.26 kg.
   a. What is its weight in newtons on the moon, where the acceleration due to gravity is one-sixth that on Earth?
   b. What is its weight on Jupiter, where the acceleration due to gravity is 2.64 times that on Earth?

3. A 2.0 kg block on an incline at a 60.0° angle is held in equilibrium by a horizontal force.
   a. Determine the magnitude of this horizontal force. (Disregard friction.)
   b. Determine the magnitude of the normal force on the block.

4. A 55 kg ice skater is at rest on a flat skating rink. A 198 N horizontal force is needed to set the skater in motion. However, after the skater is in motion, a horizontal force of 175 N keeps the skater moving at a constant velocity. Find the coefficients of static and kinetic friction between the skates and the ice.

✔ Critical Thinking

5. The force of air resistance acting on a certain falling object is roughly proportional to the square of the object's velocity and is directed upward. If the object falls fast enough, will the force of air resistance eventually exceed the weight of the object and cause the object to move upward? Explain.

Scientific Explanations

Every day, news articles report new scientific claims, or a scientific explanation is put forth to support a new government regulation. An understanding of how to analyze and evaluate these explanations will allow you to properly critique the claims and make informed decisions.

First, analyze the evidence for the explanation. The evidence is the data obtained from observations made by the scientists or policy makers. Do the data support the explanation provided? Look from other angles. Are there any alternative explanations that can be derived from the evidence?

Second, evaluate the evidence by looking at all aspects of how it was generated. Was the evidence gathered in a well-controlled experiment and were the observations documented properly? Are there other factors not noted by the researcheers that might have caused the results? Do the data adequately support the explanation presented?

Finally, it is important to systematically critique the evidence. An organized presentation of the strengths and weaknesses of the explanations and the related evidence, as well as any alternative interpretations of the evidence, will improve your ability to make informed decisions.

Force, Mass, and Acceleration

Imagine that you are asked to push a shopping cart full of textbooks. When you apply a little bit of force, the cart accelerates slowly, but when you apply more force, the cart accelerates more quickly. Your teacher explains that the acceleration of the cart is proportional to the magnitude of the force acting on it, which is an example of Newton's Second Law. Is this an adequate explanation for the different accelerations of the cart?

- Analyze the evidence for the teacher's claim. Does the teacher have enough evidence to support the explanation? Are there any other parts of Newton's Second Law that the teacher should also examine?

- Evaluate the evidence for the teacher's explanation. Does the teacher have sufficiently high quality evidence to make a claim? If not, what additional evidence is needed? Are there any additional factors that the teacher should consider?

- Critique the evidence and the explanation. How would you gather evidence to further examine the explanation? Look at Newton's Second Law from all sides. Are there other variables that could be tested to examine Newton's Second Law? How could additional and/or different evidence help improve the quality of the explanation?

Summary

Newton's laws describe the predictable ways in which forces interact to change the motion of objects. Free-body diagrams help depict the multiple forces that are acting on an object.

SECTION 1 Changes in Motion

KEY TERM

- Force is a vector quantity that causes acceleration (when unbalanced).
- Force can act either through the physical contact of two objects (contact force) or at a distance (field force).
- A free-body diagram shows only the forces that act on one object. These forces are the only ones that affect the motion of that object.

force

SECTION 2 Newton's First Law

KEY TERMS

- The tendency of an object not to accelerate is called *inertia*. Mass is the physical quantity used to measure inertia.
- The net force acting on an object is the vector sum of all external forces acting on the object. An object is in a state of equilibrium when the net force acting on the object is zero.

inertia
net force
equilibrium

SECTION 3 Newton's Second and Third Laws

- The net force acting on an object is equal to the product of the object's mass and the object's acceleration.
- When two bodies exert force on each other, the forces are equal in magnitude and opposite in direction. These forces are called an action-reaction pair. Forces always exist in such pairs.

SECTION 4 Everyday Forces

KEY TERMS

- The weight of an object is the magnitude of the gravitational force on the object and is equal to the object's mass times the acceleration due to gravity.
- A normal force is a force that acts on an object in a direction perpendicular to the surface of contact.
- Friction is a resistive force that acts in a direction opposite to the direction of the relative motion of two contacting surfaces. The force of friction between two surfaces is proportional to the normal force.

weight
normal force
static friction
kinetic friction
coefficient of friction

VARIABLE SYMBOLS		
Quantities	**Units**	**Conversions**
F (vector) force	N newtons	$= kg \bullet m/s^2$
F (scalar) force	N newtons	$= kg \bullet m/s^2$
μ coefficient of friction	(no units)	

Problem Solving

See **Appendix D: Equations** for a summary of the equations introduced in this chapter. If you need more problem-solving practice, see **Appendix I: Additional Problems**.

Forces and Newton's First Law

▶ **REVIEWING MAIN IDEAS**

1. Is it possible for an object to be in motion if no net force is acting on it? Explain.

2. If an object is at rest, can we conclude that no external forces are acting on it?

3. An object thrown into the air stops at the highest point in its path. Is it in equilibrium at this point? Explain.

4. What physical quantity is a measure of the amount of inertia an object has?

CONCEPTUAL QUESTIONS

5. A beach ball is left in the bed of a pickup truck. Describe what happens to the ball when the truck accelerates forward.

6. A large crate is placed on the bed of a truck but is not tied down.
   a. As the truck accelerates forward, the crate slides across the bed until it hits the tailgate. Explain what causes this.
   b. If the driver slammed on the brakes, what could happen to the crate?

PRACTICE PROBLEMS

For problems 7–9, see Sample Problem A.

7. Earth exerts a downward gravitational force of 8.9 N on a cake that is resting on a plate. The plate exerts a force of 11.0 N upward on the cake, and a knife exerts a downward force of 2.1 N on the cake. Draw a free-body diagram of the cake.

8. A chair is pushed forward with a force of 185 N. The gravitational force of Earth on the chair is 155 N downward, and the floor exerts a force of 155 N upward on the chair. Draw a free-body diagram showing the forces acting on the chair.

9. Draw a free-body diagram representing each of the following objects:
   a. a ball falling in the presence of air resistance
   b. a helicopter lifting off a landing pad
   c. an athlete running along a horizontal track

For problems 10–12, see Sample Problem B.

10. Four forces act on a hot-air balloon, shown from the side in the figure below. Find the magnitude and direction of the resultant force on the balloon.

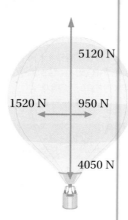

5120 N

1520 N   950 N

4050 N

11. Two lifeguards pull on ropes attached to a raft. If they pull in the same direction, the raft experiences a net force of 334 N to the right. If they pull in opposite directions, the raft experiences a net force of 106 N to the left.
    a. Draw a free-body diagram representing the raft for each situation.
    b. Find the force exerted by each lifeguard on the raft for each situation. (Disregard any other forces acting on the raft.)

12. A dog pulls on a pillow with a force of 5 N at an angle of 37° above the horizontal. Find the *x*- and *y*-components of this force.

Newton's Second and Third Laws

▶ REVIEWING MAIN IDEAS

13. The force that attracts Earth to an object is equal to and opposite the force that Earth exerts on the object. Explain why Earth's acceleration is not equal to and opposite the object's acceleration.

14. State Newton's second law ($\Sigma\mathbf{F} = m\mathbf{a}$) in your own words, and interpret the law to predict how the acceleration of an object changes if the net force on the object decreases by half.

15. An astronaut on the moon has a 110 kg crate and a 230 kg crate. How do the forces required to lift the crates straight up on the moon compare with the forces required to lift them on Earth? (Assume that the astronaut lifts with constant velocity in both cases.)

16. Draw a force diagram to identify all the action-reaction pairs that exist for a horse pulling a cart.

CONCEPTUAL QUESTIONS

17. A space explorer is moving through space far from any planet or star and notices a large rock, taken as a specimen from an alien planet, floating around the cabin of the ship. Should the explorer push it gently or kick it toward the storage compartment? Why?

18. Explain why a rope climber must pull downward on the rope in order to move upward. Discuss the force exerted by the climber's arms in relation to the weight of the climber during the various stages of each "step" up the rope.

19. An 1850 kg car is moving to the right at a constant speed of 1.44 m/s.
  a. What is the net force on the car?
  b. What would be the net force on the car if it were moving to the left?

PRACTICE PROBLEMS

For problems 20–22, see Sample Problem C.

20. What acceleration will you give to a 24.3 kg box if you push it horizontally with a net force of 85.5 N?

21. What net force is required to give a 25 kg suitcase an acceleration of 2.2 m/s^2 to the right?

22. Two forces are applied to a car in an effort to accelerate it, as shown below.
  a. What is the resultant of these two forces?
  b. If the car has a mass of 3200 kg, what acceleration does it have? (Disregard friction.)

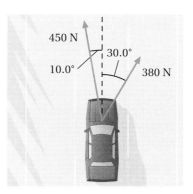

Weight, Friction, and Normal Force

▶ REVIEWING MAIN IDEAS

23. Explain the relationship between mass and weight.

24. A 0.150 kg baseball is thrown upward with an initial speed of 20.0 m/s.
  a. What is the force on the ball when it reaches half of its maximum height? (Disregard air resistance.)
  b. What is the force on the ball when it reaches its peak?

25. Draw free-body diagrams showing the weight and normal forces on a laundry basket in each of the following situations:
  a. at rest on a horizontal surface
  b. at rest on a ramp inclined 12° above the horizontal
  c. at rest on a ramp inclined 25° above the horizontal
  d. at rest on a ramp inclined 45° above the horizontal

26. If the basket in item 25 has a mass of 5.5 kg, find the magnitude of the normal force for the situations described in (a) through (d).

27. A teapot is initially at rest on a horizontal tabletop, and then one end of the table is lifted slightly. Does the normal force increase or decrease? Does the force of static friction increase or decrease?

28. Which is usually greater, the maximum force of static friction or the force of kinetic friction?

29. A 5.4 kg bag of groceries is in equilibrium on an incline of angle $\theta = 15°$. Find the magnitude of the normal force on the bag.

CONCEPTUAL QUESTIONS

30. Imagine an astronaut in space at the midpoint between two stars of equal mass. If all other objects are infinitely far away, what is the weight of the astronaut? Explain your answer.

31. A ball is held in a person's hand.
   a. Identify all the external forces acting on the ball and the reaction force to each.
   b. If the ball is dropped, what force is exerted on it while it is falling? Identify the reaction force in this case. (Disregard air resistance.)

32. Explain why pushing downward on a book as you push it across a table increases the force of friction between the table and the book.

33. Analyze the motion of a rock dropped in water in terms of its speed and acceleration. Assume that a resistive force acting on the rock increases as the speed increases.

34. A skydiver falls through the air. As the speed of the skydiver increases, what happens to the skydiver's acceleration? What is the acceleration when the skydiver reaches terminal speed?

PRACTICE PROBLEMS

For problems 35–37, see Sample Problem D.

35. A 95 kg clock initially at rest on a horizontal floor requires a 650 N horizontal force to set it in motion. After the clock is in motion, a horizontal force of 560 N keeps it moving with a constant velocity. Find μ_s and μ_k between the clock and the floor.

36. A box slides down a 30.0° ramp with an acceleration of 1.20 m/s². Determine the coefficient of kinetic friction between the box and the ramp.

37. A 4.00 kg block is pushed along the ceiling with a constant applied force of 85.0 N that acts at an angle of 55.0° with the horizontal, as in the figure. The block accelerates to the right at 6.00 m/s². Determine the coefficient of kinetic friction between the block and the ceiling.

For problems 38–39, see Sample Problem E.

38. A clerk moves a box of cans down an aisle by pulling on a strap attached to the box. The clerk pulls with a force of 185.0 N at an angle of 25.0° with the horizontal. The box has a mass of 35.0 kg, and the coefficient of kinetic friction between box and floor is 0.450. Find the acceleration of the box.

39. A 925 N crate is being pulled across a level floor by a force **F** of 325 N at an angle of 25° above the horizontal. The coefficient of kinetic friction between the crate and floor is 0.25. Find the magnitude of the acceleration of the crate.

Mixed Review

▶ REVIEWING MAIN IDEAS

40. A block with a mass of 6.0 kg is held in equilibrium on an incline of angle $\theta = 30.0°$ by a horizontal force, **F**, as shown in the figure. Find the magnitudes of the normal force on the block and of **F**. (Ignore friction.)

41. A 2.0 kg mass starts from rest and slides down an inclined plane 8.0×10^{-1} m long in 0.50 s. What net force is acting on the mass along the incline?

42. A 2.26 kg book is dropped from a height of 1.5 m.
   a. What is its acceleration?
   b. What is its weight in newtons?

43. A 5.0 kg bucket of water is raised from a well by a rope. If the upward acceleration of the bucket is 3.0 m/s², find the force exerted by the rope on the bucket of water.

44. A 3.46 kg briefcase is sitting at rest on a level floor.
  a. What is the briefcases's acceleration?
  b. What is its weight in newtons?

45. A boat moves through the water with two forces acting on it. One is a 2.10×10^3 N forward push by the motor, and the other is a 1.80×10^3 N resistive force due to the water.
  a. What is the acceleration of the 1200 kg boat?
  b. If it starts from rest, how far will it move in 12 s?
  c. What will its speed be at the end of this time interval?

46. A girl on a sled coasts down a hill. Her speed is 7.0 m/s when she reaches level ground at the bottom. The coefficient of kinetic friction between the sled's runners and the hard, icy snow is 0.050, and the girl and sled together weigh 645 N. How far does the sled travel on the level ground before coming to rest?

47. A box of books weighing 319 N is shoved across the floor by a force of 485 N exerted downward at an angle of 35° below the horizontal.
  a. If μ_k between the box and the floor is 0.57, how long does it take to move the box 4.00 m, starting from rest?
  b. If μ_k between the box and the floor is 0.75, how long does it take to move the box 4.00 m, starting from rest?

48. A 3.00 kg block starts from rest at the top of a 30.0° incline and accelerates uniformly down the incline, moving 2.00 m in 1.50 s.
  a. Find the magnitude of the acceleration of the block.
  b. Find the coefficient of kinetic friction between the block and the incline.
  c. Find the magnitude of the frictional force acting on the block.
  d. Find the speed of the block after it has slid a distance of 2.00 m.

49. A hockey puck is hit on a frozen lake and starts moving with a speed of 12.0 m/s. Exactly 5.0 s later, its speed is 6.0 m/s. What is the puck's average acceleration? What is the coefficient of kinetic friction between the puck and the ice?

50. The parachute on a racecar that weighs 8820 N opens at the end of a quarter-mile run when the car is traveling 35 m/s. What net retarding force must be supplied by the parachute to stop the car in a distance of 1100 m?

51. A 1250 kg car is pulling a 325 kg trailer. Together, the car and trailer have an acceleration of 2.15 m/s² directly forward.
  a. Determine the net force on the car.
  b. Determine the net force on the trailer.

52. The coefficient of static friction between the 3.00 kg crate and the 35.0° incline shown here is 0.300. What is the magnitude of the minimum force, F, that must be applied to the crate perpendicularly to the incline to prevent the crate from sliding down the incline?

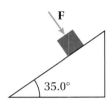

53. The graph below shows a plot of the speed of a person's body during a chin-up. All motion is vertical, and the mass of the person (excluding the arms) is 64.0 kg. Find the magnitude of the net force exerted on the body at 0.50 s intervals.

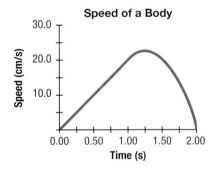

54. A machine in an ice factory is capable of exerting 3.00×10^2 N of force to pull a large block of ice up a slope. The block weighs 1.22×10^4 N. Assuming there is no friction, what is the maximum angle that the slope can make with the horizontal if the machine is to be able to complete the task?

ALTERNATIVE ASSESSMENT

1. Predict what will happen in the following test of the laws of motion. You and a partner face each other, each holding a bathroom scale. Place the scales back to back, and slowly begin pushing on them. Record the measurements of both scales at the same time. Perform the experiment. Which of Newton's laws have you verified?

2. Research how the work of scientists Antoine Lavoisier, Isaac Newton, and Albert Einstein related to the study of mass. Which of these scientists might have said the following?
   a. The mass of a body is a measure of the quantity of matter in the body.
   b. The mass of a body is the body's resistance to a change in motion.
   c. The mass of a body depends on the body's velocity.

   To what extent are these statements compatible or contradictory? Present your findings to the class for review and discussion.

3. Imagine an airplane with a series of special instruments anchored to its walls: a pendulum, a 100 kg mass on a spring balance, and a sealed half-full aquarium. What will happen to each instrument when the plane takes off, makes turns, slows down, lands, and so on? If possible, test your predictions by simulating airplane motion in elevators, car rides, and other situations. Use instruments similar to those described above, and also observe your body sensations. Write a report comparing your predictions with your experiences.

4. With a small group, determine which of the following statements is correct. Use a diagram to explain your answer.
   a. Rockets cannot travel in space because there is nothing for the gas exiting the rocket to push against.
   b. Rockets can travel because gas exerts an unbalanced force on the rocket.
   c. The action and reaction forces are equal and opposite. Therefore, they balance each other, and no movement is possible.

GRAPHING CALCULATOR PRACTICE

Static Friction

The force of static friction depends on two factors: the coefficient of static friction for the two surfaces in contact and the normal force between the two surfaces. The relationship can be represented on a graphing calculator by the following equation:

$$Y_1 = SX$$

Given a value for the coefficient of static friction (S), the graphing calculator can calculate and graph the force of static friction (Y_1) as a function of normal force (X).

In this activity, you will use a graphing calculator program to compare the force of static friction of wood boxes on a wood surface with that of steel boxes on a steel surface.

Go online to HMHScience.com to find the skillsheet and program for this graphing calculator activity.

Standards-Based Assessment

MULTIPLE CHOICE

Use the passage below to answer questions 1–2.

A truck driver slams on the brakes and skids to a stop through a displacement Δx.

1 If the truck's mass doubles, find the truck's skidding distance in terms of Δx. (Hint: Increasing the mass increases the normal force.)

- **A** $\Delta x/4$
- **B** Δx
- **C** $2\Delta x$
- **D** $4\Delta x$

2 If the truck's initial velocity were halved, what would be the truck's skidding distance?

- **A** $\Delta x/4$
- **B** Δx
- **C** $2\Delta x$
- **D** $4\Delta x$

3 Two blocks of masses m_1 and m_2 are placed in contact with each other on a smooth, horizontal surface. Block m_1 is on the left of block m_2. A constant horizontal force F to the right is applied to m_1.

What is the acceleration of the two blocks?

- **A** $a = \dfrac{F}{m_1}$
- **B** $a = \dfrac{F}{m_2}$
- **C** $a = \dfrac{F}{m_1 + m_2}$
- **D** $a = \dfrac{F}{(m_1)(m_2)}$

4 You can keep a 3 kg book from falling to the ground by placing it on a horizontal surface. What reaction force is resisting the force of the book on the surface?

- **A** air resistance
- **B** friction
- **C** normal
- **D** tension

5 A crate is pulled to the right (positive x-axis) with a force of 82.0 N, to the left with a force of 115 N, upward with a force of 565 N, and downward with a force of 236 N. Find the magnitude and direction of the net force on the crate.

- **A** 3.30 N at 96° counterclockwise from the positive x-axis
- **B** 3.30 N at 6° counterclockwise from the positive x-axis
- **C** 3.30×10^2 N at 96° counterclockwise from the positive x-axis
- **D** 3.30×10^2 N at 6° counterclockwise from the positive x-axis

6 A ball with a mass of m is thrown into the air. What is the force exerted on Earth by the ball?

- **A** $m_{ball}g$, directed down
- **B** $m_{ball}g$, directed up
- **C** $m_{Earth}g$, directed down
- **D** $m_{Earth}g$, directed up

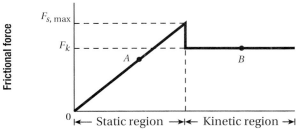

7 The graph above shows the relationship between the applied force and the force of friction.

What is the relationship between the forces at point A?

- **A** $F_s = F_{applied}$
- **B** $F_k = F_{applied}$
- **C** $F_s < F_{applied}$
- **D** $F_k > F_{applied}$

GRIDDED RESPONSE

8 A freight train has a mass of 1.5×10^7 kg. If the train can exert a constant pull of 7.5×10^5 N, how long, in seconds, would it take to increase the speed of the train from rest to 85 km/h? (Disregard friction.)

TALL ROADS
Roads that help people walk over deep holes

You know that all structures have forces acting on them—and that forces always exist in pairs. What forces must engineers consider when designing and building a bridge? As you read this explanation of how bridges are built, keep Newton's third law of motion (action-reaction forces) in mind.

THE STORY OF GETTING FROM HERE TO THERE

THE EARTH'S PULL HOLDS PEOPLE TO THE GROUND.

HEY, GET BACK HERE!

WE LIKE TO WALK AROUND, BUT SOMETIMES THE GROUND GOES PLACES WE DON'T WANT TO GO, LIKE INTO A DEEP HOLE.

OR UNDER A RIVER.

WE CAN'T GET PAST THOSE PLACES BECAUSE WE HAVE TO FOLLOW THE GROUND.

(BIRDS DON'T, SINCE THEY CAN FLY BY PUSHING ON THE AIR. SOMEONE IN A MOVIE ONCE SANG, "IF BIRDS FLY OVER THE SKY, WHY CAN'T I?" THE ANSWER IS, "YOU ARE TOO BIG AND DON'T HAVE WINGS.")

If we want to go somewhere, we can make a road that goes straight across, high above the ground. Making short roads over holes and rivers is pretty easy, but making long ones can be very hard.

HOLE
Sometimes, you want to walk somewhere, but you don't want to go where the ground goes.

ROAD
If the hole is small enough, you can put a board over the hole to make a new road. Then you can walk across the board.

LONG ROAD
If you find a bigger hole, you can try to find a bigger board. Bigger boards are longer and stronger, but they're also heavier—and bigger things get heavier faster than they get stronger.

LONGER ROAD
All boards bend a little, and longer boards bend more. A long enough board will break under your weight, and a very long board will break under its *own*.

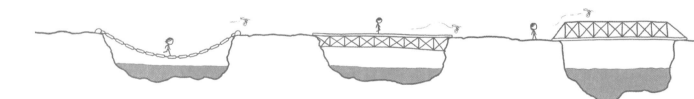

BENDY ROAD
You can cross a larger hole with a road that's allowed to bend. If you tie many small boards together and let it hang, bending won't hurt it, and that will let it hold more weight.

This kind of road gets stronger the more you let it hang down, but it also gets harder to walk across. If it hangs down *too* far, it's no better than just walking down into the hole.

THICK ROAD
You can cross a bigger hole if you make the board thicker. Thicker things are harder to bend, so this kind of road is stronger.

TALL ROAD
It might seem like it would make more sense to put the extra-thick part below the road, because it's "holding" the road up, and we usually hold things from below.

But if it's strong mostly because it's thick, then it works just as well if you add the thickness above the road.

TALL ROADS

ROAD HANGING UNDER A STRONGER SHAPE

ROAD HANGING FROM STICKS

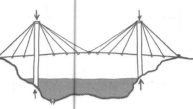

Since all this stuff you're adding is just there to hold the road up, that stuff doesn't need to be near the road. You can make a strong metal piece that goes high up over the hole—which gives it a stronger shape, but would be harder to walk on if the road went that way—and then use strong metal lines to hang the road straighter across under it.

HANGING ROAD PROBLEMS

When you hold up a road by hanging it, you have to be very careful. These tall roads keep the road from being moved by the Earth's pull—which is always straight down—but wind can make the road swing side-to-side.

Some roads have fallen down because the builders didn't understand wind well enough.

Another way to hold up a road is to build very strong sticks, then hang the road from the top ends of the sticks. The lines need to be a little stronger than the lines in the other hanging road, and the sticks need to be *really* strong. On the other hand, there are only two sticks, so that can make building easier.

THIS IS THE BEST KIND OF TALL ROAD.

That's not really true. Different tall roads are good for different things.

But a lot of the time, when you need to cross a big hole, this kind of shape will let your road reach farther than any other shape would.

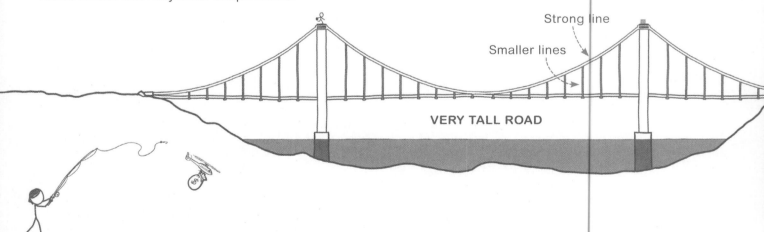

Strong line

Smaller lines

VERY TALL ROAD

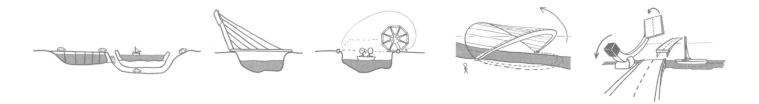

TALL ROADS ON OTHER WORLDS

A very bright person (who was known for calling the Earth a "pale blue point") once said something interesting about these kinds of roads in one of his books.

He pointed out that everything about the shape of very tall roads is decided by the laws of space and time—the laws that say how a world's weight pulls things—and those laws are the same everywhere.

That means that if there's life on other worlds, the road shape that works best for them should be the same one that works best for us. Our tall roads may look familiar to them.

Maybe that's true; maybe it's not. We don't know if there's life on other worlds, and if there is, maybe they don't build roads at all. Maybe their way of living is different from ours in ways we can't even think about.

But if they have holes they need to get across...

. . . and if, in their world, they build things out of different shapes, like us . . .

. . . and if they have problems with holding their roads up . . .

. . . then they very well may build tall roads that look just like ours.

I like that idea, because now, when I look at one of these tall roads, I always feel a little happier. It makes me think about how maybe, somewhere far across space and time, there's someone looking at another tall road, thinking about how the shape might be found across many worlds, and—maybe—wondering about me.

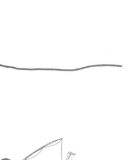

1543

Andries van Wesel, better known as Andreas Vesalius, completes his *Seven Books on the Structure of the Human Body*. It is the first work on anatomy to be based on the dissection of human bodies.

1556

Akbar becomes ruler of the Moghul Empire in North India, Pakistan, and Afghanistan. By ensuring religious tolerance, he establishes greater unity in India, making it one of the world's great powers.

1588

Queen Elizabeth I of England sends the English fleet to repel the invasion by the Spanish Armada. The success of the English navy marks the beginning of Great Britain's status as a major naval power.

1603

Kabuki theater achieved broad popularity in Japan.

1609

New Astronomy, by **Johannes Kepler**, is published. In it, Kepler demonstrates that the orbit of Mars is elliptical rather than circular.

$$T^2 \propto a^3$$

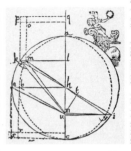

1540　1550　1560　1570　1580　1590　1600

1543

Nicholas Copernicus's *On the Revolutions of the Heavenly Bodies* is published. It is the first work on astronomy to provide an analytical basis for the motion of the planets, including Earth, around the sun.

1564

English writers **Christopher Marlowe** and **William Shakespeare** are born.

$$\Delta x = v_i \, \Delta t + \frac{1}{2} a (\Delta t)^2$$

1592

Galileo Galilei is appointed professor of mathematics at the University of Padua. While there, he performs experiments on the motions of bodies.

1608

The first telescopes are constructed in the Netherlands. Using these instruments as models, **Galileo** constructs his first telescope the following year.

1605

The first part of **Miguel de Cervantes'** *Don Quixote* is published.

1637

René Descartes' *Discourse on Method* is published. According to Descartes' philosophy of rationalism, the laws of nature can be deduced by reason.

1655

The first paintings of Dutch artist **Jan Vermeer** are produced around this time. Vermeer's paintings portray middle- and working-class people in everyday situations.

1678

$v = f\lambda$

Christiaan Huygens completes the bulk of his *Treatise on Light*, in which he presents his model of secondary wavelets, known today as Huygens's principle. The completed book is published 12 years later.

| 1630 | 1640 | 1650 | 1660 | 1670 | 1680 | 1690 |

1644

The Qing, or Manchu, Dynasty is established in China. China becomes the most prosperous nation in the world but declines until the Qing Dynasty is replaced by the Chinese Republic in 1911.

1669

Danish geologist **Niclaus Steno** correctly determines the structure of crystals and identifies fossils as organic remains.

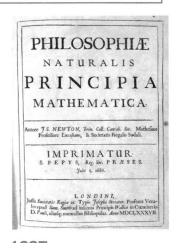

1687

$\mathbf{F} = m\mathbf{a}$

Isaac Newton's masterpiece, *Mathematical Principles of Natural Philosophy*, is published. In this extensive work, Newton systematically presents a unified model of mechanics.

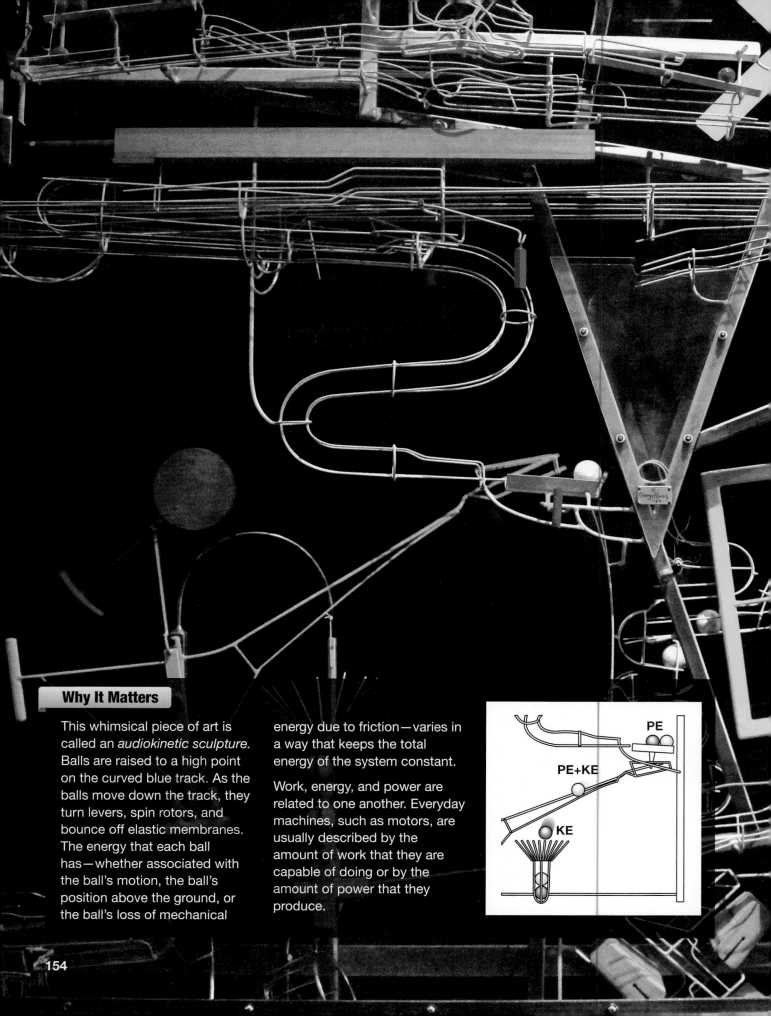

Why It Matters

This whimsical piece of art is called an *audiokinetic sculpture.* Balls are raised to a high point on the curved blue track. As the balls move down the track, they turn levers, spin rotors, and bounce off elastic membranes. The energy that each ball has—whether associated with the ball's motion, the ball's position above the ground, or the ball's loss of mechanical energy due to friction—varies in a way that keeps the total energy of the system constant.

Work, energy, and power are related to one another. Everyday machines, such as motors, are usually described by the amount of work that they are capable of doing or by the amount of power that they produce.

CHAPTER 5

Work and Energy

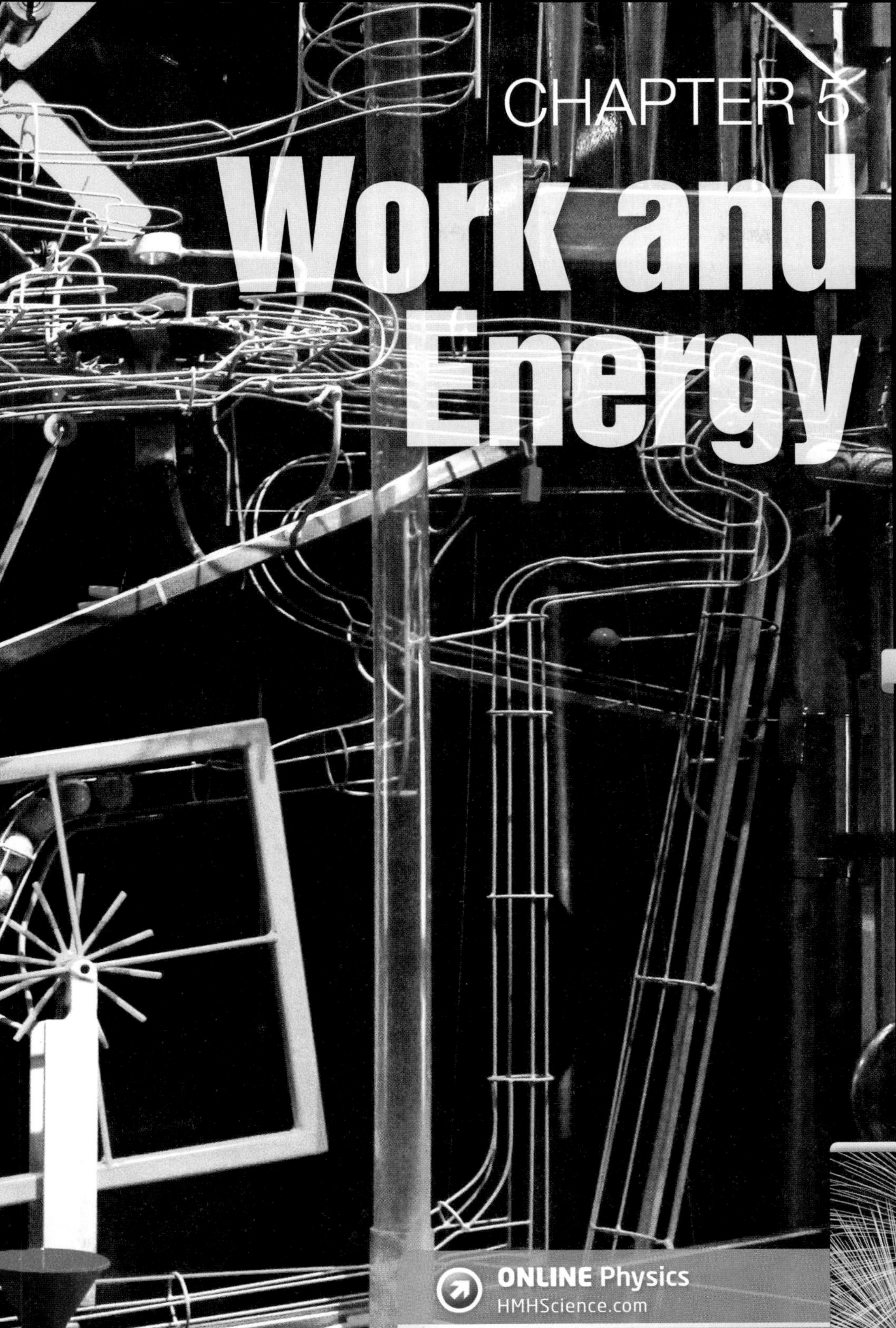

BIG IDEA

Work, energy, and power are related to each other. Although energy can change from one form to another, it is always conserved.

(➜) **ONLINE** Physics
HMHScience.com

ONLINE LABS
- Exploring Work and Energy
- Conservation of Mechanical Energy
- S.T.E.M. Lab Power Programming

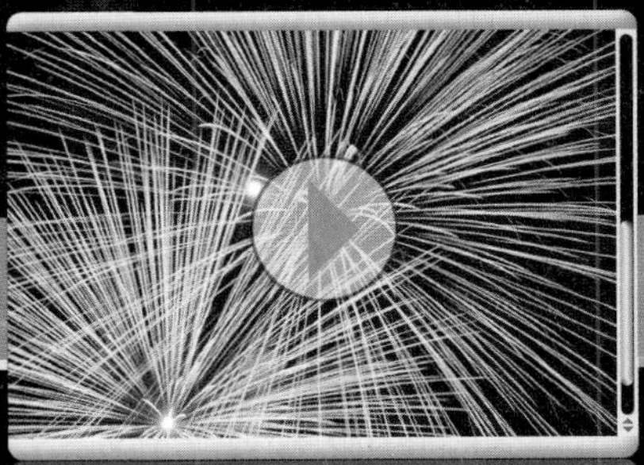

GO ONLINE **Animated Physics**
(➜) HMHScience.com

Kinetic Energy

(t) ©Corbis

Work

Key Term
work

Objectives

▶ Recognize the difference between the scientific and ordinary definitions of *work*.

▶ Define *work* by relating it to force and displacement.

▶ Identify where work is being performed in a variety of situations.

▶ Calculate the net work done when many forces are applied to an object.

SC.912.P.10.3 Compare and contrast work and power qualitatively and quantitatively.

work the product of the component of a force along the direction of displacement and the magnitude of the displacement

Definition of Work

Many of the terms you have encountered so far in this book have meanings in physics that are similar to their meanings in everyday life. In its everyday sense, the term *work* means to do something that takes physical or mental effort. But in physics, work has a distinctly different meaning. Consider the following situations:

- A student holds a heavy chair at arm's length for several minutes.
- A student carries a bucket of water along a horizontal path while walking at constant velocity.

It might surprise you to know that as the term *work* is used in physics, there is no work done on the chair or the bucket, even though effort is required in both cases. We will return to these examples later.

Work is done on an object when a force causes a displacement of the object.

Imagine that your car, like the car shown in **Figure 1.1**, has run out of gas and you have to push it down the road to the gas station. If you push the car with a constant horizontal force, the **work** you do on the car is equal to the magnitude of the force, F, times the magnitude of the displacement of the car. Using the symbol d instead of Δx for displacement, we define work for a constant force as

$$W = Fd$$

Work is not done on an object unless the object is moved with the action of a force. The application of a force alone does not constitute work. For this reason, no work is done on the chair when a student holds the chair at arm's length. Even though the student exerts a force to support the chair, the chair does not move. The student's tired arms suggest that work is being done, which is indeed true. The quivering muscles in the student's arms go through many small displacements and do work within the student's body. However, work is not done on the chair.

Work is done only when components of a force are parallel to a displacement.

When the force on an object and the object's displacement are in different directions, only the component of the force that is parallel to the object's displacement does work. Components of the force perpendicular to a displacement do not do work.

FIGURE 1.1

Work Done When Pushing a Car This person exerts a constant force on the car and displaces it to the left. The work done on the car by the person is equal to the force the person exerts times the displacement of the car.

For example, imagine pushing a crate along the ground. If the force you exert is horizontal, all of your effort moves the crate. If your force is at an angle, only the horizontal component of your applied force causes a displacement and contributes to the work. If the angle between the force and the direction of the displacement is θ, as in **Figure 1.2**, work can be expressed as follows:

$$W = Fd \cos \theta$$

If $\theta = 0°$, then $\cos 0° = 1$ and $W = Fd$, which is the definition of work given earlier. If $\theta = 90°$, however, then $\cos 90° = 0$ and $W = 0$. So no work is done on a bucket of water being carried by a student walking horizontally. The upward force exerted by the student to support the bucket is perpendicular to the displacement of the bucket, which results in no work done on the bucket.

Finally, if many constant forces are acting on an object, you can find the *net* work done on the object by first finding the net force on the object.

FIGURE 1.2

Definition of Work The work done on this crate is equal to the force times the displacement times the cosine of the angle between them.

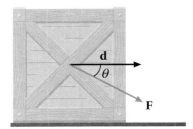

$$W = Fd \cos \theta$$

Net Work Done by a Constant Net Force

$$W_{net} = F_{net}d \cos \theta$$

**net work =
net force × displacement × cosine of the angle between them**

Work has dimensions of force times length. In the SI system, work has a unit of newtons times meters (N•m), or joules (J). To give you an idea of how large a joule is, consider that the work done in lifting an apple from your waist to the top of your head is about 1 J.

Did YOU Know?

The joule is named for the British physicist James Prescott Joule (1818–1889). Joule made major contributions to the understanding of energy, heat, and electricity.

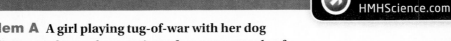

GO ONLINE

Interactive Demo
HMHScience.com

Work

Sample Problem A A girl playing tug-of-war with her dog pulls the dog a distance of 8.0 m by exerting a force at an angle of 18° with the horizontal. If the amount of work the girl does in pulling the dog is 190 J, what is the magnitude of the force?

① ANALYZE

Given: $W = 190 \text{ J}$ $d = 8.0 \text{ m}$ $\theta = 18°$

Unknown: $F = ?$

② SOLVE

Use the equation for work done by a constant force, and rearrange it to solve for F.

$$W = Fd \, (\cos \theta)$$

$$F = \frac{W}{d \, (\cos \theta)} = \frac{190 \text{ J}}{(8.0 \text{ m}) \, (\cos 18°)}$$

$$\boxed{F = 25 \text{ N}}$$

Continued

Work (continued)

Practice

1. Your car has run out of gas. Fortunately, there is a gas station nearby. You must exert a force of 715 N on the car in order to move it. By the time you reach the station, you have done 2.72×10^4 J of work. How far have you pushed the car?

2. A weightlifter lifts a set of weights a vertical distance of 2.00 m. If a constant net force of 350 N is exerted on the weights, what is the net work done on the weights?

3. A shopper in a supermarket pushes a cart with a force of 35 N directed at an angle of 25° downward from the horizontal. Find the work done by the shopper on the cart as the shopper moves along a 50.0 m length of aisle.

4. If 2.0 J of work is done in raising a 180 g apple, how far is it lifted?

The sign of work is important.

Work is a scalar quantity and can be positive or negative, as shown in **Figure 1.3.** Work is positive when the component of force is in the same direction as the displacement. For example, when you lift a box, the work done by the force you exert on the box is positive because that force is upward, in the same direction as the displacement.

Work is negative when the force is in the direction opposite the displacement. For example, the force of kinetic friction between a sliding box and the floor is opposite to the displacement of the box, so the work done by the force of friction on the box is negative.

If you are very careful in applying the equation for work, your answer will have the correct sign: cos θ is negative for angles greater than 90° but less than 270°.

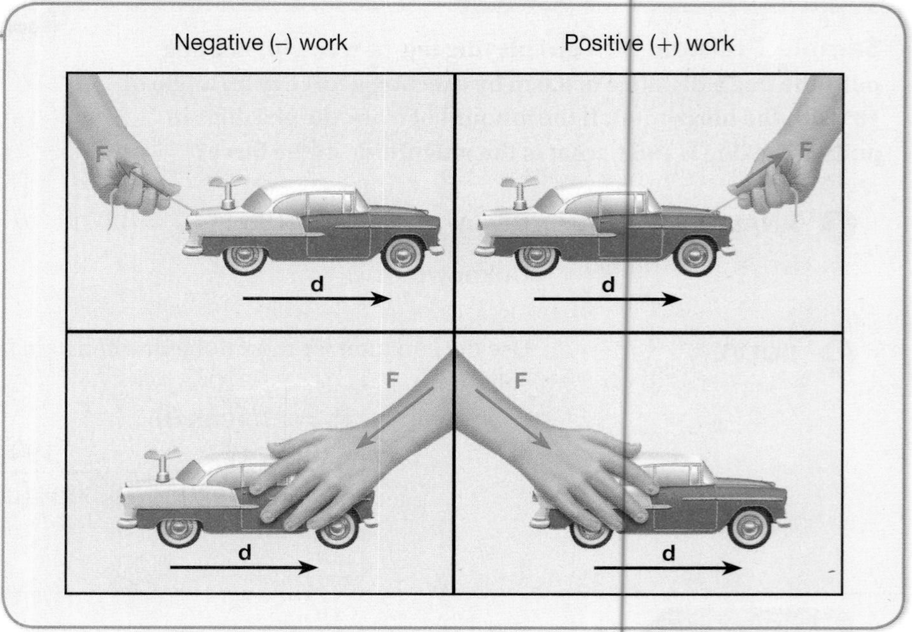

FIGURE 1.3

Positive and Negative Values of Work Depending on the angle, an applied force can either cause a moving car to slow down (left), which results in negative work done on the car, or speed up (right), which results in positive work done on the car.

Negative (−) work   Positive (+) work

If the work done on an object results only in a change in the object's speed, the sign of the net work on the object tells you whether the object's speed is increasing or decreasing. If the net work is positive, the object speeds up, and work is done *on* the object. If the net work is negative, the object slows down, and work is done *by* the object on something else.

SECTION 1 FORMATIVE ASSESSMENT

▶ Reviewing Main Ideas

1. For each of the following cases, indicate whether the work done on the second object in each example will have a positive or a negative value.

   a. The road exerts a friction force on a speeding car skidding to a stop.

   b. A rope exerts a force on a bucket as the bucket is raised up a well.

   c. Air exerts a force on a parachute as the parachutist falls to Earth.

2. If a neighbor pushes a lawnmower four times as far as you do but exerts only half the force, which one of you does more work and by how much?

3. A worker pushes a 1.50×10^3 N crate with a horizontal force of 345 N a distance of 24.0 m. Assume the coefficient of kinetic friction between the crate and the floor is 0.220.

   a. How much work is done by the worker on the crate?

   b. How much work is done by the floor on the crate?

   c. What is the net work done on the crate?

4. A 0.075 kg ball in a kinetic sculpture moves at a constant speed along a motorized vertical conveyor belt. The ball rises 1.32 m above the ground. A constant frictional force of 0.350 N acts in the direction opposite the conveyor belt's motion. What is the net work done on the ball?

✓ Critical Thinking

5. For each of the following statements, identify whether the everyday or the scientific meaning of *work* is intended.

   a. Jack had to work against time as the deadline neared.

   b. Jill had to work on her homework before she went to bed.

   c. Jack did work carrying the pail of water up the hill.

6. Determine whether work is being done in each of the following examples:

   a. a train engine pulling a loaded boxcar initially at rest

   b. a tug of war that is evenly matched

   c. a crane lifting a car

SC.912.P.10.1 Differentiate among the various forms of energy and recognize that they can be transformed from one form to others.

kinetic energy the energy of an object that is associated with the object's motion

Energy

Key Terms

kinetic energy
gravitational potential energy

work–kinetic energy theorem
elastic potential energy

potential energy
spring constant

Kinetic Energy

Kinetic energy is energy associated with an object in motion. **Figure 2.1** shows a cart of mass m moving to the right on a frictionless air track under the action of a constant net force, **F**, acting to the right. Because the force is constant, we know from Newton's second law that the cart moves with a constant acceleration, **a**. While the force is applied, the cart accelerates from an initial velocity v_i to a final velocity v_f. If the cart is displaced a distance of Δx, the work done by **F** during this displacement is

$$W_{net} = F\Delta x = ma\Delta x$$

When you studied one-dimensional motion, you learned that the following relationship holds when an object undergoes constant acceleration:

$$v_f^2 = v_i^2 + 2a\Delta x$$

$$a\Delta x = \frac{v_f^2 - v_i^2}{2}$$

Substituting this result into the equation $W_{net} = ma\Delta x$ gives

$$W_{net} = m\left(\frac{v_f^2 - v_i^2}{2}\right)$$

$$W_{net} = \frac{1}{2}mv_f^2 - \frac{1}{2}mv_i^2$$

The quantity $\frac{1}{2}mv^2$ has a special name in physics: **kinetic energy.** The kinetic energy of an object with mass m and speed v, when treated as a particle, is given by the expression shown on the next page.

Work by a Constant Force The work done on an object by a constant force equals the object's mass times its acceleration times its displacement.

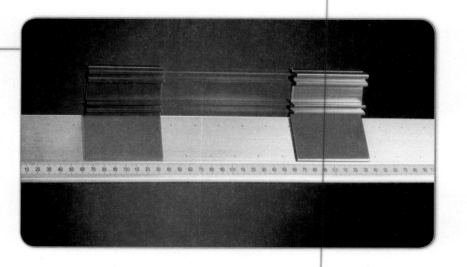

> ### Kinetic Energy
>
> $$KE = \tfrac{1}{2}\, mv^2$$
>
> **kinetic energy** $= \tfrac{1}{2} \times$ **mass** $\times$ **(speed)^2**

Kinetic energy is a scalar quantity, and the SI unit for kinetic energy (and all other forms of energy) is the joule. Recall that a joule is also used as the basic unit for work.

Kinetic energy depends on both an object's speed and its mass. If a bowling ball and a volleyball are traveling at the same speed, which do you think has more kinetic energy? You may think that because they are moving with identical speeds they have exactly the same kinetic energy. However, the bowling ball has more kinetic energy than the volleyball traveling at the same speed, because the bowling ball has more mass than the volleyball.

GO ONLINE

Interactive Demo
HMHScience.com

Kinetic Energy

Sample Problem B Silvana Cruciata from Italy ran 18.084 km in 1.000 h, a world record at the time. If Cruciata's kinetic energy was 694 J, what was her mass?

① ANALYZE

Given:
$\Delta x = 18.084 \text{ km} = 1.8084 \times 10^4 \text{ m}$

$\Delta t = 1.000 \text{ h} = 3.600 \times 10^3 \text{ s}$

$KE = 694 \text{ J}$

Unknown: $m = ?$

② PLAN

Choose an equation or situation: Use the definition of *average velocity* to calculate Cruciata's speed.

$$v_{avg} = \frac{\Delta x}{\Delta t}$$

Use the equation for kinetic energy, using v_{avg} for the velocity term, to solve for m.

$$KE = \frac{1}{2}\, m{v_{avg}}^2$$

Rearrange the equation to isolate the unknowns: Substitute the average velocity equation into the equation for kinetic energy and solve for m.

$$m = \frac{2KE}{{v_{avg}}^2} = \frac{2KE}{\left(\dfrac{\Delta x}{\Delta t}\right)^2} = \frac{2KE\Delta t^2}{\Delta x^2}$$

③ SOLVE

Substitute the values into the equation and solve:

$$m = \frac{(2)(694 \text{ J})(3.600 \times 10^3 \text{ s})^2}{(1.8084 \times 10^4 \text{ m})^2}$$

$$\boxed{m = 55.0 \text{ kg}}$$

 Continued

Kinetic Energy (continued)

④ CHECK YOUR WORK

If the average speed is rounded to 5.0 m/s and the kinetic energy is rounded to 700 J, the estimated mass is 56 kg, which is close to the calculated value.

Practice

1. Calculate the speed of an 8.0×10^4 kg airliner with a kinetic energy of 1.1×10^9 J.

2. What is the speed of a 0.145 kg baseball if its kinetic energy is 109 J?

3. Two bullets have masses of 3.0 g and 6.0 g, respectively. Both are fired with a speed of 40.0 m/s. Which bullet has more kinetic energy? What is the ratio of their kinetic energies?

4. The brightest, hottest, and most massive stars are the brilliant blue stars designated as spectral class O. If a class O star with a mass of 3.38×10^{31} kg has a kinetic energy of 1.10×10^{42} J, what is its speed? Express your answer in km/s (a typical unit for describing the speed of stars).

5. One of the world's fastest helicopters, the Westland Lynx, has a top speed of 4.00×10^2 km/h. If its kinetic energy at this speed is 2.10×10^7 J, what is the helicopter's mass?

work–kinetic energy theorem the net work done by all the forces acting on an object is equal to the change in the object's kinetic energy

The net work done on a body equals its change in kinetic energy.

The equation $W_{net} = \frac{1}{2}mv_f^2 - \frac{1}{2}mv_i^2$ derived at the beginning of this section says that the net work done by a *net* force acting on an object is equal to the *change* in the kinetic energy of the object. This important relationship, known as the **work–kinetic energy theorem,** is often written as follows:

> **Work–Kinetic Energy Theorem**
> $$W_{net} = \Delta KE$$
> **net work = change in kinetic energy**

When you use this theorem, you must include all the forces that do work on the object in calculating the net work done. From this theorem, we see that the speed of the object increases if the net work done on it is positive, because the final kinetic energy is greater than the initial kinetic energy. The object's speed decreases if the net work is negative, because the final kinetic energy is less than the initial kinetic energy.

The work–kinetic energy theorem allows us to think of kinetic energy as the work that an object can do while the object changes speed or as the amount of energy stored in the motion of an object. For example, the moving hammer in the ring-the-bell game in **Figure 2.2** has kinetic energy and can therefore do work on the puck. The puck can do work against gravity by moving up and striking the bell. When the bell is struck, part of the energy is converted into sound.

FIGURE 2.2

Work and Kinetic Energy

The moving hammer has kinetic energy and can do work on the puck, which can rise against gravity and ring the bell.

Work–Kinetic Energy Theorem

Sample Problem C The Great Pyramid of Khufu in Egypt used to have a height of 147 m and sides that sloped at an angle of 52.0° with respect to the ground. Stone blocks with masses of 1.37×10^4 kg were used to construct the pyramid. Suppose that a block with this mass at rest on top of the pyramid begins to slide down the side. Calculate the block's kinetic energy at ground level if the coefficient of kinetic friction is 0.45.

① ANALYZE

Given:

$m = 1.37 \times 10^4$ kg $h = 147$ m $g = 9.81$ m/s^2
$\theta = 52°$ $\mu_k = 0.45$ $v_i = 0$ m/s

Unknown: $KE_f = ?$

② PLAN

Choose an equation or situation:
The net work done by the block as it slides down the side of the pyramid can be expressed by using the definition of *work* in terms of net force. Because the net force is parallel to the displacement, the net work is simply the net force multiplied by the displacement. It can also be expressed in terms of changing kinetic energy by using the work-kinetic energy theorem.

$$W_{net} = F_{net}\, d$$
$$W_{net} = \Delta KE$$

The net force on the block equals the difference between the component of the force due to free-fall acceleration along the side of the pyramid and the frictional force resisting the downward motion of the block.

$$F_{net} = mg(\sin \theta) - F_k = mg\,(\sin \theta) - \mu_k\, mg\,(\cos \theta)$$

The distance the block travels along the side of the pyramid equals the height of the pyramid divided by the sine of the angle of the side's slope.

$$h = d(\sin \theta)$$
$$d = \frac{h}{\sin \theta}$$

Because the block is initially at rest, its initial kinetic energy is zero, and the change in kinetic energy equals the final kinetic energy.

$$\Delta KE = KE_f - KE_i = KE_f$$

Rearrange the equation to isolate the unknown: Combining these equations yields the following expression for the final kinetic energy.

$$KE_f = F_{net}\, d = mg\,(\sin \theta - \mu_k \cos \theta)\left(\frac{h}{\sin \theta}\right)$$
$$KE_f = mgh\left(1 - \frac{\mu_k}{\tan \theta}\right)$$

③ SOLVE

Substitute the values into the equation and solve:

$$KE_f = (1.37 \times 10^4 \text{ kg})(9.81 \text{ m/s}^2)(147 \text{ m})\left(1 - \frac{0.45}{\tan 52.0°}\right)$$

$$KE_f = (1.37 \times 10^4 \text{ kg})(9.81 \text{ m/s}^2)(147 \text{ m})(1.00 - 0.35)$$

$$KE_f = (1.37 \times 10^4 \text{ kg})(9.81 \text{ m/s}^2)(147 \text{ m})(0.65)$$

$$\boxed{KE_f = 1.3 \times 10^7 \text{ J}}$$

Continued

④ CHECK YOUR WORK
Note that the net force, and thus the final kinetic energy, is about two-thirds of what it would be if the side of the pyramid were frictionless.

Practice

1. A hockey puck with an initial speed of 8.0 m/s coasts 45 m to a stop across the ice. If the force of friction on the puck has a magnitude 0.12 N, what is the puck's mass?

2. The summit of Mount Everest is 8848.0 m above sea level, making it the highest summit on Earth. In 1953, Edmund Hillary was the first person to reach the summit. Suppose upon reaching there, Hillary slid a rock with a 45.0 g mass down the side of the mountain. If the rock's speed was 27.0 m/s when it was 8806.0 m above sea level, how much work was done on the rock by air resistance?

3. A 2.1×10^3 kg car starts from rest at the top of a driveway that is sloped at an angle of 20.0° with the horizontal. An average friction force of 4.0×10^3 N impedes the car's motion so that the car's speed at the bottom of the driveway is 3.8 m/s. What is the length of the driveway?

4. A 75 kg bobsled is pushed along a horizontal surface by two athletes. After the bobsled is pushed a distance of 4.5 m starting from rest, its speed is 6.0 m/s. Find the magnitude of the net force on the bobsled.

WHY IT MATTERS

The Energy in Food

The food that you eat provides your body with energy. Your body needs this energy to move your muscles, to maintain a steady internal temperature, and to carry out many other bodily processes. The energy in food is stored as a kind of *potential energy* in the chemical bonds within sugars and other organic molecules.

When you digest food, some of this energy is released. The energy is then stored again in sugar molecules, usually as glucose. When cells in your body need energy to carry out cellular processes, the cells break down the glucose molecules through a process called *cellular respiration*. The primary product of cellular respiration is a high-energy molecule called *adenosine triphosphate* (ATP), which has a significant role in many chemical reactions in cells.

Nutritionists and food scientists use units of Calories to quantify the energy in food. A standard calorie (cal) is defined as the amount of energy required to increase the temperature of 1 mL of water by 1°C, which equals 4.186 joules (J). A *food* Calorie is actually 1 kilocalorie, or 4186 J.

People who are trying to lose weight often monitor the number of Calories that they eat each day. These people count Calories because the body stores unused energy as fat. Most food labels show the number of Calories in each serving of food. The amount of energy that your body needs each day depends on many factors, including your age, your weight, and the amount of exercise that you get. A typically healthy and active person requires about 1500 to 2000 Calories per day.

Potential Energy

Consider the balanced boulder shown in **Figure 2.3.** As long as the boulder remains balanced, it has no kinetic energy. If it becomes unbalanced, it will fall vertically to the desert floor and will gain kinetic energy as it falls. What is the origin of this kinetic energy?

Potential energy is stored energy.

Potential energy is associated with an object that has the potential to move because of its position relative to some other location. Unlike kinetic energy, potential energy depends not only on the properties of an object but also on the object's interaction with its environment.

Gravitational potential energy depends on height from a zero level.

You learned earlier how gravitational forces influence the motion of a projectile. If an object is thrown up in the air, the force of gravity will eventually cause the object to fall back down. Similarly, the force of gravity will cause the unbalanced boulder in the previous example to fall. The energy associated with an object due to the object's position relative to a gravitational source is called **gravitational potential energy.**

Imagine an egg falling off a table. As it falls, it gains kinetic energy. But where does the egg's kinetic energy come from? It comes from the gravitational potential energy that is associated with the egg's initial position on the table relative to the floor. Gravitational potential energy can be determined using the following equation:

> **Gravitational Potential Energy**
> $$PE_g = mgh$$
> **gravitational potential energy = mass × free-fall acceleration × height**

The SI unit for gravitational potential energy, like for kinetic energy, is the joule. Note that the definition for gravitational potential energy given here is valid only when the free-fall acceleration is constant over the entire height, such as at any point near Earth's surface. Furthermore, gravitational potential energy depends on both the height and the free-fall acceleration, neither of which is a property of an object.

Also note that the height, h, is measured from an arbitrary zero level. In the example of the egg, if the floor is the zero level, then h is the height of the table, and mgh is the gravitational potential energy relative to the floor. Alternatively, if the table is the zero level, then h is zero. Thus, the potential energy associated with the egg relative to the table is zero.

Suppose you drop a volleyball from a second-floor roof and it lands on the first-floor roof of an adjacent building (see **Figure 2.4**). If the height is measured from the ground, the gravitational potential energy is not zero, because the ball is still above the ground. But if the height is measured from the first-floor roof, the potential energy is zero when the ball lands on the roof.

FIGURE 2.3

Stored Energy Energy is present in this example, but it is not kinetic energy because there is no motion. What kind of energy is it?

potential energy the energy associated with an object because of its interaction with the environment

gravitational potential energy the potential energy associated with an object's position relative to a gravitational source

FIGURE 2.4

Defining Potential Energy with Respect to Position If B is the zero level, then all the gravitational potential energy is converted to kinetic energy as the ball falls from A to B. If C is the zero level, then only part of the total gravitational potential energy at A is converted to kinetic energy during the fall from A to B.

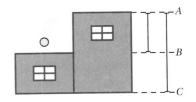

(tr) ©George Schwartz

Gravitational potential energy is associated with an object's position, so it must be measured relative to some *zero level*. The zero level is the vertical coordinate at which gravitational potential energy is defined to be zero. This zero level is arbitrary, and it is chosen to make a specific problem easier to solve. In many cases, the statement of the problem suggests what to use as a zero level.

Elastic potential energy depends on distance compressed or stretched.

Imagine you are playing with a spring on a tabletop. You push a block into the spring, compressing the spring, and then release the block. The block slides across the tabletop. The kinetic energy of the block came from the stored energy in the compressed spring. This potential energy is called **elastic potential energy.** Elastic potential energy is stored in any compressed or stretched object, such as a spring or the stretched strings of a tennis racket or guitar.

The length of a spring when no external forces are acting on it is called the *relaxed length* of the spring. When an external force compresses or stretches the spring, elastic potential energy is stored in the spring. The amount of energy depends on the distance the spring is compressed or stretched from its relaxed length, as shown in **Figure 2.5.** Elastic potential energy can be determined using the following equation:

elastic potential energy the energy stored in any deformed elastic object, such as a compressed spring or stretched rubber band

---

Elastic Potential Energy

$$PE_{elastic} = \frac{1}{2} kx^2$$

elastic potential energy =

$$\frac{1}{2} \times \textbf{spring constant} \times \left(\frac{\textbf{distance compressed}}{\textbf{or stretched}} \right)^2$$

The symbol k is called the **spring constant,** or force constant. For a flexible spring, the spring constant is small, whereas for a stiff spring, the spring constant is large. Spring constants have units of newtons divided by meters (N/m).

spring constant a parameter that is a measure of a spring's resistance to being compressed or stretched

---

FIGURE 2.5

Elastic Potential Energy The distance to use in the equation for elastic potential energy is the distance the spring is compressed or stretched from its relaxed length.

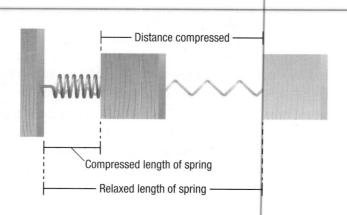

Potential Energy

GO ONLINE

Interactive Demo
HMHScience.com

Sample Problem D A 70.0 kg stuntman is attached to a bungee cord with an unstretched length of 15.0 m. He jumps off a bridge spanning a river from a height of 50.0 m. When he finally stops, the cord has a stretched length of 44.0 m. Treat the stuntman as a point mass, and disregard the weight of the bungee cord. Assuming the spring constant of the bungee cord is 71.8 N/m, what is the total potential energy relative to the water when the man stops falling?

① ANALYZE

Given: $m = 70.0$ N $k = 71.8$ N/m $g = 9.81$ m/s²
$h = 50.0$ m $-$ 44.0 m $= 6.0$ m
$x = 44.0$ m $-$ 15.0 m $= 29.0$ m
$PE = 0$ J at river level

Unknown: $PE_{tot} = ?$

Diagram:

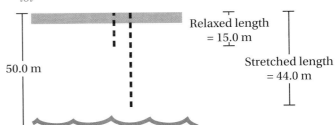

② PLAN

Choose an equation or situation:
The zero level for gravitational potential energy is chosen to be at the surface of the water. The total potential energy is the sum of the gravitational and elastic potential energy.

$$PE_{tot} = PE_g + PE_{elastic}$$

$$PE_g = mgh$$

$$PE_{elastic} = \frac{1}{2}kx^2$$

Tips and Tricks
Choose the zero potential energy location that makes the problem easiest to solve.

③ SOLVE

Substitute the values into the equations and solve:

$$PE_g = (70.0 \text{ kg})(9.81 \text{ m/s}^2)(6.0 \text{ m}) = 4.1 \times 10^3 \text{ J}$$

$$PE_{elastic} = \frac{1}{2}(71.8 \text{ N/m})(29.0 \text{ m})^2 = 3.02 \times 10^4 \text{ J}$$

$$PE_{tot} = 4.1 \times 10^3 \text{ J} + 3.02 \times 10^4 \text{ J}$$

$$\boxed{PE_{tot} = 3.43 \times 10^4 \text{ J}}$$

④ CHECK YOUR WORK

One way to evaluate the answer is to make an order-of-magnitude estimate. The gravitational potential energy is on the order of 10^2 kg $\times$ 10 m/s² $\times$ 10 m $= 10^4$ J. The elastic potential energy is on the order of 1×10^2 N/m $\times$ 10^2 m² $= 10^4$ J. Thus, the total potential energy should be on the order of 2×10^4 J. This number is close to the actual answer.

Continued ▶

Potential Energy (continued)

Practice

1. A spring with a force constant of 5.2 N/m has a relaxed length of 2.45 m. When a mass is attached to the end of the spring and allowed to come to rest, the vertical length of the spring is 3.57 m. Calculate the elastic potential energy stored in the spring.

2. The staples inside a stapler are kept in place by a spring with a relaxed length of 0.115 m. If the spring constant is 51.0 N/m, how much elastic potential energy is stored in the spring when its length is 0.150 m?

3. A 40.0 kg child is in a swing that is attached to ropes 2.00 m long. Find the gravitational potential energy associated with the child relative to the child's lowest position under the following conditions:

   a. when the ropes are horizontal

   b. when the ropes make a 30.0° angle with the vertical

   c. at the bottom of the circular arc

SECTION 2 FORMATIVE ASSESSMENT

▶ Reviewing Main Ideas

1. A pinball bangs against a bumper, giving the ball a speed of 42 cm/s. If the ball has a mass of 50.0 g, what is the ball's kinetic energy in joules?

2. A student slides a 0.75 kg textbook across a table, and it comes to rest after traveling 1.2 m. Given that the coefficient of kinetic friction between the book and the table is 0.34, use the work–kinetic energy theorem to find the book's initial speed.

3. A spoon is raised 21.0 cm above a table. If the spoon and its contents have a mass of 30.0 g, what is the gravitational potential energy associated with the spoon at that height relative to the surface of the table?

✔ Critical Thinking

4. What forms of energy are involved in the following situations?
   a. a bicycle coasting along a level road
   b. heating water
   c. throwing a football
   d. winding the mainspring of a clock

5. How do the forms of energy in item 4 differ from one another? Be sure to discuss mechanical versus nonmechanical energy, kinetic versus potential energy, and gravitational versus elastic potential energy.

Conservation of Energy

Key Term
mechanical energy

Conserved Quantities

When we say that something is *conserved*, we mean that it remains constant. If we have a certain amount of a conserved quantity at some instant of time, we will have the same amount of that quantity at a later time. This does not mean that the quantity cannot change form during that time, but if we consider all the forms that the quantity can take, we will find that we always have the same amount.

For example, the amount of money you now have is not a conserved quantity because it is likely to change over time. For the moment, however, let us assume that you do not spend the money you have, so your money is conserved. This means that if you have a dollar in your pocket, you will always have that same amount, although it may change form. One day it may be in the form of a bill. The next day you may have a hundred pennies, and the next day you may have an assortment of dimes and nickels. But when you total the change, you always have the equivalent of a dollar. It would be nice if money were like this, but of course it isn't. Because your money is often acquired and spent, it is not a conserved quantity.

An example of a conserved quantity that you are already familiar with is mass. For instance, imagine that a light bulb is dropped on the floor and shatters into many pieces. No matter how the bulb shatters, the total mass of all of the pieces together is the same as the mass of the intact light bulb, because mass is conserved.

Mechanical Energy

We have seen examples of objects that have either kinetic or potential energy. The description of the motion of many objects, however, often involves a combination of kinetic and potential energy as well as different forms of potential energy. Situations involving a combination of these different forms of energy can often be analyzed simply. For example, consider the motion of the different parts of a pendulum clock. The pendulum swings back and forth. At the highest point of its swing, there is only gravitational potential energy associated with its position. At other points in its swing, the pendulum is in motion, so it has kinetic energy as well. Elastic potential energy is also present in the many springs that are part of the inner workings of the clock. The motion of the pendulum in a clock is shown in **Figure 3.1**.

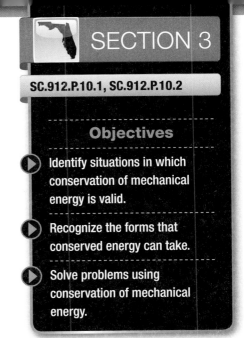
Objectives

▶ Identify situations in which conservation of mechanical energy is valid.

▶ Recognize the forms that conserved energy can take.

▶ Solve problems using conservation of mechanical energy.

SC.912.P.10.1 Differentiate among the various forms of energy and recognize that they can be transformed from one form to others.
SC.912.P.10.2 Explore the Law of Conservation of Energy by differentiating among open, closed, and isolated systems and explain that the total energy in an isolated system is a conserved quantity.

FIGURE 3.1

Motion of a Clock Pendulum
Total potential and kinetic energy must be taken into account in order to describe the total energy of the pendulum in a clock.

FIGURE 3.2

Classification of Energy

Energy can be classified in a number of ways.

Analyzing situations involving kinetic, gravitational potential, and elastic potential energy is relatively simple. Unfortunately, analyzing situations involving other forms of energy—such as chemical potential energy—is not as easy.

We can ignore these other forms of energy if their influence is negligible or if they are not relevant to the situation being analyzed. In most situations that we are concerned with, these forms of energy are not involved in the motion of objects. In ignoring these other forms of energy, we will find it useful to define a quantity called **mechanical energy.** The mechanical energy is the sum of kinetic energy and all forms of potential energy associated with an object or group of objects.

mechanical energy the sum of kinetic energy and all forms of potential energy

$$ME = KE + \Sigma PE$$

All energy, such as nuclear, chemical, internal, and electrical, that is not mechanical energy is classified as *nonmechanical energy*. Do not be confused by the term *mechanical energy*. It is not a unique form of energy. It is merely a way of classifying energy, as shown in **Figure 3.2.** As you learn about new forms of energy in this book, you will be able to add them to this chart.

Mechanical energy is often conserved.

Imagine a 75 g egg located on a countertop 1.0 m above the ground, as shown in **Figure 3.3.** The egg is knocked off the edge and falls to the ground. Because the acceleration of the egg is constant as it falls, you can use the kinematic formulas to determine the speed of the egg and the distance the egg has fallen at any subsequent time. The distance fallen can then be subtracted from the initial height to find the height of the egg above the ground at any subsequent time. For example, after 0.10 s, the egg has a speed of 0.98 m/s and has fallen a distance of 0.05 m, corresponding to a height above the ground of 0.95 m. Once the egg's speed and its height above the ground are known as a function of time, you can use what you have learned in this chapter to calculate both the kinetic energy of the egg and the gravitational potential energy associated with the position of the egg at any subsequent time. Adding the kinetic and potential energy gives the total mechanical energy at each position.

FIGURE 3.3

Conservation of Mechanical Energy The total mechanical energy, potential energy plus kinetic energy, is conserved as the egg falls.

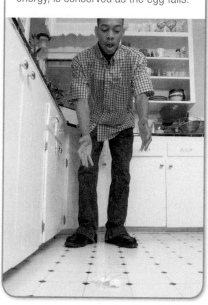

FIGURE 3.4

ENERGY OF A FALLING 75 g EGG					
Time (s)	Height (m)	Speed (m/s)	PE_g (J)	KE (J)	ME (J)
0.00	1.0	0.00	0.74	0.00	0.74
0.10	0.95	0.98	0.70	0.036	0.74
0.20	0.80	2.0	0.59	0.15	0.74
0.30	0.56	2.9	0.41	0.33	0.74
0.40	0.22	3.9	0.16	0.58	0.74

In the absence of friction, the total mechanical energy remains the same. This principle is called *conservation of mechanical energy*. Although the amount of mechanical energy is constant, mechanical energy itself can change form. For instance, consider the forms of energy for the falling egg, as shown in **Figure 3.4**. As the egg falls, the potential energy is continuously converted into kinetic energy. If the egg were thrown up in the air, kinetic energy would be converted into gravitational potential energy. In either case, mechanical energy is conserved. The conservation of mechanical energy can be written symbolically as follows:

Conservation of Mechanical Energy

$$ME_i = ME_f$$

**initial mechanical energy = final mechanical energy
(in the absence of friction)**

Quick LAB — MECHANICAL ENERGY

First, determine the mass of each of the balls. Then, tape the ruler to the side of a tabletop so that the ruler is vertical. Place the spring vertically on the tabletop near the ruler, and compress the spring by pressing down on one of the balls.

Release the ball, and measure the maximum height it achieves in the air. Repeat this process five times, and be sure to compress the spring by the same amount each time. Average the results. From the data, can you predict how high each of the other balls will rise? Test your predictions. (Hint: Assume mechanical energy is conserved.)

MATERIALS
- medium-sized spring (spring balance)
- assortment of small balls, each having a different mass
- ruler
- tape
- scale or balance

SAFETY

Students should wear goggles to perform this lab.

The mathematical expression for the conservation of mechanical energy depends on the forms of potential energy in a given problem. For instance, if the only force acting on an object is the force of gravity, as in the egg example, the conservation law can be written as follows:

$$\frac{1}{2}mv_i^2 + mgh_i = \frac{1}{2}mv_f^2 + mgh_f$$

If other forces (except friction) are present, simply add the appropriate potential energy terms associated with each force. For instance, if the egg happened to compress or stretch a spring as it fell, the conservation law would also include an elastic potential energy term on each side of the equation.

In situations in which frictional forces are present, the principle of mechanical energy conservation no longer holds, because kinetic energy is not simply converted to a form of potential energy. This special situation will be discussed more thoroughly later in this section.

GO ONLINE

Interactive Demo
HMHScience.com

Conservation of Mechanical Energy

Sample Problem E **Starting from rest, a child zooms down a frictionless slide from an initial height of 3.00 m. What is her speed at the bottom of the slide? Assume she has a mass of 25.0 kg.**

1 ANALYZE

Given: $h = h_i = 3.00 \text{ m} \quad m = 25.0 \text{ kg}$
$v_i = 0.0 \text{ m/s} \quad h_f = 0 \text{ m}$

Unknown: $v_f = ?$

2 PLAN

Choose an equation or situation:
The slide is frictionless, so mechanical energy is conserved. Kinetic energy and gravitational potential energy are the only forms of energy present.

$$KE = \frac{1}{2}mv^2 \qquad PE = mgh$$

The zero level chosen for gravitational potential energy is the bottom of the slide. Because the child ends at the zero level, the final gravitational potential energy is zero.

$$PE_{g,f} = 0$$

The initial gravitational potential energy at the top of the slide is

$$PE_{g,i} = mgh_i = mgh$$

Because the child starts at rest, the initial kinetic energy at the top is zero.

$$KE_i = 0$$

Therefore, the final kinetic energy is as follows:

$$KE_f = \frac{1}{2}mv_f^2$$

Continued

©Tony Freeman/PhotoEdit

Conservation of Mechanical Energy (continued)

③ SOLVE

Substitute the values into the equation:

$$PE_{g,i} = (25.0 \text{ kg})(9.81 \text{ m/s}^2)(3.00 \text{ m}) = 736 \text{ J}$$

$$KE_f = \left(\frac{1}{2}\right)(25.0 \text{ kg})v_f^2$$

Now use the calculated quantities to evaluate the final velocity.

$$ME_i = ME_f$$

$$PE_i + KE_i = PE_f + KE_f$$

$$736 \text{ J} + 0 \text{ J} = 0 \text{ J} + (0.500)(25.0 \text{ kg})v_f^2$$

$$\boxed{v_f = 7.67 \text{ m/s}}$$

Calculator Solution

Your calculator should give an answer similar to 7.67333, but because the answer is limited to three significant figures, it should be rounded to 7.67.

④ CHECK YOUR WORK

The expression for the square of the final speed can be written as follows:

$$v_f^2 = \frac{2mgh}{m} = 2gh$$

Notice that the masses cancel, so the final speed does not depend on the mass of the child. This result makes sense because the acceleration of an object due to gravity does not depend on the mass of the object.

Practice

1. A bird is flying with a speed of 18.0 m/s over water when it accidentally drops a 2.00 kg fish. If the altitude of the bird is 5.40 m and friction is disregarded, what is the mechanical energy of the system, and what is the speed of the fish when it hits the water?

2. A 755 N diver drops from a board 10.0 m above the water's surface. Find the mechanical energy of the system, and find the diver's speed 5.00 m above the water's surface. Then find the diver's speed just before striking the water.

3. If the diver in item 2 leaves the board with an initial upward speed of 2.00 m/s, find the diver's speed when striking the water.

4. An Olympic runner leaps over a hurdle. If the runner's initial vertical speed is 2.2 m/s, how much will the runner's center of mass be raised during the jump?

5. A pendulum bob is released from some initial height such that the speed of the bob at the bottom of the swing is 1.9 m/s. What is the initial height of the bob?

Energy conservation occurs even when acceleration varies.

If the slope of the slide in Sample Problem E were constant, the acceleration along the slide would also be constant, and the one-dimensional kinematic formulas could have been used to solve the problem. However, you do not know the shape of the slide. Thus, the acceleration may not be constant, and the kinematic formulas could not be used.

FIGURE 3.5

Friction and the Non-Conservation of Mechanical Energy

(a) As the block slides, its kinetic energy tends to decrease because of friction. The force from the hand keeps it moving. **(b)** Kinetic energy is dissipated into the block and surface.

(a)

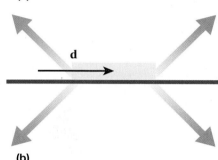

(b)

But now we can apply a new method to solve such a problem. Because the slide is frictionless, mechanical energy is conserved. We simply equate the initial mechanical energy to the final mechanical energy and ignore all the details in the middle. The shape of the slide is not a contributing factor to the system's mechanical energy as long as friction can be ignored.

Mechanical energy is not conserved in the presence of friction.

If you have ever used a sanding block to sand a rough surface, such as in **Figure 3.5**, you may have noticed that you had to keep applying a force to keep the block moving. The reason is that kinetic friction between the moving block and the surface causes the kinetic energy of the block to be converted into a nonmechanical form of energy. As you continue to exert a force on the block, you are replacing the kinetic energy that is lost because of kinetic friction. The observable result of this energy dissipation is that the sanding block and the tabletop become warmer.

In the presence of kinetic friction, nonmechanical energy is no longer negligible, and mechanical energy is no longer conserved. This does not mean that energy in general is not conserved—total energy is *always* conserved. However, the mechanical energy is converted into forms of energy that are much more difficult to account for, and the mechanical energy is therefore considered to be "lost."

✔ SECTION 3 FORMATIVE ASSESSMENT

▶ Reviewing Main Ideas

1. If the spring of a jack-in-the-box is compressed a distance of 8.00 cm from its relaxed length and then released, what is the mechanical energy of the system, and what is the speed of the toy head when the spring returns to its natural length? Assume the mass of the toy head is 50.0 g, the spring constant is 80.0 N/m, and the toy head moves only in the vertical direction. Also disregard the mass of the spring. (Hint: Remember that there are two forms of potential energy in the problem.)

2. You are designing a roller coaster in which a car will be pulled to the top of a hill of height h and then, starting from a momentary rest, will be released to roll freely down the hill and toward the peak of the next hill, which is 1.1 times as high. Will your design be successful? Explain your answer.

3. Is conservation of mechanical energy likely to hold in these situations?
   a. a hockey puck sliding on a frictionless surface of ice
   b. a toy car rolling on a carpeted floor
   c. a baseball being thrown into the air

✔ Critical Thinking

4. What parts of the kinetic sculpture on the opening pages of this chapter involve the conversion of one form of energy to another? Is mechanical energy conserved in these processes?

Power

Key Term
power

Rate of Energy Transfer

The rate at which work is done is called **power.** More generally, power is the rate of energy transfer by any method. Like the concepts of energy and work, *power* has a specific meaning in science that differs from its everyday meaning.

Imagine you are producing a play and you need to raise and lower the curtain between scenes in a specific amount of time. You decide to use a motor that will pull on a rope connected to the top of the curtain rod. Your assistant finds three motors but doesn't know which one to use. One way to decide is to consider the power output of each motor.

If the work done on an object is W in a time interval Δt, then the average power delivered to the object over this time interval is written as follows:

> **Power**
>
> $$P = \frac{W}{\Delta t}$$
>
> **power = work ÷ time interval**

It is sometimes useful to rewrite this equation in an alternative form by substituting the definition of work into the definition of power.

$$W = Fd$$

$$P = \frac{W}{\Delta t} = F\frac{d}{\Delta t}$$

The distance moved per unit time is just the speed of the object.

Objectives

▶ Relate the concepts of energy, time, and power.

▶ Calculate power in two different ways.

▶ Explain the effect of machines on work and power.

SC.912.P.10.1 Differentiate among the various forms of energy and recognize that they can be transformed from one form to others.
SC.912.P.10.3 Compare and contrast work and power qualitatively and quantitatively.

power a quantity that measures the rate at which work is done or the rate of energy transfer by any method

Conceptual Challenge

Mountain Roads Many mountain roads are built so that they zigzag up the mountain rather than go straight up toward the peak. Discuss the advantages of such a design from the viewpoint of energy conservation and power.

Light Bulbs A light bulb is described as *having* 60 watts. What's wrong with this statement?

©Werner H. Muller/Peter Arnold, Inc.

FIGURE 4.1

Light Bulbs of Varying Power Levels The power of each of these bulbs tells you the rate at which energy is converted by the bulb. The bulbs in this photo have power ratings that range from 0.7 W to 200 W.

Power (Alternative Form)

$$P = Fv$$

power = force × speed

The SI unit of power is the *watt*, W, which is defined to be one joule per second. The *horsepower*, hp, is another unit of power that is sometimes used. One horsepower is equal to 746 watts.

The watt is perhaps most familiar to you from your everyday experience with light bulbs (see **Figure 4.1**). A dim light bulb uses about 40 W of power, while a bright bulb can use up to 500 W. Decorative lights use about 0.7 W each for indoor lights and 7.0 W each for outdoor lights.

In Sample Problem F, the three motors would lift the curtain at different rates because the power output for each motor is different. So each motor would do work on the curtain at different rates and would thus transfer energy to the curtain at different rates.

GO ONLINE

Interactive Demo
HMHScience.com

Power

Sample Problem F A 193 kg curtain needs to be raised 7.5 m, at constant speed, in as close to 5.0 s as possible. The power ratings for three motors are listed as 1.0 kW, 3.5 kW, and 5.5 kW. Which motor is best for the job?

① ANALYZE

Given: $m = 193 \text{ kg}$ $\Delta t = 5.0 \text{ s}$ $d = 7.5 \text{ m}$

Unknown: $P = ?$

② SOLVE

Use the definition of power. Substitute the equation for work.

$$P = \frac{W}{\Delta t} = \frac{Fd}{\Delta t} = \frac{mgd}{\Delta t}$$

$$= \frac{(193 \text{ kg})(9.81 \text{ m/s}^2)(7.5 \text{ m})}{5.0 \text{ s}}$$

$$\boxed{P = 2.8 \times 10^3 \text{ W} = 2.8 \text{ kW}}$$

The best motor to use is the 3.5 kW motor. The 1.0 kW motor will not lift the curtain fast enough, and the 5.5 kW motor will lift the curtain too fast.

Continued

Power (continued)

1. A 1.0×10^3 kg elevator carries a maximum load of 800.0 kg. A constant frictional force of 4.0×10^3 N retards the elevator's motion upward. What minimum power, in kilowatts, must the motor deliver to lift the fully loaded elevator at a constant speed of 3.00 m/s?

2. A car with a mass of 1.50×10^3 kg starts from rest and accelerates to a speed of 18.0 m/s in 12.0 s. Assume that the force of resistance remains constant at 400.0 N during this time. What is the average power developed by the car's engine?

3. A rain cloud contains 2.66×10^7 kg of water vapor. How long would it take for a 2.00 kW pump to raise the same amount of water to the cloud's altitude, 2.00 km?

4. How long does it take a 19 kW steam engine to do 6.8×10^7 J of work?

5. A 1.50×10^3 kg car accelerates uniformly from rest to 10.0 m/s in 3.00 s.

   a. What is the work done on the car in this time interval?

   b. What is the power delivered by the engine in this time interval?

 SECTION 4 **FORMATIVE ASSESSMENT**

▶ **Reviewing Main Ideas**

1. A 50.0 kg student climbs up a 5.00 m rope at a constant speed. The student has a power output of 200.0 W. How long does it take the student to climb the rope? How much work does the student do?

2. A motor-driven winch pulls the 50.0 kg student from the previous problem up the 5.00 m rope at a constant speed of 1.25 m/s. How much power does the motor use in raising the student? How much work does the motor do on the student?

✔ **Critical Thinking**

3. How are energy, time, and power related?

4. People often use the word *powerful* to describe the engines in some automobiles. In this context, how does the word relate to the definition of *power*? How does this word relate to the alternative definition of *power*?

The Equivalence of Mass and Energy

Einstein's $E_R = mc^2$ is one of the most famous equations of the twentieth century. Einstein discovered this equation through his work with relative velocity and kinetic energy.

Relativistic Kinetic Energy

In the feature "Special Relativity and Velocities," you learned how Einstein's special theory of relativity modifies the classical addition of velocities. The classical equation for kinetic energy $\left(KE = \frac{1}{2}mv^2\right)$ must also be modified for relativity. In 1905, Einstein derived a new equation for kinetic energy based on the principles of special relativity:

$$KE = \frac{mc^2}{\sqrt{1 - \left(\dfrac{v^2}{c^2}\right)}} - mc^2$$

In this equation, m is the mass of the object, v is the velocity of the object, and c is the speed of light. Although it isn't immediately obvious, this equation reduces to the classical equation $KE = \frac{1}{2}mv^2$ for speeds that are small relative to the speed of light, as shown in **Figure 1**. The graph also illustrates that velocity can never be greater than $1.0c$ in the theory of special relativity.

Einstein's relativistic expression for kinetic energy has been confirmed by experiments in which electrons are accelerated to extremely high speeds in particle accelerators. In all cases, the experimental data correspond to Einstein's equation rather than to the classical equation. Nonetheless, the difference between the two theories at low speeds (relative to c) is so minimal that the classical equation can be used in all such cases when the speed is much less than c.

Rest Energy

The second term of Einstein's equation for kinetic energy, $-mc^2$, is required so that $KE = 0$ when $v = 0$. Note that this term is independent of velocity. This suggests that the *total* energy of an object equals its kinetic energy plus some additional form of energy equal to mc^2. The mathematical expression of this additional energy is the familiar Einstein equation:

$$E_R = mc^2$$

FIGURE 1

Graph of Velocity versus Kinetic Energy

This graph of velocity versus kinetic energy for both the classical and relativistic equations shows that the two theories are in agreement when v is much less than c. Note that v is always less than c in the relativistic case.

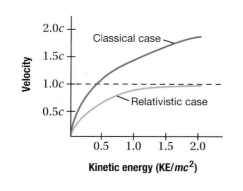

This equation shows that an object has a certain amount of energy (E_R), known as *rest energy*, simply by virtue of its mass. The rest energy of a body is equal to its mass, m, multiplied by the speed of light squared, c^2. Thus, the mass of a body is a measure of its rest energy. This equation is significant because rest energy is an aspect of special relativity that was not predicted by classical physics.

Experimental Verification

The magnitude of the conversion factor between mass and rest energy ($c^2 = 9 \times 10^{16} \, \text{m}^2/\text{s}^2$) is so great that even a very small mass has a huge amount of rest energy. Nuclear reactions utilize this relationship by converting mass (rest energy) into other forms of energy. In nuclear fission, which is the energy source of nuclear power plants, the nucleus of an atom is split into two or more nuclei. Taken together, the mass of these nuclei is slightly less than the mass of the original nucleus, and a very large amount of energy is released. In typical nuclear reactions, about one-thousandth of the initial mass is converted from rest energy into other forms of energy. This change in mass, although very small, can be detected experimentally.

Another type of nuclear reaction that converts mass into energy is fusion, which is the source of energy for our sun and other stars. About 4.5 million tons of the sun's mass is converted into other forms of energy every second, by fusing hydrogen into helium. Fortunately, the sun has enough mass to continue to fuse hydrogen into helium for approximately 5 billion more years.

Most of the energy changes encountered in your typical experiences are much smaller than the energy changes that occur in nuclear reactions and are far too small to be detected experimentally. Thus, for typical cases, the classical equation still holds, and mass and energy can be thought of as separate.

Before Einstein's theory of relativity, conservation of energy and conservation of mass were regarded as two separate laws. The equivalence between mass and energy reveals that in fact these two laws are one. In the words of Einstein, "Prerelativity physics contains two conservation laws of fundamental importance. . . . Through relativity theory, they melt together into *one* principle."

FIGURE 2

Stanford Linear Accelerator Electrons in the Stanford Linear Accelerator in California (SLAC) reach 99.999999967 percent of the speed of light. At such great speeds, the difference between classical and relativistic theories becomes significant.

FIGURE 3

Nuclear Fusion in the Sun Our sun uses a nuclear reaction called *fusion* to convert mass to energy. About 90 percent of the stars, including our sun, fuse hydrogen, and some older stars fuse helium.

Roller-Coaster Designer

A s the name states, the cars of a roller coaster really do coast along the tracks. A motor pulls the cars up a high hill at the beginning of the ride. After the hill, however, the motion of the car is a result of gravity and inertia. As the cars roll down the hill, they must pick up the speed that they need to whiz through the rest of the curves, loops, twists, and bumps in the track. To learn more about designing roller coasters, read the interview with Steve Okamoto.

The roller coaster pictured here is named Wild Thing and is located in Minnesota. The highest point on the track is 63 m off the ground, and the cars' maximum speed is 118 km/h.

How did you become a roller coaster designer?

I have been fascinated with roller coasters ever since my first ride on one. I remember going to Disneyland as a kid. My mother was always upset with me because I kept looking over the sides of the rides, trying to figure out how they worked. My interest in finding out how things worked led me to study mechanical engineering.

What sort of training do you have?

I earned a degree in product design. For this degree, I studied mechanical engineering and studio art. Product designers consider an object's form as well as its function. They also take into account the interests and abilities of the product's consumer. Most rides and parks have some kind of theme, so I must consider marketing goals and concerns in my designs.

What is the nature of your work?

To design a roller coaster, I study site maps of the location. Then, I go to the amusement park to look at the actual site. Because most rides I design are for older parks (few parks are built from scratch), fitting a coaster around, above, and in between existing rides and buildings is one of my biggest challenges. I also have to design how the parts of the ride will work together. The towers and structures that support the ride have to be strong enough to hold up a track and speeding cars that are full of people. The cars themselves need special wheels to keep them locked onto the track and

seat belts or bars to keep the passengers safely inside. It's like putting together a puzzle, except the pieces haven't been cut out yet.

What advice do you have for a student who is interested in designing roller coasters?

Studying math and science is very important. To design a successful coaster, I have to understand how energy is converted from one form to another as the cars move along the track. I have to calculate speeds and accelerations of the cars on each part of the track. They have to go fast enough to make it up the next hill! I rely on my knowledge of geometry and physics to create the roller coaster's curves, loops, and dips.

Steve Okamoto

Product Labels

Manufacturers use labels on their products to provide information about their products. Some of the information is just for the purpose of advertising, but often, regulations require that warnings or specific information about ingredients be provided. As citizens and consumers, it is important to look beyond catchy slogans and bold manufacturer claims to carefully examine the product and make good decisions.

Comparing Food Labels

Food labels provide a consistent set of information for consumers. Beyond a basic ingredient list, specific quantities of key components, such as fat, cholesterol, sodium, carbohydrates, and protein, are provided. With this information, you can make inferences about how a food item fits into your diet, or whether you have a nutrition-related reason to prefer one brand over another.

This chart provides a hypothetical sample of nutrition information from the labels of two different granola/cereal bars. Use the information to address the question that follows.

NUTRITION FACTS		
Component	Bar 1	Bar 2
Total Fat (g)	3	6
Dietary Fiber (g)	3	3
Sugar (g)	12	12
Protein (g)	2	4

- Imagine that you are looking for a hearty granola/cereal bar for a quick breakfast each morning. In the store, you see the two options detailed above. Assuming the bars are the same size and cost, based on the information provided, which bar seems more likely to satisfy your hunger throughout the morning?

Conceptual Challenge

The ability to make assumptions and generate rough estimates is a valuable skill to scientists. Quick estimates allow scientists to narrow the range of possibilities and focus on the most reasonable hypotheses.

Calorie Consumption How many calories do the students in your school consume, total, over an entire school year?

You can begin addressing the scenario by asking questions such as the following:

- How many students are in your class?
- How many classes are there in your school?
- How many days long is the school year?
- How many calories, on average, does each student consume per day?

Summary

SECTION 1 Work

KEY TERM

- Work is done on an object only when a net force acts on the object to displace it in the direction of a component of the net force.
- The amount of work done on an object by a force is equal to the component of the force along the direction of motion times the distance the object moves.

work

SECTION 2 Energy

KEY TERMS

- Objects in motion have kinetic energy because of their mass and speed.
- The net work done on or by an object is equal to the change in the kinetic energy of the object.
- Potential energy is energy associated with an object's position. Two forms of potential energy discussed in this chapter are gravitational potential energy and elastic potential energy.

kinetic energy
work–kinetic energy theorem
potential energy
gravitational potential energy
elastic potential energy
spring constant

SECTION 3 Conservation of Energy

KEY TERM

- Energy can change form but can never be created or destroyed.
- Mechanical energy is the sum of the kinetic energy and total potential energy associated with a system.
- In the absence of friction, mechanical energy is conserved, so the amount of mechanical energy remains constant.

mechanical energy

SECTION 4 Power

KEY TERM

- Power is the rate at which work is done or the rate of energy transfer.
- Machines with different power ratings do the same amount of work in different time intervals.

power

VARIABLE SYMBOLS			
Quantities		**Units**	**Conversions**
W	work	J joule	$= \text{N} \bullet \text{m}$
KE	kinetic energy	J joule	$= \text{kg} \bullet \text{m}^2/\text{s}^2$
PE_g	gravitational potential energy	J joule	
$PE_{elastic}$	elastic potential energy	J joule	
P	power	W watt	$= \text{J/s}$

Problem Solving

See **Appendix D: Equations** for a summary of the equations introduced in this chapter. If you need more problem-solving practice, see **Appendix I: Additional Problems.**

Work

▶ REVIEWING MAIN IDEAS

1. Can the speed of an object change if the net work done on it is zero?

2. Discuss whether any work is being done by each of the following agents and, if so, whether the work is positive or negative.
   a. a chicken scratching the ground
   b. a person reading a sign
   c. a crane lifting a bucket of concrete
   d. the force of gravity on the bucket in (c)

3. Furniture movers wish to load a truck using a ramp from the ground to the rear of the truck. One of the movers claims that less work would be required if the ramp's length were increased, reducing its angle with the horizontal. Is this claim valid? Explain.

CONCEPTUAL QUESTIONS

4. A pendulum swings back and forth, as shown at right. Does the tension force in the string do work on the pendulum bob? Does the force of gravity do work on the bob? Explain your answers.

5. The drivers of two identical cars heading toward each other apply the brakes at the same instant. The skid marks of one of the cars are twice as long as the skid marks of the other vehicle. Assuming that the brakes of both cars apply the same force, what conclusions can you draw about the motion of the cars?

6. When a punter kicks a football, is he doing work on the ball while his toe is in contact with it? Is he doing work on the ball after the ball loses contact with his toe? Are any forces doing work on the ball while the ball is in flight?

PRACTICE PROBLEMS

For problems 7–10, see Sample Problem A.

7. A person lifts a 4.5 kg cement block a vertical distance of 1.2 m and then carries the block horizontally a distance of 7.3 m. Determine the work done by the person and by the force of gravity in this process.

8. A plane designed for vertical takeoff has a mass of 8.0×10^3 kg. Find the net work done by all forces on the plane as it accelerates upward at 1.0 m/s^2 through a distance of 30.0 m after starting from rest.

9. When catching a baseball, a catcher's glove moves by 10 cm along the line of motion of the ball. If the baseball exerts a force of 475 N on the glove, how much work is done by the ball?

10. A flight attendant pulls her 70.0 N flight bag a distance of 253 m along a level airport floor at a constant velocity. The force she exerts is 40.0 N at an angle of 52.0° above the horizontal. Find the following:
    a. the work she does on the flight bag
    b. the work done by the force of friction on the flight bag
    c. the coefficient of kinetic friction between the flight bag and the floor

Energy

▶ REVIEWING MAIN IDEAS

11. A person drops a ball from the top of a building while another person on the ground observes the ball's motion. Each observer chooses his or her own location as the level for zero potential energy. Will they calculate the same values for:
    a. the potential energy associated with the ball?
    b. the change in potential energy associated with the ball?
    c. the ball's kinetic energy?

12. Can the kinetic energy of an object be negative? Explain your answer.

13. Can the gravitational potential energy associated with an object be negative? Explain your answer.

14. Two identical objects move with speeds of 5.0 m/s and 25.0 m/s. What is the ratio of their kinetic energies?

CONCEPTUAL QUESTIONS

15. A satellite is in a circular orbit above Earth's surface. Why is the work done on the satellite by the gravitational force zero? What does the work–kinetic energy theorem predict about the satellite's speed?

16. A car traveling at 50.0 km/h skids a distance of 35 m after its brakes lock. Predict how far it will skid if its brakes lock when its initial speed is 100.0 km/h. What happens to the car's kinetic energy as it comes to rest?

17. Explain why more energy is needed to walk up stairs than to walk horizontally at the same speed.

18. How can the work–kinetic energy theorem explain why the force of sliding friction reduces the kinetic energy of a particle?

PRACTICE PROBLEMS

For problems 19–20, see Sample Problem B.

19. What is the kinetic energy of an automobile with a mass of 1250 kg traveling at a speed of 11 m/s?

20. What speed would a fly with a mass of 0.55 g need in order to have the same kinetic energy as the automobile in item 19?

For problems 21–22, see Sample Problem C.

21. A 50.0 kg diver steps off a diving board and drops straight down into the water. The water provides an upward average net force of 1500 N. If the diver comes to rest 5.0 m below the water's surface, what is the total distance between the diving board and the diver's stopping point underwater?

22. In a circus performance, a monkey on a sled is given an initial speed of 4.0 m/s up a 25° incline. The combined mass of the monkey and the sled is 20.0 kg, and the coefficient of kinetic friction between the sled and the incline is 0.20. How far up the incline does the sled move?

For problems 23–25, see Sample Problem D.

23. A 55 kg skier is at the top of a slope, as shown in the illustration below. At the initial point **A**, the skier is 10.0 m vertically above the final point **B**.
- **a.** Set the zero level for gravitational potential energy at **B**, and find the gravitational potential energy associated with the skier at **A** and at **B**. Then find the difference in potential energy between these two points.
- **b.** Repeat this problem with the zero level at point **A**.
- **c.** Repeat this problem with the zero level midway down the slope, at a height of 5.0 m.

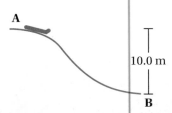

24. A 2.00 kg ball is attached to a ceiling by a string. The distance from the ceiling to the center of the ball is 1.00 m, and the height of the room is 3.00 m. What is the gravitational potential energy associated with the ball relative to each of the following?
- **a.** the ceiling
- **b.** the floor
- **c.** a point at the same elevation as the ball

25. A spring has a force constant of 500.0 N/m. Show that the potential energy stored in the spring is as follows:
- **a.** 0.400 J when the spring is stretched 4.00 cm from equilibrium
- **b.** 0.225 J when the spring is compressed 3.00 cm from equilibrium
- **c.** zero when the spring is unstretched

Conservation of Mechanical Energy

▶ REVIEWING MAIN IDEAS

26. Each of the following objects possesses energy. Which forms of energy are mechanical, which are nonmechanical, and which are a combination?
    a. glowing embers in a campfire
    b. a strong wind
    c. a swinging pendulum
    d. a person sitting on a mattress
    e. a rocket being launched into space

27. Discuss the energy transformations that occur during the pole-vault event shown in the photograph below. Disregard rotational motion and air resistance.

28. A strong cord suspends a bowling ball from the center of a lecture hall's ceiling, forming a pendulum. The ball is pulled to the tip of a lecturer's nose at the front of the room and is then released. If the lecturer remains stationary, explain why the lecturer is not struck by the ball on its return swing. Would this person be safe if the ball were given a slight push from its starting position at the person's nose?

CONCEPTUAL QUESTIONS

29. Discuss the work done and change in mechanical energy as an athlete does the following:
    a. lifts a weight
    b. holds the weight up in a fixed position
    c. lowers the weight slowly

30. A ball is thrown straight up. At what position is its kinetic energy at its maximum? At what position is gravitational potential energy at its maximum?

31. Advertisements for a toy ball once stated that it would rebound to a height greater than the height from which it was dropped. Is this possible?

32. A weight is connected to a spring that is suspended vertically from the ceiling. If the weight is displaced downward from its equilibrium position and released, it will oscillate up and down. How many forms of potential energy are involved? If air resistance and friction are disregarded, will the total mechanical energy be conserved? Explain.

PRACTICE PROBLEMS

For problems 33–34, see Sample Problem E.

33. A child and sled with a combined mass of 50.0 kg slide down a frictionless hill that is 7.34 m high. If the sled starts from rest, what is the mechanical energy of the system, and what is the sled's speed at the bottom of the hill?

34. Tarzan swings on a 30.0 m long vine initially inclined at an angle of 37.0° with the vertical. What is his speed at the bottom of the swing if he does the following?
    a. starts from rest
    b. starts with an initial speed of 4.00 m/s

Power

▶ REVIEWING MAIN IDEAS

PRACTICE PROBLEMS

For problems 35–36, see Sample Problem F.

35. If an automobile engine delivers 50.0 hp of power, how much time will it take for the engine to do 6.40×10^5 J of work? (Hint: Note that one horsepower, 1 hp, is equal to 746 watts.)

36. Water flows over a section of Niagara Falls at the rate of 1.2×10^6 kg/s and falls 50.0 m. How much power is generated by the falling water?

Mixed Review

REVIEWING MAIN IDEAS

37. A 215 g particle is released from rest at point **A** inside a smooth hemispherical bowl of radius 30.0 cm, as shown at right. Calculate the following:

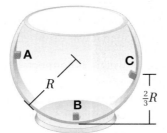

    a. the gravitational potential energy at **A** relative to **B**
    b. the particle's kinetic energy at **B**
    c. the particle's speed at **B**
    d. the potential energy and kinetic energy at **C**

38. A person doing a chin-up weighs 700.0 N, disregarding the weight of the arms. During the first 25.0 cm of the lift, each arm exerts an upward force of 355 N on the torso. If the upward movement starts from rest, what is the person's speed at this point?

39. A 50.0 kg pole vaulter running at 10.0 m/s vaults over the bar. If the vaulter's horizontal component of velocity over the bar is 1.0 m/s and air resistance is disregarded, how high was the jump?

40. An 80.0 N box of clothes is pulled 20.0 m up a 30.0° ramp by a force of 115 N that points along the ramp. If the coefficient of kinetic friction between the box and ramp is 0.22, calculate the change in the box's kinetic energy.

41. Tarzan and Jane, whose total mass is 130.0 kg, start their swing on a 5.0 m long vine when the vine is at an angle of 30.0° with the horizontal. At the bottom of the arc, Jane, whose mass is 50.0 kg, releases the vine. What is the maximum height at which Tarzan can land on a branch after his swing continues? (Hint: Treat Tarzan's and Jane's energies as separate quantities.)

42. A 0.250 kg block on a vertical spring with a spring constant of 5.00×10^3 N/m is pushed downward, compressing the spring 0.100 m. When released, the block leaves the spring and travels upward vertically. How high does it rise above the point of release?

43. Three identical balls, all with the same initial speed, are thrown by a juggling clown on a tightrope. The first ball is thrown horizontally, the second is thrown at some angle above the horizontal, and the third is thrown at some angle below the horizontal. Disregarding air resistance, describe the motions of the three balls and compare the speeds of the balls as they reach the ground.

44. A 0.60 kg rubber ball has a speed of 2.0 m/s at point A and kinetic energy of 7.5 J at point B. Determine the following:

    a. the ball's kinetic energy at A
    b. the ball's speed at B
    c. the total work done on the ball from A to B

45. Starting from rest, a 5.0 kg block slides 2.5 m down a rough 30.0° incline in 2.0 s. Determine the following:

    a. the work done by the force of gravity
    b. the mechanical energy lost due to friction
    c. the work done by the normal force between the block and the incline

46. A skier of mass 70.0 kg is pulled up a slope by a motor-driven cable. How much work is required to pull the skier 60.0 m up a 35° slope (assumed to be frictionless) at a constant speed of 2.0 m/s?

47. An acrobat on skis starts from rest 50.0 m above the ground on a frictionless track and flies off the track at a 45.0° angle above the horizontal and at a height of 10.0 m. Disregard air resistance.

    a. What is the skier's speed when leaving the track?
    b. What is the maximum height attained?

48. Starting from rest, a 10.0 kg suitcase slides 3.00 m down a frictionless ramp inclined at 30.0° from the floor. The suitcase then slides an additional 5.00 m along the floor before coming to a stop. Determine the following:

    a. the suitcase's speed at the bottom of the ramp
    b. the coefficient of kinetic friction between the suitcase and the floor
    c. the change in mechanical energy due to friction

49. A light horizontal spring has a spring constant of 105 N/m. A 2.00 kg block is pressed against one end of the spring, compressing the spring 0.100 m. After the block is released, the block moves 0.250 m to the right before coming to rest. What is the coefficient of kinetic friction between the horizontal surface and the block?

50. A 5.0 kg block is pushed 3.0 m at a constant velocity up a vertical wall by a constant force applied at an angle of 30.0° with the horizontal, as shown at right. If the coefficient of kinetic friction between the block and the wall is 0.30, determine the following:

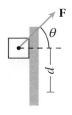

   a. the work done by the force on the block
   b. the work done by gravity on the block
   c. the magnitude of the normal force between the block and the wall

51. A 25 kg child on a 2.0 m long swing is released from rest when the swing supports make an angle of 30.0° with the vertical.
   a. What is the maximum potential energy associated with the child?
   b. Disregarding friction, find the child's speed at the lowest position.
   c. What is the child's total mechanical energy?
   d. If the speed of the child at the lowest position is 2.00 m/s, what is the change in mechanical energy due to friction?

52. A ball of mass 522 g starts at rest and slides down a frictionless track, as shown in the diagram. It leaves the track horizontally, striking the ground.
   a. At what height above the ground does the ball start to move?
   b. What is the speed of the ball when it leaves the track?
   c. What is the speed of the ball when it hits the ground?

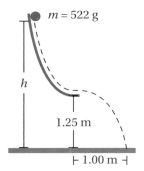

GRAPHING CALCULATOR PRACTICE

Work of Displacement

Work done, as you learned earlier in this chapter, is a result of the net applied force, the distance of the displacement, and the angle of the applied force relative to the direction of displacement. Work done is described by the following equation:

$$W_{net} = F_{net}\, d \cos \theta$$

The equation for work done can be represented on a graphing calculator as follows:

$$Y_1 = FXCOS(\theta)$$

In this activity, you will use this equation and your graphing calculator to produce a table of results for various values of θ. Column one of the table will be the displacement (X) in meters, and column two will be the work done (Y_1) in joules.

Go online to HMHScience.com to find the skillsheet and program for this graphing calculator activity.

ALTERNATIVE ASSESSMENT

1. Design experiments for measuring your power output when doing pushups, running up a flight of stairs, pushing a car, loading boxes onto a truck, throwing a baseball, or performing other energy-transferring activities. What data do you need to measure or calculate? What equipment and/or technology is needed to make these measurements or calculations? Form groups to present and discuss your plans. If your teacher approves your plans, perform the experiments.

2. Investigate the amount of kinetic energy involved when your car's speed is 60 km/h, 50 km/h, 40 km/h, 30 km/h, 20 km/h, and 10 km/h. (Hint: Find your car's mass in the owner's manual.) How much work does the brake system have to do to stop the car at each speed?

   If the owner's manual includes a table of braking distances at different speeds, determine the force the braking system must exert. Organize your findings in charts and graphs to study the questions and to present your conclusions.

3. Investigate the energy transformations of your body as you swing on a swing set. Working with a partner, measure the height of the swing at the high and low points of your motion. What points involve a maximum gravitational potential energy? What points involve a maximum kinetic energy? For three other points in the path of the swing, calculate the gravitational potential energy, the kinetic energy, and the velocity. Organize your findings in bar graphs.

4. Design an experiment to test the conservation of mechanical energy for a toy car rolling down a ramp. Use a board propped up on a stack of books as the ramp. To find the final speed of the car, use the equation:
   final speed = 2(average speed) = 2(length/time)
   Before beginning the experiment, formulate hypotheses about what you expect. Will the kinetic energy at the bottom equal the potential energy at the top? If not, which might be greater? Test your predictions with various ramp heights, and write a report describing your experiment and your results.

5. In order to save fuel, an airline executive recommended the following changes in the airline's largest jet flights:
   a. restrict the weight of personal luggage
   b. remove pillows, blankets, and magazines from the cabin
   c. lower flight altitudes by 5 percent
   d. reduce flying speeds by 5 percent

   Research the information necessary to calculate the approximate kinetic and potential energy of a large passenger aircraft. Which of the measures described above would result in significant savings? What might be their other consequences? Summarize your conclusions in a presentation or report.

6. Make a chart of the kinetic energies your body can have. First, measure your mass. Then, measure your speed when walking, running, sprinting, riding a bicycle, and driving a car. Make a poster graphically comparing these findings.

7. You are trying to find a way to bring electricity to a remote village in order to run a water-purifying device. A donor is willing to provide battery chargers that connect to bicycles. Assuming the water-purification device requires 18.6 kW•h daily, how many bicycles would a village need if a person can average 100 W while riding a bicycle? Is this a useful way to help the village? Evaluate your findings for strengths and weaknesses. Summarize your comments and suggestions in a letter to the donor.

8. Many scientific units are named after famous scientists or inventors. The SI unit of power, the watt, was named for the Scottish scientist James Watt. The SI unit of energy, the joule, was named for the English scientist James Prescott Joule. Use the Internet or library resources to learn about the contributions of these two scientists. Write a report to explain the impact of their scientific contributions on society, and then present your report to the class.

Standards-Based Assessment

Record your answers on a separate piece of paper.

MULTIPLE CHOICE

1 In which of the following situations is work not being done?

A A chair is lifted vertically with respect to the floor.
B A bookcase is slid across carpeting.
C A table is dropped onto the ground.
D A stack of books is carried at waist level across a room.

Use the graph below to answer questions 2–4. The graph shows the energy of a 75 g yo-yo at different times as the yo-yo moves up and down on its string.

Energy of Yo-Yo versus Time

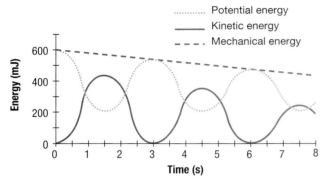

2 By what amount does the mechanical energy of the yo-yo change after 6.0 s?

A 500 mJ
B 0 mJ
C −100 mJ
D −600 mJ

3 What is the speed of the yo-yo after 4.5 s?

A 3.1 m/s
B 2.3 m/s
C 3.6 m/s
D 1.6 m/s

4 What is the maximum height of the yo-yo?

A 0.27 m
B 0.54 m
C 0.75 m
D 0.82 m

5 A car of mass m requires 5.0 kJ of work to move from rest to a final speed v. If the same amount of work is performed during the same amount of time on a car with a mass of $2m$, what is the final speed of the second car?

A $2v$ **C** $\dfrac{v}{2}$

B $\sqrt{2v}$ **D** $\dfrac{v}{\sqrt{2}}$

6 A 70.0 kg base runner moving at a speed of 4.0 m/s begins his slide into second base. The coefficient of friction between his clothes and Earth is 0.70. His slide lowers his speed to zero just as he reaches the base.

How much mechanical energy is lost because of friction acting on the runner?

A 1100 J
B 560 J
C 140 J
D 0 J

7 A spring scale has a spring with a force constant of 250 N/m and a weighing pan with a mass of 0.075 kg. During one weighing, the spring is stretched a distance of 12 cm from equilibrium. During a second weighing, the spring is stretched a distance of 18 cm.

How many times greater is the elastic potential energy of the stretched spring during the second weighing than during the first weighing?

A $\dfrac{9}{4}$ **C** $\dfrac{2}{3}$

B $\dfrac{3}{2}$ **D** $\dfrac{4}{9}$

GRIDDED RESPONSE

8 A student with a mass of 66.0 kg climbs a staircase in 44.0 s. If the distance between the base and the top if the staircase is 14.0 m, how much power, in watts, will the student deliver by climbing the stairs?

Why It Matters

Collisions in which there are transfers of momentum occur frequently in life. Examples in sports include the motion of balls against rackets in tennis and the motion of players' bodies against each other in football.

Soccer players must consider a lot of information about the ball and their own bodies in order to play effectively. Momentum is conserved in collisions, such as when a player kicks a ball. This figure shows momentum vectors for the foot and the ball.

CHAPTER 6

Momentum and Collisions

BIG IDEA

Momentum is proportional to the mass and velocity of an object. In a closed system, momentum is conserved.

ONLINE Physics
HMHScience.com

ONLINE LABS
- Conservation of Momentum
- Collisions
- Impulse and Momentum

GO ONLINE
Animated Physics
HMHScience.com

Conservation of Momentum

(br) ©Photodisc/Getty Images

191

▶ Compare the momentum of different moving objects.

▶ Compare the momentum of the same object moving with different velocities.

▶ Identify examples of change in the momentum of an object.

▶ Describe changes in momentum in terms of force and time.

Momentum and Impulse

Key Terms

momentum   impulse

Linear Momentum

When a soccer player heads a moving ball during a game, the ball's velocity changes rapidly. After the ball is struck, the ball's speed and the direction of the ball's motion change. The ball moves across the soccer field with a different speed than it had and in a different direction than it was traveling before the collision.

The quantities and kinematic equations describing one-dimensional motion predict the motion of the ball before and after the ball is struck. The concept of force and Newton's laws can be used to calculate how the motion of the ball changes when the ball is struck. In this chapter, we will examine how the force and the duration of the collision between the ball and the soccer player affect the motion of the ball.

Momentum is mass times velocity.

momentum a vector quantity defined as the product of the mass and velocity of an object

To address such issues, we need a new concept, **momentum.** *Momentum* is a word we use every day in a variety of situations. In physics, this word has a specific meaning. The linear momentum of an object of mass m moving with a velocity $\mathbf{v}$ is defined as the product of the mass and the velocity. Momentum is represented by the symbol $\mathbf{p}$.

Momentum

$$\mathbf{p} = m\mathbf{v}$$

momentum = mass × velocity

As its definition shows, momentum is a vector quantity, with its direction matching that of the velocity. Momentum has dimensions mass × length/time, and its SI units are kilogram-meters per second (kg•m/s).

If you think about some examples of the way the word *momentum* is used in everyday speech, you will see that the physics definition conveys a similar meaning. Imagine coasting down a hill of uniform slope on your bike without pedaling or using the brakes, as shown in **Figure 1.1**. Because of the force of gravity, you will accelerate; that is, your velocity will increase with time. This idea is often expressed by saying that you are "picking up speed" or "gathering momentum." The faster you move, the more momentum you have and the more difficult it is to come to a stop.

Did YOU Know?

Momentum is so fundamental in Newton's mechanics that Newton called it simply "quantity of motion." The symbol for momentum, **p**, comes from German mathematician Gottfried Leibniz. Leibniz used the term *progress* to mean "the quantity of motion with which a body proceeds in a certain direction."

Imagine rolling a bowling ball down one lane at a bowling alley and rolling a playground ball down another lane at the same speed. The more massive bowling ball exerts more force on the pins than the playground ball exerts on the pins because the bowling ball has more momentum than the playground ball. When we think of a massive object moving at a high velocity, we often say that the object has a large momentum. A less massive object with the same velocity has a smaller momentum.

On the other hand, a small object moving with a very high velocity may have a larger momentum than a more massive object that is moving slowly does. For example, small hailstones falling from very high clouds can have enough momentum to hurt you or cause serious damage to cars and buildings.

FIGURE 1.1

Momentum of a Bicycle A bicycle rolling downhill has momentum. An increase in either mass or speed will increase the momentum.

GO ONLINE

Interactive Demo
HMHScience.com

Momentum

Sample Problem A An ostrich with a mass of 146 kg is running with a momentum of 2480 kg•m/s to the right. What is the velocity of the ostrich?

❶ ANALYZE

Given: $m = 146$ kg

$\mathbf{p} = 2480$ kg•m/s to the right

Unknown: $v = ?$

❷ SOLVE

Use the equation for momentum to solve for v.

$$\mathbf{p} = mv$$
$$v = \frac{\mathbf{p}}{m}$$
$$v = \frac{2480 \text{ kg•m/s}}{146 \text{ kg}} = \boxed{17.0 \text{ m/s to the right}}$$

Practice

1. A deer with a mass of 146 kg is running head-on toward you with a speed of 17 m/s. You are going north. Find the momentum of the deer.

2. A 21 kg child on a 5.9 kg bike is riding with a velocity of 4.5 m/s to the northwest.

   a. What is the total momentum of the child and the bike together?

   b. What is the momentum of the child?

   c. What is the momentum of the bike?

3. If a blue whale has a mass of 1.46×10^5 kg and momentum of 9.73×10^5 kg•m/s to the south, what is its velocity?

FIGURE 1.2

Change in Momentum When the ball is moving very fast, the player must exert a large force over a short time to change the ball's momentum and quickly bring the ball to a stop.

impulse the product of the force and the time interval over which the force acts on an object

A change in momentum takes force and time.

Figure 1.2 shows a player stopping a moving soccer ball. In a given time interval, he must exert more force to stop a fast ball than to stop a ball that is moving more slowly. Now imagine a toy truck and a real dump truck rolling across a smooth surface with the same velocity. It would take much more force to stop the massive dump truck than to stop the toy truck in the same time interval. You have probably also noticed that a ball moving very fast stings your hands when you catch it, while a slow-moving ball causes no discomfort when you catch it. The fast ball stings because it exerts more force on your hand than the slow-moving ball does.

From examples like these, we see that a change in momentum is closely related to force. In fact, when Newton first expressed his second law mathematically, he wrote it not as $\mathbf{F} = m\mathbf{a}$, but in the following form.

$$\mathbf{F} = \frac{\Delta \mathbf{p}}{\Delta t}$$

$$\text{force} = \frac{\text{change in momentum}}{\text{time interval}}$$

We can rearrange this equation to find the change in momentum in terms of the net external force and the time interval required to make this change.

Impulse-Momentum Theorem

$$\mathbf{F}\Delta t = \Delta \mathbf{p} \quad \text{or} \quad \mathbf{F}\Delta t = \Delta \mathbf{p} = m\mathbf{v_f} - m\mathbf{v_i}$$

force × time interval = change in momentum

This equation states that a net external force, **F**, applied to an object for a certain time interval, Δt, will cause a change in the object's momentum equal to the product of the force and the time interval. In simple terms, a small force acting for a long time can produce the same change in momentum as a large force acting for a short time. In this book, all forces exerted on an object are assumed to be constant unless otherwise stated.

The expression $\mathbf{F}\Delta t = \Delta \mathbf{p}$ is called the impulse-momentum theorem. The term on the left side of the equation, $\mathbf{F}\Delta t$, is called the **impulse** of the force **F** for the time interval Δt.

The equation $\mathbf{F}\Delta t = \Delta \mathbf{p}$ explains why proper technique is important in so many sports, from karate and billiards to softball and croquet. For example, when a batter hits a ball, the ball will experience a greater change in momentum if the batter keeps the bat in contact with the ball for a longer time. Extending the time interval over which a constant force is applied allows a smaller force to cause a greater change in momentum than would result if the force were applied for a very short time. You may have noticed this fact when pushing a full shopping cart or moving furniture.

Force and Impulse

GO ONLINE

Interactive Demo
HMHScience.com

Sample Problem B A 1400 kg car moving westward with a velocity of 15 m/s collides with a utility pole and is brought to rest in 0.30 s. Find the force exerted on the car during the collision.

1 ANALYZE

Given: $m = 1400$ kg

$\mathbf{v_i} = 15$ m/s to the west, $v_i = -15$ m/s

$\Delta t = 0.30$ s

$\mathbf{v_f} = 0$ m/s

Unknown: $\mathbf{F} = ?$

Tips and Tricks

Create a simple convention for describing the direction of vectors. For example, always use a negative speed for objects moving west or south and a positive speed for objects moving east or north.

2 SOLVE

Use the impulse-momentum theorem.

$$\mathbf{F}\Delta t = \Delta \mathbf{p} = m\mathbf{v_f} - m\mathbf{v_i}$$

$$\mathbf{F} = \frac{m\mathbf{v_f} - m\mathbf{v_i}}{\Delta t}$$

$$\mathbf{F} = \frac{(1400 \text{ kg})(0 \text{ m/s}) - (1400 \text{ kg})(-15 \text{ m/s})}{0.30 \text{ s}} = \frac{21\,000 \text{ kg·m/s}}{0.30 \text{ s}}$$

$$\boxed{\mathbf{F} = 7.0 \times 10^4 \text{ N to the east}}$$

Practice

1. A 0.50 kg football is thrown with a velocity of 15 m/s to the right. A stationary receiver catches the ball and brings it to rest in 0.020 s. What is the force exerted on the ball by the receiver?

2. An 82 kg man drops from rest on a diving board 3.0 m above the surface of the water and comes to rest 0.55 s after reaching the water. What is the net force on the diver as he is brought to rest?

3. A 0.40 kg soccer ball approaches a player horizontally with a velocity of 18 m/s to the north. The player strikes the ball and causes it to move in the opposite direction with a velocity of 22 m/s. What impulse was delivered to the ball by the player?

4. A 0.50 kg object is at rest. A 3.00 N force to the right acts on the object during a time interval of 1.50 s.

   a. What is the velocity of the object at the end of this interval?

   b. At the end of this interval, a constant force of 4.00 N to the left is applied for 3.00 s. What is the velocity at the end of the 3.00 s?

FIGURE 1.3

Stopping Distances The loaded truck must undergo a greater change in momentum in order to stop than the truck without a load.

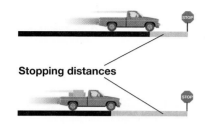

Stopping distances

Stopping times and distances depend on the impulse-momentum theorem.

Highway safety engineers use the impulse-momentum theorem to determine stopping distances and safe following distances for cars and trucks. For example, the truck hauling a load of bricks in **Figure 1.3** has twice the mass of the other truck, which has no load. Therefore, if both are traveling at 48 km/h, the loaded truck has twice as much momentum as the unloaded truck. If we assume that the brakes on each truck exert about the same force, we find that the stopping time is two times longer for the loaded truck than for the unloaded truck, and the stopping distance for the loaded truck is two times greater than the stopping distance for the truck without a load.

GO ONLINE

Interactive Demo
HMHScience.com

Stopping Distance

Sample Problem C A high-speed train with a total mass of 9.25×10^5 kg travels north at a speed of 220 km/h. Suppose it takes 16.0 s of constant acceleration for the train to come to rest at a station platform. Calculate the force acting on the train during this time. What is the train's stopping distance?

1 ANALYZE

Given:

$$m = 9.25 \times 10^5 \text{ kg}$$

$$\mathbf{v_i} = 220 \text{ km/h to the north}$$

$$\mathbf{v_f} = 0 \text{ km/h}$$

$$\Delta t = 16.0 \text{ s}$$

Unknown: $F = ?$ $\Delta x = ?$

2 SOLVE

Use the impulse-momentum theorem to solve for **F**. Use the kinematic equation for Δx in terms of initial velocity, final velocity, and time to solve for Δx.

$$\mathbf{F}\Delta t = \Delta\mathbf{p}$$

$$\mathbf{F} = \frac{\Delta\mathbf{p}}{\Delta t} = \frac{m\mathbf{v_f} - m\mathbf{v_i}}{\Delta t}$$

$$\mathbf{F} = \frac{(9.25 \times 10^5 \text{ kg})(0 \text{ km/h}) - (9.25 \times 10^5 \text{ kg})(220 \text{ km/h})(10^3 \text{ m/km})(1 \text{ h}/3600 \text{ s})}{16.0 \text{ s}}$$

$$\mathbf{F} = \frac{-(9.25 \times 10^5 \text{ kg})(220 \text{ km/h})(10^3 \text{ m/km})(1 \text{ h}/3600 \text{ s})}{16.0 \text{ s}}$$

$$\mathbf{F} = -3.5 \times 10^6 \text{ N} = \boxed{3.5 \times 10^6 \text{ N to the south}}$$

$$\Delta x = \tfrac{1}{2}(\mathbf{v_i} + \mathbf{v_f})\Delta t$$

$$\Delta x = \tfrac{1}{2}(220 \text{ km/h} + 0 \text{ km/h})(10^3 \text{ m/km})(1 \text{ h}/3600 \text{ s})(16.0 \text{ s})$$

$$\Delta x = \boxed{490 \text{ m to the north}}$$

Continued

Stopping Distance (continued)

Practice

1. How long will it take a 2.30×10^3 kg truck to go from 22.2 m/s to a complete stop if acted on by a force of -1.26×10^4 N? What would be its stopping distance?

2. A 2500 kg car is slowed down uniformly from an initial velocity of 20.0 m/s to the north by a 6250 N braking force acting opposite the car's motion. Use the impulse-momentum theorem to answer the following questions:
   a. What is the car's velocity after 2.50 s?
   b. How far does the car move during 2.50 s?
   c. How long does it take the car to come to a complete stop?

3. A 63 kg astronaut drifting 7.0 m/s to the right with respect to a spacecraft uses a jet pack to slow down. If it takes 14.0 s to come to a stop with respect to the spacecraft, what is the force exerted by the jet pack? How far does the astronaut travel before stopping?

Force is reduced when the time interval of an impact is increased.

The impulse-momentum theorem is used to design safety equipment that reduces the force exerted on the human body during collisions. Examples of this are the nets and giant air mattresses firefighters use to catch people who must jump out of tall burning buildings. The relationship is also used to design sports equipment and games.

Figure 1.4 shows an Inupiat family playing a traditional game. Common sense tells us that it is much better for the girl to fall onto the outstretched blanket than onto the hard ground. In both cases, however, the change in momentum of the falling girl is exactly the same. The difference is that the blanket "gives way" and extends the time of collision so that the change in the girl's momentum occurs over a longer time interval. A longer time interval requires a smaller force to achieve the same change in the girl's momentum. Therefore, the force exerted on the girl when she lands on the outstretched blanket is less than the force would be if she were to land on the ground.

FIGURE 1.4

Increasing the Time of Impact In this game, the girl is protected from injury because the blanket reduces the force of the collision by allowing it to take place over a longer time interval.

FIGURE 1.5

Impact Time Changes Force A large force exerted over a short time **(a)** causes the same change in the egg's momentum as a small force exerted over a longer time **(b)**.

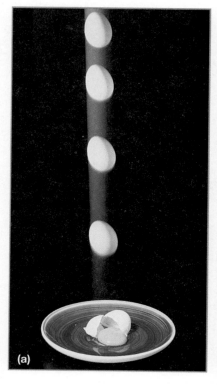

(a)

(b)

Consider a falling egg. When the egg hits a hard surface, like the plate in **Figure 1.5(a)**, the egg comes to rest in a very short time interval. The force the hard plate exerts on the egg due to the collision is large. When the egg hits a floor covered with a pillow, as in **Figure 1.5(b)**, the egg undergoes the same change in momentum but over a much longer time interval. In this case, the force required to accelerate the egg to rest is much smaller. By applying a small force to the egg over a longer time interval, the pillow causes the same change in the egg's momentum as the hard plate, which applies a large force over a short time interval. Because the force in the second situation is smaller, the egg can withstand it without breaking.

✓ SECTION 1 FORMATIVE ASSESSMENT

▶ Reviewing Main Ideas

1. The speed of a particle is doubled.
  a. By what factor is its momentum changed?
  b. What happens to its kinetic energy?

2. A pitcher claims he can throw a 0.145 kg baseball with as much momentum as a speeding bullet. Assume that a 3.00 g bullet moves at a speed of 1.50×10^3 m/s.
  a. What is the momentum of a bullet?
  b. What must the baseball's speed be if the pitcher's claim is valid?
  c. Which has greater kinetic energy, the ball or the bullet?

3. A 0.42 kg soccer ball is moving with a velocity of 12 m/s downfield. A player kicks the ball so that it has a final velocity of 18 m/s downfield.
  a. What impulse, or change in momentum, did the ball experience?
  b. Find the constant force exerted by the player's foot on the ball if the two are in contact for 0.020 s.

✓ Critical Thinking

4. When exerted on an object, does a large force always produce a larger change in the object's momentum than a smaller force does? Explain.

5. What is the relationship between impulse and momentum?

Conservation of Momentum

Momentum Conservation

So far in this chapter, we have considered the momentum of only one object at a time. Now we will consider the momentum of two or more objects interacting with each other. **Figure 2.1** shows a stationary billiard ball set into motion by a collision with a moving billiard ball. Assume that both balls are on a smooth table and that neither ball rotates before or after the collision. Before the collision, the momentum of ball B is equal to zero, because the ball is stationary. During the collision, ball B gains momentum, while ball A loses momentum. The momentum that ball A loses is exactly equal to the momentum that ball B gains.

Objectives

▶ Describe the interaction between two objects in terms of change in momentum of each.

▶ Compare the total momentum of two objects before and after they interact.

▶ Predict the final velocities of objects after collisions.

SC.912.P.12.5 Apply the law of conservation of linear momentum to interactions, such as collisions between objects.

FIGURE 2.1

Conservation of Momentum **(a)** Before the collision, the momentum of ball A is $p_{A,i}$ and of ball B is zero. **(b)** During the collision, ball A loses momentum, and ball B gains momentum. **(c)** After the collision, ball B has momentum $p_{B,f}$.

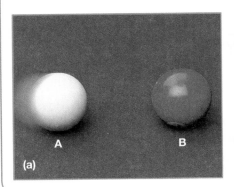
(a)

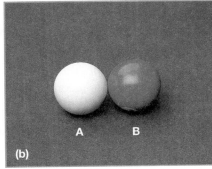
(b)

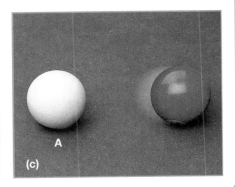
(c)

Figure 2.2 shows the velocity and momentum of each billiard ball both before and after the collision. The momentum of each ball changes due to the collision, but the *total* momentum of both the balls remains constant.

FIGURE 2.2

MOMENTUM IN A COLLISION					
Ball A			**Ball B**		
Mass	**Velocity**	**Momentum**	**Mass**	**Velocity**	**Momentum**
before collision	0.16 kg	4.50 m/s	0.72 kg•m/s	0.16 kg	0 m/s	0 kg•m/s
after collision	0.16 kg	0.11 m/s	0.018 kg•m/s	0.16 kg	4.39 m/s	0.70 kg•m/s

In other words, the momentum of ball A plus the momentum of ball B before the collision is equal to the momentum of ball A plus the momentum of ball B after the collision.

$$p_{A,i} + p_{B,i} = p_{A,f} + p_{B,f}$$

This relationship is true for all interactions between isolated objects and is known as the *law of conservation of momentum.*

Conservation of Momentum

$$m_1v_{1,i} + m_2v_{2,i} = m_1v_{1,f} + m_2v_{2,f}$$

total initial momentum = total final momentum

For an isolated system, the law of conservation of momentum can be stated as follows:

The total momentum of all objects interacting with one another remains constant regardless of the nature of the forces between the objects.

Momentum is conserved in collisions.

In the billiard-ball example, we found that the momentum of ball A does not remain constant and the momentum of ball B does not remain constant, but the total momentum of ball A and ball B does remain constant. In general, the total momentum remains constant for a system of objects that interact with one another. In this case, in which the table is assumed to be frictionless, the billiard balls are the only two objects interacting. If a third object exerted a force on either ball A or ball B during the collision, the total momentum of ball A, ball B, and the third object would remain constant.

In this book, most conservation-of-momentum problems deal with only two isolated objects. However, when you use conservation of momentum to solve a problem or investigate a situation, it is important to include all objects that are involved in the interaction. Frictional forces—such as the frictional force between the billiard balls and the table—will be disregarded in most conservation-of-momentum problems in this book.

Momentum is conserved for objects pushing away from each other.

Another example of conservation of momentum occurs when two or more interacting objects that initially have no momentum begin moving away from each other. Imagine that you initially stand at rest and then jump up, leaving the ground with a velocity **v**. Obviously, *your* momentum is not conserved; before the jump, it was zero, and it became *m***v** as you began to rise. However, the total momentum remains constant if you include Earth in your analysis. The total momentum for you and Earth remains constant.

NASA

If your momentum after you jump is 60 kg•m/s upward, then Earth must have a corresponding momentum of 60 kg•m/s downward, because total momentum is conserved. However, because Earth has an enormous mass (6×10^{24} kg), its change in momentum corresponds to a tiny velocity change (1×10^{-23} m/s).

Imagine two skaters pushing away from each other, as shown in **Figure 2.3**. The skaters are both initially at rest with a momentum of $\mathbf{p_{1,i}} = \mathbf{p_{2,i}} = 0$. When they push away from each other, they move in opposite directions with equal but opposite momentum so that the total final momentum is also zero ($\mathbf{p_{1,f}} + \mathbf{p_{2,f}} = 0$).

FIGURE 2.3

Momentum of Objects Pushing Away from Each Other (a) When the skaters stand facing each other, both skaters have zero momentum, so the total momentum of both skaters is zero. (b) When the skaters push away from each other, their momentum is equal but opposite, so the total momentum is still zero.

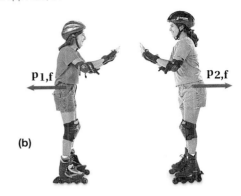

(a)

(b)

$p_{1,f}$

$p_{2,f}$

WHY IT MATTERS S.T.E.M.

Surviving a Collision

Pucks and carts collide in physics labs all the time with little damage. But when cars collide on a freeway, the resulting rapid change in speed can cause injury or death to the drivers and any passengers.

Many types of collisions are dangerous, but head-on collisions involve the greatest accelerations and thus the greatest forces. When two cars going 100 km/h (62 mi/h) collide head-on, each car dissipates the same amount of kinetic energy that it would dissipate if it hit the ground after being dropped from the roof of a 12-story building.

The key to many automobile-safety features is the concept of impulse. One way today's cars make use of the concept of impulse is by crumpling during impact. Pliable sheet metal and frame structures absorb energy until the force reaches the passenger compartment, which is built of rigid metal for protection. Because the crumpling slows the car gradually, it is an important factor in keeping the driver alive.

Even taking into account this built-in safety feature, the National Safety Council estimates that high-speed collisions involve accelerations of 20 times the free-fall acceleration. In other words, an 89 N (20 lb) infant could experience a force of 1780 N (400 lb) in a high-speed collision.

Seat belts are necessary to protect a body from forces of such large magnitudes. They stretch and extend the time it takes a passenger's body to stop, thereby reducing the force on the person. Air bags further extend the time over which the momentum of a passenger changes, decreasing the force even more. All new cars have air bags on both the driver and passenger sides. Many cars now have air bags in the door frames. Seat belts also prevent passengers from hitting the inside frame of the car. During a collision, a person not wearing a seat belt is likely to hit the windshield, the steering wheel, or the dashboard—often with traumatic results.

Sample Problem D A 76 kg boater, initially at rest in a stationary 45 kg boat, steps out of the boat and onto the dock. If the boater moves out of the boat with a velocity of 2.5 m/s to the right, what is the final velocity of the boat?

① ANALYZE

Given: $m_1 = 76$ kg $m_2 = 45$ kg

$\mathbf{v_{1,i}} = 0$ $\mathbf{v_{2,i}} = 0$

$\mathbf{v_{1,f}} = 2.5$ m/s to the right

Unknown: $\mathbf{v_{2,f}} = ?$

Diagram:

$m_1 = 76$ kg $\mathbf{v_{1,f}} = 2.5$ m/s

$m_2 = 45$ kg

② PLAN

Choose an equation or situation: Because the total momentum of an isolated system remains constant, the total initial momentum of the boater and the boat will be equal to the total final momentum of the boater and the boat.

$$m_1\mathbf{v_{1,i}} + m_2\mathbf{v_{2,i}} = m_1\mathbf{v_{1,f}} + m_2\mathbf{v_{2,f}}$$

Because the boater and the boat are initially at rest, the total initial momentum of the system is equal to zero. Therefore, the final momentum of the system must also be equal to zero.

$$m_1\mathbf{v_{1,f}} + m_2\mathbf{v_{2,f}} = 0$$

Rearrange the equation to solve for the final velocity of the boat.

$$m_2\mathbf{v_{2,f}} = -m_1\mathbf{v_{1,f}}$$

$$\mathbf{v_{2,f}} = -\frac{m_1}{m_2}\mathbf{v_{1,f}}$$

③ SOLVE

Substitute the values into the equations and solve:

$$\mathbf{v_{2,f}} = -\frac{76 \text{ kg}}{45 \text{ kg}}(2.5 \text{ m/s to the right})$$

$$\mathbf{v_{2,f}} = -4.2 \text{ m/s to the right}$$

The negative sign for $\mathbf{v_{2,f}}$ indicates that the boat is moving to the left, in the direction *opposite* the motion of the boater. Therefore,

$$\boxed{\mathbf{v_{2,f}} = 4.2 \text{ m/s to the left}}$$

④ CHECK YOUR WORK

It makes sense that the boat should move away from the dock, so the answer seems reasonable.

Conservation of Momentum (continued)

Practice

1. A 63.0 kg astronaut is on a space walk when the tether line to the shuttle breaks. The astronaut is able to throw a spare 10.0 kg oxygen tank in a direction away from the shuttle with a speed of 12.0 m/s, propelling the astronaut back to the shuttle. Assuming that the astronaut starts from rest with respect to the shuttle, find the astronaut's final speed with respect to the shuttle after the tank is thrown.

2. An 85.0 kg fisherman jumps from a dock into a 135.0 kg rowboat at rest on the west side of the dock. If the velocity of the fisherman is 4.30 m/s to the west as he leaves the dock, what is the final velocity of the fisherman and the boat?

3. Each croquet ball in a set has a mass of 0.50 kg. The green ball, traveling at 12.0 m/s, strikes the blue ball, which is at rest. Assuming that the balls slide on a frictionless surface and all collisions are head-on, find the final speed of the blue ball in each of the following situations:

   a. The green ball stops moving after it strikes the blue ball.

   b. The green ball continues moving after the collision at 2.4 m/s in the same direction.

4. A boy on a 2.0 kg skateboard initially at rest tosses an 8.0 kg jug of water in the forward direction. If the jug has a speed of 3.0 m/s relative to the ground and the boy and skateboard move in the opposite direction at 0.60 m/s, find the boy's mass.

Newton's third law leads to conservation of momentum.

Consider two isolated bumper cars, m_1 and m_2, before and after they collide. Before the collision, the velocities of the two bumper cars are $\mathbf{v}_{1,i}$ and $\mathbf{v}_{2,i}$, respectively. After the collision, their velocities are $\mathbf{v}_{1,f}$ and $\mathbf{v}_{2,f}$, respectively. The impulse-momentum theorem, $\mathbf{F}\Delta t = \Delta \mathbf{p}$, describes the change in momentum of one of the bumper cars. Applied to m_1, the impulse-momentum theorem gives the following:

$$\mathbf{F}_1 \Delta t = m_1 \mathbf{v}_{1,f} - m_1 \mathbf{v}_{1,i}$$

Likewise, for m_2 it gives the following:

$$\mathbf{F}_2 \Delta t = m_2 \mathbf{v}_{2,f} - m_2 \mathbf{v}_{2,i}$$

$\mathbf{F}_1$ is the force that m_2 exerts on m_1 during the collision, and $\mathbf{F}_2$ is the force that m_1 exerts on m_2 during the collision. Because the only forces acting in the collision are the forces the two bumper cars exert on each other, Newton's third law tells us that the force on m_1 is equal to and opposite the force on m_2 ($\mathbf{F}_1 = -\mathbf{F}_2$). Additionally, the two forces act over the same time interval, Δt. Therefore, the force m_2 exerts on m_1 multiplied by the time interval is equal to the force m_1 exerts on m_2 multiplied by the time interval, or $\mathbf{F}_1 \Delta t = -\mathbf{F}_2 \Delta t$. That is, the impulse on m_1 is equal to and opposite the impulse on m_2. This relationship is true in every collision or interaction between two isolated objects.

FIGURE 2.4

Force and Change in Momentum During the collision, the force exerted on each bumper car causes a change in momentum for each car. The total momentum is the same before and after the collision.

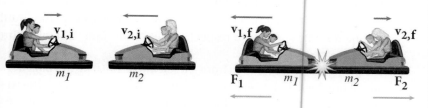

Figure **2.4** illustrates the forces acting on each bumper car. Because impulse is equal to the change in momentum, and the impulse on m_1 is equal to and opposite the impulse on m_2, the change in momentum of m_1 is equal to and opposite the change in momentum of m_2. This means that in every interaction between two isolated objects, the change in momentum of the first object is equal to and opposite the change in momentum of the second object. In equation form, this is expressed by the following equation.

$$m_1\mathbf{v_{1,f}} - m_1\mathbf{v_{1,i}} = -(m_2\mathbf{v_{2,f}} - m_2\mathbf{v_{2,i}})$$

This equation means that if the momentum of one object increases after a collision, then the momentum of the other object in the situation must decrease by an equal amount. Rearranging this equation gives the following equation for the conservation of momentum.

$$m_1\mathbf{v_{1,i}} + m_2\mathbf{v_{2,i}} = m_1\mathbf{v_{1,f}} + m_2\mathbf{v_{2,f}}$$

Forces in real collisions are not constant during the collisions.

In this book, the forces involved in a collision are treated as though they are constant. In a real collision, however, the forces may vary in time in a complicated way. **Figure 2.5** shows the forces acting during the collision of the two bumper cars. At all times during the collision, the forces on the two cars at any instant during the collision are equal in magnitude and opposite in direction. However, the magnitudes of the forces change throughout the collision—increasing, reaching a maximum, and then decreasing.

When solving impulse problems, you should use the average force over the time of the collision as the value for force. Recall that the average velocity of an object undergoing a constant acceleration is equal to the constant velocity required for the object to travel the same displacement in the same time interval. The time-averaged force during a collision is equal to the constant force required to cause the same change in momentum as the real, changing force.

FIGURE 2.5

Force on Two Bumper Cars This graph shows the force on each bumper car during the collision. Although both forces vary with time, F_1 and F_2 are always equal in magnitude and opposite in direction.

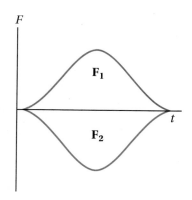

▶ **Reviewing Main Ideas**

1. A 44 kg student on in-line skates is playing with a 22 kg exercise ball. Disregarding friction, explain what happens during the following situations.

  a. The student is holding the ball, and both are at rest. The student then throws the ball horizontally, causing the student to glide back at 3.5 m/s.

  b. Explain what happens to the ball in part (a) in terms of the momentum of the student and the momentum of the ball.

  c. The student is initially at rest. The student then catches the ball, which is initially moving to the right at 4.6 m/s.

  d. Explain what happens in part (c) in terms of the momentum of the student and the momentum of the ball.

2. A boy stands at one end of a floating raft that is stationary relative to the shore. He then walks in a straight line to the opposite end of the raft, away from the shore.

  a. Does the raft move? Explain.

  b. What is the total momentum of the boy and the raft before the boy walks across the raft?

  c. What is the total momentum of the boy and the raft after the boy walks across the raft?

3. High-speed stroboscopic photographs show the head of a 215 g golf club traveling at 55.0 m/s just before it strikes a 46 g golf ball at rest on a tee. After the collision, the club travels (in the same direction) at 42.0 m/s. Use the law of conservation of momentum to find the speed of the golf ball just after impact.

✓ **Critical Thinking**

4. Two isolated objects have a head-on collision. For each of the following questions, explain your answer.

  a. If you know the change in momentum of one object, can you find the change in momentum of the other object?

  b. If you know the initial and final velocity of one object and the mass of the other object, do you have enough information to find the final velocity of the second object?

  c. If you know the masses of both objects and the final velocities of both objects, do you have enough information to find the initial velocities of both objects?

  d. If you know the masses and initial velocities of both objects and the final velocity of one object, do you have enough information to find the final velocity of the other object?

  e. If you know the change in momentum of one object and the initial and final velocities of the other object, do you have enough information to find the mass of either object?

Objectives

▶ Identify different types of collisions.

▶ Determine the changes in kinetic energy during perfectly inelastic collisions.

▶ Compare conservation of momentum and conservation of kinetic energy in perfectly inelastic and elastic collisions.

▶ Find the final velocity of an object in perfectly inelastic and elastic collisions.

SC.912.P.12.5 Apply the law of conservation of linear momentum to interactions, such as collisions between objects.

perfectly inelastic collision a collision in which two objects stick together after colliding

Elastic and Inelastic Collisions

Key Terms
perfectly inelastic collision   elastic collision

Collisions

As you go about your day-to-day activities, you probably witness many collisions without really thinking about them. In some collisions, two objects collide and stick together so that they travel together after the impact. An example of this action is a collision between football players during a tackle, as shown in **Figure 3.1.** In an isolated system, the two football players would both move together after the collision with a momentum equal to the sum of their *momenta* (plural of *momentum*) before the collision. In other collisions, such as a collision between a tennis racket and a tennis ball, two objects collide and bounce so that they move away with two different velocities.

The total momentum remains constant in any type of collision. However, the total kinetic energy is generally not conserved in a collision, because some kinetic energy is converted to internal energy when the objects deform. In this section, we will examine different types of collisions and determine whether kinetic energy is conserved in each type. We will primarily explore two extreme types of collisions: perfectly inelastic collisions and elastic collisions.

Perfectly inelastic collisions can be analyzed in terms of momentum.

When two objects, such as the two football players, collide and move together as one mass, the collision is called a **perfectly inelastic collision.** Likewise, if a meteorite collides head on with Earth, it becomes buried in Earth, and the collision is perfectly inelastic.

FIGURE 3.1

Perfectly Inelastic Collision
When one football player tackles another, they both continue to fall together. This is one familiar example of a perfectly inelastic collision.

©Nathan Bilow/Getty Images

Perfectly inelastic collisions are easy to analyze in terms of momentum, because the objects become essentially one object after the collision. The final mass is equal to the combined masses of the colliding objects. The combination moves with a predictable velocity after the collision.

Consider two cars of masses m_1 and m_2 moving with initial velocities of $\mathbf{v_{1,i}}$ and $\mathbf{v_{2,i}}$ along a straight line, as shown in **Figure 3.2**. The two cars stick together and move with some common velocity, $\mathbf{v_f}$, along the same line of motion after the collision. The total momentum of the two cars before the collision is equal to the total momentum of the two cars after the collision.

Perfectly Inelastic Collision
$$m_1\mathbf{v_{1,i}} + m_2\mathbf{v_{2,i}} = (m_1 + m_2)\,\mathbf{v_f}$$

This simplified version of the equation for conservation of momentum is useful in analyzing perfectly inelastic collisions. When using this equation, it is important to pay attention to signs that indicate direction. In **Figure 3.2**, $\mathbf{v_{1,i}}$ has a positive value (m_1 moving to the right), while $\mathbf{v_{2,i}}$ has a negative value (m_2 moving to the left).

FIGURE 3.2

Inelastic Collision
The total momentum of the two cars before the collision (a) is the same as the total momentum of the two cars after the inelastic collision (b).

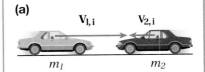

(a)

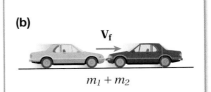

(b)

GO ONLINE

Interactive Demo
HMHScience.com

Perfectly Inelastic Collisions

Sample Problem E A 1850 kg luxury sedan stopped at a traffic light is struck from the rear by a compact car with a mass of 975 kg. The two cars become entangled as a result of the collision. If the compact car was moving at a velocity of 22.0 m/s to the north before the collision, what is the velocity of the entangled mass after the collision?

1 ANALYZE

Given:
$m_1 = 1850$ kg
$m_2 = 975$ kg
$\mathbf{v_{1,i}} = 0$ m/s
$\mathbf{v_{2,i}} = 22.0$ m/s to the north

Unknown: $\mathbf{v_f} = ?$

2 SOLVE

Use the equation for a perfectly inelastic collision.

$$m_1\mathbf{v_{1,i}} + m_2\mathbf{v_{2,i}} = (m_1 + m_2)\,\mathbf{v_f}$$

$$\mathbf{v_f} = \frac{m_1\mathbf{v_{1,i}} + m_2\mathbf{v_{2,i}}}{m_1 + m_2}$$

$$\mathbf{v_f} = \frac{(1850\ \text{kg})(0\ \text{m/s}) + (975\ \text{kg})(22.0\ \text{m/s north})}{1850\ \text{kg} + 975\ \text{kg}}$$

$$\boxed{\mathbf{v_f} = 7.59\ \text{m/s to the north}}$$

Continued

Practice

1. A 1500 kg car traveling at 15.0 m/s to the south collides with a 4500 kg truck that is initially at rest at a stoplight. The car and truck stick together and move together after the collision. What is the final velocity of the two-vehicle mass?

2. A grocery shopper tosses a 9.0 kg bag of rice into a stationary 18.0 kg grocery cart. The bag hits the cart with a horizontal speed of 5.5 m/s toward the front of the cart. What is the final speed of the cart and bag?

3. A 1.50×10^4 kg railroad car moving at 7.00 m/s to the north collides with and sticks to another railroad car of the same mass that is moving in the same direction at 1.50 m/s. What is the velocity of the joined cars after the collision?

4. A dry cleaner throws a 22 kg bag of laundry onto a stationary 9.0 kg cart. The cart and laundry bag begin moving at 3.0 m/s to the right. Find the velocity of the laundry bag before the collision.

5. A 47.4 kg student runs down the sidewalk and jumps with a horizontal speed of 4.20 m/s onto a stationary skateboard. The student and skateboard move down the sidewalk with a speed of 3.95 m/s. Find the following:

   a. the mass of the skateboard

   b. how fast the student would have to jump to have a final speed of 5.00 m/s

Kinetic energy is not conserved in inelastic collisions.

In an inelastic collision, the total kinetic energy does not remain constant when the objects collide. Some of the kinetic energy is converted to sound energy and internal energy as the objects deform during the collision.

This phenomenon helps make sense of the special use of the words *elastic* and *inelastic* in physics. We normally think of *elastic* as referring to something that always returns to, or keeps, its original shape. In physics, an elastic material is one in which the work done to deform the material during a collision is equal to the work the material does to return to its original shape. During a collision, some of the work done on an *inelastic* material is converted to other forms of energy, such as heat and sound.

The decrease in the total kinetic energy during an inelastic collision can be calculated by using the formula for kinetic energy, as shown in Sample Problem F. It is important to remember that not all of the initial kinetic energy is necessarily lost in a perfectly inelastic collision.

Kinetic Energy in Perfectly Inelastic Collisions

Sample Problem F Two clay balls collide head-on in a perfectly inelastic collision. The first ball has a mass of 0.500 kg and an initial velocity of 4.00 m/s to the right. The second ball has a mass of 0.250 kg and an initial velocity of 3.00 m/s to the left. What is the decrease in kinetic energy during the collision?

1 ANALYZE

Given: $m_1 = 0.500$ kg $m_2 = 0.250$ kg

$\mathbf{v_{1,i}} = 4.00$ m/s to the right, $v_{1,i} = +4.00$ m/s

$\mathbf{v_{2,i}} = 3.00$ m/s to the left, $v_{2,i} = -3.00$ m/s

Unknown: $\Delta KE = ?$

2 PLAN

Choose an equation or situation:
The change in kinetic energy is simply the initial kinetic energy subtracted from the final kinetic energy.

$$\Delta KE = KE_f - KE_i$$

Determine both the initial and final kinetic energy.

Initial: $KE_i = KE_{1,i} + KE_{2,i} = \frac{1}{2}m_1 v_{1,i}^2 + \frac{1}{2}m_2 v_{2,i}^2$

Final: $KE_f = KE_{1,f} + KE_{2,f} = \frac{1}{2}(m_1 + m_2)v_f^2$

As you did in Sample Problem E, use the equation for a perfectly inelastic collision to calculate the final velocity.

$$\mathbf{v_f} = \frac{m_1 \mathbf{v_{1,i}} + m_2 \mathbf{v_{2,i}}}{m_1 + m_2}$$

3 SOLVE

Substitute the values into the equation and solve:
First, calculate the final velocity, which will be used in the final kinetic energy equation.

$$v_f = \frac{(0.500 \text{ kg})(4.00 \text{ m/s}) + (0.250 \text{ kg})(-3.00 \text{ m/s})}{0.500 \text{ kg} + 0.250 \text{ kg}}$$

$\mathbf{v_f} = 1.67$ m/s to the right

Next calculate the initial and final kinetic energy.

$$KE_i = \frac{1}{2}(0.500 \text{ kg})(4.00 \text{ m/s})^2 + \frac{1}{2}(0.250 \text{ kg})(-3.00 \text{ m/s})^2 = 5.13 \text{ J}$$

$$KE_f = \frac{1}{2}(0.500 \text{ kg} + 0.250 \text{ kg})(1.67 \text{ m/s})^2 = 1.05 \text{ J}$$

Finally, calculate the change in kinetic energy.

$$\Delta KE = KE_f - KE_i = 1.05 \text{ J} - 5.13 \text{ J}$$

$$\boxed{\Delta KE = -4.08 \text{ J}}$$

4 CHECK YOUR WORK

The negative sign indicates that kinetic energy is lost.

Kinetic Energy in Perfectly Inelastic Collisions (continued)

Practice

1. A 0.25 kg arrow with a velocity of 12 m/s to the west strikes and pierces the center of a 6.8 kg target.

   a. What is the final velocity of the combined mass?

   b. What is the decrease in kinetic energy during the collision?

2. During practice, a student kicks a 0.40 kg soccer ball with a velocity of 8.5 m/s to the south into a 0.15 kg bucket lying on its side. The bucket travels with the ball after the collision.

   a. What is the final velocity of the combined mass of the bucket and the ball?

   b. What is the decrease in kinetic energy during the collision?

3. A 56 kg ice skater traveling at 4.0 m/s to the north meets and joins hands with a 65 kg skater traveling at 12.0 m/s in the opposite direction. Without rotating, the two skaters continue skating together with joined hands.

   a. What is the final velocity of the two skaters?

   b. What is the decrease in kinetic energy during the collision?

Elastic Collisions

When a player kicks a soccer ball, the collision between the ball and the player's foot is much closer to elastic than the collisions we have studied so far. In this case, *elastic* means that the ball and the player's foot remain separate after the collision.

elastic collision a collision in which the total momentum and the total kinetic energy are conserved

In an **elastic collision**, two objects collide and return to their original shapes with no loss of total kinetic energy. After the collision, the two objects move separately. In an elastic collision, both the total momentum and the total kinetic energy are conserved.

Most collisions are neither elastic nor perfectly inelastic.

In the everyday world, most collisions are not perfectly inelastic. Colliding objects do not usually stick together and continue to move as one object. Most collisions are not elastic, either. Even *nearly* elastic collisions, such as those between billiard balls, result in some decrease in kinetic energy. For example, a football deforms when it is kicked. During this deformation, some of the kinetic energy is converted to internal elastic potential energy. In most collisions, some kinetic energy is also converted into sound, such as the click of billiard balls colliding. In fact, any collision that produces sound is not elastic; the sound signifies a decrease in kinetic energy.

Elastic and perfectly inelastic collisions are limiting cases; most collisions actually fall into a category between these two extremes. In this third category of collisions, called *inelastic collisions*, the colliding objects bounce and move separately after the collision, but the total kinetic energy decreases in the collision. *For the problems in this book, we will* consider all collisions in which the objects do not stick together to be elastic *collisions.* Therefore, we will assume that the total momentum and the total kinetic energy will each stay the same before and after a collision in all collisions that are not perfectly inelastic.

Kinetic energy is conserved in elastic collisions.

Figure 3.3 shows an elastic head-on collision between two soccer balls of equal mass. Assume, as in earlier examples, that the balls are isolated on a frictionless surface and that they do not rotate. The first ball is moving to the right when it collides with the second ball, which is moving to the left. When considered as a whole, the entire system has momentum to the left.

After the elastic collision, the first ball moves to the left, and the second ball moves to the right. The magnitude of the momentum of the first ball, which is now moving to the left, is greater than the magnitude of the momentum of the second ball, which is now moving to the right. The entire system still has momentum to the left, just as before the collision.

Another example of a nearly elastic collision is the collision between a golf ball and a club. After a golf club strikes a stationary golf ball, the golf ball moves at a very high speed in the same direction as the golf club. The golf club continues to move in the same direction, but its velocity decreases so that the momentum lost by the golf club is equal to and opposite the momentum gained by the golf ball. *The total momentum is always constant throughout the collision. In addition, if the collision is perfectly elastic, the value of the total kinetic energy after the collision is equal to the value before the collision.*

Momentum and Kinetic Energy Are Conserved in an Elastic Collision

$$m_1\mathbf{v_{1,i}} + m_2\mathbf{v_{2,i}} = m_1\mathbf{v_{1,f}} + m_2\mathbf{v_{2,f}}$$

$$\tfrac{1}{2}m_1v_{1,i}^2 + \tfrac{1}{2}m_2v_{2,i}^2 = \tfrac{1}{2}m_1v_{1,f}^2 + \tfrac{1}{2}m_2v_{2,f}^2$$

Remember that v is positive if an object moves to the right and negative if it moves to the left.

FIGURE 3.3

Elastic Collision In an elastic collision like this one **(b),** both objects return to their original shapes and move separately after the collision **(c).**

(a) Initial **(b)** Impulse **(c)** Final

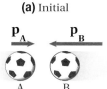

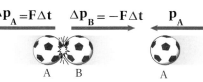

$\mathbf{p_A}$ $\mathbf{p_B}$ $\Delta\mathbf{p_A} = \mathbf{F}\Delta t$ $\Delta\mathbf{p_B} = -\mathbf{F}\Delta t$ $\mathbf{p_A}$ $\mathbf{p_B}$

A   B   A   B   A   B

GO ONLINE

Interactive Demo
HMHScience.com

Sample Problem G A talented juggler can keep as many as 12 identical balls in the air at one time. Suppose each ball has a mass of 0.20 kg and two balls have an elastic head-on collision during the act. The first ball moves away from the collision with a velocity of 3.0 m/s to the right, and the second ball moves away with a velocity of 4.0 m/s to the left. If the first ball's velocity before the collision is 4.0 m/s to the left, what is the velocity of the second ball before the collision?

1 ANALYZE

Given:

$m_1 = m_2 = 0.20$ kg

$\mathbf{v_{1,i}} =$ initial velocity of ball 1 = 4.0 m/s to the left
$\qquad = -4.0$ m/s to the right

$\mathbf{v_{1,f}} =$ final velocity of ball 1 = 3.0 m/s to the right

$\mathbf{v_{2,f}} =$ final velocity of ball 2 = 4.0 m/s to the left
$\qquad = -4.0$ m/s to the right

Unknown: $\mathbf{v_{2,i}} =$ **initial velocity of ball 2 = ?**

2 PLAN

Choose the equation or situation:
Use the equation for the conservation of momentum to determine the initial velocity of ball 2. Because both balls have identical masses, the mass terms cancel.

$$m_1\mathbf{v_{1,i}} + m_2\mathbf{v_{2,i}} = m_1\mathbf{v_{1,f}} + m_2\mathbf{v_{2,f}}$$

$$\mathbf{v_{1,i}} + \mathbf{v_{2,i}} = \mathbf{v_{1,f}} + \mathbf{v_{2,f}}$$

Rearrange the equation to isolate the unknowns:

$$\mathbf{v_{2,i}} + \mathbf{v_{1,f}} + \mathbf{v_{2,f}} - \mathbf{v_{1,i}}$$

3 SOLVE

Substitute the values into the equation and solve:
$$\mathbf{v_{2,i}} = 3.0 \text{ m/s} - 4.0 \text{ m/s} - (-4.0 \text{ m/s})$$

$$\boxed{\mathbf{v_{2,i}} = 3.0 \text{ m/s to the right}}$$

4 CHECK YOUR WORK

Confirm your answer by making sure that kinetic energy is also conserved.

$$\tfrac{1}{2}m_1 v_{1,i}^2 + \tfrac{1}{2}m_2 v_{2,i}^2 = \tfrac{1}{2}m_1 v_{1,f}^2 + \tfrac{1}{2}m_2 v_{2,f}^2$$

$$v_{1,i}^2 + v_{2,i}^2 = v_{1,f}^2 + v_{1,f}^2$$

$$(-4.0 \text{ m/s})^2 + (3.0 \text{ m/s})^2 = (3.0 \text{ m/s})^2 + (-4.0 \text{ m/s})^2$$

$$16 \text{ m}^2/\text{s}^2 + 9.0 \text{ m}^2/\text{s}^2 = 9.0 \text{ m}^2/\text{s}^2 + 16 \text{ m}^2/\text{s}^2$$

$$25 \text{ m}^2/\text{s}^2 = 25 \text{ m}^2/\text{s}^2$$

©Tony Anderson/Getty Images

Continued

Elastic Collisions (continued)

Practice

1. A 0.015 kg marble sliding to the right at 22.5 cm/s on a frictionless surface makes an elastic head-on collision with a 0.015 kg marble moving to the left at 18.0 cm/s. After the collision, the first marble moves to the left at 18.0 cm/s.

   a. Find the velocity of the second marble after the collision.

   b. Verify your answer by calculating the total kinetic energy before and after the collision.

2. Speeds as high as 273 km/h have been recorded for golf balls. Suppose a golf ball whose mass is 45.0 g is moving to the right at 273 km/h and strikes another ball that is at rest. If after the perfectly elastic collision, the first golf ball moves 91 km/h to the left and the second ball moves 182 km/h to the right, what is the mass of the second ball?

3. A 4.0 kg bowling ball sliding to the right at 8.0 m/s has an elastic head-on collision with another 4.0 kg bowling ball initially at rest. The first ball stops after the collision.

   a. Find the velocity of the second ball after the collision.

   b. Verify your answer by calculating the total kinetic energy before and after the collision.

4. A dump truck has a mass of 5.50×10^5 kg when loaded and 2.30×10^5 kg when empty. Suppose two such trucks, one loaded and one empty, crash into each other at a monster truck show. The trucks are supplied with special bumpers that make a collision almost perfectly elastic. If the trucks hit each other at equal speeds of 5.00 m/s and the empty truck recoils to the right with a speed of 9.10 m/s, what is the velocity of the full truck after the collision?

FIGURE 3.4

TYPES OF COLLISIONS

Type of Collision	Diagram	What Happens	Conserved Quantity
perfectly inelastic	m_1 $v_{1,i}$ $v_{2,i}$ m_2 $m_1 + m_2$ v_f $P_{1,i}$ $P_{2,i}$ P_f	The two objects stick together after the collision so that their final velocities are the same.	momentum
elastic	m_1 $v_{1,i}$ $v_{2,i}$ m_2 m_1 $v_{1,f}$ m_2 $v_{2,f}$ $P_{1,i}$ $P_{2,i}$ $P_{1,f}$ $P_{2,f}$	The two objects bounce after the collision so that they move separately.	momentum kinetic energy
inelastic	m_1 $v_{1,i}$ $v_{2,i}$ m_2 m_1 $v_{1,f}$ m_2 $v_{2,f}$ $P_{1,i}$ $P_{2,i}$ $P_{1,f}$ $P_{2,f}$	The two objects deform during the collision so that the total kinetic energy decreases, but the objects move separately after the collision.	momentum

SECTION 3 FORMATIVE ASSESSMENT

▶ **Reviewing Main Ideas**

1. Give two examples of elastic collisions and two examples of perfectly inelastic collisions.

2. A 95.0 kg fullback moving south with a speed of 5.0 m/s has a perfectly inelastic collision with a 90.0 kg opponent running north at 3.0 m/s.
   a. Calculate the velocity of the players just after the tackle.
   b. Calculate the decrease in total kinetic energy after the collision.

3. Two 0.40 kg soccer balls collide elastically in a head-on collision. The first ball starts at rest, and the second ball has a speed of 3.5 m/s. After the collision, the second ball is at rest.
   a. What is the final speed of the first ball?
   b. What is the kinetic energy of the first ball before the collision?
   c. What is the kinetic energy of the second ball after the collision?

✔ **Critical Thinking**

4. If two automobiles collide, they usually do not stick together. Does this mean the collision is elastic?

5. A rubber ball collides elastically with the sidewalk.
   a. Does each object have the same kinetic energy after the collision as it had before the collision? Explain.
   b. Does each object have the same momentum after the collision as it had before the collision? Explain.

High School Physics Teacher

P hysics teachers help students understand this branch of science both inside and outside the classroom. To learn more about teaching physics as a career, read this interview with Linda Rush, who teaches high school physics at Southside High School in Fort Smith, Arkansas.

Linda Rush enjoys working with students, particularly with hands-on activities.

What does a physics teacher do every day?

I teach anywhere from 100 to 130 students a day. I also take care of the lab and equipment, which is sometimes difficult but necessary. In addition, physics teachers have to attend training sessions to stay current in the field.

What schooling did you take in order to become a physics teacher?

I have two college degrees: a bachelor's in physical science education and a master's in secondary education.

At first, I planned to go into the medical field but changed my mind and decided to become a teacher. I started out as a math teacher, but I changed to science because I enjoy the practical applications.

Did your family influence your career choice?

Neither of my parents went to college, but they both liked to tinker. They built an experimental solar house back in the 1970s. My dad rebuilt antique cars. My mom was a computer programmer. When we moved from the city to the country, my parents were determined that my sister and I wouldn't be helpless, so we learned how to do and fix everything.

What is your favorite thing about your job?

I like to watch my students learn—seeing that light bulb of understanding go on. Students can learn so much from one another. I hope that more students will take physics classes. So many students are afraid to try and don't have confidence in themselves.

What are your students surprised to learn about you?

My students are often surprised to learn that I am a kayaker, a hiker, and the mother of five daughters. Sometimes they forget that teachers are real people.

What advice do you have for students who are interested in teaching physics?

Take as many lab classes in college as possible. Learn as many hands-on activities as you can to use in the classroom. Also, get a broad background in other sciences. Don't be limited to only one field. I think what has helped me is that I'm not *just* a physics person. I have a well-rounded background, having taught all kinds of science and math classes.

Linda Rush

Designing Helmets for Safety

Collisions in sports, particularly football, have always been a safety concern. Today, that concern is heightened as doctors learn more about the dangers of concussions and as players become bigger, faster, and more capable of delivering punishing collisions. Engineers are playing an important role in addressing this safety issue.

Define the Problem

Centers for Disease Control and Prevention (CDC) reports that more than 170 000 youths (age 19 and younger) are seen annually in emergency rooms for sports- or recreation-related traumatic brain injuries. A concussion occurs when a violent shaking or movement of the brain results in a disturbance of brain function. Protective helmets, such as those worn by football players, prevent or reduce head injury. Based on statistics from the CDC, however, it is clear that football helmets do not provide enough protection during collisions.

Research the Problem and Propose Solutions

Reducing the number of concussions can be done in several ways. One approach would be to change how football is played. To some extent, this is already being implemented as rules change to make the game safer, for example, by banning helmet-to-helmet collisions.

Along with rules that promote safety, another solution is to design improved helmets that address both linear and rotational forces in collisions. Some companies have introduced padded helmet covers, but the effectiveness of the covers is not certain. Another design incorporates a thin layer of plastic that forms a cap between the padding and hard outer shell. The cap connects to the helmet in a way that allows the helmet to move slightly relative to the cap during an impact. This action reduces rotational forces. One of the safest helmets includes a facemask that flexes on impact, absorbing energy that would otherwise transfer to the front of the head.

Test and Refine Solutions

Experts agree that there will likely never be a concussion-free football helmet. However, testing and refining designs can lead to helmets that minimize the risks.

The National Operating Committee on Standards for Athletic Equipment (NOCSAE) provides standards on how helmets are tested. The current test for a football helmet, for example, involves dropping it from a height of 60 inches onto a flat pad. Certified helmets meet NOCSAE standards, but their tests do not account for glancing collisions in which forces cause angular rotation of the head.

A Swedish engineer has designed a test that re-creates real-life collisions. A helmet is dropped at various angles onto a pneumatic sled that moves horizontally, which takes into account a helmet's ability to reduce rotational forces.

Improved testing and further understanding of head and brain injuries will help engineers design safer helmets.

Design Your Own

Conduct Research

Use the Internet to research the Multi-directional Impact Protection System (MIPS). Find several sports helmets that use MIPS in their products.

Communicate

Write a paragraph explaining how the MIPS design is inspired by the fluids that surround the human brain.

Design a Prototype

Draw a series of sketches that demonstrate how MIPS reduces impact forces that cause angular rotation of the head.

SECTION 1 Momentum and Impulse

KEY TERMS

- Momentum is a vector quantity defined as the product of an object's mass and velocity.

- A net external force applied constantly to an object for a certain time interval will cause a change in the object's momentum equal to the product of the force and the time interval during which the force acts.

- The product of the constant applied force and the time interval during which the force is applied is called the impulse of the force for the time interval.

momentum

impulse

SECTION 2 Conservation of Momentum

- In all interactions between isolated objects, momentum is conserved.

- In every interaction between two isolated objects, the change in momentum of the first object is equal to and opposite the change in momentum of the second object.

SECTION 3 Elastic and Inelastic Collisions

KEY TERMS

- In a perfectly inelastic collision, two objects stick together and move as one mass after the collision.

- In a perfectly inelastic collision, momentum is conserved, but kinetic energy is not conserved.

- In an inelastic collision, kinetic energy is converted to internal elastic potential energy when the objects deform. Some kinetic energy is also converted to sound energy and internal energy.

- In an elastic collision, two objects return to their original shapes and move away from the collision separately.

- Both momentum and kinetic energy are conserved in an elastic collision.

- Few collisions are elastic or perfectly inelastic.

perfectly inelastic collision

elastic collision

VARIABLE SYMBOLS	
Quantities	**Units**
p momentum	kg•m/s kilogram-meters per second
$F\Delta t$ impulse	N•s Newton-seconds = kilogram-meters per second

Problem Solving

See **Appendix D: Equations** for a summary of the equations introduced in this chapter. If you need more problem-solving practice, see **Appendix I: Additional Problems.**

CHAPTER 6 Review

Momentum and Impulse

▶ **REVIEWING MAIN IDEAS**

1. If an object is not moving, what is its momentum?

2. If two particles have equal kinetic energies, must they have the same momentum? Explain.

3. Show that $\mathbf{F} = m\mathbf{a}$ and $\mathbf{F} = \dfrac{\Delta \mathbf{p}}{\Delta t}$ are equivalent.

CONCEPTUAL QUESTIONS

4. A truck loaded with sand is moving down the highway in a straight path.
   a. What happens to the momentum of the truck if the truck's velocity is increasing?
   b. What happens to the momentum of the truck if sand leaks at a constant rate through a hole in the truck bed while the truck maintains a constant velocity?

5. Gymnasts always perform on padded mats. Use the impulse-momentum theorem to discuss how these mats protect the athletes.

6. When a car collision occurs, an air bag is inflated, protecting the passenger from serious injury. How does the air bag soften the blow? Discuss the physics involved in terms of momentum and impulse.

7. If you jump from a table onto the floor, are you more likely to be hurt if your knees are bent or if your legs are stiff and your knees are locked? Explain.

8. Consider a field of insects, all of which have essentially the same mass.
   a. If the total momentum of the insects is zero, what does this imply about their motion?
   b. If the total kinetic energy of the insects is zero, what does this imply about their motion?

9. Two students hold an open bed sheet loosely by its corners to form a "catching net." The instructor asks a third student to throw an egg into the middle of the sheet as hard as possible. Why doesn't the egg's shell break?

10. How do car bumpers that collapse on impact help protect a driver?

PRACTICE PROBLEMS

For problem 11, see Sample Problem A.

11. Calculate the linear momentum for each of the following cases:
    a. a proton with mass 1.67×10^{-27} kg moving with a velocity of 5.00×10^{6} m/s straight up
    b. a 15.0 g bullet moving with a velocity of 325 m/s to the right
    c. a 75.0 kg sprinter running with a velocity of 10.0 m/s southwest
    d. Earth ($m = 5.98 \times 10^{24}$ kg) moving in its orbit with a velocity equal to 2.98×10^{4} m/s forward

For problems 12–13, see Sample Problem B.

12. A 2.5 kg ball strikes a wall with a velocity of 8.5 m/s to the left. The ball bounces off with a velocity of 7.5 m/s to the right. If the ball is in contact with the wall for 0.25 s, what is the constant force exerted on the ball by the wall? What impulse was delivered to the ball?

13. A football punter accelerates a 0.55 kg football from rest to a speed of 8.0 m/s in 0.25 s. What constant force does the punter exert on the ball? What impulse was delivered to the ball?

For problem 14, see Sample Problem C.

14. A 0.15 kg baseball moving at +26 m/s is slowed to a stop by a catcher who exerts a constant force of −390 N. How long does it take this force to stop the ball? How far does the ball travel before stopping?

Conservation of Momentum

▶ **REVIEWING MAIN IDEAS**

15. Two skaters initially at rest push against each other so that they move in opposite directions. What is the total momentum of the two skaters when they begin moving? Explain.

16. In a collision between two soccer balls, momentum is conserved. Is momentum conserved for each soccer ball? Explain.

17. Explain how momentum is conserved when a ball bounces against a floor.

CONCEPTUAL QUESTIONS

18. As a ball falls toward Earth, the momentum of the ball increases. How would you reconcile this observation with the law of conservation of momentum?

19. In the early 1900s, Robert Goddard proposed sending a rocket to the moon. Critics took the position that in a vacuum such as exists between Earth and the moon, the gases emitted by the rocket would have nothing to push against to propel the rocket. To settle the debate, Goddard placed a gun in a vacuum and fired a blank cartridge from it. (A blank cartridge fires only the hot gases of the burning gunpowder.) What happened when the gun was fired? Explain your answer.

20. An astronaut carrying a camera in space finds herself drifting away from a space shuttle after her tether becomes unfastened. If she has no propulsion device, what should she do to move back to the shuttle?

21. When a bullet is fired from a gun, what happens to the gun? Explain your answer using the principles of momentum discussed in this chapter.

PRACTICE PROBLEMS

For problems 22–23, see Sample Problem D.

22. A 65.0 kg ice skater moving to the right with a velocity of 2.50 m/s throws a 0.150 kg snowball to the right with a velocity of 32.0 m/s relative to the ground.
 a. What is the velocity of the ice skater after throwing the snowball? Disregard the friction between the skates and the ice.

b. A second skater initially at rest with a mass of 60.0 kg catches the snowball. What is the velocity of the second skater after catching the snowball in a perfectly inelastic collision?

23. A tennis player places a 55 kg ball machine on a frictionless surface, as shown below. The machine fires a 0.057 kg tennis ball horizontally with a velocity of 36 m/s toward the north. What is the final velocity of the machine?

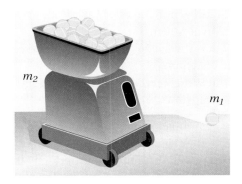

Elastic and Inelastic Collisions

▶ **REVIEWING MAIN IDEAS**

24. Consider a perfectly inelastic head-on collision between a small car and a large truck traveling at the same speed. Which vehicle has a greater change in kinetic energy as a result of the collision?

25. Given the masses of two objects and their velocities before and after a head-on collision, how could you determine whether the collision was elastic, inelastic, or perfectly inelastic? Explain.

26. In an elastic collision between two objects, do both objects have the same kinetic energy after the collision as before? Explain.

27. If two objects collide and one is initially at rest, is it possible for both to be at rest after the collision? Is it possible for one to be at rest after the collision? Explain.

PRACTICE PROBLEMS

For problems 28–29, see Sample Problem E.

28. Two carts with masses of 4.0 kg and 3.0 kg move toward each other on a frictionless track with speeds of 5.0 m/s and 4.0 m/s, respectively. The carts stick together after colliding head-on. Find the final speed.

29. A 1.20 kg skateboard is coasting along the pavement at a speed of 5.00 m/s when a 0.800 kg cat drops from a tree vertically downward onto the skateboard. What is the speed of the skateboard-cat combination?

For problems 30–31, see Sample Problem F.

30. A railroad car with a mass of 2.00×10^4 kg moving at 3.00 m/s collides and joins with two railroad cars already joined together, each with the same mass as the single car and initially moving in the same direction at 1.20 m/s.
  a. What is the speed of the three joined cars after the collision?
  b. What is the decrease in kinetic energy during the collision?

31. An 88 kg fullback moving east with a speed of 5.0 m/s is tackled by a 97 kg opponent running west at 3.0 m/s, and the collision is perfectly inelastic. Calculate the following:
  a. the velocity of the players just after the tackle
  b. the decrease in kinetic energy during the collision

For problems 32–34, see Sample Problem G.

32. A 5.0 g coin sliding to the right at 25.0 cm/s makes an elastic head-on collision with a 15.0 g coin that is initially at rest. After the collision, the 5.0 g coin moves to the left at 12.5 cm/s.
  a. Find the final velocity of the other coin.
  b. Find the amount of kinetic energy transferred to the 15.0 g coin.

33. A billiard ball traveling at 4.0 m/s has an elastic head-on collision with a billiard ball of equal mass that is initially at rest. The first ball is at rest after the collision. What is the speed of the second ball after the collision?

34. A 25.0 g marble sliding to the right at 20.0 cm/s overtakes and collides elastically with a 10.0 g marble moving in the same direction at 15.0 cm/s. After the collision, the 10.0 g marble moves to the right at 22.1 cm/s. Find the velocity of the 25.0 g marble after the collision.

Mixed Review

 REVIEWING MAIN IDEAS

35. If a 0.147 kg baseball has a momentum of $\mathbf{p} = 6.17$ kg•m/s as it is thrown from home to second base, what is its velocity?

36. A moving object has a kinetic energy of 150 J and a momentum with a magnitude of 30.0 kg•m/s. Determine the mass and speed of the object.

37. A 0.10 kg ball of dough is thrown straight up into the air with an initial speed of 15 m/s.
  a. Find the momentum of the ball of dough at its maximum height.
  b. Find the momentum of the ball of dough halfway to its maximum height on the way up.

38. A 3.00 kg mud ball has a perfectly inelastic collision with a second mud ball that is initially at rest. The composite system moves with a speed equal to one-third the original speed of the 3.00 kg mud ball. What is the mass of the second mud ball?

39. A 5.5 g dart is fired into a block of wood with a mass of 22.6 g. The wood block is initially at rest on a 1.5 m tall post. After the collision, the wood block and dart land 2.5 m from the base of the post. Find the initial speed of the dart.

40. A 730 N student stands in the middle of a frozen pond having a radius of 5.0 m. He is unable to get to the other side because of a lack of friction between his shoes and the ice. To overcome this difficulty, he throws his 2.6 kg physics textbook horizontally toward the north shore at a speed of 5.0 m/s. How long does it take him to reach the south shore?

41. A 0.025 kg golf ball moving at 18.0 m/s crashes through the window of a house in 5.0×10^{-4} s. After the crash, the ball continues in the same direction with a speed of 10.0 m/s. Assuming the force exerted on the ball by the window was constant, what was the magnitude of this force? What impulse was delivered to the ball?

42. A 1550 kg car moving south at 10.0 m/s collides with a 2550 kg car moving north. The cars stick together and move as a unit after the collision at a velocity of 5.22 m/s to the north. Find the velocity of the 2550 kg car before the collision.

43. The bird perched on the swing shown in the diagram has a mass of 52.0 g, and the base of the swing has a mass of 153 g. The swing and bird are originally at rest, and then the bird takes off horizontally at 2.00 m/s. How high will the base of the swing rise above its original level? Disregard friction.

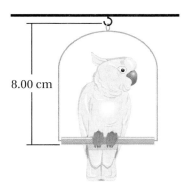

8.00 cm

44. An 85.0 kg astronaut is working on the engines of a spaceship that is drifting through space with a constant velocity. The astronaut turns away to look at Earth and several seconds later is 30.0 m behind the ship, at rest relative to the spaceship. The only way to return to the ship without a thruster is to throw a wrench directly away from the ship. If the wrench has a mass of 0.500 kg, and the astronaut throws the wrench with a speed of 20.0 m/s, how long does it take the astronaut to reach the ship?

45. A 2250 kg car traveling at 10.0 m/s collides with a 2750 kg car that is initially at rest at a stoplight. The cars stick together and move 2.50 m before friction causes them to stop. Determine the coefficient of kinetic friction between the cars and the road, assuming that the negative acceleration is constant and that all wheels on both cars lock at the time of impact.

46. A constant force of 2.5 N to the right acts on a 1.5 kg mass for 0.50 s.
  a. Find the final velocity of the mass if it is initially at rest.
  b. Find the final velocity of the mass if it is initially moving along the *x*-axis with a velocity of 2.0 m/s to the left.

47. Two billiard balls with identical masses and sliding in opposite directions have an elastic head-on collision. Before the collision, each ball has a speed of 22 cm/s. Find the speed of each billiard ball immediately after the collision. (See **Appendix A** for hints on solving simultaneous equations.)

GRAPHING CALCULATOR PRACTICE

Momentum

As you learned earlier in this chapter, the linear momentum, **p**, of an object of mass *m* moving with a velocity **v** is defined as the product of the mass and the velocity. A change in momentum requires force and time. This fundamental relationship between force, momentum, and time is shown in Newton's second law of motion.

$$\mathbf{F} = \frac{\Delta \mathbf{p}}{\Delta t}, \text{ where } \Delta \mathbf{p} = m\mathbf{v_f} - m\mathbf{v_i}$$

In this graphing calculator activity, you will determine the force that must be exerted to change the momentum of an object in various time intervals. This activity will help you better understand

- the relationship between time and force
- the consequences of the signs of the force and the velocity

Go online to HMHScience.com to find the skillsheet and program for this graphing calculator activity.

48. A 7.50 kg laundry bag is dropped from rest at an initial height of 3.00 m.

   a. What is the speed of Earth toward the bag just before the bag hits the ground? Use the value 5.98×10^{24} kg as the mass of Earth.

   b. Use your answer to part **(a)** to justify disregarding the motion of Earth when dealing with the motion of objects on Earth.

49. A 55 kg pole-vaulter falls from rest from a height of 5.0 m onto a foam-rubber pad. The pole-vaulter comes to rest 0.30 s after landing on the pad.

   a. Calculate the athlete's velocity just before reaching the pad.

   b. Calculate the constant force exerted on the pole-vaulter due to the collision.

50. An unstable nucleus with a mass of 17.0×10^{-27} kg initially at rest disintegrates into three particles. One of the particles, of mass 5.0×10^{-27} kg, moves along the positive y-axis with a speed of 6.0×10^6 m/s. Another particle, of mass 8.4×10^{-27} kg, moves along the positive x-axis with a speed of 4.0×10^6 m/s. Determine the third particle's speed and direction of motion. (Assume that mass is conserved.)

ALTERNATIVE ASSESSMENT

1. Design an experiment to test the conservation of momentum. You may use dynamics carts, toy cars, coins, or any other suitable objects. Explore different types of collisions, including perfectly inelastic collisions and elastic collisions. If your teacher approves your plan, perform the experiment. Write a report describing your results.

2. Design an experiment that uses a dynamics cart with other easily found equipment to test whether it is safer to crash into a steel railing or into a container filled with sand. How can you measure the forces applied to the cart as it crashes into the barrier? If your teacher approves your plan, perform the experiment.

3. Obtain a videotape of one of your school's sports teams in action. Create a play-by-play description of a short segment of the videotape, explaining how momentum and kinetic energy change during impacts that take place in the segment.

4. Use your knowledge of impulse and momentum to construct a container that will protect an egg dropped from a two-story building. The container should prevent the egg from breaking when it hits the ground. Do not use a device that reduces air resistance, such as a parachute. Also avoid using any packing materials. Test your container. If the egg breaks, modify your design and then try again.

5. An inventor has asked an Olympic biathlon team to test his new rifles during the target-shooting segment of the event. The new 0.75 kg guns shoot 25.0 g bullets at 615 m/s. The team's coach has hired you to advise him about how these guns could affect the biathletes' accuracy. Prepare figures to justify your answer. Be ready to defend your position.

Standards-Based Assessment

Record your answers on a separate piece of paper.

MULTIPLE CHOICE

1 If a particle's kinetic energy is zero, what is the momentum?

A zero

B 1 kg·m/s

C 15 kg·m/s

D negative

2 The vector below represents the momentum of a car traveling along a road.

The car strikes another car, which is at rest, and the result is an inelastic collision. Which of the following vectors represents the momentum of the first car after the collision?

A ←————————

B ————————→

C ←—————

D —————→

3 What is the momentum of a 0.148 kg baseball thrown with a velocity of 35 m/s toward home plate?

A 5.1 kg·m/s toward home plate

B 5.1 kg·m/s away from home plate

C 5.2 kg·m/s toward home plate

D 5.2 kg·m/s away from home plate

4 After being struck by a bowling ball, a 1.5 kg bowling pin slides to the right at 3.0 m/s and collides head-on with another 1.5 kg bowling pin initially at rest.

What is the final velocity of the second pin if the first pin moves to the right at 0.5 m/s after the collision?

A 2.5 m/s to the left

B 2.5 m/s to the right

C 3.0 m/s to the left

D 3.0 m/s to the right

5 For a given change in momentum, if the net force that is applied to an object increases, what happens to the time interval over which the force is applied?

A The time interval increases.

B The time interval decreases.

C The time interval stays the same.

D It is impossible to determine the answer from the given information.

6 Which equation expresses the law of conservation of momentum?

A $p = m\mathbf{v}$

B $m_1\mathbf{v_{1,i}} + m_2\mathbf{v_{2,i}} = m_1\mathbf{v_{1,f}} + m_2\mathbf{v_{2,f}}$

C $\frac{1}{2}m_1{v_{1,i}}^2 + m_2{v_{2,i}}^2 = \frac{1}{2}(m_1 + m_2)v_f^2$

D $KE = \mathbf{p}$

7 Two shuffleboard disks of equal mass, one of which is orange and one of which is yellow, are involved in an elastic collision. The yellow disk is initially at rest and is struck by the orange disk, which is moving initially to the right at 5.00 m/s. After the collision, the orange disk is at rest. What is the velocity of the yellow disk after the collision?

A zero

B 5.00 m/s to the left

C 2.50 m/s to the right

D 5.00 m/s to the right

GRIDDED RESPONSE

8 An 8.0 g bullet is fired into a 2.5 kg pendulum bob, which is initially at rest, and becomes embedded in the bob. The pendulum then rises a vertical distance of 6.0 cm. What was the initial speed, in m/s, of the bullet?

A BOOK EXPLAINING COMPLEX IDEAS USING ONLY THE 1,000 MOST COMMON WORDS

RANDALL MUNROE
XKCD.COM

SKY BOAT PUSHER
Machines that push other machines through the air

You've learned about momentum and how it is conserved. How does a jet engine increase an aircraft's momentum, moving it forward? Here's an explanation in simple language.

THE STORY OF MOVING MACHINES THROUGH AIR

SKY BOATS, LIKE CARS AND SEA BOATS, ARE PUSHED BY MACHINES THAT BURN FIRE WATER. FIRE WATER NEEDS AIR TO BURN, AND SKY BOAT PUSHERS USE SPECIAL BLOWERS THAT USE THE AIR THEY'RE MOVING THROUGH TO FEED THEIR FIRE.

MOST MACHINES THAT BURN FIRE WATER USE THESE FOUR STEPS:

FIRST, PULL AIR IN.

WHY DID I THINK THIS WAS THE BEST IDEA?

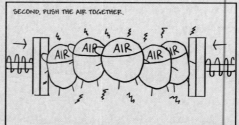

SECOND, PUSH THE AIR TOGETHER.

THIRD, BURN FIRE WATER IN THE AIR, HEATING IT AND MAKING IT GET BIGGER.

LAST, USE THAT GROWING AIR TO PUSH ON SOMETHING.

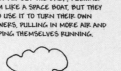

SKY BOAT PUSHERS USE THE FORCE FROM THE HOT AIR IN TWO WAYS: THEY LET IT FLY OUT THE BACK, PUSHING THEM LIKE A SPACE BOAT, BUT THEY ALSO USE IT TO TURN THEIR OWN BLOWERS, PULLING IN MORE AIR AND KEEPING THEMSELVES RUNNING.

KINDS OF PUSHERS

Small sky boats and large ones all work by pushing air, but different kinds of sky boats use different kinds of pushers.

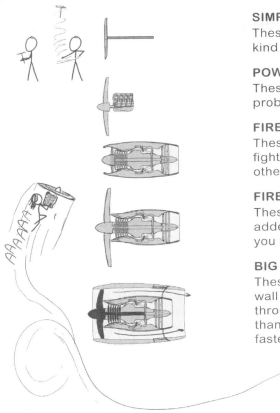

SIMPLE PUSHER
These are fun to play with, but if you try to push any kind of boat with them, your arms get tired.

POWERED PUSHER
These are even more fun to play with (though you probably want to put them on a sky boat first).

FIRE PUSHER
These are used to push fast boats, like the kind that fight in wars. They go fast, but use more fire water than other kinds.

FIRE-POWERED BLOWER
These are like the fire pushers, but with a big blower added to the front. This kind of pusher is very good if you don't want to go too fast. They're very loud.

BIG SKY BOAT PUSHER
These are like fire-powered blowers, but they have a wall around the whole thing to control how the air goes through. They only work well when you're going slower than sound, which is why almost no big sky boats go faster than that.

HOW DO THEY WORK?

To understand how air pushers work, it can help to start by looking at space pushers.

To make a fire, you need air and something to burn. Space boats pour fire water and air into a little room that's open on one side. Then the water and air is set on fire. The fire blows up and flies out the hole, pushing the boat.

Since there's no air in space, but fires need air, a space boat has to carry air with it. Sky boats can use the air around them, so they only need to carry the fire water. They can take in air, add fire water to it, and burn it.

You can make the pusher better by using a blower in the front to force more air together into the burning room. If there's more air, the fire can burn faster and hotter.

Running the blower in front takes power. You could get that power by burning fire water in a different machine and running power to the blower with power lines. But it's better to just use a little of the power from the fire you're already making.

If you put a blower in back, in the path of the fire, it can turn a stick that turns the blower in the front. This blower slows down the burning air so it doesn't push you as well. But the blower makes the fire work so much better that it more than makes up for it.

There's one last idea that makes this work better. Instead of just using the hot air to power the blowers that press the air into the burning room, you can also use it to power a big blower.

This big blower (which sometimes has a wall around it) is what really pushes the sky boat. Once you add this blower, all the rest of the parts are just there to get lots of air together, start a fire, and get power from it.

SKY BOAT PUSHER

STEP ONE: GET AIR

Air comes in from this side, the first step in making power.

STEP TWO: PUSH

These blowers push the air into a smaller and smaller space, which will help the fire burn faster and hotter.

STEP THREE: BURN

The air from the pushers comes into this burning room, where little drops of fire water are thrown into it and set on fire.

The fire water and air get hot and blow up. The walls make it hard to blow up in any direction except out the back, so that's where the burning air goes.

BLOCKER

If there's stuff in the air, like sticks or rocks, it gets pushed through here so it doesn't hurt the blowers.

POINT

This thing helps to start pushing the air together before it goes inside.

BIG BLOWER

The fire in the back turns this big blower using the stick in the middle. This blower is what really does most of the work of pushing a big sky boat; everything else is just there to turn it.

Not all sky boats have a big blower like this. Some of them just use the hot air itself, which works well for very fast boats. But for boats going slower than sound, it turns out that using the hot air to power big blowers takes less fire water than using the air itself as a pusher.

SPIN STOPPERS

The blowers that push the air together all work by spinning, but since they're all spinning in the same direction, they can start the air spinning around instead of going toward the burning room. To keep that from happening, there are little wings in between each blower to make the river of air go straight and keep it from turning too much.

POWER MAKER

This machine uses the turning stick to make a little extra power for the rest of the sky boat to use (for things like lights and computers).

AIR GETTER

The air up high is too thin to breathe. This thing grabs some of the air that the blowers pushed together and sends it to the inside of the sky boat so people can breathe.

FIRE-WATER CARRIERS

These carry fire water into the burning room.

STEP FOUR: MAKE POWER

The force of the air coming out would help push the sky boat on its own, but sky boat pushers do something cooler: They put extra blowers in the path of the air. Instead of turning those blowers to push air, they let the *air* turn the *blowers*. The blowers turn the stick in the middle of the pusher, which turns all the blowers at the start, powering the machine.

That might seem like it shouldn't work, since it's using a blower to power another blower. But the power is coming from the burning fire water pushing its way out. These blowers are just a cool way to use some of that fire to keep the machine running.

WAIT A SECOND!

One thing a lot of people wonder is "How does the force from the fire know to go out the back? Why doesn't it push on the blowers in front just as much, and slow them back down?"

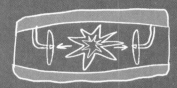

The answer is that the shape of the room and the size of the blowers make it so the easier way out is through the back. It just has to push through a few blowers on the way.

BACK PUSHER

If the sky boat needs to stop, it can use these doors to send the air out the sides and toward the front, which makes it push back instead of forward.

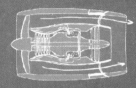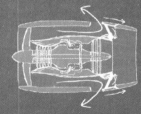

POINT

BIG BLOWER

Why It Matters

Circular motion is present all around you—from a rotating Ferris wheel in an amusement park to a space shuttle's orbit around Earth.

This photograph shows astronauts on a space walk. They are replacing gyroscopes, contained in rate sensor units, inside the Hubble Space Telescope. An expanse of water, partially covered by clouds, is in the background.

CHAPTER 7
Circular Motion and Gravitation

SECTION 1
Circular Motion

SECTION 2
Newton's Law of Universal Gravitation

SECTION 3
Motion in Space

SECTION 4
Torque and Simple Machines

BIG IDEA

Objects move in a circular path when there is a centrally directed force. The concept of circular motion helps to explain phenomena such as orbital motion or torque.

ONLINE Physics
HMHScience.com

ONLINE LABS
- Circular Motion
- Torque and Center of Mass
- Machines and Efficiency
- S.T.E.M. Lab Centripetal Roller Coaster

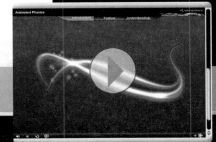

GO ONLINE
Animated
Physics
HMHScience.com

Torque

Objectives

▶ Solve problems involving centripetal acceleration.

▶ Explain how the apparent existence of an outward force in circular motion can be explained as inertia resisting the centripetal force.

Circular Motion

Key Term

centripetal acceleration

Centripetal Acceleration

Consider a spinning Ferris wheel, as shown in **Figure 1.1**. The cars on the rotating Ferris wheel are said to be in *circular motion*. Any object that revolves about a single axis undergoes circular motion. The line about which the rotation occurs is called the *axis of rotation*. In this case, it is a line perpendicular to the side of the Ferris wheel and passing through the wheel's center.

Tangential speed depends on distance.

Tangential speed (v_t) can be used to describe the speed of an object in circular motion. The tangential speed of a car on the Ferris wheel is the car's speed along an imaginary line drawn tangent to the car's circular path. This definition can be applied to any object moving in circular motion. When the tangential speed is constant, the motion is described as *uniform circular motion*.

The tangential speed depends on the distance from the object to the center of the circular path. For example, consider a pair of horses side by side on a carousel. Each completes one full circle in the same time period, but the horse on the outside covers more distance than the inside horse does, so the outside horse has a greater tangential speed.

Centripetal acceleration is due to a change in direction.

Suppose a car on a Ferris wheel is moving at a constant speed as the wheel turns. Even though the tangential speed is constant, the car still has an acceleration. To see why, consider the equation that defines acceleration:

$$\mathbf{a} = \frac{\mathbf{v_f} - \mathbf{v_i}}{t_f - t_i}$$

Acceleration depends on a change in the velocity. Because velocity is a vector, acceleration can be produced by a change in the *magnitude* of the velocity, a change in the *direction* of the velocity, or both. If the Ferris wheel car is moving at a constant speed, then there is no change in the magnitude of the velocity vector. However, think about the way the car is moving. It is not traveling in a straight line. The velocity vector is continuously changing direction.

FIGURE 1.1

Circular Motion Any point on a Ferris wheel spinning about a fixed axis undergoes circular motion.

The acceleration of a Ferris wheel car moving in a circular path and at constant speed is due to a change in direction. An acceleration of this nature is called a **centripetal acceleration**. The magnitude of a centripetal acceleration is given by the following equation:

> **Centripetal Acceleration**
> $$a_c = \frac{v_t^2}{r}$$
> $$\text{centripetal acceleration} = \frac{(\text{tangential speed})^2}{\text{radius of circular path}}$$

What is the direction of centripetal acceleration? To answer this question, consider **Figure 1.2(a)**. At time t_i, an object is at point A and has tangential velocity $\mathbf{v_i}$. At time t_f, the object is at point B and has tangential velocity $\mathbf{v_f}$. Assume that $\mathbf{v_i}$ and $\mathbf{v_f}$ differ in direction but have the same magnitudes.

The change in velocity ($\Delta\mathbf{v} = \mathbf{v_f} - \mathbf{v_i}$) can be determined graphically, as shown by the vector triangle in **Figure 1.2(b)**. Note that when Δt is very small, $\mathbf{v_f}$ will be almost parallel to $\mathbf{v_i}$. The vector $\Delta\mathbf{v}$ will be approximately perpendicular to $\mathbf{v_f}$ and $\mathbf{v_i}$ and will be pointing toward the center of the circle. Because the acceleration is in the direction of $\Delta\mathbf{v}$, the acceleration will also be directed toward the center of the circle. Centripetal acceleration is always directed toward the center of a circle. In fact, the word *centripetal* means "center seeking." This is the reason that the acceleration of an object in uniform circular motion is called *centripetal acceleration*.

centripetal acceleration the acceleration directed toward the center of a circular path

FIGURE 1.2

Centripetal Acceleration
(a) As the object moves from A to B, the direction of the object's velocity vector changes. **(b)** For short time intervals, $\Delta\mathbf{v}$ is directed toward the center of the circle.

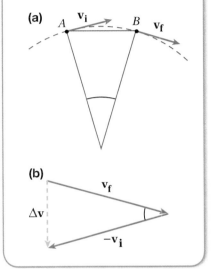

Centripetal Acceleration

GO ONLINE

Interactive Demo
HMHScience.com

Sample Problem A Calculate the orbital radius of Earth, if its tangential speed is 29.7 km/s and the centripetal acceleration acting on Earth is 5.9×10^{-3} m/s².

① ANALYZE

Given: $v_t = 29.7$ km/s $a_c = 5.9 \times 10^{-3}$ m/s²

Unknown: $r = ?$

② SOLVE

Use the centripetal acceleration equation written in terms of tangential speed. Rearrange the equation to solve for r:

$$a_c = \frac{v_t^2}{r}$$

$$r = \frac{v_t^2}{a_c} = \frac{(29.7 \times 10^3 \text{ m/s})^2}{5.9 \times 10^{-3} \text{ m/s}^2}$$

$$\boxed{r = 1.5 \times 10^{11} \text{ m} = 1.5 \times 10^8 \text{ km}}$$

Continued

Centripetal Acceleration (continued)

Practice

1. A rope attaches a tire to an overhanging tree limb. A girl swinging on the tire has a centripetal acceleration of 3.0 m/s². If the length of the rope is 2.1 m, what is the girl's tangential speed?

2. As a young boy swings a yo-yo parallel to the ground and above his head, the yo-yo has a centripetal acceleration of 250 m/s². If the yo-yo's string is 0.50 m long, what is the yo-yo's tangential speed?

3. A waterwheel built in Hamah, Syria, has a radius of 20.0 m. If the tangential velocity at the wheel's edge is 7.85 m/s, what is the centripetal acceleration of the wheel?

4. A salami is more than 20 m long. If a hungry mouse runs around the salami's circumference with a tangential speed of 0.17 m/s, the centripetal acceleration of the mouse is 0.29 m/s². What is the radius of the salami?

Tangential acceleration is due to a change in speed.

You have seen that centripetal acceleration results from a change in direction. In circular motion, an acceleration due to a change in speed is called *tangential acceleration*. To understand the difference between centripetal and tangential acceleration, consider a car traveling in a circular track. Because the car is moving in a circle, the car has a centripetal component of acceleration. If the car's speed changes, the car also has a tangential component of acceleration.

FIGURE 1.3

Force on a Ball When a ball is whirled in a circle, it is acted on by a force directed toward the center of the ball's circular path.

Centripetal Force

Consider a ball of mass m that is tied to a string of length r and that is being whirled in a horizontal circular path, as shown in **Figure 1.3**. Assume that the ball moves with constant speed. Because the velocity vector, **v**, continuously changes direction during the motion, the ball experiences a centripetal acceleration that is directed toward the center of motion. As seen earlier, the magnitude of this acceleration is given by the following equation:

$$a_c = \frac{v_t^2}{r}$$

The inertia of the ball tends to maintain the ball's motion in a straight path. However, the string exerts a force that overcomes this tendency. The forces acting on the ball are gravitational force and the force exerted by the string, as shown in **Figure 1.4(a)** on the next page. The force exerted by the string has horizontal and vertical components. The vertical component is equal and opposite to the gravitational force. Thus, the horizontal component is the net force. This net force is directed toward the center of the circle, as shown in **Figure 1.4(b)**. The net force that is directed toward the center of an object's circular path is called *centripetal force*. Newton's second law can be applied to find the magnitude of this force.

$$F_c = ma_c$$

FIGURE 1.4

Centripetal Force The net force on a ball whirled in a circle **(a)** is directed toward the center of the circle **(b)**.

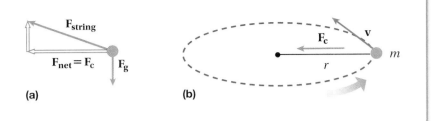

(a)   (b)

The equation for centripetal acceleration can be combined with Newton's second law to obtain the following equation for centripetal force:

Centripetal Force

$$F_c = \frac{mv_t^2}{r}$$

$$\text{centripetal force} = \text{mass} \times \frac{(\text{tangential speed})^2}{\text{radius of circular path}}$$

Centripetal force is simply the name given to the net force toward the center of the circular path followed by an object moving in uniform circular motion. Any type of force or combination of forces can provide this net force. For example, friction between a racecar's tires and a circular track is a centripetal force that keeps the car in a circular path. As another example, gravitational force is a centripetal force that keeps the moon in its orbit.

GO ONLINE

Interactive Demo
HMHScience.com

Centripetal Force

Sample Problem B A pilot is flying a small plane at 56.6 m/s in a circular path with a radius of 188.5 m. The centripetal force needed to maintain the plane's circular motion is 1.89×10^4 N. What is the plane's mass?

① ANALYZE

Given: $v_t = 56.6$ m/s $r = 188.5$ m $F_c = 1.89 \times 10^4$ N

Unknown: $m = ?$

② SOLVE

Use the equation for centripetal force. Rearrange to solve for m.

$$F_c = \frac{mv_t^2}{r}$$

$$m = \frac{F_c r}{v_t^2} = \frac{(1.89 \times 10^4 \text{ N})(188.5 \text{ m})}{(56.6 \text{ m/s})^2}$$

$$m = 1110 \text{ kg}$$

Centripetal Force (continued)

Practice

1. A 2.10 m rope attaches a tire to an overhanging tree limb. A girl swinging on the tire has a tangential speed of 2.50 m/s. If the magnitude of the centripetal force is 88.0 N, what is the girl's mass?

2. A bicyclist is riding at a tangential speed of 13.2 m/s around a circular track. The magnitude of the centripetal force is 377 N, and the combined mass of the bicycle and rider is 86.5 kg. What is the track's radius?

3. A dog sits 1.50 m from the center of a merry-go-round and revolves at a tangential speed of 1.80 m/s. If the dog's mass is 18.5 kg, what is the magnitude of the centripetal force on the dog?

4. A 905 kg car travels around a circular track with a circumference of 3.25 km. If the magnitude of the centripetal force is 2140 N, what is the car's tangential speed?

FIGURE 1.5

Removal of Centripetal Force
A ball that is on the end of a string is whirled in a vertical circular path. If the string breaks at the position shown in **(a)**, the ball will move vertically upward in free fall. **(b)** If the string breaks at the top of the ball's path, the ball will move along a parabolic path.

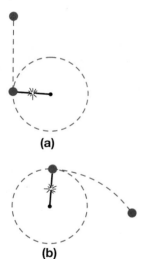

(a)

(b)

Centripetal force is necessary for circular motion.

Because centripetal force acts at right angles to an object's circular motion, the force changes the direction of the object's velocity. If this force vanishes, the object stops moving in a circular path. Instead, the object moves along a straight path that is tangent to the circle.

For example, consider a ball that is attached to a string and that is whirled in a vertical circle, as shown in **Figure 1.5**. If the string breaks when the ball is at the position shown in **Figure 1.5(a)**, the centripetal force will vanish. Thus, the ball will move vertically upward, as if it has been thrown straight up in the air. If the string breaks when the ball is at the top of its circular path, as shown in **Figure 1.5(b)**, the ball will fly off horizontally in a direction tangent to the path. The ball will then move in the parabolic path of a projectile.

Describing a Rotating System

To better understand the motion of a rotating system, consider a car traveling at high speed and approaching an exit ramp that curves to the left. As the driver makes the sharp left turn, the passenger slides to the right and hits the door. At that point, the force of the door keeps the passenger from being ejected from the car. What causes the passenger to move toward the door? A popular explanation is that a force must push the passenger outward. This force is sometimes called the *centrifugal force*, but that term often creates confusion, so it is not used in this textbook.

Inertia is often misinterpreted as a force.

The phenomenon is correctly explained as follows: Before the car enters the ramp, the passenger is moving in a straight path. As the car enters the ramp and travels along a curved path, the passenger, because of inertia, tends to move along the original straight path. This movement is in accordance with Newton's first law, which states that the natural tendency of a body is to continue moving in a straight line.

However, if a sufficiently large centripetal force acts on the passenger, the person will move along the same curved path that the car does. The origin of the centripetal force is the force of friction between the passenger and the car seat. If this frictional force is not sufficient, the passenger slides across the seat as the car turns underneath, as shown in **Figure 1.6**. Eventually, the passenger encounters the door, which provides a large enough force to enable the passenger to follow the same curved path as the car does. The passenger does not slide toward the door because of some mysterious outward force. Instead, the frictional force exerted on the passenger by the seat is not great enough to keep the passenger moving in the same circle as the car.

FIGURE 1.6

Path of Car and Passenger The force of friction on the passenger is not enough to keep the passenger on the same curved path as the car.

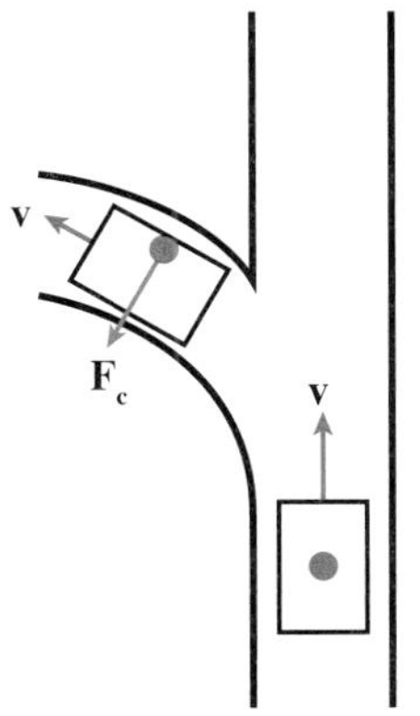

SECTION 1 FORMATIVE ASSESSMENT

▶ Reviewing Main Ideas

1. What are three examples of circular motion?

2. A girl on a spinning amusement park ride is 12 m from the center of the ride and has a centripetal acceleration of 17 m/s². What is the girl's tangential speed?

3. Use an example to describe the difference between tangential and centripetal acceleration.

4. Identify the forces that contribute to the centripetal force on the object in each of the following examples:
   a. a *bicyclist* moving around a flat, circular track
   b. a *bicycle* moving around a flat, circular track
   c. a *racecar* turning a corner on a steeply banked curve

5. A 90.0 kg person rides a spinning amusement park ride that has a radius of 11.5 m. If the person's tangential speed is 13.2 m/s, what is the magnitude of the centripetal force acting on the person?

6. Explain what makes a passenger in a turning car slide toward the door.

✔ Critical Thinking

7. A roller coaster's passengers are suspended upside down as it moves at a constant speed through a vertical loop. What is the direction of the force that causes the coaster and its passengers to move in a circle? What provides this force?

Objectives

▷ Explain how Newton's law of universal gravitation accounts for various phenomena, including satellite and planetary orbits, falling objects, and the tides.

▷ Apply Newton's law of universal gravitation to solve problems.

SC.912.E.5.2 Identify patterns in the organization and distribution of matter in the universe and the forces that determine them.
SC.912.E.5.6 Develop logical connections through physical principles, including Kepler's and Newton's Laws about the relationships and the effects of Earth, Moon, and Sun on each other.
SC.912.P.12.4 Describe how the gravitational force between two objects depends on their masses and the distance between them.

gravitational force the mutual force of attraction between particles of matter

Newton's Law of Universal Gravitation

Key Term
gravitational force

Gravitational Force

Earth and many of the other planets in our solar system travel in nearly circular orbits around the sun. Thus, a centripetal force must keep them in orbit. One of Isaac Newton's great achievements was the realization that the centripetal force that holds the planets in orbit is the very same force that pulls an apple toward the ground—**gravitational force.**

Orbiting objects are in free fall.

To see how this idea is true, we can use a thought experiment that Newton developed. Consider a cannon sitting on a high mountaintop, as shown in **Figure 2.1.** The path of each cannonball is a parabola, and the horizontal distance that each cannonball covers increases as the cannonball's initial speed increases. Newton realized that if an object were projected at just the right speed, the object would fall down toward Earth in just the same way that Earth curved out from under it. In other words, it would orbit Earth. In this case, the gravitational force between the cannonball and Earth is a centripetal force that keeps the cannonball in orbit. Satellites stay in orbit for this same reason. Thus, the force that pulls an apple toward Earth is the same force that keeps the moon and other satellites in orbit around Earth. Similarly, a gravitational attraction between Earth and our sun keeps Earth in its orbit around the sun.

FIGURE 2.1

Newton's Thought Experiment

Each successive cannonball has a greater initial speed, so the horizontal distance that the ball travels increases. If the initial speed is great enough, the curvature of Earth will cause the cannonball to continue falling without ever landing.

Gravitational force depends on the masses and the distance.

Newton developed the following equation to describe quantitatively the magnitude of the gravitational force if distance r separates masses m_1 and m_2:

Newton's Law of Universal Gravitation

$$F_g = G\frac{m_1 m_2}{r^2}$$

$$\text{gravitational force} = \text{constant} \times \frac{\text{mass 1} \times \text{mass 2}}{(\text{distance between masses})^2}$$

G is called the *constant of universal gravitation*. The value of G was unknown in Newton's day, but experiments have since determined the value to be as follows:

$$G = 6.673 \times 10^{-11} \frac{\text{N} \cdot \text{m}^2}{\text{kg}^2}$$

Newton demonstrated that the gravitational force that a spherical mass exerts on a particle outside the sphere would be the same if the entire mass of the sphere were concentrated at the sphere's center. When calculating the gravitational force between Earth and our sun, for example, you use the distance between their centers.

Gravitational force acts between all masses.

Gravitational force always attracts objects to one another, as shown in **Figure 2.2.** The force that the moon exerts on Earth is equal and opposite to the force that Earth exerts on the moon. This relationship is an example of Newton's third law of motion. Note that the gravitational forces shown in **Figure 2.2** are centripetal forces. Also, note that the gravitational force shown in **Figure 2.2** that acts on the moon is the centripetal force that causes the moon to move in its almost circular path around Earth. The centripetal force on Earth, however, is less obvious, because Earth is much more massive than the moon. Rather than orbiting the moon, Earth moves in a small circular path around a point inside Earth.

Gravitational force exists between any two masses, regardless of size. For instance, desks in a classroom have a mutual attraction because of gravitational force. The force between the desks, however, is negligibly small relative to the force between each desk and Earth because of the differences in mass.

If gravitational force acts between all masses, why doesn't Earth accelerate up toward a falling apple? In fact, it does! But Earth's acceleration is so tiny that you cannot detect it. Because Earth's mass is so large and acceleration is inversely proportional to mass, the Earth's acceleration is negligible. The apple has a much smaller mass and thus a much greater acceleration.

FIGURE 2.2

Gravitational Force The gravitational force attracts Earth and the moon to each other. According to Newton's third law, $F_{Em} = -F_{mE}$.

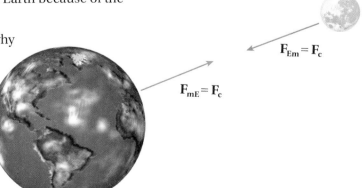

$$F_{Em} = F_c$$

$$F_{mE} = F_c$$

Gravitational Force

Sample Problem C The sun has a mass of 2.0×10^{30} kg and a radius of 7.0×10^5 km. What mass must be located at the sun's surface for a gravitational force of 470 N to exist between the mass and the sun?

1 ANALYZE

Given:
$$m_1 = 2.0 \times 10^{30} \text{ kg}$$
$$r = 7.0 \times 10^5 \text{ km} = 7.0 \times 10^8 \text{ m}$$
$$G = 6.673 \times 10^{-11} \text{ N·m}^2/\text{kg}^2$$
$$F_g = 470 \text{ N}$$

Unknown: $m_2 = ?$

2 SOLVE

Use Newton's universal law of gravitation, and rearrange it to solve for the second mass.

$$F_g = G\frac{m_1 m_2}{r^2}$$

$$m_2 = \frac{F_g r^2}{G m_1} = \frac{(470 \text{ N})(7.0 \times 10^8 \text{ m})^2}{\left(6.673 \times 10^{-11} \frac{\text{N·m}^2}{\text{kg}^2}\right)(2.0 \times 10^{30} \text{ kg})}$$

$$m_2 = \boxed{1.7 \text{ kg}}$$

Practice

1. The passenger liners *Carnival Destiny* and *Grand Princess* have a mass of about 1.0×10^8 kg each. How far apart must these two ships be to exert a gravitational attraction of 1.0×10^{-3} N on each other?

2. Jupiter, the largest planet in the solar system, has a mass 318 times that of Earth and a volume that is 1323 times greater than Earth's. Calculate the magnitude of the gravitational force exerted on a 50.0 kg mass on Jupiter's surface.

3. Predict the magnitude of the gravitational force a 66.5 kg person would experience while standing on the surface of each of the following celestial bodies:

Celestial Body	Mass	Radius
a. Earth	5.97×10^{24} kg	6.38×10^6 m
b. Mars	6.42×10^{23} kg	3.40×10^6 m
c. Pluto	1.25×10^{22} kg	1.20×10^6 m

Black Holes

This artist's conception shows a disk of material orbiting a black hole. Such disks provide indirect evidence of black holes within our own galaxy.

A black hole is an object that is so massive that nothing, not even light, can escape the pull of its gravity. In 1916, Karl Schwarzschild was the first person to suggest the existence of black holes. He used his solutions to Einstein's general-relativity equations to explain the properties of black holes. In 1967, the physicist John Wheeler coined the term *black hole* to describe these objects.

In order for an object to escape the gravitational pull of a planet, such as Earth, the object must be moving away from the planet faster than a certain threshold speed, which is called the *escape velocity*. The escape velocity at the surface of Earth is about 1.1×10^4 m/s, or about 25 000 mi/h.

The escape velocity for a black hole is greater than the speed of light. And according to Einstein's special theory of relativity, no object can move at a speed greater than or equal to the speed of light. Thus, no object that is within a certain distance of a black hole can move fast enough to escape the gravitational pull of the black hole. That distance, called the *Schwarzschild radius*, defines the edge, or *horizon*, of a black hole.

Newton's laws say that only objects with mass can be subject to forces. How can a black hole trap light if light has no mass? According to Einstein's general theory of relativity, any object with mass bends the fabric of space and time itself. When an object that has mass or even when a ray of light passes near another object, the path of the moving object or ray curves because space-time itself is curved. The curvature is so great inside a black hole that the path of any light that might be emitted from the black hole bends back toward the black hole and remains trapped inside the horizon.

Because black holes trap light, they cannot be observed directly. Instead, astronomers must look for indirect evidence of black holes. For example, astronomers have observed stars orbiting very rapidly around the centers of some galaxies. By measuring the speed of the orbits, astronomers can calculate the mass of the dark object—the black hole—that must be at the galaxy's center. Black holes at the centers of galaxies typically have masses millions or billions of times the mass of the sun.

The figure above shows a disk of material orbiting a black hole. Material that orbits a black hole can move at such high speeds and have so much energy that the material emits x-rays. From observations of the x-rays coming from such disks, scientists have discovered several black holes within our own galaxy.

This image from NASA's Chandra X-ray Observatory is of Sagittarius A*, which is a supermassive black hole at the center of our galaxy. Astronomers are studying the image to learn more about Sagittarius A* and about black holes in the centers of other galaxies.

Applying the Law of Gravitation

For about six hours, water slowly rises along the shoreline of many coastal areas and culminates in a high tide. The water level then slowly lowers for about six hours and returns to a low tide. This cycle then repeats. Tides take place in all bodies of water but are most noticeable along seacoasts. In the Bay of Fundy, shown in **Figure 2.3,** the water rises as much as 16 m from its low point. Because a high tide happens about every 12 hours, there are usually two high tides and two low tides each day. Before Newton developed the law of universal gravitation, no one could explain why tides occur in this pattern.

Newton's law of gravitation accounts for ocean tides.

High and low tides are partly due to the gravitational force exerted on Earth by its moon. The tides result from the *difference* between the gravitational force at Earth's surface and at Earth's center. A full explanation is beyond the scope of this text, but we will briefly examine this relationship.

The two high tides take place at locations on Earth that are nearly in line with the moon. On the side of Earth that is nearest to the moon, the moon's gravitational force is *greater* than it is at Earth's center (because gravitational force decreases with distance). The water is pulled toward the moon, creating an outward bulge. On the opposite side of Earth, the gravitational force is *less* than it is at the center. On this side, all mass is still pulled toward the moon, but the water is pulled least. This creates another outward bulge. Two high tides take place each day at a given point because when Earth rotates one full time, that point will pass through both bulges.

The moon's gravitational force is not the only factor that affects ocean tides. Other influencing factors include the depths of the ocean basins, Earth's tilt and rotation, and friction between the ocean water and the ocean floor. The sun also contributes to Earth's ocean tides, but the sun's effect is not as significant as the moon's is. Although the sun exerts a much greater gravitational force on Earth than the moon does, the *difference* between the force on the far and near sides of Earth is what affects the tides.

FIGURE 2.3

High and Low Tides Some of the world's highest tides occur at the Bay of Fundy, which is between New Brunswick and Nova Scotia, Canada. These photographs show a river outlet to the Bay of Fundy at low and high tide.

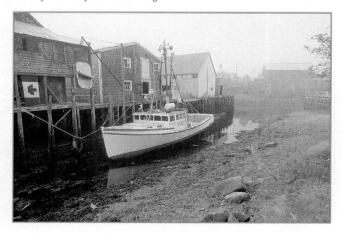
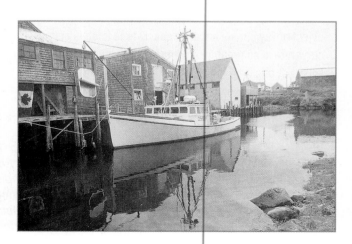

FIGURE 2.4

Gravity Experiment Henry Cavendish used an experiment similar to this one to determine the value of *G*.

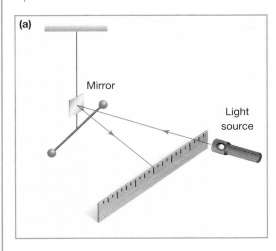

(a) Mirror
Light source

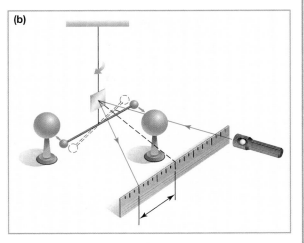

(b)

Cavendish finds the value of *G* and Earth's mass.

In 1798, Henry Cavendish conducted an experiment that determined the value of the constant *G*. This experiment is illustrated in **Figure 2.4.** As shown in **Figure 2.4(a),** two small spheres are fixed to the ends of a suspended light rod. These two small spheres are attracted to two larger spheres by the gravitational force, as shown in **Figure 2.4(b).** The angle of rotation is measured with a light beam and is then used to determine the gravitational force between the spheres. When the masses, the distance between them, and the gravitational force are known, Newton's law of universal gravitation can be used to find *G*. Once the value of *G* is known, the law can be used again to find Earth's mass.

Gravity is a field force.

Newton was not able to explain how objects can exert forces on one another without coming into contact. His mathematical theory described gravity but didn't explain how it worked. Later work also showed that Newton's laws are not accurate for very small objects or for those moving near the speed of light. Scientists later developed a theory of fields to explain how gravity and other field forces operate. According to this theory, masses create a gravitational field in space. A gravitational force is an interaction between a mass and the gravitational field created by other masses.

When you raise a ball to a certain height above Earth, the ball gains potential energy. Where is this potential energy stored? The physical properties of the ball and of Earth have not changed. However, the gravitational field between the ball and Earth *has* changed since the ball has changed position relative to Earth. According to field theory, the gravitational energy is stored in the gravitational field itself.

*Quick*LAB

MATERIALS
- spring scale
- hook (of a known mass)
- various masses

GRAVITATIONAL FIELD STRENGTH

You can attach a mass to a spring scale to find the gravitational force that is acting on that mass. Attach various combinations of masses to the hook, and record the force in each case. Use your data to calculate the gravitational field strength for each trial ($g = F_g/m$). Be sure that your calculations account for the mass of the hook. Average your values to find the gravitational field strength at your location on Earth's surface. Do you notice anything about the value you obtained?

FIGURE 2.5

Earth's Gravitational Field

The gravitational field vectors represent Earth's gravitational field at each point. Note that the field has the same strength at equal distances from Earth's center.

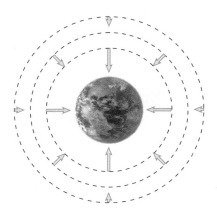

Conceptual Challenge

Gravity on the Moon The magnitude of g on the moon's surface is about $\frac{1}{6}$ of the value of g on Earth's surface. Can you infer from this relationship that the moon's mass is $\frac{1}{6}$ of Earth's mass? Why or why not?

Selling Gold A scam artist hopes to make a profit by buying and selling gold at different altitudes for the same price per weight. Should the scam artist buy or sell at the higher altitude? Explain.

At any point, Earth's gravitational field can be described by the *gravitational field strength*, abbreviated g. The value of g is equal to the magnitude of the gravitational force exerted on a unit mass at that point, or $g = F_g/m$. The gravitational field (**g**) is a vector with a magnitude of g that points in the direction of the gravitational force.

Gravitational field strength equals free-fall acceleration.

Consider an object that is free to accelerate and is acted on only by gravitational force. According to Newton's second law, $\mathbf{a} = \mathbf{F}/m$. As seen earlier, **g** is defined as $\mathbf{F_g}/m$, where $\mathbf{F_g}$ is gravitational force. Thus, the value of g at any given point is equal to the acceleration due to gravity. For this reason, $g = 9.81 \text{ m/s}^2$ on Earth's surface. Although gravitational field strength and free-fall acceleration are equivalent, they are not the same thing. For instance, when you hang an object from a spring scale, you are measuring gravitational field strength. Because the mass is at rest (in a frame of reference fixed to Earth's surface), there is no measurable acceleration.

Figure 2.5 shows gravitational field vectors at different points around Earth. As shown in the figure, gravitational field strength rapidly decreases as the distance from Earth increases, as you would expect from the inverse-square nature of Newton's law of universal gravitation.

Weight changes with location.

In the chapter about forces, you learned that weight is the magnitude of the force due to gravity, which equals mass times free-fall acceleration. We can now refine our definition of weight as mass times gravitational field strength. The two definitions are mathematically equivalent, but our new definition helps to explain why your weight changes with your location in the universe.

Newton's law of universal gravitation shows that the value of g depends on mass and distance. For example, consider a tennis ball of mass m. The gravitational force between the tennis ball and Earth is as follows:

$$F_g = \frac{Gmm_E}{r^2}$$

Combining this equation with the definition for gravitational field strength yields the following expression for g:

$$g = \frac{F_g}{m} = \frac{Gmm_E}{mr^2} = \frac{Gm_E}{r^2}$$

This equation shows that gravitational field strength depends only on mass and distance. Thus, as your distance from Earth's center increases, the value of g decreases, so your weight also decreases. On the surface of any planet, the value of g, as well as your weight, will depend on the planet's mass and radius.

Gravitational mass equals inertial mass.

Because gravitational field strength equals free-fall acceleration, free-fall acceleration on the surface of Earth likewise depends only on Earth's mass and radius. Free-fall acceleration does not depend on the falling object's mass, because *m* cancels from each side of the equation, as shown on the previous page.

Although we are assuming that the *m* in each equation is the same, this assumption was not always an accepted scientific fact. In Newton's second law, *m* is sometimes called *inertial mass*, because this *m* refers to the property of an object to resist acceleration. In Newton's gravitation equation, *m* is sometimes called *gravitational mass*, because this *m* relates to how objects attract one another.

How do we know that inertial and gravitational mass are equal? The fact that the acceleration of objects in free fall on Earth's surface is always the same confirms that the two types of masses are equal. A more massive object experiences a greater gravitational force, but the object resists acceleration by just that amount. For this reason, all masses fall with the same acceleration (disregarding air resistance).

There is no obvious reason that the two types of masses should be equal. For instance, the property of electric charges that causes them to be attracted or repelled was originally called *electrical mass*. Even though this term has the word *mass* in it, electrical *mass* has no connection to gravitational or inertial mass. The equality between inertial and gravitational mass has been continually tested and has thus far always held up.

 SECTION 2 **FORMATIVE ASSESSMENT**

▶ Reviewing Main Ideas

1. Explain how the force due to gravity keeps a satellite in orbit.

2. Is there gravitational force between two students sitting in a classroom? If so, explain why you don't observe any effects of this force.

3. Earth has a mass of 5.97×10^{24} kg and a radius of 6.38×10^6 m, while Saturn has a mass of 5.68×10^{26} kg and a radius of 6.03×10^7 m. Predict the weight of a 65.0 kg person at the following locations:
   a. on the surface of Earth
   b. 1000 km above the surface of Earth
   c. on the surface of Saturn
   d. 1000 km above the surface of Saturn

4. What is the magnitude of *g* at a height above Earth's surface where free-fall acceleration equals 6.5 m/s²?

✔ Critical Thinking

5. Suppose the value of *G* has just been discovered. Use the value of *G* and an approximate value for Earth's radius (6.38×10^6 m) to find an approximation for Earth's mass.

Motion in Space

Kepler's Laws

People have studied the motions of the planets since ancient times. Until the middle of the 16th century, most people believed that Earth was at the center of the universe. Originally, it was believed that the sun and other planets orbited Earth in perfect circles. However, this model did not account for all of the observations of planetary motion.

In the second century CE, Claudius Ptolemy developed an elaborate theory of planetary motion. Ptolemy's theory attempted to reconcile observation with theory and to keep Earth at the center of the universe. In this theory, planets travel in small circles called *epicycles* while simultaneously traveling in larger circular orbits. Even Ptolemy's complex model did not fully agree with observation, although the model did explain more than previous theories.

In 1543, the Polish astronomer Nicolaus Copernicus (1473–1543) published *On the Revolutions of the Heavenly Spheres*, in which he proposed that Earth and other planets orbit the sun in perfect circles. **Figure 3.1** shows a sun-centered planetary model that is believed to have been made for King George III of England. The idea of a sun-centered universe was not completely new in the 16th century. A Greek named Aristarchus theorized 1700 years before Copernicus did that Earth revolved around the sun, but most other scientists did not accept his theory.

Kepler's three laws describe the motion of the planets.

The astronomer Tycho Brahe (1546–1601) made many precise observations of the planets and stars. However, some of Brahe's data did not agree with the Copernican model. The astronomer Johannes Kepler (1571–1630) worked for many years to reconcile Copernican theory with Brahe's data. Kepler's analysis led to three laws of planetary motion, which were developed a generation before Newton's law of universal gravitation. Kepler's three laws can be summarized as follows.

FIGURE 3.1

Planetary Model This elaborate planetary model—called an *orrery*—shows the motions of Mercury, Venus, and Earth around the sun. The model also shows the moon's inclined orbit around Earth.

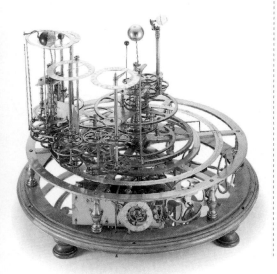

Kepler's Laws of Planetary Motion

First Law: Each planet travels in an elliptical orbit around the sun, and the sun is at one of the focal points.

Second Law: An imaginary line drawn from the sun to any planet sweeps out equal areas in equal time intervals.

Third Law: The square of a planet's orbital period (T^2) is proportional to the cube of the average distance (r^3) between the planet and the sun, or $T^2 \propto r^3$.

Kepler's first law states that the planets' orbits are ellipses rather than circles. Kepler discovered this law while working with Brahe's data for the orbit of Mars. While trying to explain the data, Kepler experimented with 70 different circular orbits and generated numerous pages of calculations. He finally realized that if the orbit is an ellipse rather than a circle and the sun is at one focal point of the ellipse, the data fit perfectly.

Kepler's second law states that an imaginary line from the sun to any planet sweeps out equal areas in equal times, as shown in **Figure 3.2**. In other words, if the time a planet takes to travel the arc on the left (Δt_1) is equal to the time the planet takes to cover the arc on the right (Δt_2), then the area A_1 is equal to the area A_2. It is easy to see from **Figure 3.2** that planets travel faster when they are closer to the sun.

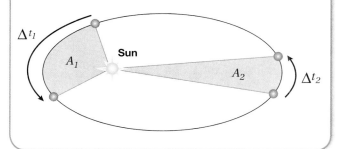

FIGURE 3.2

Kepler's Second Law This diagram illustrates a planet moving in an elliptical orbit around the sun. If Δt_1 equals Δt_2, then the two shaded areas are equal. Thus, the planet travels faster when it is closer to the sun and slower when it is farther away.

While Kepler's first two laws describe the motion of each planet individually, his third law relates the orbital periods and distances of one planet to those of another planet. The orbital period (T) is the time a planet takes to finish one full revolution, and the distance (r) is the mean distance between the planet and the sun. Kepler's third law relates the orbital period and mean distance for two orbiting planets as follows:

$$\frac{T_1^{\,2}}{T_2^{\,2}} = \frac{r_1^{\,3}}{r_2^{\,3}}, \text{ or } T^2 \propto r^3$$

This law also applies to satellites orbiting Earth, including our moon. In that case, r is the distance between the orbiting satellite and Earth. The proportionality constant depends on the mass of the central object.

Kepler's laws are consistent with Newton's law of gravitation.

Newton used Kepler's laws to support his law of gravitation. For example, Newton proved that if force is inversely proportional to distance squared, as stated in the law of universal gravitation, the resulting orbit must be an ellipse or a circle. He also demonstrated that his law of gravitation could be used to derive Kepler's third law. (Try a similar derivation yourself in the QuickLab below.) The fact that Kepler's laws closely matched observations gave additional support for Newton's theory of gravitation.

QuickLAB | **KEPLER'S THIRD LAW**

You can mathematically show how Kepler's third law can be derived from Newton's law of universal gravitation (assuming circular orbits). To begin, recall that the centripetal force is provided by the gravitational force. Set the equations for gravitational and centripetal force equal to one another, and solve for v_t^2. Because speed equals distance divided by time and because the distance for one period is the circumference ($2\pi r$), $v_t = 2\pi r/T$. Square this value, substitute the squared value into your previous equation, and then isolate T^2. How does your result relate to Kepler's third law?

Did YOU Know?

We generally speak of the moon orbiting Earth, but they are actually both in orbit around a point in the Earth-moon system. Because Earth is so much more massive than the moon, the point they orbit around lies inside Earth. Thus, the moon appears to orbit Earth. The point around which two bodies orbit does not always lie inside one of the bodies, however. For example, Pluto and its moon Charon orbit a point that lies between them. Also, many binary star systems have two stars that orbit a common center between the stars.

Kepler's third law describes orbital period.

According to Kepler's third law, $T^2 \propto r^3$. The constant of proportionality between these two variables turns out to be $4\pi^2/Gm$, where m is the mass of the object being orbited. (To learn why this is the case, try the QuickLab on the previous page.) Thus, Kepler's third law can also be stated as follows:

$$T^2 = \left(\frac{4\pi^2}{Gm}\right) r^3$$

The square root of the above equation, which is shown below on the left, describes the period of any object that is in a circular orbit. The speed of an object that is in a circular orbit depends on the same factors that the period does, as shown in the equation on the right. The assumption of a circular orbit provides a close approximation for real orbits in our solar system, because all planets except Mercury have orbits that are nearly circular.

Period and Speed of an Object in Circular Orbit

$$T = 2\pi\sqrt{\frac{r^3}{Gm}} \qquad v_t = \sqrt{G\frac{m}{r}}$$

$$\textbf{orbital period} = 2\pi\sqrt{\frac{\textbf{(mean radius)}^3}{\textbf{(constant)(mass of central object)}}}$$

$$\textbf{orbital speed} = \sqrt{\textbf{(constant)}\left(\frac{\textbf{mass of central object}}{\textbf{mean radius}}\right)}$$

Note that m in both equations is the mass of the central object that is being orbited. The mass of the planet or satellite that is in orbit does not affect its speed or period. The mean radius (r) is the distance between the centers of the two bodies. For an artificial satellite orbiting Earth, r is equal to Earth's mean radius plus the satellite's distance from Earth's surface (its "altitude"). **Figure 3.3** gives planetary data that can be used to calculate orbital speeds and periods.

FIGURE 3.3

CELESTIAL BODY DATA

Body	Mass (kg)	Mean radius (m)	Mean distance from sun (m)	Body	Mass (kg)	Mean radius (m)	Mean distance from sun (m)
Earth	5.97×10^{24}	6.38×10^{6}	1.50×10^{11}	**Neptune**	1.02×10^{26}	2.48×10^{7}	4.50×10^{12}
Earth's moon	7.35×10^{22}	1.74×10^{6}	—	**Saturn**	5.68×10^{26}	6.03×10^{7}	1.43×10^{12}
Jupiter	1.90×10^{27}	7.15×10^{7}	7.79×10^{11}	**Sun**	1.99×10^{30}	6.96×10^{8}	—
Mars	6.42×10^{23}	3.40×10^{6}	2.28×10^{11}	**Uranus**	8.68×10^{25}	2.56×10^{7}	2.87×10^{12}
Mercury	3.30×10^{23}	2.44×10^{6}	5.79×10^{10}	**Venus**	4.87×10^{24}	6.05×10^{6}	1.08×10^{11}

Period and Speed of an Orbiting Object

GO ONLINE

SOLUTION TUTOR

HMHScience.com

Sample Problem D The color-enhanced image of Venus shown here was compiled from data taken by *Magellan*, the first planetary spacecraft to be launched from a space shuttle. During the spacecraft's fifth orbit around Venus, *Magellan* traveled at a mean altitude of 361 km. If the orbit had been circular, what would *Magellan's* period and speed have been?

① ANALYZE

Given: $r_1 = 361 \text{ km} = 3.61 \times 10^5 \text{ m}$

Unknown: $T = ?$

$v_t = ?$

② PLAN

Choose an equation or situation: Use the equations for the period and speed of an object in a circular orbit.

$$T = 2\pi \sqrt{\frac{r^3}{Gm}} \qquad v_t = \sqrt{G\frac{m}{r}}$$

Use **Figure 3.3** to find the values for the radius (r_2) and mass (m) of Venus.

$$r_2 = 6.05 \times 10^6 \text{ m} \qquad m = 4.87 \times 10^{24} \text{ kg}$$

Find r by adding the distance between the spacecraft and Venus's surface (r_1) to Venus's radius (r_2).

$$r = r_1 + r_2 = (3.61 \times 10^5 \text{ m}) + (6.05 \times 10^6 \text{ m}) = 6.41 \times 10^6 \text{ m}$$

③ SOLVE

Substitute the values into the equations, and solve:

$$T = 2\pi \sqrt{\frac{(6.41 \times 10^6 \text{ m})^3}{\left(6.673 \times 10^{-11} \frac{\text{N} \cdot \text{m}^2}{\text{kg}^2}\right)(4.87 \times 10^{24} \text{ kg})}} = \boxed{5.66 \times 10^3 \text{ s}}$$

$$v_t = \sqrt{\left(6.673 \times 10^{-11} \frac{\text{N} \cdot \text{m}^2}{\text{kg}^2}\right)\left(\frac{4.87 \times 10^{24} \text{ kg}}{6.41 \times 10^6 \text{ m}}\right)} = \boxed{7.12 \times 10^3 \text{ m/s}}$$

④ CHECK YOUR WORK

Magellan takes $(5.66 \times 10^3 \text{ s})(1 \text{ min}/60 \text{ s}) \approx 94 \text{ min}$ to complete one orbit.

Practice

1. Find the orbital speed and period that the *Magellan* satellite from Sample Problem D would have at the same mean altitude above Earth, Jupiter, and Earth's moon.

2. At what distance above Earth would a satellite have a period of 125 min?

Weight and Weightlessness

In the chapter about forces, you learned that weight is the magnitude of the force due to gravity. When you step on a bathroom scale, it does not actually measure your weight. The scale measures the downward force exerted on it. When your weight is the only downward force acting on the scale, the scale reading equals your weight. If a friend pushes down on you while you are standing on the scale, the scale reading will go up. However, your weight has not changed; the scale reading equals your weight plus the extra applied force. Because of Newton's third law, the downward force you exert on the scale equals the upward force exerted on you by the scale (the normal force). Thus, the scale reading is equal to the normal force acting on you.

For example, imagine you are standing in an elevator, as illustrated in **Figure 3.4.** When the elevator is at rest, as in **Figure 3.4(a),** the magnitude of the normal force is equal to your weight. A scale in the elevator would record your weight. When the elevator begins accelerating downward, as in **Figure 3.4(b),** the normal force will be smaller. The scale would now record an amount that is less than your weight. If the elevator's acceleration were equal to free-fall acceleration, as shown in **Figure 3.4(c),** you would be falling at the same rate as the elevator and would not feel the force of the floor at all. In this case, the scale would read zero. You still have the same weight, but you and the elevator are both falling with free-fall acceleration. In other words, no normal force is acting on you. This situation is called *apparent weightlessness*.

Astronauts in orbit experience apparent weightlessness.

Astronauts floating in a space shuttle are experiencing apparent weightlessness. Because the shuttle is accelerating at the same rate as the astronauts are, this example is similar to the elevator in **Figure 3.4(c).**

FIGURE 3.4

Normal Force in an Elevator When this elevator accelerates, the normal force acting on the person changes. If the elevator were in free fall, the normal force would drop to zero, and the person would experience a sensation of apparent weightlessness.

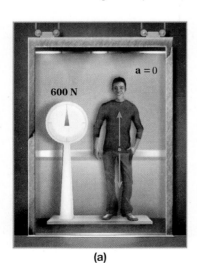

(a)

(b)

(c)

The force due to gravity keeps the astronauts and shuttle in orbit, but the astronauts *feel* weightless because no normal force is acting on them.

The human body relies on gravitational force. For example, this force pulls blood downward so that the blood collects in the veins of your legs when you are standing. Because the body of an astronaut in orbit accelerates along with the space shuttle, gravitational force has no effect on the body. This state can initially cause nausea and dizziness. Over time, it can pose serious health risks, such as weakened muscles and brittle bones. When astronauts return to Earth, their bodies need time to readjust to the effects of the gravitational force.

So far, we have been describing apparent weightlessness. Actual weightlessness occurs only in deep space, far from stars and planets. Gravitational force is never entirely absent, but it can become negligible at distances that are far enough away from any masses. In this case, a star or astronaut would not be pulled into an orbit but would instead drift in a straight line at constant speed.

SECTION 3 FORMATIVE ASSESSMENT

▶ Reviewing Main Ideas

1. Compare Ptolemy's model of the solar system with Copernicus's. How does Kepler's first law of planetary motion refine Copernicus's model?

2. Does a planet in orbit around the sun travel at a constant speed? How do you know?

3. Suppose you know the mean distance between both Mercury and the sun and Venus and the sun. You also know the period of Venus's orbit around the sun. How can you find the period of Mercury's orbit?

4. Explain how Kepler's laws of planetary motion relate to Newton's law of universal gravitation.

5. Find the orbital speed and period of Earth's moon. The average distance between the centers of Earth and of the moon is 3.84×10^8 m.

✔ Critical Thinking

6. An amusement park ride raises people high into the air, suspends them for a moment, and then drops them at the rate of free-fall acceleration. Is a person in this ride experiencing apparent weightlessness, true weightlessness, or neither? Explain.

7. Suppose you went on the ride described in item 6, held a penny in front of you, and released the penny at the moment the ride started to drop. What would you observe?

Objectives

- Distinguish between torque and force.

- Calculate the magnitude of a torque on an object.

- Identify the six types of simple machines.

- Calculate the mechanical advantage of a simple machine.

Torque and Simple Machines

Key Terms

torque   lever arm

Rotational Motion

Earlier you studied various examples of uniform circular motion, such as a spinning Ferris wheel or an orbiting satellite. During uniform circular motion, an object moves in a circular path and at constant speed. An object that is in circular motion is accelerating, because the direction of the object's velocity is constantly changing. This centripetal acceleration is directed toward the center of the circle. The net force causing the acceleration is a centripetal force, which is also directed toward the center of the circle.

In this section, we will examine a related type of motion: the motion of a rotating rigid object. For example, consider a football that is spinning as it flies through the air. If gravity is the only force acting on the football, the football spins around a point called its *center of mass*. As the football moves through the air, its center of mass follows a parabolic path. Note that the center of mass is not always at the center of the object.

Rotational and translational motion can be separated.

Imagine that you roll a strike while bowling. When the bowling ball strikes the pins, as shown in **Figure 4.1**, the pins spin in the air as they fly backward. Thus, they have both rotational and linear motion. These types of motion can be analyzed separately. In this section, we will isolate rotational motion. In particular, we will explore how to measure the ability of a force to rotate an object.

FIGURE 4.1

Types of Motion Pins that are spinning and flying through the air exhibit both rotational and translational motion.

©Doable/A. collection/Getty Images

The Magnitude of a Torque

Imagine a cat trying to leave a house by pushing perpendicularly on a cat-flap door. **Figure 4.2** shows a cat-flap door hinged at the top. In this configuration, the door is free to rotate around a line that passes through the hinge. This is the door's *axis of rotation*. When the cat pushes at the bottom edge of the door with a force that is perpendicular to the door, the door opens. The ability of a force to rotate an object around some axis is measured by a quantity called **torque**.

Torque depends on the force and the lever arm.

If a cat pushed on the door with the same force but at a point closer to the hinge, the door would be more difficult to rotate. How easily an object rotates depends not only on how much force is applied but also on where the force is applied. The farther the force is from the axis of rotation, the easier it is to rotate the object and the more torque is produced. The perpendicular distance from the axis of rotation to a line drawn along the direction of the force is called the **lever arm.**

Figure 4.3 shows a diagram of the force **F** applied by the pet perpendicular to the cat-flap door. If you examine the definition of *lever arm*, you will see that in this case the lever arm is the distance d shown in the figure, the distance from the pet's nose to the hinge. That is, d is the perpendicular distance from the axis of rotation to the line along which the applied force acts. If the pet pressed on the door at a higher point, the lever arm would be shorter. As a result, the cat would need to exert a greater force to apply the same torque.

FIGURE 4.2

Hinge Rotation The cat-flap door rotates on a hinge, allowing pets to enter and leave a house at will.

torque a quantity that measures the ability of a force to rotate an object around some axis

lever arm the perpendicular distance from the axis of rotation to a line drawn along the direction of the force

FIGURE 4.3

Torque A force applied to an extended object can produce a torque. This torque, in turn, causes the object to rotate. The axis of rotation is perpendicular to the page and passes through the black dot.

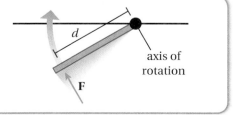

axis of rotation

QuickLAB | CHANGING THE LEVER ARM

In this activity, you will explore how the amount of force required to open a door changes when the lever arm changes. Using only perpendicular forces, open a door several times by applying a force at different distances from the hinge. You may have to tape the latch so that the door will open

when you push without turning the knob. Because the angle of the applied force is kept constant, decreasing the distance to the hinge decreases the lever arm. Compare the relative effort required to open the door when pushing near the edge to that required when pushing near

the hinged side of the door. Summarize your findings in terms of torque and the lever arm.

MATERIALS
- door
- masking tape

FIGURE 4.4

Torque and Angles In each example, the cat is pushing on the door at the same distance from the axis. To produce the same torque, the cat must apply greater force for smaller angles.

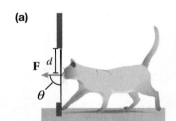

(a)

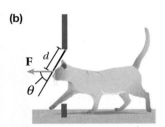

(b)

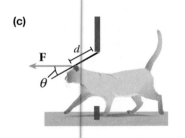

(c)

The lever arm depends on the angle.

Forces do not have to be perpendicular to an object to cause the object to rotate. Imagine the cat-flap door again. In **Figure 4.4(a),** the force exerted by the cat is perpendicular to d. When the angle is less than 90°, as in **(b)** and **(c),** the door will still rotate, but not as easily. The symbol for torque is the Greek letter *tau* (τ), and the magnitude of the torque is given by the following equation:

FIGURE 4.5

Torque and Its Sign The torque on the wrench about an axis through the bolt is positive because the applied force tends to rotate the wrench counterclockwise.

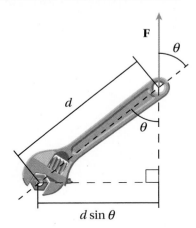

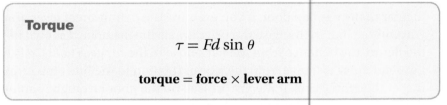

Torque

$$\tau = Fd \sin \theta$$

torque = force × lever arm

The SI unit of torque is the N•m. Notice that the inclusion of the factor $\sin \theta$ in this equation takes into account the changes in torque shown in **Figure 4.4.**

Figure 4.5 shows a wrench pivoted around a bolt. In this case, the applied force acts at an angle to the wrench. The quantity d is the distance from the axis of rotation to the point where force is applied. The quantity $d \sin \theta$, however, is the *perpendicular* distance from the axis of rotation to a line drawn along the direction of the force. Thus, $d \sin \theta$ is the lever arm. Note that the perpendicular distance between the door hinge and the point of application of force **F** in **Figure 4.4** decreases as the cat goes further through the door.

Tips and Tricks

To determine the sign of a torque, imagine that the force is the only force acting on the object and that the object is free to rotate. Visualize the direction that the object would rotate. If more than one force is acting, treat each force separately. Be careful to associate the correct sign with each torque.

The Sign of a Torque

Torque, like displacement and force, is a vector quantity. In this textbook, we will assign each torque a positive or negative sign, depending on the direction the force tends to rotate an object. We will use the convention that the sign of the torque resulting from a force is positive if the rotation is counterclockwise and negative if the rotation is clockwise. In calculations, remember to assign positive and negative values to forces and displacements according to the sign convention established in the chapter "Motion in One Dimension."

For example, imagine that you are pulling on a wishbone with a perpendicular force F_1 and that a friend is pulling in the opposite direction with a force F_2. If you pull the wishbone so that it would rotate counterclockwise, then you exert a positive torque of magnitude F_1d_1. Your friend, on the other hand, exerts a negative torque, $-F_2d_2$. To find the net torque acting on the wishbone, simply add up the individual torques.

$$\tau_{net} = \Sigma\tau = \tau_1 + \tau_2 = F_1d_1 + (-F_2d_2)$$

When you properly apply the sign convention, the sign of the net torque will tell you which way the object will rotate, if at all.

GO ONLINE

Interactive Demo
HMHScience.com

Torque

Sample Problem E A basketball is being pushed by two players during tip-off. One player exerts an upward force of 15 N at a perpendicular distance of 14 cm from the axis of rotation. The second player applies a downward force of 11 N at a perpendicular distance of 7.0 cm from the axis of rotation. Find the net torque acting on the ball about its center of mass.

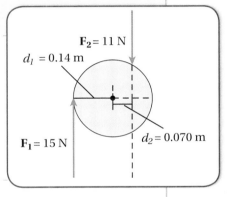

1 ANALYZE

Given: $F_1 = 15\text{ N}$ $F_2 = 11\text{ N}$
$d_1 = 0.14\text{ m}$ $d_2 = 0.070\text{ m}$

Unknown: $\tau_{net} = ?$

Diagram: see right

2 PLAN

Choose an equation or situation:
Apply the definition of torque to each force, and add up the individual torques.

$$\tau = Fd$$
$$\tau_{net} = \tau_1 + \tau_2 = F_1d_1 + F_2d_2$$

Tips and Tricks
The factor $\sin\theta$ is not included, because each given distance is the perpendicular distance from the axis of rotation to a line drawn along the direction of the force.

3 SOLVE

Substitute the values into the equations, and solve:
First, determine the torque produced by each force. Use the standard convention for signs.

$$\tau_1 = F_1d_1 = (15\text{ N})(-0.14\text{ m}) = -2.1\text{ N}\bullet\text{m}$$
$$\tau_2 = F_2d_2 = (-11\text{ N})(0.070\text{ m}) = -0.77\text{ N}\bullet\text{m}$$
$$\tau_{net} = -2.1\text{ N}\bullet\text{m} - 0.77\text{ N}\bullet\text{m}$$
$$\boxed{\tau_{net} = -2.9\text{ N}\bullet\text{m}}$$

4 CHECK YOUR WORK

The net torque is negative, so the ball rotates in a clockwise direction.

Continued

Practice

1. Find the magnitude of the torque produced by a 3.0 N force applied to a door at a perpendicular distance of 0.25 m from the hinge.

2. A simple pendulum consists of a 3.0 kg point mass hanging at the end of a 2.0 m long light string that is connected to a pivot point.

   a. Calculate the magnitude of the torque (due to gravitational force) around this pivot point when the string makes a 5.0° angle with the vertical.

   b. Repeat this calculation for an angle of 15.0°.

3. If the torque required to loosen a nut on the wheel of a car has a magnitude of 40.0 N•m, what *minimum* force must be exerted by a mechanic at the end of a 30.0 cm wrench to loosen the nut?

Types of Simple Machines

FIGURE 4.6

A Lever Because this bottle opener makes work easier, it is an example of a machine.

What do you do when you need to pry a cap off a bottle of soda? You probably use a bottle opener, as shown in **Figure 4.6**. Similarly, you would probably use scissors to cut paper or a hammer to drive a nail into a board. All of these devices make your task easier. These devices are all examples of *machines*.

The term *machine* may bring to mind intricate systems with multicolored wires and complex gear-and-pulley systems. Compared with internal-combustion engines or airplanes, simple devices such as hammers, scissors, and bottle openers may not seem like machines, but they are.

A machine is any device that transmits or modifies force, usually by changing the force applied to an object. All machines are combinations or modifications of six fundamental types of machines, called *simple machines*. These six simple machines are the lever, pulley, inclined plane, wheel and axle, wedge, and screw, as shown in **Figure 4.7** on the next page.

Using simple machines.

Because the purpose of a simple machine is to change the direction or magnitude of an input force, a useful way of characterizing a simple machine is to compare how large the output force is relative to the input force. This ratio, called the machine's *mechanical advantage*, is written as follows:

$$MA = \frac{\text{output force}}{\text{input force}} = \frac{F_{out}}{F_{in}}$$

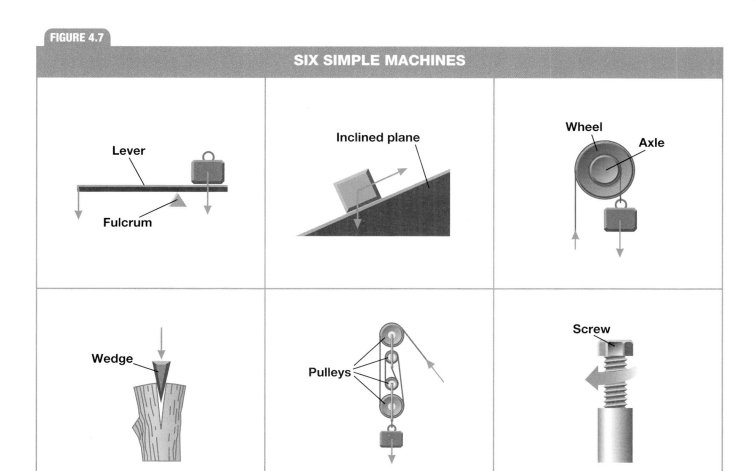

FIGURE 4.7

SIX SIMPLE MACHINES

Lever

Fulcrum

Inclined plane

Wheel

Axle

Wedge

Pulleys

Screw

One example of mechanical advantage is the use of the back of a hammer to pry a nail from a board. In this example, the hammer is a type of lever. A person applies an input force to one end of the handle. The handle, in turn, exerts an output force on the head of a nail stuck in a board. If friction is disregarded, the input torque will equal the output torque. This relation can be written as follows:

$$\tau_{in} = \tau_{out}$$

$$F_{in}d_{in} = F_{out}d_{out}$$

Substituting this expression into the definition of mechanical advantage gives the following result:

$$MA = \frac{F_{out}}{F_{in}} = \frac{d_{in}}{d_{out}}$$

The longer the input lever arm as compared with the output lever arm, the greater the mechanical advantage is. This in turn indicates the factor by which the input force is amplified. If the force of the board on the nail is 99 N and if the mechanical advantage is 10, then an input force of 10 N is enough to pull out the nail. Without a machine, the nail could not be removed unless the input force was greater than 99 N.

Tips and Tricks

This equation can be used to predict the output force for a given input force if there is no friction. The equation is not valid if friction is taken into account. With friction, the output force will be less than expected, and thus $\frac{d_{in}}{d_{out}}$ will not equal $\frac{F_{out}}{F_{in}}$.

FIGURE 4.8

An Inclined Plane Lifting this trunk directly up requires more force than pushing it up the ramp, but the same amount of work is done in both cases.

FIGURE 4.9

Changing Force or Distance
Simple machines can alter both the force needed to perform a task and the distance through which the force acts.

Small distance—Large force

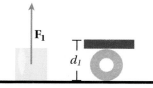

F_1 d_1

Large distance—Small force

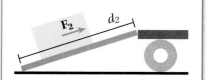

F_2 d_2

Machines can alter the force and the distance moved.

You have learned that mechanical energy is conserved in the absence of friction. This law holds for machines as well. A machine can increase (or decrease) the force acting on an object at the expense (or gain) of the distance moved, but the product of the two—the work done on the object—is constant.

For example, **Figure 4.8** shows two examples of a trunk being loaded onto a truck. **Figure 4.9** illustrates both examples schematically. In one example, the trunk is lifted directly onto the truck. In the other example, the trunk is pushed up an incline into the truck.

In the first example, a force (F_1) of 360 N is required to lift the trunk, which moves through a distance (d_1) of 1.0 m. This requires 360 N•m of work (360 N × 1 m). In the second example, a lesser force (F_2) of only 120 N would be needed (ignoring friction), but the trunk must be pushed a greater distance (d_2) of 3.0 m. This also requires 360 N•m of work (120 N × 3 m). As a result, the two methods require the same amount of energy.

Efficiency is a measure of how well a machine works.

The simple machines we have considered so far are ideal, frictionless machines. Real machines, however, are not frictionless. They dissipate energy. When the parts of a machine move and contact other objects, some of the input energy is dissipated as sound or heat. The *efficiency* of a machine is the ratio of useful work output to work input. It is defined by the following equation:

$$eff = \frac{W_{out}}{W_{in}}$$

If a machine is frictionless, then mechanical energy is conserved. This means that the work done on the machine (input work) is equal to the work done by the machine (output work) because work is a measure of energy transfer. Thus, the mechanical efficiency of an ideal machine is 1, or 100 percent. This is the best efficiency a machine can have. Because all real machines have at least a little friction, the efficiency of real machines is always less than 1.

▶ Reviewing Main Ideas

1. Determine whether each of the following situations involves linear motion, rotational motion, or a combination of the two.
   a. a baseball dropped from the roof of a house
   b. a baseball rolling toward third base
   c. a pinwheel in the wind
   d. a door swinging open

2. What quantity describes the ability of a force to rotate an object? How does it differ from a force? On what quantities does it depend?

3. How would the force needed to open a door change if you put the handle in the middle of the door?

4. What are three ways that a cat pushing on a cat-flap door can change the amount of torque applied to the door?

5. The efficiency of a squeaky pulley system is 73 percent. The pulleys are used to raise a mass to a certain height. What force is exerted on the machine if a rope is pulled 18.0 m in order to raise a 58 kg mass a height of 3.0 m?

6. A person lifts a 950 N box by pushing it up an incline. If the person exerts a force of 350 N along the incline, what is the mechanical advantage of the incline?

7. You are attempting to move a large rock by using a long lever. Will the work you do on the lever be greater than, the same as, or less than the work done by the lever on the rock? Explain.

Interpreting Graphics

8. Calculate the torque for each force acting on the bar in **Figure 4.10.** Assume the axis is perpendicular to the page and passes through point *O*. In what direction will the object rotate?

FIGURE 4.10

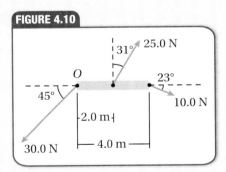

9. **Figure 4.11** shows an example of a Rube Goldberg machine. Identify two types of simple machines that are included in this compound machine.

☑ Critical Thinking

10. A bicycle can be described as a combination of simple machines. Identify two types of simple machines that are used to propel a typical bicycle.

FIGURE 4.11

Tangential Speed and Acceleration

This feature explores the concepts of tangential speed and acceleration in greater detail. Be sure you have also read the feature titled "Angular Kinematics."

Tangential Speed

Imagine an amusement-park carousel rotating about its center. Because a carousel is a rigid object, any two horses attached to the carousel have the same angular speed and angular acceleration. However, if the two horses are different distances from the axis of rotation, they have different **tangential speed.** The tangential speed of a horse on the carousel is its speed along a line drawn tangent to its circular path.

The tangential speeds of two horses at different distances from the center of a carousel are represented in **Figure 1.** Note that the two horses travel the same angular displacement during the same time interval. To achieve this, the horse on the outside must travel a greater distance (Δs) than the horse on the inside. Thus, the outside horse at point B has a greater tangential speed than the inside horse at point A. In general, an object that is farther from the axis of a rigid rotating body must travel at a higher tangential speed to cover the same angular displacement as would an object closer to the axis.

If the carousel rotates through an angle θ, a horse rotates through an arc length Δs in the interval Δt. To find the tangential speed, start with the equation for angular displacement:

$$\Delta\theta = \frac{\Delta s}{r}$$

Next, divide both sides of the equation by the time it takes to travel Δs:

$$\frac{\Delta\theta}{\Delta t} = \frac{\Delta s}{r\Delta t}$$

The left side of the equation equals ω_{avg}. Also, Δs is a linear distance, so Δs divided by Δt is a linear speed along an arc length. If Δt is very short, then Δs is so small that it is nearly tangent to the circle; therefore, $\Delta s/\Delta t$ is the tangential speed, v_t.

> **Tangential Speed**
>
> $$v_t = r\omega$$
>
> **tangential speed = distance from axis × angular speed**

FIGURE 1

Tangential Speed Horses on a carousel move at the same angular speed but different tangential speeds.

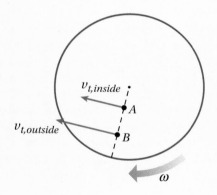

Here, ω is the instantaneous angular speed, rather than the average angular speed, because the time interval is so short. This equation is valid only when ω is measured in radians per unit of time. Other measures of angular speed must not be used in this equation.

Tangential Acceleration

If a carousel speeds up, the horses experience an angular acceleration. The linear acceleration related to this angular acceleration is tangent to the circular path and is called the **tangential acceleration.** If an object rotating about a fixed axis changes its angular speed by $\Delta\omega$ in the interval Δt, the tangential speed of a point on the object has changed by the amount Δv_t. Dividing the equation for tangential speed by Δt results in

$$\Delta v_t = r\Delta\omega$$

$$\frac{\Delta v_t}{\Delta t} = r\frac{\Delta\omega}{\Delta t}$$

If the time interval Δt is very small, then the left side of this relationship gives the tangential acceleration of the point. The angular speed divided by the time interval on the right side is the angular acceleration. Thus, the tangential acceleration (a_t) of a point on a rotating object is given by the following relationship:

Tangential Acceleration

$$a_t = r\alpha$$

tangential acceleration = distance from axis $\times$ angular acceleration

---

The angular acceleration in this equation refers to the instantaneous angular acceleration. This equation must use the unit radians to be valid. In SI, angular acceleration is expressed as radians per second per second.

Finding Total Acceleration

Any object moving in a circle has a centripetal acceleration. When both components of acceleration exist simultaneously, the tangential acceleration is tangent to the circular path, and the centripetal acceleration points toward the center of the circular path. Because these components of acceleration are perpendicular to each other, the magnitude of the *total acceleration* can be found using the Pythagorean theorem, as follows:

$$a_{total} = \sqrt{a_t^2 + a_c^2}$$

The direction of the total acceleration, as shown in **Figure 2,** depends on the magnitude of each component of acceleration and can be found using the inverse of the tangent function. Note that when there is a tangential acceleration, the tangential speed is changing, and thus this situation is *not* an example of uniform circular motion.

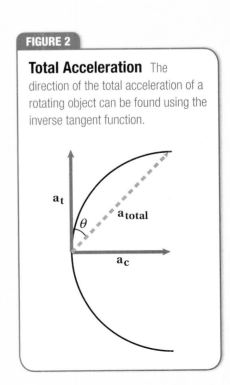

FIGURE 2

Total Acceleration The direction of the total acceleration of a rotating object can be found using the inverse tangent function.

Rotation and Inertia

In this feature, you will explore the concept of rotational inertia.

Center of Mass

You have learned that torque measures the ability of a force to rotate an object around some axis, such as a cat-flap door rotating on a hinge. Locating the axis of rotation for a cat-flap door is simple: It rotates on its hinges, because the house applies a force that keeps the hinges in place.

Now imagine you are playing fetch with your dog, and you throw a stick up into the air for the dog to retrieve. Unlike the cat-flap door, the stick is not attached to anything. There is a special point around which the stick rotates if gravity is the only force acting on the stick. This point is called the stick's **center of mass.**

The center of mass is also the point at which all the mass of the body can be considered to be concentrated (for translational motion). This means that the complete motion of the stick is a combination of both translational and rotational motion. The stick rotates in the air around its center of mass. The center of mass, in turn, moves as if the stick were a point mass, with all of its mass concentrated at that point for purposes of analyzing its translational motion. For example, the hammer in **Figure 1** rotates about its center of mass as it moves through the air. As the rest of the hammer spins, the center of mass moves along the parabolic path of a projectile.

For regularly shaped objects, such as a sphere or a cube, the center of mass is at the geometric center of the object. For more complicated objects, finding the center of mass is more difficult. Although the center of mass is the position at which an extended object's mass can be treated as a point mass, the *center of gravity* is the position at which the gravitational force acts on the extended object as if it were a point mass. For many situations, the center of mass and the center of gravity are equivalent.

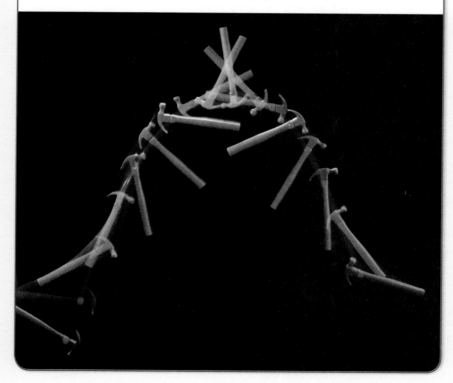

FIGURE 1

Center of Mass The point around which this hammer rotates is the hammer's center of mass. The center of mass traces out the parabola that is characteristic of projectile motion.

Moment of Inertia

You may have noticed that it is easier to rotate a baseball bat around some axes than others. The resistance of an object to changes in rotational motion is measured by a quantity called the **moment of interia.**

The moment of inertia, which is abbreviated as I, is similar to mass because they are both forms of inertia. However, there is an important difference between them. Mass is an intrinsic property of an object, and the moment of inertia is not. The moment of inertia depends on the object's mass and the distribution of that mass around the axis of rotation. The farther the mass of an object is, on average, from the axis of rotation, the greater is the object's moment of inertia and the more difficult it is to rotate the object.

According to Newton's second law, when a net force acts on an object, the resulting acceleration of the object depends on the object's mass. Similarly, when a net torque acts on an object, the resulting change in the rotational motion of the object depends on the object's moment of inertia. (This law is covered in more detail in the feature "Rotational Dynamics.")

Some simple formulas for calculating the moment of inertia of common shapes are shown in **Figure 2.** The units for moment of inertia are kg•m^2. To get an idea of the size of this unit, note that bowling balls typically have moments of inertia about an axis through their centers ranging from about 0.7 kg•m^2 to 1.8 kg•m^2, depending on the mass and size of the ball.

Did YOU Know?

A baseball bat can be modeled as a rotating thin rod. When a bat is held at its end, its length is greatest with respect to the rotation axis, so its moment of inertia is greatest. Thus, the bat is easier to swing if you hold the bat closer to the center. Baseball players sometimes do this either because a bat is too heavy (large M) or too long (large ℓ).

FIGURE 2

THE MOMENT OF INERTIA FOR VARIOUS RIGID OBJECTS OF MASS M

Shape		Moment of inertia	Shape		Moment of inertia
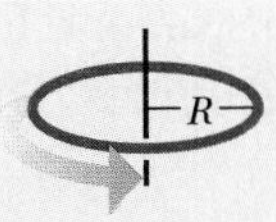	thin hoop about symmetry axis	MR^2	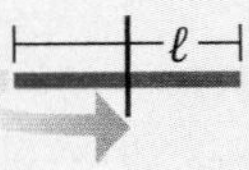	thin rod about perpendicular axis through center	$\frac{1}{12}M\ell^2$
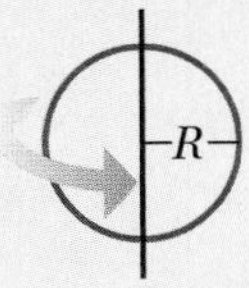	thin hoop about diameter	$\frac{1}{2}MR^2$	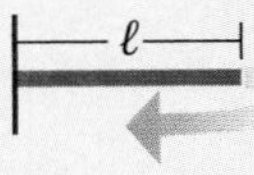	thin rod about perpendicular axis through end	$\frac{1}{3}M\ell^2$
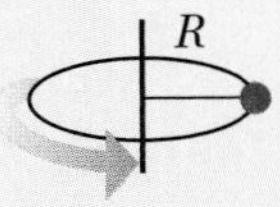	point mass about vertical axis	MR^2	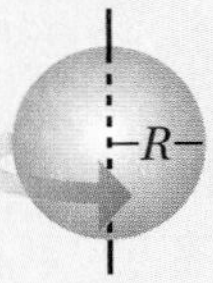	solid sphere about diameter	$\frac{2}{5}MR^2$
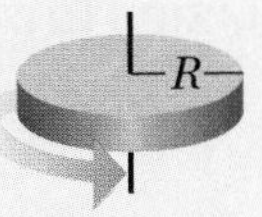	disk or cylinder about symmetry axis	$\frac{1}{2}MR^2$	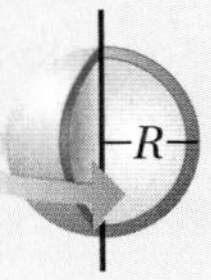	thin spherical shell about diameter	$\frac{2}{3}MR^2$

Rotational Dynamics

The feature "Angular Kinematics" developed the kinematic equations for rotational motion. Similarly, the feature "Rotation and Inertia" applied the concept of inertia to rotational motion. In this feature, you will see how torque relates to rotational equilibrium and angular acceleration. You will also learn how momentum and kinetic energy are described in rotational motion.

Rotational Equilibrium

Equal and Opposite Forces
The two forces exerted on this table are equal and opposite, yet the table moves. How is this possible?

If you and a friend push on opposite sides of a table, as shown in **Figure 1**, the two forces acting on the table are equal in magnitude and opposite in direction. You might think that the table won't move, because the two forces balance each other. But it does; it rotates in place.

The piece of furniture can move even though the net force acting on it is zero because the net torque acting on it is not zero. If the net force on an object is zero, the object is in *translational equilibrium*. If the net torque on an object is zero, the object is in *rotational equilibrium*. For an object to be completely in equilibrium, both rotational and translational, there must be both zero net force and zero net torque. The dependence of equilibrium on the absence of net torque is called the *second condition for equilibrium*.

Newton's Second Law for Rotation

Just as net force is related to translational acceleration according to Newton's second law, there is a relationship between the net torque on an object and the angular acceleration given to the object. Specifically, the net torque on an object is equal to the moment of inertia times the angular acceleration. This relationship is parallel to Newton's second law of motion and is known as Newton's second law for rotating objects. This law is expressed mathematically as follows:

Newton's Second Law for Rotating Objects
$$\tau_{net} = I\alpha$$

net torque = moment of inertia × angular acceleration

This equation shows that a net positive torque corresponds to a positive angular acceleration, and a net negative torque corresponds to a negative angular acceleration. Thus, it is important to keep track of the signs of the torques acting on the object when using this equation to calculate an object's angular acceleration.

Angular Momentum

Because a rotating object has inertia, it also possesses momentum associated with its rotation. This momentum is called **angular momentum.** Angular momentum is defined by the following equation:

> **Angular Momentum**
> $$L = I\omega$$
> **angular momentum = moment of inertia × angular speed**

The unit of angular momentum is kg•m^2/s. When the net external torque acting on an object or objects is zero, the angular momentum of the object(s) does not change. This is the law of *conservation of angular momentum*. For example, assuming the friction between the skates and the ice is negligible, there is no torque acting on the skater in **Figure 2,** so his angular momentum is conserved. When he brings his hands and feet closer to his body, more of his mass, on average, is nearer to his axis of rotation. As a result, the moment of inertia of his body decreases. Because his angular momentum is constant, his angular speed increases to compensate for his smaller moment of inertia.

Angular Kinetic Energy

Rotating objects possess kinetic energy associated with their angular speed. This is called **rotational kinetic energy** and is expressed by the following equation:

> **Rotational Kinetic Energy**
> $$KE_{rot} = \tfrac{1}{2} I\omega^2$$
> **rotational kinetic energy = $\dfrac{1}{2}$× moment of inertia × (angular speed)^2**

As shown in **Figure 3,** rotational kinetic energy is analogous to the translational kinetic energy of a particle, given by the expression $\frac{1}{2}mv^2$. The unit of rotational kinetic energy is the joule, the SI unit for energy.

FIGURE 2

Conserving Angular Momentum

When this skater brings his hands and feet closer to his body, his moment of inertia decreases, and his angular speed increases to keep total angular momentum constant

FIGURE 3

COMPARING TRANSLATIONAL AND ROTATIONAL MOTION

	Translational motion	Rotational motion
Equilibrium	$\sum F = 0$	$\sum \tau = 0$
Newton's second law	$\sum F = ma$	$\sum \tau = I\alpha$
Momentum	$p = mv$	$L = I\omega$
Kinetic energy	$KE = \frac{1}{2}mv^2$	$KE = \frac{1}{2}I\omega^2$

General Relativity

Special relativity applies only to nonaccelerating reference frames. Einstein expanded his special theory of relativity into the general theory to cover all cases, including accelerating reference frames.

Gravitational Attraction and Accelerating Reference Frames

Einstein began with a simple question: "If we pick up a stone and then let it go, why does it fall to the ground?" You might answer that it falls because it is attracted by gravitational force. As usual, Einstein was not satisfied with this typical answer. He was also intrigued by the fact that in a vacuum, all objects in free fall have the same acceleration, regardless of their mass. As you learned in the chapter on gravity, the reason is that gravitational mass is equal to inertial mass. Because the two masses are equivalent, the extra gravitational force from a larger gravitational mass is exactly canceled out by its larger inertial mass, thus producing the same acceleration. Einstein considered this equivalence to be a great puzzle.

To explore these questions, Einstein used a thought experiment similar to the one shown in **Figure 1**. In **Figure 1(a)**, a person in an elevator at rest on Earth's surface drops a ball. The ball is in free fall and accelerates downward, as you would expect. In **Figure 1(b)**, a similar elevator in space is moving upward with a constant acceleration. If an astronaut in this elevator releases a ball, the floor accelerates up toward the ball. To the astronaut, the ball appears to be accelerating downward, and this situation is identical to the situation described in **(a)**. In other words, the astronaut may *think* that his space-ship is on Earth and that the ball falls because of gravitational attraction. Because gravitational mass equals inertial mass, the astronaut cannot conduct any experiments to distinguish between the two cases. Einstein described this realization as "the happiest thought of my life."

FIGURE 1

Equivalence Einstein discovered that there is no way to distinguish between **(a)** a gravitational field and **(b)** an accelerating reference frame.

(a)

(b)

Gravity and Light

Now, imagine a ray of light crossing the accelerating elevator. Suppose that the ray of light enters the elevator from the left side. As the light ray travels across the elevator from left to right, the floor of the elevator accelerates upward. Thus, to an astronaut in the elevator, the light ray would appear to follow a parabolic path.

If Einstein's theory of the equivalence between gravitational fields and accelerating reference frames is correct, then light must also bend this way in a gravitational field. Einstein proposed using the sun's gravitational field to test this idea. The effect is small and difficult to measure, but Einstein predicted that it could be done during a solar eclipse. Einstein published the theory of general relativity in 1916. Just three years later, in 1919, the British astronomer Arthur S. Eddington conducted observations of the light from stars during an eclipse. This experiment provided support for Einstein's theory of general relativity.

Curved Space-Time

Although light traveling near a massive object such as the sun appears to bend, is it possible that the light is actually following the straightest path? Einstein theorized that the answer to this question is yes. In general relativity, the three dimensions of space and the one dimension of time are considered together as four-dimensional space-time. When no masses are present, an object moves through "flat" space-time. Einstein proposed that masses change the shape of space-time, as shown in **Figure 2**. A light ray that bends near the sun is following the new shape of the distorted space-time.

For example, imagine rolling a tennis ball across a water bed. If the water bed is flat, the tennis ball will roll straight across. If you place a heavy bowling ball in the center, the bowling ball changes the shape of the water bed. As a result, the tennis ball will then follow a curved path, which, in Newton's theory, is due to the gravitational force between the two. In general relativity, the tennis ball is simply following the curved path of space-time, which is distorted by the bowling ball. Unlike Newton's *mathematical* theory of gravitation, Einstein's theory of curved space-time offers a *physical* explanation for gravitational force.

Today, Einstein's theory of general relativity is well accepted. However, scientists have not yet been able to incorporate it with another well-accepted theory that describes things at the microscopic level: quantum mechanics. Many scientists are now working toward a unification of these two theories.

FIGURE 2

A Mass in Space-Time In the theory of general relativity, masses distort four-dimensional space-time, as illustrated here. This distortion creates the effect we describe as gravitational attraction.

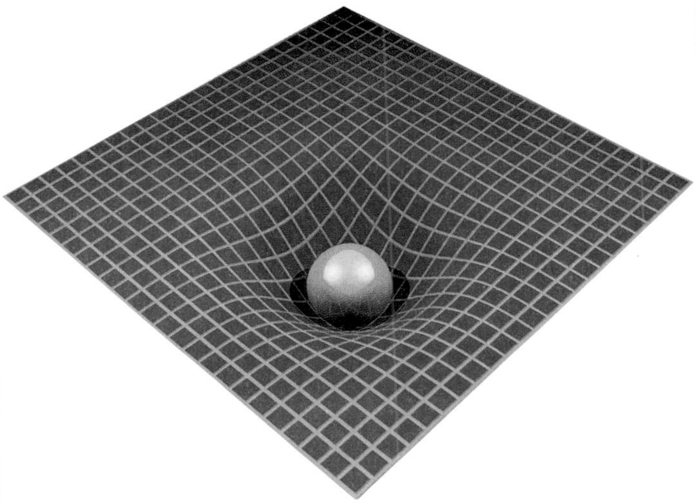

Theories Through Time

Scientists develop theories to explain natural phenomena. A scientific theory is a substantiated idea—that is, an idea that is supported by evidence—based on the results of many experiments and observations. Theories can be used to explain how the world works and predict the results of future experiments. Scientists accept theories that have been tested and are supported by strong evidence and reject those that fail to match experimental results. Advances in science, new technologies, and new discoveries may result in old theories being supported or replaced by new ones.

Gravitational Waves

Since its introduction in 1916, Einstein's theory of general relativity has stimulated further scientific inquiry and experimentation. One surprising consequence of the theory is the possibility of moving ripples in space-time. According to Einstein, large masses undergoing acceleration should produce gravitational waves, disturbances in space-time that transfer energy at the speed of light. Other phenomena predicted by the theory were experimentally verified shortly after it was introduced. However, gravitational waves cause distortions on the scale of one ten-thousandth the width of a proton, which were far too minute to be detected with the technology available at the time. In fact, it was not until 2015 that scientists working at the Laser Interferometer Gravitational-Wave Observatory (LIGO) developed the technology to sense these tiny perturbations in space-time through the use of laser interferometers. These optical devices are capable of measuring changes in distance smaller than 10^{-18} m. In February 2016, researchers announced that they had observed the gravitational waves generated during the collision of two black holes roughly 1.3 billion light years from Earth. Through careful analysis of the wave data, scientists were able to confirm that the waves generated by the collision matched the predictions made by Einstein in his theory of general relativity a century before.

- What do you think would have happened if the LIGO team made observations that didn't match the predictions made by general relativity?

- How did the advancement of technology contribute to the acceptance of the theory of general relativity?

CHAPTER 7 Summary

BIG IDEA Objects move in a circular path when there is a centrally directed force. The concept of circular motion helps to explain phenomena such as orbital motion or torque.

SECTION 1 Circular Motion

- An object that revolves about a single axis undergoes circular motion.
- An object in circular motion has a centripetal acceleration and a centripetal force, which are both directed toward the center of the circular path.

KEY TERM

centripetal acceleration

SECTION 2 Newton's Law of Universal Gravitation

- Every particle in the universe is attracted to every other particle by a force that is directly proportional to the product of the particles' masses and inversely proportional to the square of the distance between the particles.
- Gravitational field strength is the gravitational force that would be exerted on a unit mass at any given point in space and is equal to free-fall acceleration.

KEY TERM

gravitational force

SECTION 3 Motion in Space

- Kepler developed three laws of planetary motion.
- Both the period and speed of an object that is in a circular orbit around another object depend on two quantities: the mass of the central object and the distance between the centers of the objects.

SECTION 4 Torque and Simple Machines

- Torque is a measure of a force's tendency to rotate an object.
- The torque on an object depends on the magnitude of the applied force and on the lever arm.
- Simple machines provide a mechanical advantage.

KEY TERMS

torque
lever arm

VARIABLE SYMBOLS

Quantities		Units	
v_t	tangential speed	m/s	meters/second
a_c	centripetal acceleration	m/s^2	meters/second^2
F_c	centripetal force	N	newtons
F_g	gravitational force	N	newtons
g	gravitational field strength	N/kg	newtons/kilogram
T	orbital period	s	seconds
τ	torque	N•m	newton meter

Problem Solving

See **Appendix D: Equations** for a summary of the equations introduced in this chapter. If you need more problem-solving practice, see **Appendix I: Additional Problems.**

Circular Motion

▶ **REVIEWING MAIN IDEAS**

1. When a solid wheel rotates about a fixed axis, do all of the points of the wheel have the same tangential speed?

2. Correct the following statement: The racing car rounds the turn at a constant velocity of 145 km/h.

3. Describe the path of a moving body whose acceleration is constant in magnitude at all times and is perpendicular to the velocity.

4. Give an example of a situation in which an automobile driver can have a centripetal acceleration but no tangential acceleration.

CONCEPTUAL QUESTIONS

5. The force exerted by a spring increases as the spring stretches. Imagine that you attach a heavy object to one end of a spring and then, while holding the spring's other end, whirl the spring and object in a horizontal circle. Does the spring stretch? Explain.

6. Can a car move around a circular racetrack so that the car has a tangential acceleration but no centripetal acceleration?

7. Why does mud fly off a rapidly turning wheel?

PRACTICE PROBLEMS

For problems 8–9, see Sample Problem A.

8. A building superintendent twirls a set of keys in a circle at the end of a cord. If the keys have a centripetal acceleration of 145 m/s^2 and the cord has a length of 0.34 m, what is the tangential speed of the keys?

9. A sock stuck to the side of a clothes-dryer barrel has a centripetal acceleration of 28 m/s^2. If the dryer barrel has a radius of 27 cm, what is the tangential speed of the sock?

For problems 10–11, see Sample Problem B.

10. A roller-coaster car speeds down a hill past point A and then rolls up a hill past point B, as shown below.
    a. The car has a speed of 20.0 m/s at point A. If the track exerts a normal force on the car of 2.06×10^4 N at this point, what is the mass of the car? (Be sure to account for gravitational force.)
    b. What is the maximum speed the car can have at point B for the gravitational force to hold it on the track?

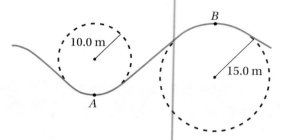

11. Tarzan tries to cross a river by swinging from one bank to the other on a vine that is 10.0 m long. His speed at the bottom of the swing is 8.0 m/s. Tarzan does not know that the vine has a breaking strength of 1.0×10^3 N. What is the largest mass that Tarzan can have and still make it safely across the river?

Newton's Law of Universal Gravitation

▶ **REVIEWING MAIN IDEAS**

12. Identify the influence of mass and distance on gravitational forces.

13. If a satellite orbiting Earth is in free fall, why does the satellite not fall and crash into Earth?

14. How does the gravitational force exerted by Earth on the sun compare with the gravitational force exerted by the sun on Earth?

15. Describe two situations in which Newton's laws are not completely accurate.

CONCEPTUAL QUESTIONS

16. Would you expect tides to be higher at the equator or at the North Pole? Why?

17. Given Earth's radius, how could you use the value of G to calculate Earth's mass?

PRACTICE PROBLEMS

For problems 18–19, see Sample Problem C.

18. The gravitational force of attraction between two students sitting at their desks in physics class is 3.20×10^{-8} N. If one student has a mass of 50.0 kg and the other has a mass of 60.0 kg, how far apart are the students sitting?

19. If the gravitational force between the electron $(9.11 \times 10^{-31}$ kg) and the proton $(1.67 \times 10^{-27}$ kg) in a hydrogen atom is 1.0×10^{-47} N, how far apart are the two particles?

Motion in Space

▶ **REVIEWING MAIN IDEAS**

20. Compare and contrast Kepler's model of the solar system with Copernicus's model.

21. How do Kepler's laws help support Newton's theory of gravitation?

22. You are standing on a scale in an elevator. For a brief time, the elevator descends with free-fall acceleration. What does the scale show your weight to be during that time interval?

23. Astronauts floating around inside the space shuttle are not actually in a zero-gravity environment. What is the real reason astronauts seem weightless?

CONCEPTUAL QUESTIONS

24. A tiny alien spaceship ($m = 0.25$ kg) and the *International Space Station* are both orbiting Earth in circular orbits and at the same distance from Earth. Which one has a greater orbital speed?

25. The planet shown below sweeps out Area 1 in half the time that the planet sweeps out Area 2. How much bigger is Area 2 than Area 1?

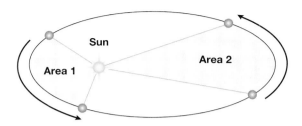

26. Comment on the statement, "There is no gravity in outer space."

PRACTICE PROBLEMS

For problems 27–29, see Sample Problem D.

27. What would be the orbital speed and period of a satellite in orbit 1.44×10^8 m above Earth?

28. A satellite with an orbital period of exactly 24.0 h is always positioned over the same spot on Earth. This is known as a *geosynchronous* orbit. Television, communication, and weather satellites use geosynchronous orbits. At what distance would a satellite have to orbit Earth in order to have a geosynchronous orbit?

29. The distance between the centers of a small moon and a planet in our solar system is 2.0×10^8 m. If the moon's orbital period is 5.0×10^4 s, what is the planet? (See **Figure 3.3** of the chapter for planet masses.)

Torque and Simple Machines

▶ **REVIEWING MAIN IDEAS**

30. Why is it easier to loosen the lid from the top of a paint can with a long-handled screwdriver than with a short-handled screwdriver?

31. If a machine cannot multiply the amount of work, what is the advantage of using such a machine?

32. In the equation for the magnitude of a torque, what does the quantity $d \sin \theta$ represent?

CONCEPTUAL QUESTIONS

33. Which of the forces acting on the rod shown below will produce a torque about the axis at the left end of the rod?

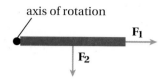

axis of rotation

F_1

F_2

34. Two forces equal in magnitude but opposite in direction act at the same point on an object. Is it possible for there to be a net torque on the object? Explain.

35. You are attempting to move a large rock by using a long lever. Is it more effective to place the lever's axis of rotation nearer to your hands or nearer to the rock? Explain.

36. A perpetual motion machine is a machine that, when set in motion, will never come to a halt. Why is such a machine not possible?

PRACTICE PROBLEMS

For problems 37–38, see Sample Problem E.

37. A bucket filled with water has a mass of 54 kg and is hanging from a rope that is wound around a 0.050 m radius stationary cylinder. If the cylinder does not rotate and the bucket hangs straight down, what is the magnitude of the torque the bucket produces around the center of the cylinder?

38. A mechanic jacks up the front of a car to an angle of 8.0° with the horizontal in order to change the front tires. The car is 3.05 m long and has a mass of 1130 kg. Gravitational force acts at the center of mass, which is located 1.12 m from the front end. The rear wheels are 0.40 m from the back end. Calculate the magnitude of the torque exerted by the jack.

Mixed Review

▶ REVIEWING MAIN IDEAS

39. A 2.00×10^3 kg car rounds a circular turn of radius 20.0 m. If the road is flat and the coefficient of static friction between the tires and the road is 0.70, how fast can the car go without skidding?

40. During a solar eclipse, the moon, Earth, and the sun lie on the same line, with the moon between Earth and the sun. What force is exerted on
a. the moon by the sun?
b. the moon by Earth?
c. Earth by the sun?

(See the table in **Appendix F** for data on the sun, moon, and Earth.)

41. A wooden bucket filled with water has a mass of 75 kg and is attached to a rope that is wound around a cylinder with a radius of 0.075 m. A crank with a turning radius of 0.25 m is attached to the end of the cylinder. What minimum force directed perpendicularly to the crank handle is required to raise the bucket?

42. If the torque required to loosen a nut that holds a wheel on a car has a magnitude of 58 N•m, what force must be exerted at the end of a 0.35 m lug wrench to loosen the nut when the angle is 56°? (Hint: See **Figure 4.5** for an example, and assume that θ is 56°.)

43. In a canyon between two mountains, a spherical boulder with a radius of 1.4 m is just set in motion by a force of 1600 N. The force is applied at an angle of 53.5° measured with respect to the vertical radius of the boulder. What is the magnitude of the torque on the boulder?

44. The hands of the clock in the famous Parliament Clock Tower in London are 2.7 m and 4.5 m long and have masses of 60.0 kg and 100.0 kg, respectively. Calculate the torque around the center of the clock due to the weight of these hands at 5:20. The weight of each hand acts at the center of mass (the midpoint of the hand).

45. The efficiency of a pulley system is 64 percent. The pulleys are used to raise a mass of 78 kg to a height of 4.0 m. What force is exerted on the rope of the pulley system if the rope is pulled for 24 m in order to raise the mass to the required height?

46. A crate is pulled 2.0 m at constant velocity along a 15° incline. The coefficient of kinetic friction between the crate and the plane is 0.160. Calculate the efficiency of this procedure.

47. A pulley system is used to lift a piano 3.0 m. If a force of 2200 N is applied to the rope as the rope is pulled in 14 m, what is the efficiency of the machine? Assume the mass of the piano is 750 kg.

48. A pulley system has an efficiency of 87.5 percent. How much of the rope must be pulled in if a force of 648 N is needed to lift a 150 kg desk 2.46 m? (Disregard friction.)

49. Jupiter's four large moons—Io, Europa, Ganymede, and Callisto—were discovered by Galileo in 1610. Jupiter also has dozens of smaller moons. Jupiter's rocky, volcanically active moon Io is about the size of Earth's moon. Io has a radius of about 1.82×10^6 m, and the mean distance between Io and Jupiter is 4.22×10^8 m.
  a. If Io's orbit were circular, how many days would it take for Io to complete one full revolution around Jupiter?
  b. If Io's orbit were circular, what would its orbital speed be?

50. A 13 500 N car traveling at 50.0 km/h rounds a curve of radius 2.00×10^2 m. Find the following:
  a. the centripetal acceleration of the car
  b. the centripetal force
  c. the minimum coefficient of static friction between the tires and the road that will allow the car to round the curve safely

51. The arm of a crane at a construction site is 15.0 m long, and it makes an angle of 20.0° with the horizontal. Assume that the maximum load the crane can handle is limited by the amount of torque the load produces around the base of the arm.
  a. What is the magnitude of the maximum torque the crane can withstand if the maximum load the crane can handle is 450 N?
  b. What is the maximum load for this crane at an angle of 40.0° with the horizontal?

52. At the sun's surface, the gravitational force between the sun and a 5.00 kg mass of hot gas has a magnitude of 1370 N. Assuming that the sun is spherical, what is the sun's mean radius?

53. An automobile with a tangential speed of 55.0 km/h follows a circular road that has a radius of 40.0 m. The automobile has a mass of 1350 kg. The pavement is wet and oily, so the coefficient of kinetic friction between the car's tires and the pavement is only 0.500. How large is the available frictional force? Is this frictional force large enough to maintain the automobile's circular motion?

GRAPHING CALCULATOR PRACTICE

Torque

Torque is a measure of the ability of a force to rotate an object around an axis. How does the angle and application distance of the applied force affect torque?

Torque is described by the following equation:

$$\tau = Fd \sin \theta$$

In this equation, F is the applied force, d is the distance from the axis of rotation, and θ is the angle at which the force is applied. A mechanic using a long wrench to loosen a "frozen" bolt is a common illustration of this equation.

In this graphing calculator activity, you will determine how torque relates to the angle of the applied force and to the distance of application.

Go online to HMHScience.com to find the skillsheet and program for this graphing calculator activity.

54. A force is applied to a door at an angle of 60.0° and 0.35 m from the hinge. The force exerts a torque with a magnitude of 2.0 N•m. What is the magnitude of the force? How large is the maximum torque this force can exert?

55. Imagine a balance with unequal arms. An earring placed in the left basket was balanced by 5.00 g of standard masses on the right. When placed in the right basket, the same earring required 15.00 g on the left to balance. Which was the longer arm? Do you need to know the exact length of each arm to determine the mass of the earring? Explain.

ALTERNATIVE ASSESSMENT

1. Research the historical development of the concept of gravitational force. Find out how scientists' ideas about gravity have changed over time. Identify the contributions of different scientists, such as Galileo, Kepler, Newton, and Einstein. How did each scientist's work build on the work of earlier scientists? What were the impacts of the scientific contributions of each of these scientists on scientific thought? Analyze, review, and critique the different scientific explanations of gravity. Focus on each scientist's hypotheses and theories. What are their strengths? What are their weaknesses? What do scientists think about gravity now? Use scientific evidence and other information to support your answers. Write a report or prepare an oral presentation to share your conclusions.

2. In the reduced gravity of space, called *microgravity*, astronauts lose bone and muscle mass, even after a short time. These effects happen more gradually on Earth as people age. Scientists are studying this phenomenon so that they can find ways to counteract it, in space and on Earth. Such studies are essential for future plans that involve astronauts spending significant time on space stations or for distant missions such as a trip to Mars. Research the causes of this phenomenon and possible methods of prevention, including NASA's current efforts to minimize bone density loss for astronauts on the *International Space Station*. Create a poster or brochure displaying the results of your research.

3. Research the life and scientific contributions of one of the astronomers discussed in the chapter: Claudius Ptolemy, Nicolaus Copernicus, Tycho Brahe, or Johannes Kepler. On a posterboard, create a visual timeline that summarizes key events in the atsronomer's life and work, including astronomical discoveries and other scientific advances or inventions. Add images to some of the events on the timeline. You may also want to include historical events on the timeline to provide context for the scientific works.

4. Describe exactly which measurements you would need to make in order to identify the torques at work during a ride on a specific bicycle. Your plans should include measurements you can make with equipment available to you. If others in the class analyzed different bicycle models, compare the models for efficiency and mechanical advantage.

5. Prepare a poster or a series of models of simple machines, explaining their use and how they work. Include a schematic diagram next to each sample or picture to identify the fulcrum, lever arm, and resistance. Add your own examples to the following list: nail clipper, wheelbarrow, can opener, nutcracker, electric drill, screwdriver, tweezers, and key in lock.

Standards-Based Assessment

Record your answers on a separate piece of paper.

MULTIPLE CHOICE

1 An object moves in a circle at a constant speed. Which of the following is *not* true of the object?

A Its centripetal acceleration points toward the center of the circle.

B Its tangential speed is constant.

C Its velocity is constant.

D A centripetal force acts on the object.

2 A car traveling at 15 m/s on a flat surface turns in a circle with a radius of 25 m.

What is the centripetal acceleration of the car?

A 2.4×10^{-2} m/s^2

B 0.60 m/s^2

C 9.0 m/s^2

D zero

3 Earth ($m = 5.97 \times 10^{24}$ kg) orbits the sun ($m = 1.99 \times 10^{30}$) at a mean distance of 1.50×10^{11} m. What is the gravitational force of the sun on Earth? ($G = 6.673 \times 10^{-11}$ N·m^2/kg^2)

A 5.29×10^{32} N

B 3.52×10^{22} N

C 5.90×10^{-2} N

D 1.77×10^{-8} N

4 Which of the following is a correct interpretation of the expression $a_g = g = G\dfrac{m_E}{r^2}$?

A Gravitational field strength changes with an object's distance from Earth.

B Free-fall acceleration changes with an object's distance from Earth.

C Free-fall acceleration is independent of the falling object's mass.

D All of the above are correct interpretations.

5 What data do you need to calculate the orbital speed of a satellite?

A mass of satellite, radius of planet, radius of orbit

B mass of satellite, radius of planet, area of orbit

C mass of satellite and radius of orbit only

D mass of planet and radius of orbit only

6 Which of the following choices correctly describes the orbital relationship between Earth and the sun?

A The sun orbits Earth in a perfect circle.

B Earth orbits the sun in a perfect circle.

C The sun orbits Earth in an ellipse, with Earth at one focus.

D Earth orbits the sun in an ellipse, with the sun at one focus.

7 Which astronomer discovered that planets travel in elliptical rather than circular orbits?

A Johannes Kepler

B Nicolaus Copernicus

C Tycho Brahe

D Claudius Ptolemy

GRIDDED RESPONSE

8 Mars orbits the sun ($m = 1.99 \times 10^{30}$ kg) at a mean distance of 2.28×10^{11} m. Calculate the length of the Martian year in Earth days. ($G = 6.673 \times 10^{-11}$ N·m^2/kg^2)

A BOOK EXPLAINING
COMPLEX IDEAS USING
ONLY THE 1,000 MOST
COMMON WORDS

RANDALL MUNROE
XKCD.COM

US SPACE TEAM'S
UP GOER FIVE
The space boat that took people
to the moon and back

You've learned the velocity required to attain orbit. Have
you ever wondered how engineers design a vehicle
capable of putting astronauts and cargo into orbit? Here's
an explanation of what they designed and why it works.

THE STORY OF TRAVELING TO OTHER WORLDS

THIS IS THE ONLY SPACE BOAT
THAT'S LANDED PEOPLE ON
ANOTHER WORLD.

PEOPLE LANDED ON
THE MOON WITH IT
SIX TIMES . . .

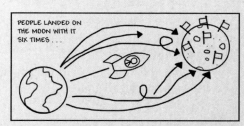

...ALL ABOUT HALF
A HUNDRED YEARS
BEFORE THIS BOOK
WAS WRITTEN.

AFTER THOSE VISITS TO
THE MOON, WE STOPPED
USING THIS SPACE BOAT
TO GO TO OTHER WORLDS.

THE US SPACE TEAM
USED THE BOAT, ONE
LAST TIME, TO SEND
UP THEIR FIRST
SPACE HOUSE.

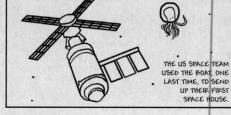

AFTER PEOPLE VISITED THE
HOUSE A FEW TIMES, IT FELL
BACK DOWN. PIECES OF IT
LANDED IN A SMALL TOWN.

THE TOWN TOLD THE US SPACE TEAM
TO PAY A FINE FOR DROPPING STUFF
ON THE GROUND.

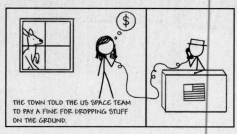

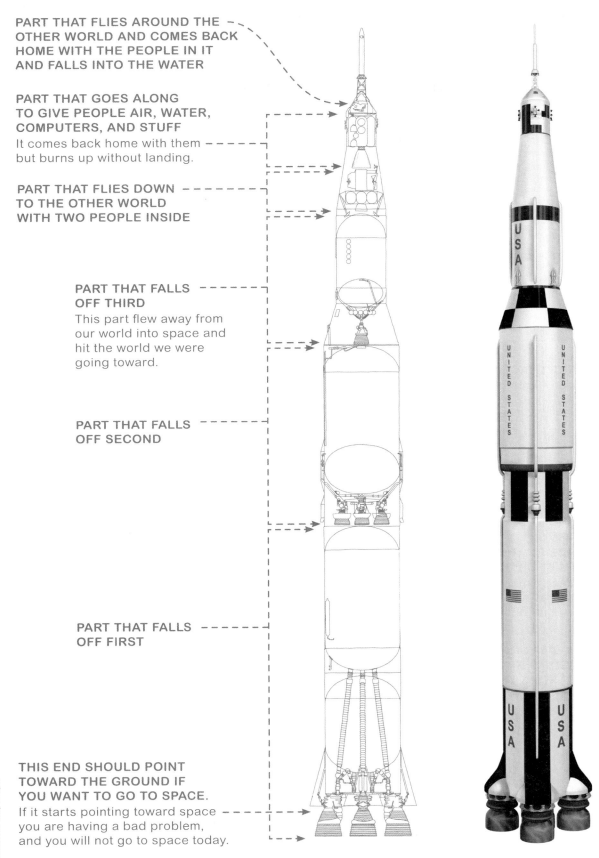

PART THAT FLIES AROUND THE
OTHER WORLD AND COMES BACK
HOME WITH THE PEOPLE IN IT
AND FALLS INTO THE WATER

PART THAT GOES ALONG
TO GIVE PEOPLE AIR, WATER,
COMPUTERS, AND STUFF
It comes back home with them
but burns up without landing.

PART THAT FLIES DOWN
TO THE OTHER WORLD
WITH TWO PEOPLE INSIDE

PART THAT FALLS
OFF THIRD
This part flew away from
our world into space and
hit the world we were
going toward.

PART THAT FALLS
OFF SECOND

PART THAT FALLS
OFF FIRST

THIS END SHOULD POINT
TOWARD THE GROUND IF
YOU WANT TO GO TO SPACE.
If it starts pointing toward space
you are having a bad problem,
and you will not go to space today.

US SPACE TEAM'S UP GOER FIVE

YOU ARE HERE

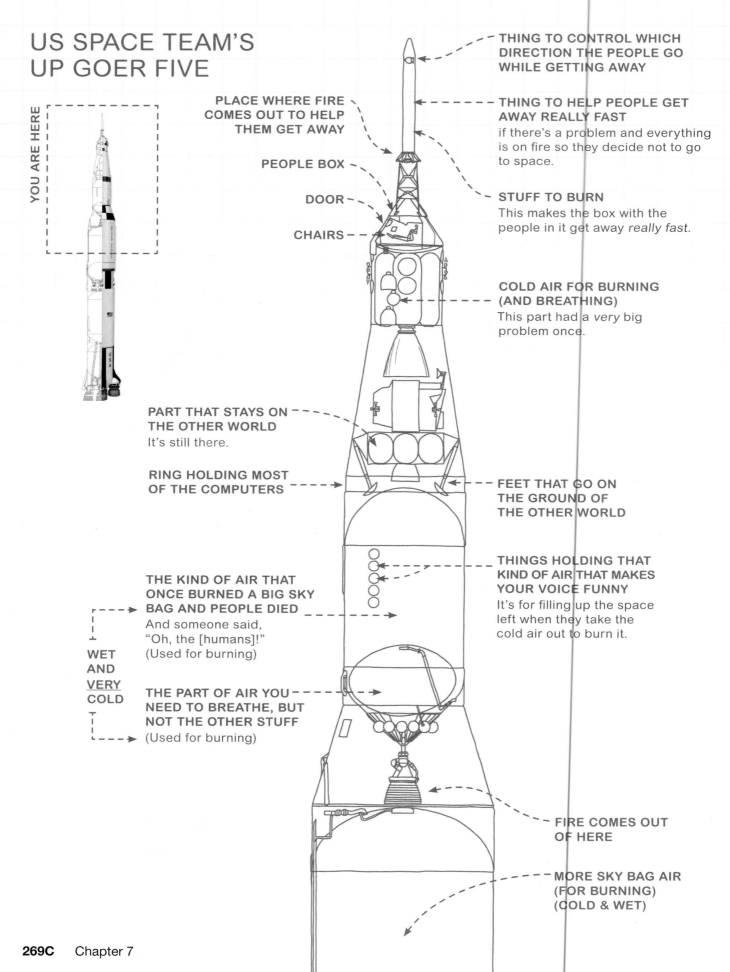

THING TO CONTROL WHICH DIRECTION THE PEOPLE GO WHILE GETTING AWAY

THING TO HELP PEOPLE GET AWAY REALLY FAST
if there's a problem and everything is on fire so they decide not to go to space.

PLACE WHERE FIRE COMES OUT TO HELP THEM GET AWAY

STUFF TO BURN
This makes the box with the people in it get away *really fast*.

PEOPLE BOX

DOOR

CHAIRS

COLD AIR FOR BURNING (AND BREATHING)
This part had a *very* big problem once.

PART THAT STAYS ON THE OTHER WORLD
It's still there.

RING HOLDING MOST OF THE COMPUTERS

FEET THAT GO ON THE GROUND OF THE OTHER WORLD

THINGS HOLDING THAT KIND OF AIR THAT MAKES YOUR VOICE FUNNY
It's for filling up the space left when they take the cold air out to burn it.

THE KIND OF AIR THAT ONCE BURNED A BIG SKY BAG AND PEOPLE DIED
And someone said, "Oh, the [humans]!" (Used for burning)

WET AND VERY COLD

THE PART OF AIR YOU NEED TO BREATHE, BUT NOT THE OTHER STUFF
(Used for burning)

FIRE COMES OUT OF HERE

MORE SKY BAG AIR (FOR BURNING) (COLD & WET)

©jamesbenet/E+/Getty Images

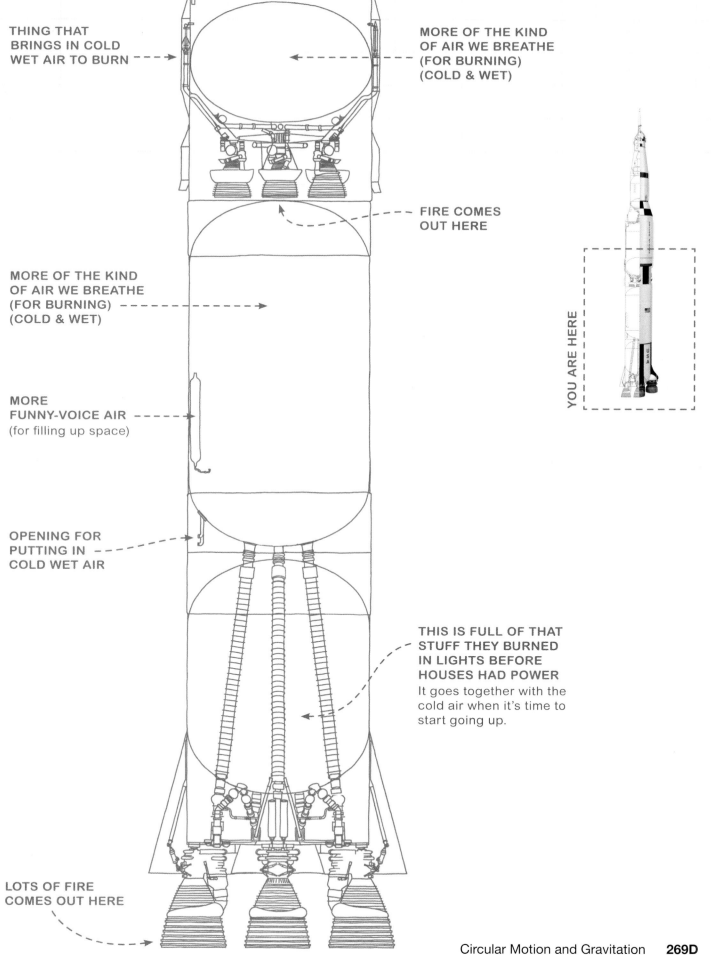

THING THAT
BRINGS IN COLD
WET AIR TO BURN

MORE OF THE KIND
OF AIR WE BREATHE
(FOR BURNING)
(COLD & WET)

FIRE COMES
OUT HERE

MORE OF THE KIND
OF AIR WE BREATHE
(FOR BURNING)
(COLD & WET)

MORE
FUNNY-VOICE AIR
(for filling up space)

YOU ARE HERE

OPENING FOR
PUTTING IN
COLD WET AIR

THIS IS FULL OF THAT
STUFF THEY BURNED
IN LIGHTS BEFORE
HOUSES HAD POWER
It goes together with the
cold air when it's time to
start going up.

LOTS OF FIRE
COMES OUT HERE

Why It Matters

Many kinds of hydraulic devices, such as the brakes in a car and the lifts that move heavy equipment, make use of the properties of fluids. An understanding of the properties of fluids is needed to design such devices.

The properties of fluids are also important for kayakers like the one pictured here. If a kayaker's weight ($\mathbf{F_g}$) exceeds the upward, buoyant force ($\mathbf{F_B}$) that causes them to float, they are sunk— literally! For an object, such as a kayak, that is immersed in a fluid, buoyant force equals the weight of the fluid that the object displaces. Buoyant force causes a kayak to pop to the surface after a plunge down a waterfall.

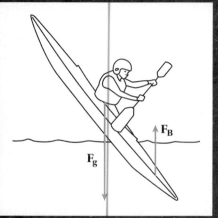

270

CHAPTER 8
Fluid Mechanics

BIG IDEA

A fluid applies a pressure
on objects that are in
contact with the fluid.

ONLINE Physics
HMHScience.com

ONLINE LABS
- **S.T.E.M. Lab** Buoyant
  Vehicle
- Buoyancy
- Archimedes' Principle

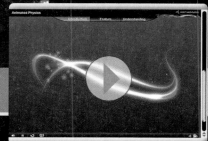

GO ONLINE
Animated
Physics
HMHScience.com

Buoyant Force

Fluids and Buoyant Force

Objectives

▶ Define a fluid.

▶ Distinguish a gas from a liquid.

▶ Determine the magnitude of the buoyant force exerted on a floating object or a submerged object.

▶ Explain why some objects float and some objects sink.

SC.912.P.8.1 Differentiate among the four states of matter.
MAFS.912.G-MG.1.2 Apply concepts of density based on area and volume in modeling situations (e.g., persons per square mile, BTUs per cubic foot). ★

fluid a nonsolid state of matter in which the atoms or molecules are free to move past each other, as in a gas or a liquid

Key Terms

fluid   mass density   buoyant force

Defining a Fluid

Matter is normally classified as being in one of three states—solid, liquid, or gaseous. Up to this point, this book's discussion of motion and the causes of motion has dealt primarily with the behavior of solid objects. This chapter concerns the mechanics of liquids and gases.

Figure 1.1(a) is a photo of a liquid; **Figure 1.1(b)** shows an example of a gas. Pause for a moment, and see if you can identify a common trait between them. One property they have in common is the ability to flow and to alter their shape in the process. Materials that exhibit these properties are called **fluids.** Solid objects are not considered to be fluids because they cannot flow and therefore have a definite shape.

Liquids have a definite volume; gases do not.

Even though both gases and liquids are fluids, there is a difference between them: One has a definite volume, and the other does not. Liquids, like solids, have a definite volume, but unlike solids, they do not have a definite shape. Imagine filling the tank of a lawn mower with gasoline. The gasoline, a liquid, changes its shape from that of its original container to that of the tank. If there is a gallon of gasoline in the container before you pour, there will be a gallon in the tank after you pour. Gases, on the other hand, have neither a definite volume nor a definite shape. When a gas is poured from a smaller container into a larger one, the gas not only changes its shape to fit the new container but also spreads out and changes its volume within the container.

FIGURE 1.1

Fluids Both **(a)** liquids and **(b)** gases are considered fluids because they can flow and change shape.

(a)

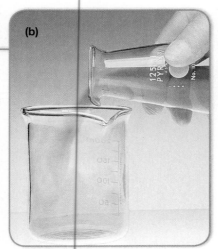

(b)

Density and Buoyant Force

Have you ever felt confined in a crowded elevator? You probably felt that way because there were too many people in the elevator for the amount of space available. In other words, the density of people was too high. In general, density is a measure of a quantity in a given space. The quantity can be anything from people or trees to mass or energy.

Mass density is mass per unit volume of a substance.

When the word *density* is used to describe a fluid, what is really being measured is the fluid's **mass density.** Mass density is the mass per unit volume of a substance. It is often represented by the Greek letter ρ (rho).

Mass Density

$$\rho = \frac{m}{V}$$

$$\text{mass density} = \frac{\text{mass}}{\text{volume}}$$

The SI unit of mass density is kilograms per cubic meter (kg/m^3). In this book, we will follow the convention of using the word *density* to refer to mass density. **Figure 1.2** lists the densities of some fluids and a few important solids.

Solids and liquids tend to be almost incompressible, meaning that their density changes very little with changes in pressure. Thus, the densities listed in **Figure 1.2** for solids and liquids are approximately independent of pressure. Gases, on the other hand, are compressible and can have densities over a wide range of values. Thus, there is not a standard density for a gas, as there is for solids and liquids. The densities listed for gases in **Figure 1.2** are the values of the density at a stated temperature and pressure. For deviations of temperature and pressure from these values, the density of the gas will vary significantly.

Buoyant forces can keep objects afloat.

Have you ever wondered why things feel lighter underwater than they do in air? The reason is that a fluid exerts an upward force on objects that are partially or completely submerged in it. This upward force is called a **buoyant force.** If you have ever rested on an air mattress in a swimming pool, you have experienced a buoyant force. The buoyant force kept you and the mattress afloat.

Because the buoyant force acts in a direction opposite the force of gravity, the net force acting on an object submerged in a fluid, such as water, is smaller than the object's weight. Thus, the object appears to weigh less in water than it does in air. The weight of an object immersed in a fluid is the object's *apparent weight*. In the case of a heavy object, such as a brick, its apparent weight is less in water than its actual weight is in air, but it may still sink in water because the buoyant force is not enough to keep it afloat.

mass density the concentration of matter of an object, measured as the mass per unit volume of a substance

buoyant force the upward force exerted by a liquid on an object immersed in or floating on the liquid

FIGURE 1.2

DENSITIES OF SOME COMMON SUBSTANCES*

Substance	ρ (kg/m³)
Hydrogen	0.0899
Helium	0.179
Steam (100°C)	0.598
Air	1.29
Oxygen	1.43
Carbon dioxide	1.98
Ethanol	0.806×10^3
Ice	0.917×10^3
Fresh water (4°C)	1.00×10^3
Seawater (15°C)	1.025×10^3
Iron	7.86×10^3
Mercury	13.6×10^3
Gold	19.3×10^3

*All densities are measured at 0°C and 1 atm unless otherwise noted.

FIGURE 1.3

Archimedes' Principle **(a)** A brick is being lowered into a container of water. **(b)** The brick displaces water, causing the water to flow into a smaller container. **(c)** When the brick is completely submerged, the volume of the displaced water **(d)** is equal to the volume of the brick.

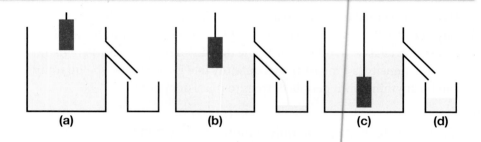

(a) (b) (c) (d)

Archimedes' principle describes the magnitude of a buoyant force.

Imagine that you submerge a brick in a container of water, as shown in **Figure 1.3.** A spout on the side of the container at the water's surface allows water to flow out of the container. As the brick sinks, the water level rises, and water flows through the spout into a smaller container. The total volume of water that collects in the smaller container is the *displaced volume* of water from the large container. The displaced volume of water is equal to the volume of the portion of the brick that is underwater.

The magnitude of the buoyant force acting on the brick at any given time can be calculated by using a rule known as *Archimedes' principle.* This principle can be stated as follows: *Any object completely or partially submerged in a fluid experiences an upward buoyant force equal in magnitude to the weight of the fluid displaced by the object.* Most people have experienced Archimedes' principle. For example, recall that it is relatively easy to lift someone if you are both standing in a swimming pool, even if lifting that same person on dry land would be difficult.

Using m_f to represent the mass of the displaced fluid, Archimedes' principle can be written symbolically as follows:

Buoyant Force

$$F_B = F_g \text{ (displaced fluid)} = m_f g$$

magnitude of buoyant force = weight of fluid displaced

Whether an object will float or sink depends on the net force acting on it. This net force is the object's apparent weight and can be calculated as follows:

$$F_{net} = F_B - F_g \text{(object)}$$

Now we can apply Archimedes' principle, using m_o to represent the mass of the submerged object.

$$F_{net} = m_f g - m_o g$$

Remember that $m = \rho V$, so the expression can be rewritten as follows:

$$F_{net} = (\rho_f V_f - \rho_o V_o)g$$

Note that in this expression, the fluid quantities refer to the *displaced* fluid.

For a floating object, the buoyant force equals the object's weight.

Imagine a cargo-filled raft floating on a lake. There are two forces acting on the raft and its cargo: the downward force of gravity and the upward buoyant force of the water. Because the raft is floating in the water, the raft is in equilibrium, and the two forces are balanced, as shown in **Figure 1.4.** For floating objects, the buoyant force and the weight of the object are equal in magnitude.

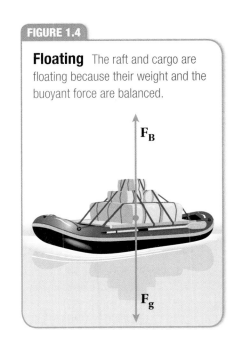

Floating The raft and cargo are floating because their weight and the buoyant force are balanced.

F_B

F_g

> **Buoyant Force on Floating Objects**
> $$F_B = F_g \, (object) = m_o g$$
> **buoyant force = weight of floating object**

Notice that Archimedes' principle is not required to find the buoyant force on a floating object if the weight of the object is known.

The apparent weight of a submerged object depends on density.

Imagine that a hole is accidentally punched in the raft shown in **Figure 1.4** and that the raft begins to sink. The cargo and raft eventually sink below the water's surface, as shown in **Figure 1.5.** The net force on the raft and cargo is the vector sum of the buoyant force and the weight of the raft and cargo. As the volume of the raft decreases, the volume of water displaced by the raft and cargo also decreases, as does the magnitude of the buoyant force. This can be written by using the expression for the net force:

$$F_{net} = (\rho_f V_f - \rho_o V_o)g$$

Because the raft and cargo are completely submerged, V_f and V_o are equal:

$$F_{net} = (\rho_f - \rho_o)Vg$$

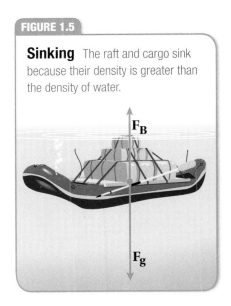

Sinking The raft and cargo sink because their density is greater than the density of water.

F_B

F_g

Notice that both the direction and the magnitude of the net force depend on the difference between the density of the object and the density of the fluid in which it is immersed. If the object's density is greater than the fluid density, the net force is negative (downward), and the object sinks. If the object's density is less than the fluid density, the net force is positive (upward), and the object rises to the surface and floats. If the densities are the same, the object hangs suspended underwater.

A simple relationship between the weight of a submerged object and the buoyant force on the object can be found by considering their ratio as follows:

$$\frac{F_g \, (object)}{F_B} = \frac{\rho_o \cancel{V} \cancel{g}}{\rho_f \cancel{V} \cancel{g}}$$

$$\frac{F_g \, (object)}{F_B} = \frac{\rho_o}{\rho_f}$$

This last expression is often useful in solving buoyancy problems.

Sample Problem A A bargain hunter purchases a "gold" crown at a flea market. After she gets home, she hangs the crown from a scale and finds its weight to be 7.84 N. She then weighs the crown while it is immersed in water, and the scale reads 6.86 N. Is the crown made of pure gold? Explain.

① ANALYZE

Given: $F_g = 7.84$ N   apparent weight = 6.86 N
$\rho_f = \rho_{water} = 1.00 \times 10^3$ kg/m³

Unknown: $\rho_o = ?$

Diagram:

In air   In water

Tips and Tricks

The use of a diagram can help clarify a problem and the variables involved. In this diagram, $F_{T,1}$ equals the actual weight of the crown, and $F_{T,2}$ is the apparent weight of the crown when immersed in water.

② PLAN

Choose an equation or situation:
Because the object is completely submerged, consider the ratio of the weight to the buoyant force.

$$F_B - F_g = \text{apparent weight}$$

$$\frac{F_g}{F_B} = \frac{\rho_o}{\rho_f}$$

Rearrange the equation to isolate the unknown:

$$F_B = F_g - (\text{apparent weight})$$

$$\rho_o = \frac{F_g}{F_B} \rho_f$$

③ SOLVE

Substitute the values into the equation, and solve:

$$F_B = 7.84 \text{ N} - 6.86 \text{ N} = 0.98 \text{ N}$$

$$\rho_o = \frac{F_g}{F_B} \rho_f = \frac{7.84 \text{ N}}{0.98 \text{ N}} (1.00 \times 10^3 \text{ kg/m}^3)$$

$$\boxed{\rho_o = 8.0 \times 10^3 \text{ kg/m}^3}$$

From **Figure 1.2**, the density of gold is 19.3×10^3 kg/m³. Because 8.0×10^3 kg/m³ $< 19.3 \times 10^3$ kg/m³, the crown cannot be pure gold.

Buoyant Force (continued)

Practice

1. A piece of metal weighs 50.0 N in air, 36.0 N in water, and 41.0 N in an unknown liquid. Find the densities of the following:

   a. the metal

   b. the unknown liquid

2. A 2.8 kg rectangular air mattress is 2.00 m long, 0.500 m wide, and 0.100 m thick. What mass can it support in water before sinking?

3. A ferry boat is 4.0 m wide and 6.0 m long. When a truck pulls onto it, the boat sinks 4.00 cm in the water. What is the weight of the truck?

4. An empty rubber balloon has a mass of 0.0120 kg. The balloon is filled with helium at 0°C, 1 atm pressure, and a density of 0.179 kg/m³. The filled balloon has a radius of 0.500 m.

   a. What is the magnitude of the buoyant force acting on the balloon? (Hint: See **Figure 1.2** for the density of air.)

   b. What is the magnitude of the net force acting on the balloon?

SECTION 1 FORMATIVE ASSESSMENT

▶ Reviewing Main Ideas

1. What is the difference between a solid and a fluid? What is the difference between a gas and a liquid?

2. Which of the following objects will float in mercury?
   a. a solid gold bead
   b. an ice cube
   c. an iron bolt
   d. 5 mL of water

3. A 650 kg weather balloon is designed to lift a 4600 kg package. What volume should the balloon have after being inflated with helium at 0°C and 1 atm pressure to lift the total load? (Hint: Use the density values in **Figure 1.2.**)

4. A submerged submarine alters its buoyancy so that it initially accelerates upward at 0.325 m/s². What is the submarine's average density at this time? (Hint: the density of sea water is 1.025×10^3 kg/m³.)

✔ Critical Thinking

5. Many kayaks are made of plastics and other composite materials that are denser than water. How are such kayaks able to float in water?

Fluid Pressure

Key Term

pressure

Pressure

Deep-sea explorers wear atmospheric diving suits like the one shown in **Figure 2.1** to resist the forces exerted by water in the depths of the ocean. You experience the effects of similar forces on your ears when you dive to the bottom of a swimming pool, drive up a mountain, or ride in an airplane.

Pressure is force per unit area.

pressure the magnitude of the force on a surface per unit area

In the examples above, the fluids exert **pressure** on your eardrums. Pressure is a measure of how much force is applied over a given area. It can be written as follows:

Pressure

$$P = \frac{F}{A}$$

$$\text{pressure} = \frac{\text{force}}{\text{area}}$$

The SI unit of pressure is the *pascal* (Pa), which is equal to 1 N/m^2. The pascal is a small unit of pressure. The pressure of the atmosphere at sea level is about 1.01×10^5 Pa. This amount of air pressure under normal conditions is the basis for another unit, the *atmosphere* (atm). For the purpose of calculating pressure, 10^5 Pa is about the same as 1 atm. The absolute air pressure inside a typical automobile tire is about 3×10^5 Pa, or 3 atm.

Applied pressure is transmitted equally throughout a fluid.

When you pump a bicycle tire, you apply a force on the pump that in turn exerts a force on the air inside the tire. The air responds by pushing not only against the pump but also against the walls of the tire. As a result, the pressure increases by an equal amount throughout the tire.

In general, if the pressure in a fluid is increased at any point in a container (such as at the valve of the tire), the pressure increases at all points inside the container by exactly the same amount. Blaise Pascal (1623–1662) noted this fact in what is now called *Pascal's principle* (or *Pascal's law*):

Pascal's Principle

Pressure applied to a fluid in a closed container is transmitted equally to every point of the fluid and to the walls of the container.

FIGURE 2.1

Protection from Pressure

Atmospheric diving suits allow divers to withstand the pressure exerted by the fluid in the ocean at depths of up to 610 m.

©Alexis Rosenfeld/Photo Researchers, Inc.

A hydraulic lift, such as the one shown in **Figure 2.2,** makes use of Pascal's principle. A small force F_1 applied to a small piston of area A_1 causes a pressure increase in a fluid, such as oil. According to Pascal's principle, this increase in pressure, P_{inc}, is transmitted to a larger piston of area A_2, and the fluid exerts a force F_2 on this piston. Applying Pascal's principle and the definition of pressure gives the following equation:

$$P_{inc} = \frac{F_1}{A_1} = \frac{F_2}{A_2}$$

Rearranging this equation to solve for F_2 produces the following:

$$F_2 = \frac{A_2}{A_1} F_1$$

This second equation shows that the output force, F_2, is larger than the input force, F_1, by a factor equal to the ratio of the areas of the two pistons. However, the input force must be applied over a longer distance; the work required to lift the truck is not reduced by the use of a hydraulic lift.

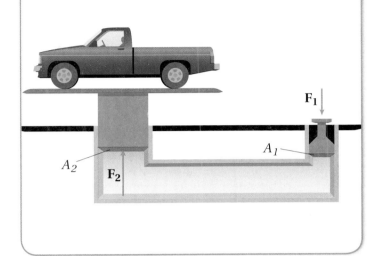

FIGURE 2.2

Hydraulic Lift The pressure is the same on both sides of the enclosed fluid, allowing a small force to lift a heavy object.

GO ONLINE

Interactive Demo
HMHScience.com

Pressure

Sample Problem B The surface of the planet Jupiter is believed to consist of liquid hydrogen. Above this surface lies a thick atmosphere that exerts a pressure of 1.00×10^7 Pa on Jupiter's surface. If the total force exerted by this atmosphere is 6.41×10^{23} N, what is the area of Jupiter's surface?

   ANALYZE

Given: $P = 1.00 \times 10^7$ Pa

$F = 6.41 \times 10^{23}$ N

Unknown: $A = ?$

   SOLVE

Use the equation for pressure, and rearrange it to solve for the area.

$$P = \frac{F}{A} \qquad\qquad A = \frac{F}{P}$$

$$A = \frac{6.41 \times 10^{23}\ \text{N}}{1.00 \times 10^7\ \text{Pa}} = \boxed{6.41 \times 10^{16}\ \text{m}^2}$$

Continued

Practice

1. In a car lift, compressed air exerts a force on a piston with a radius of 5.00 cm. This pressure is transmitted to a second piston with a radius of 15.0 cm.

   a. How large a force must the compressed air exert to lift a 1.33×10^4 N car?

   b. What pressure produces this force? Neglect the weight of the pistons.

2. A ball strikes the pavement with a force of 5.0 N. If the pressure exerted on the pavement is 9.6×10^3 Pa, what is the area of contact between the ball and the pavement?

3. Atmospheric pressure is often given in units of millimeters of mercury. This refers to the height of a mercury column above the mercury's surface at the base of a barometer. The force exerted by the atmosphere on the surface of the mercury in the reservoir equals the weight of the mercury in the column. If the mercury column extends 760 mm above the mercury's surface in the reservoir, what is the atmosphere's pressure over the mercury? Use 13.6×10^3 kg/m^3 for the density of mercury.

Pressure varies with depth in a fluid.

As a submarine dives deeper in the water, the pressure of the water against the hull of the submarine increases, so the hull must be strong enough to withstand large pressures. Water pressure increases with depth, because the water at a given depth must support the weight of the water above it.

Imagine a small area on the hull of a submarine. The weight of the entire column of water above that area exerts a force on the area. The column of water has a volume equal to Ah, where A is the cross-sectional area of the column and h is its height. Hence the mass of this column of water is $m = \rho V = \rho Ah$. Using the definitions of density and pressure, the pressure at this depth due to the weight of the column of water can be calculated as follows:

$$P = \frac{F}{A} = \frac{mg}{A} = \frac{\rho Vg}{A} = \frac{\rho Ahg}{A} = \rho hg$$

This equation is valid only if the density is the same throughout the fluid.

The pressure in the equation above is referred to as *gauge pressure*. It is not the total pressure at this depth because the atmosphere itself also exerts a pressure at the surface. Thus, the gauge pressure is actually the total pressure minus the atmospheric pressure. By using the symbol P_0 for the atmospheric pressure at the surface, we can express the total pressure, or *absolute pressure*, at a given depth in a fluid of uniform density ρ as follows:

> ### Fluid Pressure as a Function of Depth
>
> $$P = P_0 + \rho g h$$
>
> **absolute pressure =**
> **atmospheric pressure + (density × free-fall acceleration × depth)**

FIGURE 2.3

Pressure and Depth The fluid pressure at the bottom of the box is greater than the fluid pressure at the top of the box.

This expression for pressure in a fluid can be used to help understand buoyant forces. Consider a rectangular box submerged in a container of water, as shown in **Figure 2.3**. The water pressure at the top of the box is $P_0 + \rho g h_1$, and the water pressure at the bottom of the box is $P_0 + \rho g h_2$. The downward force on the box is in the negative direction and given by $-A(P_0 + \rho g h_1)$, where A is the area of the top of the box. The upward force on the box is in the positive direction and given by $A(P_0 + \rho g h_2)$. The net force on the box is the sum of these two forces.

$$F_{net} = A(P_0 + \rho g h_2) - A(P_0 + \rho g h_1) = \rho g(h_2 - h_1)A = \rho g V = m_f g$$

Note that this is an expression of Archimedes' principle. In general, we can say that buoyant forces arise from the differences in fluid pressure between the top and the bottom of an immersed object.

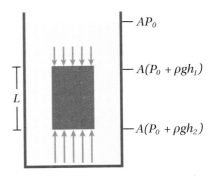

SECTION 2 FORMATIVE ASSESSMENT

▶ Reviewing Main Ideas

1. Which of the following exerts the most pressure while resting on a floor?
   a. a 25 N cube with 1.5 m sides
   b. a 15 N cylinder resting vertically with a base radius of 1.0 m
   c. a 25 N cube with 2.0 m sides
   d. a 25 N cylinder resting vertically with a base radius of 1.0 m

2. Water is to be pumped to the top of the Empire State Building, which is 366 m high. What gauge pressure is needed in the water line at the base of the building to raise the water to this height? (Hint: See **Figure 1.2** for the density of water.)

3. When a submarine dives to a depth of 5.0×10^2 m, how much pressure, in Pa, must its hull be able to withstand? How many times larger is this pressure than the pressure at the surface? (Hint: See **Figure 1.2** for the density of seawater.)

✓ Critical Thinking

4. Calculate the depth in the ocean at which the pressure is three times atmospheric pressure. (Hint: Use the value for the density of seawater given in **Figure 1.2**.)

Objectives

▶ Examine the motion of a fluid using the continuity equation.

▶ Recognize the effects of Bernoulli's principle on fluid motion.

Fluids in Motion

Key Term
ideal fluid

Fluid Flow

Have you ever gone canoeing or rafting down a river? If so, you may have noticed that part of the river flowed smoothly, allowing you to float calmly or to simply paddle along. At other places in the river, there may have been rocks or dramatic bends that created foamy white-water rapids.

When a fluid, such as river water, is in motion, the flow can be characterized in one of two ways. The flow is said to be *laminar* if every particle that passes a particular point moves along the same smooth path traveled by the particles that passed that point earlier. The smooth stretches of a river are regions of laminar flow.

In contrast, the flow of a fluid becomes irregular, or *turbulent*, above a certain velocity or under conditions that can cause abrupt changes in velocity, such as where there are obstacles or sharp turns in a river. Irregular motions of the fluid, called *eddy currents*, are characteristic of turbulent flow.

Figure 3.1 shows a photograph of water flowing past a rock. Notice the dramatic difference in flow patterns between the laminar flow and the turbulent flow. Laminar flow is much easier to model, because it is predictable. Turbulent flow is extremely chaotic and unpredictable.

FIGURE 3.1

Fluid Flow The water flowing around this rock exhibits laminar flow and turbulent flow.

Laminar flow   Turbulent flow

ideal fluid a fluid that has no internal friction or viscosity and is incompressible

The ideal fluid model simplifies fluid-flow analysis.

Many features of fluid motion can be understood by considering the behavior of an **ideal fluid.** Although no real fluid has all the properties of an ideal fluid, the ideal fluid model does help explain many properties of real fluids, so the model is a useful tool for analysis. While discussing density and buoyancy, we assumed all of the fluids used in problems were practically incompressible. A fluid is incompressible if the density of the fluid always remains constant.

The term *viscosity* refers to the amount of internal friction within a fluid. A fluid with a high viscosity flows more slowly than does a fluid with a low viscosity. As a viscous fluid flows, part of the kinetic energy of the fluid is transformed into internal energy due to the friction of the fluid particles sliding past each other. Ideal fluids are considered *nonviscous*, so they lose no kinetic energy due to friction as they flow. Ideal fluids are also characterized by a *steady flow*. In other words, the velocity, density, and pressure at each point in the fluid are constant. Ideal flow of an ideal fluid is also *nonturbulent*, which means that there are no eddy currents in the moving fluid.

Principles of Fluid Flow

Fluid behavior is often very complex. Several general principles describing the flow of fluids can be derived relatively easily from basic physical laws.

The continuity equation results from mass conservation.

Imagine that an ideal fluid flows into one end of a pipe and out the other end, as shown in **Figure 3.2.** The diameter of the pipe is different at each end. How does the speed of fluid flow change as the fluid passes through the pipe?

Because mass is conserved and because the fluid is incompressible, we know that the mass flowing into the bottom of the pipe, m_1, must equal the mass flowing out of the top of the pipe, m_2, during any given time interval:

$$m_1 = m_2$$

This simple equation can be expanded by recalling that $m = \rho V$ and by using the formula for the volume of a cylinder, $V = A\Delta x$.

$$\rho_1 V_1 = \rho_2 V_2$$

$$\rho_1 A_1 \Delta x_1 = \rho_2 A_2 \Delta x_2$$

The length of the cylinder, Δx, is also the distance the fluid travels, which is equal to the speed of flow multiplied by the time interval ($\Delta x = v\Delta t$).

$$\rho_1 A_1 v_1 \Delta t = \rho_2 A_2 v_2 \Delta t$$

The time interval and, for an ideal fluid, the density are the same on each side of the equation, so they cancel each other out. The resulting equation is called the continuity equation:

Continuity Equation
$$A_1 v_1 = A_2 v_2$$

area × speed in region 1 = area × speed in region 2

The speed of fluid flow depends on cross-sectional area.

Note in the continuity equation that A_1 and A_2 can represent any two different cross-sectional areas of the pipe, not just the ends. This equation implies that the fluid speed is faster where the pipe is narrow and slower where the pipe is wide. The product Av, which has units of volume per unit time, is called the *flow rate*. The flow rate is constant throughout the pipe.

The continuity equation explains an effect you may have observed as water flows slowly from a faucet, as shown in **Figure 3.3.** Because the water speeds up due to gravity as it falls, the stream narrows, satisfying the continuity equation. The continuity equation also explains why a river tends to flow more rapidly in places where the river is shallow or narrow than in places where the river is deep and wide.

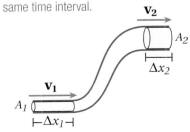

FIGURE 3.2

Mass Conservation in a Pipe
The mass flowing into the pipe must equal the mass flowing out of the pipe in the same time interval.

FIGURE 3.3

Narrowing of Falling Water
The width of a stream of water narrows as the water falls and speeds up.

FIGURE 3.4

Pressure and Speed A leaf speeds up as it passes into a constriction in a drainage pipe. The water pressure on the right is less than the pressure on the left.

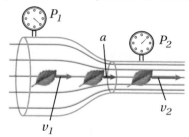

FIGURE 3.5

Bernoulli's Principle As air flows around an airplane wing, air above moves faster than air below, producing lift.

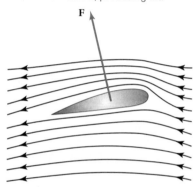

The pressure in a fluid is related to the speed of flow.

Suppose there is a water-logged leaf carried along by the water in a drainage pipe, as shown in **Figure 3.4**. The continuity equation shows that the water moves faster through the narrow part of the tube than through the wider part of the tube. Therefore, as the water carries the leaf into the constriction, the leaf speeds up.

If the water and the leaf are accelerating as they enter the constriction, an unbalanced force must be causing the acceleration, according to Newton's second law. This unbalanced force is a result of the fact that the water pressure in front of the leaf is less than the water pressure behind the leaf. The pressure difference causes the leaf and the water around it to accelerate as it enters the narrow part of the tube. This behavior illustrates a general principle known as *Bernoulli's principle*, which can be stated as follows:

Bernoulli's Principle

The pressure in a fluid decreases as the fluid's velocity increases.

The lift on an airplane wing can be explained, in part, with Bernoulli's principle. As an airplane flies, air flows around the wings and body of the plane, as shown in **Figure 3.5**. Airplane wings are designed to direct the flow of air so that the air speed above the wing is greater than the air speed below the wing. Therefore, the air pressure above the wing is less than the pressure below, and there is a net upward force on the wing, called *lift*. The tilt of an airplane wing also adds to the lift on the plane. The front of the wing is tilted upward so that air striking the bottom of the wing is deflected downward.

✓ SECTION 3 FORMATIVE ASSESSMENT

▶ Reviewing Main Ideas

1. Water at a pressure of 3.00×10^5 Pa flows through a horizontal pipe at a speed of 1.00 m/s. The pipe narrows to one-fourth its original diameter. What is the speed of the flow in the narrow section?

2. A 2.0 cm diameter faucet tap fills a 2.5×10^{-2} m³ container in 30.0 s. What is the speed at which the water leaves the faucet?

✓ Critical Thinking

3. The time required to fill a glass with water from a large container with a spigot is 30.0 s. If you replace the spigot with a smaller one so that the speed of the water leaving the nozzle doubles, how long does it take to fill the glass?

Interpreting Graphics

4. For this problem, refer back to **Figure 3.2**. Assume that the cross-sectional area A_2 in the tube is increased. Would the length Δx_2 need to be longer or shorter for the mass of liquid in both sections to still be equal?

Properties of Gases

When the density of a gas is sufficiently low, the pressure, volume, and temperature of the gas tend to be related to one another in a fairly simple way. This relationship is a good approximation for the behavior of many real gases over a wide range of temperatures and pressures, provided their particles are not charged, as in a plasma. These observations have led scientists to develop the concept of an *ideal gas*.

Volume, pressure, and temperature are the three variables that completely describe the macroscopic state of an ideal gas. One of the most important equations in fluid mechanics relates these three quantities to each other.

The Ideal Gas Law

The *ideal gas law* is an expression that relates the volume, pressure, and temperature of a gas. This relationship can be written as follows:

Ideal Gas Law

$$PV = Nk_BT$$

**pressure × volume =
number of gas particles × Boltzmann's constant × temperature**

The symbol k_B represents *Boltzmann's constant*. Its value has been experimentally determined to be approximately 1.38×10^{-23} J/K. Note that when applying the ideal gas law, you must express the temperature in the Kelvin scale. (See the chapter "Heat" to learn about the Kelvin scale.) Also, the ideal gas law makes no mention of the composition of the gas. The gas particles could be oxygen, carbon dioxide, or any other gas. In this sense, the ideal gas law is universally applicable to all gases.

If a gas undergoes a change in volume, pressure, or temperature (or any combination of these), the ideal gas law can be expressed in a particularly useful form. If the number of particles in the gas is constant, the initial and final states of the gas are related as follows:

$$N_1 = N_2$$

$$\frac{P_1V_1}{T_1} = \frac{P_2V_2}{T_2}$$

This relation is illustrated in the experiment shown in **Figure 1**. In this experiment, a flask filled with air (V_1 equals the volume of the flask) at room temperature (T_1) and atmospheric pressure ($P_1 = P_0$) is placed over a heat source, with a balloon placed over the opening of the flask. As the flask sits over the burner, the temperature of the air inside it increases from T_1 to T_2.

©Richard Megna/Fundamental Photographs, New York

FIGURE 1

Temperature, Pressure, and Volume The balloon is inflated because the volume and pressure of the air inside are both increasing.

IDEAL GAS LAW

Make sure the bottle is empty, and remove the cap. Place the bottle in the freezer for at least 10 min. Wet the quarter with water, and place the quarter over the bottle's opening as you take the bottle out of the freezer. Set the bottle on a nearby tabletop; then observe the bottle and quarter while the air in the bottle warms up. As the air inside the bottle begins to return to room temperature, the quarter begins to jiggle around on top of the bottle. What does this movement tell you about the pressure inside the bottle? What causes this change in pressure? Hypothesize as to why you need to wet the quarter before placing it on top of the bottle.

According to the ideal gas law, when the temperature increases, either the pressure or the volume—or both—must also increase. Thus, the air inside the flask exerts a pressure (P_2) on the balloon that serves to inflate the balloon. Because the balloon is expandable, the air expands to a larger volume (V_2) to fill the balloon. When the flask is taken off the burner, the pressure, volume, and temperature of the air inside will slowly return to their initial states.

Another alternative form of the ideal gas law indicates the law's dependence on mass density. Assuming each particle in the gas has a mass m, the total mass of the gas is $N \times m = M$. The ideal gas law can then be written as follows:

$$PV = Nk_BT = \frac{Mk_BT}{m}$$

$$P = \frac{Mk_BT}{mV} = \left(\frac{M}{V}\right)\frac{k_BT}{m} = \frac{\rho k_BT}{m}$$

A Real Gas

An ideal gas is defined as a gas whose behavior is accurately described by the ideal gas law. Although no real gas obeys the ideal gas law exactly for all temperatures and pressures, the ideal gas law holds for a broad range of physical conditions for all gases. The behavior of real gases departs from the behavior of an ideal gas at high pressures or low temperatures, conditions under which the gas nearly liquefies. However, when a real gas has a relatively high temperature and a relatively low pressure, such as at room temperature and atmospheric pressure, its behavior approximates that of an ideal gas.

For problems involving the motion of fluids, we have assumed that all gases and liquids are ideal fluids. An ideal fluid is a liquid or gas that is assumed to be incompressible. This is usually a good assumption, because it is difficult to compress a fluid—even a gas—when it is not confined to a container. A fluid will tend to flow under the action of a force, changing its shape while maintaining a constant volume, rather than compress.

This feature, however, considers confined gases whose pressure, volume, and temperature may change. For example, when a force is applied to a piston, the gas inside the cylinder below the piston is compressed. Even though an ideal gas behaves like an ideal fluid in many situations, it cannot be treated as incompressible when confined to a container.

Did YOU Know?

A third way of writing the ideal gas law may be familiar to you from your study of chemistry:

$$PV = nRT$$

In this equation, n is the number of moles of gas (one mole is equal to 6.02×10^{23} particles). The quantity R is a number called the *molar (universal) gas constant* and has a value of 8.31 J/(mol·K).

Fluid Pressure

This feature discusses some topics related to fluid pressure, including atmospheric pressure and the kinetic theory of gases. It also covers Bernoulli's equation, which is a more general form of Bernoulli's principle.

Atmospheric Pressure

The weight of the air in the upper portion of Earth's atmosphere exerts pressure on the layers of air below. This pressure is called *atmospheric pressure*. The force that atmospheric pressure exerts on our bodies is extremely large. (Assuming a body area of 2 m², this force is on the order of 200 000 N, or 40 000 lb.) How can we exist under such tremendous forces without our bodies collapsing? The answer is that our body cavities and tissues are permeated with fluids and gases that are pushing outward with a pressure equal to that of the atmosphere. Consequently, our bodies are in equilibrium—the force of the atmosphere pushing in equals the internal force pushing out.

An instrument that is commonly used to measure atmospheric pressure is the *mercury barometer*. **Figure 1** shows a very simple mercury barometer. A long tube that is open at one end and closed at the other is filled with mercury and then inverted into a dish of mercury. Once the tube is inverted, the mercury does not empty into the bowl. Instead, the atmosphere exerts a pressure on the mercury in the bowl. This atmospheric pressure pushes the mercury in the tube to some height above the bowl. In this way, the force exerted on the bowl of mercury by the atmosphere is equal to the weight of the column of mercury in the tube. Any change in the height of the column of mercury means that the atmosphere's pressure has changed.

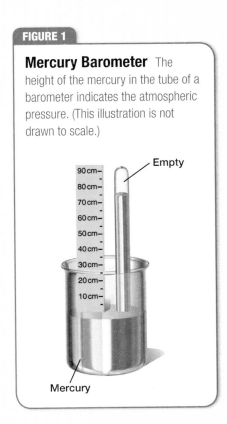

Mercury Barometer The height of the mercury in the tube of a barometer indicates the atmospheric pressure. (This illustration is not drawn to scale.)

Empty

90 cm—
80 cm—
70 cm—
60 cm—
50 cm—
40 cm—
30 cm—
20 cm—
10 cm—

Mercury

Kinetic Theory of Gases

Many models of a gas have been developed over the years. Almost all of these models attempt to explain the macroscopic properties of a gas, such as pressure, in terms of events occurring in the gas on a microscopic scale. The most successful model by far is the *kinetic theory of gases*.

In kinetic theory, gas particles are likened to a collection of billiard balls that constantly collide with one another. This simple model is successful in explaining many of the macroscopic properties of a gas. For instance, as these particles strike a wall of a container, they transfer some of their momentum during the collision. The rate of transfer of momentum to the container wall is equal to the force exerted by the gas on the container wall, in accordance with the impulse-momentum theorem. This force per unit area is the gas pressure.

Bernoulli's Equation

Imagine a fluid moving through a pipe of varying cross-sectional area and elevation, as shown in **Figure 2**. When the cross-sectional area changes, the pressure and speed of the fluid can change. This change in kinetic energy may be compensated for by a change in gravitational potential energy or by a change in pressure (so energy is still conserved). The expression for the conservation of energy in fluids is called *Bernoulli's equation*. Bernoulli's equation is expressed mathematically as follows:

> **Bernoulli's Equation**
> $$P + \tfrac{1}{2}\rho v^2 + \rho g h = \text{constant}$$
>
> **pressure + kinetic energy per unit volume + gravitational potential energy per unit volume = constant along a given streamline**

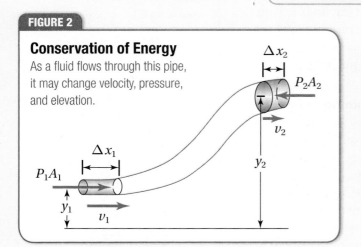

FIGURE 2

Conservation of Energy
As a fluid flows through this pipe, it may change velocity, pressure, and elevation.

Bernoulli's equation differs slightly from the law of conservation of energy. For example, two of the terms on the left side of the equation look like the terms for kinetic energy and gravitational potential energy, but they contain density, ρ, instead of mass, m. The reason is that the conserved quantity in Bernoulli's equation is energy per unit volume, not just energy. This statement of the conservation of energy in fluids also includes an additional term: pressure, P. If you wish to compare the energy in a given volume of fluid at two different points, Bernoulli's equation takes the following equivalent form:

$$P_1 + \tfrac{1}{2}\rho v_1^2 + \rho g h_1 = P_2 + \tfrac{1}{2}\rho v_2^2 + \rho g h_2$$

Comparing Bernoulli's Principle and Equation

Two special cases of Bernoulli's equation are worth mentioning here. First, if the fluid is at rest, then both speeds are zero. This case is a static situation, such as a column of water in a cylinder. If the height at the top of the column, h_1, is defined as zero and h_2 is the depth, then Bernoulli's equation reduces to the equation for pressure as a function of depth, introduced in the chapter on fluids:

$$P_1 = P_2 + \rho g h_2 \quad \text{(static fluid)}$$

Second, imagine again a fluid flowing through a horizontal pipe with a constriction. Because the height of the fluid is constant, the gravitational potential energy does not change. Bernoulli's equation then reduces to:

$$P_1 + \tfrac{1}{2}\rho v_1^2 = P_2 + \tfrac{1}{2}\rho v_2^2 \quad \text{(horizontal pipe)}$$

This equation suggests that if v_1 is greater than v_2 at two different points in the flow, then P_1 must be less than P_2. In other words, the pressure decreases as speed increases—Bernoulli's principle. Thus, Bernoulli's principle is a special case of Bernoulli's equation and is strictly true only when elevation is constant.

Modeling Bat Flight

Scientists and engineers develop models to explain phenomena and analyze systems. Models can be mathematical relationships, physical replicas, diagrams, or simulations that simplify the system and highlight the features that are of interest. Scientists use models to develop explanations and to make predictions about the behavior of the system. These predictions are then compared with the real world so that corrections to the model or current theories can be made. Engineers use models to test and refine designs. This allows them to make and test design improvements without having to construct full-scale prototypes or conduct impractical or dangerous tests on the system itself.

Developing a Working Model

Bat wings are much more complex than those of insects and birds, consisting of 25 specialized joints. Bats also use their hind limbs, back feet, and forelimb digits to control the shape of the wing and the angle of flight. Their stretchy wings allow them to capture air on the downstroke like a parachute and to release that air on the upstroke. This makes a bat wing two to three times more efficient than the rigid airfoil wing of an airplane. To gain flying speed, bats contract the thin, flexible membrane of their wings so that the entire wing is shorter and straighter. This reduces drag, which is the friction between the wing and the air through which it travels. The specialized structure of bat wings also makes it possible for bats to carry relatively heavy loads, fly long distances, and maneuver through tight spots between tree branches.

Engineers are interested in learning more about how bats fly so they can design and build aircraft that are more flexible and better able to withstand impact. One goal is to use what they learn about bat flight to build bat-sized drones. To this end, scientists and engineers at Brown University are collaborating to reveal some of the secrets of bat flight. They have observed the motion of bat wings by placing sensors on the underside of the wings and filming them with high-resolution cameras. Using the information they gathered about how bats move in flight, they have designed a "robobat," which is a simplified version of a bat wing, consisting of only seven joints. The engineers used a 3D printer to build a model consisting of a skeleton and a thin sheet of rubber for the wing membrane. The 20-centimeter-long model wing folds and expands just like a bat's wing.

The scientists learned as much when their model failed as they did when it worked. For example, they learned that the elbow joint of the wing had to be held together by very strong ligaments in order to withstand the forces from flight. They used a network of elastic fibers to mimic the strong and stretchy wing membrane of the bat.

Robot motors that flap the model wings measure power output and the energy required for each flap. Scientists observed the robobat in a wind tunnel to measure the aerodynamics of bat flight, including the lift and thrust generated by the motion of the wing. Since the model is easier to observe and work with than a live bat, the robobat helps scientists understand the aerodynamics of a bat's flight, and will hopefully help engineers design better aircraft.

- Describe the characteristics of a bat wing that make it especially adapted for flight.

- What do scientists hope to achieve by modeling bat flight? How about engineers?

SECTION 1 **Fluids and Buoyant Force**

KEY TERMS

- Force is a vector quantity that causes acceleration.
- A fluid is a material that can flow, and thus it has no definite shape. Both gases and liquids are fluids.
- Buoyant force is an upward force exerted by a fluid on an object floating on or submerged in the fluid.
- The magnitude of a buoyant force for a submerged object is determined by Archimedes' principle and is equal to the weight of the displaced fluid.
- The magnitude of a buoyant force for a floating object is equal to the weight of the object, because the object is in equilibrium.

fluid

mass density

buoyant force

SECTION 2 **Fluid Pressure**

KEY TERM

- Pressure in a fluid is the force per unit area exerted by the fluid on the surface.
- According to Pascal's principle, pressure applied to a fluid in a closed container is transmitted equally to every point of the fluid and to the walls of the container.
- The pressure in a fluid increases with depth.

pressure

SECTION 3 **Fluids in Motion**

KEY TERM

- Moving fluids can exhibit laminar (smooth) flow or turbulent flow.
- An ideal fluid is incompressible, nonviscous, and, when undergoing ideal flow, nonturbulent.
- The continuity equation is derived from the fact that the amount of fluid leaving a pipe during some time interval equals the amount entering the pipe during that same time interval.
- According to Bernoulli's principle, the pressure of an ideal fluid flowing horizontally through some region decreases as the speed of the fluid increases.

ideal fluid

VARIABLE SYMBOLS			
Quantities	**Units**		**Conversions**
ρ density	kg/m^3	kilogram per meter^3	$= 10^{-3}$ g/cm^3
P pressure	Pa	pascal	$= $ N/m^2 $= 10^{-5}$ atm

Problem Solving

See **Appendix D: Equations** for a summary of the equations introduced in this chapter. If you need more problem-solving practice, see **Appendix I: Additional Problems.**

Density and Buoyancy

▶ REVIEWING MAIN IDEAS

1. How is weight affected by buoyant force?

2. Buoyant force equals what for any floating object?

CONCEPTUAL QUESTIONS

3. If an inflated beach ball is placed beneath the surface of a pool of water and released, the ball shoots upward. Why?

4. An ice cube is submerged in a glass of water. What happens to the level of the water as the ice melts?

5. Will a ship ride higher in an inland freshwater lake or in the ocean? Why?

6. Steel is much denser than water. How, then, do steel boats float?

7. A small piece of steel is tied to a block of wood. When the wood is placed in a tub of water with the steel on top, half of the block is submerged. If the block is inverted so that the steel is underwater, will the amount of the wooden block that is submerged increase, decrease, or remain the same?

PRACTICE PROBLEMS

For problems 8–9, see Sample Problem A.

8. An object weighs 315 N in air. When tied to a string, connected to a balance, and immersed in water, it weighs 265 N. When it is immersed in oil, it weighs 269 N. Find the following:
   a. the density of the object
   b. the density of the oil

9. A sample of an unknown material weighs 300.0 N in air and 200.0 N when submerged in an alcohol solution with a density of 0.70×10^3 kg/m³. What is the density of the material?

Pressure

▶ REVIEWING MAIN IDEAS

10. Is a large amount of pressure always caused by a large force? Explain your answer.

11. What is the SI unit of pressure? What is it equal to in terms of other SI units?

CONCEPTUAL QUESTIONS

12. After a long class, a physics teacher stretches out for a nap on a bed of nails. How is this possible?

13. When drinking through a straw, you reduce the pressure in your mouth, and the atmosphere moves the liquid. Could you use a straw to drink on the moon?

PRACTICE PROBLEMS

For problems 14–16, see Sample Problem B.

14. The four tires of an automobile are inflated to an absolute pressure of 2.0×10^5 Pa. Each tire has an area of 0.024 m² in contact with the ground. Determine the weight of the automobile.

15. A pipe contains water at 5.00×10^5 Pa above atmospheric pressure. If you patch a 4.00 mm diameter hole in the pipe with a piece of bubble gum, how much force must the gum be able to withstand?

16. A piston, A, as shown at right, has a diameter of 0.64 cm. A second piston, B, has a diameter of 3.8 cm. Determine the force, $\mathbf{F}$, necessary to support the 500.0 N weight in the absence of friction.

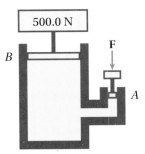

Fluid Flow

CONCEPTUAL QUESTIONS

17. Prairie dogs live in underground burrows with at least two entrances. They ventilate their burrows by building a mound around one entrance, which is open to a stream of air. A second entrance at ground level is open to almost stagnant air. Use Bernoulli's principle to explain how this construction creates air flow through the burrow.

18. Municipal water supplies are often provided by reservoirs built on high ground. Why does water from such a reservoir flow more rapidly out of a faucet on the ground floor of a building than out of an identical faucet on a higher floor?

19. If air from a hair dryer is blown over the top of a table-tennis ball, the ball can be suspended in air. Explain how this suspension is possible.

Mixed Review

▶ **REVIEWING MAIN IDEAS**

20. An engineer weighs a sample of mercury ($\rho = 13.6 \times 10^3$ kg/m^3) and finds that the weight of the sample is 4.5 N. What is the sample's volume?

21. About how much force is exerted by the atmosphere on 1.00 km^2 of land at sea level?

22. A 70.0 kg man sits in a 5.0 kg chair so that his weight is evenly distributed on the legs of the chair. Assume that each leg makes contact with the floor over a circular area with a radius of 1.0 cm. What is the pressure exerted on the floor by each leg?

23. A frog in a hemispherical bowl, as shown below, just floats in a fluid with a density of 1.35×10^3 kg/m^3. If the bowl has a radius of 6.00 cm and negligible mass, what is the mass of the frog?

24. When a load of 1.0×10^6 N is placed on a battleship, the ship sinks only 2.5 cm in the water. Estimate the cross-sectional area of the ship at water level. (Hint: See **Figure 1.2** for the density of sea water.)

25. A 1.0 kg beaker containing 2.0 kg of oil with a density of 916 kg/m^3 rests on a scale. A 2.0 kg block of iron is suspended from a spring scale and completely submerged in the oil, as shown at right. Find the equilibrium readings of both scales. (Hint: See **Figure 1.2** for the density of iron.)

26. A raft is constructed of wood having a density of 600.0 kg/m^3. The surface area of the bottom of the raft is 5.7 m^2, and the volume of the raft is 0.60 m^3. When the raft is placed in fresh water having a density of 1.0×10^3 kg/m^3, how deep is the bottom of the raft below water level?

27. A physics book has a height of 26 cm, a width of 21 cm, and a thickness of 3.5 cm.
  a. What is the density of the physics book if it weighs 19 N?
  b. Find the pressure that the physics book exerts on a desktop when the book lies face up.
  c. Find the pressure that the physics book exerts on the surface of a desktop when the book is balanced on its spine.

28. A natural-gas pipeline with a diameter of 0.250 m delivers 1.55 m^3 of gas per second. What is the flow speed of the gas?

29. A 2.0 cm thick bar of soap is floating in water, with 1.5 cm of the bar underwater. Bath oil with a density of 900.0 kg/m^3 is added and floats on top of the water. How high on the side of the bar will the oil reach when the soap is floating in only the oil?

30. Which dam must be stronger, one that holds back 1.0×10^5 m^3 of water 10 m deep or one that holds back 1.0×10^3 m^3 of water 20 m deep?

31. A light spring with a spring constant of 90.0 N/m rests vertically on a table, as shown in (**a**) below. A 2.00 g balloon is filled with helium (0°C and 1 atm pressure) to a volume of 5.00 m³ and connected to the spring, causing the spring to stretch, as shown in (**b**). How much does the spring stretch when the system is in equilibrium? (Hint: See **Figure 1.2** for the density of helium. The magnitude of the spring force equals $k\Delta x$.)

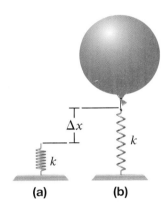

(a)   (b)

32. The aorta in an average adult has a cross-sectional area of 2.0 cm².
   a. Calculate the flow rate (in grams per second) of blood ($\rho = 1.0$ g/cm³) in the aorta if the flow speed is 42 cm/s.
   b. Assume that the aorta branches to form a large number of capillaries with a combined cross-sectional area of 3.0×10^3 cm². What is the flow speed in the capillaries?

33. A 1.0 kg hollow ball with a radius of 0.10 m is filled with air and is released from rest at the bottom of a 2.0 m deep pool of water. How high above the surface of the water does the ball rise? Disregard friction and the ball's motion when the ball is only partially submerged.

34. In testing a new material for shielding spacecraft, 150 ball bearings each moving at a supersonic speed of 400.0 m/s collide head-on and elastically with the material during a 1.00 min interval. If the ball bearings each have a mass of 8.0 g and the area of the tested material is 0.75 m², what is the pressure exerted on the material?

35. A thin, rigid, spherical shell with a mass of 4.00 kg and diameter of 0.200 m is filled with helium (adding negligible mass) at 0°C and 1 atm pressure. It is then released from rest on the bottom of a pool of water that is 4.00 m deep.
   a. Determine the upward acceleration of the shell.
   b. How long will it take for the top of the shell to reach the surface? Disregard frictional effects.

36. A student claims that if the strength of Earth's gravity doubled, people would be unable to float on water. Do you agree or disagree with this statement? Why?

37. A light spring with a spring constant of 16.0 N/m rests vertically on the bottom of a large beaker of water, as shown in (**a**) below. A 5.00×10^{-3} kg block of wood with a density of 650.0 kg/m³ is connected to the spring, and the mass-spring system is allowed to come to static equilibrium, as shown in (**b**) below. How much does the spring stretch?

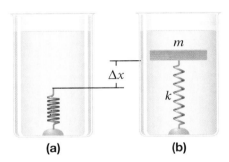

(a)   (b)

38. Astronauts sometimes train underwater to simulate conditions in space. Explain why.

39. Explain why some balloonists use helium instead of air in balloons.

ALTERNATIVE ASSESSMENT

1. Build a hydrometer from a long test tube with some sand at the bottom and a stopper. Adjust the amount of sand as needed so that the tube floats in most liquids. Calibrate it, and place a label with markings on the tube. Measure the densities of the following liquid foods: skim milk, whole milk, vegetable oil, pancake syrup, and molasses. Summarize your findings in a chart or table.

2. The owner of a fleet of tractor-trailers has contacted you after a series of accidents involving tractor-trailers passing each other on the highway. The owner wants to know how drivers can minimize the pull exerted as one tractor-trailer passes another going in the same direction. Should the passing tractor-trailer try to pass as quickly as possible or as slowly as possible? Design experiments to determine the answer by using model motor boats in a swimming pool. Indicate exactly what you will measure and how. If your teacher approves your plan and you are able to locate the necessary equipment, perform the experiment.

3. Record any examples of pumps in the tools, machines, and appliances you encounter in one week, and briefly describe the appearance and function of each pump. Research how one of these pumps works, and evaluate the explanation of the pump's operation for strengths and weaknesses. Share your findings in a group meeting, and create a presentation, model, or diagram that summarizes the group's findings.

GRAPHING CALCULATOR PRACTICE

Flow Rates

Flow rate, as you learned earlier in this chapter, is described by the following equation:

$$\text{flow rate} = Av$$

Flow rate is a measure of the volume of a fluid that passes through a tube per unit time. A is the cross-sectional area of the tube, and v is the flow speed of the fluid. If A has units of centimeters squared and v has units of centimeters per second, flow rate will have units of cubic centimeters per second.

The graphing calculator will use the following equation to determine flow rate.

$$Y_1 = \pi * V(X/2)^2$$

You will use this equation to study the flow rates (Y_1) for various hose diameters (X) and flow speeds (V). The calculator will produce a table of flow rates in cubic centimeters per second versus hose diameters in centimeters.

In this graphing calculator activity, you will learn how to read a table on the calculator and to use that table to make predictions about flow rates.

Go online to HMHScience.com to find the skillsheet and program for this graphing calculator activity.

Standards-Based Assessment

Record your answers on a separate piece of paper.

MULTIPLE CHOICE

1 The approximate inside diameter of the aorta is 1.6 cm, and that of a capillary is 1.0×10^{-6} m. The average flow speed of blood is about 1.0 m/s in the aorta and 1.0 cm/s in the capillaries. Which of the following is a possible explanation of why blood flows faster in the aorta? (Note: The continuity equation does not apply in this case because blood from the aorta moves into multiple capillaries, not just one.)

  A The aorta has a longer distance than the average capillary.

  B The aorta has a larger diameter so has more area for the blood to flow through.

  C The capillary has a smaller diameter, so the blood has less resistance to flow.

  D There are many capillaries and only one aorta, so the blood flows faster there.

2 The density of water is 1.00 g/cm^3, and the density of mercury is 13.53 g/mL. In which substance would an ice cube float higher, water or mercury, and why?

  A An ice cube would float higher in water because of the air spaces trapped in the ice cube.

  B An ice cube would float higher in water because the ice cube is much less dense than water.

  C An ice cube would float higher in mercury because it is much less dense than mercury.

  D An ice cube would float higher in mercury because mercury is usually solid like other metals.

3 A 70 kg man sits in a 5.0 kg chair so that his weight is evenly distributed on the legs of the chair. Assume that each leg makes contact with the floor over a circular area with a radius of 1.0 cm. What is the pressure exerted on the floor by each leg? (Hint: Pressure = force/area; unit of pressure = Pascals, Pa.)

  A 5.5×10^3 Pa

  B 5.5×10^5 Pa

  C 5.9×10^3 Pa

  D 5.9×10^5 Pa

4 What is the name of the force that is exerted upwards on an object floating in a fluid?

  A buoyant force

  B normal force

  C spring force

  D tension force

5 Water flows at a speed of 5.25 m/s through a garden hose with a diameter of 2.50 cm. What is the speed of the water when it sprays out of a nozzle that has a diameter of 0.120 cm? (Hint: Use the formula $A_1 v_1 = A_2 v_2$ where A is area and v is velocity.)

  A 1.21×10^{-2} m/s

  B 2.52×10^{-1} m/s

  C 1.09×10^2 m/s

  D 2.28×10^3 m/s

6 A solid sphere has a radius of 22.0 cm and a mass of 1.05 kg. It sinks to the bottom of the ocean to a depth of 9,550 m. What forces are acting on this sphere that would need to be included in a free-body diagram of the sphere?

  A buoyant force only

  B buoyant force and weight

  C buoyant force, weight, and normal force

  D buoyant force and normal force only

7 Which of the substances listed are *not* considered a fluid based on the following definition?

"A fluid is a material that can flow, and thus it has no definite shape."

  A helium

  B mercury

  C sodium

  D water

GRIDDED RESPONSE

8 A sheet of paper lies on a table. The paper measures 20.0 cm by 30.0 cm. Calculate the force, in Newtons, exerted on the paper by the atmosphere. Assume the pressure exerted by the atmosphere is 1.013×10^5 Pa. (Hint: Use the formula, pressure = force/area.)

1698

The Ashanti Empire, the last of the major African kingdoms, emerges in what is now Ghana. The Ashanti's strong centralized government and effective bureaucracy enable them to control the region for nearly two centuries.

1715 (approx.)

Chinese writer **Cao Xueqin** is born. The book *The Dream of the Red Chamber*, attributed to him and another writer, is widely regarded today as the greatest Chinese novel.

1735

John Harrison

constructs the first of four chronometers that will allow navigators to accurately determine a ship's longitude.

1738

Daniel Bernoulli's

Hydrodynamics, which includes his research on the mechanical behavior of fluids, is published.

$$P + \tfrac{1}{2}\rho v^2 + \rho g h = \text{constant}$$

| 1690 | 1700 | 1710 | 1720 | 1730 | 1740 |

1712

Thomas Newcomen invents the first practical steam engine. Over 50 years later, **James Watt** makes significant improvements to the Newcomen engine.

$$eff = \frac{W_{net}}{Q_h}$$

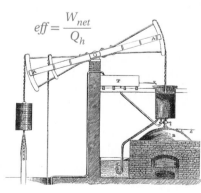

1721

Johann Sebastian Bach completes the six *Brandenburg Concertos*.

1738

Under the leadership of **Nadir Shah,** the Persian Empire expands into India as the Moghul Empire enters a stage of decline.

1747

Contrary to the favored idea that heat is a fluid, Russian chemist **Mikhail V. Lomonosov** publishes his hypothesis that heat is the result of motion. Several years later, Lomonosov formulates conservation laws for mass and energy.

1752

Benjamin Franklin performs the dangerous "kite experiment," in which he demonstrates that lightning consists of electric charge. He would build on the first studies of electricity performed earlier in the century by describing electricity as having positive and negative charge.

1770

Antoine Laurent Lavoisier begins his research on chemical reactions, notably oxidation and combustion.

1775

The American Revolution begins.

| 1740 | 1750 | 1760 | 1770 | 1780 | 1790 |

1756

The Seven Years' War begins. British general **James Wolfe** leads the capture of Fort Louisburg, in Canada, in 1758.

1757

German musician **William Herschel** emigrates to England to avoid fighting in the Seven Years' War. Over the next 60 years, he pursues astronomy, constructing the largest reflecting telescopes of the era and discovering new objects, such as binary stars and the planet Uranus.

1772

Caroline Herschel, sister of astronomer **William Herschel,** joins her brother in England. She compiles the most comprehensive star catalog of the era and discovers several nebulae—regions of glowing gas—within our galaxy.

1785

Charles Augustin de Coulomb publishes the results of experiments that will systematically and conclusively prove the inverse-square law for electric force. The law has been suggested for over 30 years by other scientists, such as **Daniel Bernoulli, Joseph Priestley,** and **Henry Cavendish.**

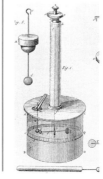

$$F_{electric} = k_C \left(\frac{q_1 q_2}{r^2} \right)$$

Why It Matters

Whether you make popcorn in a pan of hot oil or in a microwave oven, water molecules inside the hard kernels will absorb energy, as shown in the diagram. When the kernels reach a high enough pressure and temperature, they rupture. At this point, superheated water suddenly turns into steam and rushes outward, and the kernels burst open to form the fluffy, edible puffs of starch.

This type of energy transfer affects many things in the world around you, including making popcorn, turning water into ice cubes, swimming in a sun-warmed pool, and keeping warm in a sleeping bag while camping.

CHAPTER 9
Heat

BIG IDEA

Heat is the transfer of
energy due to differences
in temperature.

ONLINE Physics
HMHScience.com

ONLINE LABS
- Temperature and Internal
  Energy
- Specific Heat Capacity
- S.T.E.M. Lab Thermal
  Expansion
- S.T.E.M. Lab Thermal
  Conduction

GO ONLINE *Animated*
Physics
HMHScience.com

Specific Heat and Latent Heat

(bl) ©David Chasey/Photodisc/Getty Images

299

SECTION 1

SC.912.P.10.4, SC.912.P.10.5

Objectives

▷ Relate temperature to the kinetic energy of atoms and molecules.

▷ Describe the changes in the temperatures of two objects reaching thermal equilibrium.

▷ Identify the various temperature scales, and convert from one scale to another.

SC.912.P.10.5 Relate temperature to the average molecular kinetic energy.

Temperature and Thermal Equilibrium

Key Terms

temperature   internal energy   thermal equilibrium

Defining Temperature

When you hold a glass of lemonade with ice, such as that shown in **Figure 1.1,** you feel a sharp sensation in your hand that we describe as "cold." Likewise, you experience a "hot" feeling when you touch a cup of hot chocolate. We often associate temperature with how hot or cold an object feels when we touch it. Our sense of touch serves as a qualitative indicator of temperature. However, this sensation of hot or cold also depends on the temperature of the skin and therefore can be misleading. The same object may feel warm or cool, depending on the properties of the object and on the conditions of your body.

Determining an object's temperature with precision requires a standard definition of temperature and a procedure for making measurements that establish how "hot" or "cold" objects are.

Adding or removing energy usually changes temperature.

Consider what happens when you use an electric range to cook food. By turning the dial that controls the electric current delivered to the heating element, you can adjust the element's temperature. As the current is increased, the temperature of the element increases. Similarly, as the current is reduced, the temperature of the element decreases. In general, energy must be either added to or removed from a substance to change its temperature.

FIGURE 1.1

Hot and Cold Objects at low temperatures feel cold to the touch, while objects at high temperatures feel hot. However, the sensation of hot and cold can be misleading.

*Quick*LAB   SENSING TEMPERATURE

Fill one basin with hot tap water. Fill another with cold tap water, and add ice until about one-third of the mixture is ice. Fill the third basin with an equal mixture of hot and cold tap water.

Place your left hand in the hot water and your right hand in the cold water for 15 s. Then place both hands in the basin of lukewarm water for 15 s. Describe whether the water feels hot or cold to either of your hands.

MATERIALS
- 3 identical basins
- hot and cold tap water
- ice

SAFETY

 The temperature of the hot water must not exceed 50°C (122°F).

Temperature is proportional to the kinetic energy of atoms and molecules.

The **temperature** of a substance is proportional to the average kinetic energy of particles in the substance. A substance's temperature increases as a direct result of added energy being distributed among the particles of the substance, as shown in **Figure 1.2**.

A *monatomic* gas contains only one type of atom. For a monatomic gas, temperature can be understood in terms of the translational kinetic energy of the atoms in the gas. For other kinds of substances, molecules can rotate or vibrate, so other types of energy are also present, as shown in **Figure 1.3**.

The energies associated with atomic motion are referred to as **internal energy,** which is proportional to the substance's temperature (assuming no phase change). For an ideal gas, the internal energy depends only on the temperature of the gas. For nonideal gases, as well as for liquids and solids, other properties contribute to the internal energy. The symbol U stands for internal energy, and ΔU stands for a change in internal energy.

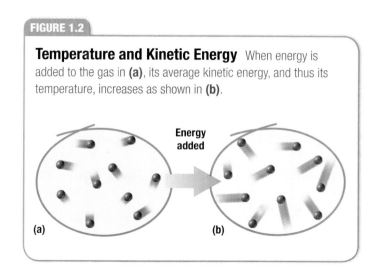

temperature a measure of the average kinetic energy of the particles in a substance

internal energy the energy of a substance due to both the random motions of its particles and to the potential energy that results from the distances and alignments between the particles

FIGURE 1.3

EXAMPLES OF DIFFERENT FORMS OF ENERGY			
Form of energy	Macroscopic examples	Microscopic examples	Energy type
translational	airplane in flight, roller coaster at bottom of rise	CO_2 molecule in linear motion	kinetic energy
rotational	spinning top	CO_2 molecule spinning about its center of mass	kinetic energy
vibrational	plucked guitar string	bending and stretching of bonds between atoms in a CO_2 molecule	kinetic and potential energy

Conceptual Challenge

1. Hot Chocolate If two cups of hot chocolate, one at 50°C and the other at 60°C, are poured together in a large container, will the final temperature of the double batch be

a. less than 50°C?

b. between 50°C and 60°C?

c. greater than 60°C?

Explain your answer.

2. Hot and Cold Liquids A cup of hot tea is poured from a teapot, and a swimming pool is filled with cold water. Which one has a higher total internal energy? Explain.

Temperature is meaningful only when it is stable.

Imagine a can of warm fruit juice immersed in a large beaker of cold water. After about 15 minutes, the can of fruit juice will be cooler, and the water surrounding it will be slightly warmer. Eventually, both the can of fruit juice and the water will be at the same temperature. That temperature will not change as long as conditions remain unchanged in the beaker. Another way of expressing this is to say that the water and can of juice are in **thermal equilibrium** with each other.

Thermal equilibrium is the basis for measuring temperature with thermometers. By placing a thermometer in contact with an object and waiting until the column of liquid in the thermometer stops rising or falling, you can find the temperature of the object. The reason is that the thermometer is in thermal equilibrium with the object. Just as in the case of the can of fruit juice in the cold water, the temperature of any two objects in thermal equilibrium always lies between their initial temperatures.

Matter expands as its temperature increases.

Increasing the temperature of a gas at constant pressure causes the volume of the gas to increase. This increase occurs not only for gases, but also for liquids and solids. In general, if the temperature of a substance increases, so does its volume. This phenomenon is known as *thermal expansion*.

You may have noticed that the concrete roadway segments of a sidewalk are separated by gaps. This is necessary because concrete expands with increasing temperature. Without these gaps, thermal expansion would cause the segments to push against each other, and they would eventually buckle and break apart.

Different substances undergo different amounts of expansion for a given temperature change. The thermal expansion characteristics of a material are indicated by a quantity called the *coefficient of volume expansion*. Gases have the largest values for this coefficient. Liquids have much smaller values.

In general, the volume of a liquid tends to decrease with decreasing temperature. However, the volume of water increases with decreasing temperature in the range between 0°C and 4°C. Also, as the water freezes, it forms a crystal that has more empty space between the molecules than does liquid water. This explains why ice floats in liquid water. It also explains why a pond freezes from the top down instead of from the bottom up. If this did not happen, fish would likely not survive in freezing temperatures.

Solids typically have the smallest coefficient of volume expansion values. For this reason, liquids in solid containers expand more than the container. This property allows some liquids to be used to measure changes in temperature.

Measuring Temperature

In order for a device to be used as a thermometer, it must make use of a change in some physical property that corresponds to changing temperature, such as the volume of a gas or liquid or the pressure of a gas at constant volume. The most common thermometers use a glass tube containing a thin column of mercury, colored alcohol, or colored mineral spirits. When the thermometer is heated, the volume of the liquid expands. (The cross-sectional area of the tube remains nearly constant during temperature changes.) The change in length of the liquid column is proportional to the temperature change, as shown in **Figure 1.4.**

Calibrating thermometers requires fixed temperatures.

A thermometer must be more than an unmarked, thin glass tube of liquid; the length of the liquid column at different temperatures must be known. One reference point is etched on the tube and refers to when the thermometer is in thermal equilibrium with a mixture of water and ice at one atmosphere of pressure. This temperature is called the *ice point* or *melting point* of water and is defined as zero degrees Celsius, or 0°C. A second reference mark is made at the point when the thermometer is in thermal equilibrium with a mixture of steam and water at one atmosphere of pressure. This temperature is called the *steam point* or *boiling point* of water and is defined as 100°C.

A temperature scale can be made by dividing the distance between the reference marks into equally spaced units, called *degrees*. This process is based on the assumption that the expansion of the mercury is linear (proportional to the temperature difference), which is a very good approximation.

Temperature units depend on the scale used.

The temperature scales most widely used today are the Fahrenheit, Celsius, and Kelvin scales. The Fahrenheit scale is commonly used in the United States. The Celsius scale is used in countries that have adopted the metric system and by the scientific community worldwide. Celsius and Fahrenheit temperature measurements can be converted to each other using this equation.

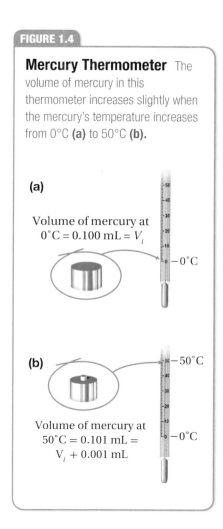

FIGURE 1.4

Mercury Thermometer The volume of mercury in this thermometer increases slightly when the mercury's temperature increases from 0°C **(a)** to 50°C **(b).**

(a)

Volume of mercury at 0°C = 0.100 mL = V_i

−0°C

(b)

−50°C

Volume of mercury at 50°C = 0.101 mL = V_i + 0.001 mL

−0°C

> **Celsius-Fahrenheit Temperature Conversion**
>
> $$T_F = \frac{9}{5}T_C + 32.0$$
>
> **Fahrenheit temperature** $= \left(\frac{9}{5} \times \textbf{Celsius temperature}\right) + \textbf{32.0}$

The number 32.0 in the equation indicates the difference between the ice-point value in each scale. The point at which water freezes is 0.0 degrees on the Celsius scale and 32.0 degrees on the Fahrenheit scale.

FIGURE 1.5

Determining Absolute Zero for an Ideal Gas This graph suggests that if the gas's temperature could be lowered to −273.15°C, or 0 K, the gas's pressure would be zero.

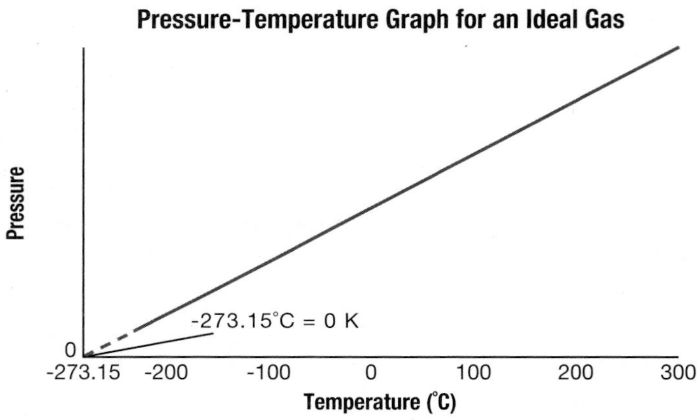

Pressure-Temperature Graph for an Ideal Gas

−273.15°C = 0 K

Pressure

Temperature (°C)

Temperature values in the Celsius and Fahrenheit scales can have positive, negative, or zero values. But because the kinetic energy of the atoms in a substance must be positive, the absolute temperature that is proportional to that energy should be positive also. A temperature scale with only positive values is suggested in the graph of pressure versus temperature for an ideal gas at constant volume, shown in **Figure 1.5.** As the gas's temperature decreases, so does its pressure. The graph suggests that if the temperature could be lowered to −273.15°C, the pressure of the sample would be zero. This temperature is designated in the Kelvin scale as 0.00 K, where K is the symbol for the temperature unit called the *kelvin*. Temperatures in this scale are indicated by the symbol T.

A temperature difference of one degree is the same on the Celsius and Kelvin scales. The two scales differ only in the choice of zero point. Thus, the ice point (0.00°C) equals 273.15 K, and the steam point (100.00°C) equals 373.15 K (see **Figure 1.6**). The Celsius temperature can therefore be converted to the Kelvin temperature by adding 273.15.

Celsius-Kelvin Temperature Conversion
$$T = T_C + 273.15$$
Kelvin temperature = Celsius temperature + 273.15

Kelvin temperatures for various physical processes can range from around 1 000 000 000 K (10^9 K), which is the temperature of the interiors of the most massive stars, to less than 1 K, which is slightly cooler than the boiling point of liquid helium. The temperature 0 K is often referred to as *absolute zero*. Absolute zero has never been reached, although laboratory experiments have reached temperatures of just a half-billionth of a degree above absolute zero.

FIGURE 1.6

TEMPERATURE SCALES AND THEIR USES			
Scale	Ice point	Steam point	Applications
Fahrenheit	32°F	212°F	meteorology, medicine, and nonscientific uses (United States)
Celsius	0°C	100°C	meteorology, medicine, and nonscientific uses (outside United States); other sciences (international)
Kelvin (absolute)	273.15 K	373.15 K	physical chemistry, gas laws, astrophysics, thermodynamics, low-temperature physics

Temperature Conversion

GO ONLINE

Interactive Demo
HMHScience.com

Sample Problem A What are the equivalent Celsius and
Kelvin temperatures of 72.0°F?

1 ANALYZE

Given: $T_F = 72.0°F$

Unknown: $T_C = ?$

$T = ?$

2 SOLVE

Use the Celsius-Fahrenheit equation to convert Fahrenheit into Celsius.

$$T_F = \frac{9}{5} T_C + 32.0$$

$$T_C = \frac{5}{9} (T_F - 32.0)$$

$$T_C = \frac{5}{9} (72.0 - 32.0)°C$$

$$= 22.2°C$$

$$\boxed{T_C = 22.2°C}$$

Use the Celsius-Kelvin equation to convert Celsius into Kelvin.

$$T = T_C + 273.15$$

$$T = (22.2 + 273.15) \text{ K}$$

$$= 295.4 \text{ K}$$

$$\boxed{T = 295.4 \text{ K}}$$

Practice

1. The lowest outdoor temperature ever recorded on Earth is −128.6°F, recorded at Vostok Station, Antarctica, in 1983. What is this temperature on the Celsius and Kelvin scales?

2. On January 21 in 1918, Granville, North Dakota, had a surprising change in temperature. Within 12 hours, the temperature changed from 237 K to 283 K. What is this change in temperature in the Celsius and Fahrenheit scales?

3. The normal human body temperature is 98.6°F. A person with a fever may record 102°F. Express these temperatures in degrees Celsius.

4. A pan of water is heated from 23°C to 78°C. What is the change in its temperature on the Kelvin and Fahrenheit scales?

5. Some volcanic lavas in Hawaii reach very high temperatures. Express the temperature 2192°F in degrees Celsius.

▶ **Reviewing Main Ideas**

1. A hot copper pan is dropped into a tub of water. If the water's temperature rises, what happens to the temperature of the pan? How will you know when the water and copper pan reach thermal equilibrium?

2. Oxygen condenses into a liquid at approximately 90.2 K. To what temperature does this correspond on both the Celsius and Fahrenheit temperature scales?

3. The boiling point of sulfur is 444.6°C. Sulfur's melting point is 586.1°F lower than its boiling point.
   a. Determine the melting point of sulfur in degrees Celsius.
   b. Find the melting and boiling points in degrees Fahrenheit.
   c. Find the melting and boiling points in kelvins.

4. Which of the following are true for popcorn kernels and the water molecules inside them during cooking, just before the kernels pop?
   a. The temperature of the kernels increases.
   b. The water molecules are destroyed.
   c. The kinetic energy of the water molecules increases.
   d. The mass of the water molecules changes.

Interpreting Graphics

5. Two gases that are in physical contact with each other consist of particles of identical mass. In what order should the images shown in **Figure 1.7** be placed to correctly describe the changing distribution of kinetic energy among the gas particles? Which group of particles has the highest temperature at any time? Explain.

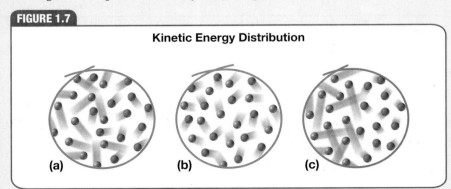

FIGURE 1.7

Kinetic Energy Distribution

(a) (b) (c)

✔ **Critical Thinking**

6. Have you ever tried to make popcorn and found that most of the kernels did not pop? What might be the reason that they did not pop? What could you do to try to make more of the kernels pop?

Defining Heat

Key Term
heat

Heat and Energy

Thermal physics often appears mysterious at the macroscopic level. Hot objects become cool without any obvious cause. To understand thermal processes, it is helpful to shift attention to the behavior of atoms and molecules. Mechanics can be used to explain much of what is happening at the molecular, or microscopic, level. This in turn accounts for what you observe at the macroscopic level. Throughout this chapter, the focus will shift between these two viewpoints.

What happens when you immerse a warm fruit juice bottle in a container of cold water, as shown in **Figure 2.1**? As the temperatures of the bottle and of the juice decrease, the water's temperature increases slightly until both final temperatures are the same. Energy is transferred from the bottle of juice to the water because the two objects are at different temperatures. This energy that is transferred is defined as **heat.**

The word *heat* is sometimes used to refer to the *process* by which energy is transferred between objects because of a difference in their temperatures. This textbook will use *heat* to refer only to the energy itself.

Energy is transferred between substances as heat.

From a macroscopic viewpoint, energy transferred as heat tends to move from an object at higher temperature to an object at lower temperature. This is similar to the mechanical behavior of objects moving from a higher gravitational potential energy to a lower gravitational potential energy. Just as a pencil will drop from your desk to the floor but will not jump from the floor to your desk, so energy will travel spontaneously from an object at higher temperature to one at lower temperature and not the other way around.

Objectives

- Explain heat as the energy transferred between substances that are at different temperatures.

- Relate heat and temperature change on the macroscopic level to particle motion on the microscopic level.

- Apply the principle of energy conservation to calculate changes in potential, kinetic, and internal energy.

SC.912.P.10.4 Describe heat as the energy transferred by convection, conduction, and radiation, and explain the connection of heat to change in temperature or states of matter.
SC.912.P.10.5 Relate temperature to the average molecular kinetic energy.

heat the energy transferred between objects because of a difference in their temperatures

FIGURE 2.1

Energy Transfer as Heat Energy is transferred as heat from objects with higher temperatures (the fruit juice and bottle) to those with lower temperatures (the cold water).

FIGURE 2.2

Transfer of Particles' Kinetic Energy as Heat Energy is transferred as heat from the higher-energy particles to lower-energy particles **(a).** The net energy transferred is zero when thermal equilibrium is reached **(b).**

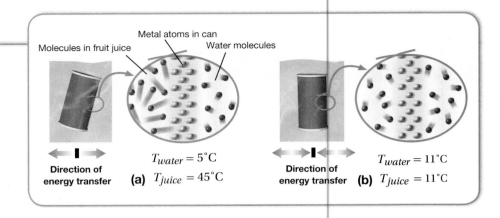

Molecules in fruit juice   Metal atoms in can   Water molecules

Direction of energy transfer   **(a)** $T_{water} = 5°C$ $T_{juice} = 45°C$

Direction of energy transfer   **(b)** $T_{water} = 11°C$ $T_{juice} = 11°C$

The direction in which energy travels as heat can be explained at the atomic level. Consider a warm can of fruit juice in cold water. At first, the molecules in the fruit juice have a higher average kinetic energy than do the water molecules that surround the can, as shown in **Figure 2.2(a).** This energy is transferred from the juice to the can by the juice molecules colliding with the metal atoms of the can. The atoms vibrate more because of their increased energy. This energy is then transferred to the surrounding water molecules, as shown in **Figure 2.2(b).**

As the energy of the water molecules gradually increases, the energy of the fruit juice's molecules and of the can's atoms decreases until all of the particles have, on the average, equal kinetic energies. In individual collisions, energy may be transferred from the lower-energy water molecules to the higher-energy metal atoms and fruit juice particles. That is, energy can be transferred in either direction. However, because the average kinetic energy of particles is higher in the object at higher temperature, more energy moves out of the object as heat than moves into it. Thus, the net transfer of energy as heat is in only one direction.

The transfer of energy as heat alters an object's temperature.

Thermal equilibrium may be understood in terms of energy exchange between two objects at equal temperature. When the can of fruit juice and the surrounding water are at the same temperature, as depicted in **Figure 2.3,** the quantity of energy transferred from the can of fruit juice to the water is the same as the energy transferred from the water to the can of juice. The net energy transferred between the two objects is zero.

This reveals the difference between temperature and heat. The atoms of all objects are in continuous motion, so all objects have some internal energy. Because temperature is a measure of that energy, all objects have some temperature. Heat, on the other hand, is the energy transferred from one object to another because of the temperature difference between them. When there is no temperature difference between a substance and its surroundings, no net energy is transferred as heat.

Energy transfer as heat depends on the difference of the temperatures of the two objects. The greater the temperature difference is between two objects, the greater the rate of energy transfer between them as heat (other factors being the same).

FIGURE 2.3

Equilibrium At thermal equilibrium, the net energy exchanged between two objects equals zero.

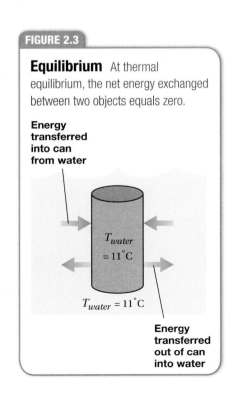

Energy transferred into can from water

$T_{water} = 11°C$

$T_{water} = 11°C$

Energy transferred out of can into water

For example, in winter, energy is transferred as heat from a car's surface at 30°C to a cold raindrop at 5°C. In the summer, energy is transferred as heat from a car's surface at 45°C to a warm raindrop at 20°C. In each case, the amount of energy transferred each second is the same, because the substances and the temperature difference (25°C) are the same. See **Figure 2.4.**

The concepts of heat and temperature help to explain why hands held in separate bowls containing hot and cold water subsequently sense the temperature of lukewarm water differently. The nerves in the outer skin of your hand detect energy passing through the skin from objects with temperatures different from your body temperature. If one hand is at thermal equilibrium with cold water, more energy is transferred from the outer layers of your hand than can be replaced by the blood, which has a temperature of about 37.0°C (98.6°F). When the hand is immediately placed in water that is at a higher temperature, energy is transferred from the water to the cooler hand. The energy transferred into the skin causes the water to feel warm. Likewise, the hand that has been in hot water temporarily gains energy from the water. The loss of this energy to the lukewarm water makes that water feel cool.

Heat has the units of energy.

Before scientists arrived at the modern model for heat, several different units for measuring heat had already been developed. These units are still widely used in many applications and therefore are listed in **Figure 2.5.** Because heat, like work, is energy in transit, all heat units can be converted to joules, the SI unit for energy.

Just as other forms of energy have a symbol that identifies them (*PE* for potential energy, *KE* for kinetic energy, *U* for internal energy, *W* for work), heat is indicated by the symbol *Q*.

Rate of Energy Transfer The energy transferred each second as heat from the car's surface to the raindrop is the same for low temperatures **(a)** as for high temperatures **(b),** provided the temperature differences are the same.

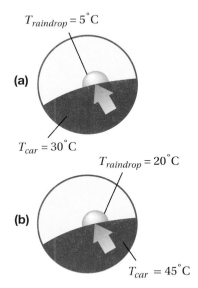

$T_{raindrop} = 5\,°C$

(a)

$T_{car} = 30\,°C$

$T_{raindrop} = 20\,°C$

(b)

$T_{car} = 45\,°C$

FIGURE 2.5

THERMAL UNITS AND THEIR VALUES IN JOULES		
Heat unit	**Equivalent value**	**Uses**
joule (J)	equal to $1 \text{ kg} \bullet \left(\dfrac{m^2}{s^2}\right)$	SI unit of energy
calorie (cal)	4.186 J	non-SI unit of heat; found especially in older works of physics and chemistry
kilocalorie (kcal)	4.186×10^3 J	non-SI unit of heat
Calorie, or dietary Calorie	4.186×10^3 J = 1 kcal	food and nutritional science
British thermal unit (Btu)	1.055×10^3 J	English unit of heat; used in engineering, air conditioning, and refrigeration
therm	1.055×10^8 J	equal to 100 000 Btu; used to measure natural-gas usage

If you were to hold a metal pan filled with water over a flame, the metal handle would initially feel comfortable to the touch. After a few minutes, however, the handle would become too hot to touch without a cooking mitt, as shown in **Figure 2.6.** The handle is hot because energy was transferred from the high-temperature fire to the pan. The added energy increased the temperature of the pan and its contents. This type of energy transfer is called *thermal conduction.*

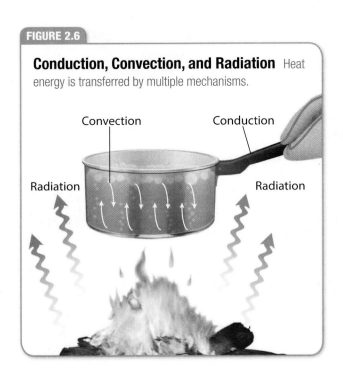

FIGURE 2.6

Conduction, Convection, and Radiation Heat energy is transferred by multiple mechanisms.

Convection

Conduction

Radiation

Radiation

The rate of thermal conduction depends on the substance.

Thermal conduction can be understood by the behavior of atoms in a metal. As the pan is heated, the atoms nearest to the flame vibrate with greater energy. These vibrating atoms jostle their less-energetic neighbors and transfer some of their energy in the process. Gradually, atoms farther away from the fire gain more energy.

The rate of thermal conduction depends on the properties of the substance being heated. A metal ice tray and a cardboard package of frozen food removed from the freezer are at the same temperature. However, the metal tray feels colder than the package because metal conducts energy more easily and more rapidly than cardboard does. Substances that rapidly transfer energy as heat are called *thermal conductors.* Substances that slowly transfer energy as heat are called *thermal insulators.* In general, metals are good thermal conductors. Materials such as asbestos, cork, ceramic, cardboard, and fiberglass are poor thermal conductors (and therefore good thermal insulators).

Did YOU Know?

Cooking oil is useful for transferring energy uniformly around the surface of the food being cooked. When popping popcorn, for instance, coating the kernels with oil improves the energy transfer to each kernel, so a higher percentage of them pop.

Convection is another mechanism through which heat energy is transferred directly.

Convection involves the movement of cold and hot matter, such as the water circulating in the pan in **Figure 2.6.** This mechanism does not involve heat alone. Instead, it uses the combined effects of pressure differences, conduction, and buoyancy. In the case of the water in the pan, the water is heated through particle collisions (conduction), causing it to expand and its density to decrease. The warm water is then displaced by denser, colder water, which will be heated in turn. Thus, the flame heats the water faster than by conduction alone. The air surrounding a fire is also subjected to convection. The current of air that rises after being heated and then cools and falls is called a *convection current.* Such currents are important beyond the circulation of air around a fire or in a room. Convection currents that extend over Earth's surface play an important role in the formation of global wind patterns.

Radiation transfers heat energy over a distance.

The other principal energy transfer mechanism is *electromagnetic radiation*. Unlike convection, energy moved in this form does not involve the transfer of matter, and in contrast to conduction, there is no direct transfer of energy between vibrating atoms. Instead, objects reduce their internal energy by giving off electromagnetic radiation of a particular wavelength. The waves in **Figure 2.6** indicate electromagnetic radiation leaving the fire. If that radiation contacts the skin of the person holding the pot, the energy of those waves will be absorbed, increasing the internal energy and, thus, the temperature of the skin. Because radiation does not depend upon the movement of matter, it can take place even in a vacuum. This property makes it possible for energy from the sun to travel through space and warm Earth.

Heat and Work

Hammer a nail into a block of wood. After several minutes, pry the nail loose from the block and touch the side of the nail. It feels warm to the touch, indicating that energy is being transferred from the nail to your hand. Work is done in pulling the nail out of the wood. The nail encounters friction with the wood, and most of the energy required to overcome this friction is transformed into internal energy. The increase in the internal energy of the nail raises the nail's temperature, and the temperature difference between the nail and your hand results in the transfer of energy to your hand as heat.

Friction is just one way of increasing a substance's internal energy. In the case of solids, internal energy can be increased by deforming their structure. Common examples of this deformation are stretching a rubber band or bending a piece of metal.

Total energy is conserved.

When the concept of mechanical energy was introduced, you discovered that whenever friction between two objects exists, not all of the work done appears as mechanical energy. Similarly, when objects collide inelastically, not all of their initial kinetic energy remains as kinetic energy after the collision. Some of the energy is absorbed as internal energy by the objects. For this reason, in the case of the nail pulled from the wood, the nail (and if you could touch it, the wood inside the hole) feels warm. If changes in internal energy are taken into account along with changes in mechanical energy, the total energy is a universally conserved property. In other words, the sum of the changes in potential, kinetic, and internal energy is equal to zero.

Conservation of Energy

$$\Delta PE + \Delta KE + \Delta U = 0$$

the change in potential energy + the change in kinetic energy + the change in internal energy = 0

QuickLAB

MATERIALS
- 1 large rubber band about 7–10 mm wide

SAFETY

To avoid breaking the rubber band, do not stretch it more than a few inches. Do not point a stretched rubber band at another person.

WORK AND HEAT

Hold the rubber band between your thumbs. Touch the middle section of the rubber band to your lip and note how it feels. Rapidly stretch the rubber band and keep it stretched. Touch the middle section of the rubber band to your lip again. Notice whether the rubber band's temperature has changed. (You may have to repeat this procedure several times before you can clearly distinguish the temperature difference.)

Conservation of Energy

Sample Problem B An arrangement similar to the one used to demonstrate energy conservation is shown at right. A vessel contains water. Paddles that are propelled by falling masses turn in the water. This agitation warms the water and increases its internal energy. The temperature of the water is then measured, giving an indication of the water's internal-energy increase. If a total mass of 11.5 kg falls 1.3 m and all of the mechanical energy is converted to internal energy, by how much will the internal energy of the water increase? (Assume no energy is transferred as heat out of the vessel to the surroundings or from the surroundings to the vessel's interior.)

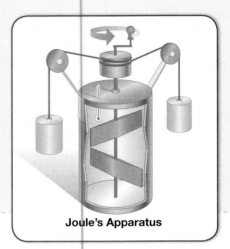

Joule's Apparatus

① ANALYZE

Given: $m = 11.5 \text{ kg}$

$h = 1.3 \text{ m}$

$g = 9.81 \text{ m/s}^2$

Unknown: $\Delta U = ?$

② PLAN

Choose an equation or situation:
Use the conservation-of-energy equation, and solve for ΔU.

$$\Delta PE + \Delta KE + \Delta U = 0$$

> **Tips and Tricks**
> Don't forget that a change in any quantity, indicated by the symbol Δ, equals the final value minus the initial value.

$$(PE_f - PE_i) + (KE_f - KE_i) + \Delta U = 0$$

$$\Delta U = -PE_f + PE_i - KE_f + KE_i$$

Because the masses begin at rest, KE_i equals zero. If we assume that KE_f is small compared to the loss of PE, we can set KE_f equal to zero also.

$$KE_f = 0 \qquad KE_i = 0$$

Because all of the potential energy is assumed to be converted to internal energy, PE_i can be set equal to mgh if PE_f is set equal to zero.

$$PE_i = mgh \qquad PE_f = 0$$

Substitute each quantity into the equation for ΔU:

$$\Delta U = 0 + mgh + 0 + 0 = mgh$$

③ SOLVE

Substitute the values into the equation, and solve:

$$\Delta U = (11.5 \text{ kg})(9.81 \text{ m/s}^2)(1.3 \text{ m})$$

$$\boxed{\Delta U = 1.5 \times 10^2 \text{ J}}$$

> **Calculator Solution**
> Because the minimum number of significant figures in the data is two, the calculator answer, 146.6595 J, should be rounded to two digits.

Continued

Conservation of Energy (continued)

4 CHECK YOUR WORK

The answer can be estimated using rounded values for m and g. If $m \approx 10$ kg and $g \approx 10$ m/s^2, then $\Delta U \approx 130$ J, which is close to the actual value calculated.

Practice

1. In the arrangement described in Sample Problem B, how much would the water's internal energy increase if the mass fell 6.69 m?

2. A worker drives a 0.500 kg spike into a rail tie with a 2.50 kg sledgehammer. The hammer hits the spike with a speed of 65.0 m/s. If one-third of the hammer's kinetic energy is converted to the internal energy of the hammer and spike, how much does the total internal energy increase?

3. A 3.0×10^{-3} kg copper penny drops a distance of 50.0 m to the ground. If 65 percent of the initial potential energy goes into increasing the internal energy of the penny, determine the magnitude of that increase.

4. The amount of internal energy needed to raise the temperature of 0.25 kg of water by 0.2°C is 209.3 J. How fast must a 0.25 kg baseball travel in order for its kinetic energy to equal this internal energy?

SECTION 2 FORMATIVE ASSESSMENT

▶ Reviewing Main Ideas

1. Use the microscopic interpretations of temperature and heat to explain how you can blow on your hands to warm them and also blow on a bowl of hot soup to cool it.

2. If a bottle of water is shaken vigorously, will the internal energy of the water change? Why or why not?

3. At Niagara Falls, if 505 kg of water falls a distance of 50.0 m, what is the increase in the internal energy of the water at the bottom of the falls? Assume that all of the initial potential energy goes into increasing the water's internal energy and that the final kinetic energy is zero.

✔ Critical Thinking

4. A bottle of water at room temperature is placed in a freezer for a short time. An identical bottle of water that has been lying in the sunlight is placed in a refrigerator for the same amount of time. What must you know to determine which situation involves more energy transfer?

5. Popcorn is routinely cooked by any of three different methods, each of which relies predominantly on a different mode of heat transfer (conduction, convection, or radiation). Find three methods for cooking popcorn, and identify the types of heat transfer that are critical for each.

Climate and Clothing

To remain healthy, the human body must maintain a temperature of about 37.0°C (98.6°F), which becomes increasingly difficult as the surrounding air becomes hotter or colder than body temperature.

Unless the body is properly insulated, its temperature will drop in its attempt to reach thermal equilibrium with very cold surroundings. If this situation is not corrected in time, the body will enter a state of hypothermia, which lowers pulse, blood pressure, and respiration. Once body temperature reaches 32.2°C (90.0°F), a person can lose consciousness. When body temperature reaches 25.6°C (78.1°F), hypothermia is almost always fatal.

To prevent hypothermia, the transfer of energy from the human body to the surrounding air must be hindered, which is done by surrounding the body with heat-insulating material. An extremely effective and common thermal insulator is air. Like most gases, air is a very poor thermal conductor, so even a thin layer of air near the skin provides a barrier to energy transfer.

The Inupiaq people of northern Alaska have designed clothing to protect them from the severe Arctic climate, where average air temperatures range from 10°C (50°F) to −37°C (−35°F). The Inupiaq clothing is made from animal skins that make use of air's insulating properties. Until recently, the traditional parka (*atigi*) was made from caribou skins. Two separate parkas are worn in layers, with the fur

The Bedouin headcloth, called a kefiyah, *employs evaporation to remove energy from the air close to the head, which cools the wearer.*

The Inupiat parka, called an atigi, *consists today of a canvas shell over sheepskin. The wool provides layers of insulating air between the wearer and the cold.*

lining the inside of the inner parka and the outside of the outer parka. Insulation is provided by air that is trapped between the short inner hairs and within the long, hollow hairs of the fur. Today, inner parkas are made from sheepskin, as shown on the left.

At the other extreme, the Bedouins of the Arabian Desert have developed clothing that permits them to survive another of the harshest environments on Earth. Bedouin garments cover most of the body, which protects the wearer from direct sunlight and prevents excessive loss of body water from evaporation. These clothes are also designed to cool the wearer. The Bedouins must keep their body temperatures from becoming too high in desert temperatures, which often are in excess of 38°C (100°F). Heat exhaustion or heat stroke will result if the body's temperature becomes too high.

Although members of different tribes, as well as men and women within the same tribes, wear different types of clothing, a few basic garments are common to all Bedouins. One such garment is the *kefiyah*, a headcloth worn by Bedouin men, as shown in the photograph above. A similar garment made of two separate cloths, which are called a *mandil* and a *hatta*, is worn by Bedouin women. Firmly wrapped around the head of the wearer, the cloth absorbs perspiration and cools the wearer during evaporation. This same garment is also useful during cold periods in the desert. The garment, wound snugly around the head, has folds that trap air and provide an insulating layer to keep the head warm.

Changes in Temperature and Phase

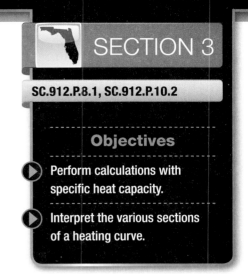
Key Terms
specific heat capacity
calorimetry
phase change
latent heat

Objectives

▶ Perform calculations with specific heat capacity.

▶ Interpret the various sections of a heating curve.

SC.912.P.8.1 Differentiate among the four states of matter.
SC.912.P.10.2 Explore the Law of Conservation of Energy by differentiating among open, closed, and isolated systems and explain that the total energy in an isolated system is a conserved quantity.

Specific Heat Capacity

On a hot day, the water in a swimming pool, such as the one shown in **Figure 3.1,** may be cool, even if the air around it is hot. This may seem odd, because both the air and water receive energy from sunlight. One reason that the water may be cooler than the air is evaporation, which is a cooling process.

However, evaporation is not the only reason for the difference. Experiments have shown that the change in temperature due to adding or removing a given amount of energy depends on the particular substance. In other words, the same change in energy will cause a different temperature change in equal masses of different substances.

The **specific heat capacity** of a substance is defined as the energy required to change the temperature of 1 kg of that substance by 1°C. (This quantity is also sometimes known as just *specific heat.*) Every substance has a unique specific heat capacity. This value tells you how much the temperature of a given mass of that substance will increase or decrease, based on how much energy is added or removed as heat. This relationship is expressed mathematically as follows:

FIGURE 3.1

Temperature Differences
The air around the pool and the water in the pool receive energy from sunlight. However, the increase in temperature is greater for the air than for the water.

specific heat capacity the quantity of heat required to raise a unit mass of homogeneous material 1 K or 1°C in a specified way given constant pressure and volume

Specific Heat Capacity

$$c_p = \frac{Q}{m\Delta T}$$

$$\text{specific heat capacity} = \frac{\text{energy transferred as heat}}{\text{mass} \times \text{change in temperature}}$$

The subscript p indicates that the specific heat capacity is measured at constant pressure. Maintaining constant pressure is an important detail when determining certain thermal properties of gases, which are much more affected by changes in pressure than are solids or liquids. Note that a temperature change of 1°C is equal in magnitude to a temperature change of 1 K, so ΔT gives the temperature change in either scale.

FIGURE 3.2

SPECIFIC HEAT CAPACITIES

Substance	c_p (J/kg•°C)	Substance	c_p (J/kg•°C)	Substance	c_p (J/kg•°C)
aluminum	8.99×10^2	ice	2.09×10^3	silver	2.34×10^2
copper	3.87×10^2	iron	4.48×10^2	steam	2.01×10^3
glass	8.37×10^2	lead	1.28×10^2	water	4.186×10^3
gold	1.29×10^2	mercury	1.38×10^2		

The equation for specific heat capacity applies to both substances that absorb energy from their surroundings and those that transfer energy to their surroundings. When the temperature increases, ΔT and Q are taken to be positive—which corresponds to energy transferred into the substance. Likewise, when the temperature decreases, ΔT and Q are negative, and energy is transferred from the substance. **Figure 3.2** lists specific heat capacities that have been determined for several substances.

Calorimetry is used to determine specific heat capacity.

To measure the specific heat capacity of a substance, it is necessary to measure mass, temperature change, and energy transferred as heat. Mass and temperature change are directly measurable, but the direct measurement of heat is difficult. However, the specific heat capacity of water is known, so the energy transferred as heat between an object of unknown specific heat capacity and a known quantity of water can be measured.

If a hot substance is placed in an insulated container of cool water, energy conservation requires that the energy the substance gives up must equal the energy absorbed by the water. Although some energy is transferred to the surrounding container, this effect is small and will be ignored. Energy conservation can be used to calculate the specific heat capacity, $c_{p,x}$, of the substance (indicated by the subscript x) as follows:

energy absorbed by water = energy released by the substance

$$Q_w = -Q_x$$

$$c_{p,w}m_w\Delta T_w = -c_{p,x}m_x\Delta T_x$$

For simplicity, a subscript w will always stand for "water" in specific heat capacity problems. The energy gained by a substance is expressed as a positive quantity, and the energy released is expressed as a negative quantity. The first equation above can be rewritten as $Q_w + Q_x = 0$, which shows that the net change in energy transferred as heat equals zero. Note that ΔT equals the final temperature minus the initial temperature.

This approach to determining a substance's specific heat capacity is called **calorimetry,** and devices that are used for making this measurement are called *calorimeters*. A calorimeter, shown in **Figure 3.3,** contains both a thermometer to measure the final temperature of substances at thermal equilibrium and a stirrer to ensure the uniform mixture of energy.

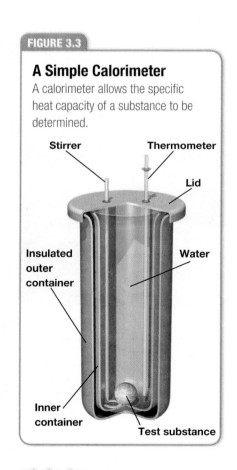

FIGURE 3.3

A Simple Calorimeter

A calorimeter allows the specific heat capacity of a substance to be determined.

Stirrer

Thermometer

Lid

Insulated outer container

Water

Inner container

Test substance

calorimetry an experimental procedure used to measure the energy transferred from one substance to another as heat

Calorimetry

Sample Problem C A 0.050 kg metal bolt is heated to an unknown initial temperature. It is then dropped into a calorimeter containing 0.15 kg of water with an initial temperature of 21.0°C. The bolt and the water then reach a final temperature of 25.0°C. If the metal has a specific heat capacity of 899 J/kg•°C, find the initial temperature of the metal.

① ANALYZE

Given:

$$m_{metal} = m_m = 0.050 \text{ kg} \qquad c_{p,m} = 899 \text{ J/kg•°C}$$

$$m_{water} = m_w = 0.15 \text{ kg} \qquad c_{p,w} = 4186 \text{ J/kg•°C}$$

$$T_{water} = T_w = 21.0°C \qquad T_{final} = T_f = 25.0°C$$

Unknown: $T_{metal} = T_m = ?$

Diagram:

Before placing hot sample in calorimeter

After thermal equilibrium has been reached

$$m_m = 0.050 \text{ kg} \qquad m_w = 0.15 \text{ kg} \qquad T_f = 25.0° \text{ C}$$
$$T_w = 21.0° \text{ C}$$

② PLAN

Choose an equation or situation:

The energy absorbed by the water equals the energy removed from the bolt.

$$Q_w = -Q_m$$

$$c_{p,w} m_w \Delta T_w = -c_{p,m} m_m \Delta T_m$$

$$c_{p,w} m_w (T_f - T_w) = -c_{p,m} m_m (T_f - T_m)$$

Rearrange the equation to isolate the unknown:

$$T_m = \frac{c_{p,w} m_w (T_f - T_w)}{c_{p,m} m_m} + T_f$$

Tips and Tricks

Because T_w is less than T_f, you know that T_m must be greater than T_f.

③ SOLVE

Substitute the values into the equation, and solve:

$$T_m = \frac{(4186 \text{ J/kg•°C})(0.15 \text{ kg})(25.0°C - 21.0°C)}{(899 \text{ J/kg•°C})(0.050 \text{ kg})} + 25.0°C$$

$$\boxed{T_m = 81°C}$$

④ CHECK YOUR WORK

T_m is greater than T_f, as expected.

Continued

1. What is the final temperature when a 3.0 kg gold bar at 99°C is dropped into 0.22 kg of water at 25°C?

2. A 0.225 kg sample of tin initially at 97.5°C is dropped into 0.115 kg of water. The initial temperature of the water is 10.0°C. If the specific heat capacity of tin is 230 J/kg•°C, what is the final equilibrium temperature of the tin-water mixture?

3. Brass is an alloy made from copper and zinc. A 0.59 kg brass sample at 98.0°C is dropped into 2.80 kg of water at 5.0°C. If the equilibrium temperature is 6.8°C, what is the specific heat capacity of brass?

4. A hot, just-minted copper coin is placed in 101 g of water to cool. The water temperature changes by 8.39°C, and the temperature of the coin changes by 68.0°C. What is the mass of the coin?

WHY IT MATTERS S.T.E.M.

Earth-Coupled Heat Pumps

As the earliest cave dwellers knew, a good way to stay warm in the winter and cool in the summer is to go underground. Now, scientists and engineers are using the same premise—and using existing technology in a new, more efficient way—to heat and cool above-ground homes for a fraction of the cost of conventional systems.

The average specific heat capacity of earth is smaller than the average specific heat capacity of air. However, earth has a greater density than air does, which means that near a house, there are more kilograms of earth than of air. So a 1°C change in temperature involves transferring more energy to or from the ground than to or from the air. Thus, the temperature of the ground in the winter will probably be higher than the temperature of the air above it. In the summer, the temperature of the ground will likely be lower than the temperature of the air.

An earth-coupled heat pump enables homeowners to tap the temperature just below the ground to heat their homes in the winter or cool them in the summer. The system includes a network of plastic pipes placed in trenches or inserted in holes drilled 2 to 3 m (6 to 10 ft) beneath the ground's surface. To heat a home, a fluid circulates through the pipe, absorbs energy from the surrounding earth, and transfers this energy to a heat pump inside the house. Although the system can function anywhere on Earth's surface, it is most appropriate in severe climates, where dramatic temperature swings may not be ideal for air-based systems.

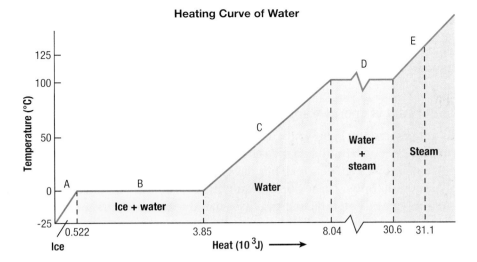

Heating Curve of Water

FIGURE 3.4

Heating Curve of Water
This idealized graph shows the temperature change of 10.0 g of ice as it is heated from −25°C in the ice phase to steam above 125°C at atmospheric pressure. (Note that the horizontal scale of the graph is not uniform.)

Latent Heat

Suppose you place an ice cube with a temperature of −25°C in a glass and then you place the glass in a room. The ice cube slowly warms, and the temperature of the ice will increase until the ice begins to melt at 0°C. The graph in **Figure 3.4** and data in **Figure 3.5** show how the temperature of 10.0 g of ice changes as energy is added.

You can see that temperature steadily increases from −25°C to 0°C (segment A of the graph). You could use the mass and the specific heat capacity of ice to calculate how much energy is added to the ice during this segment.

At 0°C, the temperature stops increasing. Instead, the ice begins to melt and to change into water (segment B). The ice-and-water mixture remains at this temperature until all of the ice melts. Suppose that you now heat the water in a pan on a stovetop. From 0°C to 100°C, the water's temperature steadily increases (segment C). At 100°C, however, the temperature stops rising, and the water turns into steam (segment D). Once the water has completely vaporized, the temperature of the steam increases (segment E).

FIGURE 3.5

CHANGES OCCURRING DURING THE HEATING OF 10.0 g OF ICE			
Segment of graph	Type of change	Amount of energy transferred as heat	Temperature range of segment
A	temperature of ice increases	522 J	−25°C to 0°C
B	ice melts; becomes water	3.33×10^3 J	0°C
C	temperature of water increases	4.19×10^3 J	0°C to 100°C
D	water boils; becomes steam	2.26×10^4 J	100°C
E	temperature of steam increases	500 J	100°C to 125°C

When substances melt, freeze, boil, condense, or sublime (change from a solid to vapor or from vapor to a solid), the energy added or removed changes the internal energy of the substance without changing the substance's temperature. These changes in matter are called **phase changes.**

phase change the physical change of a substance from one state (solid, liquid, or gas) to another at constant temperature and pressure

Latent heat is energy transferred during phase changes.

To understand the behavior of a substance undergoing a phase change, you need to consider the changes in potential energy. Potential energy is present among a collection of particles in a solid or in a liquid in the form of attractive bonds. These bonds result from the charges within atoms and molecules. Potential energy is associated with the electric forces between these charges.

Phase changes result from a change in the potential energy between particles of a substance. When energy is added to or removed from a substance that is undergoing a phase change, the particles of the substance rearrange themselves to make up for their change of energy. This rearrangement occurs without a change in the average kinetic energy of the particles. The energy that is added or removed per unit mass is called **latent heat,** abbreviated as L. Note that according to this definition, the energy transferred as heat during a phase change simply equals the mass multiplied by the latent heat, as follows:

latent heat the energy per unit mass that is transferred during a phase change of a substance

$$Q = mL$$

During melting, the energy that is added to a substance equals the difference between the total potential energies for particles in the solid and the liquid phases. This type of latent heat is called the *heat of fusion.* During vaporization, the energy that is added to a substance equals the difference in the potential energy of attraction between the liquid particles and between the gas particles. In this case, the latent heat is called the *heat of vaporization.* The heat of fusion and the heat of vaporization are abbreviated as L_f and L_v, respectively. **Figure 3.6** lists latent heats for a few substances.

FIGURE 3.6				
LATENT HEATS OF FUSION AND VAPORIZATION AT STANDARD PRESSURE				
Substance	Melting point (°C)	L_f (J/kg)	Boiling point (°C)	L_v (J/kg)
nitrogen	−209.97	2.55×10^4	−195.81	2.01×10^5
oxygen	−218.79	1.38×10^4	−182.97	2.13×10^5
ethyl alcohol	−114	1.04×10^5	78	8.54×10^5
water	0.00	3.33×10^5	100.00	2.26×10^6
lead	327.3	2.45×10^4	1745	8.70×10^5
aluminum	660.4	3.97×10^5	2467	1.14×10^7

SECTION 3 **FORMATIVE ASSESSMENT**

▶ Reviewing Main Ideas

1. A jeweler working with a heated 47 g gold ring must lower the ring's temperature to make it safe to handle. If the ring is initially at 99°C, what mass of water at 25°C is needed to lower the ring's temperature to 38°C?

2. How much energy must be added to a bowl of 125 popcorn kernels in order for them to reach a popping temperature of 175°C? Assume that their initial temperature is 21°C, that the specific heat capacity of popcorn is 1650 J/kg•°C, and that each kernel has a mass of 0.105 g.

3. Because of the pressure inside a popcorn kernel, water does not vaporize at 100°C. Instead, it stays liquid until its temperature is about 175°C, at which point the kernel ruptures and the superheated water turns into steam. How much energy is needed to pop 95.0 g of corn if 14 percent of a kernel's mass consists of water? Assume that the latent heat of vaporization for water at 175°C is 0.90 times its value at 100°C and that the kernels have an initial temperature of 175°C.

✔ Critical Thinking

4. Using the concepts of latent heat and internal energy, explain why it is difficult to build a fire with damp wood.

5. Why does steam at 100°C cause more severe burns than does liquid water at 100°C?

Interpreting Graphics

6. From the heating curve for a 15 g sample, as shown in **Figure 3.7,** estimate the following properties of the substance.
   a. the specific heat capacity of the liquid
   b. the latent heat of fusion
   c. the specific heat capacity of the solid
   d. the specific heat capacity of the vapor
   e. the latent heat of vaporization

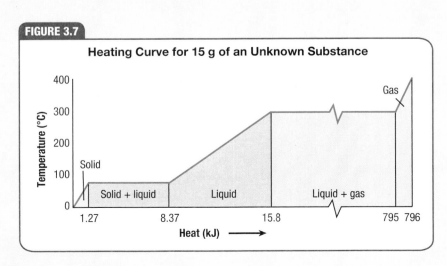

FIGURE 3.7

Heating Curve for 15 g of an Unknown Substance

HVAC Technician

H VAC stands for "heating, ventilation, and air conditioning." An HVAC technician knows what it takes to keep buildings warm in winter and cool in summer. To learn more about working with HVAC as a career, read the interview with contractor and business owner Doug Garner.

Doug Garner is checking a potential relay. This relay is connected to a capacitor that starts the compressor.

What does an HVAC technician do?

Basically, we sell, replace, and repair air-conditioning and heating equipment. We replace obsolete A/C and heating units in older homes and buildings, we install new units in new homes and buildings, and we repair units when they break down.

How did you become an HVAC technician?

There are numerous ways to get into the business. When I was about 17 years old, I was given an opportunity to work for a man with whom I went to church. I worked as an apprentice for three years after high school, and I learned from him and a couple of very good technicians. I also took some business courses at a local community college to help with the business end.

What about HVAC made it more interesting than other fields?

There were other things that I was interested in doing, but realistically HVAC was more practical. In other words, that's where the money and opportunities were for me.

What is the nature of your work?

I have a company with two service technicians and an apprentice. Most of my duties involve getting jobs secured, bidding on and designing the different systems to suit the needs of the customer. I have to have a basic understanding of advertising, marketing, and sales as well as of the technical areas as they apply to this field. Our technicians must be able to communicate well and have a good mechanical aptitude.

What do you like most about your job?

You get to work in a lot of different places and situations. It is never boring, and you meet a lot of people. You can make as much money as you are willing to work for.

What advice would you give to students who are interested in your field?

Take a course in HVAC at a technical institute or trade school, and then work as an apprentice for a few years. Mechanical engineering, sales, communication, and people skills are all important in this field; the more education you have, the more attractive you can be to a company.

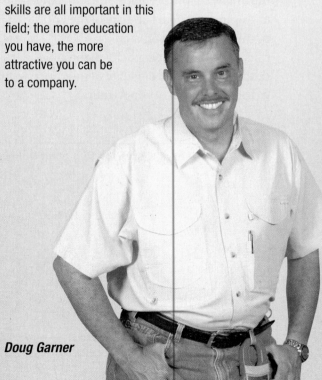

Doug Garner

Thermal Energy Transfer

Energy is transferred between substances as heat. This transfer of energy can occur via three methods: conduction, convection, and radiation. Thermal energy transfer by the collisions between particles with higher average kinetic energies and particles with lower average kinetic energies is called conduction. Conduction can only occur between objects when the two objects of different temperatures are touching. Convection involves the movement of cold and hot liquid or gas. Convection is dictated by factors such as pressure differences, conduction, and buoyancy. Radiation, on the other hand, does not require a material medium to transfer energy; instead, energy is transferred across space in the form of electromagnetic waves.

Identifying and Comparing Examples

Often, more than one type of energy transfer occurs at the same time. For instance, a pot of water on the stove is heated by both conduction and convection. At the same time, although it does not necessarily contribute to the heating of the water, energy is transferred from the stove in the form of radiation. Consider other everyday examples of the transfer of thermal energy.

- Compare and contrast the three processes of thermal energy transfer.

- Give examples of each kind of energy transfer.

- Draw a diagram of a campfire. Where does each type of energy transfer occur? Draw and label each method of transfer.

BIG IDEA   Heat is the transfer of energy due to differences in temperature.

SECTION 1 Temperature and Thermal Equilibrium

- Temperature can be changed by transferring energy to or from a substance.
- Thermal equilibrium is the condition in which the temperature of two objects in physical contact with each other is the same.
- The most common temperature scales are the Fahrenheit, Celsius, and Kelvin (or absolute) scales.

temperature
internal energy
thermal
  equilibrium

SECTION 2 Defining Heat

KEY TERM

- Heat is energy that is transferred from objects at higher temperatures to objects at lower temperatures.
- Energy is transferred by thermal conduction through particle collisions.
- Energy is conserved when mechanical energy and internal energy are taken into account. Thus, for a closed system, the sum of the changes in kinetic energy, potential energy, and internal energy must equal zero.

heat

SECTION 3 Changes in Temperature and Phase

KEY TERMS

- Specific heat capacity is a measure of the energy needed to change a substance's temperature.
- By convention, the energy that is gained by a substance is positive, and the energy that is released by a substance is negative.
- Latent heat is a measure of the energy required to change the phase of a substance.

specific heat
  capacity
calorimetry
phase change
latent heat

VARIABLE SYMBOLS			
Quantities		**Units**	
T	temperature (Kelvin)	K	kelvins
T_C	temperature (Celsius)	°C	degrees Celsius
T_F	temperature (Fahrenheit)	°F	degrees Fahrenheit
ΔU	change in internal energy	J	joules
Q	heat	J	joules
c_p	specific heat capacity at constant pressure	$\dfrac{\text{J}}{\text{kg} \bullet °\text{C}}$	
L	latent heat	$\dfrac{\text{J}}{\text{kg}}$	

Problem Solving

See **Appendix D: Equations** for a summary of the equations introduced in this chapter. If you need more problem-solving practice, see **Appendix I: Additional Problems.**

Temperature and Thermal Equilibrium

▶ **REVIEWING MAIN IDEAS**

1. What is the relationship between temperature and internal energy?

2. What must be true of two objects if the objects are in a state of thermal equilibrium?

3. What are some physical properties that could be used in developing a temperature scale?

CONCEPTUAL QUESTIONS

4. What property must a substance have in order to be used for calibrating a thermometer?

5. Which object in each of the following pairs has greater total internal energy, assuming that the two objects in each pair are in thermal equilibrium? Explain your reasoning in each case.
   a. a metal knife in thermal equilibrium with a hot griddle
   b. a 1 kg block of ice at −25°C or seven 12 g ice cubes at −25°C

6. Assume that each pair of objects in item 5 has the same internal energy instead of the same temperature. Which item in each pair will have the higher temperature? Why?

7. Why are the steam and ice points of water better fixed points for a thermometer than the temperature of a human body?

8. How does the temperature of a tub of hot water as measured by a thermometer differ from the water's temperature before the measurement is made? What property of a thermometer is necessary for the difference between these two temperatures to be minimized?

PRACTICE PROBLEMS

For problems 9–10, see Sample Problem A.

9. The highest recorded temperature on Earth was 134°F, at Death Valley, California, in 1913. Express this temperature in degrees Celsius and in kelvins.

10. The melting point of gold is 1947°F. Express this temperature in degrees Celsius and in kelvins.

Defining Heat

▶ **REVIEWING MAIN IDEAS**

11. Which drawing below shows the direction in which net energy is transferred as heat between an ice cube and the freezer walls when the temperature of both is −10°C? Explain your answer.

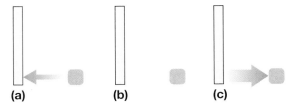

   (a)   (b)   (c)

12. A glass of water has an initial temperature of 8°C. In which situation will the rate of energy transfer be greater, when the air's temperature is 25°C or 35°C?

13. How much energy is transferred between a piece of toast and an oven when both are at a temperature of 55°C? Explain.

14. How does a metal rod conduct energy from one end, which has been placed in a fire, to the other end, which is at room temperature?

15. How does air within winter clothing keep you warm on cold winter days?

CONCEPTUAL QUESTIONS

16. If water in a sealed, insulated container is stirred, is its temperature likely to increase slightly, decrease slightly, or stay the same? Explain your answer.

17. Given your answer to item 16, why does stirring a hot cup of coffee cool it down?

18. Given any two bodies, the one with the higher temperature contains more heat. What is wrong with this statement?

19. Explain how conduction causes water on the surface of a bridge to freeze sooner than water on the road surface on either side of the bridge.

20. A tile floor may feel uncomfortably cold to your bare feet, but a carpeted floor in an adjoining room at the same temperature feels warm. Why?

21. Why is it recommended that several items of clothing be worn in layers on cold days?

22. Why does a fan make you feel cooler on a hot day?

23. A paper cup is filled with water and then placed over an open flame, as shown at right. Explain why the cup does not catch fire and burn.

PRACTICE PROBLEMS

For problems 24–25, see Sample Problem B.

24. A force of 315 N is applied horizontally to a crate in order to displace the crate 35.0 m across a level floor at a constant velocity. As a result of this work, the crate's internal energy is increased by an amount equal to 14 percent of the crate's initial internal energy. Calculate the initial internal energy of the crate. (Disregard the work done on the floor, and assume that all work goes into the crate.)

25. A 0.75 kg spike is hammered into a railroad tie. The initial speed of the spike is equal to 3.0 m/s.
  a. If the tie and spike together absorb 85 percent of the spike's initial kinetic energy as internal energy, calculate the increase in internal energy of the tie and spike.
  b. What happens to the remaining energy?

Changes in Temperature and Phase

▶ **REVIEWING MAIN IDEAS**

26. What principle permits calorimetry to be used to determine the specific heat capacity of a substance? Explain.

27. Why does the temperature of melting ice not change even though energy is being transferred as heat to the ice?

CONCEPTUAL QUESTIONS

28. Why does the evaporation of water cool the air near the water's surface?

29. Until refrigerators were invented, many people stored fruits and vegetables in underground cellars. Why was this more effective than keeping them in the open air?

30. During the winter, the people mentioned in item 29 would often place an open barrel of water in the cellar alongside their produce. Explain why this was done and why it would be effective.

PRACTICE PROBLEMS

For problems 31–32, see Sample Problem C.

31. A 25.5 g silver ring ($c_p = 234$ J/kg•°C) is heated to a temperature of 84.0°C and then placed in a calorimeter containing 5.00×10^{-2} kg of water at 24.0°C. The calorimeter is not perfectly insulated, however, and 0.140 kJ of energy is transferred to the surroundings before a final temperature is reached. What is the final temperature?

32. When a driver brakes an automobile, friction between the brake disks and the brake pads converts part of the car's translational kinetic energy to internal energy. If a 1500 kg automobile traveling at 32 m/s comes to a halt after its brakes are applied, how much can the temperature rise in each of the four 3.5 kg brake disks? Assume the disks are made of iron ($c_p = 448$ J/kg•°C) and that all of the kinetic energy is distributed in equal parts to the internal energy of the brakes.

Mixed Review

▶ REVIEWING MAIN IDEAS

33. Absolute zero on a temperature scale called the *Rankine* scale is $T_R = 0$°R, and the scale's unit is the same size as the Fahrenheit degree.
   a. Write a formula that relates the Rankine scale to the Fahrenheit scale.
   b. Write a formula that relates the Rankine scale to the Kelvin scale.

34. A 3.0 kg rock is initially at rest at the top of a cliff. Assuming the rock falls into the sea at the foot of the cliff and that its kinetic energy is transferred entirely to the water, how high is the cliff if the temperature of 1.0 kg of water is raised 0.10°C? (Neglect the heat capacity of the rock.)

35. The freezing and boiling points of water on the imaginary "Too Hot" temperature scale are selected to be exactly 50 and 200 degrees TH.
   a. Derive an equation relating the Too Hot scale to the Celsius scale. (Hint: Make a graph of one temperature scale versus the other, and solve for the equation of the line.)
   b. Calculate absolute zero in degrees TH.

36. A hot-water heater is operated by solar power. If the solar collector has an area of 6.0 m^2 and the power delivered by sunlight is 550 W/m^2, how long will it take to increase the temperature of 1.0 m^3 of water from 21°C to 61°C?

GRAPHING CALCULATOR PRACTICE

Specific Heat Capacity

Specific heat capacity (c_p), as you learned earlier in this chapter, is equal to the amount of energy required to change the temperature of 1 kg of a substance by 1°C. This relationship is expressed by the following equation:

$$\Delta T = \frac{Q}{mc_p}$$

In this equation, ΔT is the change in temperature, Q is the amount of energy absorbed by the substance as heat, c_p is the specific heat capacity of the substance, and m is the mass of the substance.

This equation can be represented on a graphing calculator as follows:

$$Y_1 = T + (X/(MC))$$

A graph of this equation will illustrate the relationship between energy absorbed as heat and temperature.

In this graphing calculator activity, you will enter various values for the energy absorbed and will determine the resulting temperature. Then, you can explore how changing the specific heat capacity, mass, and initial temperature changes your results.

Go online to HMHScience.com to find the skillsheet and program for this graphing calculator activity.

37. A student drops two metallic objects into a 120 g steel container holding 150 g of water at 25°C. One object is a 253 g cube of copper that is initially at 85°C, and the other is a chunk of aluminum that is initially at 5°C. To the surprise of the student, the water reaches a final temperature of 25°C, its initial temperature. What is the mass of the aluminum chunk?

38. At what Fahrenheit temperature are the Kelvin and Fahrenheit temperatures numerically equal?

ALTERNATIVE ASSESSMENT

1. According to legend, Archimedes determined whether the king's crown was pure gold by comparing its water displacement with the displacement of a piece of pure gold of equal mass. But this procedure is difficult to apply to very small objects. Use the concept of specific heat capacity to design a method for determining whether a ring is pure gold. Present your plan to the class, and ask others to suggest improvements to your design. Discuss each suggestion's advantages and disadvantages.

2. The host of a cooking show on television claims that you can greatly reduce the baking time for potatoes by inserting a nail through each potato. Explain whether this advice has a scientific basis. Would this approach be more efficient than wrapping the potatoes in aluminum foil? List all arguments, and discuss their strengths and weaknesses.

3. The graph of decreasing temperature versus time of a hot object is called its cooling curve. Design and perform an experiment to determine the cooling curve of water in containers of various materials and shapes. Draw cooling curves for each one. Which trends represent good insulation? Use your findings and graphs to design a lunch box that keeps food warm or cold.

39. A 250 g aluminum cup holds and is in thermal equilibrium with 850 g of water at 83°C. The combination of cup and water is cooled uniformly so that the temperature decreases by 1.5°C per minute. At what rate is energy being removed?

40. A jar of tea is placed in sunlight until it reaches an equilibrium temperature of 32°C. In an attempt to cool the liquid, which has a mass of 180 g, 112 g of ice at 0°C is added. At the time at which the temperature of the tea (and melted ice) is 15°C, determine the mass of the remaining ice in the jar. Assume the specific heat capacity of the tea to be that of pure liquid water.

4. Research the life and work of James Prescott Joule, who is best known for his apparatus demonstrating the equivalence of work and heat and the conservation of energy. Many scientists initially did not accept Joule's conclusions. Research the reasoning behind their objections. Prepare a presentation for a class discussion either supporting the objections of Joule's critics or defending Joule's conclusion before England's Royal Academy of Sciences.

5. Research how scientists measure the temperature of the following: the sun, a flame, a volcano, outer space, liquid hydrogen, mice, and insects. Find out what instruments are used in each case and how they are calibrated to known temperatures. Using what you learn, prepare a chart or other presentation on the tools used to measure temperature and the limitations on their ranges.

6. Get information on solar water heaters that are available where you live. How does each type work? Compare prices and operating expenses for solar water heaters versus gas water heaters. What are some of the other advantages and limitations of solar water heaters? Prepare an informative brochure for homeowners who are interested in this technology.

Standards-Based Assessment

Record your answers on a separate piece of paper.

MULTIPLE CHOICE

1 A metal spoon is placed in one of two identical cups of hot coffee. Why does the cup with the spoon have a lower temperature after a few minutes?

  A Energy is removed from the coffee mostly by conduction through the spoon.

  B Energy is removed from the coffee mostly by convection through the spoon.

  C Energy is removed from the coffee mostly by radiation through the spoon.

  D The metal in the spoon has an extremely large specific heat capacity.

2 The boiling point of liquid hydrogen is −252.87°C. What is the value of this temperature on the Fahrenheit scale?

  A 20.28°F

  B −220.87°F

  C −423.17°F

  D 0°F

3 Heat can be transferred by the movement of particles in a material, by the bulk motion of a heated fluid, or through a vacuum as electromagnetic waves. What is the name of each process of thermal energy transfer, in the order given?

  A conduction, convection, radiation

  B convection, conduction, radiation

  C radiation, convection, conduction

  D conduction, radiation, convection

4 A cup of hot chocolate with a temperature of 40°C is placed inside a refrigerator at 5°C. An identical cup of hot chocolate at 90°C is placed on a table in a room at 25°C. A third identical cup of hot chocolate at 80°C is placed on an outdoor table, where the surrounding air has a temperature of 0°C. For which of the three cups has the most energy been transferred as heat when equilibrium has been reached?

  A The first cup has the largest energy transfer.

  B The second cup has the largest energy transfer.

  C The third cup has the largest energy transfer.

  D The same amount of energy is transferred as heat for all three cups.

5 The graph below shows the change in average kinetic energy, as represented by temperature, of a 23 g sample of a substance as energy is added to the substance as heat.

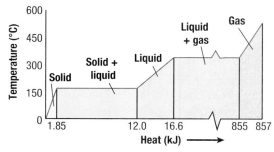

What is the specific heat capacity of the solid?

  A 1.85×10^3 J/kg•°C

  B 4.0×10^2 J/kg•°C

  C 5.0×10^2 J/kg•°C

  D 1.1×10^3 J/kg•°C

6 At the beach in the daytime, a cool breeze generally blows from the water to the shore. What is the name of this process of thermal energy transfer?

  A radiation

  B insolation

  C conduction

  D convection

7 In restaurants, heat lamps often are used to keep prepared food hot for serving. Which process of thermal energy transfer is represented by the heat lamp?

  A radiation

  B insolation

  C conduction

  D convection

GRIDDED RESPONSE

8 The freezing point of nitrogen is −346°F. What is the value of this temperature in kelvins?

Global Climate Change

Global average temperatures have warmed by 0.85°C since 1880. The years between 2000 and 2015 included nine of the ten warmest years ever recorded. Greenland and Antarctic ice sheets, as well as glaciers around the world, have been shrinking at ever-faster rates. The increased temperatures and melting ice have caused the average sea level to rise 19 cm since 1901. Do these changes represent a trend toward global warming, or is it simply part of a natural cyclic variation in climate? The answer from climate scientists around the world is virtually unanimous that Earth's climate is warming, and that the rates of ice melting and sea level rise are increasing.

Identify a Problem: Concentrations of Greenhouse Gases

If you have ever felt the sun warm the inside of a car even while the air outside was cold, then you have experienced the greenhouse effect. Visible light from the sun travels through the clear walls of a greenhouse. The light is absorbed within and is transformed into thermal energy, which causes the air temperature to increase. Thermal energy is trapped, resulting in the warm interior. Earth's thick atmosphere acts as a greenhouse. The water vapor, carbon dioxide (CO_2), methane, and nitrous oxides that are a natural part of Earth's atmosphere allow sunlight to pass through. These greenhouse gases, as they are called, trap thermal energy and prevent it from radiating back into space. Without the greenhouse effect, Earth's average temperature would be an unbearable −18°C.

The levels of atmospheric carbon dioxide and methane have increased rapidly over the past 150 years. This increase has been determined by analyzing air trapped in the ice layers of Greenland. Deeper sections of the ice contain air from earlier times. Since the beginning of human civilization, our atmosphere contained about 275 ppm (parts per million) of CO_2. In the past 150 years, human activity has increased the concentrations of greenhouse gases. In 2015, the levels of CO_2 were 402 ppm. Most of this increase is from burning fossil fuels such as coal, petroleum, and natural gas. Increases in greenhouse gas concentrations have already changed our climate.

Thermal energy in the atmosphere drives weather patterns. It determines the rate of evaporation of water and fuels the intensity of storms and other weather events. Global warming has already affected many natural systems through changes in patterns of rain and snowfall. Many regions have become more arid, and some now experience more intense rainfall. As a result, many plants and animals have been affected, shifting their habitable regions and changing migration patterns. Humans depend on a stable climate for our food supply. Changes in weather patterns have already had a negative

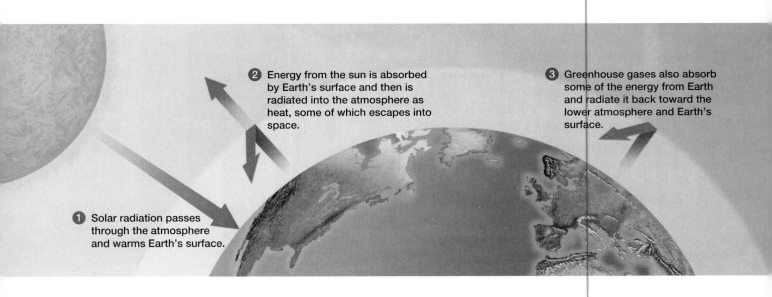

1 Solar radiation passes through the atmosphere and warms Earth's surface.

2 Energy from the sun is absorbed by Earth's surface and then is radiated into the atmosphere as heat, some of which escapes into space.

3 Greenhouse gases also absorb some of the energy from Earth and radiate it back toward the lower atmosphere and Earth's surface.

impact on crop yields around the world. Increasingly intense weather has led to more frequent heat waves, droughts, floods, cyclones, and wildfires. The rise in sea level due to global warming has also increased the risks of floods along coastal areas.

Scientists around the world agree that without a change in greenhouse gas emissions, the global climate will continue changing at ever-increasing rates, causing the extinction of many species, as well as severe food and water shortages.

Brainstorm Solutions

What are some ways to reduce greenhouse gases? One solution is to decrease the output of these gases. This can be done by replacing coal-burning power plants with renewable energy sources such as wind, solar, and hydroelectricity. Another way to reduce greenhouse gas emissions is to use vehicles that are more fuel-efficient and to ride bicycles or walk when possible. Other alternatives include reducing energy used for heating and cooling and buying products that last longer. Another solution for reducing greenhouse gases is through thoughtful land use. Planting trees and reducing deforestation allow carbon dioxide to be captured and stored. Agriculture, forestry, and other forms of land use contribute about 25 percent our total greenhouse gas emissions. Scientists agree that changes in land use can reduce emissions and even capture CO_2 from the atmosphere, making it a "sink" for CO_2 over time.

Select a Solution

The generation of greenhouse gases is as much a local issue as it is a global challenge. Solutions are likewise found at many levels. People's daily habits and choices have an effect across international borders. Lasting solutions can be based on international agreements to limit emissions on a global scale. There are many questions to consider. Which solutions are most effective? What are the costs associated with each technology? Are financial incentives available? How easy is it to apply each solution? Many practical solutions also have other benefits, such as reducing pollution, being more cost-effective, or promoting good health.

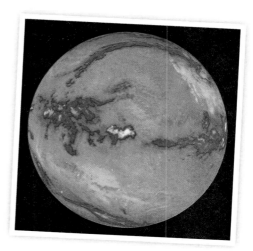

This false-color image shows the energy radiating from Earth's upper atmosphere. The blue areas are the coldest. The American southwest is in the upper right-hand corner.

Communicate

The potential impact of climate change on natural and human systems is too great to ignore. Sometimes a change in habits and behaviors happens only when people understand the long-term effects of their choices. Communication is key. Through education and community outreach programs, people can make informed decisions about the effects of climate change and the solutions they can put into action.

Design Your Own

Conduct Research

Carbon dioxide levels in the atmosphere have varied throughout Earth's history. Research the roles volcanoes, plants, and limestone formation play in the levels of CO_2 in the atmosphere. Determine whether these processes have any bearing on the recent increase in CO_2 concentrations.

Brainstorm Solutions

Can you think of any practical means of using these formation processes to reduce CO_2 concentrations?

Evaluate

Pick one of the solutions you brainstormed. What would be the advantages and disadvantages? Can it be easily implemented? Would people support it?

Why It Matters

The principles of thermodynamics explain thermodynamic systems, from complicated cyclic processes, such as those in refrigerators and internal-combustion engines, to simple thermodynamic systems like the balloon pictured in this photograph.

This balloon is used to lift scientific instruments into the upper atmosphere. Changes in temperature outside the balloon may cause energy transfers between the gas in the balloon and the outside air. This transfer of energy as heat changes the balloon's internal energy.

CHAPTER 10
Thermodynamics

SECTION 1
Relationships Between Heat and Work

SECTION 2
The First Law of Thermodynamics

SECTION 3
The Second Law of Thermodynamics

BIG IDEA

Thermodynamic systems are defined by the relationships between heat, work, and energy.

ONLINE Physics
HMHScience.com

ONLINE LABS
- Relationship Between Heat and Work

GO ONLINE

Animated **Physics**

HMHScience.com

First Law of Thermodynamics

(b) ©Digital Vision/Getty Images

▶ Recognize that a system can absorb or release energy as heat in order for work to be done on or by the system and that work done on or by a system can result in the transfer of energy as heat.

▶ Compute the amount of work done during a thermodynamic process.

▶ Distinguish between isovolumetric, isothermal, and adiabatic thermodynamic processes.

Relationships Between Heat and Work

Key Terms

system
environment

isovolumetric process
isothermal process

adiabatic process

Heat, Work, and Internal Energy

Pulling a nail from a piece of wood causes the temperature of the nail and the wood to increase. Work is done by the frictional forces between the nail and the wood fibers. This work increases the internal energy of the iron atoms in the nail and the molecules in the wood.

The increase in the nail's internal energy corresponds to an increase in the nail's temperature, which is higher than the temperature of the surrounding air. Thus, energy is transferred as heat from the nail to the air. When they are at the same temperature, this energy transfer stops.

Internal energy can be used to do work.

The example of the hammer and nail illustrates that work can increase the internal energy of a substance. This internal energy can then decrease through the transfer of energy as heat. The reverse is also possible. Energy can be transferred to a substance as heat, and this internal energy can then be used to do work.

Consider a flask of water. A balloon is placed over the mouth of the flask, and the flask is heated until the water boils. Energy transferred as heat from the flame of the gas burner to the water increases the internal energy of the water. When the water's temperature reaches the boiling point, the water changes phase and becomes steam. At this constant temperature, the volume of the steam increases. This expansion provides a force that pushes the balloon outward and does work on the atmosphere, as shown in **Figure 1.1.** Thus, the steam does work, and the steam's internal energy decreases as predicted by the principle of energy conservation.

Heat and work are energy transferred to or from a system.

On a microscopic scale, heat and work are similar. In this textbook, both are defined as energy that is transferred to or from a substance. This changes the substance's internal energy (and thus its temperature or phase). In other words, the terms *heat* and *work* always refer to energy in transit. An object never has "heat" or "work" in it; it has only internal energy.

FIGURE 1.1

Steam Doing Work Energy transferred as heat turns water into steam. Energy from the steam does work on the air outside the balloon.

In the previous examples, the internal energy of a substance or combination of substances has been treated as a single quantity to which energy is added or from which energy is taken away. Such a substance or combination of substances is called a **system.**

An example of a system would be the flask, balloon, water, and steam that were heated over the burner. As the burner transferred energy as heat to the system, the system's internal energy increased. When the expanding steam did work on the air outside the balloon by pushing it back (as the balloon expanded), the system's internal energy decreased. Some of the energy transferred to the system as heat was transferred out of the system as work done on the air.

A system is rarely completely isolated from its surroundings. In the example above, a heat interaction occurs between the burner and the system, and work is done by the system on the surroundings (the balloon moves the outside air outward). Energy is also transferred as heat to the air surrounding the flask because of the temperature difference between the flask and the surrounding air. In such cases, we must account for all of the interactions between the system and its **environment** that could affect the system's internal energy.

Work done on or by a gas is pressure multiplied by volume change.

In thermodynamic systems, work is defined in terms of pressure and volume change. Pressure is a measure of how much force is applied over a given area ($P = F/A$). Change in volume is equal to area multiplied by displacement ($\Delta V = Ad$). These expressions can be substituted into the definition of work introduced in the chapter "Work and Energy" to derive a new definition for the work done on or by a gas, as follows:

$$W = Fd$$

$$W = Fd\left(\frac{A}{A}\right) = \left(\frac{F}{A}\right)(Ad) = P\Delta V$$

Work Done by a Gas

$$W = P\Delta V$$

work = pressure × volume change

This chapter will use only this new definition of work. Note that this definition assumes that P is constant.

If the gas expands, as in **Figure 1.2**, ΔV is positive, and the work done by the gas on the piston is positive. If the gas is compressed, ΔV is negative, and the work done by the gas on the piston is negative. (In other words, the piston does work on the gas.) When the gas volume remains constant, there is no displacement, and no work is done on or by the system.

Although the pressure can change during a process, work is done only if the volume changes. A situation in which pressure increases and volume remains constant is comparable to one in which a force does not displace a mass even as the force is increased. Work is not done in either situation.

FIGURE 1.2

Gas Expanding Work done on or by the gas is the product of the volume change (area A multiplied by the displacement d) and the pressure of the gas.

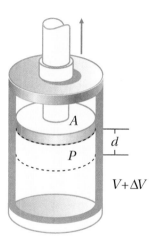

Work Done on or by a Gas

Sample Problem A An engine cylinder has a cross-sectional area of 0.010 m². How much work can be done by a gas in the cylinder if the gas exerts a constant pressure of 7.5×10^5 Pa on the piston and moves the piston a distance of 0.040 m?

① ANALYZE

Given:
$$A = 0.010 \text{ m}^2 \qquad d = 0.040 \text{ m}$$
$$P = 7.5 \times 10^5 \text{ Pa} = 7.5 \times 10^5 \text{ N/m}^2$$

Unknown: $W = ?$

② SOLVE

Use the equation for the work done on or by a gas.

$$W = P\Delta V = PAd$$

$$W = (7.5 \times 10^5 \text{ N/m}^2)(0.010 \text{ m}^2)(0.040 \text{ m})$$

$$\boxed{W = 3.0 \times 10^2 \text{ J}}$$

Tips and Tricks

Because *W* is positive, we can conclude that the work is done by the gas rather than on the gas.

Practice

1. Gas in a container is at a pressure of 1.6×10^5 Pa and a volume of 4.0 m³. What is the work done by the gas if

    a. it expands at constant pressure to twice its initial volume?

    b. it is compressed at constant pressure to one-quarter of its initial volume?

2. A gas is enclosed in a container fitted with a piston. The applied pressure is maintained at 599.5 kPa as the piston moves inward, which changes the volume of the gas from 5.317×10^{-4} m³ to 2.523×10^{-4} m³. How much work is done? Is the work done *on* or *by* the gas? Explain your answer.

3. A balloon is inflated with helium at a constant pressure that is 4.3×10^5 Pa in excess of atmospheric pressure. If the balloon inflates from a volume of 1.8×10^{-4} m³ to 9.5×10^{-4} m³, how much work is done on the surrounding air by the helium-filled balloon during this expansion?

4. Steam moves into the cylinder of a steam engine at a constant pressure and does 0.84 J of work on a piston. The diameter of the piston is 1.6 cm, and the piston travels 2.1 cm. What is the pressure of the steam?

Thermodynamic Processes

In this section, three distinct quantities have been related to each other: internal energy (U), heat (Q), and work (W). Processes that involve only work or only heat are rare. In most cases, energy is transferred as both heat and work. However, in many processes, one type of energy transfer is dominant, and the other type negligible. In these cases, the real process can be approximated with an ideal process. For example, if the dominant form of energy transfer is work and the energy transferred as heat is extremely small, we can neglect the heat transfer and still obtain an accurate model. In this way, many real processes can be approximated by one of three ideal processes.

Later, you will learn about ideal processes in gases. All objects have internal energy, which is the sum of the kinetic and potential energies of their molecules. However, monatomic gases present a simpler situation because their molecules are too far apart to interact with each other significantly. Thus, all of their internal energy is kinetic.

No work is done in a constant-volume process.

In general, when a gas undergoes a change in temperature but no change in volume, no work is done on or by the system. Such a process is called a constant-volume process, or **isovolumetric process.**

One example of an isovolumetric process takes place inside a *bomb calorimeter*, shown in **Figure 1.3.** In the container, a small quantity of a substance undergoes a combustion reaction. The energy released by the reaction increases the pressure and temperature of the gaseous products. Because the walls are thick, there is no change in the volume of the gas. Energy can be transferred to or from the container as only heat. The temperature increase of water surrounding the bomb calorimeter provides information for calculating the amount of energy produced by the reaction.

isovolumetric process a thermodynamic process that takes place at constant volume so that no work is done on or by the system

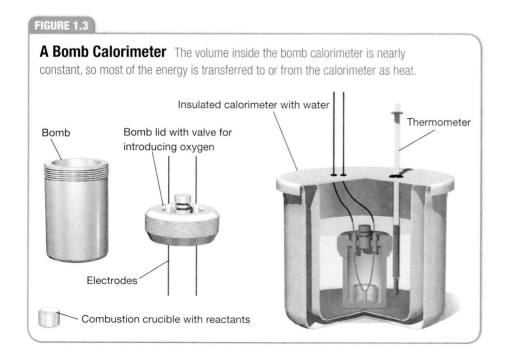

FIGURE 1.3

A Bomb Calorimeter The volume inside the bomb calorimeter is nearly constant, so most of the energy is transferred to or from the calorimeter as heat.

Insulated calorimeter with water

Thermometer

Bomb

Bomb lid with valve for introducing oxygen

Electrodes

Combustion crucible with reactants

isothermal process a thermody-namic process that takes place at constant temperature

Internal energy is constant in a constant-temperature process.

During an **isothermal process**, the temperature of the system does not change. In an ideal gas, internal energy depends only on temperature; therefore, if temperature does not change, then internal energy cannot change either. Thus, in an isothermal process, internal energy does not change when energy is transferred to or from the system as heat or work.

One example of an isothermal process is illustrated in **Figure 1.4.** Although you may think of a balloon that has been inflated and sealed as a static system, it is subject to continuous thermodynamic effects. Consider what happens to such a balloon during an approaching storm. (To simplify this example, we will assume that the balloon is only partially inflated and thus does not store elastic energy.) During the few hours before the storm arrives, the barometric pressure of the atmosphere steadily decreases by about 2000 Pa. If you are indoors and the temperature of the building is controlled, any change in outside temperature will not occur indoors. But because no building is perfectly sealed, changes in the pressure of the air outside also occur inside.

As the atmospheric pressure inside the building slowly decreases, the balloon expands and slowly does work on the air outside the balloon. At the same time, energy is slowly transferred into the balloon as heat. The net result is that the air inside the balloon stays at the same temperature as the air outside the balloon. Thus, the internal energy of the balloon's air does not change. The energy transferred out of the balloon as work is matched by the energy transferred into the balloon as heat.

You may wonder how energy can be transferred as heat from the air outside the balloon to the air inside when both gases are at the same constant temperature. The reason is that energy can be transferred as heat in an isothermal process if you consider the process as consisting of a large number of very gradual, very small sequential changes, as shown in **Figure 1.5.**

An Isothermal Process

An isothermal process can be approximated if energy is slowly removed from a system as work while an equivalent amount of energy is added as heat.

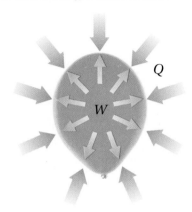

Small Energy Transfers In an isothermal process in a partially inflated balloon, **(a)** small amounts of energy are removed as work. **(b)** Energy is added to the gas within the balloon's interior as heat so that **(c)** thermal equilibrium is quickly restored.

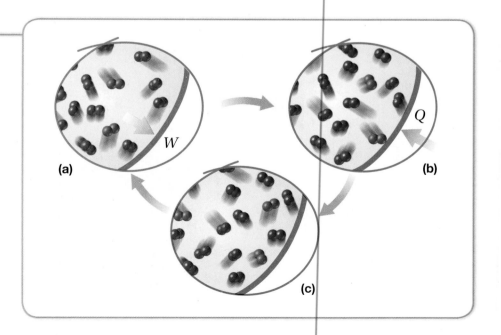

Energy is not transferred as heat in an adiabatic process.

When a tank of compressed gas is opened to fill a toy balloon, the process of inflation occurs rapidly. The internal energy of the gas does not remain constant. Instead, as the pressure of the gas in the tank decreases, so do the gas's internal energy and temperature.

If the balloon and the tank are thermally insulated, no energy can be transferred from the expanding gas as heat. A process in which changes occur but no energy is transferred to or from a system as heat is called an **adiabatic process.** The decrease in internal energy must therefore be equal to the energy transferred from the gas as work. This work is done by the confined gas as it pushes the wall of the balloon outward, overcoming the pressure exerted by the air outside the balloon. As a result, the balloon inflates, as shown in **Figure 1.6.** Note that unlike an isothermal process, which must happen slowly, an adiabatic process must happen rapidly.

As mentioned earlier, the three processes described here rarely occur ideally, but many situations can be approximated by one of the three processes. This allows you to make predictions. For example, both refrigerators and internal-combustion engines require that gases be compressed or expanded rapidly. By making the approximation that these processes are adiabatic, one can make quite good predictions about how these machines will operate.

adiabatic process a thermodynamic process during which no energy is transferred to or from the system as heat

FIGURE 1.6

Adiabatic Process As the gas inside the tank and balloon rapidly expands, its internal energy decreases. This energy leaves the system by means of work done against the outside air.

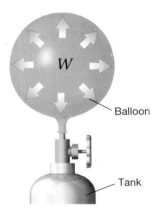

Balloon

Tank

✔ SECTION 1 **FORMATIVE ASSESSMENT**

▶ Reviewing Main Ideas

1. In which of the situations listed below is energy being transferred as heat to the system in order for the system to do work?
   a. Two sticks are rubbed together to start a fire.
   b. A firecracker explodes.
   c. A red-hot iron bar is set aside to cool.

2. A gasoline vapor and air mixture is placed in an engine cylinder. The piston has an area of 7.4×10^{-3} m^2 and is displaced inward by 7.2×10^{-2} m. If 9.5×10^5 Pa of pressure is placed on the piston, how much work is done during this process? Is work being done *on* or *by* the gas mixture?

3. A weather balloon slowly expands as energy is transferred as heat from the outside air. If the average net pressure is 1.5×10^3 Pa and the balloon's volume increases by 5.4×10^{-5} m^3, how much work is done by the expanding gas?

✔ Critical Thinking

4. Identify the following processes as isothermal, isovolumetric, or adiabatic:
   a. a tire being rapidly inflated
   b. a tire expanding gradually at a constant temperature
   c. a steel tank of gas being heated

The First Law of Thermodynamics

Key Term
cyclic process

Objectives

▶ Illustrate how the first law of thermodynamics is a statement of energy conservation.

▶ Calculate heat, work, and the change in internal energy by applying the first law of thermodynamics.

SC.912.P.10.2 Explore the Law of Conservation of Energy by differentiating among open, closed, and isolated systems and explain that the total energy in an isolated system is a conserved quantity.

Energy Conservation

Imagine a roller coaster that operates without friction. The car is raised against gravitational force by work. Once the car is freely moving, it will have a certain kinetic energy (KE) and a certain potential energy (PE). Because there is no friction, the mechanical energy ($KE + PE$) remains constant throughout the ride's duration. Thus, when the car is at the top of the rise, it moves relatively slowly (larger PE + smaller KE). At lower points in the track, the car has less potential energy and so moves more quickly (smaller PE + larger KE).

If friction is taken into account, mechanical energy is no longer conserved, as shown in **Figure 2.1.** A steady decrease in the car's total mechanical energy occurs because of work being done against the friction between the car's axles and its bearings and between the car's wheels and the coaster track. Mechanical energy is transferred to the atoms and molecules throughout the entire roller coaster (both the car and the track). Thus, the roller coaster's internal energy increases by an amount equal to the decrease in the mechanical energy. Most of this energy is then gradually dissipated to the air surrounding the roller coaster as heat. If the internal energy for the roller coaster (the system) and the energy dissipated to the surrounding air (the environment) are taken into account, then the total energy will be constant.

FIGURE 2.1

Conservation of Total Energy

In the presence of friction, the internal energy (U) of the roller coaster increases as $KE + PE$ decreases.

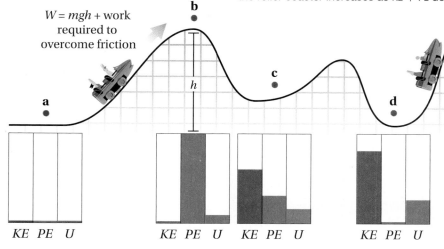

©Rafael Macia/Photo Researchers, Inc.

The principle of energy conservation that takes into account a system's internal energy as well as work and heat is called the *first law of thermodynamics.*

Imagine that the isothermally expanding toy balloon in the previous section is squeezed rapidly. The process is no longer isothermal. Instead, it is a combination of two processes. On the one hand, work (W) is done on the system. The balloon and the air inside it (the system) are compressed, so the air's internal energy and temperature increase. Work is being done on the system, so W is a negative quantity. The rapid squeezing of the balloon can be treated as an adiabatic process, so $Q = 0$ and, therefore, $\Delta U = -W$.

After the compression step, energy is transferred from the system as heat (Q). Some of the internal energy of the air inside the balloon is transferred to the air outside the balloon. During this step, the internal energy of the gas decreases, so ΔU has a negative value. Similarly, because energy is removed from the system, Q has a negative value. The change in internal energy for this step can be expressed as $-\Delta U = -Q$, or $\Delta U = Q$.

The signs for heat and work for a system are summarized in **Figure 2.2**. To remember whether a system's internal energy increases or decreases, you may find it helpful to visualize the system as a circle, as shown in **Figure 2.3**. When work is done on the system or energy is transferred as heat into the system, an arrow points into the circle. This shows that internal energy increases. When work is done by the system or energy is transferred as heat out of the system, the arrow points out of the circle. This shows that internal energy decreases.

FIGURE 2.3

Representing a System If visualizing a system as a circle, arrows represent work and heat.

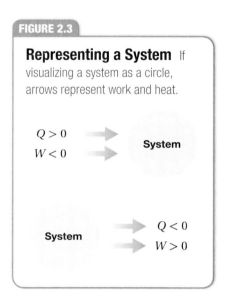

FIGURE 2.2

SIGNS OF Q AND W FOR A SYSTEM	
$Q > 0$	energy added to system as heat
$Q < 0$	energy removed from system as heat
$Q = 0$	no transfer of energy as heat
$W > 0$	work done by system (expansion of gas)
$W < 0$	work done on system (compression of gas)
$W = 0$	no work done

The first law of thermodynamics can be expressed mathematically.

In all the thermodynamic processes described so far, energy has been conserved. To describe the overall change in the system's internal energy, one must account for the transfer of energy to or from the system as heat and work. The total change in the internal energy is the difference between the final internal energy value (U_f) and the initial internal energy value (U_i). That is, $\Delta U = U_f - U_i$. Energy conservation requires that the total change in internal energy from its initial to its final equilibrium conditions be equal to the net transfer of energy as both heat and work. This statement of total energy conservation, shown mathematically, is the first law of thermodynamics.

> ### The First Law of Thermodynamics
> $$\Delta U = Q - W$$
>
> **Change in system's internal energy = energy transferred to or from system as heat − energy transferred to or from system as work**

When this equation is used, all quantities must have the same energy units. Throughout this chapter, the SI unit for energy, the joule, will be used.

According to the first law of thermodynamics, a system's internal energy can be changed by transferring energy as either work, heat, or a combination of the two. The thermodynamic processes discussed in Section 1 can therefore be expressed using the equation for the first law of thermodynamics, as shown in **Figure 2.4**.

FIGURE 2.4

FIRST LAW OF THERMODYNAMICS FOR SPECIAL PROCESSES

Process	Conditions	First law of thermodynamics	Interpretation
Isovolumetric	no work done	$\Delta V = 0$, so $P\Delta V = 0$ and $W = 0$; therefore, $\Delta U = Q$	Energy added to the system as heat ($Q > 0$) increases the system's internal energy. Energy removed from the system as heat ($Q < 0$) decreases the system's internal energy.
Isothermal	no change in temperature or internal energy	$\Delta T = 0$, so $\Delta U = 0$; therefore, $\Delta U = Q - W = 0$, or $Q = W$	Energy added to the system as heat is removed from the system as work done by the system. Energy added to the system by work done on it is removed from the system as heat.
Adiabatic	no energy transferred as heat	$Q = 0$, so $\Delta U = -W$	Work done on the system ($W < 0$) increases the system's internal energy. Work done by the system ($W > 0$) decreases the system's internal energy.
Isolated system	no energy transferred as heat and no work done on or by the system	$Q = 0$ and $W = 0$, so $\Delta U = 0$ and $U_i = U_f$	There is no change in the system's internal energy.

The First Law of Thermodynamics

GO ONLINE

Interactive Demo
HMHScience.com

Sample Problem B A total of 135 J of work is done on a gaseous refrigerant as it undergoes compression. If the internal energy of the gas increases by 114 J during the process, what is the total amount of energy transferred as heat? Has energy been added to or removed from the refrigerant as heat?

① ANALYZE

Given:

$$W = -135 \text{ J}$$
$$\Delta U = 114 \text{ J}$$

Unknown: $Q = ?$

Diagram:

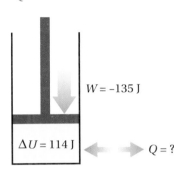

Tips and Tricks

Work is done on the gas, so work (W) has a negative value. The internal energy increases during the process, so the change in internal energy (ΔU) has a positive value.

② PLAN

Choose an equation or situation:
Apply the first law of thermodynamics using the values for ΔU and W in order to find the value for Q.

$$\Delta U = Q - W$$

Rearrange the equation to isolate the unknown:

$$Q = \Delta U + W$$

③ SOLVE

Substitute the values into the equation, and solve:

$$Q = 114 \text{ J} + (-135 \text{ J}) = -21 \text{ J}$$

$$\boxed{Q = -21 \text{ J}}$$

Tips and Tricks

The sign for the value of Q is negative. From **Figure 2.2**, $Q < 0$ indicates that energy is transferred as heat from the refrigerant.

④ CHECK YOUR WORK

Although the internal energy of the refrigerant increases under compression, more energy is added as work than can be accounted for by the increase in the internal energy. This energy is removed from the gas as heat, as indicated by the minus sign preceding the value for Q.

Continued

The First Law of Thermodynamics (continued)

1. Heat is added to a system, and the system does 26 J of work. If the internal energy increases by 7 J, how much heat was added to the system?

2. The internal energy of the gas in a gasoline engine's cylinder decreases by 195 J. If 52.0 J of work is done by the gas, how much energy is transferred as heat? Is this energy added to or removed from the gas?

3. A 2.0 kg quantity of water is held at constant volume in a pressure cooker and heated by a range element. The system's internal energy increases by 8.0×10^3 J. However, the pressure cooker is not well insulated, and as a result, 2.0×10^3 J of energy is transferred to the surrounding air. How much energy is transferred from the range element to the pressure cooker as heat?

4. The internal energy of a gas decreases by 344 J. If the process is adiabatic, how much energy is transferred as heat? How much work is done on or by the gas?

5. A steam engine's boiler completely converts 155 kg of water to steam. This process involves the transfer of 3.50×10^8 J as heat. If steam escaping through a safety valve does 1.76×10^8 J of work expanding against the outside atmosphere, what is the net change in the internal energy of the water-steam system?

Cyclic Processes

cyclic process a thermodynamic process in which a system returns to the same conditions under which it started

A refrigerator performs mechanical work to create temperature differences between its closed interior and its environment (the air in the room). This process leads to the transfer of energy as heat. A heat engine does the opposite: it uses heat to do mechanical work. Both of these processes have something in common: they are examples of **cyclic processes.**

In a cyclic process, the system's properties at the end of the process are identical to the system's properties before the process took place. The final and initial values of internal energy are the same, and the change in internal energy is zero.

$$\Delta U_{net} = 0 \text{ and } Q_{net} = W_{net}$$

A cyclic process resembles an isothermal process in that all energy is transferred as work and heat. But now the process is repeated with no net change in the system's internal energy.

Heat engines use heat to do work.

A heat engine is a device that uses heat to do mechanical work. A heat engine is similar to a water wheel, which uses a difference in potential energy to do work. A water wheel uses the energy of water falling from one level above Earth's surface to another. The change in potential energy increases the water's kinetic energy so that the water can do work on one side of the wheel and thus turn it.

Instead of using the difference in potential energy to do work, heat engines do work by transferring energy from a high-temperature substance to a lower-temperature substance, as indicated for the steam engine shown in **Figure 2.5.** For each complete cycle of the heat engine, the net work done will equal the difference between the energy transferred as heat from a high-temperature substance to the engine (Q_h) and the energy transferred as heat from the engine to a lower-temperature substance (Q_c).

$$W_{net} = Q_h - Q_c$$

The larger the difference between the energy transferred as heat into the engine and out of the engine, the more work it can do in each cycle.

The internal-combustion engine found in most vehicles is an example of a heat engine. Internal-combustion engines burn fuel within a closed chamber (the cylinder). The potential energy of the chemical bonds in the reactant gases is converted to kinetic energy of the particle products of the reaction. These gaseous products push against a piston and thus do work on the environment. In this case, a crankshaft transforms the linear motion of the piston to the rotational motion of the axle and wheels.

Although the basic operation of any internal-combustion engine resembles that of an ideal cyclic heat engine, certain steps do not fit the idealized model. When gas is taken in or removed from the cylinder, matter enters or leaves the system so that the matter in the system is not isolated. No heat engine operates perfectly. Only part of the available internal energy leaves the engine as work done on the environment; most of the energy is removed as heat.

FIGURE 2.5

Heat Engine   A heat engine is able to do work **(b)** by transferring energy from a high-temperature substance (the boiler) at T_h **(a)** to a substance at a lower temperature (the air surrounding the engine) at T_c **(c).**

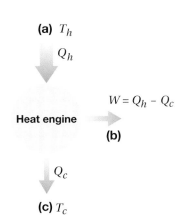

(a) T_h

Q_h

$W = Q_h - Q_c$

Heat engine

(b)

Q_c

(c) T_c

Gasoline Engines

A gasoline engine is one type of internal-combustion engine. The diagram below illustrates the steps in one cycle of operation for a gasoline engine. During compression, shown in **(a)**, work is done by the piston as it adiabatically compresses the fuel-and-air mixture in the cylinder. Once maximum compression of the gas is reached, combustion takes place. The chemical potential energy released during combustion increases the internal energy of the gas, as shown in **(b)**. The hot, high-pressure gases from the combustion reaction expand in volume, pushing the piston and turning the crankshaft, as shown in **(c)**. Once all of the work is done by the piston, some energy is transferred as heat through the walls of the cylinder. Even more energy is transferred by the physical removal of the hot exhaust gases from the cylinder, as shown in **(d)**. A new fuel-air mixture is then drawn through the intake valve into the cylinder by the downward-moving piston, as shown in **(e)**.

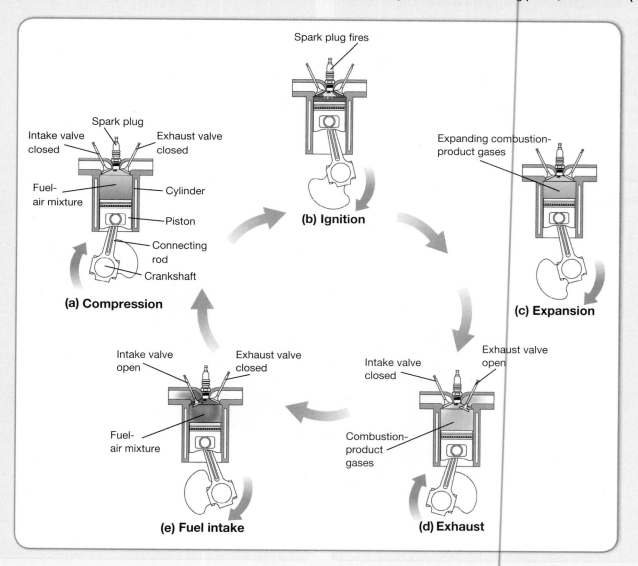

▶ Reviewing Main Ideas

1. Use the first law of thermodynamics to show that the internal energy of an isolated system is always conserved.

2. In the systems listed below, identify where energy is transferred as heat and work and where changes in internal energy occur. Is energy conserved in each case?

  a. the steam in a steam engine consisting of a boiler, a firebox, a cylinder, a piston, and a flywheel

  b. the drill bit of a power drill and a metal block into which a hole is being drilled

3. Express the first law of thermodynamics for the following processes:

  a. isothermal

  b. adiabatic

  c. isovolumetric

4. A compressor for a jackhammer expands the air in the hammer's cylinder at a constant pressure of 8.6×10^5 Pa. The increase in the cylinder's volume is $4.0^5 \times 10^{-4}$ m^3. During the process, 9.5 J of energy is transferred out of the cylinder as heat.

  a. What is the work done by the air?

  b. What is the change in the air's internal energy?

  c. What type of ideal thermodynamic process does this approximate?

5. A mixture of fuel and air is enclosed in an engine cylinder fitted with a piston. The gas pressure is maintained at 7.07×10^5 Pa as the piston moves slowly inward. If the gas volume decreases by 1.1×10^{-4} m^3 and the internal energy of the gas increases by 62 J, how much energy is added to or removed from the system as heat?

6. Over several cycles, a refrigerator does 1.51×10^4 J of work on the refrigerant. The refrigerant in turn removes 7.55×10^4 J as heat from the air inside the refrigerator.

  a. How much energy is transferred as heat to the outside air?

  b. What is the net change in the internal energy of the refrigerant?

  c. What is the amount of work done on the air inside the refrigerator?

  d. What is the net change in the internal energy of the air inside the refrigerator?

7. If a weather balloon in flight gives up 15 J of energy as heat and the gas within it does 13 J of work on the outside air, by how much does its internal energy change?

✓ Critical Thinking

8. After reading the feature on the next page, explain why opening the refrigerator door on a hot day does not cause your kitchen to become cooler.

Refrigerators

You've seen how an engine works by converting the internal energy of a gas into work. Now let's see how a refrigerator uses work to transfer heat to the internal energy of a gas. The workings of a refrigerator can be understood through simple principles of thermodynamics.

You have already learned about the concept of adiabatic heating and cooling. By mechanically compressing and expanding a gas, it is possible to raise or lower its temperature. Consider what a spray can and a bike pump do to the temperature of air. As you hold down the nozzle of a spray can, the gas leaving the can expands quickly, absorbing heat from the surrounding air. You feel that as a cooling process. When you pump air into a tire, the gas is compressed, so it heats up. Refrigerators operate much like a bike pump and spray-can nozzle put together in one system.

As shown in the image below, a refrigerator can be represented schematically as a system in which an electric motor does work (b) to compress a gas called a refrigerant. A refrigerant is a substance that turns into a gas at a low

temperature. The refrigerant releases heat (a) as it passes through a series of coils, and then absorbs the heat (c) from air and food on the inside.

The process by which a refrigerator operates consists of four basic steps, as illustrated in the diagram on the next page. The system is defined here as the refrigerant that is conveyed counterclockwise through the tubing. Heat is transferred into and out of this system. Initially, the refrigerant is at a low temperature and pressure so that it is colder than the air inside the refrigerator. The refrigerant absorbs thermal energy from inside the refrigerator (a), which lowers the refrigerator's interior temperature. This transfer of energy as heat increases the temperature of the liquid refrigerant until it becomes a gas. The refrigerant continues to absorb energy until it has completely vaporized.

Once it is in the vapor phase, the refrigerant passes through the compressor. Like a bike pump, the compressor does mechanical work (b) on the gas by rapidly decreasing its volume. This change in volume heats the refrigerant adiabatically. Next, the heated refrigerant moves to the outer coils behind the refrigerator, where thermal contact is made with outside air. Thermal energy in the refrigerant is transferred to the air (c), which is at a lower temperature. As the refrigerant passes through the coils, it cools and condenses into a liquid.

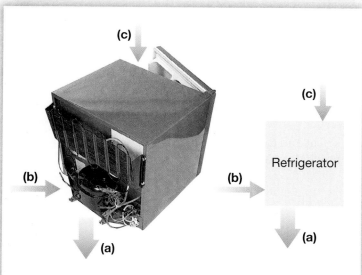

A refrigerator does work (b) in order to transfer energy as heat from the inside of the refrigerator (c) to the air outside the refrigerator (a).

The liquefied refrigerant then flows back into the refrigerator. Just outside the freezer compartment of the refrigerator, the refrigerant passes through an expansion valve. The expansion valve acts like the valve in a spray can. It rapidly expands the refrigerant, cooling it adiabatically. The refrigerant now has the same internal energy and phase as it did at the start of the process. As long as the temperature of the air inside the refrigerator is higher than the temperature of the refrigerant, the cycle repeats. Because the final internal energy is equal to the initial internal energy, this process is cyclic.

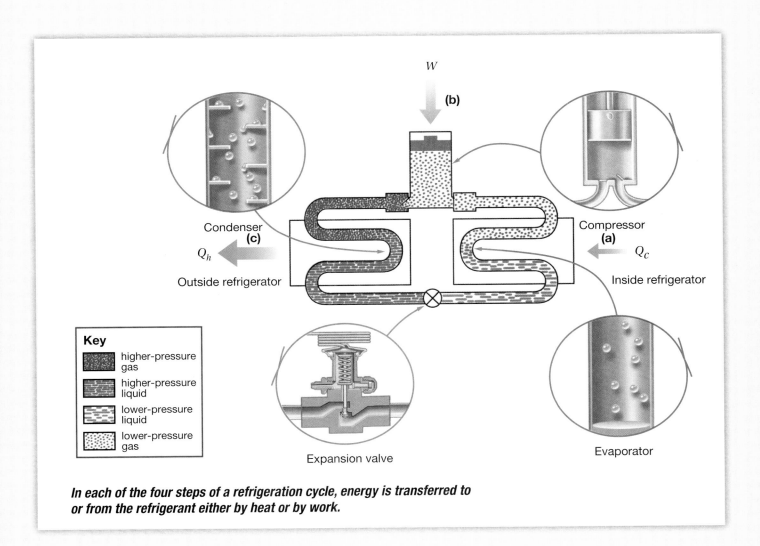

Key

	higher-pressure gas
	higher-pressure liquid
	lower-pressure liquid
	lower-pressure gas

In each of the four steps of a refrigeration cycle, energy is transferred to or from the refrigerant either by heat or by work.

- ► Recognize why the second law of thermodynamics requires two bodies at different temperatures for work to be done.

- ► Calculate the efficiency of a heat engine.

- ► Relate the disorder of a system to its ability to do work or transfer energy as heat.

The Second Law of Thermodynamics

Key Term
entropy

Efficiency of Heat Engines

In the previous section, you learned how a heat engine absorbs a quantity of energy from a high-temperature body as heat, does work on the environment, and then gives up energy to a low-temperature body as heat. The work derived from each cycle of a heat engine equals the difference between the heat input and heat output during the cycle, as follows:

$$W_{net} = Q_{net} = Q_h - Q_c$$

This equation, obtained from the first law of thermodynamics, indicates that all energy entering and leaving the system is accounted for and is thus conserved. The equation also suggests that more work is gained by taking more energy at a higher temperature and giving up less energy at a lower temperature. If no energy is given up at the lower temperature ($Q_c = 0$), then it seems that work could be obtained from energy transferred as heat from any body, such as the air around the engine. Such an engine would be able to do more work on hot days than on cold days, but it would always do work as long as the engine's temperature was less than the temperature of the surrounding air.

A heat engine cannot transfer all energy as heat to do work.

Unfortunately, it is impossible to make such an engine. As we have seen, a heat engine carries some substance through a cyclic process during which (1) the substance absorbs energy as heat from a high-temperature reservoir, (2) work is done by the engine, and (3) energy is expelled as heat to a lower-temperature reservoir. In practice, all heat engines operating in a cycle must expel some energy to a lower-temperature reservoir. In other words, it is impossible to construct a heat engine that, operating in a cycle, absorbs energy from a hot reservoir and does an equivalent amount of work.

The requirement that a heat engine give up some energy at a lower temperature in order to do work does not follow from the first law of thermodynamics. This requirement is the basis of what is called the *second law of thermodynamics.* The second law of thermodynamics can be stated as follows: *No cyclic process that converts heat entirely into work is possible.*

According to the second law of thermodynamics, W can never be equal to Q_h in a cyclic process. In other words, some energy must always be transferred as heat to the system's surroundings ($Q_c > 0$).

Efficiency measures how well an engine operates.

A cyclic process cannot completely convert energy transferred as heat into work, nor can it transfer energy as heat from a low-temperature body to a high-temperature body without work being done in the process. However, we can measure how closely a cyclic process approaches these ideal situations. A measure of how well an engine operates is given by the engine's *efficiency* (*eff*). In general, efficiency is a measure of the useful energy taken out of a process relative to the total energy that is put into the process. Efficiencies for different types of engines are listed in **Figure 3.1**.

Recall from the first law of thermodynamics that the work done on the environment by the engine is equal to the difference between the energy transferred to and from the system as heat. For a heat engine, the efficiency is the ratio of work done by the engine to the energy added to the system as heat during one cycle.

FIGURE 3.1

TYPICAL EFFICIENCIES FOR ENGINES

Engine type	eff (calculated maximum values)
steam engine	0.29
steam turbine	0.40
gasoline engine	0.60
diesel engine	0.56

Engine type	eff (measured values)
steam engine	0.17
steam turbine	0.30
gasoline engine	0.25
diesel engine	0.35

Equation for the Efficiency of a Heat Engine

$$eff = \frac{W_{net}}{Q_h} = \frac{Q_h - Q_c}{Q_h} = 1 - \frac{Q_c}{Q_h}$$

$$\text{efficiency} = \frac{\text{net work done by engine}}{\text{energy added to engine as heat}}$$

$$= \frac{\text{energy added as heat} - \text{energy removed as heat}}{\text{energy added as heat}}$$

$$= 1 - \frac{\text{energy removed as heat}}{\text{energy added as heat}}$$

Notice that efficiency is a unitless quantity that can be calculated using only the *magnitudes* for the energies added to and taken away from the engine.

This equation confirms that a heat engine has 100 percent efficiency (*eff* = 1) only if there is no energy transferred away from the engine as heat ($Q_c = 0$). Unfortunately, there can be no such heat engine, so the efficiencies of all engines are less than 1.0. The smaller the fraction of usable energy that an engine can provide, the lower its efficiency is.

Conceptual Challenge

1. Cooling Engines Use the second law of thermodynamics to explain why an automobile engine requires a cooling system to operate.

2. Power Plants Why are many coal-burning and nuclear power plants located near rivers?

©Leroy Francis/hemis.fr/Getty Images

The equation also provides some important information for increasing engine efficiency. If the amount of energy added to the system as heat is increased or the amount of energy given up by the system is reduced, the ratio of Q_c/Q_h becomes much smaller, and the engine's efficiency comes closer to 1.0.

The efficiency equation gives only a maximum value for an engine's efficiency. Friction, thermal conduction, and the inertia of moving parts in the engine hinder the engine's performance, and experimentally measured efficiencies are significantly lower than the calculated efficiencies. Several examples of these differences can be found in **Figure 3.1.**

Heat-Engine Efficiency

Sample Problem C Find the efficiency of a diesel engine that, during one cycle, receives 462 J of energy from combustion and loses 254 J as heat to the exhaust.

① ANALYZE

Given: $Q_h = 462 \text{ J}$ $Q_c = 254 \text{ J}$

Unknown: $eff = ?$

Diagram:

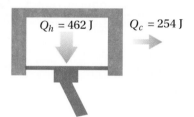

② PLAN

Choose an equation or situation:
The efficiency of a heat engine is the ratio of the work done by the engine to the energy transferred to it as heat.

$$eff = \frac{W_{net}}{Q_h} = 1 - \frac{Q_c}{Q_h}$$

③ SOLVE

Substitute the values into the equation, and solve:

$$eff = 1 - \frac{462 \text{ J}}{254 \text{ J}} = 0.450$$

$$\boxed{eff = 0.450}$$

④ CHECK YOUR WORK

Only 45 percent of the energy added as heat is used by the engine to do work. As expected, the efficiency is less than 1.0.

Continued

Heat-Engine Efficiency (continued)

Practice

1. If a steam engine takes in 2.254×10^4 kJ from the boiler and gives up 1.915×10^4 kJ in exhaust during one cycle, what is the engine's efficiency?

2. A test model for an experimental gasoline engine does 45 J of work in one cycle and gives up 31 J as heat. What is the engine's efficiency?

3. A fairly efficient steam engine was built in 1840. It required burning only 0.80 kg of coal to perform 2.6 MJ of net work. Calculate the engine's efficiency if burning coal releases 32.6 MJ of energy per kilogram of coal.

4. If a gasoline engine has an efficiency of 21 percent and loses 780 J to the cooling system and exhaust during each cycle, how much work is done by the engine?

5. Suppose a steam engine has an efficiency of 19 percent and performs 998 J of work each cycle. How much energy is received by the steam engine as heat?

6. The first working steam engine was designed in the 1700s by James Watt. Suppose this engine's efficiency is 8.0 percent. How much energy must be transferred by heat to the engine's surroundings if 2.5 kJ is transferred by heat into the engine? How much work is done?

Entropy

When you shuffle a deck of cards, it is highly improbable that the cards will end up separated by suit and in numerical sequence. Such a highly ordered arrangement can be formed in only a few ways, but there are more than 8×10^{67} ways to arrange 52 cards.

In thermodynamics, a system left to itself tends to go from a state with a very ordered set of energies to one in which there is less order. In other words, the system tends to go from one that has only a small probability of being randomly formed to one that has a high probability of being randomly formed. The measure of a system's disorder is called the **entropy** of the system. The greater the entropy of a system is, the greater the system's disorder.

entropy a measure of the randomness or disorder of a system

The greater probability of a disordered arrangement indicates that an ordered system is likely to become disordered. Put another way, the entropy of a system tends to increase. This greater probability also reduces the chance that a disordered system will become ordered at random. Thus, once a system has reached a state of the greatest disorder, it will tend to remain in that state and have *maximum entropy*.

Did YOU Know?

Entropy decreases in many systems on Earth. For example, atoms and molecules become incorporated into complex and orderly biological structures such as cells and tissues. These appear to be spontaneous because we think of the Earth as a closed system. So much energy comes from the sun that the disorder in chemical and biological systems is reduced, while the total entropy of Earth, the sun, and intervening space increases.

FIGURE 3.2

Low- and High-Entropy Systems

If all gas particles moved toward the piston, all of the internal energy could be used to do work. This extremely well-ordered situation is highly improbable.

a)

Well ordered; high efficiency and highly improbable distribution of velocities

b)

Highly disordered; average efficiency and highly probable distribution of velocities

Greater disorder means there is less energy to do work.

Heat engines are limited because only some of the energy added as heat can be used to do work. Not all of the gas particles move in an orderly fashion toward the piston and give up all of their energy in collision with the piston, as shown in **Figure 3.2(a).** Instead, they move in all available directions, as shown in **Figure 3.2(b).** They transfer energy through collisions with the walls of the engine cylinder as well as with each other. Although energy is conserved, not all of it is available to do useful work. The motion of the particles of a system is not well ordered and therefore is less useful for doing work.

Because of the connection between a system's entropy, its ability to do work, and the direction of energy transfer, the second law of thermodynamics can also be expressed in terms of entropy change. This law applies to the entire universe, not only to a system that interacts with its environment. So the second law can be stated as follows: *The entropy of the universe increases in all natural processes.*

Note that entropy can decrease for parts of systems, such as the water in the freezer shown in **Figure 3.3,** provided this decrease is offset by a greater increase in entropy elsewhere in the universe. The water's entropy decreases as it becomes ice, but the entropy of the air in the room is increased by a greater amount as energy is transferred by heat from the refrigerator. The result is that the total entropy of the refrigerator and the room together has increased.

FIGURE 3.3

Entropy in a Refrigerator

Because of the refrigerator's imperfect efficiency, the entropy of the outside air molecules increases more than the entropy of the freezing water decreases.

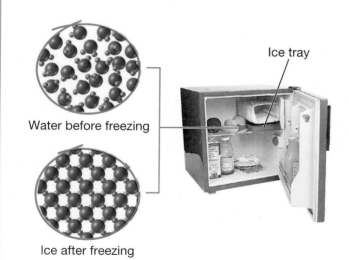

Water before freezing

Ice tray

Ice after freezing

Small decrease in entropy

Air before water freezes

Heat exhaust

Air after ice is frozen

Large increase in entropy

Take two dice from a board game. Record all the possible ways to obtain the numbers 2 through 12 on the sheet of paper. How many possible dice combinations can be rolled? How many combinations of both dice will produce the number 5? the number 8? the number 11? Which number(s) from 2 through 12 is most probable? How many ways out of the total number of ways can this number(s) be rolled? Which number(s) from 2 through 12 is least probable? How many ways out of the total number of ways can this number(s) be rolled?

Repeat the experiment with three dice. Write down all of the possible combinations that will produce the numbers 3 through 18. What number is most probable?

MATERIALS
- 3 dice
- a sheet of paper
- a pencil

SECTION 3 FORMATIVE ASSESSMENT

1. Is it possible to construct a heat engine that doesn't transfer energy to its surroundings? Explain.

2. An engineer claims to have built an engine that takes in 7.5×10^4 J and expels 3.5×10^4 J.
   a. How much energy can the engine provide by doing work?
   b. What is the efficiency of the engine?
   c. Is this efficiency possible? Explain your answer.

3. Of the items listed below, which ones have high entropy?
   a. papers scattered randomly across a desk
   b. papers organized in a report
   c. a freshly opened pack of cards
   d. a mixed deck of cards
   e. a room after a party
   f. a room before a party

4. Some compounds have been observed to form spontaneously, even though they are more ordered than their components. Explain how this is consistent with the second law of thermodynamics.

5. Discuss three common examples of natural processes that involve decreases in entropy. Identify the corresponding entropy increases in the environments of these processes.

✔ Critical Thinking

6. A steam-driven turbine is one major component of an electric power plant. Why is it advantageous to increase the steam's temperature as much as possible?

7. Show that three purple marbles and three light-blue marbles in two groups of three marbles each can be arranged in four combinations: two with only one possible arrangement each and two with nine possible arrangements each.

Deep-Sea Air Conditioning

Deep beneath the ocean, about half a mile down, sunlight barely penetrates the still waters. Scientists at Makai Ocean Engineering in Hawaii are now tapping into that pitch-dark region as a resource for air conditioning.

In tropical locations where buildings are cooled year-round, air-conditioning systems operate with cold water. Refrigeration systems cool the water, and pumps circulate it throughout the walls of a building, where the water absorbs heat from the rooms. Unfortunately, powering these compressors is neither cheap nor efficient.

Instead of cooling the water in their operating systems, the systems designed by Makai use frigid water from the ocean's depths. First, engineers install a pipeline that reaches deep into the ocean, where the water is nearly freezing. Then, powerful pumps on the shoreline move the water directly into a building's air-conditioning system. There, a system of heat exchangers uses the seawater to cool the fresh water in the air-conditioning system.

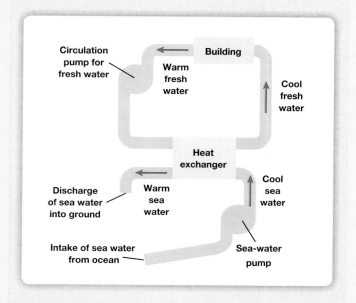

One complicating factor is that the water must also be returned to the ocean in a manner that will not disrupt the local ecosystem. It must be either piped to a depth of a few hundred feet, where its temperature is close to that of the ocean at that level, or poured into onshore pits, where it eventually seeps through the land and comes to an acceptable temperature by the time it reaches the ocean.

"This deep-sea air conditioning benefits the environment by operating with a renewable resource instead of Freon," said Dr. Van Ryzin, the founder of Makai. "Because the system eliminates the need for compressors, it uses only about 10 percent of the electricity of current methods, saving fossil fuels and a lot of money." However, deep-sea air-conditioning technology works only for buildings within a few kilometers of the shore and carries a hefty installation cost of several million dollars. For this reason, Dr. Van Ryzin thinks this type of system is most appropriate for large central air-conditioning systems, such as those necessary to cool resorts or large manufacturing plants, where the electricity savings can eventually make up for the installation costs. Under the right circumstances, air conditioning with seawater can be provided at one-third to one-half the cost of conventional air conditioning.

Scientific Evaluations

The ability to evaluate scientific explanations is an essential skill for science literacy. When you hear a new scientific claim in the news, how can you evaluate the explanation and determine the validity of the claim? The evidence that supports a scientific claim must meet several criteria. First of all, the evidence must be empirical—that is, based on observation or experimentation, not on opinion or subjective impression. In addition, the evidence must be relevant to the claim. Finally, the evidence must be sufficient to persuade another person. For this reason, explanations that cite evidence from multiple data sets or the results from multiple experiments or studies are more persuasive than arguments that rely upon only one or two pieces of evidence. Examining all sides of the evidence, including the quality and quantity of the evidence, is a key part of a scientific evaluation.

Evaluating Thermodynamics

We have learned that there is no heat engine capable of transferring all of the energy in its system to work. To operate in a cycle, a heat engine must expel a certain amount of energy relative to the heat of the lower-temperature reservoir. Because of this, every engine is designed with a cooling system to transfer heat away from the engine. This relationship between work and heat energy for a heat engine is described as *efficiency* by the second law of thermodynamics. How might you go about evaluating the efficiency of a heat engine and the second law of thermodynamics in general?

- Design a hypothetical test to evaluate the energy added and the energy removed from a heat engine. The experiment can generate empirical evidence through observational or experimental tests.

- Assume that the results of the test you proposed above confirm that heat energy is lost from the engine. According to the second law of thermodynamics, a cooling system that surrounds the engine with a cool reservoir can affect an engine's efficiency. Why would an engine's efficiency be affected by cooler surroundings? Explain your reasoning.

CHAPTER 10 **Summary**

SECTION 1 **Relationships Between Heat and Work**

KEY TERMS

- A thermodynamic system is an object or set of objects considered to be a distinct physical entity to or from which energy is added or removed. The surroundings make up the system's environment.
- Energy can be transferred to or from a system as heat and/or work, changing the system's internal energy in the process.
- For gases at constant pressure, work is defined as the product of gas pressure and the change in the volume of the gas.

system
environment
isovolumetric process
isothermal process
adiabatic process

SECTION 2 **The First Law of Thermodynamics**

KEY TERM

- Energy is conserved for any system and its environment and is described by the first law of thermodynamics.
- A cyclic process returns a system to conditions identical to those it had before the process began, so its internal energy is unchanged.

cyclic process

SECTION 3 **The Second Law of Thermodynamics**

KEY TERM

- The second law of thermodynamics states that no machine can transfer all of its absorbed energy as work.
- The efficiency of a heat engine depends on the amount of energy transferred as heat to and from the engine.
- Entropy is a measure of the disorder of a system. As a system becomes more disordered, less of its energy is available to do work.
- The entropy of a system can increase or decrease, but the total entropy of the universe is always increasing.

entropy

VARIABLE SYMBOLS			
Quantities		**Units**	
ΔU	change in internal energy	J	joules
Q	heat	J	joules
W	work	J	joules
eff	efficiency	(unitless)	

DIAGRAM SYMBOLS
Energy transferred as heat
Energy transferred as work
Thermodynamic cycle

Problem Solving

See **Appendix D: Equations** for a summary of the equations introduced in this chapter. If you need more problem-solving practice, see **Appendix I: Additional Problems.**

Heat, Work, and Internal Energy

REVIEWING MAIN IDEAS

1. Define a thermodynamic system and its environment.

2. In what two ways can the internal energy of a system be increased?

3. Which of the following expressions have units that are equivalent to the units of work?
   a. mg **d.** Fd
   b. $\frac{1}{2}mv^2$ **e.** $P\Delta V$
   c. mgh **f.** $V\Delta T$

4. For each of the following, which thermodynamic quantities (ΔU, Q, and W) have values equal to zero?
   a. an isothermal process
   b. an adiabatic process
   c. an isovolumetric process

CONCEPTUAL QUESTIONS

5. When an ideal gas expands adiabatically, it does work on its surroundings. Describe the various transfers of energy that take place.

6. In each of the following cases, trace the chain of energy transfers (as heat or as work) as well as changes in internal energy.
   a. You rub your hands together to warm them on a cold day, and they soon become cold again.
   b. A hole is drilled into a block of metal. When a small amount of water is placed in the drilled hole, steam rises from the hole.

7. Paint from an aerosol can is sprayed continuously for 30 s. The can was initially at room temperature, but now it feels cold to the touch. What type of thermodynamic process occurs for a small sample of gas as it leaves the high-pressure interior of the can and moves to the outside atmosphere?

8. The can of spray paint in item 7 is set aside for an hour. During this time, the contents of the can return to room temperature. What type of thermodynamic process takes place in the can during the time the can is not in use?

PRACTICE PROBLEMS

For problems 9–10, see Sample Problem A.

9. How much work is done when a tire's volume increases from 35.25×10^{-3} m^3 to 39.47×10^{-3} m^3 at a pressure of 2.55×10^5 Pa in excess of atmospheric pressure? Is work done on or by the gas?

10. Helium in a toy balloon does work on its surroundings as it expands with a constant pressure of 2.52×10^5 Pa in excess of atmospheric pressure. The balloon's initial volume is 1.1×10^{-4} m^3, and its final volume is 1.50×10^{-3} m^3. Determine the amount of work done by the gas in the balloon.

Energy Conservation and Cyclic Processes

REVIEWING MAIN IDEAS

11. Write the equation for the first law of thermodynamics, and explain why it is an expression of energy conservation.

12. Rewrite the equation for the first law of thermodynamics for each of the following special thermodynamic processes:
    a. an isothermal process
    b. an adiabatic process
    c. an isovolumetric process

13. How is energy conserved if more energy is transferred as heat from a refrigerator to the outside air than is removed from the inside air of the refrigerator?

CONCEPTUAL QUESTIONS

14. A bomb calorimeter is placed in a water bath, and a mixture of fuel and oxygen is burned inside it. The temperature of the water is observed to rise during the combustion reaction. The calorimeter and the water remain at constant volume.

   a. If the reaction products are the system, which thermodynamic quantities—ΔU, Q, or W—are positive, and which are negative?

   b. If the water bath is the system, which thermodynamic quantities—ΔU, Q, or W—are positive, and which are negative?

15. Which of the thermodynamic values (ΔU, Q, or W) would be negative for the following systems?

   a. A steel rail (system) undergoing slow thermal expansion on a hot day displaces the spikes and ties that hold the rail in place.

   b. the interior of a closed refrigerator (system)

   c. The helium in a thermally insulated weather balloon (system) expands during inflation.

PRACTICE PROBLEMS

For problems 16–17, see Sample Problem B.

16. Heat is added to an open pan of water at 100.0°C, vaporizing the water. The expanding steam that results does 43.0 kJ of work, and the internal energy of the system increases by 604 kJ. How much energy is transferred to the system as heat?

17. A 150 kg steel rod in a building under construction supports a load of 6050 kg. During the day, the rod's temperature increases from 22°C to 47°C. This temperature increase causes the rod to thermally expand and raise the load 5.5 mm.

   a. Find the energy transferred as heat to or from the rod. (Hint: Assume the specific heat capacity of steel is the same as for iron.)

   b. Find the work done in this process. Is work done on or by the rod?

   c. How great is the change in the rod's internal energy? Does the rod's internal energy increase or decrease?

Efficiency and Entropy

▶ **REVIEWING MAIN IDEAS**

18. The first law of thermodynamics states that you cannot obtain more energy from a process than you originally put in. The second law states that you cannot obtain as much usable energy from a system as you put into it. Explain why these two statements do not contradict each other.

19. What conditions are necessary for a heat engine to have an efficiency of 1.0?

20. In which of the following systems is entropy increasing? (Do not include the surroundings as part of the system.)

   a. An egg is broken and scrambled.

   b. A cluttered room is cleaned and organized.

   c. A thin stick is placed in a glass of sugar-saturated water, and sugar crystals form on the stick.

21. Why is it not possible for all of the energy transferred as heat from a high-temperature source to be expelled from an engine by work?

CONCEPTUAL QUESTIONS

22. If a cup of very hot water is used as an energy source and a cup of cold water is used as an energy "sink," the cups can, in principle, be used to do work, as shown below. If the contents are mixed together and the resulting lukewarm contents are separated into two cups, no work can be done. Use the second law of thermodynamics to explain this. Has the first law of thermodynamics been violated by mixing and separating the contents of the two cups?

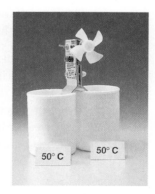

23. Suppose the waste heat at a power plant is exhausted to a pond of water. Could the efficiency of the plant be increased by refrigerating the water in the pond?

24. A salt solution is placed in a bowl and set in sunlight. The salt crystals that remain after the water has evaporated are more highly ordered than the randomly dispersed sodium and chloride ions in the solution. Has the requirement that total entropy increases been violated? Explain your answer.

25. Use a discussion of internal energy and entropy to explain why the statement "Energy is not conserved in an inelastic collision" is not true.

PRACTICE PROBLEMS

For problems 26–28, see Sample Problem C.

26. In one cycle, an engine burning a mixture of air and methanol (methyl alcohol) absorbs 525 J and expels 415 J. What is the engine's efficiency?

27. The energy provided each hour as heat to the turbine in an electric power plant is 9.5×10^{12} J. If 6.5×10^{12} J of energy is exhausted each hour from the engine as heat, what is the efficiency of this heat engine?

28. A heat engine absorbs 850 J of energy per cycle from a high-temperature source. The engine does 3.5×10^2 J of work during each cycle, expelling 5.0×10^2 J as heat. What is the engine's efficiency?

Mixed Review

▶ REVIEWING MAIN IDEAS

29. A gas expands when 606 J of energy is added to it as heat. The expanding gas does 418 J of work on its surroundings.
    a. What is the overall change in the internal energy of the gas?
    b. If the work done by the gas were equal to 1212 J (rather than 418 J), how much energy would need to be added as heat in order for the change in internal energy to equal the change in internal energy in part (a)?

GRAPHING CALCULATOR PRACTICE

Carnot Efficiency

Sadi Carnot (1796–1832), a French engineer, studied the efficiencies of heat engines. He described an ideal engine—now called the *Carnot engine*—that consists of an ideal gas inside a thermally nonconductive cylinder that has a piston and a replaceable base.

In the Carnot engine, the piston moves upward as the cylinder's conductive base is brought in contact with a heat reservoir, T_h. The piston continues to rise when the base is replaced by a nonconductive base. Then, the energy is transferred to a cooler reservoir at a temperature T_c, followed by further compression when the base is again replaced. Carnot discovered that the efficiency of such an engine can be determined by the following equation:

$$\text{highest theoretical efficiency} = 1 - \frac{T_c}{T_h}$$

In this graphing calculator activity, you will enter various values for T_h and T_c to calculate the highest theoretical efficiency of a heat engine. Because of friction and other problems, the actual efficiency of a heat engine will be lower than the calculated efficiency.

Go online to HMHScience.com to find the skillsheet and program for this graphing calculator activity.

30. The lid of a pressure cooker forms a nearly airtight seal. Steam builds up pressure and increases temperature within the pressure cooker so that food cooks faster than it does in an ordinary pot. The system is defined as the pressure cooker and the water and steam within it. Suppose that 2.0 g of water is sealed in a pressure cooker and then vaporized by heating.

a. What happens to the water's internal energy?
b. Is energy transferred as heat to or from the system?
c. Is energy transferred as work to or from the system?
d. If 5175 J must be added as heat to completely vaporize the water, what is the change in the water's internal energy?

ALTERNATIVE ASSESSMENT

1. Imagine that an inventor is asking you to invest your savings in the development of a new turbine that will produce cheap electricity. The turbine will take in 1000 J of energy from fuel to supply 650 J of work, which can then be used to power a generator. The energy removed as heat to a cooling system will raise the temperature of 0.10 kg of water by 1.2°C. Are these figures consistent with the first and second laws of thermodynamics? Would you consider investing in this project? Write a business letter to the inventor explaining how your analysis affected your decision.

2. Talk to someone who works on air conditioners or refrigerators to find out what fluids are used in these systems. What properties should refrigerant fluids have? Research the use of Freon and Freon substitutes. Why is using Freon forbidden by international treaty? What fluids are now used in refrigerators and car air conditioners? For what temperature ranges are these fluids appropriate? What are the advantages and disadvantages of each fluid? Summarize your research in the form of a presentation or report.

3. Research how an internal-combustion engine operates. Describe the four steps of a combustion cycle. What materials go in and out of the engine during each step? How many cylinders are involved in one cycle? What energy processes take place during each stroke? In which steps is work done? Summarize your findings with diagrams or in a report. Contact an expert auto mechanic, and ask the mechanic to review your report for accuracy.

4. The law of entropy can also be called the law of increasing disorder, but this law seems to contradict the existence of living organisms that are able to organize chemicals into organic molecules. Prepare for a class debate on the validity of the following arguments:

a. Living things are not subject to the laws of thermodynamics.
b. The increase in the universe's entropy due to life processes is greater than the decrease in entropy within a living organism.

5. Work in groups to create a classroom presentation on the life, times, and work of James Watt, inventor of the first commercially successful steam engine in the early nineteenth century. Include material about how this machine affected transportation and industry in the United States.

6. Most major appliances are required by law to have an EnergyGuide label attached to them. The label indicates the average amount of energy used by the appliance in a year and gives the average cost of using the appliance based on a national average of cost per energy unit. In a store, look at the EnergyGuide labels attached to three different models of one brand of a major appliance. Create a graph showing the total yearly cost of each appliance over ten years (including the initial cost of the appliance with year one). Determine which model you would purchase, and write a paragraph defending your choice.

Standards-Based Assessment

Record your answers on a separate piece of paper.

MULTIPLE CHOICE

1 In which of these processes is no work done?

A Water is boiled in a pressure cooker.

B A refrigerator is used to freeze water.

C An automobile engine operates for several minutes.

D A tire is inflated with an air pump.

2 If energy is transferred to a gas as heat and work but there is no change in its internal energy, what thermodynamic process has the gas undergone?

A adiabatic

B isothermal

C isovolumetric

D isobaric

3 Gas is compressed adiabatically in a cylinder with a cross-sectional area of 0.5 m^2 by a piston moving 0.1 m as it does 150 J of work. How much pressure does the gas exert at the end of the piston's travel?

A 7.5 N/m^2

B 750 N/m^2

C 1500 N/m^2

D 3000 N/m^2

4 Using an air pump to compress air in a cylinder does work on the air in the cylinder. The result is

A the air molecules lose kinetic energy, increasing the pressure in the cylinder.

B the air molecules gain kinetic energy, increasing the pressure in the cylinder.

C the air molecules lose kinetic energy, decreasing the pressure in the cylinder.

D the air molecules gain kinetic energy, decreasing the pressure in the cylinder.

5 To calculate the efficiency of a heat engine, which thermodynamic property do you *not* need to know?

A the energy transferred as heat to the engine

B the energy transferred as heat from the engine

C the change in the internal energy of the engine

D the work done by the engine

Use the passage and diagrams for questions 6 and 7. The figures below depict steam within the cylinder and piston of a steam engine.

Steam from boiler added to empty cylinder

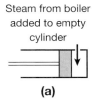

(a)

Steam expands rapidly within cylinder, moving piston outward

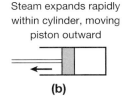

(b)

Steam condenses to hot water and is removed from cylinder

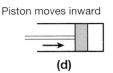

(c)

Piston moves inward

(d)

6 Which of the figures describes a situation in which $\Delta U < 0$, $Q = 0$, and $W < 0$?

A (a)   **C** (c)

B (b)   **D** (d)

7 Which of the figures describes a situation in which $\Delta U < 0$, $Q = 0$, and $W > 0$?

A (a)   **C** (c)

B (b)   **D** (d)

GRIDDED RESPONSE

8 A steam shovel raises 450.0 kg of dirt a vertical distance of 8.6 m. The engine provides 2.00×10^5 J of energy as heat for the steam shovel to lift the dirt.

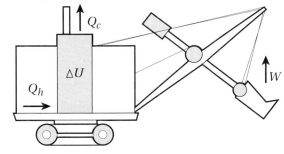

How much work, in Joules, is done by the steam shovel?

UNDER A CAR'S FRONT COVER

How a fire box turns the wheels that move a car

You've learned about complicated cyclic processes, such as those in internal-combustion engines. A car's internal-combustion engine uses heat from combustion to do work. Here's a look at all the parts and what they do.

THE STORY OF WHAT MAKES CARS MOVE

THERE'S LOTS OF STUFF UNDER THE FRONT COVER OF A CAR.

THE BIGGEST THING IS USUALLY THE FIRE BOX, WHICH TURNS THE WHEELS TO PUSH THE CAR.

BUT THERE'S A LOT OF OTHER STUFF, TOO, AND EVEN SOME-ONE WHO KNOWS A LOT ABOUT CARS CAN HAVE A HARD TIME TELLING WHAT EVERY PART IS.

This picture shows some of the things you might see if you open a car's front cover.

NOTE:
Before opening the car to look under the cover, you should stop driving.

FIRE BOX

This fire box is the car's pusher. Like sky boat pushers, it makes power by burning fire water using air from outside.

To get pushing power from the fire water, the car burns it in little closed boxes. When the water burns, it gets hot, which makes it get bigger and push on the walls of the box. One of the walls of the box can move, and it has a stick that joins it to a wheel.

When the sides of the little boxes move, their sticks push their wheels around. Those wheels are all joined by a turning stick. That stick turns more wheels, and those wheels turn the wheels that touch the ground.

POWER BOX

This box holds power to run different parts of the car. To start the fire box turning, you need a lot of power at once, so this power box is built to let out its power very fast.

You have to be careful, because if you let the two lines from the power box touch, they will let out all their power at once. This is enough power to start a fire or turn a small piece of metal to water.

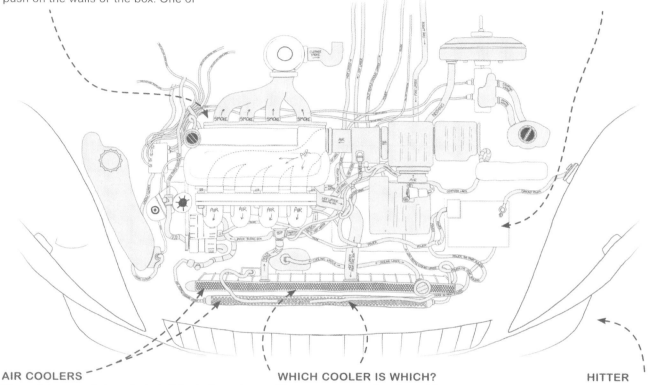

AIR COOLERS

These things cool down hot stuff by letting air blow over them. The air comes in from holes in the front of the car as it moves, but there are also blowers that pull air through the coolers even if you're not moving very fast.

WHICH COOLER IS WHICH?

There are two coolers here. The one in back cools the fire box, and the one in front cools the cooling water for the people in the car. (The people-cooler is in front because you need colder air to cool people. A fire box is so hot that warm and cold person-air are almost the same to it.)

HITTER

If the car runs into something, this part hits it first.

HOW COOLERS WORK

Some coolers work by just using water to carry away heat from hot things. But some machines can use power to make things colder than the air around them.

You need some cooling stuff. The best kind of cooling stuff is something that's air when it's as warm as a room, but turns to water when it gets cold. There are a few kinds of air that work for this.

The cooling air starts off as warm as the air outside.

To start the cooling, first you push the air into a smaller space. This makes it get hot ("Making air smaller makes it hotter" is an important air law). For some coolers, this turns them to water.

Next, you let the stuff cool down while holding it in the smaller space. When it's done cooling, it's back to being as warm as the air again, but it's smaller.

Last, you let it get big again. (If it's water now, it will turn back to air.) Because of the air law, this means it will get colder, just like making it smaller made it hotter. You use the cold air to cool things down. You keep doing this until it warms back up, then send it back and do the whole thing again.

UNDER A CAR'S FRONT COVER

FIRE STARTERS (INSIDE)
These use power to make little flashes that light the fire water.

SLIDING WATER
This water helps the parts of the fire box spin without getting stuck. If you run out of it, your engine stops turning, and sometimes the parts get stuck together and it can never turn again.

This water gets dirty, so you have to change it sometimes.

SLIDE FIXER
If you stop too hard, your wheels can stop turning and start to slide. Once wheels start sliding, they become less good at stopping the car.

When the computer feels that one of the wheels has started sliding, this box lifts the stoppers away from the wheel enough that it grabs the ground and starts turning again. Then it presses the stopper back down. It can do this many times each second. This box makes cars much, much better at stopping.

SMOKE BURNER
When cars burn fire water, the smoke it makes has lots of stuff in it that can make people and animals sick. This machine helps the smoke finish burning so it turns to air and water.

(The kind of air it turns into isn't good for the world, either, but at least it's better than the kinds in the smoke.)

LINE FROM COOLER IN SEAT AREA

SMOKE CARRIER
This carries the air out of the fire box after it's done burning.

OUT THE BACK
This line takes the cleaner smoke and sends it out through a hole in the back of the car.

POWER CHANGERS
These sit on top of the fire starters. They take the kind of power made by the power box and turn it into a kind of power that works better for starting tiny fires in the fire box.

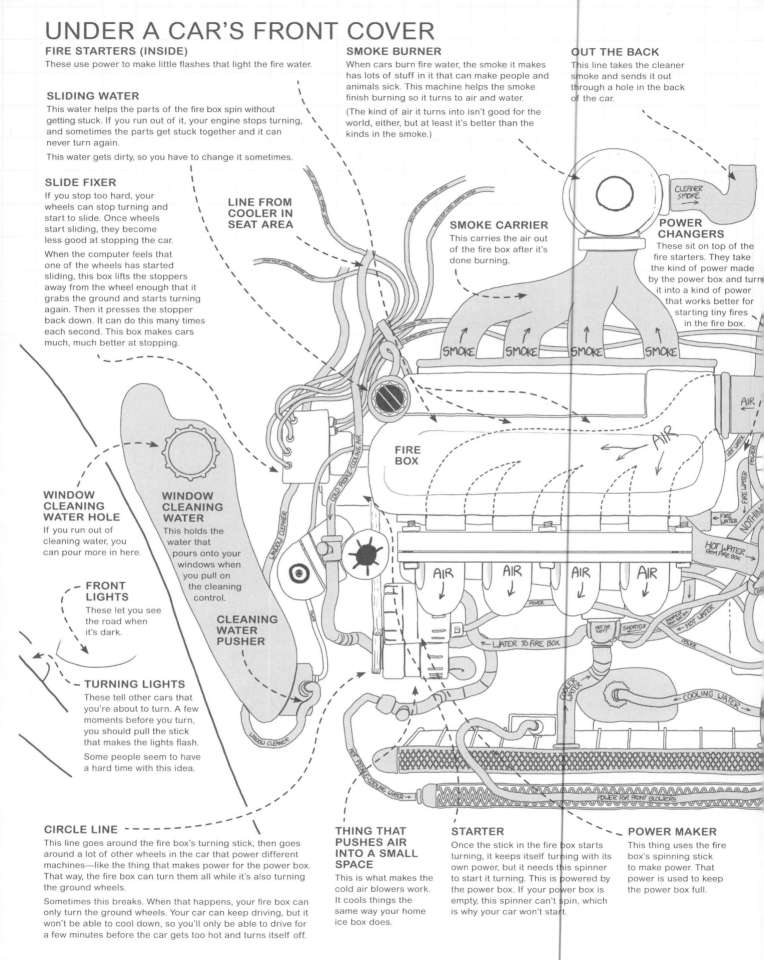

WINDOW CLEANING WATER HOLE
If you run out of cleaning water, you can pour more in here.

WINDOW CLEANING WATER
This holds the water that pours onto your windows when you pull on the cleaning control.

CLEANING WATER PUSHER

FRONT LIGHTS
These let you see the road when it's dark.

TURNING LIGHTS
These tell other cars that you're about to turn. A few moments before you turn, you should pull the stick that makes the lights flash.

Some people seem to have a hard time with this idea.

CIRCLE LINE
This line goes around the fire box's turning stick, then goes around a lot of other wheels in the car that power different machines—like the thing that makes power for the power box. That way, the fire box can turn them all while it's also turning the ground wheels.

Sometimes this breaks. When that happens, your fire box can only turn the ground wheels. Your car can keep driving, but it won't be able to cool down, so you'll only be able to drive for a few minutes before the car gets too hot and turns itself off.

THING THAT PUSHES AIR INTO A SMALL SPACE
This is what makes the cold air blowers work. It cools things the same way your home ice box does.

STARTER
Once the stick in the fire box starts turning, it keeps itself turning with its own power, but it needs this spinner to start it turning. This is powered by the power box. If your power box is empty, this spinner can't spin, which is why your car won't start.

POWER MAKER
This thing uses the fire box's spinning stick to make power. That power is used to keep the power box full.

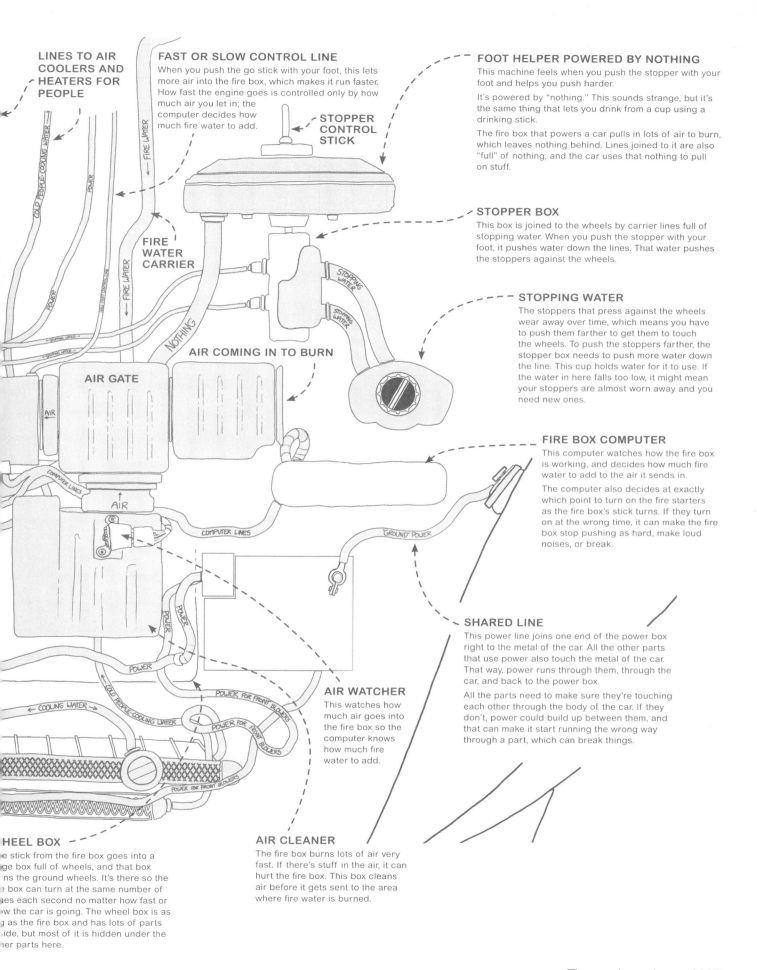

LINES TO AIR COOLERS AND HEATERS FOR PEOPLE

FAST OR SLOW CONTROL LINE
When you push the go stick with your foot, this lets more air into the fire box, which makes it run faster. How fast the engine goes is controlled only by how much air you let in; the computer decides how much fire water to add.

STOPPER CONTROL STICK

FIRE WATER CARRIER

AIR COMING IN TO BURN

AIR GATE

FOOT HELPER POWERED BY NOTHING
This machine feels when you push the stopper with your foot and helps you push harder.

It's powered by "nothing." This sounds strange, but it's the same thing that lets you drink from a cup using a drinking stick.

The fire box that powers a car pulls in lots of air to burn, which leaves nothing behind. Lines joined to it are also "full" of nothing, and the car uses that nothing to pull on stuff.

STOPPER BOX
This box is joined to the wheels by carrier lines full of stopping water. When you push the stopper with your foot, it pushes water down the lines. That water pushes the stoppers against the wheels.

STOPPING WATER
The stoppers that press against the wheels wear away over time, which means you have to push them farther to get them to touch the wheels. To push the stoppers farther, the stopper box needs to push more water down the line. This cup holds water for it to use. If the water in here falls too low, it might mean your stoppers are almost worn away and you need new ones.

FIRE BOX COMPUTER
This computer watches how the fire box is working, and decides how much fire water to add to the air it sends in.

The computer also decides at exactly which point to turn on the fire starters as the fire box's stick turns. If they turn on at the wrong time, it can make the fire box stop pushing as hard, make loud noises, or break.

SHARED LINE
This power line joins one end of the power box right to the metal of the car. All the other parts that use power also touch the metal of the car. That way, power runs through them, through the car, and back to the power box.

All the parts need to make sure they're touching each other through the body of the car. If they don't, power could build up between them, and that can make it start running the wrong way through a part, which can break things.

AIR WATCHER
This watches how much air goes into the fire box so the computer knows how much fire water to add.

HEEL BOX
e stick from the fire box goes into a
ge box full of wheels, and that box
ns the ground wheels. It's there so the
e box can turn at the same number of
es each second no matter how fast or
w the car is going. The wheel box is as
g as the fire box and has lots of parts
ide, but most of it is hidden under the
her parts here.

AIR CLEANER
The fire box burns lots of air very fast. If there's stuff in the air, it can hurt the fire box. This box cleans air before it gets sent to the area where fire water is burned.

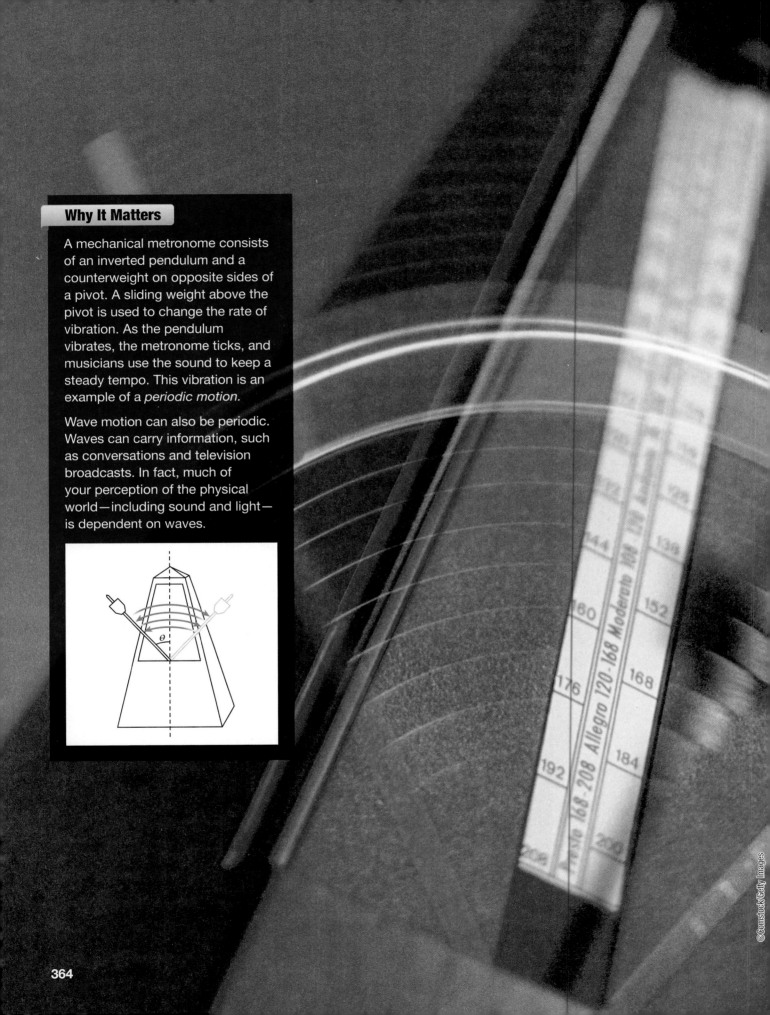

A mechanical metronome consists of an inverted pendulum and a counterweight on opposite sides of a pivot. A sliding weight above the pivot is used to change the rate of vibration. As the pendulum vibrates, the metronome ticks, and musicians use the sound to keep a steady tempo. This vibration is an example of a *periodic motion.*

Wave motion can also be periodic. Waves can carry information, such as conversations and television broadcasts. In fact, much of your perception of the physical world—including sound and light—is dependent on waves.

CHAPTER 11
Vibrations and Waves

BIG IDEA

Some events are periodic in nature. The principles of periodic motion can help us understand everything from the motion of a pendulum to the motion of a wave.

 ONLINE Physics
HMHScience.com

ONLINE LABS
- Pendulums and Spring Waves
- Simple Harmonic Motion of a Pendulum
- Pendulum Trials
- S.T.E.M. Lab Tensile Strength and Hooke's Law

 GO ONLINE **Animated Physics**
HMHScience.com

Characteristics of a Wave

(bi) ©Digital Vision/Getty Images

Objectives

- Identify the conditions of simple harmonic motion.

- Explain how force, velocity, and acceleration change as an object vibrates with simple harmonic motion.

- Calculate the spring force using Hooke's law.

Simple Harmonic Motion

Key Term
simple harmonic motion

Hooke's Law

A repeated motion, such as that of an acrobat swinging on a trapeze, is called a periodic motion. Other periodic motions include those made by a child on a playground swing, a wrecking ball swaying to and fro, and the pendulum of a grandfather clock or a metronome. In each of these cases, the periodic motion is back and forth over the same path.

One of the simplest types of back-and-forth periodic motion is the motion of a mass attached to a spring, as shown in **Figure 1.1.** Let us assume that the mass moves on a frictionless horizontal surface. When the spring is stretched or compressed and then released, it vibrates back and forth about its unstretched position. We will begin by considering this example, and then we will apply our conclusions to the swinging motion of a trapeze acrobat.

At the equilibrium position, speed reaches a maximum.

In **Figure 1.1(a)**, the spring is stretched away from its unstretched, or equilibrium, position ($x = 0$). In this stretched position, the spring exerts a force on the mass toward the equilibrium position. This spring force decreases as the spring moves toward the equilibrium position, and it reaches zero at equilibrium, as illustrated in **Figure 1.1(b)**. The mass's acceleration also becomes zero at equilibrium.

Though the spring force and acceleration decrease as the mass moves toward the equilibrium position, the speed of the mass increases. At the equilibrium position, when acceleration reaches zero, the speed reaches a maximum. At that point, although the spring force is zero, the mass's momentum causes it to overshoot the equilibrium position and compress the spring.

At maximum displacement, spring force and acceleration reach a maximum.

As the mass moves beyond equilibrium, the spring force and the acceleration increase. But the direction of the spring force and of the acceleration (toward equilibrium) is opposite the mass's direction of motion (away from equilibrium), and the mass begins to slow down.

FIGURE 1.1

A Mass-Spring System The direction of the force acting on the mass ($\mathbf{F_{elastic}}$) is always opposite the direction of the mass's displacement from equilibrium ($x = 0$). **(a)** When the spring is stretched to the right, the spring force pulls the mass to the left. **(b)** When the spring is unstretched, the spring force is zero. **(c)** When the spring is compressed to the left, the spring force is directed to the right.

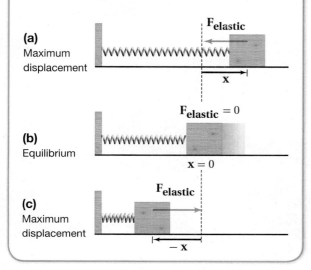

(a)
Maximum displacement

$\mathbf{F_{elastic}}$

x

(b)
Equilibrium

$\mathbf{F_{elastic}} = 0$

$x = 0$

(c)
Maximum displacement

$\mathbf{F_{elastic}}$

$-x$

When the spring's compression is equal to the distance the spring was originally stretched away from the equilibrium position (x), as shown in **Figure 1.1(c)**, the mass is at maximum displacement, and the spring force and acceleration of the mass reach a maximum. At this point, the speed of the mass becomes zero. The spring force acting to the right causes the mass to change its direction, and the mass begins moving back toward the equilibrium position. Then the entire process begins again, and the mass continues to oscillate back and forth over the same path.

In an ideal system, the mass-spring system would oscillate indefinitely. But in the physical world, friction retards the motion of the vibrating mass, and the mass-spring system eventually comes to rest. This effect is called *damping*. In most cases, the effect of damping is minimal over a short period of time, so the ideal mass-spring system provides an approximation for the motion of a physical mass-spring system.

In simple harmonic motion, restoring force is proportional to displacement.

As you have seen, the spring force always pushes or pulls the mass toward its original equilibrium position. For this reason, it is sometimes called a *restoring force*. Measurements show that the restoring force is directly proportional to the displacement of the mass. This relationship was determined in 1678 by Robert Hooke and is known as *Hooke's law*. The following equation mathematically describes Hooke's law:

Hooke's Law

$$F_{elastic} = -kx$$

spring force $= -$(**spring constant** $\times$ **displacement**)

The negative sign in the equation signifies that the direction of the spring force is always opposite the direction of the mass's displacement from equilibrium. In other words, the negative sign shows that the spring force will tend to move the object back to its equilibrium position.

As mentioned in the chapter "Work and Energy," the quantity k is a positive constant called the *spring constant*. The value of the spring constant is a measure of the stiffness of the spring. A greater value of k means a stiffer spring, because a greater force is needed to stretch or compress that spring a given amount. The SI units of k are N/m. As a result, N is the unit of the spring force when the spring constant (N/m) is multiplied by the displacement (m). The motion of a vibrating mass-spring system is an example of **simple harmonic motion.** Simple harmonic motion describes any periodic motion that is the result of a restoring force that is proportional to displacement. Because simple harmonic motion involves a restoring force, every simple harmonic motion is a back-and-forth motion over the same path.

Conceptual Challenge

Earth's Orbit The motion of Earth orbiting the sun is periodic. Is this motion simple harmonic? Why or why not?

Pinball In pinball games, the force exerted by a compressed spring is used to release a ball. If the distance the spring is compressed is doubled, how will the force exerted on the ball change? If the spring is replaced with one that is half as stiff, how will the force acting on the ball change?

simple harmonic motion vibration about an equilibrium position in which a restoring force is proportional to the displacement from equilibrium

Hooke's Law

Sample Problem A If a mass of 2.1 kg attached to a vertical spring stretches the spring 6.2 cm from its original equilibrium position, what is the spring constant?

1 ANALYZE

Given:

$m = 2.1$ kg
$x = -6.2$ cm $= -0.062$ m
$g = 9.81$ m/s^2

Unknown: $k = ?$

Diagram:

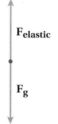

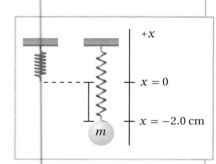

2 PLAN

Choose an equation or situation:

When the mass is attached to the spring, the equilibrium position changes. At the new equilibrium position, the net force acting on the mass is zero. So the spring force (given by Hooke's law) must be equal and opposite to the weight of the mass.

$$\mathbf{F_{net}} = 0 = \mathbf{F_{elastic}} + \mathbf{F_g}$$

$$F_{elastic} = -kx$$

$$F_g = -mg$$

$$-kx - mg = 0$$

Rearrange the equation to isolate the unknown:

$$kx = -mg$$

$$k = \frac{-mg}{x}$$

3 SOLVE

Substitute the values into the equation and solve:

$$k = \frac{-(2.1 \text{ kg})(9.81 \text{ m/s}^2)}{-0.062 \text{ m}}$$

$$\boxed{k = 330 \text{ N/m}}$$

Calculator Solution

The calculator answer for k is 332.274. This answer is rounded to two significant figures, 330 N/m.

4 CHECK YOUR ANSWER

The value of k implies that a force of 330 N is required to displace the spring 1 m.

Continued

Hooke's Law (continued)

Practice

1. Suppose the spring in Sample Problem A is replaced with a spring that stretches 36 cm from its equilibrium position.

   a. What is the spring constant in this case?

   b. Is this spring stiffer or less stiff than the one in Sample Problem A?

2. A mass of 3.0 kg is attached to a spring scale with a spring constant of 36 N/m. What is the spring's displacement?

3. A child exerts a force of 12 N to shoot a rubber band across the room. If the rubber band has a spring constant of 180 N/m, what is the rubber band's displacement?

4. How much force is required to pull a spring 3.0 cm from its equilibrium position if the spring constant is 2.7×10^3 N/m?

A stretched or compressed spring has elastic potential energy.

As you saw in the chapter "Work and Energy," a stretched or compressed spring stores elastic potential energy. To see how mechanical energy is conserved in an ideal mass-spring system, consider an archer shooting an arrow from a bow, as shown in **Figure 1.2**. Bending the bow by pulling back the bowstring is analogous to stretching a spring. To simplify this situation, we will disregard friction and internal energy.

Once the bowstring has been pulled back, the bow stores elastic potential energy. Because the bow, arrow, and bowstring (the system) are now at rest, the kinetic energy of the system is zero, and the mechanical energy of the system is solely elastic potential energy.

When the bowstring is released, the bow's elastic potential energy is converted to the kinetic energy of the arrow. At the moment the arrow leaves the bowstring, it gains most of the elastic potential energy originally stored in the bow. (The rest of the elastic potential energy is converted to the kinetic energy of the bow and the bowstring.) Thus, once the arrow leaves the bowstring, the mechanical energy of the bow-and-arrow system is solely kinetic. Because mechanical energy must be conserved, the total kinetic energy of the bow, arrow, and bowstring is equal to the elastic potential energy originally stored in the bow.

FIGURE 1.2

Conservation of Mechanical Energy The elastic potential energy stored in this stretched bow is converted into the kinetic energy of the arrow.

©Alistair Scott/Alamy Images

Shock Absorbers

Bumps in the road are certainly a nuisance, but without strategic use of damping devices, they may also prove deadly. To control a car going 110 km/h (70 mi/h), a driver needs all the wheels on the ground. Bumps in the road lift the wheels off the ground and rob the driver of control. A good solution is to fit the car with springs at each wheel. The springs absorb energy as the wheels rise over the bumps and push the wheels back to the pavement to keep the wheels on the road. Once set in motion, springs tend to continue to go up and down in simple harmonic motion. This affects the driver's control of the car and can also be uncomfortable.

One way to cut down on unwanted vibrations is to use stiff springs that compress only a few centimeters under thousands of newtons of force. Such springs have very high spring constants and thus do not vibrate as freely as softer springs with lower constants. However, this solution reduces the driver's ability to keep the car's wheels on the road.

To solve the problem, energy-absorbing devices known as *shock absorbers* are placed parallel to the springs in some automobiles, as shown in **(a)** of the illustration below. Shock absorbers are fluid-filled tubes that turn the simple harmonic motion of the springs into damped harmonic motion. In damped harmonic motion, each cycle of stretch and compression of the spring is much smaller than the previous cycle. Modern auto suspensions are set up so that all of a spring's energy is absorbed by the shock absorbers, eliminating vibrations in just one up-and-down cycle. This keeps the car from bouncing without sacrificing the spring's ability to keep the wheels on the road.

Different spring constants and shock absorber damping are combined to give a wide variety of road responses. For example, larger vehicles have heavy-duty leaf springs made of stacks of steel strips, which have a larger spring constant than coil springs do. In this type of suspension system, the shock absorber is perpendicular to the spring, as shown in **(b)** of the illustration below. The stiffness of the spring can affect steering response time, traction, and the general feel of the car.

As a result of the variety of combinations that are possible, your driving experiences can range from the luxurious floating of a limousine to the bone-rattling road feel of a sports car.

Shock Absorbers

Shock absorbers are placed differently in **(a)** some automobiles and **(b)** heavy-duty vehicles.

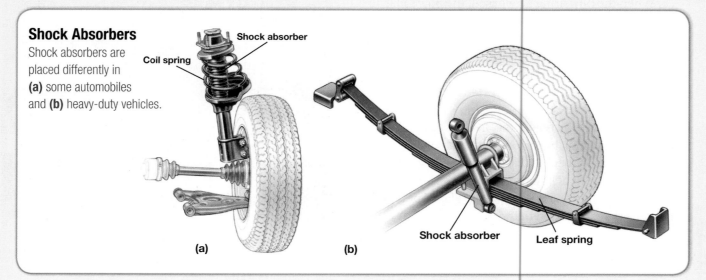

Shock absorber

Coil spring

(a)

Shock absorber   Leaf spring

(b)

The Simple Pendulum

As you have seen, the periodic motion of a mass-spring system is one example of simple harmonic motion. Now consider the trapeze acrobats shown in **Figure 1.3(a).** Like the vibrating mass-spring system, the swinging motion of a trapeze acrobat is a periodic vibration. Is a trapeze acrobat's motion an example of simple harmonic motion?

To answer this question, we will use a simple pendulum as a model of the acrobat's motion, which is a physical pendulum. A simple pendulum consists of a mass called a *bob,* which is attached to a fixed string, as shown in **Figure 1.3(b).** When working with a simple pendulum, we assume that the mass of the bob is concentrated at a point and that the mass of the string is negligible. Furthermore, we disregard the effects of friction and air resistance. For a physical pendulum, on the other hand, the distribution of the mass must be considered, and friction and air resistance also must be taken into account. To simplify our analysis, we will disregard these complications and use a simple pendulum to approximate a physical pendulum in all of our examples.

(tl) ©David Madison/Photographer's Choice/Getty Images

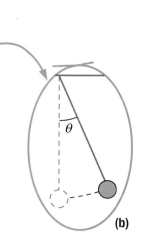

FIGURE 1.3

A Simple Pendulum **(a)** The motion of these trapeze acrobats is modeled by **(b)** a simple pendulum.

(a)

(b)

The restoring force of a pendulum is a component of the bob's weight.

To see whether the pendulum's motion is simple harmonic, we must first examine the forces exerted on the pendulum's bob to determine which force acts as the restoring force. If the restoring force is proportional to the displacement, then the pendulum's motion is simple harmonic. Let us select a coordinate system in which the x-axis is tangent to the direction of motion and the y-axis is perpendicular to the direction of motion. Because the bob is always changing its position, these axes will change at each point of the bob's motion.

The forces acting on the bob at any point include the force exerted by the string and the gravitational force. The force exerted by the string always acts along the y-axis, which is along the string. The gravitational force can be resolved into two components along the chosen axes, as shown in **Figure 1.4.** Because both the force exerted by the string and the y-component of the gravitational force are perpendicular to the bob's motion, the x-component of the gravitational force is the net force acting on the bob in the direction of its motion. In this case, the x-component of the gravitational force always pulls the bob toward its equilibrium position and hence is the restoring force. Note that the restoring force $(F_{g,x} = F_g \sin \theta)$ is zero at equilibrium, because θ equals zero at this point.

FIGURE 1.4

Components of Gravitational Force At any displacement from equilibrium, the weight of the bob $(\mathbf{F_g})$ can be resolved into two components. The x-component $(\mathbf{F_{g,x}})$, which is perpendicular to the string, is the only force acting on the bob in the direction of its motion.

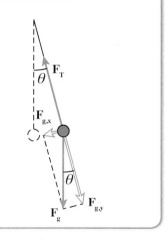

MATERIALS
- pendulum bob and string
- tape
- toy car
- protractor
- meterstick or tape measure

ENERGY OF A PENDULUM

Tie one end of a string around the pendulum bob, and tape it securely in place. Set the toy car on a smooth surface, and hold the string of the pendulum directly above the car so that the bob rests on the car. Use your other hand to pull back the bob of the pendulum. Have your partner measure the angle of the pendulum with a protractor.

Release the pendulum so that the bob strikes the car. Measure the displacement of the car. What happened to the pendulum's potential energy after you released the bob? Repeat the process using different angles. How can you account for your results?

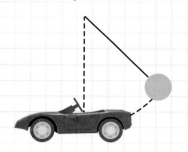

For small angles, the pendulum's motion is simple harmonic.

As with a mass-spring system, the restoring force of a simple pendulum is not constant. Instead, the magnitude of the restoring force varies with the bob's distance from the equilibrium position. The magnitude of the restoring force is proportional to sin θ. When the maximum angle of displacement θ is relatively small (<15°), sin θ is approximately equal to θ in radians. As a result, the restoring force is very nearly proportional to the displacement, and the pendulum's motion is an excellent approximation of simple harmonic motion. We will assume small angles of displacement unless otherwise noted.

Because a simple pendulum vibrates with simple harmonic motion, many of our earlier conclusions for a mass-spring system apply here. At maximum displacement, the restoring force and acceleration reach a maximum, while the speed becomes zero. Conversely, at equilibrium, the restoring force and acceleration become zero, and speed reaches a maximum. **Figure 1.6** on the next page illustrates the analogy between a simple pendulum and a mass-spring system.

Gravitational potential energy increases as a pendulum's displacement increases.

As with the mass-spring system, the mechanical energy of a simple pendulum is conserved in an ideal (frictionless) system. However, the spring's potential energy is elastic, while the potential energy associated with the pendulum is gravitational. We define the gravitational potential energy associated with a pendulum to be zero when it is at the lowest point of its swing.

Figure 1.5 illustrates how a pendulum's mechanical energy changes as the pendulum oscillates. At maximum displacement from equilibrium, a pendulum's energy is entirely gravitational potential energy. As the pendulum swings toward equilibrium, it gains kinetic energy and loses potential energy. At the equilibrium position, its energy becomes solely kinetic.

As the pendulum swings past its equilibrium position, the kinetic energy decreases, while the gravitational potential energy increases. At maximum displacement from equilibrium, the pendulum's energy is once again entirely gravitational potential energy.

FIGURE 1.5

Changes in Mechanical Energy for Simple Harmonic Motion Whether at maximum displacement **(a)**, equilibrium **(b)**, or maximum displacement in the other direction **(c)**, the pendulum's total mechanical energy remains the same. However, as the graph shows, the pendulum's kinetic energy and potential energy are constantly changing.

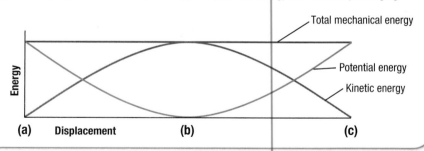

FIGURE 1.6

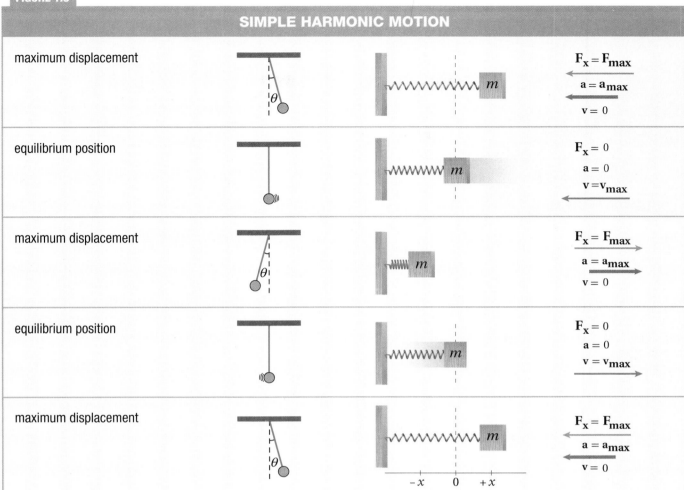

SIMPLE HARMONIC MOTION

maximum displacement

equilibrium position

maximum displacement

equilibrium position

maximum displacement

✔ SECTION 1 **FORMATIVE ASSESSMENT**

▶ Reviewing Main Ideas

1 Which of these periodic motions are simple harmonic?
  a. a child swinging on a playground swing ($\theta = 45°$)
  b. a CD rotating in a player
  c. an oscillating clock pendulum ($\theta = 10°$)

2. To launch a ball, a pinball machine compresses a spring 4.0 cm. The spring constant is 13 N/m. What is the force of the spring on the ball when the spring is released?

3. How does the restoring force acting on a pendulum bob change as the bob swings toward the equilibrium position? How do the bob's acceleration (along the direction of motion) and velocity change?

✔ Critical Thinking

4. When an acrobat swinging on a trapeze reaches the equilibrium position, the net force acting along the direction of motion is zero. Why does the acrobat swing past the equilibrium position?

Objectives

- Identify the amplitude of vibration.

- Recognize the relationship between period and frequency.

- Calculate the period and frequency of an object vibrating with simple harmonic motion.

Measuring Simple Harmonic Motion

Key Terms

amplitude   period   frequency

Amplitude, Period, and Frequency

In the absence of friction, a moving trapeze always returns to the same maximum displacement after each swing. This maximum displacement from the equilibrium position is the **amplitude.** A pendulum's amplitude can be measured by the angle between the pendulum's equilibrium position and its maximum displacement. For a mass-spring system, the amplitude is the maximum amount the spring is stretched or compressed from its equilibrium position.

amplitude the maximum displacement from equilibrium

Period and frequency measure time.

Imagine the ride shown in **Figure 2.1** swinging from maximum displacement on one side of equilibrium to maximum displacement on the other side and then back again. This cycle is considered one complete cycle of motion. The **period,** T, is the time it takes for this complete cycle of motion. For example, if one complete cycle takes 20 s, then the period of this motion is 20 s. Note that after the time T, the object is back where it started.

period the time that it takes a complete cycle to occur

The number of complete cycles the ride swings through in a unit of time is the ride's **frequency,** f. If one complete cycle takes 20 s, then the ride's frequency is $\frac{1}{20}$ cycle/s, or 0.05 cycle/s. The SI unit of frequency is s^{-1}, known as hertz (Hz). In this case, the ride's frequency is 0.05 Hz.

frequency the number of cycles or vibrations per unit of time

Period and frequency can be confusing, because both are concepts involving time in simple harmonic motion. Notice that the period is the time per cycle and that the frequency is the number of cycles per unit time, so they are inversely related.

$$f = \frac{1}{T} \text{ or } T = \frac{1}{f}$$

This relationship was used to determine the frequency of the ride.

$$f = \frac{1}{T} = \frac{1}{20 \text{ s}} = 0.05 \text{ Hz}$$

In any problem where you have a value for period or frequency, you can calculate the other value. These terms are summarized in **Figure 2.2.**

FIGURE 2.1

Period and Frequency For any periodic motion—such as the motion of this amusement park ride in Helsinki, Finland—period and frequency are inversely related.

FIGURE 2.2

MEASURES OF SIMPLE HARMONIC MOTION

Term	Example	Definition	SI unit
amplitude	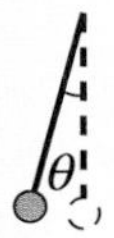	maximum displacement from equilibrium	radian, rad meter, m
period, T	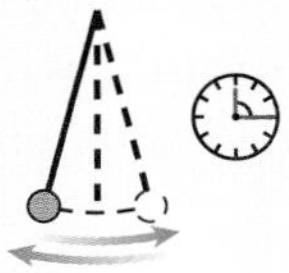	time that it takes to complete a full cycle	second, s
frequency, f	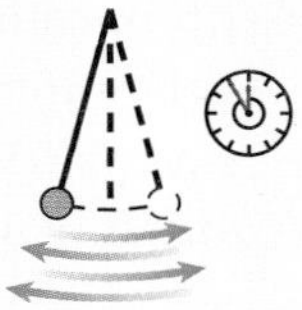	number of cycles or vibrations per unit of time	hertz, Hz ($\text{Hz} = \text{s}^{-1}$)

Did YOU Know?

Galileo is credited as the first person to notice that the motion of a pendulum depends on its length and is independent of its amplitude (for small angles). He supposedly observed this while attending church services at a cathedral in Pisa. The pendulum he studied was a swinging chandelier that was set in motion when someone bumped it while lighting the candles. Galileo is said to have measured its frequency, and hence its period, by timing the swings with his pulse.

The period of a simple pendulum depends on pendulum length and free-fall acceleration.

Although both a simple pendulum and a mass-spring system vibrate with simple harmonic motion, calculating the period and frequency of each requires a separate equation. This is because in each, the period and frequency depend on different physical factors.

Consider an experimental setup of two pendulums of the same length but with bobs of different masses. The length of a pendulum is measured from the pivot point to the center of mass of the pendulum bob. If you were to pull each bob aside the same small distance and then release them at the same time, each pendulum would complete one vibration in the same amount of time. If you then changed the amplitude of one of the pendulums, you would find that they would still have the same period. Thus, for small amplitudes, the period of a pendulum does not depend on the mass or on the amplitude.

However, changing the length of a pendulum *does* affect its period. A change in the free-fall acceleration also affects the period of a pendulum. The exact relationship between these variables can be derived mathematically or found experimentally.

Period of a Simple Pendulum in Simple Harmonic Motion

$$T = 2\pi \sqrt{\frac{L}{a_g}}$$

period = 2π × square root of (length divided by free-fall acceleration)

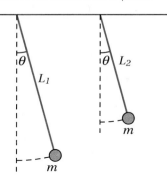

FIGURE 2.3

Pendulums When the length of one pendulum is decreased, the distance that the pendulum travels to equilibrium is also decreased. Because the accelerations of the two pendulums are equal, the shorter pendulum will have a smaller period.

Why does the period of a pendulum depend on pendulum length and free-fall acceleration? When two pendulums have different lengths but the same amplitude, the shorter pendulum will have a smaller arc to travel through, as shown in **Figure 2.3.** Because the distance from maximum displacement to equilibrium is less while the acceleration caused by the restoring force remains the same, the shorter pendulum will have a shorter period.

Why don't mass and amplitude affect the period of a pendulum? When the bobs of two pendulums differ in mass, the heavier mass provides a larger restoring force, but it also needs a larger force to achieve the same acceleration. This is similar to the situation for objects in free fall, which all have the same acceleration regardless of their mass. Because the acceleration of both pendulums is the same, the period for both is also the same.

For small angles (less than 15°), when the amplitude of a pendulum increases, the restoring force also increases proportionally. Because force is proportional to acceleration, the initial acceleration will be greater. However, the distance this pendulum must cover is also greater. For small angles, the effects of the two increasing quantities cancel, and the pendulum's period remains the same.

Simple Harmonic Motion of a Simple Pendulum

Sample Problem B You need to know the height of a tower, but darkness obscures the ceiling. You note that a pendulum extending from the ceiling almost touches the floor and that its period is 12 s. How tall is the tower?

❶ ANALYZE

Given: $T = 12 \text{ s}$ $a_g = g = 9.81 \text{ m/s}^2$

Unknown: $L = ?$

Use the equation for the period of a simple pendulum, and solve for L.

Tips and Tricks
Remember that on Earth's surface, $a_g = g = 9.81 \text{ m/s}^2$. Use this value in the equation for the period of a pendulum if a problem does not specify otherwise. At higher altitudes or on different planets, use the given value of a_g instead.

❷ PLAN

$$T = 2\pi \sqrt{\frac{L}{a_g}}$$

$$\frac{T\sqrt{a_g}}{2\pi} = \sqrt{L}$$

$$\frac{T^2 a_g}{4\pi^2} = L$$

❸ SOLVE

$$L = \frac{(12 \text{ s})^2 (9.81 \text{ m/s}^2)}{4\pi^2}$$

$$\boxed{L = 36 \text{ m}}$$

Continued ▶

Practice

1. If the period of the pendulum in the preceding sample problem were 24 s, how tall would the tower be?

2. You are designing a pendulum clock to have a period of 1.0 s. How long should the pendulum be?

3. A trapeze artist swings in simple harmonic motion with a period of 3.8 s. Calculate the length of the cables supporting the trapeze.

4. Calculate the period and frequency of a 3.500 m long pendulum at the following locations:
   a. the North Pole, where $a_g = 9.832$ m/s^2
   b. Chicago, where $a_g = 9.803$ m/s^2
   c. Jakarta, Indonesia, where $a_g = 9.782$ m/s^2

Period of a mass-spring system depends on mass and spring constant.

Now consider the period of a mass-spring system. In this case, according to Hooke's law, the restoring force acting on the mass is determined by the displacement of the mass and by the spring constant ($F_{elastic} = -kx$). The magnitude of the mass does not affect the restoring force.

So, unlike in the case of the pendulum, in which a heavier mass increased both the force on the bob and the bob's inertia, a heavier mass attached to a spring increases inertia without providing a compensating increase in force. Because of this increase in inertia, a heavy mass has a smaller acceleration than a light mass has. Thus, a heavy mass will take more time to complete one cycle of motion. In other words, the heavy mass has a greater period. Thus, as mass increases, the period of vibration increases when there is no compensating increase in force.

Conceptual Challenge

Pendulum on the Moon The free-fall acceleration on the surface of the moon is approximately one-sixth of the free-fall acceleration on the surface of Earth. Compare the period of a pendulum on the moon with that of an identical pendulum set in motion on Earth.

Pendulum Clocks Why is a wound mainspring often used to provide energy to a pendulum clock in order to prevent the amplitude of the pendulum from decreasing?

The greater the spring constant (k), the stiffer the spring; hence a greater force is required to stretch or compress the spring. When force is greater, acceleration is greater, and the amount of time required for a single cycle should decrease (assuming that the amplitude remains constant). Thus, for a given amplitude, a stiffer spring will take less time to complete one cycle of motion than one that is less stiff.

As with the pendulum, the equation for the period of a mass-spring system can be derived mathematically or found experimentally.

Period of a Mass-Spring System in Simple Harmonic Motion

$$T = 2\pi \sqrt{\frac{m}{k}}$$

period $= 2\pi \times$ square root of (mass divided by spring constant)

Note that changing the amplitude of the vibration does not affect the period. This statement is true only for systems and circumstances in which the spring obeys Hooke's law.

GO ONLINE

Interactive Demo
HMHScience.com

Simple Harmonic Motion of a Mass-Spring System

Sample Problem C A large pearl was found in the Philippines in 1934. Suppose the pearl is placed on a spring scale whose spring constant is 362 N/m. If the scale's platform oscillates with a frequency of 1.20 Hz, what is the mass of the pearl?

① ANALYZE

Given: $k = 362 \text{ N/m}$ $f = 1.20 \text{ Hz}$

Unknown: $m = ?$

Use the equation for the period of a mass-spring system. Then express the period in terms of frequency ($T = 1/f$).

② SOLVE

$$T = 2\pi \sqrt{\frac{m}{k}} = \frac{1}{f}$$

$$m = \frac{k}{4\pi^2 f^2}$$

$$m = \frac{362 \text{ N/m}}{4\pi^2 (1.20 \text{ Hz})^2}$$

$$\boxed{m = 6.37 \text{ kg}}$$

Continued

Simple Harmonic Motion of a Mass-Spring System (continued)

Practice

1. A mass of 0.30 kg is attached to a spring and is set into motion with a period of 0.24 s. What is the spring constant of the spring?

2. On Halloween, you see an "alien" that has one antenna made of a glittery foam ball connected to a spring. The spring oscillates with a period of 0.079 s and has a spring constant of 63 N/m. Find the mass of the ball.

3. A 125 N object vibrates with a period of 3.56 s when hanging from a spring. What is the spring constant of the spring?

4. Suppose a 2662 kg giant seal is placed on a scale and produces a 20.0 cm compression. If the seal and spring system are set into simple harmonic motion, what is the period of the oscillations?

5. A spring of spring constant 30.0 N/m is attached to different masses, and the system is set in motion. Find the period and frequency of vibration for masses of the following magnitudes:

   a. 2.3 kg

   b. 15 g

   c. 1.9 kg

SECTION 2 FORMATIVE ASSESSMENT

Reviewing Main Ideas

1. The reading on a metronome indicates the number of oscillations per minute. What are the frequency and period of the metronome's vibration when the metronome is set at 180?

2. A child swings with a small amplitude on a playground swing with a 2.5 m long chain.

   a. What is the period of the child's motion?

   b. What is the frequency of vibration?

3. A 0.75 kg mass attached to a vertical spring stretches the spring 0.30 m.

   a. What is the spring constant?

   b. The mass-spring system is now placed on a horizontal surface and set vibrating. What is the period of the vibration?

Critical Thinking

4. Two mass-spring systems vibrate with simple harmonic motion. If the spring constants are equal and the mass of one system is twice that of the other, which system has a greater period?

SECTION 3

SC.912.P.10.20

Objectives

▶ Distinguish local particle movement from overall wave motion.

▶ Interpret waveforms of transverse and longitudinal waves.

▶ Apply the relationship among wave speed, frequency, and wavelength to solve problems.

SC.912.P.10.20 Describe the measurable properties of waves and explain the relationships among them and how these properties change when the wave moves from one medium to another.

medium a physical environment through which a disturbance can travel

mechanical wave a wave that requires a medium through which to travel

Properties of Waves

Key Terms

medium	crest	longitudinal wave
mechanical wave	trough	
transverse wave	wavelength	

Wave Motion

Consider what happens to the surface of a pond when you drop a pebble into the water. The disturbance created by the pebble generates water waves that travel away from the disturbance, as seen in **Figure 3.1.** If you examined the motion of a leaf floating near the disturbance, you would see that the leaf moves up and down and back and forth about its original position. However, the leaf does not undergo any net displacement from the motion of the waves.

The leaf's motion indicates the motion of the particles in the water. The water molecules move locally, like the leaf does, but they do not travel across the pond. That is, the water wave moves from one place to another, but the water itself is not carried with it.

FIGURE 3.1

Ripple Waves A pebble dropped into a pond creates ripple waves similar to those shown here.

A wave is the motion of a disturbance.

Ripple waves in a pond start with a disturbance at some point in the water. This disturbance causes water on the surface near that point to move, which in turn causes points farther away to move. In this way, the waves travel outward in a circular pattern away from the original disturbance.

In this example, the water in the pond is the **medium** through which the disturbance travels. Particles in the medium—in this case, water molecules—move in vertical circles as waves pass. Note that the medium does not actually travel with the waves. After the waves have passed, the water returns to its original position.

Most types of waves require a material medium in which to travel. Sound waves, for example, cannot travel through outer space, because space is very nearly a vacuum. In order for sound waves to travel, they must have a medium such as air or water. Waves that require a material medium are called **mechanical waves.**

However, not all wave propagation requires a medium. Waves that are electromagnetic waves, such as visible light, radio waves, microwaves, and x-rays, can travel through a vacuum.

©Yagi Studio/SuperStock

380 Chapter 11

Wave Types

One of the simplest ways to demonstrate wave motion is to flip one end of a taut rope whose opposite end is fixed, as shown in **Figure 3.2.** The flip of your wrist creates a pulse that travels to the fixed end with a definite speed. A wave that consists of a single traveling pulse is called a *pulse wave*.

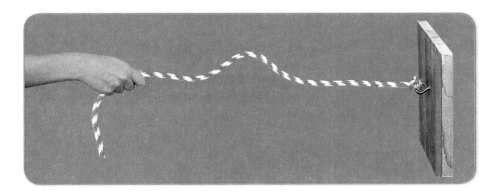

FIGURE 3.2

Wave Motion A single flip of the wrist creates a pulse wave on a taut rope.

Now imagine that you continue to generate pulses at one end of the rope. Together, these pulses form what is called a *periodic wave*. Whenever the source of a wave's motion is a periodic motion, such as the motion of your hand moving up and down repeatedly, a periodic wave is produced.

Sine waves describe particles vibrating with simple harmonic motion.

Figure 3.3 depicts a blade that vibrates with simple harmonic motion and thus makes a periodic wave on a string. As the wave travels to the right, any single point on the string vibrates up and down. Because the blade is vibrating with simple harmonic motion, the vibration of each point of the string is also simple harmonic. A wave whose source vibrates with simple harmonic motion is called a *sine wave*. A sine wave is a special case of a periodic wave in which the periodic motion is simple harmonic. The wave in **Figure 3.3** is called a sine wave because a graph of the trigonometric function $y = \sin x$ produces this curve when plotted.

A close look at a single point on the string illustrated in **Figure 3.3** shows that its motion resembles the motion of a mass hanging from a vibrating spring. As the wave travels to the right, the point vibrates around its equilibrium position with simple harmonic motion. This relationship between simple harmonic motion and wave motion enables us to use some of the terms and concepts from simple harmonic motion in our study of wave motion.

FIGURE 3.3

Sine Waves and Simple Harmonic Motion As the sine wave created by this vibrating blade travels to the right, a single point on the string vibrates up and down with simple harmonic motion.

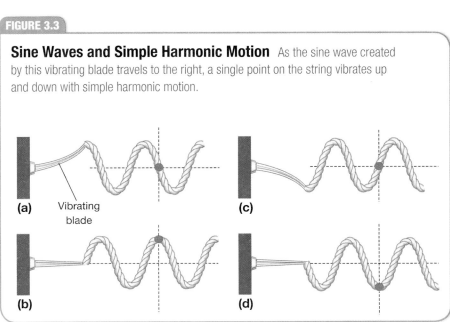

(a) Vibrating blade

(b)

(c)

(d)

Vibrations of a transverse wave are perpendicular to the wave motion.

Figure 3.4(a) is a representation of the wave shown in **Figure 3.3** at a specific instant of time, *t*. This wave travels to the right as the particles of the rope vibrate up and down. Thus, the vibrations are perpendicular to the direction of the wave's motion. A wave such as this, in which the particles of the disturbed medium move perpendicularly to the wave motion, is called a **transverse wave.**

The wave shown in **Figure 3.4(a)** can be represented on a coordinate system, as shown in **Figure 3.4 (b).** A picture of a wave like the one in **Figure 3.4 (b)** is sometimes called a *waveform.* A waveform can represent either the displacement of each point of the wave at a single moment in time or the displacements of a single particle as time passes.

In this case, the waveform depicts the displacements at a single instant. The *x*-axis represents the equilibrium position of the string, and the *y*-coordinates of the curve represent the displacement of each point of the string at time *t*. For example, points where the curve crosses the *x*-axis (where *y* = 0) have zero displacement. Conversely, at the highest and lowest points of the curve, where displacement is greatest, the absolute values of *y* are greatest.

Wave measures include crest, trough, amplitude, and wavelength.

A wave can be measured in terms of its displacement from equilibrium. The highest point above the equilibrium position is called the wave **crest.** The lowest point below the equilibrium position is the **trough** of the wave. As in simple harmonic motion, amplitude is a measure of maximum displacement from equilibrium. The amplitude of a wave is the distance from the equilibrium position to a crest or to a trough, as shown in **Figure 3.4(b).**

As a wave passes a given point along its path, that point undergoes cyclical motion. The point is displaced first in one direction and then in the other direction. Finally, the point returns to its original equilibrium position, thereby completing one cycle. The distance the wave travels along its path during one cycle is called the **wavelength**, λ (the Greek letter *lambda*). A simple way to find the wavelength is to measure the distance between two adjacent similar points of the wave, such as from crest to crest or from trough to trough. Notice in **Figure 3.4(b)** that the distances between adjacent crests or troughs in the waveform are equal.

transverse wave a wave whose particles vibrate perpendicularly to the direction the wave is traveling

crest the highest point above the equilibrium position

trough the lowest point below the equilibrium position

wavelength the distance between two adjacent similar points of a wave, such as from crest to crest or from trough to trough

---

FIGURE 3.4

Representing a Transverse Wave (a) A picture of a transverse wave at some instant *t* can be turned into (b) a graph. The *x*-axis represents the equilibrium position of the string. The curve shows the displacements of the string at time *t*.

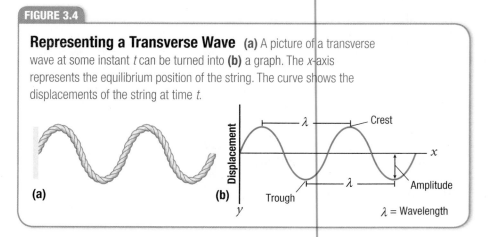

Longitudinal Wave As this wave travels to the right, the coils of the spring are tighter in some regions and looser in others. The displacement of the coils is parallel to the direction of wave motion, so this wave is longitudinal.

Compressed   Stretched   Compressed   Stretched

Vibrations of a longitudinal wave are parallel to the wave motion.

You can create another type of wave with a spring. Suppose that one end of the spring is fixed and that the free end is pumped back and forth along the length of the spring. This action produces compressed and stretched regions of the coil that travel along the spring as shown in **Figure 3.5**. The displacement of the coils is in the direction of wave motion. In other words, the vibrations are parallel to the motion of the wave.

When the particles of the medium vibrate parallel to the direction of wave motion, the wave is called a **longitudinal wave.** Sound waves in the air are longitudinal waves because air particles vibrate back and forth in a direction parallel to the direction of wave motion.

A longitudinal wave can also be described by a sine curve. Consider a longitudinal wave traveling on a spring. **Figure 3.6(a)** is a snapshot of the longitudinal wave at some instant t, and **Figure 3.6(b)** shows the sine curve representing the wave. The compressed regions correspond to the crests of the waveform, and the stretched regions correspond to troughs.

The type of wave represented by the curve in **Figure 3.6(b)** is often called a *density wave* or a *pressure wave*. The crests, where the spring coils are compressed, are regions of high density and pressure (relative to the equilibrium density or pressure of the medium). Conversely, the troughs, where the coils are stretched, are regions of low density and pressure.

longitudinal wave a wave whose particles vibrate parallel to the direction the wave is traveling

Representing a Longitudinal Wave **(a)** A longitudinal wave at some instant t can also be represented by **(b)** a graph. The crests of this waveform correspond to compressed regions, and the troughs correspond to stretched regions.

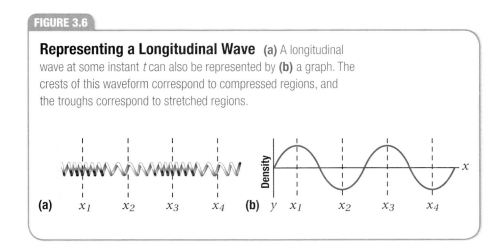

(a) x_1 x_2 x_3 x_4 (b) y x_1 x_2 x_3 x_4

Period, Frequency, and Wave Speed

Sound waves may begin with the vibrations of your vocal cords, a guitar string, or a taut drumhead. In each of these cases, the source of wave motion is a vibrating object. The vibrating object that causes a sine wave always has a characteristic frequency. Because this motion is transferred to the particles of the medium, the frequency of vibration of the particles is equal to the frequency of the source.

When the vibrating particles of the medium complete one full cycle, one complete wavelength passes any given point. Thus, wave frequency describes the number of waves that pass a given point in a unit of time.

The period of a wave is the time required for one complete cycle of vibration of the medium's particles. As the particles of the medium complete one full cycle of vibration at any point of the wave, one wavelength passes by that point. Thus, the period of a wave describes the time it takes for a complete wavelength to pass a given point.

The relationship between period and frequency seen earlier in this chapter holds true for waves as well; the period of a wave is inversely related to its frequency.

Wave speed equals frequency times wavelength.

We can now derive an expression for the speed, or velocity, of a wave in terms of its period or frequency. We know that speed is equal to displacement divided by the time it takes to undergo that displacement.

$$v = \frac{\Delta x}{\Delta t}$$

For waves, a displacement of one wavelength (λ) occurs in a time interval equal to one period of the vibration (T).

$$v = \frac{\lambda}{T}$$

As you saw earlier in this chapter, frequency and period are inversely related.

$$f = \frac{1}{T}$$

Substituting this frequency relationship into the previous equation for speed gives a new equation for the speed of a wave.

$$v = \frac{\lambda}{T} = f\lambda$$

Speed of a Wave

$$v = f\lambda$$

speed of a wave = frequency × wavelength

The speed of a mechanical wave is constant for any given medium. For example, at a concert, sound waves from different instruments reach your ears at the same moment, even when the frequencies of the sound waves are different. Thus, although the frequencies and wavelengths of the sounds produced by each instrument may be different, the product of the frequency and wavelength is always the same at the same temperature. As a result, when a mechanical wave's frequency is increased, its wavelength must decrease in order for its speed to remain constant. The speed of a wave changes only when the wave moves from one medium to another or when certain properties of the medium (such as temperature) are varied.

Wave Speed

Sample Problem D A piano string tuned to middle C vibrates with a frequency of 262 Hz. Assuming the speed of sound in air is 343 m/s, find the wavelength of the sound waves produced by the string.

1 ANALYZE

Given: $v = 343 \text{ m/s}$ $\quad f = 262 \text{ Hz}$

Unknown: $\lambda = ?$

2 SOLVE

Use the equation relating speed, wavelength, and frequency for a wave.

$$v = f\lambda$$

$$\lambda = \frac{v}{f} = \frac{343 \text{ m/s}}{262 \text{ Hz}} = \frac{343 \text{ m·s}^{-1}}{262 \text{ s}^{-1}}$$

$$\boxed{\lambda = 1.31 \text{ m}}$$

Practice

1. A piano emits frequencies that range from a low of about 28 Hz to a high of about 4200 Hz. Find the range of wavelengths in air attained by this instrument when the speed of sound in air is 340 m/s.

2. The speed of all electromagnetic waves in empty space is 3.00×10^8 m/s. Calculate the wavelength of electromagnetic waves emitted at the following frequencies:

   a. radio waves at 88.0 MHz

   b. visible light at 6.0×10^8 MHz

   c. x-rays at 3.0×10^{12} MHz

3. The red light emitted by a He-Ne laser has a wavelength of 633 nm in air and travels at 3.00×10^8 m/s. Find the frequency of the laser light.

4. A tuning fork produces a sound with a frequency of 256 Hz and a wavelength in air of 1.35 m.

   a. What value does this give for the speed of sound in air?

   b. What would be the wavelength of this same sound in water in which sound travels at 1500 m/s?

Waves transfer energy.

When a pebble is dropped into a pond, the water wave that is produced carries a certain amount of energy. As the wave spreads to other parts of the pond, the energy likewise moves across the pond. Thus, the wave transfers energy from one place in the pond to another, while the water remains in essentially the same place. In other words, waves transfer energy by the vibration of matter rather than by the transfer of matter itself.

The rate at which a wave transfers energy depends on the amplitude at which the particles of the medium are vibrating. For example, analyze the compressions and rarefactions of a wave on a spring. A greater amplitude means greater compression and stretching, which means greater potential energy in each cycle. Thus, a greater amplitude means that the wave carries more energy in a given time interval. For a mechanical wave, the energy transferred is proportional to the square of the wave's amplitude. When the amplitude of a mechanical wave is doubled, the energy it carries in a given time interval increases by a factor of four. Conversely, when the amplitude is halved, the energy decreases by a factor of four.

As with a mass-spring system or a simple pendulum, the amplitude of a wave gradually diminishes over time as its energy is dissipated. This effect, called *damping*, is usually minimal over relatively short distances. For simplicity, we have disregarded damping in our analysis of wave motions.

SECTION 3 FORMATIVE ASSESSMENT

▶ Reviewing Main Ideas

1. As waves pass by a duck floating on a lake, the duck bobs up and down but remains in essentially one place. Explain why the duck is not carried along by the wave motion.

2. Compare various wave types by sketching each of the following waves that are on a spring:
   a. a pulse wave that is longitudinal
   b. a periodic wave that is longitudinal
   c. a pulse wave that is transverse
   d. a periodic wave that is transverse

3. Draw a graph for each of the waves described in items (**b**) and (**d**) above, and label the *y*-axis of each graph with the appropriate variable. Label the following on each graph: crest, trough, wavelength, and amplitude. Compare the two graphs.

4. If the amplitude of a sound wave is increased by a factor of four, how does the energy carried by the sound wave in a given time interval change?

5. The smallest insects that a bat can detect are approximately the size of one wavelength of the sound the bat makes. What is the minimum frequency of sound waves required for the bat to detect an insect that is 0.57 cm long? (Assume the speed of sound is 340 m/s.)

Wave Interactions

Key Terms

constructive interference   standing wave   antinode
destructive interference   node

SECTION 4

Objectives

▶ Apply the superposition principle.

▶ Differentiate between constructive and destructive interference.

▶ Predict when a reflected wave will be inverted.

▶ Predict whether specific traveling waves will produce a standing wave.

▶ Identify nodes and antinodes of a standing wave.

Wave Interference

When two bumper boats collide, as shown in **Figure 4.1**, each bounces back in another direction. The two bumper boats cannot occupy the same space, and so they are forced to change the direction of their motion. This is true not just of bumper boats but of all matter. Two different material objects can never occupy the same space at the same time.

FIGURE 4.1

Bumper Boats Two of these bumper boats cannot be in the same place at one time. Waves, on the other hand, can pass through one another.

When two waves come together, they do not bounce back, as bumper boats do. If you listen carefully at a concert, you can distinguish the sounds of different instruments. Trumpet sounds are different from flute sounds, even when the two instruments are played at the same time. The sound waves of each instrument are unaffected by the other waves that are passing through the same space at the same moment. Because mechanical waves are not matter but rather are displacements of matter, two waves can occupy the same space at the same time. The combination of two overlapping waves is called *superposition*.

Figure 4.2 shows two sets of water waves in a ripple tank. As the waves move outward from their respective sources, they pass through one another. As they pass through one another, the waves interact to form an *interference pattern* of light and dark bands. Although this superposition of mechanical waves is fairly easy to observe, these are not the only kind of waves that can pass through the same space at the same time. Visible light and other forms of electromagnetic radiation also undergo superposition, and they can interact to form interference patterns.

FIGURE 4.2

Wave Interference This ripple tank demonstrates the interference of water waves.

FIGURE 4.3

Constructive
Interference When these two wave pulses meet, the displacements at each point add up to form a resultant wave. This is an example of constructive interference.

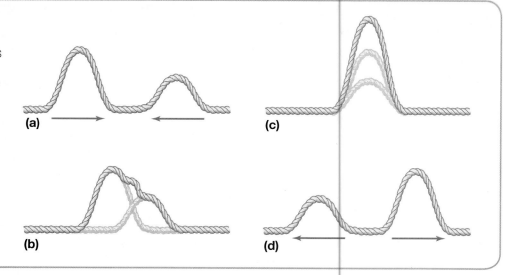

(a)

(b)

(c)

(d)

Displacements in the same direction produce constructive interference.

In **Figure 4.3(a),** two wave pulses are traveling toward each other on a stretched rope. The larger pulse is moving to the right, while the smaller pulse moves toward the left. At the moment the two wave pulses meet, a resultant wave is formed, as shown in **Figure 4.3(b).**

At each point along the rope, the displacements due to the two pulses are added together, and the result is the displacement of the resultant wave. For example, when the two pulses exactly coincide, as they do in **Figure 4.3(c),** the amplitude of the resultant wave is equal to the sum of the amplitudes of each pulse. This method of summing the displacements of waves is known as the *superposition principle.* According to this principle, when two or more waves travel through a medium at the same time, the resultant wave is the sum of the displacements of the individual waves at each point. Ideally, the superposition principle holds true for all types of waves, both mechanical and electromagnetic. However, experiments show that in reality the superposition principle is valid only when the individual waves have small amplitudes—an assumption we make in all our examples.

Notice that after the two pulses pass through each other, each pulse has the same shape it had before the waves met and each is still traveling in the same direction, as shown in **Figure 4.3(d).** This is true for sound waves at a concert, water waves in a pond, light waves, and other types of waves. Each wave maintains its own characteristics after interference, just as the two pulses do in our example above.

You have seen that when more than one wave travels through the same space at the same time, the resultant wave is equal to the sum of the individual displacements. If the displacements are on the same side of equilibrium, as in **Figure 4.3,** they have the same sign. When added together, the resultant wave is larger than the individual displacements. This is called **constructive interference.**

constructive interference
a superposition of two or more waves in which individual displacements on the same side of the equilibrium position are added together to form the resultant wave

FIGURE 4.4

Destructive Interference In this case, known as destructive interference, the displacement of one pulse is subtracted from the displacement of the other.

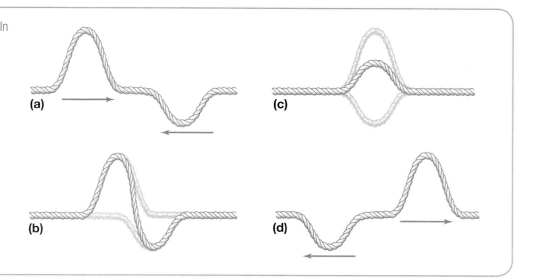

(a)

(b)

(c)

(d)

Displacements in opposite directions produce destructive interference.

What happens if the pulses are on opposite sides of the equilibrium position, as they are in **Figure 4.4(a)**? In this case, the displacements have different signs, one positive and one negative. When the positive and negative displacements are added, as shown in **Figure 4.4(b)** and **(c)**, the resultant wave is the difference between the pulses. This is called **destructive interference.** After the pulses separate, their shapes are unchanged, as seen in **Figure 4.4(d).**

Figure 4.5 shows two pulses of equal amplitude but with displacements of opposite signs. When the two pulses coincide and the displacements are added, the resultant wave has a displacement of zero. In other words, at the instant the two pulses overlap, they completely cancel each other; it is as if there were no disturbance at all. This situation is known as *complete destructive interference.*

If these waves were water waves coming together, one of the waves would be acting to pull an individual drop of water upward at the same instant and with the same force that another wave would be acting to pull it downward. The result would be no net force on the drop, and there would be no net displacement of the water at that moment.

Thus far, we have considered the interference produced by two transverse pulse waves. The superposition principle is valid for longitudinal waves as well. In a *compression*, particles are moved closer together, while in a *rarefaction*, particles are spread farther apart. So, when a compression and a rarefaction interfere, there is destructive interference.

In our examples, we have considered constructive and destructive interference separately, and we have dealt only with pulse waves. With periodic waves, complicated patterns arise that involve regions of constructive and destructive interference. The locations of these regions may remain fixed or may vary with time as the individual waves travel.

destructive interference
a superposition of two or more waves in which individual displacements on opposite sides of the equilibrium position are added together to form the resultant wave

FIGURE 4.5

Complete Destructive Interference The resultant displacement at each point of the string is zero, so the two pulses cancel one another. This is complete destructive interference.

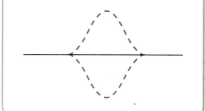

Reflection

In our discussion of waves so far, we have assumed that the waves being analyzed could travel indefinitely without striking anything that would stop them or otherwise change their motion. But what happens to the motion of a wave when it reaches a boundary?

At a free boundary, waves are reflected.

Consider a pulse wave traveling on a stretched rope whose end forms a ring around a post, as shown in **Figure 4.6(a)**. We will assume that the ring is free to slide along the post without friction.

As the pulse travels to the right, each point of the rope moves up once and then back down. When the pulse reaches the boundary, the rope is free to move up as usual, and it pulls the ring up with it. Then, the ring is pulled back down by the tension in the rope. The movement of the rope at the post is similar to the movement that would result if someone were to whip the rope upward to send a pulse to the left, which would cause a pulse to travel back along the rope to the left. This is called *reflection*. Note that the reflected pulse is upright and has the same amplitude as the incident pulse.

At a fixed boundary, waves are reflected and inverted.

Now consider a pulse traveling on a stretched rope that is fixed at one end, as in **Figure 4.6(b)**. When the pulse reaches the wall, the rope exerts an upward force on the wall, and the wall in turn exerts an equal and opposite reaction force on the rope. This downward force on the rope causes a displacement in the direction opposite the displacement of the original pulse. As a result, the pulse is inverted after reflection.

FIGURE 4.6

Reflection of a Pulse Wave
(a) When a pulse travels down a rope whose end is free to slide up the post, the pulse is reflected from the free end.
(b) When a pulse travels down a rope that is fixed at one end, the reflected pulse is inverted.

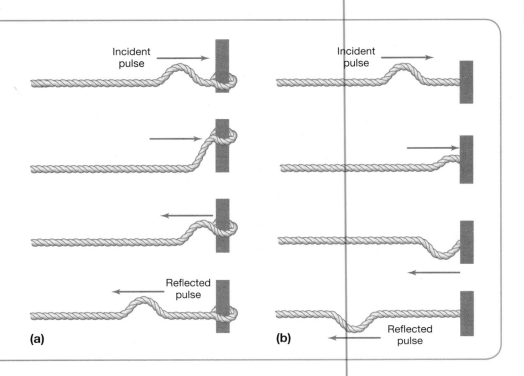

Incident pulse

Reflected pulse

(a)

Incident pulse

Reflected pulse

(b)

Standing Waves

Consider a string that is attached on one end to a rigid support and that is shaken up and down in a regular motion at the other end. The regular motion produces waves of a certain frequency, wavelength, and amplitude traveling down the string. When the waves reach the other end, they are reflected back toward the oncoming waves. If the string is vibrated at exactly the right frequency, a **standing wave**—a resultant wave pattern that appears to be stationary on the string—is produced. The standing wave consists of alternating regions of constructive and destructive interference.

standing wave a wave pattern that results when two waves of the same frequency, wavelength, and amplitude travel in opposite directions and interfere

Standing waves have nodes and antinodes.

Figure 4.7(a) shows four possible standing waves for a given string length. The points at which complete destructive interference happens are called **nodes.** There is no motion in the string at the nodes. But midway between two adjacent nodes, the string vibrates with the largest amplitude. These points are called **antinodes.**

Figure 4.7(b) shows the oscillation of the second case shown in **Figure 4.7(a)** during half a cycle. All points on the string oscillate vertically with the same frequency, except for the nodes, which are stationary. In this case, there are three nodes (N) and two antinodes (A), as illustrated in the figure.

node a point in a standing wave that maintains zero displacement

antinode a point in a standing wave, halfway between two nodes, at which the largest displacement occurs

---

FIGURE 4.7

Standing Waves **(a)** This photograph shows four possible standing waves that can exist on a given string.

(b) The diagram shows the progression of the second standing wave for one-half of a cycle.

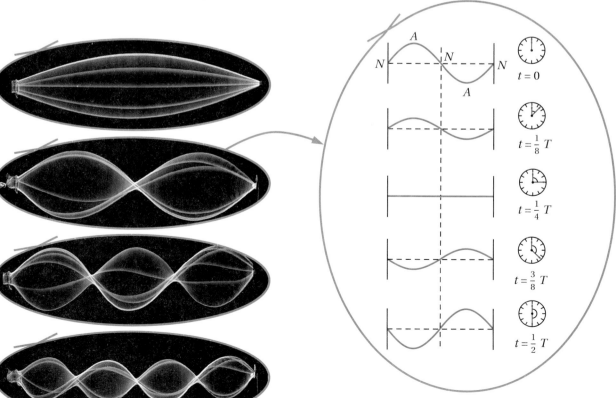

FIGURE 4.8

Frequency and Standing Waves

Only certain frequencies produce standing waves on this fixed string. The wavelength of these standing waves depends on the string length. Possible wavelengths include $2L$ **(b)**, L **(c)**, and $\frac{2}{3}L$ **(d)**.

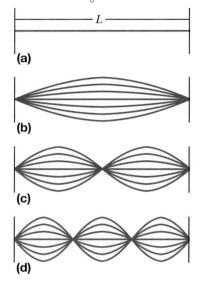

Only certain frequencies, and therefore wavelengths, produce standing wave patterns. **Figure 4.8** shows standing waves for a given string length. In each case, the curves represent the position of the string at different instants of time. If the string were vibrating rapidly, the several positions would blur together and give the appearance of loops, like those shown in the diagram. A single loop corresponds to either a crest or trough alone, while two loops correspond to a crest and a trough together, or one wavelength.

The ends of the string must be nodes, because these points cannot vibrate. As you can see in **Figure 4.8,** a standing wave can be produced for any wavelength that allows both ends of the string to be nodes. For example, in **Figure 4.8(b),** each end is a node, and there are no nodes in between. Because a single loop corresponds to either a crest or trough alone, this standing wave corresponds to one-half of a wavelength. Thus, the wavelength in this case is equal to twice the string length ($2L$).

The next possible standing wave, shown in **Figure 4.8(c),** has three nodes: one at either end and one in the middle. In this case, there are two loops, which correspond to a crest and a trough. Thus, this standing wave has a wavelength equal to the string length (L). The next case, shown in **Figure 4.8(d),** has a wavelength equal to two-thirds of the string length $\left(\frac{2}{3}L\right)$, and the pattern continues. Wavelengths between the values shown here do not produce standing waves, because they allow only one end of the string to be a node.

✔ SECTION 4 **FORMATIVE ASSESSMENT**

▶ Reviewing Main Ideas

1. A wave of amplitude 0.30 m interferes with a second wave of amplitude 0.20 m. What is the largest resultant displacement that may occur?

2. A string is rigidly attached to a post at one end. Several pulses of amplitude 0.15 m sent down the string are reflected at the post and travel back down the string without a loss of amplitude. What is the amplitude at a point on the string where the maximum displacement points of two pulses cross? What type of interference is this?

3. How would your answer to item 2 change if the same pulses were sent down a string whose end is free? What type of interference is this?

4. A stretched string fixed at both ends is 2.0 m long. What are three wavelengths that will produce standing waves on this string? Name at least one wavelength that would not produce a standing wave pattern, and explain your answer.

Interpreting Graphics

5. Look at the standing wave shown in **Figure 4.9.** How many nodes does this wave have? How many antinodes?

FIGURE 4.9

A Standing Wave

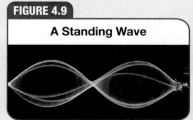

De Broglie Waves

We often treat waves and particles as if there were a clear distinction between the two. For most of the history of science, this was believed to be the case. However, in the early twentieth century, scientists were confronted with experimental evidence suggesting that the properties of matter are not always as clear-cut as everyone had assumed.

The Dual Nature of Light

This scientific revolution began in 1900, when Max Planck introduced the possibility that energy could come in discrete units. In 1905, Einstein extended Planck's theory, suggesting that all electromagnetic waves (such as light) sometimes behave like particles. According to this theory, light can behave both like a wave and like a particle; some experiments reveal its wave nature, and other experiments display its particle nature. Although this idea was initially greeted with skepticism, it explained certain phenomena that the wave theory of light could not account for and was soon confirmed empirically in a variety of experiments.

Matter Waves

The idea that light has a dual nature led Louis de Broglie to hypothesize that perhaps all matter has wavelike characteristics. De Broglie believed that there should not be two separate branches of physics, one for electromagnetic waves and another for matter. In his doctoral thesis, submitted in 1924, he proposed a theory of matter waves to reconcile this discrepancy. At that time, there was no experimental evidence to support his theory.

De Broglie's calculations suggested that matter waves had a wavelength, λ, often called the de Broglie wavelength, given by the following equation:

$$\lambda = \frac{h}{p} = \frac{h}{mv}$$

The variable h in this equation is called Planck's constant, which is approximately equal to 6.63×10^{-34} J•s. The variable p is the object's momentum, which is equivalent to its mass, m, times its velocity, v. Note that the dual nature of matter suggested by de Broglie is evident in this equation, which includes both a wave concept (λ) and a particle concept (mv).

De Broglie's equation shows that the smaller the momentum of an object, the larger its de Broglie wavelength. But even when the momentum of an object is very small from our perspective, h is so small that the wavelength is still much too small for us to detect. In order to detect a wavelength, one must use an opening comparable in size to the wavelength because waves passing through such an opening will display patterns of constructive and destructive interference. When the opening is much larger than the wavelength, waves travel through it without being affected.

FIGURE 1

Cat Hairs This image of cat hair is magnified 500 times. It was produced by an electron microscope and relies on principles from de Broglie's equation.

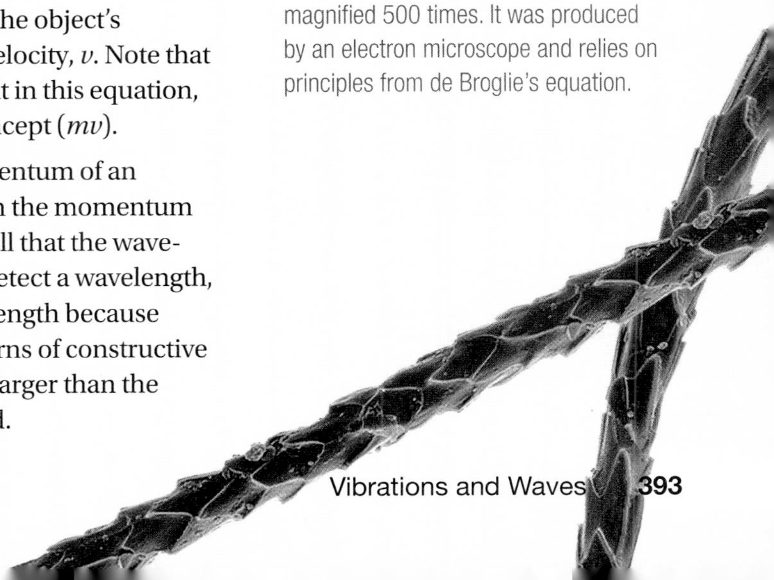

The de Broglie wavelength of a 0.15 kg baseball moving at 30 m/s is about 1.5×10^{-34} m. This is almost a trillion trillion times smaller than the diameter of a typical air molecule—much smaller than any possible opening through which we could observe interference effects. This explains why the de Broglie wavelength of objects cannot be observed in our everyday experience.

However, in the microscopic world, the wave effects of matter can be observed. Electrons ($m = 9.109 \times 10^{-31}$ kg) accelerated to a speed of 1.4×10^7 m/s have a de Broglie wavelength of about 10^{-10} m, which is approximately equal to the distance between atoms in a crystal. Thus, the atoms in a crystal can act as a three-dimensional grating that should diffract electron waves. Such an experiment was performed by Clinton J. Davisson and Lester H. Germer three years after de Broglie's thesis, and the electrons did create patterns of constructive and destructive interference, such as the pattern in **Figure 2**. This experiment gave confirmation of de Broglie's theory of the dual nature of matter.

The Electron Microscope

A practical device that relies on the wave characteristics of matter is the electron microscope. In principle, the electron microscope is similar to an ordinary compound microscope. But while ordinary microscopes use lenses to bend rays of light that are reflected from a small object, electron microscopes use electric and magnetic fields to accelerate and focus a beam of electrons. Rather than examining the image through an eyepiece, as in an ordinary microscope, a magnetic lens forms an image on a fluorescent screen. Without the fluorescent screen, the image would not be visible.

Electron microscopes are able to distinguish details about 100 times smaller than optical microscopes. Because of their great resolving power, electron microscopes are used in many areas of research. **Figure 3** shows some examples of images created by electron microscopes.

Diffracted Electron Waves In this photograph, electron waves are diffracted by a crystal. Experiments such as this show the wave nature of electrons and thereby provide empirical evidence for de Broglie's theory of the dual nature of matter.

FIGURE 3

Scanning Electron Microscope Images These color-enhanced images from a scanning electron microscope show, from left to right, a flour mite, two strips of Velcro fastened together, and pollen grains.

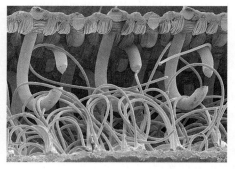

What Is a Hypothesis?

Recall that a hypothesis is a tentative, testable statement based on observations made by a scientist or group of scientists. These observations lead to the development of research questions. Scientists develop experiments to test their hypotheses. Evidence gathered from an experiment either supports or does not support a hypothesis. A hypothesis must be tested multiple times.

In Chapter 2, you read that Galileo questioned accepted theories about the motion of falling objects. Galileo's early work involved the study of pendulums. Objects in free fall moved too rapidly to measure accurately using the instruments available at the time. It has been said that Galileo began his study of pendulums while watching a suspended lamp swing back and forth from a high cathedral ceiling in Italy. He measured the motion in pendulums using his own pulse as a timekeeper, and observed the factors that affected the time it took for one period of the pendulum's swing. Galileo's discovery led to the development of pendulum clocks.

Periodic Motion

Consider the motion of a pendulum and the factors that affect that motion.

- Write a tentative statement—a hypothesis—describing how changing the mass of a pendulum bob may (or may not) affect the period of a pendulum.

- Is your hypothesis testable? Briefly describe how you might test this hypothesis.

Conceptual Challenge

The ability to make assumptions and generate rough estimates is a valuable skill to scientists. Quick estimates allow scientists to narrow the range of possibilities and focus on the most reasonable hypotheses.

Tick Tock Over the course of one year, what distance is traveled by the bob of a pendulum in a grandfather clock?

You can begin addressing the scenario by asking questions such as the following:

- How long is the pendulum?

- What is the maximum displacement of the pendulum bob?

- Approximately how far does the pendulum travel during each period?

- How many seconds are in a year?

BIG IDEA Some events are periodic in nature. The principles of periodic motion can help us understand everything from the motion of a pendulum to the motion of a wave.

SECTION 1 Simple Harmonic Motion

KEY TERM

- In simple harmonic motion, restoring force is proportional to displacement.
- A mass-spring system vibrates with simple harmonic motion, and the spring force is given by Hooke's law.
- For small angles of displacement (<15°), a simple pendulum swings with simple harmonic motion.
- In simple harmonic motion, restoring force and acceleration are maximum at maximum displacement, and speed is maximum at equilibrium.

simple harmonic motion

SECTION 2 Measuring Simple Harmonic Motion

KEY TERMS

- The period of a mass-spring system depends only on the mass and the spring constant. The period of a simple pendulum depends only on the string length and the free-fall acceleration.
- Frequency is the inverse of period.

amplitude
period
frequency

SECTION 3 Properties of Waves

KEY TERMS

- As a wave travels, the particles of the medium vibrate around an equilibrium position.
- In a transverse wave, vibrations are *perpendicular* to the direction of wave motion. In a longitudinal wave, vibrations are *parallel* to the direction of wave motion.
- Wave speed equals frequency times wavelength.

medium
mechanical wave
transverse wave
crest
trough
wavelength
longitudinal wave

SECTION 4 Wave Interactions

KEY TERMS

- If two or more waves are moving through a medium, the resultant wave is found by adding the individual displacements together point by point.
- Standing waves are formed when two waves that have the same frequency, amplitude, and wavelength travel in opposite directions and interfere.

constructive interference
destructive interference
standing wave
node
antinode

VARIABLE SYMBOLS		
Quantities	**Units**	
$F_{elastic}$ spring force	N	newtons
k spring constant	N/m	newtons/meter
T period	s	seconds
f frequency	Hz	hertz = s^{-1}
λ wavelength	m	meters

Problem Solving

See **Appendix D: Equations** for a summary of the equations introduced in this chapter. If you need more problem-solving practice, see **Appendix I: Additional Problems.**

Simple Harmonic Motion

▶ **REVIEWING MAIN IDEAS**

1. What characterizes an object's motion as simple harmonic?

2. List four examples of simple harmonic motion.

3. Does the acceleration of a simple harmonic oscillator remain constant during its motion? Is the acceleration ever zero? Explain.

4. A pendulum is released 40° from its resting position. Is its motion simple harmonic?

5. April is about to release the bob of a pendulum. Before she lets go, what sort of potential energy does the bob have? How does the energy of the bob change as it swings through one full cycle of motion?

CONCEPTUAL QUESTIONS

6. An ideal mass-spring system vibrating with simple harmonic motion would oscillate indefinitely. Explain why.

7. In a simple pendulum, the weight of the bob can be divided into two components: one tangent to the direction of motion of the bob and the other perpendicular to the direction of motion of the bob. Which of these is the restoring force, and why?

PRACTICE PROBLEMS

For problems 8–9, see Sample Problem A.

8. Janet wants to find the spring constant of a given spring, so she hangs the spring vertically and attaches a 0.40 kg mass to the spring's other end. If the spring stretches 3.0 cm from its equilibrium position, what is the spring constant?

9. In preparing to shoot an arrow, an archer pulls a bowstring back 0.40 m by exerting a force that increases uniformly from 0 to 230 N. What is the equivalent spring constant of the bow?

Period and Frequency

▶ **REVIEWING MAIN IDEAS**

10. A child swings on a playground swing. How many times does the child swing through the swing's equilibrium position during the course of a single period of motion?

11. What is the total distance traveled by an object moving back and forth in simple harmonic motion in a time interval equal to its period when its amplitude is equal to A?

12. How is the period of a simple harmonic vibration related to its frequency?

CONCEPTUAL QUESTIONS

13. What happens to the period of a simple pendulum when the pendulum's length is doubled? What happens when the suspended mass is doubled?

14. A pendulum bob is made with a ball filled with water. What would happen to the frequency of vibration of this pendulum if a hole in the ball allowed water to slowly leak out? (Treat the pendulum as a simple pendulum.)

15. If a pendulum clock keeps perfect time at the base of a mountain, will it also keep perfect time when moved to the top of the mountain? Explain.

16. If a grandfather clock is running slow, how can you adjust the length of the pendulum to correct the time?

17. A simple pendulum can be used as an altimeter on a plane. How will the period of the pendulum vary as the plane rises from the ground to its final cruising altitude?

18. Will the period of a vibrating mass-spring system on Earth be different from the period of an identical mass-spring system on the moon? Why or why not?

PRACTICE PROBLEMS

For problems 19–20, see Sample Problem B.

19. Find the length of a pendulum that oscillates with a frequency of 0.16 Hz.

20. A pendulum that moves through its equilibrium position once every 1.000 s is sometimes called a *seconds pendulum.*
    a. What is the period of any seconds pendulum?
    b. In Cambridge, England, a seconds pendulum is 0.9942 m long. What is the free-fall acceleration in Cambridge?
    c. In Tokyo, Japan, a seconds pendulum is 0.9927 m long. What is the free-fall acceleration in Tokyo?

For problem 21, see Sample Problem C.

21. A spring with a spring constant of 1.8×10^2 N/m is attached to a 1.5 kg mass and then set in motion.
    a. What is the period of the mass-spring system?
    b. What is the frequency of the vibration?

Properties of Waves

 **REVIEWING MAIN IDEAS**

22. What is common to all waves?

23. How do transverse and longitudinal waves differ?

24. The figure below depicts a pulse wave traveling on a spring.
    a. In which direction are the particles of the medium vibrating?

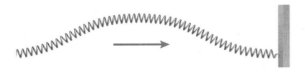

    b. Is this wave transverse or longitudinal?

25. In a stretched spring, several coils are pinched together, and others are spread farther apart than usual. What sort of wave is this?

26. How far does a wave travel in one period?

27. If you shook the end of a rope up and down three times each second, what would be the period of the waves set up in the rope? What would be the frequency?

28. Give three examples of mechanical waves. How are these different from electromagnetic waves, such as light waves?

CONCEPTUAL QUESTIONS

29. How does a single point on a string move as a transverse wave passes by that point?

30. What happens to the wavelength of a wave on a string when the frequency is doubled? What happens to the speed of the wave?

31. Why do sound waves need a medium through which to travel?

32. Two tuning forks with frequencies of 256 Hz and 512 Hz are struck. Which of the sounds will move faster through the air?

33. What is one advantage of transferring energy by electromagnetic waves?

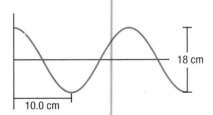

34. A wave traveling in the positive *x* direction with a frequency of 25.0 Hz is shown in the figure above. Find the following values for this wave:
    a. amplitude
    b. wavelength
    c. period
    d. speed

PRACTICE PROBLEMS

For problem 35, see Sample Problem D.

35. Microwaves travel at the speed of light, 3.00×10^8 m/s. When the frequency of microwaves is 9.00×10^9 Hz, what is their wavelength?

Wave Interactions

36. Using the superposition principle, draw the resultant waves for each of the examples below.

(a)    **(b)**

37. What is the difference between constructive interference and destructive interference?

38. Which one of the waveforms shown below is the resultant waveform?

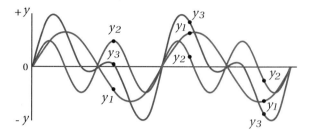

39. Anthony sends a series of pulses of amplitude 24 cm down a string that is attached to a post at one end. Assuming the pulses are reflected with no loss of amplitude, what is the amplitude at a point on the string where two pulses are crossing if:
  a. the string is rigidly attached to the post?
  b. the end at which reflection occurs is free to slide up and down?

CONCEPTUAL QUESTIONS

40. Can more than two waves interfere in a given medium?

41. What is the resultant displacement at a position where destructive interference is complete?

42. When two waves interfere, can the resultant wave be larger than either of the two original waves? If so, under what conditions?

43. Which of the following wavelengths will produce standing waves on a string that is 3.5 m long?
  a. 1.75 m
  b. 3.5 m
  c. 5.0 m
  d. 7.0 m

Mixed Review

44. In an arcade game, a 0.12 kg disk is shot across a frictionless horizontal surface by being compressed against a spring and then released. If the spring has a spring constant of 230 N/m and is compressed from its equilibrium position by 6.0 cm, what is the magnitude of the spring force on the disk at the moment it is released?

45. A child's toy consists of a piece of plastic attached to a spring, as shown at right. The spring is compressed against the floor a distance of 2.0 cm and released. If the spring constant is 85 N/m, what is the magnitude of the spring force acting on the toy at the moment it is released?

46. You dip your finger into a pan of water twice each second, producing waves with crests that are separated by 0.15 m. Determine the frequency, period, and speed of these water waves.

47. A sound wave traveling at 343 m/s is emitted by the foghorn of a tugboat. An echo is heard 2.60 s later. How far away is the reflecting object?

48. The notes produced by a violin range in frequency from approximately 196 Hz to 2637 Hz. Find the possible range of wavelengths in air produced by this instrument when the speed of sound in air is 340 m/s.

49. What is the free-fall acceleration in a location where the period of a 0.850 m long pendulum is 1.86 s?

50. Yellow light travels through a certain glass block at a speed of 1.97×10^8 m/s. The wavelength of the light in this particular type of glass is 3.81×10^{-7} m (381 nm). What is the frequency of the yellow light?

51. A certain pendulum clock that works perfectly on Earth is taken to the moon, where $a_g = 1.63$ m/s². If the clock is started at 12:00 A.M., what will it read after 24.0 h have passed on Earth?

ALTERNATIVE ASSESSMENT

1. Design an experiment to compare the spring constant and period of oscillation of a system built with two (or more) springs connected in two ways: in series (attached end to end) and in parallel (one end of each spring anchored to a common point). If your teacher approves your plan, obtain the necessary equipment and perform the experiment.

2. The rule that the period of a pendulum is determined by its length is a good approximation for amplitudes below 15°. Design an experiment to investigate how amplitudes of oscillation greater than 15° affect the motion of a pendulum. List what equipment you would need, what measurements you would perform, what data you would record, and what you would calculate. If your teacher approves your plan, obtain the necessary equipment and perform the experiment.

3. Research earthquakes and different kinds of seismic waves. Create a presentation about earthquakes that includes answers to the following questions as well as additional information: Do earthquakes travel through oceans? What is transferred from place to place as seismic waves propagate? What determines their speed?

4. Identify examples of periodic motion in nature. Create a chart describing the objects involved, their paths of motion, their periods, and the forces involved. Which of the periodic motions are harmonic, and which are not?

5. Research the active noise reduction (ANR) technology used in noise-cancelling headphones. How does it work? What are some other applications that use ANR technology? Choose one application, and create a brochure to explain how it works.

GRAPHING CALCULATOR PRACTICE

Pendulum

Would a pendulum have the same period of oscillation on Mars, Venus, or Neptune? A pendulum's period, as you learned earlier in this chapter, is described by the following equation:

$$T = 2\pi \sqrt{\frac{L}{a_g}}$$

In this equation, T is the period, L is the length of the pendulum, and a_g is the free-fall acceleration (9.81 m/s^2 on Earth's surface). This equation can be rearranged to solve for L if T is known.

$$L = \frac{a_g T^2}{4\pi^2}$$

In this graphing calculator activity, you will enter the period of a pendulum on Earth's surface. The calculator will use the previous equation to determine L, the length of the pendulum. The calculator will then use this length to display a graph showing how the period of this pendulum changes as free-fall acceleration changes. You will use this graph to find the period of a pendulum on various planets.

Go online to HMHScience.com to find the skillsheet and program for this graphing calculator activity.

Standards-Based Assessment

Record your answers on a separate piece of paper.

MULTIPLE CHOICE

Use the following image and paragraph to answer questions 1 and 2.

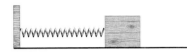

A mass is attached to a spring and moves with simple harmonic motion on a frictionless horizontal surface, as shown above.

1 In what form is the energy in the system when the mass passes through the equilibrium position?

A elastic potential energy

B gravitational potential energy

C kinetic energy

D a combination of two or more of the above

2 If the mass is displaced -0.35 m from its equilibrium position, the restoring force is 7.0 N. What is the spring constant?

A -5.0×10^{-2} N/m

B -2.0×10^{1} N/m

C 5.0×10^{-2} N/m

D 2.0×10^{1} N/m

Use the following image and information for questions 3 and 4.

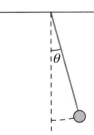

A pendulum bob hangs from a string and moves with simple harmonic motion as shown above.

3 Which of the following does *not* affect the period of the pendulum?

A length of the string

B mass of the pendulum bob

C free-fall acceleration at the pendulum's location

D All of the above affect the period.

4 If the pendulum's length is 2.00 m and $a_g = 9.80$ m/s^2, how many complete oscillations does the pendulum make in 5.00 min?

A 1.76

B 21.6

C 106

D 239

Use the paragraph below to answer questions 5 and 6.

A wave with an amplitude of 0.75 m has the same wavelength as a second wave with an amplitude of 0.53 m. The two waves interfere.

5 What is the amplitude of the resultant wave if the interference is constructive?

A 0.22 m

B 0.53 m

C 0.75 m

D 1.28 m

6 What is the amplitude of the resultant wave if the interference is destructive?

A 0.22 m

B 0.53 m

C 0.75 m

D 1.28 m

7 Two successive crests of a transverse wave are 1.20 m apart. Eight crests pass a given point every 12.0 s. What is the wave speed?

A 0.667 m/s

B 0.800 m/s

C 1.80 m/s

D 9.60 m/s

GRIDDED RESPONSE

8 A visitor to a lighthouse wishes to find out the height of the tower. The visitor ties a spool of thread to a small rock to make a simple pendulum. Then, the visitor hangs the pendulum down a spiral staircase in the center of the tower. The period of oscillation is 9.49 s. What is the height, in meters, of the tower?

1798

Benjamin Thompson (Count Rumford) demonstrates that energy transferred as heat results from mechanical processes, rather than the release of caloric, the heat fluid that has been widely believed to exist in all substances.

$$Q = mc_p\Delta T$$

1800

Alessandro Volta develops the first current-electricity cell using alternating plates of silver and zinc.

$$\Delta V = \frac{\Delta PE_{electric}}{q}$$

1804

Saint-Domingue, under the control of the French-African majority led by **Toussaint-Louverture,** becomes the independent Republic of Haiti. Over the next two decades, most of Europe's western colonies become independent.

1789

The storming of the Bastille marks the climax of the French Revolution.

| 1780 | 1790 | 1800 | 1810 |

1796

Edward Jenner develops the smallpox vaccine.

1801

Thomas Young demonstrates that light rays interfere, providing the first substantial support for a wave theory of light.

$$m\lambda = d(sin\ \theta)$$

1804

Richard Trevithick builds and tests the first steam locomotive. It pulls 10 tons along a distance of 15 km at a speed of 8 km/h.

1810

Kamehameha I unites the Hawaiian islands under a monarchy.

1811

Mathematician **Sophie Germain** writes the first of three papers on the mathematics of vibrating surfaces. She later addresses one of the most famous problems in mathematics—Fermat's last theorem—proving it to be true for a wide range of conditions.

1818

Mary Shelley writes *Frankenstein, or the Modern Prometheus*. Primarily thought of as a horror novel, the book's emphasis on science and its moral consequences also qualifies it as the first "science fiction" novel.

1830

Hector Berlioz composes his *Symphonie Fantastique*, one of the first Romantic works for large orchestra that tells a story with music.

| 1800 | 1810 | 1820 | 1830 |

1814

Augustin Fresnel begins his research in optics, the results of which will confirm and explain **Thomas Young's** discovery of interference and will firmly establish the wave model of light first suggested by **Christiaan Huygens** over a century earlier.

$$sin\ \theta = \frac{m\lambda}{a}$$

1820

Hans Christian Oersted demonstrates that an electric current produces a magnetic field. (**Gian Domenico Romagnosi,** an amateur scientist, discovered the effect 18 years earlier but, at the time, attracted no attention.) **André Marie Ampère** repeats Oersted's experiment and formulates the law of electromagnetism that today bears his name.

$$F_{magnetic} = BI\ell$$

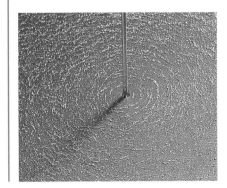

1826

Katsushika Hokusai begins his series of prints *Thirty-Six Views of Mount Fuji.*

403

Bats use sound waves to navigate and to learn about their prey. Musical instruments create a variety of pleasing sounds through different harmonics.

Some marine mammals, such as the dolphins pictured here, use sound waves to locate distant objects. In this process, called *echolocation,* a dolphin produces a rapid train of short sound pulses that travel through the water, bounce off distant objects, and reflect back to the dolphin. From these echoes, dolphins can determine the size, shape, speed, and distance of their potential prey.

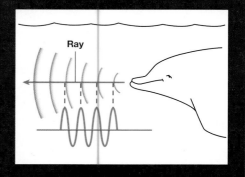

Ray

CHAPTER 12
Sound

SECTION 1
Sound Waves

SECTION 2
Sound Intensity and Resonance

SECTION 3
Harmonics

BIG IDEA

Sound waves transfer energy through vibrations. Characteristics of the sounds we perceive are due to properties of the sound waves and the medium through which they travel.

 ONLINE Physics
HMHScience.com

ONLINE LABS
- Resonance and the Nature of Sound
- Speed of Sound
- Standing Waves
- S.T.E.M. Lab Building a Musical Instrument

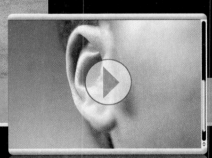

GO ONLINE **Animated Physics**
HMHScience.com

Resonance

(bl) ©Jupiter Images/Getty Images

- Explain how sound waves are produced.

- Relate frequency to pitch.

- Compare the speed of sound in various media.

- Recognize the Doppler effect, and determine the direction of a frequency shift when there is relative motion between a source and an observer.

SC.912.P.10.21 Qualitatively describe the shift in frequency in sound or electromagnetic waves due to the relative motion of a source or a receiver.

Sound Waves

Key Terms

compression   pitch
rarefaction   Doppler effect

The Production of Sound Waves

Whether a sound wave conveys the shrill whine of a jet engine or the melodic whistling of a bird, it begins with a vibrating object. We will explore how sound waves are produced by considering a vibrating tuning fork, as shown in **Figure 1.1(a)**.

The vibrating prong of a tuning fork, shown in **Figure 1.1(b)**, sets the air molecules near it in motion. As the prong swings to the right, as in **Figure 1.1(c)**, the air molecules in front of the movement are forced closer together. (This situation is exaggerated in the figure for clarity.) Such a region of high molecular density and high air pressure is called a **compression.** As the prong moves to the left, as in **Figure 1.1(d)**, the molecules to the right spread apart, and the density and air pressure in this region become lower than normal. This region of lower density and pressure is called a **rarefaction.**

As the tuning fork continues to vibrate, a series of compressions and rarefactions forms and spreads away from each prong. These compressions and rarefactions spread out in all directions, like ripple waves on a pond. When the tuning fork vibrates with simple harmonic motion, the air molecules move in a pattern that can be treated as simple harmonic motion.

FIGURE 1.1

Compressions and Rarefactions

(a) The sound from a tuning fork is produced by **(b)** the vibrations of each of its prongs. **(c)** When a prong swings to the right, there is a region of high density and pressure. **(d)** When the prong swings back to the left, a region of lower density and pressure exists.

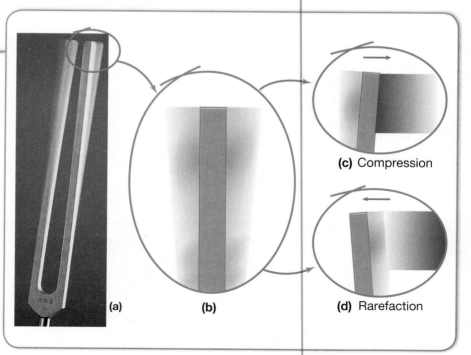

(a)   (b)   (c) Compression

(d) Rarefaction

FIGURE 1.2

Representing Sound Waves **(a)** As this tuning fork vibrates, **(b)** a series of compressions and rarefactions moves away from each prong. **(c)** The crests of this sine wave correspond to compressions, and the troughs correspond to rarefactions.

(a)

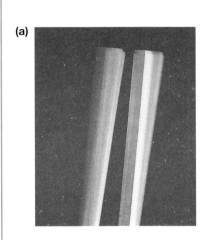

(b)

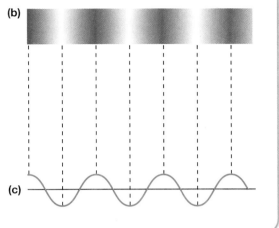

(c)

Sound waves are longitudinal.

In sound waves, the vibrations of air molecules are parallel to the direction of wave motion. Thus, sound waves are longitudinal. The simplest longitudinal wave produced by a vibrating object can be represented by a sine curve. In **Figure 1.2,** the crests correspond to compressions (regions of higher pressure), and the troughs correspond to rarefactions (regions of lower pressure). Thus, the sine curve represents the changes in air pressure due to the propagation of the sound waves. Note that **Figure 1.2** shows an idealized case. This example disregards energy losses that would decrease the wave amplitude.

Characteristics of Sound Waves

As discussed earlier, *frequency* is defined as the number of cycles per unit of time. Sound waves that the average human ear can hear, called *audible* sound waves, have frequencies between 20 and 20 000 Hz. (An individual's hearing depends on a variety of factors, including age and experiences with loud noises.) Sound waves with frequencies less than 20 Hz are called *infrasonic* waves, and those above 20 000 Hz are called *ultrasonic* waves.

It may seem confusing to use the term *sound waves* for infrasonic or ultrasonic waves, because humans cannot hear these sounds, but these waves consist of the same types of vibrations as the sounds that we can hear. The range of audible sound waves depends on the ability of the average human ear to detect their vibrations. Dogs can hear ultrasonic waves that humans cannot.

Did YOU Know?

Elephants use infrasonic sound waves to communicate with one another. Their large ears enable them to detect these low-frequency sound waves, which have relatively long wavelengths. Elephants can effectively communicate in this way, even when they are separated by many kilometers.

Sound **407**

Frequency determines pitch.

The frequency of an audible sound wave determines how high or low we perceive the sound to be, which is known as **pitch.** As the frequency of a sound wave increases, the pitch rises. The frequency of a wave is an objective quantity that can be measured, while pitch refers to how different frequencies are perceived by the human ear. Pitch depends not only on frequency but also on other factors, such as background noise and loudness.

Speed of sound depends on the medium.

Sound waves can travel through solids, liquids, and gases. Because waves consist of particle vibrations, the speed of a wave depends on how quickly one particle can transfer its motion to another particle. For example, solid particles respond more rapidly to a disturbance than gas particles do, because the molecules of a solid are closer together than those of a gas are. As a result, sound waves generally travel faster through solids than through gases. **Figure 1.3** shows the speed of sound waves in various media.

WHY IT MATTERS S.T.E.M.

Ultrasound Images

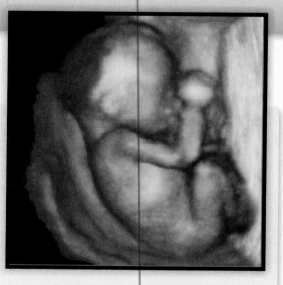

Ultrasonic waves can be used to produce images of objects inside the body. Such imaging is possible because sound waves are partially reflected when they reach a boundary between two materials of different densities. The images produced by ultrasonic waves are clearer and more detailed than those that can be produced by lower-frequency sound waves, because the short wavelengths of ultrasonic waves are easily reflected off small objects. Audible and infrasonic sound waves are not as effective, because their longer wavelengths pass around small objects.

In order for ultrasonic waves to "see" an object inside the body, the wavelength of the waves used must be about the same size as or smaller than the object. A typical frequency used in an ultrasonic device is about 10 MHz. The speed of an ultrasonic wave in human tissue is about 1500 m/s, so the wavelength of 10 MHz waves is $\lambda = v/f = 0.15$ mm. A 10 MHz ultrasonic device will not detect objects smaller than this size.

Physicians commonly use ultrasonic waves to observe fetuses. In this process, a crystal emits ultrasonic pulses. The same crystal acts as a receiver and detects the reflected sound waves. These reflected sound waves are converted to an electrical signal, which forms an image on a fluorescent screen. By repeating this process for different portions of the mother's abdomen, a physician can obtain a complete picture of the fetus, as shown above. These images allow doctors to detect some types of fetal abnormalities.

The speed of sound also depends on the temperature of the medium. As temperature rises, the particles of a gas collide more frequently. Thus, in a gas, the disturbance can spread faster at higher temperatures than at lower temperatures. In liquids and solids, the particles are close enough together that the difference due to temperature changes is less noticeable.

Sound waves propagate in three dimensions.

Sound waves actually travel away from a vibrating source in all three dimensions. When a musician plays a saxophone in the middle of a room, the resulting sound can be heard throughout the room, because the sound waves spread out in all directions. The wave fronts of sound waves spreading in three dimensions are approximately spherical. To simplify, we shall assume that the wave fronts are exactly spherical unless stated otherwise.

Spherical waves can be represented graphically in two dimensions with a series of circles surrounding the source, as shown in **Figure 1.4.** The circles represent the centers of compressions, called *wave fronts*. Because we are considering a three-dimensional phenomenon in two dimensions, each circle represents a spherical area.

Because each wave front locates the center of a compression, the distance between adjacent wave fronts is equal to one wavelength, λ. The radial lines perpendicular to the wave fronts are called *rays*.

FIGURE 1.3

SPEED OF SOUND IN VARIOUS MEDIA

Medium	v (m/s)
Gases	
air (0°C)	331
air (25°C)	346
air (100°C)	366
helium (0°C)	972
hydrogen (0°C)	1290
oxygen (0°C)	317
Liquids at 25°C	
methyl alcohol	1140
seawater	1530
water	1490
Solids	
aluminum	5100
copper	3560
iron	5130
lead	1320
vulcanized rubber	54

FIGURE 1.4

Spherical Waves In this representation of a spherical wave, the wave fronts represent compressions, and the rays show the direction of wave motion. Each wave front corresponds to a crest of the sine curve. In turn, the sine curve corresponds to a single ray.

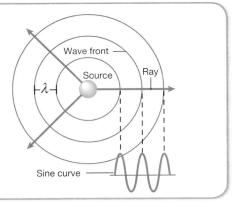

Conceptual Challenge

Music from a Trumpet Suppose you hear music being played from a trumpet that is across the room from you. Compressions and rarefactions from the sound wave reach your ear, and you interpret these vibrations as sound. Were the air particles that are vibrating near your ear carried across the room by the sound wave? How do you know?

Lightning and Thunder Light waves travel nearly 1 million times faster than sound waves in air. With this in mind, explain how the distance to a lightning bolt can be determined by counting the seconds between the flash and the sound of the thunder.

FIGURE 1.5

Spherical Waves Spherical wave fronts that are a great distance from the source can be approximated with parallel planes known as *plane waves.*

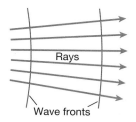

Rays

Wave fronts

Rays indicate the direction of the wave motion. The sine curve used in our previous representation of sound waves, also shown in **Figure 1.4**, corresponds to a single ray. Because crests of the sine curve represent compressions, each wave front crossed by this ray corresponds to a crest of the sine curve.

Consider a small portion of a spherical wave front that is many wavelengths away from the source, as shown in **Figure 1.5**. In this case, the rays are nearly parallel lines, and the wave fronts are nearly parallel planes. Thus, at distances from the source that are great relative to the wavelength, we can approximate spherical wave fronts with parallel planes. Such waves are called *plane waves.* Any small portion of a spherical wave that is far from the source can be considered a plane wave. Plane waves can be treated as one-dimensional waves all traveling in the same direction, as in the chapter "Vibrations and Waves."

The Doppler Effect

If you stand on the street while an ambulance speeds by with its siren on, you will notice the pitch of the siren change. The pitch will be higher as the ambulance approaches and will be lower as it moves away. As you read earlier in this section, the pitch of a sound depends on its frequency. But in this case, the siren is not changing its frequency. How can we account for this change in pitch?

Relative motion creates a change in frequency.

If a siren sounds in a parked ambulance, an observer standing on the street hears the same frequency that the driver hears, as you would expect. When an ambulance is moving, as shown in **Figure 1.6,** there is relative motion between the moving ambulance and a stationary observer. This relative motion affects the way the wave fronts of the sound waves produced by the siren are perceived by an observer. (For simplicity's sake, assume that the sound waves produced by the siren are spherical.)

Although the frequency of the siren remains constant, the wave fronts reach an observer in front of the ambulance (Observer A) more often than they would if the ambulance were stationary. The reason is that the source of the sound waves is moving toward the observer. The speed of sound in the air does not change, because the speed depends only on the temperature of the air. Thus, the product of wavelength and frequency remains constant. Because the wavelength is less, the frequency heard by Observer A is *greater* than the source frequency.

FIGURE 1.6

Doppler Effect As this ambulance moves to the left, Observer A hears the siren at a higher frequency than the driver does, while Observer B hears a lower frequency.

Observer A

Observer B

For the same reason, the wave fronts reach an observer behind the ambulance (Observer B) less often than they would if the ambulance were stationary. As a result, the frequency heard by Observer B is *less* than the source frequency. This frequency shift is known as the **Doppler effect.** The Doppler effect is named for the Austrian physicist Christian Doppler (1803–1853), who first described it.

We have considered a moving source with respect to a stationary observer, but the Doppler effect also occurs when the observer is moving with respect to a stationary source or when both are moving at different velocities. In other words, the Doppler effect occurs whenever there is *relative motion* between the source of waves and an observer. (If the observer is moving instead of the source, the wavelength in air does not change, but the frequency at which waves arrive at the ear is altered by the motion of the ear relative to the medium.) Although the Doppler effect is most commonly experienced with sound waves, it is a phenomenon common to all waves, including electromagnetic waves, such as visible light.

Doppler effect an observed change in frequency when there is relative motion between the source of waves and an observer

---

✔ SECTION 1 **FORMATIVE ASSESSMENT**

▶ Reviewing Main Ideas

1. What is the relationship between frequency and pitch?

2. Dolphin echolocation is similar to ultrasound. Reflected sound waves allow a dolphin to form an image of the object that reflected the waves. Dolphins can produce sound waves with frequencies ranging from 0.25 kHz to 220 kHz, but only those at the upper end of this spectrum are used in echolocation. Explain why high-frequency waves work better than low-frequency waves.

3. Sound pulses emitted by a dolphin travel through 20°C ocean water at a rate of 1450 m/s. In 20°C air, these pulses would travel 342.9 m/s. How can you account for this difference in speed?

Interpreting Graphics

4. Could a portion of the innermost wave front shown in **Figure 1.7** be approximated by a plane wave? Why or why not?

5. **Figure 1.8** is a diagram of the Doppler effect in a ripple tank. In which direction is the source of these ripple waves moving?

6. If the source of the waves in **Figure 1.8** is stationary, which way must the ripple tank be moving?

✔ Critical Thinking

7. As a dolphin swims toward a fish, the dolphin sends out sound waves to determine the direction the fish is moving. If the frequency of the reflected waves is higher than that of the emitted waves, is the dolphin catching up to the fish or falling behind?

Figure 1.7

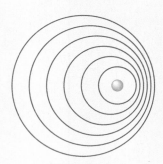

Figure 1.8

Sound Intensity and Resonance

Key Terms

intensity   decibel   resonance

Sound Intensity

When a piano player strikes a piano key, a hammer inside the piano strikes a wire and causes it to vibrate, as shown in **Figure 2.1.** The wire's vibrations are then transferred to the piano's soundboard. As the soundboard vibrates, it exerts a force on air molecules around it, causing the air molecules to move. Because this force is exerted through displacement of the soundboard, the soundboard does work on the air. Thus, as the soundboard vibrates back and forth, its kinetic energy is converted into sound waves. This is one reason that the vibration of the soundboard gradually dies out.

Intensity is the rate of energy flow through a given area.

As described in Section 1, sound waves traveling in air are longitudinal waves. As the sound waves travel outward from the source, energy is transferred from one air molecule to the next. The rate at which this energy is transferred through a unit area of the plane wave is called the **intensity** of the wave. Because power, P, is defined as the rate of energy transfer, intensity can also be described in terms of power.

$$\text{intensity} = \frac{\Delta E/\Delta t}{\text{area}} = \frac{P}{\text{area}}$$

The SI unit for power is the watt. Thus, intensity has units of watts per square meter (W/m^2). In a spherical wave, energy propagates equally in all directions; no one direction is preferred over any other. In this case, the power emitted by the source (P) is distributed over a spherical surface (area = $4\pi r^2$), assuming that there is no absorption in the medium.

> **Intensity of a Spherical Wave**
>
> $$\text{intensity} = \frac{P}{4\pi r^2}$$
>
> $$\textbf{intensity} = \frac{\textbf{(power)}}{(4\pi)\textbf{(distance from the source)}^2}$$

This equation shows that the intensity of a sound wave decreases as the distance from the source (r) increases. This occurs because the same amount of energy is spread over a larger area.

FIGURE 2.1

Inside a Piano As a piano wire vibrates, it transfers energy to the piano's soundboard, which in turn transfers energy into the air in the form of sound.

intensity the rate at which energy flows through a unit area perpendicular to the direction of wave motion

Intensity of Sound Waves

GO ONLINE

Interactive Demo
HMHScience.com

Sample Problem A What is the intensity of the sound waves produced by a trumpet at a distance of 3.2 m when the power output of the trumpet is 0.20 W? Assume that the sound waves are spherical.

 SOLVE

Given: $P = 0.20$ W $r = 3.2$ m

Unknown: Intensity = ?

Use the equation for the intensity of a spherical wave.

$$\text{Intensity} = \frac{P}{4\pi r^2}$$

$$\text{Intensity} = \frac{0.20 \text{ W}}{4\pi(3.2 \text{ m})^2}$$

Calculator Solution

The calculator answer for intensity is 0.0015542. This is rounded to 1.6×10^{-3} because each of the given quantities has two significant figures.

$$\boxed{\text{Intensity} = 1.6 \times 10^{-3} \text{ W/m}^2}$$

Practice

1. Calculate the intensity of the sound waves from an electric guitar's amplifier at a distance of 5.0 m when its power output is equal to each of the following values:

   a. 0.25 W

   b. 0.50 W

   c. 2.0 W

2. At a maximum level of loudness, the power output of a 75-piece orchestra radiated as sound is 70.0 W. What is the intensity of these sound waves to a listener who is sitting 25.0 m from the orchestra?

3. If the intensity of a person's voice is 4.6×10^{-7} W/m^2 at a distance of 2.0 m, how much sound power does that person generate?

4. How much power is radiated as sound from a band whose intensity is 1.6×10^{-3} W/m^2 at a distance of 15 m?

5. The power output of a tuba is 0.35 W. At what distance is the sound intensity of the tuba 1.2×10^{-3} W/m^2?

FIGURE 2.2

Range of Human Hearing

Range of Human Hearing Human hearing depends on both the frequency and the intensity of sound waves. Sounds in the middle of the spectrum of frequencies can be heard more easily (at lower intensities) than those at lower and higher frequencies.

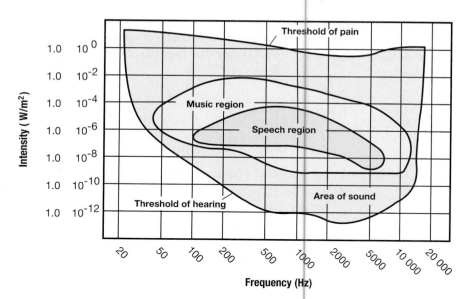

Range of Audibility of an Average Human Ear

Intensity and frequency determine which sounds are audible.

The frequency of sound waves heard by the average human ranges from 20 to 20 000 Hz. Intensity is also a factor in determining which sound waves are audible. **Figure 2.2** shows how the range of audibility of the average human ear depends on both frequency and intensity. Sounds at low frequencies (those below 50 Hz) or high frequencies (those above 12 000 Hz) must be relatively intense to be heard, whereas sounds in the middle of the spectrum are audible at lower intensities.

The softest sounds that can be heard by the average human ear occur at a frequency of about 1000 Hz and an intensity of 1.0×10^{-12} W/m^2. Such a sound is said to be at the *threshold of hearing*. The threshold of hearing at each frequency is represented by the lowest curve in **Figure 2.2.**

For frequencies near 1000 Hz and at the threshold of hearing, the changes in pressure due to compressions and rarefactions are about three ten-billionths of atmospheric pressure. The maximum displacement of an air molecule at the threshold of hearing is approximately 1×10^{-11} m. Comparing this number to the diameter of a typical air molecule (about 1×10^{-10} m) reveals that the ear is an extremely sensitive detector of sound waves.

The loudest sounds that the human ear can tolerate have an intensity of about 1.0 W/m^2. This is known as the *threshold of pain*, because sounds with greater intensities can produce pain in addition to hearing. The highest curve in **Figure 2.2** represents the threshold of pain at each frequency. Exposure to sounds above the threshold of pain can cause immediate damage to the ear, even if no pain is felt. Prolonged exposure to sounds of lower intensities can also damage the ear. Note that the threshold of hearing and the threshold of pain merge at both high and low ends of the spectrum.

Did YOU Know?

A 75-piece orchestra produces about 75 W at its loudest. This is comparable to the power required to keep one medium-sized electric light bulb burning. Speech has even less power. It would take the conversation of about 2 million people to provide the amount of power required to keep a 50 W light bulb burning.

Relative intensity is measured in decibels.

Just as the frequency of a sound wave determines its pitch, the intensity of a wave approximately determines its perceived loudness. However, loudness is not directly proportional to intensity. The reason is that the sensation of loudness is approximately logarithmic in the human ear.

Relative intensity is the ratio of the intensity of a given sound wave to the intensity at the threshold of hearing. Because of the logarithmic dependence of perceived loudness on intensity, using a number equal to 10 times the logarithm of the relative intensity provides a good indicator for human perceptions of loudness. This measure of loudness is referred to as the *decibel level.* The decibel level is dimensionless because it is proportional to the logarithm of a ratio. A dimensionless unit called the **decibel** (dB) is used for values on this scale.

The conversion of intensity to decibel level is shown in **Figure 2.3.** Notice in **Figure 2.3** that when the intensity is multiplied by ten, 10 dB are added to the decibel level. A given difference in decibels corresponds to a fixed difference in perceived loudness. Although much more intensity (0.9 W/m^2) is added between 110 and 120 dB than between 10 and 20 dB (9×10^{-11} W/m^2), in each case the perceived loudness increases by the same amount.

decibel a dimensionless unit that describes the ratio of two intensities of sound; the threshold of hearing is commonly used as the reference intensity

FIGURE 2.3

CONVERSION OF INTENSITY TO DECIBEL LEVEL

Intensity (W/m^2)	Decibel level (dB)	Examples
1.0×10^{-12}	0	threshold of hearing
1.0×10^{-11}	10	rustling leaves
1.0×10^{-10}	20	quiet whisper
1.0×10^{-9}	30	whisper
1.0×10^{-8}	40	mosquito buzzing
1.0×10^{-7}	50	normal conversation
1.0×10^{-6}	60	air conditioner at 6 m
1.0×10^{-5}	70	vacuum cleaner
1.0×10^{-4}	80	busy traffic, alarm clock
1.0×10^{-3}	90	lawn mower
1.0×10^{-2}	100	subway, power motor
1.0×10^{-1}	110	auto horn at 1 m
1.0×10^{0}	120	threshold of pain
1.0×10^{1}	130	thunderclap, machine gun
1.0×10^{3}	150	nearby jet airplane

Did YOU Know?

The original unit of decibel level is the *bel,* named in honor of Alexander Graham Bell, the inventor of the telephone. The decibel is equivalent to 0.1 bel.

FIGURE 2.4

Forced Vibrations and Resonance

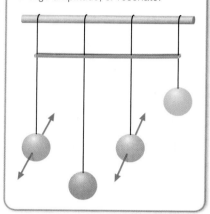

Forced Vibrations If one blue pendulum is set in motion, only the other blue pendulum, whose length is the same, will eventually oscillate with a large amplitude, or resonate.

When an isolated guitar string is held taut and plucked, hardly any sound is heard. When the same string is placed on a guitar and plucked, the intensity of the sound increases dramatically. What is responsible for this difference? To find the answer to this question, consider a set of pendulums suspended from a beam and bound by a loose rubber band, as shown in **Figure 2.4.** If one of the pendulums is set in motion, its vibrations are transferred by the rubber band to the other pendulums, which will also begin vibrating. This is called a *forced vibration.*

The vibrating strings of a guitar force the bridge of the guitar to vibrate, and the bridge in turn transfers its vibrations to the guitar body. These forced vibrations are called *sympathetic vibrations.* Because the guitar body has a larger area than the strings do, it enables the strings' vibrations to be transferred to the air more efficiently. As a result, the intensity of the sound is increased, and the strings' vibrations die out faster than they would if they were not attached to the body of the guitar. In other words, the guitar body allows the energy exchange between the strings and the air to happen more efficiently, thereby increasing the intensity of the sound produced.

In an electric guitar, string vibrations are translated into electrical impulses, which can be amplified as much as desired. An electric guitar can produce sounds that are much more intense than those of an unamplified acoustic guitar, which uses only the forced vibrations of the guitar's body to increase the intensity of the sound from the vibrating strings.

Vibration at the natural frequency produces resonance.

As you saw in the chapter on waves, the frequency of a pendulum depends on its string length. Thus, every pendulum will vibrate at a certain frequency, known as its *natural frequency.* In **Figure 2.4,** the two blue pendulums have the same natural frequency, while the red and green pendulums have different natural frequencies. When the first blue pendulum is set in motion, the red and green pendulums will vibrate only slightly, but the second blue pendulum will oscillate with a much larger amplitude, because its natural frequency matches the frequency of the pendulum that was initially set in motion. This system is said to be in

Quick LAB | RESONANCE

Go to a playground, and swing on one of the swings. Try pumping (or being pushed) at different rates—faster than, slower than, and equal to the natural frequency of the swing. Observe whether the rate at which you pump (or are pushed) affects how easily the amplitude of

the vibration increases. Are some rates more effective at building your amplitude than others? You should find that the pushes are most effective when they match the swing's natural frequency. Explain how your results support the statement that resonance

works best when the frequency of the applied force matches the system's natural frequency.

MATERIALS
• swing set

resonance. Because energy is transferred from one pendulum to the other, the amplitude of vibration of the first blue pendulum will decrease as the second blue pendulum's amplitude increases.

A striking example of structural resonance occurred in 1940, when the Tacoma Narrows bridge in Washington, shown in **Figure 2.5,** was set in motion by the wind. High winds set up standing waves in the bridge, causing the bridge to oscillate at one of its natural frequencies. The amplitude of the vibrations increased until the bridge collapsed. A more recent example of structural resonance occurred during the Loma Prieta earthquake near Oakland, California, in 1989, when part of the upper deck of a freeway collapsed. The collapse of this particular section of roadway has been traced to the fact that the earthquake waves had a frequency of 1.5 Hz, very close to the natural frequency of that section of the roadway.

resonance a phenomenon that occurs when the frequency of a force applied to a system matches the natural frequency of vibration of the system, resulting in a large amplitude of vibration

FIGURE 2.5

Effects of Resonance On November 7, 1940, the Tacoma Narrows suspension bridge collapsed, just four months after it opened. Standing waves caused by strong winds set the bridge in motion and led to its collapse.

Conceptual Challenge

Concert If a 15-person musical ensemble gains 15 new members, so that its size doubles, will a listener perceive the music created by the ensemble to be twice as loud? Why or why not?

A Noisy Factory Federal regulations require that no office or factory worker be exposed to noise levels that average above 90 dB over an 8 h day. Thus, a factory that currently averages 100 dB must reduce its noise level by 10 dB. Assuming that each piece of machinery produces the same amount of noise, what percentage of equipment must be removed? Explain your answer.

Broken Crystal Opera singers have been known to set crystal goblets in vibration with their powerful voices. In fact, an amplified human voice can shatter the glass, but only at certain fundamental frequencies. Speculate about why only certain fundamental frequencies will break the glass.

Electric Guitars Electric guitars, which use electric amplifiers to magnify their sound, can have a variety of shapes, but acoustic guitars all have the same basic shape. Explain why.

FIGURE 2.6

The Human Ear Sound waves travel through the three regions of the ear and are then transmitted to the brain as impulses through nerve endings on the basilar membrane.

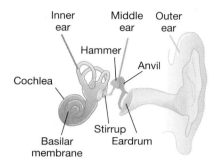

The human ear transmits vibrations that cause nerve impulses.

The human ear is divided into three sections—outer, middle, and inner—as shown in **Figure 2.6**. Sound waves travel down the ear canal of the outer ear. The ear canal terminates at a thin, flat piece of tissue called the *eardrum*.

The eardrum vibrates with the sound waves and transfers these vibrations to the three small bones of the middle ear, known as the *hammer*, the *anvil*, and the *stirrup*. These bones in turn transmit the vibrations to the inner ear, which contains a snail-shaped tube about 2 cm long called the *cochlea*.

The *basilar membrane* runs through the coiled cochlea, dividing it roughly in half. The basilar membrane has different natural frequencies at different positions along its length, according to the width and thickness of the membrane at that point. Sound waves of varying frequencies resonate at different spots along the basilar membrane, creating impulses in hair cells—specialized nerve cells—embedded in the membrane. These impulses are then sent to the brain, which interprets them as sounds of varying frequencies.

SECTION 2 FORMATIVE ASSESSMENT

Reviewing Main Ideas

1. When the decibel level of traffic in the street goes from 40 to 60 dB, how much greater is the intensity of the noise?

2. If two flutists play their instruments together at the same intensity, is the sound twice as loud as that of either flutist playing alone at that intensity? Why or why not?

3. A tuning fork consists of two metal prongs that vibrate at a single frequency when struck lightly. What will happen if a vibrating tuning fork is placed near another tuning fork of the same frequency? Explain.

4. A certain microphone placed in the ocean is sensitive to sounds emitted by dolphins. To produce a usable signal, sound waves striking the microphone must have a decibel level of 10 dB. If dolphins emit sound waves with a power of 0.050 W, how far can a dolphin be from the microphone and still be heard? (Assume the sound waves propagate spherically, and disregard absorption of the sound waves.)

Critical Thinking

5. Which of the following factors change when a sound gets louder? Which change when a pitch gets higher?
   a. intensity
   b. speed of the sound waves
   c. frequency
   d. decibel level
   e. wavelength
   f. amplitude

Hearing Loss

About 10 percent of all Americans have some degree of hearing loss. There are three basic types of hearing loss. *Conductive hearing loss* is an impairment of the transmission of sound waves in the outer ear or transmission of vibrations in the middle ear. Conductive hearing loss is most often caused by improper development of the parts of the outer or middle ear or by damage to these parts of the ear by physical trauma or disease. Conductive hearing loss can often be corrected with medicine or surgery. *Neural hearing loss* is caused by problems with the auditory nerve, which carries signals from the inner ear to the brain. One common cause of neural hearing loss is a tumor pressing against the auditory nerve. *Sensory hearing loss* is caused by damage to the inner ear, particularly the microscopic hair cells in the cochlea.

Sensory hearing loss can be present at birth and may be genetic or due to disease or developmental disorders. However, the most common source of damage to hair cells is exposure to loud noise. Short-term exposure to loud noise can cause ringing in the ears and temporary hearing impairment. Frequent or long-term exposure to noise above 80 dB—including noise from familiar sources such as hair dryers or lawn mowers—can damage the hair cells permanently.

The hair cells in the cochlea are not like the hair on your head or skin. They are highly specialized nerve cells that cannot be repaired or replaced by the body when they are severely damaged or destroyed. Cochlear hair cells can recover from minor damage, but if the source of the damage recurs frequently, even if it is only moderately loud noise, the hair cells can become permanently damaged. It is therefore important to protect yourself from sensory hearing loss by reducing your exposure to loud noise or by using a noise-dampening headset or earplugs that fully block the ear canal when you must be exposed to loud noise.

To prevent damage to their ears, people should wear ear protection when working with power tools.

Permanent sensory hearing loss usually occurs gradually, sometimes over 20 years or more. Because the hair cells that respond to higher-pitched sounds are smaller and more delicate, sensitivity to sounds with frequencies around 20 kHz is usually the first to be lost. Loss of sensitivity to sounds with frequencies around 4 kHz is often the first to be noticed, because these frequencies are in the upper range of human speech. People who are starting to lose their hearing often have trouble hearing higher-pitched voices or hearing consonant sounds such as *s, t, p, d,* and *f.* As the hearing loss advances, loss of sensitivity to a wider range of sounds follows.

Birds can regrow damaged hair cells. Scientists are studying this process to see if a similar process can be triggered in humans. For now, however, there is no "cure" for hearing loss, but some remedies are available. *Hearing aids* make any sounds that reach the ear louder. *Assistive listening devices* serve to amplify a specific small range of frequencies for people who have only partial hearing loss in that range. *Cochlear implants* use an electrode that is surgically implanted into the cochlea through a hole behind the outer ear. Electrical signals to the electrode stimulate the auditory nerve directly, in effect bypassing the hair cells altogether.

▶ Differentiate between the harmonic series of open and closed pipes.

▶ Calculate the harmonics of a vibrating string and of open and closed pipes.

▶ Relate the frequency difference between two waves to the number of beats heard per second.

Harmonics

Key Terms

fundamental frequency   timbre
harmonic series   beat

Standing Waves on a Vibrating String

As discussed in the chapter "Vibrations and Waves," a variety of standing waves can occur when a string is fixed at both ends and set into vibration. The vibrations on the string of a musical instrument, such as the violin in **Figure 3.1,** usually consist of many standing waves together at the same time, each of which has a different wavelength and frequency. So the sounds you hear from a stringed instrument, even those that sound like a single pitch, actually consist of multiple frequencies.

Figure 3.2, on the next page, shows several possible vibrations on an idealized string. The ends of the string, which cannot vibrate, must always be nodes (N). The simplest vibration that can occur is shown in the first row of **Figure 3.2.** In this case, the center of the string experiences the most displacement, and so it is an antinode (A). Because the distance from one node to the next is always half a wavelength, the string length (L) must equal $\lambda_1/2$. Thus, the wavelength is twice the string length ($\lambda_1 = 2L$).

As described in the chapter on waves, the speed of a wave equals the frequency times the wavelength, which can be rearranged as shown.

$$v = f\lambda, \text{ so } f = \frac{v}{\lambda}$$

By substituting the value for wavelength found above into this equation for frequency, we see that the frequency of this vibration is equal to the speed of the wave divided by twice the string length.

$$\text{fundamental frequency} = f_1 = \frac{v}{\lambda_1} = \frac{v}{2L}$$

This frequency of vibration is called the **fundamental frequency** of the vibrating string. Because frequency is inversely proportional to wavelength and because we are considering the greatest possible wavelength, the fundamental frequency is the lowest possible frequency of a standing wave on this string.

Harmonics are integral multiples of the fundamental frequency.

The next possible standing wave for a string is shown in the second row of **Figure 3.2.** In this case, there are three nodes instead of two, so the string length is equal to one wavelength. Because this wavelength is half the previous wavelength, the frequency of this wave is twice that of the fundamental frequency.

$$f_2 = 2f_1$$

FIGURE 3.1

Stringed Instruments The vibrating strings of a violin produce standing waves whose frequencies depend on the string lengths.

fundamental frequency the lowest frequency of vibration of a standing wave

FIGURE 3.2

THE HARMONIC SERIES

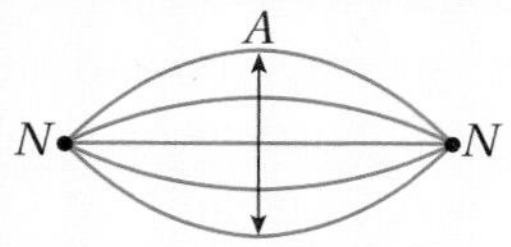	$\lambda_1 = 2L$	f_1	fundamental frequency, or first harmonic
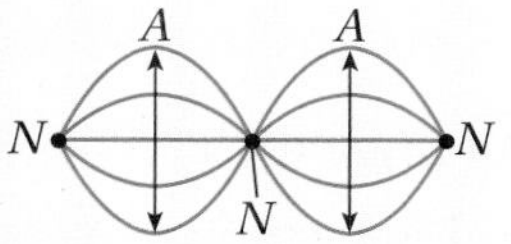	$\lambda_2 = L$	$f_2 = 2f_1$	second harmonic
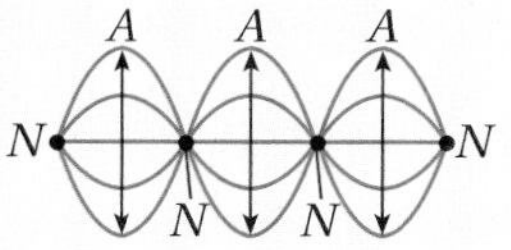	$\lambda_3 = \frac{2}{3}L$	$f_3 = 3f_1$	third harmonic
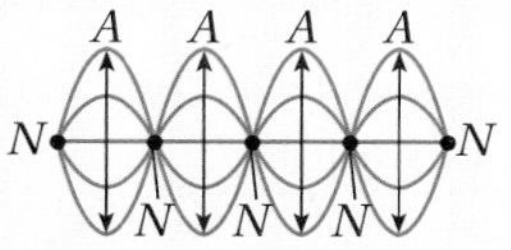	$\lambda_4 = \frac{1}{2}L$	$f_4 = 4f_1$	fourth harmonic

This pattern continues, and the frequency of the standing wave shown in the third row of **Figure 3.2** is three times the fundamental frequency. More generally, the frequencies of the standing wave patterns are all integral multiples of the fundamental frequency. These frequencies form what is called a **harmonic series.** The fundamental frequency (f_1) corresponds to the first harmonic, the next frequency (f_2) corresponds to the second harmonic, and so on.

Because each harmonic is an integral multiple of the fundamental frequency, the equation for the fundamental frequency can be generalized to include the entire harmonic series. Thus, $f_n = nf_1$, where f_1 is the fundamental frequency $(f_1 = \frac{v}{2L})$ and f_n is the frequency of the nth harmonic. The general form of the equation is written as follows:

Harmonic Series of Standing Waves on a Vibrating String

$$f_n = n\frac{v}{2L} \quad n = 1, 2, 3, \ldots$$

$$\text{frequency} = \text{harmonic number} \times \frac{\text{(speed of waves on the string)}}{\text{(2)(length of vibrating string)}}$$

Note that v in this equation is the speed of waves on the vibrating string and not the speed of the resultant sound waves in air. If the string vibrates at one of these frequencies, the sound waves produced in the surrounding air will have the same frequency. However, the speed of these waves will be the speed of sound waves in air, and the wavelength of these waves will be that speed divided by the frequency.

harmonic series a series of frequencies that includes the fundamental frequency and integral multiples of the fundamental frequency

Did YOU Know?

When a guitar player presses down on a guitar string at any point, that point becomes a node, and only a portion of the string vibrates. As a result, a single string can be used to create a variety of fundamental frequencies. In the equation on this page, L refers to the portion of the string that is vibrating.

Sound **421**

FIGURE 3.3

Waves in a Pipe The harmonic series present in each of these organ pipes depends on whether the end of the pipe is open or closed.

Standing Waves in an Air Column

Standing waves can also be set up in a tube of air, such as the inside of a trumpet, the column of a saxophone, or the pipes of an organ like those shown in **Figure 3.3.** While some waves travel down the tube, others are reflected back upward. These waves traveling in opposite directions combine to produce standing waves. Many brass instruments and woodwinds produce sound by means of these vibrating air columns.

If both ends of a pipe are open, all harmonics are present.

The harmonic series present in an organ pipe depends on whether the reflecting end of the pipe is open or closed. When the reflecting end of the pipe is open, as is illustrated in **Figure 3.4,** the air molecules have complete freedom of motion, so an antinode (of displacement) exists at this end. If a pipe is open at both ends, each end is an antinode. This situation is the exact opposite of a string fixed at both ends, where both ends are nodes.

Because the distance from one node to the next ($\frac{1}{2}\lambda$) equals the distance from one antinode to the next, the pattern of standing waves that can occur in a pipe open at both ends is the same as that of a vibrating string. Thus, the entire harmonic series is present in this case, as shown in **Figure 3.4,** and our earlier equation for the harmonic series of a vibrating string can be used.

> **Harmonic Series of a Pipe Open at Both Ends**
>
> $$f_n = n\frac{v}{2L} \quad n = 1, 2, 3, \ldots$$
>
> $$\text{frequency} = \text{harmonic number} \times \frac{\text{(speed of sound in the pipe)}}{\text{(2)(length of vibrating air column)}}$$

Did YOU Know?

A flute is similar to a pipe open at both ends. When all keys of a flute are closed, the length of the vibrating air column is approximately equal to the length of the flute. As the keys are opened one by one, the length of the vibrating air column decreases, and the fundamental frequency increases.

In this equation, L represents the length of the vibrating air column. Just as the fundamental frequency of a string instrument can be varied by changing the string length, the fundamental frequency of many woodwind and brass instruments can be varied by changing the length of the vibrating air column.

FIGURE 3.4

Harmonics in an Open-Ended Pipe
In a pipe open at both ends, each end is an antinode of displacement, and all harmonics are present.

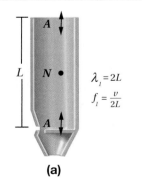

$\lambda_1 = 2L$

$f_1 = \frac{v}{2L}$

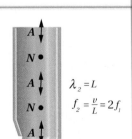

$\lambda_2 = L$

$f_2 = \frac{v}{L} = 2f_1$

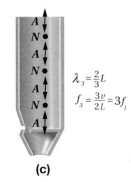

$\lambda_3 = \frac{2}{3}L$

$f_3 = \frac{3v}{2L} = 3f_1$

(a)

(b)

(c)

(a) First harmonic

(b) Second harmonic

(c) Third harmonic

(tl) ©Joseph Barnell/SuperStock

FIGURE 3.5

Harmonics in a Pipe Closed at One End In a pipe closed at one end, the closed end is a node of displacement, and the open end is an antinode of displacement. In this case, only the odd harmonics are present.

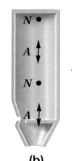

(a)

(b)

(c)

(a) First harmonic

(b) Second harmonic

(c) Third harmonic

If one end of a pipe is closed, only odd harmonics are present.

When one end of an organ pipe is closed, as is illustrated in **Figure 3.5,** the movement of air molecules is restricted at this end, making this end a node. In this case, one end of the pipe is a node, and the other is an antinode. As a result, a different set of standing waves can occur.

As shown in **Figure 3.5(a),** the simplest possible standing wave that can exist in this pipe is one for which the length of the pipe is equal to one-fourth of a wavelength. Hence, the wavelength of this standing wave equals four times the length of the pipe. Thus, in this case, the fundamental frequency equals the velocity divided by four times the pipe length.

$$f_1 = \frac{v}{\lambda_1} = \frac{v}{4L}$$

For the case shown in **Figure 3.5(b),** the length of the pipe is equal to three-fourths of a wavelength, so the wavelength is four-thirds the length of the pipe ($\lambda_3 = \frac{4}{3}L$). Substituting this value into the equation for frequency gives the frequency of this harmonic.

$$f_3 = \frac{v}{\lambda_3} = \frac{v}{\frac{4}{3}L} = \frac{3v}{4L} = 3f_1$$

The frequency of this harmonic is *three* times the fundamental frequency. Repeating this calculation for the case shown in **Figure 3.5(c)** gives a frequency equal to *five* times the fundamental frequency. Thus, only the odd-numbered harmonics vibrate in a pipe closed at one end. We can generalize the equation for the harmonic series of a pipe closed at one end as follows:

Harmonic Series of a Pipe Closed at One End

$$f_n = n\frac{v}{4L} \quad n = 1, 3, 5, \ldots$$

$$\text{frequency} = \text{harmonic number} \times \frac{\text{(speed of sound in the pipe)}}{\text{(4)(length of vibrating air column)}}$$

A PIPE CLOSED AT ONE END

Snip off the corners of one end of the straw so that the end tapers to a point, as shown below. Chew on this end to flatten it, and you create a double-reed instrument! Put your lips around the tapered end of the straw, press them together tightly, and blow through the straw. When you hear a steady tone, slowly snip off pieces of the straw at the other end. Be careful to keep about the same amount of pressure with your lips. How does the pitch change as the straw becomes shorter? How can you account for this change in pitch? You may be able to produce more than one tone for any given length of the straw. How is this possible?

Sample Problem B What are the first three harmonics in a 4.65 m long bass flute that is open at both ends? What are the first three harmonics of this pipe when one end of the pipe is closed? Assume that the speed of sound in air is 345 m/s.

① ANALYZE

Given: $L = 4.65$ m $\qquad v = 345$ m/s

Unknown: Pipe open at both ends: $f_1 \qquad f_2 \qquad f_3$

Pipe closed at one end: $f_1 \qquad f_3 \qquad f_5$

③ PLAN

Choose an equation or situation:
When the pipe is open at both ends, the fundamental frequency can be found by using the equation for the entire harmonic series:

$$f_n = n\frac{v}{2L}, n = 1, 2, 3, \ldots$$

When the pipe is closed at one end, use the following equation:

$$f_n = n\frac{v}{4L}, n = 1, 3, 5, \ldots$$

In both cases, the second two harmonics can be found by multiplying the harmonic numbers by the fundamental frequency.

③ SOLVE

Substitute the values into the equations and solve:
For a pipe open at both ends:

$$f_1 = n\frac{v}{2L} = (1)\left(\frac{345 \text{ m/s}}{(2)(4.65 \text{ m})}\right) = \boxed{37.1 \text{ Hz}}$$

The next two harmonics are the second and the third:

$$f_2 = 2f_1 = (2)(37.1 \text{ Hz}) = \boxed{74.2 \text{ Hz}}$$

$$f_3 = 3f_1 = (3)(37.1 \text{ Hz}) = \boxed{111 \text{ Hz}}$$

For a pipe closed at one end:

$$f_1 = n\frac{v}{4L} = (1)\left(\frac{345 \text{ m/s}}{(4)(4.65 \text{ m})}\right) = \boxed{18.5 \text{ Hz}}$$

The next possible harmonics are the third and the fifth:

$$f_3 = 3f_1 = (3)(18.5 \text{ Hz}) = \boxed{55.6 \text{ Hz}}$$

$$f_5 = 5f_1 = (5)(18.5 \text{ Hz}) = \boxed{92.7 \text{ Hz}}$$

Tips and Tricks

Be sure to use the correct harmonic numbers for each situation. For a pipe open at both ends, $n = 1, 2, 3$, etc. For a pipe closed at one end, only odd harmonics are present, so $n = 1, 3, 5$, etc.

Continued ▶

Harmonics (continued)

Practice

1. What is the fundamental frequency of a 0.20 m long organ pipe that is closed at one end, when the speed of sound in the pipe is 352 m/s?

2. A flute is essentially a pipe open at both ends. The length of a flute is approximately 66.0 cm. What are the first three harmonics of a flute when all keys are closed, making the vibrating air column approximately equal to the length of the flute? The speed of sound in the flute is 340 m/s.

3. A saxophonist plays a tune in the key of B-flat. The saxophone has a second harmonic frequency of 466.2 Hz when the speed of sound in air is 331m/s. What is the length of the pipe that makes up the saxophone? A saxophone should be treated as a pipe closed at one end.

4. What is the fundamental frequency of a mandolin string that is 42.0 cm long when the speed of waves on this string is 329 m/s?

Trumpets, saxophones, and clarinets are similar to a pipe closed at one end. For example, although the trumpet shown in **Figure 3.6** has two open ends, the player's mouth effectively closes one end of the instrument. In a saxophone or a clarinet, the reed closes one end.

Despite the similarity between these instruments and a pipe closed at one end, our equation for the harmonic series of pipes does not directly apply to such instruments. One reason the equation does not apply is that any deviation from the cylindrical shape of a pipe affects the harmonic series of an instrument. Another reason is that the open holes in many instruments affect the harmonics. For example, a clarinet is primarily cylindrical, but there are some even harmonics in a clarinet's tone at relatively small intensities. The shape of a saxophone is such that the harmonic series in a saxophone is similar to that in a cylindrical pipe open at both ends even though only one end of the saxophone is open. These deviations are in part responsible for the variety of sounds that can be produced by different instruments.

FIGURE 3.6

Shape and Harmonic Series Variations in shape give each instrument a different harmonic series.

Harmonics account for sound quality, or timbre.

Figure 3.7 shows the harmonics present in a tuning fork, a clarinet, and a viola when each sounds the musical note A-natural. Each instrument has its own characteristic mixture of harmonics at varying intensities.

The harmonics shown in the second column of **Figure 3.7** add together according to the principle of superposition to give the resultant waveform shown in the third column. Since a tuning fork vibrates at only its fundamental frequency, its waveform is simply a sine wave. (Some tuning forks also vibrate at higher frequencies when they are struck hard enough.) The waveforms of the other instruments are more complex because they consist of many harmonics, each at different intensities. Each individual harmonic waveform is a sine wave, but the resultant wave is more complex than a sine wave because each individual waveform has a different frequency.

In music, the mixture of harmonics that produces the characteristic sound of an instrument is referred to as the *spectrum of the sound.* From the perspective of the listener, this spectrum results in *sound quality,* or **timbre.** A clarinet sounds different from a viola because of differences in timbre, even when both instruments are sounding the same note at the same volume. The rich harmonics of most instruments provide a much fuller sound than that of a tuning fork.

The intensity of each harmonic varies within a particular instrument, depending on frequency, amplitude of vibration, and a variety of other factors. With a violin, for example, the intensity of each harmonic

timbre the musical quality of a tone resulting from the combination of harmonics present at different intensities

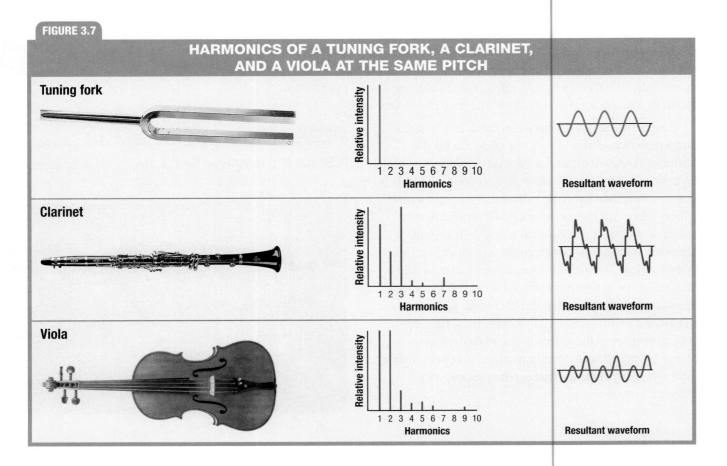

FIGURE 3.7

HARMONICS OF A TUNING FORK, A CLARINET, AND A VIOLA AT THE SAME PITCH

Tuning fork	Relative intensity / Harmonics 1 2 3 4 5 6 7 8 9 10	Resultant waveform
Clarinet	Relative intensity / Harmonics 1 2 3 4 5 6 7 8 9 10	Resultant waveform
Viola	Relative intensity / Harmonics 1 2 3 4 5 6 7 8 9 10	Resultant waveform

Reverberation

Auditoriums, churches, concert halls, libraries, and music rooms are designed with specific functions in mind. One auditorium may be made for rock concerts, while another is constructed for use as a lecture hall. Your school's auditorium, for instance, may allow you to hear a speaker well but make a band sound damped and muffled.

Rooms are often constructed so that sounds made by a speaker or a musical instrument bounce back and forth against the ceiling, walls, floor, and other surfaces. This repetitive echo is called *reverberation*. The reverberation time is the amount of time it takes for a sound's intensity to decrease by 60 dB.

For speech, the auditorium should be designed so that the reverberation time is relatively short. A repeated echo of each word could become confusing to listeners.

Music halls may differ in construction depending on the type of music usually played there. For example, rock music is generally less pleasing with a large amount of reverberation, but more reverberation is sometimes desired for orchestral and choral music.

For these reasons, you may notice a difference in the way ceilings, walls, and furnishings are designed in different rooms. Ceilings designed for a lot of reverberation are flat and hard. Ceilings in libraries and other quiet places are often made of soft or textured material to muffle sounds. Padded furnishings and plants can also be strategically arranged to absorb sound. All of these different factors are considered and combined to accommodate the auditory function of a room.

depends on where the string is bowed, the speed of the bow on the string, and the force the bow exerts on the string. Because there are so many factors involved, most instruments can produce a wide variety of tones.

Even though the waveforms of a clarinet and a viola are more complex than those of a tuning fork, note that each consists of repeating patterns. Such waveforms are said to be *periodic*. These repeating patterns occur because each frequency is an integral multiple of the fundamental frequency.

Fundamental frequency determines pitch.

The frequency of a sound determines its pitch. In musical instruments, the fundamental frequency of a vibration typically determines pitch. Other harmonics are sometimes referred to as *overtones*. In the chromatic (half-step) musical scale, there are 12 notes, each of which has a characteristic frequency. The frequency of the thirteenth note is exactly twice that of the first note, and together the 13 notes constitute an *octave*. For stringed instruments and open-ended wind instruments, the frequency of the second harmonic of a note corresponds to the frequency of the octave above that note.

FIGURE 3.8

Superposition and Beats

Beats are formed by the interference of two waves of slightly different frequencies traveling in the same direction. In this case, constructive interference is greatest at t_2, when the two waves are in phase.

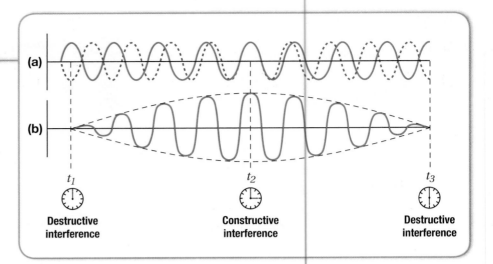

(a)

(b)

t_1 — Destructive interference

t_2 — Constructive interference

t_3 — Destructive interference

Beats

So far, we have considered the superposition of waves in a harmonic series, where each frequency is an integral multiple of the fundamental frequency. When two waves of *slightly* different frequencies interfere, the interference pattern varies in such a way that a listener hears an alternation between loudness and softness. The variation from soft to loud and back to soft is called a **beat.**

beat the periodic variation in the amplitude of a wave that is the superposition of two waves of slightly different frequencies

Sound waves at slightly different frequencies produce beats.

Figure 3.8 shows how beats occur. In **Figure 3.8(a),** the waves produced by two tuning forks of different frequencies start exactly opposite one another. These waves combine according to the superposition principle, as shown in **Figure 3.8(b).** When the two waves are exactly opposite one another, they are said to be *out of phase,* and complete destructive interference occurs. For this reason, no sound is heard at t_1.

Because these waves have different frequencies, after a few more cycles, the crest of the blue wave matches up with the crest of the red wave, as at t_2. At this point, the waves are said to be *in phase.*

Conceptual Challenge

Concert Violins Before a performance, musicians tune their instruments to match their fundamental frequencies. If a conductor hears the number of beats decreasing as two violin players are tuning, are the fundamental frequencies of these violins becoming closer together or farther apart? Explain.

Tuning Flutes How could two flute players use beats to ensure that their instruments are in tune with each other?

Sounds from a Guitar Will the speed of waves on a vibrating guitar string be the same as the speed of the sound waves in the air that are generated by this vibration? How will the frequency and wavelength of the waves on the string compare with the frequency and wavelength of the sound waves in the air?

Now constructive interference occurs, and the sound is louder. Because the blue wave has a higher frequency than the red wave, the waves are out of phase again at t_3, and no sound is heard.

As time passes, the waves continue to be in and out of phase, the interference constantly shifts between constructive interference and destructive interference, and the listener hears the sound getting softer and louder and then softer again. You may have noticed a similar phenomenon on a playground swing set. If two people are swinging next to one another at different frequencies, the two swings may alternate between being in phase and being out of phase.

The number of beats per second corresponds to the difference between frequencies.

In our previous example, there is one beat, which occurs at t_2. One beat corresponds to the blue wave gaining one entire cycle on the red wave. This is because to go from one destructive interference to the next, the red wave must lag one entire cycle behind the blue wave. If the time that lapses from t_1 to t_3 is one second, then the blue wave completes one more cycle per second than the red wave. In other words, its frequency is greater by 1 Hz. By generalizing this, you can see that the frequency difference between two sounds can be found by the number of beats heard per second.

 SECTION 3 **FORMATIVE ASSESSMENT**

▶ Reviewing Main Ideas

1. On a piano, the note middle C has a fundamental frequency of 262 Hz. What is the second harmonic of this note?

2. If the piano wire in item 1 is 66.0 cm long, what is the speed of waves on this wire?

3. A piano tuner using a 392 Hz tuning fork to tune the wire for G-natural hears four beats per second. What are the two possible frequencies of vibration of this piano wire?

4. In a clarinet, the reed end of the instrument acts as a node, and the first open hole acts as an antinode. Because the shape of the clarinet is nearly cylindrical, its harmonic series approximately follows that of a pipe closed at one end. What harmonic series is predominant in a clarinet?

✔ Critical Thinking

5. Which of the following are different for a trumpet and a banjo when both play notes at the same fundamental frequency?
   a. wavelength in air of the first harmonic
   b. which harmonics are present
   c. intensity of each harmonic
   d. speed of sound in air

The Doppler Effect and the Big Bang

You learned that relative motion between the source of sound waves and an observer creates a frequency shift known as the Doppler effect. For visible light, the Doppler effect is observed as a change in color because the frequency of light waves determines color.

Frequency Shifts

Of the colors of the visible spectrum, red light has the lowest frequency, and violet light has the highest. When a source of light waves is moving toward an observer, the frequency detected is higher than the source frequency. This corresponds to a shift toward the blue end of the spectrum, which is called a *blue shift*. When a source of light waves is moving away from an observer, the observer detects a lower frequency, which corresponds to a shift toward the red end of the spectrum, called a *red shift*. Visible light is one form of electromagnetic radiation. Blue shift and red shift can occur with any type of electromagnetic radiation, not just visible light. **Figure 1** illustrates blue shift and red shift.

In astronomy, the light from distant stars or galaxies is analyzed by a process called *spectroscopy*. In this process, starlight is passed through a prism or diffraction grating to produce a spectrum. Dark lines appear in the spectrum at specific frequencies determined by the elements present in the atmospheres of stars. When these lines are shifted toward the blue end of the spectrum, astronomers know the star is moving toward Earth; when the lines are shifted toward the red end, the star is moving away from Earth.

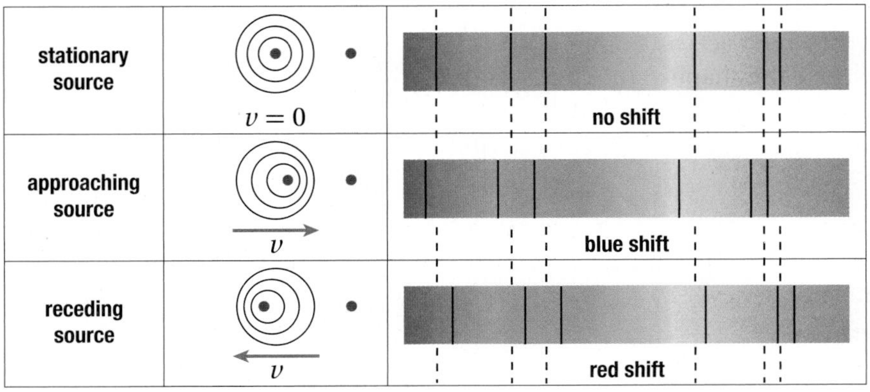

The Expansion of the Universe

As scientists began to study other galaxies with spectroscopy, the results were astonishing: nearly all of the galaxies that were observed exhibited a red shift, which suggested that they were moving away from Earth. If all galaxies are moving away from Earth, the universe must be expanding. This does not imply that Earth is at the

FIGURE 1

The Doppler Effect for Light

stationary source	$v = 0$	no shift
approaching source	v	blue shift
receding source	v	red shift

center of the expansion; the same phenomenon would be observed from any other point in the universe.

The expansion of the universe suggests that at some point in the past, the universe must have had infinite density. The eruption of the universe is often referred to as the *big bang,* which is generally considered to have occurred between about 13 billion and 15 billion years ago. Current models indicate that the big bang involved such great amounts of energy in such a small space that matter could not form clumps or even individual atoms. It took about 380 000 years for the universe to cool from around 10^{32} K to around 3000 K, a temperature cool enough for atoms to begin forming.

Experimental Verification

In the 1960s, a group of scientists at Princeton predicted that the explosion of the big bang was so momentous that a small amount of radiation—the leftover glow from the big bang—should still be found in the universe. Around this time, Arno Penzias and Robert Wilson of Bell Labs noticed a faint background hiss interfering with satellite-communications experiments they were conducting. This signal, which was detected in equal amounts in all directions, remained despite all attempts to remove it. Penzias and Wilson learned of the Princeton group's work and realized that the interference they were experiencing matched the characteristics of the radiation expected from the big bang. Subsequent experiments have confirmed the existence of this radiation, known as *cosmic microwave background radiation.* This background radiation is considered to be the most conclusive evidence for the big bang theory.

The big bang theory is generally accepted by scientists today. Research now focuses on more detailed issues. However, there are certain phenomena that the standard big bang model cannot account for, such as the uniform distribution of matter on a large scale and the large-scale clustering of galaxies. As a result, some scientists are currently working on modifications and refinements to the standard big bang theory.

In March of 2004, astronomers released a new image from the *Hubble Space Telescope.* This image, called the *Hubble Ultra Deep Field* (HUDF), looks further back in time than any previously recorded images. The image contains an estimated 10 000 galaxies. Scientists will study the HUDF to search for galaxies that existed from 400 million to 800 million years after the big bang. Because galaxies evolved quickly, many important changes happened within a billion years of the big bang. Scientists hope that studies of the HUDF image will resolve some of the current questions regarding the origin and evolution of the universe.

(tr) ©Bettmann/Corbis; (b) NASA, ESA, S. Beckwith (STScI) and the HUDF Team

FIGURE 2

Penzias and Wilson Penzias and Wilson detected microwave background radiation, presumably left over from the big bang, with the horn antenna (in the background) at Bell Telephone Laboratories in New Jersey.

FIGURE 3

Hubble Ultra Deep Field This image, called the *Hubble Ultra Deep Field*, is a compilation of images taken by two cameras on the *Hubble Space Telescope* between September 2003 and January 2004. It shows the youngest galaxies ever to be seen. These galaxies may have formed as early as 400 million years after the big bang.

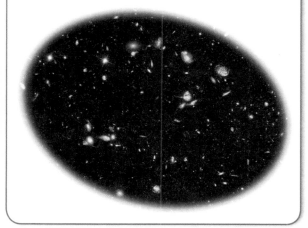

Song of the Dunes

In the 1200s, the explorer Marco Polo was startled by the strange sound he heard as he traveled through the Gobi Desert in Asia. Looking around him, he saw nothing but sand dunes stretching as far as the eye could see. Marco Polo attributed the sound to evil spirits roaming in the sand dunes. Perhaps he believed this because the noise he heard in the desert sounded like a song. The "song of the dunes" consists of a powerful, monotonous sound that can last for several minutes and be heard more than a mile away.

Some 800 years later, scientists still do not completely know how sand dunes make sound. They do know that the strong winds that blow across a desert are not the main cause, because a person in a lab can generate the same sound simply by moving sand around with the hands. Also, scientists know that sand dunes do not produce sounds by resonating like a musical instrument. Rather, the vibrations of individual sand grains are responsible. However, understanding the behavior of sand grains is a challenge. Despite its tiny size, a sand grain can be quite complex.

For example, in a stationary pile of sand, each grain interacts with five to nine adjacent grains at the same time. When the sand grains begin to move, each grain is simultaneously interacting with about three to five neighbors. However, those neighbors keep changing as the grains keep moving. Imagine all the interactions taking place between the enormous numbers of sand grains in a migrating dune. It should be no surprise that even a supercomputer cannot keep track of all these interactions.

How some sand dunes sing is still something of a mystery to science.

In 2009, two French scientists published the results of their investigation into the sound made by sand dunes. They stated that friction between the layer of moving sand grains and the underlying layer of stationary sand creates elastic waves. To test their hypothesis, the scientists set off tiny avalanches in the sand dunes of a desert.

The scientists found that elastic waves can propagate off the underlying stationary region of a sand dune in all directions. The waves emitted at the rear layer penetrate through the sides of the moving sand dune, creating constructive interference and amplifying the waves. The reflection of an elastic wave on a frictional interface results in coherent acoustic waves, which are the source of the booming sound. As the scientists explained, the principle is similar to the light from a laser. In both cases, there is a spontaneous emission of coherent waves. Other scientists are not convinced that the emission of coherent waves is responsible for the sound created by sand dunes.

There is no disagreement, however, on a danger posed by some sand dunes. Migrating sand dunes are threatening villages and cities. For example, in northern China, sand dunes are advancing on some villages at a rate of 20 meters per year. Parts of Africa and the Middle East are also threatened. In fact, sand dunes are advancing on the capital city of Mauritania. While wind may not be the main cause of singing sand dunes, it does make sand dunes move.

Wave Propagation

Sound is transmitted by vibrations in matter. For the energy of these vibrations to be conveyed over space, particles of matter are needed to receive and further transfer the energy. The movement of sound waves is affected by the medium through which the wave travels.

Different Media

Specific characteristics of media have different effects on the propagation of sound waves. For instance, for a sound wave travelling in a gas, the speed of the wave will increase with an increase in the temperature of the gas. Sound waves also travel more quickly through liquid media, compared with gases, because the particles in a liquid are closer together, which allows particles to transfer vibrations more quickly.

- Why do you think the speed of a sound wave travelling through a gas will increase as the temperature of the medium increases?

- Predict whether a sound wave travels more quickly in a solid medium than in a gas. Plan and implement a procedure to test your prediction.

- Would changes in the temperature of a solid medium have a significant impact on the speed of a wave travelling through that medium?

Conceptual Challenge

The ability to make assumptions and generate rough estimates is a valuable skill to scientists. Quick estimates allow scientists to narrow the range of possibilities and focus on the most reasonable hypotheses.

Noisy Monkeys Howler Monkeys are among the loudest animals on earth, capable of producing screams with a sound intensity of nearly 90 decibels! About how far away could a human be and still hear a Howler Monkey screaming?

You can begin addressing the scenario by asking questions such as the following:

- What is the threshold of human hearing?
- What is the nature of the medium through which the sound will travel?
- What happens to sound intensity as the sound waves travel over a distance?

CHAPTER 12 **Summary**

BIG IDEA Sound waves transfer energy through vibrations. Characteristics of the sounds we perceive are due to properties of the sound waves and the medium through which they travel.

SECTION 1 **Sound Waves**

- The frequency of a sound wave determines its pitch.
- The speed of sound depends on the medium.
- The relative motion between the source of waves and an observer creates an apparent frequency shift known as the Doppler effect.

KEY TERMS

compression
rarefaction
pitch
Doppler effect

SECTION 2 **Sound Intensity and Resonance**

- The sound intensity of a spherical wave is the power per area.
- Sound intensity is inversely proportional to the square of the distance from the source because the same energy is spread over a larger area.
- Intensity and frequency determine which sounds are audible.
- Decibel level is a measure of relative intensity on a logarithmic scale.
- A given difference in decibels corresponds to a fixed difference in perceived loudness.
- A forced vibration at the natural frequency produces resonance.
- The human ear transmits vibrations that cause nerve impulses. The brain interprets these impulses as sounds of varying frequencies.

KEY TERMS

intensity
decibel
resonance

SECTION 3 **Harmonics**

- Harmonics are integral multiples of the fundamental frequency.
- A vibrating string or a pipe open at both ends produces all harmonics.
- A pipe closed at one end produces only odd harmonics.
- The number and intensity of harmonics account for the sound quality of an instrument, also known as timbre.

KEY TERMS

fundamental frequency
harmonic series
timbre
beat

VARIABLE SYMBOLS		
Quantities	**Units**	
sound intensity	W/m^2	watts/meters squared
decibel level	dB	decibels
f_n frequency of the nth harmonic	Hz	Hertz = s^{-1}
L length of a vibrating string or an air column	m	meters

Problem Solving

See **Appendix D: Equations** for a summary of the equations introduced in this chapter. If you need more problem-solving practice, see **Appendix I: Additional Problems.**

Sound Waves

▶ **REVIEWING MAIN IDEAS**

1. Why are sound waves in air characterized as longitudinal?

2. Draw the sine curve that corresponds to the sound wave depicted below.

3. What is the difference between frequency and pitch?

4. What are the differences between infrasonic, audible, and ultrasonic sound waves?

5. Explain why the speed of sound depends on the temperature of the medium. Why is this temperature dependence more noticeable in a gas than in a solid or a liquid?

6. You are at a street corner and hear an ambulance siren. Without looking, how can you tell when the ambulance passes by?

7. Why do ultrasound waves produce images of objects inside the body more effectively than audible sound waves do?

CONCEPTUAL QUESTIONS

8. If the wavelength of a sound source is reduced by a factor of 2, what happens to the wave's frequency? What happens to its speed?

9. As a result of a distant explosion, an observer first senses a ground tremor and then hears the explosion. What accounts for this time lag?

10. By listening to a band or an orchestra, how can you determine that the speed of sound is the same for all frequencies?

11. A fire engine is moving at 40 m/s and sounding its horn. A car in front of the fire engine is moving at 30 m/s, and a van in front of the car is stationary. Which observer hears the fire engine's horn at a higher pitch, the driver of the car or the driver of the van?

12. A bat flying toward a wall emits a chirp at 40 kHz. Is the frequency of the echo received by the bat greater than, less than, or equal to 40 kHz?

Sound Intensity and Resonance

▶ **REVIEWING MAIN IDEAS**

13. What is the difference between intensity and decibel level?

14. Using **Figure 2.3** as a guide, estimate the decibel levels of the following sounds: a cheering crowd at a football game, background noise in a church, the pages of this textbook being turned, and light traffic.

15. Why is the threshold of hearing represented as a curve in **Figure 2.2** rather than as a single point?

16. Under what conditions does resonance occur?

CONCEPTUAL QUESTIONS

17. The decibel level of an orchestra is 90 dB, and a single violin achieves a level of 70 dB. How does the sound intensity from the full orchestra compare with that from the violin alone?

18. A noisy machine in a factory produces a decibel rating of 80 dB. How many identical machines could you add to the factory without exceeding the 90 dB limit set by federal regulations?

19. Why is the intensity of an echo less than that of the original sound?

20. Why are pushes given to a playground swing more effective if they are given at certain, regular intervals than if they are given at random positions in the swing's cycle?

21. Although soldiers are usually required to march together in step, they must break their march when crossing a bridge. Explain the possible danger of crossing a rickety bridge without taking this precaution.

PRACTICE PROBLEMS

For problems 22–23, see Sample Problem A.

22. A baseball coach shouts loudly at an umpire standing 5.0 m away. If the sound power produced by the coach is 3.1×10^{-3} W, what is the decibel level of the sound when it reaches the umpire? (Hint: Use **Figure 2.3** in this chapter.)

23. A stereo speaker represented by P in the figure on the right emits sound waves with a power output of 100.0 W. What is the intensity of the sound waves at point x when $r = 10.0$ m?

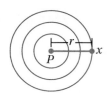

Harmonics

 REVIEWING MAIN IDEAS

24. What is fundamental frequency? How are harmonics related to the fundamental frequency?

25. The figures below show a stretched string vibrating in several of its modes. If the length of the string is 2.0 m, what is the wavelength of the wave on the string in **(a)**, **(b)**, **(c)**, and **(d)**?

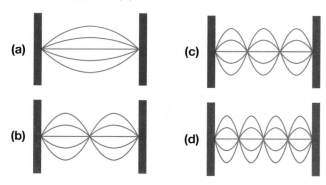

(a)

(b)

(c)

(d)

26. Why does a pipe closed at one end have a different harmonic series than an open pipe?

27. Explain why a saxophone sounds different from a clarinet, even when they sound the same fundamental frequency at the same decibel level.

CONCEPTUAL QUESTIONS

28. Why does a vibrating guitar string sound louder when it is on the instrument than it does when it is stretched on a workbench?

29. Two violin players tuning their instruments together hear six beats in 2 s. What is the frequency difference between the two violins?

30. What is the purpose of the slide on a trombone and the valves on a trumpet?

31. A student records the first 10 harmonics for a pipe. Is it possible to determine whether the pipe is open or closed by comparing the difference in frequencies between the adjacent harmonics with the fundamental frequency? Explain.

32. A flute is similar to a pipe open at both ends, while a clarinet is similar to a pipe closed at one end. Explain why the fundamental frequency of a flute is about twice that of the clarinet, even though the length of these two instruments is approximately the same.

33. The fundamental frequency of any note produced by a flute will vary slightly with temperature changes in the air. For any given note, will an increase in temperature produce a slightly higher fundamental frequency or a slightly lower one?

PRACTICE PROBLEMS

For problems 34–35, see Sample Problem B.

34. What are the first three harmonics of a note produced on a 31.0 cm long violin string if waves on this string have a speed of 274.4 m/s?

35. The human ear canal is about 2.8 cm long and can be regarded as a tube open at one end and closed at the eardrum. What is the frequency around which we would expect hearing to be best when the speed of sound in air is 340 m/s? (Hint: Find the fundamental frequency for the ear canal.)

Mixed Review

▶ REVIEWING MAIN IDEAS

36. A pipe that is open at both ends has a fundamental frequency of 320 Hz when the speed of sound in air is 331 m/s.
   a. What is the length of this pipe?
   b. What are the next two harmonics?

37. When two tuning forks of 132 Hz and 137 Hz, respectively, are sounded simultaneously, how many beats per second are heard?

38. The range of human hearing extends from approximately 20 Hz to 20 000 Hz. Find the wavelengths of these extremes when the speed of sound in air is equal to 343 m/s.

39. A dolphin in 25°C seawater emits a sound directed toward the bottom of the ocean 150 m below. How much time passes before it hears an echo? (See **Figure 1.3** in this chapter for the speed of the sound.)

40. An open organ pipe is 2.46 m long, and the speed of the air in the pipe is 345 m/s.
   a. What is the fundamental frequency of this pipe?
   b. How many harmonics are possible in the normal hearing range, 20 Hz to 20 000 Hz?

41. The fundamental frequency of an open organ pipe corresponds to the note middle C ($f = 261.6$ Hz on the chromatic musical scale). The third harmonic (f_3) of another organ pipe that is closed at one end has the same frequency. Compare the lengths of these two pipes.

42. Some studies indicate that the upper frequency limit of hearing is determined by the diameter of the eardrum. The wavelength of the sound wave and the diameter of the eardrum are approximately equal at this upper limit. If this is so, what is the diameter of the eardrum of a person capable of hearing 2.0×10^4 Hz? Assume 378 m/s is the speed of sound in the ear.

43. The decibel level of the noise from a jet aircraft is 130 dB when measured 20.0 m from the aircraft.
   a. How much sound power does the jet aircraft emit?
   b. How much sound power would strike the eardrum of an airport worker 20.0 m from the aircraft? (Use the diameter found in item 42 to calculate the area of the eardrum.)

GRAPHING CALCULATOR PRACTICE

Doppler Effect

As you learned earlier in this chapter, relative motion between a source of sound and an observer can create changes in the observed frequency. This frequency shift is known as the *Doppler effect*. The frequencies heard by the observer can be described by the following two equations, where f' represents the apparent frequency and f represents the actual frequency.

$$f' = f\left(\frac{v_{sound}}{v_{sound} - v_{source}}\right)$$

$$f' = f\left(\frac{v_{sound}}{v_{sound} + v_{source}}\right)$$

The first equation applies when the source of sound is approaching the observer, and the second equation applies when the source of sound is moving away from the observer.

In this graphing calculator activity, you will graph these two equations and will analyze the graphs to determine the apparent frequencies for various situations.

Go online to HMHScience.com to find the skillsheet and program for this graphing calculator activity.

ALTERNATIVE ASSESSMENT

1. A new airport is being built 750 m from your school. The noise level 50 m from planes that will land at the airport is 130 dB. In open spaces, such as the fields between the school and the airport, the level decreases by 20 dB each time the distance increases tenfold. Work in a cooperative group to research the options for keeping the noise level tolerable at the school. How far away would the school have to be moved to make the sound manageable? Research the cost of land near your school. What options are available for soundproofing the school's buildings? How expensive are these options? Have each member in the group present the advantages and disadvantages of such options.

2. Use soft-drink bottles and water to make a musical instrument. Adjust the amount of water in different bottles to create musical notes. Play them as percussion instruments (by tapping the bottles) or as wind instruments (by blowing over the mouths of individual bottles). What media are vibrating in each case? What affects the fundamental frequency? Use a microphone and an oscilloscope to analyze your performance and to demonstrate the effects of tuning your instrument.

3. Interview members of the medical profession to learn about human hearing. What are some types of hearing disabilities? How are hearing disabilities related to disease, age, and occupational or environmental hazards? What procedures and instruments are used to test hearing? How do hearing aids help? What are the limitations of hearing aids? Present your findings to the class.

4. Do research on the types of architectural acoustics that would affect a restaurant. What are some of the acoustics problems in places where many people gather? How do odd-shaped ceilings, decorative panels, draperies, and glass windows affect echo and noise? Find the shortest wavelengths of sounds that should be absorbed, considering that conversation sounds range from 500 to 5000 Hz. Prepare a plan or a model of your school cafeteria, and show what approaches you would use to keep the level of noise to a minimum.

5. Doppler radar systems use the Doppler effect to identify the speed of objects such as aircraft, ships, automobiles, and weather systems. For example, meteorologists use Doppler radar to track the movement of storm systems. Police use Doppler radar to determine whether a motorist is speeding. Doppler radar systems use electromagnetic waves, rather than sound waves. Choose an application of Doppler radar to research. Create a poster showing how the application works.

6. How does a piano produce sound? Why do grand pianos sound different from upright pianos? How are harpsichords and early pianos different from modern pianos? What types of tuning systems were used in the past, and which are used today? Use library and/or Internet sources to answer these questions. If possible, try playing notes on different pianos, and compare the resulting sounds. Create a presentation to share your results with the class.

7. Research the speed of sound in different media (including solids, liquids, and gases) and at different temperatures. Also investigate the concept of *supersonic* speed, and find some examples of objects that can move at supersonic speeds. Create a bar chart to compare your results.

8. Bats rely on echolocation to find and track prey. Conduct research to find out how this works. Which species of bats use echolocation? What type of sounds do bats emit? What can a bat learn from reflected sounds, and how do bats process the information? Write a paper with the results of your research.

Standards-Based Assessment

Record your answers on a separate piece of paper.

MULTIPLE CHOICE

1 Light waves and sound waves have many similar behaviors, such as reflection and refraction. One behavior they do not share is

  A polarization, because sound waves are longitudinal.

  B diffraction, because sound waves are longitudinal.

  C pressure, because light waves are transverse.

  D speed, because light waves are transverse.

2 When a part of a sound wave travels from air into water, what property of the wave remains unchanged?

  A speed

  B frequency

  C wavelength

  D amplitude

3 What is the wavelength of the sound wave shown in the figure below?

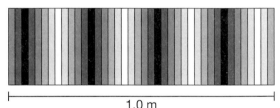

1.0 m

  A 1.00 m

  B 0.75 m

  C 0.50 m

  D 0.25 m

4 The greatest value ever achieved for the speed of sound in air is about 1.0×10^4 m/s, and the highest frequency ever produced is about 2.0×10^{10} Hz. If a single sound wave with this speed and frequency were produced, what would its wavelength be?

  A 5.0×10^{-6} m

  B 5.0×10^{-7} m

  C 2.0×10^{6} m

  D 2.0×10^{14} m

5 If the distance from a point source of sound is tripled, by what factor is the sound intensity changed?

  A $\frac{1}{9}$

  B $\frac{1}{3}$

  C 3

  D 9

6 The Doppler effect occurs in all but which of the following situations?

  A A source of sound moves toward a listener.

  B A listener moves toward a source of sound.

  C A listener and a source of sound remain at rest with respect to each other.

  D A listener and a source of sound move toward or away from each other.

7 The second harmonic of a guitar string has a frequency of 165 Hz. If the speed of waves on the string is 120 m/s, what is the string's length?

  A 0.36 m

  B 0.73 m

  C 1.1 m

  D 1.4 m

GRIDDED RESPONSE

8 The power output of a certain loudspeaker is 250.0 W. If a person listening to the sound produced by the speaker is sitting 6.5 m away, what is the intensity (in W/m^2) of the sound?

Noise Pollution

Suppose you are spending some quiet time alone—reading, studying, or just daydreaming. Suddenly your peaceful mood is shattered by the sound of a lawn mower, loud music, or an airplane taking off. If this has happened to you, then you have experienced noise pollution.

Noise is defined as any loud, discordant, or disagreeable sound, so classifying sounds as noise is often a matter of personal opinion. When you are at a party, you might enjoy listening to loud music, but when you are at home trying to sleep, you may find the same music very disturbing. Sometimes reducing noise pollution is simply a matter of turning down the volume. Other times, it's an engineering problem.

Identify a Problem: Hearing Loss

There are two kinds of noise pollution, both of which can result in long-term hearing problems and even physical damage to the ear. The small bones and hairlike cells of the inner ear are delicate and very sensitive to the compression waves we interpret as sounds.

The first type of noise pollution involves noises that are so loud they endanger the sensitive parts of the ear. Prolonged exposure to sounds of about 85 dB can begin to damage hearing irreversibly. Certain sounds above 120 dB can cause immediate damage. The sound level produced by a food blender or by diesel truck traffic is about 85 dB. A jet engine heard from a few meters away is about 140 dB. Have you ever noticed the "headphones" worn by the ground crew at an airport? These are ear protectors worn to prevent the hearing loss brought on by damage to the inner ear.

The second kind of noise pollution is more controversial because it involves noises that are considered annoyances. No one knows for sure how to measure levels of annoyance, but sometimes annoying noise becomes intolerable. Lack of sleep due to noise causes people to have slow reaction times and poor judgment, which can result in mistakes at work or school and accidents on the job or on the road. Scientists have found that continuous, irritating noise can raise blood pressure, which leads to other health problems.

Brainstorm Solutions

A major debate involves noise made by aircraft. The U.S. Department of Transportation reported that in September 2014, U.S. airlines alone carried more than 67 million domestic and international passengers. Airport traffic is expected to continue to grow at a rapid pace. People who live near airports once found aircraft noise an occasional annoyance, but because of increased traffic and runways added to accommodate growth, they now suffer sleep disruptions and other health effects.

Many people have organized groups to oppose airport expansion. Their primary concerns are the increase in noise and the decrease in property values associated with airport expansion. City governments, however, argue that an airport benefits the entire community both socially and economically and that airports must expand to meet the needs of increased populations. Officials have also argued that people knew they were taking chances by building or buying near an airport and that the community cannot compensate for their losses. Airlines contend that attempts to reduce noise by using less power during takeoffs or by veering away from populated areas can pose a serious threat to passenger safety.

Besides airports, people currently complain most about noise pollution from nearby construction sites, personal watercraft, loud stereos in homes and cars, all-terrain vehicles, snowmobiles, and power lawn equipment such as mowers and leaf blowers. Many people want to control such noise by passing laws to limit the use of this equipment to certain times of the day or by requiring that sound-muffling devices be used.

Opponents of these measures argue that much of this activity takes place on private property and that, in the case of building sites and industries, noise limitation would increase costs. Some public officials would like to control annoying noise but point out that laws to do so fall under the category of nuisance laws, which are notoriously difficult to enforce.

Noise pollution is also a problem in areas where few or no people live. Unwanted noise in wilderness areas can affect animal behavior and reproduction. Sometimes animals are simply scared away from their habitats. For this reason, the government has taken action in some national parks to reduce sightseeing flights, get rid of noisy campers, and limit or eliminate certain noisy vehicles. Some parks have even limited the number of people who can be in a park at any one time.

Select a Solution

At one particularly loud and busy airport in the Netherlands, residents complained when an additional runway was constructed in 2003. The noise from the aircraft could be heard from 29 km away. It was noted that the landscape around the airport, which was flat and open, amplified the noise like a megaphone. A commission was set up to research possible solutions. They noticed that noise levels decreased every autumn after nearby farmers had plowed and shaped the soil in their fields. They observed that the ridges absorbed the sound waves. The commission decided to reshape the land around the airport to drown out some of the noise.

By 2014, the airport had built a park just past the edge of one of the runways, called the Buitenschot Land Art Park. Workers dug 150 furrows in a large diamond-shaped pattern. Pointed ridges separated each furrow, and small parks and bike paths were added along the valleys. By the time it was finished, the park had cut earlier noise levels in half. The airport also worked with airlines on other measures to reduce noise from some of the louder airplanes.

Design Your Own

Conduct Research

1. Obtain a sound-level meter (available as an app on some smartphones), and measure the noise level at places where you and your friends might be during an average week. Also make some measurements at locations where sound is annoyingly loud. Be sure to hold the meter at head level and read the meter for 30 seconds to obtain an average. Present your findings to the class in a graphic display.

Test and Evaluate

2. Measure the sound levels at increasing distances from two sources of steady, loud noise. Then repeat your measurements, placing a layer of sound-absorbing material between the noise and the meter. Record all of your locations and measurements. Graph your data, and write an interpretation describing how sound level varies with distance from the source and how the sound level is affected by use of sound-absorbing materials.

Redesign to Improve

3. Try a different material from the one you just tested. Does a different material do a better job at absorbing sound? Does a combination of two materials work better? Does the distance between the sound source and the sound-absorbing layer change its effectiveness?

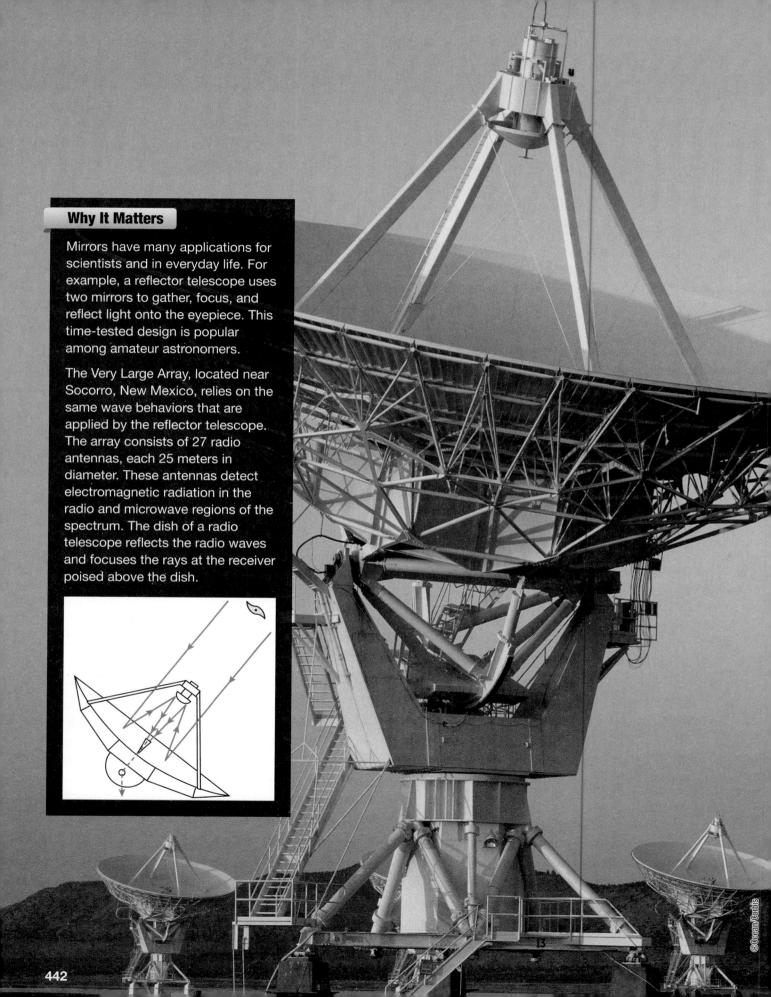

Why It Matters

Mirrors have many applications for scientists and in everyday life. For example, a reflector telescope uses two mirrors to gather, focus, and reflect light onto the eyepiece. This time-tested design is popular among amateur astronomers.

The Very Large Array, located near Socorro, New Mexico, relies on the same wave behaviors that are applied by the reflector telescope. The array consists of 27 radio antennas, each 25 meters in diameter. These antennas detect electromagnetic radiation in the radio and microwave regions of the spectrum. The dish of a radio telescope reflects the radio waves and focuses the rays at the receiver poised above the dish.

CHAPTER 13
Light and Reflection

SECTION 1
Characteristics of Light

SECTION 2
Flat Mirrors

SECTION 3
Curved Mirrors

SECTION 4
Color and Polarization

BIG IDEA

The electromagnetic spectrum includes all light waves, not just those visible to humans. Ray diagrams can be used to describe light waves and to predict the results of interactions with surfaces.

ONLINE Physics
HMHScience.com

ONLINE LABS
- Light and Mirrors
- Brightness of Light
- Designing a Device to Trace Drawings
- S.T.E.M. Lab Curved Mirrors

GO ONLINE
Animated
Physics
HMHScience.com

Curved Mirrors

SECTION 1

Objectives

▶ Identify the components of the electromagnetic spectrum.

▶ Calculate the frequency or wavelength of electromagnetic radiation.

▶ Recognize that light has a finite speed.

▶ Describe how the brightness of a light source is affected by distance.

Characteristics of Light

Key Term
electromagnetic wave

Electromagnetic Waves

When most people think of light, they think of the light that they can see. Some examples include the bright, white light that is produced by a light bulb or the sun. However, there is more to light than these examples. When you hold a piece of green plastic in front of a source of white light, you see green light pass through. This phenomenon is also true for other colors. What your eyes recognize as "white" light is actually light that can be separated into six elementary colors of the visible *spectrum*: red, orange, yellow, green, blue, and violet. If you examine a glass prism, such as the one in **Figure 1.1,** or any thick, triangular-shaped piece of glass, you will see sunlight pass through the glass and emerge as a band of colors.

The spectrum includes more than visible light.

Not all light is visible to the human eye. If you were to use certain types of photographic film to examine the light dispersed through a prism, you would find that the film records a much wider spectrum than the one you see. A variety of forms of radiation—including x-rays, micro-waves, and radio waves—have many of the same properties as visible light. The reason is that they are all examples of **electromagnetic waves.**

Light has been described as a particle, a wave, and even a combination of the two. The current model incorporates aspects of both particle and wave theories, but the wave model will be used in this section.

electromagnetic wave a wave that consists of oscillating electric and magnetic fields, which radiate outward from the source at the speed of light

FIGURE 1.1

Prism A prism separates light into its component colors.

©Photo Researchers, Inc.

Electromagnetic waves vary depending on frequency and wavelength.

In classical electromagnetic wave theory, light is considered to be a wave composed of oscillating electric and magnetic fields. These fields are perpendicular to the direction in which the wave moves, as shown in **Figure 1.2**. Therefore, electromagnetic waves are transverse waves. The electric and magnetic fields are also at right angles to each other.

Electromagnetic waves are distinguished by their different frequencies and wavelengths. In visible light, these differences in frequency and wavelength account for different colors. The difference in frequencies and wavelengths also distinguishes visible light from invisible electromagnetic radiation, such as x-rays.

Types of electromagnetic waves are listed in **Figure 1.3**. Note the wide range of wavelengths and frequencies. Although specific ranges are indicated in the table, the electromagnetic spectrum is, in reality, continuous. There is no sharp division between one kind of wave and the next. Some types of waves even have overlapping ranges.

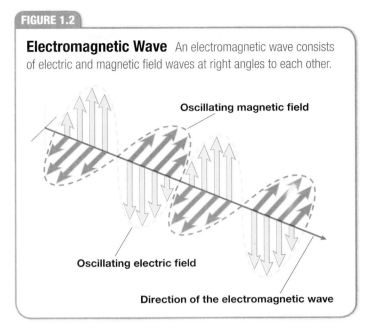

FIGURE 1.2

Electromagnetic Wave An electromagnetic wave consists of electric and magnetic field waves at right angles to each other.

Oscillating magnetic field

Oscillating electric field

Direction of the electromagnetic wave

FIGURE 1.3

THE ELECTROMAGNETIC SPECTRUM		
Classification	**Range**	**Applications**
radio waves	$\lambda > 30$ cm $f < 1.0 \times 10^9$ Hz	AM and FM radio; television
microwaves	30 cm $> \lambda > 1$ mm 1.0×10^9 Hz $< f < 3.0 \times 10^{11}$ Hz	radar; atomic and molecular research; aircraft navigation; microwave ovens
infrared (IR) waves	1 mm $> \lambda > 700$ nm 3.0×10^{11} Hz $< f < 4.3 \times 10^{14}$ Hz	molecular vibrational spectra; infrared photography; physical therapy
visible light	700 nm (red) $> \lambda > 400$ nm (violet) 4.3×10^{14} Hz $< f < 7.5 \times 10^{14}$ Hz	visible-light photography; optical microscopy; optical astronomy
ultraviolet (UV) light	400 nm $> \lambda > 60$ nm 7.5×10^{14} Hz $< f < 5.0 \times 10^{15}$ Hz	sterilization of medical instruments; identification of fluorescent minerals
x-rays	60 nm $> \lambda > 10^{-4}$ nm 5.0×10^{15} Hz $< f < 3.0 \times 10^{21}$ Hz	medical examination of bones, teeth, and vital organs; treatment for types of cancer
gamma rays	0.1 nm $> \lambda > 10^{-5}$ nm 3.0×10^{18} Hz $< f < 3.0 \times 10^{22}$ Hz	examination of thick materials for structural flaws; treatment for types of cancer; food irradiation

All electromagnetic waves move at the speed of light.

All forms of electromagnetic radiation travel at a single high speed in a vacuum. Early experimental attempts to determine the speed of light failed because this speed is so great. As experimental techniques improved, especially during the nineteenth and early twentieth centuries, the speed of light was determined with increasing accuracy and precision. By the mid-twentieth century, the experimental error was less than 0.001 percent. The currently accepted value for light traveling in a vacuum is $2.997\,924\,58 \times 10^8$ m/s. Light travels slightly slower in air, with a speed of $2.997\,09 \times 10^8$ m/s. For calculations in this book, the value used for both situations will be 3.00×10^8 m/s.

The relationship between frequency, wavelength, and speed described in the chapter on vibrations and waves also holds true for light waves.

Wave Speed Equation

$$c = f\lambda$$

speed of light = frequency × wavelength

GO ONLINE

Interactive Demo
HMHScience.com

Electromagnetic Waves

Sample Problem A A range of 6.98×10^8 Hz to 7.46×10^8 Hz once used for analog TV channels is now used for some 3G and 4G cell phones. What are the longest and shortest wavelengths in this frequency range?

❶ ANALYZE

Given: $f_1 = 6.98 \times 10^8$ Hz $f_2 = 7.46 \times 10^8$ Hz

$c = 3.00 \times 10^8$ m/s

Unknown: $\lambda_1 = ?$ $\lambda_2 = ?$

❷ SOLVE

Use the wave speed equation on this page to find the wavelengths:

$$c = f\lambda \qquad \lambda = \frac{c}{f}$$

$$\lambda_1 = \frac{3.00 \times 10^8 \text{ m/s}}{6.98 \times 10^8 \text{ Hz}}$$

$$\boxed{\lambda_1 = 0.430 \text{ m}}$$

$$\lambda_2 = \frac{3.00 \times 10^8 \text{ m/s}}{7.46 \times 10^8 \text{ Hz}}$$

$$\boxed{\lambda_2 = 0.420 \text{ m}}$$

Calculator Solution

Although the calculator solutions are 0.429799427 m and 0.402144772 m, both answers must be rounded to three digits because the frequencies have only three significant figures.

Continued

Electromagnetic Waves (continued)

1. Gamma-ray bursters are objects in the universe that emit pulses of gamma rays with high energies. The frequency of the most energetic bursts has been measured at around 3.0×10^{21} Hz. What is the wavelength of these gamma rays?

2. What is the wavelength range for the FM radio band (88 MHz–108 MHz)?

3. A radio wave traveling through Earth's atmosphere has a frequency of 7.6270×10^8 Hz and a wavelength of 39.296 cm. How fast does this radio wave travel?

4. Microwave radiation traveling in space has a frequency of 1.17306×10^{11} Hz and a wavelength of 2.5556 mm. How fast does this radiation travel?

5. The portion of the visible spectrum that appears brightest to the human eye is around 560 nm in wavelength, which corresponds to yellow-green. What is the frequency of 560 nm light?

6. What is the frequency of highly energetic ultraviolet radiation that has a wavelength of 125 nm?

Waves can be approximated as rays.

Consider an ocean wave coming toward the shore. The broad crest of the wave that is perpendicular to the wave's motion consists of a line of water particles. Similarly, another line of water particles forms a low-lying trough in the wave, and still another line of particles forms the crest of a second wave. In any type of wave, these lines of particles are called *wave fronts.*

All the points on the wave front of a plane wave can be treated as point sources, that is, coming from a source of negligible size. A few of these points are shown on the initial wave front in **Figure 1.4.** Each of these point sources produces a circular or spherical secondary wave, or *wavelet.* The radii of these wavelets are indicated by the blue arrows in **Figure 1.4.** The line that is tangent to each of these wavelets at some later time determines the new position of the initial wave front (the new wave front in **Figure 1.4**). This approach to analyzing waves is called *Huygens's principle,* named for the physicist Christiaan Huygens, who developed it.

Huygens's principle can be used to derive the properties of any wave (including light) that interacts with matter, but the same results can be obtained by treating the propagating wave as a straight line perpendicular to the wave front. This line is called a *ray,* and this simplification is called the *ray approximation.*

FIGURE 1.4

Huygens's Principle According to Huygens's principle, a wave front can be divided into point sources. The line tangent to the wavelets from these sources marks the wave front's new position.

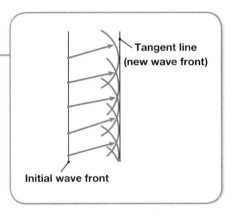

Tangent line (new wave front)

Initial wave front

Illuminance decreases as the square of the distance from the source.

You have probably noticed that it is easier to read a book beside a lamp using a 100 W bulb rather than a 25 W bulb. It is also easier to read nearer to a lamp than farther from a lamp. These experiences suggest that the intensity of light depends on both the amount of light energy emitted from a source and the distance from the light source.

Light bulbs are rated by their power input (measured in watts) and their light output. The rate at which light is emitted from a source is called the *luminous flux* and is measured in *lumens* (lm). Luminous flux is a measure of power output but is weighted to take into account the response of the human eye to light. Luminous flux helps us understand why the illumination on a book page is reduced as you move away from a light. Imagine spherical surfaces of different sizes with a point light source at the center of the sphere, shown in **Figure 1.5.** A point source provides light equally in all directions. The principle of conservation of energy requires that the luminous flux is the same on each sphere. However, the luminous flux divided by the area of the surface, which is called the *illuminance* (measured in lm/m^2, or *lux*), decreases as the radius squared when you move away from a light source.

FIGURE 1.5

Luminous Flux Less light falls on each unit square as the distance from the source increases.

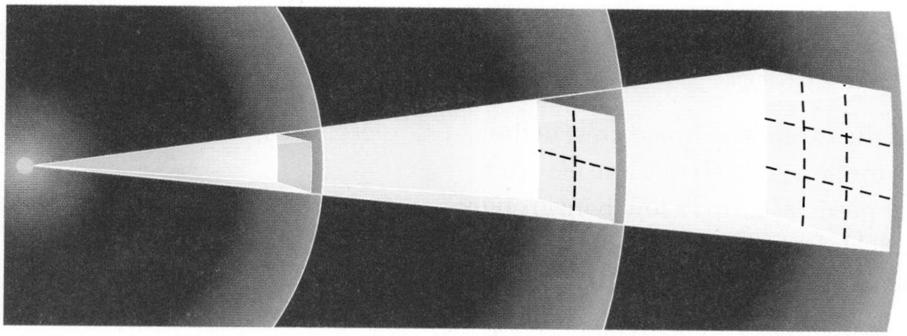

1 m   2 m   3 m

SECTION 1 FORMATIVE ASSESSMENT

Reviewing Main Ideas

1. Identify which portions of the electromagnetic spectrum are used in each of the devices listed.
   a. a microwave oven
   b. a television set
   c. a single-lens reflex camera

2. If an electromagnetic wave has a frequency of 7.57×10^{14} Hz, what is its wavelength? To what part of the spectrum does this wave belong?

3. Galileo performed an experiment to measure the speed of light by timing how long it took light to travel from a lamp he was holding to an assistant about 1.5 km away and back again. Why was Galileo unable to conclude that light had a finite speed?

Critical Thinking

4. How bright would the sun appear to an observer on Earth if the sun were four times farther from Earth than it actually is? Express your answer as a fraction of the sun's brightness on Earth's surface.

Flat Mirrors

Key Terms

reflection
angle of incidence

angle of reflection
virtual image

Reflection of Light

Suppose you have just had your hair cut and you want to know what the back of your head looks like. You can do this seemingly impossible task by using two mirrors to direct light from behind your head to your eyes. Redirecting light with mirrors reveals a basic property of light's interaction with matter.

Light traveling through a uniform substance, whether it is air, water, or a vacuum, always travels in a straight line. However, when the light encounters a different substance, its path will change. If a material is opaque to the light, such as the dark, highly polished surface of a wooden table, the light will not pass into the material more than a few wavelengths. Part of the light is absorbed, and the rest of it is deflected at the surface. This change in the direction of the light is called **reflection.** All substances absorb at least some incoming light and reflect the rest. A good mirror can reflect about 90 percent of the incident light, but no surface is a perfect reflector. Notice in **Figure 2.1** that the images of the golf ball get successively darker.

The texture of a surface affects how it reflects light.

The manner in which light is reflected from a surface depends on the surface's smoothness. Light that is reflected from a rough, textured surface, such as paper, cloth, or unpolished wood, is reflected in many different directions, as shown in **Figure 2.2(a).** This type of reflection is called *diffuse reflection* and is covered later in the chapter.

Light reflected from smooth, shiny surfaces, such as a mirror or water in a pond, is reflected in one direction only, as shown in **Figure 2.2(b).** This type of reflection is called *specular reflection*. A surface is considered smooth if its surface variations are small compared with the wavelength of the incoming light. For our discussion, reflection will be used to mean only specular reflection.

reflection the change in direction of an electromagnetic wave at a surface that causes it to move away from the surface

FIGURE 2.1

Reflection Mirrors reflect most incoming light; multiple images of an object between two mirrors can form.

FIGURE 2.2

Diffuse and Specular Reflection Diffusely reflected light is reflected in many directions **(a),** whereas specularly reflected light is reflected in the same forward direction only **(b).**

(a)

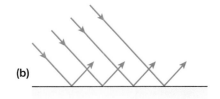

(b)

FIGURE 2.3

Symmetry of Reflected Light The symmetry of reflected light **(a)** is described by the law of reflection, which states that the angles of the incoming and reflected rays are equal **(b)**.

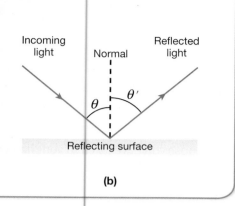

Incoming light   Normal   Reflected light

θ θ'

Reflecting surface

(a)   **(b)**

Incoming and reflected angles are equal.

You probably have noticed that when incoming rays of light strike a smooth reflecting surface, such as a polished table or mirror, at an angle close to the surface, the reflected rays are also close to the surface. When the incoming rays are high above the reflecting surface, the reflected rays are also high above the surface. An example of this similarity between incoming and reflected rays is shown in **Figure 2.3(a)**.

If a straight line is drawn perpendicular to the reflecting surface at the point where the incoming ray strikes the surface, the **angle of incidence** and the **angle of reflection** can be defined with respect to the line. Careful measurements of the incident and reflected angles, θ and θ', respectively, reveal that the angles are equal, as illustrated in **Figure 2.3(b)**.

$$\theta = \theta'$$

angle of incoming light ray = angle of reflected light ray

The line perpendicular to the reflecting surface is referred to as the *normal* to the surface. It therefore follows that the angle between the incoming ray and the surface equals $90° − \theta$, and the angle between the reflected ray and the surface equals $90° − \theta'$.

angle of incidence the angle between a ray that strikes a surface and the line perpendicular to that surface at the point of contact

angle of reflection the angle formed by the line perpendicular to a surface and the direction in which a reflected ray moves

FIGURE 2.4

Flat Mirror Light reflecting off of a flat mirror creates an image that appears to be behind the mirror.

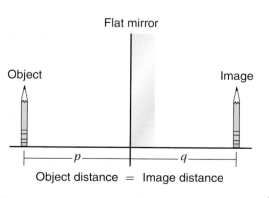

Flat mirror

Object   Image

p q

Object distance = Image distance

Flat Mirrors

The simplest mirror is the *flat mirror*, also called a *plane mirror*. If an object, such as a pencil, is placed at a distance in front of a flat mirror and light is bounced off the object, light rays will spread out from the object and reflect from the mirror's surface. To an observer looking at the mirror, these rays appear to come from a location on the other side of the mirror. As a convention, an object's image is said to be at this location behind the mirror because the light appears to come from that point. The relationship between the *object distance* from the mirror, represented as p, and the *image distance*, represented as q, is such that the object and image distances are equal, as shown in **Figure 2.4**. Similarly, the image of the object is the same size as the object.

A **virtual image** occurs when rays appear to come from a location, such as from behind a mirror, but do not actually converge at that location. As shown in **Figure 2.5(a)**, a flat mirror always forms a virtual image, which always appears as if it is behind the surface of the mirror. For this reason, a virtual image can never be displayed on a physical surface.

virtual image an image from which light rays appear to diverge, even though they are not actually focused there; a virtual image cannot be projected on a screen

Image location can be predicted with ray diagrams.

Ray diagrams, such as the one shown in **Figure 2.5(b)**, are drawings that use simple geometry to locate an image formed by a mirror. Suppose you want to make a ray diagram for a pencil placed in front of a flat mirror. First, sketch the situation. Draw the location and arrangement of the mirror and the position of the pencil with respect to the mirror. Construct the drawing so that the object and the image distances (p and q, respectively) are proportional to their actual sizes. To simplify matters, we will consider only the tip of the pencil.

To pinpoint the location of the pencil tip's image, draw two rays on your diagram. Draw the first ray from the pencil tip perpendicular to the mirror's surface. Because this ray makes an angle of 0° with a line perpendicular (or *normal*) to the mirror, the angle of reflection also equals 0°, causing the ray to reflect back on itself. In **Figure 2.5(b)**, this ray is denoted by the number 1 and is shown with arrows pointing in both directions because the incident ray reflects back on itself.

Draw the second ray from the tip of the pencil to the mirror, but this time place the ray at an angle that is not perpendicular to the surface of the mirror. The second ray is denoted in **Figure 2.5(b)** by the number 2. Then, draw the reflected ray, keeping in mind that it will reflect away from the surface of the mirror at an angle, θ', equal to the angle of incidence, θ.

Next, trace both reflected rays back to the point from which they appear to have originated, that is, behind the mirror. Use dotted lines when drawing these rays that appear to emerge from behind the mirror to distinguish them from the rays of light in front of the mirror. The point at which these dotted lines meet is the image point, which in this case is where the image of the pencil's tip forms.

By continuing this process for all of the other parts of the pencil, you can locate the complete virtual image of the pencil. Note that the pencil's image appears as far behind the mirror as the pencil is in front of the mirror ($p = q$). Likewise, the object height, h, equals the image height, h'.

FIGURE 2.5

Ray Diagram The position and size of the virtual image that forms in a flat mirror **(a)** can be predicted by constructing a ray diagram **(b)**.

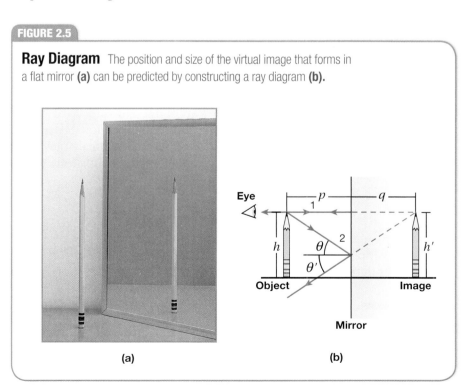

(a)

(b)

FIGURE 2.6

Mirror Reversal The front of an object becomes the back of its image.

reflection

This ray-tracing procedure will work for any object placed in front of a flat mirror. By selecting a single point on the object (usually its uppermost tip or edge), you can use ray tracing to locate the same point on the image. The rest of the image can be added once the image point and image distance have been determined.

The image formed by a flat mirror appears reversed to an observer in front of the mirror. You can easily observe this effect by placing a piece of writing in front of a mirror, as shown in **Figure 2.6**. In the mirror, each of the letters is reversed. You may also notice that the angle the word and its reflection make with respect to the mirror is the same.

✔ SECTION 2 FORMATIVE ASSESSMENT

● Reviewing Main Ideas

1. Which of the following are examples of specular reflection, and which are examples of diffuse reflection?
   a. reflection of light from the surface of a lake on a calm day
   b. reflection of light from a plastic trash bag
   c. reflection of light from the lens of eyeglasses
   d. reflection of light from a carpet

2. Suppose you are holding a flat mirror and standing at the center of a giant clock face built into the floor. Someone standing at 12 o'clock shines a beam of light toward you, and you want to use the mirror to reflect the beam toward an observer standing at 5 o'clock. What should the angle of incidence be to achieve this? What should the angle of reflection be?

3. Some department-store windows are slanted inward at the bottom. This is to decrease the glare from brightly illuminated buildings across the street, which would make it difficult for shoppers to see the display inside and near the bottom of the window. Sketch a light ray reflecting from such a window to show how this technique works.

Interpreting Graphics

4. The photograph in **Figure 2.1** shows multiple images that were created by multiple reflections between two flat mirrors. What conclusion can you make about the relative orientation of the mirrors? Explain your answer.

✔ Critical Thinking

5. If one wall of a room consists of a large flat mirror, how much larger will the room appear to be? Explain your answer.

6. Why does a flat mirror appear to reverse the person looking into a mirror left to right but not up and down?

Curved Mirrors

Key Terms

concave spherical mirror   real image   convex spherical mirror

Concave Spherical Mirrors

Small, circular mirrors, such as those used on dressing tables, may appear at first glance to be the same as flat mirrors. However, the images they form differ from those formed by flat mirrors. The images for objects close to the mirror are larger than the object, as shown in **Figure 3.1(a),** whereas the images of objects far from the mirror are smaller and upside down, as shown in **Figure 3.1(b).** Images such as these are characteristic of curved mirrors. The image in **Figure 3.1(a)** is a virtual image like those created by flat mirrors. In contrast, the image in **Figure 3.1(b)** is a *real* image.

Concave mirrors can be used to form real images.

One basic type of curved mirror is the spherical mirror. A spherical mirror, as its name implies, has the shape of part of a sphere's surface. A spherical mirror with light reflecting from its silvered, concave surface (that is, the inner surface of a sphere) is called a **concave spherical mirror.** Concave mirrors are used whenever a magnified image of an object is needed, as in the case of the dressing-table mirror.

One factor that determines where the image will appear in a concave spherical mirror and how large that image will be is the radius of curvature, *R,* of the mirror. The radius of curvature is the same as the radius of the spherical shell of which the mirror is a small part; *R* is therefore the distance from the mirror's surface to the center of curvature, *C.*

Objectives

▶ Calculate distances and focal lengths using the mirror equation for concave and convex spherical mirrors.

▶ Draw ray diagrams to find the image distance and magnification for concave and convex spherical mirrors.

▶ Distinguish between real and virtual images.

▶ Describe how parabolic mirrors differ from spherical mirrors.

SC.912.P.10.22 Construct ray diagrams and use thin lens and mirror equations to locate the images formed by lenses and mirrors.

concave spherical mirror a mirror whose reflecting surface is a segment of the inside of a sphere

---

FIGURE 3.1

Concave Spherical Mirror Curved mirrors can be used to form images that are larger **(a)** or smaller **(b)** than the object.

(a)   (b)

FIGURE 3.2

Images and Concave Mirrors

(a) The rays from a light bulb converge to form a real image in front of a concave mirror.

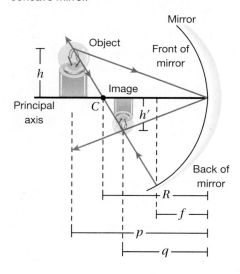

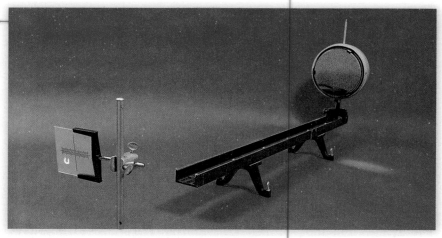

(b) In this lab setup, the real image of a light-bulb filament appears on a glass plate in front of a concave mirror.

real image an image that is formed by the intersection of light rays; a real image can be projected on a screen

Imagine a light bulb placed upright at a distance p from a concave spherical mirror, as shown in **Figure 3.2(a).** The base of the bulb is along the mirror's principal axis, which is the line that extends infinitely from the center of the mirror's surface through the center of curvature, C. Light rays diverge from the light bulb, reflect from the mirror's surface, and converge at some distance (q) in front of the mirror. Because the light rays reflected by the mirror actually pass through the image point—which in this case is below the principal axis—the image forms in front of the mirror.

If you place a piece of paper at the image point, you will see on the paper a sharp and clear image of the light bulb. As you move the paper in either direction away from the image point, the rays diverge, and the image becomes unfocused. An image of this type is called a **real image.** Unlike the virtual images that appear behind a flat mirror, real images can be displayed on a surface, like the images on a movie screen. **Figure 3.2(b)** shows a real image of a light-bulb filament on a glass plate in front of a concave mirror. This light bulb itself is outside the photograph, to the left.

Images created by spherical mirrors suffer from spherical aberration.

As you draw ray diagrams, you may notice that certain rays do not exactly intersect at the image point. This phenomenon is particularly noticeable for rays that are far from the principal axis and for mirrors with a small radius of curvature. This situation, called *spherical aberration,* also occurs with real light rays and real spherical mirrors and will be discussed further at the end of this section when we introduce *parabolic mirrors.* In the next pages of this section, you will learn about the mirror equation and ray diagrams. Both of these concepts are valid only for *paraxial rays,* but they do provide quite useful approximations. Paraxial rays are those light rays that are very near the principal axis of the mirror. We will assume that all of the rays used in our drawings and calculations with spherical mirrors are paraxial, even though they may not appear to be so in all of the diagrams accompanying the text.

Image location can be predicted with the mirror equation.

Looking at **Figure 3.2(a),** you can see that object distance, image distance, and radius of curvature are interdependent. If the object distance and radius of curvature of the mirror are known, you can predict where the image will appear. Alternatively, the radius of curvature of a mirror can be calculated if you know where the image is for a given object distance. The following equation relates object distance, p, image distance, q, and the radius of curvature, R, and is called the *mirror equation.*

$$\frac{1}{p} + \frac{1}{q} = \frac{2}{R}$$

If the light bulb is placed very far from the mirror, the object distance, p, is great enough compared with R that $1/p$ is almost 0. In this case, q is almost $R/2$, so the image forms about halfway between the center of curvature and the center of the mirror's surface. The image point, as shown in **Figure 3.3,** is in this special case called the *focal point* of the mirror and is denoted by the capital letter F. Because the light rays are reversible, the reflected rays from a light source at the focal point will emerge parallel to each other and will not form an image.

For light emerging from a source very far away from a mirror, the light rays are essentially parallel to one another. In this case, an image forms at the focal point, F, and the image distance is called the *focal length,* denoted by the lowercase letter f. For a spherical mirror, the focal length is equal to half the radius of curvature of the mirror. The mirror equation can therefore be expressed in terms of the focal length.

Mirror Equation

$$\frac{1}{p} + \frac{1}{q} = \frac{1}{f}$$

$$\frac{1}{\textbf{object distance}} + \frac{1}{\textbf{image distance}} = \frac{1}{\textbf{focal length}}$$

FIGURE 3.3

Parallel Light Rays Light rays that are parallel converge at a single point **(a),** which can be represented in a diagram **(b),** when the rays are assumed to be from a distant object ($p \approx \infty$).

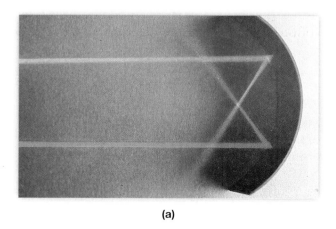

(a)

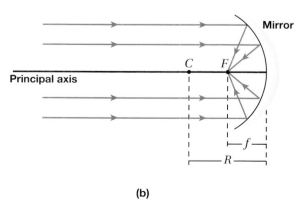

(b)

A set of sign conventions for the three variables must be established for use with the mirror equation. The region in which light rays reflect and form real images is called the front side of the mirror. The other side, where light rays do not exist—and where virtual images are formed—is called the back side of the mirror.

Object and image distances have a positive sign when measured from the center of the mirror to any point on the mirror's front side. Distances for images that form on the back side of the mirror always have a negative sign. Because the mirrored surface is on the front side of a concave mirror, its focal length always has a positive sign. The object and image heights are positive when above the principal axis and negative when below.

Magnification relates image and object sizes.

Unlike flat mirrors, curved mirrors form images that are not the same size as the object. The measure of how large or small the image is with respect to the original object's size is called the *magnification* of the image.

If you know where an object's image will form for a given object distance, you can determine the magnification of the image. Magnification, *M,* is defined as the ratio of the height of the object's image to the object's actual height. *M* also equals the negative of the ratio of the image distance to the object distance. If an image is smaller than the object, the magnitude of its magnification is less than 1. If the image is larger than the object, the magnitude of its magnification is greater than 1. Magnification is a unitless quantity.

Equation for Magnification

$$M = \frac{h'}{h} = -\frac{q}{p}$$

$$\text{magnification} = \frac{\text{image height}}{\text{object height}} = -\frac{\text{image distance}}{\text{object distance}}$$

M is negative for an image that is upside down, or *inverted,* with respect to the object. The image is also in front of the mirror. When the image is *upright* with respect to the object, *M* is positive and the image is behind the mirror. The conventions for magnification are listed in **Figure 3.4**.

FIGURE 3.4

SIGN CONVENTIONS FOR MAGNIFICATION		
Orientation of image with respect to object	Sign of *M*	Type of image this applies to
upright	+	virtual
inverted	−	real

Ray diagrams can be used for concave spherical mirrors.

Ray diagrams are useful for checking values calculated from the mirror and magnification equations. The techniques for ray diagrams that were used to locate the image for an object in front of a flat mirror can also be used for concave spherical mirrors. When drawing ray diagrams for concave mirrors, follow the basic procedure for a flat mirror but also measure all distances along the principal axis and mark the center of curvature, C, and the focal point, F. As with a flat mirror, draw the diagram to scale. For instance, if the object distance is 50 cm, you can draw the object distance as 5 cm.

For spherical mirrors, three reference rays are used to find the image point. The intersection of any *two* rays locates the image. The third ray should intersect at the same point and can be used to check the diagram. These reference rays are described in **Figure 3.5.**

FIGURE 3.5

RULES FOR DRAWING REFERENCE RAYS

Ray	Line drawn from object to mirror	Line drawn from mirror to image after reflection
1	parallel to principal axis	through focal point F
2	through focal point F	parallel to principal axis
3	through center of curvature C	back along itself through C

The image distance in the diagram should agree with the value for q calculated from the mirror equation. However, the image distance may differ because of inaccuracies that arise from drawing the ray diagrams at a reduced scale and far from the principal axis. Ray diagrams should therefore be used to obtain *approximate* values only; they should not be relied on for the best quantitative results.

Concave mirrors can produce both real and virtual images.

When an object is moved toward a concave spherical mirror, its image changes, as shown in **Figure 3.6**. If the object is very far from the mirror, the light rays converge very near the focal point, F, of the mirror and form an image there. For objects at a finite distance greater than the radius of curvature, C, the image is real, smaller than the object, inverted, and located between C and F. When the object is at C, the image is real, located at C, and inverted. For an object at C, the image is the same size as the object. If the object is located between C and F, the image will be real, inverted, larger than the object, and located outside of C. When the object is at the focal point, no image is formed. When the object lies between F and the mirror surface, the image forms again, but now it becomes virtual, upright, and larger.

FIGURE 3.6

IMAGES CREATED BY CONCAVE MIRRORS

Ray Diagrams

1.

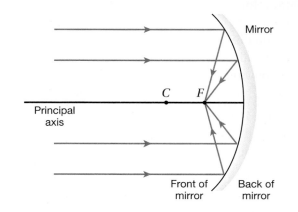

Configuration: object at infinity
Image: real image at F

2.

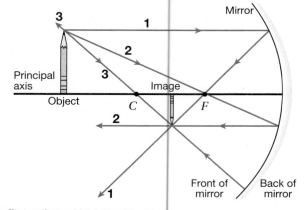

Configuration: object outside C
Image: real image between C and F, inverted with magnification < 1

3.

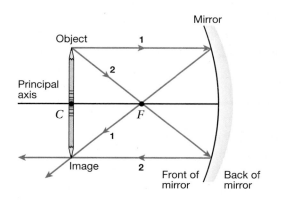

Configuration: object at C
Image: real image at C, inverted with magnification $= 1$

4.

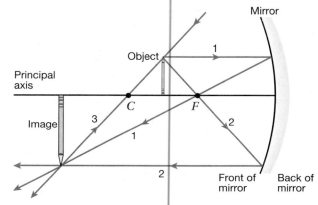

Configuration: object between C and F
Image: real image outside C, inverted with magnification > 1

5.

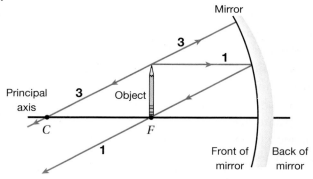

Configuration: object at F
Image: image at infinity (no image)

6.

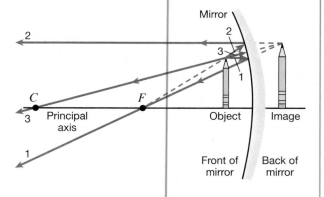

Configuration: object inside F
Image: virtual, upright image at C with magnification > 1

GO ONLINE

Interactive Demo
HMHScience.com

Sample Problem B A concave spherical mirror has a focal length of 10.0 cm. Locate the image of a pencil that is placed upright 30.0 cm from the mirror. Find the magnification of the image. Draw a ray diagram to confirm your answer.

 ANALYZE

Determine the sign and magnitude of the focal length and object size.

$$f = +10.0 \text{ cm} \qquad p = +30.0 \text{ cm}$$

The mirror is concave, so f is positive. The object is in front of the mirror, so p is positive.

Unknown: $q = ?$
$M = ?$

Diagram: Draw a ray diagram using the rules given in **Figure 3.5.**

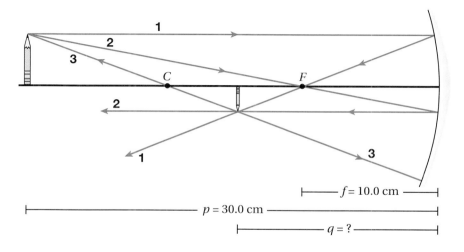

 PLAN

Use the mirror equation to relate the object and image distances to the focal length.

$$\frac{1}{p} + \frac{1}{q} = \frac{1}{f}$$

Use the magnification equation in terms of object and image distances.

$$M = -\frac{q}{p}$$

Rearrange the equation to isolate the image distance, and calculate.

Subtract the reciprocal of the object distance from the reciprocal of the focal length to obtain an expression for the unknown image distance.

$$\frac{1}{q} = \frac{1}{f} - \frac{1}{p}$$

Continued

Imaging with Concave Mirrors (continued)

③ SOLVE

Substitute the values for f and p into the mirror equation and the magnification equation to find the image distance and magnification.

$$\frac{1}{q} = \frac{1}{10.0 \text{ cm}} - \frac{1}{30.0 \text{ cm}} = \frac{0.100}{1 \text{ cm}} - \frac{0.033}{1 \text{ cm}} = \frac{0.067}{1 \text{ cm}}$$

$$\boxed{q = 15 \text{ cm}}$$

$$\boxed{M = -\frac{q}{p} = -\frac{15 \text{ cm}}{30.0 \text{ cm}} = -0.50}$$

④ CHECK YOUR WORK

Evaluate your answer in terms of the image location and size.
The image appears between the focal point (10.0 cm) and the center of curvature (20.0 cm), as confirmed by the ray diagram. The image is smaller than the object and inverted ($-1 < M < 0$), as is also confirmed by the ray diagram. The image is therefore real.

Practice

1. Find the image distance and magnification of the mirror in the sample problem when the object distances are 10.0 cm and 5.00 cm. Are the images real or virtual? Are the images inverted or upright? Draw a ray diagram for each case to confirm your results.

2. A concave shaving mirror has a focal length of 33 cm. Calculate the image position of a cologne bottle placed in front of the mirror at a distance of 93 cm. Calculate the magnification of the image. Is the image real or virtual? Is the image inverted or upright? Draw a ray diagram to show where the image forms and how large it is with respect to the object.

3. A concave makeup mirror is designed so that a person 25.0 cm in front of it sees an upright image at a distance of 50.0 cm behind the mirror. What is the radius of curvature of the mirror? What is the magnification of the image? Is the image real or virtual?

4. A pen placed 11.0 cm from a concave spherical mirror produces a real image 13.2 cm from the mirror. What is the focal length of the mirror? What is the magnification of the image? If the pen is placed 27.0 cm from the mirror, what is the new position of the image? What is the magnification of the new image? Is the new image real or virtual? Draw ray diagrams to confirm your results.

Convex Spherical Mirrors

On recent models of automobiles, there is a side-view mirror on the passenger's side of the car. Unlike the flat mirror on the driver's side, which produces unmagnified images, the passenger's mirror bulges outward at the center. Images in this mirror are distorted near the mirror's edges, and the image is smaller than the object. This type of mirror is called a **convex spherical mirror.**

A convex spherical mirror is a segment of a sphere that is silvered so that light is reflected from the sphere's outer, convex surface. This type of mirror is also called a diverging mirror because the incoming rays diverge after reflection as though they were coming from some point behind the mirror. The resulting image is therefore always virtual, and the image distance is always negative. Because the mirrored surface is on the side opposite the radius of curvature, a convex spherical mirror also has a negative focal length. The sign conventions for all mirrors are summarized in **Figure 3.8.**

The technique for drawing ray diagrams for a convex mirror differs slightly from that for concave mirrors. The focal point and center of curvature are situated behind the mirror's surface. Dotted lines are extended along the reflected reference rays to points behind the mirror, as shown in **Figure 3.7(a).** A virtual, upright image forms where the three rays apparently intersect. Magnification for convex mirrors is always less than 1, as shown in **Figure 3.7(b).**

Convex spherical mirrors take the objects in a large field of view and produce a small image, so they are well suited for providing a fixed observer with a complete view of a large area. Convex mirrors are often placed in stores to help employees monitor customers and at the intersections of busy hallways so that people in both hallways can tell when others are approaching.

The side-view mirror on the passenger's side of a car is another application of the convex mirror. This mirror usually carries the warning "objects are closer than they appear." Without this warning, a driver might think that he or she is looking into a flat mirror, which does not alter the size of the image. The driver could therefore be fooled into believing that a vehicle is farther away than it is because the image is smaller than the actual object.

convex spherical mirror a mirror whose reflecting surface is an outward-curved segment of a sphere

---

FIGURE 3.7

Reflection from a Convex Mirror Light rays diverge upon reflection from a convex mirror **(a),** forming a virtual image that is always smaller than the object **(b).**

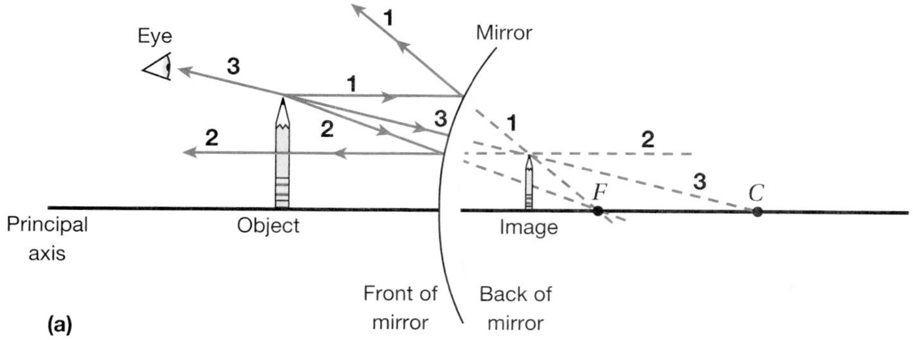

(a)

(b)

Did YOU Know?

There are certain circumstances in which the object for one mirror is the image that appears behind another mirror. In these cases, the object is virtual and has a negative object distance. Because of the rarity of these situations, virtual object distance ($p < 0$) has not been listed in **Figure 3.8**.

FIGURE 3.8

SIGN CONVENTIONS FOR MIRRORS

Symbol	Situation	Sign	
p	object is in front of the mirror (real object)	+	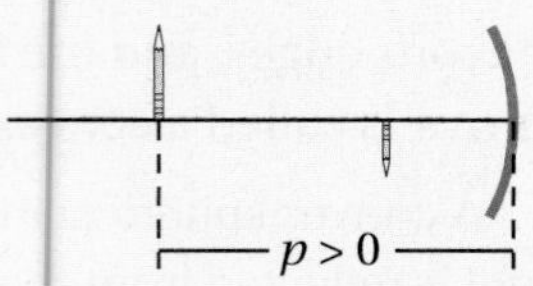 $p > 0$
q	image is in front of the mirror (real image)	+	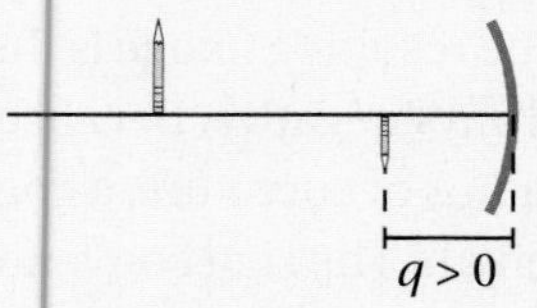 $q > 0$
q	image is behind the mirror (virtual image)	−	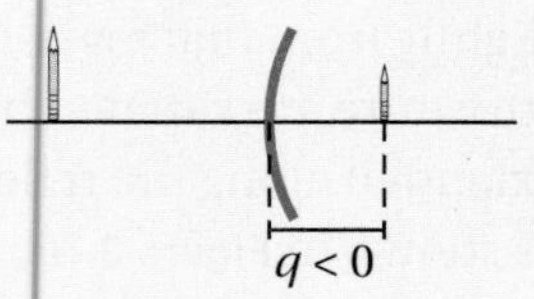 $q < 0$
R, f	center of curvature is in front of the mirror (concave spherical mirror)	+	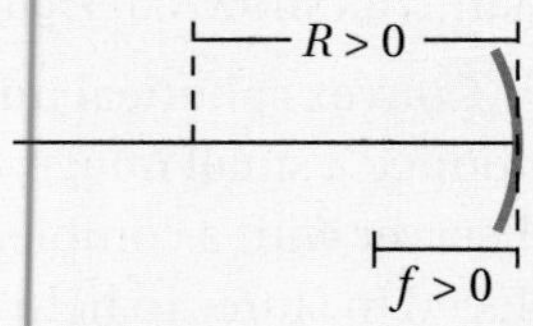 $R > 0$ $f > 0$
R, f	center of curvature is behind the mirror (convex spherical mirror)	−	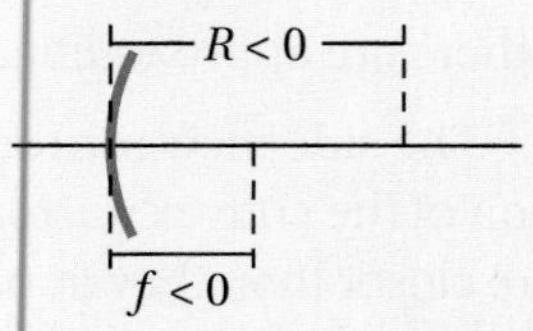 $R < 0$ $f < 0$
R, f	mirror has no curvature (flat mirror)	∞	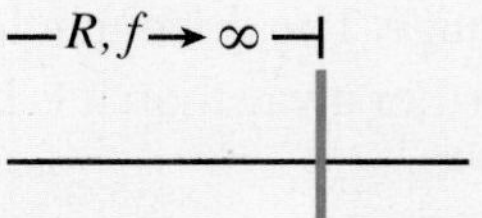 $R, f \rightarrow \infty$
h'	image is above the principal axis	+	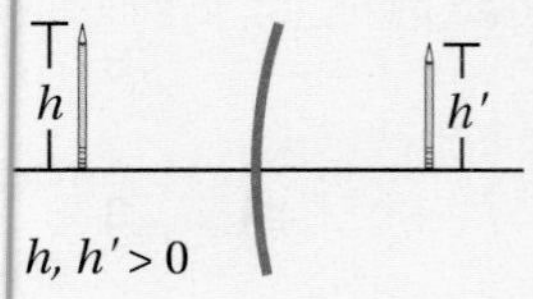 $h, h' > 0$
h'	image is below the principal axis	−	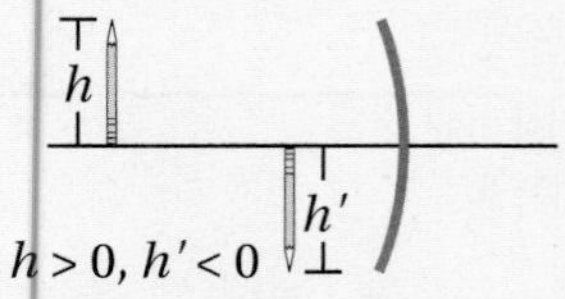 $h > 0, h' < 0$

GO ONLINE

Interactive Demo
HMHScience.com

Sample Problem C A pencil with a length of 9.50 cm is placed on its end in front of a convex spherical mirror with a focal length of 12.0 cm. An erect image is formed 8.88 cm behind the mirror. Find the position of the pencil, the magnification of the image, and the height of the image.

1 ANALYZE

Given: $f = -12.0$ cm $q = -8.88$ cm $h = 9.50$ cm

Because the mirror is convex, the focal length is negative. The image is behind the mirror, so q is also negative.

Unknown: $p = ?$ $h' = ?$ $M = ?$

Diagram: Construct a ray diagram.

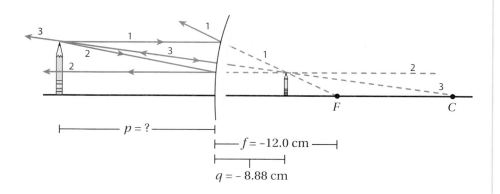

2 PLAN

Choose an equation or situation: Use the mirror equation.

$$\frac{1}{p} + \frac{1}{q} = \frac{1}{f}$$

Use the magnification formula.

$$M = \frac{h'}{h} = -\frac{q}{p}$$

Rearrange the equation to isolate the unknown:

$$\frac{1}{p} = \frac{1}{f} - \frac{1}{q} \text{ and } h' = -Mh$$

3 SOLVE

Substitute the values into the first equation above, and solve for p:

$$\frac{1}{p} = \frac{1}{-12.0 \text{ cm}} - \frac{1}{-8.88 \text{ cm}}$$

$$\frac{1}{p} = \frac{-0.0833}{1 \text{ cm}} - \frac{-0.112}{1 \text{ cm}} = \frac{0.296}{1 \text{ cm}}$$

$$\boxed{p = 33.8 \text{ cm}}$$

Continued

Substitute the values for p and q to find the magnification of the image.

$$M = -\frac{q}{p} = -\frac{-8.88 \text{ cm}}{33.8 \text{ cm}}$$

$$\boxed{M = 0.262}$$

Substitute the values for p, q, and h to find the height of the image.

$$h' = -Mh = 0.262 \times 9.50 \text{ cm}$$

$$\boxed{h' = 2.50 \text{ cm}}$$

Practice

1. The image of a crayon appears to be 23.0 cm behind the surface of a convex mirror and is 1.70 cm tall. If the mirror's focal length is 46.0 cm, how far in front of the mirror is the crayon positioned? What is the magnification of the image? Is the image virtual or real? Is the image inverted or upright? How tall is the actual crayon?

2. The passenger side of your car has a side-view mirror with a convex spherical mirror. When you pass a car, you see its reflection. If the image is 9.0 cm tall and the car is 1.5 m tall, what is the mirror's magnification? If the car is 3 m from the mirror, what is the focal length of the mirror? What is the mirror's radius of curvature?

3. A convex mirror of focal length 33 cm forms an image of a soda bottle at a distance of 19 cm behind the mirror. If the height of the image is 7.0 cm, where is the bottle located, and how tall is it? What is the magnification of the image? Is the image virtual or real? Is the image inverted or upright? Draw a ray diagram to confirm your results.

4. A convex mirror with a radius of curvature of 0.450 m is placed above the aisles in a store. Determine the image distance and magnification of a cardboard box on the floor 2.75 m below the mirror. Is the image virtual or real? Is the image inverted or upright?

5. Sitting beside a spherical glass ornament, you notice that your face is reflected in the sphere. The image appears 5.2 cm behind the ornament when you are 17 cm in front of it. What is the ornament's focal length and radius of curvature?

6. A candle is 49 cm in front of a convex spherical mirror that has a focal length of 35 cm. What are the image distance and magnification? Is the image virtual or real? Is the image inverted or upright? Draw a ray diagram to confirm your results.

Parabolic Mirrors

You have probably noticed that certain rays in ray diagrams do not intersect exactly at the image point. This occurs especially with rays that reflect at the mirror's surface far from the principal axis. The situation also occurs with real light rays and real spherical mirrors.

If light rays from an object are near the principal axis, all of the reflected rays pass through the image point. Rays that reflect at points on the mirror far from the principal axis converge at slightly different points on the principal axis, as shown in **Figure 3.9.** This produces a blurred image. This effect, called *spherical aberration,* is present to some extent in any spherical mirror.

Parabolic mirrors eliminate spherical aberration.

A simple way to reduce the effect of spherical aberration is to use a mirror with a small diameter; that way, the rays are never far from the principal axis. If the mirror is large to begin with, shielding its outer portion will limit how much of the mirror is used and thus will accomplish the same effect. However, many concave mirrors, such as those used in astronomical telescopes, are made large so that they will collect a large amount of light. An alternative approach is to use a mirror that is not a segment of a sphere but still focuses light rays in a manner similar to a small spherical concave mirror. This is accomplished with a parabolic mirror.

Parabolic mirrors are segments of a paraboloid (a three-dimensional parabola) whose inner surface is reflecting. All rays parallel to the principal axis converge at the focal point regardless of where on the mirror's surface the rays reflect. Thus, a real image forms without spherical aberration, as illustrated in **Figure 3.10.** Similarly, light rays from an object at the focal point of a parabolic mirror will be reflected from the mirror in parallel rays. Parabolic reflectors are ideal for flashlights and automobile headlights. (Spherical mirrors are extensively used because they are easier to manufacture than parabolic mirrors and thus are less expensive.)

Reflecting telescopes use parabolic mirrors.

A telescope permits you to view distant objects, whether they are buildings a few kilometers away or galaxies that are millions of light-years from Earth. Not all telescopes are intended for visible light. Because all electromagnetic radiation obeys the law of reflection, parabolic surfaces can be constructed to reflect and focus electromagnetic radiation of different wavelengths. For instance, a radio telescope consists of a large metal parabolic surface that reflects radio waves in order to receive radio signals from objects in space.

There are two types of telescopes that use visible light. One type, called a *refracting telescope,* uses a combination of lenses to form an image. The other kind uses a curved mirror and small lenses to form an image. This type of telescope is called a *reflecting telescope.*

FIGURE 3.9

Spherical Aberration

Spherical aberration occurs when parallel rays far from the principal axis converge away from the mirror's focal point.

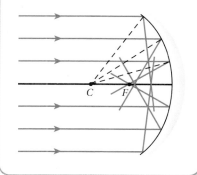

FIGURE 3.10

Parabolic Mirror All parallel rays converge at a parabolic mirror's focal point. The curvature in this figure is much greater than it is in real parabolic mirrors.

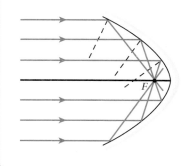

FIGURE 3.11

Reflecting Telescope The parabolic objective mirror in a Cassegrain reflector focuses incoming light.

F

Small mirror

Parabolic objective mirror

Eyepiece

A

Reflecting telescopes employ a parabolic mirror (called an *objective mirror*) to focus light. One type of reflecting telescope, called a *Cassegrain reflector,* is shown in **Figure 3.11.** Parallel light rays pass down the barrel of the telescope and are reflected by the parabolic objective mirror at the telescope's base. These rays converge toward the objective mirror's focal point, *F,* where a real image would normally form. However, a small curved mirror that lies in the path of the light rays reflects the light back toward the center of the objective mirror. The light then passes through a small hole in the center of the objective mirror and comes to a focus at point *A.* An eyepiece near point *A* magnifies the image.

You may wonder how a hole can be placed in the objective mirror without affecting the final image formed by the telescope. Each part of the mirror's surface reflects light from distant objects, so a complete image is always formed. The presence of the hole merely reduces the amount of light that is reflected. Even that is not severely affected by the hole, because the light-gathering capacity of an objective mirror is dependent on the mirror's area. For instance, a 1 m diameter hole in a mirror that is 4 m in diameter reduces the mirror's reflecting surface by only $\frac{1}{16}$, or 6.25 percent.

✔ SECTION 3 FORMATIVE ASSESSMENT

▶ Reviewing Main Ideas

1. A steel ball bearing with a radius of 1.5 cm forms an image of an object that has been placed 1.1 cm away from the bearing's surface. Determine the image distance and magnification. Is the image virtual or real? Is the image inverted or upright? Draw a ray diagram to confirm your results.

2. A spherical mirror is to be used in a motion-picture projector to form an inverted, real image 95 times as tall as the picture in a single frame of film. The image is projected onto a screen 13 m from the mirror. What type of mirror is required, and how far should it be from the film?

3. Which of the following images are real, and which are virtual?
   a. the image of a distant illuminated building projected onto a piece of heavy, white cardboard by a small reflecting telescope
   b. the image of an automobile in a flat rearview mirror
   c. the image of shop aisles in a convex observation mirror

✔ Critical Thinking

4. Why is an image formed by a parabolic mirror sharper than the image of the same object formed by a concave spherical mirror?

5. The reflector of the radio telescope at Arecibo Observatory has a radius of curvature of 265.0 m. How far above the reflector must the radio-detecting equipment be placed in order to obtain clear radio images?

Color and Polarization

Key Term
linear polarization

SECTION 4

Objectives

- Recognize how additive colors affect the color of light.
- Recognize how pigments affect the color of reflected light.
- Explain how linearly polarized light is formed and detected.

Color

You have probably noticed that the color of an object can appear different under different lighting conditions. These differences are due to differences in the reflecting and light-absorbing properties of the object being illuminated.

So far, we have assumed that objects are either like mirrors, which reflect almost all light uniformly, or like rough objects, which reflect light diffusely in several directions. However, objects absorb certain wavelengths from the light striking them and reflect the rest. The color of an object depends on which wavelengths of light shine on the object and which wavelengths are reflected (see **Figure 4.1**).

If all wavelengths of incoming light are completely reflected by an object, that object appears to have the same color as the light illuminating it. This gives the object the same appearance as a white object illuminated by the light. An object of a particular color, such as the green leaf in **Figure 4.1,** absorbs light of all colors except the light whose color is the same as the object's color. By contrast, an object that reflects no light appears black. In truth, leaves appear green only when their primary pigment, chlorophyll, is present. In the autumn, when the green pigment is destroyed, other colors are reflected by the leaves.

Additive primary colors produce white light when combined.

Because white light can be dispersed into its elementary colors, it is reasonable to suppose that elementary colors can be combined to form white light. One way of doing this is to use a lens to recombine light that has been dispersed by a prism. Another way is to combine light that has been passed through red, green, and blue filters. These colors are called the *additive primary colors* because when they are added in varying proportions, they can form all of the colors of the spectrum.

FIGURE 4.1

Color and Reflection A leaf appears green under white light because the primary pigment in the leaf reflects only green light.

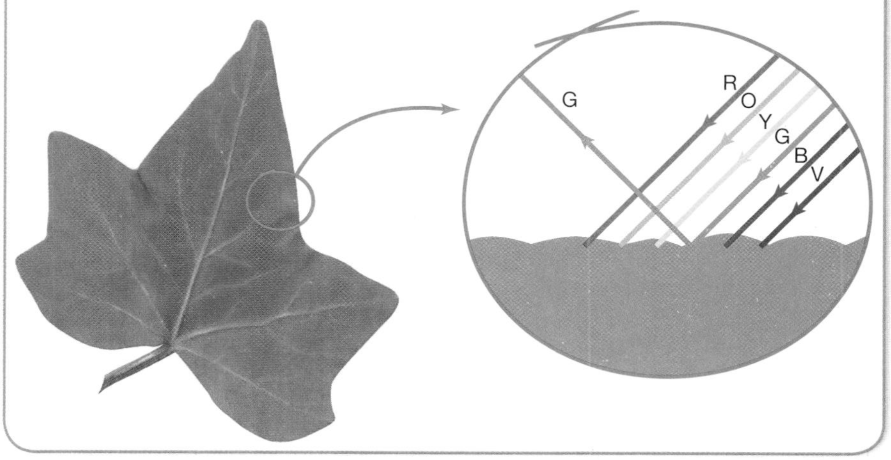

FIGURE 4.2

Combining Additive Primary Colors

The combination of the additive primary colors in any two circles produces the complementary color of the third additive primary color.

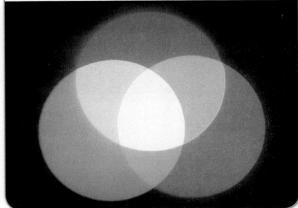

When light passed through a red filter is combined with green light produced with a green filter, a patch of yellow light appears. When two primary colors are combined, a color *complementary* to the third primary is formed. If this yellow light is combined with blue light, the resulting light will be colorless, or "white," as shown in **Figure 4.2**. The additive primary colors of red, green, and blue produce the complementary colors cyan, magenta, and yellow, as indicated in **Figure 4.3**.

One application of additive primary colors is the use of certain chemical compounds to give color to glass. Iron compounds give glass a green color. Manganese compounds give glass a magenta, or reddish-blue, color. Green and magenta are complementary colors, so the right proportion of these compounds produces an equal combination of green and magenta light, and the resulting glass appears colorless.

Another example of additive colors is the image produced on a color television screen. A television screen consists of small, luminous dots, or *pixels*, that glow either red, green, or blue. Varying the brightness of different pixels in different parts of the picture produces a picture that appears to have many colors present at the same time.

Humans can see in color because there are three kinds of color receptors in the eye. Each receptor, called a *cone cell*, is sensitive to either red, green, or blue light. Light of different wavelengths stimulates a combination of these receptors so that a wide range of colors can be perceived.

FIGURE 4.3

ADDITIVE AND SUBTRACTIVE PRIMARY COLORS

Colors	Additive (mixing light)	Subtractive (mixing pigments)
red	primary	complementary to cyan
green	primary	complementary to magenta
blue	primary	complementary to yellow
cyan (blue green)	complementary to red	primary
magenta (red blue)	complementary to green	primary
yellow	complementary to blue	primary

Subtractive primary colors filter out all light when combined.

When blue light and yellow light are mixed, white light results. However, if you mix a blue pigment (such as paint or the colored wax of a crayon) with a yellow pigment, the resulting color is green, not white. This difference is due to the fact that pigments rely on colors of light that are absorbed, or subtracted, from the incoming light.

For example, yellow pigment subtracts blue and violet colors from white light and reflects red, orange, yellow, and green light. Blue pigment subtracts red, orange, and yellow from the light and reflects green, blue, and violet. When yellow and blue pigments are combined, only green light is reflected.

When pigments are mixed, each one subtracts certain colors from white light, and the resulting color depends on the frequencies that are not absorbed. The primary pigments (or *primary subtractive colors*, as they are sometimes called) are cyan, magenta, and yellow. These are the same colors that are complementary to the additive primary colors (see **Figure 4.3**). When two primary pigments are combined, they produce either red, green, or blue. When the three primary pigments are mixed together in the proper proportions, all of the colors are subtracted from white light, and the mixture is black, as shown in **Figure 4.4.**

Combining yellow pigment and its complementary color, blue, should produce a black pigment. Yet earlier, blue and yellow were combined to produce green. The difference between these two situations is explained by the broad use of color names. The "blue" pigment that is added to a "yellow" pigment to produce green is not a pure blue. If it were, only blue light would be reflected from it. Similarly, a pure yellow pigment will reflect only yellow light. Because most pigments found in paints and dyes are combinations of different substances, they reflect light from nearby parts of the visible spectrum. Without knowledge of the light-absorption characteristics of these pigments, it is hard to predict exactly what colors will result from different combinations.

FIGURE 4.4

Combining Subtractive Primary Colors

The combination of the subtractive primary colors by any two filters produces the complementary color of the third subtractive primary color.

Conceptual Challenge

Colors in a Blanket Brown is a mixture of yellow with small amounts of red and green. If you shine red light on a brown woolen blanket, what color will the blanket appear? Will it appear lighter or darker than it would under white light? Explain your answers.

Blueprints If a blueprint (a blue drawing on a white background) is viewed under blue light, will you still be able to perceive the drawing? What will the blueprint look like under yellow light?

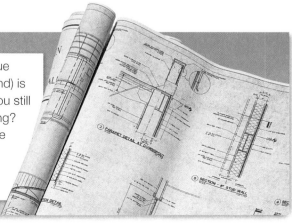

FIGURE 4.5

Unpolarized Light

Randomly oscillating electric fields produce unpolarized light.

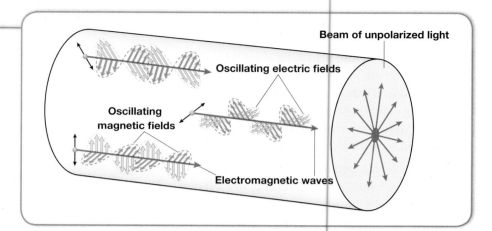

FIGURE 4.6

Linearly Polarized Light

Light waves with aligned electric fields are linearly polarized.

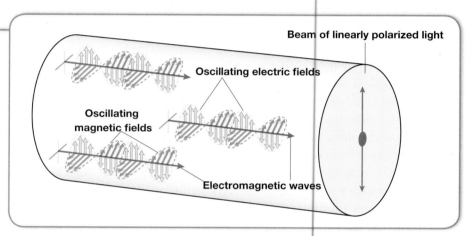

Polarization of Light Waves

You have probably seen sunglasses with polarized lenses that reduce glare without blocking the light entirely. There is a property of light that allows some of the light to be filtered by certain materials in the lenses.

In an electromagnetic wave, the electric field is at right angles to both the magnetic field and the direction of propagation. Light from a typical source consists of waves that have electric fields oscillating in random directions, as shown in **Figure 4.5.** Light of this sort is said to be *unpolarized*.

Electric-field oscillations of unpolarized light waves can be treated as combinations of vertical and horizontal electric-field oscillations. There are certain processes that separate waves with electric-field oscillations in the vertical direction from those in the horizontal direction, producing a beam of light with electric field waves oriented in the same direction, as shown in **Figure 4.6.** These waves are said to have **linear polarization.**

linear polarization the alignment of electromagnetic waves in such a way that the vibrations of the electric fields in each of the waves are parallel to each other

Light can be linearly polarized through transmission.

Certain transparent crystals cause unpolarized light that passes through them to become linearly polarized. The direction in which the electric fields are polarized is determined by the arrangement of the atoms or molecules in the crystal. For substances that polarize light by transmission, the line along which light is polarized is called the *transmission axis* of the substance. Only light waves that are linearly polarized with respect to the transmission axis of the polarizing substance can pass freely through the substance. All light that is polarized at an angle of 90° to the transmission axis does not pass through.

When two polarizing films are held with the transmission axes parallel, light will pass through the films, as shown in **Figure 4.7(a).** If they are held with the transmission axes perpendicular to each other, as in **Figure 4.7(b),** no light will pass through the films.

A polarizing substance can be used not only to linearly polarize light but also to determine if and how light is linearly polarized. By rotating a polarizing substance as a beam of polarized light passes through it, a change in the intensity of the light can be seen (see **Figure 4.8**). The light is brightest when its plane of polarization is parallel to the transmission axis. The larger the angle is between the electric-field waves and the transmission axis, the smaller the component of light that passes through the polarizer will be and the less bright the light will be. When the transmission axis is perpendicular to the plane of polarization for the light, no light passes through.

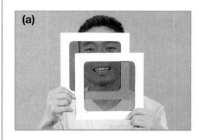

(a)

(b)

FIGURE 4.8

Polarization and Brightness The brightness of the polarized light decreases as the angle, θ, increases between the transmission axis of the second polarizer and the plane of polarization of the light.

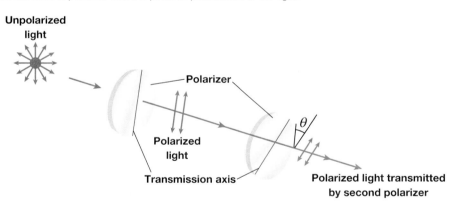

Unpolarized light

Polarizer

Polarized light

Transmission axis

θ

Polarized light transmitted by second polarizer

Quick LAB POLARIZATION OF SUNLIGHT

During mid-morning or mid-afternoon, when the sun is well above the horizon but not directly overhead, look directly up at the sky through the polarizing filter. Note how the light's intensity is reduced.

Rotate the polarizer. Take note of which orientations of the

polarizer make the sky darker and thus best reduce the amount of transmitted light.

Repeat the test with light from other parts of the sky. Test light reflected off a table near a window. Compare the results of these various experiments.

MATERIALS
• a sheet of polarizing filter or sunglasses with polarizing lenses

SAFETY

Never look directly at the sun.

FIGURE 4.9

Polarized Sunglasses At a particular angle, reflected light is polarized horizontally. This light can be blocked by aligning the transmission axes of the sunglasses vertically.

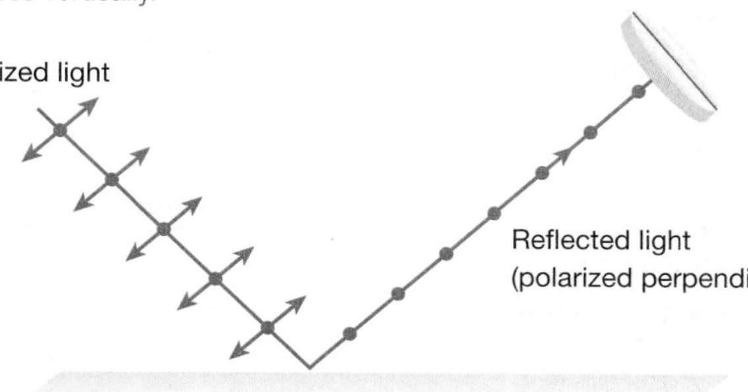

Unpolarized light

Polarizer with transmission axis in vertical orientation

Reflected light (polarized perpendicular to page)

Reflecting surface

FIGURE 4.10

Polarized Sunlight The sunlight scattered by air molecules is polarized for an observer on Earth's surface.

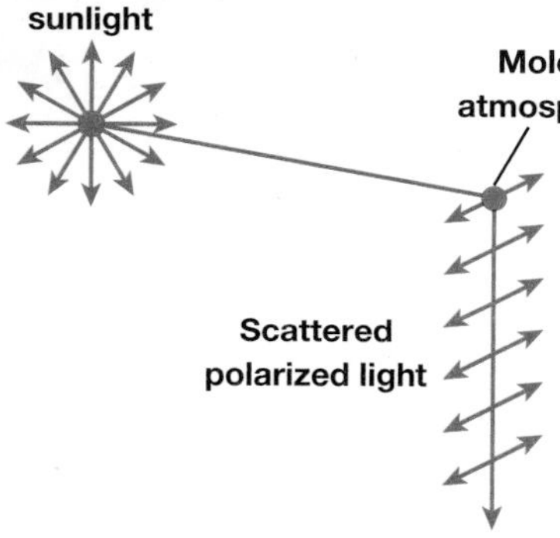

Unpolarized sunlight

Molecule of atmospheric gas

Scattered polarized light

Observer

Light can be polarized by reflection and scattering.

When light is reflected at a certain angle from a surface, the reflected light is completely polarized parallel to the reflecting surface. If the surface is parallel to the ground, the light is polarized horizontally. This is the case with glaring light that reflects at a low angle from bodies of water.

Because the light that causes glare is in most cases horizontally polarized, it can be filtered out by a polarizing substance whose transmission axis is oriented vertically (perpendicular to the direction of the reflected light). This is the case with polarizing sunglasses. As shown in **Figure 4.9,** the angle between the polarized reflected light and the transmission axis of the polarizer is 90°. Thus, none of the polarized light passes through.

In addition to reflection and absorption, scattering can also polarize light. Scattering, or the absorption and reradiation of light by particles in the atmosphere, causes sunlight to be polarized, as shown in **Figure 4.10.** When an unpolarized beam of sunlight strikes air molecules, the electrons in the molecules begin vibrating with the electric field of the incoming wave. A horizontally polarized wave is emitted by the electrons as a result of their horizontal motion, and a vertically polarized wave is emitted as a result of their vertical motion. The polarization is most noticeable when the sun is low in the sky and to the left or right of the observer.

✓ SECTION 4 **FORMATIVE ASSESSMENT**

▶ Reviewing Main Ideas

1. A lens for a spotlight is coated so that it does not transmit yellow light. If the light source is white, what color is the spotlight?

2. A house is painted with pigments that reflect red and blue light but absorb all other colors. What color does the house appear to be when it is illuminated by white light? What color does it appear to be under red light?

3. What primary pigments would an artist need to mix to obtain a pale yellow green color? What primary additive colors would a theater-lighting designer need to mix in order to produce the same color with light?

✔ Critical Thinking

4. The light reflected from the surface of a pool of water is observed through a polarizer. How can you tell if the reflected light is polarized?

Longitudinal and Transverse Waves

Longitudinal waves, such as sound waves, are characterized by particles that vibrate parallel to the direction the wave is traveling. In contrast, particles associated with transverse waves, such as electromagnetic waves, vibrate perpendicular to the direction of travel. This distinction significantly impacts how the two different types of waves behave, as you have learned in the chapters about vibrations and waves, sound, and light.

Both longitudinal and transverse waves are described in terms of their ranges. Sound ranges from infrasound, through audible sound, to ultrasound. Audible sound is the range of frequencies that humans can hear. The electromagnetic (EM) spectrum ranges in frequency from radio waves to gamma rays. A small part of the range is the visible spectrum, which is the range of frequencies that humans can see. Comparing and contrasting longitudinal and transverse waves can help you develop a deeper understanding about each type of wave.

- What part of a longitudinal wave corresponds to a crest in a transverse wave?

- Electromagnetic waves, which are transverse waves, are often described in terms of wavelength. An electromagnetic wave's wavelength determines where it fits on the electromagnetic spectrum. How is the wavelength of an electromagnetic wave measured differently than the wavelength of a longitudinal wave, such as a sound wave?

- Explain how polarization of electromagnetic waves can occur. Can sound waves undergo polarization? Why or why not?

- Both transverse and longitudinal waves can undergo complete destructive interference upon interaction of two waves of identical wavelength. Compare the result of complete destructive interference for two visible electromagnetic waves with that for two sound waves.

Conceptual Challenge

The ability to make assumptions and generate rough estimates is a valuable skill to scientists. Quick estimates allow scientists to narrow the range of possibilities and focus on the most reasonable hypotheses.

Wavelength Measurement What is the thickness of a piece of cardboard, measured in terms of wavelengths of visible light?

You can begin addressing the scenario by asking questions such as the following:

- Approximately how thick is a piece of cardboard?

- What is the average wavelength of an electromagnetic wave in the visible spectrum?

SECTION 1 **Characteristics of Light**

KEY TERM

- Light is electromagnetic radiation that consists of oscillating electric and magnetic fields with different wavelengths.
- The frequency times the wavelength of electromagnetic radiation is equal to *c*, the speed of light.
- The brightness of light is inversely proportional to the square of the distance from the light source.

electromagnetic wave

SECTION 2 **Flat Mirrors**

KEY TERMS

- Light obeys the law of reflection, which states that the incident and reflected angles of light are equal.
- Flat mirrors form virtual images that are the same distance from the mirror's surface as the object is.

reflection

angle of incidence

angle of reflection

virtual image

SECTION 3 **Curved Mirrors**

KEY TERMS

- The mirror equation relates object distance, image distance, and focal length of a spherical mirror.
- The magnification equation relates image height or distance to object height or distance, respectively.

concave spherical mirror

real image

convex spherical mirror

SECTION 4 **Color and Polarization**

KEY TERM

- Light of different colors can be produced by adding light consisting of the primary additive colors (red, green, and blue).
- Pigments can be treated as subtractive colors (magenta, yellow, and cyan).
- Light can be linearly polarized by transmission, reflection, or scattering.

linear polarization

VARIABLE SYMBOLS		
Quantities	**Units**	
p object distance	m	meters
q image distance	m	meters
R radius of curvature	m	meters
f focal length	m	meters
M magnification	(unitless)	

DIAGRAM SYMBOLS	
Light rays (real)	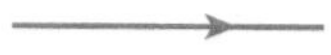
Light rays (apparent)	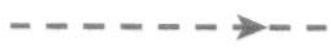
Normal lines	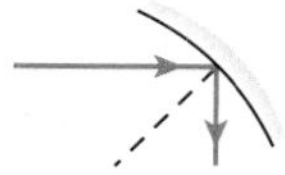
Flat mirror	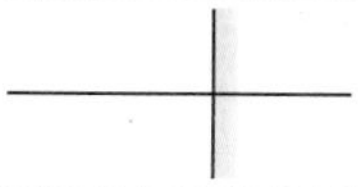
Concave mirror	Convex mirror

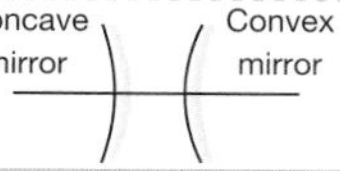

Problem Solving

See **Appendix D: Equations** for a summary of the equations introduced in this chapter. If you need more problem-solving practice, see **Appendix I: Additional Problems.**

Characteristics of Light

▶ **REVIEWING MAIN IDEAS**

1. Which band of the electromagnetic spectrum has
   a. the lowest frequency?
   b. the shortest wavelength?

2. Which of the following electromagnetic waves has the highest frequency?
   a. radio
   b. ultraviolet radiation
   c. blue light
   d. infrared radiation

3. Why can light be used to measure distances accurately? What must be known in order to make distance measurements?

4. For the diagram below, use Huygens's principle to show what the wave front at point *A* will look like at point *B*. How would you represent this wave front in the ray approximation?

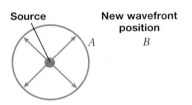

5. What is the relationship between the actual brightness of a light source and its apparent brightness from where you see it?

CONCEPTUAL QUESTIONS

6. Suppose an intelligent society capable of receiving and transmitting radio signals lives on a planet orbiting Procyon, a star 11.5 light-years away from Earth. If a signal were sent toward Procyon in 1999, what is the earliest year that Earth could expect to receive a return message? (Hint: A light-year is the distance light travels in one year.)

7. How fast do x-rays travel in a vacuum?

8. Why do astronomers observing distant galaxies talk about looking backward in time?

9. Do the brightest stars that you see in the night sky necessarily give off more light than dimmer stars? Explain your answer.

PRACTICE PROBLEMS

For problems 10–13, see Sample Problem A.

10. The compound eyes of bees and other insects are highly sensitive to light in the ultraviolet portion of the spectrum, particularly light with frequencies between 7.5×10^{14} Hz and 1.0×10^{15} Hz. To what wavelengths do these frequencies correspond?

11. The brightest light detected from the star Antares has a frequency of about 3×10^{14} Hz. What is the wavelength of this light?

12. What is the wavelength for an FM radio signal if the number on the dial reads 99.5 MHz?

13. What is the wavelength of a radar signal that has a frequency of 33 GHz?

Flat Mirrors

▶ **REVIEWING MAIN IDEAS**

14. For each of the objects listed below, identify whether light is reflected diffusely or specularly.
    a. a concrete driveway
    b. an undisturbed pond
    c. a polished silver tray
    d. a sheet of paper
    e. a mercury column in a thermometer

15. If you were stranded on an island, where would you align a mirror to use sunlight to signal a searching aircraft?

16. If you are standing 2 m in front of a flat mirror, how far behind the mirror is your image? What is the magnification of the image?

CONCEPTUAL QUESTIONS

17. When you shine a flashlight across a room, you see the beam of light on the wall. Why do you not see the light in the air?

18. How can an object be a specular reflector for some electromagnetic waves yet be diffuse for others?

19. A flat mirror that is 0.85 m tall is attached to a wall so that its upper edge is 1.7 m above the floor. Use the law of reflection and a ray diagram to predict whether this mirror will show a person who is 1.7 m tall his or her complete reflection.

20. Two flat mirrors make an angle of 90.0° with each other, as diagrammed at right. An incoming ray makes an angle of 35° with the normal of mirror A. Use the law of reflection to determine the angle of reflection from mirror B. What is unusual about the incoming and reflected rays of light for this arrangement of mirrors?

$\theta = 35°$

Mirror A

Mirror B

21. If you walk 1.2 m/s toward a flat mirror, how fast does your image move with respect to the mirror? In what direction does your image move with respect to you?

22. Why do the images produced by two opposing flat mirrors appear to be progressively smaller?

Curved Mirrors

▶ REVIEWING MAIN IDEAS

23. Which type of mirror should be used to project movie images on a large screen?

24. If an object is placed outside the focal length of a concave mirror, which type of image will be formed? Will it appear in front of or behind the mirror?

25. Can you use a convex mirror to burn a hole in paper by focusing light rays from the sun at the mirror's focal point?

26. A convex mirror forms an image from a real object. Can the image ever be larger than the object?

27. Why are parabolic mirrors preferred over spherical concave mirrors for use in reflecting telescopes?

CONCEPTUAL QUESTIONS

28. Where does a ray of light that is parallel to the principal axis of a concave mirror go after it is reflected at the mirror's surface?

29. What happens to the real image produced by a concave mirror if you move the original object to the location of the image?

30. Consider a concave spherical mirror and a real object. Is the image always inverted? Is the image always real? Give conditions for your answers.

31. Explain why enlarged images seem dimmer than the original objects.

32. What test could you perform to determine if an image is real or virtual?

33. You've been given a concave mirror that may or may not be parabolic. What test could you perform to determine whether it is parabolic?

PRACTICE PROBLEMS

For problems 34–35, see Sample Problem B.

34. A concave shaving mirror has a radius of curvature of 25.0 cm. For each of the following cases, find the magnification and determine whether the image formed is real or virtual and upright or inverted.
 a. an upright pencil placed 45.0 cm from the mirror
 b. an upright pencil placed 25.0 cm from the mirror
 c. an upright pencil placed 5.00 cm from the mirror

35. A concave spherical mirror can be used to project an image onto a sheet of paper, allowing the magnified image of an illuminated real object to be accurately traced. If you have a concave mirror with a focal length of 8.5 cm, where would you place a sheet of paper so that the image projected onto it is twice as far from the mirror as the object is? Is the image upright or inverted, real or virtual? What would the magnification of the image be?

For problem 36, see Sample Problem C.

36. A convex mirror with a radius of curvature of 45.0 cm forms a 1.70 cm tall image of a pencil at a distance of 15.8 cm behind the mirror. Calculate the object distance for the pencil and its height. Is the image real or virtual? What is the magnification? Is the image inverted or upright?

Color and Polarization

▶ **REVIEWING MAIN IDEAS**

37. What are the three primary additive colors? What happens when you mix them?

38. What are the three primary subtractive colors (or primary pigments)? What happens when you mix them?

39. Explain why a polarizing disk used to analyze light can block light from a beam that has been passed through another polarizer. What is the relative orientation of the two polarizing disks?

CONCEPTUAL QUESTIONS

40. Explain what could happen when you mix the following:
  a. cyan and yellow pigment
  b. blue and yellow light
  c. pure blue and pure yellow pigment
  d. green and red light
  e. green and blue light

41. What color would an opaque magenta shirt appear to be under the following colors of light?
  a. white   **d.** green
  b. red   **e.** yellow
  c. cyan

42. A substance is known to reflect green and blue light. What color would it appear to be when it is illuminated by white light? By blue light?

43. How can you tell if a pair of sunglasses has polarizing lenses?

44. Why would sunglasses with polarizing lenses remove the glare from your view of the hood of your car or a distant body of water but not from a tall metal tank used for storing liquids?

45. Is light from the sky polarized? Why do clouds seen through polarizing glasses stand out in bold contrast to the sky?

Mixed Review

▶ **REVIEWING MAIN IDEAS**

46. The real image of a tree is magnified −0.085 times by a telescope's primary mirror. If the tree's image forms 35 cm in front of the mirror, what is the distance between the mirror and the tree? What is the focal length of the mirror? What is the value for the mirror's radius of curvature? Is the image virtual or real? Is the image inverted or upright?

47. A candlestick holder has a concave reflector behind the candle, as shown below. The reflector magnifies a candle −0.75 times and forms an image 4.6 cm away from the reflector's surface. Is the image inverted or upright? What are the object distance and the reflector's focal length? Is the image virtual or real?

48. A child holds a candy bar 15.5 cm in front of the convex side-view mirror of an automobile. The image height is reduced by one-half. What is the radius of curvature of the mirror?

49. A glowing electric light bulb placed 15 cm from a concave spherical mirror produces a real image 8.5 cm from the mirror. If the light bulb is moved to a position 25 cm from the mirror, what is the position of the image? Is the final image real or virtual? What are the magnifications of the first and final images? Are the two images inverted or upright?

50. A convex mirror is placed on the ceiling at the intersection of two hallways. If a person stands directly underneath the mirror, the person's shoe is a distance of 195 cm from the mirror. The mirror forms an image of the shoe that appears 12.8 cm behind the mirror's surface. What is the mirror's focal length? What is the magnification of the image? Is the image real or virtual? Is the image upright or inverted?

51. The side-view mirror of an automobile has a radius of curvature of 11.3 cm. The mirror produces a virtual image one-third the size of the object. How far is the object from the mirror?

52. An object is placed 10.0 cm in front of a mirror. What type must the mirror be to form an image of the object on a wall 2.00 m away from the mirror? What is the magnification of the image? Is the image real or virtual? Is the image inverted or upright?

53. The reflecting surfaces of two intersecting flat mirrors are at an angle of θ ($0° < \theta < 90°$), as shown in the figure below. A light ray strikes the horizontal mirror. Use the law of reflection to show that the emerging ray will intersect the incident ray at an angle of $\phi = 180° - 2\theta$.

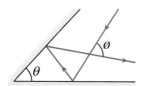

54. Show that if a flat mirror is assumed to have an "infinite" radius of curvature, the mirror equation reduces to $q = -p$.

55. A real object is placed at the zero end of a meterstick. A large concave mirror at the 100.0 cm end of the meterstick forms an image of the object at the 70.0 cm position. A small convex mirror placed at the 20.0 cm position forms a final image at the 10.0 cm point. What is the radius of curvature of the convex mirror? (Hint: The first image created by the concave mirror acts as an object for the convex mirror.)

56. A dedicated sports-car enthusiast polishes the inside and outside surfaces of a hubcap that is a section of a sphere. When he looks into one side of the hubcap, he sees an image of his face 30.0 cm behind the hubcap. He then turns the hubcap over and sees another image of his face 10.0 cm behind the hubcap.
   a. How far is his face from the hubcap?
   b. What is the radius of curvature of the hubcap?
   c. What is the magnification for each image?
   d. Are the images real or virtual?
   e. Are the images upright or inverted?

57. An object 2.70 cm tall is placed 12.0 cm in front of a mirror. What type of mirror and what radius of curvature are needed to create an upright image that is 5.40 cm in height? What is the magnification of the image? Is the image real or virtual?

58. A "floating coin" illusion consists of two parabolic mirrors, each with a focal length of 7.5 cm, facing each other so that their centers are 7.5 cm apart (see the figure below). If a few coins are placed on the lower mirror, an image of the coins forms in the small opening at the center of the top mirror. Use the mirror equation, and draw a ray diagram to show that the final image forms at that location. Show that the magnification is 1 and that the image is real and upright. (Note: A flashlight beam shined on these images has a very startling effect. Even at a glancing angle, the incoming light beam is seemingly reflected off the images of the coins. Do you understand why?)

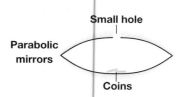

59. Use the mirror equation and the equation for magnification to prove that the image of a real object formed by a convex mirror is always upright, virtual, and smaller than the object. Use the same equations to prove that the image of a real object placed in front of any spherical mirror is always virtual and upright when $p < |f|$.

60. Use trigonometry to derive the mirror and magnification equations. (Hint: Note that the incoming ray between the object and the mirror forms the hypotenuse of a right triangle. The reflected ray between the image point and the mirror is also the hypotenuse of a right triangle.)

ALTERNATIVE ASSESSMENT

1. Suntan lotions include compounds that absorb the ultraviolet radiation in sunlight and therefore prevent the ultraviolet radiation from damaging skin cells. Design experiments to test the properties of varying grades (SPFs) of suntan lotions. Plan to use blueprint paper, film, plants, or other light-sensitive items. Write down the questions that will guide your inquiry, the materials you will need, the procedures you plan to follow, and the measurements you will take. If your teacher approves your plan, perform the experiments and report or demonstrate your findings in class.

2. The Egyptian scholar Alhazen studied lenses, mirrors, rainbows, and other light phenomena early in the Middle Ages. Research his scholarly work, his life, and his relationship with the Caliph al-Hakim. How advanced were Alhazen's inventions and theories? Summarize your findings, and report them to the class.

3. Work in cooperative groups to explore the use of corner and ceiling mirrors as low-tech surveillance devices. Make a floor plan of an existing store, or devise a floor plan for an imaginary one. Determine how much of the store could be monitored by a clerk if flat mirrors were placed in the corners. If you could use curved mirrors in such a system, would you use concave or convex mirrors? Where would you place them? Identify which parts of the store could be observed with the curved mirrors in place. Note any disadvantages that your choice of mirrors may have.

4. Research the characteristics, effects, and applications of a specific type of electromagnetic wave in the spectrum. Find information about the range of wavelengths, frequencies, and energies; natural and artificial sources of the waves; and the methods used to detect them. Find out how they were discovered and how they affect matter. Learn about any dangers associated with them and about their uses in technology. Work together with others in the class who are researching other parts of the spectrum to build a group presentation, brochure, chart, or webpage that covers the entire spectrum.

5. The Chinese astronomer Chang Heng (78–139 CE) recognized that moonlight was a reflection of sunlight. He applied this theory to explain lunar eclipses. Make diagrams showing how Chang might have represented the moon's illumination and the path of light when Earth, the moon, and the sun were in various positions on ordinary nights and on nights when there were lunar eclipses. Find out more about Chang's other scientific work, and report your findings to the class.

6. Explore how many images are produced when you stand between two flat mirrors whose reflecting surfaces face each other. What are the locations of the images? Are they identical? Investigate these questions with diagrams and calculations. Then test your predicted results with parallel mirrors, perpendicular mirrors, and mirrors at angles in between. Which angles produce one, two, three, five, and seven images? Summarize your results with a chart, diagram, or computer presentation.

GRAPHING CALCULATOR PRACTICE

Mirrors

Mirrors produce many types of images: virtual or real, enlarged or reduced, and upright or inverted. The mirror equation and the magnification equation can help sort things out. The mirror equation relates the object distance (p), image distance (q), and focal length (f) to one another.

$$\frac{1}{p} + \frac{1}{q} = \frac{1}{f}$$

Image size can be determined from the magnification equation.

$$M = \frac{h'}{h} = -\frac{q}{p}$$

Magnification values that are greater than 1 or less than −1 indicate that the image of an object is larger than the object itself. Negative magnification values indicate that an image is real and inverted, while positive magnification values indicate that an image is virtual and upright.

In this graphing calculator activity, the calculator will produce a table of image distance and magnification for various object distances for a mirror with a known focal length. You will use this table to determine the characteristics of the images produced by a variety of mirrors and object distances.

Go online to HMHScience.com to find the skillsheet and program for this graphing calculator activity.

Standards-Based Assessment

Record your answers on a separate piece of paper.

MULTIPLE CHOICE

1 Which of the following statements is true about the speeds of gamma rays and radio waves in a vacuum?

A Gamma rays travel faster than radio waves.

B Radio rays travel faster than gamma rays.

C Gamma rays and radio waves travel at the same speed in a vacuum.

D The speed of gamma rays and radio waves in a vacuum depends on their frequencies.

2 Which of the following correctly states the law of reflection?

A The angle between an incident ray of light and the normal to the mirror's surface equals the angle between the mirror's surface and the reflected light ray.

B The angle between an incident ray of light and the mirror's surface equals the angle between the normal to the mirror's surface and the reflected light ray.

C The angle between an incident ray of light and the normal to the mirror's surface equals the angle between the normal and the reflected light ray.

D The angle between an incident ray of light and the normal to the mirror's surface is complementary to the angle between the normal and the reflected light ray.

3 Which of the following processes does not linearly polarize light?

A scattering

B transmission

C refraction

D reflection

4 Which of the following kinds of waves cannot be polarized?

A microwaves

B ultrasonic waves

C infrared waves

D gamma waves

5 If a hummingbird hovers 30 cm in front of a window, what will it see?

A the image of a very large hummingbird 5 cm in front of the window.

B the image of a very small upside-down hummingbird 30 cm behind the window.

C the image of a normal-sized upside-down hummingbird 30 cm behind the window.

D the image of a normal-sized right-side-up hummingbird 30 cm behind the window.

6 What kind of mirror is shown in this ray diagram?

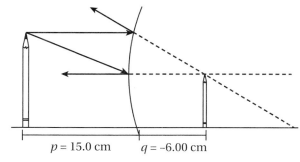

$p = 15.0$ cm $q = -6.00$ cm

A flat

B convex

C concave

D Not enough information to draw a conclusion

GRIDDED RESPONSE

7 The clothing department of a store has a mirror that consists of three flat mirrors, arranged symmetrically so that a person standing before the mirrors can see how an article of clothing looks from the side and back. Suppose a ray from a flashlight shines on the mirror on the left. If the incident ray makes an angle of 65° with respect to the normal to the mirror's surface, what will be the angle θ, in degrees, of the ray reflected from the mirror on the right?

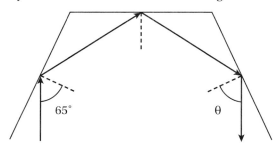

65°   θ

A BOOK EXPLAINING
COMPLEX IDEAS USING
ONLY THE 1,000 MOST
COMMON WORDS

RANDALL MUNROE
XKCD.COM

COLORS OF LIGHT
Light we can see and light we can't see

You know that the electromagnetic spectrum includes all light waves, not just those visible to the human eye. Electromagnetic waves have different properties due to their different wavelengths and frequencies. Here's a look at the different kinds of light.

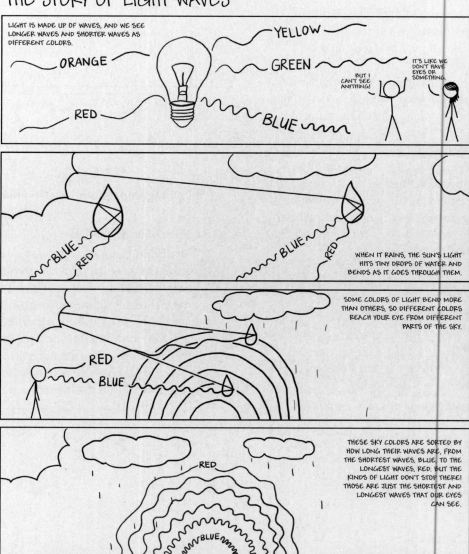

In real life, even if you could see longer and shorter light waves, you wouldn't see these colors spread out in the sky. There are three reasons for this.

FIRST
The Sun gives off most of its light in colors that we can see, and light that's a little shorter or longer. In colors that are *much* shorter or longer, the Sun is pretty dark!

SECOND
Lots of these kinds of light don't go through water, so they wouldn't go through the rain.

THIRD
The colors are sorted from long to short because short waves (blue) bend more than long waves (red). But there are some colors, kinds we can't see, where it goes the other way! That means that these colors wouldn't be spread out like they're shown on the next pages; they'd be laid in sheets over themselves—some parts top to bottom and other parts bottom to top—all in the same area of the sky.

COLORS OF LIGHT

HOW LONG ARE THESE WAVES?

A big country ----------------|

A small country --------------|

A city --------------------------|

A small town -----------------|

A building ----------------------|

A truck ------------------------|

A dog --------------------------|

A finger -----------------------|

A computer key ---------------|

These two black spots: ----|

A hair (the short way) ------|

A single bag of water
from your blood -----------|

A small thing that
takes over your body's
bags of water -------------|

The dust in smoke --------|

The larger pieces
everything is made of ----|

The smaller pieces
everything is made of ----|

The heavy centers
of those pieces -----------|

WHAT ARE THEY?

LONG WAVES

RADIO

Radio waves and light are the same stuff. Radio is just longer. Our eyes can't see light that long, but we can build machines that can.

POWER WAVES

When you stick the end of something into the wall to power it, the power comes out in waves.

They're very long, slow waves, taking so long to change that our power lines aren't long enough to hold the "high" part of the wave and the "low" part at the same time. It might make more sense to say that the power turns on for a while, then turns off.

Light "turns on and off" too fast to count, but power waves only turn on and off a few dozen times each second.

OLD RADIO

Cars use space radios for a few different things like . . .

NEWER RADIO

. . . finding where they are . . .
. . . and playing music

Phones
Computer
hot spots

"SMALL" WAVES

REAL SIZE – ⌐

Food-heating boxes are named after these waves. They use this color.

WARM LIGHT

Everything gives off light because everything is at least a little warm, and warm things give off light. Warmer things give off more light made of shorter waves.

Our bodies give off these colors of light because we're kind of warm, but not warm enough to give off light you can see.

If you wear special computer glasses that help you see these colors of light, you can see where people are in the dark using the light from their bodies.

LIGHT WE CAN SEE

RAIN COLORS

People say those rain lights in the sky show all the colors, but they don't really; there's no deep pink.

The more you learn about color, the more you find that almost everything people say about color is only sort of true.

LIGHT CARRYING A LOT OF POWER

These very "short" colors of light aren't really like waves at all. They're more like tiny rocks going very fast.

Not very many things make this kind of light.

LIGHT FROM WARM THINGS

Space heat from the start of time

Body heat

Sun light

BLACK LIGHT

This is the kind of light that burns your skin if you stay out in the Sun.

SPACE BITS

Sometimes, tiny rocks—going almost as fast as light—hit Earth. The air keeps us safe, but when they hit the air, they make a flash of high-power light. The air keeps us safe from that, too.

If any of these hit you, they could break down the things in your bags of water that tell your body how to grow. If you got enough of them, it could make your body start growing wrong.

When people go into space, where there's no air to stop these things, they sometimes see little flashes of light as the things from space hit their eyes.

That's one reason we don't let people stay in space too long—if they stay too long, their bodies might get hit in enough places that they start growing wrong.

CAN THEY REACH US FROM SPACE?

This side shows which kinds of light can get through Earth's air.

These long waves go through normal air, but can't get through a special layer of air near the edge of space. The air in that layer acts kind of like a mirror for radio, which is why you can pick up some kinds of radio messages from other parts of the Earth.

These radio waves go through air just fine. We use them for looking at stars and talking to our space boats.

These colors are stopped by the water in the air.

FROM THESE IMAGES, IT LOOKS LIKE YOUR BODY IS FULL OF BONES.

OH NO! IS THERE ANY CURE?

LIGHT THAT DOCTORS USE TO SEE THROUGH YOU

These kinds of light can't get through air.

FAR-AWAY FLASHES

About once every day, our space boats see flashes of very, very high-power light from somewhere far off in space.

We're pretty sure they come from huge stars dying, but we aren't sure exactly what happens in the stars to make the light.

This picture shows what other colors you would see if the rain colors kept going. (The picture isn't in color, but that's okay—they're not real colors, anyway!)

Light from the Sun can get through air. That's good, since we need it to see.

The Sun gives off light in these colors. The colors our eyes can see are right in the middle of that, which makes sense; eyes grew to fit the Sun's light.

A special layer stops some of the light that burns your skin. A while back, we learned that we had made a hole in that layer.

We didn't mean to. We're fixing it.

Most of us have seen a rainbow when sunlight hits droplets of water in the air. Sunlight is bent, or *refracted,* as it passes through a raindrop, as shown in the diagram below. Longer wavelengths of light (red) are bent the least, and shorter wavelengths of light (violet) are bent the most.

Refraction is also key to understanding how artificial lenses function. Lenses are essential to many artistic and scientific applications—from microscopes, to cameras, to the practice of optometry.

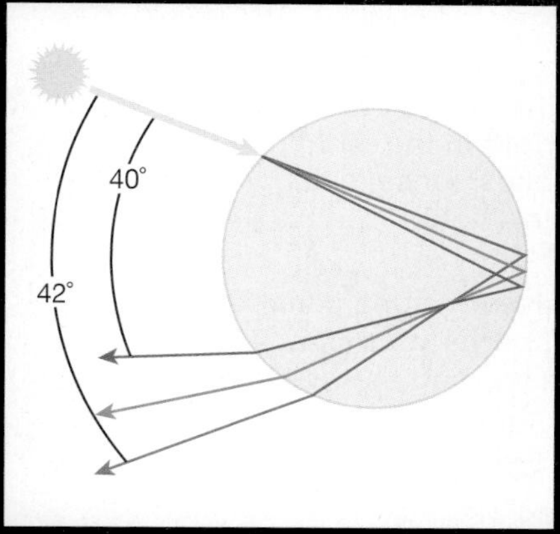

CHAPTER 14
Refraction

BIG IDEA

Patterns of refraction demonstrate the wave behavior of light. This predictable behavior is important for the design of any device involving lenses.

ONLINE Physics
HMHScience.com

ONLINE LABS
- Refraction and Lenses
- Converging Lenses
- S.T.E.M. Lab Fiber Optics
- S.T.E.M. Lab Camera Design

GO ONLINE **Animated Physics**
HMHScience.com

Lenses

Objectives

▶ Recognize situations in which refraction will occur.

▶ Identify which direction light will bend when it passes from one medium to another.

▶ Use Snell's law.

SC.912.P.12.7 Recognize that nothing travels faster than the speed of light in vacuum which is the same for all observers no matter how they or the light source are moving.

FIGURE 1.1

Refraction through a Water Droplet
The flower looks small when viewed through the water droplet. The light from the flower is bent because of the shape of the water droplet and the change in material as the light passes through the water.

Refraction

Key Terms

refraction   index of refraction

Refraction of Light

Look at the tiny image of the flower that appears in the water droplet in **Figure 1.1.** The blurred flower (the object) can be seen in the background of the photo. Why does the flower look different when viewed through the droplet? This phenomenon occurs because light is bent at the boundary between the water and the air around it. The bending of light as it travels from one medium to another is called **refraction.**

If light travels from one transparent medium to another at any angle other than straight on (normal to the surface), the light ray changes direction when it meets the boundary. As in the case of reflection, the angles of the incoming and refracted rays are measured with respect to the normal. For studying refraction, the normal line is extended into the refracting medium, as shown in **Figure 1.2.** The angle between the refracted ray and the normal is called the *angle of refraction, θ_r,* and the angle of incidence is designated as θ_i.

Refraction occurs when light's velocity changes.

Glass, water, ice, diamonds, and quartz are all examples of transparent media through which light can pass. The speed of light in each of these materials is different. The speed of light in water, for instance, is less than the speed of light in air. And the speed of light in glass is less than the speed of light in water.

When light moves from a material in which its speed is higher to a material in which its speed is lower, such as from air to glass, the ray is bent toward the normal, as shown in **Figure 1.2(a).** If the ray moves from

FIGURE 1.2

Refraction When light moves from one medium to another, part of it is reflected, and part is refracted. **(a)** When the light ray moves from air into glass, the refracted portion is bent toward the normal, **(b)** When the light ray moves from glass into air, the refracted portion is bent away from the normal. θ_i is the angle of incidence, and θ_r is the angle of refraction.

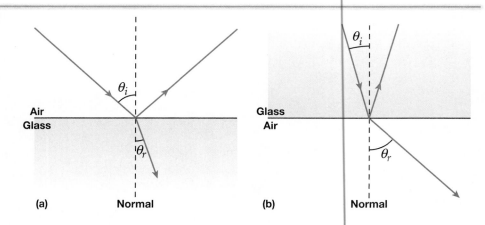

(cl) ©Christopher Burki/Getty Images

a material in which its speed is lower to one in which its speed is higher, as in **Figure 1.2(b),** the ray is bent away from the normal. If the incident ray of light is parallel to the normal, then no refraction (bending) occurs in either case.

Note that the path of a light ray that crosses a boundary between two different media is reversible. If the ray in **Figure 1.2(a)** originated inside the glass block, it would follow the same path as shown in the figure, but the reflected ray would be inside the block.

Refraction can be explained in terms of the wave model of light.

You have learned how to use wave fronts and light rays to approximate light waves. This analogy can be extended to light passing from one medium into another. In **Figure 1.3,** the wave fronts are shown in red and are assumed to be spherical. The combined wave front (dotted line connecting the individual wave fronts) is a superposition of all the spherical wave fronts. The direction of propagation of the wave is perpendicular to the wave front and is what we call the *light ray.*

Consider wave fronts of a plane wave of light traveling at an angle to the surface of a block of glass, as shown in **Figure 1.3.** As the light enters the glass, the wave fronts slow down, but the wave fronts that have not yet reached the surface of the glass continue traveling at the speed of light in air. During this time, the slower wave fronts travel a smaller distance than do the wave fronts in the air, so the entire plane wave changes directions.

Note the difference in wavelength (the space between the wave fronts) between the plane wave in air and the plane wave in the glass. Because the wave fronts inside the glass are traveling more slowly, in the same time interval they move through a shorter distance than the wave fronts that are still traveling in air. Thus, the wavelength of the light in the glass, λ_{glass}, is shorter than the wavelength of the incoming light, λ_{air}. The frequency of the light does *not* change when the light passes from one medium to another.

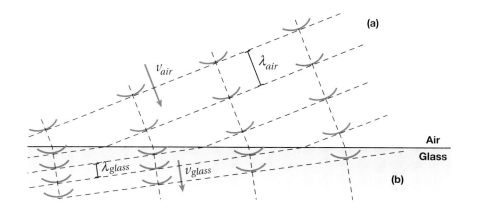

FIGURE 1.3

Refraction and the Wave Model of Light A plane wave traveling in air **(a)** has a wavelength of λ_{air} and velocity of ν_{air}. Each wave front turns as it strikes the glass. Because the speed of the wave fronts in the glass **(b)**, ν_{glass}, is slower, the wavelength of the light becomes shorter, and the wave fronts change direction.

The Law of Refraction

index of refraction the ratio of the speed of light in a vacuum to the speed of light in a given transparent medium

An important property of transparent substances is the **index of refraction.** The index of refraction for a substance is the ratio of the speed of light in a vacuum to the speed of light in that substance.

> **Index of Refraction**
>
> $$n = \frac{c}{v}$$
>
> $$\text{index of refraction} = \frac{\text{speed of light in vacuum}}{\text{speed of light in medium}}$$

From this definition, we see that the index of refraction is a dimensionless number that is always greater than 1 because light always travels slower in a substance than in a vacuum. **Figure 1.4** lists the indices of refraction for different substances. Note that the larger the index of refraction is, the slower light travels in that substance and the more a light ray will bend when it passes from a vacuum into that material.

Imagine, as an example, light passing between air and water. When light begins in the air (high speed of light and low index of refraction) and travels into the water (lower speed of light and higher index of refraction), the light rays are bent toward the normal. Conversely, when light passes from the water to the air, the light rays are bent away from the normal.

Note that the value for the index of refraction of air is nearly that of a vacuum. For simplicity, *use the value n = 1.00 for air when solving problems.*

Did YOU Know?

The index of refraction of any medium can also be expressed as the ratio of the wavelength of light in a vacuum, λ_0, to the wavelength of light in that medium, λ_n, as shown in the following relation.

$$n = \frac{\lambda_0}{\lambda_n}$$

FIGURE 1.4

INDICES OF REFRACTION FOR VARIOUS SUBSTANCES*

Solids at 20°C	*n*	Liquids at 20°C	*n*
cubic zirconia	2.20	benzene	1.501
diamond	2.419	carbon disulfide	1.628
fluorite	1.434	carbon tetrachloride	1.461
fused quartz	1.458	ethyl alcohol	1.361
glass, crown	1.52	glycerine	1.473
glass, flint	1.66	water	1.333
ice (at 0°C)	1.309	**Gases at 0°C, 1 atm**	***n***
polystyrene	1.49	air	1.000 293
sodium chloride	1.544	carbon dioxide	1.000 450
zircon	1.923		

*measured with light of vacuum wavelength = 589 nm

FIGURE 1.5

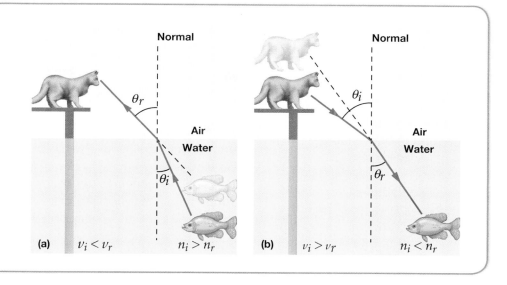

Image Position for Objects in Different Media **(a)** To the cat on the pier, the fish looks closer to the surface than it really is. **(b)** To the fish, the cat seems to be farther from the surface than it actually is.

Objects appear to be in different positions due to refraction.

When looking at a fish underwater, a cat sitting on a pier perceives the fish to be closer to the water's surface than it actually is, as shown in **Figure 1.5(a).** Conversely, the fish perceives the cat on the pier to be farther from the water's surface than it actually is, as shown in **Figure 1.5(b).**

Because of the reversibility of refraction, both the fish and the cat see along the same path, as shown by the solid lines in both figures. However, the light ray that reaches the fish forms a smaller angle with respect to the normal than does the light ray from the cat to the water's surface. The reason is that light is bent toward the normal when it travels from a medium with a lower index of refraction (the air) to one with a higher index of refraction (the water). Extending this ray along a straight line shows the cat's image to be above the cat's actual position.

On the other hand, the light ray that reaches the cat from the water's surface forms a larger angle with respect to the normal instead of a smaller one. This is because the light from the fish travels from a medium with a higher index of refraction to one with a lower index of refraction.

Conceptual Challenge

The Invisible Man H. G. Wells wrote a famous novel about a man who made himself invisible by changing his index of refraction. What would his index of refraction have to be to accomplish this?

Visibility for the Invisible Man Would the invisible man be able to see anything?

Fishing When trying to catch a fish, should a pelican dive into the water horizontally in front of or behind the image of the fish it sees?

Note that the fish's image is closer to the water's surface than the fish actually is. An underwater object seen from the air above appears larger than its actual size because the image, which is the same size as the object, is closer to the observer.

Wavelength affects the index of refraction.

Note that the indices of refraction listed in **Figure 1.4** are only valid for light that has a wavelength of 589 nm in a vacuum. The reason is that the amount that light bends when entering a different medium depends on the wavelength of the light as well as the speed, as shown in **Figure 1.6**. Each color of light has a different wavelength, so each color of the spectrum is refracted by a different amount. This explains why a spectrum is produced when white light passes through a prism.

Snell's law determines the angle of refraction.

The index of refraction of a material can be used to figure out how much a ray of light will be refracted as it passes from one medium to another. As mentioned, the greater the index of refraction, the more refraction occurs. But how can the angle of refraction be found?

In 1621, Willebrord Snell experimented with light passing through different media. He developed a relationship called Snell's law, which can be used to find the angle of refraction for light traveling between any two media.

> **Snell's Law**
>
> $$n_i \sin \theta_i = n_r \sin \theta_r$$
>
> **index of refraction of first medium × sine of the angle of incidence = index of refraction of second medium × sine of the angle of refraction**

GO ONLINE

Interactive Demo
HMHScience.com

Snell's Law

Sample Problem A A light ray of wavelength 589 nm (produced by a sodium lamp) traveling through air strikes a smooth, flat slab of crown glass at an angle of 30.0° to the normal. Find the angle of refraction, θ_r.

 ANALYZE

Given:
$$\theta_i = 30.0°$$
$$n_i = 1.00$$
$$n_r = 1.52$$

Unknown: $\theta_r = ?$

Continued

Snell's Law (continued)

2 SOLVE

Use the equation for Snell's law.

$$n_i \sin \theta_i = n_r \sin \theta_r$$

$$\theta_r = \sin^{-1}\left[\frac{n_i}{n_r}(\sin \theta_i)\right] = \sin^{-1}\left[\frac{1.00}{1.52}(\sin 30.0°)\right]$$

$$\boxed{\theta_r = 19.2°}$$

Practice

1. Find the angle of refraction for a ray of light that enters a bucket of water from air at an angle of 25.0° to the normal. (Hint: Use **Figure 1.4.**)

2. For an incoming ray of light of vacuum wavelength 589 nm, fill in the unknown values in the following table. (Hint: Use **Figure 1.4.**)

	from (medium)	to (medium)	θ_i	θ_r
a.	flint glass	crown glass	25.0°	?
b.	air	?	14.5°	9.80°
c.	air	diamond	31.6°	?

3. A ray of light of vacuum wavelength 550 nm traveling in air enters a slab of transparent material. The incoming ray makes an angle of 40.0° with the normal, and the refracted ray makes an angle of 26.0° with the normal. Find the index of refraction of the transparent material. (Assume that the index of refraction of air for light of wavelength 550 nm is 1.00.)

SECTION 1 FORMATIVE ASSESSMENT

▶ Reviewing Main Ideas

1. Sunlight passes into a raindrop at an angle of 22.5° from the normal at one point on the droplet. What is the angle of refraction?

2. For each of the following cases, will light rays be bent toward or away from the normal?
   a. $n_i > n_r$, where $\theta_i = 20°$
   b. $n_i < n_r$, where $\theta_i = 20°$
   c. from air to glass with an angle of incidence of 30°
   d. from glass to air with an angle of incidence of 30°

3. Find the angle of refraction of a ray of light that enters a diamond from air at an angle of 15.0° to the normal. (Hint: Use **Figure 1.4.**)

✓ Critical Thinking

4. In which of the following situations will light from a laser be refracted?
   a. traveling from air into a diamond at an angle of 30° to the normal
   b. traveling from water into ice along the normal
   c. upon striking a metal surface
   d. traveling from air into a glass of iced tea at an angle of 25° to the normal

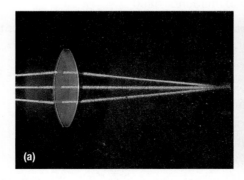
Objectives

▶ Use ray diagrams to find the position of an image produced by a converging or diverging lens, and identify the image as real or virtual.

▶ Solve problems using the thin-lens equation.

▶ Calculate the magnification of lenses.

▶ Describe the positioning of lenses in compound microscopes and refracting telescopes.

SC.912.P.10.22 Construct ray diagrams and use thin lens and mirror equations to locate the images formed by lenses and mirrors.

lens a transparent object that refracts light rays such that the light rays converge or diverge to create an image

Thin Lenses

Key Term
lens

Types of Lenses

When light traveling in air enters a pane of glass, it is bent toward the normal. As the light exits the pane of glass, it is bent again. When the light exits, however, its speed increases as it enters the air, so the light bends away from the normal. Because the amount of refraction is the same regardless of whether light is entering or exiting a medium, the light rays are bent as much on exiting the pane of glass as they were on entering.

Curved surfaces change the direction of light.

With curved surfaces, the direction of the normal line differs for each spot on the medium. When light passes through a medium that has one or more curved surfaces, the change in the direction of the light rays varies from point to point. This principle is applied in media called **lenses**. Like mirrors, lenses form images, but lenses do so by refraction instead of reflection. The images formed can be real or virtual, depending on the type of lens and the placement of the object. Recall that real images form when rays of light actually intersect to form the image. Virtual images form at a point from which light rays appear to come but do not actually come. Real images can be projected onto a screen; virtual images cannot be projected.

Lenses are commonly used to form images in optical instruments, such as cameras, telescopes, and microscopes. In fact, transparent tissue in the front of the human eye acts as a lens, converging light toward the light-sensitive retina at the back of the eye.

A typical lens consists of a piece of glass or plastic ground so that each of its surfaces is a segment of either a sphere or a plane. **Figure 2.1** shows examples of lenses. Notice that the lenses are shaped differently. The lens

(l), (r) ©Richard Megna/Fundamental Photographs, New York

FIGURE 2.1

Converging and Diverging Lenses **(a)** When rays of light pass through a converging lens (thicker at the middle), they are bent inward. **(b)** When they pass through a diverging lens (thicker at the edge), they are bent outward.

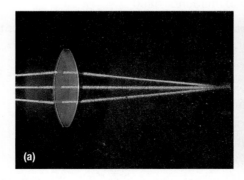

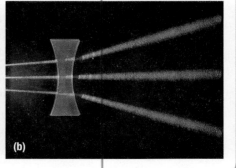

(a)

(b)

that is thicker at the middle than it is at the rim, shown in **Figure 2.1(a)**, is a *converging* lens. The lens that is thinner at the middle than it is at the rim, shown in **Figure 2.1(b)**, is a *diverging* lens. The light rays show why the names *converging* and *diverging* are applied to these lenses.

Focal length is the image distance for an infinite object distance.

As with mirrors, it is convenient to define a point called the *focal point* for a lens. Note that light rays from an object far away are nearly parallel. The focal point of a converging lens is the location where the image of an object at an infinite distance from the lens is focused. In **Figure 2.2(a)**, a group of rays parallel to the principal axis passes through a focal point, *F*, after being bent inward by the lens. Unlike mirrors, lenses have two focal points, one on each side of the lens because light can pass through the lens from either side, as shown in **Figure 2.2**. The distance from the focal point to the center of the lens is called the *focal length, f*. The focal length is the image distance that corresponds to an infinite object distance.

Rays parallel to the principal axis diverge after passing through a diverging lens, as shown in **Figure 2.2(b)**. In this case, the focal point is defined as the point from which the diverged rays appear to originate. Again, the focal length is defined as the distance from the center of the lens to the focal point.

Ray diagrams of thin-lens systems help identify image height and location.

Earlier, we used a set of rays and ray diagrams to predict the images formed by mirrors. A similar approach can be used for lenses. As shown in **Figure 2.1**, refraction occurs at a boundary between two materials with different indexes of refraction. However, for *thin lenses* (lenses for which the thickness of the lens is small compared to the radius of curvature of the lens or the distance of the object from the lens), we can represent the front and back boundaries of the lens as a line segment passing through the center of the lens. To draw ray diagrams, we will use a line segment with arrow ends to indicate a converging lens, as in **Figure 2.2(a)**.

To show a diverging lens, we will draw a line segment with "upside-down" arrow ends, as illustrated in **Figure 2.2(b)**. We can then draw ray diagrams using the set of rules outlined in **Figure 2.3**.

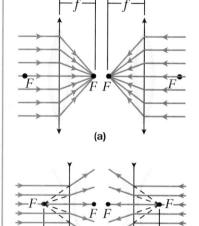

FIGURE 2.2

Focal Points Both **(a)** converging lenses and **(b)** diverging lenses have two focal points but only one focal length.

(a)

(b)

FIGURE 2.3

		RULES FOR DRAWING REFERENCE RAYS	
Ray	From object to lens	From *converging* lens to image	From *diverging* lens to image
parallel ray	parallel to principal axis	passes through focal point, *F*	directed away from focal point, *F*
central ray	to the center of the lens	from the center of the lens	from the center of the lens
focal ray	passes through focal point, *F*	parallel to principal axis	parallel to principal axis

The reasons that these rules work relate to concepts already covered in this textbook. From the definition of a focal point, we know that light traveling parallel to the principal axis (parallel ray) will be focused at the focal point. For a converging lens, this means that light will come together at the focal point in back of the lens. (In this book, the *front* of the lens is defined as the side of the lens that the light rays first encounter. The *back* of the lens refers to the side of the lens opposite where the light rays first encounter the lens.) But a similar ray passing through a diverging lens will exit the lens as if it originated from the focal point in front of the lens. Because refraction is reversible, a ray entering a converging lens from either focal point will be refracted so that it is parallel to the principal axis.

For both lenses, a ray passing through the center of the lens will continue in a straight line with no net refraction. This occurs because the sides of a lens are parallel to one another along any path through the center of the lens. As with a pane of glass, the exiting ray will be parallel to the ray that entered the lens. For ray diagrams, the usual assumption is that the lens is negligibly thin, so it is assumed that the ray is not displaced sideways but instead continues in a straight line.

Characteristics of Lenses

Figure 2.4 on the next page summarizes the possible relationships between object and image positions for converging lenses. The rules for drawing reference rays were used to create each of these diagrams. Note that applications are listed along with each ray diagram to show the varied uses of the different configurations.

Converging lenses can produce real or virtual images of real objects.

An object infinitely far away from a converging lens will create a point image at the focal point distance, as shown in the first diagram in **Figure 2.4.** This image is real, and can be projected on a screen.

As a distant object approaches the focal point distance, the image becomes larger and farther away, as shown in the second, third, and fourth diagrams in **Figure 2.4.** When the object is at the focal point, as shown in the fifth diagram, the light rays from the object are refracted so that they exit the lens parallel to each other. (Because the object is at the focal point, it is impossible to draw a third ray that passes through that focal point, the lens, and the tip of the object.)

When the object is between a converging lens and its focal point, the light rays from the object diverge when they pass through the lens, as shown in the sixth diagram in **Figure 2.4.** This image appears to an observer in back of the lens as being on the same side of the lens as the object. In other words, the brain interprets these diverging rays as coming from an object directly along the path of the rays that reach the eye. The ray diagram for this final case is less straightforward than those drawn for the other cases in the table. The first two rays (parallel to the axis and through the center of the lens) are drawn in the usual fashion. The third ray, however, is drawn so that if it were extended, it would connect the focal point in front of the lens, the

FIGURE 2.4

IMAGES CREATED BY CONVERGING LENSES

Ray diagrams

1.

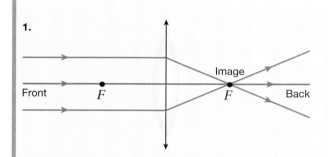

Configuration: object at infinity; point image at *F*
Applications: burning a hole in paper with a magnifying glass

2.

Configuration: object outside 2*F*; real, smaller image between *F* and 2*F*
Applications: lens of a camera, human eyeball lens, and objective lens of a refracting telescope

3.

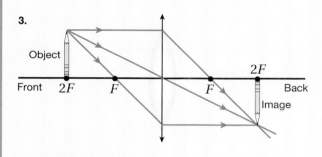

Configuration: object at 2*F*; real, inverted image at 2*F* same size as object
Applications: inverting lens of a field telescope

4.

Configuration: object between *F* and 2*F*; magnified real, inverted image outside 2*F*
Applications: motion-picture or slide projector and objective lens in a compound microscope

5.

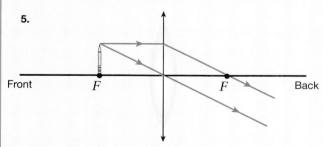

Configuration: object at *F*; image at infinity
Applications: lenses used in lighthouses and searchlights

6.

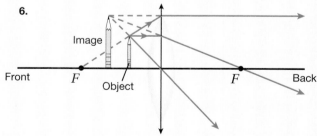

Configuration: object inside *F*; magnified virtual, upright image on the same side of the lens as the object
Applications: magnifying with a magnifying glass; eyepiece lens of microscope, binoculars, and telescope

tip of the object, and the lens in a straight line. To determine where the image is, draw lines extending from the rays exiting the lens back to the point where they would appear to have originated to an observer on the back side of the lens (these lines are dashed in the sixth diagram in **Figure 2.4**).

Diverging lenses produce virtual images from real objects.

A diverging lens creates a virtual image of a real object placed anywhere with respect to the lens. The image is upright, and the magnification is always less than one; that is, the image size is reduced. Additionally, the image appears inside the focal point for any placement of the real object.

FIGURE 2.5

Ray Diagram for a Diverging Lens The image created by a diverging lens is always a virtual, smaller image.

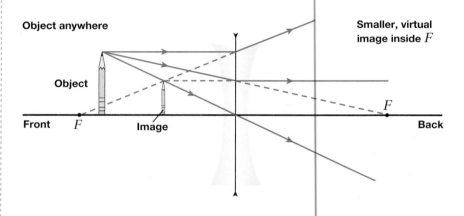

The ray diagram shown in **Figure 2.5** for diverging lenses was created using the rules given in **Figure 2.3**. The first ray, parallel to the axis, appears to come from the focal point on the same side of the lens as the object. This ray is indicated by the oblique dashed line. The second ray passes through the center of the lens and is not refracted. The third ray is drawn as if it were going to the focal point in back of the lens. As this ray passes through the lens, it is refracted parallel to the principal axis and must be extended backward, as shown by the dashed line. The location of the tip of the image is the point at which the three rays appear to have originated.

The Thin-Lens Equation and Magnification

Ray diagrams for lenses give a good estimate of image size and distance, but it is also possible to calculate these values. The equation that relates object and image distances for a lens is called the *thin-lens equation*, because it is derived using the assumption that the lens is very thin. In other words, this equation applies when the lens thickness is much smaller than its focal length.

Thin-Lens Equation

$$\frac{1}{p} + \frac{1}{q} = \frac{1}{f}$$

$$\frac{1}{\text{object distance}} + \frac{1}{\text{image distance}}$$

$$= \frac{1}{\text{focal length}}$$

When using the thin-lens equation, we often illustrate it using the ray diagram model in which we magnify the vertical axis and show the lens position as a thin line. Remember that actual light rays bend at the lens surfaces while our diagram shows bending at a single central line in an idealized model, which is quite good for thin lenses. But the model, and the equation, must be modified to deal properly with thick lenses, systems of lenses, and object and image points far from the principal axis.

The thin-lens equation can be applied to both converging and diverging lenses if we adhere to a set of sign conventions. **Figure 2.6** gives the sign conventions for lenses. Under this convention, an object in front of the lens has a positive object distance, and an object in back of the lens, or a virtual object, has a negative object distance. Note that virtual objects only occur in multiple-lens systems. Similarly, an image in back of the lens (that is, a real image) has a positive image distance, and an image in front of the lens, or a virtual image, has a negative image distance. A converging lens has a positive focal length, and a diverging lens has a negative focal length. Therefore, converging lenses are sometimes called *positive lenses*, and diverging lenses are sometimes called *negative lenses*.

FIGURE 2.6

SIGN CONVENTIONS FOR LENSES

	+	−
p	real object in front of the lens	virtual object in back of the lens
q	real image in back of the lens	virtual image in front of the lens
f	converging lens	diverging lens

Magnification by a lens depends on object and image distances.

Recall that magnification (M) is defined as the ratio of image height to object height. The following equation can be used to calculate the magnification of both converging and diverging lenses.

Magnification of a Lens

$$M = \frac{h'}{h} = -\frac{q}{p}$$

$$\text{magnification} = \frac{\text{image height}}{\text{object height}} = -\frac{\text{image distance}}{\text{object distance}}$$

If close attention is given to the sign conventions defined in **Figure 2.6,** then the magnification will describe the image's size and orientation. When the magnitude of the magnification of an object is less than one, the image is smaller than the object. Conversely, when the magnitude of the magnification is greater than one, the image is larger than the object.

Additionally, a negative sign for the magnification indicates that the image is real and inverted. A positive magnification signifies that the image is upright and virtual.

Lenses

Sample Problem B An object is placed 30.0 cm in front of a converging lens and then 12.5 cm in front of a diverging lens. Both lenses have a focal length of 10.0 cm. For both cases, find the image distance and the magnification. Describe the images.

---

① ANALYZE

Given:

$$f_{converging} = 10.0 \text{ cm} \qquad f_{diverging} = -10.0 \text{ cm}$$
$$p_{converging} = 30.0 \text{ cm} \qquad p_{diverging} = 12.5 \text{ cm}$$

Unknown:

$$q_{converging} = ? \qquad M_{converging} = ?$$
$$q_{diverging} = ? \qquad M_{diverging} = ?$$

Diagrams:

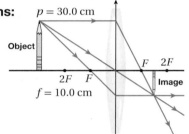

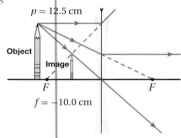

---

② PLAN

Choose an equation or situation:
The thin-lens equation can be used to find the image distance, and the equation for magnification will serve to describe the size and orientation of the image.

$$\frac{1}{p} + \frac{1}{q} = \frac{1}{f} \qquad M = -\frac{q}{p}$$

Rearrange the equation to isolate the unknown:

$$\frac{1}{q} = \frac{1}{f} - \frac{1}{p}$$

---

③ SOLVE

For the converging lens:

$$\frac{1}{q} = \frac{1}{f} - \frac{1}{p} = \frac{1}{10.0 \text{ cm}} - \frac{1}{30.0 \text{ cm}} = \frac{2}{30.0 \text{ cm}}$$

$$\boxed{q = 15.0 \text{ cm}}$$

$$M = -\frac{q}{p} = -\frac{15.0 \text{ cm}}{30.0 \text{ cm}}$$

$$\boxed{M = -0.500}$$

Continued ▶

For the diverging lens:

$$\frac{1}{q} = \frac{1}{f} - \frac{1}{p} = \frac{1}{-10.0 \text{ cm}} - \frac{1}{12.5 \text{ cm}} = -\frac{22.5}{125 \text{ cm}}$$

$$\boxed{q = -5.56 \text{ cm}}$$

$$M = -\frac{q}{p} = -\frac{-5.56 \text{ cm}}{12.5 \text{ cm}}$$

$$\boxed{M = 0.445}$$

4 CHECK YOUR WORK

These values and signs for the converging lens indicate a real, inverted, smaller image. This is expected because the object distance is longer than twice the focal length of the converging lens. The values and signs for the diverging lens indicate a virtual, upright, smaller image formed inside the focal point. This is the only kind of image diverging lenses form.

Practice

1. Predict how an object will appear if it is placed 20.0 cm in front of a converging lens of focal length 10.0 cm. Find the image distance and the magnification. Describe the image.

2. Sherlock Holmes examines a clue by holding his magnifying glass at arm's length and 10.0 cm away from an object. The magnifying glass has a focal length of 15.0 cm. Find the image distance and the magnification. Describe the image that he observes.

3. An object is placed 20.0 cm in front of a diverging lens of focal length 10.0 cm. Find the image distance and the magnification. Describe the image.

4. Fill in the missing values in the following table.

	f	p	q	M
Converging lens				
a.	6.0 cm	?	−3.0 cm	?
b.	2.9 cm	?	7.0 cm	?
Diverging lens				
c.	−6.0 cm	4.0 cm	?	?
d.	?	5.0 cm	?	0.50

Eyeglasses and Contact Lenses

The transparent front of the eye, called the *cornea*, acts like a lens, directing light rays toward the light-sensitive *retina* in the back of the eye. Although most of the refraction of light occurs at the cornea, the eye also contains a small lens, called the *crystalline lens*, that refracts light as well.

When the eye attempts to produce a focused image of a nearby object but the image position is behind the retina, the abnormality is known as *hyperopia*, and the person is said to be *farsighted*. With this defect, distant objects are seen clearly, but near objects are blurred. Either the hyperopic eye is too short, or the ciliary muscle that adjusts the shape of the lens cannot adjust enough to properly focus the image. **Figure 2.7** shows how hyperopia can be corrected with a converging lens.

Another condition, known as *myopia*, or *nearsightedness*, occurs either when the eye is longer than normal or when the maximum focal length of the lens is insufficient to produce a clear image on the retina. In this case, light from a distant object is focused in front of the retina. The distinguishing feature of this imperfection is that distant objects are not seen clearly. Nearsightedness can be corrected with a diverging lens, as shown in **Figure 2.7.**

A contact lens is simply a lens worn directly over the cornea of the eye. The lens floats on a thin layer of tears.

FIGURE 2.7

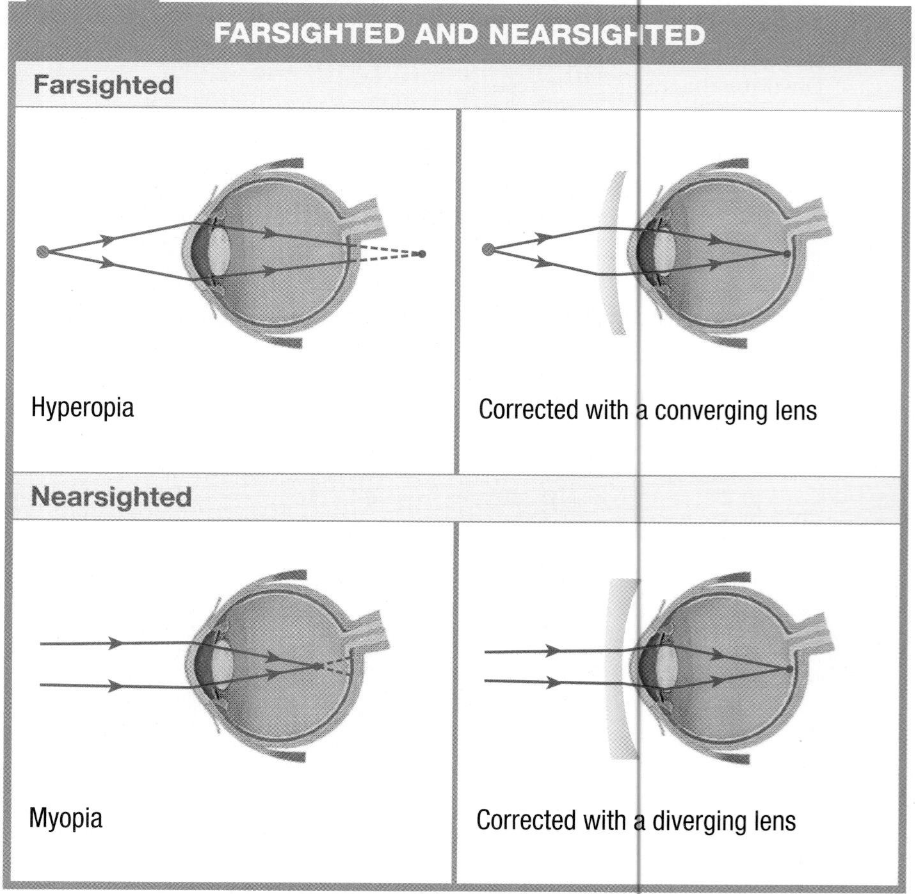

FARSIGHTED AND NEARSIGHTED

Farsighted

Hyperopia

Corrected with a converging lens

Nearsighted

Myopia

Corrected with a diverging lens

Combination of Thin Lenses

If two lenses are used to form an image, the system can be treated in the following manner. First, the image of the first lens is calculated as though the second lens were not present. The light then approaches the second lens as if it had come from the image formed by the first lens. Hence, *the image formed by the first lens is treated as the object for the second lens.* The image formed by the second lens is the final image of the system. The overall magnification of a system of lenses is the product of the magnifications of the separate lenses. If the image formed by the first lens is in back of the second lens, then the image is treated as a virtual object for the second lens (that is, *p* is negative). The same procedure can be extended to a system of three or more lenses.

Compound microscopes use two converging lenses.

A simple magnifier, such as a magnifying glass, provides only limited assistance when inspecting the minute details of an object. Greater magnification can be achieved by combining two lenses in a device called a *compound microscope.* It consists of two lenses: an objective lens (near the object) with a focal length of less than 1 cm and an eyepiece with a focal length of a few centimeters. As shown in **Figure 2.8,** the object placed just outside the focal point of the objective lens forms a real, inverted, and enlarged image that is at or just inside the focal point of the eyepiece. The eyepiece, which serves as a simple magnifier, uses this enlarged image as its object and produces an even more enlarged virtual image. The image viewed through a microscope is upside down with respect to the actual orientation of the specimen, as shown in **Figure 2.8.**

The microscope has extended our vision into the previously unknown realm of incredibly small objects. A question that is often asked about microscopes is, "With extreme patience and care, would it be possible to construct a microscope that would enable us to see an atom?" As long as visible light is used to illuminate the object, the answer is no. In order to be seen, the object under a microscope must be at least as large as a wavelength of light. An atom is many times smaller than a wavelength of visible light, so its mysteries must be probed through other techniques.

FIGURE 2.8

Compound Microscope In a compound microscope, the real, inverted image produced by the objective lens is used as the object for the eyepiece lens.

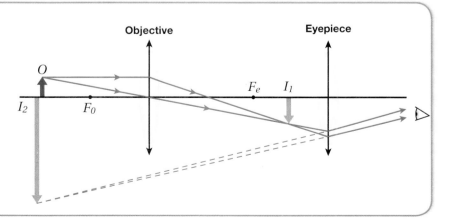

CAMERAS

This cross-sectional view of a DSLR camera shows the many optical elements used to form an image on the digital imager.

Cameras come in many types and sizes, from the small and simple camera on your cell phone to the large and complex video camera used to film a Hollywood motion picture. Most cameras have at least one lens, and more complex cameras may have 30 or more lenses and may even contain mirrors and prisms. Up until relatively recently, cameras used film to record an image. The film would undergo a chemical change when exposed to light.

Today, however, most cameras are digital and no longer require film. Instead, they use an imager, which is an array of tiny electronic sensors that can sense light. The imager lies on the wall opposite the lens and creates an electrical impulse when hit by incoming photons. A microchip in the camera then translates these data into an image that is then stored on a memory storage device like a hard drive.

The simplest camera, called a pinhole camera, consists of a closed light-tight box with a small hole, about 0.5 mm, in it. A surprisingly good image can be made with a pinhole camera. The hole bends the light so that it forms an image on the back of the box that is captured by a light-sensing device, either film or a digital imager. More sophisticated cameras use lenses. The simplest of these cameras, called a fixed-focus camera, includes a single, converging lens and a shutter, which opens and closes quickly to allow light to pass through the lens and expose the light sensor. Phones and webcams are of this kind. This type of camera usually gives good images only for objects far from the camera but can't focus on nearby objects. For this reason, fixed-focus cameras are of limited use.

The simplest form of a camera consists of a box with a very small hole in the front. Light is projected onto the inside back of the box.

Even more sophisticated cameras, such as point-and-shoot cameras or digital single-lens-reflex cameras (DSLR, for short), include a series of lenses that can allow the user to zoom in and out and to focus on the object. They are able to focus the image of the object onto the imager by making slight changes in the distance between the lenses. Zooming also works by moving the lenses in certain ways.

The most complex lenses can be found on single-lens reflex (SLR) cameras. Although named single-lens, these cameras in fact have multiple lenses that are interchangeable, meaning that one can be removed and replaced with another. Some lenses are fixed, in that they don't zoom.

An example of such a lens is a normal lens that provides about the same field of view as a human eye. On the other hand, a wide-angle lens has a very short focal length and can capture a larger field of view than a normal lens. A telephoto lens has a long focal length and increases magnification. Telephoto lenses have a narrow angle of view. Sometimes, however, a photographer wants to photograph distant objects with more detail or capture a larger object without taking multiple shots. Zoom lenses allow the photographer to change the focal length without changing lenses. As you might imagine, zoom lenses require multiple lenses and are therefore bulkier and heavier than fixed lenses.

High-quality cameras contain quite a few lenses, both converging and diverging, to minimize the distortions and aberrations, or imperfect focusing of light rays, that are created by a single converging lens. The most prevalent aberration occurs because lenses bend light of different colors by different amounts, causing, in effect, rainbows to appear in the image. Therefore, the quality of the final image depends not only on the type of material used to manufacture the lens, but also on the design of lenses that reduce these aberrations.

Refracting telescopes also use two converging lenses.

As mentioned in the chapter on light and reflection, there are two types of telescopes, reflecting and refracting. In a refracting telescope, an image is formed at the eye in much the same manner as is done with a microscope. A small, inverted image is formed at the focal point of the objective lens, F_0, because the object is essentially at infinity. The eyepiece is positioned so that its focal point lies very close to the focal point of the objective lens, where the image is formed, as shown in **Figure 2.9**. Because the image is now just inside the focal point of the eyepiece, F_e, the eyepiece acts like a simple magnifier and allows the viewer to examine the object in detail.

FIGURE 2.9

Refracting Telescope The image produced by the objective lens of a refracting telescope is a real, inverted image that is at its focal point. This inverted image, in turn, is the object from which the eyepiece creates a magnified, virtual image.

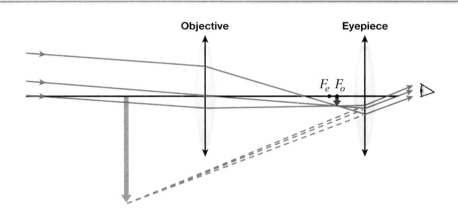

SECTION 2 FORMATIVE ASSESSMENT

▶ Reviewing Main Ideas

1. What type of image is produced by the cornea and the lens on the retina?

2. Predict the type of image, virtual or real, produced in the following cases:
   a. an object inside the focal point of a camera lens
   b. an object outside the focal point of a refracting telescope's objective lens
   c. an object outside the focal point of a camera's viewfinder

3. Predict the image position for an object placed 3.0 cm outside the focal point of a converging lens with a 4.0 cm focal length.

4. What is the magnification of the object from item 3?

Interpreting Graphics

5. Using a ray diagram, find the position and height of an image produced by a viewfinder in a camera with a focal length of 5.0 cm if the object is 1.0 cm tall and 10.0 cm in front of the lens. A camera viewfinder is a diverging lens.

✔ Critical Thinking

6. Compare the length of a refracting telescope with the sum of the focal lengths of its two lenses.

▷ Predict whether light will be refracted or undergo total internal reflection.

▷ Recognize atmospheric conditions that cause refraction.

▷ Explain dispersion and phenomena such as rainbows in terms of the relationship between the index of refraction and the wavelength.

Optical Phenomena

Key Terms

total internal reflection   dispersion
critical angle   chromatic aberration

Total Internal Reflection

An interesting effect called **total internal reflection** can occur when light moves along a path from a medium with a *higher* index of refraction to one with a *lower* index of refraction. Consider light rays traveling from water into air, as shown in **Figure 3.1(a).** Four possible directions of the rays are shown in the figure.

At some particular angle of incidence, called the **critical angle,** the refracted ray moves parallel to the boundary, making the angle of refraction equal to 90°, as shown in **Figure 3.1(b).** For angles of incidence greater than the critical angle, the ray is entirely reflected at the boundary, as shown in **Figure 3.1.** This ray is reflected at the boundary as though it had struck a perfectly reflecting surface. Its path and the path of all rays like it can be predicted by the law of reflection; that is, the angle of incidence equals the angle of reflection.

In optical equipment, prisms are arranged so that light entering the prism is totally internally reflected off the back surface of the prism. Prisms are used in place of silvered or aluminized mirrors because they reflect light more efficiently and are more scratch resistant.

Snell's law can be used to find the critical angle. As mentioned above, when the angle of incidence, θ_i, equals the critical angle, θ_c, then the angle of refraction, θ_r, equals 90°. Substituting these values into Snell's law gives the following relation.

$$n_i \sin \theta_c = n_r \sin 90°$$

total internal reflection the complete reflection that takes place within a substance when the angle of incidence of light striking the surface boundary is greater than the critical angle

critical angle the angle of incidence at which the refracted light makes an angle of 90° with the normal

FIGURE 3.1

Internal Reflection

(a) This photo demonstrates several different paths of light radiated from the bottom of an aquarium.

(b) At the critical angle, θ_c, a light ray will travel parallel to the boundary. Any rays with an angle of incidence greater than θ_c will be totally internally reflected at the boundary.

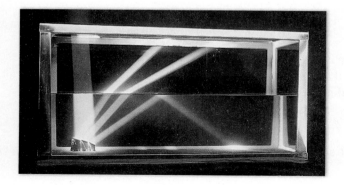

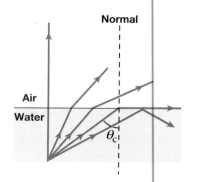

Because the sine of 90° equals 1, the following relationship results.

> **Critical Angle**
>
> $$\sin \theta_c = \frac{n_r}{n_i} \qquad \text{for } n_i > n_r$$
>
> $$\text{sine (critical angle)} = \frac{\text{index of refraction of second medium}}{\text{index of refraction of first medium}}$$
>
> **but only if index of refraction of first medium >
> index of refraction of second medium**

Note that this equation can be used only when n_i is greater than n_r. In other words, *total internal reflection occurs only when light moves along a path from a medium of higher index of refraction to a medium of lower index of refraction.* If n_i were less than n_r, this equation would give $\sin \theta_c > 1$, which is an impossible result, because by definition the sine of an angle can never be greater than 1.

When the second substance is air, the critical angle is small for substances with large indices of refraction. Diamonds, which have an index of refraction of 2.419, have a critical angle of 24.4°. By comparison, the critical angle for crown glass, a very clear optical glass, where $n = 1.52$, is 41.0°.

Because diamonds have such a small critical angle, most of the light that enters a cut diamond is totally internally reflected. The reflected light eventually exits the diamond from the most-visible faces of the diamond. Jewelers cut diamonds so that the maximum light entering the upper surface is reflected back to these faces.

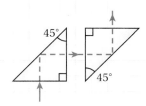

Critical Angle

Sample Problem C Find the critical angle for a crystal glass-air boundary if the index of refraction of a certain glass crystal is 1.65.

1 ANALYZE

Given: $n_i = 1.65$ $n_r = 1.00$

Unknown: $\theta_c = ?$

> **Tips and Tricks**
> Remember that the critical-angle equation is valid only if the light is moving from a higher to a lower index of refraction.

2 SOLVE

Use the equation for critical angle on this page.

$$\sin \theta_c = \frac{n_r}{n_i}$$

$$\theta_c = \sin^{-1}\left(\frac{n_r}{n_i}\right) = \sin^{-1}\left(\frac{1.00}{1.65}\right)$$

$$\boxed{\theta_c = 37.3°}$$

Continued

Critical Angle (continued)

Practice

1. Glycerine is used to make soap and other personal-care products. Find the critical angle for light traveling from glycerine ($n = 1.473$) into air.

2. A company makes optical fibers that are 13.6 km in length. If the critical angle for the fibers in air is 42.1°, what is the index of refraction of the material?

3. Light moves from a clear andalusite ($n = 1.64$) crystal into ivory. If the critical angle for andalusite is 69.9°, what is the index of refraction for ivory?

4. Which has a smaller critical angle in air, diamond ($n = 2.419$) or cubic zirconia ($n = 2.20$)? Show your work.

Fiber Optics

Another interesting application of total internal reflection is the use of glass or transparent plastic rods, like the ones shown in the photograph, to transfer light from one place to another. As indicated in the illustration, light is confined to traveling within the rods, even around gentle curves, as a result of successive internal reflections. Such a *light pipe* can be flexible if thin fibers rather than thick rods are used. If a bundle of parallel fibers is used to construct an optical transmission line, images can be transferred from one point to another.

This technique is used in a technology known as *fiber optics*. Very little light intensity is lost in these fibers as a result of reflections on the sides. Any loss of intensity is due essentially to reflections from the two ends and absorption by the fiber material. Fiber-optic devices are particularly useful for viewing images produced at inaccessible locations. For example, a fiber-optic cable can be threaded through the esophagus and into the stomach to look for ulcers.

Fiber-optic cables are used in telecommunications because the fibers can carry much higher volumes of telephone calls and computer signals than can electrical wires.

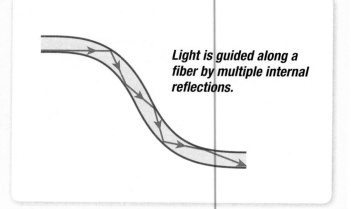

Light is guided along a fiber by multiple internal reflections.

Atmospheric Refraction

We see an example of refraction every day: the sun can be seen even after it has passed below the horizon. Rays of light from the sun strike Earth's atmosphere and are bent because the atmosphere has an index of refraction different from that of the near-vacuum atmosphere of space. The bending in this situation is gradual and continuous because the light moves through layers of air that have a continuously changing index of refraction. Our eyes follow them back along the direction from which they appear to have come. This effect is pictured in **Figure 3.2** in the observation of a star.

Refracted light produces mirages.

The *mirage* is another phenomenon of nature produced by refraction in the atmosphere. A mirage can be observed when the ground is so hot that the air directly above it is warmer than the air at higher elevations.

These layers of air at different heights above Earth have different densities and different refractive indices. The effect this can have is pictured in **Figure 3.3.** In this situation, the observer sees a tree in two different ways. One group of light rays reaches the observer by the straight-line path *A*, and the eye traces these rays back to see the tree in the normal fashion. A second group of rays travels along the curved path *B*. These rays are directed toward the ground and are then bent as a result of refraction. Consequently, the observer also sees an inverted image of the tree by tracing these rays back to the point at which they appear to have originated. Because both an upright image and an inverted image are seen when the image of a tree is observed in a reflecting pool of water, the observer subconsciously calls upon this past experience and concludes that a pool of water must be in front of the tree.

Dispersion

An important property of the index of refraction is that its value in anything but a vacuum depends on the wavelength of light. Because the index of refraction is a function of wavelength, Snell's law indicates that incoming light of different wavelengths is bent at different angles as it moves into a refracting material. This phenomenon is called **dispersion.** As mentioned in Section 1, the index of refraction decreases with increasing wavelength. For instance, blue light ($\lambda \approx 470$ nm) bends more than red light ($\lambda \approx 650$ nm) when passing into refracting material.

White light passed through a prism produces a visible spectrum.

To understand how dispersion can affect light, consider what happens when light strikes a prism, as in **Figure 3.4.** Because of dispersion, the blue component of the incoming ray is bent more than the red component, and the rays that emerge from the second face of the prism fan out in a series of colors known as a *visible spectrum.* These colors, in order of decreasing wavelength, are red, orange, yellow, green, blue, and violet.

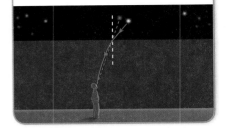

FIGURE 3.2

Atmospheric Refraction
The atmosphere of the Earth bends the light of a star and causes the viewer to see the star in a slightly different location.

FIGURE 3.3

Mirage A mirage is produced by the bending of light rays in the atmosphere when there are large temperature differences between the ground and the air.

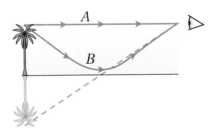

dispersion the process of separating polychromatic light into its component wavelengths

FIGURE 3.4

Dispersion When white light enters a prism, the blue light is bent more than the red, and the prism disperses the white light into its various spectral components.

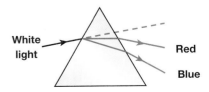

FIGURE 3.5

Rainbows and Raindrops
(a) Rainbows are produced because of dispersion of light in raindrops. **(b)** Sunlight is spread into a spectrum upon entering a spherical raindrop and then internally reflected on the back side of the raindrop. The perceived color of each water droplet then depends on the angle at which that drop is viewed.

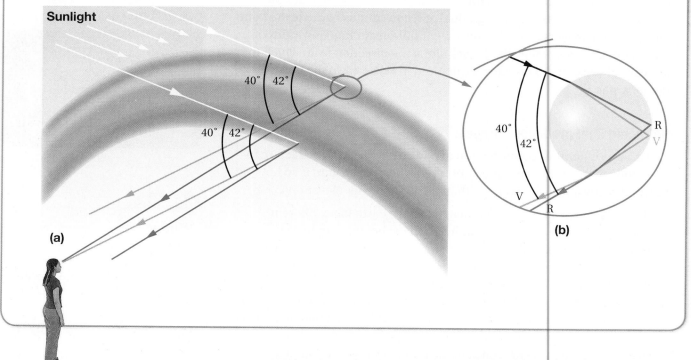

Rainbows are created by dispersion of light in water droplets.

The dispersion of light into a spectrum is demonstrated most vividly in nature by a rainbow, often seen by an observer positioned between the sun and a rain shower. When a ray of sunlight strikes a drop of water in the atmosphere, it is first refracted at the front surface of the drop, with the violet light refracting the most and the red light the least. Then, at the back surface of the drop, the light is reflected and returns to the front surface, where it again undergoes refraction as it moves from water into air. The rays leave the drop so that the angle between the incident white light and the returning violet ray is 40° and the angle between the white light and the returning red ray is 42°, as shown in **Figure 3.5(b).**

Now, consider **Figure 3.5(a).** When an observer views a raindrop high in the sky, the red light reaches the observer, but the violet light, like the other spectral colors, passes over the observer because it deviates from the path of the white light more than the red light does. Hence, the observer sees this drop as being red. Similarly, a drop lower in the sky would direct violet light toward the observer and appear to be violet. (The red light from this drop would strike the ground and not be seen.) The remaining colors of the spectrum would reach the observer from raindrops lying between these two extreme positions.

Note that rainbows are most commonly seen above the horizon, where the ends of the rainbow disappear into the ground. However, if an observer is at an elevated vantage point, such as on an airplane or at the rim of a canyon, a complete circular rainbow can be seen.

Lens Aberrations

One of the basic problems of lenses and lens systems is the imperfect quality of the images. The simple theory of mirrors and lenses assumes that rays make small angles with the principal axis and that all rays reaching the lens or mirror from a point source are focused at a single point, producing a sharp image. Clearly, this is not always true in the real world. Where the approximations used in this theory do not hold, imperfect images are formed.

As with spherical mirrors, *spherical aberration* occurs for lenses also. It results from the fact that the focal points of light rays far from the principal axis of a spherical lens are different from the focal points of rays with the same wavelength passing near the axis. Rays near the middle of the lens are focused farther from the lens than rays at the edges.

Another type of aberration, called **chromatic aberration,** arises from the wavelength dependence of refraction. Because the index of refraction of a material varies with wavelength, different wavelengths of light are focused at different focal points by a lens. For example, when white light passes through a lens, violet light is refracted more than red light, as shown in **Figure 3.6;** thus, the focal length for red light is greater than that for violet light. Other colors' wavelengths have intermediate focal points. Because a diverging lens has the opposite shape, the chromatic aberration for a diverging lens is opposite that for a converging lens. Chromatic aberration can be greatly reduced by the use of a combination of converging and diverging lenses made from two different types of glass.

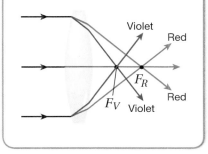

FIGURE 3.6

Chromatic Aberration
Because of dispersion, white light passing through a converging lens is focused at different focal points for each wavelength of light. (The angles in this figure are exaggerated for clarity.)

chromatic aberration the focusing of different colors of light at different distances behind a lens

---

 SECTION 3 **FORMATIVE ASSESSMENT**

▶ Reviewing Main Ideas

1. Find the critical angle for light traveling from water ($n = 1.333$) into ice ($n = 1.309$).

2. Which of the following describe places where a mirage is likely to appear?
   a. above a warm lake on a warm day
   b. above an asphalt road on a hot day
   c. above a ski slope on a cold day
   d. above the sand on a beach on a hot day
   e. above a black car on a sunny day

3. When white light passes through a prism, which will be bent more, the red or green light?

✓ Critical Thinking

4. After a storm, a man walks out onto his porch. Looking to the east, he sees a rainbow that has formed above his neighbor's house. What time of day is it, morning or evening?

Optometrist

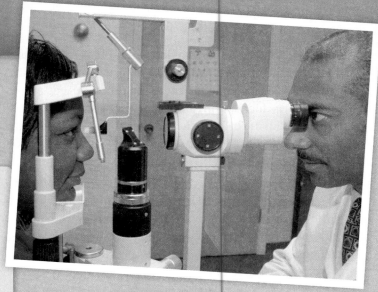

Dr. Dewey Handy uses optical devices to test the vision of a patient.

The job of an optometrist is to correct imperfect vision using optical devices such as eyeglasses or contact lenses. Optometrists also treat diseases of the eye such as glaucoma. To learn more about optometry as a career, read the interview with Dewey Handy, O.D.

How did you decide to become an optometrist?

For a while, I didn't know what career I was going to choose. In high school, I had a great love for geometry and an interest in science and anatomy. In college, I was looking for a challenge, so I ended up majoring in physics—almost by accident.

In college, I decided to apply my abilities in science to directly help people. I wasn't excited about dentistry or general medicine, but I was looking for something in a health career that would allow me to use physics.

What education is required to become an optometrist?

I have a bachelor of science in physics, and I attended optometry school for four years.

What sort of work does an optometrist do?

After taking a complete eye and medical history, the doctor may use prisms and/or lenses to determine the proper prescription for the patient. Then, a series of neurological, health, and binocular vision tests are done. After the history and data have been collected, a diagnosis and treatment plan are developed. This treatment may include glasses, contact lenses, low-vision aids, vision training, or medication for treatment of eye disease.

What do you enjoy most about your job?

I like the problem-solving nature of the work, putting the data together to come up with solutions. We read the problem, compile data, develop a formula, and solve the problem—just as in physics, but with people instead of abstract problems. I also like helping people.

What advice do you have for students who are interested in optometry?

You definitely need to have a good background in basic science: chemistry, biology, and physics. Even if you don't major in science, you need to have a good grasp of it by the time you get to optometry school.

Being well rounded will help you get into optometry school—and get out, too. You have to be comfortable doing the science; you also have to be comfortable dealing with people.

Dr. Dewey Handy

Scientific Critiques

Analyzing and evaluating a scientific explanation can help you determine whether the explanation is valid and supported by sufficient evidence. However, that carefully gathered detail and reasoning must be reviewed critically and organized to effectively communicate your own criticisms of the explanation. It is important to articulate strengths, weaknesses, and suggestions when critiquing scientific studies and explanations.

Snell's Law

Suppose a group of students wishes to observe the refraction of light and experimentally examine Snell's Law. To accomplish this, the students design an experiment to gather empirical evidence about the refraction of light through a glass block. In the experiment, the students pass light through a glass block at different angles of incidence, while measuring the angle of refraction as the light exits the other side. After making five measurements at different angles of incidence, the students determine that the angle of refraction increases as the angle of incidence increases, consistent with Snell's Law.

Answer the following questions as a critical observer of the experiment described. Recall that a critique might include comments on observation or experiment procedures, quality of empirical evidence, and whether all sides of the evidence were considered.

- Given the limited detail provided, do you feel that the students likely generated enough data to logically arrive at any conclusions?

- Critique the experimental methods used. List possible sources of error that a group of students performing this type of experiment might encounter.

- Research other information on Snell's Law. Did the students address all aspects of the law? Aside from obtaining additional data, are there any other ways to improve on the experiment by evaluating the existing data to further examine Snell's Law?

- Recommend another experiment that could be performed using the same glass block that would help further verify Snell's Law.

Conceptual Challenge

The ability to make assumptions and generate rough estimates is a valuable skill to scientists. Quick estimates allow scientists to narrow the range of possibilities and focus on the most reasonable hypotheses.

In the Deep Imagine looking straight down into a pool of water that is 2 meters deep and seeing a light on the bottom of the pool. Assume that the light is approximately the size of a quarter. How large would the diameter of the light appear at the surface of the pool?

You can begin addressing the scenario by asking questions such as the following:

- What is the diameter of a quarter?

- What is the angle of refraction as light exits the water?

SECTION 1 **Refraction**

- According to Snell's law, as a light ray travels from one medium into another medium where its speed is different, the light ray will change its direction unless it travels along the normal.

- When light passes from a medium with a smaller index of refraction to one with a larger index of refraction, the ray bends toward the normal. For the opposite situation, the ray bends away from the normal.

KEY TERMS

refraction
index of refraction

SECTION 2 **Thin Lenses**

- The image produced by a converging lens is real and inverted when the object is outside the focal point and virtual and upright when the object is inside the focal point. Diverging lenses always produce upright, virtual images.

- The location of an image created by a lens can be found using either a ray diagram or the thin-lens equation.

KEY TERM

lens

SECTION 3 **Optical Phenomena**

- Total internal reflection can occur when light attempts to move from a material with a higher index of refraction to one with a lower index of refraction. If the angle of incidence of a ray is greater than the critical angle, the ray is totally reflected at the boundary.

- Mirages and the visibility of the sun after it has physically set are natural phenomena that can be attributed to refraction of light in Earth's atmosphere.

KEY TERMS

total internal reflection
critical angle
dispersion
chromatic aberration

VARIABLE SYMBOLS		
Quantities	**Units**	
θ_i angle of incidence	°	degrees
θ_r angle of refraction	°	degrees
n index of refraction	(unitless)	
p distance from object to lens	m	meters
q distance from image to lens	m	meters
h' image height	m	meters
h object height	m	meters
θ_c critical angle	°	degrees

Problem Solving

See **Appendix D: Equations** for a summary of the equations introduced in this chapter. If you need more problem-solving practice, see **Appendix I: Additional Problems**.

Refraction and Snell's Law

▶ **REVIEWING MAIN IDEAS**

1. Does a light ray traveling from one medium into another always bend toward the normal?

2. As light travels from a vacuum ($n = 1$) to a medium such as glass ($n > 1$), does its wavelength change? Does its speed change? Does its frequency change?

3. What is the relationship between the speed of light and the index of refraction of a transparent substance?

4. Why does a clear stream always appear to be shallower than it actually is?

5. What are the three conditions that must be met for refraction to occur?

CONCEPTUAL QUESTIONS

6. Two colors of light (X and Y) are sent through a glass prism, and X is bent more than Y. Which color travels more slowly in the prism?

7. Why does an oar appear to be bent when part of it is in the water?

8. A friend throws a coin into a pool. You close your eyes and dive toward the spot where you saw it from the edge of the pool. When you reach the bottom, will the coin be in front of you or behind you?

9. The level of water ($n = 1.33$) in a clear glass container is easily observed with the naked eye. The level of liquid helium ($n = 1.03$) in a clear glass container is extremely difficult to see with the naked eye. Explain why.

PRACTICE PROBLEMS

For problems 10–14, see Sample Problem A.

10. Light passes from air into water at an angle of incidence of 42.3°. Determine the angle of refraction in the water.

11. A ray of light enters the top of a glass of water at an angle of 36° with the vertical. What is the angle between the refracted ray and the vertical?

12. A narrow ray of yellow light from glowing sodium ($\lambda_0 = 589$ nm) traveling in air strikes a smooth surface of water at an angle of $\theta_i = 35.0°$. Determine the angle of refraction, θ_r.

13. A ray of light traveling in air strikes a flat 2.00 cm thick block of glass ($n = 1.50$) at an angle of 30.0° with the normal. Trace the light ray through the glass, and find the angles of incidence and refraction at each surface.

14. The light ray shown in the figure below makes an angle of 20.0° with the normal line at the boundary of linseed oil and water. Determine the angles θ_1 and θ_2. Note that $n = 1.48$ for linseed oil.

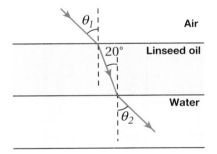

Ray Diagrams and Thin Lenses

▶ **REVIEWING MAIN IDEAS**

15. Which type of lens can focus the sun's rays?

16. Why is no image formed when an object is at the focal point of a converging lens?

17. Consider the image formed by a thin converging lens. Under what conditions will the image be
    a. inverted?
    b. upright?
    c. real?
    d. virtual?
    e. larger than the object?
    f. smaller than the object?

18. Repeat a–f of item 17 for a thin diverging lens.

19. Explain this statement: The focal point of a converging lens is the location of an image of a point object at infinity. Based on this statement, can you think of a quick method for determining the focal length of a positive lens?

CONCEPTUAL QUESTIONS

20. If a glass converging lens is submerged in water, will its focal length be longer or shorter than when the lens is in air?

21. In order to get an image that is right-side up, slides must be placed upside down in a slide projector. What type of lens must the slide projector have? Predict whether the slide is inside or outside the focal point of the lens.

22. If there are two converging lenses in a compound microscope, why is the image still inverted?

23. In a Jules Verne novel, a piece of ice is shaped into the form of a magnifying lens to focus sunlight and thereby start a fire. Is this possible?

PRACTICE PROBLEMS

For problems 24–26, see Sample Problem B.

24. An object is placed in front of a diverging lens with a focal length of 20.0 cm. For each object distance, find the image distance and the magnification. Describe each image.
    a. 40.0 cm
    b. 20.0 cm
    c. 10.0 cm

25. A person looks at a gem using a converging lens with a focal length of 12.5 cm. The lens forms a virtual image 30.0 cm from the lens. Determine the magnification. Is the image upright or inverted?

26. An object is placed in front of a converging lens with a focal length of 20.0 cm. For each object distance, predict the image distance and the magnification. Describe each image.
    a. 40.0 cm
    b. 10.0 cm

Total Internal Reflection, Atmospheric Refraction, and Aberrations

▶ REVIEWING MAIN IDEAS

27. Is it possible to have total internal reflection for light incident from air on water? Explain.

28. What are the conditions necessary for the occurrence of a mirage?

29. On a hot day, what is it that we are seeing when we observe a "water on the road" mirage?

30. Why does the arc of a rainbow appear with red colors on top and violet colors on the bottom?

31. What type of aberration is involved in each of the following situations?
    a. The edges of the image appear reddish.
    b. The central portion of the image cannot be clearly focused.
    c. The outer portion of the image cannot be clearly focused.
    d. The central portion of the image is enlarged relative to the outer portions.

CONCEPTUAL QUESTIONS

32. A laser beam passing through a nonhomogeneous sugar solution follows a curved path. Explain.

33. On a warm day, the image of a boat floating on cold water appears above the boat. Explain.

34. Explain why a mirror cannot give rise to chromatic aberration.

35. Why does a diamond show flashes of color when observed under ordinary white light?

PRACTICE PROBLEMS

For problems 36–38, see Sample Problem C.

36. Calculate the critical angle for light going from glycerine into air.

37. Assuming that $\lambda = 589$ nm, calculate the critical angles for the following materials when they are surrounded by air:
  a. zircon
  b. fluorite
  c. ice

38. Light traveling in air enters the flat side of a prism made of crown glass ($n = 1.52$), as shown at right. Will the light pass through the other side of the prism, or will it be totally internally reflected? Be sure to show your work.

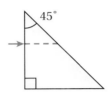

Mixed Review

▶ **REVIEWING MAIN IDEAS**

39. The angle of incidence and the angle of refraction for light going from air into a material with a higher index of refraction are 63.5° and 42.9°, respectively. What is the index of refraction of this material?

40. A person standing beside a pool shines a light at a friend who is swimming underwater. If the ray in the water makes an angle of 36.2° with the normal, what is the angle of incidence?

41. What is the index of refraction of a material in which the speed of light is 1.85×10^8 m/s? Look at the indices of refraction in **Figure 1.4** to identify this material.

42. Light moves from flint glass into water at an angle of incidence of 28.7°.
  a. What is the angle of refraction?
  b. At what angle would the light have to be incident to give an angle of refraction of 90.0°?

43. A magnifying glass has a converging lens of focal length 15.0 cm. At what distance from a nickel should you hold this lens to get an image with a magnification of +2.00?

44. The image of the United States postage stamps in the figure above is 1.50 times the size of the actual stamps in front of the lens. Determine the focal length of the lens if the distance from the lens to the stamps is 2.84 cm.

45. Where must an object be placed to have a magnification of 2.00 in each of the following cases? Show your work.
  a. a converging lens of focal length 12.0 cm
  b. a diverging lens of focal length 12.0 cm

46. A diverging lens is used to form a virtual image of an object. The object is 80.0 cm in front of the lens, and the image is 40.0 cm in front of the lens. Determine the focal length of the lens.

47. A microscope slide is placed in front of a converging lens with a focal length of 2.44 cm. The lens forms an image of the slide 12.9 cm from the slide.
  a. How far is the lens from the slide if the image is real?
  b. How far is the lens from the slide if the image is virtual?

48. Where must an object be placed to form an image 30.0 cm from a diverging lens with a focal length of 40.0 cm? Determine the magnification of the image.

49. The index of refraction for red light in water is 1.331, and that for blue light is 1.340. If a ray of white light traveling in air enters the water at an angle of incidence of 83.0°, what are the angles of refraction for the red and blue components of the light?

50. A ray of light traveling in air strikes the surface of mineral oil at an angle of 23.1° with the normal to the surface. If the light travels at 2.17×10^8 m/s through the oil, what is the angle of refraction? (Hint: Remember the definition of the index of refraction.)

51. A ray of light traveling in air strikes the surface of a liquid. If the angle of incidence is 30.0° and the angle of refraction is 22.0°, find the critical angle for light traveling from the liquid back into the air.

52. The laws of refraction and reflection are the same for sound and for light. The speed of sound is 340 m/s in air and 1510 m/s in water. If a sound wave that is traveling in air approaches a flat water surface with an angle of incidence of 12.0°, what is the angle of refraction?

53. A jewel thief decides to hide a stolen diamond by placing it at the bottom of a crystal-clear fountain. He places a circular piece of wood on the surface of the water and anchors it directly above the diamond at the bottom of the fountain, as shown below. If the fountain is 2.00 m deep, find the minimum diameter of the piece of wood that would prevent the diamond from being seen from outside the water.

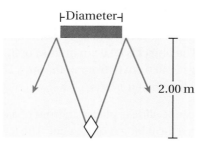

54. A ray of light traveling in air strikes the surface of a block of clear ice at an angle of 40.0° with the normal. Part of the light is reflected, and part is refracted. Find the angle between the reflected and refracted light.

55. An object's distance from a converging lens is 10 times the focal length. How far is the image from the lens? Express the answer as a fraction of the focal length.

56. A fiber-optic cable used for telecommunications has an index of refraction of 1.53. For total internal reflection of light inside the cable, what is the minimum angle of incidence to the inside wall of the cable if the cable is in the following:
    a. air
    b. water

57. A ray of light traveling in air strikes the midpoint of one face of an equiangular glass prism ($n = 1.50$) at an angle of exactly 30.0°, as shown below.
    a. Trace the path of the light ray through the glass, and find the angle of incidence of the ray at the bottom of the prism.
    b. Will the ray pass through the bottom surface of the prism, or will it be totally internally reflected?

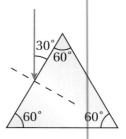

58. Light strikes the surface of a prism, $n = 1.8$, as shown in the figure below. If the prism is surrounded by a fluid, what is the maximum index of refraction of the fluid that will still cause total internal reflection within the prism?

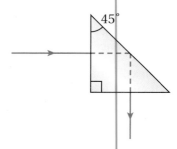

59. A fiber-optic rod consists of a central strand of material surrounded by an outer coating. The interior portion of the rod has an index of refraction of 1.60. If all rays striking the interior walls of the rod with incident angles greater than 59.5° are subject to total internal reflection, what is the index of refraction of the coating?

60. A flashlight on the bottom of a 4.00 m deep swimming pool sends a ray upward and at an angle so that the ray strikes the surface of the water 2.00 m from the point directly above the flashlight. What angle (in air) does the emerging ray make with the water's surface? (Hint: To determine the angle of incidence, consider the right triangle formed by the light ray, the pool bottom, and the imaginary line straight down from where the ray strikes the surface of the water.)

61. A submarine is 325 m horizontally out from the shore and 115 m beneath the surface of the water. A laser beam is sent from the submarine so that it strikes the surface of the water at a point 205 m from the shore. If the beam strikes the top of a building standing directly at the water's edge, find the height of the building. (Hint: To determine the angle of incidence, consider the right triangle formed by the light beam, the horizontal line drawn at the depth of the submarine, and the imaginary line straight down from where the beam strikes the surface of the water.)

62. A laser beam traveling in air strikes the midpoint of one end of a slab of material, as shown in the figure in the next column. The index of refraction of the slab is 1.48. Determine the number of internal reflections of the laser beam before it finally emerges from the opposite end of the slab.

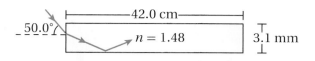

63. A nature photographer is using a camera that has a lens with a focal length of 4.80 cm. The photographer is taking pictures of ancient trees in a forest and wants the lens to be focused on a very old tree that is 10.0 m away.
  a. How far must the lens be from the film in order for the resulting picture to be clearly focused?
  b. Predict how much the lens would have to be moved to take a picture of another tree that is only 1.75 m away.

64. The distance from the front to the back of your eye is approximately 1.90 cm. If you can see a clear image of a book when it is 35.0 cm from your eye, what is the focal length of the lens/cornea system?

65. Suppose you look out the window and see your friend, who is standing 15.0 m away. To what focal length must your eye muscles adjust the lens of your eye so that you may see your friend clearly? Remember that the distance from the front to the back of your eye is about 1.90 cm.

GRAPHING CALCULATOR PRACTICE

Snell's Law

What happens to a light ray that passes from air into a medium whose index of refraction differs from that of air? Snell's law, as you learned earlier in this chapter, describes the relationship between the angle of refraction and the index of refraction.

$$n_i \sin \theta_i = n_r \sin \theta_r$$

In this equation, n_i is the index of refraction of the medium of the incident light ray, and θ_i is the angle of incidence; n_r is the index of refraction of the medium of the refracted light, and θ_r is the angle of refraction.

In this graphing calculator activity, you will enter the angle of incidence and will view a graph of the index of refraction versus the angle of refraction. You can use this graph to better understand the relationship between the index of refraction and the angle of refraction.

Go online to HMHScience.com to find the skillsheet and program for this graphing calculator activity.

ALTERNATIVE ASSESSMENT

1. Interview an optometrist, optician, or ophthalmologist. Find out what equipment and tools each uses. What kinds of eye problems is each able to correct? What training is necessary for each career?

2. Obtain permission to use a microscope and slides from your school's biology teacher. Identify the optical components (lenses, mirror, object, and light source) and knobs. Find out how they function at different magnifications and what adjustments must be made to obtain a clear image. Sketch a ray diagram for the microscope's image formation. Estimate the size of the images you see, and predict the approximate size of the actual cells or microorganisms you observe. How closely do your estimates match the magnification indicated on the microscope?

3. Construct your own telescope with mailing tubes (one small enough to slide inside the other), two lenses, cardboard disks for mounting the lenses, glue, and masking tape. Test your instrument at night. Try to combine different lenses and explore ways to improve your telescope's performance. Keep records of your results to make a brochure documenting the development of your telescope.

4. Study the history of the camera. Possible topics include the following: How did the camera obscura work? What discovery made the first permanent photograph possible? How do instant cameras work? How do modern digital cameras differ from film cameras? Give a short presentation to the class to share the information.

5. Create a pinhole camera with simple household materials. Find instructions on the Internet for constructing a pinhole camera, and follow them to make your own pinhole camera. Partner with a photography student to develop the pictures in your school's darkroom. Create a visual presentation to share your photographs with the class.

6. Research how phone, television, and radio signals are transmitted over long distances through fiber-optic devices. Obtain information from companies that provide telephone or cable television service. What materials are fiber-optic cables made of? What are their most important properties? Are there limits on the kind of light that travels in these cables? What are the advantages of fiber-optic technology over broadcast transmission? Produce a brochure or informational video to explain this technology to consumers.

7. When the Indian physicist Venkata Raman first saw the Mediterranean Sea, he proposed that its blue color was due to the structure of water molecules rather than to the scattering of light from suspended particles. Later, he won the Nobel Prize for work relating to the implications of this hypothesis. Research Raman's life and work. Find out about his background and the challenges and opportunities he met on his way to becoming a physicist. Create a presentation about him in the form of a report, poster, short video, or computer presentation.

8. Choose a radio telescope to research. Possibilities include the Very Large Array in New Mexico, the Arecibo telescope in Puerto Rico, or the Green Bank Telescope in West Virginia. Use the Internet to learn about observations that have been made with the telescope. How long has the telescope been operating? How large is the telescope? What discoveries have been made with it? Has the telescope been used for any SETI (search for extraterrestrial intelligence) investigations? After your research is complete, write a list of questions that you still have about the telescope. If possible, call the observatory and interview a member of the staff. Write a magazine article with the results of your research.

Standards-Based Assessment

Record your answers on a separate piece of paper.

MULTIPLE CHOICE

1 How is light affected by an increase in the index of refraction?

   A Its frequency increases.
   B Its frequency decreases.
   C Its speed increases.
   D Its speed decreases.

Use the ray diagram below to answer questions 2–3.

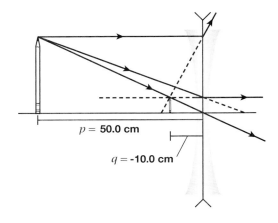

$p = $ **50.0 cm**

$q = $ **-10.0 cm**

2 What is the focal length of the lens?

   A -12.5 cm
   B -8.33 cm
   C 8.33 cm
   D 12.5 cm

3 What is true of the image formed by the lens?

   A real, inverted, and enlarged
   B real, inverted, and diminished
   C virtual, upright, and enlarged
   D virtual, upright, and diminished

4 A block of flint glass with an index of refraction of 1.66 is immersed in oil with an index of refraction of 1.33. How does the critical angle for a refracted light ray in the glass vary from when the glass is surrounded by air?

   A It remains unchanged.
   B It increases.
   C It decreases.
   D No total internal reflection takes place when the glass is placed in the oil.

5 If an object in air is viewed from beneath the surface of water below, where does the object appear to be?

   A The object appears above its true position.
   B The object appears exactly at its true position.
   C The object appears below its true position.
   D The object cannot be viewed from beneath the water's surface.

6 The phenomenon called "looming" is similar to a mirage, except that the inverted image appears above the object instead of below it. What must be true if looming is to occur?

   A The temperature of the air must increase with distance above the surface.
   B The temperature of the air must decrease with distance above the surface.
   C The mass of the air must increase with distance above the surface.
   D The mass of the air must increase with distance above the surface.

7 Medical doctors use a variety of equipment making use of a variety of types of waves to diagnose conditions within the human body. The type of wave they choose for a given diagnosis depends largely on the behaviors of the types of waves. Which type of waves would be chosen for looking directly into a patient's eye with an ophthalmoscope?

   A sound waves
   B light waves
   C x-rays
   D gamma waves

GRIDDED RESPONSE

8 A layer of glycerine ($n = 1.47$) covers a zircon slab ($n = 1.92$). At what angle, given in degrees, to the normal must a beam of light pass through the zircon toward the glycerine so that the light undergoes total internal reflection?

PICTURE TAKER
Machines that turn light into pictures

You've learned that cameras convert straight lines (light) into images (photos) using basic principles of optics and chemical reactions. From simple pinhole cameras to sophisticated digital cameras, all use refraction to produce images. Here's an explanation that presents some complex ideas about photography in simple language.

A BOOK EXPLAINING COMPLEX IDEAS USING ONLY THE 1,000 MOST COMMON WORDS

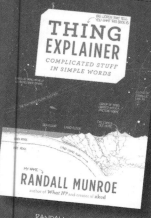

RANDALL MUNROE
XKCD.COM

THE STORY OF MAKING PICTURES

WHEN YOU LOOK AT SOMETHING, THE LIGHT FROM IT GOES INTO YOUR EYE AND MAKES A PICTURE INSIDE YOUR HEAD.

THE PICTURE GIVES YOU AN IDEA ABOUT THE THING'S SHAPE AND COLOR.

THAT WAS STRANGE!

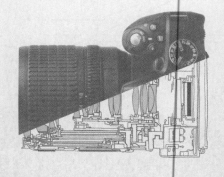

SINCE BEFORE HUMANS LEARNED TO WRITE, WE'VE BEEN USING PAINTING TO TURN OUR IDEAS BACK INTO PICTURES. PICTURES LET US REMEMBER THE THINGS WE SAW AND IDEAS WE HAD, AND TO PUT THOSE IDEAS IN OTHER PEOPLE'S HEADS, TOO.

A FEW HUNDRED YEARS AGO, WE STARTED MAKING MACHINES THAT TURNED LIGHT STRAIGHT INTO PICTURES.

SMILE!

PICTURE MAKING HAS BECOME A BIG PART OF HOW WE TALK AND SHARE.

SHAPE

To make a picture of something, you need to control the light so that each part of the paper sees light from just one part of it.

One way to do this is by blocking almost all the light paths using a wall with a hole in it. (This makes a picture that's turned over, but that's okay—you can just turn it back.)

MORE LIGHT

The hole idea works, but a tiny hole doesn't let very much light through, so it takes a long time for enough light to hit the paper to make a picture.

To let in more light, you could make the hole bigger, but then the light from one spot starts to spread out on the paper, clouding the picture.

BENDING LIGHT

To make the picture less clouded, we need to bend lots of light from each part of the thing toward the spot on the picture that goes with it. We can do this by using things that bend light—like water and glass.

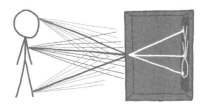
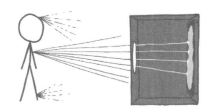
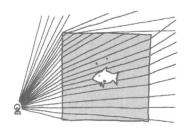

SPECIAL SHAPES

By cutting glass into the right shapes, we can make light benders that catch lots of light and send the light from each direction to a different part of the picture. This machine is good enough to take a simple picture, but it will be a little clouded and not very sharp or bright. To take a clearer picture, we have to add more benders to control the path the light takes more carefully. Most picture takers use glass, since it's easier to cut it into a shape than water.

Some people are trying to build computer-controlled benders that use water, which would let the benders change shape to control the light without using as many parts.

NOT AGAIN...

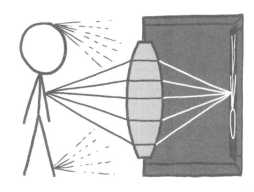

LIGHT PAPER

Some kinds of paper change color when light hits them. Picture takers used these for a long time.

This paper alone isn't enough to make a picture, though. When you hold the paper up to someone, light from every part of them hits every part of the paper, so your whole page will be all one color. (Unless you hold the paper so close to the thing that each part of the paper only sees light from one part of the thing, but that doesn't work very well.)

OKAY, SMILE!

BIG PICTURE TAKER

This machine is used to take sharp pictures, even of things that are small or far away.

Our eyes are better than most picture takers at seeing small and far-away things, but thanks to its very large benders that take in lots of light, this kind of picture taker can see even better.

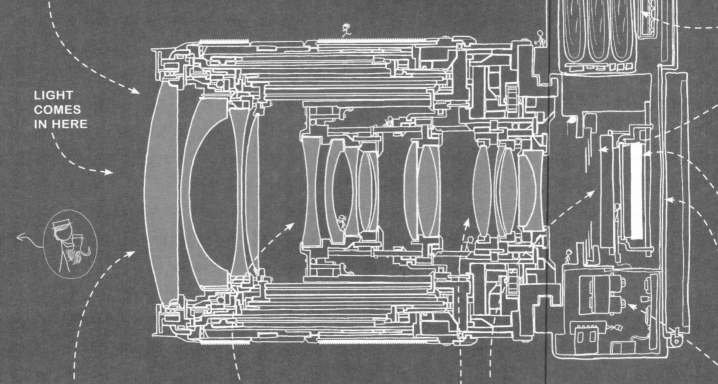

LOOKER

The whole front end of the picture taker is for gathering light. The whole thing can come off, so you can use different lookers for different kinds of pictures.

LIGHT COMES IN HERE

WHY ARE THERE SO MANY BENDERS?

These light benders are here for different reasons, but one of the big ones is that some colors of light bend more than others when they go through glass. This can make some colors in a picture sharp while others are spread out. Different kinds of glass break up colors in different ways, so by sending the light through one kind of glass and then another, groups of benders can get the different colors to the same place.

FRONT BENDERS

These grab all the light and start bringing it together so the other benders can do things with it.

FROM YOUR PICTURES, WE FIGURED YOU WERE JUST BAD AT USING CAMERAS.

NO, I'M ACTUALLY LIKE THIS.

CLOSE-OR-FAR BENDERS

These benders control how close up or far away the things in the picture look. They slide forward to look at small things far away, and back to see a wider view of the whole area.

PICTURE BENDERS

These light benders are the ones that bring the light together to make a picture on the light catcher in the back.

DUST SHAKER WINDOW

Even a tiny piece of dust stuck to the picture window can make the machine take bad pictures. In small picture takers, the picture window is locked inside and safe from dust. But on ones where you can take the big looker off to put on a different one, dust can get in. To keep dust from being a problem, there's a window in front of the picture window with a shaker on it. The shaker shakes the window very fast, throwing off any dust that sticks to it.

NO MIRROR

Nice picture takers used to have a mirror here, so you could look through a hole in the top and see through the looker, to see what would be in the picture. The loud "picture-taking sound" is the mirror moving out of the way to let light reach the back. Now, more and more picture takers are using screens to show you the view instead.

POWER BOX

Taking pictures can use lots of power, so picture takers usually need special power boxes.

MEMORY

This holds the pictures you take.

PICTURE WINDOW

This window opens and closes to let light through to the light catcher and take a picture. It has two sheets. When it starts taking a picture, the bottom sheet pulls down out of the way. When it's done gathering light, the top screen comes down to cover it. It uses two screens; if it used a screen that came up and then pulled back, then the top half of the light catcher would spend more time catching light than the bottom.

LIGHT CATCHER

This used to be made of paper, but on computer picture takers like this one, it's a flat sheet of computer light feelers. Each one checks how much light is hitting it, then tells the computer. The computer puts the messages together to make a picture.

SCREEN

This screen shows you what the light catcher is seeing. It also lets you look at the pictures you took and decide whether you want to keep them. Some picture takers have a hole you can look through, too, which shows you a view out the looker using a mirror (or pretends to, using another screen).

FLASH

If there's not enough light to make a good picture, this can light up the area for a moment while the picture window is open. The light can make the shadows in a picture look strange, though, so some people try not to use it very much.

CHANGING SHAPE

Picture takers have changed shape over time. The back parts are smaller, but some of the front parts of good picture takers have stayed big. The jobs done by the back parts, like saving pictures and storing power, are now being done by small computers. The front parts bend light, and computers can't do that yet. Soon, people might just use their hand computers as the back part, sticking them to a looker to take nice pictures.

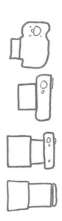

HAND COMPUTER

LOOKER

Devices called *diffraction gratings* use the principle of interference to separate light into a spectrum of wavelengths. Diffraction gratings are used in instruments called *spectrometers*, which are used to study the chemical composition and temperature of stars.

The streaks of colored light you see coming from a compact disc are a product of *constructive interference.* A compact disc disperses light in a manner similar to that of a diffraction grating.

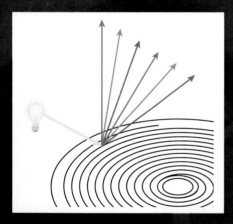

CHAPTER 15

Interference and Diffraction

BIG IDEA

Like mechanical waves, light waves can interact with each other and with obstacles. The patterns formed by these interactions depend on wavelength.

ONLINE Physics
HMHScience.com

ONLINE LAB
- Diffraction
- Double-Slit Interference

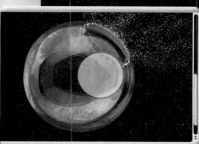

GO ONLINE
Animated
Physics
HMHScience.com

Diffraction

(br) ©Don Farrall/Photodisc/Getty Images

▶ Describe how light waves interfere with each other to produce bright and dark fringes.

▶ Identify the conditions required for interference to occur.

▶ Predict the location of interference fringes using the equation for double-slit interference.

Interference

Key Terms

coherence   path difference   order number

Combining Light Waves

You have probably noticed the bands of color that form on the surface of a soap bubble, as shown in **Figure 1.1**. Unlike the colors that appear when light passes through a refracting substance, these colors are the result of light waves combining with each other.

Interference takes place only between waves with the same wavelength.

To understand how light waves combine with each other, let us review how other kinds of waves combine. If two waves with identical wavelengths interact, they combine to form a resultant wave. This resultant wave has the same wavelength as the component waves, but according to the superposition principle, its displacement at any instant equals the sum of the displacements of the component waves. The resultant wave is the consequence of the *interference* between the two waves.

Figure 1.2 can be used to describe pairs of mechanical waves or electromagnetic waves with the same wavelength. A light source that has a single wavelength is called *monochromatic*, which means single colored. In the case of *constructive interference,* as in **Figure 1.2(a)**, the component waves combine to form a resultant wave with the same wavelength but with an amplitude that is greater than the amplitude of either of the individual component waves. For light, the result of constructive interference is light that is brighter than the light from the contributing waves. In the case of *destructive interference,* as in **Figure 1.2(b)**, the resultant amplitude is less than the amplitude of the larger component wave. For light, the result of destructive interference is dimmer light or dark spots.

FIGURE 1.1

Interference on a Soap Bubble Light waves interfere to form bands of color on a soap bubble's surface.

FIGURE 1.2

Wave Interference Two waves can interfere **(a)** constructively or **(b)** destructively. In interference, energy is not lost but is instead redistributed.

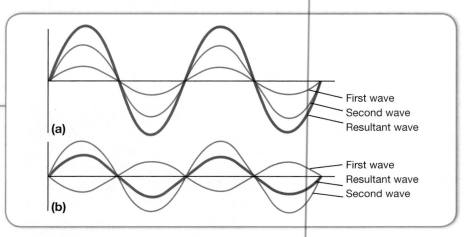

(a)
First wave
Second wave
Resultant wave

First wave
Resultant wave
Second wave
(b)

FIGURE 1.3

Comparison of Waves In Phase and 180° Out of Phase

(a) The features of two waves in phase completely match, whereas **(b)** they are opposite each other in waves that are 180° out of phase.

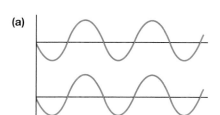

(a)

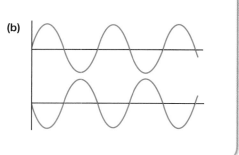

(b)

Waves must have a constant phase difference for interference to be observed.

For two waves to produce a stable interference pattern, the phases of the individual waves must remain unchanged relative to one another. If the crest of one wave overlaps the crest of another wave, as in **Figure 1.3(a),** the two have a phase difference of 0° and are said to be *in phase*. If the crest of one wave overlaps the trough of the other wave, as in **Figure 1.3(b),** the two waves have a phase difference of 180° and are said to be *out of phase*.

Waves are said to have **coherence** when the phase difference between two waves is constant and the waves do not shift relative to each other as time passes. Sources of such waves are said to be *coherent*.

coherence the correlation between the phases of two or more waves

When two light bulbs are placed side by side, no interference is observed. The reason is that the light waves from one bulb are emitted independently of the waves from the other bulb. Random changes occurring in the light from one bulb do not necessarily occur in the light from the other bulb. Thus, the phase difference between the light waves from the two bulbs is not constant. The light waves still interfere, but the conditions for the interference change with each phase change, and therefore, no single interference pattern is observed. Light sources of this type are said to be *incoherent*.

Demonstrating Interference

Interference in light waves from two sources can be demonstrated in the following way. Light from a single source is passed through a narrow slit and then through two narrow parallel slits. The slits serve as a pair of coherent light sources because the waves emerging from them come from the same source. Any random change in the light emitted by the source will occur in the two separate beams at the same time.

If monochromatic light is used, the light from the two slits produces a series of bright and dark parallel bands, or *fringes*, on a distant viewing screen, as shown in **Figure 1.4.** When the light from the two slits arrives at a point on the viewing screen where constructive interference occurs, a bright fringe appears at that location. When the light from the two slits combines destructively at a point on the viewing screen, a dark fringe appears at that location.

FIGURE 1.4

Monochromatic Light Interference
An interference pattern consists of alternating light and dark fringes.

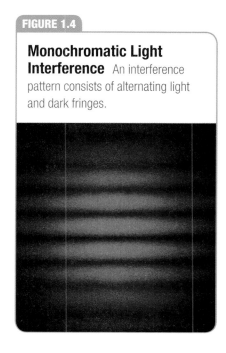

FIGURE 1.5

White-Light Interference

When waves of white light from two coherent sources interfere, the pattern is indistinct because different colors interfere constructively and destructively at different positions.

When a white-light source is used to observe interference, the situation becomes more complicated. The reason is that white light includes waves of many wavelengths. An example of a white-light interference pattern is shown in **Figure 1.5.** The interference pattern is stable or well defined at positions where there is constructive interference between light waves of the same wavelength. This explains the color bands on either side of the center band of white light.

Figure 1.6 shows some of the ways that two coherent waves leaving the slits can combine at the viewing screen. When the waves arrive at the central point of the screen, as in **Figure 1.6(a)**, they have traveled equal distances. Thus, they arrive in phase at the center of the screen, constructive interference occurs, and a bright fringe forms at that location.

When the two light waves combine at a specific point off the center of the screen, as in **Figure 1.6(b)**, the wave from the more distant slit must travel one wavelength farther than the wave from the nearer slit. Because the second wave has traveled exactly one wavelength farther than the first wave, the two waves are in phase when they combine at the screen. Constructive interference therefore occurs, and a second bright fringe appears on the screen.

If the waves meet midway between the locations of the two bright fringes, as in **Figure 1.6(c)**, the first wave travels half a wavelength farther than the second wave. In this case, the trough of the first wave overlaps the crest of the second wave, giving rise to destructive interference. Consequently, a dark fringe appears on the viewing screen between the bright fringes.

FIGURE 1.6

Conditions for Interference of Light Waves

(a) When both waves of light travel the same distance (l_1), they arrive at the screen in phase and interfere constructively. **(b)** If the difference between the distances traveled by the light from each source equals a whole wavelength (λ), the waves still interfere constructively. **(c)** If the distances traveled by the light differ by a half wavelength, the waves interfere destructively.

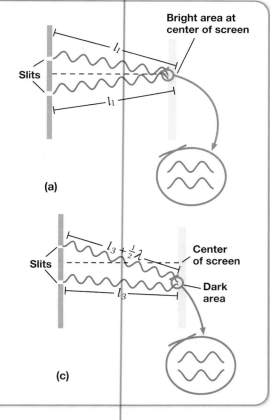

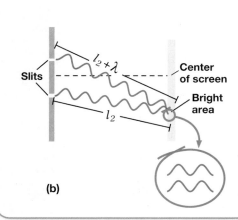

(b)

(c)

Predicting the location of interference fringes.

Consider two narrow slits separated by a distance d, as shown in **Figure 1.7**, and through which two coherent, monochromatic light waves, l_1 and l_2, pass and are projected onto a screen. If the distance from the slits to the screen is very large compared with the distance between the slits, then l_1 and l_2 are nearly parallel. As a result of this approximation, l_1 and l_2 make the same angle, θ, with the horizontal dotted lines that are perpendicular to the slits. Angle θ also indicates the position where waves combine with respect to the central point of the screen.

The difference in the distance traveled by the two waves is called their **path difference.** Study the right triangle shown in **Figure 1.7**, and note that the path difference between the two waves is equal to $d \sin \theta$. Note carefully that the value for the path difference varies with angle θ and that each value of θ defines a specific position on the screen.

The value of the path difference determines whether the two waves are in or out of phase when they arrive at the viewing screen. If the path difference is either zero or some whole-number multiple of the wavelength, the two waves are in phase, and constructive interference results. The condition for bright fringes (constructive interference) is given by:

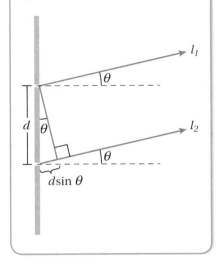

FIGURE 1.7

Path Difference for Light Waves from Two Slits

The path difference for two light waves equals $d \sin \theta$. In order to emphasize the path difference, the figure is not drawn to scale.

path difference the difference in the distance traveled by two beams when they are scattered in the same direction from different points

order number the number assigned to interference fringes with respect to the central bright fringe

---

Equation for Constructive Interference

$$d \sin \theta = \pm m\lambda \quad m = 0, 1, 2, 3, \ldots$$

the path difference between two waves = an integer multiple of the wavelength

In this equation, m is the **order number** of the fringe. The central bright fringe at $\theta = 0$ ($m = 0$) is called the *zeroth-order maximum*, or the *central maximum*; the first maximum on either side of the central maximum, which occurs when $m = 1$, is called the *first-order maximum*; and so forth.

Similarly, when the path difference is an odd multiple of $\frac{1}{2}\lambda$, the two waves arriving at the screen are 180° out of phase, giving rise to destructive interference. The condition for dark fringes is given by the following equation:

Equation for Destructive Interference

$$d \sin \theta = \pm\left(m + \frac{1}{2}\right)\lambda \quad m = 0, 1, 2, 3, \ldots$$

the path difference between two waves = an odd number of half wavelengths

If $m = 0$ in this equation, the path difference is $\pm \frac{1}{2}\lambda$, which is the condition required for the first dark fringe on either side of the bright central maximum. Likewise, if $m = 1$, the path difference is $\pm \frac{3}{2}\lambda$, which is the condition for the second dark fringe on each side of the central maximum. This pattern continues.

FIGURE 1.8

Position of Higher-Order Interference Fringes

The higher-order ($m = 1, 2$) maxima appear on either side of the central maximum ($m = 0$).

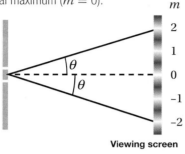

Viewing screen

A representation of the interference pattern formed by double-slit interference is shown in **Figure 1.8**. The numbers indicate the two *maxima* (the plural of *maximum*) that form on either side of the central (zeroth-order) maximum. The darkest areas indicate the positions of the dark fringes, or *minima* (the plural of *minimum*), that also appear in the pattern.

Because the separation between interference fringes varies for light of different wavelengths, double-slit interference provides a method of measuring the wavelength of light. In fact, this technique was used to make the first measurement of the wavelength of light.

GO ONLINE

Interactive Demo
HMHScience.com

Interference

Sample Problem A The distance between the two slits is 0.030 mm. The second-order bright fringe ($m = 2$) is measured on a viewing screen at an angle of 2.33° from the central maximum. Determine the wavelength of the light.

1 ANALYZE

Given: $d = 3.0 \times 10^{-5}$ m $m = 2$ $\theta = 2.33°$

Unknown: $\lambda = ?$

Diagram:

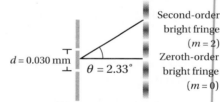

$d = 0.030$ mm $\theta = 2.33°$

Second-order bright fringe ($m = 2$)
Zeroth-order bright fringe ($m = 0$)

Diagram not to scale

2 PLAN

Choose an equation or situation:
Use the equation for constructive interference.

$$d \sin \theta = m\lambda$$

Rearrange the equation to isolate the unknown:

$$\lambda = \frac{d \sin \theta}{m}$$

3 SOLVE

Substitute the values into the equation and solve:

$$\lambda = \frac{(3.0 \times 10^{-5} \text{ m})(\sin 2.33°)}{2}$$

$$\lambda = 6.1 \times 10^{-7} \text{ m} = 6.1 \times 10^2 \text{ nm}$$

$$\boxed{\lambda = 6.1 \times 10^2 \text{ nm}}$$

Calculator Solution

Because the minimum number of significant figures for the data is two, the calculator answer 6.098245×10^{-7} should be rounded to two significant figures.

4 CHECK YOUR WORK

This wavelength of light is in the visible spectrum. The wavelength corresponds to light of the color orange.

 Continued

Interference (continued)

1. Lasers are devices that can emit light at a specific wavelength. A double-slit interference experiment is performed with blue-green light from an argon-gas laser. The separation between the slits is 0.50 mm, and the first-order maximum of the interference pattern is at an angle of 0.059° from the center of the pattern. What is the wavelength of argon laser light?

2. Light falls on a double slit with slit separation of 2.02×10^{-6} m, and the first bright fringe is seen at an angle of 16.5° relative to the central maximum. Find the wavelength of the light.

3. A pair of narrow parallel slits separated by a distance of 0.250 mm is illuminated by the green component from a mercury vapor lamp ($\lambda = 546.1$ nm). Calculate the angle from the central maximum to the first bright fringe on either side of the central maximum.

4. Using the data from item 2, determine the angle between the central maximum and the second dark fringe in the interference pattern.

SECTION 1 FORMATIVE ASSESSMENT

▶ Reviewing Main Ideas

1. What is the necessary condition for a path-length difference between two waves that interfere constructively? Destructively?

2. If white light is used instead of monochromatic light to demonstrate interference, how does the interference pattern change?

3. If the distance between two slits is 0.0550 mm, find the angle between the first-order and second-order bright fringes for yellow light with a wavelength of 605 nm.

Interpreting Graphics

4. Two radio antennas simultaneously transmit identical signals with a wavelength of 3.35 m, as shown in **Figure 1.9.** A radio several miles away in a car traveling parallel to the straight line between the antennas receives the signals. If the second maximum is located at an angle of 1.28° north of the central maximum for the interfering signals, what is the distance, d, between the two antennas?

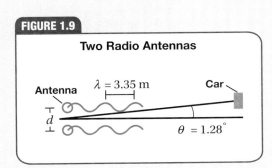

FIGURE 1.9

Two Radio Antennas

Antenna
$\lambda = 3.35$ m
Car
d
$\theta = 1.28°$

Objectives

▶ Describe how light waves bend around obstacles and produce bright and dark fringes.

▶ Calculate the positions of fringes for a diffraction grating.

▶ Describe how diffraction determines an optical instrument's ability to resolve images.

Diffraction

Key Terms

diffraction   resolving power

The Bending of Light Waves

If you stand near the corner of a building, you can hear someone who is talking around the corner, but you cannot see the person. The reason is that sound waves are able to bend around the corner. In a similar fashion, water waves bend around obstacles, such as the barriers shown in **Figure 2.1.** Light waves can also bend around obstacles, but because of their short wavelengths, the amount they bend is too small to be easily observed.

If light traveled in straight lines, you would not be able to observe an interference pattern in the double-slit demonstration. Instead, you would see two thin strips of light where each slit and the source were lined up. The rest of the screen would be dark. The edges of the slits would appear on the screen as sharply defined shadows. But this does not happen. Some of the light bends to the right and left as it passes through each slit.

The bending of light as it passes through each of the two slits can be understood using Huygens's principle, which states that any point on a wave front can be treated as a point source of waves. Because each slit serves as a point source of light, the waves spread out from the slits. The result is that light deviates from a straight-line path and enters the region that would otherwise be shadowed. This divergence of light from its initial direction of travel is called **diffraction.**

diffraction a change in the direction of a wave when the wave encounters an obstacle, an opening, or an edge

In general, diffraction occurs when waves pass through small openings, around obstacles, or by sharp edges. When a wide slit (1 mm or more) is placed between a distant light source and a screen, the light produces a bright rectangle with clearly marked edges on the screen. But if the slit is

©Fundamental Photographs, New York

FIGURE 2.1

Water Waves and Diffraction

A property of all waves is that they bend, or *diffract*, around objects.

gradually narrowed, the light eventually begins to spread out and produce a *diffraction pattern,* such as that shown in **Figure 2.2.** Like the
interference fringes in the double-slit demonstration, this pattern of light
and dark bands arises from the combination of light waves.

Wavelets in a wave front interfere with each other.

Diffraction patterns resemble interference patterns because they also
result from constructive and destructive interference. In the case of
interference, it is assumed that the slits behave as point sources of light.
For diffraction, the actual width of a single slit is considered.

According to Huygens's principle, each portion of a slit acts as a
source of waves. Thus, light from one portion of the slit can interfere with
light from another portion of the slit. The resultant intensity of the
diffracted light on the screen depends on the angle, θ, through which the
light is diffracted.

To understand the single-slit diffraction pattern, consider **Figure 2.3(a),**
which shows an incoming plane wave passing through a slit of width a.
Each point (or, more accurately, each infinitely thin slit) within the wide slit
is a source of Huygens wavelets. The figure is simplified by showing only
five among this infinite number of sources. As with double-slit interference, the viewing screen is assumed to be so far from the slit that the rays
emerging from the slit are nearly parallel. At the viewing screen's midpoint,
all rays from the slit travel the same distance, so a bright fringe appears.

The wavelets from the five sources can also interfere destructively
when they arrive at the screen, as shown in **Figure 2.3(b).** When the extra
distance traveled by the wave originating at point 3 is half a wavelength
longer than the wave from point 1, these two waves interfere destructively
at the screen. At the same time, the wave from point 5 travels half a
wavelength farther than the wave from point 3, so these waves also
interfere destructively. With all pairs of points interfering destructively,
this point on the screen is dark.

For angles other than those at which destructive interference completely
occurs, some of the light waves remain uncanceled. At these angles light
appears on the screen as part of a bright band. The brightest band appears
in the pattern's center, while the bands to either side are much dimmer.

FIGURE 2.3

Destructive Interference in Single-Slit Diffraction

(a) By treating the light coming through
the slit as a line of infinitely thin sources
along the slit's width, one can determine
(b) the conditions at which destructive
interference occurs between the waves
from the upper half of the slit and the
waves from the lower half.

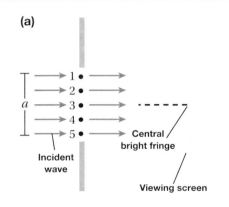

(a)

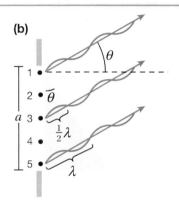

(b)

(tr) ©Houghton Mifflin Harcourt

FIGURE 2.4

Diffraction Pattern from a Single Slit

In a diffraction pattern, the central maximum is twice as wide as the secondary maxima.

FIGURE 2.5

Shadow of a Washer A diffraction pattern forms in the washer's shadow when light is diffracted at the washer's edge. Note the dark and light stripes both around the washer and inside the washer.

Light diffracted by an obstacle also produces a pattern.

The diffraction pattern that results from monochromatic light passing through a single slit consists of a broad, intense central band—the *central maximum*—flanked by a series of narrower, less intense secondary bands (called *secondary maxima*) and a series of dark bands, or *minima*.

An example of such a pattern is shown in **Figure 2.4.** The points at which maximum constructive interference occurs lie approximately halfway between the dark fringes. Note that the central bright fringe is quite a bit brighter and about twice as wide as the next brightest maximum.

Diffraction occurs around the edges of all objects. **Figure 2.5** shows the diffraction pattern that appears in the shadow of a washer. The pattern consists of the shadow and a series of bright and dark bands of light that continue around the edge of the shadow. The washer is large compared with the wavelength of the light, and a magnifying glass is required to observe the pattern.

Diffraction Gratings

FIGURE 2.6

Constructive Interference on a CD Compact discs disperse light into its component colors in a manner similar to that of a diffraction grating.

You have probably noticed that if white light is incident on a compact disc, streaks of color are visible. These streaks appear because the digital information (alternating pits and smooth reflecting surfaces) on the disc forms closely spaced rows. These rows of data do not reflect nearly as much light as the thin portions of the disc that separate them. These areas consist entirely of reflecting material, so light reflected from them undergoes constructive interference in certain directions.

This constructive interference depends on the direction of the incoming light, the orientation of the disc, and the light's wavelength. Each wavelength of light can be seen at a particular angle with respect to the disc's surface, causing you to see a "rainbow" of color, as shown in **Figure 2.6.**

This phenomenon has been put to practical use in a device called a *diffraction grating*. A diffraction grating, which can be constructed to either transmit or reflect light, uses diffraction and interference to disperse light into its component colors with an effect similar to that of a glass prism. A transmission grating consists of many equally spaced parallel slits. Gratings are made by ruling equally spaced lines on a piece

FIGURE 2.7

Constructive Interference by a Diffraction Grating

Light of a single wavelength passes through each of the slits of a diffraction grating to constructively interfere at a particular angle θ.

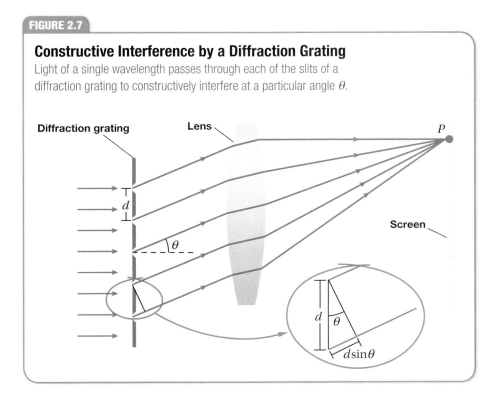

Conceptual Challenge

Spiked Stars Photographs of stars always show spikes extending from the stars. Given that the aperture of a camera's rectangular shutter has straight edges, explain how diffraction accounts for the spikes.

Radio Diffraction Visible light waves are not observed diffracting around buildings or other obstacles. However, radio waves can be detected around buildings or mountains, even when the transmitter is not visible. Explain why diffraction is more evident for radio waves than for visible light.

of glass using a diamond cutting point driven by an elaborate machine called a *ruling engine*. Replicas are then made by pouring liquid plastic on the grating and then peeling it off once it has set. This plastic grating is then fastened to a flat piece of glass or plastic for support.

Figure 2.7 shows a schematic diagram of a section of a diffraction grating. A monochromatic plane wave is incoming from the left, normal to the plane of the grating. The waves that emerge nearly parallel from the grating are brought together at a point P on the screen by the lens. The intensity of the pattern on the screen is the result of the combined effects of interference and diffraction. Each slit produces diffraction, and the diffracted beams in turn interfere with one another to produce the pattern.

For some arbitrary angle, θ, measured from the original direction of travel of the wave, the waves must travel *different* path lengths before reaching point P on the screen. Note that the path difference between waves from any two adjacent slits is $d \sin \theta$. If this path difference equals one wavelength or some integral multiple of a wavelength, waves from all slits will be in phase at P, and a bright line will be observed. The condition for bright-line formation at angle θ is therefore given by the equation for constructive interference:

$$d \sin \theta = \pm m\lambda \quad m = 0, 1, 2, 3, \ldots$$

This equation can be used to calculate the wavelength of light if you know the grating spacing and the angle of deviation. The integer m is the order number for the bright lines of a given wavelength. If the incident radiation contains several wavelengths, each wavelength deviates by a specific angle, which can be determined from the equation.

FIGURE 2.8

Maxima from a Diffraction Grating

Light is dispersed by a diffraction grating. The angle of deviation for the first-order maximum is smaller for blue light than for yellow light.

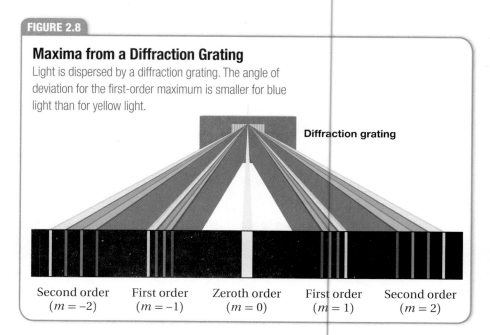

Diffraction grating

| Second order $(m = -2)$ | First order $(m = -1)$ | Zeroth order $(m = 0)$ | First order $(m = 1)$ | Second order $(m = 2)$ |

FIGURE 2.9

Spectrometer The spectrometer uses a grating to disperse the light from a source.

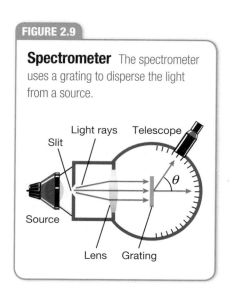

Note in **Figure 2.8** that all wavelengths combine at $\theta = 0$, which corresponds to $m = 0$. This is called the *zeroth-order maximum*. The *first-order maximum*, corresponding to $m = 1$, is observed at an angle that satisfies the relationship $\sin \theta = \lambda/d$. The *second-order maximum*, corresponding to $m = 2$, is observed at an angle where $\sin \theta = 2\lambda/d$.

The sharpness of the principal maxima and the broad range of the dark areas depend on the number of lines in a grating. The number of lines per unit length in a grating is the inverse of the line separation d. For example, a grating ruled with 5000 lines/cm has a slit spacing, d, equal to the inverse of this number; hence, $d = (1/5000)$ cm $= 2 \times 10^{-4}$ cm. The greater the number of lines per unit length in a grating, the less separation between the slits and the farther spread apart the individual wavelengths of light.

Diffraction gratings are frequently used in devices called *spectrometers*, which separate the light from a source into its monochromatic components. A diagram of the basic components of a spectrometer is shown in **Figure 2.9.** The light to be analyzed passes through a slit and is formed into a parallel beam by a lens. The light then passes through the grating. The diffracted light leaves the grating at angles that satisfy the diffraction-grating equation. A telescope with a calibrated scale is used to observe the first-order maxima and to measure the angles at which they appear. From these measurements, the wavelengths of the light can be determined, and the chemical composition of the light source can be identified. An example of a spectrum produced by a spectrometer is shown in **Figure 2.10.** Spectrometers are used in astronomy to study the chemical compositions and temperatures of stars, interstellar gas clouds, and galaxies.

FIGURE 2.10

Spectrum of Mercury Vapor

The light from mercury vapor is passed through a diffraction grating, producing the spectrum shown.

Sample Problem B Monochromatic light from a helium-neon laser ($\lambda = 632.8$ nm) shines at a right angle to the surface of a diffraction grating that contains 150 500 lines/m. Find the angles at which one would observe the first-order and second-order maxima.

① ANALYZE

Given: $\lambda = 632.8$ nm $= 6.328 \times 10^{-7}$ m $\quad m = 1$ and 2

$$d = \frac{1}{150\,500\,\dfrac{\text{lines}}{\text{m}}} = \frac{1}{150\,500}\,\text{m}$$

Unknown: $\theta_1 = ?$ $\quad \theta_2 = ?$

Diagram:

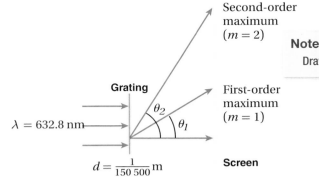

Second-order maximum ($m = 2$)

Note
Drawing is not to scale

Grating

θ_2

θ_1

$\lambda = 632.8$ nm

First-order maximum ($m = 1$)

$d = \frac{1}{150\,500}$ m

Screen

② PLAN

Choose an equation or situation: Use the equation for a diffraction grating.

$$d \sin \theta = \pm m\lambda$$

Rearrange the equation to isolate the unknown:

$$\theta = \sin^{-1}\left(\frac{m\lambda}{d}\right)$$

③ SOLVE

Substitute the values into the equation, and solve:

For the first-order maximum, $m = 1$:

$$\theta_1 = \sin^{-1}\left(\frac{\lambda}{d}\right) = \sin^{-1}\left(\frac{6.328 \times 10^{-7}\,\text{m}}{\dfrac{1}{150\,500}\,\text{m}}\right)$$

$$\boxed{\theta_1 = 5.465°}$$

For $m = 2$:

$$\theta_2 = \sin^{-1}\left(\frac{2\lambda}{d}\right)$$

$$\theta_2 = \sin^{-1}\left(\frac{2(6.328 \times 10^{-7}\,\text{m})}{\dfrac{1}{150\,500}\,\text{m}}\right)$$

$$\boxed{\theta_2 = 10.98°}$$

Calculator Solution
Because the minimum number of significant figures for the data is four, the calculator answers 5.464926226 and 10.98037754 should be rounded to four significant figures.

Continued

Diffraction Gratings (continued)

④ CHECK YOUR WORK

The second-order maximum is spread slightly more than twice as far from the center as the first-order maximum. This diffraction grating does not have high dispersion, and it can produce spectral lines up to the tenth-order maxima (where $\sin \theta = 0.9524$).

Practice

1. A diffraction grating with 5.000×10^3 lines/cm is used to examine the sodium spectrum. Calculate the angular separation of the two closely spaced yellow lines of sodium (588.995 nm and 589.592 nm) in each of the first three orders.

2. A diffraction grating with 4525 lines/cm is illuminated by direct sunlight. The first-order solar spectrum is spread out on a white screen hanging on a wall opposite the grating.

   a. At what angle does the first-order maximum for blue light with a wavelength of 422 nm appear?

   b. At what angle does the first-order maximum for red light with a wavelength of 655 nm appear?

3. A grating with 1555 lines/cm is illuminated with light of wavelength 565 nm. What is the highest-order number that can be observed with this grating? (Hint: Remember that $\sin \theta$ can never be greater than 1 for a diffraction grating.)

4. Repeat item 3 for a diffraction grating with 15 550 lines/cm that is illuminated with light of wavelength 565 nm.

5. A diffraction grating is calibrated by using the 546.1 nm line of mercury vapor. The first-order maximum is found at an angle of 21.2°. Calculate the number of lines per centimeter on this grating.

Diffraction and Instrument Resolution

The ability of an optical system, such as a microscope or a telescope, to distinguish between closely spaced objects is limited by the wave nature of light. To understand this limitation, consider **Figure 2.11,** which shows two light sources far from a narrow slit. The sources can be taken as two point sources that are not coherent. For example, they could be two distant stars that appear close to each other in the night sky.

If no diffraction occurred, you would observe two distinct bright spots (or images) on the screen at the far right. However, because of diffraction, each source is shown to have a bright central region flanked by weaker bright and dark rings. What is observed on the screen is the resultant from the superposition of two diffraction patterns, one from each source.

FIGURE 2.11

Limits of an Optical System Each of two distant point sources produces a diffraction pattern.

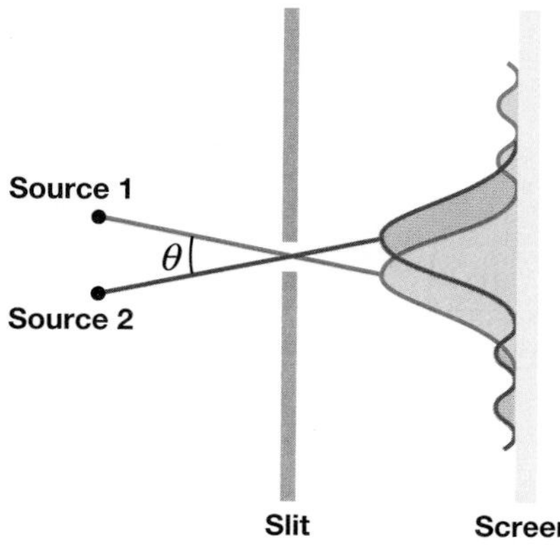

Source 1

θ

Source 2

Slit   Screen

Resolution depends on wavelength and aperture width.

If the two sources are separated so that their central maxima do not overlap, as in **Figure 2.12**, their images can just be distinguished and are said to be barely *resolved*. To achieve high resolution or **resolving power,** the angle between the resolved objects, θ, should be as small as possible, as shown in **Figure 2.11**. The shorter the wavelength of the incoming light or the wider the opening, or *aperture,* through which the light passes, the smaller the angle of resolution, θ, will be and the greater the resolving power will be. For visible-light telescopes, the aperture width, D, is approximately equal to the diameter of the mirror or lens. The equation to determine the limiting angle of resolution *in radians* for an optical instrument with a circular aperture is as follows:

$$\theta = 1.22 \frac{\lambda}{D}$$

The constant 1.22 comes from the derivation of the equation for circular apertures and is absent for long slits. Note that one radian equals $(180/\pi)°$. The equation indicates that for light with a short wavelength, such as an x-ray, a small aperture is sufficient for high resolution. On the other hand, if the wavelength of the light is long, as in the case of a radio wave, the aperture must be large in order to resolve distant objects. This is one reason that radio telescopes have large dishlike antennas.

Yet even with their large sizes, radio telescopes cannot resolve sources as easily as visible-light telescopes resolve visible-light sources. At the shortest radio wavelength (1 mm), the largest single antenna for a radio telescope—the 305 m dish at Arecibo, Puerto Rico—has a resolution angle of 4×10^{-6} rad. The same resolution angle can be obtained for the longest visible light waves (700 nm) by an optical telescope with a 21 cm mirror.

resolving power the ability of an optical instrument to form separate images of two objects that are close together

---

FIGURE 2.12

Resolution Two point sources are barely resolved if the central maxima of their diffraction patterns do not overlap.

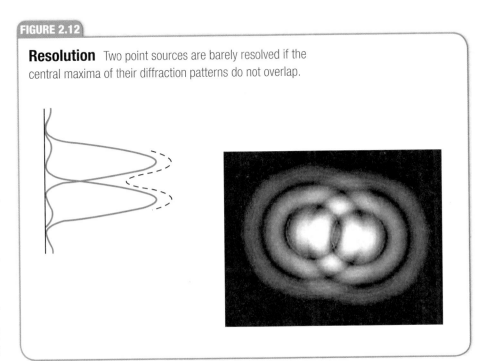

FIGURE 2.13

Combining Many Telescopes The 27 antennas at the Very Large Array in New Mexico are used together to provide improved resolution for observing distant radio sources. The antennas can be arranged to have the resolving power of a 36 km wide radio telescope.

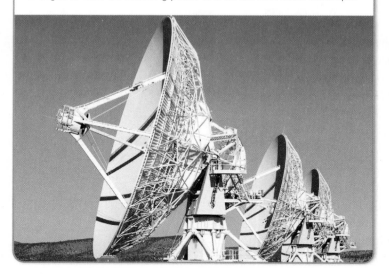

To compensate for the poor resolution of radio waves, one can combine several radio telescopes so that they will function like a much larger telescope. An example of this is shown in **Figure 2.13.** If the radio antennas are arranged in a line and computers are used to process the signals that each antenna receives, the resolution of the radio "images" is the same as it would be if the radio telescope had a diameter of several kilometers.

It should be noted that the resolving power for optical telescopes on Earth is limited by the constantly moving layers of air in the atmosphere, which blur the light from objects in space. The images from the *Hubble Space Telescope* are of superior quality largely because the telescope operates in the vacuum of space. Under these conditions, the actual resolving power of the telescope is close to the telescope's theoretical resolving power.

✔ SECTION 2 FORMATIVE ASSESSMENT

▶ Reviewing Main Ideas

1. Light passes through a diffraction grating with 3550 lines/cm and forms a first-order maximum at an angle of 12.07°.
   a. What is the wavelength of the light?
   b. At what angle will the second maximum appear?

2. Describe the change in width of the central maximum of the single-slit diffraction pattern as the width of the slit is made smaller.

3. Which object would produce the most distinct diffraction pattern: an apple, a pencil lead, or a human hair? Explain your answer.

4. Would orange light or blue light produce a wider diffraction pattern? Explain why.

✔ Critical Thinking

5. A point source of light is inside a container that is opaque except for a single hole. Discuss what happens to the image of the point source projected onto a screen as the hole's width is reduced.

6. Would it be easier to resolve nearby objects if you detected them using ultraviolet radiation rather than visible light? Explain.

Lasers

SECTION 3
Objectives

▶ Describe the properties of laser light.

▶ Explain how laser light has particular advantages in certain applications.

Key Term
laser

Lasers and Coherence

At this point, you are familiar with electromagnetic radiation that is produced by glowing, or *incandescent*, light sources. This includes light from light bulbs, candle flames, or the sun. You may have seen another form of light that is very different from the light produced by incandescent sources. The light produced by a **laser** has unique properties that make it very useful for many applications.

To understand how laser light is different from conventional light, consider the light produced by an incandescent light bulb, as shown in **Figure 3.1.** When electric charges move through the filament, electromagnetic waves are emitted in the form of visible light. In a typical light bulb, there are variations in the structure of the filament and in the way charges move through it. As a result, electromagnetic waves are emitted at different times from different parts of the filament. These waves have different intensities and move in different directions. The light also covers a wide range of the electromagnetic spectrum because it includes light of different wavelengths. Because so many different wavelengths exist, and because the light is changing almost constantly, the light produced is incoherent. That is, the component waves do not maintain a constant phase difference at all times. The wave fronts of incoherent light are like the wave fronts that result when rain falls on the surface of a pond. No two wave fronts are caused by the same event, and they therefore do not produce a stable interference pattern.

laser a device that produces coherent light at a single wavelength

Did YOU Know?

The light from an ordinary electric lamp undergoes about 100 million (10^8) random changes every second.

FIGURE 3.1

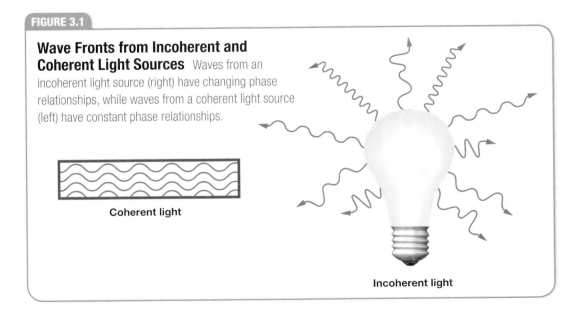

Wave Fronts from Incoherent and Coherent Light Sources Waves from an incoherent light source (right) have changing phase relationships, while waves from a coherent light source (left) have constant phase relationships.

Coherent light

Incoherent light

Lasers, on the other hand, typically produce a narrow beam of coherent light. The waves emitted by a laser are in phase, and they do not shift relative to each other as time progresses. Because all the waves are in phase, they interfere constructively at all points. The individual waves effectively behave like a single wave with a very large amplitude. In addition, the light produced by a laser is monochromatic, so all the waves have exactly the same wavelength. As a result of these properties, the intensity, or brightness, of laser light can be made much greater than that of incoherent light. For light, intensity is a measure of the energy transferred per unit time over a given area.

Lasers transform energy into coherent light.

A laser is a device that converts light, electrical energy, or chemical energy into coherent light. The word *laser* is an acronym (a word made from the first letters of several words) that stands for "*l*ight *a*mplification by *s*timulated *e*mission of *r*adiation." There are a variety of different types of lasers, but they all have some common features. They all use a substance called the *active medium* to which energy is added to produce coherent light. The active medium can be a solid, liquid, or gas. The composition of the active medium determines the wavelength of the light produced by the laser.

The basic operation of a laser is shown in **Figure 3.2.** When high-energy light or electrical or chemical energy is added to the active medium, as in **Figure 3.2(a),** the atoms in the active medium absorb some of the energy.

FIGURE 3.2

Operation of a Laser

(a) Atoms or molecules in the active medium of a laser absorb energy from an external source.

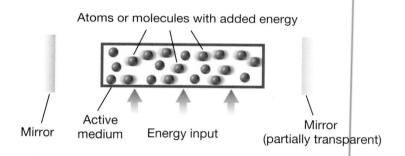

Atoms or molecules with added energy

Mirror   Active medium   Energy input   Mirror (partially transparent)

(b) When a spontaneously emitted light wave interacts with an atom, it may cause the atom to emit an identical light wave.

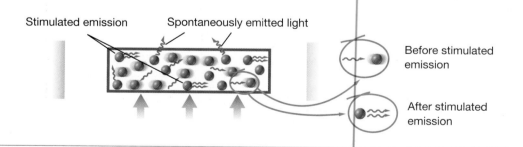

Stimulated emission   Spontaneously emitted light

Before stimulated emission

After stimulated emission

(c) Stimulated emission increases the amount of coherent light in the active medium, and the coherent waves behave as a single wave.

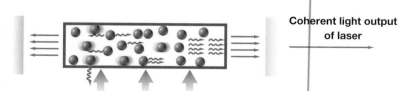

Coherent light output of laser

You will learn that atoms exist at different *energy states* in the chapter "Atomic Physics." When energy is added to an atom that is at a lower energy state, the atom can be excited to a higher energy state. These *excited* atoms then release their excess energy in the form of electromagnetic radiation when they return to their original, lower energy states.

When light of a certain wavelength is applied to excited atoms, the atoms can be induced to release light waves of the same wavelength. After one atom spontaneously releases its energy in the form of a light wave, this initial wave can cause other energized atoms to release their excess energy as light waves with the same wavelength, phase, and direction as the initial wave, as shown in **Figure 3.2(b).** This process is called *stimulated emission*.

Most of the light produced by stimulated emission escapes out the sides of the glass tube. However, some of the light moves along the length of the tube, producing more stimulated emission as it goes. Mirrors on the ends of the material return these coherent light waves into the active medium, where they stimulate the emission of more coherent light waves, as shown in **Figure 3.2(c).** As the light passes back and forth through the active medium, it becomes more and more intense. One of the mirrors is slightly transparent, which allows the intense coherent light to be emitted by the laser.

Applications of Lasers

There are a wide variety of laser types, with wavelengths ranging from the far infrared to the x-ray region of the spectrum. Scientists have also created *masers*, devices similar to lasers but that operate in the microwave region of the spectrum. Lasers are used in many ways, from common household uses to a wide variety of industrial uses and very specialized medical applications.

Lasers are used to measure distances with great precision.

Of the properties of laser light, the one that is most evident is that it emerges from the laser as a narrow beam. Unlike the light from a light bulb or even the light that is focused by a parabolic reflector, the light from a laser undergoes very little spreading with distance. One reason is that all the light waves emitted by the laser have the same direction. As a result, a laser can be used to measure large distances, because it can be pointed at distant reflectors and the reflected light can be detected.

As shown in **Figure 3.3,** astronomers direct laser light at particular points on the moon's surface to determine the Earth-to-moon distance. A pulse of light is directed toward one of several 0.25 m^2 reflectors that were placed on the moon's surface by astronauts during the *Apollo* missions. By knowing the speed of light and measuring the time the light takes to travel to the moon and back, scientists have measured the Earth-to-moon distance to be about 3.84×10^5 km. Geologists use repeated measurements to record changes in the height of Earth's crust from geological processes. Lasers can be used for these measurements even when the height changes by only a few centimeters.

FIGURE 3.3

Distance to the Moon The laser at the Observatoire de la Côte d'Azur is aimed at mirrors on the moon left behind by U.S. and Russian lunar missions. Timing of the laser's trip yields a distance accurate to 3 centimeters out of a total of 380 000 km.

Optical Storage Devices

A useful application of the laser is the digital optical disc player, which is a device that plays digital media stored onto discs such as the compact disc (CD), the digital versatile disc (DVD), and other high-definition discs. In a digital optical disc player, light from a laser is directed through a series of optics toward a videodisc on which data have been digitally recorded. The player "reads" the data in the way the laser light is reflected from the disc.

In digital recording, a video or audio signal is sampled at regular intervals of time, almost 50,000 times per second. Each sampling is converted to an electrical signal, which in turn is converted into a series of binary numbers. Binary numbers consist only of zeros and ones. The binary

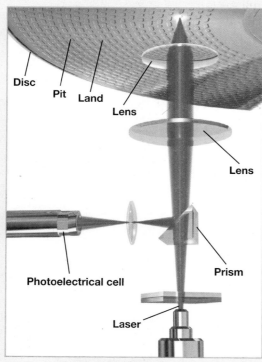

Disc
Pit Land
Lens
Lens
Prism
Photoelectrical cell
Laser

Light from a laser is directed toward the surface of the disc. Smooth parts of the disc reflect the light back to the photoelectric cell.

numbers are coded to contain information about the signal, including the sound and image, as well as the speed of the motor that rotates the disc. These binary data in a digital optical disc are stored as a series of pits and smooth areas (called *lands*) etched onto the surface of the disc. The series of pits and lands is recorded starting at the center of the disc and spiraling outward along tracks in the disc. In a DVD, these tracks are 320 nm wide and spaced 740 nm apart. If you could stretch out the data track of a DVD, it would be 12 km long!

When you play a digital optical disc, a laser light is reflected off this series of pits and lands into a detector. In fact, the depth of the pit is designed so that destructive interference occurs when the laser transitions from a pit to a land or from a land to a pit. The detector records the changes in light reflection between the pits and lands as ones and smooth areas as zeros—binary data that are then converted back to the analog signal you see as video or hear as music. This step is called digital-to-analog (d-a) conversion, and the analog signal can then be amplified through a speaker system.

The size of the pits and lands limits how much data can be stored on a disc. The wavelength of the laser light in the disc player corresponds to the size of the pits and lands. The first form of optical disc was the CD, which stores enough data for 74 minutes of music. A CD player uses an infrared laser beam (with a wavelength of 780 nm) to read the data. A DVD stores seven times more data than a CD. To read the smaller pits and lands, a DVD player uses a red laser beam (650 nm). A Blu-ray Disc™ stores six times more data than a DVD. A blue laser beam (405 nm) is used to read the small pits and lands on a Blu-ray Disc.

Blu-ray Disc™ is a trademark of the Blu-ray Disc Association.

Lasers have many applications in medicine.

Lasers are also used for many medical procedures by making use of the fact that specific body tissues absorb different wavelengths of laser light. For example, lasers can be used to lighten or remove scars and certain types of birthmarks without affecting surrounding tissues. The scar tissue responds to the wavelength of light used in the laser, but other body tissues are protected.

Many medical applications of lasers take advantage of the fact that water can be vaporized by high-intensity infrared light produced by carbon dioxide lasers having a wavelength of 10 μm. Carbon dioxide lasers can cut through muscle tissue by heating and evaporating the water contained in the cells. One advantage of a laser is that the energy from the laser also coagulates blood in the newly opened blood vessels, thereby reducing blood loss and decreasing the risk of infection. A laser beam can also be trapped in an optical fiber endoscope, which can be inserted through an orifice and directed to internal body structures. As a result, surgeons can stop internal bleeding or remove tumors without performing massive surgery.

Lasers can also be used to treat tissues that cannot be reached by conventional surgical methods. For example, some very specific wavelengths of lasers can pass through certain structures at the front of the eye—the cornea and lens—without damaging them. Therefore, lasers can be effective at treating lesions of the retina, inside the eye.

Lasers are used for other eye surgeries, including surgery to correct *glaucoma*, a condition in which the fluid pressure within the eye is too great. Left untreated, glaucoma can lead to damage of the optic nerve and eventual blindness. Focusing a laser at the clogged drainage port allows a tiny hole to be burned in the tissue, which relieves the pressure. Lasers can also be used to correct nearsightedness by focusing the beam on the central portion of the cornea to cause it to become flatter.

Did YOU Know?

The principle behind reading the information stored on a compact disc is also the basis for the reading of bar codes found on many products. When these products are scanned, laser light reflected from the bars and spaces of the bar code reproduces the binary codes that represent the product's inventory number. This information is transmitted to the store's computer system, which returns the product's name and price to the cash register.

✓ SECTION 3 FORMATIVE ASSESSMENT

▶ Reviewing Main Ideas

1. How does light from a laser differ from light whose waves all have the same wavelength but are not coherent?

2. The process of stimulated emission involves producing a second wave that is identical to the first. Does this gaining of a second wave violate the principle of energy conservation? Explain your answer.

✔ Critical Thinking

3. Fiber-optic systems transmit light by means of internal reflection within thin strands of extremely pure glass. In these fiber-optic systems, laser light is used instead of white light to transmit the signal. Apply your knowledge of refraction to explain why.

Laser Surgeon

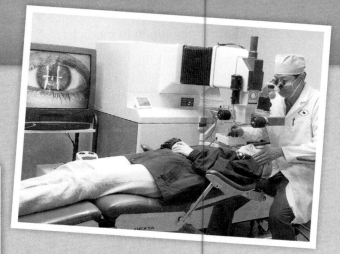

Dr. Wong makes measurements of the eye in preparation for laser surgery.

Laser surgery combines two fields—eye care and engineering—to give perfect vision to people who otherwise need glasses or contacts. To learn more about this career, read the interview with ophthalmologist Dr. L. Shawn Wong, who runs a laser center in Austin, Texas.

What sort of education helped you become a laser surgeon?

Besides using my medical school training, I use a lot of engineering in my work; physics and math courses are very helpful. In high school, even in junior high, having a love of math and science is extremely helpful.

Who helped you find your career path?

Of all my teachers, my junior high earth science teacher made the biggest impression on me. What I learned in those classes I actually still use today: problem solving. Interestingly, I work in the town where I grew up; a lot of my former teachers are my patients today.

What makes laser surgery interesting to you?

It's nice to be able to help people. Unlike glasses and contacts, laser surgery is not a correction; it's a cure. When you are improving people's vision, everybody in the room gets to see the results. I don't need to tell patients they're doing well—they can tell.

What is the nature of your work?

A typical patient is somebody born with poor vision. We make these patients undergo a lot of formal diagnostic testing and informal screening to be sure they are good candidates. Lasers are used for diagnosing as well as treating. Laser tolerances are extremely small—we're talking in terms of submicrons, the individual cells of the eye.

What is the favorite thing about your job? What part would you most like to change?

My favorite thing is making people visually free. I would like to be able to solve an even wider range of problems. We can't solve everything.

How does your work relate to the physics of interference and diffraction?

Measuring diffraction and interference is part of every aspect of what we do. The approach is based on doing many small things correctly. Applying small physics principles in the right order can solve very big problems.

What advice would you give to somebody who is considering a career in laser surgery?

My education didn't start in medical school; it started by asking questions as a kid. You need a genuine love of taking on complex problems. A background in physics and math is extremely helpful. Technology in medicine is based on engineering.

Being well rounded will help you get into medical school —and get out, too. You have to be comfortable doing the science, but you also have to be comfortable dealing with people.

Shawn Wong

Quantum Phenomena

One branch of physics involves the study of quantum mechanics. A *quantum* is the smallest amount of something. A quantum of light or any other electromagnetic radiation is called a photon. The concept of the photon as a discrete quantity of light came from the observations of the photoelectric effect, in which electrons are emitted from a metal surface when light shines on that surface. Scientists observed that the electrons emitted from the surface of a metal all had similar energy when the same wavelength of light was used. And, the emission of the electrons did not depend on the intensity of the light or the length of time it fell on the metal surface. For a given material, the effect only occurred when the light was at a certain wavelength or a shorter one. Shorter wavelengths carry more energy than longer ones. Later studies showed that a single photon releases a single electron and that the number of electrons released is always equal to the number of photons. Quantum mechanics models how electrons behave and examines phenomena that occur at submicroscopic scales. You will read more about the history and implications of quantum mechanics in the chapter about atomic physics.

Applications of Quantum Phenomena

Quantum phenomena have many applications, including any technology that relies on the variable conductivity of a semiconductor. In addition, you rely on quantum phenomena when you use a digital camera. When photons strike a digital imager in a camera, the imager captures information electronically. An imager consists of many tiny capacitors in a grid arrangement. The electronic circuits repeatedly charge these capacitors and then measure the charge on them. If light falls on the capacitor, the charge diminshes proportionally to the intensity of the light. No light leaves the charge undisturbed, and an intense light will totally discharge the capacitor. The photons of light cause the release of electrons from parts of the capacitor and those electrons travel between the plates of the capacitor, slowly discharging it. The circuitry determines the brightness of the light from each capacitor but not the light's color. Each capacitor is covered with one of three colored filters. The filter colors are chosen to allow the detection of red, green, and blue light. The electronic circuits "know" the color associated with each location. Then, all the intensity and color information is processed to form a full-color image.

- Research the use of semiconductors in other applications. In what way does the function of semiconductors rely on a quantum phenomenon? Provide an example of an industrial or consumer application for semiconductor technology.

- There are a variety of consumer, industrial, and medical applications for quantum phenomena. Conduct research to find at least two examples of applications of quantum phenomena not discussed here. How is a quantum phenomenon key to the functions of the applications you have chosen? Write a report with your findings.

BIG IDEA Like mechanical waves, light waves can interact with each other and with obstacles. The patterns formed by these interactions depend on wavelength.

SECTION 1 Interference

- Light waves with the same wavelength and constant phase differences interfere with each other to produce light and dark interference patterns.
- In double-slit interference, the position of a bright fringe requires that the path difference between two interfering point sources be equal to a whole number of wavelengths.
- In double-slit interference, the position of a dark fringe requires that the path difference between two interfering point sources be equal to an odd number of half wavelengths.

coherence
path difference
order number

SECTION 2 Diffraction

- Light waves form a diffraction pattern by passing around an obstacle or bending through a slit and interfering with each other.
- The position of a maximum in a pattern created by a diffraction grating depends on the separation of the slits in the grating, the order of the maximum, and the wavelength of the light.

diffraction
resolving power

SECTION 3 Lasers

- A laser is a device that transforms energy into a beam of coherent monochromatic light.

laser

VARIABLE SYMBOLS	
Quantities	**Units**
λ wavelength	m meters
θ angle from the center of an interference pattern	° degrees
d slit separation	m meters
m order number	(unitless)

Problem Solving

See **Appendix D: Equations** for a summary of the equations introduced in this chapter. If you need more problem-solving practice, see **Appendix I: Additional Problems.**

Interference

 REVIEWING MAIN IDEAS

1. What happens if two light waves with the same amplitude interfere constructively? What happens if they interfere destructively?

2. Interference in sound is recognized by differences in volume; how is interference in light recognized?

3. A double-slit interference experiment is performed with red light and then again with blue light. In what ways do the two interference patterns differ? (Hint: Consider the difference in wavelength for the two colors of light.)

4. What data would you need to collect to correctly calculate the wavelength of light in a double-slit interference experiment?

CONCEPTUAL QUESTIONS

5. If a double-slit experiment were performed underwater, how would the observed interference pattern be affected? (Hint: Consider how light changes in a medium with a higher index of refraction.)

6. Because of their great distance from us, stars are essentially point sources of light. If two stars were near each other in the sky, would the light from them produce an interference pattern? Explain your answer.

7. Assume that white light is provided by a single source in a double-slit experiment. Describe the interference pattern if one slit is covered with a red filter and the other slit is covered with a blue filter.

8. An interference pattern is formed by using green light and an apparatus in which the two slits can move. If the slits are moved farther apart, will the separation of the bright fringes in the pattern decrease, increase, or remain unchanged? Why?

PRACTICE PROBLEMS

For problems 9–11, see Sample Problem A.

9. Light falls on two slits spaced 0.33 mm apart. If the angle between the first dark fringe and the central maximum is 0.055°, what is the wavelength of the light?

10. A sodium-vapor street lamp produces light that is nearly monochromatic. If the light shines on a wooden door in which there are two straight, parallel cracks, an interference pattern will form on a distant wall behind the door. The slits have a separation of 0.3096 mm, and the second-order maximum occurs at an angle of 0.218° from the central maximum. Determine the following quantities:
    a. the wavelength of the light
    b. the angle of the third-order maximum
    c. the angle of the fourth-order maximum

11. All but two gaps within a set of venetian blinds have been blocked off to create a double-slit system. These gaps are separated by a distance of 3.2 cm. Infrared radiation is then passed through the two gaps in the blinds. If the angle between the central and the second-order maxima in the interference pattern is 0.56°, what is the wavelength of the radiation?

Diffraction

 REVIEWING MAIN IDEAS

12. Why does light produce a pattern similar to an interference pattern when it passes through a single slit?

13. How does the width of the central region of a single-slit diffraction pattern change as the wavelength of the light increases?

14. Why is white light separated into a spectrum of colors when it is passed through a diffraction grating?

15. Why might orbiting telescopes be problematic for the radio portion of the electromagnetic spectrum?

CONCEPTUAL QUESTIONS

16. Monochromatic light shines through two different diffraction gratings. The second grating produces a pattern in which the first-order and second-order maxima are more widely spread apart. Use this information to tell if there are more or fewer lines per centimeter in the second grating than in the first.

17. Why is the resolving power of your eye better at night than during the day?

18. Globular clusters, such as the one shown below, are spherical groupings of stars. Because there can be millions of stars in a single cluster and because they are distant, resolving individual stars within the cluster is a challenge. Of the following conditions, which would make it easier to resolve the component stars? Which would make it more difficult?

   a. The number of stars per unit volume is half as great.
   b. The cluster is twice as far away.
   c. The cluster is observed in the ultraviolet portion instead of in the visible region of the electromagnetic spectrum.
   d. The telescope's mirror or lens is twice as wide.

PRACTICE PROBLEMS

For problems 19–21, see Sample Problem B.

19. Light with a wavelength of 707 nm is passed through a diffraction grating with 795 slits/cm. Find the angle at which one would observe the first-order maximum.

20. If light with a wavelength of 353 nm is passed through the diffraction grating with 795 slits/cm, find the angle at which one would observe the second-order maximum.

21. By attaching a diffraction-grating spectroscope to an astronomical telescope, one can measure the spectral lines from a star and determine the star's chemical composition. Assume the grating has 3661 lines/cm.
   a. If the wavelengths of the star's light are 478.5 nm, 647.4 nm, and 696.4 nm, what are the angles at which the first-order spectral lines occur?
   b. At what angles are these lines found in the second-order spectrum?

Lasers

▶ **REVIEWING MAIN IDEAS**

22. What properties does laser light have that are not found in the light used to light your home?

23. Laser light is commonly used to demonstrate double-slit interference. Explain why laser light is preferable to light from other sources for observing interference.

24. Give two examples in which the uniform direction of laser light is advantageous. Give two examples in which the high intensity of laser light is advantageous.

25. Laser light is often linearly polarized. How would you show that this statement is true?

Mixed Review

▶ **REVIEWING MAIN IDEAS**

26. The 546.1 nm line in mercury is measured at an angle of 81.0° in the third-order spectrum of a diffraction grating. Calculate the number of lines per centimeter for the grating.

27. Recall from your study of heat and entropy that the entropy of a system is a measure of that system's disorder. Why is it appropriate to describe a laser as an entropy-reducing device?

28. A double-slit interference experiment is performed using blue light from a hydrogen discharge tube ($\lambda = 486$ nm). The fifth-order bright fringe in the interference pattern is 0.578° from the central maximum. How far apart are the two slits separated?

29. A beam containing light of wavelengths λ_1 and λ_2 passes through a set of parallel slits. In the interference pattern, the fourth bright line of the λ_1 light occurs at the same position as the fifth bright line of the λ_2 light. If λ_1 is known to be 540.0 nm, what is the value of λ_2?

30. Visible light from an incandescent light bulb ranges from 400.0 nm to 700.0 nm. When this light is focused on a diffraction grating, the entire first-order spectrum is seen, but none of the second-order spectrum is seen. What is the maximum spacing between lines on this grating?

31. In an arrangement to demonstrate double-slit interference, $\lambda = 643$ nm, $\theta = 0.737°$, and $d = 0.150$ mm. For light from the two slits interfering at this angle, what is the path difference both in millimeters and in terms of the number of wavelengths? Will the interference correspond to a maximum, a minimum, or an intermediate condition?

ALTERNATIVE ASSESSMENT

1. Simulate interference patterns. Use a computer to draw concentric circles at regular distances to represent waves traveling from a point source. Photocopy the page onto two transparencies, and lay them on an overhead projector. Vary the distances between "source points," and observe how these variations affect interference patterns. Design transparencies with thicker lines with larger separations to explore the effect of wavelength on interference.

2. Investigate the effect of slit separation on interference patterns. Wrap a flashlight or a pen light tightly with tinfoil and make pinholes in the foil. First, record the pattern you see on a screen a few inches away with one hole; then, do the same with two holes. How does the distance between the holes affect the distance between the bright parts of the pattern? Draw schematic diagrams of your observations, and compare them with the results of double-slit interference. How would you improve your equipment?

3. Soap bubbles exhibit different colors because light that is reflected from the outer layer of the soap film interferes with light that is refracted and then reflected from the inner layer of the soap film. Given a refractive index of $n = 1.35$ and thicknesses ranging from 600 nm to 1000 nm for a soap film, can you predict the colors of a bubble? Test your answer by making soap bubbles and observing the order in which the colors appear. Can you tell the thickness of a soap bubble from its colors? Organize your findings into a chart, or create a computer program to predict the thicknesses of a bubble based on the wavelengths of light it reflects.

4. Thomas Young's 1803 experiment provided crucial evidence for the wave nature of light, but it was met with strong opposition in England until Augustin Fresnel presented his wave theory of light to the French Academy of Sciences in 1819. Research the lives and careers of these two scientists. Create a presentation about one of them. The presentation can be in the form of a report, poster, short video, or computer presentation.

5. Research waves that surround you, including those used in commercial, medicinal, and industrial applications. Interpret how the waves' characteristics and behaviors make them useful. For example, investigate what kinds of waves are used in medical procedures such as MRI and ultrasound. What are their wavelengths? Research how lasers are used in medicine. How are they used in industry? Prepare a poster or chart describing your findings, and present it to the class.

GRAPHING CALCULATOR PRACTICE

Double-Slit Experiment

One of the classic experiments that demonstrate the wave nature of light is the double-slit experiment. In this experiment, light from a single source is passed through a narrow slit and then through two narrow parallel slits. When the light appears on a viewing screen behind the slits, you see a pattern of alternating bright and dark fringes corresponding to constructive and destructive interference of the light.

As you studied earlier in the chapter, the bright fringes are described by the following equation.

$$d \sin \theta = \pm m\lambda$$

In this equation, d is the slit separation, θ is the fringe angle, m is the order number, and λ is the wavelength of the incident wave. Typically, only the first few fringes ($m = 0, 1, 2, 3$) are bright enough to see.

In this graphing calculator activity, you will calculate a table of fringe angles. By analyzing this table, you will gain a better understanding of the relationship between fringe angles, wavelength, and slit separation.

Go online to HMHScience.com to find the skillsheet and program for this graphing calculator activity.

Standards-Based Assessment

Record your answers on a separate piece of paper.

MULTIPLE CHOICE

1 Which of the following must be true for two waves with identical amplitudes and wavelengths to undergo complete destructive interference?

  A The waves must be in phase at all times.

  B The waves must be 90° out of phase at all times.

  C The waves must be 180° out of phase at all times.

  D The waves must be 270° out of phase at all times.

2 Why is the diffraction of sound easier to observe than the diffraction of visible light?

  A Sound waves are easier to detect than visible light waves.

  B Sound waves have longer wavelengths than visible light waves and so bend more around barriers.

  C Sound waves are longitudinal waves, which diffract more than transverse waves.

  D Sound waves have greater amplitude than visible light waves.

3

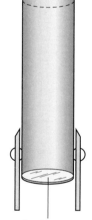

Area of mirror = 80 m²   Area of mirror = 20 m²

For observing the same object, how many times better is the resolution of the telescope shown on the left in the figure above than that of the telescope shown on the right?

  A 4   **C** $\frac{1}{2}$

  B 2   **D** $\frac{1}{4}$

4 Which equation correctly describes the condition for observing the third dark fringe in an interference pattern?

  A $d \sin \theta = \frac{\lambda}{2}$

  B $d \sin \theta = \frac{3\lambda}{2}$

  C $d \sin \theta = \frac{5\lambda}{2}$

  D $d \sin \theta = 3\lambda$

5 Medical applications such as the electrocardiogram (EKG) make use of the wave characteristics of the electrical waves produced by the heart. Which wave characteristic is most important in analyzing the electrocardiogram?

  A frequency

  B wavelength

  C speed

  D waveform

6 Airport workers such as baggage handlers wear special ear protection employing ANC (active noise control) technology. What kind of wave behavior is used in these ear protectors to prevent hearing loss due to the loud sound of jet engines?

  A refraction

  B interference

  C diffraction

  D dispersion

7 Cell phones communicate by means of waves. What are the primary characteristics of those waves that make them suitable for use in cell-phone networks?

  A long wavelengths

  B low frequencies

  C short wavelengths

  D high speed

GRIDDED RESPONSE

8 A diffraction grating used in a spectrometer causes the third-order maximum of blue light with a wavelength of 490 nm to form at an angle of 6.33° from the central maximum ($m = 0$). What is the ruling of the grating in lines/cm?

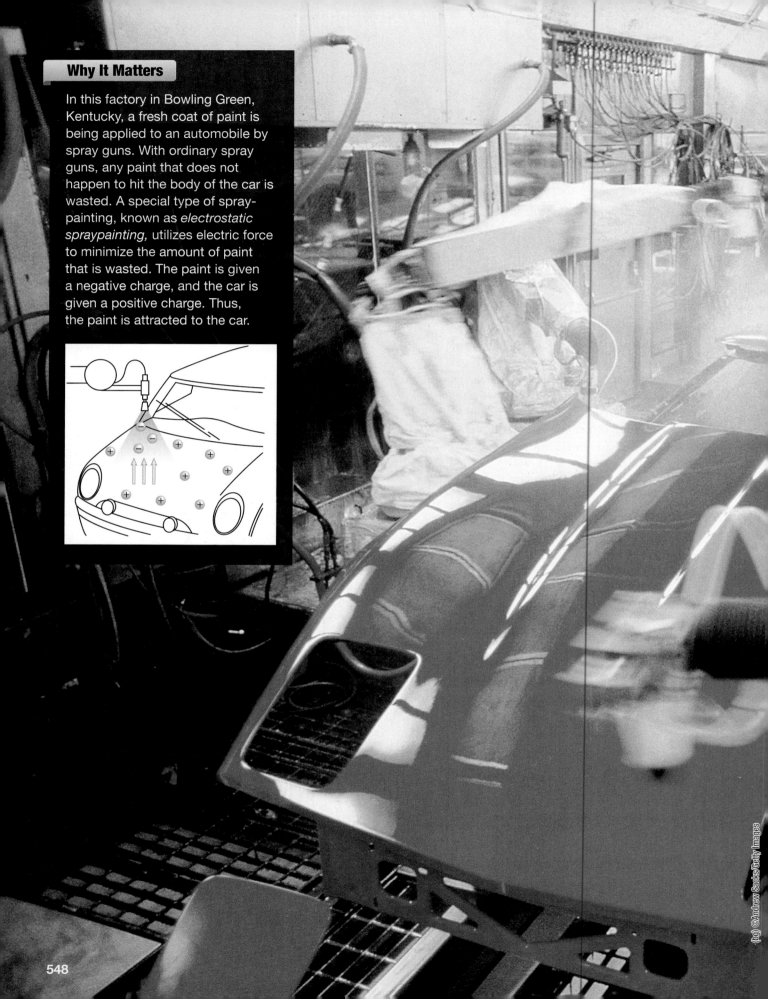

Why It Matters

In this factory in Bowling Green, Kentucky, a fresh coat of paint is being applied to an automobile by spray guns. With ordinary spray guns, any paint that does not happen to hit the body of the car is wasted. A special type of spray-painting, known as *electrostatic spraypainting,* utilizes electric force to minimize the amount of paint that is wasted. The paint is given a negative charge, and the car is given a positive charge. Thus, the paint is attracted to the car.

CHAPTER 16

Electric Forces and Fields

BIG IDEA

Electric force is the force between charged particles and acts at a distance. The magnitude of the electric force between two objects depends on the electric charge each has and the distance between them.

ONLINE Physics
HMHScience.com

ONLINE LABS
- Charges and Electrostatics
- Electrostatics
- Electric Force
- **S.T.E.M. Lab** Levitating Toys

GO ONLINE **Animated**
Physics
HMHScience.com

Coulomb's Law

Objectives

▶ Understand the basic properties of electric charge.

▶ Differentiate between conductors and insulators.

▶ Distinguish between charging by contact, by induction, and by polarization.

FIGURE 1.1

Attraction and Repulsion

(a) If you rub a balloon across your hair on a dry day, the balloon and your hair become charged and attract each other. **(b)** Two charged balloons, on the other hand, repel each other.

(a)

(b)

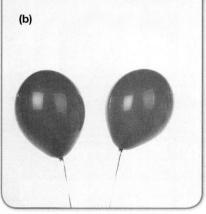

Electric Charge

Key Terms

electrical conductor   electrical insulator   induction

Properties of Electric Charge

You have probably noticed that after running a plastic comb through your hair on a dry day, the comb attracts strands of your hair or small pieces of paper. A simple experiment you might try is to rub an inflated balloon back and forth across your hair. You may find that the balloon is attracted to your hair, as shown in **Figure 1.1(a).** On a dry day, a rubbed balloon will stick to the wall of a room, often for hours. When materials behave this way, they are said to be *electrically charged.* Experiments such as these work best on a dry day because excessive moisture can provide a pathway for charge to leak off a charged object.

You can give your body an electric charge by vigorously rubbing your shoes on a wool rug or by sliding across a car seat. You can then remove the charge on your body by lightly touching another person. Under the right conditions, you will see a spark just before you touch, and both of you will feel a slight tingle.

Another way to observe static electricity is to rub two balloons across your hair and then hold them near one another, as shown in **Figure 1.1(b).** In this case, you will see the two balloons pushing each other apart. Why is a rubbed balloon attracted to your hair but repelled by another rubbed balloon?

There are two kinds of electric charge.

The two balloons in **Figure 1.1(b)** must have the same kind of charge, because each became charged in the same way. Because the two charged balloons repel one another, we see that *like charges repel.* Conversely, a rubbed balloon and your hair, which do not have the same kind of charge, are attracted to one another. Thus, *unlike charges attract.*

Benjamin Franklin (1706–1790) named the two different kinds of charge *positive* and *negative.* By convention, when you rub a balloon across your hair, the charge on your hair is referred to as *positive,* and that on the balloon is referred to as *negative,* as shown in **Figure 1.3.** Positive and negative charges are said to be *opposite* because an object with an equal amount of positive and negative charge has no net charge.

Electrostatic spraypainting utilizes the principle of attraction between unlike charges. Paint droplets are given a negative charge, and the object to be painted is given a positive charge. In ordinary spraypainting, many paint droplets drift past the object being painted. But in electrostatic spraypainting, the negatively charged paint droplets are attracted to the positively charged target object, so more of the paint droplets hit the object being painted and less paint is wasted.

FIGURE 1.2

CONVENTIONS FOR REPRESENTING CHARGES AND ELECTRIC FIELD VECTORS

positive charge	$\oplus$ $+q$
negative charge	$\ominus$ $-q$
electric field vector	$\longrightarrow$ **E**
electric field lines	

Did YOU Know?

Some cosmetic products contain an organic compound called *chitin*, which is found in crabs and lobsters and in butterflies and other insects. Chitin is positively charged, so it helps cosmetic products stick to human hair and skin, which are usually slightly negatively charged.

Electric charge is conserved.

When you rub a balloon across your hair, how do the balloon and your hair become electrically charged? To answer this question, you'll need to know a little about the atoms that make up the matter around you. Every atom contains even smaller particles. Positively charged particles, called *protons*, and uncharged particles, called *neutrons*, are located in the center of the atom, called the *nucleus*. Negatively charged particles, known as *electrons*, are located outside the nucleus and move around it.

Protons and neutrons are relatively fixed in the nucleus of the atom, but electrons are easily transferred from one atom to another. When the electrons in an atom are balanced by an equal number of protons, the atom has no net charge. If an electron is transferred from one neutral atom to another, the second atom gains a negative charge, and the first atom loses a negative charge, thereby becoming positive. Atoms that are positively or negatively charged are called *ions*.

Both a balloon and your hair contain a very large number of neutral atoms. Charge has a natural tendency to be transferred between unlike materials. Rubbing the two materials together serves to increase the area of contact and thus enhance the charge-transfer process. When a balloon is rubbed against your hair, some of your hair's electrons are transferred to the balloon. Thus, the balloon gains a certain amount of negative charge, while your hair loses an equal amount of negative charge and hence is left with a positive charge. In this and similar experiments, only a small portion of the total available charge is transferred from one object to another.

The positive charge on your hair is equal in magnitude to the negative charge on the balloon. Electric charge is conserved in this process; no charge is created or destroyed. This principle of conservation of charge is one of the fundamental laws of nature.

FIGURE 1.3

Charges on a Balloon

(a) This negatively charged balloon is attracted to positively charged hair because the two have opposite charges. **(b)** Two negatively charged balloons repel one another because they have the same charge.

(a)

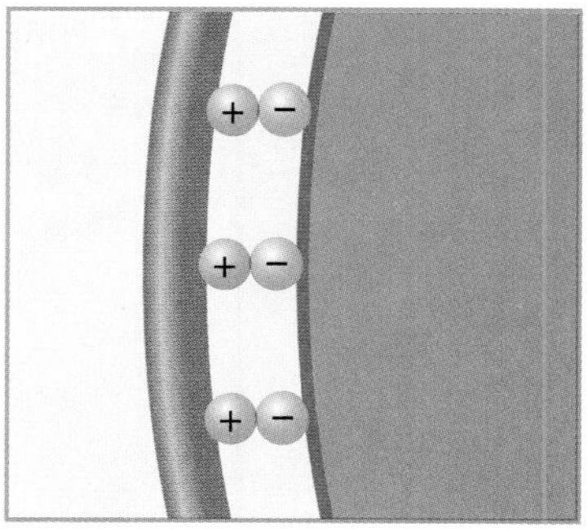

(b)

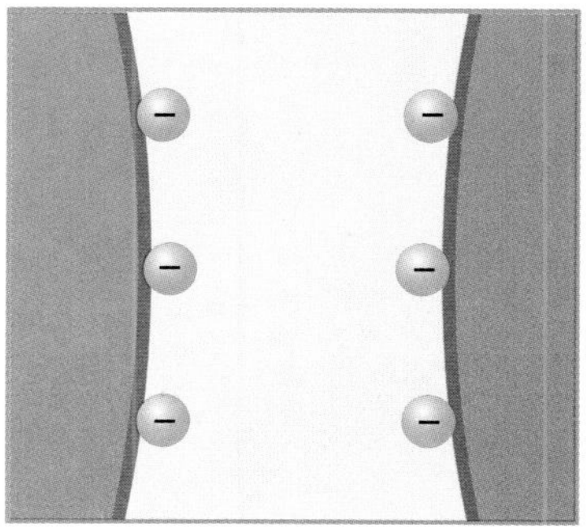

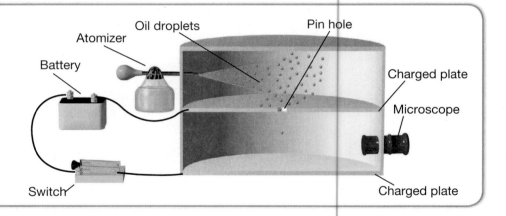

FIGURE 1.4

The Millikan Experiment

This is a schematic view of an apparatus similar to that used by Millikan in his oil-drop experiment. In his experiment, Millikan found that there is a fundamental unit of charge.

Did YOU Know?

In typical electrostatic experiments, in which an object is charged by rubbing, a net charge on the order of 10^{-6} C (= 1 μC) is obtained. This is a very small fraction of the total amount of charge within each object.

Electric charge is quantized.

In 1909, Robert Millikan (1868–1953) performed an experiment at the University of Chicago in which he observed the motion of tiny oil droplets between two parallel metal plates, as shown in **Figure 1.4.** The oil droplets were charged by friction in an atomizer and allowed to pass through a hole in the top plate. Initially, the droplets fell due to their weight. The top plate was given a positive charge as the droplets fell, and the droplets with a negative charge were attracted back upward toward the positively charged plate. By turning the charge on this plate on and off, Millikan was able to watch a single oil droplet for many hours as it alternately rose and fell.

After repeating this process for thousands of drops, Millikan found that when an object is charged, its charge is always a multiple of a fundamental unit of charge, symbolized by the letter e. In modern terms, charge is said to be *quantized*. This means that charge occurs as integer multiples of e in nature. Thus, an object may have a charge of $\pm e$, or $\pm 2e$, or $\pm 3e$, and so on.

Other experiments in Millikan's time demonstrated that the electron has a charge of $-e$ and the proton has an equal and opposite charge, $+e$. The value of e has since been determined to be $1.602\ 176 \times 10^{-19}$ C, where the coulomb (C) is the SI unit of electric charge. For calculations, this book will use the approximate value given in **Figure 1.5.** A total charge of -1.0 C contains 6.2×10^{18} electrons. Comparing this with the number of free electrons in 1 cm^3 of copper, which is on the order of 10^{23}, shows that 1.0 C is a substantial amount of charge.

FIGURE 1.5		
CHARGE AND MASS OF ATOMIC PARTICLES		
Particle	**Charge (C)**	**Mass (kg)**
electron	-1.60×10^{-19}	9.109×10^{-31}
proton	$+1.60 \times 10^{-19}$	1.673×10^{-27}
neutron	0	1.675×10^{-27}

Transfer of Electric Charge

When a balloon and your hair are charged by rubbing, only the rubbed areas become charged, and there is no tendency for the charge to move into other regions of the material. In contrast, when materials such as copper, aluminum, and silver are charged in some small region, the charge readily distributes itself over the entire surface of the material. For this reason, it is convenient to classify substances in terms of their ability to transfer electric charge.

Materials in which electric charges move freely, such as copper and aluminum, are called **electrical conductors.** Most metals are conductors. Materials in which electric charges do not move freely, such as glass, rubber, silk, and plastic, are called **electrical insulators.**

Semiconductors are a third class of materials characterized by electrical properties that are somewhere between those of insulators and conductors. In their pure state, semiconductors are insulators. But the carefully controlled addition of specific atoms as impurities can dramatically increase a semiconductor's ability to conduct electric charge. Silicon and germanium are two well-known semiconductors that are used in a variety of electronic devices.

Certain metals and compounds belong to a fourth class of materials, called *superconductors.* Superconductors have zero electrical resistance when they are at or below a certain temperature. Thus, superconductors can conduct electricity indefinitely without heating.

Insulators and conductors can be charged by contact.

In the experiments discussed above, a balloon and hair become charged when they are rubbed together. This process is known as *charging by contact.* Another example of charging by contact is a common experiment in which a glass rod is rubbed with silk and a rubber rod is rubbed with wool or fur. The two rods become oppositely charged and attract one another, as a balloon and your hair do. If two glass rods are charged, the rods have the same charge and repel each other, just as two charged balloons do. Likewise, two charged rubber rods repel one another. All of the materials used in these experiments—glass, rubber, silk, wool, and fur—are insulators. Can conductors also be charged by contact?

If you try a similar experiment with a copper rod, the rod does not attract or repel another charged rod. This result might suggest that a metal cannot be charged by contact. However, if you hold the copper rod with an insulating handle and then rub it with wool or fur, the rod attracts a charged glass rod and repels a charged rubber rod.

In the first case, the electric charges produced by rubbing readily move from the copper through your body and finally to Earth, because copper and the human body are both conductors. The copper rod does become charged, but it soon becomes neutral again. In the second case, the insulating handle prevents the flow of charge to Earth, and the copper rod remains charged. Thus, both insulators and conductors can become charged by contact.

electrical conductor a material in which charges can move freely

electrical insulator a material in which charges cannot move freely

Conceptual Challenge

Plastic Wrap Plastic wrap becomes electrically charged as it is pulled from its container, and as a result, it is attracted to objects such as food containers. Explain why plastic is a good material for this purpose.

Charge Transfer If a glass rod is rubbed with silk, the glass becomes positively charged, and the silk becomes negatively charged. Compare the mass of the glass rod before and after it is charged.

Electrons Many objects in the large-scale world have no net charge, even though they contain an extremely large number of electrons. How is this possible?

FIGURE 1.6

Charging by Induction

Charging by Induction **(a)** When a charged rubber rod is brought near a metal sphere, the electrons move away from the rod, and the charge on the sphere becomes redistributed. **(b)** If the sphere is grounded, some of the electrons travel through the wire to the ground. **(c)** When this wire is removed, the sphere has an excess of positive charge. **(d)** The electrons become evenly distributed on the surface of the sphere when the rod is removed.

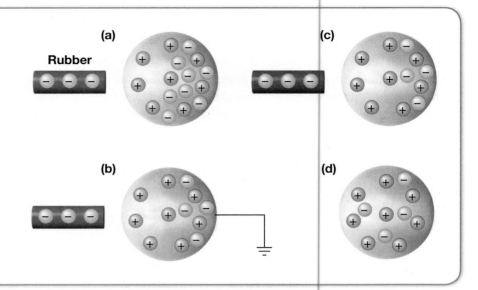

QuickLAB

MATERIALS
- plastic comb
- water faucet

POLARIZATION

Turn on a water faucet, and adjust the flow of water so that you have a small but steady stream. The stream should be as slow as possible without producing individual droplets. Comb your hair vigorously. Hold the charged end of the comb near the stream without letting the comb get wet. What happens to the stream of water? What might be causing this to happen?

induction the process of charging a conductor by bringing it near another charged object and grounding the conductor

Conductors can be charged by induction.

When a conductor is connected to Earth by means of a conducting wire or copper pipe, the conductor is said to be *grounded*. Earth can be considered to be an infinite reservoir for electrons because it can accept an unlimited number of electrons. This fact is the key to understanding another method of charging a conductor.

Consider a negatively charged rubber rod brought near a neutral (uncharged) conducting sphere that is insulated so that there is no conducting path to ground. The repulsive force between the electrons in the rod and those in the sphere causes a redistribution of negative charge on the sphere, as shown in **Figure 1.6(a).** As a result, the region of the sphere nearest the negatively charged rod has an excess of positive charge.

If a grounded conducting wire is then connected to the sphere, as shown in **Figure 1.6(b),** some of the electrons leave the sphere and travel to Earth. If the wire to ground is then removed while the negatively charged rod is held in place, as shown in **Figure 1.6(c),** the conducting sphere is left with an excess of induced positive charge. Finally, when the rubber rod is removed from the vicinity of the sphere, as in **Figure 1.6(d),** the induced net positive charge remains on the ungrounded sphere. The motion of negative charges on the sphere causes the charge to become uniformly distributed over the outside surface of the ungrounded sphere. This process is known as **induction,** and the charge is said to be *induced* on the sphere.

Notice that charging an object by induction requires no contact with the object inducing the charge but does require contact with a third object, which serves as either a *source* or a *sink* of electrons. A sink is a system which can absorb a large number of charges, such as Earth, without becoming locally charged itself. In the process of inducing a charge on the sphere, the charged rubber rod did not come in contact with the sphere and thus did not lose any of its negative charge. This is in contrast to charging an object by contact, in which charges are transferred directly from one object to another.

A surface charge can be induced on insulators by polarization.

A process very similar to charging by induction in conductors takes place in insulators. In most neutral atoms or molecules, the center of positive charge coincides with the center of negative charge. In the presence of a charged object, these centers may shift slightly, resulting in more positive charge on one side of a molecule than on the other. This is known as *polarization*.

This realignment of charge within individual molecules produces an induced charge on the surface of the insulator, as shown in **Figure 1.7(a)**. When an object becomes polarized, it has no net charge but is still able to attract or repel objects due to this realignment of charge. This explains why a plastic comb can attract small pieces of paper that have no net charge, as shown in **Figure 1.7(b)**. As with induction, in polarization one object induces a charge on the surface of another object with no physical contact.

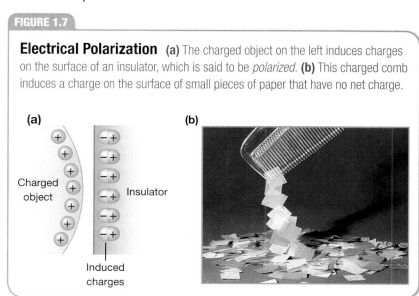

FIGURE 1.7

Electrical Polarization (a) The charged object on the left induces charges on the surface of an insulator, which is said to be *polarized*. (b) This charged comb induces a charge on the surface of small pieces of paper that have no net charge.

(a)

Charged object

Insulator

Induced charges

(b)

 SECTION 1 **FORMATIVE ASSESSMENT**

▶ Reviewing Main Ideas

1. When a rubber rod is rubbed with wool, the rod becomes negatively charged. What can you conclude about the magnitude of the wool's charge after the rubbing process? Why?

2. What did Millikan's oil-drop experiment reveal about the nature of electric charge?

3. A typical lightning bolt has about 10.0 C of charge. How many excess electrons are in a typical lightning bolt?

4. If you stick a piece of transparent tape on your desk and then quickly pull it off, you will find that the tape is attracted to other areas of your desk that are not charged. Why does this happen?

✔ Critical Thinking

5. Metals, such as copper and silver, can become charged by induction, while plastic materials cannot. Explain why.

6. Why is an electrostatic spray gun more efficient than an ordinary spray gun?

Objectives

▶ Calculate electric force using Coulomb's law.

▶ Compare electric force with gravitational force.

▶ Apply the superposition principle to find the resultant force on a charge and to find the position at which the net force on a charge is zero.

SC.912.N.3.5 Describe the function of models in science, and identify the wide range of models used in science.
SC.912.P.10.13 Relate the configuration of static charges to the electric field, electric force, electric potential, and electric potential energy.

Electric Force

Coulomb's Law

Two charged objects near one another may experience acceleration either toward or away from each other because each object exerts a force on the other object. This force is called the *electric force*. The two balloon experiments described in the first section demonstrate that the electric force is attractive between opposite charges and repulsive between like charges. What determines how small or large the electric force will be?

The closer two charges are, the greater is the force on them.

It seems obvious that the distance between two objects affects the magnitude of the electric force between them. Further, it is reasonable that the amount of charge on the objects will also affect the magnitude of the electric force. What is the precise relationship between distance, charge, and the electric force?

In the 1780s, Charles Coulomb conducted a variety of experiments in an attempt to determine the magnitude of the electric force between two charged objects. Coulomb found that the electric force between two charges is proportional to the product of the two charges. Hence, if one charge is doubled, the electric force likewise doubles, and if both charges are doubled, the electric force increases by a factor of four. Coulomb also found that the electric force is inversely proportional to the square of the distance between the charges. Thus, when the distance between two charges is halved, the force between them increases by a factor of four. The following equation, known as Coulomb's law, expresses these conclusions mathematically for two charges separated by a distance, r.

Coulomb's Law

$$F_{electric} = k_C \left(\frac{q_1 q_2}{r^2} \right)$$

electric force = Coulomb constant × $\dfrac{(\text{charge 1})(\text{charge 2})}{(\text{distance})^2}$

The symbol k_C, called the *Coulomb constant*, has SI units of N•m^2/C^2 because this gives N as the unit of electric force. The value of k_C depends on the choice of units. Experiments have determined that in SI units, k_C has the value 8.9875×10^9 N•m^2/C^2. When dealing with Coulomb's law, remember that force is a vector quantity and must be treated accordingly. The electric force between two objects always acts along the line that connects their centers of charge. Also, note that Coulomb's law applies exactly only to point charges or particles and to spherical distributions of charge. When applying Coulomb's law to spherical distributions of charge, use the distance between the centers of the spheres as r.

Coulomb's Law

GO ONLINE

Interactive Demo
HMHScience.com

Sample Problem A The electron and proton of a hydrogen atom are separated, on average, by a distance of about 5.3×10^{-11} m. Find the magnitudes of the electric force and the gravitational force that each particle exerts on the other.

1 ANALYZE

Given: $r = 5.3 \times 10^{-11}$ m $\qquad q_e = -1.60 \times 10^{-19}$ C

$k_C = 8.99 \times 10^9$ N•m^2/C^2 $\qquad q_p = +1.60 \times 10^{-19}$ C

$m_e = 9.109 \times 10^{-31}$ kg $\qquad m_p = 1.673 \times 10^{-2}$ kg

$G = 6.673 \times 10^{-11}$ N•m^2/kg^2

Unknown: $F_{electric} = ?$ $\qquad F_g = ?$

2 PLAN

Choose an equation or situation:
Find the magnitude of the electric force using Coulomb's law and the magnitude of the gravitational force using Newton's law of gravitation (introduced in the chapter "Circular Motion and Gravitation" in this book).

$$F_{electric} = k_C \frac{q_1 q_2}{r^2} \qquad F_g = G \frac{m_e m_p}{r^2}$$

3 SOLVE

Substitute the values into the equations, and solve:
Because we are finding the magnitude of the electric force, which is a scalar, we can disregard the sign of each charge in our calculation.

$$F_{electric} = k_C \frac{q_e q_p}{r^2} = \left(8.99 \times 10^9 \frac{\text{N•m}^2}{\text{C}^2}\right)\left(\frac{(1.60 \times 10^{-19} \text{ C})^2}{(5.3 \times 10^{-11} \text{ m})^2}\right)$$

$$\boxed{F_{electric} = 8.2 \times 10^{-8} \text{ N}}$$

$$F_g = G \frac{m_e m_p}{r^2}$$

$$= \left(6.673 \times 10^{-11} \frac{\text{N•m}^2}{\text{kg}^2}\right)\left(\frac{(9.109 \times 10^{-31} \text{ kg})(1.673 \times 10^{-27} \text{ kg})}{(5.3 \times 10^{-11} \text{ m})^2}\right)$$

$$\boxed{F_g = 3.6 \times 10^{-47} \text{ N}}$$

4 CHECK YOUR WORK

The electron and the proton have opposite signs, so the electric force between the two particles is attractive. The ratio $F_{electric}/F_g \approx 2 \times 10^{39}$; hence, the gravitational force between the particles is negligible compared with the electric force between them. Because each force is inversely proportional to distance squared, their ratio is independent of the distance between the two particles.

Continued

Coulomb's Law (continued)

Practice

1. A balloon rubbed against denim gains a charge of $-8.0\ \mu C$. What is the electric force between the balloon and the denim when the two are separated by a distance of 5.0 cm? (Assume that the charges are located at a point.)

2. Two identical conducting spheres are placed with their centers 0.30 m apart. One is given a charge of $+12 \times 10^{-9}\ C$, and the other is given a charge of $-18 \times 10^{-9}\ C$.

   a. Find the electric force exerted on one sphere by the other.

   b. The spheres are connected by a conducting wire. After equilibrium has occurred, find the electric force between the two spheres.

3. Two stationary point charges of $+60.0\ \mu C$ and $+50.0\ \mu C$ exert a repulsive force on each other of 175 N. What is the distance between the two charges?

Resultant force on a charge is the vector sum of the individual forces on that charge.

Frequently, more than two charges are present, and it is necessary to find the net electric force on one of them. As demonstrated in Sample Problem A, Coulomb's law gives the electric force between any pair of charges. Coulomb's law also applies when more than two charges are present. Thus, the resultant force on any single charge equals the vector sum of the individual forces exerted on that charge by all of the other individual charges that are present. This is an example of the *principle of superposition*. Once the magnitudes of the individual electric forces are found, the vectors are added together exactly as you learned earlier. This process is demonstrated in Sample Problem B.

Conceptual Challenge

Electric Force The electric force is significantly stronger than the gravitational force. However, although we feel our attraction to Earth by gravity, we do not usually feel the effects of the electric force. Explain why.

Electrons in a Coin An ordinary nickel contains about 10^{24} electrons, all repelling one

another. Why don't these electrons fly off the nickel?

Charged Balloons When the distance between two negatively charged balloons is doubled, by what factor does the repulsive force between them change?

The Superposition Principle

Sample Problem B A large movie screen is 24.7 m high and 33.3 m wide. Consider the arrangement of charges shown below. If $q_1 = 2.00$ nC, $q_2 = -3.00$ nC, and $q_3 = 4.00$ nC, find the magnitude and direction of the resultant electric force on q_1.

 ANALYZE

Define the problem, and identify the known variables.

Given: $q_1 = 2.00$ nC $= 2.00 \times 10^{-9}$ C $\qquad r_{1,2} = 24.7$ m

$\qquad\qquad q_2 = -3.00$ nC $= -3.00 \times 10^{-9}$ C $\quad r_{1,3} = 33.3$ m

$\qquad\qquad q_3 = 4.00$ nC $= 4.00 \times 10^{-9}$ C $\qquad k_c = 8.99 \times 10^9$ N•m^2/C^2

Unknown: $F_{1,tot} = ?$

Diagram:

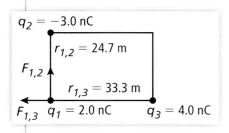

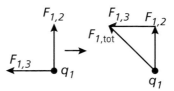

Tips and Tricks

According to the superposition principle, the resultant force on the charge q_1 is the vector sum of the forces exerted by q_2 and q_3 on q_1. First find the force exerted on q_1 by each charge, then use the Pythagorean theorem to find the magnitude of the resultant force on q_1. Take the ratio of the resultant y-component to the resultant x-component, and then take the arc tangent of that quantity to find the direction of the resultant force on q_1.

 PLAN

Calculate the magnitude of the forces with Coulomb's law:

$$F_{2,1} = k_C \frac{q_2 q_1}{(r_{2,1})^2} = \left(8.99 \times 10^9 \, \frac{\text{N•m}^2}{\text{C}^2}\right)\left(\frac{(3.00 \times 10^{-9} \, \text{C})\,(2.00 \times 10^{-9} \, \text{C})}{(24.7 \, \text{m})^2}\right)$$

$$F_{2,1} = 8.84 \times 10^{-11} \, \text{N}$$

$$F_{3,1} = k_C \frac{q_3 q_1}{(r_{3,1})^2} = \left(8.99 \times 10^9 \, \frac{\text{N•m}^2}{\text{C}^2}\right)\left(\frac{(4.00 \times 10^{-9} \, \text{C})\,(2.00 \times 10^{-9} \, \text{C})}{(33.3 \, \text{m})^2}\right)$$

$$F_{3,1} = 6.49 \times 10^{-11} \, \text{N}$$

Determine the direction of the forces by analyzing the signs of the charges:

The force $\mathbf{F_{2,1}}$ is attractive because q_1 and q_2 have opposite signs.
$\mathbf{F_{2,1}}$ is directed along the positive y-axis, so its sign is positive.
The force $\mathbf{F_{3,1}}$ is repulsive because q_1 and q_3 have the same sign. $\mathbf{F_{3,1}}$ is directed toward the negative x-axis, so its sign is negative.

Find the x-component and y-component of each force:

For $\mathbf{F_{2,1}}$: $\qquad F_x = F_{3,1} = -6.49 \times 10^{-11}$ N; $F_y = 0$

For $\mathbf{F_{3,1}}$: $\qquad F_y = F_{2,1} = 8.84 \times 10^{-11}$ N; $F_x = 0$

Calculate the magnitude of the total force acting in both directions:

$$F_{x,tot} = F_x = -6.49 \times 10^{-11} \, \text{N}$$

$$F_{y,tot} = F_y = 8.84 \times 10^{-11} \, \text{N}$$

Continued

The Superposition Principle (continued)

③ SOLVE   **Use the Pythagorean theorem to find the magnitude of the resultant force:**

$$F_{1,tot} = \sqrt{(F_{x,tot})^2 + (F_{y,tot})^2} = \sqrt{(-6.49 \times 10^{-11}\ \text{N})^2 + (8.84 \times 10^{-11}\ \text{N})^2}$$

$$\boxed{F_{1,tot} = 1.10 \times 10^{-10}\ \text{N}}$$

Use a suitable trigonometric function to find the direction of the resultant force.

In this case, you can use the inverse tangent function:

$$\tan\theta = \frac{F_{y,tot}}{F_{x,tot}} = \frac{(8.84 \times 10^{-11}\ \text{N})}{(-6.49 \times 10^{-11}\ \text{N})} = -1.36$$

$$\theta = \tan^{-1}(-1.36)$$

$$\boxed{\theta = -53.7°}$$

Evaluate your answer:

The resultant force makes an angle of 53.7° to the left and above the x-axis.

Practice

1. Consider three point charges, $q_1 = 4.50$ C, $q_2 = 4.50$ C, and $q_3 = 6.30$ C, located at the corners of an isosceles triangle. The charges q_1 and q_2 are 5.00 m apart and form the base. The triangle is 3.50 m high, and q_3 is located at the top. Calculate the magnitude and direction of the resultant force on q_3.

2. Four charged particles are placed so that each particle is at the corner of a square. The sides of the square are 15 cm. The charge at the upper-left corner is $+3.0\ \mu$C, the charge at the upper-right corner is $-6.0\ \mu$C, the charge at the lower-left corner is $-2.4\ \mu$C, and the charge at the lower-right corner is $-9.0\ \mu$C.

   a. What is the net electric force on the $+3.0\ \mu$C charge?

   b. What is the net electric force on the $-6.0\ \mu$C charge?

   c. What is the net electric force on the $-9.0\ \mu$C charge?

Forces are equal when charged objects are in equilibrium.

Consider an object that is in equilibrium. According to Newton's first law, the net external force acting on a body in equilibrium must equal zero. In electrostatic situations, the equilibrium position of a charge is the location at which the net electric force on the charge is zero. To find this location, you must find the position at which the electric force from one charge is equal and opposite the electric force from another charge. This can be done by setting the forces (found by Coulomb's law) equal and then solving for the distance between either charge and the equilibrium position. This is demonstrated in Sample Problem C.

Equilibrium

Sample Problem C A well is 2231 m deep. Consider two charges, $q_2 = 1.60$ mC and q_1, separated by a distance equal to the depth of the well. If a third charge, $q_3 = 1.998$ μC, is placed 888 m from q_2 and is between q_2 and q_1, this third charge will be in equilibrium. What is the value of q_1?

 ANALYZE

Given:

$q_2 = 1.60$ mC $= 1.60 \times 10^{-3}$ C

$q_3 = 1.998$ μC $= 1.998 \times 10^{-6}$ C

$r_{3,2} = 888$ m

$r_{3,1} = 2231$ m $- 888$ m $= 1342$ m

$r_{2,1} = 2231$ m

$k_C = 8.99 \times 10^9$ N·m²/C²

Unknown: $q_1 = ?$

Diagram:

$\vdash\!\!\!-----r_{2,1} = 2231 \text{ m}-----\!\!\!\dashv$

$\vdash\!\!-r_{3,1} = 1342 \text{ m}-\!\!\dashv\vdash r_{3,2} = 888 \text{ m}-\!\!\dashv$

$\bullet$ $\bullet$ $\bullet$

q_1 $q_3 = 1.998$ μC $q_2 = 1.60$ mC

 PLAN

Choose the equation or situation: The force exerted on q_3 by q_2 will be opposite the force exerted on q_3 by q_1. The resultant force on q_3 must be zero in order for the charge to be in equilibrium. This indicates that $F_{3,1}$ and $F_{3,2}$ must be equal to each other.

$$F_{3,1} = k_C \left(\frac{q_3 q_1}{(r_{3,1})^2} \right) \text{ and } F_{3,2} = k_C \left(\frac{q_3 q_2}{(r_{3,2})^2} \right)$$

$$F_{3,1} = F_{3,2}$$

$$k_C \left(\frac{q_3 q_1}{(r_{3,1})^2} \right) = k_C \left(\frac{q_3 q_2}{(r_{3,2})^2} \right)$$

> **Tips and Tricks**
> Because k_C and q_3 are common terms, they can be canceled from both sides of the equation.

Rearrange the equation to isolate the unknowns: q_3 and k_C cancel.

$$q_1 = q_2 \left(\frac{r_{3,1}}{r_{3,2}} \right)^2$$

 SOLVE

Substitute the values into the equation and solve:

$$q_1 = (1.60 \times 10^{-3} \text{ C}) \left(\frac{1342 \text{ m}}{888 \text{ m}} \right)^2 = 3.65 \times 10^{-3} \text{ C}$$

$$\boxed{q_1 = 3.65 \text{ mC}}$$

Because q_1 is a little more than twice as large as q_2, the third charge (q_3) must be farther from q_1 for the forces on q_3 to balance.

Continued

Practice

1. Over a period of more than 30 years, Albert Klein of California drove 2.5×10^6 km in one automobile. Consider two charges, $q_1 = 2.0$ C and $q_2 = 6.0$ C, separated by Klein's total driving distance. A third charge, $q_3 = 4.0$ C, is placed on the line connecting q_1 and q_2. How far from q_1 should q_3 be placed for q_3 to be in equilibrium?

2. A charge q_1 of -5.00×10^{-9} C and a charge q_2 of -2.00×10^{-9} C are separated by a distance of 40.0 cm. Find the equilibrium position for a third charge of $+15.0 \times 10^{-9}$ C.

3. An electron is released above Earth's surface. A second electron directly below it exerts just enough of an electric force on the first electron to cancel the gravitational force on it. Find the distance between the two electrons.

Electric force is a field force.

The Coulomb force is the second example we have studied of a force that is exerted by one object on another even though there is no physical contact between the two objects. Such a force is known as a *field force*. Recall that another example of a field force is gravitational attraction. Notice that the mathematical form of the Coulomb force is very similar to that of the gravitational force. Both forces are inversely proportional to the square of the distance of separation.

However, there are some important differences between electric and gravitational forces. First of all, as you have seen, electric forces can be either attractive or repulsive. Gravitational forces, on the other hand, are always attractive. The reason is that charge comes in two types—positive and negative—but mass comes in only one type, which results in an attractive gravitational force.

Another difference between the gravitational force and the electric force is their relative strength. As shown in Sample Problem A, the electric force is significantly stronger than the gravitational force. As a result, the electric force between charged atomic particles is much stronger than their gravitational attraction to Earth and between each other.

In the large-scale world, the relative strength of these two forces can be seen by noting that the amount of charge required to overcome the gravitational force is relatively small. For example, if you rub a balloon against a dog or cat's fur and hold the balloon directly above the fur, the fur will stand on end because it is attracted toward the balloon. Although only a small amount of charge is transferred from the fur to the balloon, the electric force between the two is nonetheless stronger than the gravitational force that pulls the fur toward the ground.

Coulomb quantified electric force with a torsion balance.

Earlier in this chapter, you learned that Charles Coulomb was the first person to quantify the electric force and establish the inverse-square law for electric charges. Coulomb measured electric forces between charged objects with a torsion balance, as shown in **Figure 2.1**. A torsion balance consists of two small spheres fixed to the ends of a light horizontal rod. The rod is made of an insulating material and is suspended by a silk thread.

In this experiment, one of the spheres is given a charge, and another charged object is brought near the charged sphere. The attractive or repulsive force between the two causes the rod to rotate and to twist the suspension. The angle through which the rod rotates is measured by the deflection of a light beam reflected from a mirror attached to the suspension. The rod rotates through some angle against the restoring force of the twisted thread before reaching equilibrium. The value of the angle of rotation increases as the charge increases, thereby providing a quantitative measure of the electric force. With this experiment, Coulomb established the equation for electric force introduced at the beginning of this section. More recent experiments have verified these results to within a very small uncertainty.

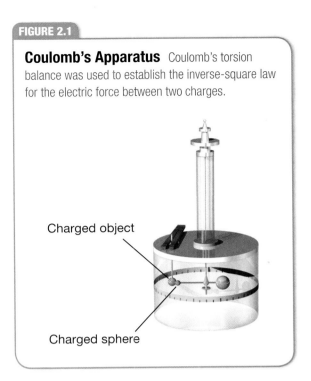

FIGURE 2.1

Coulomb's Apparatus Coulomb's torsion balance was used to establish the inverse-square law for the electric force between two charges.

Charged object

Charged sphere

✔ SECTION 2 FORMATIVE ASSESSMENT

1. A small glass ball rubbed with silk gains a charge of $+2.0 \ \mu C$. The glass ball is placed 12 cm from a small charged rubber ball that carries a charge of $-3.5 \ \mu C$.
   a. What is the magnitude of the electric force between the two balls?
   b. Is this force attractive or repulsive?
   c. How many electrons has the glass ball lost in the rubbing process?

2. The electric force between a negatively charged paint droplet and a positively charged automobile body is increased by a factor of two, but the charges on each remain constant. How has the distance between the two changed? (Assume that the charge on the automobile is located at a single point.)

3. A $+2.2 \times 10^{-9} \ C$ charge is on the x-axis at $x = 1.5$ m, a $+5.4 \times 10^{-9} \ C$ charge is on the x-axis at $x = 2.0$ m, and a $+3.5 \times 10^{-9} \ C$ charge is at the origin. Find the net force on the charge at the origin.

4. A charge q_1 of $-6.00 \times 10^{-9} \ C$ and a charge q_2 of $-3.00 \times 10^{-9} \ C$ are separated by a distance of 60.0 cm. Where could a third charge be placed so that the net electric force on it is zero?

✔ Critical Thinking

5. What are some similarities between the electric force and the gravitational force? What are some differences between the two forces?

Objectives

▶ Calculate electric field strength.

▶ Draw and interpret electric field lines.

▶ Identify the four properties associated with a conductor in electrostatic equilibrium.

The Electric Field

Key Term
electric field

Electric Field Strength

As discussed earlier in this chapter, electric force, like gravitational force, is a field force. Unlike contact forces, which require physical contact between objects, field forces are capable of acting through space, producing an effect even when there is no physical contact between the objects involved. The concept of a field is a model that is frequently used to understand how two objects can exert forces on each other at a distance. For example, a charged object sets up an **electric field** in the space around it. When a second charged object enters this field, forces of an electrical nature arise. In other words, the second object interacts with the field of the first object.

electric field a region where a test charge experiences an electric force

To define an electric field more precisely, consider **Figure 3.1(a),** which shows an object with a small positive charge, q_0, placed near a second object with a larger positive charge, Q. The strength of the electric field, E, at the location of q_0 is defined as the magnitude of the electric force acting on q_0 divided by the charge of q_0:

$$E = \frac{F_{electric}}{q_0}$$

Note that this is the electric field at the location of q_0 produced by the charge Q and *not* the field produced by q_0.

Because electric field strength is a ratio of force to charge, the SI units of E are newtons per coulomb (N/C). The electric field is a vector quantity. By convention, the direction of **E** at a point is defined as the direction of the electric force that would be exerted on a small *positive* charge (called a test charge) placed at that point. Thus, in **Figure 3.1(a),** the direction of the electric field is horizontal and away from the sphere because a positive charge would be repelled by the positive sphere. In **Figure 3.1(b),** the direction of the electric field is toward the sphere because a positive charge would be attracted toward the negatively charged sphere. In other words, the direction of **E** depends on the sign of the charge producing the field.

FIGURE 3.1

Electric Fields **(a)** A small object with a positive charge q_0 placed in the field, **E,** of an object with a larger positive charge experiences an electric force away from the object. **(b)** A small object with a positive charge q_0 placed in the field, **E,** of a negatively charged object experiences an electric force toward the object.

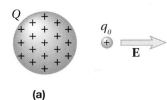

(a)
(b)

Now, consider the positively charged conducting sphere in **Figure 3.2(a)**. The field in the region surrounding the sphere could be explored by placing a positive test charge, q_0, in a variety of places near the sphere. To find the electric field at each point, you would first find the electric force on this charge and then divide this force by the magnitude of the test charge.

However, when the magnitude of the test charge is great enough to influence the charge on the conducting sphere, a difficulty with our definition arises. According to Coulomb's law, a strong test charge will cause a rearrangement of the charges on the sphere, as shown in **Figure 3.2(b).** As a result, the force exerted on the test charge is different from what the force would be if the movement of charge on the sphere had not taken place. Furthermore, the strength of the measured electric field is different from what it would be in the absence of the test charge. To eliminate this problem, we assume that the test charge is small enough to have a negligible effect on the location of the charges on the sphere, the situation shown in **Figure 3.2(a).**

FIGURE 3.2

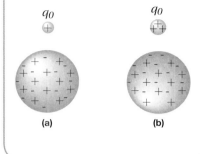

Test Charges We must assume a small test charge, as in **(a),** because a larger test charge, as in **(b),** can cause a redistribution of the charge on the sphere, which changes the electric field strength.

Electric field strength depends on charge and distance.

To reformulate our equation for electric field strength from a point charge, consider a small test charge, q_0, located a distance, r, from a charge, q. According to Coulomb's law, the magnitude of the force on the test charge is given by the following equation:

$$F_{electric} = k_C \frac{q q_0}{r^2}$$

We can find the magnitude of the electric field due to the point charge q at the position of q_0 by substituting this value into our previous equation for electric field strength.

$$E = \frac{F_{electric}}{q_0} = k_C \frac{q \cancel{q_0}}{r^2 \cancel{q_0}}$$

Notice that q_0 cancels, and we have a new equation for electric field strength due to a point charge.

Electric Field Strength Due to a Point Charge

$$E = k_C \frac{q}{r^2}$$

electric field strength = Coulomb constant × $\dfrac{\textbf{charge producing the field}}{\textbf{(distance)}^2}$

As stated above, electric field, **E,** is a vector. If q is positive, the field due to this charge is directed outward radially from q. If q is negative, the field is directed toward q. As with electric force, the electric field due to more than one charge is calculated by applying the principle of superposition. A strategy for solving superposition problems is given in Sample Problem D.

FIGURE 3.3

ELECTRIC FIELDS

Examples	E, N/C
in a fluorescent lighting tube	10
in the atmosphere during fair weather	100
under a thundercloud or in a lightning bolt	10 000
at the electron in a hydrogen atom	5.1×10^{11}

Our new equation for electric field strength points out an important property of electric fields. As the equation indicates, an electric field at a given point depends only on the charge, q, of the object setting up the field and on the distance, r, from that object to a specific point in space. As a result, we can say that an electric field exists at any point near a charged body even when there is no test charge at that point. The examples in **Figure 3.3** show the magnitudes of various electric fields.

Electric Field Strength

GO ONLINE

Interactive Demo
HMHScience.com

Sample Problem D The Seto-Ohashi bridge, linking the two Japanese islands of Honshu and Shikoku, is the longest "rail and road" bridge, with an overall length of 12.3 km. Suppose two equal charges are placed at opposite ends of the bridge. If the resultant electric field strength due to these charges at the point exactly 12.3 km above one of the bridge's ends is 3.99×10^{-2} N/C and is directed at $75.3°$ above the positive x-axis, what is the magnitude of each charge?

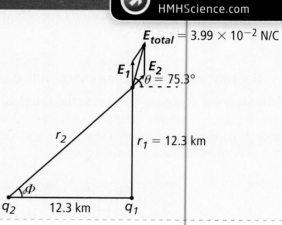

1 ANALYZE

Define the problem, and identify the known variables.

Given: $E_{tot} = 3.99 \times 10^{-2}$ N/C

$\theta = 75.3°$

$r_1 = 12.3 \text{ km} = 1.23 \times 10^4 \text{ m}$

$k_C = 8.99 \times 10^9 \text{ N·m}^2/\text{C}^2$

Unknown: $q_1 = ?$ $q_2 = ?$

2 PLAN

Tips and Tricks

According to the superposition principle, the resultant electric field strength at the point above the bridge is the vector sum of the electric field strengths produced by q_1 and q_2. First, find the components of the electric field strengths produced by each charge, then combine components in the x- and y-directions to find the electric field strength components of the resultant vector. Equate this to the components in the x- and y-directions of the electric field vector. Finally, rearrange the equation to solve for the charge.

The distance r_2 must be calculated from the information in the diagram. Because r_2 forms the hypotenuse of a right triangle whose sides equal r_1, it follows that

$$r_2 = \sqrt{(r_1)^2 + (r_1)^2} = \sqrt{2(r_1)^2} = 1.74 \times 10^4 \text{ m}$$

The angle that r_2 makes with the coordinate system equals the inverse tangent of the ratio of the vertical to the horizontal components. Because these components are equal,

$$\tan \phi = 1.00, \text{ or } \phi = 45.0°$$

Find the x- and y-components of each electric field strength vector:
At this point, the direction of each component must be taken into account.

For **E₁**: $E_{x,1} = 0$

Continued

$$E_{y,1} = E_1 = \frac{k_C q_1}{(r_1)^2}$$

For $\mathbf{E}_2$:

$$E_{x,2} = E_2 \cos(45.0°) = \frac{k_C q_2}{\sqrt{2}(r_2)^2}$$

$$E_{y,2} = E_2 \sin(45.0°) = \frac{k_C q_2}{\sqrt{2}(r_2)^2}$$

Calculate the magnitude of the total electric field strength in both the x and y directions:

$$E_{x,tot} = E_{x,1} + E_{x,2} = \frac{k_C q_2}{\sqrt{2}(r_2)^2} E_{tot} \cos(75.3°)$$

$$E_{y,tot} = E_{y,1} + E_{y,2} = \frac{k_C q_1}{(r_1)^2} + \frac{k_C q_2}{\sqrt{2}(r_2)^2} E_{tot} \sin(75.3°)$$

③ SOLVE

Rearrange the equation to isolate the unknowns:

$$q_2 = \frac{E_{tot} \cos(75.3°) \sqrt{2}\,(r_2)^2}{k_c}$$

$$= \frac{(3.99 \times 10^{-2}\,\text{N/C}) \cos(75.3°)\ \sqrt{2}\,(1.74 \times 10^4\,\text{m})^2}{8.99 \times 10^9\,\text{N·m}^2/\text{C}^2}$$

$$\boxed{q_2 = q_1 = 4.82 \times 10^{-4}\,\text{C}}$$

Practice

1. A charge, $q_1 = 5.00\ \mu\text{C}$, is at the origin, and a second charge, $q_2 = -3.00\ \mu\text{C}$, is on the x-axis 0.800 m from the origin. Find the electric field at a point on the y-axis 0.500 m from the origin.

2. Suppose three charges of 3.6 μC each are placed at three corners of the Imperial Palace in Beijing, China, which has a length of 960 m and a width of 750 m. What is the strength of the electric field at the fourth corner?

3. An electric field of 2.0×10^4 N/C is directed along the positive x-axis.

   a. What is the electric force on an electron in this field?

   b. What is the electric force on a proton in this field?

Electric Field Lines

A convenient aid for visualizing electric field patterns is to draw lines pointing in the direction of the electric field, called *electric field lines.* Although electric field lines do not really exist, they offer a useful means of analyzing fields by representing both the strength and the direction of the field at different points in space. This is useful because the field at each point is often the result of more than one charge, as seen in Sample Problem D. Field lines make it easier to visualize the net field at each point.

The number of field lines is proportional to the electric field strength.

By convention, electric field lines are drawn so that the electric field vector, **E,** is tangent to the lines at each point. Further, the number of lines per unit area through a surface perpendicular to the lines is proportional to the strength of the electric field in a given region. Thus, E is stronger where the field lines are close together and weaker where they are far apart.

Figure 3.4(a) shows some representative electric field lines for a positive point charge. Note that this two-dimensional drawing contains only the field lines that lie in the plane containing the point charge. The lines are actually directed outward radially from the charge in all directions, somewhat like quills radiate from the body of a porcupine. Because a positive test charge placed in this field would be repelled by the positive charge q, the lines are directed away from the positive charge, extending to infinity. Similarly, the electric field lines for a single negative point charge, which begin at infinity, are directed inward toward the charge, as shown in Figure 3.4(b). Note that the lines are closer together as they get near the charge, indicating that the strength of the field is increasing. This is consistent with our equation for electric field strength, which is inversely proportional to distance squared. Figure 3.4(c) shows grass seeds in an insulating liquid. When a small charged conductor is placed in the center, these seeds align with the electric field produced by the charged body.

The rules for drawing electric field lines are summarized in Figure 3.5. Note that no two field lines from the same field can cross one another. The reason is that at every point in space, the electric field vector points in a single direction and any field line at that point must also point in that direction.

(bl) ©2011 Richard Megna/Fundamental Photographs, NYC

FIGURE 3.4

Electric Field Lines for a Single Charge The diagrams **(a)** and **(b)** show some representative electric field lines for a positive and a negative point charge. In **(c),** grass seeds align with a similar field produced by a charged body.

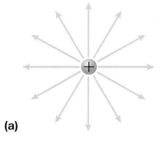

(a)

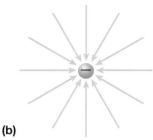

(b)

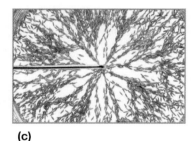

(c)

FIGURE 3.5

RULES FOR DRAWING ELECTRIC FIELD LINES

The lines must begin on positive charges or at infinity and must terminate on negative charges or at infinity.
The number of lines drawn leaving a positive charge or approaching a negative charge is proportional to the magnitude of the charge.
No two field lines from the same field can cross each other.

FIGURE 3.6

Electric Field Lines for Two Opposite

Charges **(a)** This diagram shows the electric field lines for two equal and opposite point charges. Note that the number of lines leaving the positive charge equals the number of lines terminating on the negative charge. **(b)** In this photograph, grass seeds in an insulating liquid align with an electric field produced by two oppositely charged conductors.

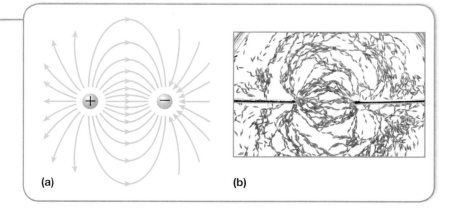

(a) (b)

FIGURE 3.7

Electric Field Lines for Two Positive

Charges **(a)** This diagram shows the electric field lines for two positive point charges. **(b)** The photograph shows the analogous case for grass seeds in an insulating liquid around two conductors with the same charge.

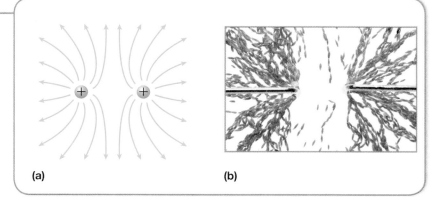

(a) (b)

Figure 3.6 shows the electric field lines for two point charges of equal magnitudes but opposite signs. This charge configuration is called an *electric dipole*. In this case, the number of lines that begin at the positive charge must equal the number of lines that terminate on the negative charge. At points very near the charges, the lines are nearly radial. The high density of lines between the charges indicates a strong electric field in this region.

In electrostatic spraypainting, field lines between a negatively charged spray gun and a positively charged target object are similar to those shown in **Figure 3.6.** As you can see, the field lines suggest that paint droplets that narrowly miss the target object still experience a force directed toward the object, sometimes causing them to wrap around from behind and hit it. This does happen and increases the efficiency of an electrostatic spray gun.

Figure 3.7 shows the electric field lines in the vicinity of two equal positive point charges. Again, close to either charge, the lines are nearly radial. The same number of lines emerges from each charge because the charges are equal in magnitude. At great distances from the charges, the field approximately equals that of a single point charge of magnitude $2q$.

Finally, **Figure 3.8** is a sketch of the electric field lines associated with a positive charge $+2q$ and a negative charge $-q$. In this case, the number of lines leaving the charge $+2q$ is twice the number terminating on the charge $-q$. Hence, only half the lines that leave the positive charge end at the negative charge. The remaining half terminate at infinity. At distances that are great compared with the separation between the charges, the pattern of electric field lines is equivalent to that of a single charge, $+q$.

FIGURE 3.8

Electric Field Lines for Two

Unequal Charges In this case, only half the lines originating from the positive charge terminate on the negative charge, because the positive charge is twice as great as the negative charge.

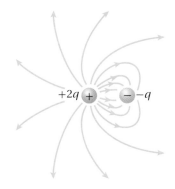

Conductors in Electrostatic Equilibrium

A good electric conductor, such as copper, contains charges (electrons) that are only weakly bound to the atoms in the material and are free to move about within the material. When no net motion of charge is occurring within a conductor, the conductor is said to be in *electrostatic equilibrium*. As we shall see, such a conductor that is isolated has the four properties summarized in **Figure 3.9.**

FIGURE 3.9

CONDUCTORS IN ELECTROSTATIC EQUILIBRIUM

The electric field is zero everywhere inside the conductor.

Any excess charge on an isolated conductor resides entirely on the conductor's outer surface.

The electric field just outside a charged conductor is perpendicular to the conductor's surface.

On an irregularly shaped conductor, charge tends to accumulate where the radius of curvature of the surface is smallest, that is, at sharp points.

The first property, which states that the electric field is zero inside a conductor in electrostatic equilibrium, can be understood by examining what would happen if this were not true. If there were an electric field inside a conductor, the free charges would move, and a flow of charge, or current, would be created. However, if there were a net movement of charge, the conductor would no longer be in electrostatic equilibrium.

The fact that any excess charge resides on the outer surface of the conductor is a direct result of the repulsion between like charges described by Coulomb's law. If an excess of charge is placed inside a conductor, the repulsive forces arising between the charges force them as far apart as possible, causing them to quickly migrate to the surface.

We can understand why the electric field just outside a conductor must be perpendicular to the conductor's surface by considering what would happen if this were not true. If the electric field were *not* perpendicular to the surface, the field would have a component along the surface. This would cause the free negative charges within the conductor to move on the surface of the conductor. But if the charges moved, a current would be created, and there would no longer be electrostatic equilibrium. Hence, **E** must be perpendicular to the surface.

To see why charge tends to accumulate at sharp points, consider a conductor that is fairly flat at one end and relatively pointed at the other. Any excess charge placed on the object moves to its surface. **Figure 3.10** shows the forces between two charges at each end of such an object. At the flatter end, these forces are predominantly directed parallel to the surface. Thus, the charges move apart until repulsive forces from other nearby charges create a state of equilibrium.

At the sharp end, however, the forces of repulsion between two charges are directed predominantly perpendicular to the surface. As a result, there is less tendency for the charges to move apart along the surface, and the amount of charge per unit area is greater than at the flat end. The cumulative effect of many such outward forces from nearby charges at the sharp end produces a large electric field directed away from the surface.

FIGURE 3.10

Irregularly Shaped Conductor

When one end of a conductor is more pointed than the other, excess charge tends to accumulate at the sharper end, resulting in a larger charge per unit area and therefore a larger repulsive electric force between charges at this end.

Microwave Ovens

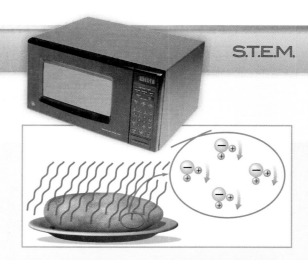

It would be hard to find a place in America that does not have a microwave oven. Most homes, convenience stores, and restaurants have this marvelous invention that somehow heats only the soft parts of the food and leaves the inorganic and hard materials, like ceramic and the surfaces of bone, at approximately the same temperature. A neat trick, indeed, but how is it done?

Microwave ovens take advantage of a property of water molecules called *bipolarity.* Water molecules are considered bipolar because each molecule has a positive and a negative end. In other words, more of the electrons in these molecules are at one end of the molecule than the other.

Because microwaves are a high-frequency form of electromagnetic radiation, they supply an electric field that changes polarity billions of times a second. As this electric field passes a bipolar molecule, the positive side of the molecule experiences a force in one direction, and the negative side of the molecule is pushed or pulled in the other direction. When the field changes polarity, the directions of these forces are reversed. Instead of tearing apart, the molecules swing around and line up with the electric field.

As the bipolar molecules rotate, they rub against one another, producing friction. This friction in turn increases the internal energy of the food. Energy is transferred to the food by radiation (the microwaves) as opposed to conduction from hot air, as in a conventional oven.

Depending on the microwave oven's power and design, this rotational motion can generate up to about 3 J of internal energy each second in 1 g of water. At this rate, a top-power microwave oven can boil a cup (250 mL) of water in 2 min using about 0.033 kW•h of electricity.

Items such as dry plates and the air in the oven are unaffected by the fluctuating electric field because they are not polarized. Because energy is not wasted on heating these nonpolar items, the microwave oven cooks food faster and more efficiently than other ovens.

✓ SECTION 3 FORMATIVE ASSESSMENT

1. Find the electric field at a point midway between two charges of $+40.0 \times 10^{-9}$ C and $+60.0 \times 10^{-9}$ C separated by a distance of 30.0 cm.

2. Two point charges are a small distance apart.
   a. Sketch the electric field lines for the two if one has a charge four times that of the other and if both charges are positive.
   b. Repeat **(a)**, but assume both charges are negative.

Interpreting Graphics

3. Figure 3.11 shows the electric field lines for two point charges separated by a small distance.
   a. Determine the ratio q_1/q_2.
   b. What are the signs of q_1 and q_2?

✓ Critical Thinking

4. Explain why you're more likely to get a shock from static electricity by touching a metal object with your finger instead of with your entire hand.

FIGURE 3.11

Field Lines for Unknown Charges

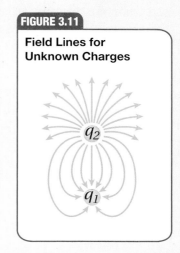

q_2

q_1

Electric Air Cleaners

Engineers use scientific principles to solve practical problems. Those problems sometimes involve issues of safety and health, like indoor air pollution.

Define the Problem

The Environmental Protection Agency (EPA) has identified indoor air pollution as one of the top five environmental health risks. Indoor air pollutants fall into two categories: particulate matter (PM) and gaseous pollutants.

PM includes solid and liquid particles such as dust, smoke, bacteria, viruses, molds, insect body parts, and animal dander. Gaseous pollutants include carbon monoxide, radon, and fumes from tobacco smoke, paints, dyes, cleaners, hobby materials, food cooking, and laser printers.

Design Solutions

One way to reduce indoor PM pollutants is to trap and remove them. As you have learned, charged particles are attracted to oppositely charged objects and are repelled by like charged objects. An electronic air filter could give a charge to PM and then use electric forces and fields to trap the pollutants.

Two designs of electronic air filters are electrostatic precipitators and ion generators. An electrostatic precipitator draws air through it, as shown in the diagram. First, the particulates are charged in an ion charging section. Next, the charged particulates pass through a charged plate area, where they experience electric forces that attract them onto an oppositely charged collector plate.

Ion generators release charged particles into the air to attach themselves to neutrally charged PM. Once the particulates are charged, they stick to nearby neutral surfaces, such as walls, curtains, furniture, and floors.

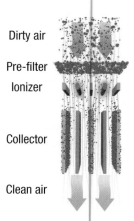

Dirty air

Pre-filter

Ionizer

Collector

Clean air

Design Your Own

Optimize Solutions

Which design solution to indoor PM pollution do you think is best? Continue the engineering design process to find out.

Conduct Research

Research pros and cons of electrostatic precipitators and ion generators.

Evaluate

What is the EPA's stance on the effectiveness of each? What is the difference between efficiency and effectiveness?

Build a Prototype

Use the Internet or other sources to find out more about how these electronic air cleaners work. Create a physical or virtual model to demonstrate the operation of the air cleaner you think works best. If you can think of a way to improve the mechanism, include the improvement in your model.

Communicate

Present your model to the class. Be open to challenging questions and suggestions for further improvements to the model.

BIG IDEA Electric force is the force between charged particles and acts at a distance. The magnitude of the electric force between two objects depends on the electric charge each has and the distance between them.

SECTION 1 Electric Charge

- There are two kinds of electric charge: positive and negative. Like charges repel, and unlike charges attract.
- Electric charge is conserved.
- The fundamental unit of charge, e, is the magnitude of the charge of a single electron or proton.
- Conductors and insulators can be charged by contact. Conductors can also be charged by induction. A surface charge can be induced on an insulator by polarization.

KEY TERMS

electrical conductor
electrical insulator
induction

SECTION 2 Electric Force

- According to Coulomb's law, the electric force between two point charges is proportional to the magnitude of each of the charges and inversely proportional to the square of the distance between them.
- The electric force is a field force.
- The resultant electric force on any charge is the vector sum of the individual electric forces on that charge.

SECTION 3 The Electric Field

- An electric field exists in the region around a charged object.
- Electric field strength depends on the magnitude of the charge producing the field and the distance between that charge and a point in the field.
- The direction of the electric field vector, **E,** is the direction in which an electric force would act on a positive test charge.
- Field lines are tangent to the electric field vector at any point, and the number of lines is proportional to the magnitude of the field strength.

KEY TERM

electric field

VARIABLE SYMBOLS

Quantities		Units		Conversions
$F_{electric}$	electric force	N	newtons	$= kg \bullet m/s^2$
q	charge	C	coulomb (SI unit of charge)	$= 6.3 \times 10^{18} \ e$
		e	fundamental unit of charge	$= 1.60 \times 10^{-19} \ C$
k_C	Coulomb constant	$N \bullet \dfrac{m^2}{C^2}$	newtons $\times \dfrac{meters^2}{coulombs^2}$	$= 8.99 \times 10^9 \ N \bullet m^2$
E	electric field strength	N/C	newtons/coulomb	

DIAGRAM SYMBOLS

positive charge	$\bigoplus$ $+q$
negative charge	$\ominus$ $-q$
electric field vector	$\longrightarrow$ **E**
electric field lines	

Problem Solving

See **Appendix D: Equations** for a summary of the equations introduced in this chapter. If you need more problem-solving practice, see **Appendix I: Additional Problems.**

Electric Charge

▶ REVIEWING MAIN IDEAS

1. How are conductors different from insulators?

2. When a conductor is charged by induction, is the induced surface charge on the conductor the same as or opposite the charge of the object inducing the surface charge?

3. A negatively charged balloon has 3.5 μC of charge. How many excess electrons are on this balloon?

CONCEPTUAL QUESTIONS

4. Would life be different if the electron were positively charged and the proton were negatively charged? Explain your answer.

5. Explain from an atomic viewpoint why charge is usually transferred by electrons.

6. Because of a higher moisture content, air is a better conductor of charge in the summer than in the winter. Would you expect the shocks from static electricity to be more severe in summer or winter? Explain your answer.

7. A balloon is negatively charged by rubbing and then clings to a wall. Does this mean that the wall is positively charged?

8. Which effect proves more conclusively that an object is charged, attraction to or repulsion from another object? Explain.

Electric Force

▶ REVIEWING MAIN IDEAS

9. What determines the direction of the electric force between two charges?

10. In which direction will the electric force from the two equal positive charges move the negative charge shown below?

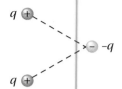

11. The gravitational force is always attractive, while the electric force is both attractive and repulsive. What accounts for this difference?

12. When more than one charged object is present in an area, how can the total electric force on one of the charged objects be predicted?

13. Identify examples of electric forces in everyday life.

CONCEPTUAL QUESTIONS

14. According to Newton's third law, every action has an equal and opposite reaction. When a comb is charged and held near small pieces of paper, the comb exerts an electric force on the paper pieces and pulls them toward it. Why don't you observe the comb moving toward the paper pieces as well?

PRACTICE PROBLEMS

For problems 15–17, see Sample Problem A.

15. At the point of fission, a nucleus of ^{235}U that has 92 protons is divided into two smaller spheres, each of which has 46 protons and a radius of 5.90×10^{-15} m. What is the magnitude of the repulsive force pushing these two spheres apart?

16. What is the electric force between a glass ball that has $+2.5$ μC of charge and a rubber ball that has -5.0 μC of charge when they are separated by a distance of 5.0 cm?

17. An alpha particle (charge $= +2.0e$) is sent at high speed toward a gold nucleus (charge $= +79e$). What is the electric force acting on the alpha particle when the alpha particle is 2.0×10^{-14} m from the gold nucleus?

For problems 18–19, see Sample Problem B.

18. Three positive point charges of 3.0 nC, 6.0 nC, and 2.0 nC, respectively, are arranged in a triangular pattern, as shown at right. Find the magnitude and direction of the electric force acting on the 6.0 nC charge.

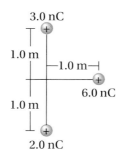

3.0 nC

1.0 m

—1.0 m—

6.0 nC

1.0 m

2.0 nC

19. Two positive point charges, each of which has a charge of 2.5×10^{-9} C, are located at $y = +0.50$ m and $y = -0.50$ m. Find the magnitude and direction of the resultant electric force acting on a charge of 3.0×10^{-9} C located at $x = 0.70$ m.

For problems 20–21, see Sample Problem C.

20. Three point charges lie in a straight line along the y-axis. A charge of $q_1 = -9.0$ μC is at $y = 6.0$ m, and a charge of $q_2 = -8.0$ μC is at $y = -4.0$ m. The net electric force on the third point charge is zero. Where is this charge located?

21. A charge of $+3.5$ nC and a charge of $+5.0$ nC are separated by 40.0 cm. Find the equilibrium position for a -6.0 nC charge.

The Electric Field

▶ **REVIEWING MAIN IDEAS**

22. What is an electric field?

23. Show that the definition of electric field strength $(E = F_{electric}/q_0)$ is equivalent to the equation $E = k_C q/r^2$ for point charges.

24. As you increase the potential on an irregularly shaped conductor, a bluish purple glow called a *corona* forms around a sharp end sooner than around a smoother end. Explain why.

25. Draw some representative electric field lines for two charges of $+q$ and $-3q$ separated by a small distance.

26. When electric field lines are being drawn, what determines the number of lines originating from a charge? What determines whether the lines originate from or terminate on a charge?

27. Consider the electric field lines in the figure below.
 a. Where is charge density the highest? Where is it the lowest?
 b. If an opposite charge were brought into the vicinity, where would charge on the pear-shaped object "leak off" most readily?

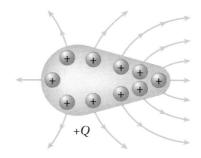

$+Q$

28. Do electric field lines actually exist?

CONCEPTUAL QUESTIONS

29. When defining the electric field, why must the magnitude of the test charge be very small?

30. Why can't two field lines from the same field cross one another?

31. A "free" electron and "free" proton are placed in an identical electric field. Compare the electric force on each particle. How do their accelerations compare?

PRACTICE PROBLEMS

For problems 32–33, see Sample Problem D.

32. Find the electric field at a point midway between two charges of $+30.0 \times 10^{-9}$ C and $+60.0 \times 10^{-9}$ C separated by a distance of 30.0 cm.

33. A $+5.7$ μC point charge is on the x-axis at $x = -3.0$ m, and a $+2.0$ μC point charge is on the x-axis at $x = +1.0$ m. Determine the net electric field (magnitude and direction) on the y-axis at $y = +2.0$ m.

Mixed Review

▶ **REVIEWING MAIN IDEAS**

34. Calculate the net charge on a substance consisting of a combination of 7.0×10^{13} protons and 4.0×10^{13} electrons.

35. An electron moving through an electric field experiences an acceleration of 6.3×10^3 m/s^2.
   a. Find the electric force acting on the electron.
   b. What is the strength of the electric field?

36. One gram of copper has 9.48×10^{21} atoms, and each copper atom has 29 electrons.
   a. How many electrons are contained in 1.00 g of copper?
   b. What is the total charge of these electrons?

37. Consider three charges arranged as shown below.
   a. What is the electric field strength at a point 1.0 cm to the left of the middle charge?
   b. What is the magnitude of the force on a $-2.0\ \mu$C charge placed at this point?

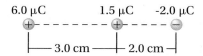

38. Consider three charges arranged in a triangle as shown below.
   a. What is the net electric force acting on the charge at the origin?
   b. What is the net electric field at the position of the charge at the origin?

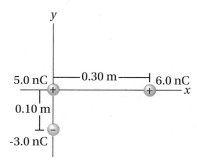

39. Sketch the electric field pattern set up by a positively charged hollow conducting sphere. Include regions both inside and outside the sphere.

40. The moon ($m = 7.36 \times 10^{22}$ kg) is bound to Earth ($m = 5.98 \times 10^{24}$ kg) by gravity. If, instead, the force of attraction were the result of each having a charge of the same magnitude but opposite in sign, find the quantity of charge that would have to be placed on each to produce the required force.

41. Two small metallic spheres, each with a mass of 0.20 g, are suspended as pendulums by light strings from a common point. They are given the same electric charge, and the two come to equilibrium when each string is at an angle of 5.0° with the vertical. If the string is 30.0 cm long, what is the magnitude of the charge on each sphere?

42. What are the magnitude and the direction of the electric field that will balance the weight of an electron? What are the magnitude and direction of the electric field that will balance the weight of a proton?

43. An electron and a proton are each placed at rest in an external uniform electric field of magnitude 520 N/C. Calculate the speed of each particle after 48 ns.

44. A Van de Graaff generator is charged so that the magnitude of the electric field at its surface is 3.0×10^4 N/C.
   a. What is the magnitude of the electric force on a proton released at the surface of the generator?
   b. Find the proton's acceleration at this instant.

45. Thunderstorms can have an electric field of up to 3.4×10^5 N/C. What is the magnitude of the electric force on an electron in such a field?

46. An object with a net charge of 24 μC is placed in a uniform electric field of 610 N/C, directed vertically. What is the mass of this object if it floats in this electric field?

47. Three identical point charges, with mass $m = 0.10$ kg, hang from three strings, as shown below. If $L = 30.0$ cm and $\theta = 45°$, what is the value of q?

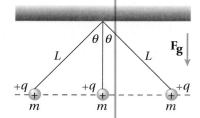

48. In a laboratory experiment, five equal negative point charges are placed symmetrically around the circumference of a circle of radius r. Calculate the electric field at the center of the circle.

49. An electron and a proton both start from rest and from the same point in a uniform electric field of 370.0 N/C. How far apart are they 1.00 μs after they are released? Ignore the attraction between the electron and the proton. (Hint: Imagine the experiment performed with the proton only, and then repeat with the electron only.)

50. An electron is accelerated by a constant electric field of magnitude 300.0 N/C.
  a. Find the acceleration of the electron.
  b. Find the electron's speed after 1.00×10^{-8} s, assuming it starts from rest.

51. If the electric field strength is increased to about 3.0×10^6 N/C, air breaks down and loses its insulating quality. Under these conditions, sparking results.
  a. What acceleration does an electron experience when the electron is placed in such an electric field?
  b. If the electron starts from rest when it is placed in an electric field under these conditions, in what distance does it acquire a speed equal to 10.0 percent of the speed of light?
  c. What acceleration does a proton experience when the proton is placed in such an electric field?

52. Each of the protons in a particle beam has a kinetic energy of 3.25×10^{-15} J. What are the magnitude and direction of the electric field that will stop these protons in a distance of 1.25 m?

53. A small 2.0 g plastic ball is suspended by a 20.0 cm string in a uniform electric field of 1.0×10^4 N/C, as shown below.
  a. Is the ball's charge positive or negative?
  b. If the ball is in equilibrium when the string makes a 15° angle with the vertical as indicated, what is the net charge on the ball?

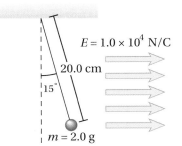

$E = 1.0 \times 10^4$ N/C

20.0 cm

15°

$m = 2.0$ g

GRAPHING CALCULATOR PRACTICE

Coulomb's Law

One of the most important and fundamental laws of physics—and of all science—is Coulomb's law. As you learned earlier in this chapter, this law states that the electric force, $F_{electric}$, between two charges, q_1 and q_2, which are separated by a distance, r, is given by the following equation.

$$F_{electric} = k_C \left(\frac{q_1 q_2}{r^2} \right)$$

In this graphing calculator activity, you will enter the charges and will observe a graph of electric force versus distance. By analyzing graphs for various sets of charges (positive with positive, negative with negative, and positive with negative), you will better understand Coulomb's law and how charge and distance affect electric force.

Go online to HMHScience.com to find the skillsheet and program for this graphing calculator activity.

54. A constant electric field directed along the positive x-axis has a strength of 2.0×10^3 N/C.
  a. Find the electric force exerted on a proton by the field.
  b. Find the acceleration of the proton.
  c. Find the time required for the proton to reach a speed of 1.00×10^6 m/s, if it starts from rest.

55. Consider an electron that is released from rest in a uniform electric field.
  a. If the electron is accelerated to 1.0 percent of the speed of light after traveling 2.0 mm, what is the strength of the electric field?`
  b. What speed does the electron have after traveling 4.0 mm from rest?

ALTERNATIVE ASSESSMENT

1. A metal can is placed on a wooden table. If a positively charged ball suspended by a thread is brought close to the can, the ball will swing toward the can, make contact, and move away. Hypothesize about why this happens, and predict whether the ball is likely to make contact a second time. Sketch diagrams showing the charges on the ball and on the can at each phase. How can you test whether your hypothesis is correct? If your teacher approves of your plan, try testing your explanation.

2. The common copying machine was designed in the 1960s, after the American inventor Chester Carlson developed a practical device for attracting carbon-black to paper using localized electrostatic action. Research how this process works, and determine why the last copy made when several hundred copies are made can be noticeably less sharp than the first copy. Create a report, poster, or brochure for office workers containing tips for using copiers.

3. The *triboelectric series* is an ordered list of materials that can be charged by friction. Use the Internet to find a copy of the triboelectric series and to learn about how it works. Design a series of demonstrations to illustrate charging by friction, and use the triboelectric series to determine the resulting charges for each material. Select a sample of the materials spread across the series, and indicate whether each material is an insulator or a conductor. Is a material's position in the triboelectric series related to its conductivity? If your teacher approves of your plan, conduct your demonstrations for the class. Explain to the class how the triboelectric series works, and discuss whether it is always completely accurate.

56. A DNA molecule (deoxyribonucleic acid) is 2.17 μm long. The ends of the molecule become singly ionized so that there is -1.60×10^{-19} C on one end and $+1.60 \times 10^{-19}$ C on the other. The helical molecule acts as a spring and compresses 1.00 percent upon becoming charged. Find the effective spring constant of the molecule.

4. Research how an electrostatic precipitator works to remove smoke and dust particles from the polluting emissions of fuel-burning industries. Find out what industries use precipitators. What are their advantages and costs? What alternatives are available? Summarize your findings in a brochure.

5. Imagine you are a member of a research team interested in lightning and you are preparing a grant proposal. Research information about the frequency, location, and effects of thunderstorms. Write a proposal that includes background information, research questions, a description of necessary equipment, and recommended locations for data collection.

6. Electric force is also known as the *Coulomb force*. Research the historical development of the concept of electric force. Describe the work of Coulomb and other scientists such as Priestley, Cavendish, and Faraday.

7. Benjamin Franklin (1706–1790) first suggested the terms *positive* and *negative* for the two different types of electric charge. Franklin was the first person to realize that lightning is a huge electric discharge. He demonstrated this with a dangerous experiment in which he used a kite to gather charges during a thunderstorm. Franklin also invented the first lightning rod. Conduct research to find out more about one of these discoveries or about another one of Franklin's famous inventions. Create a poster showing how the invention works or how the discovery was made.

Standards-Based Assessment

Record your answers on a separate piece of paper.

MULTIPLE CHOICE

1 In which way is the electric force similar to the gravitational force?

A Electric force is proportional to the mass of the object.

B Electric force is similar in strength to gravitational force.

C Electric force is both attractive and repulsive.

D Electric force decreases in strength as the distance between the charges increases.

2 What must the charges be for A and B in the figure below so that they produce the electric field lines shown below?

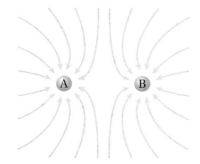

A A and B must both be positive.

B A and B must both be negative.

C A must be negative, and B must be positive.

D A must be positive, and B must be negative.

3 By how much does the electric force between two charges change when the distance between them is doubled?

A 4   **C** $\frac{1}{2}$

B 2   **D** $\frac{1}{4}$

4 A negatively charged object is brought close to the surface of a conductor, whose opposite side is then grounded. What is this process of charging called?

A charging by contact

B charging by induction

C charging by conduction

D charging by polarization

5 Which of the following is an example of an electric force?

A plastic wrap sticks to a glass bowl containing leftovers

B a frozen dinner is heated in a microwave oven

C a diver falls into the water while executing a swan dive

D a compass needle swings around to point north

6 A student is given a small object that is hanging from a ring stand on a nylon thread. The student attempts to charge the object electrically in several ways. Based upon his results, he concludes the object is made of an insulating material. Which set of results must he have collected?

A The object could be charged only by contact.

B The object could be charged by either contact or induction.

C The object could be charged by either contact or polarization.

D The object could be charged only by polarization.

GRIDDED RESPONSE

7 Three identical charges ($q = +5.0$ mC) are along a circle with a radius of 2.0 m at angles of 30°, 150°, and 270°, as shown in the figure below.

What is the resultant electric field at the center in N/C?

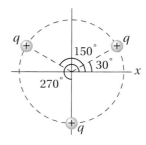

A BOOK EXPLAINING COMPLEX IDEAS USING ONLY THE 1,000 MOST COMMON WORDS

FOOD-HEATING RADIO BOX

Waves that make pieces of water move faster

You know that microwaves are a high-frequency form of electromagnetic radiation. How does a microwave oven cook food faster and more efficiently than other types of ovens? Here's a look at what makes microwaves so useful.

RANDALL MUNROE
XKCD.COM

THE STORY OF HEATING FOOD WITH RADIO WAVES

THESE BOXES USE RADIO WAVES TO HEAT FOOD.

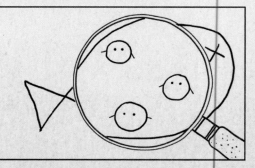

RADIO WAVES PUSH ON THE TINY PIECES WATER IS MADE OF AND MAKE THEM GO FASTER.

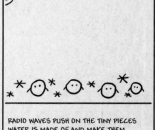

WHEN TINY PIECES IN SOMETHING MOVE FASTER, THAT THING GETS HOTTER. IF YOU SEND ENOUGH RADIO WAVES THROUGH WATER, THE WATER HEATS UP.

FOOD-HEATING RADIO BOXES CAN HEAT UP COLD FOOD YOU SAVED, AND LET YOU BUY FOOD THAT'S FULL OF ICE, KEEP IT FOR A LONG TIME, AND THEN HEAT IT AND GET RID OF THE ICE.

MINE DOESN'T LOOK GOOD...

THESE BOXES MADE IT MUCH EASIER FOR PEOPLE TO EAT WITHOUT SPENDING A LONG TIME MAKING THEIR FOOD.

GREAT... NOW WHAT DO I DO WITH THE OTHER TEN HUNDRED OR SO MINUTES?

YOU CAN ALSO USE A RADIO BOX TO TAKE FRESH FOOD (LIKE FISH) AND HEAT IT UP AND TURN IT INTO DIFFERENT KINDS OF FOOD, JUST LIKE YOU DO WITH THE OTHER HEATING BOXES IN YOUR KITCHEN.

BUT IT CAN BE HARD TO USE FOR THAT, SO BE CAREFUL, ESPECIALLY WITH FOOD MADE FROM ANIMALS.

OK, WHO HEATED UP THE FISH IN THE FOOD-HEATING RADIO BOX??

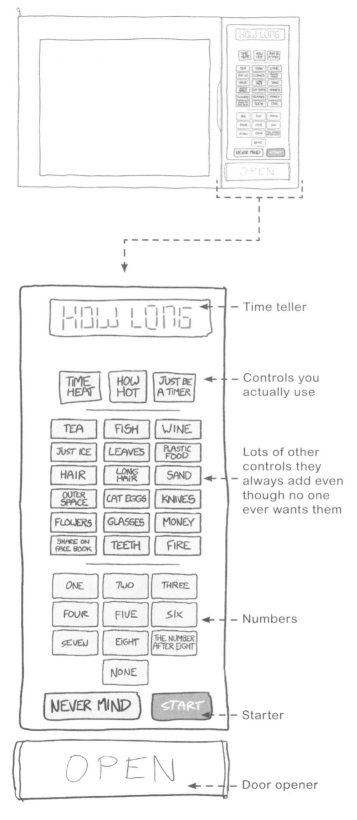

— Time teller

— Controls you
  actually use

Lots of other
controls they
— always add even
though no one
ever wants them

— Numbers

— Starter

— Door opener

RADIO

These radio boxes use exactly the same size of wave as the computer "hot spots" in your house. Different kinds of radio machines use different sizes of waves, but these two use the same size. There's a reason for that.

At the same time food-heating radio boxes started being used a lot, people were building more and more radios to send messages. Countries decided to leave the wave size used by radio boxes (about hand-sized) open for anyone to use, since radio boxes everywhere were already using it. When people started making computer radios, they used that size, since it was one of the few sizes of wave that anyone was allowed to use at home.

Now, the whole world sends messages from their computers using the food-heating radio box wave size. It works fine—the only problem is that if there's a hole in your radio box, it can make the movie on your computer stop for a moment while you make food.

COMPUTER
"HOT SPOTS"

WHY IS THERE ICE IN HOT FOOD?

Radio boxes are good at heating water but bad at heating ice. They *can* heat ice, but it takes a long time.

When you put iced food in a radio box, after a while, parts of it start to turn to water. But since radio boxes are really good at heating water, those parts start to get hot really fast. They can even get so hot they start turning to air—before all the ice is even gone!

To get around this problem, you can run the radio box on low power, which will heat the food with lots of pauses in between. That gives time for the hot parts to spread out, and no one spot will get too warm.

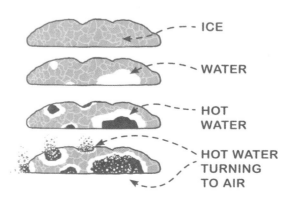

- - - ICE

- - - WATER

- - - HOT
      WATER

- - - HOT WATER
      TURNING
      TO AIR

FOOD-HEATING RADIO BOX

RADIO WAVE STOPPER
This stuff, which you see if you look inside the door, stops radio waves from getting out. They can't really hurt you—other than by slowly warming you up—but they could hurt other radios or make little flashes of light.

SPINNER
This spinner waves a metal stick to change the shape of the radio waves so the warm spots, which are places where the waves are strong, move around a little.

RADIO HALLWAY
This hallway carries the radio waves into the food box.

LIGHT

RADIO WAVES
The shapes they make are why food gets hot and cold spots.

REAL SIZE
This is about how big food radio waves are

This spinner turns the plate to try to give each piece of food some time in the hot areas.

FOOD PLATE

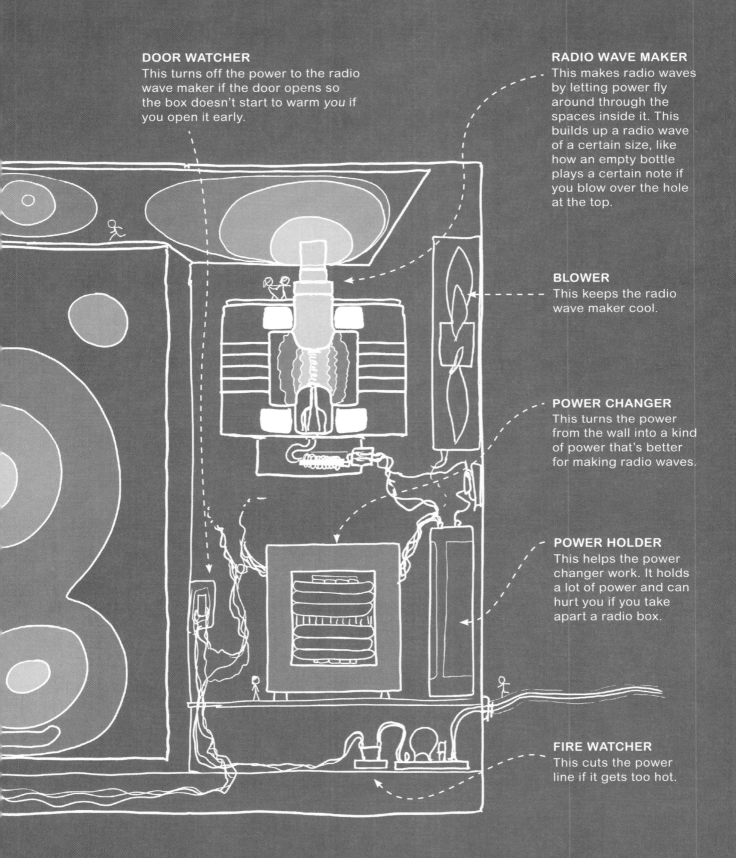

DOOR WATCHER
This turns off the power to the radio wave maker if the door opens so the box doesn't start to warm *you* if you open it early.

RADIO WAVE MAKER
This makes radio waves by letting power fly around through the spaces inside it. This builds up a radio wave of a certain size, like how an empty bottle plays a certain note if you blow over the hole at the top.

BLOWER
This keeps the radio wave maker cool.

POWER CHANGER
This turns the power from the wall into a kind of power that's better for making radio waves.

POWER HOLDER
This helps the power changer work. It holds a lot of power and can hurt you if you take apart a radio box.

FIRE WATCHER
This cuts the power line if it gets too hot.

The use of electrical energy is universal in modern society. An understanding of electrical energy can help us use electric power more wisely.

Not all electrical energy transfers are under our control. During a thunderstorm, different charges accumulate in different parts of a cloud to create an electric field between the cloud and the ground. Eventually, a critical *breakdown voltage* is reached. At this point, the molecules in the air are broken down into charged particles, forming a state of matter called a *plasma*. Because a plasma conducts electricity, an electric charge flows between the cloud and the ground; this is known as lightning.

CHAPTER 17

Electrical Energy and Current

SECTION 1
Electric Potential

SECTION 2
Capacitance

SECTION 3
Current and Resistance

SECTION 4
Electric Power

BIG IDEA

Electrical energy is the energy associated with charged particles. Current, the flow of electric charge, transfers electrical energy from one location to another.

 ONLINE Physics
HMHScience.com

ONLINE LABS
- Resistors and Current
- Current and Resistance
- S.T.E.M. Lab Battery-Operated Portable Heater

GO ONLINE
Animated
Physics
HMHScience.com

Ohm's Law

581

©Photodisc/Getty Images

Objectives

▶ Distinguish between electrical potential energy, electric potential, and potential difference.

▶ Solve problems involving electrical energy and potential difference.

▶ Describe the energy conversions that occur in a battery.

Electric Potential

Key Terms

electrical potential energy   electric potential   potential difference

Electrical Potential Energy

You have learned that when two charges interact, there is an electric force between them. As with the gravitational force associated with an object's position relative to Earth, there is a potential energy associated with the electric force. This kind of potential energy is called **electrical potential energy.** Unlike gravitational potential energy, electrical potential energy results from the interaction of two objects' charges, not their masses.

Electrical potential energy is a component of mechanical energy.

Mechanical energy is conserved as long as friction and radiation are not present. As with gravitational and elastic potential energy, electrical potential energy can be included in the expression for mechanical energy. If a gravitational force, an elastic force, and an electric force are all acting on an object, the mechanical energy can be written as follows:

$$ME = KE + PE_{grav} + PE_{elastic} + PE_{electric}$$

electrical potential energy potential energy associated with a charge due to its position in an electric field

FIGURE 1.1

Tesla Coil
As the charges in these sparks move, the electrical potential energy decreases, just as gravitational potential energy decreases as an object falls.

To account for the forces (except friction) that may also be present in a problem, the appropriate potential-energy terms associated with each force are added to the expression for mechanical energy.

Recall from your study of work and energy that any time a force is used to move an object, work is done on that object. This statement is also true for charges moved by an electric force. Whenever a charge moves—because of the electric field produced by another charge or group of charges—work is done on that charge.

For example, negative electric charges build up on the plate in the center of the device, called a *Tesla coil,* shown in **Figure 1.1.** The electrical potential energy associated with each charge decreases as the charge moves from the central plate to the walls (and through the walls to the ground).

©Arthur S. Aubry/Photodisc/Getty Images

Electrical potential energy can be associated with a charge in a uniform field.

Consider a positive charge in a uniform electric field. (A uniform field is a field that has the same value and direction at all points.) Assume the charge is displaced at a constant velocity *in the same direction as the electric field,* as shown in **Figure 1.2.**

There is a change in the electrical potential energy associated with the charge's new position in the electric field. The change in the electrical potential energy depends on the charge, q, as well as the strength of the electric field, E, and the displacement, d. It can be written as follows:

$$\Delta PE_{electric} = -qEd$$

The negative sign indicates that the electrical potential energy will increase if the charge is negative and decrease if the charge is positive.

As with other forms of potential energy, it is the *difference* in electrical potential energy that is physically important. If the displacement in the expression above is chosen so that it is the distance in the direction of the field from the reference point, or zero level, then the initial electrical potential energy is zero and the expression can be rewritten as shown below. As with other forms of energy, the SI unit for electrical potential energy is the joule (J).

> **Electrical Potential Energy in a Uniform Electric Field**
>
> $$PE_{electric} = -qEd$$
>
> **electrical potential energy =**
> **−(charge × electric field strength × displacement from the**
> **reference point in the direction of the field)**

This equation is valid only for a uniform electric field, such as that between two oppositely charged parallel plates. In contrast, the electric field lines for a point charge are farther apart as the distance from the charge increases. Thus, the electric field of a point charge is an example of a nonuniform electric field.

Electrical potential energy is similar to gravitational potential energy.

When electrical potential energy is calculated, d is the magnitude of the displacement's component *in the direction of the electric field.* The electric field does work on a positive charge by moving the charge in the direction of **E** (just as Earth's gravitational field does work on a mass by moving the mass toward Earth). After such a movement, the system's final potential energy is less than its initial potential energy. A negative charge behaves in the opposite manner, because a negative charge undergoes a force in the direction opposite **E**. Moving a charge in a direction that is perpendicular to **E** is analogous to moving an object horizontally in a gravitational field: no work is done, and the potential energy of the system remains constant.

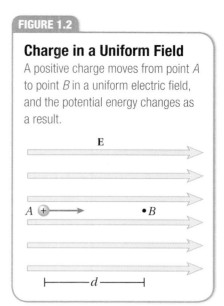

FIGURE 1.2

Charge in a Uniform Field
A positive charge moves from point *A* to point *B* in a uniform electric field, and the potential energy changes as a result.

Potential Difference

The concept of electrical potential energy is useful in solving problems, particularly those involving charged particles. But at any point in an electric field, as the magnitude of the charge increases, the magnitude of the associated electrical potential energy increases. It is more convenient to express the potential in a manner independent of the charge at that point, a concept called **electric potential.**

The electric potential V at some point is defined as the electrical potential energy associated with a charged particle in an electric field divided by the charge of the particle.

$$V = \frac{PE_{electric}}{q}$$

The electric potential at a point is the result of the electric fields due to all *other* charges near enough and large enough to contribute force on a charge at that point. In other words, the electric potential at a point *is independent of the charge at that point.* The force that a test charge at the point in question experiences is proportional to the magnitude of the charge.

electric potential the work that must be performed against electric forces to move a charge from a reference point to the point in question, divided by the charge

Potential difference is a change in electric potential.

The **potential difference** between two points in an electric field can be expressed as follows:

potential difference the work that must be performed against electric forces to move a charge between the two points in question, divided by the charge

> **Potential Difference**
>
> $$\Delta V = \frac{\Delta PE_{electric}}{q}$$
>
> $$\text{potential difference} = \frac{\text{change in electrical potential energy}}{\text{electric charge}}$$

FIGURE 1.3

Car Battery For a typical car battery, there is a potential difference of 13.2 V between the negative (black) and the positive (red) terminals.

Potential difference is a measure of the difference in the electrical potential energy between two positions in space divided by the charge. The SI unit for potential difference (and for electric potential) is the *volt,* V, and is equivalent to one joule per coulomb. As a 1 C charge moves through a potential difference of 1 V, the charge gains 1 J of energy. The potential difference between the two terminals of a battery can range from about 1.5 V for a small battery to about 13.2 V for a car battery like the one the student is looking at in **Figure 1.3.**

Because the reference point for measuring electrical potential energy is arbitrary, the reference point for measuring electric potential is also arbitrary. Thus, only changes in electric potential are significant.

Remember that electrical potential energy is a quantity of energy, with units in joules. However, electric potential and potential difference are both measures of energy per unit charge (measured in units of volts), and potential difference describes a change in energy per unit charge.

The potential difference in a uniform field varies with the displacement from a reference point.

The expression for potential difference can be combined with the expressions for electrical potential energy. The resulting equations are often simpler to apply in certain situations. For example, consider the electrical potential energy of a charge in a uniform electric field.

$$PE_{electric} = -qEd$$

This expression can be substituted into the equation for potential difference.

$$\Delta V = \frac{\Delta(-qEd)}{q}$$

As the charge moves in a uniform electric field, the quantity in the parentheses does not change from the reference point. Thus, the potential difference in this case can be rewritten as follows:

> **Potential Difference in a Uniform Electric Field**
>
> $$\Delta V = -Ed$$
>
> **potential difference =**
> **−(magnitude of the electric field × displacement)**

Keep in mind that d is the displacement *parallel* to the field and that motion perpendicular to the field does not change the electrical potential energy.

The reference point for potential difference near a point charge is often at infinity.

To determine the potential difference between two points in the field of a point charge, first calculate the electric potential associated with each point charge. Imagine a point charge q_2 at point A in the electric field of a point charge q_1 at point B some distance, r, away as shown in **Figure 1.4**. The electric potential at point A due to q_1 can be expressed as follows:

$$V_A = \frac{PE_{electric}}{q_2}$$

$$= k_C \frac{q_1 q_2}{r q_2}$$

$$= k_C \frac{q_1}{r}$$

Do not confuse the two charges in this example. The charge q_1 is responsible for the electric potential at point A. Therefore, *an electric potential exists at some point in an electric field regardless of whether there is a charge at that point.* In this case, the electric potential at a point depends on only two quantities: the charge responsible for the electric potential (in this case, q_1) and the distance, r, from this charge to the point in question.

FIGURE 1.4

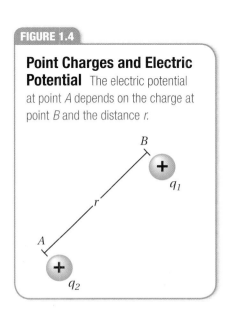

Point Charges and Electric Potential The electric potential at point A depends on the charge at point B and the distance r.

To determine the potential difference between any two points near the point charge q_1, first note that the electric potential at each point depends only on the distance from each point to the charge q_1. If the two distances are r_1 and r_2, then the potential difference between these two points can be written as follows:

$$\Delta V = k_C \frac{q_1}{r_2} - k_C \frac{q_1}{r_1} = k_C q_1 \left(\frac{1}{r_2} - \frac{1}{r_1} \right)$$

If the distance r_1 between the point and q_1 is large enough, it is assumed to be infinitely far from the charge q_1. In that case, the quantity $1/r_1$ is zero. The expression then simplifies to the following (dropping the subscripts):

This result for the potential difference associated with a point charge appears identical to the electric potential associated with a point charge. The two expressions look the same only because we have chosen a special reference point from which to measure the potential difference.

One common application of the concept of potential difference is in the operation of electric circuits. Recall that the reference point for determining the electric potential at some point is arbitrary and must be defined. Earth is frequently designated to have an electric potential of zero and makes a convenient reference point. Thus, *grounding* an electrical device (connecting it to Earth) creates a possible reference point, which is commonly used to measure the electric potential in an electric circuit.

The superposition principle can be used to calculate the electric potential for a group of charges.

The electric potential at a point near two or more charges is obtained by applying a rule called the *superposition principle.* This rule states that the total electric potential at some point near several point charges is the algebraic sum of the electric potentials resulting from each of the individual charges. While this is similar to the method used previously to find the resultant electric field at a point in space, here the summation is much easier to evaluate because the electric potentials are scalar quantities, not vector quantities. There are no vector components to consider.

To evaluate the electric potential at a point near a group of point charges, you simply take the algebraic sum of the potentials resulting from all charges. Remember that you must keep track of signs. The electric potential at some point near a positive charge is positive, and the potential near a negative charge is negative.

Potential Energy and Potential Difference

GO ONLINE

Interactive Demo
HMHScience.com

Sample Problem A A charged oil droplet gains 1.9×10^{-19} J of electrical potential energy while moving 3.0 cm in a uniform electric field. What is the charge on the droplet if the strength of the electric field is 2.0×10^4 N/C?

① ANALYZE

Given: $\Delta PE_{electric} = 1.9 \times 10^{-19}$ J

$d = 3.0 \text{ cm} = 3.0 \times 10^{-2}$ m

$E = 2.0 \times 10^4$ N/C

Unknown: $q = ?$

② SOLVE

Use the equation for the change in electrical potential energy.

$$\Delta PE_{electric} = -qEd$$

Rearrange to solve for q, and insert values.

$$q = -\frac{\Delta PE_{electric}}{Ed}$$

$$q = -\frac{(1.9 \times 10^{-19} \text{ J})}{(2.0 \times 10^4 \text{ N/C})(3.0 \times 10^{-2} \text{ m})}$$

$$\boxed{q = -3.2 \times 10^{-19} \text{ C}}$$

Practice

1. What would be the charge on the droplet in the Sample Problem above if the increase in electrical potential energy was 4.8×10^{-16} J?

2. Two charged plates separated by 15 cm create a uniform electric field of 360 N/C. What is the potential difference between the plates?

3. An electron moves 4.5 m in the direction of an electric field of strength 325 N/C. Determine the change in electrical potential energy associated with the electron.

A battery does work to move charges.

A good illustration of the concepts of electric potential and potential difference is the way in which a battery powers an electrical device, such as a flashlight, a motor, or a clock. A battery is an energy-storage device that provides a constant potential difference between two locations, called *terminals,* inside the battery.

Recall that the reference point for determining the electric potential at a location is arbitrary. For example, consider a typical 1.5 V alkaline battery. This type of battery maintains a potential difference across its terminals such that the positive terminal has an electric potential that is 1.5 V higher than the electric potential of the negative terminal. If we designate that the negative terminal of the battery is at zero potential, the positive terminal would have a potential of 1.5 V. We could just as correctly choose the potential of the negative terminal to be −0.75 V and the positive terminal to be +0.75 V. The potential difference is still 1.5 V.

Inside a battery, a chemical reaction produces electrons (negative charges) that collect on the negative terminal of the battery. Negative charges move inside the battery from the positive terminal to the negative terminal, through a potential difference of $\Delta V = -1.5$ V. The chemical reaction inside the battery does work on—that is, provides energy to—the charges when moving them from the positive terminal to the negative terminal. This transit increases the magnitude of the electrical potential energy associated with the charges. The result of this motion is that every coulomb of charge that leaves the positive terminal of the battery is associated with a total of 1.5 J of electrical potential energy.

Now, consider the movement of electrons in an electrical device that is connected to a battery. As 1 C of charge moves through the device toward the positive terminal of the battery, the charge gives up its 1.5 J of electrical energy to the device. When the charge reaches the positive terminal, the charge's electrical potential energy is again zero. Electrons must travel to the positive terminal for the chemical reaction in a battery to occur. For this reason, a battery can be unused for a period of time and still have power available.

*Quick*LAB — A VOLTAIC PILE

Dissolve as much salt as possible in the water. Soak the paper towel in the saltwater, and then tear it into small circles that are slightly bigger than a nickel. Make a stack alternating one penny, a piece of paper towel, and then one nickel. Repeat this stack by placing the second penny on top of the first nickel. Measure the voltage between the first penny and the last nickel by placing the leads of the voltmeter at each end of the stack. Be sure to have your voltmeter on the lowest dc voltage setting. Try stacking additional layers of penny, paper towel, and nickel, and measure the voltage again. What happens if you replace the nickels or pennies with dimes or quarters?

MATERIALS
- salt
- water
- paper towel
- pennies
- nickels
- voltmeter (1 V range)

▶ **Reviewing Main Ideas**

1. What is the difference between $\Delta PE_{electric}$ and $PE_{electric}$?

2. In a uniform electric field, what factors does the electrical potential energy depend on?

3. Describe the conditions that are necessary for mechanical energy to be a conserved quantity.

4. Is there a single correct reference point from which all electrical potential energy measurements must be taken?

5. A uniform electric field with a magnitude of 250 N/C is directed in the positive x direction. A 12 μC charge moves from the origin to the point (20.0 cm, 50.0 cm). What is the change in the electrical potential energy of the system as a result of the change in position of this charge?

6. What is the change in the electrical potential energy in a lightning bolt if 35 C of charge travels to the ground from a cloud 2.0 km above the ground in the direction of the field? Assume the electric field is uniform and has a magnitude of 1.0×10^6 N/C.

7. The gap between electrodes in a spark plug is 0.060 cm. Producing an electric spark in a gasoline-air mixture requires an electric field of 3.0×10^6 V/m. What minimum potential difference must be supplied by the ignition circuit to start a car?

8. A proton is released from rest in a uniform electric field with a magnitude of 8.0×10^4 V/m. The proton is displaced 0.50 m as a result.
   a. Find the potential difference between the proton's initial and final positions.
   b. Find the change in electrical potential energy of the proton as a result of this displacement.

9. In a thunderstorm, the air must be ionized by a high voltage before a conducting path for a lightning bolt can be created. An electric field of about 1.0×10^6 V/m is required to ionize dry air. What would the breakdown voltage in air be if a thundercloud were 1.60 km above ground? Assume that the electric field between the cloud and the ground is uniform.

10. Explain how electric potential and potential difference are related. What units are used for each one?

✓ **Critical Thinking**

11. Given the electrical potential energy, how do you calculate electric potential?

12. Why is electric potential a more useful quantity for most calculations than electrical potential energy is?

Objectives

▶ Relate capacitance to the storage of electrical potential energy in the form of separated charges.

▶ Calculate the capacitance of various devices.

▶ Calculate the energy stored in a capacitor.

Capacitance

Key Term

capacitance

Capacitors and Charge Storage

A *capacitor* is a device that is used to store electrical potential energy. It has many uses, including tuning the frequency of radio receivers, eliminating sparking in automobile ignition systems, and storing energy in electronic flash units.

An *energized* (or charged) capacitor is useful because energy can be reclaimed from the capacitor when needed for a specific application. A simple design for a capacitor consists of two parallel metal plates separated by a small distance. This type of capacitor is called a *parallel-plate capacitor.* When we speak of *the charge on a capacitor,* we mean the magnitude of the charge on either plate.

The capacitor is energized by connecting the plates to the two terminals of a battery or other sources of potential difference, as **Figure 2.1** shows. When this connection is made, charges are removed from one of the plates, leaving the plate with a net charge. An equal and opposite amount of charge accumulates on the other plate. Charge transfer between the plates stops when the potential difference between the plates is equal to the potential difference between the terminals of the battery. This charging process is shown in **Figure 2.1(b).**

FIGURE 2.1

Charging a Capacitor When connected to a battery, the plates of a parallel-plate capacitor become oppositely charged.

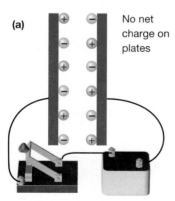

(a) No net charge on plates

Before charging

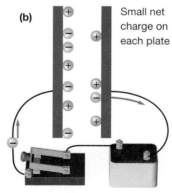

(b) Small net charge on each plate

During charging

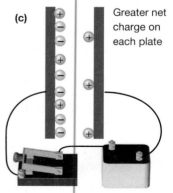

(c) Greater net charge on each plate

After charging

Capacitance is the ratio of charge to potential difference.

The ability of a conductor to store energy in the form of electrically separated charges is measured by the **capacitance** of the conductor. Capacitance is defined as the ratio of the net charge on each plate to the potential difference created by the separated charges.

Capacitance

$$C = \frac{Q}{\Delta V}$$

$$\text{capacitance} = \frac{\text{magnitude of charge on each plate}}{\text{potential difference}}$$

The SI unit for capacitance is the *farad,* F, which is equivalent to a coulomb per volt (C/V). In practice, most typical capacitors have capacitances ranging from microfarads ($1\ \mu F = 1 \times 10^{-6}$ F) to picofarads ($1\ pF = 1 \times 10^{-12}$ F).

Capacitance depends on the size and shape of the capacitor.

The capacitance of a parallel-plate capacitor with no material between its plates is given by the following expression:

Capacitance for a Parallel-Plate Capacitor in a Vacuum

$$C = \varepsilon_0 \frac{A}{d}$$

$$\text{capacitance} = \text{permittivity of a vacuum} \times \frac{\text{area of one of the plates}}{\text{distance between the plates}}$$

In this expression, the Greek letter ε (*epsilon*) represents a constant called the *permittivity* of the medium. When it is followed by a subscripted zero, it refers to a vacuum. It has a magnitude of 8.85×10^{-12} C^2/N•m^2.

We can combine the two equations for capacitance to find an expression for the charge stored on a parallel-plate capacitor.

$$Q = \frac{\varepsilon_0 A}{d} \Delta V$$

This equation tells us that for a given potential difference, ΔV, the charge on a plate is proportional to the area of the plates and inversely proportional to the separation of the plates.

Suppose an isolated conducting sphere has a radius R and a charge Q. The potential difference between the surface of the sphere and infinity is the same as it would be for an equal point charge at the center of the sphere.

$$\Delta V = k_C \frac{Q}{R}$$

Substituting this expression into the definition of capacitance results in the following expression:

$$C_{sphere} = \frac{Q}{\Delta V} = \frac{R}{k_C}$$

This equation indicates that the capacitance of a sphere increases as the size of the sphere increases. Because Earth is so large, it has an extremely large capacitance. Thus, Earth can provide or accept a large amount of charge without its electric potential changing too much. This is the reason that Earth is often used as a reference point for measuring potential differences in electric circuits.

The material between a capacitor's plates can change its capacitance.

So far, we have assumed that the space between the plates of a parallel-plate capacitor is a vacuum. However, in many parallel-plate capacitors, the space is filled with a material called a *dielectric*. A dielectric is an insulating material, such as air, rubber, glass, or waxed paper. When a dielectric is inserted between the plates of a capacitor, the capacitance increases. The capacitance increases because the molecules in a dielectric can align with the applied electric field, causing an excess negative charge near the surface of the dielectric at the positive plate and an excess positive charge near the surface of the dielectric at the negative plate. The surface charge on the dielectric effectively reduces the charge on the capacitor plates, as shown in **Figure 2.2**. Thus, the plates can store more charge for a given potential difference. According to the expression $Q = C\Delta V$, if the charge increases and the potential difference is constant, the capacitance must increase. A capacitor with a dielectric can store more charge and energy for a given potential difference than can the same capacitor without a dielectric. In this book, problems will assume that capacitors are in a vacuum, with no dielectrics.

Discharging a capacitor releases its charge.

Once a capacitor is charged, the battery or other source of potential difference that charged it can be removed from the circuit. The two plates of the capacitor will remain charged unless they are connected with a material that conducts. Once the plates are connected, the capacitor will *discharge*. This process is the opposite of charging. The charges move back from one plate to another until both plates are uncharged again, because this is the state of lowest potential energy.

FIGURE 2.2

A Capacitor with a Dielectric
The effect of a dielectric is to reduce the strength of the electric field in a capacitor.

Conceptual Challenge

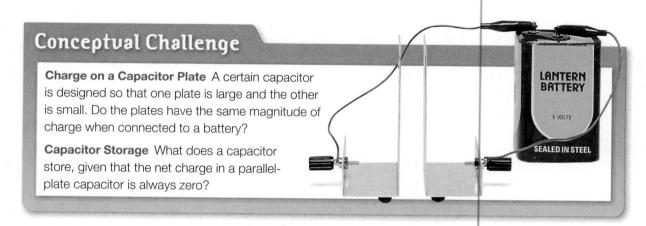

Charge on a Capacitor Plate A certain capacitor is designed so that one plate is large and the other is small. Do the plates have the same magnitude of charge when connected to a battery?

Capacitor Storage What does a capacitor store, given that the net charge in a parallel-plate capacitor is always zero?

One device that uses a capacitor is the flash attachment of a camera. A battery is used to charge the capacitor, and this stored charge is then released when the shutter-release button is pressed to take a picture. One advantage of using a discharging capacitor instead of a battery to power a flash is that with a capacitor, the stored charge can be delivered to a flash tube much faster, illuminating the subject at the instant more light is needed.

Computers make use of capacitors in many ways. For example, one type of computer keyboard has capacitors at the base of its keys, as shown in **Figure 2.3.** Each key is connected to a movable plate, which represents one side of the capacitor. The fixed plate on the bottom of the keyboard represents the other side of the capacitor. When a key is pressed, the capacitor spacing decreases, causing an increase in capacitance. External electronic circuits recognize that a key has been pressed when its capacitance changes.

Because the capacitance between plates is easily measurable and changes depending on the distance and material between them, capacitors are ideal for use as sensors.

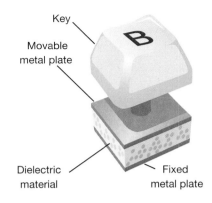

FIGURE 2.3

Capacitors in Keyboards

A parallel-plate capacitor is often used in keyboards.

Key

Movable metal plate

Dielectric material

Fixed metal plate

Energy and Capacitors

A charged capacitor stores electrical potential energy because it requires work to move charges through a circuit to the opposite plates of a capacitor. The work done on these charges is a measure of the transfer of energy.

For example, if a capacitor is initially uncharged so that the plates are at the same electric potential, that is, if both plates are neutral, then almost no work is required to transfer a small amount of charge from one plate to the other. However, once a charge has been transferred, a small potential difference appears between the plates. As additional charge is transferred through this potential difference, the electrical potential energy of the system increases. This increase in energy is the result of work done on the charge. The electrical potential energy stored in a capacitor that is charged from zero to some charge, Q, is given by the following expression:

Electrical Potential Energy Stored in a Charged Capacitor

$$PE_{electric} = \tfrac{1}{2}Q\Delta V$$

electrical potential energy $= \tfrac{1}{2}$ (charge on one plate) (final potential difference)

Note that this equation is also an expression for the work required to charge the capacitor.

FIGURE 2.4

Electrical Breakdown The markings caused by electrical breakdown in this material look similar to the lightning bolts produced when air undergoes electrical breakdown to form a plasma of charged particles.

By substituting the definition of capacitance ($C = Q/\Delta V$), we can see that these alternative forms are also valid:

$$PE_{electric} = \tfrac{1}{2}C(\Delta V)^2$$

$$PE_{electric} = \frac{Q^2}{2C}$$

These results apply to any capacitor. In practice, there is a limit to the maximum energy (or charge) that can be stored, because electrical breakdown ultimately occurs between the plates of the capacitor for a sufficiently large potential difference. So capacitors are usually labeled with a maximum operating potential difference. Electrical breakdown in a capacitor is like a lightning discharge in the atmosphere. **Figure 2.4** shows a pattern created in a block of plastic resin that has undergone electrical breakdown. This book's problems assume that all potential differences are below the maximum.

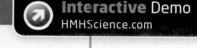

GO ONLINE

Interactive Demo
HMHScience.com

Capacitance

Sample Problem B A capacitor, connected to a 12 V battery, holds 36 μC of charge on each plate. What is the capacitance of the capacitor? How much electrical potential energy is stored in the capacitor?

1 ANALYZE

Given: $Q = 36 \ \mu C = 3.6 \times 10^{-5} \ C$ $\Delta V = 12 \ V$

Unknown: $C = ?$ $PE_{electric} = ?$

2 SOLVE

To determine the capacitance, use the definition of capacitance.

$$C = \frac{Q}{\Delta V} = \frac{3.6 \times 10^{-5} \ C}{12 \ V}$$

$$\boxed{C = 3.0 \times 10^{-6} \ F = 3.0 \ \mu F}$$

To determine the electrical potential energy, use the alternative form of the equation for the potential energy stored in the charged capacitor:

$$PE_{electric} = \tfrac{1}{2}C(\Delta V)^2$$

$$PE_{electric} = (0.5)(3.0 \times 10^{-6} \ F)(12 \ V)^2$$

$$\boxed{PE_{electric} = 2.2 \times 10^{-4} \ J}$$

Continued

Capacitance (continued)

Practice

1. A 4.00 μF capacitor is connected to a 12.0 V battery.

   a. What is the charge on each plate of the capacitor?

   b. If this same capacitor is connected to a 1.50 V battery, how much electrical potential energy is stored?

2. A parallel-plate capacitor has a charge of 6.0 μC when charged by a potential difference of 1.25 V.

   a. Find its capacitance.

   b. How much electrical potential energy is stored when this capacitor is connected to a 1.50 V battery?

3. A capacitor has a capacitance of 2.00 pF.

   a. What potential difference would be required to store 18.0 pC?

   b. How much charge is stored when the potential difference is 2.5 V?

4. You are asked to design a parallel-plate capacitor having a capacitance of 1.00 F and a plate separation of 1.00 mm. Calculate the required surface area of each plate. Is this a realistic size for a capacitor?

SECTION 2 FORMATIVE ASSESSMENT

▶ Reviewing Main Ideas

1. Assume Earth and a cloud layer 800.0 m above Earth can be treated as plates of a parallel-plate capacitor.
   a. If the cloud layer has an area of $1.00 \times 10^6 \text{ m}^2$, what is the capacitance?
   b. If an electric field strength of 2.0×10^6 N/C causes the air to conduct charge (lightning), what charge can the cloud hold?
   c. Describe what must happen to its molecules for air to conduct electricity.

2. A parallel-plate capacitor has an area of 2.0 cm², and the plates are separated by 2.0 mm.
   a. What is the capacitance?
   b. How much charge does this capacitor store when connected to a 6.0 V battery?

3. A parallel-plate capacitor has a capacitance of 1.35 pF. If a 12.0 V battery is connected to this capacitor, how much electrical potential energy would it store?

✔ Critical Thinking

4. Explain why two metal plates near each other will not become charged until connected to a source of potential difference.

SC.912.P.10.15 Investigate and explain the relationships among current, voltage, resistance, and power.

electric current the rate at which electric charges pass through a given area

Current The current in this wire is defined as the rate at which electric charges pass through a cross-sectional area of the wire.

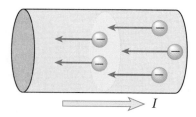

Current and Resistance

Key Terms

electric current   drift velocity   resistance

Current and Charge Movement

Although many practical applications and devices are based on the principles of static electricity, electricity did not become an integral part of our daily lives until scientists learned to control the movement of electric charge, known as *current*. Electric currents power our lights, radios, television sets, air conditioners, and refrigerators. Currents also are used in automobile engines, travel through miniature components that make up the chips of computers, and perform countless other invaluable tasks.

Electric currents are even part of the human body. This connection between physics and biology was discovered by Luigi Galvani (1737–1798). While conducting electrical experiments near a frog he had recently dissected, Galvani noticed that electrical sparks caused the frog's legs to twitch and even convulse. After further research, Galvani concluded that electricity was present in the frog. Today, we know that electric currents are responsible for transmitting messages between body muscles and the brain. In fact, every function involving the nervous system is initiated by electrical activity.

Current is the rate of charge movement.

A current exists whenever there is a net movement of electric charge through a medium. To define *current* more precisely, suppose electrons are moving through a wire, as shown in **Figure 3.1**. The **electric current** is the rate at which these charges move through the cross section of the wire. If ΔQ is the amount of charge that passes through this area in a time interval, Δt, then the current, I, is the ratio of the amount of charge to the time interval. Note that the direction of current is *opposite* the movement of the negative charges. We will further discuss this detail later in this section.

Electric Current

$$I = \frac{\Delta Q}{\Delta t}$$

$$\text{electric current} = \frac{\text{charge passing through a given area}}{\text{time interval}}$$

The SI unit for current is the *ampere,* A. One ampere is equivalent to one coulomb of charge passing through a cross-sectional area in a time interval of one second (1 A = 1 C/s).

Current

Sample Problem C The current in a light bulb is 0.835 A. How long does it take for a total charge of 1.67 C to pass through the filament of the bulb?

1 ANALYZE

Given: $\Delta Q = 1.67 \text{ C}$

$I = 0.835 \text{ A}$

Unknown: $\Delta t = ?$

2 SOLVE

Use the definition of electric current. Rearrange to solve for the time interval.

$$I = \frac{\Delta Q}{\Delta t}$$

$$\Delta t = \frac{\Delta Q}{I}$$

$$\Delta t = \frac{1.67 \text{ C}}{0.835 \text{ A}} = \boxed{2.00 \text{ s}}$$

Practice

1. If the current in a wire of a CD player is 5.00 mA, how long would it take for 2.00 C of charge to pass through a cross-sectional area of this wire?

2. In a particular television tube, the beam current is 60.0 μA. How long does it take for 3.75×10^{14} electrons to strike the screen? (Hint: Recall that an electron has a charge of -1.60×10^{-19} C.)

3. If a metal wire carries a current of 80.0 mA, how long does it take for 3.00×10^{20} electrons to pass a given cross-sectional area of the wire?

4. The compressor on an air conditioner draws 40.0 A when it starts up. If the start-up time is 0.50 s, how much charge passes a cross-sectional area of the circuit in this time?

5. A total charge of 9.0 mC passes through a cross-sectional area of a nichrome wire in 3.5 s.

   a. What is the current in the wire?

   b. How many electrons pass through the cross-sectional area in 10.0 s?

   c. If the number of charges that pass through the cross-sectional area during the given time interval doubles, what is the resulting current?

Conventional current is defined in terms of positive charge movement.

The moving charges that make up a current can be positive, negative, or a combination of the two. In a common conductor, such as copper, current is due to the motion of negatively charged electrons, because the atomic structure of solid conductors allows many electrons to be freed from their atoms and to move freely through the material. In contrast, the protons are relatively fixed inside the nucleus of the atom. In certain particle accelerators, a current exists when positively charged protons are set in motion. In some cases—in gases and dissolved salts, for example—current is the result of positive charges moving in one direction and negative charges moving in the opposite direction.

Positive and negative charges in motion are sometimes called *charge carriers. Conventional current* is defined in terms of the flow of positive charges. Thus, negative charge carriers, such as electrons, would have a conventional current in the direction opposite their physical motion. The three possible cases of charge flow are shown in **Figure 3.2.** We will use conventional current in this book unless stated otherwise.

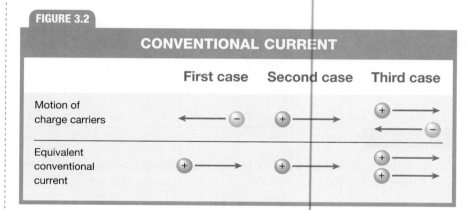

FIGURE 3.2

CONVENTIONAL CURRENT

	First case	Second case	Third case
Motion of charge carriers			
Equivalent conventional current			

As you have learned, an electric field in a material sets charges in motion. For a material to be a good conductor, charge carriers in the material must be able to move easily through the material. Many metals are good conductors because metals usually contain a large number of free electrons. Body fluids and saltwater are able to conduct electric charge because they contain charged atoms called *ions.* Because dissolved ions can move through a solution easily, they can be charge carriers. A solute that dissolves in water to give a solution that conducts electric current is called an *electrolyte.*

Drift Velocity

When you turn on a light switch, the light comes on almost immediately. For this reason, many people think that electrons flow very rapidly from the switch to the light bulb. However, this is not the case. When you turn on the switch, electron motion near the switch changes the electric field there, and the change propagates throughout the wire very quickly. Such changes travel through the wire at nearly the speed of light. The charges themselves, however, travel much more slowly.

Drift velocity is the net velocity of charge carriers.

To see how the electrons move, consider a solid conductor in which the charge carriers are free electrons. When the conductor is in electrostatic equilibrium, the electrons move randomly, similar to the movement of molecules in a gas. When a potential difference is applied across the conductor, an electric field is set up inside the conductor. The force due to that field sets the electrons in motion, thereby creating a current.

These electrons do not move in straight lines along the conductor in a direction opposite the electric field. Instead, they undergo repeated collisions with the vibrating metal atoms of the conductor. If these collisions were charted, the result would be a complicated zigzag pattern like the one shown in **Figure 3.3.** The energy transferred from the electrons to the metal atoms during the collisions increases the vibrational energy of the atoms, and the conductor's temperature increases.

The electrons gain kinetic energy as they are accelerated by the electric field in the conductor. They also lose kinetic energy because of the collisions described above. However, despite the internal collisions, the individual electrons move slowly along the conductor in a direction opposite the electric field, **E,** with a velocity known as the **drift velocity, v_{drift}.**

Drift speeds are relatively small.

The magnitudes of drift velocities, or drift speeds, are typically very small. In fact, the drift speed is much less than the average speed between collisions. For example, in a copper wire that has a current of 10.0 A, the drift speed of electrons is only 2.46×10^{-4} m/s. These electrons would take about 68 min to travel 1 m. The electric field, on the other hand, reaches electrons throughout the wire at a speed approximately equal to the speed of light.

FIGURE 3.3

Drift Velocity When an electron moves through a conductor, collisions with the vibrating metal atoms of the conductor force the electron to change its direction constantly.

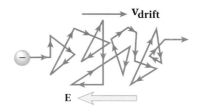

drift velocity the net velocity of a charge carrier moving in an electric field

Conceptual Challenge

Electric Field Inside a Conductor
We concluded in our study of electrostatics that the field inside a conductor is zero, yet we have seen that an electric field exists inside a conductor that carries a current. How is this zero electric field possible?

Turning on a Light If charges travel very slowly through a metal (approximately 10^{-4} m/s), why doesn't it take several hours for a light to come on after you flip a switch?

Particle Accelerator
The positively charged dome of a Van de Graaff generator can be used to accelerate positively charged protons. A current exists due to the motion of these protons. In this case, how does the direction of conventional current compare with the direction in which the charge carriers move?

Resistance to Current

When a light bulb is connected to a battery, the current in the bulb depends on the potential difference across the battery. For example, a 9.0 V battery connected to a light bulb generates a greater current than a 6.0 V battery connected to the same bulb. But potential difference is not the only factor that determines the current in the light bulb. The materials that make up the connecting wires and the bulb's filament also affect the current in the bulb. Even though most materials can be classified as conductors or insulators, some conductors allow charges to move through them more easily than others. The opposition to the motion of charge through a conductor is the conductor's **resistance.** Quantitatively, resistance is defined as the ratio of potential difference to current, as follows:

resistance the opposition presented to electric current by a material or device

---

Resistance

$$R = \frac{\Delta V}{I}$$

$$\text{resistance} = \frac{\text{potential difference}}{\text{current}}$$

The SI unit for resistance, the *ohm*, is equal to one volt per ampere and is represented by the Greek letter Ω (*omega*).

Resistance is constant over a range of potential differences.

For many materials, including most metals, experiments show that *the resistance is constant over a wide range of applied potential differences.* This statement, known as Ohm's law, is named for Georg Simon Ohm (1789–1854), who was the first to conduct a systematic study of electrical resistance. Mathematically, Ohm's law is stated as follows:

$$\frac{\Delta V}{I} = \text{constant}$$

As can be seen by comparing the definition of resistance with Ohm's law, the constant of proportionality in the Ohm's law equation is resistance. It is common practice to express Ohm's law as $\Delta V = IR$.

Ohm's law does not hold for all materials.

Ohm's law is not a fundamental law of nature like the conservation of energy or the universal law of gravitation. Instead, it is a behavior that is valid only for certain materials. Materials that have a constant resistance over a wide range of potential differences are said to be *ohmic*. A graph of current versus potential difference for an ohmic material is linear, as shown in **Figure 3.4(a).** This is because the slope of such a graph ($I/\Delta V$) is inversely proportional to resistance. When resistance is constant, the current is proportional to the potential difference, and the resulting graph is a straight line.

Materials that do not function according to Ohm's law are said to be *non-ohmic*. **Figure 3.4(b)** shows a graph of current versus potential difference for a non-ohmic material. In this case, the slope is not constant, because resistance varies. Hence, the resulting graph is nonlinear. One common semiconducting device that is non-ohmic is the *diode*. Its resistance is small for currents in one direction and large for currents in the reverse direction. Diodes are used in circuits to control the direction of current. This book assumes that all resistors function according to Ohm's law unless stated otherwise.

Resistance depends on length, area, material, and temperature.

Earlier in this section, you learned that electrons do not move in straight-line paths through a conductor. Instead, they undergo repeated collisions with the metal atoms. These collisions affect the motion of charges somewhat as a force of internal friction would. This is the origin of a material's resistance. Thus, any factors that affect the number of collisions will also affect a material's resistance. Some of these factors are shown in **Figure 3.5.**

Two of these factors—length and cross-sectional area—are purely geometrical. It is intuitive that a longer length of wire provides more resistance than a shorter length of wire does. Similarly, a wider wire allows charges to flow more easily than a thinner wire does, much as a larger pipe allows water to flow more easily than a smaller pipe does. The material effects have to do with the structure of the atoms making up the material. Finally, for most materials, resistance increases as the temperature of the metal increases. When a material is hot, its atoms vibrate fast, and it is more difficult for an electron to flow through the material.

FIGURE 3.5

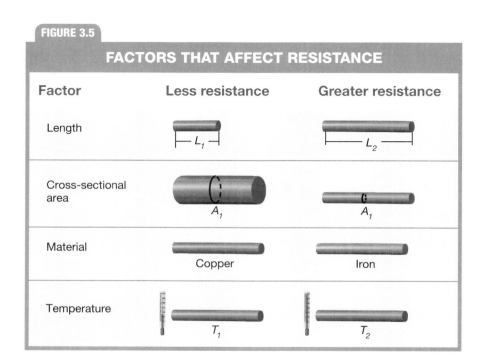

FACTORS THAT AFFECT RESISTANCE

Factor	Less resistance	Greater resistance
Length	L_1	L_2
Cross-sectional area	A_1	A_1
Material	Copper	Iron
Temperature	T_1	T_2

FIGURE 3.6

Resistors Resistors, such as those shown here, are used to control current. The colors of the bands represent a code for the values of the resistances.

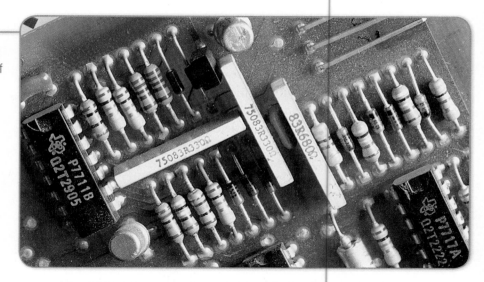

Resistors can be used to control the amount of current in a conductor.

One way to change the current in a conductor is to change the potential difference across the ends of the conductor. But in many cases, such as in household circuits, the potential difference does not change. How can the current in a certain wire be changed if the potential difference remains constant?

According to the definition of resistance, if ΔV remains constant, current decreases when resistance increases. Thus, the current in a wire can be decreased by replacing the wire with one of higher resistance. The same effect can be accomplished by making the wire longer or by connecting a *resistor* to the wire. A resistor is a simple electrical element that provides a specified resistance. **Figure 3.6** shows a group of resistors in a circuit board. Resistors are sometimes used to control the current in an attached conductor, because this is often more practical than changing the potential difference or the properties of the conductor.

GO ONLINE

Interactive Demo
HMHScience.com

Resistance

Sample Problem D A medical belt pack with a portable laser for in-the-field medical purposes has been constructed. The laser draws a current of 2.5 A and the circuitry resistance is 0.6 Ω. What is the potential difference across the laser?

1 ANALYZE

Given: $I = 2.5 \text{ A}$ $R = 0.6 \text{ Ω}$

Unknown: $\Delta V = ?$

2 SOLVE

Use the definition of resistance.

$$\Delta V = IR = (2.5 \text{ A})(0.6 \text{ Ω}) = \boxed{1.5 \text{ V}}$$

Continued

Resistance (continued)

1. A 1.5 V battery is connected to a small light bulb with a resistance of 3.5 Ω. What is the current in the bulb?

2. A stereo with a resistance of 65 Ω is connected across a potential difference of 120 V. What is the current in this device?

3. Electric eels, found in South America, can provide a potential difference of 440 V that draws a current of 0.80 A through the eel's prey. Calculate the resistance of the circuit (the eel and its prey).

4. The current in a microwave oven is 6.25 A. If the resistance of the oven's circuitry is 17.6 Ω, what is the potential difference across the oven?

5. A refrigerator's circuit carries a current equal to 0.65 A when the voltage across the circuit equals 117 V. How large is the resistance of the refrigerator's circuit?

6. The current in a certain resistor is 0.50 A when it is connected to a potential difference of 110 V. What is the current in this same resistor if

   a. the operating potential difference is 90.0 V?

   b. the operating potential difference is 130 V?

Saltwater and perspiration lower the body's resistance.

The human body's resistance to current is on the order of 100 000 Ω when the skin is dry. However, the body's resistance decreases when the skin is wet. If the body is soaked with saltwater, its resistance can be as low as 300 Ω. This is because ions in saltwater readily conduct electric charge. Such low resistances can be dangerous if a large potential difference is applied between parts of the body, because current increases as resistance decreases. Currents in the body that are less than 0.01 A either are imperceptible or generate a slight tingling feeling. Greater currents are painful and can disturb breathing, and currents above 0.15 A disrupt the electrical activity of the heart and can be fatal.

Perspiration also contains ions that conduct electric charge. In a *galvanic skin response* (GSR) test, commonly used as a stress test and as part of some so-called lie detectors, a very small potential difference is set up across the body. Perspiration increases when a person is nervous or stressed, thereby decreasing the resistance of the body. In GSR tests, a state of low stress and high resistance, or "normal" state, is used as a control, and a state of higher stress is reflected as a decreased resistance compared with the normal state.

FIGURE 3.7

Potentiometer Rotating the knob of a potentiometer changes the resistance.

Resistive Element

Rotating Dial

Potentiometers have variable resistance.

A *potentiometer,* shown in **Figure 3.7,** is a special type of resistor that has a fixed contact on one end and an adjustable, sliding contact that allows the user to tap off different potential differences. The sliding contact is frequently mounted on a rotating shaft, and the resistance is adjusted by rotating a knob. Potentiometers (frequently called *pots* for short) have many applications. In fact, most of the knobs on everyday items, such as the volume control on a stereo, are potentiometers. Potentiometers may also be mounted linearly. One example is a dimmer switch to control the light output of a light fixture. The joystick on a video game controller uses two potentiometers, one for motion in the *x*-direction and one for motion in the *y*-direction, to tell the computer the movements that you make when playing a game.

✔ SECTION 3 FORMATIVE ASSESSMENT

● Reviewing Main Ideas

1. Can the direction of conventional current ever be opposite the direction of charge movement? If so, when?

2. The charge that passes through the filament of a certain light bulb in 5.00 s is 3.0 C.
   a. What is the current in the light bulb?
   b. How many electrons pass through the filament of the light bulb in a time interval of 1.0 min?

3. How much current would a 10.2 Ω toaster oven draw when connected to a 120 V outlet?

4. An ammeter registers 2.5 A of current in a wire that is connected to a 9.0 V battery. What is the wire's resistance?

5. In a particular diode, the current triples when the applied potential difference is doubled. What can you conclude about the diode?

6. What is the function of resistors in a circuit board? What is the function of diodes in a circuit board?

7. Calculate the current in a 75 Ω resistor when a potential difference of 115 V is placed across it. What will the current be if the resistor is replaced with a 47 Ω resistor?

✔ Critical Thinking

8. Which is less in a conductor that carries a current, the drift speed of an electron or the average speed of the electron between collisions? Explain your answer.

9. You have only one type of wire. If you are connecting a battery to a light bulb with this wire, how could you decrease the current in the wire?

Superconductors

Take a moment to imagine the many things that could be created with materials that conduct electricity with *zero* resistance. There would be no heating or reduction in the current when conducting electricity with such a material. These materials exist and are called *superconductors.*

Superconductors have zero resistance below a certain temperature, called the *critical temperature.* The graph of resistance as a function of temperature for a superconductor resembles that of a normal metal at temperatures well above the critical temperature. But when the temperature is near or below the critical temperature, the resistance suddenly drops to zero, as the graph below shows. This graph shows the resistance of mercury just above and below its critical temperature of 4.15 K.

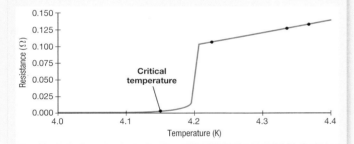

Today, there are thousands of known superconductors, including common metals such as aluminum, tin, lead, and zinc. However, for common metals that exhibit superconductivity, the critical temperature is extremely low—near absolute zero. For example, the critical temperature of aluminum is 1.19 K, just a little more than one degree above absolute zero. Temperatures near absolute zero are difficult to achieve and maintain. Interestingly, copper, silver, and gold, which are excellent conductors at room temperature, do not exhibit superconductivity.

An important recent development in physics is the discovery of high-temperature superconductors. The excitement began with a 1986 publication by scientists at the IBM Zurich Research Laboratory in Switzerland. In this publication, scientists reported evidence for superconductivity at a temperature near 30 K. More recently, scientists have

This express train in Shanghai, China, which utilizes the Meissner effect, levitates above the track and travels at up to 430 km/h in normal operations.

found superconductivity at temperatures as high as 150 K. However, 150 K is still −123°C, which is much colder than room temperature. The search continues for a material that has superconducting qualities at room temperature. This search has both scientific and practical applications.

One of the truly remarkable features of superconductors is that once a current is established in them, the current continues even if the applied potential difference is removed. In fact, steady currents have been observed to persist for many years in superconducting loops with no apparent decay. This feature makes superconducting materials attractive for a wide variety of applications.

Because electric currents produce magnetic effects, current in a superconductor can be used to float a magnet in the air over a superconductor. This effect, known as the Meissner effect, is used with high-speed express trains, such as the one shown in the figure above. This type of train levitates a few inches above the track.

One useful application of superconductivity is superconducting magnets. Such magnets are being considered for storing energy. The idea of using superconducting power lines to transmit power more efficiently is also being researched. Modern superconducting electronic devices that consist of two thin-film superconductors separated by a thin insulator have been constructed. They include magnetometers (magnetic-field measuring devices) and various microwave devices.

SECTION 4

Objectives

▶ Differentiate between direct current and alternating current.

▶ Relate electric power to the rate at which electrical energy is converted to other forms of energy.

▶ Calculate electric power and the cost of running electrical appliances.

Electric Power

Sources and Types of Current

When you drop a ball, it falls to the ground, moving from a place of higher gravitational potential energy to one of lower gravitational potential energy. As discussed in Section 1, charges behave in similar ways. For example, free electrons in a conductor move randomly when all points in the conductor are at the same potential. But when a potential difference is applied across the conductor, they will move from a position of higher electric potential to a position of lower electric potential. Thus, a potential difference maintains current in a circuit.

Batteries and generators supply energy to charge carriers.

Batteries maintain a potential difference across their terminals by converting *chemical* energy to electrical potential energy. **Figure 4.1** shows students measuring the potential difference of a battery created using a lemon, copper, and tin.

As charge carriers move from higher to lower electrical potential energy, this energy is converted into kinetic energy. This motion allows collisions to occur between the moving charges and the remaining material in the circuit elements. These collisions transfer energy (in the form of heat) back to the circuit.

A battery stores energy in the form of chemical energy, and its energy is released through a chemical reaction that occurs inside the battery. The battery continues to supply electrical energy to the charge carriers until its chemical energy is depleted. At this point, the battery must be replaced or recharged.

Because batteries must often be replaced or recharged, generators are sometimes preferable. Generators convert *mechanical* energy into electrical energy. For example, a hydroelectric power plant converts the kinetic energy of falling water into electrical potential energy. Generators are the source of the current to a wall outlet in your home and supply the electrical energy to operate your appliances. When you plug an appliance into an outlet, an effective potential difference of 120 V is applied to the device.

Current can be direct or alternating.

There are two different types of current: *direct current* (dc) and *alternating current* (ac). In direct current, charges move in only one direction with negative charges moving from a lower to higher electric potential. Hence, the conventional current is directed from the positive terminal to the negative terminal of a battery. Note, however, that the electrons actually move in the opposite direction.

FIGURE 4.1

Batteries Batteries maintain electric current by converting chemical energy into electrical energy.

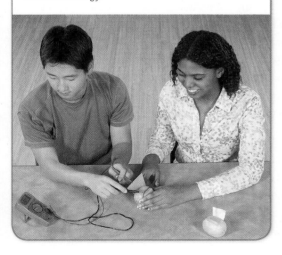

FIGURE 4.2

Alternating Current

(a) The direction of direct current does not change, while **(b)** the direction of alternating current continually changes.

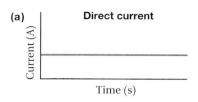

(a) Direct current

(b) Alternating current

Consider a light bulb connected to a battery. The potential difference between the terminals of a battery is fixed, so batteries always generate a direct current.

In alternating current, the terminals of the source of potential difference are constantly changing sign. Hence, there is no net motion of the charge carriers in alternating current; they simply vibrate back and forth. If this vibration were slow enough, you would notice flickering in lights and similar effects in other appliances. To eliminate this problem, alternating current is made to change direction rapidly. In the United States, alternating current oscillates 60 times every second. Thus, its frequency is 60 Hz. The graphs in **Figure 4.2** compare direct and alternating current. Alternating current has advantages that make it more practical for use in transferring electrical energy. For this reason, the current supplied to your home by power companies is alternating current rather than direct current.

Energy Transfer

When a battery is used to maintain an electric current in a conductor, chemical energy stored in the battery is continuously converted to the electrical energy of the charge carriers. As the charge carriers move through the conductor, this electrical energy is converted to internal energy due to collisions between the charge carriers and other particles in the conductor.

For example, consider a light bulb connected to a battery, as shown in **Figure 4.3(a).** Imagine a charge Q moving from the battery's terminal to the light bulb and then back to the other terminal. The changes in electrical potential energy are shown in **Figure 4.3(b).** If we disregard the resistance of the connecting wire, no loss in energy occurs as the charge moves through the wire (A to B). But when the charge moves through the filament of the light bulb (B to C), which has a higher resistance than the wire has, it loses electrical potential energy due to collisions. This electrical energy is converted into internal energy, and the filament warms up and glows.

When the charge first returns to the battery's terminal (D), its potential energy is, by convention, zero, and the battery must do work on the charge. As the charge moves between the terminals of the battery (D to A), its electrical potential energy increases by $Q\Delta V$ (where ΔV is the potential difference across the two terminals). The battery's chemical energy must decrease by the same amount.

FIGURE 4.3

Changes in Electrical Potential Energy
A charge leaves the battery at A with a certain amount of electrical potential energy. The charge loses this energy while moving from B to C, and then regains the energy as it moves through the battery from D to A.

(a)

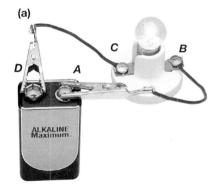

(b)

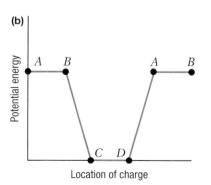

Electric power is the rate of conversion of electrical energy.

Earlier in the text, power was described as the rate at which work is done. *Electric power,* then, is the rate at which charge carriers do work. Put another way, electric power is the rate at which charge carriers convert electrical potential energy to nonelectrical forms of energy.

$$P = \frac{W}{\Delta t} = \frac{\Delta PE}{\Delta t}$$

Potential difference is the change in potential energy per unit of charge.

$$\Delta V = \frac{\Delta PE}{q}$$

This equation can be rewritten in terms of potential energy.

$$\Delta PE = q\Delta V$$

We can then substitute this expression for potential energy into the equation for power.

$$P = \frac{\Delta PE}{\Delta t} = \frac{q\Delta V}{\Delta t}$$

Because current, I, is defined as the rate of charge movement ($q/\Delta t$), we can express electric power as current multiplied by potential difference.

Electric Power

$$P = I\Delta V$$

electric power = current × potential difference

This equation describes the rate at which charge carriers lose electrical potential energy. In other words, power is the rate of conversion of electrical energy. Recall that the SI unit of power is the *watt*, W. In terms of the dissipation of electrical energy, 1 W is equivalent to 1 J of electrical energy being converted to other forms of energy per second.

Most light bulbs are labeled with their power ratings. The amount of heat and light given off by a bulb is related to the power rating, also known as *wattage*, of the bulb.

Because $\Delta V = IR$ for ohmic resistors, we can express the power dissipated by a resistor in the following alternative forms:

$$P = I\Delta V = I(IR) = I^2R$$

$$P = I\Delta V = \left(\frac{\Delta V}{R}\right)\Delta V = \frac{(\Delta V)^2}{R}$$

The conversion of electrical energy to internal energy in a resistant material is called *joule heating*, also often referred to as an I^2R loss.

Electric Power

GO ONLINE

Interactive Demo
HMHScience.com

Sample Problem E In 1994, a group of students at Lawrence Technological University, in Southfield, Michigan, built a car that combines a conventional diesel engine and an electric direct-current motor. The power delivered by the motor is 32 kW. If the resistance of the car's circuitry is 8.0 Ω, find the current drawn by the motor.

① ANALYZE

Given: $P = 32 \text{ kW} = 3.2 \times 10^4 \text{ W}$

$R = 8.0 \ \Omega$

Unknown: $I = ?$

② SOLVE

Because power and resistance are known, use the second form of the power equation to solve for I.

$$P = I^2 R$$

$$I = \sqrt{\frac{P}{R}}$$

$$I = \sqrt{\frac{(3.2 \times 10^4 \text{ W})}{(8.0 \ \Omega)}}$$

$$\boxed{I = 63 \text{ A}}$$

Practice

1. A 1050 W electric toaster operates on a household circuit of 120 V. What is the resistance of the wire that makes up the heating element of the toaster?

2. A small electronic device is rated at 0.25 W when connected to 120 V. What is the resistance of this device?

3. A calculator is rated at 0.10 W and has an internal resistance of 22 Ω. What battery potential difference is required for this device?

4. In 1995, Los Alamos National Lab developed a model electric power plant that used geothermal energy. Find the plant's projected power output if the plant produces a current of 6.40×10^3 A at 4.70×10^3 V.

5. An electric heater is operated by applying a potential difference of 50.0 V across a wire of total resistance 0.100 Ω. Find the current in the wire and the power rating of the heater.

Electric companies measure energy consumed in kilowatt-hours.

Electric power, as discussed previously, is the rate of energy transfer. Power companies charge for energy, not power. However, the unit of energy used by electric companies to calculate consumption, the *kilowatt-hour,* is defined in terms of power. One kilowatt-hour (kW•h) is the energy delivered in 1 h at the constant rate of 1 kW. The following equation shows the relationship between the kilowatt-hour and the SI unit of energy, the joule:

$$1 \text{ kW}\bullet\text{h} \times \frac{10^3 \text{ W}}{1 \text{ kW}} \times \frac{60 \text{ min}}{1 \text{ h}} \times \frac{60 \text{ s}}{1 \text{ min}} = 3.6 \times 10^6 \text{ W}\bullet\text{s} = 3.6 \times 10^6 \text{ J}$$

On an electric bill, the electrical energy used in a given period is usually stated in multiples of kilowatt-hours. An electric meter, such as the one outside your home, is used by the electric company to determine how much energy is consumed over some period of time. So the electric company does not charge for the amount of power delivered but instead charges for the amount of energy used.

Household Appliance Power Usage

Hair dryers contain a resistive coil that becomes hot when there is an electric current in the coil.

The electrical energy supplied by power companies is used to generate electric currents. These currents are used to operate household appliances. When the charge carriers that make up an electric current encounter resistance, some of the electrical energy is converted to internal energy by collisions, and the conductor warms up. This effect is used in many appliances, such as hair dryers, electric heaters, electric clothes dryers, steam irons, and toasters.

Hair dryers contain a long, thin heating coil that becomes very hot when there is an electric current in the coil. This coil is commonly made of an alloy of the two metals nickel and chromium. This nickel-chromium alloy conducts electricity poorly.

In a hair dryer, a fan behind the heating coil blows air through the hot coils. The air is then heated and blown out of the hair dryer. The same principle is also used in clothes dryers and electric heaters.

In a steam iron, a heating coil warms the bottom of the iron and also turns water into steam. An electric toaster has heating elements around the edges and in the center. When bread is loaded into the toaster, the heating coils turn on, and a timer controls how long the elements remain on before the bread is popped out of the toaster.

Appliances that use resistive heater coils consume a relatively large amount of electric energy. This energy consumption occurs because a large amount of current is required to heat the coils to a useful level. Because power is proportional to the current squared times the resistance, energy consumption is high.

Electrical energy is transferred at high potential differences to minimize energy loss.

When transporting electrical energy by power lines, such as those shown in **Figure 4.4**, power companies want to minimize the I^2R loss and maximize the energy delivered to a consumer. This can be done by decreasing either current or resistance. Although wires have little resistance, recall that resistance is proportional to length. Hence, resistance becomes a factor when power is transported over long distances. Even though power lines are designed to minimize resistance, some energy will be lost due to the length of the power lines.

As expressed by the equation $P = I^2R$, energy loss is proportional to the *square* of the current in the wire. For this reason, decreasing current is even more important than decreasing resistance. Because $P = I\Delta V$, the same amount of power can be transported either at high currents and low potential differences or at low currents and high potential differences. Thus, transferring electrical energy at low currents, thereby minimizing the I^2R loss, requires that electrical energy be transported at very high potential differences. Power plants transport electrical energy at potential differences of up to 765 000 V. Locally, this potential difference is reduced by a transformer to about 4000 V. At your home, this potential difference is reduced again to about 120 V by another transformer.

FIGURE 4.4

Electrical Power Lines Power companies transfer electrical energy at high potential differences in order to minimize the I^2R loss.

✔ SECTION 4 FORMATIVE ASSESSMENT

▶ Reviewing Main Ideas

1. What does the power rating on a light bulb describe?

2. If the resistance of a light bulb is increased, how will the electrical energy used by the light bulb over the same time period change?

3. The potential difference across a resting neuron in the human body is about 70 mV, and the current in it is approximately 200 µA. How much power does the neuron release?

4. How much does it cost to watch an entire World Series (21 h) on a 90.0 W black-and-white television set? Assume that electrical energy costs $0.070/kW•h.

5. Explain why it is more efficient to transport electrical energy at high potential differences and low currents rather than at low potential differences and high currents.

Electron Tunneling

Current is related to the motion of charge carriers, which can be treated as particles. But the electron has both particle and wave characteristics. The wave nature of the electron leads to some strange consequences that cannot be explained in terms of classical physics. One example is *tunneling*, a phenomenon whereby electrons can pass into regions that, according to classical physics, they do not have the energy to reach.

Probability Waves

To see how tunneling is possible, we must explore matter waves in greater detail. De Broglie's revolutionary idea that particles have a wave nature raised the question of how matter waves behave. In 1926, Erwin Schrödinger proposed a wave equation that described the manner in which de Broglie matter waves change in space and time. Two years later, in an attempt to relate the wave and particle natures of matter, Max Born suggested that the square of the amplitude of a matter wave is proportional to the probability of finding the corresponding particle at that location. This theory is called *quantum mechanics*.

Tunneling

Born's interpretation makes it possible for a particle to be found in a location that is not allowed by classical physics. Consider an electron with a potential energy of zero in the region between 0 and L (region II) of **Figure 1.** We call this region the *potential well.* The electron has a potential energy of some finite value U outside this area (regions I and III). If the energy of the electron is less than U, then according to classical physics, the electron cannot escape the well without first acquiring additional energy.

The probability wave for this electron (in its lowest energy state) is shown in **Figure 2** on the next page. Between any two points of this curve, the area under the corresponding part of the curve is proportional to the probability of finding the electron in that region. The highest point of the curve corresponds to the most probable location of the electron, while the lower points correspond to less probable locations. Note that the curve never actually meets the *x*-axis. This means that the electron has some finite probability of being anywhere in space. Hence, there is a probability that the electron will actually be found outside the potential well. In other words, according to quantum mechanics, the electron is no longer confined to strict boundaries because of its energy. When the electron is found outside the boundaries established by classical physics, it is said to have *tunneled* to its new location.

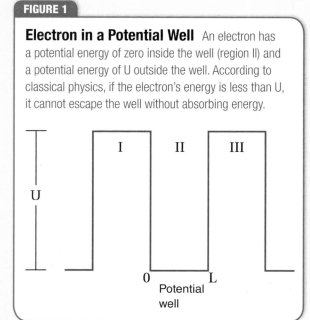

FIGURE 1

Electron in a Potential Well An electron has a potential energy of zero inside the well (region II) and a potential energy of U outside the well. According to classical physics, if the electron's energy is less than U, it cannot escape the well without absorbing energy.

Scanning Tunneling Microscopes

In 1981, Gerd Binnig and Heinrich Rohrer, at IBM Zurich, discovered a practical application of tunneling current: a powerful microscope called the *scanning tunneling microscope,* or *STM.* The STM can produce highly detailed images with resolution comparable to the size of a single atom. The image of the surface of graphite shown in **Figure 3** demonstrates the power of the STM. Note that individual carbon atoms are recognizable. The smallest detail that can be discerned is about 0.2 nm, or approximately the size of an atom's radius. A typical optical microscope has a resolution no better than 200 nm, or about half the wavelength of visible light, so it could never show the detail seen in **Figure 3.**

In the STM, a conducting probe with a very sharp tip is brought near the surface to be studied. According to classical physics, electrons cannot move between the surface and the tip because they lack the energy to escape either material. But according to quantum theory, electrons can tunnel across the barrier, provided the distance is small enough (about 1 nm). Scientists can apply a potential difference between the surface and the tip to make electrons tunnel preferentially from surface to tip. In this way, the tip samples the distribution of electrons just above the surface.

The STM works because the probability of tunneling decreases exponentially with distance. By monitoring changes in the tunneling current as the tip is scanned over the surface, scientists obtain a sensitive measure of the topography of the electron distribution on the surface. The result is used to make images such as the one in **Figure 3.** The STM can measure the height of surface features to within 0.001 nm, approximately 1/100 of an atomic diameter.

Although the STM was originally designed for imaging atoms, other practical applications are being developed. Engineers have greatly reduced the size of the STM and hope to someday develop a computer in which every piece of data is held by a single atom or by small groups of atoms and then read by an STM.

(b) ©Colin Cuthbert/Photo Researchers, Inc.

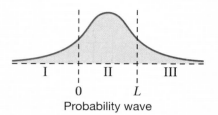

FIGURE 2

Probability Wave of an Electron in a Potential Well The probability curve for an electron in its lowest energy state shows that there is a certain probability of finding the electron outside the potential well.

Probability wave

FIGURE 3

Surface of Graphite A scanning tunneling microscope (STM) was used to produce this image of the surface of graphite, a form of carbon. The contours represent the arrangement of individual carbon atoms on the surface. An STM enables scientists to see small details on surfaces with a lateral resolution of 0.2 nm and a vertical resolution of 0.001 nm.

Superconductors and BCS Theory

The resistance of many solids (other than semiconductors) increases with increasing temperature. The reason is that at a nonzero temperature, the atoms in a solid are always vibrating, and the higher the temperature, the larger the amplitude of the vibrations. It is more difficult for electrons to move through the solid when the atoms are moving with large amplitudes. This situation is somewhat similar to walking through a crowded room. It is much harder to do so when the people are in motion than when they are standing still.

If the resistance depended only on atomic vibrations, we would expect the resistance of the material that is cooled to absolute zero to go gradually to zero. Experiments have shown, however, that this does not happen. In fact, the resistances of very cold solids behave in two very different ways—either the substance suddenly begins superconducting at temperatures above absolute zero, or it never superconducts, no matter how cold it gets.

Resistance from Lattice Imperfections

The graph in **Figure 1** shows the temperature dependence of the resistance of two similar objects, one made of silver and the other made of tin. The temperature dependence of the resistance of the silver object is similar to that of a typical metal. At higher temperatures, the resistance decreases as the metal is cooled. This decrease in resistance suggests that the amplitude of the lattice vibrations is decreasing, as expected. But at a temperature of about 10 K, the curve levels off, and the resistance becomes constant. Cooling the metal further does not appreciably lower the resistance, even though the vibrations of the metal's atoms have been lessened.

Part of the cause of this nonzero resistance, even at absolute zero, is *lattice imperfection*. The regular, geometric pattern of the crystal, or lattice, in a solid is often flawed. A lattice imperfection occurs when some of the atoms do not line up perfectly.

Imagine you are walking through a crowded room in which the people are standing in perfect rows. It would be easy to walk through the room between two rows. Now imagine that occasionally one person stands in the middle of the aisle instead of in the row, making it harder for you to pass. This is similar to the effect of a lattice imperfection. Even in the absence of thermal vibrations, many materials exhibit a *residual resistance* due to the imperfect geometric arrangement of their atoms.

Figure 1 shows that the resistance of tin jumps to zero below a certain temperature that is well above absolute zero. A solid whose resistance is zero below a certain nonzero temperature is called a **superconductor.** The temperature at which the resistance goes to zero is the critical temperature of the superconductor.

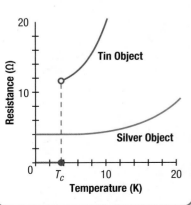

FIGURE 1

Resistance and Temperature The resistance of silver exhibits the behavior of a normal metal. The resistance of tin goes to zero at temperature T_c, the temperature at which tin becomes a superconductor.

Temperature Dependence of Resistance

BCS Theory

Before the discovery of superconductivity, it was thought that all materials should have some nonzero resistance due to lattice vibrations and lattice imperfections, much like the behavior of the silver in **Figure 1.**

The first complete microscopic theory of superconductivity was not developed until 1957. This theory is called *BCS theory* after the three scientists who first developed it: John Bardeen, Leon Cooper, and Robert Schrieffer. The crucial breakthrough of BCS theory is a new understanding of the special way that electrons traveling in pairs move through the lattice of a superconductor. According to BCS theory, electrons do suffer collisions in a superconductor, just as they do in any other material. However, the collisions do not alter the total momentum of a pair of electrons. The net effect is as if the electrons moved unimpeded through the lattice.

Cooper Pairs

Imagine an electron moving through a lattice, such as electron 1 in **Figure 2.** There is an attractive force between the electron and the nearby positively charged atoms in the lattice. As the electron passes by, the attractive force causes the lattice atoms to be pulled toward the electron. The result is a concentration of positive charge near the electron. If a second electron is nearby, it can be attracted to this excess positive charge in the lattice before the lattice has had a chance to return to its equilibrium position.

Through the process of deforming the lattice, the first electron gives up some of its momentum. The deformed region of the lattice attracts the second electron, transferring excess momentum to the second electron. The net effect of this two-step process is a weak, delayed attractive force between the two electrons, resulting from the motion of the lattice as it is deformed by the first electron. The two electrons travel through the lattice acting as if they were a single particle. This particle is called a *Cooper pair.* In BCS theory, Cooper pairs are responsible for superconductivity.

The reason superconductivity has been found at only low temperatures so far is that Cooper pairs are weakly bound. Random thermal motions in the lattice tend to destroy the bonds between Cooper pairs. Even at very low temperatures, Cooper pairs are constantly being formed, destroyed, and reformed in a superconducting material, usually with different pairings of electrons.

Calculations of the properties of a Cooper pair have shown that this peculiar bound state of two electrons has zero total momentum in the absence of an applied electric field. When an external electric field is applied, the Cooper pairs move through the lattice under the influence of the field. However, the center of mass for every Cooper pair has exactly the same momentum. This crucial feature of Cooper pairs explains superconductivity. If one electron scatters, the other electron in a pair also scatters in a way that keeps the total momentum constant. The net result is that scattering due to lattice imperfections and lattice vibrations has no net effect on Cooper pairs.

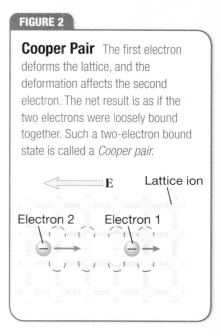

FIGURE 2

Cooper Pair The first electron deforms the lattice, and the deformation affects the second electron. The net result is as if the two electrons were loosely bound together. Such a two-electron bound state is called a *Cooper pair.*

Image Credits:

Electrician

David Ellison teaches electrician skills to students at a local community college.

Electricity enables us to see at night, to cook, to have heat and hot water, to communicate, to be entertained, and to do many other things. Without electricity, our lives would be unimaginably different. To learn more about being an electrician, read the interview with master electrician David Ellison.

How did you become an electrician?

I went to junior college to learn electronics—everything from TVs and radios to radio towers and television stations. But I didn't particularly like that sort of work. While working in a furniture factory, I got to know the master electrician for the factory, and I began working with him. Eventually he got me a job with a master electrician in town.

Most of my experience has been on the job—very little schooling. But back then, there wasn't a lot of schooling. Now they have some good classes.

What about electrical work made it more interesting than other fields?

I enjoy working with something you can't see or smell—but if you do touch it, it'll let you know. And if you flip a light switch, there it is. I also enjoy wiring up the switches and safeties, and solving problems when they don't work.

Where do you currently work?

I have been self-employed since 1989. About three years ago, I was invited to teach at the community college. I enjoy it. My students seem to relate better to the fact that I'm still working in the field. When I explain something to them, I can talk from recent experience. Teaching helps me stay on top of the field, too.

Are there any drawbacks to your work?

Electricity is dangerous. I've been burned twice over 30 percent of my body. Also, the hours can be bad.

Since I own my business, I go from 6:00 in the morning until 9:00 or 10:00 at night. I am on call at the local hospital—I was there on Thanksgiving Day. But that's the nature of my relationship with my customers.

What advice do you have for a student who is interested in becoming an electrician?

If you know a local electrical contractor, go talk or visit for the day. Or take a class at the local community college to see if it interests you. Some companies have their own classes, usually one night a week. Going to school gives you some technical knowledge, but getting out and doing it is still the best way to learn.

David Ellison

Electrical Energy

Electrical energy is used for many household activities, from heating and cooling to cooking. The amount of electrical energy used depends on how much energy each individual appliance uses and how long each appliance is used.

Understanding the Cost of Electrical Energy Service

Consumers typically pay electrical energy suppliers a certain cost for each kilowatt-hour of energy consumed. Find an electrical energy service bill from home or find an example on the Internet. By looking at a series of electrical energy bills, we can infer information about a consumer's energy consumption habits. We may even be able to infer information about the electrical energy service supplier and how the energy is generated. Consider the following scenarios:

- Using your example bill, determine how many kilowatt-hours of energy the consumer has used for the bill's time period in kilowatt-hours. How much electrical energy does the consumer use each day?

- Consider a consumer who is looking at her electrical energy bills for an entire year. For each month, she knows how many kilowatt-hours were consumed and how much the supplier charged per kilowatt-hour of service. The consumer notices that the total bill costs are higher in the winter and summer months. What might we infer about the consumer's electrical energy consumption habits?

- A consumer notices that his electrical energy service bill is fluctuating significantly each month, despite consistent energy consumption. We can infer that the cost per kilowatt-hour is changing each month and causing the fluctuation in the customer's bills. What factors might affect the cost of electrical energy service provided by a supplier?

Conceptual Challenge

The ability to make assumptions and generate rough estimates is a valuable skill to scientists. Quick estimates allow scientists to narrow the range of possibilities and focus on the most reasonable hypotheses.

New York Lights How many kilowatt-hours of electrical energy are used in New York City residences each year?

You can begin addressing the scenario by asking questions such as the following:

- How many residences are there in New York City?

- In a typical home, how much electrical energy does each appliance use on a weekday? On a weekend?

- How many appliances, on average, does each residence have?

- How does electrical energy consumption vary by season?

BIG IDEA Electrical energy is the energy associated with charged particles. Current, the flow of electric charge, transfers electrical energy from one location to another.

SECTION 1 Electric Potential

KEY TERMS

- Electrical potential energy is energy that is associated with a charged object because of its shape and its position in an electric field.
- Electric potential is electrical potential energy divided by charge.
- Only differences in electric potential (potential differences) from one position to another are useful in calculations.

electrical potential energy
electric potential
potential difference

SECTION 2 Capacitance

KEY TERM

- The capacitance, C, of an object is the magnitude of the charge, Q, on each of a capacitor's plates divided by the potential difference, ΔV, between the plates.
- A capacitor is a device that is used to store electrical potential energy. The potential energy stored in a charged capacitor depends on the charge and the potential difference between the capacitor's two plates.

capacitance

SECTION 3 Current and Resistance

KEY TERMS

- Current is the rate at which charge passes through a conductor.
- Resistance equals potential difference divided by current.
- Resistance depends on length, cross-sectional area, temperature, and material.

electric current
drift velocity
resistance

SECTION 4 Electric Power

- In direct current, charges move in a single direction; in alternating current, the direction of charge movement continually alternates.
- Electric power is the rate of conversion of electrical energy.
- The power dissipated by a resistor equals current squared times resistance.
- Electric companies measure energy consumed in kilowatt-hours.

VARIABLE SYMBOLS		
Quantities	**Units**	**Conversions**
$PE_{electric}$ electrical potential energy	J joule	$= N \bullet m = kg \bullet m^2/s^2$
ΔV potential difference	V volt	$= J/C$
C capacitance	F farad	$= C/V$
I current	A ampere	$= C/s$
R resistance	Ω ohm	$= V/A$
P electric power	W watt	$= J/s$

DIAGRAM SYMBOLS	
electric field	$\overrightarrow{\quad}$ **E**
current	$\overrightarrow{\quad}$ *I*
positive charge	+
negative charge	−

Problem Solving

See **Appendix D: Equations** for a summary of the equations introduced in this chapter. If you need more problem-solving practice, see **Appendix I: Additional Problems.**

Electrical Potential Energy and Potential Difference

▶ **REVIEWING MAIN IDEAS**

1. Describe the motion and explain the energy conversions that are involved when a positive charge is placed in a uniform electric field. Be sure your discussion includes the following terms: *electrical potential energy*, *work*, and *kinetic energy*.

2. If a point charge is displaced perpendicular to a uniform electric field, which of the following expressions is likely to be equal to the change in electrical potential energy?
   a. $-qEd$
   b. 0
   c. $-k_C \left(\dfrac{q^2}{r^2} \right)$

3. Differentiate between electrical potential energy and electric potential.

4. Differentiate between electric potential and potential difference.

5. At what location in relationship to a point charge is the electric potential considered by convention to be zero?

CONCEPTUAL QUESTIONS

6. If the electric field in some region is zero, must the electric potential in that same region also be zero? Explain your answer.

7. If a proton is released from rest in a uniform electric field, does the corresponding electric potential at the proton's changing locations increase or decrease? What about the electrical potential energy?

PRACTICE PROBLEMS

For problems 8–9, see Sample Problem A.

8. The magnitude of a uniform electric field between two plates is about 1.7×10^6 N/C. If the distance between these plates is 1.5 cm, find the potential difference between the plates.

9. In the figure below, find the electric potential at point *P* due to the grouping of charges at the other corners of the rectangle.

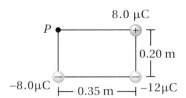

Capacitance

▶ **REVIEWING MAIN IDEAS**

10. What happens to the charge on a parallel-plate capacitor if the potential difference doubles?

11. You want to increase the maximum potential difference of a parallel-plate capacitor. Describe how you can do this for a fixed plate separation.

12. Why is Earth considered a "ground" in electric terms? Can any other object act as a ground?

CONCEPTUAL QUESTIONS

13. If the potential difference across a capacitor is doubled, by what factor is the electrical potential energy stored in the capacitor multiplied?

14. Two parallel plates are uncharged. Does the set of plates have a capacitance? Explain.

15. If you were asked to design a small capacitor with high capacitance, what factors would be important in your design?

16. A parallel-plate capacitor is charged and then disconnected from a battery. How much does the stored energy change when the plate separation is doubled?

17. Why is it dangerous to touch the terminals of a high-voltage capacitor even after the potential difference has been removed? What can be done to make the capacitor safe to handle?

PRACTICE PROBLEMS

For problems 18–19, see Sample Problem B.

18. A 12.0 V battery is connected to a 6.0 pF parallel-plate capacitor. What is the charge on each plate?

19. Two devices with capacitances of 25 µF and 5.0 µF are each charged with separate 120 V power supplies. Calculate the total energy stored in the two capacitors.

Electric Current

▶ REVIEWING MAIN IDEAS

20. What is electric current? What is the SI unit for electric current?

21. In a metal conductor, current is the result of moving electrons. Can charge carriers ever be positive?

22. What is meant by the term *conventional current*?

23. What is the difference between the drift speed of an electron in a metal wire and the average speed of the electron between collisions with the atoms of the metal wire?

24. There is a current in a metal wire due to the motion of electrons. Sketch a possible path for the motion of a single electron in this wire, the direction of the electric field vector, and the direction of conventional current.

25. What is an electrolyte?

26. What is the direction of conventional current in each case shown below?

      (a)   (b)

CONCEPTUAL QUESTIONS

27. In an analogy between traffic flow and electric current, what would correspond to the charge, Q? What would correspond to the current, I?

28. Is current ever "used up"? Explain your answer.

29. Why do wires usually warm up when an electric current is in them?

30. When a light bulb is connected to a battery, charges begin moving almost immediately, although each electron travels very slowly across the wire. Explain why the bulb lights up so quickly.

31. What is the net drift velocity of an electron in a wire that has alternating current in it?

PRACTICE PROBLEMS

For problems 32–33, see Sample Problem C.

32. How long does it take a total charge of 10.0 C to pass through a cross-sectional area of a copper wire that carries a current of 5.0 A?

33. A hair dryer draws a current of 9.1 A.
    a. How long does it take for 1.9×10^3 C of charge to pass through the hair dryer?
    b. How many electrons does this amount of charge represent?

Resistance

▶ REVIEWING MAIN IDEAS

34. What factors affect the resistance of a conductor?

35. Each of the wires shown below is made of copper. Assuming each piece of wire is at the same temperature, which has the greatest resistance? Which has the least resistance?

  (a)

  (b)

  (c)

  (d)

36. Why are resistors used in circuit boards?

CONCEPTUAL QUESTIONS

37. For a constant resistance, how are potential difference and current related?

38. If the potential difference across a conductor is constant, how is current dependent on resistance?

39. Using the atomic theory of matter, explain why the resistance of a material should increase as its temperature increases.

PRACTICE PROBLEMS

For problems 40–42, see Sample Problem D.

40. A nichrome wire with a resistance of 15 Ω is connected across the terminals of a 3.0 V flashlight battery. How much current is in the wire?

41. How much current is drawn by a television with a resistance of 35 Ω that is connected across a potential difference of 120 V?

42. Calculate the current that each resistor shown below would draw when connected to a 9.0 V battery.

(a) ——[ ]—— 5.0 Ω

(b) ——[ ]—— 2.0 Ω

(c) ——[ ]—— 20.0 Ω

Electric Power

▶ **REVIEWING MAIN IDEAS**

43. Why must energy be continuously pumped into a circuit by a battery or a generator to maintain an electric current?

44. Name at least two differences between batteries and generators.

45. What is the difference between direct current and alternating current? Which type of current is supplied to the appliances in your home?

46. Compare and contrast mechanical power with electric power.

47. What quantity is measured in kilowatt-hours? What quantity is measured in kilowatts?

48. If electrical energy is transmitted over long distances, the resistance of the wires becomes significant. Why?

49. How many joules are in a kilowatt-hour?

CONCEPTUAL QUESTIONS

50. A student in your class claims that batteries work by supplying the charges that move in a conductor, generating a current. What is wrong with this reasoning?

51. A 60 W light bulb and a 75 W light bulb operate from 120 V. Which bulb has a greater current in it?

52. Two conductors of the same length and radius are connected across the same potential difference. One conductor has twice as much resistance as the other. Which conductor dissipates more power?

53. It is estimated that in Nation Z (population 250 million) there is one electric clock per person, with each clock using energy at a rate of 2.5 W. Using this estimate, how much energy is consumed by all of the electric clocks in Nation Z in a year?

54. When a small lamp is connected to a battery, the filament becomes hot enough to emit electromagnetic radiation in the form of visible light, while the wires do not. What does this tell you about the relative resistances of the filament and the wires?

PRACTICE PROBLEMS

For problems 55–56, see Sample Problem E.

55. A computer is connected across a 110 V power supply. The computer dissipates 130 W of power in the form of electromagnetic radiation and heat. Calculate the resistance of the computer.

56. The operating potential difference of a light bulb is 120 V. The power rating of the bulb is 75 W. Find the current in the bulb and the bulb's resistance.

Mixed Review

▶ **REVIEWING MAIN IDEAS**

57. At some distance from a point charge, the electric potential is 600.0 V, and the magnitude of the electric field is 200.0 N/C. Determine the distance from the charge and the charge.

58. A circular parallel-plate capacitor with a spacing of 3.0 mm is charged to produce a uniform electric field with a strength of 3.0×10^6 N/C. What plate radius is required if the stored charge is -1.0 μC?

59. A 12 V battery is connected across two parallel metal plates separated by 0.30 cm. Find the magnitude of the electric field.

60. A parallel-plate capacitor has an area of 5.00 cm², and the plates are separated by 1.00 mm. The capacitor stores a charge of 400.0 pC.
 a. What is the potential difference across the plates of the capacitor?
 b. What is the magnitude of the uniform electric field in the region that is located between the plates?

61. A proton is accelerated from rest through a potential difference of 25 700 V.
   a. What is the kinetic energy of this proton in joules after this acceleration?
   b. What is the speed of the proton after this acceleration?

62. A proton is accelerated from rest through a potential difference of 120 V. Calculate the final speed of this proton.

63. A pair of oppositely charged parallel plates are separated by 5.33 mm. A potential difference of 600.0 V exists between the plates.
   a. What is the magnitude of the electric field strength in the region that is located between the plates?
   b. What is the magnitude of the force on an electron that is in the region between the plates at a point that is exactly 2.90 mm from the positive plate?
   c. The electron is moved to the negative plate from an initial position 2.90 mm from the positive plate. What is the change in electrical potential energy due to the movement of this electron?

64. The three charges shown below are located at the vertices of an isosceles triangle. Calculate the electric potential at the midpoint of the base if each one of the charges at the corners has a magnitude of 5.0×10^{-9} C.

65. A charge of -3.00×10^{-9} C is at the origin of a coordinate system, and a charge of 8.00×10^{-9} C is on the x-axis at 2.00 m. At what two locations on the x-axis is the electric potential zero?
(Hint: One location is between the charges, and the other is to the left of the y-axis.)

66. An ion is displaced through a potential difference of 60.0 V and experiences an increase of electrical potential energy of 1.92×10^{-17} J. Calculate the charge on the ion.

67. A proton is accelerated through a potential difference of 4.5×10^6 V.
   a. How much kinetic energy has the proton acquired?
   b. If the proton started at rest, how fast is it moving?

68. Each plate on a 3750 pF capacitor carries a charge with a magnitude of 1.75×10^{-8} C.
   a. What is the potential difference across the plates when the capacitor has been fully charged?
   b. If the plates are 6.50×10^{-4} m apart, what is the magnitude of the electric field between the two plates?

69. A net charge of 45 mC passes through the cross-sectional area of a wire in 15 s.
   a. What is the current in the wire?
   b. How many electrons pass the cross-sectional area in 1.0 min?

70. The current in a lightning bolt is 2.0×10^5 A. How many coulombs of charge pass through a cross-sectional area of the lightning bolt in 0.50 s?

71. A person notices a mild shock if the current along a path through the thumb and index finger exceeds 80.0 µA. Determine the maximum allowable potential difference without shock across the thumb and index finger for the following:
   a. a dry-skin resistance of 4.0×10^5 Ω
   b. a wet-skin resistance of 2.0×10^3 Ω

72. A color television has a power rating of 325 W. How much current does this set draw from a potential difference of 120 V?

73. An x-ray tube used for cancer therapy operates at 4.0 MV with a beam current of 25 mA striking a metal target. Calculate the power of this beam.

74. The mass of a gold atom is 3.27×10^{-25} kg. If 1.25 kg of gold is deposited on the negative electrode of an electrolytic cell in a period of 2.78 h, what is the current in the cell in this period? Assume that each gold ion carries one elementary unit of positive charge.

75. The power supplied to a typical black-and-white television is 90.0 W when the set is connected across a potential difference of 120 V. How much electrical energy does this set consume in 1.0 h?

76. A color television set draws about 2.5 A of current when connected to a potential difference of 120 V. How much time is required for it to consume the same energy that the black-and-white model described in item 75 consumes in 1.0 h?

77. The headlights on a car are rated at 80.0 W. If they are connected to a fully charged 90.0 A•h, 12.0 V battery, how long does it take the battery to completely discharge?

78. The current in a conductor varies over time as shown in the graph below.
   a. How many coulombs of charge pass through a cross section of the conductor in the time interval $t = 0$ to $t = 5.0$ s?
   b. What constant current would transport the same total charge during the 5.0 s interval as does the actual current?

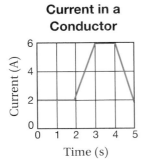

Current in a Conductor

79. Birds resting on high-voltage power lines are a common sight. A certain copper power line carries a current of 50.0 A, and its resistance per unit length is 1.12×10^{-5} Ω/m. If a bird is standing on this line with its feet 4.0 cm apart, what is the potential difference across the bird's feet?

80. An electric car is designed to run on a bank of batteries with a total potential difference of 12 V and a total energy storage of 2.0×10^7 J.
   a. If the electric motor draws 8.0 kW, what is the current delivered to the motor?
   b. If the electric motor draws 8.0 kW as the car moves at a steady speed of 20.0 m/s, how far will the car travel before it is "out of juice"?

GRAPHING CALCULATOR PRACTICE

Resistance and Current

When you install a 100 W light bulb, what is the resistance of and current passing through this light bulb? The answer to this question and similar questions is found in two equations that you learned earlier in this chapter:

$$P = \frac{(\Delta V)^2}{R} \quad \text{and} \quad P = I\Delta V$$

These equations describe the power dissipated by a resistor. In these equations, P is the power in watts, ΔV is the potential difference in volts, R is the resistance in ohms, and I is the current in amperes.

In this graphing calculator activity, you will calculate a series of tables of resistance and current versus potential difference for various values of dissipated power. By analyzing these tables, you will better understand the relationships between power, potential difference, resistance, and current. (You will also be able to answer the question about the 100 W light bulb.)

Go online to HMHScience.com to find the skillsheet and program for this graphing calculator activity.

ALTERNATIVE ASSESSMENT

1. Imagine that you are assisting nuclear scientists who need to accelerate electrons between electrically charged plates. Design and sketch a piece of equipment that could accelerate electrons to 10^7 m/s. What should the potential difference be between the plates? How would protons move inside this device? What would you change in order to accelerate the electrons to 100 m/s?

2. Tantalum is an element widely used in electrolytic capacitors. Research tantalum and its properties. Where on Earth is it found? In what form is it found? How expensive is it? Present your findings to the class in the form of a report, poster, or computer presentation.

3. Research an operational maglev train, such as the commercially operating train in Shanghai, China, or the demonstration trains in Japan or Germany. Alternatively, research a maglev system that is under construction or being proposed for development. Investigate the cost of development, major hurdles that had to be overcome or will need to be overcome, and the advantages and disadvantages of the train. Suppose that there is a proposal for a maglev train in your area. Develop an argument for or against the proposed train, based on your research. Write a paper to convince other citizens of your position.

4. Visit an electric parts or electronic parts store or consult a print or online catalog to learn about different kinds of resistors. Find out what the different resistors look like, what they are made of, what their resistance is, how they are labeled, and what they are used for. Summarize your findings in a poster or a brochure entitled *A Consumer's Guide to Resistors*.

5. The units of measurement you learned about in this chapter were named after four famous scientists: André Marie Ampère, Michael Faraday, Georg Simon Ohm, and Alessandro Volta. Research their lives, works, discoveries, and contributions. Create a presentation about one of these scientists. The presentation can be in the form of a report, poster, short video, or computer presentation.

6. A *thermistor* is a device that changes its resistance as its temperature changes. Thermistors are often used in digital thermometers. Another common temperature sensor is the *thermocouple,* which generates a potential difference that depends on its temperature. Many thermostats use thermistors or thermocouples to regulate temperature. Research how thermistors or thermocouples work and how they are used in one of the applications mentioned above. Create a computer presentation or a poster with the results of your research.

Standards-Based Assessment

Record your answers on a separate piece of paper.

MULTIPLE CHOICE

1 What changes would occur if the electron moved from point A to point B in the uniform electric field?

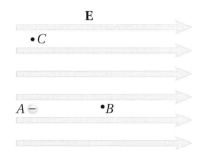

A The electron's electrical potential energy would increase; its electric potential would increase.

B The electron's electrical potential energy would increase; its electric potential would decrease.

C The electron's electrical potential energy would decrease; its electric potential would decrease.

D Neither the electron's electrical potential energy nor its electric potential would change.

2 A proton ($q = 1.6 \times 10^{-19}$ C) moves 2.0×10^{-6} m in the direction of an electric field that has a magnitude of 2.0 N/C.

What is the potential difference between the proton's starting point and ending point?

A -6.4×10^{-25} J

B -4.0×10^{-6} V

C $+6.4 \times 10^{-25}$ J

D $+4.0 \times 10^{-6}$ V

3 If the area of the plates of a parallel-plate capacitor is doubled while the spacing between the plates is halved, how is the capacitance affected?

A C is doubled.

B C is increased by four times.

C C is decreased by $\frac{1}{4}$.

D C does not change.

4 How long does it take 5.0 C of charge to pass through a cross section of a copper wire if $I = 5.0$ A?

A 0.20 s   **C** 5.0 s

B 1.0 s   **D** 25 s

5 A potential difference of 12 V produces a current of 0.40 A in a piece of copper wire. What is the resistance of the wire?

A 4.8 Ω

B 12 Ω

C 30 Ω

D 36 Ω

6 How much power is needed to operate a radio that draws 7.0 A of current when a potential difference of 115 V is applied across it?

A 6.1×10^{-2} W

B 2.3×10^{0} W

C 1.6×10^{1} W

D 8.0×10^{2} W

7 How many joules of energy are dissipated by a 50.0 W light bulb in 2.00 s?

A 25.0 J

B 50.0 J

C 100 J

D 200 J

GRIDDED RESPONSE

8 A parallel-plate capacitor is made of two circular plates, each of which has a diameter of 2.50×10^{-3} m. The plates of the capacitor are separated by a space of 1.40×10^{-4} m.

If the potential difference of 0.12 V is removed from the circuit and the circuit is allowed to discharge until the charge on the plates has decreased to 70.7 percent of its fully charged value, what will the potential difference across the capacitor be in V?

Hybrid Electric Vehicles

Charging stations for electric vehicles (EVs) are cropping up all over the United States. The EV is not new, however. It has been around since the 1800s. The first EVs were slow (14–20 mph) and had a limited range (30–40 miles). Due to the limited power infrastructure in the U.S., the EV was popular only among the wealthy in urban areas. At the beginning of the 20th century, improved road conditions gave travelers access to greater distances with more ease, but the EV still lacked range. Cars that burned gasoline in internal combustion engines (ICEs) didn't have this problem. By the 1910s, EV makers stopped production.

Defining the Problem: Range and Charging of EVs

In 1973, the Organization of Petroleum Exporting Countries (OPEC) cut off their oil exports for political and economic reasons. Gasoline shortages occurred and prices soared. In an attempt to lower our dependency on foreign oil, the U.S. began research and development programs on electric vehicles in earnest. In the 1990s, the EV started its comeback. As federal and state laws required greater fuel efficiency and lower emissions, automakers responded by developing electric and hybrid electric car models. EVs, however, were still unpopular and suffered the same design problems of limited range and lack of recharging facilities and capabilities. People had "range anxiety" about EVs: they feared that their EV would not make it to the next charging point and would strand the occupants.

In the late 2000s, a global economic depression caused many people to abandon their less fuel-efficient sport-utility vehicles (SUVs) for smaller, more fuel-efficient cars. In 2008, the first highway-capable, all-electric vehicle in serial production was released to the public. The Tesla Roadster boasted a driving range of 220 miles. The cost of this long-range EV was beyond many people's budgets. However, other EVs appeared on the market with driving ranges of 50–80 miles per charge, priced comparably with ICEs. So why aren't more people driving EVs?

Designing Solutions

Although a recent study at Columbia University indicates that 95% of daily driving needs could be met with current EV ranges, Americans are still wary. Range anxiety could be partly addressed with engineering solutions such as increased battery life and driving range. Range anxiety may also be quelled by gaining consumer trust in the range reading number that glows on the car's dashboard.

Another engineering solution would be to provide convenient charging, which takes into account charging locations and charging time. Gas stations in the U.S. outnumber EV charging stations about 10 to 1. This infrastructure will no doubt grow as the demand for EV charging stations swells. Most charging of EVs is done overnight at the owner's home, at a relatively slow charging rate. During the day and on long-distance road trips, consumers want fast recharging of their EV batteries.

Optimizing Design Solutions

Range The primary way to extend driving range in EVs is to optimize their battery packs. Through chemical reactions, batteries provide electricity to run the engine and other devices in a car. Energy density is a term that refers to a battery's amount of energy storage per mass or volume. Since the battery's invention in 1800, energy density has improved significantly through engineering design processes. Boosting the energy density of a battery requires a chemical reaction that produces a greater potential difference without adding weight to the battery pack. Lithium ion (Li ion) batteries are currently considered the best battery technology available but other battery types use different chemical reactions to produce a potential difference. Nanotechnology may provide solutions. For example, coating the anode terminal with certain nanoparticles could allow for more current.

Improved software engineering designs in EVs can address range anxiety by providing more accurate driving range estimates. Such software improvements would factor in winds, temperature, terrain, traffic conditions, driving style, and other variables.

Charging Current charging stations can charge EVs up to 80% battery capacity in 20–30 minutes. Skeptics say that EVs will never replace ICEs unless the charge time gets close to the 5-minute pump time. Faster charging methods will need to be designed that can quickly and safely deliver high electric currents.

An alternative to the charging station is a battery-swapping station where a discharged battery can be switched with a charged one. This requires a battery pack design that is easy to get to and remove from the vehicle. In the U.S., a prototype facility completed the swap in a little under 3 minutes in 2014.

It is difficult to say when or if the EV market will dominate ICEs. First, engineers must resolve the issues of range, an acceptable charging experience, and a reasonable price.

Design Your Own

Conduct Research

1. Research car dealers online, and see what information they have about EVs. Do they have any EV models available? What type of battery technology do these models use? What is the range of the battery? What is the expected lifetime of the battery? What is the typical charging time? Where are the local charging points? What are the costs at charging points? What is the source of the electricity used to charge the battery?

Evaluate and Communicate

2. The federal government and some states offer tax deductions and other incentives for people who own EVs or other alternative-fuel vehicles. With classmates, discuss the following question: "To promote the use of EVs, would it be more beneficial for the government to spend taxpayers' money to subsidize charging stations or alternative-fuel vehicles?"

Build a Prototype

3. Check the Internet for information on how a Li ion battery pack works in EVs. Use this information to draw a model to demonstrate the battery pack's operation. Research potential improvements to the battery design, and draw a model that illustrates one improvement.

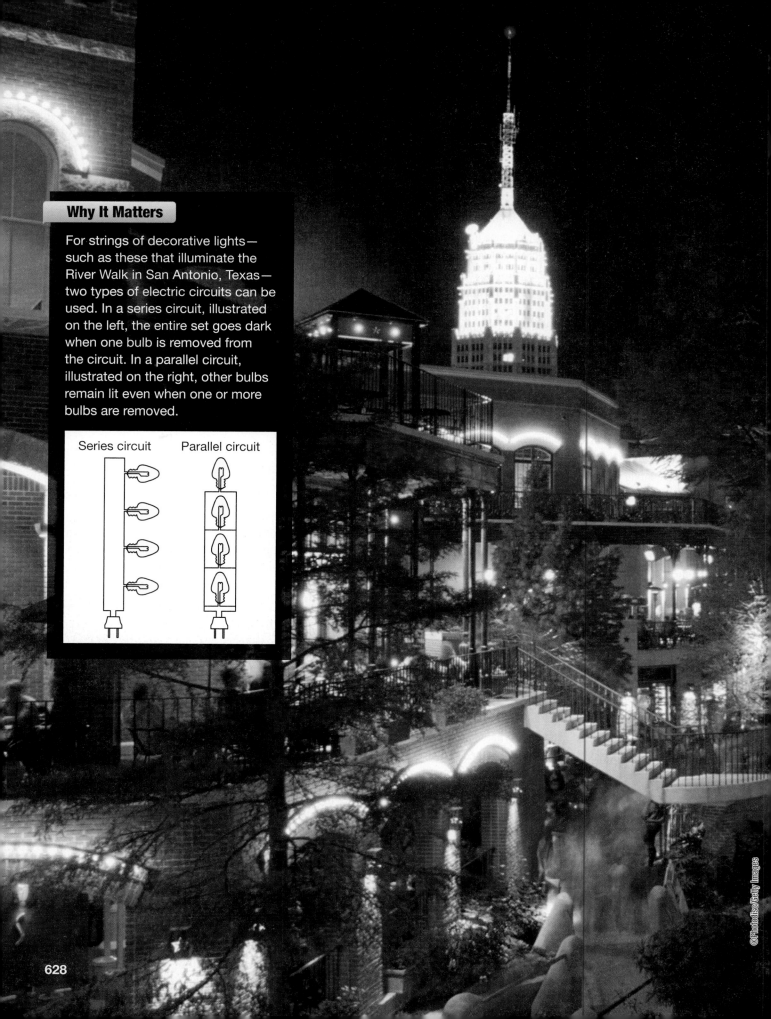

For strings of decorative lights—such as these that illuminate the River Walk in San Antonio, Texas—two types of electric circuits can be used. In a series circuit, illustrated on the left, the entire set goes dark when one bulb is removed from the circuit. In a parallel circuit, illustrated on the right, other bulbs remain lit even when one or more bulbs are removed.

Series circuit   Parallel circuit

CHAPTER 18
Circuits and Circuit Elements

BIG IDEA

Electric circuit elements control the potential differences and currents in a circuit. Circuit elements can be wired in series, parallel, or a combination of the two.

 ONLINE Physics
HMHScience.com

ONLINE LABS
- Exploring Circuit Elements
- Resistors in Series and in Parallel
- S.T.E.M. Lab Design a Circuit
- S.T.E.M. Lab Design a Dimmer Switch

GO ONLINE

Animated Physics
HMHScience.com

Resistors in Circuits

(bl) ©Photodisc/Getty Images

Objectives

▶ Interpret and construct circuit diagrams.

▶ Identify circuits as open or closed.

▶ Deduce the potential difference across the circuit load, given the potential difference across the battery's terminals.

Schematic Diagrams and Circuits

Key Terms

schematic diagram   electric circuit

Schematic Diagrams

Take a few minutes to examine the battery and light bulb in **Figure 1.1(a)**; then draw a diagram of each element in the photograph and its connection. How easily could your diagram be interpreted by someone else? Could the elements in your diagram be used to depict a string of decorative lights, such as those draped over the trees of the San Antonio River Walk?

A diagram that depicts the construction of an electrical apparatus is called a **schematic diagram.** The schematic diagram shown in **Figure 1.1(b)** uses symbols to represent the bulb, battery, and wire from **Figure 1.1(a)**. Note that these same symbols can be used to describe these elements in any electrical apparatus. This way, schematic diagrams can be read by anyone familiar with the standard set of symbols.

Reading schematic diagrams allows us to determine how the parts in an electrical device are arranged. In this chapter, you will see how the arrangement of resistors in an electrical device can affect the current in and potential difference across the other elements in the device. The ability to interpret schematic diagrams for complicated electrical equipment is an essential skill for solving problems involving electricity.

As shown in **Figure 1.2** on the next page, each element used in a piece of electrical equipment is represented by a symbol in schematic diagrams that reflects the element's construction or function. For example, the schematic-diagram symbol that represents an open switch resembles the open knife switch that is shown in the corresponding photograph. Note that **Figure 1.2** also includes other forms of schematic-diagram symbols; these alternative symbols will not be used in this book.

schematic diagram a representation of a circuit that uses lines to represent wires and different symbols to represent components

FIGURE 1.1

A Battery and Light Bulb **(a)** When this battery is connected to a light bulb, the potential difference across the battery generates a current that illuminates the bulb. **(b)** The connections between the light bulb and battery can be represented in a schematic diagram.

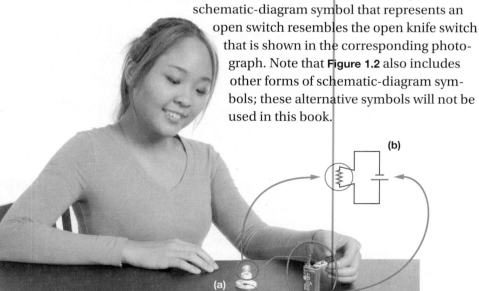

FIGURE 1.2

SCHEMATIC DIAGRAM SYMBOLS

Component	Symbol used in this book	Other forms of this symbol	Explanation
Wire or conductor 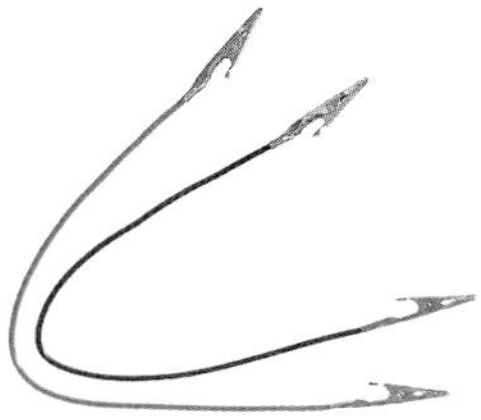			• Wires that connect elements are conductors. • Because wires offer negligible resistance, they are represented by straight lines
Resistor or circuit load 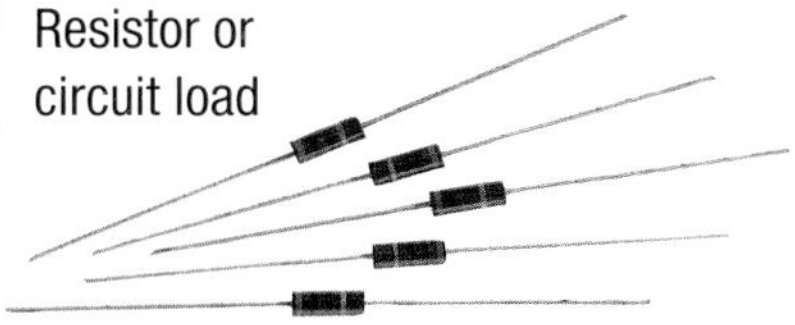			• Resistors are shown having multiple bends, illustrating resistance to the movement of charges.
Bulb or lamp 			• The multiple bends of the filament indicate that the light bulb behaves as a resistor. • The symbol for the filament of the bulb is often enclosed in a circle to emphasize the enclosure of a resistor in a bulb.
Plug 		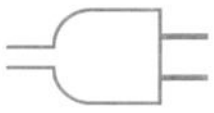	• The plug symbol looks like a container for two prongs. • The emf between the two prongs of a plug is symbolized by lines of unequal length.
Battery 	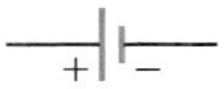	 **Multiple cells**	• Differences in line length indicate a potential difference between positive and negative terminals of the battery. • The longer line represents the positive terminal of the battery.
Switch 	 Open  Closed		• The small circles indicate the two places where the switch makes contact with the wires. Most switches work by breaking only one of the contacts, not both.
Capacitor 	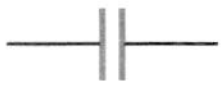		• The two parallel plates of a capacitor are symbolized by two parallel lines of equal length. • One curved line indicates that the capacitor can be used with only direct current sources with the polarity as shown.

FIGURE 1.3

A Complete Circuit When all electrical components are connected, charges can move freely in a circuit. The movement of charges in a circuit can be halted by opening the switch.

electric circuit a set of electrical components connected such that they provide one or more complete paths for the movement of charges

Electric Circuits

Think about how you get the bulb in **Figure 1.3** to light up. Will the bulb stay lit if the switch is opened? Is there any way to light the bulb without connecting the wires to the battery?

The filament of the light bulb acts as a resistor. When a wire connects the terminals of the battery to the light bulb, as shown in **Figure 1.3,** charges built up on one terminal of the battery have a path to follow to reach the opposite charges on the other terminal. Because there are charges moving through the wire, a current exists. This current causes the filament to heat up and glow.

Together, the bulb, battery, switch, and wire form an **electric circuit.** An electric circuit is a path through which charges can flow. A schematic diagram for a circuit is sometimes called a *circuit diagram.*

Any element or group of elements in a circuit that dissipates energy is called a *load.* A simple circuit consists of a source of potential difference and electrical energy, such as a battery, and a load, such as a bulb or group of bulbs. Because the connecting wire and switch have negligible resistance, we will not consider these elements as part of the load.

In **Figure 1.3,** the path from one battery terminal to the other is complete, a potential difference exists, and electrons move from one terminal to the other. In other words, there is a closed-loop path for electrons to follow. This is called a *closed circuit.* The switch in the circuit in **Figure 1.3** must be closed in order for a steady current to exist.

Without a complete path, there is no charge flow and therefore no current. This situation is an *open circuit.* If the switch in **Figure 1.3** were open, as shown in **Figure 1.2,** the circuit would be open, the current would be zero, and the bulb would not light up.

Conceptual Challenge

Bird on a Wire Why is it possible for a bird to be perched on a high-voltage wire without being electrocuted? (Hint: Consider the potential difference between the bird's two feet.)

Parachutist on a Wire Suppose a parachutist lands on a high-voltage wire and grabs the wire in preparation to be rescued. Will the parachutist be electrocuted? If the wire breaks, why should the parachutist let go of the wire as it falls to the ground? (Hint: First consider the potential difference between the parachutist's two hands holding the wire. Then consider the potential difference between the wire and the ground.)

(b) ©blickwinkel/Alamy

CFLs and LEDs

You are probably familiar with the pear-shaped lightbulbs called incandescent bulbs. Thomas Edison first invented these bulbs in 1879, and they have been in use ever since. They work by heating a small metal filament that glows and produces light. Incandescent bulbs give off a warm and pleasant light, but they are extremely inefficient. Nearly 90% of the energy they use is converted into heat, and only 10% is converted into light. Many countries, including the United States, have passed laws phasing out the most inefficient of the incandescent bulbs. There are currently two main types of replacements.

The first type of light bulb is called compact fluorescent light (or CFL for short). CFLs work by running an electric current through a long glass tube that contains a mixture of gases. The gas absorbs energy from the electricity and emits ultraviolet light. The ultraviolet light hits the surface of the tube, which has been coated with a chemical that absorbs the ultraviolet light and emits visible light.

The second type of light bulb is called light-emitting diode (or LED for short). LEDs work by moving electrons and protons in a solid piece of material called a semiconductor. As the electrons move through this material, they lose energy and release light. The electrons here release no energy as heat, so LEDs are more energy efficient than both incandescent and CFLs. In addition, because LEDs are made of solid material, they can be very small and are very durable so they last a long time.

Although both CFLs and LEDS cost considerably more than incandescent bulbs, they use much less energy to produce the same amount of light. In addition, they have a much longer life span. When both of these factors are taken into account, replacing your incandescent bulbs with CFLs or LEDs might cost more up front, but they end up saving money over the life of the bulb.

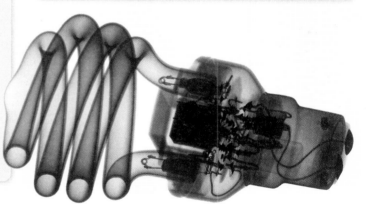

Short circuits can be hazardous.

Without a load, such as a bulb or other resistor, the circuit contains little resistance to the movement of charges. This situation is called a *short circuit.* For example, a short circuit occurs when a wire is connected from one terminal of a battery to the other by a wire with little resistance. This commonly occurs when uninsulated wires connected to different terminals come into contact with each other.

When short circuits occur in the wiring of your home, the increase in current can become unsafe. Most wires cannot withstand the increased current, and they begin to overheat. The wire's insulation may even melt or cause a fire.

The source of potential difference and electrical energy is the circuit's emf.

Will a bulb in a circuit light up if you remove the battery? Without a potential difference, there is no charge flow and no current. The battery is necessary because the battery is the source of potential difference and electrical energy for the circuit. So the bulb must be connected to the battery to be lit.

Any device that increases the potential energy of charges circulating in a circuit is a source of *emf*, or electromotive "force." The emf is the energy per unit charge supplied by a source of electric current. Think of such a source as a "charge pump" that forces electrons to move in a certain direction. Batteries and generators are examples of emf sources.

For conventional current, the terminal voltage is less than the emf.

Look at the battery attached to the light bulb in the circuit shown in **Figure 1.4.** As shown in the inset, instead of behaving only like a source of emf, the battery behaves as if it contains both an emf source and a resistor. The battery's internal resistance to current is the result of moving charges colliding with atoms inside the battery while the charges are traveling from one terminal to the other. Thus, when charges move conventionally in a battery, the potential difference across the battery's terminals, the *terminal voltage,* is actually slightly less than the emf.

Unless otherwise stated, any reference in this book to the potential difference across a battery should be thought of as the potential difference measured across the battery's terminals rather than as the emf of the battery. In other words, all examples and end-of-chapter problems will disregard the internal resistance of the battery.

FIGURE 1.4

A Battery's Internal Resistance **(a)** A battery in a circuit behaves as if it contains both **(b)** an emf source and **(c)** an internal resistance. For simplicity's sake, in problem solving it will be assumed that this internal resistance is insignificant.

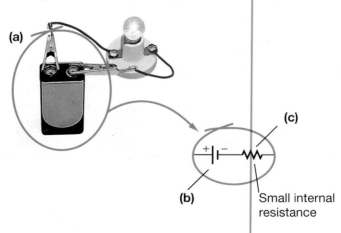

(a)

(c)

(b)   Small internal resistance

Potential difference across a load equals the terminal voltage.

When charges move within a battery from one terminal to the other, the chemical energy of the battery is converted to the electrical potential energy of the charges. As charges move through the circuit, their electrical potential energy is converted to other forms of energy. For instance, when the load is a resistor, the electrical potential energy of the charges is converted to the internal energy of the resistor and dissipated as thermal energy and light energy.

Because energy is conserved, the energy gained and the energy lost must be equal for one complete trip around the circuit (starting and ending at the same place). Thus, the electrical potential energy gained in the battery must equal the energy dissipated by the load. Because the potential difference is the measurement of potential energy per amount of charge, the potential increase across the battery must equal the potential decrease across the load.

 SECTION 1 FORMATIVE ASSESSMENT

> ### Reviewing Main Ideas

1. Identify the types of elements in the schematic diagram illustrated in **Figure 1.5** and the number of each type.

2. Using the symbols listed in **Figure 1.2,** draw a schematic diagram of a working circuit that contains two resistors, an emf source, and a closed switch.

3. In which of the circuits pictured below will there be no current?

FIGURE 1.5

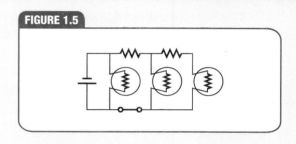

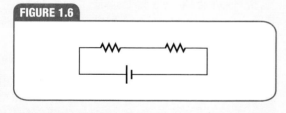

FIGURE 1.6

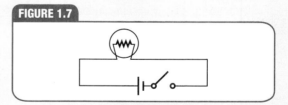

FIGURE 1.7

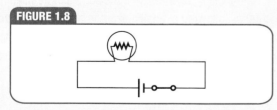

FIGURE 1.8

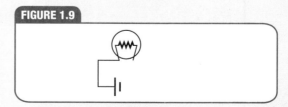

FIGURE 1.9

4. If the potential difference across the bulb in a certain flashlight is 3.0 V, what is the potential difference across the combination of batteries used to power it?

> ### ✔ Critical Thinking

5. In what forms is the electrical energy that is supplied to a string of decorative lights dissipated?

Transistors and Integrated Circuits

You may have heard about objects called *semiconductors*. Semiconductors are materials that have properties between those of insulators and conductors. They play an important role in today's world, as they are the foundation of circuits found in virtually every electronic device.

Most commercial semiconductors are made primarily of either silicon or germanium. The conductive properties of semiconductors can be enhanced by adding impurities to the base material in a process called *doping*. Depending on how a semiconductor is doped, it can be either an n-type semiconductor or a p-type semiconductor. N-type semiconductors carry negative charges (in the form of electrons), and p-type semiconductors carry positive charges. The positive charges in a p-type semiconductor are not actually positively charged particles. They are "holes" created by the absence of electrons.

The most interesting and useful properties of semiconductors emerge when more than one type of semiconductor is used in a device. One such device is a *diode,* which is made by placing a p-type semiconductor next to an n-type semiconductor. The junction where the two types meet is called a *p-n junction.* A diode has almost infinite resistance in one direction and nearly zero resistance in the other direction. One useful application of diodes is a light-emitting diode (LED), which produces light with little heat. LEDs are found in computer screens and remote controls. Another application of diodes is the conversion of alternating current to direct current.

A *transistor* is a device that contains three layers of semiconductors. Transistors can be either *pnp transistors* or *npn transistors,* depending on the order of the layers.

A transistor is like two diodes placed back-to-back. You might think this would mean that no current exists in a transistor, as there is infinite resistance at one or the other of the p-n junctions. However, if a small voltage is applied to the middle layer of the transistor, the p-n junctions are altered in such a way that a large amount of current can be in the transistor. As a result, transistors can be used as switches, allowing a small current to turn a larger current on or off. Transistor-based switches are the building blocks of computers. A single switch turned on or off can represent a binary digit, or *bit,* which is always either a one or a zero.

An *integrated circuit* is a collection of transistors, diodes, capacitors, and resistors embedded in a single piece of silicon, known as a *chip*. The earliest chips contained only one transistor. Today transistors can be made so small that billions fit onto a chip the size of your fingernail. This has made it possible for the development of smaller and more powerful computers, smartphones, and other mobile technology.

Motherboards, such as the one pictured above, include multiple transistors.

Resistors in Series or in Parallel

Key Terms
series
parallel

SECTION 2

Objectives

▶ Calculate the equivalent resistance for a circuit of resistors in series, and find the current in and potential difference across each resistor in the circuit.

▶ Calculate the equivalent resistance for a circuit of resistors in parallel, and find the current in and potential difference across each resistor in the circuit.

Resistors in Series

In a circuit that consists of a single bulb and a battery, the potential difference across the bulb equals the terminal voltage. The total current in the circuit can be found using the equation $\Delta V = IR$.

What happens when a second bulb is added to such a circuit, as shown in **Figure 2.1**? When moving through this circuit, charges that pass through one bulb must also move through the second bulb. Because all charges in the circuit must follow the same conducting path, these bulbs are said to be connected in **series.**

Resistors in series carry the same current.

Light-bulb filaments are resistors; thus, **Figure 2.1(b)** represents the two bulbs in **Figure 2.1(a)** as resistors. Because charge is conserved, charges cannot build up or disappear at a point. For this reason, the amount of charge that enters one bulb in a given time interval equals the amount of charge that exits that bulb in the same amount of time. Because there is only one path for a charge to follow, the amount of charge entering and exiting the first bulb must equal the amount of charge that enters and exits the second bulb in the same time interval.

Because the current is the amount of charge moving past a point per unit of time, the current in the first bulb must equal the current in the second bulb. This is true for any number of resistors arranged in series. *When many resistors are connected in series, the current in each resistor is the same.*

series describes two or more components of a circuit that provide a single path for current

---

FIGURE 2.1

Two Bulbs in Series These two light bulbs are connected in series. Because light-bulb filaments are resistors, **(a)** the two bulbs in this series circuit can be represented by **(b)** two resistors in the schematic diagram shown on the right.

The total current in a series circuit depends on how many resistors are present and on how much resistance each offers. Thus, to find the total current, first use the individual resistance values to find the total resistance of the circuit, called the *equivalent resistance.* Then the equivalent resistance can be used to find the current.

The equivalent resistance in a series circuit is the sum of the circuit's resistances.

As described in Section 1, the potential difference across the battery, ΔV, must equal the potential difference across the load, $\Delta V_1 + \Delta V_2$, where ΔV_1 is the potential difference across R_1 and ΔV_2 is the potential difference across R_2.

$$\Delta V = \Delta V_1 + \Delta V_2$$

According to $\Delta V = IR$, the potential difference across each resistor is equal to the current in that resistor multiplied by the resistance.

$$\Delta V = I_1 R_1 + I_2 R_2$$

Because the resistors are in series, the current in each is the same. For this reason, I_1 and I_2 can be replaced with a single variable for the current, I.

$$\Delta V = I(R_1 + R_2)$$

Finding a value for the equivalent resistance of the circuit is now possible. If you imagine the equivalent resistance replacing the original two resistors, as shown in **Figure 2.2**, you can treat the circuit as if it contains only one resistor and use $\Delta V = IR$ to relate the total potential difference, current, and equivalent resistance.

$$\Delta V = I(R_{eq})$$

Now set the last two equations for ΔV equal to each other, and divide by the current.

$$\Delta V = I(R_{eq}) = I(R_1 + R_2)$$

$$R_{eq} = R_1 + R_2$$

Thus, the equivalent resistance of the series combination is the sum of the individual resistances. An extension of this analysis shows that the equivalent resistance of two or more resistors connected in series can be calculated using the following equation.

> **Resistors in Series**
> $$R_{eq} = R_1 + R_2 + R_3 \dots$$
>
> **Equivalent resistance equals the total of individual resistances in series.**

Because R_{eq} represents the sum of the individual resistances that have been connected in series, *the equivalent resistance of a series combination of resistors is always greater than any individual resistance.*

FIGURE 2.2

Equivalent Resistance for a Series Circuit (a) The two resistors in the actual circuit have the same effect on the current in the circuit as (b) the equivalent resistor.

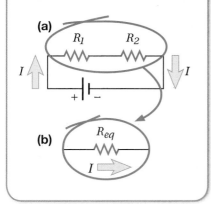

To find the total current in a series circuit, first simplify the circuit to a single equivalent resistance using the boxed equation on page 638; then use $\Delta V = IR$ to calculate the current.

$$I = \frac{\Delta V}{R_{eq}}$$

Because the current in each bulb is the same, you can also use $\Delta V = IR$ to calculate the potential difference across each resistor.

$$\Delta V_1 = IR_1 \quad \text{and} \quad \Delta V_2 = IR_2$$

The method described above can be used to find the potential difference across resistors in a series circuit containing any number of resistors.

Resistors in Series

Sample Problem A A 9.0 V battery is connected to four light bulbs, as shown at right. Find the equivalent resistance for the circuit and the current in the circuit. Use the equivalent resistance to determine the total power dissipated by the resistors in the circuit.

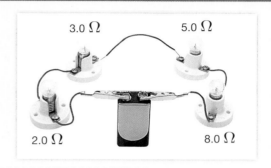

1 ANALYZE

Given:

$\Delta V = 9.0\ \text{V} \qquad R_1 = 2.0\ \Omega$

$R_2 = 3.0\ \Omega \qquad R_3 = 5.0\ \Omega$

$R_4 = 8.0\ \Omega$

Unknown: $R_{eq} = ? \qquad I = ?$

Diagram:

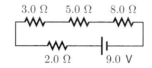

2 PLAN

Choose an equation or situation:
Because the resistors are connected end to end, they are in series. Thus, the equivalent resistance can be calculated with the equation for resistors in series.

$$R_{eq} = R_1 + R_2 + R_3 \ldots$$

The following equation can be used to calculate the current.

$$\Delta V = IR_{eq}$$

Rearrange the equation to isolate the unknown:
No rearrangement is necessary to calculate R_{eq}, but $\Delta V = IR_{eq}$ must be rearranged to calculate current.

$$I = \frac{\Delta V}{R_{eq}}$$

Continued

Resistors in Series (continued)

3 SOLVE

Substitute the values into the equation and solve:

$$R_{eq} = 2.0\ \Omega + 3.0\ \Omega + 5.0\ \Omega + 8.0\ \Omega$$

$$\boxed{R_{eq} = 18.0\ \Omega}$$

Substitute the equivalent resistance value into the equation for current.

$$I = \frac{\Delta V}{R_{eq}} = \frac{9.0\ \text{V}}{18.0\ \Omega}$$

$$\boxed{I = 0.50\ \text{A}}$$

Use the value calculated for R_{eq} to determine the total power dissipated by resistors in the circuit.

$$P = \frac{(\Delta V)^2}{R_{eq}}$$

$$P = \frac{(9.0\ \text{V})^2}{18\ \Omega}$$

$$P = 4.5\ \text{W}$$

4 CHECK YOUR WORK

For resistors connected in series, the equivalent resistance should be greater than the largest resistance in the circuit.

$$18.0\ \Omega > 8.0\ \Omega$$

Practice

1. A 12.0 V storage battery is connected to three resistors, 6.75 Ω, 15.3 Ω, and 21.6 Ω, respectively. The resistors are joined in series.

   a. Calculate the equivalent resistance of the circuit and the total power dissipated by resistors in the circuit.

   b. What is the current in the circuit?

2. A series combination of two resistors, 7.25 Ω and 4.03 Ω, is connected to a 9.00 V battery.

   a. Calculate the equivalent resistance of the circuit and the current.

   b. What is the potential difference across each resistor?

3. In case of an emergency, a corridor on an airplane has 57 lights wired in series. Each light bulb has a resistance of 2.0 Ω. Find the equivalent resistance.

4. A quadraphonic car stereo operates on electric current provided by the car's 12 V battery and is connected in series. Each channel of the stereo, which feeds the electrical signal to one of the stereo's four speakers, has a resistance of 4.1 Ω. How much current is in the circuit of each stereo channel?

Series circuits require all elements to conduct.

What happens to a series circuit when a single bulb burns out? Consider what a circuit diagram for a string of lights with one broken filament would look like. As the schematic diagram in **Figure 2.3** shows, the broken filament means that there is a gap in the conducting pathway used to make up the circuit. Because the circuit is no longer closed, there is no current in it, and all of the bulbs go dark.

Why, then, would anyone arrange resistors in series? Resistors can be placed in series with a device in order to regulate the current in that device. In the case of decorative lights, adding an additional bulb will decrease the current in each bulb. Thus, the filament of each bulb need not withstand such a high current. Another advantage to placing resistors in series is that several lesser resistances can be used to add up to a single greater resistance that is unavailable. Finally, in some cases, it is important to have a circuit that will have no current if any one of its component parts fails. This technique is used in a variety of contexts, including some burglar-alarm systems.

FIGURE 2.3

Burned-Out Filament in a Series Circuit A burned-out filament in a bulb has the same effect as an open switch. Because this series circuit is no longer complete, there is no current in the circuit.

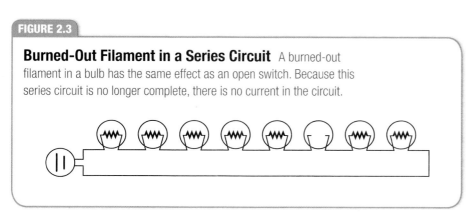

Resistors in Parallel

As discussed above, when a single bulb in a series light set burns out, the entire string of lights goes dark because the circuit is no longer closed. What would happen if there were alternative pathways for the movement of charge, as shown in **Figure 2.4**?

A wiring arrangement that provides alternative pathways for the movement of a charge is a **parallel** arrangement. The bulbs of the decorative light set shown in the schematic diagram in **Figure 2.4** are arranged in parallel with each other.

parallel describes two or more components of a circuit that provide separate conducting paths for current because the components are connected across common points or junctions

FIGURE 2.4

A Parallel Circuit These decorative lights are wired in parallel. Notice that in a parallel arrangement, there is more than one path for current.

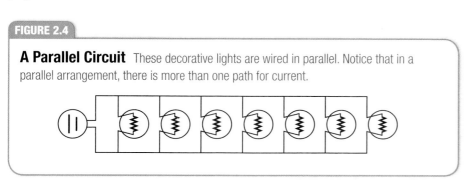

FIGURE 2.5

A Simple Parallel Circuit

(a) This simple parallel circuit with two bulbs connected to a battery can be represented by (b) the schematic diagram shown on the right.

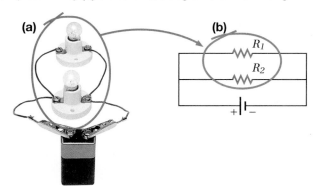

Resistors in parallel have the same potential differences across them.

To explore the consequences of arranging resistors in parallel, consider the two bulbs connected to a battery in **Figure 2.5(a)**. In this arrangement, the left side of each bulb is connected to the positive terminal of the battery, and the right side of each bulb is connected to the negative terminal. Because the sides of each bulb are connected to common points, the potential difference across each bulb is the same. If the common points are the battery's terminals, as they are in the figure, the potential difference across each resistor is also equal to the terminal voltage of the battery. The current in each bulb, however, is not always the same.

The sum of currents in parallel resistors equals the total current.

In **Figure 2.5**, when a certain amount of charge leaves the positive terminal and reaches the branch on the left side of the circuit, some of the charge moves through the top bulb, and some moves through the bottom bulb. If one of the bulbs has less resistance, more charge moves through that bulb because the bulb offers less opposition to the flow of charges.

Because charge is conserved, the sum of the currents in each bulb equals the current I delivered by the battery. This is true for all resistors in parallel.

$$I = I_1 + I_2 + I_3 \ldots$$

The parallel circuit shown in **Figure 2.5** can be simplified to an equivalent resistance with a method similar to the one used for series circuits. To do this, first show the relationship among the currents.

$$I = I_1 + I_2$$

QuickLAB   SERIES AND PARALLEL CIRCUITS

Cut the regular drinking straws and thin stirring straws into equal lengths. Tape them end to end in long tubes to form series combinations. Form parallel combinations by taping the straws together side by side.

Try several combinations of like and unlike straws. Blow through each combination of tubes, holding your fingers in front of the openings to compare the airflow (or current) that you achieve with each combination.

Rank the combinations according to how much resistance they offer. Classify them according to the amount of current created in each.

MATERIALS
- 4 regular drinking straws
- 4 stirring straws or coffee stirrers
- tape

Straws in series

Straws in parallel

Then substitute the equivalents for current according to $\Delta V = IR$.

$$\frac{\Delta V}{R_{eq}} = \frac{\Delta V_1}{R_1} + \frac{\Delta V_2}{R_2}$$

Because the potential difference across each bulb in a parallel arrangement equals the terminal voltage ($\Delta V = \Delta V_1 = \Delta V_2$), you can divide each side of the equation by ΔV to get the following equation.

$$\frac{1}{R_{eq}} = \frac{1}{R_1} + \frac{1}{R_2}$$

An extension of this analysis shows that the equivalent resistance of two or more resistors connected in parallel can be calculated using the following equation.

Resistors in Parallel

$$\frac{1}{R_{eq}} = \frac{1}{R_1} + \frac{1}{R_2} + \frac{1}{R_3} \cdots$$

The equivalent resistance of resistors in parallel can be calculated using a reciprocal relationship.

Notice that this equation does not give the value of the equivalent resistance directly. You must take the reciprocal of your answer to obtain the value of the equivalent resistance.

Because of the reciprocal relationship, *the equivalent resistance for a parallel arrangement of resistors must always be less than the smallest resistance in the group of resistors.*

The conclusions made about both series and parallel circuits are summarized in **Figure 2.6.**

FIGURE 2.6

RESISTORS IN SERIES OR IN PARALLEL		
	Series	**Parallel**
schematic diagram		
current	$I = I_1 = I_2 = I_3 \ldots$ $=$ same for each resistor	$I = I_1 + I_2 + I_3 \ldots$ $=$ sum of currents
potential difference	$\Delta V = \Delta V_1 + \Delta V_2 + \Delta V_3 \ldots$ $=$ sum of potential differences	$\Delta V = \Delta V_1 = \Delta V_2 = \Delta V_3 \ldots$ $=$ same for each resistor
equivalent resistance	$R_{eq} = R_1 + R_2 + R_3 \ldots$ $=$ sum of individual resistances	$\dfrac{1}{R_{eq}} = \dfrac{1}{R_1} + \dfrac{1}{R_2} + \dfrac{1}{R_3}$ $=$ reciprocal sum of resistances

Resistors in Parallel

Sample Problem B A 9.0 V battery is connected to four resistors, as shown at right. Find the equivalent resistance for the circuit and the total current in the circuit. Use the total current to determine the total power dissipated by the resistors in the circuit.

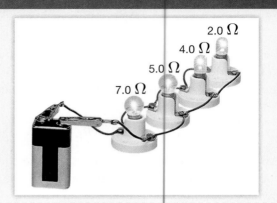

① ANALYZE

Given: $\Delta V = 9.0\ V$ $R_1 = 2.0\ \Omega$

   $R_2 = 4.0\ \Omega$ $R_3 = 5.0\ \Omega$

   $R_4 = 7.0\ \Omega$

Unknown: $R_{eq} = ?$ $I = ?$

Diagram:

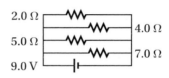

② PLAN

Choose an equation or situation:
Because both sides of each resistor are connected to common points, they are in parallel. Thus, the equivalent resistance can be calculated with the equation for resistors in parallel.

$$\frac{1}{R_{eq}} = \frac{1}{R_1} + \frac{1}{R_2} + \frac{1}{R_3} \ldots \text{ for parallel}$$

The following equation can be used to calculate the current.

$$\Delta V = IR_{eq}$$

Rearrange the equation to isolate the unknown:
No rearrangement is necessary to calculate R_{eq}; rearrange $\Delta V = IR_{eq}$ to calculate the total current delivered by the battery.

$$I = \frac{\Delta V}{R_{eq}}$$

Tips and Tricks

The equation for resistors in parallel gives you the reciprocal of the equivalent resistance. Be sure to take the reciprocal of this value in the final step to find the equivalent resistance.

③ SOLVE

Substitute the values into the equation and solve:

$$\frac{1}{R_{eq}} = \frac{1}{2.0\ \Omega} + \frac{1}{4.0\ \Omega} + \frac{1}{5.0\ \Omega} + \frac{1}{7.0\ \Omega}$$

$$\frac{1}{R_{eq}} = \frac{0.5}{1\ \Omega} + \frac{0.25}{1\ \Omega} + \frac{0.20}{1\ \Omega} + \frac{0.14}{1\ \Omega} = \frac{1.09}{1\ \Omega}$$

$$R_{eq} = \frac{1\ \Omega}{1.09}$$

$$\boxed{R_{eq} = 0.917\ \Omega}$$

Continued

Resistors in Parallel (continued)

Substitute that equivalent resistance value in the equation for current.

$$I = \frac{\Delta V_{tot}}{R_{eq}} = \frac{9.0 \text{ V}}{0.917 \text{ }\Omega}$$

$$\boxed{I = 9.8 \text{ A}}$$

Calculator Solution

The calculator answer is 9.814612868, but because the potential difference, 9.0 V, has only two significant digits, the answer is reported as 9.8 A.

Use the value calculated for I to determine the total power dissipated by resistors in the circuit.

$$P = I\Delta V$$

$$P = (9.8 \text{ A})(9.0 \text{ V})$$

$$P = 88 \text{ W}$$

④ CHECK YOUR WORK

For resistors connected in parallel, the equivalent resistance should be less than the smallest resistance.

$$0.917 \text{ }\Omega < 2.0 \text{ }\Omega$$

Practice

1. The potential difference across the equivalent resistance in Sample Problem B equals the potential difference across each of the individual parallel resistors. Calculate the value for the current in each resistor.

2. A length of wire is cut into five equal pieces. The five pieces are then connected in parallel, with the resulting resistance being 2.00 Ω. What was the resistance of the original length of wire before it was cut up?

3. A 4.0 Ω resistor, an 8.0 Ω resistor, and a 12.0 Ω resistor are connected in parallel across a 24.0 V battery.

   a. What is the equivalent resistance of the circuit and the total power dissipated by resistors in the circuit?

   b. What is the current in each resistor?

Parallel circuits do not require all elements to conduct.

What happens when a bulb burns out in a string of decorative lights that is wired in parallel? There is no current in that branch of the circuit, but each of the parallel branches provides a separate alternative pathway for current. Thus, the potential difference supplied to the other branches and the current in these branches remain the same, and the bulbs in these branches remain lit.

When resistors are wired in parallel with an emf source, the potential difference across each resistor always equals the potential difference across the source. Because household circuits are arranged in parallel, appliance manufacturers are able to standardize their design, producing devices that all operate at the same potential difference. As a result, manufacturers can choose the resistance to ensure that the current will be neither too high nor too low for the internal wiring and other components that make up the device.

Additionally, the equivalent resistance of several parallel resistors is less than the resistance of any of the individual resistors. Thus, a low equivalent resistance can be created with a group of resistors of higher resistances.

✓ SECTION 2 FORMATIVE ASSESSMENT

▶ Reviewing Main Ideas

1. Two resistors are wired in series. In another circuit, the same two resistors are wired in parallel. In which circuit is the equivalent resistance greater?

2. A 5 Ω, a 10 Ω, and a 15 Ω resistor are connected in series.
   a. Which resistor has the most current in it?
   b. Which resistor has the largest potential difference across it?

3. A 5 Ω, a 10 Ω, and a 15 Ω resistor are connected in parallel.
   a. Which resistor has the most current in it?
   b. Which resistor has the largest potential difference across it?

4. Find the current in, potential difference across, and power dissipated by each of the resistors in the following circuits:
   a. a 2.0 Ω and a 4.0 Ω resistor wired in series with a 12 V source
   b. a 2.0 Ω and a 4.0 Ω resistor wired in parallel with a 12 V source

Interpreting Graphics

5. The brightness of a bulb depends only on the bulb's resistance and on the potential difference across it. A bulb with a greater potential difference dissipates more power and thus is brighter. The five bulbs shown in **Figure 2.7** are identical, and so are the three batteries. Rank the bulbs in order of brightness from greatest to least, indicating if any are equal. Explain your reasoning. (Disregard the resistance of the wires.)

FIGURE 2.7

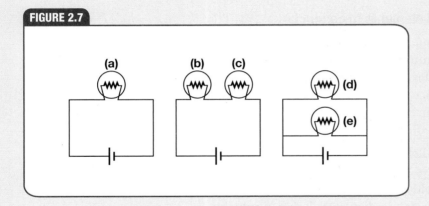

Complex Resistor Combinations

Objectives

▶ Calculate the equivalent resistance for a complex circuit involving both series and parallel portions.

▶ Calculate the current in and potential difference across individual elements within a complex circuit.

Resistors Combined Both in Parallel and in Series

Series and parallel circuits are not often encountered independent of one another. Most circuits today employ both series and parallel wiring to utilize the advantages of each type.

A common example of a complex circuit is the electrical wiring typical in a home. In a home, a fuse or circuit breaker is connected in series to numerous outlets, which are wired to one another in parallel. An example of a typical household circuit is shown in **Figure 3.1**.

As a result of the outlets being wired in parallel, all the appliances operate independently; if one is switched off, any others remain on. Wiring the outlets in parallel ensures that an identical potential difference exists across any appliance. This way, appliance manufacturers can produce appliances that all use the same standard potential difference.

To prevent excessive current, a fuse or circuit breaker must be placed in series with all of the outlets. Fuses and circuit breakers open the circuit when the current becomes too high. A fuse is a small metallic strip that melts if the current exceeds a certain value. After a fuse has melted, it must be replaced. A circuit breaker, a more modern device, triggers a switch when current reaches a certain value. The switch must be reset, rather than replaced, after the circuit overload has been removed. Both fuses and circuit breakers must be in series with the entire load to prevent excessive current from reaching any appliance. If all the devices in **Figure 3.1** were used at once, the circuit would be overloaded. The circuit breaker would interrupt the current.

Fuses and circuit breakers are carefully selected to meet the demands of a circuit. If the circuit is to carry currents as large as 30 A, an appropriate fuse or circuit breaker must be used. Because the fuse or circuit breaker is placed in series with the rest of the circuit, the current in the fuse or circuit breaker is the same as the total current in the circuit. To find this current, one must determine the equivalent resistance.

When determining the equivalent resistance for a complex circuit, you must simplify the circuit into groups of series and parallel resistors and then find the equivalent resistance for each group by using the rules for finding the equivalent resistance of series and parallel resistors.

FIGURE 3.1

A Household Circuit **(a)** When all of these devices are plugged into the same household circuit, **(b)** the result is a parallel combination of resistors in series with a circuit breaker.

(a)

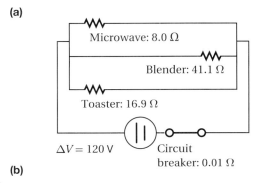

Microwave: 8.0 Ω

Blender: 41.1 Ω

Toaster: 16.9 Ω

$\Delta V = 120$ V   Circuit breaker: 0.01 Ω

(b)

Equivalent Resistance

Sample Problem C Determine the equivalent resistance of the complex circuit shown below.

① ANALYZE

The best approach is to divide the circuit into groups of series and parallel resistors. This way, the methods presented in Sample Problems A and B can be used to calculate the equivalent resistance for each group.

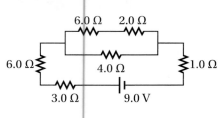

② PLAN

Redraw the circuit as a group of resistors along one side of the circuit.

Because bends in a wire do not affect the circuit, they do not need to be represented in a schematic diagram. Redraw the circuit without the corners, keeping the arrangement of the circuit elements the same, as shown at right.

Tips and Tricks
For now, disregard the emf source and work only with the resistances.

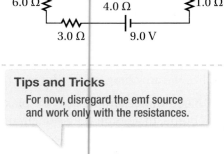

③ SOLVE

Identify components in series, and calculate their equivalent resistance.

Resistors in groups (**a**) and (**b**) are in series.
For group (**a**): $R_{eq} = 3.0\ \Omega + 6.0\ \Omega = 9.0\ \Omega$
For group (**b**): $R_{eq} = 6.0\ \Omega + 2.0\ \Omega = 8.0\ \Omega$

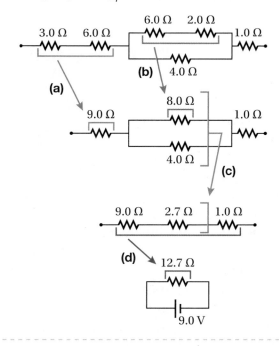

Continued

Equivalent Resistance (continued)

Identify components in parallel, and calculate their equivalent resistance.

Resistors in group (**c**) are in parallel.

For group (**c**):

$$\frac{1}{R_{eq}} = \frac{1}{8.0\ \Omega} + \frac{1}{4.0\ \Omega} = \frac{0.12\ \Omega}{1} + \frac{0.25}{1\ \Omega} = \frac{0.37}{1\ \Omega}$$

$$R_{eq} = 2.7\ \Omega$$

Repeat steps 2 and 3 until the resistors in the circuit are reduced to a single equivalent resistance.

The remainder of the resistors, group (**d**), are in series.

For group (**d**): $R_{eq} = 9.0\ \Omega + 2.7\ \Omega + 1.0\ \Omega$

$$\boxed{R_{eq} = 12.7\ \Omega}$$

Practice

1. For each of the following sets of values, determine the equivalent resistance for the circuit shown in **Figure 3.2**.

   a. $R_a = 25.0\ \Omega$ $R_b = 3.0\ \Omega$ $R_c = 40.0\ \Omega$

   b. $R_a = 12.0\ \Omega$ $R_b = 35.0\ \Omega$ $R_c = 25.0\ \Omega$

   c. $R_a = 15.0\ \Omega$ $R_b = 28.0\ \Omega$ $R_c = 12.0\ \Omega$

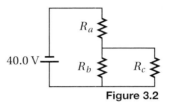

Figure 3.2

2. For each of the following sets of values, determine the equivalent resistance for the circuit shown in **Figure 3.3**.

   a. $R_a = 25.0\ \Omega$ $R_b = 3.0\ \Omega$ $R_c = 40.0\ \Omega$
       $R_d = 15.0\ \Omega$ $R_e = 18.0\ \Omega$

   b. $R_a = 12.0\ \Omega$ $R_b = 35.0\ \Omega$ $R_c = 25.0\ \Omega$
       $R_d = 50.0\ \Omega$ $R_e = 45.0\ \Omega$

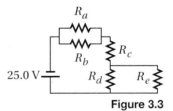

Figure 3.3

Work backward to find the current in and potential difference across a part of a circuit.

Now that the equivalent resistance for a complex circuit has been determined, you can work backward to find the current in and potential difference across any resistor in that circuit. In the household example, substitute potential difference and equivalent resistance in $\Delta V = IR$ to find the total current in the circuit. Because the fuse or circuit breaker is in series with the load, the current in it is equal to the total current. Once this total current is determined, $\Delta V = IR$ can again be used to find the potential difference across the fuse or circuit breaker.

There is no single formula for finding the current in and potential difference across a resistor buried inside a complex circuit. Instead, $\Delta V = IR$ and the rules reviewed in **Figure 3.4** must be applied to smaller pieces of the circuit until the desired values are found.

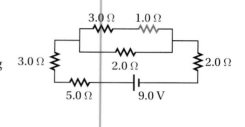

	Series	Parallel
current	same as total	add to find total
potential difference	add to find total	same as total

SERIES AND PARALLEL RESISTORS

GO ONLINE

Interactive Demo
HMHScience.com

Current in and Potential Difference Across a Resistor

Sample Problem D Determine the current in and potential difference across the 1.0 Ω resistor highlighted in the figure below.

---

① ANALYZE

First determine the total circuit current by reducing the resistors to a single equivalent resistance. Then rebuild the circuit in steps, calculating the current and potential difference for the equivalent resistance of each group until the current in and potential difference across the 1.0 Ω resistor are known.

---

② PLAN

Determine the equivalent resistance of the circuit.
The equivalent resistance of the circuit is 11.3 Ω; this value is calculated in Sample Problem C.

Calculate the total current in the circuit.
Substitute the potential difference and equivalent resistance in $\Delta V = IR$, and rearrange the equation to find the current delivered by the battery.

$$I = \frac{\Delta V}{R_{eq}} = \frac{9.0\text{ V}}{11.3\ \Omega} = 0.80\text{ A}$$

Determine a path from the equivalent resistance found in step 1 to the 1.0 Ω resistor.
Review the path taken to find the equivalent resistance in the figure at right, and work backward through this path. The equivalent resistance for the entire circuit is the same as the equivalent resistance for group (**d**). The center resistor in group (**d**) in turn is the equivalent resistance for group (**c**). The top resistor in group (**c**) is the equivalent resistance for group (**b**), and the right resistor in group (**b**) is the 1.0 Ω resistor.

> **Tips and Tricks**
> It is not necessary to solve for R_{eq} first and then work backward to find current in or potential difference across a particular resistor, as shown in this sample problem, but working through these steps keeps the mathematical operations at each step simpler.

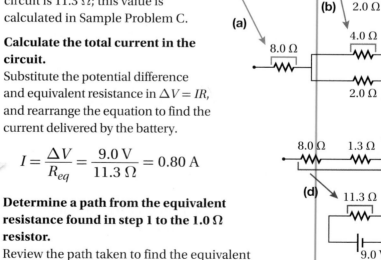

Continued

③ SOLVE

Follow the path determined in the previous step, and calculate the current in and potential difference across each equivalent resistance. Repeat this process until the desired values are found.

A. Regroup, evaluate, and calculate.
Replace the circuit's equivalent resistance with group (**d**). The resistors in group (**d**) are in series; therefore, the current in each resistor is the same as the current in the equivalent resistance, which equals 0.80 A. The potential difference across the 1.3 Ω resistor in group (**d**) can be calculated using $\Delta V = IR$.

Given: $I = 0.80$ A $R = 1.3\ \Omega$

Unknown: $\Delta V = ?$

$$\Delta V = IR = (0.80\ \text{A})(1.3\ \Omega) = \boxed{1.0\ \text{V}}$$

B. Regroup, evaluate, and calculate.
Replace the center resistor with group (**c**).
The resistors in group (**c**) are in parallel; therefore, the potential difference across each resistor is the same as the potential difference across the 1.3 Ω equivalent resistance, which equals 1.0 V. The current in the 4.0 Ω resistor in group (**c**) can be calculated using $\Delta V = IR$.

Given: $\Delta V = 1.0$ V $R = 4.0\ \Omega$

Unknown: $I = ?$

$$I = \frac{\Delta V}{R} = \frac{1.0}{4.0} = \boxed{0.25\ \text{A}}$$

C. Regroup, evaluate, and calculate.
Replace the 4.0 Ω resistor with group (**b**).

The resistors in group (**b**) are in series; therefore, the current in each resistor is the same as the current in the 4.0 Ω equivalent resistance, which equals 0.25 A.

$$\boxed{I = 0.25\ \text{A}}$$

Tips and Tricks

You can check each step in problems like Sample Problem D by using $\Delta V = IR$ for each resistor in a set. You can also check the sum of ΔV for series circuits and the sum of I for parallel circuits.

The potential difference across the 1.0 Ω resistor can be calculated using $\Delta V = IR$.

Given: $I = 0.25$ A $R = 1.0\ \Omega$

Unknown: $\Delta V = ?$

$$\Delta V = IR = (0.25\ \text{A})(1.0\ \Omega) = 0.25\ \text{V}$$

$$\boxed{\Delta V = 0.25\ \text{V}}$$

Continued

Practice

Calculate the current in and potential difference across each of the resistors shown in the schematic diagram in **Figure 3.5.**

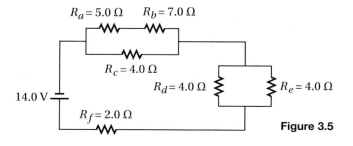

$R_a = 5.0\ \Omega$ $R_b = 7.0\ \Omega$

$R_c = 4.0\ \Omega$

$R_d = 4.0\ \Omega$ $R_e = 4.0\ \Omega$

14.0 V

$R_f = 2.0\ \Omega$

Figure 3.5

WHY IT MATTERS

Decorative Lights and Bulbs

L ight sets arranged in series cannot remain lit if a bulb burns out. Wiring in parallel can eliminate this problem, but each bulb must then be able to withstand 120 V. To eliminate the drawbacks of either approach, modern light sets typically contain two or three sections connected to each other in parallel, each of which contains bulbs in series.

When a bulb is removed from a modern light set, half or one-third of the lights in the set go dark, because the bulbs in that section are wired in series. When a bulb burns out, however, all of the other bulbs in the set remain lit. How is this possible?

Modern decorative bulbs have a short loop of insulated wire, called the *jumper,* that is wrapped around the wires connected to the filament, as shown at right. There is no current in the insulated wire when the bulb is functioning properly. When the filament breaks, however, the current in the section is zero, and the potential difference across the two wires connected to the broken filament is then 120 V. This large potential difference creates a spark

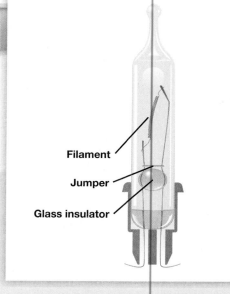

Filament

Jumper

Glass insulator

across the two wires that burns the insulation off the small loop of wire. Once that occurs, the small loop closes the circuit, and the other bulbs in the section remain lit.

Because the small loop in the burned-out bulb has very little resistance, the equivalent resistance of that portion of the light set decreases; its current increases. This increased current results in a slight increase in each bulb's brightness. As more bulbs burn out, the temperature in each bulb increases and can become a fire hazard; thus, bulbs should be replaced soon after burning out.

▶ Reviewing Main Ideas

1. Find the equivalent resistance of the complex circuit shown in **Figure 3.6.**

2. What is the current in the 1.5 Ω resistor in the complex circuit shown in **Figure 3.6?**

3. What is the potential difference across the 1.5 Ω resistor in the circuit shown in **Figure 3.6?**

4. A certain strand of miniature lights contains 35 bulbs wired in series, with each bulb having a resistance of 15.0 Ω. What is the equivalent resistance when three such strands are connected in parallel across a potential difference of 120.0 V?

5. What is the current in and potential difference across each of the bulbs in the strands of lights described in item 4?

6. If one of the bulbs in one of the three strands of lights in item 4 goes out while the other bulbs in that strand remain lit, what is the current in and potential difference across each of the lit bulbs in that strand?

FIGURE 3.6

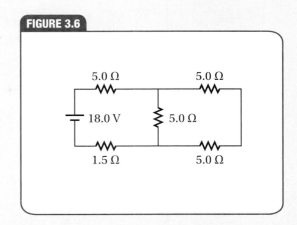

Interpreting Graphics

7. **Figure 3.7** depicts a household circuit containing several appliances and a circuit breaker attached to a 120 V source of potential difference.

   a. Is the current in the toaster equal to the current in the microwave?

   b. Is the potential difference across the microwave equal to the potential difference across the popcorn popper?

   c. Is the current in the circuit breaker equal to the total current in all of the appliances combined?

   d. Determine the equivalent resistance for the circuit.

   e. Determine how much current is in the toaster.

FIGURE 3.7

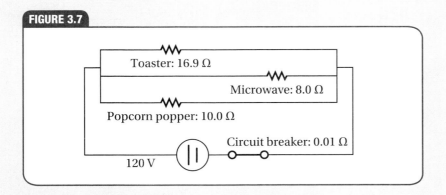

Semiconductor Technician

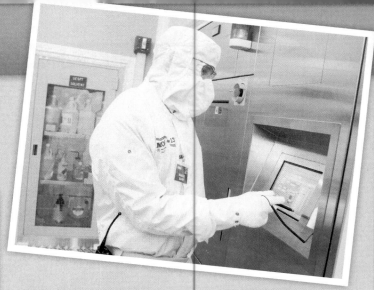

E lectronic chips are used in a wide variety of devices, from toys to phones to computers. To learn more about chip making as a career, read the interview with etch process engineering technician Brad Baker, who works for Motorola.

Brad Baker is creating a recipe on the plasma etch tool to test a new process.

What training did you receive in order to become a semiconductor technician?

My experience is fairly unique. My degree is in psychology. You have to have an associate's degree in some sort of electrical or engineering field or an undergraduate degree in any field.

What about semiconductor manufacturing made it more interesting than other fields?

While attending college, I worked at an airline. There was not a lot of opportunity to advance, which helped point me in other directions. Circuitry has a lot of parallels to the biological aspects of the brain, which is what I studied in school. We use the scientific method a lot.

What is the nature of your work?

I work on the etch process team. Device engineers design the actual semiconductor. Our job is to figure out how to make what they have requested. It's sort of like being a chef. Once you have experience, you know which ingredient to add.

What is your favorite thing about your job?

I feel like a scientist. My company gives us the freedom to try new things and develop new processes.

Has your job changed since you started it?

Each generation of device is smaller, so we have to do more in less space. As the devices get smaller, it becomes more challenging to get a design process that is powerful enough but doesn't etch too much or too little.

What advice do you have for students who are interested in semiconductor engineering?

The field is very science oriented, so choose chemical engineering, electrical engineering, or material science as majors. Other strengths are the ability to understand and meet challenges, knowledge of troubleshooting techniques, patience, and analytical skills. Also, everything is computer automated, so you have to know how to use computers.

Brad Baker

Responsible Use of Resources

Look around your classroom. What happens to all the lab materials when they are no longer needed? Some of the materials found in a lab must be disposed of with special care because they can be hazardous to people who handle them. Many lab materials, however, can be recycled or reused. Even before starting a lab activity, it is important to consider the responsible use of resources. By reducing the amount of resources used at the beginning of an activity, you will reduce the number of items to be be discarded or recycled later.

Safe Disposal and Recycling Practices

Materials that make up circuits and circuit components can often require particular disposal and/or recycling practices. Many cities offer electronics recycling programs to safely eliminate or recycle potentially hazardous electronic and circuit components. For instance, most types of batteries can be recycled, but careful handling is important. Wrapping the terminals of each battery with electrical tape can reduce fire hazards. Many recycling centers will accept automotive battery materials. However, leaking batteries should not be recycled, and instead should be disposed of as hazardous waste.

- As you look around your classroom, identify three items that could be recycled after they have been used.

- Research the recycling program in your area. Are there resources to help you recycle electronic components?

- Aside from batteries, what components in a circuit might receive special disposal or recycling treatment?

- How do CFLs and LEDs help to reduce the amount of resources used?

Conceptual Challenge

The ability to make assumptions and generate rough estimates is a valuable skill to scientists. Quick estimates allow scientists to narrow the range of possibilities and focus on the most reasonable hypotheses.

Counting the Bulbs If everyone used incandescent bulbs, how many light bulbs would the average home use over the course of one year? What if only compact fluorescent light (CFL) bulbs were used instead?

You can begin addressing the scenario by asking questions such as the following:

- How many light bulbs does the average home use each day?

- For how many hours is each light bulb turned on each day?

- How many hours does each light bulb last?

SECTION 1 Schematic Diagrams and Circuits

KEY TERMS

- Schematic diagrams use standardized symbols to summarize the contents of electric circuits.
- A circuit is a set of electrical components connected so that they provide one or more complete paths for the movement of charges.
- Any device that transforms nonelectrical energy into electrical energy, such as a battery or a generator, is a source of emf.
- If the internal resistance of a battery is neglected, the emf can be considered equal to the terminal voltage, the potential difference across the source's two terminals.

schematic diagram
electric circuit

SECTION 2 Resistors in Series or in Parallel

KEY TERMS

- Resistors in series have the same current.
- The equivalent resistance of a set of resistors connected in series is the sum of the individual resistances.
- The sum of currents in parallel resistors equals the total current.
- The equivalent resistance of a set of resistors connected in parallel is calculated using an inverse relationship.

series
parallel

SECTION 3 Complex Resistor Combinations

- Many complex circuits can be understood by isolating segments that are in series or in parallel and simplifying them to their equivalent resistances.

VARIABLE SYMBOLS

Quantities		Units		Conversions
I	current	A	amperes	= C/s = coulombs of charge per second
R	resistance	Ω	ohms	= V/A = volts per ampere of current
ΔV	potential difference	V	volts	= J/C = joules of energy per coulomb of charge

DIAGRAM SYMBOLS

wire or conductor	
resistor or circuit load	
bulb or lamp	
plug	
battery / direct-current emf source	
switch	
capacitor	

Problem Solving

See **Appendix D: Equations** for a summary of the equations introduced in this chapter. If you need more problem-solving practice, see **Appendix I: Additional Problems.**

Schematic Diagrams and Circuits

▶ REVIEWING MAIN IDEAS

1. Why are schematic diagrams useful?

2. Draw a circuit diagram for a circuit containing three 5.0 Ω resistors, a 6.0 V battery, and a switch.

3. The switch in the circuit shown below can be set to connect to points *A, B,* or *C.* Which of these connections will provide a complete circuit?

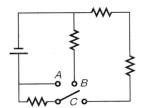

4. If the batteries in a cassette recorder provide a terminal voltage of 12.0 V, what is the potential difference across the entire recorder?

5. In a case in which the internal resistance of a battery is significant, which is greater?
   a. the terminal voltage
   b. the emf of the battery

CONCEPTUAL QUESTIONS

6. Do charges move from a source of potential difference into a load or through both the source and the load?

7. Assuming that you want to create a circuit that has current in it, why should there be no openings in the circuit?

8. Suppose a 9 V battery is connected across a light bulb. In what form is the electrical energy supplied by the battery dissipated by the light bulb?

9. Why is it dangerous to use an electrical appliance when you are in the bathtub?

10. Which of the switches in the circuit below will complete a circuit when closed? Which will cause a short circuit?

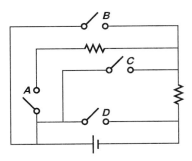

Resistors in Series or in Parallel

▶ REVIEWING MAIN IDEAS

11. If four resistors in a circuit are connected in series, which of the following is the same for the resistors in the circuit?
   a. potential difference across the resistors
   b. current in the resistors

12. If four resistors in a circuit are in parallel, which of the following is the same for the resistors in the circuit?
   a. potential difference across the resistors
   b. current in the resistors

CONCEPTUAL QUESTIONS

13. A short circuit is a circuit containing a path of very low resistance in parallel with some other part of the circuit. Discuss the effect of a short circuit on the current within the portion of the circuit that has very low resistance.

14. Fuses protect electrical devices by opening a circuit if the current in the circuit is too high. Would a fuse work successfully if it were connected in parallel with the device that it is supposed to protect?

15. What might be an advantage of using two identical resistors in parallel that are connected in series with another identical parallel pair, as shown below, instead of using a single resistor?

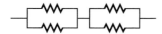

PRACTICE PROBLEMS

For problems 16–17, see Sample Problem A.

16. A length of wire is cut into five equal pieces. If each piece has a resistance of 0.15 Ω, what was the resistance of the original length of wire?

17. A 4.0 Ω resistor, an 8.0 Ω resistor, and a 12 Ω resistor are connected in series with a 24 V battery. Determine the following:
  a. the equivalent resistance for the circuit
  b. the current in the circuit

For problems 18–19, see Sample Problem B.

18. The resistors in item 17 are connected in parallel across a 24 V battery. Determine the following:
  a. the equivalent resistance for the circuit
  b. the current delivered by the battery

19. An 18.0 Ω resistor, 9.00 Ω resistor, and 6.00 Ω resistor are connected in parallel across a 12 V battery. Determine the following:
  a. the equivalent resistance for the circuit
  b. the current delivered by the battery

Complex Resistor Combinations

CONCEPTUAL QUESTIONS

20. A technician has two resistors, each of which has the same resistance, R.
  a. How many different resistances can the technician achieve?
  b. Express the effective resistance of each possibility in terms of R.

21. The technician in item 20 finds another resistor, so now there are three resistors with the same resistance.
  a. How many different resistances can the technician achieve?
  b. Express the effective resistance of each possibility in terms of R.

22. Three identical light bulbs are connected in circuit to a battery, as shown below. Compare the level of brightness of each bulb when all the bulbs are illuminated. What happens to the brightness of each bulb if the following changes are made to the circuit?
  a. Bulb A is removed from its socket.
  b. Bulb C is removed from its socket.
  c. A wire is connected directly between points D and E.
  d. A wire is connected directly between points D and F.

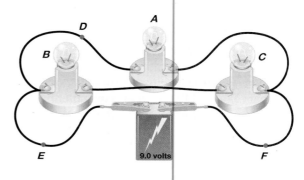

PRACTICE PROBLEMS

For problems 23–24, see Sample Problem C.

23. Find the equivalent resistance of the circuit shown in the figure below.

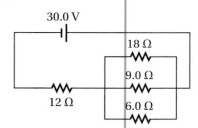

24. Find the equivalent resistance of the circuit shown in the figure below.

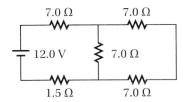

For problems 25–26, see Sample Problem D.

25. For the circuit shown below, determine the current in each resistor and the potential difference across each resistor.

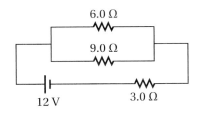

26. For the circuit shown in the figure below, determine the following:

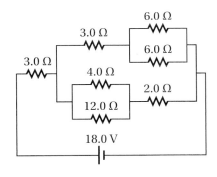

   a. the current in the 2.0 Ω resistor
   b. the potential difference across the 2.0 Ω resistor
   c. the potential difference across the 12.0 Ω resistor
   d. the current in the 12.0 Ω resistor

Mixed Review

REVIEWING MAIN IDEAS

27. An 8.0 Ω resistor and a 6.0 Ω resistor are connected in series with a battery. The potential difference across the 6.0 Ω resistor is measured as 12 V. Find the potential difference across the battery.

28. A 9.0 Ω resistor and a 6.0 Ω resistor are connected in parallel to a battery, and the current in the 9.0 Ω resistor is found to be 0.25 A. Find the potential difference across the battery.

29. A 9.0 Ω resistor and a 6.0 Ω resistor are connected in series to a battery, and the current through the 9.0 Ω resistor is 0.25 A. What is the potential difference across the battery?

30. A 9.0 Ω resistor and a 6.0 Ω resistor are connected in series with an emf source. The potential difference across the 6.0 Ω resistor is measured with a voltmeter to be 12 V. Find the potential difference across the emf source.

31. An 18.0 Ω, 9.00 Ω, and 6.00 Ω resistor are connected in series with an emf source. The current in the 9.00 Ω resistor is measured to be 4.00 A.
   a. Calculate the equivalent resistance of the three resistors in the circuit.
   b. Find the potential difference across the emf source.
   c. Find the current in the other resistors.

32. The stockroom has only 20 Ω and 50 Ω resistors.
   a. You need a resistance of 45 Ω. How can this resistance be achieved using three resistors?
   b. Describe two ways to achieve a resistance of 35 Ω using four resistors.

33. The equivalent resistance of the circuit shown below is 60.0 Ω. Use the diagram to determine the value of R.

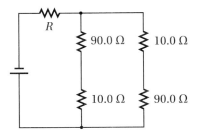

34. Two identical parallel-wired strings of 25 bulbs are connected to each other in series. If the equivalent resistance of the combination is 150.0 Ω and it is connected across a potential difference of 120.0 V, what is the resistance of each individual bulb?

35. The figures **(a)–(e)** below depict five resistance diagrams. Each individual resistance is 6.0 Ω.

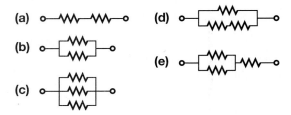

a. Which resistance combination has the greatest equivalent resistance?
b. Which resistance combination has the least equivalent resistance?
c. Which resistance combination has an equivalent resistance of 4.0 Ω?
d. Which resistance combination has an equivalent resistance of 9.0 Ω?

36. Three small lamps are connected to a 9.0 V battery, as shown below.

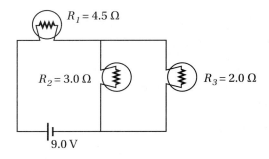

a. What is the equivalent resistance of this circuit?
b. What is the current in the battery?
c. What is the current in each bulb?
d. What is the potential difference across each bulb?

37. An 18.0 Ω resistor and a 6.0 Ω resistor are connected in series to an 18.0 V battery. Find the current in and the potential difference across each resistor.

38. A 30.0 Ω resistor is connected in parallel to a 15.0 Ω resistor. These are joined in series to a 5.00 Ω resistor and a source with a potential difference of 30.0 V.
a. Draw a schematic diagram for this circuit.
b. Calculate the equivalent resistance.
c. Calculate the current in each resistor.
d. Calculate the potential difference across each resistor.

39. A resistor with an unknown resistance is connected in parallel to a 12 Ω resistor. When both resistors are connected to an emf source of 12 V, the current in the unknown resistor is measured with an ammeter to be 3.0 A. What is the resistance of the unknown resistor?

40. The resistors described in item 37 are reconnected in parallel to the same 18.0 V battery. Find the current in each resistor and the potential difference across each resistor.

41. The equivalent resistance for the circuit shown below drops to one-half its original value when the switch, S, is closed. Determine the value of R.

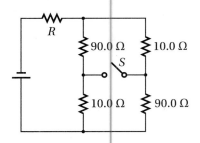

42. You can obtain only four 20.0 Ω resistors from the stockroom.
a. How can you achieve a resistance of 50.0 Ω under these circumstances?
b. What can you do if you need a 5.0 Ω resistor?

43. Four resistors are connected to a battery with a terminal voltage of 12.0 V, as shown below. Determine the following:

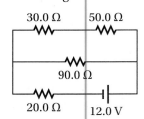

a. the equivalent resistance for the circuit
b. the current in the battery
c. the current in the 30.0 Ω resistor
d. the power dissipated by the 50.0 Ω resistor
e. the power dissipated by the 20.0 Ω resistor

(Hint: Remember that $P = \dfrac{(\Delta V)^2}{R} = I \Delta V$.)

44. Two resistors, *A* and *B*, are connected in series to a 6.0 V battery. A voltmeter connected across resistor *A* measures a potential difference of 4.0 V. When the two resistors are connected in parallel across the 6.0 V battery, the current in *B* is found to be 2.0 A. Find the resistances of *A* and *B*.

45. Draw a schematic diagram of nine 100 Ω resistors arranged in a series-parallel network so that the total resistance of the network is also 100 Ω. All nine resistors must be used.

46. For the circuit below, find the following:

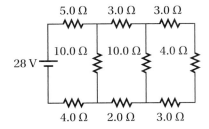

a. the equivalent resistance of the circuit
b. the current in the 5.0 Ω resistor

47. The power supplied to the circuit shown below is 4.00 W. Determine the following:

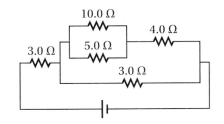

a. the equivalent resistance of the circuit
b. the potential difference across the battery

48. Your toaster oven and coffee maker each dissipate 1200 W of power. Can you operate both of these appliances at the same time if the 120 V line you use in your kitchen has a circuit breaker rated at 15 A? Explain.

49. An electric heater is rated at 1300 W, a toaster is rated at 1100 W, and an electric grill is rated at 1500 W. The three appliances are connected in parallel across a 120 V emf source.
a. Find the current in each appliance.
b. Is a 30.0 A circuit breaker sufficient in this situation? Explain.

GRAPHING CALCULATOR PRACTICE

Parallel Resistors

Electric circuits are often composed of combinations of series and parallel circuits. The overall resistance of a circuit is determined by dividing the circuit into groups of series and parallel resistors and determining the equivalent resistance of each group. As you learned earlier in this chapter, the equivalent resistance of parallel resistors is given by the following equation:

$$\frac{1}{R_{eq}} = \frac{1}{R_1} + \frac{1}{R_2} + \frac{1}{R_3} + \cdots$$

One interesting consequence of this equation is that the equivalent resistance for resistors in parallel will always be less than the smallest resistor in the group.

In this graphing calculator activity, you will determine the equivalent resistance for various resistors in parallel. You will confirm that the equivalent resistance is always less than the smallest resistor, and you will relate the number of resistors and changes in resistance to the equivalent resistance.

Go online to HMHScience.com to find the skillsheet and program for this graphing calculator activity.

ALTERNATIVE ASSESSMENT

1. How many ways can two or more batteries be connected in a circuit with a light bulb? How will the current change depending on the arrangement? First draw diagrams of the circuits you want to test. Then identify the equipment you need and measurements you need to make to answer the question. If your teacher approves your plan, obtain the equipment and perform the experiment.

2. Research the career of an electrical engineer or technician. Prepare materials for people interested in this career field. Include information on where people in this career field work, which tools and equipment they use, and the challenges of their field. Indicate what training is typically necessary to enter the field.

3. The manager of an automotive repair shop has been contacted by two competing firms that are selling ammeters to be used in testing automobile electrical systems. One firm has published claims that its ammeter is better because it has high internal resistance. The other firm has published claims that its ammeter is better because it has low resistance. Write a report with your recommendation to the manager of the automotive repair shop. Include diagrams and calculations that explain how you reached your conclusion.

4. You and your friend want to start a business exporting small electrical appliances. You have found people willing to be your partners to distribute these appliances in Germany. Write a letter to these potential partners that describes your product line and that asks for the information you will need about the electric power, sources, consumption, and distribution in Germany.

5. Contact an electrician, builder, or contractor, and ask to see a house electrical plan. Study the diagram to identify the circuit breakers, their connections to different appliances in the home, and the limitations they impose on the circuit's design. Find out how much current, on average, is in each appliance in the house. Draw a diagram of the house, showing which circuit breakers control which appliances. Your diagram should also keep the current in each of these appliances under the performance and safety limits.

Standards-Based Assessment

Record your answers on a separate piece of paper.

MULTIPLE CHOICE

1 Which of the following is the correct term for a circuit in which the load has been unintentionally bypassed?

A closed circuit
B dead circuit
C open circuit
D short circuit

Use the diagram below to answer questions 2–4.

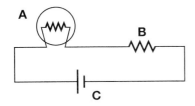

2 Which of the circuit elements contribute to the load of the circuit?

A only **A**
B **A** and **B** but not **C**
C only **C**
D **A**, **B**, and **C**

3 Which of the following is the correct equation for the equivalent resistance of the circuit?

A $R_{eq} = R_A + R_B$

B $\dfrac{1}{R_{eq}} = \dfrac{1}{R_A} + \dfrac{1}{R_B}$

C $R_{eq} = I\Delta V$

D $\dfrac{1}{R_{eq}} = \dfrac{1}{R_A} + \dfrac{1}{R_B} + \dfrac{1}{R_C}$

4 Which of the following is the correct equation for the current in the resistor?

A $I = I_A + I_B + I_C$

B $I_B = \dfrac{\Delta V}{R_{eq}}$

C $I_B = I_{total} + I_A$

D $I_B = \dfrac{\Delta V}{R_B}$

Use the following passage to answer questions 5–7.

Six light bulbs are connected in parallel to a 9.0 V battery. Each bulb has a resistance of 3.0 Ω.

5 What is the potential difference across each bulb?

A 1.5 V
B 3.0 V
C 9.0 V
D 27 V

6 What is the current in each bulb?

A 0.5 A
B 3.0 A
C 4.5 A
D 18 A

7 What is the total current in the circuit?

A 0.5 A
B 3.0 A
C 4.5 A
D 18 A

GRIDDED RESPONSE

8 For the circuit shown below, calculate the equivalent resistance of the circuit in Ω.

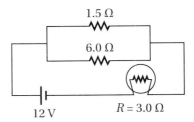

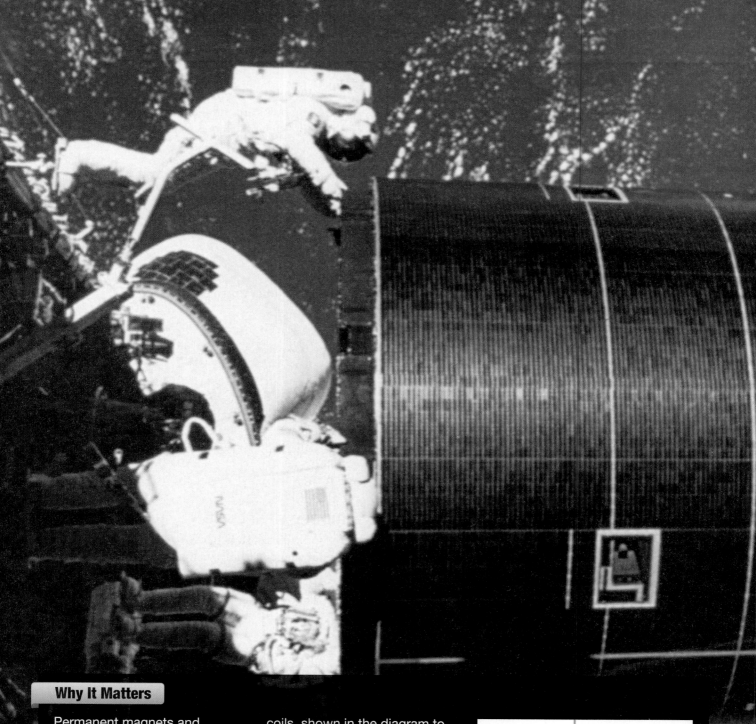

Why It Matters

Permanent magnets and electromagnets are used in many everyday and scientific applications. Huge electromagnets are used to pick up and move heavy loads, such as scrap iron at a recycling plant, and satellites sometimes contain loops of wire called *magnetic torque coils.* These coils, shown in the diagram to the right, can be activated by a satellite operator on Earth. When current is in the coil, the magnetic field of Earth exerts a torque on the loop of wire. Torque coils are used to align a satellite in the orientation needed for its instruments to work.

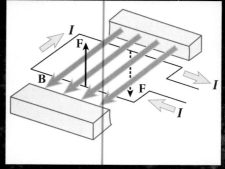

664

CHAPTER 19
Magnetism

SECTION 1
Magnets and Magnetic Fields

SECTION 2
Magnetism from Electricity

SECTION 3
Magnetic Force

BIG IDEA

Magnetic force is a force due to moving charges, such as those that produce an electric current. Like gravity and electric force, magnetic force acts at a distance.

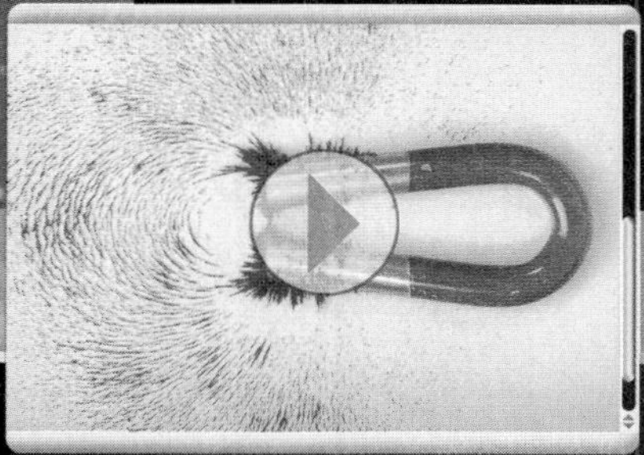

ONLINE Physics
HMHScience.com

ONLINE LABS
- Magnetism
- Magnetic Field of a Conducting Wire
- Magnetism from Electricity

GO ONLINE
Animated Physics
HMHScience.com

Magnetic Force

SECTION 1

Objectives

▶ For given situations, predict whether magnets will repel or attract each other.

▶ Describe the magnetic field around a permanent magnet.

▶ Describe the orientation of Earth's magnetic field.

Magnets and Magnetic Fields

Key Terms

magnetic domains   magnetic field

Magnets

Most people have had experience with different kinds of magnets, such as those shown in **Figure 1.1.** You have probably seen a variety of magnet shapes, such as horseshoe magnets, bar magnets, and the flat magnets frequently used to attach items to a refrigerator. All types of magnets attract iron-containing objects such as paper clips and nails. In the following discussion, we will assume that the magnet has the shape of a bar. Iron objects are most strongly attracted to the ends of such a magnet. These ends are called *poles;* one is called the *north pole*, and the other is called the *south pole*. The names derive from the behavior of a magnet on Earth. If a bar magnet is suspended from its midpoint so that it can swing freely in a horizontal plane, it will rotate until its north pole points north and its south pole points south. In fact, a compass is just a magnetized needle that swings freely on a pivot.

The list of important technological applications of magnetism is very long. For instance, large electromagnets are used to pick up heavy loads. Magnets are also used in meters, motors, generators, and loudspeakers. Magnetic tapes are routinely used in sound- and video-recording equipment, and magnetic recording material is used on computer disks. Superconducting magnets are currently being used to contain extremely high-temperature plasmas that are used in controlled nuclear fusion research. Superconducting magnets are also used to levitate modern trains. These *maglev* trains are faster and provide a smoother ride than the ordinary track system because of the absence of friction between the train and the track.

Like poles repel each other, and unlike poles attract each other.

The magnetic force between two magnets can be likened to the electric force between charged objects in that unlike poles of two magnets attract one another and like poles repel one another. Thus, the north pole of a magnet is attracted to the south pole of another magnet, and two north poles (or two south poles) brought close together repel each other. Electric charges differ from magnetic poles in that they can be isolated, whereas magnetic poles cannot.

FIGURE 1.1

Variety of Magnets Magnets come in a variety of shapes and sizes, but like poles of two magnets always repel one another.

In fact, no matter how many times a permanent magnet is cut, each piece always has a north pole and a south pole. Thus, magnetic poles always occur in pairs.

Magnetic Domains

The magnetic properties of many materials are explained in terms of a model in which an electron is said to spin on its axis much like a top does. (This classical description should not be taken literally. The property of electron spin can be understood only with the methods of quantum mechanics.) The spinning electron represents a charge that is in motion. As you will learn in the next section of this chapter, moving charges create magnetic fields.

In atoms containing many electrons, the electrons usually pair up with their spins opposite each other, causing their fields to cancel each other. For this reason, most substances, such as wood and plastic, are not magnetic. However, in materials such as iron, cobalt, and nickel, the magnetic fields produced by the electron spins do not cancel completely. Such materials are said to be *ferromagnetic*.

In ferromagnetic materials, strong coupling occurs between neighboring atoms to form large groups of atoms whose net spins are aligned; these groups are called **magnetic domains.** Domains typically range in size from about 10^{-4} cm to 10^{-1} cm. In an unmagnetized substance, the domains are randomly oriented, as shown in **Figure 1.2(a).** When an external magnetic field is applied, the orientation of the magnetic fields of each domain may change slightly to more closely align with the external magnetic field, or the domains that are already aligned with the external field may grow at the expense of the other domains. This alignment enhances the applied magnetic field.

Some materials can be made into permanent magnets.

Just as two materials, such as rubber and wool, can become charged after they are rubbed together, an unmagnetized piece of iron can become a permanent magnet by being stroked with a permanent magnet. Magnetism can be induced by other means as well. For example, if a piece of unmagnetized iron is placed near a strong permanent magnet, the piece of iron will eventually become magnetized. The process can be reversed either by heating and cooling the iron or by hammering the iron, because these actions cause the magnetic domains to jiggle and lose their alignment.

A magnetic piece of material is classified as magnetically *hard* or *soft*, depending on the extent to which it retains its magnetism. Soft magnetic materials, such as iron, are easily magnetized but also tend to lose their magnetism easily. In hard magnetic materials, domain alignment persists after the external magnetic field is removed; the result is a permanent magnet. In contrast, hard magnetic materials, such as cobalt and nickel, are difficult to magnetize, but once they are magnetized, they tend to retain their magnetism. In soft magnetic materials, once the external field is removed, the random motion of the particles in the material changes the orientation of the domains, and the material returns to an unmagnetized state.

FIGURE 1.2

Domains of Unmagnetized and Magnetized Materials

When a substance is unmagnetized its domains are randomly oriented, as shown in **(a)**. When a substance is magnetized, its domains are more closely aligned, as shown in **(b)**.

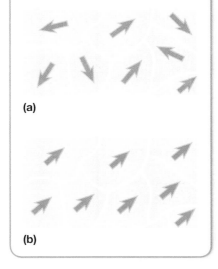

(a)

(b)

magnetic domain a region composed of a group of atoms whose spins are aligned in the same direction

Magnetic Fields

You know that the interaction between charged objects can be described using the concept of an electric field. A similar approach can be used to describe the **magnetic field** that surrounds any magnetized material. As with an electric field, a magnetic field, **B,** is a vector quantity that has both magnitude and direction.

Magnetic field lines can be drawn with the aid of a compass.

The magnetic field of a bar magnet can be explored using a compass, as illustrated in **Figure 1.4.** If a small, freely suspended bar magnet, such as the needle of a compass, is brought near a magnetic field, the compass needle will align with the magnetic field lines. The direction of the magnetic field, **B,** at any location is defined as the direction that the north pole of a compass needle points to at that location.

Magnetic field lines appear to begin at the north pole of a magnet and to end at the south pole of a magnet. However, magnetic field lines have no beginning or end. Rather, they always form a closed loop. In a permanent magnet, the field lines actually continue within the magnet itself to form a closed loop. (These lines are not shown in the illustration.)

This text will follow a simple convention to indicate the direction of **B.** An arrow will be used to show a magnetic field that is in the same plane as the page, as shown in **Figure 1.3.** When the field is directed into the page, we will use a series of blue crosses to represent the tails of arrows. If the field is directed out of the page, we will use a series of blue dots to represent the tips of arrows.

magnetic field a region in which a magnetic force can be detected

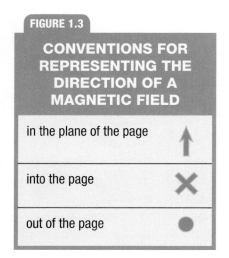

FIGURE 1.3

CONVENTIONS FOR REPRESENTING THE DIRECTION OF A MAGNETIC FIELD

in the plane of the page	↑
into the page	✕
out of the page	●

FIGURE 1.4

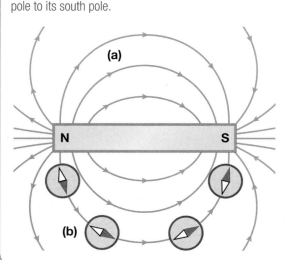

Magnetic Field of a Bar Magnet The magnetic field **(a)** of a bar magnet can be traced with a compass **(b).** Note that the north poles of the compasses point in the direction of the field lines from the magnet's north pole to its south pole.

Magnetic flux relates to the strength of a magnetic field.

One useful way to model magnetic field strength is to define a quantity called *magnetic flux*, Φ_M. It is defined as the number of field lines that cross a certain area at right angles to that area. Magnetic flux can be calculated by the following equation.

Magnetic Flux

$$\Phi_M = AB \cos \theta$$

magnetic flux = (surface area) × (magnetic field component normal to the plane of surface)

Now look again at **Figure 1.4.** Imagine two circles of the same size that are perpendicular to the axis of the magnet. One circle is located near one pole of the magnet, and the other circle is alongside the magnet. More magnetic field lines cross the circle that is near the pole of the magnet. This greater flux indicates that the magnetic field is strongest at the magnet's poles.

Earth has a magnetic field similar to that of a bar magnet.

The north and south poles of a small bar magnet are correctly described as the "north-seeking" and "south-seeking" poles. This description means that if a magnet is used as a compass, the north pole of the magnet will seek, or point to, a location near the geographic North Pole of Earth. Because unlike poles attract, we can deduce that the geographic North Pole of Earth corresponds to the magnetic south pole and the geographic South Pole of Earth corresponds to the magnetic north pole. Note that the configuration of Earth's magnetic field, pictured in **Figure 1.5,** resembles the field that would be produced if a bar magnet were buried within Earth.

If a compass needle is allowed to rotate both perpendicular to and parallel to the surface of Earth, the needle will be exactly parallel with respect to Earth's surface only near the equator. As the compass is moved northward, the needle will rotate so that it points more toward the surface of Earth. Finally, at a point just north of Hudson Bay, in Canada, the north pole of the needle will point perpendicular to Earth's surface. This site is considered to be the location of the magnetic south pole of Earth. It is approximately 1500 km from Earth's geographic North Pole. Similarly, the magnetic north pole of Earth is roughly the same distance from the geographic South Pole.

The difference between true north, which is defined by the axis of rotation of Earth, and north indicated by a compass varies from point to point on Earth. This difference is referred to as *magnetic declination*. An imaginary line running roughly north-south near the center of North America currently has zero declination. Along this line, a compass will indicate true north. However, in the state of Washington, a compass aligns about 20° east of true north. To further complicate matters, geological evidence indicates that Earth's magnetic field has changed—and even reversed—throughout Earth's history.

Although Earth has large deposits of iron ore deep beneath its surface, the high temperatures there prevent the iron from retaining permanent

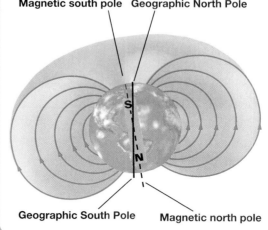

Earth's Magnetic Field Earth's magnetic field has a configuration similar to a bar magnet's. Note that the magnetic south pole is near the geographic North Pole and that the magnetic north pole is near the geographic South Pole.

Magnetic south pole   Geographic North Pole

Geographic South Pole   Magnetic north pole

Did YOU Know?

By convention, the north pole of a magnet is frequently painted red. This practice comes from the long-standing use of magnets, in the form of compasses, as navigational aids. Long before global positioning system (GPS) satellites, the compass gave humans an easy way to orient themselves.

QuickLAB   MAGNETIC FIELD OF A FILE CABINET

Stand in front of the file cabinet, and hold the compass face up and parallel to the ground. Now move the compass from the top of the file cabinet to the bottom. Making sure that the compass is parallel to the ground, check to see if the direction of the compass needle changes as it moves from the top of the cabinet to the bottom. If the compass needle changes direction, the file cabinet is magnetized. Can you explain what might have caused the file cabinet to become magnetized? Remember that Earth's magnetic field has a vertical component as well as a horizontal component.

Try tracing the field around some large metal objects around your house. Can you find an object that has been magnetized by the horizontal component of Earth's magnetic field?

MATERIALS
- compass
- metal file cabinet

magnetization. It is considered likely that the source of Earth's magnetic field is the movement of charges in *convection currents* inside Earth's liquid core. These currents occur because the temperature in Earth's core is unevenly distributed. Charged ions circling inside the interior of Earth likely produce a magnetic field. There is also evidence that the strength of a planet's magnetic field is linked to the planet's rate of rotation. Jupiter rotates at a faster rate than Earth, and recent space probes indicate that Jupiter's magnetic field is stronger than Earth's. Conversely, Venus rotates more slowly than Earth and has a weaker magnetic field than Earth. Investigations continue into the cause of Earth's magnetism.

SECTION 1 **FORMATIVE ASSESSMENT**

▶ Reviewing Main Ideas

1. For each of the cases in the figure below, identify whether the magnets will attract or repel one another.

a.

| S | N | S | N |

b.

| S | N | N | S |

c.

2. When you break a bar magnet in half, how many poles does each piece have?

Interpreting Graphics

3. Which of the compass-needle orientations in the figure below might correctly describe the magnet's field at that point?

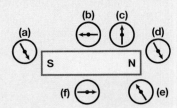

✔ Critical Thinking

4. Satellite ground operators use feedback from a device called a magnetometer, which senses the direction of Earth's magnetic field, to decide which torque coil to activate. What direction will the magnetometer read for Earth's magnetic field when the satellite passes over Earth's equator?

5. In order to protect other equipment, the body of a satellite must remain unmagnetized, even when the torque coils have been activated. Would hard or soft magnetic materials be best for building the rest of the satellite?

Magnetic Resonance Imaging

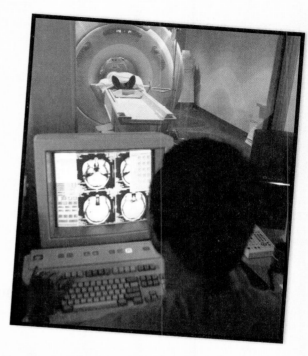

agnetic resonance imaging, or MRI, is an imaging technique that has been used in clinical medicine since the early 1980s. MRI allows doctors to make two-dimensional images or three-dimensional models of parts of the human body. The use of MRI in medicine has grown rapidly. MRI produces high-resolution images that can be tailored to study different types of tissues, depending on the application. Also, MRI procedures are generally much safer than *computerized axial tomography (CAT)* scans, which flood the body with x-rays.

A typical MRI machine looks like a giant cube, 2–3 meters on each side, with a cylindrical hollow in the center to accommodate the patient, as shown in the photo at right. The MRI machine uses electromagnets to create magnetic fields ranging in strength from 0.5–2.0 T. These fields are strong enough to erase credit cards and to pull pens out of pockets, even across the MRI exam room. Because resistance would cause normal electromagnets to dissipate a huge amount of heat when creating fields this strong, the electromagnets in most MRI machines contain superconducting wires that have zero resistance.

The creation of an image with MRI depends on the behavior of atomic nuclei within a magnetic field. In a strong magnetic field, the nucleus of an atom tends to line up along the direction of the field. This behavior is particularly true for hydrogen atoms, which are the most common atoms in the body.

The imaging magnet in most MRI machines is of the superconducting type. The magnet is the most expensive component of the MRI system.

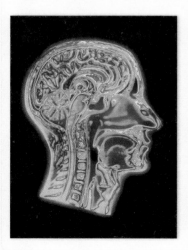

The primary magnet in an MRI system creates a strong, uniform magnetic field centered on the part of the patient that is being examined. The field causes hydrogen nuclei in the body to line up in the direction of the field. Smaller magnets, called *gradient magnets,* are then turned on and off to create small variations, or pulses, in the overall magnetic field. Each pulse causes the hydrogen nuclei to shift away from their alignment. After the pulse, the nuclei return to alignment, and as they do so, they emit radio frequency electromagnetic waves. Scanners within the MRI machine detect these radio waves, and a computer processes the waves into images.

Different types of tissues can be seen with MRI, depending on the frequency and duration of the pulses. MRI is particularly good for imaging the brain and spinal tissues and can be used to study brain function, brain tumors, multiple sclerosis, and other neurological disorders. MRI can also be used to create images of blood vessels without the surrounding tissue, which can be very useful for studying the circulatory system. The main drawbacks of MRI are that MRI systems are very expensive and that MRI cannot be used on some patients, such as those with pacemakers or certain types of metal implants.

Objectives

▶ Describe the magnetic field produced by current in a straight conductor and in a solenoid.

▶ Use the right-hand rule to determine the direction of the magnetic field in a current-carrying wire.

SC.912.P.10.15 Investigate and explain the relationships among current, voltage, resistance, and power.

Magnetism from Electricity

Key Term
solenoid

Magnetic Field of a Current-Carrying Wire

Scientists in the late 1700s suspected that there was a relationship between electricity and magnetism, but no theory had been developed to guide their experiments. In 1820, Danish physicist Hans Christian Oersted devised a method to study this relationship. Following a lecture to his advanced class, Oersted demonstrated that when brought near a current-carrying wire, a compass needle is deflected from its usual north-south orientation. He published an account of this discovery in July 1820, and his work stimulated other scientists all over Europe to repeat the experiment.

A long, straight, current-carrying wire has a cylindrical magnetic field.

The experiment shown in **Figure 2.1(a)** uses iron filings to show that a current-carrying conductor produces a magnetic field. In a similar experiment, several compass needles are placed in a horizontal plane near a long vertical wire, as illustrated in **Figure 2.2(b)**. When no current is in the wire, all needles point in the same direction (that of Earth's magnetic field). However, when the wire carries a strong, steady current, all the needles deflect in directions tangent to concentric circles around the wire. This result points out the direction of **B,** the magnetic field *induced* by the current. When the current is reversed, the needles reverse direction.

FIGURE 2.1

Magnetic Field of a Current-Carrying Wire

(a) When the wire carries a strong current, the alignments of the iron filings show that the magnetic field induced by the current forms concentric circles around the wire.
(b) Compasses can be used to show the direction of the magnetic field induced by the wire.

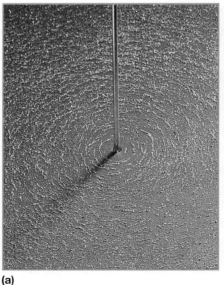

(a)

(b)

(bl), (br) ©Richard Menga/Fundamental Photographs, New York;

The right-hand rule can be used to determine the direction of the magnetic field.

These observations show that the direction of **B** is consistent with a simple rule for conventional current, known as *the right-hand rule*: If the wire is grasped in the right hand with the thumb in the direction of the current, as shown in **Figure 2.2,** the four fingers will curl in the direction of **B.**

As shown in **Figure 2.1(a),** the lines of **B** form concentric circles about the wire. By symmetry, the magnitude of **B** is the same everywhere on a circular path centered on the wire and lying in a plane perpendicular to the wire. Experiments show that **B** is proportional to the current in the wire and inversely proportional to the distance from the wire.

Magnetic Field of a Current Loop

The right-hand rule can also be applied to find the direction of the magnetic field of a current-carrying loop, such as the loop represented in **Figure 2.3(a).** Regardless of where on the loop you apply the right-hand rule, the field within the loop points in the same direction—upward. Note that the field lines of the current-carrying loop resemble those of a bar magnet, as shown in **Figure 2.3(b).** If a long, straight wire is bent into a coil of several closely spaced loops, as shown on the next page in **Figure 2.4,** the resulting device is called a **solenoid.**

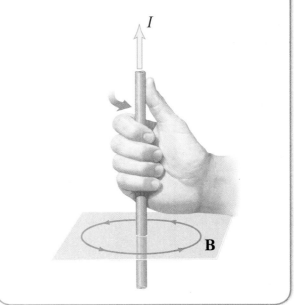

FIGURE 2.2

The Right-Hand Rule You can use the right-hand rule to find the direction of this magnetic field.

solenoid a long, helically wound coil of insulated wire

FIGURE 2.3

Current-Carrying Loop (a) The magnetic field of a current loop is similar to **(b)** that of a bar magnet.

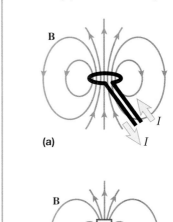

(a)

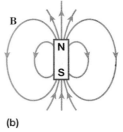

(b)

*Quick*LAB   **ELECTROMAGNETISM**

Wind the wire around the nail, as shown below. Remove the insulation from the ends of the wire, and hold these ends against the metal terminals of the battery.

Use the compass to determine whether the nail is magnetized. Next, flip the battery so that the direction of the current is reversed. Again, bring the compass toward the same part of the nail. Can you

explain why the compass needle now points in a different direction?

Bring paper clips near the nail while connected to the battery. What happens to the paper clips? How many can you pick up?

MATERIALS
- D-cell battery
- 1 m length of insulated wire
- large nail
- compass
- metal paper clips

Solenoids produce a strong magnetic field by combining several loops.

A solenoid is important in many applications because it acts as a magnet when it carries a current. The magnetic field strength inside a solenoid increases with the current and is proportional to the number of coils per unit length. The magnetic field of a solenoid can be increased by inserting an iron rod through the center of the coil; this device is often called an *electromagnet*. The magnetic field that is induced in the rod adds to the magnetic field of the solenoid, often creating a powerful magnet.

Figure 2.4 shows the magnetic field lines of a solenoid. Note that the field lines inside the solenoid point in the same direction, are nearly parallel, are uniformly spaced, and are close together. This indicates that the field inside the solenoid is strong and nearly uniform. The field outside the solenoid is nonuniform and much weaker than the interior field. Solenoids are used in a wide variety of applications, from most of the appliances in your home to very high-precision medical equipment.

FIGURE 2.4

Magnetic Field of a Solenoid The magnetic field inside a solenoid is strong and nearly uniform. Note that the field lines resemble those of a bar magnet, so a solenoid effectively has north and south poles.

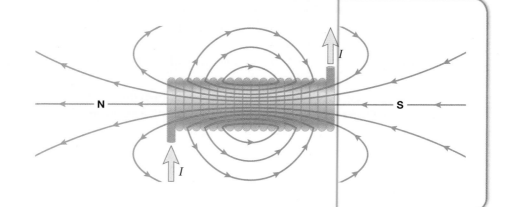

SECTION 2 FORMATIVE ASSESSMENT

▶ Reviewing Main Ideas

1. What is the shape of the magnetic field produced by a straight current-carrying wire?

2. Why is the magnetic field inside a solenoid stronger than the magnetic field outside?

3. If electrons behave like magnets, then why aren't all atoms magnets?

✔ Critical Thinking

4. In some satellites, torque coils are replaced by devices called *torque rods*. In torque rods, a ferromagnetic material is inserted inside the coil. Why does a torque rod have a stronger magnetic field than a torque coil?

Magnetic Force

Objectives

- Given the force on a charge in a magnetic field, determine the strength of the magnetic field.

- Use the right-hand rule to find the direction of the force on a charge moving through a magnetic field.

- Determine the magnitude and direction of the force on a wire carrying current in a magnetic field.

Charged Particles in a Magnetic Field

Although experiments show that a constant magnetic field does not exert a net force on a stationary charged particle, charges moving through a magnetic field do experience a magnetic force. This force has its maximum value when the charge moves perpendicular to the magnetic field, decreases in value at other angles, and becomes zero when the particle moves along the field lines. To keep the math simple in this book, we will limit our discussion to situations in which charges move parallel or perpendicular to the magnetic field lines.

A charge moving through a magnetic field experiences a force.

Recall that the electric field at a point in space is defined as the electric force per unit charge acting on some test charge placed at that point. In a similar manner, we can describe the properties of the magnetic field, **B,** in terms of the magnetic force exerted on a test charge at a given point. Our test object is assumed to be a positive charge, q, moving with velocity **v** perpendicular to **B.** It has been found experimentally that the strength of the magnetic force on the particle moving perpendicular to the field is equal to the product of the magnitude of the charge, q, the magnitude of the velocity, v, and the strength of the external magnetic field, B, as shown by the following relationship.

$$F_{magnetic} = qvB$$

This expression can be rearranged as follows:

Magnitude of a Magnetic Field

$$B = \frac{F_{magnetic}}{qv}$$

$$\text{magnetic field} = \frac{\text{magnetic force on a charged particle}}{\text{(magnitude of charge)(speed of charge)}}$$

If the force is in newtons, the charge is in coulombs, and the speed is in meters per second, the unit of magnetic field strength is the tesla (T). Thus, if a 1 C charge moving at 1 m/s perpendicular to a magnetic field experiences a magnetic force of 1 N, the magnitude of the magnetic field is equal to 1 T. Most magnetic fields are much smaller than 1 T. We can express the units of the magnetic field as follows:

$$T = \frac{N}{C \bullet m/s} = \frac{N}{A \bullet m} = \frac{V \bullet s}{m^2}$$

Conventional laboratory magnets can produce magnetic fields up to about 1.5 T. Superconducting magnets that can generate magnetic fields as great as 30 T have been constructed. For comparison, Earth's magnetic field near its surface is about 50 μT (5×10^{-5} T).

FIGURE 3.1

Alternative Right-Hand Rule

Use this alternative right-hand rule to find the direction of the magnetic force on a positive charge.

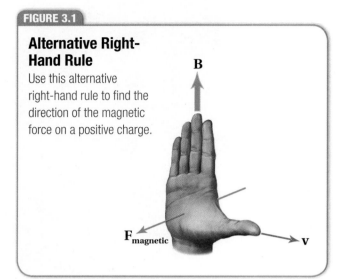

An alternative right-hand rule can be used to find the direction of the magnetic force.

Experiments show that the direction of the magnetic force on a moving charge is always perpendicular to both the velocity, **v**, and the magnetic field, **B**. To determine the direction of the force, use the right-hand rule. Similar to before, place your fingers in the direction of **B** with your thumb pointing in the direction of **v**, as illustrated in **Figure 3.1**. The magnetic force, $\mathbf{F}_{\text{magnetic}}$, on a positive charge is directed *out* of the palm of your hand.

If the charge is negative rather than positive, the force is directed *opposite* that shown in **Figure 3.1**. That is, if q is negative, simply use the right-hand rule to find the direction of $\mathbf{F}_{\text{magnetic}}$ for positive q and then reverse this direction for the negative charge.

WHY IT MATTERS

Auroras

Every so often, the sky in far north and far south latitudes lights up with a spectacular natural light show. These phenomena, called aurora borealis in the Northern Hemisphere and aurora australis in the Southern Hemisphere, are due to the interaction between charged particles and the Earth's magnetic field. The sun constantly emits charged particles, protons and electrons, which eventually make their way to Earth. Once they reach Earth, they move through its magnetic field. This in turn produces a force that causes the charges to accelerate and move toward the poles.

The charges, guided along the Earth's magnetic field, spiral toward the lower atmosphere. They eventually collide with atoms of nitrogen and oxygen. These atoms, in turn, get excited by the collision and emit light, ranging from brilliant reds to sparkling greens. The color of these lights depends on the atom being excited and its altitude. Auroras are most often seen near the poles because Earth's magnetic field lines are most concentrated there and because the field lines are at the correct height to produce these seemingly magical interactions.

Particle in a Magnetic Field

Sample Problem A A proton moving east experiences a force of 8.8×10^{-19} N upward due to the Earth's magnetic field. At this location, the field has a magnitude of 5.5×10^{-5} T to the north. Find the speed of the particle.

① ANALYZE

Given: $q = 1.60 \times 10^{-19}$ C $B = 5.5 \times 10^{-5}$ T

$F_{magnetic} = 8.8 \times 10^{-19}$ N

Unknown: $v = ?$

② SOLVE

Use the definition of magnetic field strength. Rearrange to solve for v.

$$B = \frac{F_{magnetic}}{qv}$$

$$v = \frac{F_{magnetic}}{qB}$$

Tips and Tricks

The directions given can be used to verify the right-hand rule. Imagine standing at this location and facing north. Turn the palm of your right hand upward (the direction of the force) with your thumb pointing east (the direction of the velocity). If your palm and thumb point in these directions, your fingers point directly north in the direction of the magnetic field, as they should.

$$v = \frac{8.8 \times 10^{-19} \text{ N}}{(1.60 \times 10^{-19} \text{ C})(5.5 \times 10^{-5} \text{ T})} = 1.0 \times 10^5 \text{ m/s}$$

$$\boxed{v = 1.0 \times 10^5 \text{ m/s}}$$

Practice

1. A proton moves perpendicularly to a magnetic field that has a magnitude of 4.20×10^{-2} T. What is the speed of the particle if the magnitude of the magnetic force on it is 2.40×10^{-14} N?

2. If an electron in an electron beam experiences a downward force of 2.0×10^{-14} N while traveling in a magnetic field of 8.3×10^{-2} T west, what is the direction and magnitude of the velocity?

3. A uniform 1.5 T magnetic field points north. If an electron moves vertically downward (toward the ground) with a speed of 2.5×10^7 m/s through this field, what force (magnitude and direction) will act on it?

FIGURE 3.2

Charge Moving Through a Uniform Magnetic Field

When the velocity, **v**, of a charged particle is perpendicular to a uniform magnetic field, the particle moves in a circle whose plane is perpendicular to **B**.

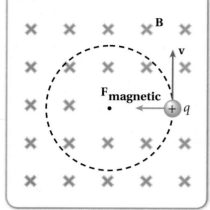

A charge moving through a magnetic field follows a circular path.

Consider a positively charged particle moving in a uniform magnetic field. Suppose the direction of the particle's initial velocity is exactly perpendicular to the field, as in **Figure 3.2**. Application of the right-hand rule for the charge q shows that the direction of the magnetic force, **F_magnetic**, at the charge's location is to the left. Furthermore, application of the right-hand rule at any point shows that the magnetic force is always directed toward the center of the circular path. Therefore, the magnetic force is, in effect, a force that maintains circular motion and changes only the direction of **v**, not its magnitude.

Now consider a charged particle traveling with its initial velocity at some angle to a uniform magnetic field. A component of the particle's initial velocity is parallel to the magnetic field. This parallel part is not affected by the magnetic field, and that part of the motion will remain the same. The perpendicular part results in a circular motion, as described above. The particle will follow a helical path, like the red stripes on a candy cane, whose axis is parallel to the magnetic field.

Magnetic Force on a Current-Carrying Conductor

FIGURE 3.3

Force on a Current-Carrying Wire in a Magnetic Field

A current-carrying conductor in a magnetic field experiences a force that is perpendicular to the direction of the current.

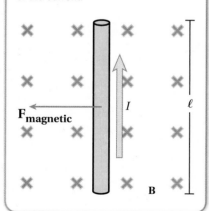

Recall that current consists of many charged particles in motion. If a force is exerted on a single charged particle when the particle moves through a magnetic field, it should be no surprise that a current-carrying wire also experiences a force when it is placed in a magnetic field. The resultant force on the wire is the sum of the individual magnetic forces on the charged particles. The force on the particles is transmitted to the bulk of the wire through collisions with the atoms making up the wire.

Consider a straight segment of wire of length ℓ carrying current, I, in a uniform external magnetic field, **B**, as in **Figure 3.3**. When the current and magnetic field are perpendicular, the magnitude of the total magnetic force on the wire is given by the following relationship.

> **Force on a Current-Carrying Conductor Perpendicular to a Magnetic Field**
>
> $$F_{magnetic} = BI\ell$$
>
> **magnitude of magnetic force = (magnitude of magnetic field) (current)(length of conductor within B)**

The direction of the magnetic force on a wire can be obtained by using the right-hand rule. However, in this case, you must place your thumb in the direction of the current rather than in the direction of the velocity, **v**. In **Figure 3.3**, the direction of the magnetic force on the wire is to the left. When the current is either in the direction of the field or opposite the direction of the field, the magnetic force on the wire is zero.

Two parallel conducting wires exert a force on one another.

Because a current in a conductor creates its own magnetic field, it is easy to understand that two current-carrying wires placed close together exert magnetic forces on each other. When the two conductors are parallel to each other, the direction of the magnetic field created by one is perpendicular to the direction of the current of the other, and vice versa. In this way, a force of $F_{magnetic} = BI\ell$ acts on each wire, where B is the magnitude of the magnetic field created by the other wire.

Consider the two long, straight, parallel wires shown in **Figure 3.4.** When the current in each is in the same direction, the two wires attract one another. Confirm this by using the right-hand rule. Point your thumb in the direction of current in one wire, and point your fingers in the direction of the field produced by the other wire. By doing this, you find that the direction of the force (pointing out from the palm of your hand) is toward the other wire. When the currents in each wire are in opposite directions, the wires repel one another.

Loudspeakers use magnetic force to produce sound.

The loudspeakers in most sound systems use a magnetic force acting on a current-carrying wire in a magnetic field to produce sound waves. One speaker design, shown in **Figure 3.5,** consists of a coil of wire, a flexible paper cone attached to the coil that acts as the speaker, and a permanent magnet. In a speaker system, a sound signal is converted to a varying electric signal by the microphone. This electrical signal is amplified and sent to the loudspeaker. At the loudspeaker, this varying electrical current causes a varying magnetic force on the coil. This alternating force on the coil results in vibrations of the attached cone, which produce variations in the density of the air in front of it. In this way, an electric signal is converted to a sound wave that closely resembles the sound wave produced by the source.

FIGURE 3.4

Force Between Parallel Conducting Wires

Two parallel wires, each carrying a steady current, exert magnetic forces on each other. The force is **(a)** attractive if the currents have the same direction and **(b)** repulsive if the two currents have opposite directions.

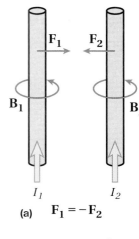

FIGURE 3.5

Loudspeaker In a loudspeaker, when the direction and magnitude of the current in the coil of wire change, the paper cone attached to the coil moves, producing sound waves.

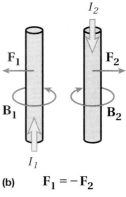

Force on a Current-Carrying Conductor

GO ONLINE

Interactive Demo
HMHScience.com

Sample Problem B A wire 25 m long carries a current of 12 A from west to east. If the magnetic force on the wire due to Earth's magnetic field is upward (away from Earth) and has a magnitude of 4.0×10^{-2} N, find the magnitude and direction of the magnetic field at this location.

① ANALYZE

Given: $\ell = 25$ m $I = 12$ A $F_{magnetic} = 4.0 \times 10^{-2}$ N

Unknown: $B = ?$

② SOLVE

Use the equation for the force on a current-carrying conductor perpendicular to a magnetic field.

$$F_{magnetic} = BI\ell$$

Rearrange to solve for B.

$$B = \frac{F_{magnetic}}{I\ell} = \frac{4.0 \times 10^{-2}\,\text{N}}{(12\,\text{A})(25\,\text{m})} = \boxed{1.3 \times 10^{-4}\,\text{T}}$$

Using the right-hand rule to find the direction of **B,** hold your hand so that your thumb is pointing to the east (in the direction of the current) and the palm of your hand up (in the direction of the force). Your fingers point north. Thus, Earth's magnetic field is from south to north.

Practice

1. A 6.0 m wire carries a current of 7.0 A toward the $+x$-direction. A magnetic force of 7.0×10^{-6} N acts on the wire in the $-y$-direction. Find the magnitude and direction of the magnetic field producing the force.

2. A printer is connected to a 1.0 m cable. If the magnetic force is 9.1×10^{-5} N, and the magnetic field is 1.3×10^{-4} T, what is the current in the cable?

3. Suppose a straight wire with a length of 2.0 m runs perpendicular to a magnetic field with a magnitude of 38 T. What current would have to pass through the wire in order for the magnetic force to equal the weight of a student with a mass of 75 kg?

4. The magnetic force acting on a wire that is perpendicular to a 1.5 T uniform magnetic field is 4.4 N. If the current in the wire is 5.0 A, what is the length of the wire that is inside the magnetic field?

Galvanometers

A *galvanometer* is a device used in the construction of both ammeters and voltmeters. Its operation is based on the fact that a torque acts on a current loop in the presence of a magnetic field. **Figure 3.6** shows a simplified arrangement of the main components of a galvanometer. It consists of a coil of wire wrapped around a soft iron core mounted so that it is free to pivot in the magnetic field provided by the permanent magnet. The torque experienced by the coil is proportional to the current in the coil. This means that the larger the current, the greater the torque and the more the coil will rotate before the spring tightens enough to stop the movement. Hence, the amount of deflection of the needle is proportional to the current in the coil. When there is no current in the coil, the spring returns the needle to zero. Once the instrument is properly calibrated, it can be used in conjunction with other circuit elements as an ammeter (to measure currents) or as a voltmeter (to measure potential differences).

FIGURE 3.6

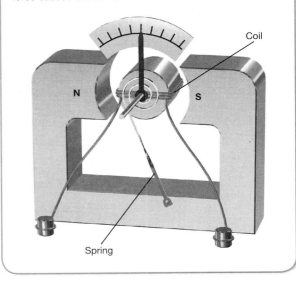

A Galvanometer In a galvanometer, when current enters the coil, which is in a magnetic field, the magnetic force causes the coil to twist.

Coil

Spring

✓ SECTION 3 FORMATIVE ASSESSMENT

▶ Reviewing Main Ideas

1. A particle with a charge of 0.030 C experiences a magnetic force of 1.5 N while moving at right angles to a uniform magnetic field. If the speed of the charge is 620 m/s, what is the magnitude of the magnetic field the particle passes through?

2. An electron moving north encounters a uniform magnetic field. If the magnetic field points east, what is the direction of the magnetic force on the electron?

3. A straight segment of wire has a length of 25 cm and carries a current of 5.0 A. If the wire is perpendicular to a magnetic field of 0.60 T, then what is the magnitude of the magnetic force on this segment of the wire?

4. Two parallel wires have charges moving in the same direction. Is the force between them attractive or repulsive?

5. Identify an object in your home or classroom that uses magnetic force, and explain how it works.

▶ Interpreting Graphics

6. Find the direction of the magnetic force on the current-carrying wire in **Figure 3.7**.

FIGURE 3.7

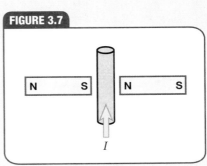

I

Magnetic Forces

Magnets are easy to come by. They are used for many purposes, from securing notes and pictures on refrigerators to complex medical applications such as magnetic resonance imaging. Everyday items such as speakers, earphones, door latches, and any devices that have electric motors all use magnets. Holding two magnets near each other is an easy way to demonstrate the forces exhibited by magnets. Magnetic force is a field force, as demonstrated by the attraction or repulsion you can feel when you hold two magnets nearby each other. Magnetic forces are the forces that act on charged particles moving through a magnetic field. These forces occur naturally, and they have also been harnessed in a variety of applications.

- Identify examples of magnetic forces in everyday life.

- Research and describe at least two applications of magnetic forces that are routinely used by consumers.

- Research at least two industrial and/or medical applications that rely on magnets. How are magnetic forces used for each application?

Conceptual Challenge

The ability to make assumptions and generate rough estimates is a valuable skill to scientists. Quick estimates allow scientists to narrow the range of possibilities and focus on the most reasonable hypotheses.

Refrigerator Magnets Refrigerator magnets come in a variety of strengths. Imagine you have one magnet that is only capable of holding up a single 4 inch by 6 inch photo, and on the same refrigerator, you have a second magnet that is capable of holding up a 12-month calendar. How much more force is the second magnet capable of applying?

You can begin addressing the scenario by asking questions such as the following:

- How much does a 4 inch by 6 inch photo weigh?
- How much does a 12-month calendar weigh?

BIG IDEA Magnetic force is a force due to moving charges, such as those that produce an electric current. Like gravity and electric force, magnetic force acts at a distance.

SECTION 1 **Magnets and Magnetic Fields**

KEY TERMS

- Like magnetic poles repel, and unlike poles attract.
- A magnetic domain is a group of atoms whose spins are aligned.
- The direction of any magnetic field is defined as the direction the north pole of a magnet would point if placed in the field. The magnetic field of a magnet points from the north pole of the magnet to the south pole.
- The magnetic north pole of Earth corresponds to the geographic South Pole, and the magnetic south pole corresponds to the geographic North Pole.

magnetic domain
magnetic field

SECTION 2 **Magnetism from Electricity**

KEY TERM

- A magnetic field exists around any current-carrying wire; the direction of the magnetic field follows a circular path around the wire.
- The magnetic field created by a solenoid or coil is similar to the magnetic field of a permanent magnet.

solenoid

SECTION 3 **Magnetic Force**

- The direction of the force on a positive charge moving through a magnetic field can be found by using the alternate right-hand rule.
- A current-carrying wire in an external magnetic field undergoes a magnetic force. The direction of the magnetic force on the wire can be found by using the alternate right-hand rule.
- Two parallel current-carrying wires exert on one another forces that are equal in magnitude and opposite in direction. If the currents are in the same direction, the two wires attract one another. If the currents are in opposite directions, the wires repel one another.

VARIABLE SYMBOLS		
Quantities	**Units**	**Conversions**
B magnetic field	T tesla	$= \dfrac{N}{C \bullet m/s} = \dfrac{N}{A \bullet m}$
$F_{magnetic}$ magnetic force	N newtons	$= \dfrac{kg \bullet m}{s^2}$
ℓ length of conductor in field	m meters	

DIAGRAM SYMBOLS	
magnetic field vector	↑
magnetic field pointing into the page	✖
magnetic field pointing out of the page	●

Problem Solving

See **Appendix D: Equations** for a summary of the equations introduced in this chapter. If you need more problem-solving practice, see **Appendix I: Additional Problems.**

Magnets and Magnetic Fields

▶ REVIEWING MAIN IDEAS

1. What is the minimum number of poles for a magnet?

2. When you break a magnet in half, how many poles does each piece have?

3. The north pole of a magnet is attracted to the geographic North Pole of Earth, yet like poles repel. Can you explain this?

4. Which way would a compass needle point if you were at the magnetic north pole?

5. What is a magnetic domain?

6. Why are iron atoms so strongly affected by magnetic fields?

7. When a magnetized steel needle is strongly heated in a Bunsen burner flame, it becomes demagnetized. Explain why.

8. If an unmagnetized piece of iron is attracted to one pole of a magnet, will it be repelled by the opposite pole?

CONCEPTUAL QUESTIONS

9. In the figure below, two permanent magnets with holes bored through their centers are placed one

over the other. Because the poles of the upper magnet are the reverse of those of the lower, the upper magnet levitates above the lower magnet. If the upper magnet were displaced slightly, either up or down, what would be the resulting motion? Explain. What would happen if the upper magnet were inverted?

10. You have two iron bars and a ball of string in your possession; one iron bar is magnetized, and one iron bar is not. How can you determine which iron bar is magnetized?

11. Why does a very strong magnet attract both poles of a weak magnet?

12. A magnet attracts a piece of iron. The iron can then attract another piece of iron. Explain, on the basis of alignment of domains, what happens in each piece of iron.

13. When a small magnet is repeatedly dropped, it becomes demagnetized. Explain what happens to the magnet at the atomic level.

Magnetism from Electricity

▶ REVIEWING MAIN IDEAS

14. A conductor carrying a current is arranged so that electrons flow in one segment from east to west. If a compass is held over this segment of the wire, in what direction is the needle deflected? (Hint: Recall that current is defined as the motion of *positive* charges.)

15. What factors does the strength of the magnetic field of a solenoid depend on?

CONCEPTUAL QUESTIONS

16. A solenoid with ends marked *A* and *B* is suspended by a thread so that the core can rotate in the horizontal plane. A current is maintained in the coil so that the electrons move clockwise when viewed from end *A* toward end *B*. How will the coil align itself in Earth's magnetic field?

17. Is it possible to orient a current-carrying loop of wire in a uniform magnetic field so that the loop will not tend to rotate?

18. If a solenoid were suspended by a string so that it could rotate freely, could it be used as a compass when it carried a direct current? Could it also be used if the current were alternating in direction?

Magnetic Force

REVIEWING MAIN IDEAS

19. Two charged particles are projected into a region where there is a magnetic field perpendicular to their velocities. If the particles are deflected in opposite directions, what can you say about them?

20. Suppose an electron is chasing a proton up this page when suddenly a magnetic field pointing into the page is applied. What would happen to the particles?

21. Why does the picture on a television screen become distorted when a magnet is brought near the screen?

22. A proton moving horizontally enters a region where there is a uniform magnetic field perpendicular to the proton's velocity, as shown below. Describe the proton's subsequent motion. How would an electron behave under the same circumstances?

$$\begin{array}{cccc}
\times & \times & \times & \\
\times & \times & \times & B_{in} \\
\times & \times & \times & \\
\times & \times & \times & \\
\times & \times & \times &
\end{array}$$

23. Explain why two parallel wires carrying currents in opposite directions repel each other.

24. Can a stationary magnetic field set a resting electron in motion? Explain.

25. At a given instant, a proton moves in the positive x-direction in a region where there is a magnetic field in the negative z-direction. What is the direction of the magnetic force? Does the proton continue to move along the x-axis? Explain.

26. For each situation below, use the movement of the positively charged particle and the direction of the magnetic force acting on it to find the direction of the magnetic field.

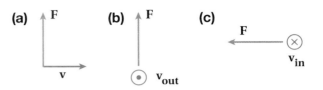

CONCEPTUAL QUESTIONS

27. A stream of electrons is projected horizontally to the right. A straight conductor carrying a current is supported parallel to and above the electron stream.
    a. What is the effect on the electron stream if the current in the conductor is left to right?
    b. What is the effect if the current is reversed?

28. If the conductor in item 27 is replaced by a magnet with a downward magnetic field, what is the effect on the electron stream?

29. Two wires carrying equal but opposite currents are twisted together in the construction of a circuit. Why does this technique reduce stray magnetic fields?

PRACTICE PROBLEMS

For problems 30–31, see Sample Problem A.

30. A duck flying due east passes over Atlanta, where the magnetic field of Earth is 5.0×10^{-5} T directed north. The duck has a positive charge of 4.0×10^{-8} C. If the magnetic force acting on the duck is 3.0×10^{-11} N upward, what is the duck's velocity?

31. A proton moves eastward in the plane of Earth's magnetic equator, where Earth's magnetic field points north and has a magnitude of 5.0×10^{-5} T. What velocity must the proton have for the magnetic force to just cancel the gravitational force?

For problems 32–33, see Sample Problem B.

32. A wire carries a 10.0 A current at an angle 90.0° from the direction of a magnetic field. If the magnitude of the magnetic force on a 5.00 m length of the wire is 15.0 N, what is the strength of the magnetic field?

33. A thin 1.00 m long copper rod in a uniform magnetic field has a mass of 50.0 g. When the rod carries a current of 0.245 A, it floats in the magnetic field. What is the field strength of the magnetic field?

Mixed Review

▶ **REVIEWING MAIN IDEAS**

34. A proton moves at 2.50×10^6 m/s horizontally at a right angle to a magnetic field.
 a. What is the strength of the magnetic field required to exactly balance the weight of the proton and keep it moving horizontally?
 b. Should the direction of the magnetic field be in a horizontal or a vertical plane?

35. Find the direction of the force on a proton moving through each magnetic field in the four figures below.

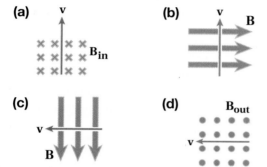

36. Find the direction of the force on an electron moving through each magnetic field in the four figures in item 35.

37. In the four figures in item 35, assume that in each case the velocity vector shown is replaced with a wire carrying a current in the direction of the velocity vector. Find the direction of the magnetic force acting on each wire.

38. A proton moves at a speed of 2.0×10^7 m/s at right angles to a magnetic field with a magnitude of 0.10 T. Find the magnitude of the acceleration of the proton.

39. A proton moves perpendicularly to a uniform magnetic field, **B**, with a speed of 1.0×10^7 m/s and experiences an acceleration of 2.0×10^{13} m/s² in the positive x-direction when its velocity is in the positive z-direction. Determine the magnitude and direction of the field.

40. A proton travels with a speed of 3.0×10^6 m/s at an angle of 37° west of north. A magnetic field of 0.30 T points to the north. Determine the following:
 a. the magnitude of the magnetic force on the proton
 b. the direction of the magnetic force on the proton
 c. the proton's acceleration as it moves through the magnetic field
 (Hint: The magnetic force experienced by the proton in the magnetic field is proportional to the component of the proton's velocity that is perpendicular to the magnetic field.)

41. In the figure below, a 15 cm length of conducting wire that is free to move is held in place between two thin conducting wires. All the wires are in a magnetic field. When a 5.0 A current is in the wire, as shown in the figure, the wire segment moves upward at a constant velocity. Assuming the wire slides without friction on the two vertical conductors and has a mass of 0.15 kg, find the magnitude and direction of the minimum magnetic field that is required to move the wire.

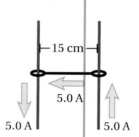

42. A current, $I = 15$ A, is directed along the positive x-axis and perpendicular to a uniform magnetic field. The conductor experiences a magnetic force per unit length of 0.12 N/m in the negative y-direction. Calculate the magnitude and direction of the magnetic field in the region through which the current passes.

43. A proton moving perpendicular to a magnetic field of strength 3.5 mT experiences a force due to the field of 4.5×10^{-21} N. Calculate the following:
 a. the speed of the proton
 b. the kinetic energy of the proton
 Recall that a proton has a charge of 1.60×10^{-19} C and a mass of 1.67×10^{-27} kg.

44. A singly charged positive ion that has a mass of 6.68×10^{-27} kg moves clockwise with a speed of 1.00×10^4 m/s. The positively charged ion moves in a circular path that has a radius of 3.00 cm. Find the direction and strength of the uniform magnetic field through which the charge is moving. (Hint: The magnetic force exerted on the positive ion is the centripetal force, and the speed given for the positive ion is its tangential speed.)

45. What speed would a proton need to achieve in order to circle Earth 1000.0 km above the magnetic equator? Assume that Earth's magnetic field is everywhere perpendicular to the path of the proton and that Earth's magnetic field has an intensity of 4.00×10^{-8} T. (Hint: The magnetic force exerted on the proton is equal to the centripetal force, and the speed needed by the proton is its tangential speed. Remember that the radius of the circular orbit should also include the radius of Earth. Ignore relativistic effects.)

46. Calculate the force on an electron in each of the following situations:
   a. moving at 2.0 percent the speed of light and perpendicular to a 3.0 T magnetic field
   b. 3.0×10^{-6} m from a proton
   c. in Earth's gravitational field at the surface of Earth
   Use the following: $q_e = -1.6 \times 10^{-19}$ C; $m_e = 9.1 \times 10^{-31}$ kg; $q_p = 1.6 \times 10^{-19}$ C; $c = 3.0 \times 10^8$ m/s; $k_C = 9.0 \times 10^9$ N•m^2/C^2

GRAPHING CALCULATOR PRACTICE

Solenoids

A solenoid consists of a long, helically wound coil of insulated wire. When it carries a current, a solenoid acts as a magnet. The magnetic field strength (B) increases linearly with the current (I) and with the number of coils per unit length. Because there is a direct relation between B and I, the following equation applies to any solenoid:

$$B = aI + b$$

In this equation, the parameters a and b are different for different solenoids. The a and b parameters can be determined if the magnetic field strength of the solenoid is known at two different currents. Once you determine a and b, you can predict the magnetic field strength of a solenoid for various currents.

The graphing calculator program that accompanies this activity uses this procedure. You will be given the magnetic field and current data for various solenoids. You will then use this information and the program to predict the magnetic field strength of each solenoid.

Go online to HMHScience.com to find the skillsheet and program for this graphing calculator activity.

ALTERNATIVE ASSESSMENT

1. During a field investigation with your class, you find a roundish chunk of metal that attracts iron objects. Design a procedure to determine whether the object is magnetic and, if so, to locate its poles. Describe the limitations of your method. What materials would you need? How would you draw your conclusions? List all the possible results you can anticipate and the conclusions you could draw from each result.

2. Imagine you have been hired by a manufacturer interested in making kitchen magnets. The manufacturer wants you to determine how to combine several magnets to get a very strong magnet. He also wants to know what protective material to use to cover the magnets. Develop a method for measuring the strength of different magnets by recording the maximum number of paper clips they can hold under various conditions. First open a paper clip to use as a hook. Test the strength of different magnets and combinations of magnets by holding up the magnet, placing the open clip on the magnet, and hooking the rest of the paper clips so that they hang below the magnet. Examine the effect of layering different materials between the magnet and the clips. Organize your data in tables and graphs to present your conclusions.

3. Research phenomena related to one of the following topics, and prepare a report or presentation with pictures and data.
   a. How does Earth's magnetic field vary with latitude, with longitude, with the distance from Earth, and in time?
   b. How do people who rely on compasses account for these differences in Earth's magnetic field?
   c. What is the Van Allen belt?
   d. How do solar flares occur?
   e. How do solar flares affect Earth?

4. Obtain old buzzers, bells, telephone receivers, speakers, motors from power or kitchen tools, and so on to take apart. Identify the mechanical and electromagnetic components. Examine their connections. How do they produce magnetic fields? Work in a cooperative group to describe and organize your findings about several devices for a display entitled "Anatomy of Electromagnetic Devices."

5. Magnetic force was first described by the ancient Greeks, who mined a magnetic mineral called magnetite. Magnetite was used in early experiments on magnetic force. Research the historical development of the concept of magnetic force. Describe the work of Peregrinus, William Gilbert, Oersted, Faraday, and other scientists.

Standards-Based Assessment

Record your answers on a separate piece of paper.

MULTIPLE CHOICE

1 Which of the following motions is the result of a magnetic force?

A bits of paper are attracted to a comb after a girl combs her hair

B a compass needle swings around to point north

C a car accelerates along a level road

D a foil balloon floats up and sticks to the ceiling

2 According to their promotional materials, CDs and DVDs are read by a laser pickup head as the discs spin rapidly. What characteristic of laser light is required for this application?

A Laser light is visible light.

B Laser light is very intense.

C Laser light is monochromatic.

D Laser light is very fast.

3 Which of the following statements is correct?

A The north pole of a freely rotating magnet points north because the magnetic pole near the geographic North Pole is like the north pole of a magnet.

B The north pole of a freely rotating magnet points north because the magnetic pole near the geographic North Pole is like the south pole of a magnet.

C The north pole of a freely rotating magnet points south because the magnetic pole near the geographic South Pole is like the north pole of a magnet.

D The north pole of a freely rotating magnet points south because the magnetic pole near the geographic South Pole is like the south pole of a magnet.

4 A wire 25 cm long carries a 12 A current from east to west. Earth's magnetic field at the wire's location has a magnitude of 4.8×10^{-5} T and is directed from south to north. What is the magnitude of the magnetic force on the wire?

A 2.3×10^{-5} N   **C** 2.3×10^{-3} N

B 1.4×10^{-4} N   **D** 1.4×10^{-2} N

5 This diagram shows a charged particle (an electron) from the sun passing into Earth's magnetic field.

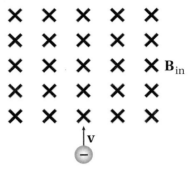

How will the electron move in the magnetic field?

A It will curve to the right and then continue moving in a straight line to the right.

B It will curve to the left and then continue moving in a straight line to the left.

C It will move in a clockwise circle.

D It will move in a counterclockwise circle.

6 Loudspeakers often use magnetic force to produce sound waves. Variations in the density of the air in front of the speaker produce sound waves that resemble the sound waves of the original source. Which of the following explanations **best** describes what produces these variations?

A Alternating magnetic forces act on a coil of wire and cause vibrations of an attached paper cone.

B Constant electrical signals are minimized and converted to sound waves when they travel through a magnetic field.

C Constant magnetic forces produce alternating sound signals that act on a coil of wire.

D Varying magnetic forces cause alternating electrical currents on a coil of wire that is picked up by an attached paper cone.

GRIDDED RESPONSE

7 A team of scientists investigates the effects of a uniform 0.25 T magnetic field on nucleons. A proton ($q = 1.6 \times 10^{-19}$ C; $m = 1.7 \times 10^{-27}$ kg) in this magnetic field moves in a clockwise circle with a tangential speed of 2.8×10^5 m/s. What is the radius of the circle in meters?

Radiation Shielding

The sun emits electromagnetic radiation across a broad spectrum. Most of this radiation is in the form of visible light, followed by infrared (radiant heat) and ultraviolet. Ultraviolet radiation can damage cells (for example, causing a sunburn), but it doesn't strip off electrons and disrupt cell processes the way bombardment by ionizing radiation can. The sun emits streams of such radiation (protons, electrons, and some heavier nuclei) in occasional solar storms. Collisions between ionizing radiation and living cells can damage the chemical bonds the cells need to function, including those in DNA. Another form of ionizing radiation in space, galactic cosmic radiation, consists of high-energy protons and nuclei thought to originate in supernovas.

Life on Earth has two principal means of protection from this radiation. One is Earth's magnetic field, which redirects charged particles toward the poles. The other is Earth's atmosphere, which absorbs most potentially damaging radiation before it can reach Earth's surface. Life underwater, or underground, is further shielded from radiation.

Identify a Problem: Shielding Astronauts from Radiation

Simply climbing a mountain or flying in an airplane measurably raises your radiation exposure. Astronauts in Low-Earth Orbit, such as those on the International Space Station, are largely outside Earth's atmosphere but inside its magnetic field. Astronauts on missions to Mars or elsewhere in the solar system will be outside both Earth's atmosphere and its magnetic field. This greatly increases their exposure to potentially damaging radiation.

Brainstorm Solutions

There are two basic approaches to radiation shielding: passive and active. Passive shielding means surrounding astronauts in a physical barrier that will absorb radiation, much as Earth's atmosphere does. One potential drawback is that the collision of a high-energy particle with a molecule of shielding can throw off secondary high-energy particles, which can be even more damaging than the primary radiation. The barrier material must therefore be thick enough to absorb most of these secondary

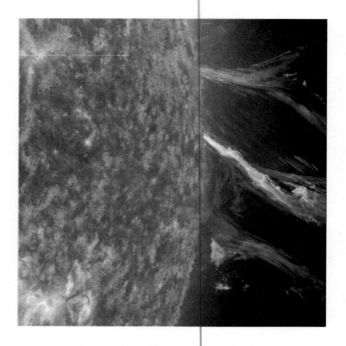

In a coronal mass ejection, plasma and magnetic fields explode from the sun's corona. The CMEs typically travel outward from the sun at speeds of around 300 km/h but can be up to ten times faster. When the CME travels faster than the solar wind, the associated shock wave accelerates charged particles ahead of the CME. These are the main component of the solar radiation storm associated with CMEs, which can damage electronics on Earth.

©NASA/Science Photo Library/Getty Images

particles. The most penetrating ionizing radiation passes through aluminum but can be stopped by materials such as concrete.

Active shielding uses electromagnetic forces to deflect incoming charged particles, much as Earth's magnetic field does. Examples of such shielding include electrostatic, plasma, and magnetic shielding. Electrostatic and plasma shielding create a strong positive electric field around the spacecraft, which would deflect positive charges. Because this would attract and accelerate electrons, a low-intensity magnetic field within the larger shield would be used to deflect the negative charges. In magnetic shielding, charged particles are diverted around the spacecraft by a strong magnetic field.

Select a Solution

Boosting mass into space is difficult and expensive. Initially, none of the active-shielding designs could be implemented in a cost-effective way, so passive shielding was adopted.

Heavier elements, such as lead, produce more secondary radiation than do lighter elements. So in addition to the challenge of lifting the shield into orbit, engineers needed a material that was lighter in weight and less inclined to produce secondary radiation than metal or concrete. They focused on hydrogen.

Water is one possible hydrogen-rich material, but it is heavy. Shielding is instead now made of a lightweight polyethylene plastic, RFX1, composed entirely of carbon and hydrogen atoms. RFX1 is 50% better than aluminum at shielding from solar eruptions and 15% better at shielding from cosmic radiation.

Delicate electronics are vulnerable to damage from radiation.

Redesign and Improve

As we look toward more missions beyond Earth, there will continue to be a need for a lightweight, reliable, broad-spectrum form of radiation shielding. Recent advances in lightweight superconductors have led engineers to reexamine the possibility of using a magnetic or electric field to shield spacecraft. Future spacecraft may employ one of these designs or some new combination of active and passive shielding.

Design Your Own

Define the Problem

Even on spacecraft with no human occupants, electronics need to be shielded from radiation. Research how radiation interacts with Random Access Memory and with microprocessors.

Brainstorm Solutions

Research methods of protecting electronics and people from radiation in space. What are some advantages and disadvantages of each? Brainstorm other possible solutions. Then choose the most promising method.

Optimize the Solution

Sketch a model of the method that might best protect a satellite and explain how the system would work. Present the system to classmates, discuss any flaws or improvements, and revise the design based on feedback.

©Science Source

Why It Matters

This diagram shows how the vibrations of the strings in an electric guitar change the magnetic field near a coil of wire called the pickup. In turn, this induces an electric current in the coil, which is then amplified to create the unique sound of an electric guitar.

Electric guitars have many different types of pickups, but all generate electric current by induction. An understanding of the induction of electromagnetic fields is essential to the design of an electric guitar.

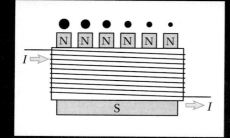

CHAPTER 20
Electromagnetic Induction

BIG IDEA
Magnetic and electric forces are actually a single force—the electromagnetic force. Changing magnetic fields produce electric fields and electric current, and changing electric fields produce magnetic fields.

ONLINE Physics
HMHScience.com

ONLINE LABS
- Electricity and Magnetism
- Electromagnetic Induction
- S.T.E.M. Lab Motors
- S.T.E.M. Lab Building a Circuit Breaker

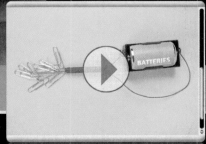

GO ONLINE
Animated Physics
HMHScience.com
Ways of Inducing Current

Objectives

▷ Recognize that relative motion between a conductor and a magnetic field induces an emf in the conductor.

▷ Describe how the change in the number of magnetic field lines through a circuit loop affects the magnitude and direction of the induced electric current.

▷ Apply Lenz's law and Faraday's law of induction to solve problems involving induced emf and current.

electromagnetic induction the process of creating a current in a circuit loop by changing the magnetic flux in the loop

Electricity from Magnetism

Key Term
electromagnetic induction

Electromagnetic Induction

Recall that when you were studying circuits, you were asked if it was possible to produce an electric current using only wires and no battery. So far, all electric circuits that you have studied have used a battery or an electrical power supply to create a potential difference within a circuit. The electric field associated with that potential difference causes charges to move through the circuit and to create a current.

It is also possible to *induce* a current in a circuit without the use of a battery or an electrical power supply. You have learned that a current in a circuit is the source of a magnetic field. Conversely, a current results when a closed electric circuit moves with respect to a magnetic field, as shown in **Figure 1.1.** The process of inducing a current in a circuit by changing the magnetic field that passes through the circuit is called **electromagnetic induction.**

Consider a closed circuit consisting of only a resistor that is in the vicinity of a magnet. There is no battery to supply a current. If neither the magnet nor the circuit is moving with respect to the other, no current will be present in the circuit. But if the circuit moves toward or away from the magnet or the magnet moves toward or away from the circuit, a current is induced. As long as there is relative motion between the two, a current is created in the circuit.

The separation of charges by the magnetic force induces an emf.

It may seem strange that there can be an induced emf and a corresponding induced current without a battery or similar source of electrical

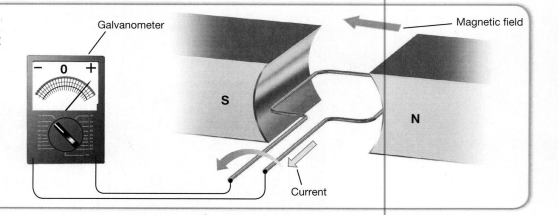

FIGURE 1.1

Electromagnetic Induction When the circuit loop crosses the lines of the magnetic field, a current is induced in the circuit, as indicated by the movement of the galvanometer needle.

Galvanometer

Magnetic field

S

N

Current

energy. Recall that a moving charge can be deflected by a magnetic field. This deflection can be used to explain how an emf occurs in a wire that moves through a magnetic field.

Consider a conducting wire pulled through a magnetic field, as shown on the left in **Figure 1.2**. You learned when studying magnetism that charged particles moving with a velocity at an angle to the magnetic field will experience a magnetic force. According to the right-hand rule, this force will be perpendicular to both the magnetic field and the motion of the charges. For free positive charges in the wire, the force is directed downward along the wire. For negative charges, the force is upward. This effect is equivalent to replacing the segment of wire and the magnetic field with a battery that has a potential difference, or emf, between its terminals, as shown on the right in **Figure 1.2**. As long as the conducting wire moves through the magnetic field, the emf will be maintained.

The polarity of the induced emf depends on the direction in which the wire is moved through the magnetic field. For instance, if the wire in **Figure 1.2** is moved to the right, the right-hand rule predicts that the negative charges will be pushed upward. If the wire is moved to the left, the negative charges will be pushed downward. The magnitude of the induced emf depends on the velocity with which the wire is moving through the magnetic field, on the length of the wire in the field, and on the strength of the magnetic field.

The angle between a magnetic field and a circuit affects induction.

One way to induce an emf in a closed loop of wire is to move all or part of the loop into or out of a constant magnetic field. No emf is induced if the loop is static and the magnetic field is constant.

The magnitude of the induced emf and current depend partly on how the loop is oriented to the magnetic field, as shown in **Figure 1.3**. The induced current is largest if the plane of the loop is perpendicular to the magnetic field, as in **(a)**; it is smaller if the plane is tilted into the field, as in **(b)**; and it is zero if the plane is parallel to the field, as in **(c)**.

The role that the orientation of the loop plays in inducing the current can be explained by the force that the magnetic field exerts on the charges in the moving loop. Only the component of the magnetic field *perpendicular* to

FIGURE 1.2

Potential Difference in a Wire The separation of positive and negative moving charges by the magnetic force creates a potential difference (emf) between the ends of the conductor.

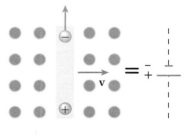

B (out of page)

FIGURE 1.3

Orientation of a Loop in a Magnetic Field These three loops of wire are moving out of a region that has a constant magnetic field. The induced emf and current are largest when the plane of the loop is perpendicular to the magnetic field **(a)**, smaller when the plane of the loop is tilted **(b)**, and zero when the plane of the loop and the magnetic field are parallel **(c)**.

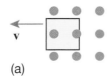
(a)

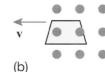
(b)

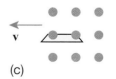
(c)

both the plane and the motion of the loop exerts a magnetic force on the charges in the loop. If the area of the loop is moved *parallel* to the magnetic field, there is no magnetic field component perpendicular to the plane of the loop and therefore no induced emf to move the charges around the circuit.

Change in the number of magnetic field lines induces a current.

So far, you have learned that moving a circuit loop into or out of a magnetic field can induce an emf and a current in the circuit. Changing the size of the loop or the strength of the magnetic field also will induce an emf in the circuit.

One way to predict whether a current will be induced in a given situation is to consider how many magnetic field lines cut through the loop. For example, moving the circuit into the magnetic field causes some lines to move into the loop. Changing the size of the circuit loop or rotating the loop changes the number of field lines passing through the loop, as does changing the magnetic field's strength or direction. **Figure 1.4** summarizes these three ways of inducing a current.

Did YOU Know?

In 1996, the space shuttle *Columbia* attempted to use a 20.7 km conducting tether to study Earth's magnetic field in space. The plan was to drag the tether through the magnetic field, inducing an emf in the tether. The magnitude of the emf would directly vary with the strength of the magnetic field. Unfortunately, the tether broke before it was fully extended, so the experiment was abandoned.

Characteristics of Induced Current

Suppose a bar magnet is pushed into a coil of wire. As the magnet moves into the coil, the strength of the magnetic field within the coil increases, and a current is induced in the circuit. This induced current in turn produces its own magnetic field, whose direction can be found by using the right-hand rule. If you were to apply this rule for several cases, you would notice that the induced magnetic field direction depends on the change in the applied field.

FIGURE 1.4

WAYS OF INDUCING A CURRENT IN A CIRCUIT

Description	Before	After
Circuit is moved into or out of magnetic field (either circuit or magnet moving).	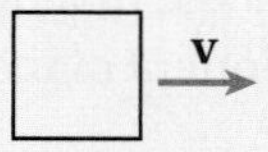	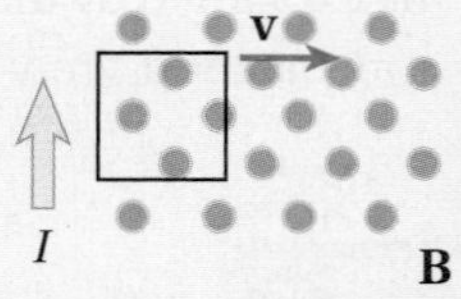
Circuit is rotated in the magnetic field (angle between area of circuit and magnetic field changes).	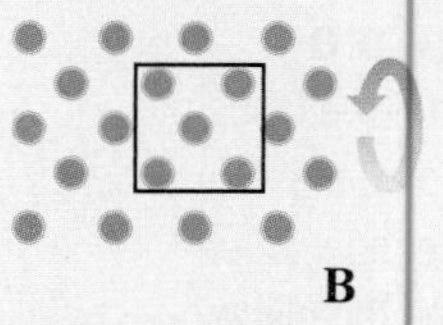	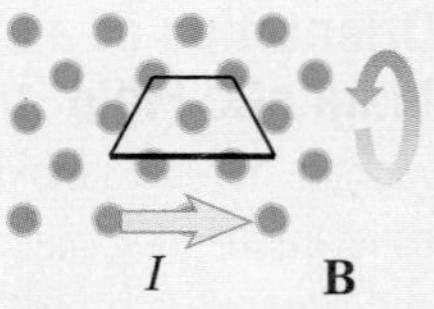
Intensity and/or direction of magnetic field is varied.	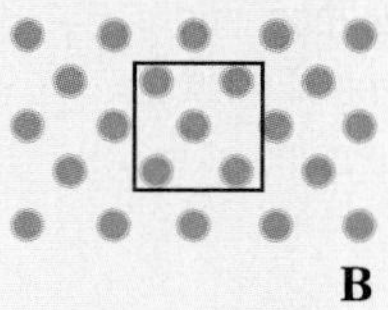	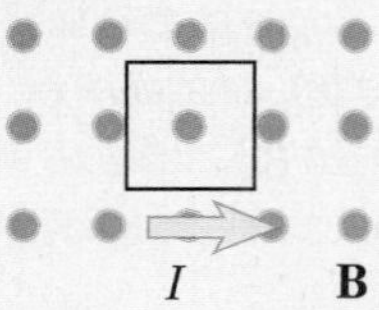

FIGURE 1.5

Magnet Moving Toward Coil When a bar magnet is moved toward a coil, the induced magnetic field is similar to the field of a bar magnet. The orientation is shown.

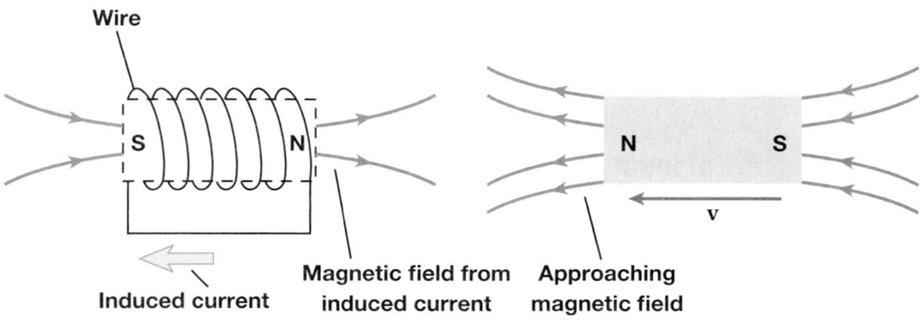

Wire

Induced current **Magnetic field from induced current** **Approaching magnetic field**

Falling Magnet A bar magnet is dropped toward the floor, on which lies a large ring of conducting metal. The magnet's length—and thus the poles of the magnet—is parallel to the direction of motion. Disregarding air resistance, does the magnet fall toward the ring with the constant acceleration of a freely falling body? Explain your answer.

Induction in a Bracelet Suppose you are wearing a bracelet that is an unbroken ring of copper. If you walk briskly into a strong magnetic field while wearing the bracelet, how would you hold your wrist with respect to the magnetic field in order to avoid inducing a current in the bracelet?

As the magnet approaches, the magnetic field passing through the coil increases in strength. The induced current in the coil is in a direction that produces a magnetic field that opposes the increasing strength of the approaching field. So the induced magnetic field is in the opposite direction of the increasing magnetic field.

The induced magnetic field is similar to the field of a bar magnet. The field is oriented as shown in **Figure 1.5.** The coil and the approaching magnet create a pair of forces that repel each other.

If the magnet is moved away from the coil, the magnetic field passing through the coil decreases in strength. Again, the current induced in the coil produces a magnetic field that opposes the decreasing strength of the receding field. This means that the magnetic field that the coil sets up is in the same direction as the receding magnetic field.

The induced magnetic field is similar to the field of a bar magnet oriented as shown in **Figure 1.6.** In this case, the coil and magnet attract each other.

FIGURE 1.6

Magnet Moving Away from Coil When a bar magnet is moved away from a coil, the induced magnetic field is similar to the field of a bar magnet with the orientation shown.

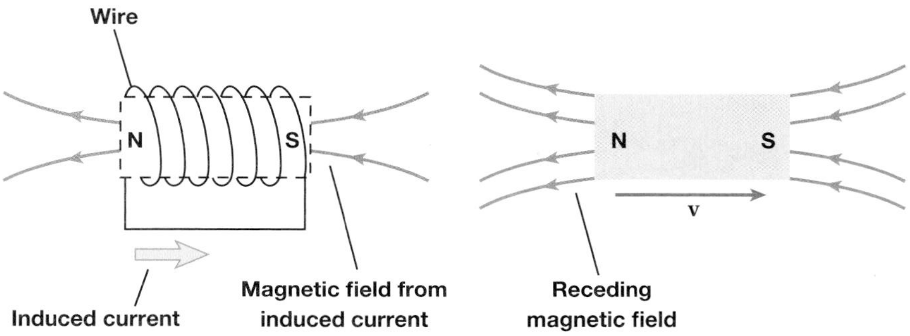

Wire

Induced current **Magnetic field from induced current** **Receding magnetic field**

The rule for finding the direction of the induced current is called *Lenz's law* and is expressed as follows:

The magnetic field of the induced current is in a direction to produce a field that opposes the change causing it.

Note that the field of the induced current does not oppose the applied field but rather the change in the applied field. If the applied field changes, the induced field tends to keep the total field strength constant.

Faraday's law of induction predicts the magnitude of the induced emf.

Lenz's law allows you to determine the direction of an induced current in a circuit. Lenz's law does not provide information on the magnitude of the induced current or the induced emf. To calculate the magnitude of the induced emf, you must use *Faraday's law of magnetic induction.* For a single loop of a circuit, this may be expressed as follows:

$$\text{emf} = -\frac{\Delta \Phi_M}{\Delta t}$$

Recall from the chapter on magnetism that the magnetic flux, Φ_M, can be written as $AB \cos \theta$. This equation means that a change with time of any of the three variables—applied magnetic field strength, B; circuit area, A; or angle of orientation, θ—can give rise to an induced emf. The term $B \cos \theta$ represents the component of the magnetic field perpendicular to the plane of the loop. The angle θ is measured between the applied magnetic field and the normal to the plane of the loop, as indicated in **Figure 1.7**.

The minus sign in front of the equation is included to indicate the polarity of the induced emf. The sign indicates that the induced magnetic field opposes the change in the applied magnetic field, as stated by Lenz's law.

If a circuit contains a number, N, of tightly wound loops, the average induced emf is simply N times the induced emf for a single loop. The equation thus takes the general form of Faraday's law of magnetic induction.

Faraday's Law of Magnetic Induction

$$\text{emf} = -N\frac{\Delta \Phi_M}{\Delta t}$$

**average induced emf = −the number of loops in the circuit ×
the time rate of change of the magnetic flux**

In this chapter, N is always assumed to be a whole number.

Recall that the SI unit for magnetic field strength is the tesla (T), which equals one newton per ampere-meter, or N/(A•m). The tesla can also be expressed in the equivalent units of one volt-second per meter squared, or (V•s)/m². Thus, the unit for emf, as for electric potential, is the volt.

FIGURE 1.7

Magnetic Field of a Conducting Loop at an Angle The angle θ is defined as the angle between the magnetic field and the normal to the plane of the loop. $B \cos \theta$ equals the component of the magnetic field perpendicular to the plane of the loop.

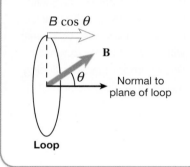

Induced emf and Current

Sample Problem A A unicycle with a wheel diameter of 2.5 cm travels 3.6 m. Suppose the wheel has 200 turns of thin wire wrapped around its rim, creating loops with the same diameter as the wheel. An emf of 9.6 mV is induced when the wheel is perpendicular to a magnetic field that steadily decreases from 0.68 T to 0.24 T. For how long is the emf induced?

1 ANALYZE

Given:

$N = 200$ turns

$D = 2.5 \text{ cm} = 2.5 \times 10^{-2} \text{ m}$

$B_i = 0.68 \text{ T}$

$B_f = 0.24 \text{ T}$

$\text{emf} = 9.6 \text{ mV} = 9.6 \times 10^{-3} \text{ V}$

$\theta = 0.0°$

Unknown: $\Delta t = ?$

2 PLAN

Choose the equation or situation: Use Faraday's law of magnetic induction to find the induced emf in the coil. Only the magnetic field strength changes with time.

$$\text{emf} = -N\frac{\Delta\Phi_M}{\Delta t} = -\frac{N\Delta[AB\cos\theta]}{\Delta t} = -NA\cos\theta\frac{\Delta B}{\Delta t}$$

Use the equation for the area of a circle to calculate the area (A).

$$A = \pi r^2 = \pi\left(\frac{D}{2}\right)^2$$

Rearrange the equation to isolate the unknowns:

$$\Delta t = -NA\cos\theta\frac{\Delta B}{\text{emf}}$$

Continued

Induced emf and Current (continued)

3 SOLVE

Substitute values into the equation and solve:

$$A = \pi \left(\frac{2.5 \times 10^{-2}\,\text{m}}{2} \right)^2 = 4.9 \times 10^{-4}\,\text{m}^2$$

$$\Delta t = -(200)(4.9 \times 10^{-4}\,\text{m}^2)[\cos 0.0°]\frac{(0.24\,\text{T} - 0.68\,\text{T})}{(9.6 \times 10^{-3}\,\text{V})}$$

$$\boxed{\Delta t = 4.5\,\text{s}}$$

4 CHECK YOUR WORK

The induced emf is directed through the coiled wire so that the magnetic field produced opposes the decrease in the applied magnetic field. The rate of this change is indicated by the positive value of time.

Practice

1. Computers store memory by spinning a stack of magnetic-coated plates beneath an electromagnetic head. Suppose a head consisting of a 148-turn coil wrapped around an iron ring with an area of $1.25 \times 10^{-8}\,\text{m}^2$. The head is parallel to a magnetic field that changes by $5.2 \times 10^{-4}\,\text{T}$ in $8.5 \times 10^{-9}\,\text{s}$. What is the induced emf in the coil?

2. A coil with 205 turns of wire, a total resistance of 23 Ω, and a cross-sectional area of 0.25 m^2 is positioned with its plane perpendicular to the field of a powerful electromagnet. What average current is induced in the coil during the 0.25 s that the magnetic field drops from 1.6 T to 0.0 T?

3. An electromagnet that has a mass of almost $8.0 \times 10^6\,\text{kg}$ was built at the CERN particle physics research facility in Switzerland. As part of the detector in one of the world's largest particle accelerators, this magnet creates a fairly large magnetic field with a magnitude of 0.50 T. Consider a coil of wire that has 880 equal turns. Suppose this loop is placed perpendicular to the magnetic field, which is gradually decreased to zero in 12 s. If an emf of 147 V is induced, what is the area of the coil?

4. A 505-turn circular-loop coil with a diameter of 15.5 cm is initially aligned so that its plane is perpendicular to Earth's magnetic field. In 2.77 ms, the coil is rotated 90.0° so that its plane is parallel to Earth's magnetic field. If an average emf of 0.166 V is induced in the coil, what is the value of Earth's magnetic field?

Electric Guitar Pickups

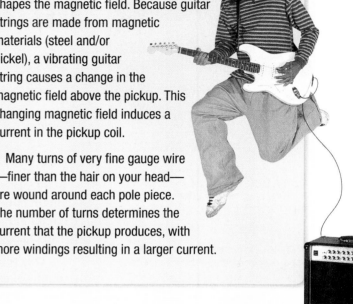

T he word *pickup* refers to a device that "picks up" the sound of an instrument and turns the sound into an electrical signal. The most common type of electric guitar pickup uses electromagnetic induction to convert string vibrations into electrical energy.

In their most basic form, magnetic pickups consist simply of a permanent magnet and a coil of copper wire. A pole piece under each guitar string concentrates and

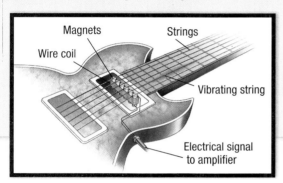

shapes the magnetic field. Because guitar strings are made from magnetic materials (steel and/or nickel), a vibrating guitar string causes a change in the magnetic field above the pickup. This changing magnetic field induces a current in the pickup coil.

Many turns of very fine gauge wire —finer than the hair on your head— are wound around each pole piece. The number of turns determines the current that the pickup produces, with more windings resulting in a larger current.

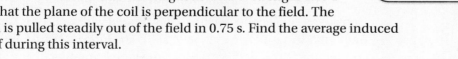

SECTION 1 FORMATIVE ASSESSMENT

▶ Reviewing Main Ideas

1. A circular current loop made of flexible wire is located in a magnetic field. Describe three ways an emf can be induced in the loop.

2. A bar magnet is positioned near a coil of wire, as shown to the right. What is the direction of the current in the resistor when the magnet is moved to the left, as in **(a)**? to the right, as in **(b)**?

3. A 256-turn coil with a cross-sectional area of 0.0025 m^2 is placed in a uniform external magnetic field of strength 0.25 T so that the plane of the coil is perpendicular to the field. The coil is pulled steadily out of the field in 0.75 s. Find the average induced emf during this interval.

✓ Critical Thinking

4. Electric guitar strings are made of ferromagnetic materials that can be magnetized. The strings lie closely over and perpendicular to a coil of wire. Inside the coil are permanent magnets that magnetize the segments of the strings overhead. Using this arrangement, explain how the vibrations of a plucked string produce an electrical signal at the same frequency as the vibration of the string.

SC.912.P.10.15 Investigate and explain the relationships among current, voltage, resistance, and power.

generator a machine that converts mechanical energy into electrical energy

FIGURE 2.1

A Simple Generator In a simple generator, the rotation of conducting loops through a constant magnetic field induces an alternating current in the loops.

Generators, Motors, and Mutual Inductance

Key Terms

generator   alternating current

back emf   mutual inductance

Generators and Alternating Current

In the previous section, you learned that a current can be induced in a circuit either by changing the magnetic field strength or by moving the circuit loop in or out of the magnetic field. Another way to induce a current is to change the orientation of the loop with respect to the magnetic field.

This second approach to inducing a current represents a practical means of generating electrical energy. In effect, the mechanical energy used to turn the loop is converted to electrical energy. A device that does this conversion is called an electric **generator.**

In most commercial power plants, mechanical energy is provided in the form of rotational motion. For example, in a hydroelectric plant, falling water directed against the blades of a turbine causes the turbine to turn. In a plant that burns coal or natural gas, energy produced by burning fuel is used to convert water to steam, and this steam is directed against the turbine blades to turn the turbine.

Basically, a generator uses the turbine's rotary motion to turn a wire loop in a magnetic field. A simple generator is shown in **Figure 2.1.** As the loop rotates, the effective area of the loop changes with time, inducing an emf and a current in an external circuit connected to the ends of the loop.

A generator produces a continuously changing emf.

Consider a single loop of wire that is rotated with a constant angular frequency in a uniform magnetic field. The loop can be thought of as four conducting wires. In this example, the loop is rotating counterclockwise within a magnetic field directed to the left.

When the area of the loop is perpendicular to the magnetic field lines, as shown in **Figure 2.2(a)** on the next page, every segment of wire in the loop is moving parallel to the magnetic field lines. At this instant, the magnetic field does not exert force on the charges in any part of the wire, so the induced emf in each segment is therefore zero.

As the loop rotates away from this position, segments *a* and *c* cross magnetic field lines, so the magnetic force on the charges in these segments, and thus the induced emf, increases. The magnetic force on the charges in segments *b* and *d* cancel each other, so the motion of these segments does not contribute to the emf or the current. The greatest magnetic force on the charges and the greatest induced emf occur at the instant when segments *a* and *c* move perpendicularly to the magnetic field lines, as in **Figure 2.2(b).** This occurs when the plane of the loop is parallel to the field lines.

Because segment *a* moves downward through the field while segment *c* moves upward, their emfs are in opposite directions, but both produce a counterclockwise current. As the loop continues to rotate, segments *a* and *c* cross fewer lines, and the emf decreases. When the plane of the loop is perpendicular to the magnetic field, the motion of segments *a* and *c* is again parallel to the magnetic lines, and the induced emf is again zero, as shown in **Figure 2.2(c).** Segments *a* and *c* now move in directions opposite those in which they moved from their positions in **(a)** to those in **(b).** As a result, the polarity of the induced emf and the direction of the current are reversed, as shown in **Figure 2.2(d).**

FIGURE 2.2

Induction of an emf in an ac Generator For a rotating loop in a magnetic field, the induced emf is zero when the loop is perpendicular to the magnetic field, as in **(a)** and **(c)**, and is at a maximum when the loop is parallel to the field, as in **(b)** and **(d)**.

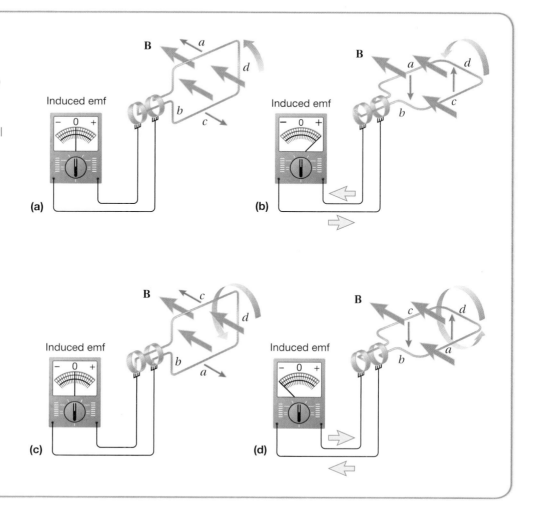

FIGURE 2.3

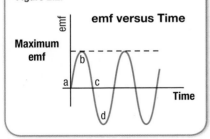

Alternating emf The change with time of the induced emf in a rotating loop is depicted by a sine wave. The letters on the plot correspond to the coil locations in **Figure 2.2.**

A graph of the change in emf versus time as the loop rotates is shown in **Figure 2.3.** Note the similarities between this graph and a sine curve. The four locations marked on the curve correspond to the orientation of the loop with respect to the magnetic field in **Figure 2.2.** At locations *a* and *c*, the emf is zero. These locations correspond to the instants when the plane of the loop is perpendicular to the direction of the magnetic field. At locations *b* and *d*, the emf is at its maximum and minimum, respectively. These locations correspond to the instants when the plane of the loop is parallel to the magnetic field.

The induced emf is the result of the steady change in the angle θ between the magnetic field lines and the normal to the loop. The following equation for the emf produced by a generator can be derived from Faraday's law of induction. The derivation is not shown here, because it requires the use of calculus. In this equation, the angle of orientation, θ, has been replaced with the equivalent expression ωt, where ω is the angular frequency of rotation $(2\pi f)$.

$$\text{emf} = NAB\omega \sin \omega t$$

The equation describes the sinusoidal variation of emf with time, as graphed in **Figure 2.3.**

The maximum emf strength can be easily calculated for a sinusoidal function. The emf has a maximum value when the plane of a loop is parallel to a magnetic field, that is, when $\sin \omega t = 1$, which occurs when $\omega t = \theta = 90°$. In this case, the expression above reduces to the following:

$$\text{maximum emf} = NAB\omega$$

Note that the maximum emf is a function of four things: the number of loops, N; the area of the loop, A; the magnetic field strength, B; and the angular frequency of the rotation of the loop, ω.

Alternating current changes direction at a constant frequency.

Note in **Figure 2.3** that the emf alternates from positive to negative. As a result, the output current from the generator changes its direction at regular intervals. This variety of current is called **alternating current,** or, more commonly, *ac.*

alternating current an electric current that changes direction at regular intervals

The rate at which the coil in an ac generator rotates determines the maximum generated emf. The frequency of the alternating current can differ from country to country. In the United States, Canada, and Central America, the frequency of rotation for commercial generators is 60 Hz. This means that the emf undergoes one full cycle of changing direction 60 times each second. In the United Kingdom, Europe, and most of Asia and Africa, 50 Hz is used. (Recall that $\omega = 2\pi f$, where f is the frequency in Hz.)

Resistors can be used in either alternating- or direct-current applications. A resistor resists the motion of charges regardless of whether they move in one continuous direction or shift direction periodically. Thus, if the definition for resistance holds for circuit elements in a dc circuit, it will also hold for the same circuit elements with alternating currents and emfs.

FIGURE 2.4

ac versus dc Generators
A simple dc generator (shown on the right) employs the same design as an ac generator (shown on the left). A split slip ring converts alternating current to direct current.

ac Generator

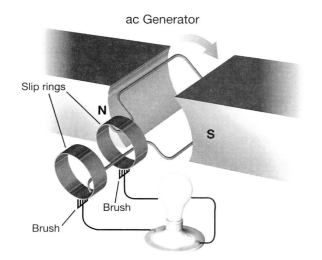

dc Generator

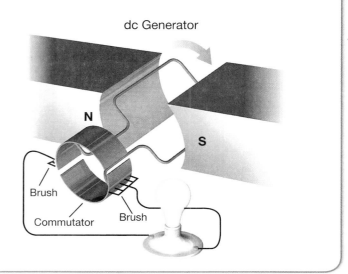

Alternating current can be converted to direct current.

The conducting loop in an ac generator must be free to rotate through the magnetic field. Yet it must also be part of an electric circuit at all times. To accomplish this, the ends of the loop are connected to conducting rings, called *slip rings,* that rotate with the loop. Connections to the external circuit are made by stationary graphite strips, called *brushes,* that make continuous contact with the slip rings. Because the current changes direction in the loop, the output current through the brushes alternates direction as well.

By varying this arrangement slightly, an ac generator can be converted to a dc generator. Note in **Figure 2.4** that the components of a dc generator are essentially the same as those of the ac generator except that the contacts to the rotating loop are made by a single split slip ring, called a *commutator.*

At the point in the loop's rotation when the current has dropped to zero and is about to change direction, each half of the commutator comes into contact with the brush that was previously in contact with the other half of the commutator. The reversed current in the loop changes directions again so that the output current has the same direction as it originally had, although it still changes from a maximum value to zero. A plot of this pulsating direct current is shown in **Figure 2.5.**

A steady direct current can be produced by using many loops and commutators distributed around the rotation axis of the dc generator. This generator uses slip rings to continually switch the output of the generator to the commutator that is producing its maximum emf. This switching produces an output that has a slight ripple but is nearly constant.

FIGURE 2.5

Current Output for a dc Generator
The output current for a dc generator with a single loop is a sine wave with the negative parts of the curve made positive.

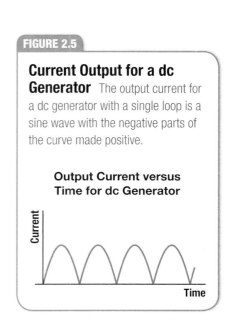

Output Current versus Time for dc Generator

Motors

Motors are machines that convert electrical energy to mechanical energy. Instead of a current being generated by a rotating loop in a magnetic field, a current is supplied to the loop by an emf source, and the magnetic force on the current loop causes it to rotate (see **Figure 2.6**).

A motor is almost identical in construction to a dc generator. The coil of wire is mounted on a rotating shaft and is positioned between the poles of a magnet. Brushes make contact with a commutator, which alternates the current in the coil. This alternation of the current causes the magnetic field produced by the current to regularly reverse and thus always be repelled by the fixed magnetic field. Thus, the coil and the shaft are kept in continuous rotational motion.

A motor can perform mechanical work when a shaft connected to its rotating coil is attached to some external device. As the coil in the motor rotates, however, the changing normal component of the magnetic field through it induces an emf that acts to reduce the current in the coil. If this were not the case, Lenz's law would be violated. This induced emf is called the **back emf.**

back emf the emf induced in a motor's coil that tends to reduce the current in the coil of the motor

The back emf increases in magnitude as the magnetic field changes at a higher rate. In other words, the faster the coil rotates, the greater the back emf becomes. The potential difference available to supply current to the motor equals the difference between the applied potential difference and the back emf. Consequently, the current in the coil is also reduced because of the presence of back emf. As the motor turns faster, both the net emf across the motor and the net current in the coil become smaller.

FIGURE 2.6

Components of a dc Motor In a motor, the current in the coil interacts with the magnetic field, causing the coil and the shaft on which the coil is mounted to turn.

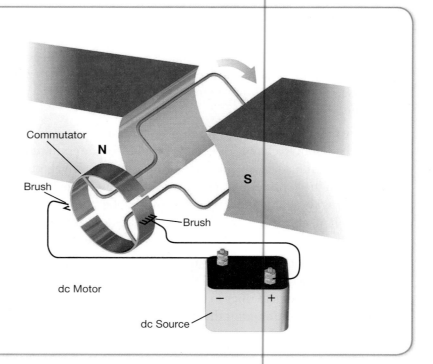

Commutator

N

Brush

S

Brush

dc Motor

dc Source

− +

Mutual Inductance

The basic principle of electromagnetic induction was first demonstrated by Michael Faraday. His experimental apparatus, which resembled the arrangement shown in **Figure 2.7**, used a coil connected to a switch and a battery instead of a magnet to produce a magnetic field. This coil is called the *primary coil,* and its circuit is called the *primary circuit.* The magnetic field is strengthened by the magnetic properties of the iron ring around which the primary coil is wrapped.

A second coil is wrapped around another part of the iron ring and is connected to a galvanometer. An emf is induced in this coil, called the *secondary coil,* when the magnetic field of the primary coil is changed. When the switch in the primary circuit is closed, the galvanometer in the secondary circuit deflects in one direction and then returns to zero. When the switch is opened, the galvanometer deflects in the opposite direction and again returns to zero. When there is a steady current in the primary circuit, the galvanometer reads zero.

The magnitude of this emf is predicted by Faraday's law of induction. However, Faraday's law can be rewritten so that the induced emf is proportional to the changing current in the primary coil. This can be done because of the direct proportionality between the magnetic field produced by a current in a coil, or solenoid, and the current itself. The form of Faraday's law in terms of changing primary current is as follows:

$$\text{emf} = -N\frac{\Delta \Phi M}{\Delta t} = -M\frac{\Delta I}{\Delta t}$$

The constant, *M,* is called the **mutual inductance** of the two-coil system. The mutual inductance depends on the geometrical properties of the coils and their orientation to each other. A changing current in the secondary coil can also induce an emf in the primary circuit. In fact, when the current through the second coil varies, the induced emf in the first coil is governed by an analogous equation *with the same value of M.*

The induced emf in the secondary circuit can be changed by changing the number of turns of wire in the secondary coil. This arrangement is the basis of an extremely useful electrical device: the transformer.

mutual inductance the ability of one circuit to induce an emf in a nearby circuit in the presence of a changing current

---

FIGURE 2.7

Induction of Current by a Fluctuating Current

Faraday's electromagnetic-induction experiment used a changing current in one circuit to induce a current in another circuit.

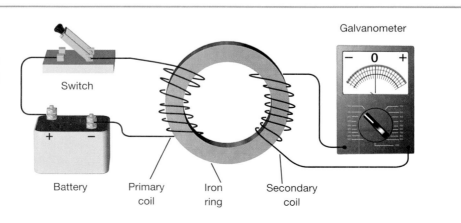

Switch

Battery

Primary coil

Iron ring

Secondary coil

Galvanometer

S.T.E.M.

Avoiding Electrocution

Y ou can receive an electric shock by touching something that is at a different electric potential than your body. For example, you might touch a high-electric-potential object while in contact with a cold-water pipe (normally at zero potential) or while standing on the floor with wet feet (because impure water is a good conductor).

Electric shock can result in fatal burns or can cause the muscles of vital organs, such as the heart, to malfunction. The degree of damage to the body depends on the magnitude of the current, the length of time it acts, and the part of the body through which it passes. A current of 100 milliamps (mA) can be fatal. If the current is larger than about 10 mA, the hand muscles contract, and the person may be unable to let go of the wire.

Any wires designed to have such currents in them are wrapped in insulation, usually plastic or rubber, to prevent electrocution. However, with frequent use, electrical cords can fray, exposing some of the conductors. In these and other situations in which electrical contact can be made, devices called a ground fault circuit interrupter (GFCI) and a ground fault interrupter (GFI) are mounted in electrical

outlets and individual appliances to prevent further electrocution.

GFCIs and GFIs provide protection by comparing the current in one side of the electrical outlet socket to the current in the other socket. The two currents are compared by induction in a device called a *differential transformer.* If there is even a 5 mA difference, the interrupter opens the circuit in a few milliseconds (thousandths of a second). The quick motion needed to open the circuit is again provided by induction, with the use of a solenoid switch.

Despite these safety devices, you can still be electrocuted. Never use electrical appliances near water or with wet hands. Use a battery-powered radio near water, because batteries cannot supply enough current to harm you. It is also a good idea to replace old outlets with GFCI-equipped units or to install GFI-equipped circuit breakers.

✔ SECTION 2 **FORMATIVE ASSESSMENT**

▶ Reviewing Main Ideas

1. A loop with 37 turns and an area of 0.33 m² is rotating at 281 rad/s. The loop's axis of rotation is perpendicular to a uniform magnetic field with a strength of 0.035 T. What is the maximum emf induced?

2. A generator coil has 25 turns of wire and a cross-sectional area of 36 cm². The maximum emf developed in the generator is 2.8 V at 60 Hz. What is the strength of the magnetic field in which the coil rotates?

3. Explain what would happen if a commutator were not used in a motor.

✔ Critical Thinking

4. Suppose a fixed distance separates the centers of two circular loops. What relative orientation of the loops will give the maximum mutual inductance? What orientation will give the minimum mutual inductance?

AC Circuits and Transformers

Key Terms
rms current   transformer

Effective Current

In the previous section, you learned that an electrical generator could produce an alternating current that varies as a sine wave with respect to time. Commercial power plants use generators to provide electrical energy to power the many electrical devices in our homes and businesses. In this section, we will investigate the characteristics of simple ac circuits.

As with the discussion about direct-current circuits, the resistance, the current, and the potential difference in a circuit are all relevant to a discussion about alternating-current circuits. The emf in ac circuits is analogous to the potential difference in dc circuits. One way to measure these three important circuit parameters is with a digital multimeter, as shown in **Figure 3.1.** The resistance, current, or emf can be measured by choosing the proper settings on the multimeter and locations in the circuit.

Effective current and effective emf are measured in ac circuits.

An ac circuit consists of combinations of circuit elements and an ac generator or an ac power supply, which provides the alternating current. As shown earlier, the emf produced by a typical ac generator is sinusoidal and varies with time. The induced emf as a function of time (Δv) can be written in terms of the maximum emf (ΔV_{max}), and the emf produced by a generator can be expressed as follows:

$$\Delta v = \Delta V_{max}\sin \omega t$$

A simple ac circuit can be treated as an equivalent resistance and an ac source. In a circuit diagram, the ac source is represented by the symbol ⊘, as shown in **Figure 3.2.**

The instantaneous current that changes with the potential difference can be determined using the definition for resistance. The instantaneous current, i, is related to maximum current by the following expression:

$$i = I_{max}\sin \omega t$$

The rate at which electrical energy is converted to internal energy in the resistor (the power, P) has the same form as in the case of direct current. The electrical energy converted to internal energy at some point in time in a resistor is proportional to the *square* of the instantaneous current and is independent of the direction of the current. However, the

SECTION 3

Objectives

▶ Solve problems involving rms and maximum values of current and emf for ac circuits.

▶ Apply the transformer equation to solve problems involving step-up and step-down transformers.

FIGURE 3.1

A Digital Multimeter
The effective current and emf of an electric circuit can be measured using a digital multimeter.

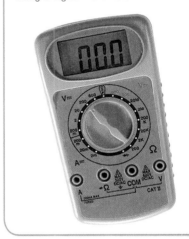

FIGURE 3.2

A Schematic of an ac Circuit
An ac circuit represented schematically consists of an ac source and an equivalent resistance.

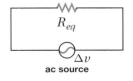

R_{eq}

Δv
ac source

energy produced by an alternating current with a maximum value of I_{max} is not the same as that produced by a direct current of the same value. The energies are different because during a cycle, the alternating current is at its maximum value for only an instant.

An important measure of the current in an ac circuit is the **rms current.** The rms (or *root-mean-square*) current is the same as the amount of direct current that would dissipate the same energy in a resistor as is dissipated by the instantaneous alternating current over a complete cycle. **Figure 3.3** shows a graph in which instantaneous and rms currents are compared. **Figure 3.4** summarizes the notations used in this chapter for these and other ac quantities.

The equation for the average power dissipated in an ac circuit has the same form as the equation for power dissipated in a dc circuit except that the dc current I is replaced by the rms current (I_{rms}).

$$P = (I_{rms})^2 R$$

This equation is identical in form to the one for direct current. However, the power dissipated in the ac circuit equals half the power dissipated in a dc circuit when the dc current equals I_{max}.

$$P = (I_{rms})^2 R = \frac{1}{2}(I_{max})^2 R$$

From this equation, you may note that the rms current is related to the maximum value of the alternating current by the following equation:

$$(I_{rms})^2 = \frac{(I_{max})^2}{2}$$

Solving the above equation for I_{rms} leads to the following:

$$I_{rms} = \frac{I_{max}}{\sqrt{2}} = 0.707\, I_{max}$$

This equation says that an alternating current with a maximum value of 5 A produces the same heating effect in a resistor as a direct current of $(5/\sqrt{2})$ A, or about 3.5 A.

Alternating emfs are also best discussed in terms of their rms values, with the relationship between rms and maximum values analogous to the one for currents. The rms and maximum values are related as follows:

$$\Delta V_{rms} = \frac{\Delta V_{max}}{\sqrt{2}} = 0.707\, V_{max}$$

FIGURE 3.3

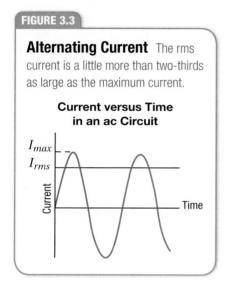

Alternating Current The rms current is a little more than two-thirds as large as the maximum current.

Current versus Time in an ac Circuit

FIGURE 3.4

	NOTATION USED FOR AC CIRCUITS	
	Induced or Applied emf	**Current**
instantaneous values	Δv	i
maximum values	ΔV_{max}	I_{max}
rms values	$\Delta V_{rms} = \dfrac{\Delta V_{max}}{\sqrt{2}}$	$I_{rms} = \dfrac{I_{rms}}{\sqrt{2}}$

GO ONLINE

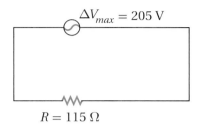

Interactive Demo
HMHScience.com

Sample Problem B A generator with a maximum output emf of 205 V is connected to a 115 Ω resistor. Calculate the rms potential difference. Find the rms current through the resistor. Find the maximum ac current in the circuit.

1 ANALYZE

Given: $\Delta V_{max} = 205$ V $R = 115$ Ω

Unknown: $\Delta V_{rms} = ?$ $I_{rms} = ?$ $I_{max} = ?$

Diagram:

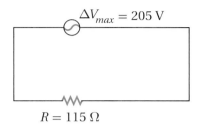

$\Delta V_{max} = 205$ V

$R = 115$ Ω

2 PLAN

Choose an equation or situation: Use the equation for the rms potential difference to find ΔV_{rms}.

$$\Delta V_{rms} = 0.707 \, \Delta V_{max}$$

Rearrange the definition for resistance to calculate I_{rms}.

$$I_{rms} = \frac{\Delta V_{rms}}{R}$$

Use the equation for rms current to find I_{max}.

$$I_{rms} = 0.707 \, I_{max}$$

Rearrange the equation to isolate the unknown:
Rearrange the equation relating rms current to maximum current so that maximum current is calculated.

$$I_{max} = \frac{I_{rms}}{0.707}$$

> **Tips and Tricks**
> Because emf is measured in volts, maximum emf is frequently abbreviated as ΔV_{max}, and rms emf can be abbreviated as ΔV_{rms}.

3 SOLVE

Substitute the values into the equation and solve:

$$\Delta V_{rms} = (0.707)(205 \text{ V}) = 145 \text{ V}$$

$$I_{rms} = \frac{145 \text{ V}}{115 \text{ Ω}} = 1.26 \text{ A}$$

$$I_{max} = \frac{1.26 \text{ A}}{0.707} = 1.78 \text{ A}$$

> $\Delta V_{rms} = 145$ V
>
> $I_{rms} = 1.26$ A
>
> $I_{max} = 1.78$ A

4 CHECK YOUR WORK

The rms values for the emf and current are a little more than two-thirds the maximum values, as expected.

rms Current and emf (continued)

1. What is the rms current in a light bulb that has a resistance of 25 Ω and an rms emf of 120 V? What are the maximum values for current and emf?

2. The current in an ac circuit is measured with an ammeter. The meter gives a reading of 5.5 A. Calculate the maximum ac current.

3. A toaster is plugged into a source of alternating emf with an rms value of 110 V. The heating element is designed to convey a current with a peak value of 10.5 A. Find the following:

   a. the rms current in the heating element

   b. the resistance of the heating element

4. An audio amplifier provides an alternating rms emf of 15.0 V. A loudspeaker connected to the amplifier has a resistance of 10.4 Ω. What is the rms current in the speaker? What are the maximum values of the current and the emf?

5. An ac generator has a maximum emf output of 155 V.

   a. Find the rms emf output.

   b. Find the rms current in the circuit when the generator is connected to a 53 Ω resistor.

6. The largest emf that can be placed across a certain capacitor at any instant is 451 V. What is the largest rms emf that can be placed across the capacitor without damaging it?

Resistance influences current in an ac circuit.

The ac potential difference (commonly called the *voltage*) of 120 V measured from an electrical outlet is actually an rms emf of 120 V. (This, too, is a simplification that assumes that the voltmeter has infinite resistance.) A quick calculation shows that such an emf has a maximum value of about 170 V.

The resistance of a circuit modifies the current in an ac circuit just as it does in a dc circuit. If the definition of resistance is valid for an ac circuit, the rms emf across a resistor equals the rms current multiplied by the resistance. Thus, all maximum and rms values can be calculated if only one current or emf value and the circuit resistance are known.

Ammeters and voltmeters that measure alternating current are calibrated to measure rms values. In this chapter, all values of alternating current and emf will be given as rms values unless otherwise noted. The equations for ac circuits have the same form as those for dc circuits when rms values are used.

Transformers

It is often desirable or necessary to change a small ac applied emf to a larger one or to change a large applied emf to a smaller one. The device that makes these conversions possible is the **transformer.**

In its simplest form, an ac transformer consists of two coils of wire wound around a core of soft iron, like the apparatus for the Faraday experiment. The coil on the left in **Figure 3.5** has N_1 turns and is connected to the input ac potential difference source. This coil is called the primary winding, or the *primary*. The coil on the right, which is connected to a resistor R and consists of N_2 turns, is the *secondary*. As in Faraday's experiment, the iron core "guides" the magnetic field lines so that nearly all of the field lines pass through both of the coils.

Because the strength of the magnetic field in the iron core and the cross-sectional area of the core are the same for both the primary and secondary windings, the measured ac potential differences across the two windings differ only because of the different number of turns of wire for each. The applied emf that gives rise to the changing magnetic field in the primary is related to that changing field by Faraday's law of induction.

$$\Delta V_1 = -N_1 \frac{\Delta \Phi_M}{\Delta t}$$

Similarly, the induced emf across the secondary coil is

$$\Delta V_2 = -N_2 \frac{\Delta \Phi_M}{\Delta t}$$

Taking the ratio of ΔV_1 to ΔV_2 causes all terms on the right side of both equations except for N_1 and N_2 to cancel. This result is the transformer equation.

FIGURE 3.5

Basic Components of an ac Transformer A transformer uses the alternating current in the primary circuit to induce an alternating current in the secondary circuit.

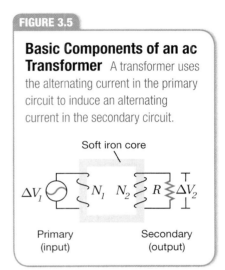

Soft iron core

ΔV_1 N_1 N_2 R ΔV_2

Primary (input)   Secondary (output)

Transformer Equation

$$\Delta V_2 = \frac{N_2}{N_1} \Delta V_1$$

induced emf in secondary =

$$\left(\frac{\textbf{number of turns in secondary}}{\textbf{number of turns in primary}} \right) \textbf{applied emf in primary}$$

Another way to express this equation is to equate the ratio of the potential differences to the ratio of the number of turns.

$$\frac{\Delta V_2}{\Delta V_1} = \frac{N_2}{N_1}$$

When N_2 is greater than N_1, the secondary emf is greater than that of the primary, and the transformer is called a *step-up transformer*. When N_2 is less than N_1, the secondary emf is less than that of the primary, and the transformer is called a *step-down transformer.*

It may seem that a transformer provides something for nothing. For example, a step-up transformer can change an applied emf from 10 V to 100 V. However, the power output at the secondary is, at best, equal to the power input at the primary. In reality, energy is lost to heating and radiation, so the output power will be *less* than the input power. Thus, an increase in induced emf at the secondary means that there must be a proportional decrease in current.

GO ONLINE

Interactive Demo
HMHScience.com

Transformers

Sample Problem C An ac generator at a central power station uses a step-up transformer to provide a potential difference of 68 kV across the secondary coil. If the primary coil has 125 turns and the secondary coil has 625 turns, what is the potential difference across the primary coil?

❶ ANALYZE

Given: $\Delta V_2 = 68 \text{ kV} = 6.8 \times 10^4 \text{ V}$ $N_1 = 125 \text{ turns}$

$N_2 = 625 \text{ turns}$

Unknown: $\Delta V_1 = ?$

❷ PLAN

Choose the equation or situation: Use the transformer equation.

$$\frac{\Delta V_1}{\Delta V_2} = \frac{N_1}{N_2}$$

Rearrange the equation to isolate the unknowns: Rearrange the equation for a transformer to solve for the potential difference in the primary coil.

$$\Delta V_1 = \frac{\Delta V_2 N_1}{N_2}$$

❸ SOLVE

Substitute the values into the equation and solve:

$$\Delta V_1 = \frac{\Delta V_2 N_1}{N_2} = \frac{(6.8 \times 10^4 \text{ V})(125)}{(625)}$$

$$\Delta V_1 = \boxed{1.4 \times 10^4 \text{ V} = 14 \text{kV}}$$

❹ CHECK YOUR WORK

The potential difference across the primary should be 14 kV. The step-up factor for the transformer is 1:5.

Continued ▶

Practice

1. A transmission line to a city has a potential difference of 6.9 kV across the secondary coil. If the primary coil has 1400 turns and the secondary coil has 140 turns, what is the potential difference across the primary coil?

2. A step-up transformer used in an automobile has a potential difference across the primary of 12 V and a potential difference across the secondary of 2.0×10^4 V. If the number of turns in the primary is 21, what is the number of turns in the secondary?

3. A step-up transformer for long-range transmission of electric power is used to create a potential difference of 119 340 V across the secondary. If the potential difference across the primary is 117 V and the number of turns in the secondary is 25 500, what is the number of turns in the primary?

4. A potential difference of 0.750 V is needed to provide a large current for arc welding. If the potential difference across the primary of a step-down transformer is 117 V, what is the ratio of the number of turns of wire on the primary to the number of turns on the secondary?

5. A step-down transformer has 525 turns in its secondary and 12 500 turns in its primary. If the potential difference across the primary is 3510 V, what is the potential difference across the secondary?

Real transformers are not perfectly efficient.

The transformer equation assumes that no power is lost between the transformer's primary and secondary coils. Real transformers typically have efficiencies ranging from 90 percent to 99 percent. Power is lost because of the small currents induced by changing magnetic fields in the transformer's iron core and because of resistance in the wires of the windings.

The power lost to resistive heating in transmission lines varies as I^2R. To minimize I^2R loss and maximize the deliverable energy, power companies use a high emf and a low current when transmitting power over long distances. By reducing the current by a factor of 10, the power loss is reduced by a factor of 100. In practice, the emf is stepped up to around 230 000 V at the generating station, is stepped down to 20 000 V at a regional distribution station, and is finally stepped down to 120 V at the customer's utility pole. The high emf in long-distance transmission lines makes the lines especially dangerous when high winds knock them down.

FIGURE 3.6

A Step-Up Transformer in an Auto Ignition System
The transformer in an automobile engine raises the potential difference across the gap in a spark plug so that sparking occurs.

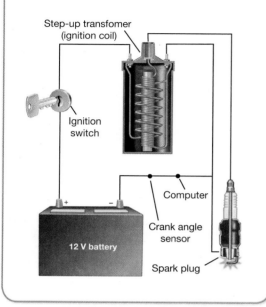

Step-up transformer (ignition coil)

Ignition switch

Computer

Crank angle sensor

+ − 12 V battery

Spark plug

The ignition coil in a gasoline engine is a transformer.

An automobile battery provides a constant emf of 12 dc volts to power various systems in your automobile. The ignition system uses a transformer, called the *ignition coil,* to convert the car battery's 12 dc volts to a potential difference that is large enough to cause sparking between the gaps of the spark plugs. The diagram in **Figure 3.6** shows a type of ignition system that has been used in automobiles since about 1990. In this arrangement, called an *electronic ignition,* each cylinder has its own transformer coil.

The ignition system on your car has to work in perfect concert with the rest of the engine. The goal is to ignite the fuel at the exact moment when the expanding gases can do the maximum amount of work. A photoelectric detector, called a *crank angle sensor,* uses the crankshaft's position to determine when the cylinder's contents are near maximum compression.

The sensor then sends a signal to the automobile's computer. Upon receiving this signal, the computer closes the primary circuit to the cylinder's coil, causing the current in the primary to rapidly increase. As we learned earlier in this chapter, the increase in current induces a rapid change in the magnetic field of the transformer. Because the change in magnetic field on the primary side is so quick, the change induces a very large emf, from 40 000 to 100 000 V. The emf is applied across the spark plug and creates a spark that ignites and burns the fuel that powers your automobile.

✓ SECTION 3 FORMATIVE ASSESSMENT

▶ Reviewing Main Ideas

1. The rms current that a single coil of an electric guitar produces is 0.025 mA. The coil's resistance is 4.3 kΩ. What is the maximum instantaneous current? What is the rms emf produced by the coil? What is the maximum emf produced by the coil?

2. A step-up transformer has exactly 50 turns in its primary and exactly 7000 turns in its secondary. If the applied emf in the primary is 120 V, what emf is induced in the secondary?

3. A television picture tube requires a high potential difference, which a step-up transformer provides in older models. The transformer has 12 turns in its primary and 2550 turns in its secondary. If 120 V is applied across the primary, what is the output emf?

✓ Critical Thinking

4. What is the average value of current over one cycle of an ac signal? Why, then, is a resistor heated by an ac current?

Electromagnetic Waves

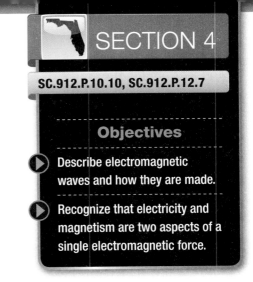
Objectives

▷ Describe electromagnetic waves and how they are made.

▷ Recognize that electricity and magnetism are two aspects of a single electromagnetic force.

Key Terms

electromagnetic radiation   photon

Propagation of Electromagnetic Waves

Light is a phenomenon known as an *electromagnetic wave*. As the name implies, oscillating electric and magnetic fields create electromagnetic waves. In this section, you will learn more about the nature and the discovery of electromagnetic waves.

The wavelength and frequency of electromagnetic waves vary widely, from radio waves with very long wavelengths to gamma rays with extremely short wavelengths. The visible light that our eyes can detect occupies an intermediate range of wavelengths. Familiar objects "look" quite different at different wavelengths. **Figure 4.1** shows how a person might appear to us if we could see beyond the red end of the visible spectrum.

In this chapter, you have learned that a changing magnetic field can induce a current in a circuit (Faraday's law of induction). From Coulomb's law, which describes the electrostatic force between two charges, you know that electric field lines start on positive charges and end at negative charges. On the other hand, magnetic field lines always form closed loops and have no beginning or end. Finally, you learned in the chapter on magnetism that a magnetic field is created around a current-carrying wire, as stated by Ampère's law.

SC.912.P.10.10 Compare the magnitude and range of the four fundamental forces (gravitational, electromagnetic, weak nuclear, strong nuclear).
SC.912.P.12.7 Recognize that nothing travels faster than the speed of light in vacuum which is the same for all observers no matter how they or the light source are moving.

Electromagnetic waves consist of changing electric and magnetic fields.

In the mid-1800s, Scottish physicist James Clerk Maxwell created a simple but sophisticated set of equations to describe the relationship between electric and magnetic fields. Maxwell's equations summarized the known phenomena of his time: the observations that were described by Coulomb, Faraday, Ampère, and other scientists of his era. Maxwell believed that nature is symmetric, and he hypothesized that a changing electric field should produce a magnetic field in a manner analogous to Faraday's law of induction.

Maxwell's equations described many of the phenomena, such as magnetic induction, that had already been observed. However, other phenomena that had not been observed could be derived from the equations. For example, Maxwell's

FIGURE 4.1

Infrared Image of a Person At normal body temperature, humans radiate most strongly in the infrared, at a wavelength of about 10 microns (10^{-5} m). The wavelength of the infrared radiation can be correlated to temperature.

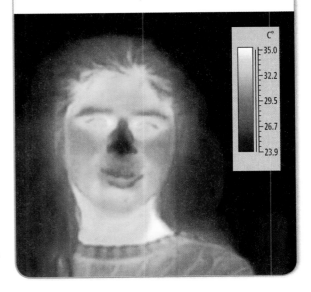

FIGURE 4.2

An Electromagnetic Wave

An electromagnetic wave consists of electric and magnetic field waves at right angles to each other. The wave moves in the direction perpendicular to both oscillating waves.

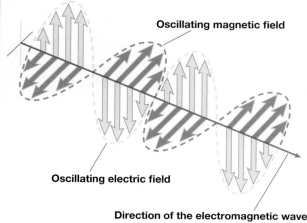

Oscillating magnetic field

Oscillating electric field

Direction of the electromagnetic wave

equations predicted that a changing magnetic field would create a changing electric field, which would, in turn, create a changing magnetic field, and so on. The predicted result of those changing fields is a wave that moves through space at the speed of light.

Maxwell predicted that light was electromagnetic in nature. The scientific community did not immediately accept Maxwell's equations. However, in 1887, a German physicist named Heinrich Hertz generated and detected electromagnetic waves in his laboratory. Hertz's experimental confirmation of Maxwell's work convinced the scientific community to accept the work.

Electromagnetic waves are simply oscillating electric and magnetic fields. The electric and magnetic fields are at right angles to each other and also at right angles to the direction that the wave is moving. **Figure 4.2** is a simple illustration of an electromagnetic wave at a single point in time. The electric field oscillates in one plane while the magnetic field oscillates in a perpendicular plane. The wave travels in the direction that is perpendicular to both of the oscillating fields. In the chapter on vibrations and waves, you learned that this kind of wave is called a *transverse wave*.

Electric and magnetic forces are aspects of a single force.

Although magnetism and electricity seem like very different things, we know that both electric and magnetic fields can produce forces on charged particles. These forces are aspects of one and the same force, called the *electromagnetic force*. Physicists have identified four *fundamental forces* in the universe: the strong force, which holds together the nucleus of an atom; the electromagnetic force, which is discussed here; the weak force, which is involved in nuclear decay; and the gravitational force, discussed in the chapter "Circular Motion and Gravitation." In the 1970s, physicists came to regard the electromagnetic and the weak force as two aspects of a single *electroweak interaction*.

The electromagnetic force obeys the *inverse-square law*. The force's magnitude decreases as one over the distance from the source squared. The inverse-square law applies to phenomena—such as gravity, light, and sound—that spread their influence equally in all directions and with an infinite range.

All electromagnetic waves are produced by accelerating charges.

The simplest radiation source is an oscillating charged particle. Consider a negatively charged particle (electron) moving back and forth beside a fixed positive charge (proton). Recall that the changing electric field induces a magnetic field perpendicular to the electric field. In this way, the wave *propagates* itself as each changing field induces the other.

The frequency of oscillation determines the frequency of the wave that is produced. In an antenna, two metal rods are connected to an alternating voltage source that is changed from positive to negative voltage at the desired frequency. The wavelength λ of the wave is related to the frequency f by the equation $\lambda = c/f$, in which c is the speed of light.

Electromagnetic waves transfer energy.

All types of waves, whether they are mechanical or electromagnetic or are longitudinal or transverse, have an energy associated with their motion. In the case of electromagnetic waves, that energy is stored in the oscillating electric and magnetic fields.

The simplest definition of energy is the capacity to do work. When work is performed on a body, a force moves the body in the direction of the force. The force that electromagnetic fields exert on a charged particle is proportional to the electric field strength, E, and the magnetic field strength, B. So we can say that energy is stored in electric and magnetic fields in much the same way that energy is stored in gravitational fields.

The energy transported by electromagnetic waves is called **electromagnetic radiation.** The energy carried by electromagnetic waves can be transferred to objects in the path of the waves or converted to other forms, such as heat. An everyday example is the use of the energy from microwave radiation to warm food. Energy from the sun reaches Earth via electromagnetic radiation across a variety of wavelengths. Some of these wavelengths are illustrated in **Figure 4.3.**

electromagnetic radiation the transfer of energy associated with an electromagnetic wave; it varies periodically and travels at the speed of light

FIGURE 4.3

The Sun at Different Wavelengths of Radiation

The sun radiates in all parts of the electromagnetic spectrum, not just in the visible light that we are accustomed to observing. These images show what the sun would look like if we could "see" at different wavelengths of electromagnetic radiation.

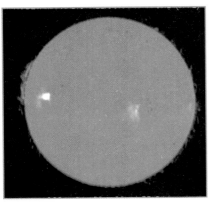

Radio

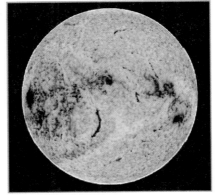

Infrared

Visible (black and white)

Ultraviolet

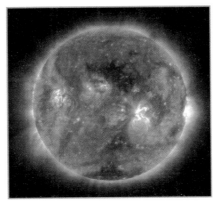

Extreme UV

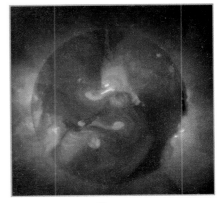

X-ray

The Search for Extraterrestrials

This is a question humans have pondered for centuries. In 1959, Philip Morrison and Guiseppe Cocconi set out to answer it by considering how electromagnetic (EM) radiation travels through space. Space is described as a vacuum, but there are regions of gas and dust between stars. Most EM frequencies are absorbed by interstellar material. However, radio waves penetrate gas and dust and are mostly unaffected. Morrison and Cocconi identified frequencies from 1 GHz to 10 GHz (microwave portion) as prime "channels" for communication.

In 1960, radio astronomer Frank Drake pioneered the first modern experiment in the search for extraterrestrials (Project Ozma) using a radio telescope at the National Radio Astronomy Observatory in West Virginia. Drake's search was unsuccessful. To stir more interest in the scientific community, Drake held the first meeting on the "search for extraterrestrial intelligence," or SETI, in 1961. He drafted an equation that could be used to estimate the number of active communicating alien civilizations in our galaxy to rouse scientific dialogue at the meeting. This equation now bears Drake's name.

Today, Drake's pioneering mission continues as the SETI Institute in California listens for signatures of alien technology. The institute is a not-for-profit research organization dedicated to scientific research, education, and public outreach. It uses the Allen Telescope Array (ATA), a series of 42 small radio dishes located in the Cascade Mountains.

Humans have already sent several symbolic messages to other worlds. In 1962, the first radio message broadcast to extraterrestrial civilizations was sent in Morse code by the former Soviet Union. In the 1970s, four American spacecraft were sent to explore the planets in the outer solar system. Astronomers included plaques etched with pictorial messages, along with songs and sounds from Earth.

Douglas Vakoch, SETI Director of Interstellar Communications, heads "Earth Speaks," a project that invites the public to submit text, images, and sounds that could be used as a response to a potential alien call. What would you submit?

photon a unit or quantum of light; a particle of electromagnetic radiation that has zero mass and carries a quantum of energy

High-energy electromagnetic waves behave like particles.

Sometimes an electromagnetic wave behaves like a particle. This notion is called the *wave-particle duality* of light. It is important to understand that there is no difference in what light *is* at different frequencies. The difference lies in how light *behaves*.

When thinking about electromagnetic waves as a stream of particles, it is helpful to utilize the concept of a **photon.** A photon is a particle that carries energy but has zero mass. You will learn more about photons in the chapter on atomic physics. The relationship between frequency and photon energy is simple: $E = hf$, in which h, Plank's constant, is a fixed number and f is the frequency of the wave.

Low-energy photons tend to behave more like waves, and high-energy photons behave more like particles. This distinction helps scientists design detectors and telescopes to distinguish different frequencies of radiation.

The Electromagnetic Spectrum

At first glance, radio waves seem completely different from visible light and gamma rays. They are produced and detected in very different ways. Though your eyes can see visible light, a large antenna is needed to detect radio waves, and sophisticated scientific equipment must be used to observe gamma rays. Even though they appear quite different, all the different parts of the *electromagnetic spectrum* are fundamentally the same thing. They are all electromagnetic waves.

The electromagnetic spectrum can be expressed in terms of wavelength, frequency, or energy. The electromagnetic spectrum is shown in **Figure 4.4.** Longer wavelengths, like radio waves, are usually described in terms of frequency. If your favorite FM radio station is 90.5, the frequency is 90.5 MHz (9.05×10^7 Hz). Infrared, visible, and ultraviolet light are usually described in terms of wavelength. We see the wavelength 670 nm (6.70×10^{-7} m) as red light. The shortest wavelength radiation is generally described in terms of the energy of one photon. For example, the element cesium-137 emits gamma rays with energy of 662 keV (10^{-13} J). (A keV is a *kilo-electron volt*, equal to 1000 eV or 1.60×10^{-16} J.)

Radio waves.

Radio waves have the longest wavelengths in the spectrum. The wavelengths range in size from the diameter of a soccer ball to the length of a soccer field and beyond. Because long wavelengths easily travel around objects, they work well for transmitting information long distances. In the United States, the FCC regulates the radio spectrum by assigning the bands that certain stations can use for radio and television broadcasting.

Objects that are far away in deep space also emit radio waves. Because these waves can pass through Earth's atmosphere, scientists can use huge antennas on land to collect the waves, which can help them understand the nature of the universe.

FIGURE 4.4

The Electromagnetic Spectrum

The electromagnetic spectrum ranges from very long radio waves, with wavelengths equal to the height of a tall building, to very short-wavelength gamma rays, with wavelengths as short as the diameter of the nucleus of an atom.

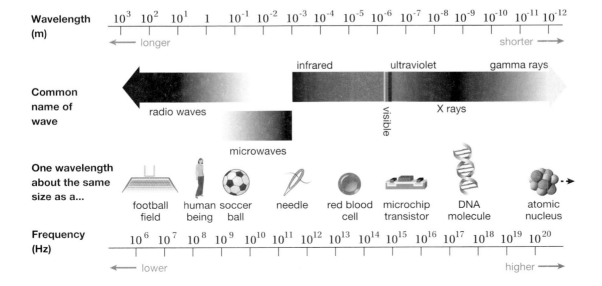

Microwaves.

The wavelengths of microwaves range from 30 cm to 1 mm in length. These waves are considered to be part of the radio spectrum and are also regulated by the FCC. Microwaves are used to study the stars, to talk with satellites in orbit, and to heat up your after-school snack.

Microwave ovens use the longer-wavelength microwaves to cook your popcorn quickly. Microwaves are also useful for transmitting information, because they can penetrate mist, clouds, smoke, and haze. Microwave towers throughout the world convey telephone calls and computer data from city to city. Shorter-wavelength microwaves are used for radar. Radar works by sending out bursts of microwaves and detecting the reflections off of objects the waves hit.

Infrared.

Infrared light lies between the microwave and the visible parts of the electromagnetic spectrum. The *far-infrared* wavelengths, which are close to the microwave end of the spectrum, are about the size of the head of a pin. Short, *near-infrared* wavelengths are microscopic. They are about the size of a cell.

You experience far-infrared radiation every day as heat given off by anything warm: sunlight, a warm sidewalk, a flame, and even your own body. Television remote controls and some burglar-alarm systems use near-infrared radiation. Night-vision goggles show the world as it looks in the infrared, which helps police officers and rescue workers to locate people, animals, and other warm objects in the dark. Mosquitoes can also "see" in the infrared, which is one of the tools in their arsenal for finding dinner.

Visible light.

The wavelengths that the human eye can see range from about 700 nm (red light) to 400 nm (violet light). This range is a very small part of the electromagnetic spectrum. We see the visible spectrum as a rainbow, as shown in **Figure 4.5.**

Visible light is produced in many ways. An incandescent light bulb gives off light—and heat—from a glowing filament. In neon lights and in lasers, atoms emit light directly. Televisions and fluorescent lights make use of *phosphors*, which are materials that emit light when they are exposed to high-energy electrons or ultraviolet radiation. Fireflies create light through a chemical reaction.

Ultraviolet.

Ultraviolet (UV) light has wavelengths that are shorter than visible light, just beyond the violet. Our sun emits light throughout the spectrum, but the ultraviolet waves are the ones responsible for causing sunburns. Even though you cannot see ultraviolet light with your eyes, this light will also damage your retina. Only a small portion of the ultraviolet waves that the sun emits actually penetrates Earth's atmosphere. Various atmospheric gases, such as ozone, block most of the UV waves.

FIGURE 4.5

The Visible Light Spectrum When white light shines through a prism or through water, such as in this rainbow, you can see the colors of the visible light spectrum.

Ultraviolet light is often used as a disinfectant to kill bacteria in city water supplies or to sterilize equipment in hospitals. Scientists use ultraviolet light to determine the chemical makeup of atoms and molecules and also the nature of stars and other celestial bodies. Ultraviolet light is also used to harden some kinds of dental fillings.

X-rays.

As the wavelengths of electromagnetic waves decrease, the associated photons increase in energy. X-rays have very short wavelengths, about the size of atoms, and are usually thought of in terms of their energy instead of their wavelength.

While the German scientist Wilhelm Conrad Roentgen was experimenting with vacuum tubes, he accidentally discovered x-rays. A week later, he took an x-ray photograph of his wife's hand, which clearly revealed her wedding ring and her bones. This first x-ray is shown in **Figure 4.6.** Roentgen called the phenomenon *x-ray* to indicate that it was an unknown type of radiation, and the name remains in use today.

You are probably familiar with the use of x-rays in medicine and dentistry. Airport security also uses x-rays to see inside luggage. Emission of x-rays from otherwise dark areas of space suggests the existence of black holes.

Gamma rays.

The shortest-wavelength electromagnetic waves are called *gamma rays*. As with x-rays, gamma rays are usually described by their energy. The highest-energy gamma rays observed by scientists come from the hottest regions of the universe.

Radioactive atoms and nuclear explosions produce gamma rays. Gamma rays can kill living cells and are used in medicine to destroy cancer cells. The universe is a huge generator of gamma rays. Because gamma rays do not fully pierce Earth's atmosphere, astronomers frequently mount gamma-ray detectors on satellites.

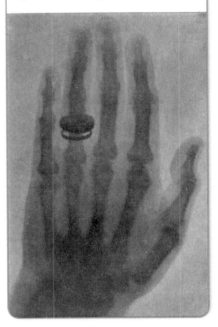

FIGURE 4.6

X-ray Image of a Hand
Wilhelm Roentgen took this x-ray image of Bertha Roentgen's hand one week after his discovery of this new type of electromagnetic radiation.

SECTION 4 **FORMATIVE ASSESSMENT**

▶ Reviewing Main Ideas

1. What concepts did Maxwell use to help create his theory of electricity and magnetism? What phenomenon did Maxwell's equations predict?

2. What do electric and magnetic forces have in common?

3. The parts of the electromagnetic spectrum are commonly described in one of three ways. What are these ways?

✔ Critical Thinking

4. Where is the energy of an electromagnetic wave stored? Describe how this energy can be used.

Theories Versus Hypotheses

If a group of related hypotheses are very well supported and explain a great amount of data, scientists may put the hypotheses together in their formulation of a theory. A theory is a general explanation for a broad range of data. A theory differs from a hypothesis in scope and reliability. A hypothesis is a specific testable prediction for a limited set of conditions. A theory is a generally accepted principle that has been well established to be highly reliable and that helps explain many observations.

James Maxwell and Electromagnetic Waves

James Maxwell generated equations describing the relationship between electric and magnetic fields. Many of the relationships predicted by the equations, such as the induction of an electric field by changing magnetic fields, were already accepted as theories. However, Maxwell's model extended additional hypotheses that a magnetic field would be induced by a changing electric field, leading to oscillating magnetic and electric fields—an electromagnetic wave. At the time, these waves could not be detected or observed. Fortunately, Heinrich Hertz devised a way to generate and detect these electromagnetic waves predicted by Maxwell's model. As the understanding of electromagnetic waves grew through the addition of reliable, empirical observations by many scientists, theories describing electromagnetic waves and their behavior were established.

- What might have happened to Maxwell's hypothesis about electromagnetic waves if scientists had been unable to detect them?

- Distinguish between scientific hypotheses and scientific theories.

- What must be highly reliable and well-established, a scientific hypothesis or a scientific theory? Explain why.

- Why is it important that many scientists and many experiments contribute to the formation of theories?

Conceptual Challenge

The ability to make assumptions and generate rough estimates is a valuable skill to scientists. Quick estimates allow scientists to narrow the range of possibilities and focus on the most reasonable hypotheses.

To the Moon If a microwave and a visible light wave both leave Earth at the same time and travel to the moon, how much of a time difference would there be between the arrival of the two waves at their destination?

You can begin addressing the scenario by asking questions such as the following:

- What is the distance from Earth to the moon?

- How fast do visible light waves travel?

- How fast do microwaves travel?

CHAPTER 20 Summary

BIG IDEA Magnetic and electric forces are actually a single force—the electromagnetic force. Changing magnetic fields produce electric fields and electric current, and changing electric fields produce magnetic fields.

SECTION 1 Electricity from Magnetism

KEY TERM

- A change in the magnetic flux through a conducting coil induces an electric current in the coil. This concept is called *electromagnetic induction.*
- Lenz's law states that the magnetic field of an induced current opposes the change that caused it.
- The magnitude of the induced emf can be calculated using Faraday's law of induction.

electromagnetic induction

SECTION 2 Generators, Motors, and Mutual Inductance

KEY TERMS

- Generators use induction to convert mechanical energy into electrical energy.
- Motors use an arrangement similar to that of generators to convert electrical energy into mechanical energy.
- *Mutual inductance* is the process by which an emf is induced in one circuit as a result of a changing current in another nearby circuit.

generator
alternating current
back emf
mutual inductance

SECTION 3 AC Circuits and Transformers

KEY TERMS

- The root-mean-square (rms) current and rms emf in an ac circuit are important measures of the characteristics of an ac circuit.
- A transformer is a device that can change a small alternating voltage to a larger one, and vice versa.

rms current
transformer

SECTION 4 Electromagnetic Waves

KEY TERMS

- Electromagnetic waves are transverse waves that are traveling at the speed of light and are associated with oscillating electric and magnetic fields.
- Electromagnetic waves transfer energy. The energy of electromagnetic waves is stored in the waves' electric and magnetic fields.
- The electromagnetic spectrum has a wide variety of applications and characteristics that cover a broad range of wavelengths and frequencies.

electromagnetic radiation
photon

VARIABLE SYMBOLS		
Quantities		**Units**
N	number of turns	(unitless)
ΔV_{max}	maximum emf	V volt
ΔV_{rms}	rms emf	V volt
I_{max}	maximum current	A ampere
I_{rms}	rms current	A ampere
M	mutual inductance	H henry = V•s/A

Problem Solving

See **Appendix D: Equations** for a summary of the equations introduced in this chapter. If you need more problem-solving practice, see **Appendix I: Additional Problems.**

Electricity from Magnetism

▶ **REVIEWING MAIN IDEAS**

1. Suppose you have two circuits. One consists of an electromagnet, a dc emf source, and a variable resistor that permits you to control the strength of the magnetic field. In the second circuit, you have a coil of wire and a galvanometer. List three ways that you can induce a current in the second circuit.

2. Explain how Lenz's law allows you to determine the direction of an induced current.

3. What four factors affect the magnitude of the induced emf in a coil of wire?

4. If you have a fixed magnetic field and a length of wire, how can you increase the induced emf across the ends of the wire?

CONCEPTUAL QUESTIONS

5. Rapidly inserting the north pole of a bar magnet into a coil of wire connected to a galvanometer causes the needle of the galvanometer to deflect to the right. What will happen to the needle if you do the following?
   a. pull the magnet out of the coil
   b. let the magnet sit at rest in the coil
   c. thrust the south end of the magnet into the coil

6. Explain how Lenz's law illustrates the principle of energy conservation.

7. Does dropping a strong magnet down a long copper tube induce a current in the tube? If so, what effect will the induced current have on the motion of the magnet?

8. Two bar magnets are placed side by side so that the north pole of one magnet is next to the south pole of the other magnet. If these magnets are then pushed toward a coil of wire, would you expect an emf to be induced in the coil? Explain your answer.

9. An electromagnet is placed next to a coil of wire in the arrangement shown below. According to Lenz's law, what will be the direction of the induced current in the resistor R in the following cases?
   a. The magnetic field suddenly decreases after the switch is opened.
   b. The coil is moved closer to the electromagnet.

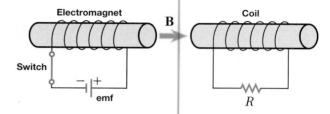

PRACTICE PROBLEMS

For problems 10–12, see Sample Problem A.

10. A flexible loop of conducting wire has a radius of 0.12 m and is perpendicular to a uniform magnetic field with a strength of 0.15 T, as in figure **(a)** below. The loop is grasped at opposite ends and stretched until it closes to an area of 3×10^{-3} m², as in figure **(b)** below. If it takes 0.20 s to close the loop, find the magnitude of the average emf induced in the loop during this time.

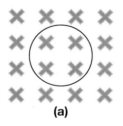
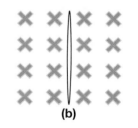

(a)   (b)

11. A rectangular coil 0.055 m by 0.085 m is positioned so that its cross-sectional area is perpendicular to the direction of a magnetic field, B. If the coil has 75 turns and a total resistance of 8.7 Ω and the field decreases at a rate of 3.0 T/s, what is the magnitude of the induced current in the coil?

12. A 52-turn coil with an area of $5.5 \times 10^{-3}\ \text{m}^2$ is dropped from a position where $B = 0.00\ \text{T}$ to a new position where $B = 0.55\ \text{T}$. If the displacement occurs in 0.25 s and the area of the coil is perpendicular to the magnetic field lines, what is the resulting average emf induced in the coil?

Generators, Motors, and Mutual Inductance

▶ REVIEWING MAIN IDEAS

13. List the essential components of an electric generator, and explain the role of each component in generating an alternating emf.

14. A student turns the handle of a small generator attached to a lamp socket containing a 15 W bulb. The bulb barely glows. What should the student do to make the bulb glow more brightly?

15. What is meant by the term *frequency* in reference to an alternating current?

16. How can an ac generator be converted to a dc generator? Explain your answer.

17. What is meant by back emf? How is it induced in an electric motor?

18. Describe how mutual induction occurs.

19. What is the difference between a step-up transformer and a step-down transformer?

20. Does a step-up transformer increase power? Explain your answer.

CONCEPTUAL QUESTIONS

21. When the plane of a rotating loop of wire is parallel to the magnetic field lines, the number of lines passing through the loop is zero. Why is the current at a maximum at this point in the loop's rotation?

22. In many transformers, the wire around one winding is thicker, and therefore has lower resistance, than the wire around the other winding. If the thicker wire is wrapped around the secondary winding, is the device a step-up or a step-down transformer? Explain.

23. A bar magnet is attached perpendicular to a rotating shaft. The magnet is then placed in the center of a coil of wire. In which of the arrangements shown below could this device be used as an electric generator? Explain your choice.

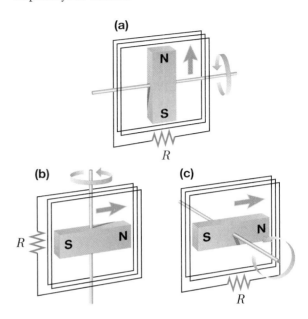

24. Would a transformer work with pulsating direct current? Explain your answer.

25. The faster the coil of loops, or *armature*, of an ac generator rotates, the harder it is to turn the armature. Use Lenz's law to explain why this happens.

PRACTICE PROBLEMS

For problems 26–29, see Sample Problem B.

26. The rms applied emf across high-voltage transmission lines in Great Britain is 220 000 V. What is the maximum emf?

27. The maximum applied emf across certain heavy-duty appliances is 340 V. If the total resistance of an appliance is 120 Ω, calculate the following:
   a. the rms applied emf
   b. the rms current

28. The maximum current that can pass through a light-bulb filament is 0.909 A when its resistance is 182 Ω.
   a. What is the rms current conducted by the filament of the bulb?
   b. What is the rms emf across the bulb's filament?
   c. How much power does the light bulb use?

29. A 996 W hair dryer is designed to carry a peak current of 11.8 A.
  a. How large is the rms current in the hair dryer?
  b. What is the rms emf across the hair dryer?

ac Circuits and Transformers

▶ **REVIEWING MAIN IDEAS**

30. Which quantities remain constant when alternating currents are generated?

31. How does the power dissipated in a resistor by an alternating current relate to the power dissipated by a direct current that has potential difference and current values that are equal to the maximum values of the alternating current?

CONCEPTUAL QUESTIONS

32. In a ground fault interrupter, would the difference in current across an outlet be measured in terms of the rms value of current or the actual current at a given moment? Explain your answer.

33. Voltmeters and ammeters that measure ac quantities are calibrated to measure the rms values of emf and current, respectively. Why would this be preferred to measuring the maximum emf or current?

PRACTICE PROBLEMS

For problems 34–37, see Sample Problem C.

34. A transformer is used to convert 120 V to 9.0 V for use in a portable CD player. If the primary, which is connected to the outlet, has 640 turns, how many turns does the secondary have?

35. Suppose a 9.00 V CD player has a transformer for converting current in Great Britain. If the ratio of the turns of wire on the primary to the secondary coils is 24.6 to 1, what is the outlet potential difference?

36. A transformer is used to convert 120 V to 6.3 V in order to power a toy electric train. If there are 210 turns in the primary, how many turns should there be in the secondary?

37. The transformer shown in the figure below is constructed so that the coil on the left has twenty times as many turns of wire as the coil on the right does.
  a. If the input potential difference is across the coil on the left, what type of transformer is this?
  b. If the input potential difference is 24 000 V, what is the output potential difference?

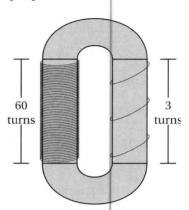

60 turns

3 turns

Electromagnetic Waves

▶ **REVIEWING MAIN IDEAS**

38. How are electric and magnetic fields oriented to each other in an electromagnetic wave?

39. How does the behavior of low-energy electromagnetic radiation differ from that of high-energy electromagnetic radiation?

CONCEPTUAL QUESTIONS

40. Why does electromagnetic radiation obey the inverse-square law?

41. Why is a longer antenna needed to produce a low-frequency radio wave than to produce a high-frequency radio wave?

Mixed Review Problems

▶ **REVIEWING MAIN IDEAS**

42. A student attempts to make a simple generator by passing a single loop of wire between the poles of a horseshoe magnet with a 2.5×10^{-2} T field. The area of the loop is 7.54×10^{-3} m^2 and is moved perpendicular to the magnetic field lines. In what time interval will the student have to move the loop out of the magnetic field in order to induce an emf of 1.5 V? Is this a practical generator?

43. The same student in item 42 modifies the simple generator by wrapping a much longer piece of wire around a cylinder with about one-fourth the area of the original loop (1.886×10^{-3} m^2). Again using a uniform magnetic field with a strength of 2.5×10^{-2} T, the student finds that by removing the coil perpendicular to the magnetic field lines during 0.25 s, an emf of 149 mV can be induced. How many turns of wire are wrapped around the coil?

44. A coil of 325 turns and an area of 19.5×10^{-4} m^2 is removed from a uniform magnetic field at an angle of 45° in 1.25 s. If the induced emf is 15 mV, what is the magnetic field's strength?

45. A transformer has 22 turns of wire in its primary and 88 turns in its secondary.
   a. Is this a step-up or step-down transformer?
   b. If 110 V ac is applied to the primary, what is the output potential difference?

46. A bolt of lightning, such as the one shown on the left side of the figure below, behaves like a vertical wire conducting electric current. As a result, it produces a magnetic field whose strength varies with the distance from the lightning. A 105-turn circular coil is oriented perpendicular to the magnetic field, as shown on the right side of the figure below. The coil has a radius of 0.833 m. If the magnetic field at the coil drops from 4.72×10^{-3} T to 0.00 T in 10.5 μs, what is the average emf induced in the coil?

GRAPHING CALCULATOR PRACTICE

Alternating Current

In alternating current (ac), the emf alternates from positive to negative. The current responds to changes in emf by oscillating with the same frequency of the emf. This relationship is shown in the following equation for instantaneous current:

$$i = I_{max} \sin \omega t$$

In this equation, ω is the ac frequency, and I_{max} is the maximum current. The effective current of an ac circuit is the root-mean-square current (rms current), I_{rms}. The rms current is related to the maximum current by the following equation:

$$I_{rms} = \frac{I_{max}}{\sqrt{2}}$$

In this graphing calculator activity, the calculator will use these two equations to make graphs of instantaneous current and rms current versus time. By analyzing these graphs, you will be able to determine what the values of the instantaneous current and the rms current are at any point in time. The graphs will give you a better understanding of current in ac circuits.

Go online to HMHScience.com to find the skillsheet and program for this graphing calculator activity.

47. The potential difference in the lines that carry electric power to homes is typically 20.0 kV. What is the ratio of the turns in the primary to the turns in the secondary of the transformer if the output potential difference is 117 V?

48. The alternating emf of a generator is represented by the equation emf = (245 V) sin 560t, in which emf is in volts and t is in seconds. Use these values to find the frequency of the emf and the maximum emf output of the source.

49. A pair of adjacent coils has a mutual inductance of 1.06 H. Determine the average emf induced in the secondary circuit when the current in the primary circuit changes from 0 A to 9.50 A in a time interval of 0.0336 s.

50. A generator supplies 5.0×10^3 kW of power. The output emf is 4500 V before it is stepped up to 510 kV. The electricity travels 410 mi (6.44×10^5 m) through a transmission line that has a resistance per unit length of 4.5×10^{-4} Ω/m.

  a. How much power is lost through transmission of the electrical energy along the line?

  b. How much power would be lost through transmission if the generator's output emf were not stepped up? What does this answer tell you about the role of large emfs (voltages) in power transmission?

ALTERNATIVE ASSESSMENT

1. Two identical magnets are dropped simultaneously from the same point. One of them passes through a coil of wire in a closed circuit. Predict whether the two magnets will hit the ground at the same time. Explain your reasoning. Then, plan an experiment to test which of the following variables measurably affect how long each magnet takes to fall: magnetic strength, coil cross-sectional area, and the number of loops the coil has. What measurements will you make? What are the limits of precision in your measurements? If your teacher approves your plan, obtain the necessary materials and perform the experiments. Report your results to the class, describing how you made your measurements, what you concluded, and what additional questions need to be investigated.

2. What do adapters do to potential difference, current, frequency, and power? Examine the input/output information on several adapters to find out. Do they contain step-up or step-down transformers? How does the output current compare to the input? What happens to the frequency? What percentage of the energy do they transfer? What are they used for?

3. Research the debate between the proponents of alternating current and those who favored direct current in the 1880s and 1890s. How were Thomas Edison and George Westinghouse involved in the controversy? What advantages and disadvantages did each side claim? What uses of electricity were anticipated? What kind of current was finally generated in the Niagara Falls hydroelectric plant? Had you been in a position to fund these projects at that time, which projects would you have funded? Prepare your arguments to reenact a meeting of businesspeople in Buffalo in 1887.

4. Research the history of telecommunication. Who invented the telegraph? Who patented it in England? Who patented it in the United States? Research the contributions of Charles Wheatstone, Joseph Henry, and Samuel Morse. How did each of these men deal with issues of fame, wealth, and credit to other people's ideas? Write a summary of your findings, and prepare a class discussion about the effect patents and copyrights have had on modern technology.

Standards-Based Assessment

Record your answers on a separate piece of paper.

MULTIPLE CHOICE

1 Which of the following equations correctly describes Faraday's law of induction?

A $\text{emf} = -N\dfrac{\Delta(AB \tan \theta)}{\Delta t}$

B $\text{emf} = N\dfrac{\Delta(AB \cos \theta)}{\Delta t}$

C $\text{emf} = -N\dfrac{\Delta(AB \cos \theta)}{\Delta t}$

D $\text{emf} = M\dfrac{\Delta(AB \cos \theta)}{\Delta t}$

2 For the coil shown in the figure below, what must be done to induce a clockwise current?

A Either move the north pole of a magnet down into the coil, or move the south pole of the

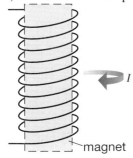

magnet up and out of the coil.

B Either move the south pole of a magnet down into the coil, or move the north pole of the magnet up and out of the coil.

C Move either pole of the magnet down into the coil.

D Move either pole of the magnet up and out of the coil.

3 A coil is moved out of a magnetic field to induce an emf. The wire of the coil is then rewound so the area of the coil is increased by 1.5 times. Extra wire is used in the coil so the number of turns is doubled. If the time in which the coil is removed from the field is reduced by half and the magnetic field strength remains unchanged, how many times greater is the new induced emf than the original induced emf?

A 1.5 times   **C** 3 times

B 2 times   **D** 6 times

4 Two transformers are connected in series, as shown.

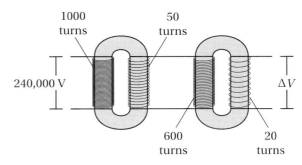

What is the output potential difference from the secondary coil of the transformer on the right?

A 400 V   **C** 160 000 V

B 12 000 V   **D** 360 000 V

5 Energy transported by electromagnetic waves is stored in the oscillating electric and magnetic fields and is called electromagnetic radiation. What particles can be used to describe this radiation?

A electrons   **C** photons

B magnetons   **D** protons

6 Which of the following *correctly* describes the composition of an electromagnetic wave?

A a transverse electric wave and a magnetic transverse wave that are parallel and are moving in the same direction

B a transverse electric wave and a magnetic transverse wave that are perpendicular and are moving in the same direction

C a transverse electric wave and a magnetic transverse wave that are parallel and are moving at right angles to each other

D a transverse electric wave and a magnetic transverse wave that are perpendicular and are moving at right angles to each other

GRIDDED RESPONSE

7 A transformer has 150 turns of wire on the primary coil and 75 000 turns on the secondary coil. If the input potential difference across the primary coil is 120 V, what is the output potential difference, in volts, across the secondary coil?

PHYSICS AND ITS WORLD

1831

Charles Darwin sets sail on the HMS *Beagle* to begin studies of life forms in South America, New Zealand, and Australia. His discoveries form the foundation for the theory of evolution by natural selection.

1837

Queen Victoria ascends the British throne at the age of 18. Her reign continues for 64 years, setting the tone for the Victorian era.

1843

Richard Wagner's first major operatic success, *The Flying Dutchman*, premieres in Dresden, Germany.

1850

Rudolf Clausius formulates the second law of thermodynamics, the first step in the transformation of thermodynamics into an exact science.

$$W = Q_h - Q_c$$

1830   1840   1850

1831

Michael Faraday begins experiments demonstrating electromagnetic induction. Similar experiments are conducted around the same time by **Joseph Henry** in the United States, but he doesn't publish the results of his work at this time.

$$\text{emf} = -N \frac{\Delta[AB(\cos\theta)]}{\Delta t}$$

1843

James Prescott Joule determines that mechanical energy is equivalent to energy transferred as heat, laying the foundation for the principle of energy conservation.

$$\Delta U = Q - W$$

1844

Samuel Morse sends the first telegraph message from Washington, D.C., to Baltimore.

1850

Harriet Tubman, an ex-slave from Maryland, becomes a "conductor" on the Underground Railroad. Over the next decade, she helps more than 300 slaves escape to northern "free" states.

1861

Benito Juárez is elected president of Mexico. During his administration, the invasion by France is repelled, and basic social reforms are implemented.

1873

James Clerk Maxwell completes his *Treatise on Electricity and Magnetism*. In this work, Maxwell gives **Michael Faraday's** discoveries a mathematical framework.

$$c = \frac{1}{\sqrt{\mu_0 \varepsilon_0}}$$

1878

The first commercial telephone exchange in the United States begins operation in New Haven, Connecticut.

1884

Adventures of Huckleberry Finn, by **Samuel L. Clemens** (better known as Mark Twain), is published.

1860   1870   1880   1890

1861

The American Civil War begins at Fort Sumter in Charleston, South Carolina.

1874

The first exhibition of impressionist paintings, including works by **Claude Monet, Camille Pissarro,** and **Pierre-Auguste Renoir,** takes place in Paris.

1888

Heinrich Hertz experimentally demonstrates the existence of electromagnetic waves, which were predicted by **James Clerk Maxwell. Oliver Lodge** makes the same discovery independently.

$$\lambda = \frac{c}{f}$$

Why It Matters

The theory of quantum mechanics has led to both technological advances and new understandings of nature. For instance, it has enabled us to use nuclear energy and to perform life-saving MRIs. It also explains how the stars shine and why the northern lights occur.

Colorful lights similar to these in Denali National Park, Alaska, are commonly seen in the sky in northern latitudes. They are known as the *aurora borealis,* or the *northern lights.* The lights can extend thousands of kilometers and appear as arcs, bands, or streaks of color, sometimes flickering or pulsating. This is caused by billions of atomic "jumps," as shown in the diagram.

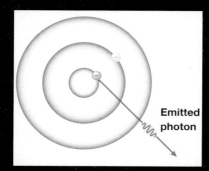

Emitted photon

CHAPTER 21
Atomic Physics

BIG IDEA

Quantum mechanics provides a framework for explaining atomic-scale phenomena, such as the photoelectric effect, the structure of atoms, and the wave-particle duality of light.

 ONLINE Physics
HMHScience.com

ONLINE LAB
- The Photoelectric Effect

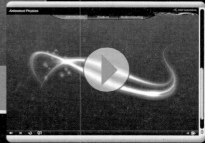

GO ONLINE **Animated Physics**
HMHScience.com

The Photoelectric Effect

Objectives

▶ Calculate energy of quanta using Planck's equation.

▶ Solve problems involving maximum kinetic energy, work function, and threshold frequency in the photoelectric effect.

Quantization of Energy

Key Terms

blackbody radiation   photoelectric effect   work function

ultraviolet catastrophe   photon   Compton shift

Blackbody Radiation

By the end of the nineteenth century, scientists thought that classical physics was nearly complete. One of the few remaining questions to be solved involved electromagnetic radiation and thermodynamics. Specifically, scientists were concerned with the glow of objects when they reach a high temperature.

All objects emit electromagnetic radiation. This radiation, which depends on the temperature and other properties of an object, typically consists of a continuous distribution of wavelengths from the infrared, visible, and ultraviolet portions of the spectrum. The distribution of the intensity of the different wavelengths varies with temperature.

At low temperatures, radiation wavelengths are mainly in the infrared region. So they cannot be seen by the human eye. As the temperature of an object increases, the range of wavelengths given off shifts into the visible region of the electromagnetic spectrum. For example, the molten metal shown in **Figure 1.1** seems to have a yellow glow. At even higher temperatures, the object appears to have a white glow, as in the hot tungsten filament of a light bulb, and then a bluish glow.

Classical physics cannot account for blackbody radiation.

One problem at the end of the 1800s was understanding the distribution of wavelengths given off by a blackbody. Most objects absorb some incoming radiation and reflect the rest. An ideal system that absorbs all incoming radiation is called a *blackbody*. Physicists study **blackbody radiation,** also known as cavity radiation, by observing a hollow object with a small opening, as shown in **Figure 1.2**. The system is a good example of how a blackbody works; it traps radiation. The light given off by the opening is in equilibrium with light from the walls of the object, because the light has been given off and reabsorbed many times.

Experimental data for the radiation given off by an object at three different temperatures are shown in **Figure 1.3(a)**. Note that as

FIGURE 1.1

Molten Metal This molten metal has a bright yellow glow because of its high temperature.

blackbody radiation the radiation emitted by a blackbody, which is a perfect radiator and absorber and emits radiation based only on its temperature

FIGURE 1.2

Light Absorption by a Blackbody Light enters this hollow object through the small opening and strikes the interior wall. Some of the energy is absorbed by the wall, but some is reflected at a random angle. After each reflection, part of the light is absorbed by the wall. After many reflections, essentially all of the incoming energy is absorbed by the cavity wall. Only a small fraction of the incident energy escapes through the opening.

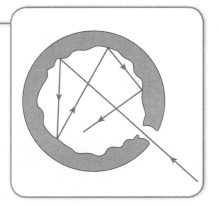

(tl) ©Volker Steger/Photo Researchers, Inc

FIGURE 1.3

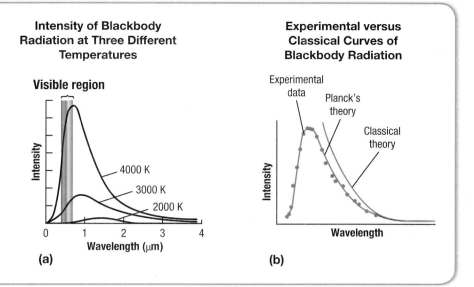

Blackbody Radiation (a) This graph shows the intensity of blackbody radiation at three different temperatures. (b) Classical theory's prediction for blackbody radiation (the blue curve) did not correspond to the experimental data (the red data points) at all wavelengths, whereas Planck's theory (the red curve) did.

Intensity of Blackbody Radiation at Three Different Temperatures

Visible region

Intensity

4000 K
3000 K
2000 K

Wavelength (μm)

(a)

Experimental versus Classical Curves of Blackbody Radiation

Experimental data
Planck's theory
Classical theory

Intensity

Wavelength

(b)

the temperature increases, the total energy given off by the body (the area under the curve) also increases. In addition, as the temperature increases, the peak of the distribution shifts to shorter wavelengths.

Scientists could not account for these experimental results with classical physics. **Figure 1.3(b)** compares an experimental plot of the blackbody radiation spectrum (the red data points) with the theoretical picture of what this curve should look like based on classical theories (the blue curve). Classical theory predicts that as the wavelength approaches zero, the amount of energy being radiated should become infinite. This prediction is contrary to the experimental data, which show that as the wavelength approaches zero, the amount of energy being radiated also approaches zero. This contradiction is often called the **ultraviolet catastrophe** because the disagreement occurs at the ultraviolet end of the spectrum.

ultraviolet catastrophe the failed prediction of classical physics that the energy radiated by a blackbody at extremely short wavelengths is extremely large and that the total energy radiated is infinite

Experimental data for blackbody radiation support the quantization of energy.

In 1900, Max Planck (1858–1947) developed a formula for blackbody radiation that was in complete agreement with experimental data at all wavelengths. Planck's original theoretical approach is rather abstract in that it involves arguments based on entropy and thermodynamics. The arguments presented in this book are easier to visualize, and they convey the spirit and revolutionary impact of Planck's original work.

Planck proposed that blackbody radiation was produced by submicroscopic electric oscillators, which he called *resonators*. He assumed that the walls of a glowing cavity were composed of billions of these resonators, all vibrating at different frequencies. Although most scientists naturally assumed that the energy of these resonators was continuous, Planck made the radical assumption that these resonators could only absorb and then give off certain discrete amounts of energy.

When he first discovered this idea, Planck was using a mathematical technique in which quantities that are known to be continuous are temporarily considered to be discrete. After the calculations are made, the discrete units are taken to be infinitesimally small. Planck found that the calculations worked if he omitted this step and considered energy to come in discrete units throughout his calculations. With this method, Planck found that the total energy (E_n) of a resonator with frequency f is an integral multiple of hf, as follows:

$$E_n = nhf$$

In this equation, n is a positive integer called a *quantum number,* and the factor h is Planck's constant, which equals $6.626\,068\,96 \times 10^{-34}$ J•s. To simplify calculations, we will use the approximate value of $h = 6.63 \times 10^{-34}$ J•s in this textbook. Because the energy of each resonator comes in discrete units, it is said to be *quantized,* and the allowed energy states are called *quantum states* or *energy levels.* With the assumption that energy is quantized, Planck was able to derive the red curve shown in **Figure 1.3(b)** on the previous page.

According to Planck's theory, the resonators absorb or give off energy in discrete multiples of hf. Einstein later applied the concept of quantized energy to light. The units of light energy called *quanta* (now called *photons*) are absorbed or given off as a result of electrons "jumping" from one quantum state to another. As seen by the equation above, if the quantum number (n) changes by one unit, the amount of energy radiated changes by hf. For this reason, the energy of a light quantum, which corresponds to the energy difference between two adjacent levels, is given by the following equation:

Energy of a Light Quantum
$$E = hf$$
energy of a quantum ($n = 1$) = Planck's constant × frequency

A resonator will radiate or absorb energy only when it changes quantum states. The idea that energy comes in discrete units marked the birth of a new theory known as *quantum mechanics.*

If Planck's constant is expressed in units of J•s, the equation $E = hf$ gives the energy in joules. However, when dealing with the parts of atoms, energy is often expressed in units of the electron volt, eV. An *electron volt* is defined as the energy that an electron or proton gains when it is accelerated through a potential difference of 1 V. Because $1\text{ V} = 1$ J/C, the relation between the electron volt and the joule is as follows:

$$1\text{ eV} = 1.60 \times 10^{-19}\text{ C•V} = 1.60 \times 10^{-19}\text{ C•J/C} = 1.60 \times 10^{-19}\text{ J}$$

Planck's idea that energy is quantized was so radical that most scientists, including Planck himself, did not consider the quantization of energy to be realistic. Planck thought of his assumption as a mathematical approach to be used in calculations rather than a physical explanation. Therefore, he and other scientists continued to search for a different explanation of blackbody radiation that was consistent with classical physics.

Quantum Energy

Sample Problem A At the peak of the sun's radiation spectrum, each photon carries an energy of about 2.7 eV. What is the frequency of this light?

① ANALYZE

Given: $E = 2.7$ eV $\quad h = 6.63 \times 10^{-34}$ J•s

Unknown: $f = ?$

② SOLVE

Use the equation for the energy of a light quantum, and isolate frequency.

$$E = hf \quad \text{or} \quad f = \frac{E}{h}$$

Tips and Tricks

Always be sure that your units cancel properly. In this problem, you need to convert energy from electron volts to joules. For this reason, 2.7 eV is multiplied by the conversion factor of 1.60×10^{-19} J/eV.

$$f = \frac{E}{h} = \frac{(2.7 \text{ eV})(1.60 \times 10^{-19} \text{ J/eV})}{6.63 \times 10^{-34} \text{ J•s}}$$

$$f = 6.5 \times 10^{14} \text{ Hz}$$

Practice

1. Assume that the pendulum of a grandfather clock acts as one of Planck's resonators. If it carries away an energy of 8.1×10^{-15} eV in a one-quantum change, what is the frequency of the pendulum? (Note that an energy this small would not be measurable. For this reason, we do not notice quantum effects in the large-scale world.)

2. A vibrating mass-spring system has a frequency of 0.56 Hz. How much energy of this vibration is carried away in a one-quantum change?

3. A photon in a laboratory experiment has an energy of 5.0 eV. What is the frequency of this photon?

4. Radiation emitted from human skin reaches its peak at $\lambda = 940$ μm.

   a. What is the frequency of this radiation?

   b. What type of electromagnetic waves are these?

   c. How much energy (in electron volts) is carried by one quantum of this radiation?

FIGURE 1.4

Light Shining on Metal

A light beam shining on a metal **(a)** may eject electrons from the metal **(b)**. Because this interaction involves both light and electrons, it is called the photoelectric effect.

(a)

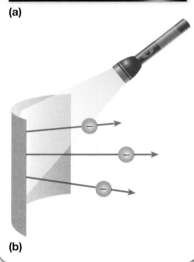

(b)

photoelectric effect the emission of electrons from a metal surface that occurs when light of certain frequencies shines on the surface of the metal

The Photoelectric Effect

As discussed in the chapter "Electromagnetic Induction," James Maxwell discovered in 1873 that light was a form of electromagnetic waves. Experiments by Heinrich Hertz provided experimental evidence of Maxwell's theories. However, the results of some later experiments by Hertz could not be explained by the wave model of the nature of light. One of these was the **photoelectric effect.** When light strikes a metal surface, the surface may emit electrons, as **Figure 1.4** illustrates. Scientists call this effect the photoelectric effect. They refer to the electrons that are emitted as *photoelectrons.*

Classical physics cannot explain the photoelectric effect.

The fact that light waves can eject electrons from a metal surface does not contradict the principles of classical physics. Light waves have energy, and if that energy is great enough, an electron could be stripped from its atom and have enough energy to escape the metal. However, the details of the photoelectric effect cannot be explained by classical theories. In order to see where the conflict arises, we must consider what should happen according to classical theory and then compare these predictions with experimental observations.

Remember that the energy of a wave increases as its intensity increases. Thus, according to classical physics, light waves of any frequency should have sufficient energy to eject electrons from the metal if the intensity of the light is high enough. Moreover, at lower intensities, electrons should be ejected if light shines on the metal for a sufficient time period. (Electrons would take time to absorb the incoming energy before acquiring enough kinetic energy to escape from the metal.) Furthermore, increasing the intensity of the light waves should increase the kinetic energy of the photoelectrons, and the maximum kinetic energy of any electron should be determined by the light's intensity. These classical predictions are summarized in the second column of **Figure 1.5.**

FIGURE 1.5

THE PHOTOELECTRIC EFFECT		
	Classical predictions	Experimental evidence
Whether electrons are ejected depends on . . .	the intensity of the light.	the frequency of the light.
The kinetic energy of ejected electrons depends on . . .	the intensity of the light.	the frequency of the light.
At low intensities, electron ejection . . .	takes time.	occurs almost instantaneously above a certain frequency.

Scientists found that *none* of these classical predictions are observed experimentally. No electrons are emitted if the frequency of the incoming light falls below a certain frequency, even if the intensity is very high. This frequency, known as the *threshold frequency* (f_t), differs from metal to metal.

If the light frequency exceeds the threshold frequency, the photoelectric effect is observed. The number of photoelectrons emitted is proportional to the light intensity, but the maximum kinetic energy of the photoelectrons is independent of the light intensity. Instead, the maximum kinetic energy of the photoelectrons increases with increasing frequency. Furthermore, electrons are emitted from the surface almost instantaneously, even at low intensities. See **Figure 1.5.**

Einstein proposed that all electromagnetic waves are quantized.

Albert Einstein resolved this conflict in his 1905 paper on the photoelectric effect, for which he received the Nobel Prize in 1921, by extending Planck's concept of quantization to electromagnetic waves. Einstein assumed that an electromagnetic wave can be viewed as a stream of particles, now called **photons.** Each photon has an energy, E, given by Planck's equation ($E = hf$). In this theory, each photon is absorbed as a unit by an electron. When a photon's energy is transferred to an electron in a metal, the energy acquired by the electron is equal to *hf.*

photon a unit or quantum of light; a particle of electromagnetic radiation that has zero mass and carries a quantum of energy

work function the minimum energy needed to remove an electron from a metal atom

Threshold frequency depends on the work function of the surface.

In order to be ejected from a metal, an electron must overcome the force that binds it to the metal. The smallest amount of energy the electron must have to escape the surface of a metal is the **work function** of the metal. The work function is equal to hf_t, where f_t is the threshold frequency for the metal. Photons with energy greater than hf_t eject electrons from the surface of and from within the metal. Because energy must be conserved, the maximum kinetic energy (of photoelectrons ejected from the surface) is the difference between the photon energy and the work function of the metal. This relationship is expressed mathematically by the following equation:

FIGURE 1.6

Maximum Kinetic Energy of Emitted Electrons
This graph shows a linear relationship between the maximum kinetic energy of emitted electrons and the frequency of incoming light. The intercept with the horizontal axis is the threshold frequency.

Maximum Kinetic Energy of a Photoelectron

$$KE_{max} = hf - hf_t$$

**maximum kinetic energy = (Planck's constant ×
frequency of incoming photon) − work function**

According to this equation, there should be a linear relationship between f and KE_{max} because h is a constant and the work function, hf_t, is constant for any given metal. Experiments have verified that this is indeed the case, as shown in **Figure 1.6,** and the slope of such a curve ($\Delta KE / \Delta f$) gives a value for h that corresponds to Planck's value.

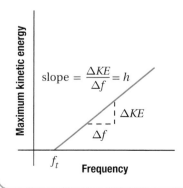

Maximum Kinetic Energy of Electrons versus Frequency of Incoming Light

$$\text{slope} = \frac{\Delta KE}{\Delta f} = h$$

The Photoelectric Effect

Sample Problem B Light of wavelength 3.5×10^{-7} m shines on a cesium surface. Cesium has a work function of 2.14 eV. What is the maximum kinetic energy of the photoelectrons?

① ANALYZE

Given: $\lambda = 3.5 \times 10^{-7}$ m $hf_t = 2.14$ eV

Unknown: $KE_{max} = ?$

② SOLVE

Use the equation for the maximum kinetic energy of a photoelectron, given on page 741.

$$KE_{max} = hf - hf_t = \frac{hc}{\lambda} - hf_t$$

$$KE_{max} = \frac{(6.63 \times 10^{-34}\,\text{J·s})\,(3.0 \times 10^{8}\,\text{m/s})}{(1.06 \times 10^{-19}\,\text{J/eV})\,(3.5 \times 10^{-7}\,\text{m})} - 2.14\,\text{eV}$$

$$\boxed{KE_{max} = 1.41\,\text{eV}}$$

Practice

1. Light of frequency 6.5×10^{14} Hz illuminates a lithium surface. The ejected photoelectrons are found to have a maximum kinetic energy of 0.20 eV. Find the threshold frequency of this metal.

2. Light of wavelength 350 nm falls on a potassium surface, and the photoelectrons have a maximum kinetic energy of 1.3 eV. What is the work function of potassium? What is the threshold frequency for potassium?

3. The threshold frequency of platinum is 1.36×10^{15} Hz. What is the work function of platinum?

4. Which of the following metals will exhibit the photoelectric effect when light of 7.0×10^{14} Hz frequency is shined on it?

    a. lithium, $hf_t = 2.3$ eV

    b. silver, $hf_t = 4.7$ eV

    c. cesium, $hf_t = 2.14$ eV

Photon theory accounts for observations of the photoelectric effect.

The photon theory of light explains features of the photoelectric effect that cannot be understood using classical concepts. The photoelectric effect is not observed below a certain threshold frequency, because the energy of the photon must be greater than or equal to the work function of the material. If the energy of each incoming photon is not equal to or greater than the work function, electrons will never be ejected from the surface, regardless of how many photons are present (how great the intensity is). Because the energy of each photon depends on the frequency of the incoming light ($E = hf$), the photoelectric effect is not observed when the incoming light is below a certain frequency (f_t).

Above the threshold frequency, if the light intensity is doubled, the number of photons is doubled. This in turn doubles the number of electrons ejected from the metal. However, the equation for the maximum kinetic energy of an electron shows that the kinetic energy depends only on the light frequency and the work function, not on the light intensity. Thus, even though there are more electrons ejected, the maximum kinetic energy of individual electrons remains the same.

Finally, the fact that the electrons are emitted almost instantaneously is consistent with the particle theory of light, in which energy appears in small packets. Because each photon affects a single electron, there is no significant time delay between shining light on the metal and observing electrons being ejected.

Einstein's success in explaining the photoelectric effect by assuming that electromagnetic waves are quantized led scientists to realize that the quantization of energy must be considered a real description of the physical world rather than a mathematical contrivance, as most had initially supposed. The discreteness of energy had not been considered a viable possibility, because the energy quantum is not detected in our everyday experiences. However, scientists began to believe that the true nature of energy is seen in the submicroscopic level of atoms and molecules, where quantum effects become important and measurable.

Conceptual Challenge

Photoelectric Effect Even though bright red light delivers more total energy per second than dim violet light, the red light cannot eject electrons from a certain metallic surface, while the dimmer violet light can. How does Einstein's photon theory explain this observation?

Photographs Suppose a photograph were made of a person's face using only a few photons. According to Einstein's photon theory, would the result be simply a very faint image of the entire face? Why or why not?

Glowing Objects The color of a hot object depends on the object's temperature. As temperature increases, the color turns from red to orange to yellow to white and finally to blue. Classical physics cannot explain this color change, while quantum mechanics can. What explanation is given by quantum mechanics?

©D. Hurst/Alamy Photos

FIGURE 1.7

Photon Colliding with an Electron
(a) When a photon collides with an electron, (b) the scattered photon has less energy and a longer wavelength than the incoming photon.

Incoming photon   Stationary electron

(a)

(b)

Recoiling electron

Scattered photon

Compton shift an increase in the wavelength of the photon scattered by an electron relative to the wavelength of the incident photon

Compton shift supports the photon theory of light.

The American physicist Arthur Compton (1892–1962) realized that if light behaves like a particle, then a collision between an electron and a photon should be similar to a collision between two billiard balls. Photons should have momentum as well as energy; both quantities should be conserved in elastic collisions. So when a photon collides with an electron initially at rest, as in **Figure 1.7**, the photon transfers some of its energy and momentum to the electron. As a result, the energy and frequency of the scattered photon are lowered; its wavelength should increase.

In 1923, to test this theory, Compton directed electromagnetic waves (x-rays) toward a block of graphite. He found that the scattered waves had less energy and longer wavelengths than the incoming waves, just as he had predicted. This change in wavelength, known as the **Compton shift,** provides support for Einstein's photon theory of light.

The amount that the wavelength shifts depends on the angle through which the photon is scattered. Note that even the largest change in wavelength is very small in relation to the wavelengths of visible light. For this reason, the Compton shift is difficult to detect using visible light, but it can be observed using electromagnetic waves with much shorter wavelengths, such as x-rays.

✓ SECTION 1 FORMATIVE ASSESSMENT

▶ Reviewing Main Ideas

1. Describe the conflict known as the ultraviolet catastrophe. How did Planck resolve this conflict? How does Planck's assumption depart from classical physics?

2. What is the energy (in eV units) carried by one photon of violet light that has a wavelength of 4.5×10^{-7} m?

3. What effects did scientists originally think that the intensity of light shining on a photosensitive surface would have on electrons ejected from that surface? How did these predictions differ from observations?

4. How does Einstein's theory that electromagnetic waves are quantized explain the fact that the frequency of light (rather than the intensity) determines whether electrons are ejected from a photosensitive surface?

5. Light with a wavelength of 1.00×10^{-7} m shines on tungsten, which has a work function of 4.6 eV. Are electrons ejected from the tungsten? If so, what is their maximum kinetic energy?

✔ Critical Thinking

6. Is the number of photons in 1 J of red light (650 nm) greater than, equal to, or less than the number of photons in 1 J of blue light (450 nm)? Explain.

Solar Cells

The amount of solar energy that strikes Earth in one hour could power the world's energy consumption for an entire year. Yet solar energy is not directly usable; it has to be converted. It has proven difficult to capture sunlight and transform it into usable forms. Over the past several decades, scientists have been busy developing technology that can capture and harness this solar energy. Solar cells, also known as photovoltaic cells, are able to convert solar energy into electrical energy. You have likely seen them on calculators and on the roofs of homes. Have you ever wondered how they work?

Solar cells are made of layers of two types of semiconductors called n-type and p-type. These semiconductors are made of pure silicon mixed with various chemicals. N-type semiconductors have an element, often phosphorus, that allows some electrons to be easily freed for motion. P-type semiconductors include an element, such as boron, that allows the equivalent of positive charges to be freed easily. When these two semiconductors are together, they can create an electric field that can, under the right conditions, produce an electric current.

The solar cell is unable to produce a current by itself; it requires energy to cause its electrons to move. This energy comes from sunlight. When photons from the sun hit silicon atoms on the surface of the solar cell, they dislodge electrons. These photons need to have enough energy to release electrons, as described by the photoelectric effect. The electrons are then free to move through the semiconductor. Because of the arrangement of the semiconductors, the electrons can only move in a very specific way—from the n-type to the p-type material. Metal wires that run between the two materials capture these moving electrons and lead them away from the cell. The current that leaves the cell is DC and can be used to do things like charge batteries. It can also be converted to AC to power the electrical grid.

The sun provides about 1000 watts of energy per square meter. The solar cells in use today convert only a fraction of this solar energy into electrical energy. Most solar panels are 12 to 18 percent efficient, which means that a vast majority of the sun's energy is never captured. Scientists have recently engineered solar cells that are more than 40 percent efficient, making solar panels a promising alternative to traditional means of electrical power production.

How large would a solar panel need to be in order to power a typical American home? Excluding things like heat and dryers, the average home in America uses about 14 kilowatt-hours of electrical energy per day. This would require a solar panel measuring about 300 square feet, or about a square measuring 17 feet per side. Because the material and installation costs for a solar panel of this size are quite high, using solar cells is currently not cost effective for most homes.

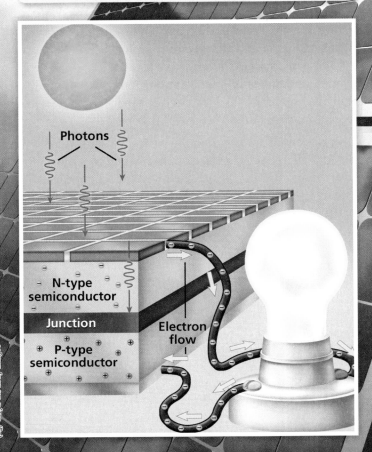

Models of the Atom

Objectives

▶ Explain the strengths and weaknesses of various models of the atom.

▶ Recognize that each element has a unique emission and absorption spectrum.

SC.912.P.8.3 Explore the scientific theory of atoms (also known as atomic theory) by describing changes in the atomic model over time and why those changes were necessitated by experimental evidence.

Key Terms

emission spectrum

absorption spectrum

Early Models of the Atom

The model of the atom in the days of Newton was that of a tiny, hard, indestructible sphere. This model was a good basis for the kinetic theory of gases. However, new models had to be devised when experiments revealed the electrical nature of atoms. The discovery of the electron in 1897 prompted J. J. Thomson (1856–1940) to suggest a new model of the atom. In Thomson's model, electrons are embedded in a spherical volume of positive charge like seeds in a watermelon, as shown in **Figure 2.1**.

Rutherford proposed a planetary model of the atom.

In 1911, Hans Geiger and Ernest Marsden, under the supervision of Ernest Rutherford (1871–1937), performed an important experiment showing that Thomson's model could not be correct. In this experiment, a beam of positively charged *alpha particles*—particles that consist of two protons and two neutrons—was projected against a thin metal foil, as shown in **Figure 2.2**. Most of the alpha particles passed through the foil as if it were empty space. Some of the alpha particles were deflected from their original direction through very large angles. Some particles were even deflected backward. Such deflections were completely unexpected on the basis of the Thomson model. Rutherford wrote, "It was quite the most incredible event that has ever happened to me in my life. It was almost as incredible as if you fired a 15-inch shell at a piece of tissue paper and it came back and hit you."

Such large deflections could not occur on the basis of Thomson's model, in which positive charge is evenly distributed throughout the atom, because the positively charged alpha particles would never come close to a positive charge concentrated enough to cause such large-angle deflections.

FIGURE 2.1

Thomson's Model of the Atom

In Thomson's model, electrons are embedded in a larger region of positive charge.

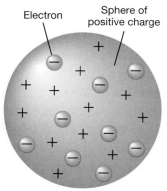

The Thomson model of the atom

FIGURE 2.2

Rutherford's Foil Experiment

In this experiment, positively charged alpha particles are directed at a thin metal foil. Because many particles pass through the foil and only a few are deflected, Rutherford concluded that the atom's positive charge is concentrated at the center of the atom.

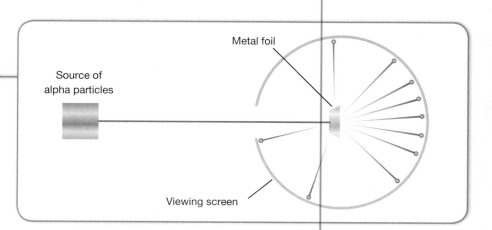

On the basis of his observations, Rutherford concluded that all of the positive charge in an atom and most of the atom's mass are found in a region that is small compared to the size of the atom. He called this concentration of positive charge and mass the *nucleus* of the atom. Any electrons in the atom were assumed to be in the relatively large volume outside the nucleus. So, according to Rutherford's theory, most alpha particles missed the nuclei of the metal atoms entirely and passed through the foil, while only a few came close enough to the nuclei to be deflected.

Rutherford's model predicts that atoms are unstable.

To explain why electrons in this outer region of the atom were not pulled into the nucleus, Rutherford viewed the electrons as moving in orbits about the nucleus, much like the planets orbit the sun, as shown in **Figure 2.3**.

However, this assumption posed a serious difficulty. If electrons orbited the nucleus, they would undergo a centripetal acceleration. According to Maxwell's theory of electromagnetism, accelerated charges should radiate electromagnetic waves, losing energy. So the radius of an atom's orbit would steadily decrease. This would lead to an ever-increasing frequency of emitted radiation and a rapid collapse of the atom as the electrons plunged into the nucleus. In fact, calculations show that according to this model, the atom would collapse in about one-billionth of a second. This difficulty with Rutherford's model led scientists to continue searching for a new model of the atom.

(bl), (bc), (br) ©Richard Megna/Fundamental Photographs, New York

FIGURE 2.3

The Rutherford Model

In Rutherford's model of the atom, electrons orbit the nucleus in a manner similar to planets orbiting the sun.

Atomic Spectra

In addition to solving the problems with Rutherford's planetary model, scientists hoped that a new model of the atom would explain another mysterious fact about gases. When an evacuated glass tube is filled with a pure atomic gas and a sufficiently high potential difference is applied between metal electrodes in the tube, a current is produced in the gas. As a result, the tube gives off light, as shown in **Figure 2.4**. The light's color is characteristic of the gas in the tube. This is how a neon sign works. The variety of colors seen in neon signs is the result of the light given off by different gases in the tubes.

FIGURE 2.4

Glowing Gases When a potential difference is applied across an atomic gas in a tube—here, hydrogen **(a)**, mercury **(b)**, and nitrogen **(c)**—the gas glows. The color of the glow depends on the type of gas.

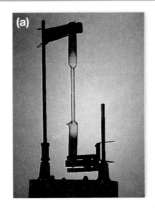  

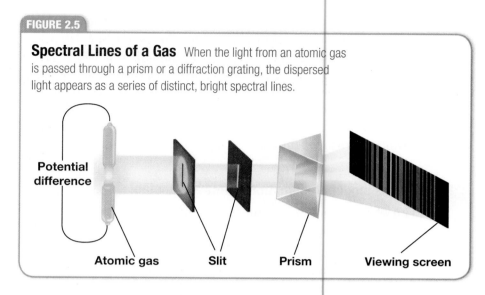

FIGURE 2.5

Spectral Lines of a Gas When the light from an atomic gas is passed through a prism or a diffraction grating, the dispersed light appears as a series of distinct, bright spectral lines.

Potential difference

Atomic gas   Slit   Prism   Viewing screen

Each gas has a unique emission and absorption spectrum.

When the light given off (emitted) by an atomic gas is passed through a prism, as shown in **Figure 2.5,** a series of distinct bright lines is seen. Each line corresponds to a different wavelength, or color, of light. Such a series of spectral lines is commonly referred to as an **emission spectrum.**

As shown in **Figure 2.6,** the emission spectra for hydrogen, mercury, and helium are each unique. Further analysis of other substances reveals that every element has a distinct emission spectrum. In other words, the wavelengths contained in a given spectrum are characteristic of the element giving off the light. Because no two elements give off the same line spectrum, it is possible to use spectroscopy to identify elements in a mixture.

In addition to giving off light at specific wavelengths, an element can also absorb light at specific wavelengths. The spectral lines corresponding to this process form what is known as an **absorption spectrum.** An absorption spectrum can be seen by passing light containing all wavelengths through a vapor of the element being analyzed. The absorption spectrum consists of a series of dark lines placed over the otherwise continuous spectrum.

emission spectrum a diagram or graph that indicates the wavelengths of radiant energy that a substance emits

absorption spectrum a diagram or graph that indicates the wavelengths of radiant energy that a substance absorbs

FIGURE 2.6

Emission Spectrums of Three Gases Each of these gases—hydrogen, mercury, and helium—has a unique emission spectrum.

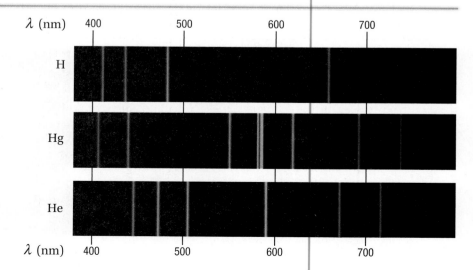

λ (nm)   400   500   600   700

H

Hg

He

λ (nm)   400   500   600   700

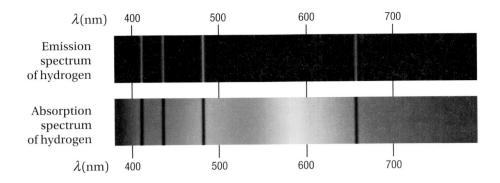

FIGURE 2.7

Emission and Absorption Spectra of Hydrogen Hydrogen's dark absorption lines occur at the same wavelengths as its bright emission lines.

Each line in the absorption spectrum of a given element coincides with a line in the emission spectrum of that element, as shown in **Figure 2.7** for hydrogen. In everyday experience, more emission lines are usually seen than absorption lines. The reason for this will be discussed shortly.

The absorption spectrum of an element has many practical applications. For example, the continuous spectrum of radiation emitted by the sun must pass through the cooler gases of the solar atmosphere and then through Earth's atmosphere. The various absorption lines seen in the solar spectrum have been used to identify elements in the solar atmosphere. Scientists are also able to examine the light from stars other than our sun in this fashion. With careful observation and analysis, astronomers have determined the proportions of various elements present in individual stars.

Historically, the occurrence of atomic spectra was of great importance to scientists attempting to find a new model of the atom. Long after atomic spectra had been discovered, their cause remained unexplained. There was nothing in Rutherford's planetary model to account for the fact that each element has a unique series of spectral lines. Scientists hoped that a new model of the atom would explain this phenomenon.

The Bohr Model of the Hydrogen Atom

In 1913, the Danish physicist Niels Bohr (1885–1962) proposed a new model of the hydrogen atom that explained atomic spectra. Bohr's model of hydrogen contains some classical features and some revolutionary principles that could not be explained by classical physics.

Bohr's model is similar to Rutherford's in that the electron moves in circular orbits about the nucleus. The electric force between the positively charged proton inside the nucleus and the negatively charged electron is the force that holds the electron in orbit. However, in Bohr's model, only certain orbits are allowed. The electron is never found between these orbits; instead, it is said to "jump" instantly from one orbit to another without ever being between orbits.

Bohr's model further departs from classical physics by assuming that the hydrogen atom does not emit energy in the form of radiation when the electron is in any of these allowed orbits. Hence, the total energy of the atom remains constant, and one difficulty with the Rutherford model (the instability of the atom) is resolved.

Quick **LAB**

MATERIALS
- a diffraction grating
- a variety of light sources, such as:
  ✓ a fluorescent light
  ✓ an incandescent light
  ✓ a clear aquarium bulb
  ✓ a sodium-vapor street light
  ✓ a gym light
  ✓ a neon sign

SAFETY

Be careful of high potential differences that may be present near some of these light sources.

ATOMIC SPECTRA

Certain types of light sources produce a continuous spectrum when viewed through a diffraction grating, while others produce discrete lines. Observe a variety of different light sources through a diffraction grating, and compare your results. Try to find at least one example of a continuous spectrum and a few examples of discrete lines.

Bohr claimed that rather than radiating energy continuously, the electron radiates energy only when it jumps from an outer orbit to an inner one. The frequency of the radiation emitted in the jump is related to the change in the atom's energy. The energy of an emitted photon (E) is equal to the energy decrease of the atom ($-\Delta E_{atom}$). The change in the atom's energy is $\Delta E_{atom} = E_{final} - E_{initial}$, and so the photon's energy is $E = -\Delta E_{atom} = E_{initial} - E_{final}$. Planck's equation can then be used to find the frequency of the emitted radiation: $E = E_{initial} - E_{final} = hf$.

In Bohr's model, transitions between stable orbits with different energy levels account for the discrete spectral lines.

The lowest energy state in the Bohr model, which corresponds to the smallest possible radius, is often called the *ground state* of the atom, and the radius of this orbit is called the *Bohr radius.* At ordinary temperatures, most electrons are in the ground state, with the electron relatively close to the nucleus. When light of a continuous spectrum shines on the atom, only the photons whose energy (hf) matches the energy separation between two levels can be absorbed by the atom. When this occurs, an electron jumps from a lower energy state to a higher energy state, which corresponds to an orbit farther from the nucleus, as shown in **Figure 2.8(a).** This is called an *excited state.* The absorbed photons account for the dark lines in the absorption spectrum.

Once an electron is in an excited state, there is a certain probability that it will jump back to a lower energy level by emitting a photon, as shown in **Figure 2.8(b).** This process is known as *spontaneous emission.* The emitted photons are responsible for the bright lines in the emission spectrum.

In both cases, there is a correlation between the "size" of an electron's jump and the energy of the photon. For example, an electron in the fourth energy level could jump to the third level, the second level, or the ground state. Because Planck's equation gives the energy from one level to the next level, a greater jump means that more energy is emitted. Thus, jumps between different levels correspond to the various spectral lines that are observed. The jumps that correspond to the four spectral lines in the visible spectrum of hydrogen are shown in **Figure 2.9.** Bohr's calculations successfully account for the wavelengths of all the spectral lines of hydrogen.

FIGURE 2.8

Energy Levels in an Atom
(a) When a photon is absorbed by an atom, an electron jumps to a higher energy level. **(b)** When the electron falls back to a lower energy level, the atom releases a photon.

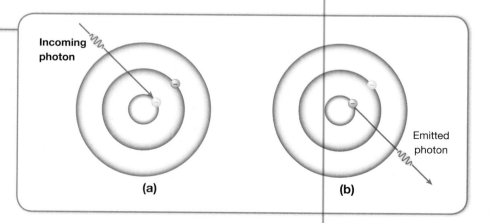

Incoming photon

Emitted photon

(a)   (b)

As noted earlier, fewer absorption lines than emission lines are typically observed. The reason is that absorption spectra are usually observed when a gas is at room temperature. Thus, most electrons are in the ground state, so all transitions observed are from a single level (E_1) to higher levels. Emission spectra, on the other hand, are seen by raising a gas to a high temperature and viewing downward transitions between any two levels. In this case, all transitions are possible, so more spectral lines are observed.

Bohr's idea of the quantum jump between energy levels provides an explanation for the aurora borealis, or northern lights. Charged particles from the sun sometimes become trapped in Earth's magnetic field and collect around the northern and southern magnetic poles. (Light shows in southern latitudes are called *aurora australis,* or *southern lights.*) As they collect, these charged particles from the sun collide with the electrons of the atoms in our atmosphere and transfer energy to these electrons, causing them to jump to higher energy levels. When an electron returns to a lower orbit, some of the energy is released as a photon. The northern lights are the result of billions of these quantum jumps happening at the same time.

The colors of the northern lights are determined by the type of gases in the atmosphere. The charged particles from the sun are most commonly released from Earth's magnetic field into a part of the atmosphere that contains oxygen, which releases green light. Red lights are the result of collisions with nitrogen atoms. Because each type of gas releases a unique color, the northern lights contain only a few distinct colors rather than a continuous spectrum.

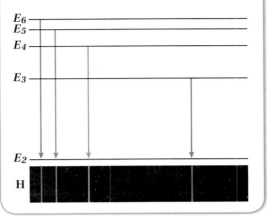

FIGURE 2.9

Spectral Lines of Hydrogen Every jump from one energy level to another corresponds to a specific spectral line. This example shows the transitions that result in the visible spectral lines of hydrogen. The lowest energy level, E_1, is not shown in this diagram.

Conceptual Challenge

Neon Signs When a potential difference is placed across electrodes at the ends of a tube that contains neon, such as a neon sign, the neon glows. Is the light emitted by a neon sign a continuous spectrum or distinct lines? Defend your answer.

Energy Levels If a certain atom has four possible energy levels and an electron can jump between any two energy levels of the atom, how many different spectral lines could be emitted?

Identifying Gases Neon is not the only type of gas used in neon signs. As you have seen, a variety of gases exhibit similar effects when there is a potential difference across them. While the colors observed are sometimes different, certain gases do glow with the same color. How could you distinguish two such gases?

Interpreting Energy-Level Diagrams

Sample Problem C An electron in a hydrogen atom drops from energy level E_4 to energy level E_2. What is the frequency of the emitted photon, and which line in the emission spectrum corresponds to this event?

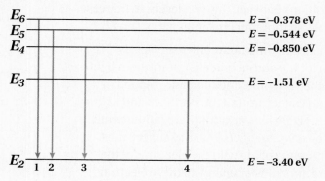

① ANALYZE

Find the energy of the photon.

The energy of the photon is equal to the change in the energy of the electron. The electron's initial energy level was E_4, and the electron's final energy level was E_2. Using the values from the energy-level diagram gives the following:

$$E = E_{initial} - E_{final}$$
$$E = (-0.850 \text{ eV}) - (-3.40 \text{ eV}) = 2.55 \text{ eV}$$

Tips and Tricks

Note that the energies for each energy level are negative. The reason is that the energy of an electron in an atom is defined with respect to the amount of work required to remove the electron from the atom. In some energy-level diagrams, the energy of E_1 is defined as zero, and the higher energy levels are positive. In either case, the difference between a higher energy level and a lower one is always positive, indicating that the electron loses energy when it drops to a lower level.

② SOLVE

Use Planck's equation to find the frequency.

$$E = hf$$
$$f = \frac{E}{h}$$
$$f = \frac{(2.55 \text{ eV})(1.60 \times 10^{-19} \text{ J/eV})}{6.63 \times 10^{-34} \text{ J} \bullet \text{s}}$$

$$\boxed{f = 6.15 \times 10^{14} \text{ Hz}}$$

Tips and Tricks

Note that electron volts were converted to joules so that the units cancel properly.

Find the corresponding line in the emission spectrum.

Examination of the diagram shows that the electron's jump from energy level E_4 to energy level E_2 corresponds to line 3 in the emission spectrum.

Continued

Interpreting Energy-Level Diagrams (continued)

Practice

1. An electron in a hydrogen atom drops from energy level E_3 to E_2. What is the frequency of the emitted photon, and which line in the emission spectrum shown in Sample Problem C corresponds to this event?

2. An electron in a hydrogen atom drops from energy level E_6 to energy level E_3. What is the frequency of the emitted photon, and in which range of the electromagnetic spectrum is this photon?

3. The energy-level diagram in **Figure 2.10** shows the first five energy levels for mercury vapor. The energy of E_1 is defined as zero. What is the frequency of the photon emitted when an electron drops from energy level E_5 to E_1 in a mercury atom?

E_5 ———————————————— $E = 6.67$ eV
E_4 ———————————————— $E = 5.43$ eV
E_3 ———————————————— $E = 4.86$ eV
E_2 ———————————————— $E = 4.66$ eV

E_1 ———————————————— $E = 0$ eV   **Figure 2.10**

4. How many different spectral lines *could* be emitted if mercury vapor were excited by photons with 6.67 eV of energy? (Hint: An electron could move, for example, from energy level E_5 to E_3, then from E_3 to E_2, and then from E_2 to E_1.)

5. The emission spectrum of hydrogen has one emission line at a frequency of 7.29×10^{14} Hz. Calculate which two energy levels electrons must jump between to produce this line, and identify the line in the energy-level diagram in Sample Problem C. (Hint: First, find the energy of the photons, and then use the energy-level diagram.)

Bohr's model is incomplete.

The Bohr model of hydrogen was a tremendous success in some respects because it explained several features of the spectra of hydrogen that had previously defied explanation. Bohr's model gave an expression for the radius of the hydrogen atom, 5.3×10^{-11} m, and predicted the energy levels of hydrogen. This model was also successful when applied to hydrogen-like atoms, that is, atoms that contain only one electron. But while many attempts were made to extend the Bohr model to multielectron atoms, the results were unsuccessful.

Bohr's model of the atom also raised new questions. For example, Bohr assumed that electrons do not radiate energy when they are in a stable orbit, but his model offered no explanation for this. Another problem with Bohr's model was that it could not explain why electrons always have certain stable orbits, while other orbits do not occur. Finally, the model followed classical physics in certain respects but radically departed from classical physics in other respects. For all of these reasons, Bohr's model was not considered to be a complete picture of the structure of the atom, and scientists continued to search for a new model that would resolve these difficulties.

 SECTION 2 FORMATIVE ASSESSMENT

▶ Reviewing Main Ideas

1. Based on the Thomson model of the atom, what did Rutherford expect to happen when he projected positively charged alpha particles against a metal foil?

2. Why did Rutherford conclude that an atom's positive charge and most of its mass are concentrated in the center of the atom?

3. What are two problems with Rutherford's model of the atom?

4. How could the atomic spectra of gases be used to identify the elements present in distant stars?

5. Bohr's model of the atom follows classical physics in some respects and quantum mechanics in others. Which assumptions of the Bohr model correspond to classical physics? Which correspond to quantum mechanics?

6. How does Bohr's model of the atom account for the emission and absorption spectra of an element?

✔ Critical Thinking

7. A Norwegian scientist, Lars Vegard, determined the different wavelengths that are part of the northern lights. He found that only a few wavelengths of light, rather than a continuous spectrum, are present in the lights. How does Bohr's model of the atom account for this observation?

Quantum Mechanics

Key Term

uncertainty principle

The Dual Nature of Light

There is considerable evidence for the photon theory of light. In this theory, all electromagnetic waves consist of photons, particle-like pulses that have energy and momentum. On the other hand, light and other electromagnetic waves exhibit interference and diffraction effects that are considered to be wave behaviors. So which model is correct? We will see that each is correct and that a specific phenomenon often exhibits only one or the other of these natures of light.

Light is both a wave and a particle.

Some experiments can be better explained or only explained by the photon concept, whereas others require a wave model. Most physicists accept both models and believe that the true nature of light is not describable in terms of a single classical picture.

For an example of how photons can be compatible with electromagnetic waves, consider radio waves at a frequency of 2.5 MHz. The energy of a photon having this frequency can be found using Planck's equation, as follows:

$$E = hf = (6.63 \times 10^{-34} \text{ J} \bullet \text{s})(2.5 \times 10^6 \text{ Hz}) = 1.7 \times 10^{-27} \text{ J}$$

From a practical viewpoint, this energy is too small to be detected as a single photon. A sensitive radio receiver might need as many as 10^{10} of these photons to produce a detectable signal. With such a large number of photons reaching the detector every second, we would not be able to detect the individual photons striking the antenna. Thus, the signal would appear as a continuous wave.

Now consider what happens as we go to higher frequencies and hence shorter wavelengths. In the visible region, it is possible to observe both the photon and the wave characteristics of light. As we mentioned earlier, a light beam can show interference phenomena and produce photoelectrons. The interference phenomena are best explained by the wave model of light, while the photoelectrons are best explained by the particle theory of light.

At even higher frequencies and correspondingly shorter wavelengths, the momentum and energy of the photons increase. Consequently, the photon nature of light becomes very evident. In addition, as the wavelength decreases, wave effects, such as interference and diffraction, become more difficult to observe. Very indirect methods are required to detect the wave nature of very high-frequency radiation, such as gamma rays.

Objectives

- Recognize the dual nature of light and matter.

- Calculate the de Broglie wavelength of matter waves.

- Distinguish between classical ideas of measurement and Heisenberg's uncertainty principle.

- Describe the quantum-mechanical picture of the atom, including the electron cloud and probability waves.

Thus, all forms of electromagnetic radiation can be described from two points of view. At one extreme, the electromagnetic wave description suits the overall interference pattern formed by a large number of photons. At the other extreme, the particle description is more suitable for dealing with highly energetic photons of very short wavelengths.

Matter Waves

In the world around us, we are accustomed to regarding things such as thrown baseballs solely as particles and things such as sound waves solely as forms of wave motion. As already noted, this rigid distinction cannot be made with light, which has both wave and particle characteristics. In 1924, the French physicist Louis de Broglie (1892–1987) extended the wave-particle duality. In his doctoral dissertation, de Broglie proposed that all forms of matter may have both wave properties and particle properties. At that time, this was a highly revolutionary idea with no experimental support. Now, however, scientists accept the concept of matter's dual nature.

The wavelength of a photon is equal to Planck's constant (h) divided by the photon's momentum (p). De Broglie speculated that this relationship might also hold for matter waves, as follows:

Wavelength of Matter Waves

$$\lambda = \frac{h}{p} = \frac{h}{mv}$$

$$\text{de Broglie wavelength} = \frac{\textbf{Planck's constant}}{\textbf{momentum}}$$

As seen by this equation, the larger the momentum of an object, the smaller its wavelength. In an analogy with photons, de Broglie postulated that the frequency of a matter wave can be found with Planck's equation as illustrated below:

Frequency of Matter Waves

$$f = \frac{E}{h}$$

$$\text{de Broglie frequency} = \frac{\textbf{energy}}{\textbf{Planck's constant}}$$

The dual nature of matter suggested by de Broglie is quite apparent in these two equations, both of which contain particle concepts (E and mv) and wave concepts (λ and f).

At first, de Broglie's proposal that all particles also exhibit wave properties was regarded as pure speculation. If particles such as electrons had wave properties, then under certain conditions they should exhibit interference phenomena. Three years after de Broglie's proposal, C. J. Davisson and L. Germer, of the United States, discovered that

FIGURE 3.1

Interference Patterns for Electrons and Light (a) Electrons show interference patterns similar to those of **(b)** light waves. This demonstrates that electrons sometimes behave like waves.

(a)
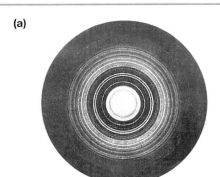

(b)
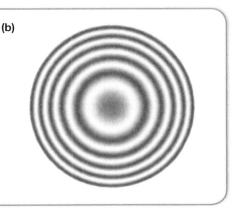

electrons can be diffracted by a single crystal of nickel. This important discovery provided the first experimental confirmation of de Broglie's theory. An example of electron diffraction compared with light diffraction is shown in **Figure 3.1.**

Electron diffraction by a crystal is possible because the de Broglie wavelength of a low-energy electron is approximately equal to the distance between atoms in a crystal. In principle, diffraction effects should be observable even for objects in our large-scale world. However, the wavelengths of material objects in our everyday world are much smaller than any possible aperture through which the object could pass.

GO ONLINE

Interactive Demo
HMHScience.com

De Broglie Waves

Sample Problem D A grain of sand blows along a seashore at a velocity of 5.2 m/s. If it has a de Broglie wavelength of 5.8×10^{-29} m, what is the mass of the sand grain?

1 ANALYZE

Given: $v = 5.2$ m/s $\qquad \lambda = 5.8 \times 10^{-32}$ m

Unknown: $m = ?$

2 SOLVE

Use the equation for the de Broglie wavelength, given on page 756.

$$\lambda = \frac{h}{mv}$$

Rearrange the equation relating wavelength, mass, and velocity to solve for mass.

$$m = \frac{h}{\lambda v} = \frac{6.63 \times 10^{-34} \text{ J} \cdot \text{s}}{(5.2 \text{ m/s})(5.8 \times 10^{-29} \text{ m})}$$

$$\boxed{m = 2.2 \times 10^{-6} \text{ kg}}$$

Continued

De Broglie Waves (continued)

Practice

1. What is the speed of a neutron with a de Broglie wavelength of 5.6×10^{-14} m?

2. If the de Broglie wavelength of an electron is equal to 5.00×10^{-7} m, how fast is the electron moving?

3. How fast would one have to throw a 0.15 kg baseball if it were to have a wavelength equal to 5.00×10^{-7} m (the same wavelength as the electron in problem 2)?

4. What is the de Broglie wavelength of a 1375 kg car traveling at 43 km/h?

5. A bacterium moving across a petri dish at 3.5 μm/s has a de Broglie wavelength of 1.9×10^{-13} m. What is the bacterium's mass?

De Broglie waves account for the allowed orbits of Bohr's model.

At first, no one could explain why only some orbits were stable. Then, de Broglie saw a connection between his theory of the wave character of matter and the stable orbits in the Bohr model. De Broglie assumed that an electron orbit would be stable only if it contained an integral (whole) number of electron wavelengths, as shown in **Figure 3.2.** The first orbit contains one wavelength, the second orbit contains two wavelengths, and so on.

De Broglie's hypothesis compares with the example of standing waves on a vibrating string of a given length, as discussed in the chapter "Vibrations and Waves." In this analogy, the circumference of the electron's orbit corresponds to the string's length. So the condition for an electron orbit is that the circumference must contain an integral multiple of electron wavelengths.

FIGURE 3.2

De Broglie's Orbits De Broglie's hypothesis that there is always an integral number of electron wavelengths around each circumference explains why only certain orbits are stable.

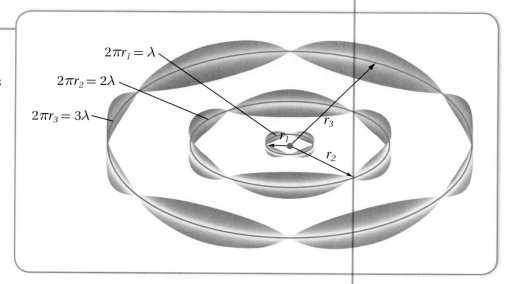

The Uncertainty Principle

In classical mechanics, there is no limitation to the accuracy of our measurements in experiments. In principle, we could always make a more precise measurement using a more finely detailed meterstick or a stronger magnifier. This unlimited precision does not hold true in quantum mechanics. The absence of such precision is not due to the limitations of our instruments. It is a fundamental limitation inherent in nature due to the wave nature of particles.

Simultaneous measurements of position and momentum cannot be completely certain.

In 1927, Werner Heisenberg argued that *it is fundamentally impossible to make simultaneous measurements of a particle's position and momentum with infinite accuracy.* In fact, the more we learn about a particle's momentum, the less we know of its position, and the reverse is also true. This principle is known as Heisenberg's **uncertainty principle.**

uncertainty principle the principle that states that it is impossible to simultaneously determine a particle's position and momentum with infinite accuracy

To understand the uncertainty principle, consider the following thought experiment. Suppose you wish to measure the position and momentum of an electron as accurately as possible. You might be able to do this by viewing the electron with a powerful microscope. In order for you to see the electron and thus determine its location, at least one photon of light must bounce off the electron and pass through the microscope into your eye. This incident photon is shown moving toward the electron in **Figure 3.3(a).** When the photon strikes the electron as in **Figure 3.3(b),** it transfers some of its energy and momentum to the electron. So in the process of attempting to locate the electron very accurately, we become less certain of its momentum. The measurement procedure limits the accuracy to which we can determine position and momentum simultaneously.

FIGURE 3.3

Heisenberg's Uncertainty Principle The images below show a thought experiment for viewing an electron with a powerful microscope. **(a)** The electron is viewed before colliding with the photon. **(b)** The electron recoils (is disturbed) as the result of the collision with the photon.

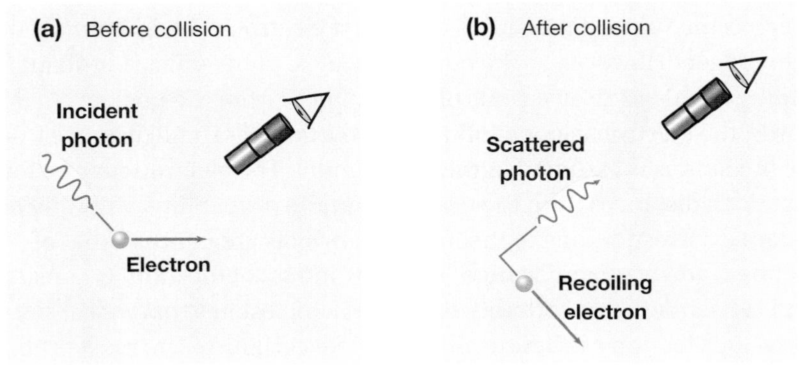

(a) Before collision

Incident photon

Electron

(b) After collision

Scattered photon

Recoiling electron

The mathematical form of the uncertainty principle states that the product of the uncertainties in position and momentum will always be larger than some minimum value. Arguments similar to those given here show that this minimum value is Planck's constant (h) divided by 4π. Thus, $\Delta x \Delta p \geq \frac{h}{4\pi}$. In this equation, Δx and Δp represent the uncertainty in the measured values of a particle's position and momentum, respectively, at some instant. This equation shows that if Δx is made very small, Δp will be large, and vice versa.

The Electron Cloud

In 1926, Erwin Schrödinger proposed a wave equation that described the manner in which de Broglie's matter waves change in space and time. Although this equation and its derivation are beyond the scope of this book, we will consider Schrödinger's equation qualitatively. Solving Schrödinger's equation yields a quantity called the *wave function,* represented by ψ (Greek letter *psi*). A particle is represented by a wave function, ψ, that depends on the position of the particle and time.

An electron's location is described by a probability distribution.

As discussed earlier, simultaneous measurements of position and momentum cannot be completely certain. Because the electron's location cannot be precisely determined, it is useful to discuss the *probability* of finding the electron at different locations. It turns out that the quantity $|\psi|^2$ is proportional to the probability of finding the electron at a given position. This interpretation of Schrödinger's wave function was first proposed by the German physicist Max Born in 1926.

Figure 3.4 shows the probability per unit distance of finding the electron at various distances from the nucleus in the ground state of hydrogen. The height of the curve at each point is proportional to the probability of finding the electron, and the x-coordinate represents the electron's distance from the nucleus. Note that there is a near-zero probability of finding the electron in the nucleus.

The peak of this curve represents the distance from the nucleus at which the electron is most likely to be found in the ground state. Schrödinger's wave equation predicts that this distance is 5.3×10^{-11} m, which is the value of the radius of the first electron orbit in Bohr's model of hydrogen. However, as the curve indicates, there is also a probability of finding the electron at various other distances from the nucleus. In other words, the electron is not confined to a particular orbital distance from the nucleus as is assumed in the Bohr model. The electron may be found at various distances from the nucleus, but the probability of finding it at a distance corresponding to the first Bohr orbit is greater than that of finding it at any other distance. This new model of the atom is consistent with Heisenberg's uncertainty principle, which states that we cannot know the electron's location with complete certainty. The most probable distance for the electron's location in the ground state is equal to the first Bohr radius.

FIGURE 3.4

Probability Distribution for an Electron The height of this curve is proportional to the probability of finding the electron at different distances from the nucleus in the ground state of hydrogen.

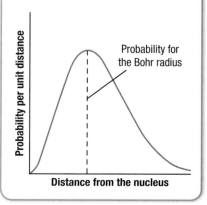

Probability of Finding an Electron at Different Distances from the Nucleus

Probability for the Bohr radius

Quantum mechanics also predicts that the wave function for the hydrogen atom in the ground state is spherically symmetrical; hence, the electron can be found in a spherical region surrounding the nucleus. This is in contrast to the Bohr theory, which confines the position of the electron to points in a plane. This result is often interpreted by viewing the electron as a cloud surrounding the nucleus, called an *electron cloud.* The density of the cloud at each location is related to the probability of finding the electron at that location.

Analysis of each of the energy levels of hydrogen reveals that the most probable electron location in each case is in agreement with each of the radii predicted by the Bohr theory. The discrete energy levels that could not be explained by Bohr's theory can be derived from Schrödinger's wave equation. In addition, the de Broglie wavelengths account for the allowed orbits that were unexplainable in Bohr's theory. Thus, the new quantum-mechanical model explains certain aspects of the structure of the atom that Bohr's model could not account for. Although probability waves and electron clouds cannot be simply visualized as Bohr's planetary model could, they offer a mathematical picture of the atom that is more accurate than Bohr's model.

The material presented in this chapter is only an introduction to quantum theory. Although we have focused on the simplest example— the hydrogen atom—quantum mechanics has been successfully applied to multielectron atomic structures. In fact, it forms the basis for understanding the structure of all known atoms and the existence of all molecules. Although most scientists believe that quantum mechanics may be nearly the final picture of the deepest levels of nature, a few continue to search for other explanations, and debates about the implications of quantum mechanics continue.

 ## SECTION 3 FORMATIVE ASSESSMENT

▶ Reviewing Main Ideas

1. Is light considered to be a wave or a particle? Explain your answer.

2. How did de Broglie account for the fact that the electrons in Bohr's model are always found at certain distinct distances from the nucleus?

3. Calculate the de Broglie wavelength of a proton moving at 1.00×10^4 m/s.

4. What is the physical significance of the square of the Schrödinger wave function, $|\psi|^2$?

5. Why is the electron sometimes viewed as an electron cloud?

✓ Critical Thinking

6. In classical physics, the accuracy of measurements has always been limited by the measuring instruments used, and no instrument is perfect. How is this limitation different from that formulated by Heisenberg in the uncertainty principle?

Semiconductor Doping

A good electrical *conductor* has a large number of free charge carriers that can move easily through a material. An *insulator* has a small number of free charge carriers that are relatively immobile. *Semiconductors* exhibit electronic properties between those of insulators and those of conductors. The development of *band theory* uses basic physical principles to explain some of the properties of these three categories of materials.

Electron Energy Levels

Electrons in an atom can possess only certain amounts of energy. For this reason, the electrons are often said to occupy specific *energy levels.* Electrons in a shell sometimes form a set of closely spaced energy levels. Normally, electrons are in the lowest energy level available to them. The specific arrangement of electrons in which all are in the lowest possible energy levels of an atom is called the atom's **ground state.**

If an atom absorbs sufficient energy from the environment, some of the atom's electrons can move to higher energy levels. The atom is then said to be in an **excited state.** If an electron absorbs so much energy that it is no longer bound to the atom, it is then called a *free electron.*

Band Theory

Band theory uses the concept of energy levels to explain the mechanisms of conduction in many solids. When identical atoms are far apart, they have identical energy-level diagrams. No two electrons in the same system can occupy the same state. As a result, when two atoms are brought closer together, the energy levels of each atom are altered by the influence of the electric field of the other atom. **Figure 1** shows how two energy levels split when there are two atoms **(a),** four atoms **(b),** and many atoms **(c)** at different separation distances. In the case of two atoms, each energy level splits into two different energy levels, as shown in **Figure 1(a).** Notice that the energy difference between two new energy levels depends on the distance between the atoms.

FIGURE 1

Energy Bands Energy levels split when two atoms are close together **(a).** Adding a few more nearby atoms causes further splitting **(b).** When many atoms interact, the energy levels are so closely spaced that they can be represented as energy bands **(c).**

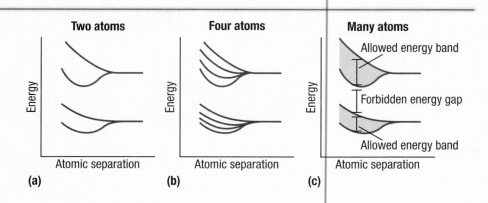

When more atoms are brought close together, each energy level splits into more levels. If there are many atoms, the energy level splits so many times and the new energy levels are so closely spaced that they may be regarded as a continuous band of energies, as in **Figure 1(c).** The highest band containing occupied energy levels is called the *valence band,* as shown in **Figure 2.** The band immediately above the valence band is called the *conduction band.*

Electron-Hole Pairs and Intrinsic Semiconductors

Imagine that a few electrons are excited from the valence band to the conduction band by an electric field, as in **Figure 3.** The electrons in the conduction band are free to move through the material. Normally, electrons in the valence band are unable to move because all nearby energy levels are occupied. But when an electron moves from the valence band into the conduction band, it leaves a vacancy, or **hole,** in an otherwise filled valence band. The hole is positively charged because it results from the removal of an electron from a neutral atom. Whenever another valence electron from this or a nearby atom moves into the hole, a new hole is created at its former location. So the net effect can be viewed as a positive hole migrating through the material in a direction opposite the motion of the electrons in the conduction band.

In a material containing only one element or compound, there are an equal number of conduction electrons and holes. Such combinations of charges are called *electron-hole pairs,* and a semiconductor that contains such pairs is called an *intrinsic semiconductor.* In the presence of an electric field, the holes move in the direction of the field, and the conduction electrons move opposite the field.

Adding Impurities to Enhance Conduction

One way to change the concentration of charge carriers is to add *impurities,* atoms that are different from those of an intrinsic semiconductor. This process is called **doping.** Even a few added impurity atoms (about one part in a million) can have a large effect on a semiconductor's resistance. The semiconductor's conductivity increases as the doping level increases. When impurities dominate conduction, the material is called an *extrinsic semiconductor.* There are two methods for doping a semiconductor: either add impurities that have extra valence electrons or add impurities that have fewer valence electrons compared with the atoms in the intrinsic semiconductor.

Semiconductors used in commercial devices are usually doped silicon or germanium. These elements have four valence electrons. Semiconductors are doped by replacing an atom of silicon or germanium with one containing either three valence electrons or five valence electrons. Note that a doped semiconductor is electrically neutral, because it is made of neutral atoms. The balance of positive and negative charges has not changed, but the number of charges that are free and able to move has. These charges are therefore able to participate in electrical conduction.

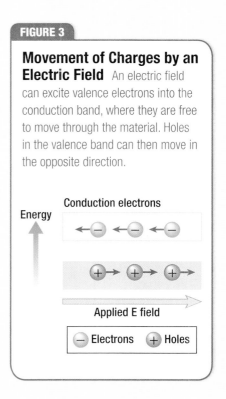

FIGURE 2

Energy Bands Energy levels of atoms become energy bands in solids. The valence band is the highest occupied band.

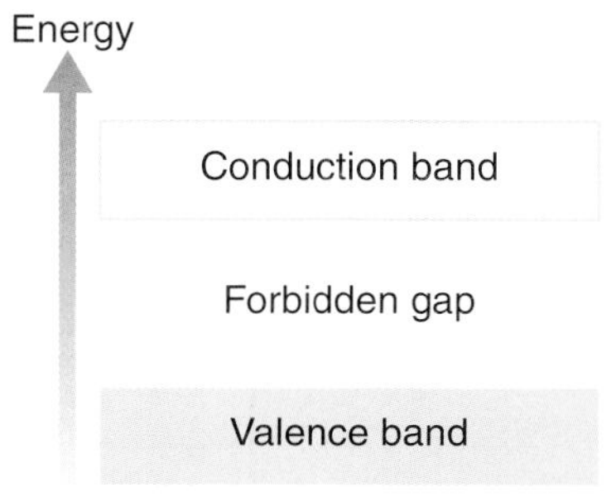

Energy

Conduction band

Forbidden gap

Valence band

FIGURE 3

Movement of Charges by an Electric Field An electric field can excite valence electrons into the conduction band, where they are free to move through the material. Holes in the valence band can then move in the opposite direction.

Conduction electrons

Energy

Applied E field

− Electrons   + Holes

New Technology and Scientific Advances

Scientific advances are inextricably linked with advances in thinking and technology. When one scientist proposes a novel hypothesis to explain a phenomenon, a new set of experimental approaches may be developed, or a contemporary scientist may examine an existing data set with a new approach. Similarly, when new technology is developed, scientists work to examine old theories in other ways, to improve on existing explanations with new information.

Models of the Atom

Many models have been proposed for the structure of atoms. With each new discovery, existing theories have been reworked by the scientists of the time, with developments continuing into the contemporary era. Scientists of Newton's time considered the atom as a simple, indestructible sphere. However, when J.J. Thomson discovered the electron in 1897, a new area of science was opened wide. New experimental techniques and technologies, ranging from Rutherford's foil experiment to observation of atomic spectra of gas, led to ever-improving models for the atomic structure, including Bohr's model. Although Bohr's theories were uniquely able to explain scientists' observations of atomic spectra, it was still incomplete. Another leap in scientific thinking was necessary.

The development of modern quantum mechanics as a new area of science led to a significant shift in scientific thought. With regard to the atomic model in particular, de Broglie extended the wave-particle duality of light to propose matter waves. A few years after his proposal, another set of scientists verified de Broglie's ideas with a new experiment. Continuing this boom of new thinking, Heisenberg and Schroedinger further honed our understanding of the quantum theory of the atom.

Beyond scientific developments, quantum theories have had significant societal impact through the development of new applications, such as the semiconductors that are key to many consumer and industrial technologies.

- How do new developments in both science and technology affect scientific theories? Give at least one example of each from the development of atomic theory.

- What new areas of science or new technologies have impacted scientists' understanding of atomic structure since Newton's time?

- How might a significant breakthrough by one scientist studying atomic structure affect other scientists who are exploring the same thing?

- Research and describe how technology and applications of quantum theories have impacted society.

BIG IDEA Quantum mechanics provides a framework for explaining atomic-scale phenomena, such as the photoelectric effect, the structure of atoms, and the wave-particle duality of light.

SECTION 1 Quantization of Energy

KEY TERMS

- Blackbody radiation and the photoelectric effect contradict classical physics, but they can be explained with the assumption that energy comes in discrete units, or is quantized.
- The energy of a light quantum, or photon, depends on the frequency of the light. Specifically, the energy of a photon is equal to frequency multiplied by Planck's constant.
- Planck's constant (h) is approximately equal to 6.63×10^{-34} J•s.
- The relation between the electron volt and the joule is as follows: 1 eV = 1.60×10^{-19} J.
- The minimum energy required for an electron to escape from a metal depends on the threshold frequency of the metal.
- The maximum kinetic energy of photoelectrons depends on the work function and the frequency of the light shining on the metal.

blackbody radiation

ultraviolet catastrophe

photoelectric effect

photon

work function

Compton shift

SECTION 2 Models of the Atom

KEY TERMS

- Rutherford's scattering experiment revealed that all of an atom's positive charge and most of an atom's mass are concentrated at its center.
- Each gas has a unique emission and absorption spectrum.
- Atomic spectra are explained by Bohr's model of the atom, in which electrons move from one energy level to another when they absorb or emit photons.

emission spectrum

absorption spectrum

SECTION 3 Quantum Mechanics

KEY TERM

- Light has both wave and particle characteristics.
- De Broglie proposed that matter has both wave and particle characteristics.
- Simultaneous measurements of position and momentum cannot be made with infinite accuracy.

uncertainty principle

VARIABLE SYMBOLS			
Quantities		**Units**	
E	photon energy	J	joules
		eV	electron volts
f_t	threshold frequency	Hz	hertz
hf_t	work function	eV	electron volts
KE_{max}	maximum kinetic energy	eV	electron volts

Problem Solving

See **Appendix D: Equations** for a summary of the equations introduced in this chapter. If you need more problem-solving practice, see **Appendix I: Additional Problems.**

Quantization of Energy

▶ **REVIEWING MAIN IDEAS**

1. Why is the term *ultraviolet catastrophe* used to describe the discrepancy between the predictions of classical physics and the experimental data for blackbody radiation?

2. What is meant by the term *quantum*?

3. What did Planck assume in order to explain the experimental data for blackbody radiation? How did Planck's assumption contradict classical physics?

4. What is the relationship between a joule and an electron volt?

5. How do observations of the photoelectric effect conflict with the predictions of classical physics?

6. What does Compton scattering demonstrate?

CONCEPTUAL QUESTIONS

7. Which has more energy, a photon of ultraviolet radiation or a photon of yellow light?

8. If the photoelectric effect is observed for one metal using light of a certain wavelength, can you conclude that the effect will also be observed for another metal under the same conditions?

9. What effect, if any, would you expect the temperature of a material to have on the ease with which electrons can be ejected from the metal in the photoelectric effect?

10. A photon is deflected by a collision with a moving electron. Can the photon's wavelength ever become shorter as a result of the collision? Explain your answer.

PRACTICE PROBLEMS

For problems 11–12, see Sample Problem A.

11. A quantum of electromagnetic radiation has an energy of 2.0 keV. What is its frequency?

12. Calculate the energy in electron volts of a photon having a wavelength in the following ranges:
 a. the microwave range, 5.00 cm
 b. the visible light range, 5.00×10^{-7} m
 c. the x-ray range, 5.00×10^{-8} m

For problems 13–14, see Sample Problem B.

13. Light of frequency 1.5×10^{15} Hz illuminates a piece of tin, and the tin emits photoelectrons of maximum kinetic energy 1.2 eV. What is the threshold frequency of the metal?

14. The threshold frequency of silver is 1.14×10^{15} Hz. What is the work function of silver?

Models of the Atom

▶ **REVIEWING MAIN IDEAS**

15. What did Rutherford's foil experiment reveal?

16. If Rutherford's planetary model were correct, atoms would be extremely unstable. Explain why.

17. How can the absorption spectrum of a gas be used to identify the gas?

18. What restriction does the Bohr model place on the movement of an electron in an atom?

19. How is Bohr's model of the hydrogen atom similar to Rutherford's planetary model? How are the two models different?

20. How does Bohr's model account for atomic spectra?

CONCEPTUAL QUESTIONS

21. Explain why all of the wavelengths in an element's absorption spectrum are also found in that element's emission spectrum.

22. More emission lines than absorption lines are usually observed in the atomic spectra of most elements. Explain why this occurs.

PRACTICE PROBLEMS

For problems 23–24, see Sample Problem C.

23. Electrons in the ground state of hydrogen (energy level E_1) have an energy of -13.6 eV. Use this value and the energy-level diagram in Sample Problem C to calculate the frequencies of photons emitted when electrons drop to the ground state from the following energy levels:
a. E_2
b. E_3
c. E_4
d. E_5

24. Sketch an emission spectrum showing the relative positions of the emission lines produced by the photons in problem 23. In what part of the electromagnetic spectrum are these lines?

Quantum Mechanics

▶ **REVIEWING MAIN IDEAS**

25. Name two situations in which light behaves like a wave and two situations in which light behaves like a particle.

26. What does Heisenberg's uncertainty principle claim?

27. How do de Broglie's matter waves account for the "allowed" electron orbits?

28. Describe the quantum-mechanical model of the atom. How is this model similar to Bohr's model? How are the two different?

CONCEPTUAL QUESTIONS

29. How does Heisenberg's uncertainty principle conflict with the Bohr model of hydrogen?

30. Why can the wave properties of an electron be observed, while those of a speeding car cannot?

31. An electron and a proton are accelerated from rest through the same potential difference. Which particle has the longer wavelength? (Hint: Note that $\Delta PE = q\Delta V = \Delta KE$.)

32. Discuss why the term *electron cloud* is used to describe the arrangement of electrons in the quantum-mechanical view of the atom.

GRAPHING CALCULATOR PRACTICE

De Broglie Wavelength

In 1924, Louis de Broglie proposed the radical new idea that all forms of matter have both wave and particle properties. As you learned earlier in this chapter, this idea is demonstrated in the de Broglie equation.

$$\lambda = \frac{h}{mv}$$

In this equation, mass (m) and velocity (v) are particle properties, and wavelength (λ) is a wave property.

In this graphing calculator activity, you will use this equation to study the de Broglie wavelengths associated with moving particles of various masses and various speeds. You will discover why this equation has very different consequences for subatomic particles, such as electrons and neutrons, than for macroscopic particles, such as baseballs.

Go online to HMHScience.com to find the skillsheet and program for graphing calculator activity.

PRACTICE PROBLEMS

For problems 33–34, see Sample Problem D.

33. How fast must an electron move if it is to have a de Broglie wavelength of 5.2×10^{-11} m?

34. Calculate the de Broglie wavelength of a 0.15 kg baseball moving at 45 m/s.

Mixed Review

▶ **REVIEWING MAIN IDEAS**

35. A light source of wavelength λ illuminates a metal and ejects photoelectrons with a maximum kinetic energy of 1.00 eV. A second light source of wavelength $\frac{1}{2}\lambda$ ejects photoelectrons with a maximum kinetic energy of 4.00 eV. What is the work function of the metal?

36. A 0.50 kg mass falls from a height of 3.0 m. If all of the energy of this mass could be converted to visible light of wavelength 5.0×10^{-7} m, how many photons would be produced?

37. Red light ($\lambda = 670.0$ nm) produces photoelectrons from a certain material. Green light ($\lambda = 520.0$ nm) produces photoelectrons from the same material with 1.50 times the previous maximum kinetic energy. What is the material's work function?

38. Find the de Broglie wavelength of a ball with a mass of 0.200 kg just before it strikes Earth after it has been dropped from a building 50.0 m tall.

ALTERNATIVE ASSESSMENT

1. Calculate the de Broglie wavelength for an electron, a neutron, a baseball, and your body, at speeds varying from 1.0 m/s to 3.0×10^7 m/s. Organize your findings in a table. The distance between atoms in a crystal is approximately 10^{-10} m. Which wavelengths could produce diffraction patterns using crystal as a diffraction grating? What can you infer about the wave characteristics of large objects? Explain your conclusions.

2. Bohr, Einstein, Planck, and Heisenberg each received the Nobel Prize for their contributions to twentieth-century physics. Their lives were also affected by the extraordinary events of World War II. Research their stories and the ways the war affected their work. What were their opinions about science and politics during and after the war? Write a report about your findings and about the opinions of your classmates regarding the involvement and responsibility of scientists in politics.

3. Conduct research on the history of atomic theory. Create a timeline that shows the development of modern atomic theory, beginning with John Dalton's contributions in 1808. Include the discoveries of J. J. Thomson, Ernest Rutherford, Niels Bohr, and Erwin Schrödinger. You may also include other significant discoveries in the history of atomic theory.

In addition, add historical events to the timeline to provide context for the scientific discoveries, and include illustrations with key entries.

4. Choose a simple element, and then create three-dimensional models of an atom of this element. Create at least three different models, corresponding to different versions of atomic theory throughout history. Include information about which historical theories you are representing in each model and which parts of those theories are no longer accepted today. Also include information about the limitations of your models.

5. As seen in this chapter, the modern atomic theory arose from many hypotheses regarding atoms. Each hypothesis was based on observational evidence and helped explain phenomena seen in the natural world. Choose one hypothesis about atoms from the chapter to research further, and explain how it (a) had durable explanatory power, and (b) was tested over a wide variety of conditions. Then describe when and how the hypothesis became an accepted part of the atomic theory.

6. Research examples of at least two applications of quantum phenomena, and prepare a report with your findings.

Standards-Based Assessment

Record your answers on a separate piece of paper.

MULTIPLE CHOICE

1 At the end of the 19th century, electromagnetic waves was the accepted theory of light. Then in 1905, Einstein explained the photoelectric effect in terms of particles of light called photons. It was not until 1922 that Compton used a new technology called x-ray scattering to show that x-rays behaved like photons and confirmed Einstein's photon theory of light. What is true of the photon theory?

A It predicts the behavior of light under all conditions.

B It explains the behavior of light under all conditions.

C It changed the accepted theory of light as a result of new technology.

D It entirely replaced the electromagnetic theory of light.

2 Two emission spectrographs are shown below. What can be said about the two elements, (a) and (b), that produced these spectra?

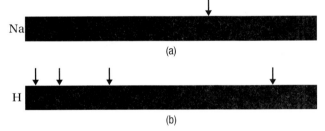

A Element (b) is more dense than (a) since it has more lines.

B Element (a) is more dense than (b) because its lines are thicker.

C Element (b) has more electrons than (a) since it has more lines.

D Element (a) emits fewer colors in the visible spectrum, compared with element (b).

3 Scientific discoveries in the fields of atomic physics, nuclear physics, and quantum physics have led to important new technological applications in the 20th century. Which of the following applications is most clearly an application of a quantum phenomenon?

A television

B solar cells

C atomic energy

D hybrid automobiles

4 What happens when an electron moves from a higher energy level to a lower energy level in an atom?

A Energy is absorbed from a source outside the atom.

B The energy contained in the electromagnetic field inside the atom increases.

C Energy is released across a continuous range of values.

D A photon is emitted with energy equal to the difference in energy between the two levels.

5 This is an energy-level diagram for hydrogen.

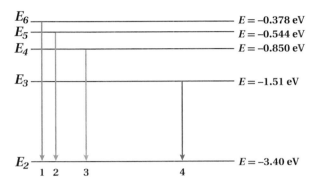

What frequency of photon would be absorbed when an electron jumps from E_2 to E_3?

A 1.89 eV

B 4.56×10^{14} Hz

C 6.89×10^{14} Hz

D 2.85×10^{33} Hz

6 What type of spectrum is created by applying a high potential difference to a pure atomic gas?

A an emission spectrum

B an absorption spectrum

C a continuous spectrum

D a visible spectrum

GRIDDED RESPONSE

7 Light of wavelength 3.0×10^{-7} m shines on a lithium metal sample, which has a work function of 2.3 eV. What is the maximum kinetic energy of the photoelectrons, in eV, emitted from the sample?

PHYSICS AND ITS WORLD

1895

In Paris, the brothers **Auguste** and **Louis Lumière** show a motion picture to the public for the first time.

1905

Vol. 17 of *Annalen der Physik* contains three extraordinarily original and important papers by **Albert Einstein.** In one paper, he introduces his special theory of relativity. In another, he presents the quantum theory of light.

$$E_0 = mc^2$$

1912

Henrietta Leavitt discovers the period-luminosity relation for variable stars, making them among the most accurate and useful objects for determining astronomical distances.

1914

World War I begins.

1890   1900   1910   1920

1898

Marie and **Pierre Curie** are the first to isolate the radioactive elements polonium and radium.

Po, Ra

1903

Wilbur and **Orville Wright** fly the first successful heavier-than-air craft.

1913

Niels Bohr—building on the discoveries of **Ernest Rutherford** and **J. J. Thomson,** and the quantum theories of **Max Planck** and **Albert Einstein**—develops a model of atomic structure based on energy levels that accounts for emission spectra.

$$E_n = \frac{13.6}{n^2}\ \text{eV}$$

1922

James Joyce's *Ulysses* is published.

1926

Erwin Schrödinger uses the wave-particle model for light and matter to develop the theory of wave mechanics, which describes atomic systems. About the same time, **Werner Heisenberg** develops a mathematically equivalent theory called *quantum mechanics*, by which the probability that matter has certain properties is determined.

$$p = \frac{h}{\lambda}$$

1937

Pablo Picasso paints *Guernica* in outraged response to the Nazi bombing of that town during the Spanish Civil War.

1942

Shin'ichiro Tomonaga proposes an important tenet of quantum electrodynamics, which describes the interactions between charged particles and light at the quantum level. The theory is later independently developed by **Richard Feynman** and **Julian Schwinger.**

1929

The New York Stock Exchange collapses, ushering in a global economic crisis known in the United States as the Great Depression.

1938

Otto Hahn and **Fritz Strassmann** achieve nuclear fission. Early the next year, **Lise Meitner** and **Otto Frisch** explain the process and introduce the term *fission* to describe the division of a nucleus into lighter nuclei.

$$_{0}^{1}n + \,_{92}^{235}U \longrightarrow \,_{56}^{141}Ba + \,_{36}^{92}Kr + 3\,_{0}^{1}n$$

1939

World War II begins with the Nazi invasion of Poland.

1948

Martin Luther King Jr. graduates from Morehouse College and enters Crozer Theological Seminary, where he becomes acquainted with the principles of **Mohandas Gandhi.** During the next two decades, he becomes one of the most forceful and articulate voices in the U.S. civil rights movement.

Nuclear fission is an important energy source today, and nuclear fusion may be an important energy source in the future. In addition, radioactive decay makes it possible to date organic materials that are 1000 to 25 000 years old.

The reindeer sled pictured here carries the tusks of a 20 000-year-old woolly mammoth found in Russia. Scientists used a process called *carbon dating* to estimate the mammoth's age. All living organisms have the same ratio of carbon-14 atoms to carbon-12 atoms. The carbon-14 atoms decay into other atoms when an organism dies. Thus, the ratio of carbon-14 to carbon-12 can be used to date the organism.

^{14}C atoms

Number of parent nuclei

Time

Subatomic Physics

BIG IDEA

Interactions of subatomic particles result in the formation of atoms and other particles. Four fundamental forces are involved in these interactions: strong force, weak force, electromagnetic force, and gravitational force.

ONLINE Physics
HMHScience.com

ONLINE LABS
- Half-Life

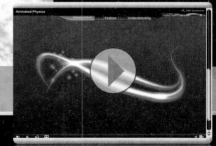

GO ONLINE *Animated* **Physics**

HMHScience.com

Alpha, Beta, and
Gamma Radiation

SECTION 1

Objectives

- Identify the properties of the nucleus of an atom.
- Explain why some nuclei are unstable.
- Calculate the binding energy of various nuclei.

The Nucleus

Key Terms

isotope | strong force | binding energy

Properties of the Nucleus

You have learned that atoms are composed of electrons, protons, and neutrons. Except for the ordinary hydrogen nucleus, which consists of a single proton, both protons and neutrons are found in the nucleus. Together, protons and neutrons are referred to as *nucleons.*

As seen in the chapter "Atomic Physics," Rutherford's scattering experiment led to the conclusion that all of an atom's positive charge and most of its mass are concentrated in the nucleus. Rutherford's calculations revealed that the nucleus has a radius no greater than about 10^{-14} m. Because such small lengths are common in nuclear physics, a convenient unit of length is the *femtometer* (fm). Sometimes called the *fermi,* this unit is equal to 10^{-15} m.

A nucleus can be specified by an atomic number and mass number.

There are a few important quantities that describe the charge and mass of the nucleus. **Figure 1.1** lists these quantities and the symbols used to represent them. The mass number (A) represents the total number of protons and neutrons—or nucleons—in the nucleus. The atomic number (Z) represents the number of protons; the neutron number (N) represents the number of neutrons. Note that A, Z, and N are always integers.

FIGURE 1.1

SYMBOLS FOR NUCLEAR QUANTITIES

Symbol	Name	Explanation
A	mass number	the number of nucleons (protons and neutrons) in the nucleus
Z	atomic number	the number of protons in the nucleus
N	neutron number	the number of neutrons in the nucleus

For example, a typical atom of aluminum has a mass number (A) of 27 and an atomic number (Z) of 13. Therefore, it has 13 protons and 14 neutrons ($27 - 13 = 14$). A periodic table of elements usually includes the atomic number of an element near the element's chemical symbol.

Frequently, the mass number and the atomic number of the nucleus of an atom are written before the atom's chemical symbol, as shown in **Figure 1.2.** The chemical symbol for aluminum is Al. The superscript refers to the mass number A (27 in the case of aluminum), and the subscript refers to the atomic number Z (13 in the case of aluminum).

An element can be identified by its atomic number, Z. Because the number of protons determines the element, the atomic number of any given element does not change. Thus, the chemical symbol, such as Al, or the name of the element, such as aluminum, can always be used to determine the atomic number. For this reason, the atomic number is sometimes omitted.

Although atomic number does not change within an element, atoms of the same element can have different mass numbers. This is because the number of neutrons in a particular element can vary. Atoms that have the same atomic number but different neutron numbers (and thus different mass numbers) are called **isotopes.** The neutron number for an isotope can be found from the following relationship:

$$A = Z + N$$

This expression says that the mass number of an atom (A) equals the number of protons (Z) plus the number of neutrons (N) in the nucleus.

The natural abundance of isotopes can vary greatly. For example, $^{11}_{6}C$, $^{12}_{6}C$, $^{13}_{6}C$, and $^{14}_{6}C$ are four isotopes of carbon. The natural abundance of the $^{12}_{6}C$ isotope is about 98.9 percent, while that of the $^{13}_{6}C$ isotope is only about 1.1 percent. Some isotopes do not occur naturally but can be produced in the laboratory. Even the simplest element, hydrogen, has isotopes: $^{1}_{1}H$, called hydrogen; $^{2}_{1}H$, called *deuterium* (or *heavy hydrogen*); and $^{3}_{1}H$, called *tritium* (or *heavy heavy hydrogen*).

A nucleus is very dense.

Experiments have shown that most nuclei are approximately spherical and that the volume of a nucleus is proportional to the total number of nucleons, and thus to the mass of the nucleus. This suggests that *all nuclei have nearly the same density*, which is about 2.3×10^{17} kg/m³, which is 2.3×10^{14} times greater than the density of water (1.0×10^{3} kg/m³). Nucleons combine to form a nucleus as though they were tightly packed spheres, as shown in **Figure 1.3.**

Unified mass unit and rest energy define the mass of a nucleus.

Because the mass of a nucleus is extremely small, the *unified mass unit,* u, is often used for atomic masses. This unit is sometimes referred to as the *atomic mass unit.* 1 u is defined so that 12 u is equal to the mass of one atom of carbon-12. The mass of a nucleus (or atom) is measured relative to the mass of an atom of the neutral carbon-12 isotope (the nucleus plus six electrons). Therefore, 1 u = 1.660 538 86 $\times$ 10⁻²⁷ kg. The proton and neutron each have a mass of about 1 u, and the electron has a mass that is only a small fraction of a unified mass unit—about 5×10^{-4} u.

FIGURE 1.2

Chemical Symbol

The chemical symbol of an element is often written with its mass number and atomic number, as shown here.

Mass number (A)

Chemical symbol

$$^{27}_{13}\text{Al}$$

Atomic number (Z)

isotope an atom that has the same number of protons (or the same atomic number) as other atoms of the same element do but that has a different number of neutrons (and thus a different atomic mass)

FIGURE 1.3

Nucleus A nucleus can be visualized as a cluster of tightly packed spherical protons and neutrons. This illustration is just a representation; nucleons actually fill very little of the volume of the nucleus and are in rapid motion.

Alternatively, the mass of the nucleus is often expressed in terms of rest energy. A particle has a certain amount of energy, called *rest energy*, associated with its mass. The following equation expresses the relationship between mass and rest energy mathematically:

Relationship Between Rest Energy and Mass

$$E_R = mc^2$$

rest energy = (mass)(speed of light)^2

This expression is often used because mass is not conserved in many nuclear processes, as we will see. Because the rest energy of a particle is given by $E_R = mc^2$, it is convenient to express a particle's mass in terms of its energy equivalent. The equation that follows is for the rest energy of a particle with a mass of exactly 1 u.

$$E_R = mc^2 = \frac{(1.660\,538\,782 \times 10^{-27}\ \text{kg})(299\,792\,458\ \text{m/s})^2}{1.602\,176\,53 \times 10^{-19}\ \text{J/eV}} \approx 931.49\ \text{MeV}$$

Thus, the conversion of 1 u of mass into energy would produce about 931.49 MeV. This book will use the value 931.49 MeV for calculations. (Recall that M is an abbreviation for the SI prefix *mega-*, which indicates 10^6.)

Did YOU Know?

The mass-energy equivalence, the relationship between mass and energy, is predicted by Einstein's special theory of relativity. Another aspect of this theory is that time and length are relative. That is, they depend on an observer's frame of reference, while the speed of light is absolute.

The masses and energy equivalent of the proton, neutron, and electron are summarized in **Figure 1.4.** Notice that in order to distinguish between the mass of the proton and the mass of the neutron, you must know their masses to at least four significant figures. The masses and some other properties of selected isotopes are given in **Appendix H**.

FIGURE 1.4

MASS AND REST ENERGY OF ATOMIC PARTICLES

Particle	*m* (kg)	*m* (u)	E_R (MeV)
proton	1.673×10^{-27}	1.007 276	938.3
neutron	1.675×10^{-27}	1.008 665	939.6
electron	9.109×10^{-31}	0.000 549	0.5110

Nuclear Stability

Given that the nucleus consists of a closely packed collection of protons and neutrons, you might be surprised that it can exist. It seems that the Coulomb repulsion between protons would cause a nucleus to fly apart. There must be some attractive force to overcome this repulsive force. This force is called the *nuclear force*, or the **strong force.**

strong force the interaction that binds nucleons together in a nucleus

The strong force has some properties that make it very much unlike other types of force. The strong force is almost completely independent of electric charge. For a given separation, the force of attraction between two protons, two neutrons, or a proton and a neutron has the same magnitude.

Another unusual property of the strong force is its very short range, only about 10^{-15} m. For longer distances, the strong force is virtually zero.

Neutrons help to stabilize a nucleus.

A plot of neutron number versus atomic number (the number of protons) for stable nuclei is shown in **Figure 1.5**. The solid line in the plot shows the location of nuclei that have an equal number of protons and neutrons ($N = Z$). Notice that only light nuclei are on this line, while all heavier nuclei fall above this line. This means that heavy nuclei are stable only when they have more neutrons than protons. This can be understood in terms of the characteristics of the strong force.

For a nucleus to be stable, the repulsion between positively charged protons must be balanced by the strong nuclear force's attraction between all the particles in the nucleus. The repulsive force exists between all protons in a nucleus because the electrostatic force is long range. But a proton or a neutron attracts only its nearest neighbors, because of the nuclear force's short range. So as the number of protons increases, the number of neutrons has to increase even more to add enough attractive forces to maintain stability.

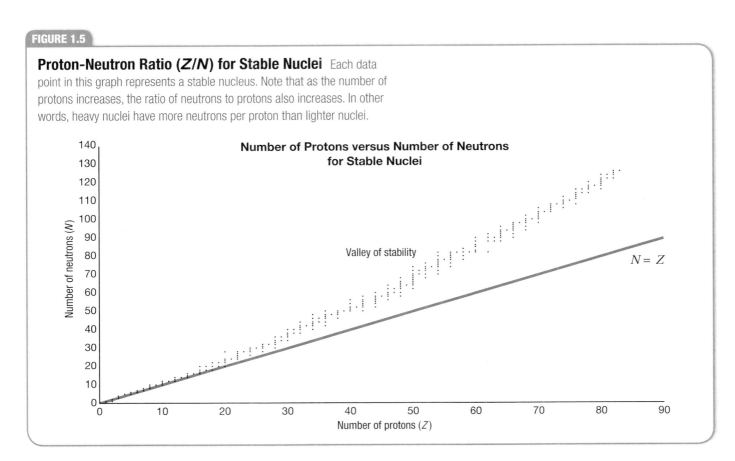

FIGURE 1.5

Proton-Neutron Ratio (Z/N) for Stable Nuclei Each data point in this graph represents a stable nucleus. Note that as the number of protons increases, the ratio of neutrons to protons also increases. In other words, heavy nuclei have more neutrons per proton than lighter nuclei.

For Z greater than 83, the repulsive forces between protons cannot be compensated by the addition of more neutrons. That is, *elements that contain more than 83 protons do not have stable nuclei.* The long, narrow region in **Figure 1.5** that contains the cluster of dots representing stable nuclei is sometimes referred to as the *valley of stability*. Nuclei that are not stable decay into other nuclei until the decay product is one of the nuclei located in the valley of stability.

A stable nucleus's mass is less than the masses of its nucleons.

The particles in a stable nucleus are held tightly together by the attractions of the strong nuclear force. In order to break such a nucleus apart into separated protons and neutrons, energy must be added to overcome this force's attraction. For most nuclei, the particles bound together in the nucleus have a lower energy state than the same set of particles would have if they were separated. Because they are so much higher in energy, isolated protons and neutrons are very rare.

The quantity of energy needed to break a nucleus into individual unbound nucleons is the same as the quantity of energy released when unbound nucleons come together to form a stable nucleus. This quantity of energy is called the **binding energy** of the nucleus. It is equal to the difference in energy between the nucleons when bound and the same nucleons when unbound. (Note that except for very small values of A, unbound nucleons do not simply combine into a full-grown nucleus.) Binding energy can be calculated from the rest energies of the particles making up a nucleus as follows:

$$E_{bind} = E_{R,unbound} - E_{R,bound}$$

Using the equation for rest energy, we can rewrite this as follows:

$$E_{bind} = m_{unbound}c^2 - m_{bound}c^2 = (m_{unbound} - m_{bound})c^2$$

The mass of the nucleons when unbound minus the mass of the nucleons when bound is called the *mass defect* and is expressed as Δm. Thus, the previous equation for binding energy can be expressed as follows:

> **Binding Energy of a Nucleus**
>
> $$E_{bind} = \Delta m c^2$$
>
> **binding energy = mass defect × (speed of light)^2**

Note that the total mass of a stable nucleus (m_{bound}) is always less than the sum of the masses of its individual nucleons ($m_{unbound}$). It is often useful to find the mass defect in terms of u so that it can be converted to energy as described earlier in this chapter (1 u = 931.49 MeV).

The mass of the unbound nucleus is the sum of the individual nucleon masses, and the mass of the bound nucleus is about equal to the atomic mass minus the mass of the electrons. Thus, the mass defect can be written as $\Delta m = (Zm_p + Nm_n) - (\text{atomic mass} - Zm_e)$. One way to rearrange this equation is $\Delta m = (Zm_p + Zm_e) + Nm_n - (\text{atomic mass})$.

binding energy the energy released when unbound nucleons come together to form a stable nucleus, which is equivalent to the energy required to break the nucleus into individual nucleons

Because a hydrogen atom contains one proton and one electron, the first term is equal to Z(atomic mass of H). The equation for mass defect can be rewritten as follows:

$$\Delta m = Z(\text{atomic mass of H}) + Nm_n - \text{atomic mass}$$

Use this equation and the atomic masses given in **Appendix H** to calculate mass defect when solving problems involving binding energy. (In this discussion, we have disregarded the binding energies of the electrons. This is reasonable because nuclear binding energies are many tens of thousands of times greater than electronic binding energies.)

The binding energy per nucleon for light nuclei ($A < 20$) is smaller than for heavier nuclei. Particles in lighter nuclei are less tightly bound on average than particles in heavier nuclei. Except for the lighter nuclei, the average binding energy per nucleon is about 8 MeV. Of all nuclei, iron-58 has the greatest binding energy per nucleon.

GO ONLINE

Interactive Demo
HMHScience.com

Binding Energy

Sample Problem A Given that the atomic mass of iron −55 is 54.938 297 u, calculate the binding energy of $^{55}_{26}$Fe.

1 ANALYZE

Given: $Z = 26$ atomic mass of iron $-55 = 54.938\ 297$ u

$N = 29$ atomic mass of H $= 1.007\ 825$ u

$m_n = 1.008\ 665$ u

Unknown: $E_{bind} = ?$

2 PLAN

Choose the equation or situation:
First, find the mass defect with the following relationship:

$$\Delta m = Z(\text{atomic mass of H}) + Nm_n - \text{atomic mass}$$

Then, find the binding energy by converting the mass defect to rest energy.

3 SOLVE

Substitute the values into the equation and solve:

$$\Delta m = 26(1.007\ 825\ \text{u}) + 29(1.008\ 665\ \text{u}) - 54.938\ 297\ \text{u}$$

$$\Delta m = 26.203\ 450\ \text{u} + 29.251\ 285\ \text{u} - 54.938\ 297\ \text{u}$$

$$\Delta m = 0.516\ 438\ \text{u}$$

$$E_{bind} = (0.516\ 438\ \text{u})\ (931.49\ \text{MeV/u})$$

$$\boxed{E_{binding} = 481.06\ \text{MeV}}$$

Continued

Binding Energy (continued)

Practice

1. Calculate the total binding energy of $^{20}_{10}\text{Ne}$ and $^{40}_{20}\text{Ca}$. (Refer to **Appendix H** for this and the following problems.)

2. Determine the difference in the binding energy of $^{107}_{47}\text{Ag}$ and $^{63}_{29}\text{Cu}$.

3. Find the mass defect of $^{32}_{16}\text{S}$.

4. Find the binding energy per nucleon of $^{238}_{92}\text{U}$ in MeV.

✔ SECTION 1 FORMATIVE ASSESSMENT

▶ Reviewing Main Ideas

1. Does the nuclear mass or the charge of the nucleus determine what element an atom is?

2. Oxygen has several isotopes. What do these isotopes have in common? How do they differ?

3. Of atomic number, mass number, and neutron number, which are the same for each isotope of an element, and which are different?

4. The protons in a nucleus repel one another with the Coulomb force. What holds these protons together?

5. Describe the relationship between the number of protons, the number of neutrons, and the stability of a nucleus.

6. Use the equation that describes mass-energy equivalence to calculate the total binding energy of the following:

   a. $^{93}_{41}\text{Nb}$

   b. $^{197}_{79}\text{Au}$

   c. $^{27}_{13}\text{Al}$

   (Refer to **Appendix H**.)

7. How many protons are there in the nucleus of $^{14}_{6}\text{C}$? How many neutrons? How many electrons are there in the neutral atom?

✔ Critical Thinking

8. Two isotopes having the same mass number are known as *isobars*. Calculate the difference in binding energy per nucleon for the isobars $^{23}_{11}\text{Na}$ and $^{23}_{12}\text{Mg}$. How do you account for this difference?

Nuclear Decay

Key Term

half-life

Objectives

▶ Describe the three modes of nuclear decay.

▶ Predict the products of nuclear decay.

▶ Calculate the decay constant and the half-life of a radioactive substance.

Nuclear Decay Modes

So far, we have considered what happens when nucleons are bound together to form stable nuclei. However, not all nuclei are stable. There are about 400 stable nuclei; hundreds of others are unstable and tend to break apart into other particles. This process is called *nuclear decay*.

The nuclear decay process can be a natural event or can be induced artificially. In either case, when a nucleus decays, radiation is emitted in the form of particles, photons, or both. The emission of particles and photons is called *radiation,* and the process is called *radioactivity.* For example, the hands and numbers of the watch shown in **Figure 2.1** contain small amounts of radium salts. The nuclei within these salts decay, releasing light energy that causes the watch to glow in the dark. The nucleus before decay is called the *parent nucleus,* and the nucleus remaining after decay is called the *daughter nucleus.* In all nuclear reactions, the energy released is found by the equation $E = \Delta mc^2$.

A radioactive material can emit three types of radiation.

Three types of radiation can be emitted by a nucleus as it undergoes radioactive decay: alpha (α) particles, in which the emitted particles are ^4_2He nuclei; beta (β) particles, in which the emitted particles are either electrons or positrons (positively charged particles with a mass equal to that of the electron); and gamma (γ) rays, in which the emitted "rays" are high-energy photons. These three types of radiation are summarized in **Figure 2.2**.

FIGURE 2.1

Radioactivity The radioactive decay of radium nuclei causes the hands and numbers of this watch to glow in the dark.

FIGURE 2.2

TYPES OF RADIATION AND RULES FOR RADIOACTIVE DECAY

Particle	Symbols	Composition	Charge	Effect on parent nucleus
alpha	α (^4_2He)	2 protons, 2 neutrons	+2	mass loss; new element produced
beta	β^- ($^{\,0}_{-1}e$)	electron	−1	no change in mass number; new element produced
	β^+ (^0_1e)	positron	+1	
gamma	γ	photon	0	energy loss

The ability of radiation to pass through a material depends on the type of radiation. Alpha particles can usually be stopped by a piece of paper, beta particles can penetrate a few millimeters of aluminum, and gamma rays can penetrate several centimeters of lead.

Helium nuclei are emitted in alpha decay.

When a nucleus undergoes alpha decay, it emits an alpha particle ($^4_2$He). Thus, the nucleus loses two protons and two neutrons. This makes the nucleus lighter and decreases its positive charge. (Because the electrons around the nuclei do not participate in nuclear reactions, they are ignored.)

For example, the nucleus of uranium-238 ($^{238}_{92}$U) can decay by alpha emission to a thorium-234 nucleus and an alpha particle, as follows:

$$^{238}_{92}\text{U} \rightarrow \,^{234}_{90}\text{Th} + \,^4_2\text{He}$$

This expression says that a parent nucleus, $^{238}_{92}$U, emits an alpha particle, $^4_2$He, and thereby changes to a daughter nucleus, $^{234}_{90}$Th (thorium-234). This nuclear reaction and all others follow the rules summarized in **Figure 2.3.** Simply put, these two rules state that the atomic numbers and mass numbers are both conserved. The rules can be used to determine the unknown daughter atom when a parent atom undergoes alpha decay.

FIGURE 2.3
RULES FOR NUCLEAR DECAY
The total of the atomic numbers on the left is the same as the total on the right, because charge must be conserved.
The total of the mass numbers on the left is the same as the total on the right, because nucleon number must be conserved.

Electrons or positrons are emitted in beta decay.

When a radioactive nucleus undergoes beta decay, the nucleus emits either an electron or a positron. (A positron has the same mass as the electron but is positively charged.) The atomic number is increased or decreased by one, with an opposite change in the neutron number. Because the daughter nucleus contains the same number of nucleons as the parent nucleus, the mass number does not change. Thus, beta decay does little to change the mass of a nucleus. Instead, the ratio of neutrons to protons in a nucleus is changed. This ratio affects the stability of the nucleus, as seen earlier.

A typical beta decay event involves carbon-14, as follows:

$$^{14}_6\text{C} \rightarrow \,^{14}_7\text{N} + \,^0_{-1}e \quad \text{(partial equation)}$$

This decay produces an electron, written as $^0_{-1}e$. In this decay, the atomic number of the daughter nucleus is increased by 1.

Another beta decay event involves nitrogen-12, as follows:

$$^{12}_{7}\text{N} \rightarrow {}^{12}_{6}\text{C} + {}^{0}_{1}e \quad \text{(partial equation)}$$

This decay produces a positron, written as ${}^{0}_{1}e$. In this decay, the atomic number of the daughter nucleus is decreased by 1.

The superscripts and subscripts on the carbon and nitrogen nuclei follow our usual conventions, but those on the electron and the positron may need some explanation. The -1 indicates that the electron has a charge whose magnitude is equal to that of the proton but is negative. Similarly, the 1 indicates that the positron has a charge that is equal to that of the proton in magnitude and sign. Thus, the subscript can be thought of as the charge of the particle. The 0 used for the mass number of the electron and the positron reflects the fact that electrons and positrons are not nucleons; thus, their emission does not change the mass number. Notice that both subscripts and superscripts must balance in the equations for beta decay, just as in alpha decay.

Beta decay transforms neutrons and protons.

A bubble-chamber image of a positron is shown in **Figure 2.4**. The emission of electrons or positrons from a nucleus is surprising because the nucleus is made of only protons and neutrons. This apparent discrepancy can be explained by noting that in beta decay, either a neutron is transformed into a proton, creating an electron in the process, or a proton is transformed into a neutron, creating a positron in the process. These two beta decays can be written as follows:

$$^{1}_{0}n \rightarrow {}^{1}_{1}p + {}^{0}_{-1}e$$
$$^{1}_{1}p \rightarrow {}^{1}_{0}n + {}^{0}_{1}e$$
$$\text{(partial equations)}$$

Decay events can be written in this way because other particles in the nucleus, much like the electrons around the nucleus, do not directly participate in the beta decay. The electrons and positrons involved in beta decay, on the other hand, are produced in the nuclear-decay process. Because they do not come from the shells around the nucleus, they cannot be ignored.

Neutrinos and antineutrinos are emitted in beta decay.

Before we conclude our discussion of beta decay, there is one problem that must be resolved. In analyzing the experimental results of beta decay reactions, scientists noticed a disturbing fact. If carbon-14 beta decay actually occurred as described on the previous page, energy, linear momentum, and angular momentum would not be conserved. In 1930, to solve this problem, Wolfgang Pauli proposed that a third particle must be missing from the equation. He reasoned that this new particle, called a *neutrino,* is necessary to conserve energy and momentum. Experimental evidence confirmed the existence of such a particle in 1956.

The Greek letter *nu* (ν) is used to represent a neutrino. When a bar is drawn above the nu ($\overline{\nu}$), the particle is an antineutrino, or the antiparticle of a neutrino. The properties of the neutrino are summarized in **Figure 2.5**.

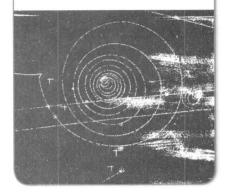

FIGURE 2.4

Positron in a Bubble-Chamber The spiral in this bubble-chamber image is the track left by a positron. This reaction took place in a magnetic field, which caused the positron to spiral as it lost energy.

FIGURE 2.5

PROPERTIES OF THE NEUTRINO

The neutrino has zero electric charge.

The neutrino's mass was once believed to be zero; recent experiments suggest a very small nonzero mass (much smaller than the mass of the electron).

The neutrino interacts very weakly with matter and is therefore very difficult to detect.

Note that the neutrino has no electric charge and that its mass is very small, perhaps even zero. As a result, the neutrino is difficult to detect experimentally.

With the neutrino, we can now describe the beta decay process of carbon-14 in a form that takes energy and momentum conservation into account, as follows:

$$^{14}_{6}C \rightarrow \,^{14}_{7}N + \,^{0}_{-1}e + \overline{\nu}$$

According to this expression, carbon-14 decays into a nitrogen nucleus, releasing an electron and an antineutrino in the process.

The decay of nitrogen-12 can also be rewritten, as follows:

$$^{12}_{7}N \rightarrow \,^{12}_{6}C + \,^{0}_{1}e + \nu$$

Here we see that when $^{12}_{7}N$ decays into $^{12}_{6}C$, a positron and a neutrino are produced. To avoid confusing these two types of beta decay, keep in mind this simple rule: *In beta decay, an electron is always accompanied by an antineutrino, and a positron is always accompanied by a neutrino.*

High-energy photons are emitted in gamma decay.

Very often, a nucleus that undergoes radioactive decay, either alpha or beta, is left in an excited energy state. The nucleus can then undergo a gamma decay in which one or more nucleons make transitions from a higher energy level to a lower energy level. In the process, one or more photons are emitted. Such photons, or *gamma rays,* have very high energy relative to the energy of visible light. The process of nuclear de-excitation, or gamma decay, is very similar to the emission of light by an atom, in which an electron makes a transition from a state of higher energy to a state of lower energy (as discussed in the chapter "Atomic Physics"). Note that in gamma decay, energy is emitted but the parts of the nucleus are left unchanged. Thus, both the atomic number and the mass number stay the same. Nonetheless, gamma decay is still considered to be a form of nuclear decay because it involves protons or neutrons in the nucleus.

Two common reasons for a nucleus being in an excited state are alpha and beta decay. The following sequence of events represents a typical situation in which gamma decay occurs:

$$^{12}_{5}B \rightarrow \,^{12}_{6}C^* + \,^{0}_{-1}e + \overline{\nu}$$

$$^{12}_{6}C^* \rightarrow \,^{12}_{6}C + \gamma$$

The first step is a beta decay in which $^{12}_{5}B$ decays to $^{12}_{6}C^*$. The asterisk indicates that the carbon nucleus is left in an excited state following the decay. The excited carbon nucleus then decays in the second step to the ground state by emitting a gamma ray.

Nuclear Decay Series

If the product of a nuclear decay is stable, the decay process ends. In other cases, the decay product—the daughter nucleus—is itself unstable. The daughter nucleus then becomes the parent nucleus for an additional decay process. Such a sequence is called a *decay series*.

Figure 2.6(a) depicts the number of protons versus neutrons for all stable nuclei. A small portion of this graph is enlarged in **Figure 2.6(b)**, which shows a naturally occurring decay series. This decay series begins with thorium, Th, and ends with lead, Pb.

Each square in **Figure 2.6(b)** corresponds to a possible nucleus. The black dots represent stable nuclei, and the red dots represent unstable nuclei. Thus, each black dot in **Figure 2.6(b)** corresponds to a data point in the circled portion of **Figure 2.6(a)**. The decay series continues until a stable nucleus is reached, in this case ^{208}Pb. Notice that there is a branch in the decay path; there are actually two ways that thorium can decay into lead.

The entire series in **Figure 2.6(b)** consists of 10 decays: 6 alpha decays and 4 beta decays. When α decay occurs, the nucleus moves down two squares and to the left two squares because it loses two protons and two neutrons. When β^- decay occurs, the nucleus moves down one square and to the right one square because it loses one neutron and gains one proton. Gamma decays are not represented in this series because they do not alter the ratio of protons to neutrons. In other words, gamma decays do not change the atomic number (Z) or the neutron number (N). Note that the result of the decay series is to lighten the nucleus.

FIGURE 2.6

Nuclear Stability and Nuclear Decay The heaviest nuclei in the graph of all stable nuclei **(a)** are represented by the black dots in the enlarged view **(b)**. Note that an unstable nucleus (represented by the red dots) will continue to decay until the daughter nucleus is stable.

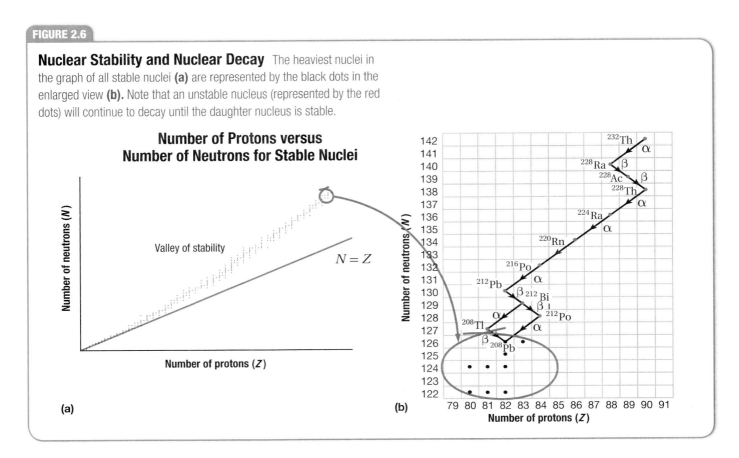

Nuclear Decay

Sample Problem B Bromine-80 decays by emitting a positron and a neutrino. Write the complete decay formula for this process.

1 ANALYZE

Given: The decay can be written symbolically as follows:

$$^{80}_{35}\text{Br} \longrightarrow \text{X} + ^{0}_{1}e + \nu$$

Unknown: The daughter element (X)

2 SOLVE

The mass numbers and atomic numbers on the two sides of the expression must be the same so that both charge and nucleon number are conserved during the course of a particular decay.

$$\text{Mass number of X} = 80 - 0 = 80$$

$$\text{Atomic number of X} = 35 - (1) = 34$$

$$^{80}_{35}\text{Br} \longrightarrow ^{80}_{34}\text{X} + ^{0}_{1}e + \nu$$

The periodic table (Appendix G) shows that the nucleus with an atomic number of 34 is selenium, Se. Thus, the process is as follows:

$$^{80}_{35}\text{Br} \longrightarrow ^{80}_{34}\text{Se} + ^{0}_{1}e + \nu$$

Practice

1. Complete this radioactive-decay formula: $^{12}_{5}\text{B} \longrightarrow ? + ^{0}_{-1}e + \overline{\nu}$
   (Refer to **Appendix G** for this problem and the following problems.)

2. Complete this radioactive-decay formula: $^{212}_{83}\text{Bi} \longrightarrow ? + ^{4}_{2}\text{He}$

3. Complete this radioactive-decay formula: $? \longrightarrow ^{131}_{54}\text{Xe} + ^{0}_{-1}e + \overline{\nu}$

4. Complete this radioactive-decay formula: $^{225}_{89}\text{Ac} \longrightarrow ^{221}_{87}\text{Fr} + ?$

5. Nickel-63 decays by β^- emission to copper-63. Write the complete decay formula for this process.

6. One of cesium's most stable isotopes undergoes beta decay (β^-) to form $^{135}_{56}\text{Ba}$. Write the equation describing this beta-decay reaction.

Measuring Nuclear Decay

Imagine that you are studying a sample of radioactive material. You know that the atoms in the material are decaying into other types of atoms. How many of the unstable parent atoms remain after a certain amount of time?

The decay constant indicates the rate of radioactive decay.

If the sample contains N radioactive parent nuclei at some instant, the number of parent nuclei that decay into daughter nuclei (ΔN) in a small time interval (Δt) is proportional to N, as follows:

$$\Delta N = -\lambda N \Delta t$$

The negative sign signifies that N decreases with time; that is, ΔN is negative. The quantity λ is called the *decay constant*. The value of λ for any isotope indicates the rate at which that isotope decays. Isotopes with a large decay constant decay quickly, and those with a small decay constant decay slowly. The number of decays per unit time, $-\Delta N/\Delta t$, is called the *decay rate,* or *activity,* of the sample. Note that the activity of a sample equals the decay constant times the number of radioactive nuclei in the sample, as follows:

$$\text{activity} = \frac{-\Delta N}{\Delta t} = \lambda N$$

The SI unit of activity is the *becquerel* (Bq). One becquerel is equal to 1 decay/s. The *curie* (Ci), which was the original unit of activity, is the approximate activity of 1 g of radium. One curie is equal to 3.7×10^{10} Bq.

Half-life measures how long it takes half a sample to decay.

Another quantity that characterizes radioactive decay is the **half-life,** written as $T_{1/2}$. The half-life of a substance is the time it takes for half of the radioactive nuclei in a sample to decay. The half-life of any substance is inversely proportional to the decay constant of the substance.

half-life the time needed for half of the original nuclei of a sample of a radioactive substance to undergo radioactive decay

Conceptual Challenge

Decay Series Suppose a radioactive parent substance with a very long half-life has a daughter with a very short half-life. Describe what happens to a freshly purified sample of the parent substance.

Probability of Decay "The more probable the decay, the shorter the half-life." Explain this statement.

Decay of Radium The radioactive nucleus $^{226}_{88}\text{Ra}$ (radium-226) has a half-life of about 1.6×10^3 years. Although the solar system is approximately 5 billion years old, we still find this radium nucleus in nature. Explain how this is possible.

Substances with large decay constants have short half-lives. The relationship between half-life and decay constant is given in the equation below. A derivation of this equation is beyond the scope of this book, but it involves the natural logarithm of 2. Because ln 2 = 0.693, this factor occurs in the final equation.

Half-Life

$$T_{1/2} = \frac{0.693}{\lambda}$$

$$\text{half-life} = \frac{0.693}{\text{decay constant}}$$

Consider a sample that begins with N radioactive nuclei. By definition, after one half-life, $\frac{1}{2}N$ radioactive nuclei remain. After two half-lives, half of these will have decayed, so $\frac{1}{4}N$ radioactive nuclei remain. After three half-lives, $\frac{1}{8}N$ will remain, and so on.

Measuring Nuclear Decay

Sample Problem C The half-life of the radioactive radium (^{226}Ra) nucleus is 5.0×10^{10} s. A sample contains 3.0×10^{16} nuclei. What is the decay constant for this decay? How many radium nuclei, in curies, will decay per second?

1 ANALYZE

Given: $T_{1/2} = 5.0 \times 10^{10}$ s $N = 3.0 \times 10^{16}$

Unknown: $\lambda = ?$ activity $= ?$ Ci

2 PLAN

Choose an equation or situation:
To find the decay constant, use the equation for half-life.

$$T_{1/2} = \frac{0.693}{\lambda}$$

The number of nuclei that decay per second is given by the equation for the activity of a sample.

$$\text{activity} = \lambda N$$

Rearrange the equation to isolate the unknown:
The first equation must be rearranged to isolate the decay constant, λ.

$$\lambda = \frac{0.693}{T_{1/2}}$$

Continued

Measuring Nuclear Decay (continued)

③ SOLVE

Substitute the values into the equations, and solve:

$$\lambda = \frac{0.693}{T_{1/2}} = \frac{0.693}{5.0 \times 10^{10}\,\text{s}}$$

$$\boxed{\lambda = 1.4 \times 10^{-11}\,\text{s}^{-1}}$$

Tips and Tricks

Always pay attention to units. Here, the activity is divided by the conversion factor $3.7 \times 10^{10}\,\text{s}^{-1}/\text{Ci}$ to convert the answer from becquerels to curies, as specified in the problem statement.

$$\text{activity} = \lambda N = \frac{(1.4 \times 10^{-11}\,\text{s}^{-1})\,(3.0 \times 10^{16})}{3.7 \times 10^{10}\,\text{s}^{-1}/\text{Ci}}$$

$$\boxed{\text{activity} = 1.1 \times 10^{-5}\,\text{Ci}}$$

④ CHECK YOUR WORK

Because the half-life is on the order of 10^{10} s, the decay constant, which approximately equals 0.7 divided by the half-life, should equal a little less than $10^{-10}\,\text{s}^{-1}$. Thus, $1.4 \times 10^{-11}\,\text{s}^{-1}$ is a reasonable answer for the decay constant.

Practice

1. The half-life of $^{214}_{84}\text{Po}$ is 164 μs. A polonium-214 sample contains 2.0×10^6 nuclei. What is the decay constant for the decay? How many polonium nuclei, in curies, will decay per second?

2. The half-life of $^{214}_{83}\text{Bi}$ is 19.7 min. A bismuth-214 sample contains 2.0×10^9 nuclei. What is the decay constant for the decay? How many bismuth nuclei, in curies, will decay per second?

3. The half-life of $^{131}_{53}\text{I}$ is 8.07 days. Calculate the decay constant for this isotope. What is the activity in Ci for a sample that contains 2.5×10^{10} iodine-131 nuclei?

4. Suppose that you start with 1.00×10^{-3} g of a pure radioactive substance and determine 2.0 h later that only 0.25×10^{-3} g of the substance is left undecayed. What is the half-life of this substance?

5. Radon-222 ($^{222}_{86}\text{Rn}$) is a radioactive gas with a half-life of 3.82 days. A gas sample contains 4.0×10^8 radon atoms initially.

   a. Estimate how many radon atoms will remain after 12 days.

   b. Estimate how many radon nuclei will have decayed by this time.

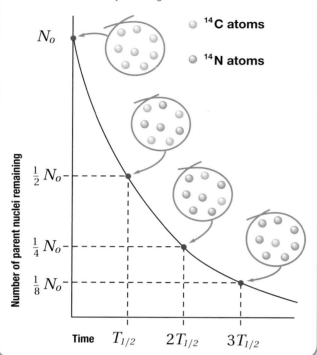

FIGURE 2.7

Half-Life of Carbon-14 The radioactive isotope carbon-14 has a half-life of 5715 years. In each successive 5715-year period, half the remaining carbon-14 nuclei decay to nitrogen-14.

- N_o
- ^{14}C atoms
- ^{14}N atoms
- $\frac{1}{2} N_o$
- $\frac{1}{4} N_o$
- $\frac{1}{8} N_o$

Number of parent nuclei remaining

Time $T_{1/2}$ $2T_{1/2}$ $3T_{1/2}$

A *decay curve* is a plot of the number of radioactive parent nuclei remaining in a sample as a function of time. A typical decay curve for a radioactive sample is shown in **Figure 2.7.** After each half-life, half the remaining parent nuclei have decayed. This is represented in the circles to the right of the decay curve. The blue spheres are the parent nuclei (carbon-14), and the red spheres are daughter nuclei (nitrogen-14). Notice that the total number of nuclei remains constant, while the number of carbon atoms continually decreases over time.

For example, the initial sample contains 8 carbon-14 atoms. After one half-life, there are 4 carbon-14 atoms and 4 nitrogen-14 atoms. By the next half-life, the number of carbon-14 atoms is reduced to 2, and the process continues. As the number of carbon-14 atoms decreases, the number of nitrogen-14 atoms increases.

Living organisms have a constant ratio of carbon-14 to carbon-12 because they continuously exchange carbon dioxide with their surroundings. When an organism dies, this ratio changes due to the decay of carbon-14. Measuring the ratio between carbon-14, which decays as shown in **Figure 2.7,** and carbon-12, which does not decay, provides an approximate date as to when the organism was alive.

✔ SECTION 2 **FORMATIVE ASSESSMENT**

▶ Reviewing Main Ideas

1. Explain the main differences between alpha, beta, and gamma decays.

2. Complete the following radioactive decay formulas:

a. $^{232}_{90}\text{Th} \rightarrow ? + ^{4}_{2}\text{He}$

b. $^{12}_{5}\text{B} \rightarrow ? + ^{0}_{-1}e + \bar{\nu}$

c. $? \rightarrow ^{4}_{2}\text{He} + ^{145}_{60}\text{Nd}$

3. A radioactive sample consists of 5.3×10^5 nuclei. There is one decay every 4.2 h.

a. What is the decay constant for the sample?

b. What is the half-life for the sample?

✔ Critical Thinking

4. The ^{14}C content decreases after the death of a living system with a half-life of 5715 years. If an archaeologist finds an ancient fire pit containing partially consumed firewood and if the ^{14}C content of the wood is only 12.5 percent that of an equal carbon sample from a present-day tree, what is the age of the ancient site?

Nuclear Reactions

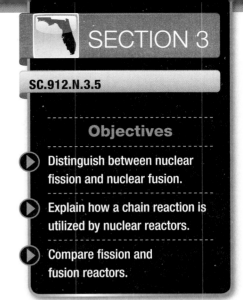

Fission and Fusion

Any process that involves a change in the nucleus of an atom is called a *nuclear reaction*. Nuclear reactions include *fission*, in which a nucleus splits into two or more nuclei, and *fusion*, in which two or more nuclei combine.

Objectives

▶ Distinguish between nuclear fission and nuclear fusion.

▶ Explain how a chain reaction is utilized by nuclear reactors.

▶ Compare fission and fusion reactors.

SC.912.N.3.5 Describe the function of models in science, and identify the wide range of models used in science.

Stable nuclei can be converted to unstable nuclei.

When a nucleus is bombarded with energetic particles, it may capture a particle, such as a neutron. As a result, the nucleus will no longer be stable and will disintegrate. For example, protons can be released when alpha particles collide with nitrogen atoms, as follows:

$$\begin{smallmatrix}4\\2\end{smallmatrix}\text{He} + \begin{smallmatrix}14\\7\end{smallmatrix}\text{N} \longrightarrow \text{X} + \begin{smallmatrix}1\\1\end{smallmatrix}\text{H}$$

According to this expression, an alpha particle ($\begin{smallmatrix}4\\2\end{smallmatrix}\text{He}$) strikes a nitrogen nucleus ($\begin{smallmatrix}14\\7\end{smallmatrix}\text{N}$) and produces an unknown product nucleus (X) and a proton ($\begin{smallmatrix}1\\1\end{smallmatrix}\text{H}$). By balancing atomic numbers and mass numbers, we can conclude that the unknown product has a mass number of 17 and an atomic number of 8. Because the element with an atomic number of 8 is oxygen, the product can be written symbolically as $\begin{smallmatrix}17\\8\end{smallmatrix}\text{O}$, and the reaction can be written as follows:

$$\begin{smallmatrix}4\\2\end{smallmatrix}\text{He} + \begin{smallmatrix}14\\7\end{smallmatrix}\text{N} \longrightarrow \begin{smallmatrix}18\\9\end{smallmatrix}\text{F} \longrightarrow \begin{smallmatrix}17\\8\end{smallmatrix}\text{O} + \begin{smallmatrix}1\\1\end{smallmatrix}\text{H}$$

This nuclear reaction starts with two stable isotopes—helium and nitrogen—that form an unstable intermediate nucleus, fluorine. The intermediate nucleus then disintegrates into two different stable isotopes, hydrogen and oxygen. This reaction, which was the first nuclear reaction to be observed, was detected by Rutherford in 1919.

Heavy nuclei can undergo nuclear fission.

Nuclear fission occurs when a heavy nucleus splits into two lighter nuclei. For fission to occur naturally, the nucleus must release energy. This means that the nucleons in the daughter nuclei must be more tightly bound and therefore have less mass than the nucleons in the parent nucleus. This decrease in mass per nucleon appears as released energy when fission occurs, often in forms such as photons or kinetic energy of the fission products. Because fission produces lighter nuclei, the binding energy per nucleon must *increase* with decreasing atomic number. **Figure 3.1** shows that this is possible only for atoms in which $A > 58$. Thus, *fission occurs naturally only for heavy atoms.*

FIGURE 3.1

Binding Energy per Nucleon

Light nuclei are very loosely bound. The binding energy of heavy nuclei is roughly the same for all nuclei.

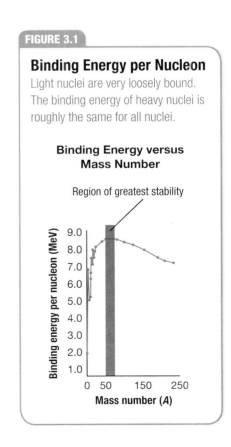

Binding Energy versus Mass Number

Region of greatest stability

One example of this process is the fission of uranium-235. First, the nucleus is bombarded with neutrons. When the nucleus absorbs a neutron, it becomes unstable and decays. The fission of ^{235}U can be represented as follows:

$$_{0}^{1}n + _{92}^{235}\text{U} \longrightarrow _{92}^{236}\text{U}^{*} \longrightarrow X + Y + \text{neutrons}$$

The isotope $_{92}^{236}\text{U}^{*}$ is an intermediate state that lasts only for about 10^{-12} s before splitting into X and Y. Many combinations of X and Y are possible. In the fission of uranium, about 90 different daughter nuclei can be formed. The process also results in the production of about two or three neutrons per fission event.

A typical reaction of this type is as follows:

$$_{0}^{1}n + _{92}^{235}\text{U} \longrightarrow _{56}^{140}\text{Ba} + _{36}^{93}\text{Kr} + 3 _{0}^{1}n$$

To estimate the energy released in a typical fission process, note that the binding energy per nucleon is about 7.6 MeV for heavy nuclei (those having a mass number of approximately 240) and about 8.5 MeV for nuclei of intermediate mass (see **Figure 3.1**). The amount of energy released in a fission event is the difference in these binding energies (8.5 MeV − 7.6 MeV, or about 0.9 MeV per nucleon). Assuming a total of 240 nucleons, this is about 220 MeV. This is a very large amount of energy relative to the energy released in typical chemical reactions. For example, the energy released in burning one molecule of the octane used in gasoline engines is about one hundred-millionth the energy released in a single fission event.

FIGURE 3.2

A Nuclear Chain Reaction A nuclear chain reaction can be initiated by the capture of a neutron.

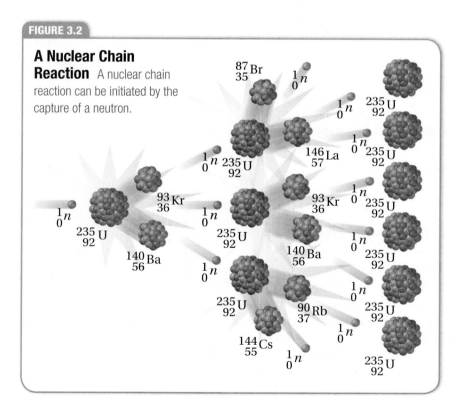

Neutrons released in fission can trigger a chain reaction.

When ^{235}U undergoes fission, an average of about 2.5 neutrons are emitted per event. The released neutrons can be captured by other nuclei, making these nuclei unstable. This triggers additional fission events, which lead to the possibility of a *chain reaction,* as shown in **Figure 3.2**. Calculations show that if the chain reaction is not controlled—that is, if it does not proceed slowly—it could result in the release of an enormous amount of energy and a violent explosion. If the energy in 1 kg of ^{235}U were released, it would equal the energy released by the detonation of about 20 000 tons of TNT. This is the principle behind the first nuclear bomb, shown in **Figure 3.3**, which was essentially an uncontrolled fission reaction.

A *nuclear reactor* is a system designed to maintain a controlled, self-sustained chain reaction. Such a system was first achieved with uranium as the fuel in 1942 by Enrico Fermi, at the University of Chicago. Primarily, it is the uranium-235 isotope that releases energy through nuclear fission. Uranium from ore typically contains only about 0.7 percent of ^{235}U, with the remaining 99.3 percent being the ^{238}U isotope. Because uranium-238 tends to absorb neutrons without fissioning, reactor fuels must be processed to increase the proportion of ^{235}U so that the reaction can sustain itself. This process is called *enrichment.*

At this time, all nuclear reactors operate through fission. One difficulty associated with fission reactors is the safe disposal of radioactive materials when the core is replaced. Transportation of reactor fuel and reactor wastes poses safety risks. As with all energy sources, the risks must be weighed against the benefits and the availability of the energy source.

Light nuclei can undergo nuclear fusion.

Nuclear fusion occurs when two light nuclei combine to form a heavier nucleus. As with fission, the product of a fusion event must have a greater binding energy than the original nuclei for energy to be released in the reaction. Because fusion reactions produce heavier nuclei, the binding energy per nucleon must increase as atomic number increases. As shown in **Figure 3.1**, this is possible only for atoms with $A < 58$. Hence, *fusion occurs naturally only for light atoms.*

One example of this process is the fusion reactions that occur in stars. All stars generate energy through fusion. About 90 percent of the stars, including our sun, fuse hydrogen and possibly helium. Some other stars fuse helium or other heavier elements. The *proton-proton cycle* is a series of three nuclear-fusion reactions that are believed to be stages in the liberation of energy in our sun and other stars rich in hydrogen. In the proton-proton cycle, four protons combine to form an alpha particle and two positrons, releasing 25 MeV of energy in the process. The first two steps in this cycle are as follows:

$$^1_1\text{H} + {}^1_1\text{H} \longrightarrow {}^2_1\text{H} + {}^0_1 e + \nu$$

$$^1_1\text{H} + {}^2_1\text{H} \longrightarrow {}^3_2\text{He} + \gamma$$

This is followed by either of the following processes:

$$^1_1\text{H} + {}^3_2\text{He} \longrightarrow {}^4_2\text{He} + {}^0_1 e + \nu$$

$$^3_2\text{He} + {}^3_2\text{He} \longrightarrow {}^4_2\text{He} + {}^1_1\text{H} + {}^1_1\text{H}$$

The released energy is carried primarily by gamma rays, positrons, and neutrinos. These energy-liberating fusion reactions are called *thermonuclear fusion reactions.* The hydrogen (fusion) bomb, first detonated in 1952, is an example of an uncontrolled thermonuclear fusion reaction.

FIGURE 3.3

Atomic Bomb The first nuclear fission bomb, often called the *atomic bomb,* was tested in New Mexico in 1945.

Did YOU Know?

What has been called the *atomic bomb* since 1945 is actually a tremendous *nuclear fission* reaction. Likewise, the so-called *hydrogen bomb* is an uncontrolled *nuclear fusion* reaction in which hydrogen nuclei merge to form helium nuclei.

Fusion reactors are being developed.

The enormous amount of energy released in fusion reactions suggests the possibility of harnessing this energy for useful purposes on Earth. Efforts are under way to create controlled thermonuclear reactions in the form of a *fusion reactor*. Because of the ready availability of its fuel source—water—controlled fusion is often called the ultimate energy source.

For example, if deuterium ($_1^2H$) were used as the fuel, 0.16 g of deuterium could be extracted from just 1 L of water at a cost of about one cent. Such rates would make the fuel costs of even an inefficient reactor almost insignificant. An additional advantage of fusion reactors is that few radioactive byproducts are formed. The proton-proton cycle shows that the end product of the fusion of hydrogen nuclei is safe, nonradioactive helium. Unfortunately, a thermonuclear reactor that can deliver a net power output for an extended time is not yet a reality. Many difficulties must be resolved before a successful device is constructed.

For example, the energy released in a gas undergoing nuclear fusion depends on the number of fusion reactions that can occur in a given amount of time. This varies with the density of the gas because collisions are more frequent in a denser gas. It also depends on the amount of time the gas is confined.

In addition, the Coulomb repulsion force between two charged nuclei must be overcome before they can fuse. The fundamental challenge is to give the nuclei enough kinetic energy to overcome this repulsive force. This can be accomplished by heating the fuel to extremely high temperatures (about 10^8 K, or about 10 times greater than the interior temperature of the sun). Such high temperatures are difficult and expensive to obtain in a laboratory or a power plant.

✓ SECTION 3 FORMATIVE ASSESSMENT

▶ Reviewing Main Ideas

1. What are the similarities and differences between fission and fusion?

2. Explain how nuclear reactors utilize chain reactions.

3. What is enrichment? Why is enrichment necessary when uranium is used as a reactor fuel?

4. A fission reaction leads to the formation of ^{141}Ba and ^{92}Kr when ^{235}U absorbs a neutron.
   a. How is this reaction expressed symbolically?
   b. How many neutrons are released in this reaction?

5. What are some advantages to fusion reactors (as opposed to fission reactors)? What are some difficulties in the development of a fusion reactor?

✓ Critical Thinking

6. Why would a fusion reactor produce less radioactive waste material than a fission reactor does?

Particle Physics

The Particle View of Nature

Particle physics seeks to discover the ultimate structure of matter: *elementary particles*. Elementary particles, which are the fundamental units that compose matter, do not appear to be divisible and have neither size nor structure.

Many new particles have been produced in accelerators.

Until 1932, scientists thought protons and electrons were elementary particles because these particles were stable. However, beginning in 1945, experiments at particle accelerators, such as the Stanford Linear Accelerator shown in **Figure 4.1,** have demonstrated that new particles are often formed in high-energy collisions between known particles. These new particles tend to be very unstable and have very short half-lives, ranging from 10^{-6} s to 10^{-23} s. So far, more than 300 new particles have been catalogued.

There are four fundamental interactions in nature.

All particles in nature are subject to four fundamental forces: *strong*, *electromagnetic*, *weak*, and *gravitational*. Let us examine each of these in turn, starting with the strongest of the four, the strong interaction.

The *strong force* is responsible for the tight binding of quarks to form neutrons and protons and for the nuclear force, a sort of residual strong force binding neutrons and protons into nuclei. This force represents the "glue" that holds the nucleons together. Without it, the Coulomb repulsion between protons would cause the nucleus to fly apart. The strong interaction is the strongest of all the fundamental forces and is a short-range force that is negligible for separations greater than about 10^{-15} m (the approximate size of the nucleus).

The *electromagnetic force,* which is about 10^{-2} times the strength of the strong force, is responsible for the binding of atoms and molecules. It is a long-range force that decreases in strength as the inverse square of the separation of the interacting particles. In the nineteenth century, it was known that a current-carrying wire produces a magnetic field, that a changing magnetic field near a loop of wire can produce a current, and that oscillating electric and magnetic fields are the building blocks of light. However, these were considered to be unrelated phenomena until James Clerk Maxwell (1831–1879) showed that these were manifestations of the underlying electromagnetic force.

The *weak force* is a short-range nuclear force that tends to produce instability in certain nuclei. It is responsible for beta decay, and its strength is only about 10^{-13} times that of the strong force. Scientists now believe that the weak and electromagnetic forces are manifestations of a

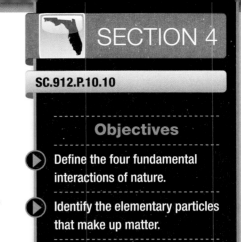

Objectives

- Define the four fundamental interactions of nature.
- Identify the elementary particles that make up matter.
- Describe the standard model of the universe.

SC.912.P.10.10 Compare the magnitude and range of the four fundamental forces (gravitational, electromagnetic, weak nuclear, strong nuclear).

FIGURE 4.1

Particle Accelerator

The Stanford Linear Accelerator, in California, creates high-energy particle collisions that provide evidence of new particles.

©David Parker/Photo Researchers, Inc.

single force called the *electroweak force*. For their work with the unification of these forces, Sheldon Glashow (b. 1932), Steven Weinberg (b. 1933), and Abdus Salam (1926–1996) received the Nobel Prize in 1979.

A theory that unifies the electromagnetic and weak interactions, called the *electroweak theory*, postulates that the weak and electromagnetic interactions have the same strength at very high particle energies. The photon and the three massive W and Z bosons play a key role in the electroweak theory. The theory makes many predictions, but the most spectacular is the predictions of the masses of the W and Z particles at about 82 GeV/c^2 and 93 GeV/c^2, respectively. These particles were subsequently discovered at the CERN Laboratory in Geneva, Switzerland, leading to the 1984 Nobel Prize in Physics for Carlo Rubbia and Simon van der Meer.

The *gravitational force* is a long-range interaction with a strength of approximately 10^{-38} times that of the strong force. Although this familiar interaction is the force that holds the planets, stars, and galaxies together, its effect on elementary particles is negligible.

A force can be thought of as mediated by an exchange of particles.

There is an obvious problem with the law of gravity as stated by Newton, and Newton, himself, recognized the flaw in his work. How does an object, such as the sun, reach out across millions of miles of space and exert a force on another object, such as Earth? Newton left the solution to that question to the consideration of others.

Scientists now believe that all of the fundamental forces are transmitted by the exchange of particles or quanta between the interacting objects. In the case of the familiar electromagnetic interaction, the field particles are photons. In the language of modern physics, it can be said that the electromagnetic force is *mediated* (carried) by photons, which are the quanta of the electromagnetic field. **Figure 4.2** is a diagram depicting the repulsion of two electrons through the exchange of a photon. Such diagrams are called Feynman diagrams, introduced by Nobel Prize–winning physicist Richard Feynman (1918–1988).

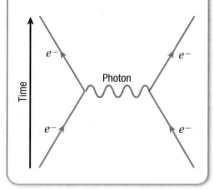

FIGURE 4.2

Feynman Diagram of Electrons Exchanging a Photon In particle physics, the electromagnetic interaction is modeled as an exchange of photons. The wavy red line represents a photon, and the blue lines represent electrons.

FIGURE 4.3

THE FUNDAMENTAL INTERACTIONS OF NATURE

Interaction (force)	Relative strength	Range of force	Mediating field particle
strong	1	≈ 1 fm	gluon
electro-magnetic	10^{-2}	proportional to $1/r^2$	photon
weak	10^{-13}	$< 10^{-3}$ fm	$W^\pm$ and Z bosons
gravitational	10^{-38}	proportional to $1/r^2$	graviton

Likewise, the strong force is mediated by field particles called *gluons*, the weak force is mediated by the W and Z *bosons*, and the gravitational force is mediated by quanta of the gravitational field called *gravitons*. All of these field quanta have been detected except for the graviton, which may never be found directly because of the weakness of the gravitational field. These interactions, their ranges, and their relative strengths are summarized in **Figure 4.3** on the previous page.

Did YOU Know?

The interaction of charged particles by the exchange of photons is described by a theory called *quantum electrodynamics*, or *QED*.

Classification of Particles

All particles other than the mediating field particles can be classified into two broad categories: *leptons* and *hadrons*. The difference between the two is whether they interact through the strong interaction. Leptons are a group of particles that participate in the weak, gravitational, and electromagnetic interactions but not in the strong interaction. Hadrons are particles that interact through all four fundamental interactions, including the strong interaction.

Leptons are thought to be elementary particles.

Electrons and neutrinos are both leptons. Like all leptons, they have no measurable size or internal structure and do not seem to break down into smaller units. Because of this, *leptons appear to be truly elementary*.

The number of known leptons is small. Currently, scientists believe there are only six leptons: the electron, the muon, the tau, and a neutrino associated with each. Each of these six leptons also has an antiparticle.

Hadrons include mesons and baryons.

Hadrons, the strongly interacting particles, can be further divided into two classes: *mesons* and *baryons*. Originally, mesons and baryons were classified according to their masses. Baryons were heavier than mesons, and both were heavier than leptons. However, this distinction no longer holds. Today, mesons and baryons are distinguished by their internal structure.

All mesons are unstable. Because of this, they are not constituents of normal, everyday matter. Baryons have masses equal to or greater than the proton mass. The most common examples of baryons are protons and neutrons, which are constituents of normal, everyday matter. A summary of this classification of particles is given in **Figure 4.4**.

Hadrons are thought to be made of quarks.

Particle-collision experiments involving hadrons seem to involve many short-lived particles, implying that hadrons are made up of more fundamental particles. Furthermore, there are numerous hadrons, and many of them are known to decay into other hadrons. These facts strongly suggest that hadrons, unlike leptons, cannot be truly elementary.

In 1963, Murray Gell-Mann and George Zweig independently proposed that hadrons have a more elementary substructure. According to

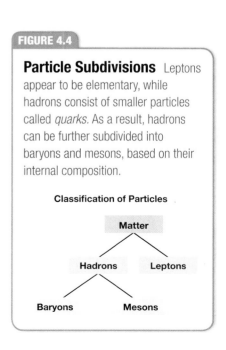

FIGURE 4.4

Particle Subdivisions Leptons appear to be elementary, while hadrons consist of smaller particles called *quarks*. As a result, hadrons can be further subdivided into baryons and mesons, based on their internal composition.

Classification of Particles

Matter

Hadrons   Leptons

Baryons   Mesons

their model, all hadrons are composed of two or three fundamental particles, which came to be called *quarks.* In the original model, there were three types of quarks, designated by the symbols *u, d,* and *s.* These were given the arbitrary names *up, down,* and *sideways* (now more commonly referred to as *strange*). Associated with each quark is an antiquark of opposite charge.

The difference between mesons and baryons is due to the number of quarks that compose them. The compositions of all hadrons known when Gell-Mann and Zweig presented their models could be completely specified by three simple rules, which are summarized in **Figure 4.5.**

Later evidence from collision experiments encouraged theorists to propose the existence of three more quarks, now known as *charm, top,* and *bottom.* These six quarks seem to fit together in pairs: up and down, charm and strange, and top and bottom.

All quarks have a charge associated with them. The charge of a hadron is equal to the sum of the charges of its constituent quarks and is either zero or a multiple of *e,* the fundamental unit of charge. This implies that quarks have a very unusual property—fractional electric charge. In other words, the charge of the electron is no longer thought to be the smallest possible nonzero charge that a particle can have. The charges for all six quarks that have been discovered and their corresponding antiquarks are summarized in **Figure 4.7.**

FIGURE 4.5

HADRONS

Particle	Composition
meson	one quark and one antiquark
baryon	three quarks
antibaryon	three antiquarks

FIGURE 4.7

CHARGES OF QUARKS AND ANTIQUARKS

Quark	Charge	Antiquark	Charge
up (*u*)	$+\frac{2}{3}e$	$\bar{u}$	$-\frac{2}{3}e$
down (*d*)	$-\frac{1}{3}e$	$\bar{d}$	$+\frac{1}{3}e$
charm (*c*)	$+\frac{2}{3}e$	$\bar{c}$	$-\frac{2}{3}e$
strange (*s*)	$-\frac{1}{3}e$	$\bar{s}$	$+\frac{1}{3}e$
top (*t*)	$+\frac{2}{3}e$	$\bar{t}$	$-\frac{2}{3}e$
bottom (*b*)	$-\frac{1}{3}e$	$\bar{b}$	$+\frac{1}{3}e$

FIGURE 4.6

Quarks Baryons contain three quarks, while mesons contain a quark and an antiquark. The baryons represented are a proton (p^+) and a neutron (*n*). The mesons shown are a pion (π^+) and a kaon (K^-), both rare particles.

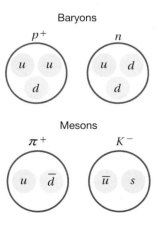

Figure 4.6 represents the quark compositions of several hadrons, both baryons and mesons. Just two of the quarks, *u* and *d,* are needed to construct the hadrons encountered in ordinary matter (protons and neutrons). The other quarks are needed only to construct rare forms of matter that are typically found only in high-energy situations, such as particle collisions.

The charges of the quarks that make up each hadron in **Figure 4.6** add up to zero or a multiple of *e.* For example, the proton contains three quarks (u, u, and d) having charges of $+\frac{2}{3}e$, $+\frac{2}{3}e$, and $-\frac{1}{3}e$. The total charge of the proton is $+e$, as you would expect. Likewise, the total charge of quarks in a neutron is zero ($+\frac{2}{3}e$, $-\frac{1}{3}e$, and $-\frac{1}{3}e$).

You may be wondering whether such discoveries will ever end. At present, physicists believe that six quarks and six leptons (and their antiparticles) are the fundamental particles. Despite many extensive efforts, no isolated quark has ever been observed. Physicists now believe that quarks are permanently confined inside ordinary particles by the strong force. This force is often called the *color force* for quarks. Of course, quarks are not really colored. Color is merely a name given to the property of quarks that allows them to attract one another and form composite particles. The attractive force between nucleons is a byproduct of the strong force between quarks.

The Standard Model

The current model used in particle physics to understand matter is called the *standard model*. This model was developed over many years by a variety of people. Although the details of the standard model are complex, the model's essential elements can be summarized by using **Figure 4.8.**

According to the standard model, the strong force is mediated by gluons. This force holds quarks together to form composite particles, such as protons, neutrons, and mesons. Leptons participate only in the electromagnetic, gravitational, and weak interactions. The combination of composite particles, such as protons and neutrons, with leptons, such as electrons, makes the constituents of all matter, which are atoms.

FIGURE 4.8

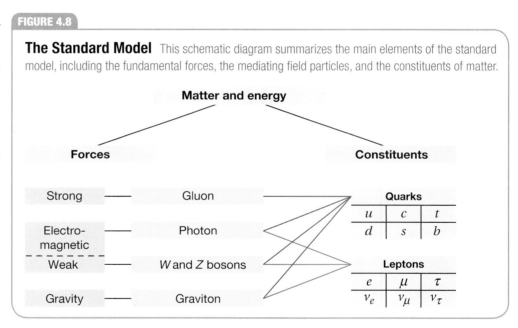

The Standard Model This schematic diagram summarizes the main elements of the standard model, including the fundamental forces, the mediating field particles, and the constituents of matter.

The standard model can help explain the early universe.

Particle physics helps us understand the evolution of the universe. If we extrapolate our knowledge of the history of the universe, we find that time itself goes back only about 13 billion to 15 billion years. At that time, the universe was inconceivably dense. In the brief instant after this singular moment, the universe expanded rapidly in an event called the *big bang*. Immediately afterward, there were such extremes in the density of matter and energy that all four fundamental interactions of physics operated in a single, unified way. The temperatures and energy present reduced everything into an undifferentiated "quark soup."

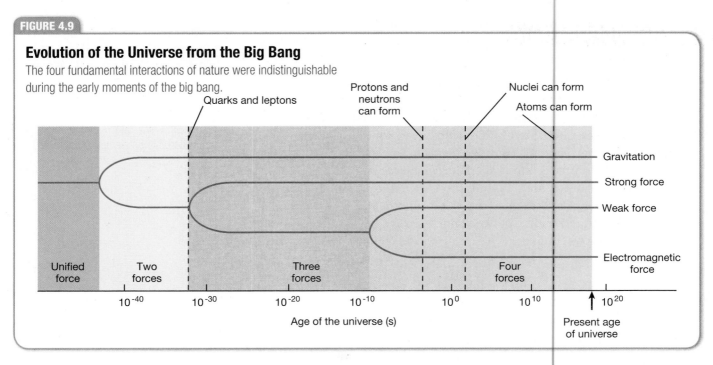

FIGURE 4.9

Evolution of the Universe from the Big Bang

The four fundamental interactions of nature were indistinguishable during the early moments of the big bang.

Quarks and leptons

Protons and neutrons can form

Nuclei can form

Atoms can form

Gravitation

Strong force

Weak force

Electromagnetic force

Unified force

Two forces

Three forces

Four forces

10^{-40} 10^{-30} 10^{-20} 10^{-10} 10^{0} 10^{10} 10^{20}

Age of the universe (s)

Present age of universe

The evolution of the four fundamental interactions from the big bang to the present is shown in **Figure 4.9**. During the first 10^{-43} s, it is presumed that the strong, electroweak (electromagnetic and weak), and gravitational interactions were joined together. From 10^{-43} s to 10^{-32} s after the big bang, gravity broke free of this unification while the strong and electroweak interactions remained as one. This was a period when particle energies were so great (greater than 10^{16} GeV) that very massive particles that are now rare, as well as quarks, leptons, and their antiparticles, existed.

Then the universe rapidly expanded and cooled, the strong and electroweak interactions parted, and the grand unification was broken. About 10^{-10} s after the big bang, as the universe continued to cool, the electroweak interaction split into the weak interaction and the electromagnetic interaction.

Until about 7×10^5 years (2×10^{13} s) after the big bang, most of the energy in the universe was in the form of radiation rather than matter. This was the era of the radiation-dominated universe. Such intense radiation prevented matter from forming even single hydrogen atoms. Matter did exist, but only in the form of ions and electrons. Electrons are strong scatterers of photons, so matter at this time was opaque to radiation. Matter continuously absorbed and reemitted photons, thereby ensuring thermal equilibrium of radiation and matter.

By the time the universe was about 380 000 years (1×10^{13} s) old, it had expanded and cooled to about 3000 K. At this temperature, protons could bind to electrons to form hydrogen atoms. Without free electrons to scatter photons, the universe suddenly became transparent. Matter and radiation no longer interacted as strongly, and each evolved separately. By this time, most of the energy in the universe was in the form of matter. Clumps of neutral matter steadily grew: first atoms, followed by molecules, gas clouds, stars, and finally galaxies. This period, referred to as the matter-dominated universe, continues to this day.

The standard model is still incomplete.

While particle physicists have been exploring the realm of the very small, cosmologists have been exploring cosmic history back to the first microsecond of the big bang. Observation of the events that occur when two particles collide in an accelerator is essential to reconstructing the early moments in cosmic history. Perhaps the key to understanding the early universe is to first understand the world of elementary particles. Cosmologists and particle physicists find that they have many common goals, and they are working together to attempt to study the physical world at its most fundamental level.

Our understanding of physics at short distances is far from complete. Particle physics still faces many questions. For example, why does the photon have no mass, while the W and Z bosons do? Because of this mass difference, the electromagnetic and weak forces are quite distinct at low energies, such as those in everyday life, but they behave in similar ways at very high energies.

To account for these changes, the standard model proposes the existence of a particle called the *Higgs boson,* which exists only at the high energies at which the electromagnetic and weak forces begin to merge. On July 4, 2012, an international team of scientists working at the Large Hadron Collider in Europe announced they had detected a new heavy particle that resembled the Higgs boson. This unstable particle was reported to have a mass of around 126 GeV, consistent with the standard model.

There are still other questions that the standard model has yet to answer. Is it possible to unify the strong and electroweak theories in a logical and consistent manner? Why do quarks and leptons form three similar but distinct families? Are muons the same as electrons (apart from their different masses), or do they have other subtle differences that have not been detected? Why are some particles charged and others neutral? Why do quarks carry a fractional charge? What determines the masses of the fundamental constituents? Can isolated quarks exist? The questions go on and on. Because of the rapid advances and new discoveries in the field of particle physics, by the time you read this book, some of these questions may have been resolved, while new questions may have emerged.

 SECTION 4 **FORMATIVE ASSESSMENT**

● Reviewing Main Ideas

1. Name the four fundamental interactions and the particles that mediate each interaction.

2. What are the differences between hadrons and leptons? What are the differences between baryons and mesons?

3. Describe the main stages of the evolution of the universe according to the big bang theory.

4. What evidence do scientists have for the existence of strong forces? weak forces? What effects do these forces have in nature?

Antimatter

Startling discoveries made in the twentieth century have confirmed that electrons and other particles of matter have *antiparticles.* Antiparticles have the same mass as their corresponding particle but an opposite charge.

The Discovery of Antiparticles

The discovery of antiparticles began in the 1920s with work by the theoretical physicist Paul Adrien Maurice Dirac (1902–1984), who developed a version of quantum mechanics that incorporated Einstein's theory of special relativity. Dirac's theory was successful in many respects, but it had one major problem: its relativistic wave equation required solutions corresponding to negative energy states. This negative set of solutions suggested the existence of something like an electron but with an opposite charge, just as the negative energy states were opposite to an electron's typical energy states. At the time, there was no experimental evidence of such antiparticles.

In 1932, shortly after Dirac's theory was introduced, evidence of the antielectron was discovered by the American physicist Carl Anderson. The antielectron, also known as the *positron,* has the same mass as the electron but is positively charged. Anderson found the positron while examining tracks created by electronlike particles in a cloud chamber placed in a magnetic field. As described in the chapter "Magnetism," such a field will cause moving particles to follow curved paths. The direction in which a particle moves depends on whether its charge is positive or negative. Anderson noted that some of the tracks had deflections typical of an electron's mass but in the opposite direction, corresponding to a positively charged particle.

Pair Production and Annihilation

Since Anderson's initial discovery, the positron has been observed in a number of experiments. In perhaps the most common process, a gamma ray with sufficiently high energy collides with a nucleus, creating an electron-positron pair. An example of this process, known as *pair production,* is shown in **Figure 1**. During pair production, the energy of the photon is completely converted into the rest energy and kinetic energy of the electron and the positron. Thus, pair production is a striking verification of the equivalence of mass (rest energy) and other forms of energy as predicted by Einstein's special theory of relativity. (This equivalence is discussed in the feature "The Equivalence of Mass and Energy.")

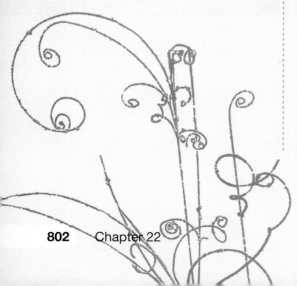

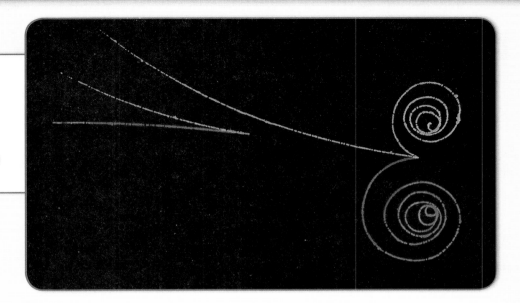

Once formed, a positron will most likely soon collide with an oppositely charged electron in a process known as *pair annihilation.* This process is the opposite of pair production—an electron-positron pair produces two photons. In the simplest example of pair annihilation, an electron and a positron initially at rest combine with each other and disappear, leaving behind two photons. Because the initial momentum of the electron-positron pair is zero, it is impossible to produce a single photon. Momentum can be conserved only if two photons moving in opposite directions, both with the same energy and magnitude of momentum, are produced.

Antimatter Produced in a Particle Accelerator

After the positron was discovered, physicists began to search for the antiproton and antineutron. However, because the proton and neutron are much more massive than the electron, a much greater amount of energy is required to produce their antiparticles. By 1955, technological advances in particle accelerators brought evidence of the antiproton, and evidence of the antineutron was found a year later.

The discovery of other antiparticles leads to the question of whether these antiparticles can be combined to form antimatter and, if so, how that antimatter would behave. In 1995, physicists at the CERN particle accelerator in Geneva, Switzerland, succeeded in producing antihydrogen atoms, that is, atoms with a single antielectron orbiting an antiproton. Researchers observed nine antihydrogen atoms during a three-week period, but the longest they were able to store them was for less than 37 billionths of a second! Clearly, more time with the atoms was needed to interact with them. In June 2011, scientists at CERN reported that they succeeded in trapping antimatter atoms for more than 16 minutes. Now that they are able to study these atoms for longer time periods, scientists hope to study the properties of antihydrogen, specifically to see if it has the same spectral lines as hydrogen.

Subatomic Physics **803**

Radiologist

A radiologist's job is to interpret many different kinds of medical images, including those from X-rays, CT scans, fluoroscopy, and angiography. To learn more about radiology as a career, read the interview with Katherine Maturen, who works in a large, university-based hospital in Michigan.

Katherine Maturen reviews a CT scan of an abdomen on a digital workstation.

What schooling did you receive in order to become a radiologist?

I attended four years of college, four years of medical school, and five years of specialty training in radiology.

What influenced your decision to become a radiologist?

During college, I studied a lot of different things and did not decide to go to medical school until my senior year. In medical school, I considered several different specialties before deciding on radiology. The fact that many radiologists seem to really enjoy their work was certainly influential.

What about radiology makes it interesting to you?

Radiology is primarily concerned with diagnosis, which can be like a fun puzzle in really challenging cases. I like the problem-solving aspect. I love anatomy, and I find the many different kinds of radiological images aesthetically pleasing. Another attraction of radiology is to see and understand disease processes.

What kinds of skills are important for a radiologist?

Good observation skills, attention to detail, and a strong knowledge of normal anatomy are essential for a radiologist. The best radiologists also have a thorough understanding of disease processes and the physics of imaging. Finally, the ability to develop rapport both with patients and medical colleagues is very important.

What is your favorite thing about your job?

My favorite thing is reading studies and making diagnoses. The only thing I don't like is long hours and working all night, for obvious reasons!

What advice do you have for students who are interested in radiology?

You should pursue what interests you, regardless of other people's expectations of you or what you have done in the past. Try new things and follow your intellectual curiosity. Remember, you want a job that is actually interesting to you, not just a way to pay the bills.

If you think medical school sounds like too much school, consider radiological technologist programs, where you will be the one working with patients and actually taking most of the pictures. If you decide to go to medical school, don't spend all of your time in college taking science classes. Broaden your horizons and learn about things outside of medicine. And in medical school, pay attention in anatomy lab!

Katherine Maturen

Applications of Atomic and Nuclear Phenomena

Atomic and nuclear phenomena involve the properties of atomic nuclei. There are many important applications of nuclear phenomena, ranging from medical technology to home consumer goods to electrical power generation. Consider applications described throughout the textbook, and perform additional research to address the following tasks:

- Describe two medical devices that rely on atomic and nuclear phenomena.

- Excluding medical applications, describe two industrial, consumer, or scientific devices that rely on atomic and nuclear phenomena.

- Provide a description of at least one future application of nuclear phenomena that is currently being researched and developed.

Conceptual Challenge

The ability to make assumptions and generate rough estimates is a valuable skill to scientists. Quick estimates allow scientists to narrow the range of possibilities and focus on the most reasonable hypotheses.

Nuclear Fission Consider the amount of electrical energy consumed by an average household for one month. With the use of nuclear fission, how many uranium atoms would be required to power an average household for one year?

You can begin addressing the scenario by asking questions such as the following:

- How much energy does an average household consume each day?

- How much energy is released from each fission event?

- How does that energy released translate into kilowatt-hours of electrical energy?

BIG IDEA Interactions of subatomic particles result in the formation of atoms and other particles. Four fundamental forces are involved in these interactions: strong force, weak force, electromagnetic force, and gravitational force.

SECTION 1 The Nucleus

KEY TERMS

- The nucleus, which consists of protons and neutrons, is the small, dense core of an atom.
- A nucleus can be characterized by a mass number, A, an atomic number, Z, and a neutron number, N.
- The binding energy of a nucleus is the difference in energy between its nucleons when bound and its nucleons when unbound.

isotope
strong force
binding energy

SECTION 2 Nuclear Decay

KEY TERM

- An unstable nucleus can decay in three ways: alpha (α) decay, beta (β) decay, or gamma (γ) decay.
- The decay constant, λ, indicates the rate of radioactive decay.
- The half-life, $T_{1/2}$, is the time required for half the original nuclei of a radioactive substance to undergo radioactive decay.

half-life

SECTION 3 Nuclear Reactions

- Nuclear reactions involve a change in the nucleus of an atom.
- In fission, a heavy nucleus splits into two lighter nuclei. In fusion, two light nuclei combine to form a heavier nucleus.

SECTION 4 Particle Physics

- There are four fundamental interactions in nature: strong, weak, gravitational, and electromagnetic.
- The constituents of matter can be classified as leptons or hadrons, and hadrons can be further divided into mesons and baryons. Electrons and neutrinos are leptons. Protons and neutrons are baryons.
- Mesons consist of a quark-antiquark pair; baryons consist of three quarks.

PARTICLE SYMBOLS	
Particle name	**Symbol**
alpha particle (helium nucleus)	α ($^4_2$He)
beta particle (electron)	β^- ($^{0}_{-1}$e)
beta particle (positron)	β^+ ($^{0}_{-1}$e)
gamma ray	γ
neutron	n ($^1_0 n$)
proton	p ($^1_1 p$)
neutrino	ν
antineutrino	$\bar{\nu}$

VARIABLE SYMBOLS				
Quantities		**Units**		**Conversions**
m	mass	u	atomic mass unit	= $1.660\,539 \times 10^{-27}$ kg = 931.49 MeV/c^2
λN	activity or decay rate	Bq Ci	becquerel curie	= 1 decay/s = 3.7×10^{10} Bq
$T_{1/2}$	half-life	s	seconds	

Problem Solving

See **Appendix D: Equations** for a summary of the equations introduced in this chapter. If you need more problem-solving practice, see **Appendix I: Additional Problems.**

The Nucleus

▶ **REVIEWING MAIN IDEAS**

1. How many protons are there in the nucleus $^{197}_{79}Au$? How many neutrons? How many electrons are there in the neutral atom?

2. What are isotopes?

3. What holds the nucleons in a nucleus together?

CONCEPTUAL QUESTIONS

4. Is it possible to accurately predict an atom's mass from its atomic number? Explain.

5. What would happen if the binding energy of a nucleus were zero?

6. Why do heavier elements require more neutrons to maintain stability?

PRACTICE PROBLEMS

For problems 7–9, see Sample Problem A and refer to Appendix H.

7. Calculate the total binding energy of $^{12}_{6}C$.

8. Calculate the total binding energy of tritium ($^{3}_{1}H$) and helium-3 ($^{3}_{2}He$).

9. Calculate the average binding energy per nucleon of $^{24}_{12}Mg$ and $^{85}_{37}Rb$.

Nuclear Decay and Reactions

▶ **REVIEWING MAIN IDEAS**

10. Explain the main differences between alpha, beta, and gamma emissions.

11. The figure below shows the steps by which $^{235}_{92}U$ decays to $^{207}_{82}Pb$. Draw this diagram, and enter the correct isotope symbol in each square.

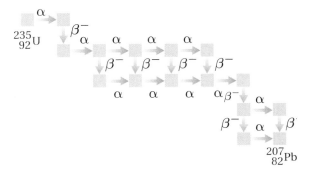

12. What factors make fusion difficult to achieve?

CONCEPTUAL QUESTIONS

13. If a film is kept in a box, alpha particles from a radioactive source outside the box cannot expose the film, but beta particles can. Explain.

14. An alpha particle has twice the charge of a beta particle. Why does the beta particle deflect more when both pass between electrically charged plates, assuming they both have the same speed?

15. Suppose you have a single atom of a radioactive material whose half-life is one year. Can you be certain that the nucleus will have decayed after two years? Explain.

16. Why is carbon dating unable to provide accurate estimates of very old materials?

17. A free neutron undergoes beta decay with a half-life of about 15 min. Can a free proton undergo a similar decay? (Hint: Compare the masses of the proton and the neutron.)

18. Is it possible for a $^{12}_{6}C$ (12.000 000 u) nucleus to spontaneously decay into three alpha particles? Explain.

19. Why is the temperature required for deuterium-tritium fusion lower than that needed for deuterium-deuterium fusion? (Hint: Consider the Coulomb repulsion and nuclear attraction for each case.)

PRACTICE PROBLEMS

For problems 20–21, see Sample Problem B.

20. Determine the product of the following reaction:
$^7_3\text{Li} + ^4_2\text{He} \rightarrow ? + ^1_0n$

21. Complete the following nuclear reactions:
a. $? + ^{14}_7\text{N} \rightarrow ^1_1\text{H} + ^{17}_8\text{O}$
b. $^7_3\text{Li} + ^1_1\text{H} \rightarrow ^4_2\text{He} + ?$

For problems 22–24, see Sample Problem C.

22. A radioactive sample contains 1.67×10^{11} atoms of $^{108}_{47}\text{Ag}$ (half-life $= 2.42$ min) at some instant. Calculate the decay constant and the activity of the sample in mCi.

23. How long will it take a sample of polonium-210 with a half-life of 140 days to decay to one-sixteenth its original strength?

24. The amount of carbon-14 ($^{14}_6\text{C}$) in a wooden artifact is measured to be 6.25 percent the amount in a fresh sample of wood from the same region. The half-life of carbon-14 is 5715 years. Assuming the same amount of carbon-14 was initially present in the artifact, determine the age of the artifact.

Particle Physics

▶ **REVIEWING MAIN IDEAS**

25. Describe the properties of quarks.

26. What is the electric charge of the particles with the following quark compositions?
a. udd
b. uud
c. $u\bar{d}$

27. What is the electric charge of the baryons with the following quark compositions?
a. $\bar{u}\bar{u}\bar{d}$
b. $\bar{u}\bar{d}\bar{d}$

28. What are each of the baryons in item 27 called?

29. How many quarks or antiquarks are there in the following particles?
a. a baryon
b. an antibaryon
c. a meson
d. an antimeson

CONCEPTUAL QUESTIONS

30. Compare a neutrino with a photon.

31. Consider the statement "All mesons are hadrons, but not all hadrons are mesons." Is this statement true? Explain.

Mixed Review

▶ **REVIEWING MAIN IDEAS**

32. Complete the following nuclear reaction:
$^{27}_{13}\text{Al} + ^4_2\text{He} \rightarrow ? + ^{30}_{15}\text{P}?$

33. Consider the hydrogen atom to be a sphere with a radius equal to the Bohr radius, 0.53×10^{-10} m, and calculate the approximate value of the ratio of atomic density to nuclear density.

34. Certain stars are thought to collapse at the end of their lives, combining their protons and electrons to form a neutron star. Such a star could be thought of as a giant atomic nucleus. If a star with a mass equal to that of the sun (1.99×10^{30} kg) were to collapse into neutrons, what would be the radius of the star?

35. Calculate the difference in binding energy for the two nuclei $^{15}_8\text{O}$ and $^{15}_7\text{N}$.

36. A piece of charcoal known to be approximately 25 000 years old contains 7.96×10^{10} C-14 atoms.
a. Determine the number of decays per minute expected from this sample. (The half-life of C-14 is 5715 years.)
b. If the radioactive background in the counter without a sample is 20.0 counts per minute and we assume 100.0 percent efficiency in counting, explain why 25 000 years is close to the limit of dating with this technique.

37. Natural gold has only one stable isotope, $^{197}_{79}Au$. If gold is bombarded with slow neutrons, β^- particles are emitted.
   a. Write the appropriate reaction equation.
   b. Calculate the maximum energy of the emitted beta particles.

38. Two ways ^{235}U can undergo fission when bombarded with a neutron are described below. In each case, neutrons are also released. Find the number of neutrons released in each of the following:
   a. ^{140}Xe and ^{94}Sr released as fission fragments
   b. ^{132}Sn and ^{101}Mo released as fission fragments

39. When a ^6_3Li nucleus is struck by a proton, an alpha particle and a product nucleus are released. What is the product nucleus?

40. Suppose $^{10}_5B$ is struck by an alpha particle, releasing a proton and a product nucleus in the reaction. What is the product nucleus?

41. An all-electric home uses about 2.0×10^3 kW•h of electrical energy per month. How many ^{235}U atoms would be required to provide this house with its energy needs for one year? Assume 100.0 percent conversion efficiency and 208 MeV released per fission.

42. When ^{18}O is struck by a proton, ^{18}F and another particle are produced. What is the other particle?

43. When a star has exhausted its hydrogen fuel, it may fuse other nuclear fuels, such as helium. At temperatures above 1.0×10^8 K, helium fusion can occur.
   a. Two alpha particles fuse to produce a nucleus, A, and a gamma ray. What is nucleus A?
   b. Nucleus A absorbs an alpha particle to produce a nucleus, B, and a gamma ray. What is nucleus B?

44. A sample of a radioactive isotope is measured to have an activity of 240.0 mCi. If the sample has a half-life of 14 days, how many nuclei of the isotope are there at this time?

GRAPHING CALCULATOR PRACTICE

Nuclear Decay

In nuclear decay, a radioactive substance is transformed into another substance that may or may not be radioactive. The amount of radioactive material remaining is given by the following equation:

$$m = m_0 e^{-\lambda t}$$

In this nuclear decay equation, m_0 is the initial mass, and λ is the decay constant. As you learned earlier in this chapter, the decay constant is related to the half-life by the following equation:

$$T_{1/2} = \frac{0.693}{\lambda}$$

One of the interesting aspects of nuclear decay is that radioactive substances have a wide range of half-lives—from femtoseconds to billions of years. And all of these radioactive substances obey both of these equations.

In this graphing calculator activity, the calculator will use these equations to make graphs of the amount of remaining mass versus time. By analyzing these graphs, you will be able to make predictions about radioactive substances that have various initial masses and various half-lives.

Go online to HMHScience.com to find the skillsheet and program for this graphing calculator activity.

45. At some instant of time, the activity of a sample of radioactive material is 5.0 μCi. If the sample contains 1.0×10^9 radioactive nuclei, what is the half-life of the material?

46. It has been estimated that Earth has 9.1×10^{11} kg of natural uranium that can be economically mined. Of this total, 0.70 percent is ^{235}U. If all the world's energy needs (7.0×10^{12} J/s) were supplied by ^{235}U fission, how long would this supply last? Assume that 208 MeV of energy is released per fission event and that the mass of ^{235}U is about 3.9×10^{-25} kg.

47. If the average energy released in a fission event is 208 MeV, find the total number of fission events required to provide enough energy to keep a 100.0 W light bulb burning for 1.0 h.

48. How many atoms of ^{235}U must undergo fission to operate a 1.0×10^3 MW power plant for one day if the conversion efficiency is 30.0 percent? Assume 208 MeV released per fission event.

ALTERNATIVE ASSESSMENT

1. You are designing a nuclear power plant for a space station to be established on Mars. Material A is radioactive and has a half-life of two years. Material B is also radioactive and has a half-life of one year. Atoms of material B have half the mass of atoms of material A. Discuss the benefits and drawbacks involved with each of these fuels.

2. Design a questionnaire to investigate what people in your community know about nuclear power and how they feel about it. Give the questionnaire to your classmates for their comments, and if your teacher approves, conduct a study with people in your community. Present your results in the form of a class presentation and discussion.

3. Investigate careers in nuclear medicine. Interview people who work with radiation or with isotopic tracers in a hospital. Find out what kind of patients they treat or test and the technology they use. What training is necessary for this type of career?

4. Research the lives and careers of female nuclear physicists such as Marie Curie, Lise Meitner, Ida Tacke Noddack, and Maria Goeppert-Mayer. Create a presentation about one of these scientists. The presentation can be in the form of a report, poster, short video, or computer presentation.

5. Research how radioactive decay is used to date archaeological remains and fossils. What nuclear reactions are involved in the carbon-14 dating technique? What assumptions are made when the carbon-14 dating technique is used? What time scale is the carbon-14 technique suitable for? Is the carbon-14 technique appropriate to determine the age of a painting suspected to be 375 years old? Summarize your findings in a brochure or poster for visitors to a science museum.

6. Research the problem of nuclear waste in the United States. How much is there? What kinds of radioactive waste are there? Where are they produced? What are the costs and hazards associated with different techniques for disposal of radioactive waste? How do other countries deal with the problem? Choose the disposal option you think is most appropriate, and write a position paper. Include information about all options and the reasons for your choice.

7. Some modern physicists have developed *string theory* in an attempt to unify the four fundamental forces. Conduct research to learn about this theory. What are the main principles of string theory? Why do some scientists oppose it? Share your results with the class in a short lecture presentation.

8. Research the work of scientists who have make key contributions to the understanding of each of the four fundamental forces. What new evidence or understanding did each of these scientists contribute?

Standards-Based Assessment

Record your answers on a separate piece of paper.

MULTIPLE CHOICE

1 One unified mass unit (u) is equivalent to a mass of 1.66×10^{-27} kg. What is the equivalent rest energy in joules?

  A 8.27×10^{-46} J

  B 4.98×10^{-19} J

  C 1.49×10^{-10} J

  D 9.31×10^{8} J

2 What kind of force holds protons and neutrons together in a nucleus?

  A electromagnetic force

  B gravitational force

  C weak force

  D strong force

3 A nuclear reaction of major historical note took place in 1932, when a beryllium target was bombarded with alpha particles. Analysis of the experiment showed that the following reaction took place: $^{4}_{2}\text{He} + ^{9}_{4}\text{Be} \rightarrow ^{12}_{6}\text{C} + \text{X}$. What is X in this reaction?

  A $^{0}_{1}e$

  B $^{0}_{-1}p$

  C $^{1}_{0}n$

  D $^{1}_{1}p$

4 A sample of organic material is found to contain 18 g of carbon-14. Based on samples of pottery found at a dig, investigators believe the material is about 23 000 years old. The half-life of carbon-14 is 5715 years. About what percentage of the material's carbon-14 has decayed?

  A 4.0%

  B 25%

  C 75%

  D 94%

5 The half-life of radium-228 is 5.76 years. At some instant, a sample contains 2.0×10^9 nuclei. What is the decay constant and the activity of the sample?

  A $\lambda = 3.81 \times 10^{-9}$ s^{-1}; activity $= 2.1 \times 10^{-10}$ Ci

  B $\lambda = 3.81 \times 10^{-9}$ s^{-1}; activity $= 7.8$ Ci

  C $\lambda = 0.120$ s^{-1}; activity $= 6.5 \times 10^{-3}$ Ci

  D $\lambda = 2.6 \times 10^8$ s^{-1}; activity $= 1.4 \times 10^7$ Ci

6 What fraction of a radioactive sample has decayed after two half-lives have elapsed?

  A ¼

  B ½

  C ¾

  D The whole sample has decayed.

7 Which of the following choices does not correctly match a fundamental interaction with its mediating particles?

  A strong: gluons

  B electromagnetic: electrons

  C weak: W and Z bosons

  D gravitational: gravitons

GRIDDED RESPONSE

8 The table below shows the atomic masses of three elements.

Nucleus	Mass
$^{238}_{92}$U	238.050 784 u
$^{234}_{90}$Th	234.043 593 u
$^{4}_{2}$He	4.002 602 u

How much energy, in MeV, is released in the alpha decay of $^{238}_{92}$U?

Nuclear Power Safety

How Does Nuclear Power Work?

Nuclear reactors may seem extremely high-tech, but they are essentially "kettles" that boil water to produce electricity. These kettles get their heat from nuclear fission. Nuclear fission occurs when a large nucleus splits into two smaller nuclei and releases heat and neutrons. In a nuclear reactor, these released neutrons strike other large nuclei, causing them to split. This reaction becomes self-sustaining, producing heat to boil water, which turns a turbine that generates electricity.

Nuclear power facilities must use radioactive materials to achieve sustained fission chain reactions. The majority of nuclear power plants use the most common naturally occurring isotope of uranium, U-238. However, since this isotope does not fission easily, the reactor is enriched with a small amount of the very fissile isotope U-235.

Identify the Problem: Nuclear Accidents

Since 1952, there have been 33 serious nuclear incidents and accidents globally. The International Nuclear and Radiological Event Scale (INES) was established by the International Atomic Energy Agency to communicate to the public the safety significance of events involving ionizing radiation. This scale goes from 1 to 7, with 7 being a major accident. Three of the most well-known nuclear accidents are Three Mile Island, Chernobyl, and Fukushima Daiichi. The Chernobyl accident, which occurred in Ukraine (part of the Soviet Union at that time) in 1986, and the 2011 Fukushima Daiichi accident in Japan both ranked a 7 on the INES (major release of radioactive material with widespread health and environmental effects). The Three Mile Island accident occurred in Pennsylvania in 1979 and ranked a 5 (limited release of radioactive material likely to require implementation of countermeasures).

The severity of a nuclear accident depends on heat. If a reactor core (where the fission takes place) contains too much heat, it will melt, and that could lead to the release of radioactive contaminates into the environment. At Three Mile Island, a pressure valve got stuck in an open position, leading to an escape of coolant. A light indicating the position of the valve malfunctioned, and an operator interpreted the reactor as having an excess of coolant when it was actually low on coolant. This led to a manual override of the emergency coolant system, causing a partial melting of the reactor core and a release of radioactive gases and iodine into the environment.

At Chernobyl, two major factors led to the accident: a flawed reactor design and inadequately trained personnel. During a test of safety systems, operators inadvertently caused the reactor to increase power output. They then tried to insert control rods to stop the fission reaction, but because of a flawed rod design, this action further raised the power output of the reactor, resulting in an explosion that blew the lid off the reactor.

At Fukushima Daiichi, natural disasters led to the demise of the nuclear power facility. After a major earthquake shook the area, most of the backup diesel generators continued to pump coolant into the reactors, but they failed after a 15-meter tsunami disabled 12 of 13 backup generators—as well as heat exchangers that dump reactor waste heat into the sea. Three of four reactor cores largely melted.

Brainstorm Solutions: Designing Fail-Safe Systems

Three basic safety functions exist in a nuclear reactor: 1) controlling reactivity, 2) controlling the cooling of the fuel, and 3) containing radioactive substances. Safety systems that satisfy these three functions must be in place.

Controlling reactivity requires stopping neutrons from hitting other nuclei. This can be achieved by adding control rods or fluids to the reactor. These materials absorb the neutrons, preventing them from hitting fissionable nuclei. Normally, cooling the fuel is achieved by circulating coolant through the reactor core using pumps that are controlled by electric power, backup diesel motors, or backup batteries. The nuclear fuel is shaped into pellets that are encased in rods made of metal alloys or ceramic. Containment vessels and the facility itself are constructed of several layers of metal, ceramic, and concrete. These layers all help shield the environment from the radioactive substances inside.

This dome was built after the Chernobyl accident to contain the nuclear reactor and prevent further leaking of radioactive material.

Redesign to Improve: Lessons Learned

After the Three Mile Island accident, the U.S. government and the nuclear power industry moved quickly to improve safety at nuclear power facilities. The Institute of Nuclear Power Operations was developed to promote the highest safety standards, and the National Academy for Nuclear Training was established.

After the Chernobyl accident, the world learned that the type of reactor used was a highly unusual design. The reactor had a "positive void coefficient," meaning the nuclear reactions in its core would increase if steam bubbles (voids) were to form in the reactor. In addition, Chernobyl did not have an effective containment vessel over the reactor core, and the control rod design was faulty. In the aftermath of the accident, the Soviet Union modified its other nuclear power facilities of the same design to remove the positive void coefficient. The control rods were also retrofitted.

In the Fukushima accident, the backup safety systems that were in place required electricity or diesel fuel motors to shut down reactors and pump coolant during emergency situations. The tsunami conditions disabled the backup systems, causing the meltdown.

The Fukushima Daiichi accident has prompted engineers to rethink current designs of nuclear power facilities. Engineers at the Center for Advanced Energy Studies are designing new ways to shut down and cool nuclear reactors without actions from an operator or electronic systems. These new methods are called *passive safety methods* and use the nature of physics to perform the safety work. One such design uses gravity rather than pumps to drive coolant systems. While electricity can go out in a disaster like Fukushima Daiichi, gravity will not.

The future of nuclear power rests on engineers who can find creative solutions that harness the nature of physics to keep nuclear facilities safe.

Design Your Own

Conduct Research

As U.S. nuclear power facilities approach retirement age, replacing them is a concern. The U.S. Department of Energy is now supporting the development and use of small, modular nuclear reactors. Research the design of small, modular reactors and their benefits.

Brainstorm Solutions

Find the location of a nuclear power facility, near you or elsewhere. List several ways in which a passive system could be implemented at the facility to use gravity to feed coolant into the reactor. If the closest facility were to shut down, what are four areas where small, modular reactors could be placed to use gravity as a passive safety measure?

Select a Solution

From the four areas you identified, choose the best location for using gravity to supply coolant to the reactor. Sketch a model of the design.

©kpzfoto/Alamy

1953

$$n\lambda = 2d \sin\theta$$

Rosalind Franklin, a crystallographer and chemist, produces an x-ray image of DNA.

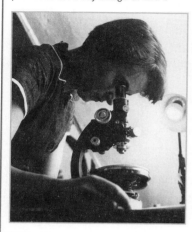

1957

The Soviet Union launches Sputnik, the world's first satellite, into space.

1969

The Woodstock Music Festival takes places on a farm in New York. Woodstock proves to be the beginning of the end of the hippie counterculture movement of the 1960s.

1975

After over a decade of war, Saigon falls to the North Vietnamese army, and United States troops leave Vietnam, ending the Vietnam War.

1950   1955   1960   1965   1970   1975

1954

In the landmark case *Brown v. Board of Education*, the United States Supreme Court unanimously rules that "separate educational facilities are inherently unequal," paving the way for school desegregation and the civil rights movement.

1968

u u d
u d d

Scientists at the **Stanford Linear Accelerator** run experiments that provide the first direct evidence of the existence of quarks.

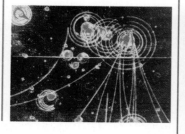

1969

On July 20, the United States sends *Apollo 11* to the moon. **Neil Armstrong** and **Buzz Aldrin** become the first two humans to walk on the moon.

1975

$$v^2 = \frac{GM}{r^2}$$

In her observations of spiral galaxies, astronomer **Vera Rubin** notices that stars on the outer edge of the galaxy move at the same speed as those closer to the center of the galaxy. Her discovery lends support to the theory of dark matter.

1981

NASA launches the first shuttle, *Columbia*, into space. After a two-day mission, *Columbia* returns to Earth.

1989–1990

Scientists at the European Organization for Nuclear Research (CERN), in an effort to facilitate the sharing of information, establish the World Wide Web.

1997

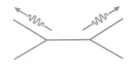

Scientist **Nicolas Gisin** sends two photons in opposite directions down a wire. When the photons are 7 miles apart, they encounter two paths. Although the photons are unable to communicate, the paths taken by both match.

2012

Scientists at CERN's Large Hadron Collider announce the discovery of the Higgs Boson, a particle predicted to exist by the Standard Model. The Higgs Boson and its associated field are what gives particles like protons and neutrons their mass.

| 1980 | 1985 | 1990 | 1995 | 2000 | 2005 | 2010 |

1971–1985

$$S_{GS} = \int C_{(2)} \hat{} X_8$$

Throughout the 1970s, scientists such as **Michael Green** theorize that even the smallest parts of matter, quarks, are made up of smaller units. They call this the superstring theory.

1986

A failure at the Chernobyl nuclear power plant triggers a huge explosion, sending radioactive material not only into the local environment, but also into the atmosphere.

1994

Apartheid ends in South Africa after nearly 50 years of forced segregation in which the minority white population denied basic rights to the majority black population. Former political prisoner **Nelson Mandela** becomes president.

2003

$$k_B T_c = 1.14 E_D \, e^{-1/N(0)V}$$

In her lab, **Deborah S. Jin** discovers a sixth form of matter, called *fermionic condensates.* This matter forms when fermions are cooled to very low temperatures close to 0 kelvin.

Contents

Mathematical Review

Scientific Notation

Positive exponents Many quantities that scientists deal with have very large or very small values. For example, the speed of light is about 300 000 000 m/s, and the ink required to make the dot over an *i* in this textbook has a mass of about 0.000 000 001 kg. Obviously, it is cumbersome to work with numbers such as these. We avoid this problem by using a method based on powers of the number 10.

$$10^0 = 1$$
$$10^1 = 10$$
$$10^2 = 10 \times 10 = 100$$
$$10^3 = 10 \times 10 \times 10 = 1000$$
$$10^4 = 10 \times 10 \times 10 \times 10 = 10\ 000$$
$$10^5 = 10 \times 10 \times 10 \times 10 \times 10 = 100\ 000$$

The number of zeros determines the power to which 10 is raised, or the *exponent* of 10. For example, the speed of light, 300 000 000 m/s, can be expressed as 3×10^8 m/s. In this case, the exponent of 10 is 8.

Negative exponents For numbers whose absolute value is less than one, we note the following:

$$10^{-1} = \frac{1}{10} = 0.1$$
$$10^{-2} = \frac{1}{10 \times 10} = 0.01$$
$$10^{-3} = \frac{1}{10 \times 10 \times 10} = 0.001$$
$$10^{-4} = \frac{1}{10 \times 10 \times 10 \times 10} = 0.0001$$
$$10^{-5} = \frac{1}{10 \times 10 \times 10 \times 10 \times 10} = 0.000\ 01$$

The value of the negative exponent equals the number of places the decimal point must be moved to be to the right of the first nonzero digit (in these cases, the digit 1). Numbers that are expressed as a number greater than or equal to 1 and less than 10 multiplied by a power of 10 are said to be in *scientific notation*. For example, 5 943 000 000 is 5.943×10^9 when expressed in scientific notation, and 0.000 0832 is 8.32×10^{-5} when expressed in scientific notation.

Multiplication and division in scientific notation When numbers expressed in scientific notation are being multiplied, the following general rule is very useful:

$$10^n \times 10^m = 10^{(n+m)}$$

Note that n and m can be any numbers; they are not necessarily integers. For example, $10^2 \times 10^5 = 10^7$, and $10^{1/4} \times 10^{1/2} = 10^{3/4}$. The rule also applies to negative exponents. For example, $10^3 \times 10^{-8} = 10^{-5}$. When dividing numbers expressed in scientific notation, note the following:

$$\frac{10^n}{10^m} = 10^n \times 10^{-m} = 10^{(n-m)}$$

For example, $\dfrac{10^3}{10^2} = 10^{(3-2)} = 10^1$.

Fractions

The rules for multiplying, dividing, adding, and subtracting fractions are summarized in **Figure 1,** where a, b, c, and d are four numbers.

FIGURE 1

BASIC OPERATIONS FOR FRACTIONS

Operation	Rule	Example
Multiplication	$\left(\dfrac{a}{b}\right)\left(\dfrac{c}{d}\right) = \dfrac{ac}{bd}$	$\left(\dfrac{2}{3}\right)\left(\dfrac{4}{5}\right) = \dfrac{(2)(4)}{(3)(5)} = \dfrac{8}{15}$
Division	$\dfrac{\left(\dfrac{a}{b}\right)}{\left(\dfrac{c}{d}\right)} = \dfrac{ad}{bc}$	$\dfrac{\left(\dfrac{2}{3}\right)}{\left(\dfrac{4}{5}\right)} = \dfrac{(2)(5)}{(3)(4)} = \dfrac{10}{12} = \dfrac{5}{6}$
Addition and Subtraction	$\dfrac{a}{b} \pm \dfrac{c}{d} = \dfrac{ad \pm bc}{bd}$	$\dfrac{2}{3} - \dfrac{4}{5} = \dfrac{(2)(5) - (3)(4)}{(3)(5)} = -\dfrac{2}{15}$

Powers

Rules of exponents When powers of a given quantity, x, are multiplied, the rule used for scientific notation applies:

$$(x^n)(x^m) = x^{(n+m)}$$

For example, $(x^2)(x^4) = x^{(2+4)} = x^6$.

When dividing the powers of a given quantity, note the following:

$$\frac{x^n}{x^m} = x^{(n-m)}$$

For example, $\dfrac{x^8}{x^2} = x^{(8-2)} = x^6$.

A power that is a fraction, such as $\frac{1}{3}$, corresponds to a root as follows:

$$x^{1/n} = \sqrt[n]{x}$$

For example, $4^{1/3} = \sqrt[3]{4} \approx 1.5874$. (A scientific calculator is useful for such calculations.)

Finally, any quantity, x^n, that is raised to the mth power is as follows:

$$(x^n)^m = x^{nm}$$

For example, $(x^2)^3 = x^{(2)(3)} = x^6$.

The basic rules of exponents are summarized in **Figure 2.**

FIGURE 2

RULES OF EXPONENTS		
$x^0 = 1$	$x^1 = x$	$(x^n)(x^m) = x^{(n+m)}$
$\frac{x^n}{x^m} = x^{(n-m)}$	$x^{(1/n)} = \sqrt[n]{x}$	$(x^n)^m = x^{(nm)}$

Algebra

Solving for unknowns When algebraic operations are performed, the laws of arithmetic apply. Symbols such as x, y, and z are usually used to represent quantities that are not specified. Such unspecified quantities are called *unknowns.*

First, consider the following equation:

$$8x = 32$$

If we wish to solve for x, we can divide each side of the equation by the same factor without disturbing the equality. In this case, if we divide both sides by 8, we have the following:

$$\frac{8x}{8} = \frac{32}{8}$$

$$x = 4$$

Next, consider the following equation:

$$x + 2 = 8$$

In this type of equation, we can add or subtract the same quantity from each side. If we subtract 2 from each side, we get the following:

$$x + 2 - 2 = 8 - 2$$

$$x = 6$$

In general, if $x + a = b$, then $x = b - a$.

Now, consider the following equation:

$$\frac{x}{5} = 9$$

If we multiply each side by 5, we are left with x isolated on the left and a value of 45 on the right.

$$(5)\left(\frac{x}{5}\right) = (9)(5)$$

$$x = 45$$

In all cases, *whatever operation is performed on the left side of the equation must also be performed on the right side.*

Factoring

Some useful formulas for factoring an equation are given in **Figure 3**. As an example of a common factor, consider the equation $5x + 5y + 5z = 0$. This equation can be expressed as $5(x + y + z) = 0$. The expression $a^2 + 2ab + b^2$, which is an example of a perfect square, is equivalent to the expression $(a + b)^2$. For example, if $a = 2$ and $b = 3$, then $2^2 + (2)(2)(3) + 3^2 = (2 + 3)^2$, or $(4 + 12 + 9) = 5^2 = 25$. Finally, for an example of the difference of two squares, let $a = 6$ and $b = 3$. In this case, $(6^2 - 3^2) = (6 + 3)(6 - 3)$, or $(36 - 9) = (9)(3) = 27$.

FIGURE 3

FACTORING EQUATIONS

$ax + ay + az = a(x + y + z)$	common factor
$a^2 + 2ab + b^2 = (a + b)^2$	perfect square
$a^2 - b^2 = (a + b)(a - b)$	difference of two squares

Quadratic Equations

The general form of a quadratic equation is as follows:

$$ax^2 + bx + c = 0$$

In this equation, x is the unknown quantity, a and b are numerical factors known as *coefficients*, and c is a *constant*. This equation has two roots, given by the following:

$$x = \frac{-b \pm \sqrt{b^2 - 4ac}}{2a}$$

If $b^2 \geq 4ac$, the value inside the square-root symbol will be positive or zero, and the roots will be real. If $b^2 < 4ac$, the value inside the square-root symbol will be negative, and the roots will be imaginary numbers. In problems in this physics book, imaginary roots should not occur.

Example

Find the solutions for the equation $x^2 + 5x + 4 = 0$.

SOLVE

The given equation can be expressed as $(1)x^2 + (5)x + (4) = 0$. In other words, $a = 1$, $b = 5$, and $c = 4$. The two roots of this equation can be found by substituting these values into the quadratic equation, as follows:

$$x = \frac{-b \pm \sqrt{b^2 - 4ac}}{2a} = \frac{-5 \pm \sqrt{5^2 - (4)(1)(4)}}{(2)(1)} = \frac{-5 \pm \sqrt{9}}{2} = \frac{-5 + 3}{2}$$

The two roots are $x = \frac{-5 + 3}{2} = -1$ and $x = \frac{-5 - 3}{2} = -4$

$$\boxed{x = -1 \text{ and } x = -4}$$

We can evaluate these answers by substituting them into the given equation and verifying that the result is zero.

$$x^2 + 5x + 4 = 0$$

For $x = -1$, $(-1)^2 + 5(-1) + 4 = 1 - 5 + 4 = 0$.

For $x = -4$, $(-4)^2 + 5(-4) + 4 = 16 - 20 + 4 = 0$.

Example

Find the solutions for the equation $2x^2 - 3x - 4 = 0$.

SOLVE

The given equation can be expressed as $(2)x^2 + (-3x) + (-4) = 0$. Thus, $a = 2$, $b = -3$, and $c = -4$. Substitute these values into the quadratic equation to find the solutions for the given equation.

$$x = \frac{-b \pm \sqrt{b^2 - 4ac}}{2a} = \frac{3 \pm \sqrt{(-3)^2 - (4)(2)(-4)}}{(2)(2)} = \frac{3 \pm \sqrt{41}}{4} \approx \frac{3 \pm 6.403}{4}$$

The two roots are $x \approx \frac{3 + 6.403}{4} \approx 2.351$ and $x \approx \frac{3 - 6.403}{4} \approx -0.851$.

$$\boxed{x \approx 2.351 \text{ and } x \approx -0.851}$$

Again, evaluate these answers by substituting them into the given equation.

$$2x^2 - 3x - 4 = 0$$

For $x = 2.351$, $2(2.351)^2 - 3(2.351) - 4 \approx 11.054 - 7.053 - 4 \approx 0$.

For $x = -0.851$, $2(-0.851)^2 - 3(-0.851) - 4 \approx 1.448 + 2.553 - 4 \approx 0$.

Linear Equations

A linear equation has the following general form:

$$y = ax + b$$

In this equation, a and b are constants. This equation is called linear because the graph of y versus x is a straight line, as shown in **Figure 4.** The constant b, called the *intercept*, represents the value of y where the straight line intersects the y-axis. The constant a is equal to the *slope* of the straight line and is also equal to the tangent of the angle that the line makes with the x-axis (θ). If any two points on the straight line are specified by the coordinates (x_1, y_1) and (x_2, y_2), as in **Figure 4,** then the slope of the straight line can be expressed as follows:

$$\text{slope} = \frac{y_2 - y_1}{x_2 - x_1} = \frac{\Delta y}{\Delta x}$$

For example, if the two points shown in **Figure 4** are $(2, 4)$ and $(6, 9)$, then the slope of the line is as follows:

$$\text{slope} = \frac{(9 - 4)}{(6 - 2)} = \frac{5}{4}$$

Note that a and b can have either positive or negative values. If $a > 0$, the straight line has a *positive* slope, as in **Figure 4.** If $a < 0$, the straight line has a *negative* slope. Furthermore, if $b > 0$, the y-intercept is positive (above the x-axis), while if $b < 0$, the y-intercept is negative (below the x-axis). **Figure 5** gives an example of each of these four possible cases, which are summarized in **Figure 6.**

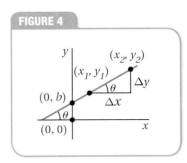

FIGURE 4

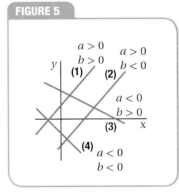

FIGURE 5

FIGURE 6

LINEAR EQUATIONS		
Constants	Slope	y-intercept
$a > 0, b > 0$	positive slope	positive y-intercept
$a > 0, b < 0$	positive slope	negative y-intercept
$a < 0, b > 0$	negative slope	positive y-intercept
$a < 0, b < 0$	negative slope	negative y-intercept

Solving Simultaneous Linear Equations

Consider the following equation:

$$3x + 5y = 15$$

This equation has two unknowns, x and y. Such an equation does not have a unique solution. That is, $(x = 0, y = 3)$, $(x = 5, y = 0)$, and $(x = 2, y = \frac{9}{5})$ are all solutions to this equation.

If a problem has two unknowns, a unique solution is possible only if there are two independent equations. In general, if a problem has n unknowns, its solution requires n independent equations. There are three basic methods that can be used to solve simultaneous equations. Each of these methods is discussed below, and an example is given for each.

First method: substitution One way to solve two simultaneous equations involving two unknowns, x and y, is to solve one of the equations for one of the unknown values in terms of the other unknown value. In other words, either solve one equation for x in terms of y, or solve one equation for y in terms of x. Once you have an expression for either x or y, substitute this expression into the other original equation. At this point, the equation has only one unknown quantity. This unknown can be found through algebraic manipulations and then can be used to determine the other unknown.

Example

Solve the following two simultaneous equations:

1. $5x + y = -8$.
2. $2x - 2y = 4$

SOLVE

First solve for either x or y in one of the equations. We'll begin by solving equation 2 for x.

2. $2x - 2y = 4$
$$2x = 4 + 2y$$
$$x = \frac{4 + 2y}{2} = 2 + y$$

Next, we substitute this expression for x into equation 1 and solve for y.

1. $5x + y = -8$
$$5(2 + y) + y = -8$$
$$10 + 5y + y = -8$$
$$6y = -18$$
$$\boxed{y = -3}$$

To find x, substitute this value for y into the equation for x derived from equation 2.

$$x = 2 + y = 2 + -3$$
$$\boxed{x = -1}$$

There is always more than one way to solve simultaneous equations by substitution. In this example, we first solved equation 2 for x. However, we could have begun by solving equation 2 for y or equation 1 for x or y. Any of these processes would result in the same answer.

Second method: canceling one term Simultaneous equations can also be solved by multiplying both sides of one of the equations by a value that will make either the x-value or the y-value in that equation equal to and opposite the corresponding value in the second equation. When the two equations are added together, that unknown value drops out, and only one of the unknown values remains. This unknown can be found through algebraic manipulations and then can be used to determine the other unknown.

Example

Solve the following two simultaneous equations:

1. $3x + y = -6$
2. $-4x - 2y = 6$

SOLVE

First, multiply each term of one of the equations by a factor that will make either the x- or the y-values cancel when the two equations are added together. In this case, we can multiply each term in equation 1 by the factor 2. The positive $2y$ in equation 1 will then cancel the negative $2y$ in equation 2.

1. $(2)(3x) + (2)(y) = -(2)(6)$
   $6x + 2y = -12$

Next, add the two equations together and solve for x.

2. $-4x - 2y = 6$
1. $6x + 2y = -12$
   $2x = -6$
   $\boxed{x = -3}$

Then, substitute this value of x into either equation to find y.

1. $3x + y = -6$
   $y = -6 - 3x = -6 - (3)(-3) = -6 + 9$
   $\boxed{y = 3}$

In this example, we multiplied both sides of equation 1 by 2 so that the y-terms would cancel when the two equations were added together. As with substitution, this is only one of many possible ways to solve the equations. For example, we could have multiplied both sides of equation 2 by $\frac{3}{4}$ so that the x-terms would cancel when the two equations were added together.

Third method: graphing the equations Two linear equations with two unknowns can also be solved by a graphical method. If the straight lines corresponding to the two equations are plotted in a conventional coordinate system, the intersection of the two lines represents the solution.

Example

Solve the following two simultaneous equations:

1. $x - y = 2$
2. $x - 2y = -1$

SOLVE

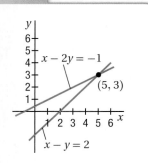

FIGURE 7

These two equations are plotted in **Figure 7**. To plot an equation, rewrite the equation in the form $y = ax + b$, where a is the slope and b is the y-intercept. In this example, the equations can be rewritten as follows:

$$y = x - 2$$

$$y = \frac{1}{2}x + \frac{1}{2}$$

Once one point of a line is known, any other point on that line can be found with the slope of the line. For example, the slope of the first line is 1, and we know that $(0, -2)$ is a point on this line. If we choose the point $x = 2$, we have $(2, y_2)$. The coordinate y_2 can be found as follows:

$$\text{slope} = \frac{y_2 - y_1}{x_2 - x_1} - \frac{y_2 - (-2)}{2 - 0} = 1$$

$$y_2 = 0$$

Connecting the two known coordinates, $(0, -2)$ and $(2, 0)$, results in a graph of the line. The second line can be plotted with the same method.

As shown in **Figure 7**, the intersection of the two lines has the coordinates $x = 5, y = 3$. This intersection represents the solution to the equations. You should check this solution using either of the analytical techniques discussed above.

Logarithms

Suppose that a quantity, x, is expressed as a power of another quantity, a.

$$x = a^y$$

The number a is called the *base number*. The *logarithm* of x with respect to the base, a, is equal to the exponent to which a must be raised in order to satisfy the expression $x = a^y$.

$$y = \log_a x$$

Conversely, the *antilogarithm* of y is the number x.

$$x = \text{antilog}_a y$$

Common and natural bases In practice, the two bases most often used are base 10, called the *common* logarithm base, and base $e = 2.718...$, called the *natural* logarithm base. When common logarithms are used, y and x are related as follows:

$$y = \log_{10} x, \text{ or } x = 10^y$$

When natural logarithms are used, the symbol ln is used to signify that the logarithm has a base of e; in other words, $\log_e x = \ln x$.

$$y = \ln x, \text{ or } x = e^y$$

For example, $\log_{10} 52 \approx 1.716$, so antilog$_{10}$ $1.716 = 10^{1.716} \approx 52$. Likewise, $\ln 52 \approx 3.951$, so antiln $3.951 = e^{3.951} \approx 52$.

Note that you can convert between base 10 and base e with the equation

$$\ln x \approx (2.302\ 585)\log_{10} x.$$

Some useful properties of logarithms are summarized in **Figure 8.**

FIGURE 8

PROPERTIES OF LOGARITHMS

Rule	Example
$\log (ab) = \log a + \log b$	$\log (2)(5) = \log 2 + \log 5$
$\log \left(\dfrac{a}{b}\right) = \log a - \log b$	$\log \dfrac{3}{4} = \log 3 - \log 4$
$\log (a^n) = n \log a$	$\log 7^3 = 3 \log 7$
$\ln e = 1$	
$\ln e^a = a$	$\ln e^5 = 5$
$\ln \left(\dfrac{1}{a}\right) = -\ln a$	$\ln \dfrac{1}{8} = -\ln 8$

Conversions Between Fractions, Decimals, and Percentages

The rules for converting numbers from fractions to decimals and percentages and from percentages to decimals are summarized in **Figure 9.**

FIGURE 9

CONVERSIONS

Conversion	Rule	Example
Fraction to decimal	divide numerator by denominator	$\dfrac{31}{45} \approx 0.69$
Fraction to percentage	convert to decimal, then multiply by 100%	$\dfrac{31}{45} \approx (0.69)(100\%) = 69\%$
Percentage to decimal	move decimal point two places to the left, and remove the percent sign	$69\% = 0.69$

Geometry

Figure 10 provides equations for the area and volume of several geometrical shapes used throughout this text.

FIGURE 10

GEOMETRICAL AREAS AND VOLUMES

Geometrical shape	Useful equations
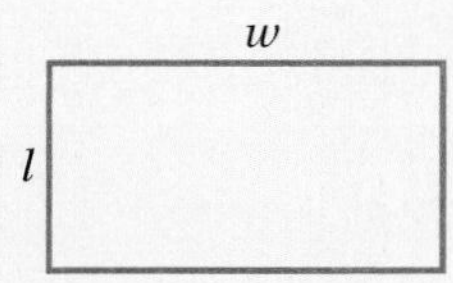 rectangle	area $= lw$ perimeter $= 2(l + w)$
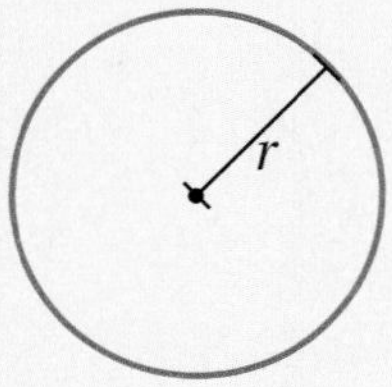 circle	area $= \pi r^2$ circumference $= 2\pi r$
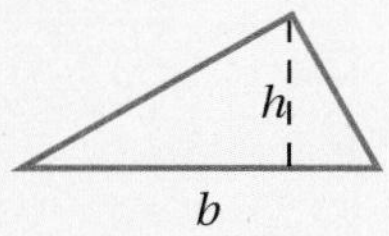 triangle	area $= \frac{1}{2}bh$
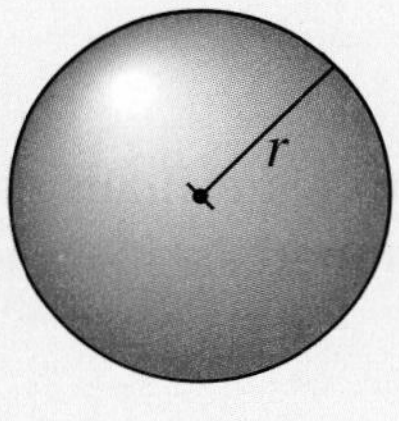 sphere	surface area $= 4\pi r^2$ volume $= \frac{4}{3}\pi r^3$
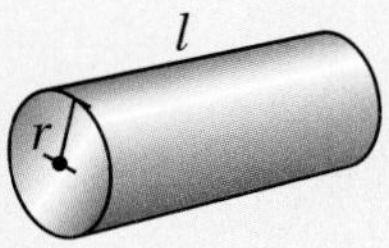 cylinder	surface area $= 2\pi r^2 + 2\pi rl$ volume $= \pi r^2 l$
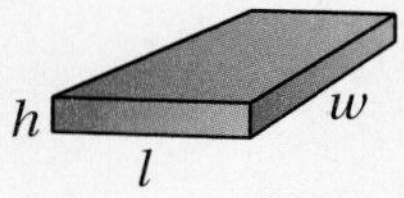 rectangular box	surface area $= 2(lh + lw + hw)$ volume $= lwh$

Trigonometry and the Pythagorean Theorem

The portion of mathematics that is based on the relationships between the sides and angles of triangles is called *trigonometry*. Many of the concepts of this branch of mathematics are of great importance in the study of physics. To review some of the basic concepts of trigonometry, consider the right triangle shown in **Figure 11**, where side a is opposite the angle θ, side b is adjacent to the angle θ, and side c is the hypotenuse of the triangle (the side opposite the right angle). The most common trigonometry functions are summarized in **Figure 12**, using **Figure 11** as an example.

FIGURE 11

$$\sin \theta = \frac{a}{c}$$
$$\cos \theta = \frac{b}{c}$$
$$\tan \theta = \frac{a}{b}$$

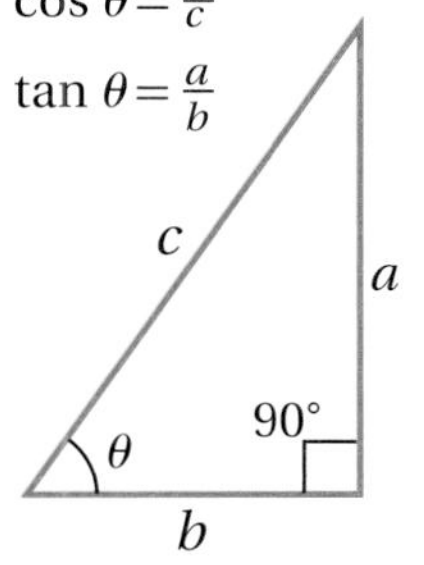

FIGURE 12

TRIGONOMETRY FUNCTIONS

sine (sin)	$\sin \theta = \dfrac{\text{side opposite } \theta}{\text{hypotenuse}} = \dfrac{a}{c}$
cosine (cos)	$\cos \theta = \dfrac{\text{side adjacent to } \theta}{\text{hypotenuse}} = \dfrac{b}{c}$
tangent (tan)	$\tan \theta = \dfrac{\text{side opposite } \theta}{\text{side adjacent to } \theta} = \dfrac{a}{b}$
inverse sine ($\sin^{-1}$)	$\theta = \sin^{-1}\left(\dfrac{\text{side opposite } \theta}{\text{hypotenuse}}\right) = \sin^{-1}\left(\dfrac{a}{c}\right)$
inverse cosine ($\cos^{-1}$)	$\theta = \cos^{-1}\left(\dfrac{\text{side adjacent to } \theta}{\text{hypotenuse}}\right) = \cos^{-1}\left(\dfrac{b}{c}\right)$
inverse tangent ($\tan^{-1}$)	$\theta = \tan^{-1}\left(\dfrac{\text{side opposite } \theta}{\text{side adjacent to } \theta}\right) = \tan^{-1}\left(\dfrac{a}{b}\right)$

When $\theta = 30°$, for example, the ratio of a to c is always 0.50. In other words, $\sin 30° = 0.50$. Sine, cosine, and tangent are quantities without units because each represents the ratio of two lengths. Furthermore, note the following trigonometry identity:

$$\frac{\sin \theta}{\cos \theta} = \frac{\dfrac{\text{side opposite } \theta}{\text{hypotenuse}}}{\dfrac{\text{side adjacent to } \theta}{\text{hypotenuse}}} = \frac{\text{side opposite } \theta}{\text{side adjacent to } \theta} = \tan \theta$$

Some additional trigonometry identities are as follows:

$$\sin^2\theta + \cos^2\theta = 1$$
$$\sin \theta = \cos(90° - \theta)$$
$$\cos \theta = \sin(90° - \theta)$$

Determining an unknown side The first three functions given in **Figure 12** can be used to determine any unknown side of a right triangle when one side and one of the non-right angles are known. For example, if $\theta = 30°$ and $a = 1.0$ m, the other two sides of the triangle can be found as follows:

$$\sin \theta = \frac{a}{c}$$

$$c = \frac{a}{\sin \theta} = \frac{1.0 \text{ m}}{\sin 30°}$$

$$\boxed{c = 2.0 \text{ m}}$$

$$\tan \theta = \frac{a}{b}$$

$$b = \frac{a}{\tan \theta} = \frac{1.0 \text{ m}}{\tan 30°}$$

$$\boxed{b \approx 1.7 \text{ m}}$$

Determining an unknown angle In some cases, you might know the value of the sine, cosine, or tangent of an angle and need to know the measure of the angle itself. The inverse sine, cosine, and tangent functions given in **Figure 12** can be used for this purpose. For example, in **Figure 11,** suppose you know that side $a = 1.0$ m and side $c = 2.0$ m. To find the angle θ, you could use the inverse sine function, $\sin^{-1}$, as follows:

$$\theta = \sin^{-1}\left(\frac{a}{c}\right) = \sin^{-1}\left(\frac{1.0 \text{ m}}{2.0 \text{ m}}\right) = \sin^{-1}(0.50)$$

$$\boxed{\theta = 30°}$$

Converting from degrees to radians The two most common units used to measure angles are degrees and radians. A full circle is represented by 360 degrees (360°) or by 2π radians (2π rad). As such, the following conversions can be used:

$$[\text{angle } (°)] = \frac{180}{\pi} [\text{angle (rad)}]$$

$$[\text{angle (rad)}] = \frac{\pi}{180} [\text{angle } (°)]$$

Pythagorean theorem Another useful equation when working with right triangles is the Pythagorean theorem. If a and b are the two legs of a right triangle and c is the hypotenuse, as in **Figure 13**, the Pythagorean theorem can be expressed as follows:

$$c^2 = a^2 + b^2$$

FIGURE 13

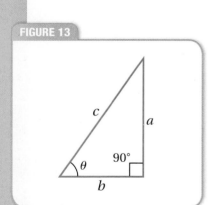

In other words, the square of the hypotenuse of a right triangle equals the sum of the squares of the other two legs of the triangle. The Pythagorean theorem is useful when two sides of a right triangle are known but the third side is not. For example, if $c = 2.0$ m and $a = 1.0$ m, you could find b using the Pythagorean theorem as follows:

$$b = \sqrt{c^2 - a^2} = \sqrt{(2.0 \text{ m})^2 - (1.0 \text{ m})^2}$$

$$b = \sqrt{4.0 \text{ m}^2 - 1.0 \text{ m}^2} = \sqrt{3.0 \text{ m}^2}$$

$$\boxed{b \approx 1.7 \text{ m}}$$

Law of sines and law of cosines The law of sines may be used to find angles of any general triangle. The law of cosines is used for calculating one side of a triangle when the angle opposite and the other two sides are known. If a, b, and c are the three sides of the triangle and θ_a, θ_b, and θ_c are the three angles opposite those sides, as shown in **Figure 14,** the following relationships hold true:

$$\frac{a}{\sin \theta_a} = \frac{b}{\sin \theta_b} = \frac{c}{\sin \theta_c}$$

$$c^2 = a^2 + b^2 - 2ab \cos \theta_c$$

FIGURE 14

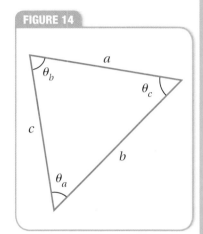

Accuracy in Laboratory Calculations

Absolute error Some laboratory experiments, such as one that measures free-fall acceleration, may involve finding a value that is already known. In this type of experiment, the accuracy of your measurements can be determined by comparing your results with the accepted value. The absolute value of the difference between your experimental or calculated result and the accepted value is called the *absolute error*. Thus, absolute error can be found with the following equation:

$$\text{absolute error} = \left| \text{experimental} - \text{accepted} \right|$$

Be sure not to confuse accuracy with precision. The *accuracy* of a measurement refers to how close that measurement is to the accepted value for the quantity being measured. *Precision* depends on the instruments used to measure a quantity. A meterstick that includes millimeters, for example, will give a more precise result than a meterstick whose smallest unit of measure is a centimeter. Thus, a measurement of 9.61 m/s² for free-fall acceleration is more precise than a measurement of 9.8 m/s², but 9.8 m/s² is more accurate than 9.61 m/s².

Relative error Note that a measurement that has a relatively large absolute error may be more accurate than a measurement that has a smaller absolute error if the first measurement involved much larger quantities. For this reason, the percentage error, or *relative error*, is often more meaningful than the absolute error. The relative error of a measured value can be found with the following equation:

$$\text{relative error} = \frac{(\text{experimental} - \text{accepted})}{\text{accepted}}$$

In other words, the relative error is the difference between the experimental value and the accepted value divided by the accepted value. Because relative error takes the size of the quantity being measured into account, the accuracy of two different measurements can be compared by comparing their relative errors.

For example, consider two laboratory experiments in which you are determining values that are fairly well known. In the first, you determine that free-fall acceleration at Earth's surface is 10.31 m/s². In the second, you find that the speed of sound in air at 25°C is 355 m/s. The accepted values for these quantities are 9.81 m/s² and 346 m/s, respectively. Now we'll find the absolute and relative errors for each experiment.

For the first experiment, the absolute and relative errors can be calculated as follows:

$$\text{absolute error} = |\text{experimental} - \text{accepted}| = |10.31 \text{ m/s}^2 - 9.81 \text{ m/s}^2|$$

$$\boxed{\text{absolute error} = 0.50 \text{ m/s}^2}$$

$$\text{relative error} = \frac{(\text{experimental} - \text{accepted})}{\text{accepted}} = \frac{(10.31 \text{ m/s}^2 - 9.81 \text{ m/s}^2)}{9.81 \text{ m/s}^2}$$

$$\boxed{\text{relative error} = 0.051 = 5.1\%}$$

For the second experiment, the absolute and relative errors can be calculated as follows:

$$\text{absolute error} = |\text{experimental} - \text{accepted}| = |355 \text{ m/s} - 346 \text{ m/s}|$$

$$\boxed{\text{absolute error} = 9 \text{ m/s}}$$

$$\text{relative error} = \frac{(\text{experimental} - \text{accepted})}{\text{accepted}} = \frac{(355 \text{ m/s} - 346 \text{ m/s})}{346 \text{ m/s}}$$

$$\boxed{\text{relative error} = 0.026 = 2.6\%}$$

Note that the *absolute* error is less in the first experiment, while the *relative* error is less in the second experiment. The absolute error is less in the first experiment because typical values for free-fall acceleration are much smaller than typical values for the speed of sound in air. The relative errors take this difference into account. Thus, comparing the relative errors shows that the speed of sound is measured with greater accuracy than is the free-fall acceleration.

The Scientific Process

Science and Its Scope

Science is a specific way of looking at and understanding the world around us. The scope of science encompasses a search for understanding natural and physical phenomena. For example, biologists explore how living things function in their environment. Geologists examine how Earth's structures and materials have changed over time. Chemists investigate the nature of matter and the changes it undergoes. Physicists search for an understanding of the interactions between matter and energy.

Often, the areas that scientists investigate overlap. As a result, there are biochemists who study the chemistry of living things, geophysicists who investigate the physical properties of Earth, and physical chemists who apply physical laws to chemical reactions. Moreover, the scope of science is not limited to investigating phenomena on Earth. In fact, the scope of science extends throughout the universe.

Science and Its Limitations

Science is limited to investigating phenomena that can be examined usefully in a scientific way. Some questions are outside the realm of science because they deal with phenomena that are not scientifically testable. In other words, scientists must be able to use scientific processes in their search for an answer or a solution. For example, they may need to design a controlled experiment, analyze the results in a logical way, or develop scientific models to explain data. As a result, the scope of science does not extend to issues of morals, values, or the supernatural. In effect, the scope of science is limited to answering the question "how," not "why."

Sometimes, technology is a limitation for scientists. For example, scientists who studied space were once limited to observing only what they could see with their eyes. In the 1600s, Galileo used his telescope to observe things the eye could not see, such as the large moons of Jupiter. Since Galileo, scientists have developed instruments that have allowed them to see even farther and fainter objects. They have even put telescopes into space, such as the *Hubble Space Telescope*, and sent probes to the edges of our solar system. However, there is still a limit to what our current technology can detect. One of the deepest mysteries in space involves dark energy, which scientists think is responsible for the expansion of the universe. To detect this dark energy, scientists will need to build a space telescope that is able to make the large number and specific types of observations that are needed.

Science and Its Methods

All scientists use certain processes in their search for explanations as to how the natural world operates. These processes include making observations, asking questions, forming a reasonable answer, evaluating the validity of the explanation, and communicating the results. Taken together, the processes constitute the scientific method. The scientific method is not a series of exact steps but rather a strategy for drawing sound conclusions. The scientific method also includes procedures that a scientist follows, such as conducting an experiment in a laboratory or using a computer to analyze data. A scientist chooses the procedures to use depending on the nature of the investigation.

There is no one correct scientific procedure. One scientist might use a field study to investigate a geologic formation, while another might do a chemical analysis on a rock sample. Another scientist might develop an experimental procedure to determine how to slow down the division of cells. Still another scientist might use a computer to create a model of a molecule.

Sometimes, different groups come to the same scientific conclusions through two different approaches. For example, in 1964, Arno Penzias and Robert Wilson were using a supersensitive antenna in their research laboratory to pick up certain radio waves coming from space. However, there was a background noise that they were picking up everywhere they pointed the antenna. Penzias and Wilson could not eliminate this steady noise. They checked their equipment and found nothing unusual. The scientists even cleaned the antenna, but the noise still persisted. They concluded that this radiation must actually be coming from space.

While these two scientists were working with their antenna, another team of scientists just 60 km away at Princeton University was about to start a search for the same cosmic radiation that Penzias and Wilson had discovered. The members of the Princeton team had reasoned that when the universe was formed, a tremendous blast of radiation must have been released into space. The Princeton team had been planning to make observations designed to find and measure this radiation. When another scientist became aware of the coincidence, he put Penzias and Wilson in touch with the Princeton team. Penzias and Wilson had observed the radiation the Princeton team had predicted.

Science and Its Investigators

Sometimes, scientists investigating the same phenomenon might interpret the results quite differently. One scientist might have one explanation, while the other scientist has a completely different explanation. One example is the behavior of light. Some scientists explained the behavior of light in terms of waves. Others explained the same behavior of light in terms of particles. Today, scientists recognize that light has a dual nature—its behavior resembles that of both waves and particles. In this case, both explanations were logically consistent. Moreover, these explanations were tested by other scientists who confirmed the results.

Science and Its Evidence

Any explanation proposed by a scientist must abide by the rules of evidence. The data must support the conclusion. If they don't, then the explanation must be modified or even discarded. For example, observational evidence of the orbit of Mercury could not be explained by Newton's law of gravity. Albert Einstein proposed a new way of thinking about gravity that explained the change in Mercury's orbit. When scientists were able to directly observe some of the results that Einstein predicted, they accepted his theory of general relativity.

Scientists also expect that all results can be replicated by other scientists working under the same conditions. For instance, in 1989, two scientists reported that they had performed "cold fusion." In effect, the scientists claimed to have carried out nuclear fusion at room temperature in a container on a countertop. People were at first hopeful that this discovery would lead to cheap and plentiful energy sources. However, a group of scientists organized that same year by the U.S. Department of Energy found no evidence to support "cold fusion." Other groups were unable to obtain the same results of the original experimenters. If no one can replicate a scientific result, then that result is usually not accepted as valid.

Science and Its Theories

Scientists hope to arrive at a conclusion about the phenomenon they investigate. They start by making observations and asking questions. Then they suggest a reasonable explanation for what they observe. This explanation is known as a hypothesis. A hypothesis is a rational explanation of a single event or phenomenon based upon what is observed but that has not been proven.

A hypothesis usually develops from observations about the natural world. Sometimes, the results of observations are expected, but sometimes they are not. Unexpected results can lead to new hypotheses. For example, in 1820, a Danish scientist named Hans Christian Oersted discovered a relationship between magnetism and electricity. While working with equipment for a lecture demonstration, Oersted placed a compass near a wire connected to an apparatus that generated an electrical current. Oersted noticed that the needle on the compass jumped and pointed toward the wire. He formed a hypothesis that electricity and magnetism were related.

A hypothesis is a testable explanation. One way to test a hypothesis is by carrying out experiments that test the predictions made by a hypothesis. Oersted conducted further experiments and found that he could control the direction in which the compass needle pointed by moving the wire. His new observations supported his hypothesis.

A good scientist recognizes that there is a chance that a test can fail to support the hypothesis. If Oersted's compass needle had jumped for some other reason, he would have gotten different results. When this occurs, the scientist needs to rethink the hypothesis and construct another explanation for the event or phenomenon.

Unlike a hypothesis, a theory is a well-established and highly reliable explanation accepted by scientists. A theory is an explanation of a set of related observations or events based upon proven hypotheses, and it is verified multiple times by different groups of scientists. A theory may also develop from a collection of hypotheses that have been tested and verified. For example, during the nineteenth century, various scientists developed hypotheses to account for observations that linked electricity and magnetism. In 1873, James Maxwell published his book *Treatise on Electricity and Magnetism*. The theory of electromagnetism is now a well-established part of science.

Science and Its Laws

In science, a law is a descriptive statement that reliably predicts events under certain conditions. A law can sometimes be expressed in terms of a single mathematical equation. Some scientific laws include Newton's laws of motion, the laws of thermodynamics, the ideal gas laws, and the laws of conservation of mass and energy. It is important to know the conditions under which a law is valid before using it. Laws can be valid over a wide range of circumstances or over a very limited range of circumstances.

A law is not the same as a theory. A law describes what is observed in nature under certain conditions. A theory is a system of ideas that explains many related observations and is supported by a large body of evidence acquired through scientific investigation. For example, Newton's law of gravitation predicts the size of the gravitational force between masses. It says nothing of what causes this force. Einstein's theory of gravity, however, explains that motion due to gravity is due to the bending of space-time caused by mass.

Laws and theories do, however, share certain features—both are supported by observational evidence, both are widely accepted by scientists, and both may need to be modified or abandoned if conflicting evidence is discovered. They are both tools that help scientists to answer questions about the world around them.

Symbols

Diagram Symbols

MECHANICS	
Symbol	Meaning
→	displacement vector, displacement component
→	velocity vector, velocity component
→	acceleration vector
→	force vector, force component
→	momentum vector
→	gravitational field vector
∠	angle marking
↰	rotational motion

THERMODYNAMICS	
Symbol	Meaning
→	energy transferred as heat
→	energy transferred as work
↻	cycle or process

WAVES AND ELECTROMAGNETISM	
Symbol	Meaning
↘	ray (light or sound)
⊕	positive charge
⊖	negative charge
	electric field lines
→	electric field vector
	electric current
	magnetic field lines
→ ✕ ●	magnetic field vector (into page, out of page)

MATHEMATICAL SYMBOLS

Symbol	Meaning	Symbol	Meaning
Δ	(Greek *delta*) change in some quantity	$\leq$	less than or equal to
$\sum$	(Greek *sigma*) sum of quantities	$\propto$	is proportional to
θ	(Greek *theta*) any angle	$\approx$	is approximately equal to
$=$	equal to	$\lvert n \rvert$	absolute value or magnitude of
$>$	greater than	sin	sine
$\geq$	greater than or equal to	cos	cosine
$<$	less than	tan	tangent

Quantity Symbols Used Throughout

Symbols that are **boldfaced** refer to vector quantities that have both a magnitude and a direction. Symbols that are *italicized* refer to quantities with only a magnitude. Symbols that are neither are usually units.

Symbol	Quantity
A	area
D	diameter
$\mathbf{F}, F$	force
m	mass
M	total mass
R	radius (of a spherical body, a curved mirror, or a curved lens)
r	radius (of sphere, shell, or disk)
t	time
V	volume

Translational Mechanics Symbols Used in This Book

Symbols that are **boldfaced** refer to vector quantities that have both a magnitude and a direction. Symbols that are *italicized* refer to quantities with only a magnitude. Symbols that are neither are usually units.

Symbol	Quantity
$\mathbf{a}$, a	acceleration
$\mathbf{a_g}$	free-fall acceleration (acceleration due to gravity)
$\mathbf{d}$, d	displacement
$\mathbf{F}\Delta t$	impulse
$\mathbf{F_g}$, F_g	gravitational force
$\mathbf{F_k}$, F_k	force of kinetic friction
$\mathbf{F_n}$, F_n	normal force
$\mathbf{F_{net}}$, F_{net}	net force
$\mathbf{F_R}$, F_R	force of air resistance
$\mathbf{F_s}$, F_s	force of static friction
$\mathbf{F_{s,max}}$, $F_{s,max}$	maximum force of static friction
h	height
k	spring constant
KE	kinetic energy
KE_{trans}	translational kinetic energy
MA	mechanical advantage
ME	mechanical energy (sum of all kinetic and potential energy)
μ_k	(Greek *mu*) coefficient of kinetic friction
μ_s	(Greek *mu*) coefficient of static friction
P	power
$\mathbf{p}$, p	momentum
PE	potential energy
$PE_{elastic}$	elastic potential energy
PE_g	gravitational potential energy
r	separation between point masses
$\mathbf{v}$, v	velocity or speed
W	work
$W_{friction}$	work done by a frictional force (or work required to overcome a frictional force)
W_{net}	net work done
$\Delta\mathbf{x}$, Δx	displacement in the x-direction
$\Delta\mathbf{y}$, Δy	displacement in the y-direction

Rotational Mechanics Symbols Used in This Book

Symbols that are **boldfaced** refer to vector quantities that have both a magnitude and a direction. Symbols that are *italicized* refer to quantities with only a magnitude. Symbols that are neither are usually units.

Symbol	Quantity
a_t	tangential acceleration
a_c	centripetal acceleration
α	(Greek *alpha*) angular acceleration
$d \sin \theta$	lever arm (for torque calculations)
$\mathbf{F_c}, F_c$	centripetal force
I	moment of inertia
KE_{rot}	rotational kinetic energy
L	angular momentum
ℓ	length of a rotating rod
s	arc length
τ	(Greek *tau*) torque
τ_{net}	(Greek *tau*) net torque
θ	(Greek *theta*) angle of rotation
$\Delta\theta$	(Greek *delta* and *theta*) angular displacement (in radians)
v_t	tangential speed
ω	(Greek *omega*) angular speed

Fluid Dynamics and Thermodynamics Symbols Used in This Book

Symbols that are **boldfaced** refer to vector quantities that have both a magnitude and a direction. Symbols that are *italicized* refer to quantities with only a magnitude. Symbols that are neither are usually units.

Symbol	Quantity
c_p	specific heat capacity
eff	efficiency of a simple machine, thermal efficiency of a heat engine
$\mathbf{F_B}, F_B$	buoyant force
L	latent heat
L_f	latent heat of fusion
L_v	latent heat of vaporization
N	number of gas particles or nuclei
P	pressure
P_0	initial pressure, atmospheric pressure
P_{net}	net pressure
ρ	(Greek *rho*) mass density
Q	heat
Q_c	energy transferred as heat to or from a low-temperature (cold) substance
Q_h	energy transferred as heat to or from a high-temperature (hot) substance
Q_{net}	net amount of energy transferred as heat to or from a system
T	temperature (absolute)
T_C	temperature in degrees Celsius
T_c	temperature of a low-temperature (cold) substance
T_F	temperature in degrees Fahrenheit
T_h	temperature of a high-temperature (hot) substance
U	internal energy

Vibrations, Waves, and Optics Symbols Used in This Book

Symbols that are **boldfaced** refer to vector quantities that have both a magnitude and a direction. Symbols that are *italicized* refer to quantities with only a magnitude. Symbols that are neither are usually units.

Symbol	Quantity
C	center of curvature for spherical mirror
d	slit separation in double-slit interference of light
$d \sin \theta$	path difference for interfering light waves
$\mathbf{F}_{elastic}, F_{elastic}$	spring force
F	focal point
f	focal length
f	frequency
f_n	nth harmonic frequency
h	object height
h'	image height
k	spring constant
L	length of a pendulum, vibrating string, or vibrating column of air
ℓ	path length of light wave
λ	(Greek *lambda*) wavelength
m	order number for interference fringes
M	magnification of image
n	harmonic number (sound)
n	index of refraction
p	object distance
q	image distance
T	period of a pendulum (simple harmonic motion)
θ	(Greek *theta*) angle of incidence of a beam of light (reflection)
θ	(Greek *theta*) angle of fringe separation from center of interference pattern
θ'	(Greek *theta*) angle of reflection
θ_c	(Greek theta) critical angle of refraction
θ_i	(Greek *theta*) angle of incidence of a beam of light (refraction)
θ_r	(Greek *theta*) angle of refraction

Electromagnetism Symbols Used in This Book

Symbols that are **boldfaced** refer to vector quantities that have both a magnitude and a direction. Symbols that are *italicized* refer to quantities with only a magnitude. Symbols that are neither are usually units.

Symbol	Quantity
$\mathbf{B}, B$	magnetic field
C	capacitance
d	separation of plates in a capacitor
$\mathbf{E}, E$	electric field
emf	emf (potential difference) produced by a battery or electromagnetic induction
$\mathbf{F}_{electric}, F_{electric}$	electric force
$\mathbf{F}_{magnetic}, F_{magnetic}$	magnetic force
I	electric current
i	instantaneous current (ac circuit)
I_{max}	maximum current (ac circuit)
I_{rms}	root-mean-square current (ac circuit)
L	self-inductance
ℓ	length of an electrical conductor in a magnetic field
M	mutual inductance
N	number of turns in a current-carrying loop or a transformer coil
$PE_{electric}$	electrical potential energy
Q	large charge or charge on a fully charged capacitor
q	charge
R	resistance
r	separation between charges
R_{eq}	equivalent resistance
V	electric potential
ΔV	potential difference
Δv	instantaneous potential difference (ac circuit)
ΔV_{max}	maximum potential difference (ac circuit)
ΔV_{rms}	root-mean-square potential difference (ac circuit)
ω	(Greek *omega*) angular frequency

Particle and Electronic Symbols Used in This Book

For this part of the book, two tables are given because some symbols refer to quantities and others refer to specific particles. The symbol's context should make clear which table should be consulted.

Symbol	Quantity
A	mass number
β	(Greek *beta*) current or potential difference gain of an amplifier
E	photon energy
E_R	rest energy
f_t	threshold frequency (photoelectric effect)
hf_t	work function (photoelectric effect)
KE_{max}	maximum energy of ejected photoelectron
λ	(Greek *lambda*) decay constant
λN	decay rate (activity)
N	neutron number, number of decayed particles
n	energy quantum number
$T_{1/2}$	half-life
Z	atomic number

Symbol	Particle
α	alpha particle
$b, \bar{b}$	bottom quark, antiquark
β^+	(Greek *beta*) positron (beta particle)
β^-	(Greek *beta*) electron (beta particle)
$c, \bar{c}$	charmed quark, antiquark
$d, \bar{d}$	down quark, antiquark
$e^+, {}^{0}_{+1}e$	positron
$e^-, {}^{0}_{-1}e$	electron
γ	(Greek *gamma*) photon (gamma rays)
${}^{4}_{2}\text{He}$	alpha particle (helium-4 nucleus)
μ	(Greek *mu*) muon
${}^{1}_{0}\text{n}$	neutron
${}^{1}_{1}\text{p}$	proton
$s, \bar{s}$	strange quark, antiquark
$t, \bar{t}$	top quark, antiquark
$u, \bar{u}$	up quark, antiquark
τ	(Greek *tau*) tauon
$\upsilon, \bar{\upsilon}$	(Greek *nu*) neutrino, antineutrino
W^+, W^-	boson (weak force)
Z	boson (weak force)

Equations

Motion in One Dimension

DISPLACEMENT

$$\Delta x = x_f - x_i$$

AVERAGE VELOCITY

$$v_{avg} = \frac{\Delta x}{\Delta t} = \frac{x_f - x_i}{t_f - t_i}$$

AVERAGE SPEED

$$\text{average speed} = \frac{\text{distance traveled}}{\text{time of travel}}$$

AVERAGE ACCELERATION

$$a_{avg} = \frac{\Delta v}{\Delta t} = \frac{v_f - v_i}{t_f - t_i}$$

DISPLACEMENT
These equations are valid only for constantly accelerated, straight-line motion.

$$\Delta x = \frac{1}{2}(v_i + v_f)\Delta t$$

$$\Delta x = v_i \Delta t + \frac{1}{2}a(\Delta t)^2$$

FINAL VELOCITY
These equations are valid only for constantly accelerated, straight-line motion.

$$v_f = v_i + a\Delta t$$

$$v_f^2 = v_i^2 + 2a\Delta x$$

Two-Dimensional Motion and Vectors

PYTHAGOREAN THEOREM
This equation is valid only for right triangles.

$$c^2 = a^2 + b^2$$

TANGENT, SINE, AND COSINE FUNCTIONS
These equations are valid only for right triangles.

$$\tan \theta = \frac{opp}{adj} \qquad \sin \theta = \frac{opp}{hyp} \qquad \tan \theta = \frac{adj}{hyp}$$

VERTICAL MOTION OF A PROJECTILE THAT FALLS FROM REST
These equations assume that air resistance is negligible and apply only when the initial vertical velocity is zero. On Earth's surface, $a_y = -g = -9.81 \text{ m/s}^2$.

$$v_{y,f} = a_y \Delta t$$

$$v_{y,f}^2 = 2a_y \Delta y$$

$$\Delta y = \frac{1}{2}a_y(\Delta t)^2$$

HORIZONTAL MOTION OF A PROJECTILE
These equations assume that air resistance is negligible.

$$v_x = v_{x,i} = \text{constant}$$

$$\Delta x = v_x \Delta t$$

PROJECTILES LAUNCHED AT AN ANGLE

These equations assume that air resistance is negligible. On Earth's surface, $a_y = -g = -9.81 \text{ m/s}^2$.

$$v_x = v_i \cos \theta = \text{constant}$$

$$\Delta x = (v_i \cos \theta)\Delta t$$

$$v_{y,f} = v_i \sin \theta + a_y \Delta t$$

$$v_{y,f}^2 = v_i^2 (\sin \theta)^2 + 2a_y \Delta y$$

$$\Delta y = (v_i \sin \theta)\Delta t + \frac{1}{2}a_y(\Delta t)^2$$

RELATIVE VELOCITY

$$\mathbf{v_{ac}} = \mathbf{v_{ab}} + \mathbf{v_{bc}}$$

Forces and the Laws of Motion

NEWTON'S FIRST LAW

An object at rest remains at rest, and an object in motion continues in motion with constant velocity (that is, constant speed in a straight line) unless the object experiences a net external force.

NEWTON'S SECOND LAW

$\sum \mathbf{F}$ is the vector sum of all external forces acting on the object.

$$\sum \mathbf{F} = m\mathbf{a}$$

NEWTON'S THIRD LAW

If two objects interact, the magnitude of the force exerted on object 1 by object 2 is equal to the magnitude of the force exerted on object 2 by object 1, and these two forces are opposite in direction.

WEIGHT

On Earth's surface, $a_g = g = 9.81 \text{ m/s}^2$.

$$F_g = ma_g$$

COEFFICIENT OF STATIC FRICTION

$$\mu_s = \frac{F_{s,max}}{F_n}$$

COEFFICIENT OF KINETIC FRICTION

The coefficient of kinetic friction varies with speed, but we neglect any such variations here.

$$\mu_k = \frac{F_k}{F_n}$$

FORCE OF FRICTION

$$F_f = \mu F_n$$

Work and Energy

NET WORK
This equation applies only when the force is constant.

$$W_{net} = F_{net}d\cos\theta$$

KINETIC ENERGY

$$KE = \frac{1}{2}mv^2$$

WORK–KINETIC ENERGY THEOREM

$$W_{net} = \Delta KE$$

GRAVITATIONAL POTENTIAL ENERGY

$$PE_g = mgh$$

ELASTIC POTENTIAL ENERGY

$$PE_{elastic} = \frac{1}{2}kx^2$$

MECHANICAL ENERGY

$$ME = KE + \Sigma PE$$

CONSERVATION OF MECHANICAL ENERGY
This equation is valid only if nonmechanical forms of energy (such as friction) are disregarded.

$$ME_i = ME_f$$

POWER

$$P = \frac{W}{\Delta t} = Fv$$

Momentum and Collisions

MOMENTUM

$$\mathbf{p} = m\mathbf{v}$$

IMPULSE-MOMENTUM THEOREM
This equation is valid only when the force is constant.

$$\mathbf{F}\Delta t = \Delta\mathbf{p} = m\mathbf{v_f} - m\mathbf{v_i}$$

CONSERVATION OF MOMENTUM
These equations are valid for a closed system, that is, when no external forces act on the system during the collision. When such external forces are either negligibly small or act for too short a time to make a significant change in the momentum, these equations represent a good approximation. The second equation is valid for two-body collisions.

$$\mathbf{p_i} = \mathbf{p_f}$$
$$m_1\mathbf{v_{1,i}} + m_2\mathbf{v_{2,i}} = m_1\mathbf{v_{1,f}} + m_2\mathbf{v_{2,f}}$$

CONSERVATION OF MOMENTUM FOR A PERFECTLY INELASTIC COLLISION

This is a simplified version of the conservation of momentum equation valid only for perfectly inelastic collisions between two bodies.

$$m_1 \mathbf{v_{1,i}} + m_2 \mathbf{v_{2,i}} = (m_1 + m_2)\, \mathbf{v_f}$$

CONSERVATION OF KINETIC ENERGY FOR AN ELASTIC COLLISION

No collision is perfectly elastic; some kinetic energy is always converted to other forms of energy. But if these losses are minimal, this equation can provide a good approximation.

$$\frac{1}{2} m_1 v_{1,i}^2 + \frac{1}{2} m_2 v_{2,i}^2 = \\ \frac{1}{2} m_1 v_{1,f}^2 + \frac{1}{2} m_2 v_{2,f}^2$$

Circular Motion and Gravitation

CENTRIPETAL ACCELERATION

$$a_c = \frac{v_t^2}{r}$$

CENTRIPETAL FORCE

$$F_c = \frac{m v_t^2}{r}$$

NEWTON'S LAW OF UNIVERSAL GRAVITATION

The constant of universal gravitation (G) equals 6.673×10^{-11} N•m^2/kg^2.

$$F_g = G \frac{m_1 m_2}{r^2}$$

KEPLER'S LAWS OF PLANETARY MOTION

First Law: Each planet travels in an elliptical orbit around the sun, and the sun is at one of the focal points.

Second Law: An imaginary line drawn from the sun to any planet sweeps out equal areas in equal time intervals.

Third Law: The square of a planet's orbital period (T^2) is proportional to the cube of the average distance (r^3) between the planet and the sun, or $T^2 \propto r^3$.

PERIOD AND SPEED OF AN OBJECT IN CIRCULAR ORBIT

The constant of universal gravitation (G) equals 6.673×10^{-11} N•m^2/kg^2.

$$T = 2\pi \sqrt{\frac{r^3}{Gm}}$$

$$v_t = \sqrt{G \frac{m}{r}}$$

TORQUE

$$\tau = Fd \sin \theta$$

MECHANICAL ADVANTAGE
This equation disregards friction.

$$MA = \frac{F_{out}}{F_{in}} = \frac{d_{in}}{d_{out}}$$

EFFICIENCY
This equation accounts for friction.

$$eff = \frac{W_{out}}{W_{in}}$$

Fluid Mechanics

MASS DENSITY

$$\rho = \frac{m}{V}$$

BUOYANT FORCE
The first equation is for an object that is completely or partially submerged. The second equation is for a floating object.

$$F_B = F_g\,(displaced\ fluid) = m_f g$$
$$F_B = F_g\,(object) = mg$$

PRESSURE

$$P = \frac{F}{A}$$

PASCAL'S PRINCIPLE

Pressure applied to a fluid in a closed container is transmitted equally to every point of the fluid and to the walls of the container.

HYDRAULIC LIFT EQUATION

$$F_2 = \frac{A_2}{A_1} F_1$$

FLUID PRESSURE AS A FUNCTION OF DEPTH

$$P = P_0 + \rho g h$$

CONTINUITY EQUATION

$$A_1 v_1 = A_2 v_2$$

BERNOULLI'S PRINCIPLE

The pressure in a fluid decreases as the fluid's velocity increases.

Heat

TEMPERATURE CONVERSIONS

$$T_F = \frac{9}{5} T_C + 32.0$$
$$T = T_C + 273.15$$

| CONSERVATION OF ENERGY | $\Delta PE + \Delta KE + \Delta U = 0$ |

| SPECIFIC HEAT CAPACITY | $c_p = \dfrac{Q}{m\Delta T}$ |

CALORIMETRY
These equations assume that the energy transferred to the surrounding container is negligible.

$$Q_w = -Q_x$$
$$c_{p,w}\, m_w \Delta T_w = -c_{p,x}\, m_x \Delta T_x$$

LATENT HEAT

$$Q = mL$$

Thermodynamics

WORK DONE BY A GAS
This equation is valid only when the pressure is constant. When the work done by the gas (W) is negative, positive work is done on the gas.

$$W = PAd = P\Delta V$$

THE FIRST LAW OF THERMODYNAMICS
Q represents the energy added to the system as heat and W represents the work done by the system.

$$\Delta U = Q - W$$

CYCLIC PROCESSES

$$\Delta U_{net} = 0 \text{ and } Q_{net} = W_{net}$$

EFFICIENCY OF A HEAT ENGINE

$$eff = \frac{W_{net}}{Q_h} = \frac{Q_h - Q_c}{Q_h} = 1 - \frac{Q_c}{Q_h}$$

Vibrations and Waves

HOOKE'S LAW

$$F_{elastic} = -kx$$

PERIOD OF A SIMPLE PENDULUM IN SIMPLE HARMONIC MOTION
This equation is valid only when the amplitude is small (less than about 15°).

$$T = 2\pi \sqrt{\frac{L}{a_g}}$$

PERIOD OF A MASS-SPRING SYSTEM IN SIMPLE HARMONIC MOTION

$$T = 2\pi \sqrt{\frac{m}{k}}$$

SPEED OF A WAVE

$$v = f\lambda$$

Sound

INTENSITY OF A SPHERICAL WAVE
This equation assumes that there is no absorption in the medium.

$$\text{intensity} = \frac{P}{4\pi r^2}$$

HARMONIC SERIES OF A VIBRATING STRING OR A PIPE OPEN AT BOTH ENDS

$$f_n = n\frac{v}{2L} \quad n = 1, 2, 3, \ldots$$

HARMONIC SERIES OF A PIPE CLOSED AT ONE END

$$f_n = n\frac{v}{4L} \quad n = 1, 3, 5, \ldots$$

BEATS

frequency difference = number of beats per second

Light and Reflection

SPEED OF ELECTROMAGNETIC WAVES
This book uses the value $c = 3.00 \times 10^8$ m/s for the speed of EM waves in a vacuum or in air.

$$c = f\lambda$$

LAW OF REFLECTION

angle of incidence (θ) = angle of reflection (θ')

MIRROR EQUATION
This equation is derived assuming that the rays incident on the mirror are very close to the principal axis of the mirror.

$$\frac{1}{p} + \frac{1}{q} = \frac{1}{f}$$

MAGNIFICATION OF A CURVED MIRROR

$$M = \frac{h'}{h} = -\frac{q}{p}$$

Refraction

INDEX OF REFRACTION
For any material other than a vacuum, the index of refraction varies with the wavelength of light.

$$n = \frac{c}{v}$$

SNELL'S LAW

$$n_i \sin \theta_i = n_r \sin \theta_r$$

THIN-LENS EQUATION

This equation is derived assuming that the thickness of the lens is much less than the focal length of the lens.

$$\frac{1}{p} + \frac{1}{q} = \frac{1}{f}$$

MAGNIFICATION OF A LENS

This equation can be used only when the index of refraction of the first medium (n_i) is greater than the index of refraction of the second medium (n_r).

$$M = \frac{h'}{h} = -\frac{q}{p} \, (\textit{for } n_i > n_r)$$

CRITICAL ANGLE

This equation can be used only when the index of refraction of the first medium (n_i) is greater than the index of refraction of the second medium (n_r).

$$\sin \theta_c = \frac{n_r}{n_i} (\textit{for } n_i > n_r)$$

Interference and Diffraction

CONSTRUCTIVE AND DESTRUCTIVE INTERFERENCE

The grating spacing multiplied by the sine of the angle of deviation is the path difference between two waves. To observe interference effects, the sources must be coherent and have identical wavelengths.

Constructive Interference:
$$d \sin \theta = \pm m\lambda$$
$$m = 0, 1, 2, 3, \ldots$$

Destructive Interference:
$$d \sin \theta = \pm(m + \frac{1}{2})\lambda$$
$$m = 0, 1, 2, 3, \ldots$$

DIFFRACTION GRATING

See the equation above for constructive interference.

LIMITING ANGLE OF RESOLUTION

This equation gives the angle θ in radians and applies only to circular apertures.

$$\theta = 1.22 \frac{\lambda}{D}$$

Electric Forces and Fields

COULOMB'S LAW

This equation assumes either point charges or spherical distributions of charge.

$$F_{electric} = k_C \left(\frac{q_1 q_2}{r^2} \right)$$

ELECTRIC FIELD STRENGTH DUE TO A POINT CHARGE

$$E = k_C \frac{q}{r^2}$$

Electrical Energy and Current

ELECTRICAL POTENTIAL ENERGY
The displacement, d, is from the reference point and is parallel to the field. This equation is valid only for a uniform electric field.

$$PE_{electric} = -qEd$$

POTENTIAL DIFFERENCE
The second half of this equation is valid only for a uniform electric field, and Δd is parallel to the field.

$$\Delta V = \frac{\Delta PE_{electric}}{q} = -E\Delta d$$

POTENTIAL DIFFERENCE BETWEEN A POINT AT INFINITY AND A POINT NEAR A POINT CHARGE

$$\Delta V = k_C \frac{q}{r}$$

CAPACITANCE

$$C = \frac{Q}{\Delta V}$$

CAPACITANCE FOR A PARALLEL-PLATE CAPACITOR IN A VACUUM
The permittivity in a vacuum (ε_0) equals 8.85×10^{-12} C^2/(N•m^2).

$$C = \varepsilon_0 \frac{A}{d}$$

ELECTRICAL POTENTIAL ENERGY STORED IN A CHARGED CAPACITOR
There is a limit to the maximum energy (or charge) that can be stored in a capacitor, because electrical breakdown ultimately occurs between the plates of the capacitor for a sufficiently large potential difference.

$$PE_{electric} = \frac{1}{2}Q\Delta V = \frac{1}{2}C(\Delta V)^2 = \frac{Q^2}{2C}$$

ELECTRIC CURRENT

$$I = \frac{\Delta Q}{\Delta t}$$

RESISTANCE

$$R = \frac{\Delta V}{I}$$

OHM'S LAW
Ohm's law is not universal, but it does apply to many materials over a wide range of applied potential differences.

$$\frac{\Delta V}{I} = \text{constant}$$

ELECTRIC POWER

$$P = I\Delta V = I^2 R = \frac{(\Delta V)^2}{R}$$

Circuits and Circuit Elements

RESISTORS IN SERIES: EQUIVALENT RESISTANCE AND CURRENT

$$R_{eq} = R_1 + R_2 + R_3 \ldots$$

The current in each resistor is the same and is equal to the total current.

RESISTORS IN PARALLEL: EQUIVALENT RESISTANCE AND CURRENT

$$\frac{1}{R_{eq}} = \frac{1}{R_1} + \frac{1}{R_2} + \frac{1}{R_3} \ldots$$

The sum of the current in each resistor equals the total current.

Magnetism

MAGNETIC FLUX

$$\Phi_M = AB \cos \theta$$

MAGNITUDE OF A MAGNETIC FIELD

The direction of $F_{magnetic}$ is always perpendicular to both B and v and can be found with the right-hand rule.

$$B = \frac{F_{magnetic}}{qv}$$

FORCE ON A CURRENT-CARRYING CONDUCTOR PERPENDICULAR TO A MAGNETIC FIELD

This equation can be used only when the current and the magnetic field are at right angles to each other.

$$F_{magnetic} = BI\ell$$

Electromagnetic Induction

FARADAY'S LAW OF MAGNETIC INDUCTION

N is assumed to be a whole number.

$$\text{emf} = -N\frac{\Delta\Phi_M}{\Delta t}$$

EMF PRODUCED BY A GENERATOR

N is assumed to be a whole number.

$$\text{emf} = NAB\omega \sin \omega t$$
$$\text{maximum emf} = NAB\omega$$

FARADAY'S LAW FOR MUTUAL INDUCTANCE

$$\text{emf} = -M\frac{\Delta I}{\Delta t}$$

RMS CURRENT AND POTENTIAL DIFFERENCE

$$I_{rms} = \frac{I_{max}}{\sqrt{2}} = 0.707\, I_{max}$$

$$\Delta V_{rms} = \frac{\Delta V_{max}}{\sqrt{2}} = 0.707\, \Delta V$$

TRANSFORMERS
N is assumed to be a whole number.

$$\Delta V_2 = \frac{N_2}{N_1} \Delta V_1$$

Atomic Physics

ENERGY OF A LIGHT QUANTUM

$$E = hf$$

MAXIMUM KINETIC ENERGY OF A PHOTOELECTRON

$$KE_{max} = hf - hf_t$$

WAVELENGTH AND FREQUENCY OF MATTER WAVES
Planck's constant (h) equals 6.63×10^{-34} J•s.

$$\lambda = \frac{h}{p} = \frac{h}{mv}$$

$$f = \frac{E}{h}$$

Subatomic Physics

RELATIONSHIP BETWEEN REST ENERGY AND MASS

$$E_R = mc^2$$

BINDING ENERGY OF A NUCLEUS

$$E_{bind} = \Delta mc^2$$

MASS DEFECT

$$\Delta m = Z(\text{atomic mass of H}) + Nm_n - \text{atomic mass}$$

ACTIVITY (DECAY RATE)

$$\text{activity} = -\frac{\Delta N}{\Delta t} = \lambda N$$

HALF-LIFE

$$T_{1/2} = \frac{0.693}{\lambda}$$

Take It Further Topics

CONVERSION BETWEEN RADIANS AND DEGREES

$$\theta \text{ (rad)} = \frac{\pi}{180°}\theta \text{ (deg)}$$

ANGULAR DISPLACEMENT
This equation gives $\Delta\theta$ in radians.

$$\Delta\theta = \frac{\Delta s}{r}$$

AVERAGE ANGULAR VELOCITY

$$\omega_{avg} = \frac{\Delta\theta}{\Delta t}$$

AVERAGE ANGULAR ACCELERATION

$$\alpha_{avg} = \frac{\Delta\omega}{\Delta t}$$

ROTATIONAL KINEMATICS
These equations apply only when the angular acceleration is constant. The symbol ω represents instantaneous rather than average angular velocity.

$$\omega f = \omega_i + \alpha\Delta t$$
$$\Delta\theta = \omega_i\Delta t + \frac{1}{2}\alpha(\Delta t)^2$$
$$\omega f^2 = \omega_i^2 + 2\alpha(\Delta\theta)$$
$$\Delta\theta = \frac{1}{2}(\omega_i + \omega_f)\Delta t$$

TANGENTIAL SPEED
For this equation to be valid, ω must be in rad/s.

$$v_t = r\omega$$

TANGENTIAL ACCELERATION
For this equation to be valid, α must be in rad/s^2.

$$a_t = r\alpha$$

NEWTON'S SECOND LAW FOR ROTATING OBJECTS

$$\tau = I\alpha$$

ANGULAR MOMENTUM

$$L = I\omega$$

ROTATIONAL KINETIC ENERGY

$$KE_{rot} = \frac{1}{2}I\omega^2$$

IDEAL GAS LAW
Boltzmann's constant (k_B) equals 1.38×10^{-23} J/K.

$$PV = Nk_BT$$

BERNOULLI'S EQUATION

$$P + \frac{1}{2}\rho v^2 + \rho gh = \text{constant}$$

APPENDIX E

SI Units

SI BASE UNITS USED IN THIS BOOK

Symbol	Name	Quantity
A	ampere	current
K	kelvin	absolute temperature
kg	kilogram	mass
m	meter	length
s	second	time

SI PREFIXES

Symbol	Name	Numerical equivalent
a	atto	10^{-18}
f	femto	10^{-15}
p	pico	10^{-12}
n	nano	10^{-9}
μ	micro	10^{-6}
m	milli	10^{-3}
c	centi	10^{-2}
d	deci	10^{-1}
k	kilo	10^{3}
M	mega	10^{6}
G	giga	10^{9}
T	tera	10^{12}
P	peta	10^{15}
E	exa	10^{18}

OTHER COMMONLY USED UNITS

Symbol	Name	Quantity	Conversions
atm	standard atmosphere	pressure	$1.013\,250 \times 10^5$ Pa
Btu	British thermal unit	energy	1.055×10^3 J
Cal	food calorie	energy	$= 1$ kcal $= 4.186 \times 10^3$ J
cal	calorie	energy	4.186 J
Ci	curie	decay rate or activity	3.7×10^{10} s^{-1}
°F	degree Fahrenheit	temperature	0.5556°C
ft	foot	length	0.3048 m
ft•lb	foot-pound	work and energy	1.356 J
g	gram	mass	0.001 kg
gal	gallon	volume	3.785×10^{-3} m^3
hp	horsepower	power	746 W
in	inch	length	2.54×10^{-2} m
kcal	kilocalorie	energy	4.186×10^3 J
lb	pound	force	4.45 N
mi	mile	length	1.609×10^3 m
rev	revolution	angular displacement	2π rad
°	degree	angular displacement	$= \left(\dfrac{2\pi}{326}\right)$ rad $= 1.745 \times 10^{-2}$ rad

OTHER UNITS ACCEPTABLE WITH SI

Symbol	Name	Quantity	Conversion
Bq	becquerel	decay rate or activity	$\dfrac{1}{s}$
C	coulomb	electric charge	$1\ A\bullet s$
°C	degree Celsius	temperature	$1\ K$
dB	decibel	relative intensity (sound)	(unitless)
eV	electron volt	energy	$1.60 \times 10^{-19}\ J$
F	farad	capacitance	$1\ \dfrac{A^2\bullet s^4}{kg\bullet m^2} = 1\ \dfrac{C}{V}$
H	henry	inductance	$1\ \dfrac{kg\bullet m^2}{A^2\bullet s^2} = 1\ \dfrac{J}{A^2}$
h	hour	time	$3.600 \times 10^3\ s$
Hz	hertz	frequency	$\dfrac{1}{s}$
J	joule	work and energy	$1\ \dfrac{kg\bullet m^2}{s^2} = 1\ N\bullet m$
kW•h	kilowatt-hour	energy	$3.60 \times 10^6\ J$
L	liter	volume	$10^{-3}\ m^3$
min	minute	time	$6.0 \times 10^1\ s$
N	newton	force	$1\ \dfrac{kg\bullet m}{s^2}$
Pa	pascal	pressure	$1\ \dfrac{kg}{m\bullet s^2} = 1\ \dfrac{N}{m^2}$
rad	radian	angular displacement	(unitless)
T	tesla	magnetic field strength	$1\ \dfrac{kg}{A\bullet s^3} = 1\ \dfrac{N}{A\bullet m} = 1\ \dfrac{V\bullet s}{m^2}$
u	unified mass unit	mass (atomic masses)	$1.660\ 538\ 782 \times 10^{-27}\ kg$
V	volt	electric potential difference	$1\ \dfrac{kg\bullet m^2}{A\bullet s^3} = 1\ \dfrac{J}{C}$
W	watt	power	$1\ \dfrac{kg\bullet m^2}{s^3} = 1\ \dfrac{J}{s}$
Ω	ohm	resistance	$1\ \dfrac{kg\bullet m^2}{A^2\bullet s^3} = 1\ \dfrac{V}{A}$

Reference Tables

FUNDAMENTAL CONSTANTS

Symbol	Quantity	Established value	Value used for calculations in this book
c	speed of light in a vacuum	299 792 458 m/s	3.00×10^8 m/s
e^-	elementary charge	$1.602\ 176\ 487 \times 10^{-19}$ C	1.60×10^{-19} C
e^1	base of natural logarithms	2.718 2818 28	2.72
ε_0	(Greek *epsilon*) permittivity of a vacuum	$8.854\ 187\ 817 \times 10^{-12}$ C^2/(N•m^2)	8.85×10^{-12} C^2/(N•m^2)
G	constant of universal gravitation	$6.672\ 59 \times 10^{-11}$ N•m^2/kg^2	6.673×10^{-11} N•m^2/kg^2
g	free-fall acceleration at Earth's surface	9.806 65 m/s^2	9.81 m/s^2
h	Planck's constant	$6.626\ 068\ 96 \times 10^{-34}$ J•s	6.63×10^{-34} J•s
k_B	Boltzmann's constant (R/N_A)	$1.380\ 6504 \times 10^{-23}$ J/K	1.38×10^{-23} J/K
k_C	Coulomb constant	$8.987\ 551\ 787 \times 10^9$ N•m^2/C^2	8.99×10^9 N•m^2/C^2
R	molar (universal) gas constant	8.314 472 J/(mol•K)	8.31 J/(mol•K)
π	(Greek *pi*) ratio of the circumference to the diameter of a circle	3.141 592 654	calculator value

COEFFICIENTS OF FRICTION (APPROXIMATE VALUES)

	μ_s	μ_k		μ_s	μ_k
steel on steel	0.74	0.57	waxed wood on wet snow	0.14	0.1
aluminum on steel	0.61	0.47	waxed wood on dry snow	–	0.04
rubber on dry concrete	1.0	0.8	metal on metal (lubricated)	0.15	0.06
rubber on wet concrete	–	0.5	ice on ice	0.1	0.03
wood on wood	0.4	0.2	Teflon on Teflon	0.04	0.04
glass on glass	0.9	0.4	synovial joints in humans	0.01	0.003

USEFUL ASTRONOMICAL DATA

Symbol	Quantity	Value used for calculations in this book
I_E	moment of inertia of Earth	8.03×10^{37} kg•m^2
M_E	mass of Earth	5.97×10^{24} kg
R_E	radius of Earth	6.38×10^6 m
	average Earth–moon distance	3.84×10^8 m
	average Earth–sun distance	1.50×10^{11} m
	mass of the moon	7.35×10^{22} kg
	mass of the sun	1.99×10^{30} kg
yr	period of Earth's orbit	3.16×10^7 s

THE MOMENT OF INERTIA FOR A FEW SHAPES

Shape		Moment of inertia
	thin hoop about symmetry axis	MR^2
	thin hoop about diameter	$\frac{1}{2}MR^2$
	point mass about axis	MR^2
	disk or cylinder about symmetry axis	$\frac{1}{2}MR^2$

THE MOMENT OF INERTIA FOR A FEW SHAPES

Shape		Moment of inertia
⊢—ℓ—⊣	thin rod about perpendicular axis through center	$\frac{1}{12}M\ell^2$
⊢—ℓ—⊣	thin rod about perpendicular axis through end	$\frac{1}{3}M\ell^2$
	solid sphere about diameter	$\frac{2}{5}MR^2$
	thin spherical shell about diameter	$\frac{2}{3}MR^2$

DENSITIES OF SOME COMMON SUBSTANCES*

Substance	$\rho\,(kg/m^3)$
hydrogen	0.0899
helium	0.179
steam (100°C)	0.598
air	1.29
oxygen	1.43
carbon dioxide	1.98
ethanol	0.806×10^3
ice	0.917×10^3
fresh water (4°C)	1.00×10^3
sea water (15°C)	1.025×10^3
glycerine	1.26×10^3
aluminum	2.70×10^3
iron	7.86×10^3
copper	8.92×10^3
silver	10.5×10^3
lead	11.3×10^3
mercury	13.6×10^3
gold	19.3×10^3

*All densities are measured at 0°C and 1 atm unless otherwise noted.

SPECIFIC HEAT CAPACITIES

Substance	$c_p\,(J/kg \cdot °C)$
aluminum	8.99×10^2
copper	3.87×10^2
glass	8.37×10^2
gold	1.29×10^2
ice	2.09×10^3
iron	4.48×10^2
lead	1.28×10^2
mercury	1.38×10^2
silver	2.34×10^2
steam	2.01×10^3
water	4.186×10^3

LATENT HEATS OF FUSION AND VAPORIZATION AT STANDARD PRESSURE

Substance	Melting point (°C)	L_f(J/kg)	Boiling point (°C)	L_v(J/kg)
nitrogen	−209.97	2.55×10^4	−195.81	2.01×10^5
oxygen	−218.79	1.38×10^4	−182.97	2.13×10^5
ethyl alcohol	−114	1.04×10^5	78	8.54×10^5
water	0.00	3.33×10^5	100.00	2.26×10^6
lead	327.3	2.45×10^4	1745	8.70×10^5
aluminum	660.4	3.97×10^5	2467	1.14×10^7

SPEED OF SOUND IN VARIOUS MEDIA

Medium	v(m/s)	Medium	v(m/s)	Medium	v(m/s)
Gases		**Liquids at 25°C**		**Solids**	
air (0°C)	331	methyl alcohol	1140	aluminum	5100
air (25°C)	346	sea water	1530	copper	3560
air (100°C)	366	water	1490	iron	5130
helium (0°C)	972			lead	1320
hydrogen (0°C)	1290			vulcanized rubber	54
oxygen (0°C)	317				

CONVERSION OF INTENSITY TO DECIBEL LEVEL

Intensity (W/m²)	Decibel level (dB)	Examples
1.0×10^{-12}	0	threshold of hearing
1.0×10^{-11}	10	rustling leaves
1.0×10^{-10}	20	quiet whisper
1.0×10^{-9}	30	whisper
1.0×10^{-8}	40	mosquito buzzing
1.0×10^{-7}	50	normal conversation
1.0×10^{-6}	60	air conditioning at 6 m
1.0×10^{-5}	70	vacuum cleaner
1.0×10^{-4}	80	busy traffic, alarm clock
1.0×10^{-3}	90	lawn mower
1.0×10^{-2}	100	subway, power motor
1.0×10^{-1}	110	auto horn at 1 m
1.0×10^{0}	120	threshold of pain
1.0×10^{1}	130	thunderclap, machine gun
1.0×10^{3}	150	nearby jet airplane

INDICES OF REFRACTION FOR VARIOUS SUBSTANCES*

Solids at 20°C	n	Liquids at 20°C	n	Gases at 0°C, 1 atm	n
cubic zirconia	2.20	benzene	1.501	air	1.000 293
diamond	2.419	carbon disulfide	1.628	carbon dioxide	1.000 450
fluorite	1.434	carbon tetrachloride	1.461		
fused quartz	1.458	ethyl alcohol	1.361		
glass, crown	1.52	glycerine	1.473		
glass, flint	1.66	water	1.333		
ice (at 0°C)	1.309				
polystyrene	1.49				
sodium chloride	1.544				
zircon	1.923				

*measured with light of vacuum wavelength = 589 nm

USEFUL ATOMIC DATA

Symbol	Quantity	Established value	Value used for calculations in this book
m_e	mass of electron	$9.109\ 382\ 15 \times 10^{-31}$ kg $5.485\ 799\ 0943 \times 10^{-4}$ u $0.510\ 998\ 910$ MeV	9.109×10^{-31} kg 5.49×10^{-4} u 5.110×10^{-1} MeV
m_n	mass of neutron	$1.674\ 927\ 211 \times 10^{-27}$ kg $1.008\ 664\ 915\ 97$ u $939.565\ 346$ MeV	1.675×10^{-27} kg $1.008\ 665$ u 9.396×10^{2} MeV
m_p	mass of proton	$1.672\ 621\ 637 \times 10^{-27}$ kg $1.007\ 276\ 466\ 77$ u $938.272\ 013$ MeV	1.673×10^{-27} kg $1.007\ 276$ u 9.383×10^{2} MeV

Periodic Table of the Elements

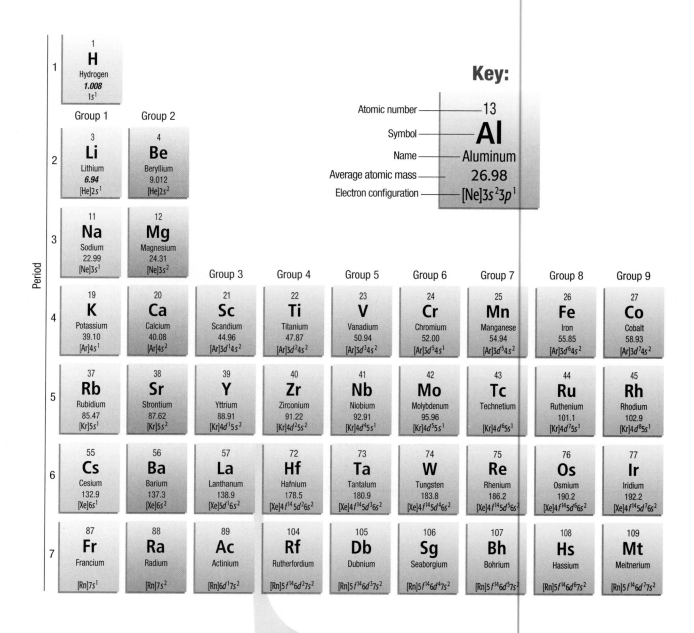

Key:

Atomic number — 13
Symbol — **Al**
Name — Aluminum
Average atomic mass — 26.98
Electron configuration — $[Ne]3s^2 3p^1$

Period

Group 1

1 | **H** | Hydrogen | *1.008* | $1s^1$

Group 2

2 | 3 **Li** Lithium *6.94* $[He]2s^1$ | 4 **Be** Beryllium 9.012 $[He]2s^2$

3 | 11 **Na** Sodium 22.99 $[Ne]3s^1$ | 12 **Mg** Magnesium 24.31 $[Ne]3s^2$

Group 3 | **Group 4** | **Group 5** | **Group 6** | **Group 7** | **Group 8** | **Group 9**

4 | 19 **K** Potassium 39.10 $[Ar]4s^1$ | 20 **Ca** Calcium 40.08 $[Ar]4s^2$ | 21 **Sc** Scandium 44.96 $[Ar]3d^1 4s^2$ | 22 **Ti** Titanium 47.87 $[Ar]3d^2 4s^2$ | 23 **V** Vanadium 50.94 $[Ar]3d^3 4s^2$ | 24 **Cr** Chromium 52.00 $[Ar]3d^5 4s^1$ | 25 **Mn** Manganese 54.94 $[Ar]3d^5 4s^2$ | 26 **Fe** Iron 55.85 $[Ar]3d^6 4s^2$ | 27 **Co** Cobalt 58.93 $[Ar]3d^7 4s^2$

5 | 37 **Rb** Rubidium 85.47 $[Kr]5s^1$ | 38 **Sr** Strontium 87.62 $[Kr]5s^2$ | 39 **Y** Yttrium 88.91 $[Kr]4d^1 5s^2$ | 40 **Zr** Zirconium 91.22 $[Kr]4d^2 5s^2$ | 41 **Nb** Niobium 92.91 $[Kr]4d^4 5s^1$ | 42 **Mo** Molybdenum 95.96 $[Kr]4d^5 5s^1$ | 43 **Tc** Technetium $[Kr]4d^6 5s^1$ | 44 **Ru** Ruthenium 101.1 $[Kr]4d^7 5s^1$ | 45 **Rh** Rhodium 102.9 $[Kr]4d^8 5s^1$

6 | 55 **Cs** Cesium 132.9 $[Xe]6s^1$ | 56 **Ba** Barium 137.3 $[Xe]6s^2$ | 57 **La** Lanthanum 138.9 $[Xe]5d^1 6s^2$ | 72 **Hf** Hafnium 178.5 $[Xe]4f^{14} 5d^2 6s^2$ | 73 **Ta** Tantalum 180.9 $[Xe]4f^{14} 5d^3 6s^2$ | 74 **W** Tungsten 183.8 $[Xe]4f^{14} 5d^4 6s^2$ | 75 **Re** Rhenium 186.2 $[Xe]4f^{14} 5d^5 6s^2$ | 76 **Os** Osmium 190.2 $[Xe]4f^{14} 5d^6 6s^2$ | 77 **Ir** Iridium 192.2 $[Xe]4f^{14} 5d^7 6s^2$

7 | 87 **Fr** Francium $[Rn]7s^1$ | 88 **Ra** Radium $[Rn]7s^2$ | 89 **Ac** Actinium $[Rn]6d^1 7s^2$ | 104 **Rf** Rutherfordium $[Rn]5f^{14} 6d^2 7s^2$ | 105 **Db** Dubnium $[Rn]5f^{14} 6d^3 7s^2$ | 106 **Sg** Seaborgium $[Rn]5f^{14} 6d^4 7s^2$ | 107 **Bh** Bohrium $[Rn]5f^{14} 6d^5 7s^2$ | 108 **Hs** Hassium $[Rn]5f^{14} 6d^6 7s^2$ | 109 **Mt** Meitnerium $[Rn]5f^{14} 6d^7 7s^2$

58 **Ce** Cerium 140.1 $[Xe]4f^1 5d^1 6s^2$ | 59 **Pr** Praseodymium 140.9 $[Xe]4f^3 6s^2$ | 60 **Nd** Neodymium 144.2 $[Xe]4f^4 6s^2$ | 61 **Pm** Promethium $[Xe]4f^5 6s^2$ | 62 **Sm** Samarium 150.4 $[Xe]4f^6 6s^2$

90 **Th** Thorium 232.0 $[Rn]6d^2 7s^2$ | 91 **Pa** Protactinium 231.0 $[Rn]5f^2 6d^1 7s^2$ | 92 **U** Uranium 238.0 $[Rn]5f^3 6d^1 7s^2$ | 93 **Np** Neptunium $[Rn]5f^4 6d^1 7s^2$ | 94 **Pu** Plutonium $[Rn]5f^6 7s^2$

Atomic masses are averages based upon the naturally occurring composition of isotopes on Earth. For elements that have slightly different isotopic composition depending on the source, IUPAC now reports a range of values for atomic masses. These atomic masses are shown here in bold italics. The atomic masses in this table have been rounded to values sufficiently accurate for everyday calculations. Per IUPAC convention, no values are listed for elements whose isotopes lack a characteristic abundance in natural samples.

Hydrogen

Semiconductors
(also known as metalloids)

Metals
- Alkali metals
- Alkaline-earth metals
- Transition metals
- Other metals

Nonmetals
- Halogens
- Noble gases
- Other nonmetals

Group 18

2
He
Helium
4.003
$1s^2$

Group 13	Group 14	Group 15	Group 16	Group 17
5	6	7	8	9	10
B	**C**	**N**	**O**	**F**	**Ne**
Boron	Carbon	Nitrogen	Oxygen	Fluorine	Neon
10.81	*12.01*	*14.007*	*15.999*	19.00	20.18
$[He]2s^22p^1$	$[He]2s^22p^2$	$[He]2s^22p^3$	$[He]2s^22p^4$	$[He]2s^22p^5$	$[He]2s^22p^6$

13	14	15	16	17	18
Al	**Si**	**P**	**S**	**Cl**	**Ar**
Aluminum	Silicon	Phosphorus	Sulfur	Chlorine	Argon
26.98	*28.085*	30.97	*32.06*	*35.45*	39.95
$[Ne]3s^23p^1$	$[Ne]3s^23p^2$	$[Ne]3s^23p^3$	$[Ne]3s^23p^4$	$[Ne]3s^23p^5$	$[Ne]3s^23p^6$

Group 10	Group 11	Group 12

28	29	30	31	32	33	34	35	36
Ni	**Cu**	**Zn**	**Ga**	**Ge**	**As**	**Se**	**Br**	**Kr**
Nickel	Copper	Zinc	Gallium	Germanium	Arsenic	Selenium	Bromine	Krypton
58.69	63.55	65.38	69.72	72.63	74.92	78.96	79.90	83.80
$[Ar]3d^84s^2$	$[Ar]3d^{10}4s^1$	$[Ar]3d^{10}4s^2$	$[Ar]3d^{10}4s^24p^1$	$[Ar]3d^{10}4s^24p^2$	$[Ar]3d^{10}4s^24p^3$	$[Ar]3d^{10}4s^24p^4$	$[Ar]3d^{10}4s^24p^5$	$[Ar]3d^{10}4s^24p^6$

46	47	48	49	50	51	52	53	54
Pd	**Ag**	**Cd**	**In**	**Sn**	**Sb**	**Te**	**I**	**Xe**
Palladium	Silver	Cadmium	Indium	Tin	Antimony	Tellurium	Iodine	Xenon
106.4	107.9	112.4	114.8	118.7	121.8	127.6	126.9	131.3
$[Kr]4d^{10}$	$[Kr]4d^{10}5s^1$	$[Kr]4d^{10}5s^2$	$[Kr]4d^{10}5s^25p^1$	$[Kr]4d^{10}5s^25p^2$	$[Kr]4d^{10}5s^25p^3$	$[Kr]4d^{10}5s^25p^4$	$[Kr]4d^{10}5s^25p^5$	$[Kr]4d^{10}5s^25p^6$

78	79	80	81	82	83	84	85	86
Pt	**Au**	**Hg**	**Tl**	**Pb**	**Bi**	**Po**	**At**	**Rn**
Platinum	Gold	Mercury	Thallium	Lead	Bismuth	Polonium	Astatine	Radon
195.1	197.0	200.6	*204.38*	207.2	209.0			
$[Xe]4f^{14}5d^96s^1$	$[Xe]4f^{14}5d^{10}6s^1$	$[Xe]4f^{14}5d^{10}6s^2$	$[Xe]4f^{14}5d^{10}6s^26p^1$	$[Xe]4f^{14}5d^{10}6s^26p^2$	$[Xe]4f^{14}5d^{10}6s^26p^3$	$[Xe]4f^{14}5d^{10}6s^26p^4$	$[Xe]4f^{14}5d^{10}6s^26p^5$	$[Xe]4f^{14}5d^{10}6s^26p^6$

110	111	112	113	114	115	116	117	118
Ds	**Rg**	**Cn**	**Nh**	**Fl**	**Mc**	**Lv**	**Ts**	**Og**
Darmstadtium	Roentgenium	Copernicium	Nihonium	Flerovium	Moscovium	Livermorium	Tennessine	Oganesson
$[Rn]5f^{14}6d^97s^1$	$[Rn]5f^{14}6d^{10}7s^1$	$[Rn]5f^{14}6d^{10}7s^2$	$[Rn]5f^{14}6d^{10}7s^27p^1$	$[Rn]5f^{14}6d^{10}7s^27p^2$	$[Rn]5f^{14}6d^{10}7s^27p^3$	$[Rn]5f^{14}6d^{10}7s^27p^4$	$[Rn]5f^{14}6d^{10}7s^27p^5$	$[Rn]5f^{14}6d^{10}7s^27p^6$

63	64	65	66	67	68	69	70	71
Eu	**Gd**	**Tb**	**Dy**	**Ho**	**Er**	**Tm**	**Yb**	**Lu**
Europium	Gadolinium	Terbium	Dysprosium	Holmium	Erbium	Thulium	Ytterbium	Lutetium
152.0	157.3	158.9	162.5	164.9	167.3	168.9	173.1	175.0
$[Xe]4f^76s^2$	$[Xe]4f^75d^16s^2$	$[Xe]4f^96s^2$	$[Xe]4f^{10}6s^2$	$[Xe]4f^{11}6s^2$	$[Xe]4f^{12}6s^2$	$[Xe]4f^{13}6s^2$	$[Xe]4f^{14}6s^2$	$[Xe]4f^{14}5d^16s^2$

95	96	97	98	99	100	101	102	103
Am	**Cm**	**Bk**	**Cf**	**Es**	**Fm**	**Md**	**No**	**Lr**
Americium	Curium	Berkelium	Californium	Einsteinium	Fermium	Mendelevium	Nobelium	Lawrencium
$[Rn]5f^77s^2$	$[Rn]5f^76d^17s^2$	$[Rn]5f^97s^2$	$[Rn]5f^{10}7s^2$	$[Rn]5f^{11}7s^2$	$[Rn]5f^{12}7s^2$	$[Rn]5f^{13}7s^2$	$[Rn]5f^{14}7s^2$	$[Rn]5f^{14}6d^17s^2$

Periodic Table of the Elements   **R45**

Abbreviated Table of Isotopes and Atomic Masses

FUNDAMENTAL CONSTANTS						
Z	Element	Symbol	Average Atomic Mass (u)	Mass Number (*indicates radioactivity) A	Atomic Mass (u)	Percent Abundance	Half-life (if radioactive) $T_{1/2}$
0	(Neutron)	n		1*	1.008 665		10.4 m
1	Hydrogen	H	1.0079	1	1.007 825	99.985	
	Deuterium	D		2	2.014 102	0.015	
	Tritium	T		3*	3.016 049		12.33 y
2	Helium	He	4.002 60	3	3.016 029	0.000 14	
				4	4.002 602	99.999 86	
				6*	6.018 886		0.81 s
3	Lithium	Li	6.941	6	6.015 121	7.5	
				7	7.016 003	92.5	
4	Beryllium	Be	9.0122	7*	7.016 928		53.3 d
				8*	8.005 305		6.7×10^{-17} s
				9	9.012 174	100	
				10*	10.013 584		1.5×10^6 y
5	Boron	B	10.81	10	10.012 936	19.9	
				11	11.009 305	80.1	
6	Carbon	C	12.011	10*	10.016 854		19.3 s
				11*	11.011 433		20.4 m
				12	12.000 000	98.9	
				13	13.003 355	1.10	
				14*	14.003 242		5715 y
7	Nitrogen	N	14.0067	13*	13.005 738		996 m
				14	14.003 074	99.63	
				15	15.000 108	0.37	
				16*	16.006 100		7.13 s
8	Oxygen	O	15.9994	15*	15.003 065		122 s
				16	15.994 915	99.761	
				17	16.999 132	0.039	
				18	17.999 160	0.200	
				19*	19.003 577		26.9 s
9	Fluorine	F	18.998 40	18*	18.000 937		109.8 m
				19	18.998 404	100	
				20*	19.999 982		11.0 s
10	Neon	Ne	20.180	19*	19.001 880		17.2 s
				20	19.992 435	90.48	
				21	20.993 841	0.27	
				22	21.991 383	9.25	
11	Sodium	Na	22.989 87	22*	21.994 434		2.61 y
				23	22.989 767	100	
				24*	23.990 961		14.96 h
12	Magnesium	Mg	24.305	23*	22.994 124		11.3 s
				24	23.985 042	78.99	
				25	24.985 838	10.00	
				26	25.982 594	11.01	

Z	Element	Symbol	Average Atomic Mass (u)	Mass Number (*indicates radioactivity) A	Atomic Mass (u)	Percent Abundance	Half-life (if radioactive) $T_{1/2}$
13	Aluminum	Al	26.981 54	26*	25.986 892		7.4×10^5 y
				27	26.981 534	100	
14	Silicon	Si	28.086	28	27.976 927	92.23	
				29	28.976 495	4.67	
				30	29.973 770	3.10	
15	Phosphorus	P	30.973 76	30*	29.978 307		2.50 m
				31	30.973 762		
				32*	31.973 907	100	14.263 d
16	Sulfur	S	32.066	32	31.972 071	95.02	
				33	32.971 459	0.75	
				34	33.967 867	4.21	
				35*	34.969 033		87.5 d
17	Chlorine	Cl	35.453	35	34.968 853	75.77	
				36*	35.968 307		3.0×10^5 y
				37	36.975 893	24.23	
18	Argon	Ar	39.948	36	35.967 547	0.337	
				37*	36.966 776		35.04 d
				38	37.962 732	0.063	
				39*	38.964 314		269 y
				40	39.962 384	99.600	
19	Potassium	K	39.0983	39	38.963 708	93.2581	
				40*	39.964 000	0.0117	1.28×10^9 y
				41	40.961 827	6.7302	
20	Calcium	Ca	40.08	40	39.962 591	96.941	
				41*	40.962 279		1.0×10^5 y
				42	41.958 618	0.647	
				43	42.958 767	0.135	
				44	43.955 481	2.086	
21	Scandium	Sc	44.9559	41*	40.969 250		0.596 s
				45	44.955 911	100	
22	Titanium	Ti	47.88	44*	43.959 691		60 y
				47	46.951 765	7.3	
				48	47.947 947	73.8	
23	Vanadium	V	50.9415	50*	49.947 161	0.25	1.5×10^{17} y
				51	50.943 962	99.75	
24	Chromium	Cr	51.996	48*	47.954 033		21.6 h
				52	51.940 511	83.79	
				53	52.940 652	9.50	
25	Manganese	Mn	54.938 05	54*	53.940 361		312.1 d
				55	54.938 048	100	
26	Iron	Fe	55.847	54	53.939 613	5.9	
				55*	54.938 297		2.7 y
				56	55.934 940	91.72	
27	Cobalt	Co	58.933 20	59	58.933 198	100	
				60*	59.933 820		5.27 y
28	Nickel	Ni	58.793	58	57.935 345	68.077	
				59*	58.934 350		7.5×10^4 y
				60	59.930 789	26.223	
29	Copper	Cu	63.54	63	62.929 599	69.17	
				65	64.927 791	30.83	

Z	Element	Symbol	Average Atomic Mass (u)	Mass Number (*indicates radioactivity) A	Atomic Mass (u)	Percent Abundance	Half-life (if radioactive) $T_{1/2}$
30	Zinc	Zn	65.39	64	63.929 144	48.6	
				66	65.926 035	27.9	
				67	66.927 129	4.1	
				68	67.924 845	18.8	
31	Gallium	Ga	69.723	69	68.925 580	60.108	
				71	70.924 703	39.892	
32	Germanium	Ge	72.61	70	69.924 250	21.23	
				72	71.922 079	27.66	
				73	72.923 462	7.73	
				74	73.921 177	35.94	
				76	75.921 402	7.44	
33	Arsenic	As	74.9216	75	74.921 594	100	
34	Selenium	Se	78.96	76	75.919 212	9.36	
				77	76.919 913	7.63	
				78	77.917 397	23.78	
				80	79.916 519	49.61	
				82*	81.916 697	8.73	1.4×10^{20} y
35	Bromine	Br	79.904	79	78.918 336	50.69	
				81	80.916 287	49.31	
36	Krypton	Kr	83.80	81*	80.916 589		2.1×10^5 y
				82	81.913 481	11.6	
				83	82.914 136	11.4	
				84	83.911 508	57.0	
				85*	84.912 531		10.76 y
				86	85.910 615	17.3	
37	Rubidium	Rb	85.468	85	84.911 793	72.17	
				87*	86.909 186	27.83	4.75×10^{10} y
38	Strontium	Sr	87.62	86	85.909 266	9.86	
				87	86.908 883	7.00	
				88	87.905 618	82.58	
				90*	89.907 737		29.1 y
39	Yttrium	Y	88.9058	89	88.905 847	100	
40	Zirconium	Zr	91.224	90	89.904 702	51.45	
				91	90.905 643	11.22	
				92	91.905 038	17.15	
				93*	92.906 473		1.5×10^6 y
				94	93.906 314	17.38	
41	Niobium	Nb	92.9064	93	92.906 376	100	
				94*	93.907 280		2×10^4 y
42	Molybdenum	Mo	95.94	92	91.906 807	14.84	
				93*	92.906 811		3.5×10^3 y
				94	93.905 085	9.25	
				95	94.905 841	15.92	
				96	95.904 678	16.68	
				97	96.906 020	9.55	
				98	97.905 407	24.13	
				100	99.907 476	9.63	
43	Technetium	Tc		97*	96.906 363		2.6×10^6 y
				98*	97.907 215		4.2×10^6 y
				99*	98.906 254		2.1×10^5 y

Z	Element	Symbol	Average Atomic Mass (u)	Mass Number (*indicates radioactivity) A	Atomic Mass (u)	Percent Abundance	Half-life (if radioactive) $T_{1/2}$
44	Ruthenium	Ru	101.07	99	98.905 939	12.7	
				100	99.904 219	12.6	
				101	100.905 558	17.1	
				102	101.904 348	31.6	
				104	103.905 558	18.6	
45	Rhodium	Rh	102.9055	103	102.905 502	100	
46	Palladium	Pd	106.42	104	103.904 033	11.14	
				105	104.905 082	22.33	
				106	105.903 481	27.33	
				108	107.903 898	26.46	
				110	109.905 158	11.72	
47	Silver	Ag	107.868	107	106.905 091	51.84	
				109	108.904 754	48.16	
48	Cadmium	Cd	112.41	109*	108.904 984		462 d
				110	109.903 004	12.49	
				111	110.904 182	12.80	
				112	111.902 760	24.13	
				113*	112.904 401	12.22	9.3×10^{15} y
				114	113.903 359	28.73	
49	Indium	In	114.82	113	112.904 060	4.3	
				115*	114.903 876	95.7	4.4×10^{14} y
50	Tin	Sn	118.71	116	115.901 743	14.53	
				117	116.902 953	7.58	
				118	117.901 605	24.22	
				119	118.903 308	8.58	
				120	119.902 197	32.59	
				121*	120.904 237		55 y
51	Antimony	Sb	121.76	121	120.903 820	57.36	
				123	122.904 215	42.64	
52	Tellurium	Te	127.60	125	124.904 429	7.12	
				126	125.903 309	18.93	
				128*	127.904 468	31.79	$> 8 \times 10^{24}$ y
				130*	129.906 228	33.87	$< 1.25 \times 10^{21}$ y
53	Iodine	I	126.9045	127	126.904 474	100	
				129*	128.904 984		1.6×10^7 y
54	Xenon	Xe	131.29	129	128.904 779	26.4	
				131	130.905 069	21.2	
				132	131.904 141	26.9	
				134	133.905 394	10.4	
				136*	135.907 214	8.9	$> 2.36 \times 10^{21}$ y
55	Cesium	Cs	132.9054	133	132.905 436	100	
				135*	134.905 891		2×10^6 y
				137*	136.907 078		30 y
56	Barium	Ba	137.33	133*	132.905 990		10.5 y
				137	136.905 816	11.23	
				138	137.905 236	71.70	
57	Lanthanum	La	138.905	138*	137.907 105	0.0902	1.05×10^{11} y
				139	138.906 346	99.9098	
58	Cerium	Ce	140.12	138	137.905 986	0.25	
				140	139.905 434	88.43	
				142*	141.909 241	11.13	$> 5 \times 10^{16}$ y
59	Praseodymium	Pr	140.9076	141	140.907 647	100	

Z	Element	Symbol	Average Atomic Mass (u)	Mass Number (*indicates radioactivity) A	Atomic Mass (u)	Percent Abundance	Half-life (if radioactive) $T_{1/2}$
60	Neodymium	Nd	144.24	142 143 144* 145 146	141.907 718 142.909 809 143.910 082 144.912 568 145.913 113	27.13 12.18 23.80 8.30 17.19	2.3×10^{15} y
61	Promethium	Pm		145* 146*	144.912 745 145.914 968		17.7 y 5.5 y
62	Samarium	Sm	150.36	147* 148* 149* 150 152 154	146.914 894 147.914 819 148.917 180 149.917 273 151.919 728 153.922 206	15.0 11.3 13.8 7.4 26.7 22.7	1.06×10^{11} y 7×10^{15} y $> 2 \times 10^{15}$ y
63	Europium	Eu	151.96	151 152* 153	150.919 846 151.921 740 152.921 226	47.8 52.2	13.5 y
64	Gadolinium	Gd	157.25	155 156 157 158 160	154.922 618 155.922 119 156.923 957 157.924 099 159.927 050	14.80 20.47 15.65 24.84 21.86	
65	Terbium	Tb	158.9253	159	158.925 345	100	
66	Dysprosium	Dy	162.5	161 162 163 164	160.926 930 161.926 796 162.928 729 163.929 172	18.9 25.5 24.9 28.2	
67	Holmium	Ho	164.9303	165	164.930 316	100	
68	Erbium	Er	167.26	166 167 168 170	165.930 292 166.932 047 167.932 369 169.935 462	33.6 22.95 27.8 14.9	
69	Thulium	Tm	168.9342	169 171*	168.934 213 170.936 428	100	1.92 y
70	Ytterbium	Yb	173.04	171 172 173 174 176	170.936 324 171.936 379 172.938 209 173.938 861 175.942 564	14.3 21.9 16.12 31.8 12.7	
71	Lutetium	Lu	174.967	175 176*	174.940 772 175.942 679	97.41 2.59	3.78×10^{10} y
72	Hafnium	Hf	178.49	177 178 179 180	176.943 218 177.943 697 178.945 813 179.946 547	18.606 27.297 13.029 35.100	
73	Tantalum	Ta	180.9479	181	180.947 993	99.988	
74	Tungsten	W	183.85	182 183 184 186	181.948 202 182.950 221 183.950 929 185.954 358	26.3 14.28 30.7 28.6	
75	Rhenium	Re	186.207	185 187*	184.952 951 186.955 746	37.40 62.60	4.4×10^{10} y

Z	Element	Symbol	Average Atomic Mass (u)	Mass Number (*indicates radioactivity) A	Atomic Mass (u)	Percent Abundance	Half-life (if radioactive) $T_{1/2}$
76	Osmium	Os	190.2	188	187.955832	13.3	
				189	188.958 139	16.1	
				190	189.958 439	26.4	
				192	191.961 468	41.0	
77	Iridium	Ir	192.2	191	190.960 585	37.3	
				193	192.962 916	62.7	
78	Platinum	Pt	195.08	194	193.962 655	32.9	
				195	194.964 765	33.8	
				196	195.964 926	25.3	
79	Gold	Au	196.9665	197	196.966 543	100	
80	Mercury	Hg	200.59	198	197.966 743	9.97	
				199	198.968 253	16.87	
				200	199.968 299	23.10	
				201	200.970 276	13.10	
				202	201.970 617	29.86	
81	Thallium	Tl	204.383	203	202.972 320	29.524	
				204*	203.073 839		3.78 y
				205	204.974 400	70.476	
				208*	207.981 992		3.053 m
82	Lead	Pb	207.2	206	205.974 440	24.1	
				207	206.974 871	22.1	
				208	207.976 627	52.4	
				212*	211.991 872		10.64 h
83	Bismuth	Bi	208.9803	209	208.980 374	100	
				212*	211.991 259		60.6 m
84	Polonium	Po		209*	208.982 405		102 y
				212*	211.988 842		0.30 μs
				216*	216.001 889		0.145 s
85	Astatine	At		218*	218.008 685		1.6 s
				219*	219.011 294		0.9 m
86	Radon	Rn		220*	220.011 369		55.6 s
				222*	222.017 571		3.823 d
87	Francium	Fr		223*	223.019 733		22 m
88	Radium	Ra		224*	224.020 187		3.66 d
				226*	226.025 402		1.6×10^3 y
				228*	228.031 064		5.75 y
89	Actinium	Ac		227*	227.027 701		18.72 y
				228*	228.028 716		1.913 y
90	Thorium	Th		232*	232.038 051	100	1.40×10^{10} y
				234*	234.043 593		24.1 d
91	Protactinium	Pa		231*	231.035 880		32.760 y
				234*	234.043 300		6.7 h
92	Uranium	U		234*	234.040 946	0.0055	2.46×10^5 y
				235*	235.043 924	0.720	7.04×10^8 y
				238*	238.050 784	99.2745	4.47×10^9 y
93	Neptunium	Np		236*	236.046 560		1.15×10^5 y
				237*	237.048 168		2.14×10^6 y
94	Plutonium	Pu		239*	239.052 157		2.412×10^5 y
				244*	244.064 200		8.1×10^7 y

Additional Problems

The Science of Physics

1. Mt. Waialeale in Hawaii gets 1.168×10^3 cm of rainfall on average per year. Express this quantity in meters.

2. An acre is equal to about 4.0469×10^3 m^2. Express this area in square kilometers.

3. A group drinks about 6.4×10^4 cm^3 of water per person per year. Express this in cubic meters.

4. The largest stone jar on the Plain of Jars in Laos has a mass of 6.0×10^3 kg. Express this mass in milligrams.

5. Half of a sample of the radioactive isotope beryllium-8 decays in 6.7×10^{-17} s. Express this time in picoseconds.

Motion in One Dimension

6. The fastest airplane is the Lockheed SR-71. If an SR-71 flies 15.0 km west in 15.3 s, what is its average velocity in kilometers per hour?

7. Except for a 22.0 min rest stop, Emily drives with a constant velocity of 89.5 km/h, north. How long does the trip take if Emily's average velocity is 77.8 km/h, north?

8. A spaceship accelerates uniformly for 1220 km. How much time is required for the spaceship to increase its speed from 11.1 km/s to 11.7 km/s?

9. A polar bear initially running at 4.0 m/s accelerates uniformly for 18 s. If the bear travels 135 m in this time, what is its maximum speed?

10. A walrus accelerates from 7.0 km/h to 34.5 km/h over a distance of 95 m. What is the magnitude of the walrus's acceleration?

11. A snail can move about 4.0 m in 5.0 min. What is the average speed of the snail?

12. A crate is accelerated at 0.035 m/s^2 for 28.0 s along a conveyor belt. If the crate's initial speed is 0.76 m/s, what is its final speed?

13. A person throws a ball vertically and catches it after 5.10 s. What is the ball's initial velocity?

14. A bicyclist accelerates -0.870 m/s^2 during a 3.80 s interval. What is the change in the velocity of the bicyclist and bicycle?

15. A hockey puck slides 55.0 m in 1.25 s with a uniform acceleration. If the puck's final speed is 43.2 m/s, what was its initial speed?

16. A small rocket launched from rest travels 12.4 m upward in 2.0 s. What is the rocket's net acceleration?

17. A jet slows uniformly from 153 km/h to 0 km/h over 42.0 m. What is the jet's acceleration?

18. A softball thrown straight up at 17.5 m/s is caught 3.60 s later. How high does the ball rise?

19. A child, starting from rest, sleds down a snow-covered slope in 5.50 s. If the child's final speed is 14.0 m/s, what the length of the slope?

20. A skydiver opens her parachute and drifts down for 34.0 s with a constant velocity of 6.50 m/s. What is the skydiver's displacement?

21. In a race, a tortoise runs at 10.0 cm/s, and a hare runs at 200.0 cm/s. Both start at the same time, but the hare stops to rest for 2.00 min. The tortoise wins by 20.0 cm. At what time does the tortoise cross the finish line?

22. What is the length of the race in problem 21?

23. The cable pulling an elevator upward at 12.5 m/s breaks. How long does it take for the elevator to come to rest?

24. A disk is uniformly accelerated from rest for 0.910 s over 7.19 km. What is its final speed?

25. A tiger accelerates 3.0 m/s^2 for 4.1 s to reach a final speed of 55.0 km/h. What was its initial speed in kilometers per hour?

26. A shark accelerates uniformly from 2.8 km/h to 32.0 km/h in 1.5 s. How large is its acceleration?

27. The 1903 Wright flyer was accelerated at 4.88 m/s^2 along a track that was 18.3 m long. How long did it take to accelerate the flyer from rest?

28. A drag racer starts at rest and reaches a speed of 386.0 km/h with an average acceleration of 16.5 m/s^2. How long does this acceleration take?

29. A hummingbird accelerates at -9.20 m/s^2 such that its velocity changes from $+50.0$ km/h to 0 km/h. What is its displacement?

30. A train backs up from an initial velocity of -4.0 m/s and an average acceleration of -0.27 m/s^2. What is the train's velocity after 17 s?

31. A cross-country skier skiing with an initial velocity of $+4.42$ m/s slows uniformly at -0.75 m/s^2. How long does it take the skier to stop?

32. What is the skier's displacement in problem 31?

33. A speedboat uniformly increases its speed from 25 m/s west to 35 m/s west. How long does it take the boat to travel 250 m west?

34. A ship accelerates at -7.6×10^{-2} m/s^2 so that it comes to rest at the dock 255 m away in 82.0 s. What is the ship's initial speed?

35. A student skates downhill with an average acceleration of 0.85 m/s^2. Her initial speed is 4.5 m/s, and her final speed is 10.8 m/s. How long does she take to skate down the hill?

36. A wrench dropped from a tall building is caught in a safety net when the wrench has a velocity of -49.5 m/s. How far did it fall?

37. A rocket sled comes to a complete stop from a speed of 320 km/h in 0.18 s. What is the sled's average acceleration?

38. A racehorse uniformly accelerates 7.56 m/s^2, reaching its final speed after running 19.0 m. If the horse starts at rest, what is its final speed?

39. An arrow is shot upward at a speed of 85.1 m/s. How long does the archer have to move from the launching spot before the arrow returns to Earth?

40. A handball strikes a wall with a forward speed of 13.7 m/s and bounces back with a speed of 11.5 m/s. If the ball changes velocity in 0.021 s, what is the handball's average acceleration?

41. A ball accelerates at 6.1 m/s^2 from 1.8 m/s to 9.4 m/s. How far does the ball travel?

42. A small sandbag is dropped from rest from a hovering hot-air balloon. After 2.0 s, what is the sandbag's displacement below the balloon?

43. A hippopotamus accelerates at 0.678 m/s^2 until it reaches a speed of 8.33 m/s. If the hippopotamus runs 46.3 m, what was its initial speed?

44. A ball is hit upward with a speed of 7.5 m/s. How long does the ball take to reach maximum height?

45. A surface probe on the planet Mercury falls 17.6 m downward from a ledge. If free-fall acceleration near Mercury is -3.70 m/s^2, what is the probe's velocity when it reaches the ground?

Two-Dimensional Motion and Vectors

46. A plane moves 599 m northeast along a runway. If the northern component of this displacement is 89 m, how large is the eastern component?

47. Find the displacement direction in problem 46.

48. A train travels 478 km southwest along a straight stretch. If the train is displaced south by 42 km, what is the train's displacement to the west?

49. Find the displacement direction in problem 48.

50. A ship's total displacement is 7400 km at 26° south of west. If the ship sails 3200 km south, what is the western component of its journey?

51. The distance from an observer on a plain to the top of a nearby mountain is 5.3 km at 8.4° above the horizontal. How tall is the mountain?

52. A skyrocket travels 113 m at an angle of 82.4° with respect to the ground and toward the south. What is the rocket's horizontal displacement?

53. A hot-air balloon descends with a velocity of 55 km/h at an angle of 37° below the horizontal. What is the vertical velocity of the balloon?

54. A stretch of road extends 55 km at 37° north of east and then continues for 66 km due east. What is a driver's resultant displacement along this road?

55. A driver travels 4.1 km west, 17.3 km north, and finally 1.2 km at an angle of 24.6° west of north. What is the driver's displacement?

56. A tornado picks up a car and hurls it horizontally 125 m with a speed of 90.0 m/s. How long does it take the car to reach the ground?

57. A squirrel knocks a nut horizontally at a speed of 10.0 cm/s. If the nut lands at a horizontal distance of 18.6 cm, how high up is the squirrel?

58. A flare is fired at an angle of 35° to the ground at an initial speed of 250 m/s. How long does it take for the flare to reach its maximum altitude?

59. A football kicked with an initial speed of 23.1 m/s reaches a maximum height of 16.9 m. At what angle was the ball kicked?

60. A bird flies north at 58.0 km/h relative to the wind. The wind is blowing at 55.0 km/h south relative to Earth. How long will it take the bird to fly 1.4 km relative to Earth?

61. A racecar moving at 286 km/h is 0.750 km behind a car moving at 252 km/h. How long will it take the faster car to catch up to the slower car?

62. A helicopter flies 165 m horizontally and then moves downward to land 45 m below. What is the helicopter's resultant displacement?

63. A toy parachute floats 13.0 m downward. If the parachute travels 9.0 m horizontally, what is the resultant displacement?

64. A billiard ball travels 2.7 m at an angle of 13° with respect to the long side of the table. What are the components of the ball's displacement?

65. A golf ball has a velocity of 1.20 m/s at 14.0° east of north. What are the velocity components?

66. A tiger leaps with an initial velocity of 55.0 km/h at an angle of 13.0° with respect to the horizontal. What are the components of the tiger's velocity?

67. A tramway extends 3.88 km up a mountain from a station 0.8 km above sea level. If the horizontal displacement is 3.45 km, how far above sea level is the mountain peak?

68. A bullet travels 850 m, ricochets, and moves another 640 m at an angle of 36° from its previous forward motion. What is the bullet's resultant displacement?

69. A bird flies 46 km at 15° south of east, then 22 km at 13° east of south, and finally 14 km at 14° west of south. What is the bird's displacement?

70. A ball is kicked with a horizontal speed of 9.37 m/s off the top of a mountain. The ball moves 85.0 m horizontally before hitting the ground. How tall is the mountain?

71. A ball is kicked with a horizontal speed of 1.50 m/s from a height of 2.50×10^2 m. What is its horizontal displacement when it hits the ground?

72. What is the velocity of the ball in problem 71 when it reaches the ground?

73. A shingle slides off a roof at a speed of 2.0 m/s and an angle of 30.0° below the horizontal. How long does it take the shingle to fall 45 m?

74. A ball is thrown with an initial speed of 10.0 m/s and an angle of 37.0° above the horizontal. What are the vertical and horizontal components of the ball's displacement after 2.5 s?

75. A rocket moves north at 55.0 km/h with respect to the air. It encounters a wind from 17.0° north of west at 40.0 km/h with respect to Earth. What is the rocket's velocity with respect to Earth?

76. How far to the north and west does the rocket in problem 75 travel after 15.0 min?

77. A cable car travels 2.00×10^2 m on level ground, then 3.00×10^2 m at an incline of 3.0°, and then 2.00×10^2 m at an incline of 8.8°. What is the final displacement of the cable car?

78. A hurricane moves 790 km at 18° north of west, then due west for 150 km, then north for 470 km, and finally 15° east of north for 240 km. What is the hurricane's resultant displacement?

79. What is the range of an arrow shot horizontally at 85.3 m/s from 1.50 m above the ground?

80. A drop of water in a fountain takes 0.50 s to travel 1.5 m horizontally. The water is projected upward at an angle of 33°. What is the drop's initial speed?

81. A golf ball is hit up a 41.0° ramp to travel 4.46 m horizontally and 0.35 m below the edge of the ramp. What is the ball's initial speed?

82. A flare is fired with a velocity of 87 km/h west from a car traveling 145 km/h north. With respect to Earth, what is the flare's resultant displacement 0.45 s after being launched?

83. A sailboat travels south at 12.0 km/h with respect to the water against a current 15.0° south of east at 4.0 km/h. What is the boat's velocity?

Forces and the Laws of Motion

84. A boat exerts a 9.5×10^4 N force 15.0° north of west on a barge. Another exerts a 7.5×10^4 N force north. What direction is the barge moved?

85. A shopper exerts a force on a cart of 76 N at an angle of 40.0° below the horizontal. How much force pushes the cart in the forward direction?

86. How much force pushes the cart in problem 85 against the floor?

87. What are the magnitudes of the largest and smallest net forces that can be produced by combining a force of 6.0 N and a force of 8.0 N?

88. A buoyant force of 790 N lifts a 214 kg sinking boat. What is the boat's net acceleration?

89. A house is lifted by a net force of 2850 N and moves from rest to an upward speed of 15 cm/s in 5.0 s. What is the mass of the house?

90. An 8.0 kg bag is lifted 20.0 cm in 0.50 s. If it is initially at rest, what is the net force on the bag?

91. A 90.0 kg skier glides at constant speed down a 17.0° slope. Find the frictional force on the skier.

92. A snowboarder slides down a 5.0° slope at a constant speed. What is the coefficient of kinetic friction between the snow and the board?

93. A 2.00 kg block is in equilibrium on a 36.0° incline. What is the normal force on the block?

94. A 1.8×10^3 kg car is parked on a hill on a 15.0° incline. A 1.25×10^4 N frictional force holds the car in place. Find the coefficient of static friction.

95. The coefficient of kinetic friction between a jar slid across a table and the table is 0.20. What is the magnitude of the jar's acceleration?

96. A force of 5.0 N to the left causes a 1.35 kg book to have a net acceleration of 0.76 m/s^2 to the left. What is the frictional force on the book?

97. A child pulls a toy by exerting a force of 15.0 N at an angle of 55.0° with respect to the floor. What are the components of the force?

98. A car is pulled by three forces: 600.0 N to the north, 750.0 N to the east, and 675 N at 30.0° south of east. What direction does the car move?

99. Suppose a catcher exerts a force of −65.0 N to stop a baseball with a mass of 0.145 kg. What is the ball's net acceleration as it is being caught?

100. A 2.0 kg fish pulled upward by a fisherman rises 1.9 m in 2.4 s, starting from rest. What is the net force on the fish during this interval?

101. An 18.0 N force pulls a cart against a 15.0 N frictional force. The speed of the cart increases 1.0 m/s every 5.0 s. What is the cart's mass?

102. A 47 kg sled carries a 33 kg load. The coefficient of kinetic friction between the sled and snow is 0.075. What is the magnitude of the frictional force on the sled as it moves up a hill with a 15° incline?

103. Ice blocks slide with an acceleration of 1.22 m/s^2 down a chute at an angle of 12.0° below the horizontal. What is the coefficient of kinetic friction between the ice and the chute?

104. A 1760 N force pulls a 266 kg load up a 17° incline. What is the coefficient of static friction between the load and the incline?

105. A 4.26 × 10^7 N force pulls a ship at a constant speed along a dry dock. The coefficient of kinetic friction between the ship and dry dock is 0.25. Find the normal force exerted on the ship.

106. If the incline of the dry dock in problem 105 is 10.0°, what is the ship's mass?

107. A 65.0 kg skier is pulled up an 18.0° slope by a force of 2.50 × 10^2 N. If the net acceleration uphill is 0.44 m/s^2, what is the frictional force between the skis and the snow?

108. Four forces are acting on a hot-air balloon:
$\mathbf{F}_1$ = 2280.0 N up, $\mathbf{F}_2$ = 2250.0 N down, $\mathbf{F}_3$ = 85.0 N west, and $\mathbf{F}_4$ = 12.0 N east. What is the direction of the net external force on the balloon?

109. A traffic signal is supported by two cables, each of which makes an angle of 40.0° with the vertical. If each cable can exert a maximum force of 7.50 × 10^2 N, what is the largest weight they can support?

110. A certain cable of an elevator is designed to exert a force of 4.5 × 10^4 N. If the maximum acceleration that a loaded car can withstand is 3.5 m/s^2, what is the combined mass of the car and its contents?

111. A frictional force of 2400 N keeps a crate of machine parts from sliding down a ramp with an incline of 30.0°. The coefficient of static friction between the box and the ramp is 0.20. What is the normal force of the ramp on the box?

112. Find the mass of the crate in problem 111.

113. A 5.1 × 10^2 kg bundle of bricks is pulled up a ramp at an incline of 14° to a construction site. The force needed to move the bricks up the ramp is 4.1 × 10^3 N. What is the coefficient of static friction between the bricks and the ramp?

Work and Energy

114. If 2.13 × 10^6 J of work must be done on a roller-coaster car to move it 3.00 × 10^2 m, how large is the net force acting on the car?

115. A force of 715 N is applied to a roller-coaster car to push it horizontally. If 2.72 × 10^4 J of work is done on the car, how far has it been pushed?

116. In 0.181 s, through a distance of 8.05 m, a test pilot's speed decreases from 88.9 m/s to 0 m/s. If the pilot's mass is 70.0 kg, how much work is done against his body?

117. What is the kinetic energy of a disk with a mass of 0.20 g and a speed of 15.8 km/s?

118. A 9.00 × 10^2 kg walrus is swimming at a speed of 35.0 km/h. What is its kinetic energy?

119. A golf ball with a mass of 47.0 g has a kinetic energy of 1433 J. What is the ball's speed?

120. A turtle, swimming at 9.78 m/s, has a kinetic energy of 6.08 × 10^4 J. What is the turtle's mass?

121. A 50.0 kg parachutist is falling at a speed of 47.00 m/s when her parachute opens. Her speed upon landing is 5.00 m/s. How much work is done by the air to reduce the parachutist's speed?

122. An 1100 kg car accelerates from 48.0 km/h to 59.0 km/h over 100.0 m. What was the magnitude of the net force acting on it?

123. What is the gravitational potential energy of a 64.0 kg person at 5334 m above sea level?

124. A spring has a force constant of 550 N/m. What is the elastic potential energy stored in the spring when the spring is compressed 1.2 cm?

125. What is the kinetic energy of a 0.500 g raindrop that falls 0.250 km? Ignore air resistance.

126. A 50.0 g projectile is fired upward at 3.00×10^2 m/s and lands at 89.0 m/s. How much mechanical energy is lost to air resistance?

127. How long does it take for 4.5×10^6 J of work to be done by a 380.3 kW engine?

128. A ship's engine has a power output of 13.0 MW. How much work can it do in 15.0 min?

129. A catcher picks up a baseball from the ground with a net upward force of 7.25×10^{-2} N so that 4.35×10^{-2} J of net work is done. How far is the ball lifted?

130. A crane does 1.31×10^3 J of net work when lifting cement 76.2 m. How large is the net force doing this work?

131. A girl exerts a force of 35.0 N at an angle of 20.0° to the horizontal to move a wagon 15.0 m along a level path. What is the net work done on it if a frictional force of 24.0 N is present?

132. The *Queen Mary* had a mass of 7.5×10^7 kg and a top cruising speed of 57 km/h. What was the kinetic energy of the ship at that speed?

133. How fast is a 55.0 kg skydiver falling when her kinetic energy is 7.81×10^4 J?

134. A hockey puck with an initial speed of 8.0 m/s coasts 45 m to a stop. If the force of friction on the puck is 0.12 N, what is the puck's mass?

135. How far does a 1.30×10^4 kg jet travel if it is slowed from 2.40×10^2 km/h to 0 km/h by an acceleration of -30.8 m/s^2?

136. An automobile is raised 7.0 m, resulting in an increase in gravitational potential energy of 6.6×10^4 J. What is the automobile's mass?

137. A spring in a pogo stick has a force constant of 1.5×10^4 N/m. How far is the spring compressed when its elastic potential energy is 120 J?

138. A 100.0 g arrow is pulled back 30.0 cm against a bowstring. The bowstring's force constant is 1250 N/m. At what speed will the arrow leave the bow?

139. A ball falls 3.0 m down a vertical pipe, the end of which bends horizontally. How fast does the ball leave the pipe if no energy is lost to friction?

140. A spacecraft's engines do 1.4×10^{13} J of work in 8.5 min. What is the power output of these engines?

141. A runner exerts a force of 334 N against the ground while using 2100 W of power. How long does it take him to run a distance of 50.0 m?

142. A high-speed boat has four 300.0 kW motors. How much work is done in 25 s by the motors?

143. A 92 N force pushes an 18 kg box of books, initially at rest, 7.6 m across a floor. The coefficient of kinetic friction between the floor and the box is 0.35. What is the final kinetic energy of the box of books?

144. A guardrail can be bent by 5.00 cm and then restore its shape. What is its force constant if struck by a car with 1.09×10^4 J of kinetic energy?

145. A 25.0 kg trunk strikes the ground with a speed of 12.5 m/s. If no energy is lost from air resistance, what is the height from which the trunk fell?

146. Sliding a 5.0 kg stone up a frictionless ramp with a 25.0° incline increases its gravitational potential energy by 2.4×10^2 J. How long is the ramp?

147. A constant 4.00×10^2 N force moves a 2.00×10^2 kg iceboat 0.90 km. Frictional force is negligible, and the boat starts at rest. Find the boat's final speed.

148. A 50.0 kg circus clown jumps from a platform into a net 1.00 m above the ground. The net is stretched 0.65 m and has a force constant of 3.4×10^4 N/m. What is the height of the platform?

Momentum and Collisions

149. If a 50.0 kg cheetah, initially at rest, runs 274 m north in 8.65 s, what is its momentum?

150. If a 1.46×10^5 kg whale has a momentum of 9.73×10^5 kg•m/s to the south, what is its velocity?

151. A star has a momentum of 8.62×10^{36} kg•m/s and a speed of 255 km/s. What is its mass?

152. A 5.00 g projectile has a velocity of 255 m/s right. Find the force to stop this projectile in 1.45 s.

153. How long does it take a 0.17 kg hockey puck to decrease its speed by 9.0 m/s if the coefficient of kinetic friction is 0.050?

154. A 705 kg racecar driven by a 65 kg driver moves with a velocity of 382 km/h right. Find the force to bring the car and driver to a stop in 12.0 s.

155. Find the stopping distance in problem 154.

156. A 50.0 g shell fired from a 3.00 kg rifle has a speed of 400.0 m/s. With what velocity does the rifle recoil in the opposite direction?

157. A twig at rest in a pond moves with a speed of 0.40 cm/s opposite a 2.5 g snail, which has a speed of 1.2 cm/s. What is the mass of the twig?

158. A 25.0 kg sled holding a 42.0 kg child has a speed of 3.50 m/s. They collide with and pick up a snowman, initially at rest. The resulting speed of the snowman, sled, and child is 2.90 m/s. What is the snowman's mass?

159. An 8500 kg railway car moves right at 4.5 m/s, and a 9800 kg railway car moves left at 3.9 m/s. The cars collide and stick together. What is the final velocity of the system?

160. What is the change in kinetic energy for the two railway cars in problem 159?

161. A 55 g clay ball moving at 1.5 m/s collides with a 55 g clay ball at rest. By what percentage does the kinetic energy change after the inelastic collision?

162. A 45 g golf ball collides elastically with an identical ball at rest and stops. If the second ball's final speed is 3.0 m/s, what was the first ball's initial speed?

163. A 5.00×10^2 kg racehorse gallops with a momentum of 8.22×10^3 kg•m/s to the west. What is the horse's velocity?

164. A 3.0×10^7 kg ship collides elastically with a 2.5×10^7 kg ship moving north at 4.0 km/h. After the collision, the first ship moves north at 3.1 km/h, and the second ship moves south at 6.9 km/h. Find the unknown velocity.

165. A high-speed train has a mass of 7.10×10^5 kg and moves at a speed of 270.0 km/h. What is the magnitude of the train's momentum?

166. A bird with a speed of 50.0 km/h has a momentum of magnitude of 0.278 kg•m/s. What is the bird's mass?

167. A 75 N force pulls a child and sled initially at rest down a snowy hill. If the combined mass of the sled and child is 55 kg, what is their speed after 7.5 s?

168. A student exerts a net force of −1.5 N over a period of 0.25 s to bring a falling 60.0 g egg to a stop. What is the egg's initial speed?

169. A 1.1×10^3 kg walrus starts swimming east from rest and reaches a velocity of 9.7 m/s in 19 s. What is the net force acting on the walrus?

170. A 12.0 kg wagon at rest is pulled by a 15.0 N force at an angle of 20.0° above the horizontal. If an 11.0 N frictional force resists the forward force, how long will the wagon take to reach a speed of 4.50 m/s?

171. A 42 g meteoroid moving forward at 7.82×10^3 m/s collides with a spacecraft. What force is needed to stop the meteoroid in 1.0×10^{-6} s?

172. A 455 kg polar bear slides for 12.2 s across the ice. If the coefficient of kinetic friction between the bear and the ice is 0.071, what is the change in the bear's momentum as it comes to a stop?

173. How far does the bear in problem 172 slide?

174. How long will it take a -1.26×10^4 N force to stop a 2.30×10^3 kg truck moving at a speed of 22.2 m/s?

175. A 63 kg skater at rest catches a sandbag moving north at 5.4 m/s. The skater and bag then move north at 1.5 m/s. Find the sandbag's mass.

176. A 1.36×10^4 kg barge is loaded with 8.4×10^3 kg of coal. What was the unloaded barge's speed if the loaded barge has a speed of 1.3 m/s?

177. A 1292 kg automobile moves east at 88.0 km/h. If all forces remain constant, what is the car's velocity if its mass is reduced to 1255 kg?

178. A 68 kg student steps into a 68 kg boat at rest, causing both to move west at a speed of 0.85 m/s. What was the student's initial velocity?

179. A 1400 kg automobile, heading north at 45 km/h, collides inelastically with a 2500 kg truck traveling east at 33 km/h. What is the vehicles' final velocity?

180. An artist throws 1.3 kg of paint onto a 4.5 kg canvas at rest. The paint-covered canvas slides backward at 0.83 m/s. What is the change in the kinetic energy of the paint and canvas?

181. Find the change in kinetic energy if a 0.650 kg fish leaping to the right at 15.0 m/s collides inelastically with a 0.950 kg fish leaping to the left at 13.5 m/s.

182. A 10.0 kg cart moving at 6.0 m/s hits a 2.5 kg cart moving at 3.0 m/s in the opposite direction. Find the carts' final speed after an inelastic collision.

183. A ball, thrown right at 6.00 m/s, hits a 1.25 kg panel at rest and then bounces back at 4.90 m/s. The panel moves right at 1.09 m/s. Find the ball's mass.

184. A 2150 kg car, moving east at 10.0 m/s, collides and joins with a 3250 kg car. The cars move east together at 5.22 m/s. What is the 3250 kg car's initial velocity?

185. Find the change in kinetic energy in problem 184.

186. A 15.0 g toy car moving to the right at 20.0 cm/s collides elastically with a 20.0 g toy car moving left at 30.0 cm/s. The 15.0 g car then moves left at 37.1 cm/s. Find the 20.0 g car's final velocity.

187. A remora swimming right at 5.0 m/s attaches to a 150.0 kg shark moving left at 7.00 m/s. Both move left at 6.25 m/s. Find the remora's mass.

188. A 6.5×10^{12} kg comet, moving at 420 m/s, catches up to and collides inelastically with a 1.50×10^{13} kg comet moving at 250 m/s. Find the change in the comets' kinetic energy.

189. A 7.00 kg ball moves east at 2.00 m/s, collides with a 7.00 kg ball at rest, and then moves 30.0° north of east at 1.73 m/s. What is the second ball's final velocity?

190. A 2.0 kg block moving at 8.0 m/s on a frictionless surface collides elastically with a block at rest. The first block moves in the same direction at 2.0 m/s. What is the second block's mass?

Circular Motion and Gravitation

191. A pebble that is 3.81 m from the eye of a tornado has a tangential speed of 124 m/s. What is the magnitude of the pebble's centripetal acceleration?

192. A racecar speeds along a curve with a tangential speed of 75.0 m/s. The centripetal acceleration on the car is 22.0 m/s^2. Find the radius of the curve.

193. A subject in a large centrifuge has a radius of 8.9 m and a centripetal acceleration of 20g (g = 9.81 m/s^2). What is the tangential speed of the subject?

194. A 1250 kg automobile with a tangential speed of 48.0 km/h follows a circular road that has a radius of 35.0 m. How large is the centripetal force?

195. A rock in a sling is 0.40 m from the axis of rotation and has a tangential speed of 6.0 m/s. What is the rock's mass if the centripetal force is 8.00×10^2 N?

196. A 7.55×10^{13} kg comet orbits the sun with a speed of 0.173 km/s. If the centripetal force on the comet is 505 N, how far is it from the sun?

197. A 2.05×10^8 kg asteroid has an orbit with a 7378 km radius. The centripetal force on the asteroid is 3.00×10^9 N. Find the asteroid's tangential speed.

198. Find the gravitational force between a 0.500 kg mass and a 2.50×10^{12} kg mountain that is 10.0 km away.

199. The gravitational force between Ganymede and Jupiter is 1.636×10^{22} N. Jupiter's mass is 1.90×10^{27} kg, and the distance between the two bodies is 1.071×10^6 km. What is Ganymede's mass?

200. At the sun's surface, the gravitational force on 1.00 kg is 274 N. The sun's mass is 1.99×10^{30} kg. If the sun is assumed spherical, what is the sun's radius?

201. At the surface of a red giant star, the gravitational force on 1.00 kg is only 2.19×10^{-3} N. If its mass equals 3.98×10^{31} kg, what is the star's radius?

202. Uranus has a mass of 8.6×10^{25} kg. The mean distance between the centers of the planet and its moon Miranda is 1.3×10^5 km. If the orbit is circular, what is Miranda's period in hours?

203. What is the tangential speed in problem 202?

204. The rod connected halfway along the 0.660 m radius of a wheel exerts a 2.27×10^5 N force. How large is the maximum torque?

205. A golfer exerts a torque of 0.46 N•m on a golf club. If the club exerts a force of 0.53 N on a stationary golf ball, what is the length of the club?

206. What is the orbital radius of the Martian moon Deimos if it orbits 6.42×10^{23} kg Mars in 30.3 h?

207. A 4.00×10^2 N•m torque is produced, applying a force 1.60 m from the fulcrum and at an angle of 80.0° to the lever. How large is the force?

208. A customer 11 m from the center of a revolving restaurant has a speed of 1.92×10^{-2} m/s. How large a centripetal acceleration acts on the customer?

209. A toy train on a circular track has a tangential speed of 0.35 m/s and a centripetal acceleration of 0.29 m/s^2. What is the radius of the track?

210. A person against the inner wall of a hollow cylinder with a 150 m radius feels a centripetal acceleration of 9.81 m/s^2. Find the cylinder's tangential speed.

211. The tangential speed of 0.20 kg toy carts is 5.6 m/s when they are 0.25 m from a turning shaft. How large is the centripetal force on the carts?

212. A 1250 kg car on a curve with a 35.0 m radius has a centripetal force from friction and gravity of 8.07×10^3 N. What is the car's tangential speed?

213. Two wrestlers, 2.50×10^{-2} m apart, exert a 2.77×10^{-3} N gravitational force on each other. One has a mass of 157 kg. What is the other's mass?

214. A 1.81×10^5 kg blue whale is 1.5 m from a 2.04×10^4 kg whale shark. What is the gravitational force between them?

215. Triton's orbit around Neptune has a radius of 3.56×10^5 km. Neptune's mass is 1.03×10^{26} kg. What is Triton's period?

216. Find the tangential speed in problem 215.

217. A moon orbits a 1.0×10^{26} kg planet in 365 days. What is the radius of the moon's orbit?

218. What force is required to produce a 1.4 N•m torque when applied to a door at a 60.0° angle and 0.40 m from the hinge?

219. What is the maximum torque that the force in problem 218 can exert?

220. A worker hanging 65.0° from the blade of a windmill exerts an 8.25×10^3 N•m torque. If the worker weighs 587 N, what is the blade's length?

Fluid Mechanics

221. A cube of volume 1.00 m³ floats in gasoline, which has a density of 675 kg/m³. How large a buoyant force acts on the cube?

222. A cube 10.0 cm on each side has a density of 2.053×10^4 kg/m³. Its apparent weight in fresh water is 192 N. Find the buoyant force.

223. A 1.47×10^6 kg steel hull has a base that is 2.50×10^3 m² in area. If it is placed in sea water ($\rho = 1.025 \times 10^3$ kg/m³), how deep does the hull sink?

224. What size force will open a door of area 1.54 m² if the net pressure on the door is 1.013×10^3 Pa?

225. Gas at a pressure of 1.50×10^6 Pa exerts a force of 1.22×10^4 N on the upper surface of a piston. What is the piston's upper surface area?

226. In a barometer, the mercury column's weight equals the force from air pressure on the mercury's surface. Mercury's density is 13.6×10^3 kg/m³. What is the air's pressure if the column is 760 mm high?

227. A cube of osmium with a volume of 166 cm³ is placed in fresh water. The cube's apparent weight is 35.0 N. What is the density of osmium?

228. A block of ebony with a volume of 2.5×10^{-3} m³ is placed in fresh water. If the apparent weight of the block is 7.4 N, what is the density of ebony?

229. One piston of a hydraulic lift holds 1.40×10^3 kg. The other holds an ice block ($\rho = 917$ kg/m³) that is 0.076 m thick. Find the first piston's area.

230. A hydraulic-lift piston raises a 4.45×10^4 N weight by 448 m. How large is the force on the other piston if it is pushed 8.00 m downward?

231. A platinum flute with a density of 21.5 g/cm³ is submerged in fresh water. If its apparent weight is 40.2 N, what is the flute's mass?

Heat

232. Surface temperature on Mercury ranges from 463 K during the day to 93 K at night. Express this temperature range in degrees Celsius.

233. Solve problem 233 for degrees Fahrenheit.

234. The temperature in Fort Assiniboine, Montana, went from −5°F to +37°F on January 19, 1892. Calculate this change in temperature in kelvins.

235. An acorn falls 9.5 m, absorbing 0.85 of its initial potential energy. If 1200 J/kg will raise the acorn's temperature 1.0°C, what is its temperature increase?

236. A bicyclist on level ground brakes from 13.4 m/s to 0 m/s. What is the cyclist's and bicycle's mass if the increase in internal energy is 5836 J?

237. A 61.4 kg roller skater on level ground brakes from 20.5 m/s to 0 m/s. What is the total change in the internal energy of the system?

238. A 0.225 kg tin can ($c_p = 2.2 \times 10^3$ J/kg•°C) is cooled in water, to which it transfers 3.9×10^4 J of energy. By how much does the can's temperature change?

239. What mass of bismuth ($c_p = 121$ J/kg•°C) increases temperature by 5.0°C when 25 J is added by heat?

240. Placing a 0.250 kg pot in 1.00 kg of water raises the water's temperature 1.00°C. The pot's temperature drops 17.5°C. Find the pot's specific heat capacity.

241. Lavas at Kilauea in Hawaii have temperatures of 2192°F. Express this quantity in degrees Celsius.

242. The present temperature of the background radiation in the universe is 2.7 K. What is this temperature in degrees Celsius?

243. The human body cannot survive at a temperature of 42°C for very long. Express this quantity in kelvins.

244. Two sticks rubbed together gain 2.15×10^4 J from kinetic energy and lose 33 percent of it to the air. How much does the sticks' internal energy change?

245. A stone falls 561.7 m. When the stone lands, the internal energy of the ground and the stone increases by 105 J. What is the stone's mass?

246. A 2.5 kg block of ice at 0.0°C slows on a level floor from 5.7 m/s to 0 m/s. If 3.3×10^5 J causes 1.0 kg of ice to melt, how much of the ice melts?

247. Placing a 3.0 kg skillet in 5.0 kg of water raises the water's temperature 2.25°C and lowers the skillet's temperature 29.6°C. Find the skillet's specific heat.

248. Air has a specific heat of 1.0×10^3 J/kg•°C. If air's temperature increases 55°C when 45×10^6 J is added to it by heat, what is the air's mass?

249. A 0.23 kg tantalum part has a specific heat capacity of 140 J/kg•°C. By how much does the part's temperature change if it gives up 3.0×10^4 J as heat?

Thermodynamics

250. A volume of air increases 0.227 m³ at a net pressure of 2.07×10^7 Pa. How much work is done on the air?

251. The air in a hot-air balloon does 3.29×10^6 J of work, increasing the balloon's volume by 2190 m³. What is the net pressure in the balloon?

252. Filling a fire extinguisher with nitrogen gas at a net pressure of 25.0 kPa requires 472.5 J of work on the gas. Find the change in the gas's volume.

253. The internal energy of air in a closed car rises 873 J. How much heat energy is transferred to the air?

254. A system's initial internal energy increases from 39 J to 163 J. If 114 J of heat is added to the system, how much work is done on the system?

255. A gas does 623 J of work on its surroundings when 867 J is added to the gas as heat. What is the change in the internal energy of the gas?

256. An engine with an efficiency of 0.29 takes in 693 J as heat. How much work does the engine do?

257. An engine with an efficiency of 0.19 does 998 J of work. How much energy is taken in by heat?

258. Find the efficiency of an engine that receives 571 J as heat and loses 463 J as heat per cycle.

259. A 5.4×10^{-4} m³ increase in steam's volume does 1.3 J of work on a piston. What is the pressure?

260. A pressure of 655 kPa does 393 J of work inflating a bike tire. Find the change in volume.

261. An engine's internal energy changes from 8093 J to 2.0920×10^4 J. If 6932 J is added as heat, how much work is done on or by the system?

262. Steam expands from a geyser to do 192 kJ of work. If the system's internal energy increases by 786 kJ, how much energy is transferred as heat?

263. If 632 kJ is added to a boiler and 102 kJ of work is done as steam escapes from a safety valve, what is the net change in the system's internal energy?

264. A power plant with an efficiency of 0.35 percent requires 7.37×10^8 J of energy as heat. How much work is done by the power plant?

265. An engine with an efficiency of 0.11 does 1150 J of work. How much energy is taken in as heat?

266. A test engine performs 128 J of work and receives 581 J of energy as heat. What is the engine's efficiency?

Vibrations and Waves

267. A scale with a spring constant of 420 N/m is compressed 4.3 cm. What is the spring force?

268. A 669 N weight attached to a giant spring stretches it 6.5 cm. What is the spring constant?

269. An archer applies a force of 52 N on a bowstring with a spring constant of 490 N/m. What is the bowstring's displacement?

270. On Mercury, a pendulum 1.14 m long would have a 3.55 s period. Calculate a_g for Mercury.

271. Find the length of a pendulum that oscillates with a frequency of 2.5 Hz.

272. Calculate the period of a 6.200 m long pendulum in Oslo, Norway, where $a_g = 9.819$ m/s².

273. Find the pendulum's frequency in problem 272.

274. A 24 kg child jumps on a trampoline with a spring constant of 364 N/m. What is the oscillation period?

275. A 32 N weight oscillates with a 0.42 s period when on a spring scale. Find the spring constant.

276. Find the mass of a ball that oscillates at a period of 0.079 s on a spring with a constant of 63 N/m.

277. A dolphin hears a 280 kHz sound with a wavelength of 0.51 cm. What is the wave's speed?

278. If a sound wave with a frequency of 20.0 Hz has a speed of 331 m/s, what is its wavelength?

279. A sound wave has a speed of 2.42×10^4 m/s and a wavelength of 1.1 m. Find the wave's frequency.

280. An elastic string with a spring constant of 65 N/m is stretched 15 cm and released. What is the spring force exerted by the string?

281. The spring in a seat compresses 7.2 cm under a 620 N weight. What is the spring constant?

282. A 3.0 kg mass is hung from a spring with a spring constant of 36 N/m. Find the displacement.

283. Calculate the period of a 2.500 m long pendulum in Quito, Ecuador, where $a_g = 9.780$ m/s^2.

284. How long is a pendulum with a frequency of 0.50 Hz?

285. A tractor seat supported by a spring with a spring constant of 2.03×10^3 N/m oscillates at a frequency of 0.79 Hz. What is the mass on the spring?

286. An 87 N tree branch oscillates with a period of 0.64 s. What is the branch's spring constant?

287. What is the oscillation period for an 8.2 kg baby in a seat that has a spring constant of 221 N/m?

288. An organ creates a sound with a speed of 331 m/s and a wavelength of 10.6 m. Find the frequency.

289. What is the speed of an earthquake S-wave with a 2.3×10^4 m wavelength and a 0.065 Hz frequency?

Sound

290. What is the distance from a sound with 5.88×10^{-5} W power if its intensity is 3.9×10^{-6} W/m^2?

291. Sound waves from a stereo have a power output of 3.5 W at 0.50 m. What is the sound's intensity?

292. What is a vacuum cleaner's power output if the sound's intensity 1.5 m away is 4.5×10^{-4} W/m^2?

293. Waves travel at 499 m/s on a 0.850 m long cello string. Find the string's fundamental frequency.

294. A mandolin string's first harmonic is 392 Hz. How long is the string if the wave speed on it is 329 m/s?

295. A 1.53 m long pipe that is closed on one end has a seventh harmonic frequency of 466.2 Hz. What is the speed of the waves in the pipe?

296. A pipe open at both ends has a fundamental frequency of 125 Hz. If the pipe is 1.32 m long, what is the speed of the waves in the pipe?

297. Traffic has a power output of 1.57×10^{-3} W. At what distance is the intensity 5.20×10^{-3} W/m^2?

298. If a mosquito's buzzing has an intensity of 9.3×10^{-8} W/m^2 at a distance of 0.21 m, how much sound power does the mosquito generate?

299. A note from a flute (a pipe with a closed end) has a first harmonic of 392.0 Hz. How long is the flute if the sound's speed is 331 m/s?

300. An organ pipe open at both ends has a first harmonic of 370.0 Hz when the speed of sound is 331 m/s. What is the length of this pipe?

Light and Reflection

301. A 7.6270×10^8 Hz radio wave has a wavelength of 39.296 cm. What is this wave's speed?

302. An x-ray's wavelength is 3.2 nm. Using the speed of light in a vacuum, calculate the frequency of the x-ray.

303. What is the wavelength of ultraviolet light with a frequency of 9.5×10^{14} Hz?

304. A concave mirror has a focal length of 17 cm. Where must a 2.7 cm tall coin be placed for its image to appear 23 cm in front of the mirror's surface?

305. How tall is the coin's image in problem 304?

306. A concave mirror's focal length is 9.50 cm. A 3.0 cm tall pin appears to be 15.5 cm in front of the mirror. How far from the mirror is the pin?

307. How tall is the pin's image in problem 306?

308. A convex mirror's magnification is 0.11. Suppose you are 1.75 m tall. How tall is your image?

309. How far in front of the mirror in problem 308 are you if your image is 42 cm behind the mirror?

310. A mirror's focal length is −12 cm. What is the object distance if an image forms 9.00 cm behind the surface of the mirror?

311. What is the magnification in problem 310?

312. A metal bowl is like a concave spherical mirror. You are 35 cm in front of the bowl and see an image at 42 cm. What is the bowl's focal length?

313. For problem 312, find the bowl's radius of curvature.

314. A concave spherical mirror on a dressing table has a focal length of 60.0 cm. If someone sits 35.0 cm in front of it, where is the image?

315. What is the magnification in problem 314?

316. An image appears 5.2 cm behind the surface of a convex mirror when the object is 17 cm in front of the mirror. What is the mirror's focal length?

317. If the object in problem 316 is 3.2 cm tall, how tall is its image?

318. In order for someone to observe an object, the wavelength of the light must be smaller than the object. The Bohr radius of a hydrogen atom is $5.291\,770 \times 10^{-11}$ m. What is the lowest frequency that can be used to locate a hydrogen atom?

319. Meteorologists use Doppler radar to watch the movement of storms. If a weather station uses electromagnetic waves with a frequency of 2.85×10^9 Hz, what is the wavelength of the radiation?

320. PCS cellular phones have antennas that use radio frequencies from 1800 to 2000 MHz. What range of wavelengths corresponds to these frequencies?

321. Suppose you have a mirror with a focal length of 32.0 cm. Where would you place your right hand so that you appear to be shaking hands with yourself?

322. A car's headlamp is made of a light bulb in front of a concave spherical mirror. If the bulb is 5.0 cm in front of the mirror, what is the radius of the mirror?

323. Suppose you are 19 cm in front of the bell of your friend's trumpet and you see your image at 14 cm. If the trumpet's bell is a concave mirror, what would be its focal length?

324. A soup ladle is like a spherical convex mirror with a focal length of 27 cm. If you are 43 cm in front of the ladle, where does the image appear?

325. What is the magnification in problem 324?

326. Just after you dry a spoon, you look into the convex part of the spoon. If the spoon has a focal length of −8.2 cm and you are 18 cm in front of the spoon, where does the image appear?

327. The base of a lamp is made of a convex spherical mirror with a focal length of −39 cm. Where does the image appear when you are 16 cm from the base?

328. Consider the lamp and location in problem 327. If your nose is 6.0 cm long, how long does the image appear?

329. How fast does microwave radiation that has a frequency of $1.173\,06 \times 10^{11}$ Hz and a wavelength of 2.5556 mm travel?

330. Suppose the microwaves in your microwave oven have a frequency of 2.5×10^{10} Hz. What is the wavelength of these microwaves?

331. You place an electric heater 3.00 m in front of a concave spherical mirror that has a focal length of 30.0 cm. Where would your hand feel warmest?

332. You see an image of your hand as you reach for a doorknob with a focal length of 6.3 cm. How far from the doorknob is your hand when the image appears at 5.1 cm behind the doorknob?

333. What is the magnification of the image in problem 332?

Refraction

334. A ray of light in air enters an amethyst crystal ($n = 1.553$). If the angle of refraction is 35°, what is the angle of incidence?

335. Light passes from air at an angle of incidence of 59.2° into a nephrite jade vase ($n = 1.61$). Determine the angle of refraction in the jade.

336. Light entering a pearl travels at a speed of 1.97×10^8 m/s. What is the pearl's index of refraction?

337. An object in front of a diverging lens of focal length 13.0 cm forms an image with a magnification of +5.00. How far from the lens is the object placed?

338. An object with a height of 18 cm is placed in front of a converging lens. The image height is −9.0 cm. What is the magnification of the lens?

339. If the focal length of the lens in problem 338 is 6.0 cm, how far in front of the lens is the object?

340. Where does the image appear in problem 339?

341. The critical angle for light traveling from a green tourmaline gemstone into air is 37.8°. What is tourmaline's index of refraction?

342. Find the critical angle for light traveling from ruby ($n = 1.766$) into air.

343. Find the critical angle for light traveling from emerald ($n = 1.576$) into air.

344. Malachite has two indices of refraction: $n_1 = 1.91$ and $n_2 = 1.66$. A ray of light in air enters malachite at an incident angle of 35.2°. Calculate both of the angles of refraction.

345. A ray of light in air enters a serpentine figurine ($n = 1.555$). If the angle of refraction is 33°, what is the angle of incidence?

346. The critical angle for light traveling from an aquamarine gemstone into air is 39.18°. What is the index of refraction for aquamarine?

347. A 15 cm tall object is placed 44 cm in front of a diverging lens. A virtual image appears 14 cm in front of the lens. What is the lens's focal length?

348. What is the image height in problem 347?

349. A lighthouse converging lens has a focal length of 4 m. What is the image distance for an object placed 4 m in front of the lens?

350. What is the magnification in problem 349?

351. Light moves from olivine ($n = 1.670$) into onyx. If the critical angle for olivine is 62.85°, what is the index of refraction for onyx?

352. When light in air enters an opal mounted on a ring, the light travels at a speed of 2.07×10^8 m/s. What is opal's index of refraction?

353. When light in air enters albite, it travels at a velocity of 1.95×10^8 m/s. What is albite's index of refraction?

354. A searchlight is constructed by placing a 500 W bulb 0.5 m in front of a converging lens. The focal length of the lens is 0.5 m. What is the image distance?

355. A microscope slide is placed in front of a converging lens with a focal length of 3.6 cm. The lens forms a real image of the slide 15.2 cm behind the lens. How far is the lens from the slide?

356. Where must an object be placed to form an image 12 cm in front of a diverging lens with a focal length of 44 cm?

357. The critical angle for light traveling from almandine garnet into air ranges from 33.1° to 35.3°. Calculate the range of almandine garnet's index of refraction.

358. Light moves from a clear andalusite ($n = 1.64$) crystal into ivory. If the critical angle for andalusite is 69.9°, what is the index of refraction for ivory?

Interference and Diffraction

359. Light with a 587.5 nm wavelength passes through two slits. A second-order bright fringe forms 0.130° from the center. Find the slit separation.

360. Light passing through two slits with a separation of 8.04×10^{-6} m forms a third bright fringe 13.1° from the center. Find the wavelength.

361. Two slits are separated by 0.0220 cm. Find the angle at which a first-order bright fringe is observed for light with a wavelength of 527 nm.

362. For 546.1 nm light, the first-order maximum for a diffraction grating forms at 75.76°. How many lines per centimeter are on the grating?

363. Infrared light passes through a diffraction grating of 3600 lines/cm. The angle of the third-order maximum is 76.54°. What is the wavelength?

364. A diffraction grating with 1950 lines/cm is used to examine light with a wavelength of 497.3 nm. Find the angle of the first-order maximum.

365. At what angle does the second-order maximum in problem 364 appear?

366. Light passes through two slits separated by 3.92×10^{-6} m to form a second-order bright fringe at an angle of 13.1°. What is the light's wavelength?

367. Light with a wavelength of 430.8 nm shines on two slits that are 0.163 mm apart. What is the angle at which a second dark fringe is observed?

368. Light of wavelength 656.3 nm passes through two slits. The fourth-order dark fringe is 0.548° from the central maximum. Find the slit separation.

369. The first-order maximum for light with a wavelength of 447.1 nm is found at 40.25°. How many lines per centimeter does the grating have?

370. Light through a diffraction grating of 9550 lines/cm forms a second-order maximum at 54.58°. What is the wavelength of the light?

Electric Forces and Fields

371. Charges of $-5.3\ \mu C$ and $+5.3\ \mu C$ are separated by 4.2 cm. Find the electric force between them.

372. A dog's fur is combed, and the comb gains a charge of 8.0 nC. Find the electric force between the fur and comb when they are 2.0 cm apart.

373. Two equal charges are separated by 6.5×10^{-11} m. If the magnitude of the electric force between the charges is 9.92×10^{-4} N, what is the value of q?

374. Two point charges of $-13.0\ \mu C$ and $-16.0\ \mu C$ exert repulsive forces on each other of 12.5 N. What is the distance between the two charges?

375. Three equal point charges of 4.00 nC lie 4.00 m apart on a line. Calculate the magnitude and direction of the net force on the middle charge.

376. Four protons are at the corners of a square with sides 1.52×10^{-9} m long. Calculate the resultant force vector on the proton at the upper-right corner.

377. Three 2.0 nC charges are located at coordinates (0 m, 0 m), (1.0 m, 0 m), and (1.0 m, 2.0 m). Find the resultant force on the first charge.

378. Charges of 7.2 nC and 6.7 nC are 32 cm apart. Find the equilibrium position for a -3.0 nC charge.

379. A $-12.0\ \mu C$ charge is between two $6.0\ \mu C$ charges, 5.0 cm away from each. What electric force keeps the central charge in equilibrium?

380. A 9.0 N/C electric field is directed along the x-axis. Find the electric force vector on a -6.0 C charge.

381. What charge experiences an electric force of 6.43×10^{-9} N in an electric field of 4.0×10^3 N/C?

382. A $5.00\ \mu C$ charge is 0.500 m above a $15.0\ \mu C$ charge. Calculate the electric field at a point 1.00 m above the 15.0 mC charge.

383. Two static point charges of $99.9\ \mu C$ and $33.3\ \mu C$ exert repulsive forces on each other of 87.3 N. What is the distance between the two charges?

384. Two particles are separated by 9.30×10^{-11} m. If the magnitude of the electric force between the charges is 2.66×10^{-8} N, what is the value of q?

385. A -23.4 nC charge is 0.500 m below a 4.65 nC charge and 1.00 m below a 0.299 nC charge. Find the resultant force vector on the -23.4 nC charge.

386. Three point charges are on the corners of a triangle: $q_1 = -9.00$ nC is at the origin; $q_2 = -8.00$ nC is at $x = 2.00$ m; and $q_3 = 7.00$ nC is at $y = 3.00$ m. Find the magnitude and direction of the resultant force on q_1.

387. Charges of -2.50 nC and -7.50 nC are 20.0 cm apart. Find a 5.0 nC charge's equilibrium position.

388. A -4.6 C charge is in equilibrium with a -2.3 C charge 2.0 m to the right and an unknown charge 4.0 m to the right. What is the unknown charge?

389. Find the electric force vector on a 5.0 nC charge in a 1500 N/C electric field directed along the y-axis.

390. What electric charge experiences an 8.42×10^{-9} N electric force in an electric field of 1663 N/C?

391. Two $3.00\ \mu C$ charges lie 2.00 m apart on the x-axis. Find the resultant electric field vector at a point 0.250 m on the y-axis, above the charge on the left.

392. Two electrons are 2.00×10^{-10} m and 3.00×10^{-10} m, respectively, from a point. Where with respect to that point must a proton be placed so that the resultant electric field strength is zero?

393. A -7.0 C charge is in equilibrium with a 49 C charge 18 m to the right and an unknown charge 25 m to the right. What is the unknown charge?

394. Suppose two pions are separated by 8.3×10^{-10} m. If the magnitude of the electric force between the charges is 3.34×10^{-10} N, what is the value of q?

395. Suppose two muons having equal but opposite charge are separated by 6.4×10^{-8} m. If the magnitude of the electric force between the charges is 5.62×10^{-14} N, what is the value of q?

396. Consider four electrons at the corners of a square. Each side of the square is 3.02×10^{-5} m. Find the magnitude and direction of the resultant force on q_3 if it is at the origin.

397. A charge of 5.5 nC and a charge of 11 nC are separated by 88 cm. Find the equilibrium position for a -22 nC charge.

398. Three charges are on the y-axis. At the origin is a charge, $q_1 = 72$ C; an unknown charge, q_2, is at $y = 15$ mm. A third charge, $q_3 = -8.0$ C, is placed at $y = -9.0$ mm so that it is in electrostatic equilibrium with q_1 and q_2. What is the charge on q_2?

Electrical Energy and Current

399. A helium-filled balloon with a 14.5 nC charge rises 290 m above Earth's surface. By how much does the electrical potential energy change if Earth's electric field is -105 N/C?

400. A charged airplane rises 7.3 km in a 3.4×10^5 N/C electric field. The electrical potential energy changes by -1.39×10^{11} J. What is the charge on the plane?

401. Earth's radius is 6.4×10^6 m. What is Earth's capacitance if it is regarded as a conducting sphere?

402. A 0.50 pF capacitor is connected across a 1.5 V battery. How much charge can this capacitor store?

403. A 76 C charge passes through a wire's cross-sectional area in 19 s. Find the current in the wire.

404. The current in a telephone is 1.4 A. How long does 98 C of charge take to pass a point in the wire?

405. What is a television's total resistance if it is plugged into a 120 V outlet and carries 0.75 A of current?

406. A motor with a resistance of 12.2 Ω is plugged into a 120.0 V outlet. What is the current in the motor?

407. The potential difference across a motor with a 0.30 Ω resistance is 720 V. How much power is used?

408. What is a microwave oven's resistance if it uses 1750 W of power at a voltage of 120.0 V?

409. A 64 nC charge moves 0.95 m with an electrical potential energy change of -3.88×10^{-5} J. What is the electric field strength?

410. A -14 nC charge travels through a 156 N/C electric field with a change of 2.1×10^{-6} J in the electrical potential energy. How far does the charge travel?

411. A 5.0×10^{-5} F polyester capacitor stores 6.0×10^{-4} C. Find the potential difference across the capacitor.

412. Some ceramic capacitors can store 3×10^{-2} C with a potential difference of 30 kV across them. What is the capacitance of such a capacitor?

413. The area of the plates in a 4550 pF parallel-plate capacitor is 6.4×10^{-3} m^2. Find the plate separation.

414. A television receiver contains a 14 μF capacitor charged across a potential difference of 1.5×10^4 V. How much charge does this capacitor store?

415. A photocopier uses 9.3 A in 15 s. How much charge passes a point in the copier's circuit in this time?

416. A 114 μC charge passes through a gold wire's cross-sectional area in 0.36 s. What is the current?

417. If the current in a blender is 7.8 A, how long do 56 C of charge take to pass a point in the circuit?

418. A computer uses 3.0 A in 2.0 min. How much charge passes a point in the circuit in this time?

419. A battery-powered lantern has a resistance of 6.4 Ω. What potential difference is provided by the battery if the total current is 0.75 A?

420. The potential difference across an electric eel is 650 V. How much current would an electric eel deliver to a body with a resistance of 1.0×10^2 Ω?

421. If a garbage-disposal motor has a resistance of 25.0 Ω and carries a current of 4.66 A, what is the potential difference across the motor's terminals?

422. A medium-sized oscillating fan draws 545 mA of current when the potential difference across its motor is 120 V. How large is the fan's resistance?

423. A generator produces a 2.5×10^4 V potential difference across power lines that carry 20.0 A of current. How much power is generated?

424. A computer with a resistance of 91.0 Ω uses 230.0 W of power. Find the current in the computer.

425. A laser uses 6.0×10^{13} W of power. What is the potential difference across the laser's circuit if the current in the circuit is 8.0×10^6 A?

426. A blender with a 75 Ω resistance uses 350 W of power. What is the current in the blender's circuit?

Circuits and Circuit Elements

427. A theater has 25 surround-sound speakers wired in series. Each speaker has a resistance of 12.0 Ω. What is the equivalent resistance?

428. In case of an emergency, a corridor on an airplane has 57 lights wired in series. Each light bulb has a resistance of 2.00 Ω. Find the equivalent resistance.

429. Four resistors with resistances of 39 Ω, 82 Ω, 12 Ω, and 42 Ω are connected in parallel across a 3.0 V potential difference. Find the equivalent resistance.

430. Four resistors with resistances of 33 Ω, 39 Ω, 47 Ω, and 68 Ω are connected in parallel across a 1.5 V potential difference. Find the equivalent resistance.

431. A 16 Ω resistor is connected in series with another resistor across a 12 V battery. The current in the circuit is 0.42 A. Find the unknown resistance.

432. A 24 Ω resistor is connected in series with another resistor across a 3.0 V battery. The current in the circuit is 62 mA. Find the unknown resistance.

433. A 3.3 Ω resistor and another resistor are connected in parallel across a 3.0 V battery. The current in the circuit is 1.41 A. Find the unknown resistance.

434. A 56 Ω resistor and another resistor are connected in parallel across a 12 V battery. The current in the circuit is 3.21 A. Find the unknown resistance.

435. Three bulbs with resistances of 56 Ω, 82 Ω, and 24 Ω are wired in series. If the voltage across the circuit is 9.0 V, what is the current in the circuit?

436. Three bulbs with resistances of 96 Ω, 48 Ω, and 29 Ω are wired in series. What is the current through the bulbs if the voltage across them is 115 V?

437. A refrigerator ($R_1 = 75$ Ω) wired in parallel with an oven ($R_2 = 91$ Ω) is plugged into a 120 V outlet. What is the current in the circuit of each appliance?

438. A computer ($R_1 = 82$ Ω) and printer ($R_2 = 24$ Ω) are wired in parallel across a 120 V potential difference. Find the current in each machine's circuit.

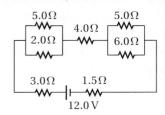

439. For the figure above, what is the equivalent resistance of the circuit?

440. For the figure above, find the current in the circuit.

441. For the figure above, what is the potential difference across the 6.0 Ω resistor?

442. For the figure above, what is the current through the 6.0 Ω resistor?

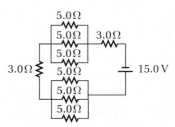

443. For the figure above, calculate the equivalent resistance of the circuit.

444. For the figure above, what is the total current in the circuit?

445. For the figure above, what is the current in the 3.0 Ω resistors?

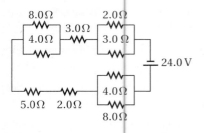

446. For the figure above, calculate the equivalent resistance of the circuit.

447. For the figure above, what is the total current in the circuit?

448. For the figure above, what is the current in either of the 8.0 Ω resistors?

Magnetism

449. A proton moves at right angles to a magnetic field of 0.8 T. If the proton's speed is 3.0×10^7 m/s, how large is the magnetic force exerted on the proton?

450. A weak magnetic field exerts a 1.9×10^{-22} N force on an electron moving 3.9×10^6 m/s perpendicular to the field. What is the magnetic field strength?

451. A 5.0×10^{-5} T magnetic field exerts a 6.1×10^{-17} N force on a 1.60×10^{-19} C charge, which moves at a right angle to the field. What is the charge's speed?

452. A 14 A current passes through a 2 m wire. A 3.6×10^{-4} T magnetic field is at right angles to the wire. What is the magnetic force on the wire?

453. A 1.0 m printer cable is perpendicular to a 1.3×10^{-4} T magnetic field. What current must the cable carry to experience a 9.1×10^{-5} N magnetic force?

454. A wire perpendicular to a 4.6×10^{-4} T magnetic field experiences a 2.9×10^{-3} N magnetic force. How long is the wire if it carries a 10.0 A current?

455. A 12 m wire carries a 12 A current. What magnetic field causes a 7.3×10^{-2} N magnetic force to act on the wire when it is perpendicular to the field?

456. A magnetic force of 3.7×10^{-13} N is exerted on an electron moving at 7.8×10^6 m/s perpendicular to a sunspot. How large is the sunspot's magnetic field?

457. An electron moves with a speed of 2.2×10^6 m/s at right angles through a 1.1×10^{-2} T magnetic field. How large is the magnetic force on the electron?

458. A pulsar's magnetic field is 1×10^{-8} T. How fast does an electron move perpendicular to this field so that a 3.2×10^{-22} N magnetic force acts on the charge?

459. A levitation device designed to suspend 75 kg uses 10.0 m of wire and a 4.8×10^{-4} T magnetic field, perpendicular to the wire. What current is needed?

460. A power line carries 1.5×10^3 A for 15 km. Earth's magnetic field is 2.3×10^{-5} T at a 45° angle to the power line. What is the magnetic force on the line?

Electromagnetic Induction

461. A coil with 540 turns and a 0.016 m² area is rotated exactly from 0° to 90.0° in 0.050 s. How strong must a magnetic field be to induce an emf of 3.0 V?

462. A 550-turn coil with an area of 5.0×10^{-5} m² is in a magnetic field that decreases by 2.5×10^{-4} T in 2.1×10^{-5} s. What is the induced emf in the coil?

463. A 246-turn coil has a 0.40 m² area in a magnetic field that increases from 0.237 T to 0.320 T. What time interval is needed to induce an emf of −9.1 V?

464. A 9.5 V emf is induced in a coil that rotates from 0.0° to 90.0° in a 1.25×10^{-2} T magnetic field for 25 ms. The coil's area is 250 cm². How many turns of wire are in the coil?

465. A generator provides an rms emf of 320 V across 100 Ω. What is the maximum emf?

466. Find the rms current in the circuit in problem 465.

467. Some wind turbines can provide an rms current of 1.3 A. What is the maximum ac current?

468. A transformer has 1400 turns on the primary and 140 turns on the secondary. What is the voltage across the primary if the secondary voltage is 6.9 kV?

469. A transformer has 140 turns on the primary and 840 turns on the secondary. What is the voltage across the secondary if the primary voltage is 5.6 kV?

470. A step-down transformer converts a 3.6 kV voltage to 1.8 kV. If the primary (input) coil has 58 turns, how many turns does the secondary have?

471. A step-up transformer converts a 4.9 kV voltage to 49 kV. If the secondary (output) coil has 480 turns, how many turns does the primary have?

472. A 320-turn coil rotates from 0° to 90.0° in a 0.046 T magnetic field in 0.25 s, which induces an average emf of 4.0 V. What is the area of the coil?

473. A 180-turn coil with a 5.0×10^{-5} m² area is in a magnetic field that decreases by 5.2×10^{-4} T in 1.9×10^{-5} s. What is the induced current if the coil's resistance is 1.0×10^2 W?

474. A generator provides a maximum ac current of 1.2 A and a maximum output emf of 211 V. Calculate the rms potential difference.

475. Calculate the rms current for problem 474.

476. A generator can provide a maximum output emf of 170 V. Calculate the rms potential difference.

477. A step-down transformer converts 240 V across the primary to 5.0 V across the secondary. What is the step-down ratio $(N_1 : N_2)$?

Atomic Physics

478. Determine the energy of a photon of green light with a wavelength of 527 nm.

479. Calculate the de Broglie wavelength of an electron with a velocity of 2.19×10^6 m/s.

480. Calculate the frequency of ultraviolet (UV) light having a photon energy of 20.7 eV.

481. X-ray radiation can have an energy of 12.4 MeV. To what wavelength does this correspond?

482. Light of wavelength 240 nm shines on a potassium surface. Potassium has a work function of 2.3 eV. What is the maximum kinetic energy of the photoelectrons?

483. Manganese has a work function of 4.1 eV. What is the wavelength of the photon that will just have the threshold energy for manganese?

484. What is the speed of a proton with a de Broglie wavelength of 2.64×10^{-14} m?

485. A cheetah can run as fast as 28 m/s. If the cheetah has a de Broglie wavelength of 8.97×10^{-37} m, what is the cheetah's mass?

486. What is the energy of a photon of blue light with a wavelength of 430.8 nm?

487. Calculate the frequency of infrared (IR) light with a photon energy of 1.78 eV.

488. Calculate the wavelength of a radio wave that has a photon energy of 3.1×10^{-6} eV.

489. Light of frequency 6.5×10^{14} Hz illuminates a lithium surface. The ejected photoelectrons are found to have a maximum kinetic energy of 0.20 eV. Find the threshold frequency of this metal.

490. Light of wavelength 519 nm shines on a rubidium surface. Rubidium has a work function of 2.16 eV. What is the maximum kinetic energy of the photoelectrons?

491. The smallest known virus moves across a petri dish at 5.6×10^{-6} m/s. If the de Broglie wavelength of the virus is 2.96×10^{-8} m, what is the virus's mass?

492. The threshold frequency of platinum is 1.36×10^{15} Hz. What is the work function of platinum?

493. The ship *Queen Elizabeth II* has a mass of 7.6×10^{7} kg. Calculate the de Broglie wavelength if this ship sails at 35 m/s.

494. Cobalt has a work function of 5.0 eV. What is the wavelength of the photon that will just have the threshold energy for cobalt?

495. Light of frequency 9.89×10^{14} Hz illuminates a calcium surface. The ejected photoelectrons are found to have a maximum kinetic energy of 0.90 eV. Find the threshold frequency of this metal.

496. What is the speed of a neutron with a de Broglie wavelength of 5.6×10^{-14} m?

Subatomic Physics

497. Calculate the binding energy of $^{39}_{19}$K.

498. Determine the difference in the binding energy of $^{107}_{47}$Ag and $^{63}_{29}$Cu.

499. Find the mass defect of $^{58}_{28}$Ni.

500. Complete this radioactive-decay formula:
$^{212}_{84}$Po $\longrightarrow$? $+ \, ^{4}_{2}$He.

501. Complete this radioactive-decay formula:
$^{16}_{7}$N $\longrightarrow$? $+ \, ^{0}_{-1}e + \overline{\nu}$.

502. Complete this radioactive-decay formula:
$^{147}_{62}$Sm $\longrightarrow \, ^{143}_{60}$Nd $+$?

503. A 3.29×10^{-3} g sample of a pure radioactive substance is found after 30.0 s to have only 8.22×10^{-4} g left undecayed. What is the half-life of the substance?

504. The half-life of $^{48}_{24}$Cr is 21.6 h. A chromium-48 sample contains 6.5×10^{6} nuclei. Calculate the activity of the sample in mCi.

505. How long will it take a sample of lead-212 (which has a half-life of 10.64 h) to decay to one-eighth its original strength?

506. Compute the binding energy of $^{120}_{50}$Sn.

507. Calculate the difference in the binding energy of $^{12}_{6}$C and $^{16}_{8}$O.

508. What is the mass defect of $^{64}_{30}$Zn?

509. Complete this radioactive-decay formula:
? $\longrightarrow \, ^{131}_{54}$Xe $+ \, ^{0}_{-1}e + \overline{\nu}$.

510. Complete this radioactive-decay formula:
$^{160}_{74}$W $\longrightarrow \, ^{156}_{72}$Hf $+$?

511. Complete this radioactive-decay formula:
? $\longrightarrow \, ^{107}_{52}$Te $+ \, ^{4}_{2}$He.

512. A 4.14×10^{-4} g sample of a pure radioactive substance is found after 1.25 days to have only 2.07×10^{-4} g left undecayed. What is the substance's half-life?

513. How long will it take a sample of cadmium-109 with a half-life of 462 days to decay to one-fourth its original strength?

514. The half-life of $^{55}_{26}$Fe is 2.7 years. What is the decay constant for the isotope?

CHAPTER 1
The Science of Physics

PRACTICE A, p. 15
1. 5×10^{-5} m
3. 1.2×10^{41} kJ
5. 6.55×10^{23} cm^3

1 REVIEW, p. 31
11. **a.** 2×10^2 mm
    b. 7.8×10^3 s
    c. 1.6×10^7 µg
    d. 7.5×10^4 cm
    e. 6.75×10^{-4} g
    f. 4.62×10^{-2} cm
    g. 9.7 m/s
13. 1.08×10^9 km
19. **a.** 3
    b. 4
    c. 3
    d. 2
21. 228.8 cm
23. b, c
29. 4×10^8 breaths
31. 5.4×10^8 s
33. 2×10^3 balls
35. 7×10^2 tuners
37. **a.** 22 cm; 38 cm^2
    b. 29.2 cm; 67.9 cm^2
39. 9.818×10^{-2} m
41. The ark (6×10^4 m^3) was about 100 times as large as a typical house (6×10^2 m^3).
43. 1.0×10^3 kg
45. **a.** 0.618 g/cm^3
    b. 4.57×10^{16} m^2

CHAPTER 2
Motion in One Dimension

PRACTICE A, p. 42
3. 680 m to the north
5. 0.43 h

PRACTICE B, p. 47
1. 2.2 s
3. 5.4 s
5. **a.** 1.4 m/s
   b. 3.1 m/s

PRACTICE C, p. 51
1. 21 m
3. 9.1 s

PRACTICE D, p. 53
1. 34 s
3. −7.5 m/s; 19 m

PRACTICE E, p. 55
1. +2.51 m/s
3. **a.** 16 m/s
   b. 7.0 s
5. +2.3 m/s^2

PRACTICE F, p. 61
1. **a.** −42 m/s
   b. 11 s
3. **a.** 8.0 m/s
   b. 1.63 s

2 REVIEW, p. 73
1. 5.0 m; +5.0 m
3. t_1: negative; t_2: positive; t_3: positive; t_4: negative; t_5: zero
7. 10.1 km to the east
9. **a.** +70.0 m
   b. +140.0 m
   c. +14 m/s
   d. +28 m/s
11. 0.2 km west of the flagpole
17. 0.0 m/s^2; +1.36 m/s^2; +0.680 m/s^2
19. 110 m
21. **a.** −15 m/s
    b. −38 m
23. 17.5 m
25. 0.99 m/s
31. 3.94 s

33. 1.51 h
35. **a.** 2.00 min
    b. 1.00 min
    c. 2.00 min
37. 931 m
39. −26 m/s; 31 m
41. 1.6 s
43. 5 s; 85 s; +60 m/s
45. -1.5×10^3 m/s^2
47. **a.** 3.40 s
    b. −9.2 m/s
    c. −31.4 m/s; −33 m/s
49. **a.** 4.6 s after stock car starts
    b. 38 m
    c. +17 m/s (stock car), +21 m/s (racecar)
51. 4.44 m/s

CHAPTER 3
Two-Dimensional Motion and Vectors

PRACTICE A, p. 88
1. **a.** 23 km
   b. 17 km to the east
3. 15.7 m at 22° to the side of downfield

PRACTICE B, p. 91
1. 95 km/h
3. 14.9 m, south

PRACTICE C, p. 93
1. 49 m at 7.3° to the right of downfield
3. 13.0 m at 57° north of east

PRACTICE D, p. 98
1. 0.66 m/s
3. 7.6 m/s

PRACTICE E, p. 100
1. $\Delta x = 0.33$ m, $\Delta y = 3.2$ cm
3. 2.0 s; 4.8 m

1. $\Delta t = 1.7$ h
3. $\Delta t = 9.00$ s

3 REVIEW, p. 111

7. **a.** 5.20 m at 60.0° above the positive x-axis
   b. 3.00 m at 30.0° below the positive x-axis
   c. 3.00 m at 150° counter-clockwise from the positive x-axis
   d. 5.20 m at 60.0° below the positive x-axis
9. 15.3 m at 58.4° south of east
19. if the vector is oriented at 45° from the axes
21. **a.** 5 blocks at 53° north of east
    b. 13 blocks
23. 61.8 m at 76.0° S of E (or S of W), 25.0 m at 53.1° S of E (or S of W)
25. 2.81 km east, 1.31 km north
31. 45.1 m/s
33. 11 m
35. **a.** clears the goal by 1 m
    b. falling
37. 80 m; 210 m
41. **a.** 70 m/s east
    b. 20 m/s
43. **a.** 10.1 m/s at 8.53° east of north
    b. 48.8 m
45. 7.5 min
47. **a.** 41.7 m/s
    b. 3.81 s
    c. $v_{y,f} = -13.5$ m/s, $v_{x,f} = 34.2$ m/s, $v_f = 36.7$ m/s
49. 10.5 m/s
51. **a.** 2.66 m/s
    b. 0.64 m
53. 157 km
55. **a.** 32.5 m
    b. 1.78 s

57. **a.** 57.7 km/h at 60.0° west of the vertical
    b. 28.8 km/h straight down
59. 18 m; 7.9 m
61. 6.19 m/s downfield

CHAPTER 4
Forces and the Laws of Motion

PRACTICE A, p. 124

1. **a.** A gravitational force pointed downward on skydiver
   b. An air resistance force pointed upward that is equal in length to a gravitational force downward on skydiver

PRACTICE B, p. 127

1. $F_x = 60.6$ N; $F_y = 35.0$ N
3. 47° north of east

PRACTICE C, p. 131

1. 2.2 m/s² forward
3. 4.50 m/s² to the east
5. 14 N

PRACTICE D, p. 139

1. 0.19
3. **a.** 8.7×10^2 N, 6.7×10^2 N
   b. 1.1×10^2 N, 84 N
   c. 1×10^3 N, 5×10^2 N
   d. 5 N, 2 N

PRACTICE E, p. 140

1. 2.7 m/s² in the positive x-direction
3. **a.** 0.061
   b. 3.61 m/s² down the ramp

4 REVIEW, p. 146

11. **a.** $\mathbf{F}_1$ (220 N) and $\mathbf{F}_2$ (114 N) both point right; $\mathbf{F}_1$ (220 N) points left, and $\mathbf{F}_2$ (114 N) points right.

b. first situation: 220 N to the right, 114 N to the right; second situation: 220 N to the left, 114 N to the right
21. 55 N to the right
29. 51 N
35. 0.70, 0.60
37. 0.816
39. 1.0 m/s²
41. 13 N down the incline
43. 64 N upward
45. **a.** 0.25 m/s² forward
    b. 18 m
    c. 3.0 m/s
47. **a.** 2 s
    b. The box will never move. The force exerted is not enough to overcome friction.
49. −1.2 m/s²; 0.12
51. **a.** 2690 N forward
    b. 699 N forward
53. 13 N, 13 N, 0 N, −26 N

CHAPTER 5
Work and Energy

PRACTICE A, p. 157

1. 38.0 m
3. 1.6×10^3

PRACTICE B, p. 161

1. 1.7×10^2 m/s
3. the bullet with the greater mass; 2 to 1
5. 3.40×10^3 kg

PRACTICE C, p. 163

1. 0.17 kg
3. 5.1 m

PRACTICE D, p. 167

1. 3.3 J
3. **a.** 785 J
   b. 105 J
   c. 0.00 J

PRACTICE E, p. 172

1. 429.9 J; 20.7 m/s
3. 14.1 m/s
5. 0.18 m

PRACTICE F, p. 176

1. 66 kW
3. 2.61×10^8 s (8.27 years)
5. **a.** 7.50×10^4 J
   b. 2.50×10^4 W

5 REVIEW, p. 183

7. 53 J, −53 J
9. 47.5 J
19. 7.6×10^4 J
21. 2.0×10^1 m
23. **a.** 5400 J, 0 J; 5400 J
    b. 0 J, −5400 J; 5400 J
    c. 2700 J, −2700 J; 5400 J
33. 3600 J; 12.0 m/s
35. 17.2 s
37. **a.** 0.633 J
    b. 0.633 J
    c. 2.43 m/s
    d. 0.422 J, 0.211 J
39. 5.0 m
41. 2.5 m
45. **a.** 61 J
    b. −45 J
    c. 0 J
47. **a.** 28.0 m/s
    b. 30.0 m above the ground
49. 0.107
51. **a.** 66 J
    b. 2.3 m/s
    c. 66 J
    d. −16 J

CHAPTER 6

Momentum and Collisions

PRACTICE A, p. 193

1. 2.5×10^3 kg•m/s to the south
3. 6.66 m/s to the south

PRACTICE B, p. 195

1. 3.8×10^2 N to the left
3. 16 kg•m/s to the south

PRACTICE C, p. 196

1. 4.06 s; 45.1 m
3. 32 N to the left; 49 m to the right

PRACTICE D, p. 202

1. 1.90 m/s
3. **a.** 12.0 m/s
   b. 9.6 m/s

PRACTICE E, p. 207

1. 3.8 m/s to the south
3. 4.25 m/s to the north
5. **a.** 3.0 kg
   b. 5.32 m/s

PRACTICE F, p. 209

1. **a.** 0.43 m/s to the west
   b. 17 J
3. **a.** 4.6 m/s to the south
   b. 3.9×10^3 J

PRACTICE G, p. 212

1. **a.** 22.5 cm/s to the right
   b. $KE_i = 6.2 \times 10^{-4}$ J $= KE_f$
3. **a.** 8.0 m/s to the right
   b. $KE_i = 1.3 \times 10^2$ J $= KE_f$

6 REVIEW, p. 218

11. **a.** 8.35×10^{-21} kg•m/s upward
    b. 4.88 kg•m/s to the right
    c. 7.50×10^2 kg•m/s to the southwest
    d. 1.78×10^{29} kg•m/s forward
13. 18 N; 4.4 kg•m/s
23. 0.037 m/s to the south
29. 3.00 m/s
31. **a.** 0.81 m/s to the east
    b. 1.4×10^3 J
33. 4.0 m/s
35. 42.0 m/s toward second base

37. **a.** 0.0 kg•m/s
    b. 1.1 kg•m/s upward
39. 23 m/s
41. 4.0×10^2 N; 0.2 kg•m/s opposite the direction the ball was traveling
43. 2.36×10^{-2} m
45. 0.413
47. −22 cm/s, 22 cm/s
49. **a.** 9.9 m/s downward
    b. 1.8×10^3 N upward

CHAPTER 7

Circular Motion and Gravitation

PRACTICE A, p. 227

1. 2.5 m/s
3. 3.08 m/s^2

PRACTICE B, p. 229

1. 29.6 kg
3. 40.0 N

PRACTICE C, p. 234

1. 26 km
3. **a.** 651 N
   b. 246 N
   c. 38.5 N

PRACTICE D, p. 243

1. Earth: 7.69×10^3 m/s, 5.51×10^3 s; Jupiter: 4.20×10^4 m/s, 1.08×10^4 s; moon: 1.53×10^3 m/s, 8.63×10^3 s

PRACTICE E, p. 249

1. 0.75 N•m
3. 133 N

7 REVIEW, p. 264

9. 2.7 m/s
11. 62 kg
19. 1.0×10^{-10} m (0.10 nm)

27. $v_t = 1630$ m/s;
$T = 5.78 \times 10^5$ s
29. Jupiter ($m = 1.9 \times 10^{27}$ kg)
33. $\mathbf{F_2}$
37. 26 N•m
39. 12 m/s
41. 220 N
43. 1800 N•m
45. 2.0×10^2 N
47. 72%
49. a. 2.25 days
b. 1.60×10^4 m/s
51. a. 6300 N•m
b. 550 N
53. 6620 N; no ($F_c = 7880$ N)

CHAPTER 8
Fluid Mechanics

PRACTICE A, p. 276

1. a. 3.57×10^3 kg/m^3
b. 6.4×10^2 kg/m^3
3. 9.4×10^3 N

PRACTICE B, p. 279

1. a. 1.48×10^3 N
b. 1.88×10^5 Pa
3. 1.0×10^5 Pa

8 REVIEW, p. 291

9. 2.1×10^3 kg/m^3
15. 6.28 N
21. 1.01×10^{11} N
23. 6.11×10^{-1} kg
25. 17 N, 31 N
27. a. 1.0×10^3 kg/m^3
b. 3.5×10^2 Pa
c. 2.1×10^3 Pa
29. 1.7×10^{-2} m
31. 0.605 m
33. 6.3 m
35. a. 0.48 m/s^2
b. 4.0 s
37. 1.7×10^{-3} m

CHAPTER 9
Heat

PRACTICE A, p. 305

1. $-89.22°$C, 183.93 K
3. 37.0°C, 39°C
5. 1.200×10^{3}°C

PRACTICE B, p. 312

1. 755 J
3. 0.96 J

PRACTICE C, p. 317

1. 47°C
3. 390 J/kg•°C

9 REVIEW, p. 325

9. 57.8°C, 331.0 K
25. a. 2.9 J
b. It goes into the air, the ground, and the hammer.
31. 25.0°C
33. a. $T_R = T_F + 459.7$, or
$T_F = T_R - 459.7$
b. $T = \dfrac{5}{9} T_R$, or $T_R = \dfrac{9}{5} T$
35. a. $T_{TH} = \dfrac{3}{2} T_C + 50$, or
$T_C = \dfrac{2}{3}(T_{TH} - 50)$
b. $-360°$ TH
37. 330 g
39. 5.7×10^3 J/min $= 95$ J/s

CHAPTER 10
Thermodynamics

PRACTICE A, p. 336

1. a. 6.4×10^5 J
b. -4.8×10^5 J
3. 3.3×10^2 J

PRACTICE B, p. 343

1. 33 J
3. 1.00×10^4 J
5. 1.74×10^8 J

PRACTICE C, p. 352

1. 0.1504
3. $0.10 = 10$ percent
5. 5.3×10^3 J

10 REVIEW, p. 359

3. b, c, d, e
9. 1.08×10^3 J; done by the gas
15. a. none (Q, W, and $\Delta U > 0$)
b. $\Delta U < 0$, $Q < 0$ for refrigerator interior ($W = 0$)
c. $\Delta U < 0$ ($Q = 0$, $W > 0$)
17. a. 1.7×10^6 J, to the rod
b. 3.3×10^2 J; by the rod
c. 1.7×10^6 J; it increases
27. 0.32
29. a. 188 J
b. 1.400×10^3 J

CHAPTER 11
Vibrations and Waves

PRACTICE A, p. 368

1. a. 57 N/m
b. less stiff
3. -6.7 cm

PRACTICE B, p. 376

1. 1.4×10^2 m
3. 3.6 m

PRACTICE C, p. 378

1. 2.1×10^2 N/m
3. 39.7 N/m
5. a. 1.7 s, 0.59 Hz
b. 0.14 s, 7.1 Hz
c. 1.6 s, 0.62 Hz

PRACTICE D, p. 385

1. 0.081 m $\leq \lambda \leq 12$ m
3. 4.74×10^{14} Hz

11 REVIEW, p. 397

9. 580 N/m
11. $4A$
19. 9.7 m
21. **a.** 0.57 s
    b. 1.8 Hz
27. 1/3 s; 3 Hz
35. 0.0333 m
39. **a.** 0.0 cm
    b. 48 cm
43. a, b, and d ($\lambda = 0.5L$, L, and $2L$, respectively)
45. 1.7 N
47. 446 m
49. 9.70 m/s^2
51. 9:48 A.M.

CHAPTER 12
Sound

PRACTICE A, p. 413

1. **a.** 8.0×10^{-4} W/m^2
   b. 1.6×10^{-3} W/m^2
   c. 6.4×10^{-3} W/m^2
3. 2.3×10^{-5} W
5. 4.8 m

PRACTICE B, p. 424

1. 440 Hz
3. 35.5 cm

12 REVIEW, p. 436

23. 7.96×10^{-2} W/m^2
25. **a.** 4.0 m
    b. 2.0 m
    c. 1.3 m
    d. 1.0 m
29. 3 Hz
35. 3.0×10^3 Hz
37. 5 beats per second
39. 0.20 s
41. $L_{closed} = 1.5 \, (L_{open})$

43. **a.** 5.0×10^4 W
    b. 2.8×10^{-3} W

CHAPTER 13
Light and Reflection

PRACTICE A, p. 446

1. 1.0×10^{-13} m
3. 2.9971×10^8 m/s
5. 5.4×10^{14} Hz

PRACTICE B, p. 459

1. $p = 10.0$ cm: no image (infinite q); $p = 5.00$ cm: $q = -10.0$ cm, $M = 2.00$; virtual, upright image
3. $R = 1.00 \times 10^2$ cm; $M = 2.00$; virtual image

PRACTICE C, p. 463

1. $p = 46.0$ cm; $M = 0.500$; virtual, upright image; $h = 3.40$ cm
3. $p = 45$ cm; $h = 17$ cm; $M = 0.41$; virtual, upright image
5. $f = -7.7$ cm; R = -15 cm

13 REVIEW, p. 475

7. 3.00×10^8 m/s
11. 1×10^{-6} m
13. 9.1×10^{-3} m (9.1 mm)
21. 1.2 m/s; The image moves toward the mirror's surface.
35. $q = 26$ cm; real, inverted; $M = -2.0$
47. inverted; $p = 6.1$ cm; $f = 2.6$ cm; real
49. $q_2 = 6.7$ cm; real; $M_1 = -0.57$, $M_2 = -0.27$; inverted

51. $p = 11.3$ cm
55. $R = -25.0$ cm
57. concave, $R = 48.1$ cm; $M = 2.00$; virtual

CHAPTER 14
Refraction

PRACTICE A, p. 488

1. 18.5°
3. 1.47

PRACTICE B, p. 496

1. 20.0 cm, $M = -1.00$; real, inverted image
3. -6.67 cm, $M = 0.333$; virtual, upright image

PRACTICE C, p. 503

1. 42.8°
3. 1.54

14 REVIEW, p. 511

11. 26°
13. 30.0°, 19.5°, 19.5°, 30.0°
23. yes, because $n_{ice} > n_{air}$
25. 3.40; upright
37. **a.** 31.3°
    b. 44.2°
    c. 49.8°
39. 1.31
41. 1.62; carbon disulfide
43. 7.50 cm
45. **a.** 6.00 cm
    b. A diverging lens cannot form an image larger than the object.
47. **a.** 3.01 cm
    b. 2.05 cm
49. blue: 47.8°, red: 48.2°
51. 48.8°
53. 4.54 m
55. $\dfrac{10}{9} f$

57. a. 24.7°
  b. It will pass through the bottom surface because $\theta_i < \theta_c$ ($\theta_c = 41.8°$).
59. 1.38
61. 58.0 m
63. a. 4.83 cm
  b. The lens must be moved 0.12 cm.
65. 1.90 cm

CHAPTER 15
Interference and Diffraction

PRACTICE A, p. 524

1. 5.1×10^{-7} m $= 5.1 \times 10^2$ nm
3. 0.125°

PRACTICE B, p. 531

1. 0.02°, 0.04°, 0.11°
3. 11
5. 6.62×10^3 lines/cm

15 REVIEW, p. 543

5. θ would decrease because λ is shorter in water.
9. 630 nm
11. 160 μm
19. 3.22°
21. a. 10.09°, 13.71°, 14.77°
  b. 20.51°, 28.30°, 30.66°
29. 432.0 nm
31. 1.93×10^{-3} mm $= 3 \lambda$; a maximum

CHAPTER 16
Electric Forces and Fields

PRACTICE A, p. 557

1. 230 N (attractive)
3. 0.393 m

PRACTICE B, p. 558

1. 2.24×10^{10} N

PRACTICE C, p. 561

1. $x = 9.3 \times 10^8$ m
3. 5.07 m

PRACTICE D, p. 566

1. 1.66×10^5 N/C, 81.1° above the positive x-axis
3. a. 3.2×10^{-15} N, along the negative x-axis
  b. 3.2×10^{-15} N, along the positive x-axis

16 REVIEW, p. 574

15. 3.50×10^3 N
17. 91 N (repulsive)
19. 1.48×10^{-7} N, along the $+x$ direction
21. 18 cm from the 3.5 nC charge
33. 5.7×10^3 N/C, 75° above the positive x-axis
35. a. 5.7×10^{-27} N, in a direction opposite $\mathbf{E}$
  b. 3.6×10^{-8} N/C
37. a. 2.0×10^7 N/C, along the positive x-axis
  b. 4.0×10^1 N
41. 7.2×10^{-9} C
43. $v_{electron} = 4.4 \times 10^6$ m/s; $v_{proton} = 2.4 \times 10^3$ m/s
45. 5.4×10^{-14} N
47. 2.0×10^{-6} C
49. 32.5 m
51. a. 5.3×10^{17} m/s^2
  b. 8.5×10^{-4} m
  c. 2.9×10^{14} m/s^2
53. a. positive
  b. 5.3×10^{-7} C
55. a. 1.3×10^4 N/C
  b. 4.2×10^6 m/s

CHAPTER 17
Electrical Energy and Current

PRACTICE A, p. 587

1. 8.0×10^{-19} C
3. 2.3×10^{-16} J

PRACTICE B, p. 594

1. a. 4.80×10^{-5} C
  b. 4.50×10^{-6} J
3. a. 9.00 V
  b. 5.0×10^{-12} C

PRACTICE C, p. 597

1. 4.00×10^2 s
3. 6.00×10^2 s
5. a. 2.6×10^{-3} A
  b. 1.6×10^{17} electrons
  c. 5.1×10^{-3} A

PRACTICE D, p. 602

1. 0.43 A
3. 5.5×10^2 Ω
5. 1.8×10^2 Ω

PRACTICE E, p. 609

1. 14 Ω
3. 1.5 V
5. 5.00×10^2 A

17 REVIEW, p. 619

9. -4.2×10^5 V
19. 0.22 J
23. $v_{avg} > v_{drift}$
33. a. 3.5 min
  b. 1.2×10^{22} electrons
41. 3.4 A
49. 3.6×10^6 J
51. the 75 W bulb
53. 2.0×10^{16} J

55. $93 \, \Omega$

57. $3.000 \, \text{m}; 2.00 \times 10^{-7} \, \text{C}$

59. $4.0 \times 10^3 \, \text{V/m}$

61. **a.** $4.11 \times 10^{-15} \, \text{J}$
 b. $2.22 \times 10^6 \, \text{m/s}$

63. **a.** $1.13 \times 10^5 \, \text{V/m}$
 b. $1.81 \times 10^{-14} \, \text{N}$
 c. $4.39 \times 10^{-17} \, \text{J}$

65. $0.545 \, \text{m}, -1.20 \, \text{m}$

67. **a.** $7.2 \times 10^{-13} \, \text{J}$
 b. $2.9 \times 10^7 \, \text{m/s}$

69. **a.** $3.0 \times 10^{-3} \, \text{A}$
 b. 1.1×10^{18} electrons/min

71. **a.** $32 \, \text{V}$
 b. $0.16 \, \text{V}$

73. $1.0 \times 10^5 \, \text{W}$

75. $3.2 \times 10^5 \, \text{J}$

77. $13.5 \, \text{h}$

79. $2.2 \times 10^{-5} \, \text{V}$

CHAPTER 18
Circuits and Circuit Elements

PRACTICE A, p. 639

1. **a.** $43.6 \, \Omega; 3.3 \, \text{W}$
 b. $0.275 \, \text{A}$
3. $0.5 \, \Omega$

PRACTICE B, p. 644

1. $4.5 \, \text{A}, 2.2 \, \text{A}, 1.8 \, \text{A}, 1.3 \, \text{A}$
3. **a.** $2.2 \, \Omega; 262 \, \text{W}$
 b. $6.0 \, \text{A}, 3.0 \, \text{A}, 2.00 \, \text{A}$

PRACTICE C, p. 648

1. **a.** $27.8 \, \Omega$
 b. $26.6 \, \Omega$
 c. $23.4 \, \Omega$

PRACTICE D, p. 650

R_a: $0.50 \, \text{A}, 2.5 \, \text{V}$
R_b: $0.50 \, \text{A}, 3.5 \, \text{V}$
R_c: $1.5 \, \text{A}, 6.0 \, \text{V}$
R_d: $1.0 \, \text{A}, 4.0 \, \text{V}$
R_e: $1.0 \, \text{A}, 4.0 \, \text{V}$
R_f: $2.0 \, \text{A}, 4.0 \, \text{V}$

18 REVIEW, p. 658

17. **a.** $24 \, \Omega$
 b. $1.0 \, \text{A}$

19. **a.** $2.99 \, \Omega$
 b. $4.0 \, \text{A}$

21. **a.** seven combinations
 b. $R, 2R, 3R, \dfrac{R}{2}, \dfrac{R}{3}, \dfrac{2R}{3}, \dfrac{3R}{2}$

23. $15 \, \Omega$

25. $3.0 \, \Omega$: $1.8 \, \text{A}, 5.4 \, \text{V}$
 $6.0 \, \Omega$: $1.1 \, \text{A}, 6.5 \, \text{V}$
 $9.0 \, \Omega$: $0.72 \, \text{A}, 6.5 \, \text{V}$

27. $28 \, \text{V}$

29. $3.8 \, \text{V}$

31. **a.** $33.0 \, \Omega$
 b. $132 \, \text{V}$
 c. $4.00 \, \text{A}, 4.00 \, \text{A}$

33. $10.0 \, \Omega$

35. **a.** a
 b. c
 c. d
 d. e

37. $18.0 \, \Omega$: $0.750 \, \text{A}, 13.5 \, \text{V}$
 $6.0 \, \Omega$: $0.750 \, \text{A}, 4.5 \, \text{V}$

39. $4.0 \, \Omega$

41. $13.96 \, \Omega$

43. **a.** $62.4 \, \Omega$
 b. $0.192 \, \text{A}$
 c. $0.102 \, \text{A}$
 d. $0.520 \, \text{W}$
 e. $0.737 \, \text{W}$

47. **a.** $5.1 \, \Omega$
 b. $4.5 \, \text{V}$

49. **a.** 11 A (heater), 9.2 A (toaster), 12 A (grill)
 b. The total current is 32.2 A, so the 30.0 A circuit breaker will open the circuit if these appliances are all on.

CHAPTER 19
Magnetism

PRACTICE A, p. 677

1. $3.57 \times 10^6 \, \text{m/s}$
3. $6.0 \times 10^{-12} \, \text{N}$ west

PRACTICE B, p. 680

1. $1.7 \times 10^{-7} \, \text{T}$ in $+z$-direction
3. $9.7 \, \text{A}$

19 REVIEW, p. 685

31. $2.1 \times 10^{-3} \, \text{m/s}$

33. $2.00 \, \text{T}$

39. $2.1 \times 10^{-2} \, \text{T}$, in the negative y-direction

41. $2.0 \, \text{T}$, out of the page

43. **a.** $8.0 \, \text{m/s}$
 b. $5.4 \times 10^{-26} \, \text{J}$

45. $2.82 \times 10^7 \, \text{m/s}$

CHAPTER 20
Electromagnetic Induction

PRACTICE A, p. 699

1. $0.11 \, \text{V}$
3. $4.0 \, \text{m}^2$

PRACTICE B, p. 711

1. $4.8 \, \text{A}; 6.8 \, \text{A}, 170 \, \text{V}$
3. **a.** $7.42 \, \text{A}$
 b. $14.8 \, \Omega$
5. **a.** $1.10 \times 10^2 \, \text{V}$
 b. $2.1 \, \text{A}$

PRACTICE C, p. 714

1. $6.9 \times 10^4 \, \text{V}$
3. 25 turns
5. $147 \, \text{V}$

20 REVIEW, p. 726

11. $0.12 \, \text{A}$
27. **a.** $2.4 \times 10^2 \, \text{V}$
 b. $2.0 \, \text{A}$

29. a. 8.34 A
   b. 119 V
35. 221 V
37. a. a step-down transformer
   b. 1.2×10^3 V
43. 790 turns
45. a. a step-up transformer
   b. 440 V
47. 171:1
49. 300 V

CHAPTER 21
Atomic Physics

PRACTICE A, p. 739

1. 2.0 Hz
3. 1.2×10^{15} Hz

PRACTICE B, p. 742

1. 6.0×10^{14} Hz
3. 5.64 eV

PRACTICE C, p. 752

1. 4.56×10^{14} Hz; line 4
3. 1.61×10^{15} Hz
5. E_6 to E_2; line 1

PRACTICE D, p. 757

1. 7.1×10^6
3. 8.84×10^{-27} m/s
5. 1.0×10^{-15} kg

21 REVIEW, p. 766

11. 4.8×10^{17} Hz
13. 1.2×10^{15} Hz
23. a. 2.46×10^{15} Hz
   b. 2.92×10^{15} Hz
   c. 3.09×10^{15} Hz
   d. 3.16×10^{15} Hz
33. 1.4×10^7 m/s
35. 2.00 eV
37. 0.80 eV

CHAPTER 22
Subatomic Physics

PRACTICE A, p. 779

1. 160.65 MeV; 342.05 MeV
3. 0.291 769 u

PRACTICE B, p. 786

1. $^{12}_{6}$C
3. $^{131}_{53}$I
5. $^{63}_{28}$Ni $\rightarrow$ $^{63}_{29}$Cu + $^{0}_{-1}e$ + $\overline{\nu}$

PRACTICE C, p. 788

1. 4.23×10^3 s^{-1}, 0.23 Ci
3. 9.94×10^{-7} s^{-1},
   6.7×10^{-7} Ci
5. a. about 5.0×10^7 atoms
   b. about 3.5×10^8 atoms

22 REVIEW, p. 807

1. 79; 118; 79
7. 92.162 MeV
9. 8.2607 MeV/nucleon; 8.6974 MeV/nucleon
21. a. $^{4}_{2}$He
   b. $^{4}_{2}$He
23. 560 days
27. a. $-e$
   b. 0
33. 1.2×10^{-14}
35. 3.53 MeV
37. a. $^{1}_{0}n$ + $^{197}_{79}$Au $\rightarrow$ $^{198}_{80}$Hg + $^{0}_{-1}e$ + $\overline{\nu}$
   b. 7.885 MeV
39. $^{3}_{2}$He
41. 2.6×10^{21} atoms
43. a. $^{8}_{4}$Be
   b. $^{12}_{6}$C
45. 3.8×10^3 s
47. 1.1×10^{16} fission events

APPENDIX I

ADDITIONAL PROBLEMS, p. R52

1. 11.68 m
3. 6.4×10^{-2} m^3
5. 6.7×10^{-5} ps
7. 2.80 h = 2 h, 48 min
9. 4.0×10^1 km/h
11. 48 m/h
13. +25.0 m/s = 25.0 m/s, upward
15. 44.8 m/s
17. -21.5 m/s^2 = 21.5 m/s^2, backward
19. 38.5 m
21. 126 s
23. 1.27 s
25. 11 km/h
27. 2.74 s
29. 10.5 m, forward
31. 5.9 s
33. 8.3 s
35. 7.4 s
37. -490 m/s^2 = 490 m/s^2, backward
39. 17.3 s
41. 7.0 m
43. 2.6 m/s
45. -11.4 m/s = 11.4 m/s, downward
47. 8.5° north of east
49. 5.0° south of west
51. 770 m
53. -33 km/h = 33 km/h, downward
55. 18.9 km, 76° north of west
57. 17.0 m
59. 52.0°
61. 79 s
63. 15.8 m, 55° below the horizontal
65. 0.290 m/s, east; 1.16 m/s, north
67. 2.6 km

69. 66 km, 46° south of east
71. 10.7 m
73. 3.0 s
75. 76.9 km/h, 60.1° west of north
77. 7.0×10^2 m, 3.8° above the horizontal
79. 47.2 m
81. 6.36 m/s
83. 13.6 km/h, 73° south of east
85. 58 N
87. 14.0 N; 2.0 N
89. 9.5×10^4 kg
91. 258 N, up the slope
93. 15.9 N
95. 2.0 m/s^2
97. $F_x = 8.60$ N; $F_y = 12.3$ N
99. -448 m/s^2 = 448 m/s^2, backward
101. 15 kg
103. 0.085
105. 1.7×10^8 N
107. 24 N, downhill
109. 1.150×10^3 N
111. 1.2×10^4 N
113. 0.60
115. 38.0 m
117. 2.5×10^4 J
119. 247 m/s
121. -5.46×10^4 J
123. 3.35×10^6 J
125. 1.23 J
127. 12 s
129. 0.600 m
131. 133 J
133. 53.3 m/s
135. 72.2 m
137. 0.13 m = 13 cm
139. 7.7 m/s
141. 8.0 s
143. 230 J
145. 7.96 m
147. 6.0×10^1 m/s

149. 1.58×10^3 kg•m/s, north
151. 3.38×10^{31} kg
153. 18 s
155. 637 m, to the right
157. 7.5 g
159. 0.0 m/s
161. -5.0×10^1 percent
163. 16.4 m/s, west
165. 5.33×10^7 kg•m/s
167. 1.0×10^1 m/s
169. 560 N, east
171. -3.3×10^8 N = 3.3×10^8 N, backward
173. 52 m
175. 24 kg
177. 90.6 km/h, east
179. 26 km/h, 37° north of east
181. -157 J
183. 0.125 kg
185. -4.1×10^4 J
187. 9.8 kg
189. 1.0 m/s, 60° south of east
191. 4.04×10^3 m/s^2
193. 42 m/s
195. 8.9 kg
197. 1.04×10^4 m/s = 10.4 km/s
199. 1.48×10^{23} kg
201. 1.10×10^{12} m
203. 6.6×10^3 m/s = 6.6 km/s
205. 0.87 m
207. 254 N
209. 0.42 m = 42 cm
211. 25 N
213. 165 kg
215. 5.09×10^5 s = 141 h
217. 5.5×10^9 m = 5.5×10^6 km
219. 1.6 N•m
221. 6.62×10^3 N
223. 0.574 m
225. 8.13×10^{-3} m^2
227. 2.25×10^4 kg/m^3

229. 2.0×10^1 m^2
231. 4.30 kg
233. 374°F to -292°F
235. 6.6×10^{-2}°C
237. 1.29×10^4 J
239. 4.1×10^{-2} kg
241. 1.200×10^3°C
243. 315 K
245. 1.91×10^{-2} kg = 19.1 g
247. 530 J/kg•°C
249. -930°C
251. 1.50×10^3 Pa = 1.50 kPa
253. 873 J
255. 244 J
257. 5.3×10^3 J
259. 2.4×10^3 Pa = 2.4 kPa
261. 5895 J
263. 5.30×10^2 kJ = 5.30×10^5 J
265. 1.0×10^4 J
267. -18 N
269. -0.11 m = -11 cm
271. 4.0×10^{-2} m = 4.0 cm
273. 0.2003 Hz
275. 730 N/m
277. 1.4×10^3 m/s
279. 2.2×10^4 Hz
281. 8.6×10^3 N/m
283. 3.177 s
285. 82 kg
287. 1.2 s
289. 1.5×10^3 m/s
291. 1.1 W/m^2
293. 294 Hz
295. 408 m/s
297. 0.155 m
299. 0.211 m = 21.1 cm
301. 2.9971×10^8 m/s
303. 3.2×10^{-7} m = 320 nm
305. -0.96 cm
307. -1.9 cm
309. 3.8 m
311. 0.25
313. 38 cm

315. 2.40

317. 0.98 cm

319. 10.5 cm

321. 64.0 cm in front of the mirror

323. 8.3 cm

325. 0.40

327. −11 cm

329. 2.9979×10^8 m/s

331. 33.3 cm

333. 0.19

335. 32.2°

337. −10.4 cm

339. 18 cm

341. 1.63

343. 39.38°

345. 58°

347. −21 cm

349. ∞

351. 1.486

353. 1.54

355. 4.8 cm

357. 1.73 to 1.83

359. 5.18×10^{-4} m = 0.518 mm

361. 0.137°

363. 9.0×10^{-7} m = 9.0×10^2 nm

365. 11.2°

367. 0.227°

369. 1.445×10^4 lines/cm

371. 140 N attractive

373. 2.2×10^{-17} C

375. 0.00 N

377. 4.0×10^{-8} N, 9.3° below the negative x-axis

379. 260 N from either charge

381. 1.6×10^{-12} C

383. 0.585 m = 58.5 cm

385. 3.97×10^{-6} N, upward

387. 0.073 m = 7.3 cm

389. 7.5×10^{-6} N, along the $+y$-axis

391. 4.40×10^5 N/C, 89.1° above the $-x$-axis

393. −7.4 C

395. 1.6×10^{-19} C

397. 36 cm

399. 4.4×10^{-4} J

401. 7.1×10^{-4} F

403. 4.0 A

405. 160 Ω

407. 1.7×10^6 W = 1.7 MW

409. 6.4×10^2 N/C

411. 12 V

413. 1.2×10^{-5} m

415. 1.4×10^2 C

417. 7.2 s

419. 4.8 V

421. 116 V

423. 5.0×10^5 W = 0.50 MW

425. 7.5×10^6 V

427. 3.00×10^2 Ω

429. 6.0 Ω

431. 13 Ω

433. 6.0 Ω

435. 0.056 A = 56 mA

437. 1.6 A (refrigerator); 1.3 A (oven)

439. 12.6 Ω

441. 2.6 V

443. 9.4 Ω

445. 1.6 A

447. 1.45 A

449. 4×10^{-12} N

451. 7.6×10^6 m/s

453. 0.70 A

455. 5.1×10^{-4} T

457. 3.9×10^{-15} N

459. 1.5×10^5 A

461. 1.7×10^{-2} T

463. 0.90 s

465. 450 V

467. 1.8 A

469. 3.4×10^4 V = 34 kV

471. 48 turns

473. 2.5×10^{-3} A = 2.5 mA

475. 0.85 A

477. 48:1

479. 3.32×10^{-10} m

481. 1.00×10^{-13} m

483. 3.0×10^{-7} m

485. 26 kg

487. 4.30×10^{14} Hz

489. 6.0×10^{14} Hz

491. 4.0×10^{-21} kg

493. 2.5×10^{-43} m

495. 7.72×10^{14} Hz

497. 333.73 MeV

499. 0.543 705 u

501. $^{16}_{8}$O

503. 15.0 s

505. 31.92 h

507. 35.46 MeV

509. $^{131}_{53}$I

511. $^{111}_{54}$Xe

513. 924 days

absorption spectrum a diagram or graph that indicates the wavelengths of radiant energy that a substance absorbs

acceleration the rate at which velocity changes over time; an object accelerates if its speed, direction, or both change

accuracy a description of how close a measurement is to the correct or accepted value of the quantity measured

adiabatic process a thermodynamic process in which no energy is transferred to or from the system as heat

alternating current an electric current that changes direction at regular intervals

amplitude the maximum displacement from equilibrium

angle of incidence the angle between a ray that strikes a surface and the line perpendicular to that surface at the point of contact

angle of reflection the angle formed by the line perpendicular to a surface and the direction in which a reflected ray moves

angular acceleration the time rate of change of angular velocity, usually expressed in radians per second per second

angular displacement the angle through which a point, line, or body is rotated in a specified direction and about a specified axis

angular momentum for a rotating object, the product of the object's moment of inertia and angular velocity about the same axis

angular velocity the rate at which a body rotates about an axis, usually expressed in radians per second

antinode a point in a standing wave, halfway between two nodes, at which the largest displacement occurs

average velocity the total displacement divided by the time interval during which the displacement occurred

back emf the emf induced in a motor's coil that tends to reduce the current in the coil of the motor

beat the periodic variation in the amplitude of a wave that is the superposition of two waves of slightly different frequencies

binding energy the energy released when unbound nucleons come together to form a stable nucleus, which is equivalent to the energy required to break the nucleus into individual nucleons

blackbody radiation the radiation emitted by a blackbody, which is a perfect radiator and absorber and emits radiation based only on its temperature

buoyant force the upward force exerted by a liquid on an object immersed in or floating on the liquid

calorimetry an experimental procedure used to measure the energy transferred from one substance to another as heat

capacitance the ability of a conductor to store energy in the form of electrically separated charges

center of mass the point in a body at which all the mass of the body can be considered to be concentrated when analyzing translational motion

centripetal acceleration the acceleration directed toward the center of a circular path

chromatic aberration the focusing of different colors of light at different distances behind a lens

coefficient of friction the ratio of the magnitude of the force of friction between two objects in contact to the magnitude of the normal force with which the objects press against each other

coherence the correlation between the phases of two or more waves

components of a vector the projections of a vector along the axes of a coordinate system

compression the region of a longitudinal wave in which the density and pressure are at a maximum

Compton shift an increase in the wavelength of the photon scattered by an electron relative to the wavelength of the incident photon

concave spherical mirror a mirror whose reflecting surface is an inward-curved segment of a sphere

constructive interference a superposition of two or more waves in which individual displacements on the same side of the equilibrium position are added together to form the resultant wave

controlled experiment an experiment that tests only one factor at a time by comparing a control group with an experimental group

convex spherical mirror a mirror whose reflecting surface is an outward-curved segment of a sphere

crest the highest point above the equilibrium position

critical angle the minimum angle of incidence for which total internal reflection occurs

cyclic process a thermodynamic process in which a system returns to the same conditions under which it started

decibel a dimensionless unit that describes the ratio of two intensities of sound; the threshold of hearing is commonly used as the reference intensity

destructive interference a superposition of two or more waves in which individual displacements on opposite sides of the equilibrium position are added together to form the resultant wave

diffraction a change in the direction of a wave when the wave encounters an obstacle, an opening, or an edge

dispersion the process of separating polychromatic light into its component wavelengths

displacement the change in position of an object

doping the addition of an impurity element to a semiconductor

Doppler effect an observed change in frequency when there is relative motion between the source of waves and an observer

drift velocity the net velocity of a charge carrier moving in an electric field

elastic collision a collision in which the total momentum and total kinetic energy remain constant

elastic potential energy the energy stored in any deformed elastic object

electrical conductor a material in which charges can move freely

electrical insulator a material in which charges cannot move freely

electrical potential energy potential energy associated with a charge due to its position in an electric field

electric circuit a set of electrical components connected such that they provide one or more complete paths for the movement of charges

electric current the rate at which charges pass through a given area

electric field a region where a test charge experiences an electric charge

electric potential the work that must be performed against electric forces to move a charge from a reference point to the point in question, divided by the charge

electromagnetic induction the process of creating a current in a circuit by a changing magnetic field

electromagnetic radiation the transfer of energy associated with an electromagnetic wave; it varies periodically and travels at the speed of light

electromagnetic wave a wave that consists of oscillating electric and magnetic fields, which radiate outward from the source at the speed of light

emission spectrum a diagram or graph that indicates the wavelengths of radiant energy that a substance emits

entropy a measure of the randomness or disorder of a system

environment the combination of conditions and influences outside a system that affect the behavior of the system

equilibrium in physics, the state in which the net force on an object is zero

excited state a state in which an atom has more energy than it does at its ground state

fluid a nonsolid state of matter in which the atoms or molecules are free to move past each other, as in a gas or liquid

force an action exerted on an object that may change the object's state of rest or motion; force has magnitude and direction

frame of reference a system for specifying the precise location of objects in space and time

free fall the motion of a body when only the force due to gravity is acting on the body

frequency the number of cycles or vibrations per unit of time; also the number of waves produced per unit of time

fundamental frequency the lowest frequency of vibration of a standing wave

G

generator a machine that converts mechanical energy into electrical energy

gravitational force the mutual force of attraction between particles of matter

gravitational potential energy the potential energy associated with an object's position relative to a gravitational source

ground state the lowest energy state of a quantized system

H

half-life the time needed for half of the original nuclei of a sample of a radioactive substance to undergo radioactive decay

harmonic series a series of frequencies that includes the fundamental frequency and integral multiples of the fundamental frequency

heat the energy transferred between objects because of a difference in their temperatures; energy is always transferred from higher-temperature objects to lower-temperature objects until thermal equilibrium is reached

hole an energy level that is not occupied by an electron in a solid

hypothesis an explanation that is based on prior scientific research or observations—one that can be tested

I

ideal fluid a fluid that has no internal friction or viscosity and is incompressible

impulse the product of the force and the time interval over which the force acts on an object

index of refraction the ratio of the speed of light in a vacuum to the speed of light in a given transparent medium

induction the process of charging a conductor by bringing it near another charged object and grounding the conductor

inertia the tendency of an object to resist being moved or, if the object is moving, to resist a change in speed or direction

instantaneous velocity the velocity of an object at some instant or at a specific point in the object's path

intensity the rate at which energy flows through a unit area perpendicular to the direction of wave motion

internal energy the energy of a substance due to both the random motions of its particles and to the potential energy that results from the distances and alignments between the particles

isothermal process a thermodynamic process that takes place at constant temperature

isotope an atom that has the same number of protons (or the same atomic number) as other atoms of the same element do but that has a different number of neutrons (and thus a different atomic mass)

isovolumetric process a thermodynamic process that takes place at constant volume so that no work is done on or by the system

kinetic energy the energy of an object that is associated with the object's motion

kinetic friction the force that opposes the movement of two surfaces that are in contact and are sliding over each other

laser a device that produces coherent light of only one wavelength

latent heat the energy per unit mass that is transferred during a phase change of a substance

lens a transparent object that refracts light rays such that the light rays converge or diverge to create an image

lever arm the perpendicular distance from the axis of rotation to a line drawn along the direction of the force

linear polarization the alignment of electromagnetic waves in such a way that the vibrations of the electric fields in each of the waves are parallel to each other

longitudinal wave a wave whose particles vibrate parallel to the direction the wave is traveling

magnetic domain a region composed of a group of atoms whose spins are aligned in the same direction

magnetic field a region where a magnetic force can be detected

mass density the concentration of matter of an object, measured as the mass per unit volume of a substance

mechanical energy the sum of kinetic energy and all forms of potential energy

mechanical wave a wave that requires a medium through which to travel

medium a physical environment through which a disturbance can travel

model a pattern, plan, representation, or description designed to show the structure or workings of an object, system, or concept

moment of inertia the tendency of a body that is rotating about a fixed axis to resist a change in this rotating motion

momentum a vector quantity defined as the product of the mass and velocity of an object

mutual inductance the ability of one circuit to induce an emf in a nearby circuit in the presence of a changing current

net force a single force whose external effects on a rigid body are the same as the effects of several actual forces acting on the body

node a point in a standing wave that maintains zero displacement

normal force a force that acts on an object lying on a surface, acting in a direction perpendicular to the surface

order number the number assigned to interference fringes relative to the central bright fringe

parallel describes two or more components of a circuit that provide separate conducting paths for current because the components are connected across common points or junctions

path difference the difference in the distance traveled by two beams when they are scattered in the same direction from different points

perfectly inelastic collision a collision in which two objects stick together after colliding

period the time that it takes a complete cycle or wave oscillation to occur

phase change the physical change of a substance from one state (solid, liquid, or gas) to another at constant temperature and pressure

photoelectric effect the emission of electrons from a metal when light of certain frequencies shines on the surface of the metal

photon a unit or quantum of light; a particle of electromagnetic radiation that has zero mass and carries a quantum of energy

pitch a measure of how high or low a sound is perceived to be, depending on the frequency of the sound wave

potential difference the work that must be performed against electric forces to move a charge between the two points in question divided by the charge

potential energy the energy associated with an object because of its interaction with the environment

power a quantity that measures the rate at which work is done or the rate of energy transfer by any method

precision the degree of exactness of a measurement

pressure the magnitude of the force on a surface per unit area

projectile motion the motion that an object exhibits when thrown, launched, or otherwise projected near the surface of Earth

radian an angle whose arc length is equal to the radius of the circle, which is approximately equal to 57.3°

rarefaction the region of a longitudinal wave in which the density and pressure are at a minimum

real image an image that is formed by the intersection of light rays; a real image can be projected on a screen

reflection the turning back of an electromagnetic wave at a surface

refraction the bending of a wave front as the wave front passes between two substances in which the speed of the wave differs

resistance the opposition presented to electric current by a material or device

resolving power the ability of an optical instrument to form separate images of two objects that are close together

resonance a phenomenon that occurs when the frequency of a force applied to a system matches the natural frequency of vibration of the system, resulting in a large amplitude of vibration

resultant a vector that represents the sum of two or more vectors

rms current the value of alternating current that gives the same heating effect that the corresponding value of direct current does

rotational kinetic energy the energy of an object that is due to the object's rotational motion

scalar a physical quantity that has magnitude but no direction

schematic diagram a representation of a circuit that uses lines to represent wires and different symbols to represent components

series describes two or more components of a circuit that provide a single path for current

significant figures those digits in a measurement that are known with certainty plus the first digit that is uncertain

simple harmonic motion vibration about an equilibrium position in which a restoring force is proportional to the displacement from equilibrium

solenoid a long, helically wound coil of insulated wire

specific heat capacity the quantity of heat required to raise a unit mass of homogeneous material 1 K or 1°C in a specified way given constant pressure and volume

spring constant the energy available for use when a deformed elastic object returns to its original configuration

standing wave a wave pattern that results when two waves of the same frequency, wavelength, and amplitude travel in opposite directions and interfere

static friction the force that resists the initiation of sliding motion between two surfaces that are in contact and at rest

strong force the interaction that binds nucleons together in a nucleus

superconductor a material whose resistance is zero at a certain critical temperature, which varies with each material

system a set of particles or interacting components considered to be a distinct physical entity for the purpose of study

tangential acceleration the acceleration of an object that is tangent to the object's circular path

tangential speed the speed of an object that is tangent to the object's circular path

temperature a measure of the average kinetic energy of the particles in an object

thermal equilibrium the state in which two bodies in physical contact with each other have identical temperatures

timbre the musical quality of a tone resulting from the combination of harmonics present at different intensities

torque a quantity that measures the ability of a force to rotate an object around some axis

total internal reflection the complete reflection that takes place within a substance when the angle of incidence of light striking the surface boundary is less than the critical angle

transformer a device that increases or decreases the emf of alternating current

transistor a semiconductor device that can amplify current and that is used in amplifiers, oscillators, and switches

transverse wave a wave whose particles vibrate perpendicularly to the direction the wave is traveling

trough the lowest point below the equilibrium position

ultraviolet catastrophe the failed prediction of classical physics that the energy radiated by a blackbody at extremely short wavelengths is extremely large and that the total energy radiated is infinite

uncertainty principle the principle that states that it is impossible to simultaneously determine a particle's position and momentum with infinite accuracy

vector a physical quantity that has both magnitude and a direction

virtual image an image from which light rays appear to diverge, even though they are not actually focused there; a virtual image cannot be projected on a screen

wavelength the distance between two adjacent similar points of a wave, such as from crest to crest or from trough to trough

weight a measure of the gravitational force exerted on an object; its value can change with the location of the object in the universe

work the product of the component of a force along the direction of displacement and the magnitude of the displacement

work function the minimum energy needed to remove an electron from a metal atom

work–kinetic energy theorem the net work done by all the forces acting on an object is equal to the change in the object's kinetic energy

dielectrics with, 592, *592f*
discharging of, 592–593
electrical breakdown in, 594, *594f*
electrical potential energy stored in, 593–594, *594f*
in integrated circuit, 636
parallel-plate, 590–591, *590f*, 592, *592f*, 593, *593f*
in schematic diagrams, *631f*
uses, 593, *593f*
carbon, isotopes of, 775
carbon-14, 775
radioactive decay of, 782, 783–784, 790, *790f*
carbon dating, 772–773, 790, *790f*
careers in physics: electrician, 616
high school physics teacher, 215
HVAC technician, 322
kinesiologist, 108
laser surgeon, 540
optometrist, 508
radiologist, 804
roller-coaster designer, 180
science writer, 70
semiconductor technician, 654
Cassegrain reflector, 466, *466f*
CAT (computerized axial tomography) scans, 671
Cavendish, Henry, 237, 296
CCDs (charge-coupled devices), 500
cellular respiration, 164
Celsius (C) scale, 303, 304, *304f*, 305
center of gravity, 256
center of mass: of orbiting pair of objects, 233, 242
of rotating object, 246, 256, *256f*
central maximum, 523–524, *524f*, 528, *528f*
resolving power and, 533, *533f*
centrifugal force, 230
centripetal acceleration, 226–228, *227f*
centripetal force, 228–230, *228f*, *229f*, *230f*
CFCs (chlorofluorocarbons), 348
chain reaction, 792–793, *792f*
charge carriers, 598, *598f* (*see also* **electric charge; electric current**)
alternating current and, 607
batteries and, 606, 607, *607f*
drift velocity of, 598–599, *599f*
power and, 608
resistance and, 601, *601f*
charge-coupled devices (CCDs), 500

charged particles (*see also* **charge carriers; electric charge**): in atoms, 551, 552, *552f*
aurora borealis and, 676, 734–735, 751
magnetic fields and, 675–678, *676f*, *678f*
oscillating, 718
charging: by contact, 553
by induction, 554, *554f*
by polarization, 555, *555f*
chemical energy: in batteries, 588, 605, 606, *606f*, 607
in food, 164
chips, 636, 654
chlorofluorocarbons (CFCs), 348
chromatic aberrations, 500, 507, *507f*
circuit. See **electric circuit**
circuit breakers, 647, *647f*, 708
circuit diagrams, 630, *630f*, *631f*, 632 (*see also* **electric circuit**)
ac sources in, 709, *709f*
circular motion, *64f*, 65, *224f*, 226–231
axis of rotation in, 226, 227
centripetal acceleration in, 226–228, *227f*, 255, *255f*
centripetal force in, 228–230, *228f*, *229f*, *230f*, 232
of charge in magnetic field, 678, *678f*
equations for, R29–R30
inertia in, 230–231, *231f*
tangential acceleration in, 228
tangential speed in, 226, 227, 228, 229, 254
Clausius, Rudolph, 732
closed circuit, *631f*, 632
cochlear implants, 419
coefficient of volume expansion, 302
coefficients of friction, 138–139, *138f*, R40
coherence, 521
lasers and, 535–537, *535f*, *536f*
"cold fusion," R18
collisions, 206–214
conservation of momentum in, 199–201, *199f*
elastic, 210–214, *211f*, *214f*
equations for, R28–R29
forces in, 122, *122f*, 194–198, *197f*, *198f*, 203–204, *204f*
inelastic, 206–211, *214f*
perfectly inelastic, 206–211, *206f*, *207f*, *214f*
types of, *214f*
color force, 799
colors, 467–469, *467f*, *468f*, *469f* (*see also* **spectrum, visible**)

complementary, 468, *468f*, *469f*
diffraction gratings and, 528–530, *528f*
lens aberration and, 507, *507f*
primary, 467–469, *468f*, *469f*
of rainbows, 482–483, 506, *506f*, 722, *722f*
reflection and, 467, *467f*
in white-light interference patterns, 522, *522f*
commutators, 705, *705f*, 706, *706f*
compact discs (CDs), 518–519, 528, *528f*
compact fluorescent light (CFL), 633
compass, 666, 668, *668f*, 669, 672, *672f*
complementary colors, 468–469, *468f*, *469f*
components, of vectors, 90–93, *90f*, *92f*, 95, *95f*
compound microscopes, 499, *499f*
compression, 389, 406–407, *406f*, *407f*
compressors, 348
Compton, Arthur, 744
Compton shift, 744, *744f*
computerized axial tomography (CAT), 671
computers, 593, *593f*, 604, 636, *636f*
concave spherical mirrors, 453–460
focal length and focal point in, 455–456, *455f*
magnification by, 456, *456f*
mirror equation, 455–456, *455f*
ray diagrams for, 457, *457f*, *458f*
real images in, 453–454, *453f*, *454f*, 457
sign conventions for, 456, *456f*, *462f*
spherical aberration, 453, 454, 465, *465f*
virtual images in, 453, *453f*, 457, *458f*
conduction, thermal, 310, *310f*
conduction band, 763, *763f*
conductors, electrical. See **electrical conductors**
conductors, thermal, 310
cone cells, 468
conservation of angular momentum, 259, *259f*
conservation of electric charge, 551, *551f*
in nuclear decay, 782, *782f*
in series circuit, 637

conservation of energy, 311–312 (*see also* **conservation of mechanical energy**)
first law of thermodynamics and, 340–342, *340f*, *341f*, *342f*
in fluids, 288, *288f*
friction and, 172, 174, *174f*
theory of relativity and, 179
conservation of mass, 179, 283, *283f*
conservation of mechanical energy, 171–174, *171f*, *174f*, 369, *369f* (*see also* **conservation of energy**)
friction and, 171, 174, *174f*
machines and, 252, *252f*
conservation of momentum, 199–204, *199f*, *201f*, *204f*
constant acceleration, 49–56, *49f*, *50f*, *56f* (*see also* **free fall; free-fall acceleration**)
displacement and, 50–56, *56f*
velocity and, 49–56, *56f*, 58, *58f*
constant of universal gravitation, 233, 237, *237f*
constants, table of, R40–R41
constant velocity: net force and, 125–126, 129
position-time graph and, 43–44, *43f*, *44f*
velocity-time graph and, 48, *48f*, *50f*
constructive interference, 388, *388f*, 520, *520f*
beats and, 428–429, *428f*
diffraction gratings and, 529, *529f*
interference fringes and, 521–524, *521f*, *522f*, *523f*, *524f*
sand dunes and, 432
standing waves and, 391
contact forces, 121 (*see also* **collisions; elastic forces; friction; normal force**)
contact lenses, 498, *498f*
in laboratory safety, xxvi
continuity equation, 283, *283f*, 284
controlled experiments, 9
convection, 310
convection currents, 670
conventional current, 598, *598f*
converging lenses, 490–491, *490f*
chromatic aberration for, 507, *507f*
of compound microscopes, 499, *499f*
of eyeglasses, 498, *498f*
image characteristics of, 492–494, *493f*
magnification of, 495, *495f*
ray diagrams for, 491–492, *491f*

FUNDAMENTAL CONSTANTS

Symbol	Quantity	Established value	Value used for calculations in this book
c	speed of light in a vacuum	299 792 458 m/s	3.00×10^8 m/s
e^-	elementary charge	$1.602\ 176\ 487 \times 10^{-19}$ C	1.60×10^{-19} C
e^l	base of natural logarithms	2.718 2818 28	2.72
ε_0	(Greek *epsilon*) permittivity of a vacuum	$8.854\ 187\ 817 \times 10^{-12}$ C²/(N•m²)	8.85×10^{-12} C²/(N•m²)
G	constant of universal gravitation	$6.672\ 59 \times 10^{-11}$ N•m²/kg²	6.673×10^{-11} N•m²/kg²
g	free-fall acceleration at Earth's surface	9.806 65 m/s²	9.81 m/s²
h	Planck's constant	$6.626\ 068\ 96 \times 10^{-34}$ J•s	6.63×10^{-34} J•s
k_B	Boltzmann's constant (R/N_A)	$1.380\ 6504 \times 10^{-23}$ J/K	1.38×10^{-23} J/K
k_C	Coulomb constant	$8.987\ 551\ 787 \times 10^9$ N•m²/C²	8.99×10^9 N•m²/C²
R	molar (universal) gas constant	8.314 472 J/(mol•K)	8.31 J/(mol•K)
π	(Greek *pi*) ratio of the circumference to the diameter of a circle	3.141 592 654	calculator value

USEFUL ASTRONOMICAL DATA

Symbol	Quantity	Value used for calculations in this book
I_E	moment of inertia of Earth	8.03×10^{37} kg•m²
M_E	mass of Earth	5.97×10^{24} kg
R_E	radius of Earth	6.38×10^6 m

USEFUL ATOMIC DATA

Symbol	Quantity	Established value	Value used for calculations in this book
m_e	mass of electron	$9.109\ 382\ 15 \times 10^{-31}$ kg $5.485\ 799\ 0943 \times 10^{-4}$ u 0.510 998 910 MeV	9.109×10^{-31} kg 5.49×10^{-4} u 5.110×10^{-1} MeV
m_n	mass of neutron	$1.674\ 927\ 211 \times 10^{-27}$ kg 1.008 664 915 97 u 939.565 346 MeV	1.675×10^{-27} kg 1.008 665 u 9.396×10^2 MeV
m_p	mass of proton	$1.672\ 621\ 637 \times 10^{-27}$ kg 1.007 276 466 77 u 938.272 013 MeV	1.673×10^{-27} kg 1.007 276 u 9.383×10^2 MeV

OCR gateway

GCSE Separate Sciences

Authors

Graham Bone

Simon Broadley

Sue Hocking

Mark Matthews

Jim Newall

Angela Saunders

Nigel Saunders

Contents

How to use this book

Welcome to the continuation of your Gateway GCSE courses in **Biology, Chemistry, and Physics**. This book has been specially written by experienced teachers and examiners to match the 2011 specification.

On these two pages you can see the types of pages you will find in this book, and the features on them. Everything in the book is designed to provide you with the support you need to help you prepare for your examinations and achieve your best.

Module openers

Specification matching grid: This shows you how the pages in the module match to the exam specifications, so you can track your progress through the module as you learn.

Why study this module: Here you can read about the reasons why the science you're about to learn is relevant to your everyday life.

B5 The living body

Why study this module?

In this module you will find out about the changes in your body as you grow up and change from a child into an adult. You will find out about menstruation and fertility, and how the stages of human life, such as adolescence and how adolescence is controlled, as many young people want a independent they are. However more of us are living longer. 'Spare-part surgery' is increasingly possible, and you will learn about organ transplants and mechanical devices that can help boost or kidney function.

You will also learn about some of your body systems and life processes, such as your skeleton, digestive system, respiratory system, circulatory system, and excretory processes.

You should remember

1. You are made of cells organised into tissues, organs, and systems – such as the reproductive system, circulatory system, and respiratory system.
2. Your joints and antagonistic muscles enable you to move.
3. The male and female reproductive systems.
4. Puberty and the menstrual cycle.

Module summary

OCR specification match	
B5a	5.1 Skeletons
B5a	5.2 Muscles and joints
B5b	5.3 The circulatory system
B5b	5.4 The cardiac cycle
B5c	5.5 Heart, valves and plumbing
B5c	5.6 Blood donation and transfusions
B5c	5.7 Gaseous exchange
B5d	5.8 The human respiratory system
B5d	5.9 Diseases of the respiratory system
B5e	5.10 Digestion
B5f	5.11 Functioning kidney
B5f	5.12 How the kidney works
B5g	5.13 Growing up
B5g	5.14 Fertility and fetal screening
B5h	5.15 Growth
B5h	5.16 New parts for old
OCR Upgrade	

Opener image: Every module starts with a picture and information on a new or interesting piece of science that relates to what you're about to learn.

You should remember: This list is a summary of the things you've already learnt that will come up again in this module. Check through them in advance and see if there is anything that you need to recap on before you get started.

Main pages

Specification matching grid: This shows you how the pages in the module match to the exam specifications, so you can track your progress through the module as you learn.

Learning objectives: You can use these objectives to understand what you need to learn to prepare for your exams. Higher Tier only objectives appear in pink text.

Key words: These are the terms you need to understand for your exams. You can look for these words in the text in bold or check the glossary to see what they mean.

Questions: Use the questions on each spread to test yourself on what you've just read.

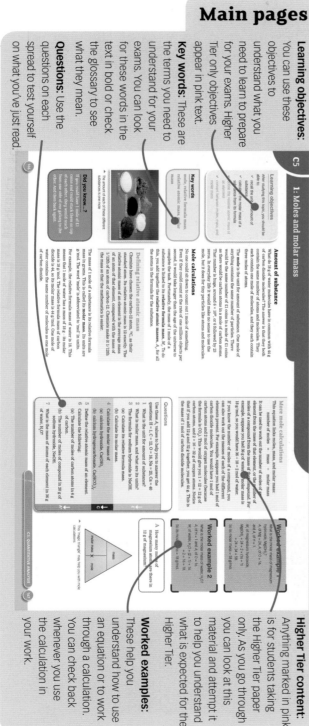

C5 1: Moles and molar mass

Learning objectives

After studying this topic, you should be able to:
✓ recall the unit for amount of substance
✓ calculate the molar mass of a substance from its formula
✓ convert between moles, mass, and molar mass

Key words
mole, relative atomic mass, relative formula mass

Amount of substance

What do 18 g of water molecules have in common with 44 g of carbon dioxide molecules? The answer is that they both contain the same number of molecules. They each contain one mole of molecules, and they each contain three moles of atoms.

The mole is the unit for the amount of substance. One mole of anything contains the same number of particles. There would be the same number of E1 coins in a mole of E1 coins as there would be carbon atoms in a mole of carbon atoms.

Mole calculations

No one could sit down to count out 1 mole of something. Even if they could count at the rate of one million objects per second, it would take longer than the age of the universe to complete the task. Fortunately, the mass of 1 mole of a substance is linked to its **relative formula mass**, M_r, for all the atoms in the formula for the substance.

Defining relative atomic mass

Chemists have chosen the carbon-12 atom, ^{12}C, as their standard atom. Its relative atomic mass is 12 exactly. The relative atomic mass of an element is the average mass of an atom of that element, compared with the mass of 1/12th of an atom of carbon-12. Chemists make it 1/12th the mass so that the mathematics is easier.

More mole calculations

This equation links moles, mass, and molar mass:

number of moles = mass / molar mass

It can be used to work out the number of moles of element from the mass of that element, or the number of moles of a compound from the mass of that compound. For example, suppose you had 36 g of water whose molar mass is 18 g/mol...

Questions

1. What is the unit for amount of substance?
2. What is molar mass, and what are its units?
3. The formula for sodium hydroxide is NaOH.
   (a) Calculate its molar mass.
   (b) Calculate its relative formula mass.
4. Calculate the molar mass of:
   (a) sodium hydroxide, NaOH,
   (b) calcium hydrogencarbonate, $Ca(HCO_3)_2$.
5. Define the relative atomic mass of an element.
6. Calculate the following:
   (a) The number of moles of carbon atoms in 6 g of carbon.
   (b) The number of atoms of each element in 36 g of water, H_2O.

Worked example 2

Higher Tier content: Anything marked in pink is for students taking the Higher Tier paper only. As you go through you can look at this material and attempt it to help you understand what is expected for the Higher Tier.

Worked examples: These help you understand how to use an equation or to work through a calculation. You can check back whenever you use the calculation in your work.

Summary and exam-style questions

Every summary question at the end of a spread includes an indication of how hard it is. You can track your own progress by seeing which of the questions you can answer easily, and which you have difficulty with.

When you reach the end of a module you can use the exam-style questions to test how well you know what you've just learnt. Each question has a grade band next to it, so you can see what you need to do for the grade you are aiming for.

↑ E — Grades G–E
↑ C — Grades D–C
↑ A* — Grades B–A*

Module summaries

Visual summary:
Another way to start revision is to use a visual summary, linking ideas together in groups so you can see how one topic relates to another. You can use this page as a start for your own summary.

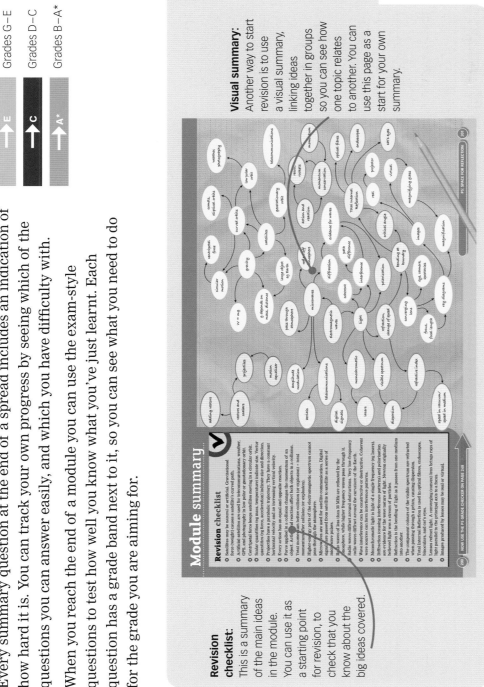

Revision checklist:
This is a summary of the main ideas in the module. You can use it as a starting point for revision, to check that you know about the big ideas covered.

OCR Upgrade

Exam-style questions:
Using these questions you can practice your exam skills, and make sure you're ready for the real thing. Each question has a grade band next to it, so you can understand what level you are working at and focus on where you need to improve to get your target grade.

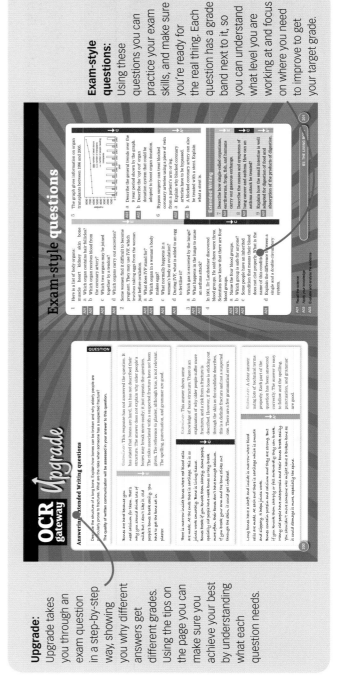

Upgrade:
Upgrade takes you through an exam question in a step-by-step way, showing you why different answers get different grades. Using the tips on the page you can make sure you achieve your best by understanding what each question needs.

Routes and assessment

Matching your course

The modules in this book have been written to match the specification so that you can take three separate GCSEs in science.

In the diagram below you can see that the modules can be used to progress from **GCSE Science B** and **GCSE Additional Science B** to **GCSE Biology B**, **GCSE Chemistry B**, and **GCSE Physics B** courses.

GCSE Biology	GCSE Chemistry	GCSE Physics
GCSE Science		
B1	C1	P1
B2	C2	P2
GCSE Additional Science		
B3	C3	P3
B4	C4	P4
B5	C5	P5
B6	C6	P6

GCSE Biology B, GCSE Chemistry B, and GCSE Physics B

The content in the modules of this book covers all the things you need to know to be able to progress from taking two GCSEs in Science and Additional Science to taking three separate GCSEs in each of Biology, Chemistry, and Physics.

Understanding exam questions

The list below explains some of the common words you will see used in exam questions.

Calculate

Work out a number. You can use your calculator to help you. You may need to use an equation. The question will say if your working must be shown. (Hint: don't confuse with 'Estimate' or 'Predict')

Compare

Write about the similarities and differences between two things.

Describe

Write a detailed answer that covers what happens, when it happens, and where it happens. Talk about facts and characteristics. (Hint: don't confuse with 'Explain')

Discuss

Write about the issues related to a topic. You may need to talk about the opposing sides of a debate, and you may need to show the difference between ideas, opinions, and facts.

Estimate

Suggest an approximate (rough) value, without performing a full calculation or an accurate measurement. Don't just guess – use your knowledge of science to suggest a realistic value. (Hint: don't confuse with 'Calculate' and 'Predict')

Explain

Write a detailed answer that covers how and why a thing happens. Talk about mechanisms and reasons. (Hint: don't confuse with 'Describe')

Evaluate

You will be given some facts, data or other information. Write about the data or facts and provide your own conclusion or opinion on them.

Justify

Give some evidence or write down an explanation to tell the examiner why you gave an answer.

Outline

Give only the key facts of the topic. You may need to set out the steps of a procedure or process – make sure you write down the steps in the correct order.

Predict

Look at some data and suggest a realistic value or outcome. You may use a calculation to help. Don't guess – look at trends in the data and use your knowledge of science. (Hint: don't confuse with 'Calculate' or 'Estimate')

Show

Write down the details, steps or calculations needed to prove an answer that you have been given.

Suggest

Think about what you've learnt and apply it to a new situation or a context. You may not know the answer. Use what you have learnt to suggest sensible answers to the question.

Write down

Give a short answer, without a supporting argument.

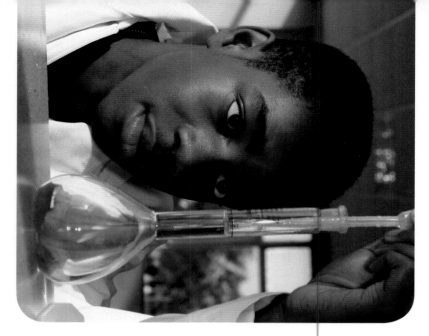

Understanding Controlled Assessment

What is Controlled Assessment?

As part of the assessment for your GCSE Biology B, Chemistry B, and Physics B courses you will undertake Controlled Assessment tasks. This section of the book includes information designed to help you understand what Controlled Assessment is, how to prepare for it, and how it will contribute towards your final mark.

Controlled Assessment has taken the place of coursework for the new 2011 GCSE Sciences specifications. The main difference between coursework and Controlled Assessment is that you will be supervised by your teacher when you carry out some of your Controlled Assessment task.

What will I have to do during my Controlled Assessment?

The Controlled Assessment task is designed to see how well you can:

- plan practical ways to answer scientific questions
- plan practical ways to test hypotheses
- think of appropriate ways to collect data
- assess and manage risks during practical work
- collect, analyse, and interpret your own data
- research, analyse, and interpret data collected by other people
- draw conclusions based on your evidence
- evaluate your method
- evaluate your data.

How do I prepare for my Controlled Assessment?

Throughout your course you will learn how to carry out investigations in a scientific way, and how to analyse and compare data properly. These skills will be covered in all the activities you work on during the course.

In addition, the scientific knowledge and understanding that you develop throughout the course will help you as you analyse information and draw your own conclusions.

How will my Controlled Assessment be structured?

Your Controlled Assessment is a task divided into three parts. You will be introduced to each part of the task by your teacher before you start.

What are the three parts of the Controlled Assessment?

Your Controlled Assessment task will be made up of three parts. These three parts make up an investigation, with each part looking at a different part of the scientific process.

	What skills will be covered in each part?
Part 1	Research and collecting secondary data
Part 2	Planning and collecting primary data
Part 3	Analysis and evaluation

Do I get marks for the way I write?

Yes. In two of the three parts of the Controlled Assessment you will see a pencil symbol (✏). This symbol is also found on your exam papers in questions where marks are given for the way you write.

These marks are awarded for quality of written communication. When your work is marked you will be assessed on:

* how easy your work is to read
* how accurate your spelling, punctuation, and grammar are
* how clear your meaning is
* whether you have presented information in a way that suits the task
* whether you have used a suitable structure and style of writing.

Part 1 – Research and collecting secondary data

At the beginning of your task your teacher will introduce Part 1. They will tell you:

* how much time you have – for Part 1 this should be about 2 hours, either in class or during your homework time
* what the task is about
* about the material you will use in Part 1 of the task
* the conditions you will work under
* your deadline.

The first part of your Controlled Assessment is all about research. You should use the stimulus material for Part 1 to learn about the topic of the task and then start your own research. Whatever you find during your research can be used during later parts of the Controlled Assessment.

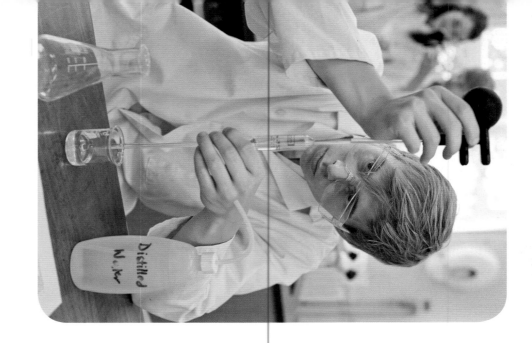

Sources, references, and plagiarism

For your research you can use a variety of sources including fieldwork, the Internet, resources from the library, audio, video, and others. Your teacher will be able to give you advice on whether a particular type of source is suitable or not.

For every piece of material you find during your research you must make sure you keep a record of where you found it, and who produced it originally. This is called referencing, and without it you might be accused of trying to pass other people's work off as your own. This is known as plagiarism.

Writing up your research

At the end of Part 1 of the Controlled Assessment you will need to write up your own individual explanation of the method you have used. This should include information on how you carried out your own research and collected your research data.

This write up will be collected in by your teacher and kept. You will get it back when it is time for you to take Part 3.

Part 2 – Planning and collecting primary data

Following Part 1 of your Controlled Assessment task your teacher will introduce Part 2. They will tell you:

- how much time you have – for Part 2 this should be about 1 hour for planning and 1 hour an experiment
- what the task is about
- about the material you will use in Part 2 of the task
- the conditions you will work under
- your deadline.

Part 2 of the Controlled Assessment is all about planning and carrying out an experiment. You will be given a hypothesis for the Controlled Assessment task. Once you have the hypothesis you will need to plan and carry out your experiment in order to test it.

Risk assessment

Part of your planning will need to include a risk assessment for your experiment. To get the maximum number of marks, you will need to make sure you have:

- evaluated all significant risks
- made reasoned judgements to come up with appropriate responses to reduce the risks you identified

- manage all of the risks during the task, making sure that you don't have any accidents and that there is no need for your teacher to come and help you.

Working in groups and writing up alone

You will be allowed to work in groups of no more than three people to develop your plan and carry out the experiment. Even though this work will be done in groups, you need to make sure you have your own individual records of your plan and results.

This write up will be collected in by your teacher and kept. You will get it back when it is time for you to take Part 3.

Part 3 – Analysis and evaluation

Following Part 2 of your Controlled Assessment task your teacher will introduce Part 3. They will tell you:

- how much time you have – for Part 3 this should be about 2 hours
- what the task is about
- about the answer booklet you will use in Part 3
- the conditions you will work under.

Part 3 of the Controlled Assessment is all about analysing and evaluating the work you carried out in Parts 1 and 2. Your teacher will give you access to the work you produced and handed in for Parts 1 and 2.

For Part 3 you will work under controlled conditions, in a similar way to an exam. It is important that for this part of the task you work alone, without any help from anyone else and without using anyone else's work from Parts 1 and 2.

The Part 3 answer booklet

For Part 3 you will do your work in an answer booklet provided for you. The questions provided for you to respond to in the answer booklet are designed to guide you through this final part of the Controlled Assessment. Using the questions you will need to:

- evaluate your data
- evaluate the methods you used to collect your data
- take any opportunities you have for using mathematical skills and producing useful graphs
- draw a conclusion
- justify your conclusion.

B5

The living body

Why study this module?

In this module you will find out about the changes in your body as you grow up and change from a child into an adult.

You will find out about menstruation and fertility, and how fertility can be controlled or assisted. You will learn about the stages of human life, such as adolescence. Today adolescence is extended, as many young people want a university education so are not ready to begin a fully independent life until they are in their mid twenties.

However, more of us are living longer. 'Spare-part surgery' is increasingly possible, and you will learn about organ transplants and mechanical devices that can help heart or kidney function.

You will also learn about some of your body systems and life processes, such as your skeleton, digestive system, respiratory system, circulatory system, and excretory processes.

You should remember

1 You are made of cells organised into tissues, organs, and systems – such as the reproductive system, circulatory system, and respiratory system.

2 Your joints and antagonistic muscles enable you to move.

3 The male and female reproductive systems.

4 Puberty and the menstrual cycle.

In 2009, UK Biobank was launched. This is a major UK medical research initiative around 500000 UK citizens aged 40–69 are taking part. They give blood, saliva, and urine samples that will be frozen and stored. Their DNA will be analysed. The participants also take tests to assess their mental faculties and answer questions about their lifestyle. As time passes, data about the participants' illnesses will be correlated with their genetic and biological data. Hopefully this information, along with the data from the Human Genome Project, will inform medical scientists about how our genes and lifestyle influence our health and life expectancy. This will help produce better treatments and medicines for people in the future. Within your lifetime, it will probably be standard medical practice for everyone to be able to have their genome sequenced.

The functions of skeletons

Skeletons provide

- support
- protection
- a framework for muscle attachment to allow movement.

A Name three functions of skeletons.

▶ The great white shark, *Carcharodon carcharias*. Its skeleton is made of cartilage.

Types of skeleton

Some animals do not have a hard skeleton

Many invertebrate animals do not have a skeleton. Those that live in water can become quite large because the water buoys them up. Earthworms are supported by the pressure of the fluid inside their body. The fluid presses outwards against their muscular body wall.

Insects have an external skeleton

Insects, along with spiders and crustaceans (lobsters, crabs, and prawns), have an external skeleton made of chitin. This gives a protective outer covering which supports the animal. It also gives a framework for muscle attachment. These animals all have jointed legs and their skeleton, muscles, and joints allow them to move. However, this hard covering can restrict growth. The animals have to shed their old skeleton at intervals and grow before the new skeleton hardens.

Some animals have an internal skeleton

Fish, amphibians, reptiles, birds, and mammals, including humans, have an internal skeleton. In some fish such as sharks, dogfish, rays, and skates, the skeleton is made solely of **cartilage** (gristle).

Your skeleton is made of **bone**, but there are places where there is still cartilage, such as:

- the tip of your nose
- your ear lobes
- at the ends of your long bones, such as limb bones and ribs.

Bone and cartilage are both living tissues. They have blood vessels and nerves and they can grow with the body. The internal skeleton forms a framework. Joints and muscles allow it to move. The many small bones of the spine give great flexibility.

More about bone

While you were growing in the womb, your skeleton was first made of cartilage, which is mainly protein. From about 6 weeks, minerals are deposited into the cartilage. These are mainly calcium phosphate. The cartilage becomes ossified – is turned into bone. Children have more cartilage at the ends of their bones than adults, because they are still growing. Forensic scientists can tell the age of a person from the skeleton, according to how much cartilage is still present. Both cartilage and bone can be infected by pathogens.

Paramedics have to be careful not to move a person who has a suspected bone fracture. Moving someone with a broken backbone could injure their spinal cord.

> **B** Why do children need to drink milk or eat cheese to make their bones strong?

The structure of a long bone

You can see from the diagram that the head of the long bone is covered with smooth cartilage. The outer part of the shaft is hardened bone. It can withstand compression. The shaft is fairly hollow. This makes the bone lighter than solid bones, but still strong. In the centre of the shaft are the bone marrow and blood vessels. Some fat is stored here, and new blood cells are made.

Bones can break

Bones are very strong, but if you knock them they can fracture (break). There are different types of fracture:

- Green stick – the bone is bent but not broken. Children with rickets are prone to this.
- Simple fracture – the bone is broken but the skin is intact.
- Compound fracture – also called an open fracture; the broken ends of the bone stick out through the skin.

Doctors use X-rays to look at the damage done to a broken bone before treating it.

Older people who have osteoporosis (soft bones) are more susceptible to fractures, which may happen in a fall.

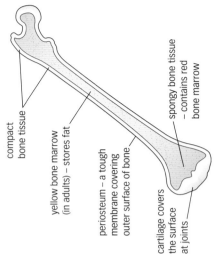

bone

cartilage growth areas

cartilage grows

most of cartilage ossified

epiphysis

diaphysis

epiphysis

epiphysis

▲ How a bone gets bigger

compact bone tissue

yellow bone marrow (in adults) – stores fat

periosteum – a tough membrane covering outer surface of bone

cartilage covers the surface at joints

spongy bone tissue – contains red bone marrow

▲ The structure of a long bone

Questions

→ E 1 List and describe three types of bone fracture.

→ C 2 Find out how long a broken limb has to be immobilised in plaster.

3 Explain how the embryo skeleton changes from being cartilage into bone.

→ A* 4 Why do you think there is a higher incidence of osteoporosis in Scandinavia?

The human arm

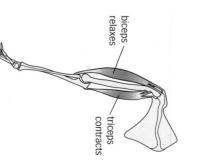

contraction of biceps raises forearm

effort

tendon

scapula

load

radius

ulna

fulcrum (pivot)

humerus

triceps contracts

biceps relaxes

biceps relaxes

triceps contracts

▶ The main bones and muscles of the human arm when bent and extended

When you bend your arm:

- Your biceps muscle contracts and your triceps muscle relaxes.

- As your biceps contracts, the **tendon** that joins it to the radius does not stretch.

- So it pulls the radius upwards and your arm bends.

When you straighten your arm:

- Your triceps muscle contracts and your biceps relaxes.

- The tendon from the triceps pulls on the ulna.

- Your arm straightens.

When a pair of muscles acts together in this way, one contracting and the other relaxing, we say they are antagonistic.

Levers

When the arm bends and straightens it acts as a lever:

- The elbow is the pivot point (fulcrum).

- The hand moves through a larger distance than the muscles.

- The muscles exert a larger force than the load that the hand lifts.

Joints

The contracting muscles provide the force to move your bones. However, you could not move if you did not have joints in your skeleton. Joints are where the end of one bone meets another bone. There are different types of joint.

Learning objectives

After studying this topic, you should be able to:

- understand how joints and muscles allow bones to move

- identify the main bones of the arm

- know that the biceps and triceps work antagonistically to bend or straighten the arm

Key words

tendon, synovial joint, ligament

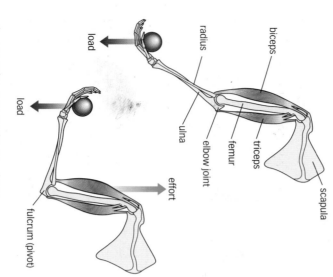

biceps

radius

ulna

triceps

femur

elbow joint

scapula

load

load

effort

fulcrum (pivot)

▶ How the arm works as a lever

A Explain how your arm muscles allow you to bend and straighten your arm.

B What are antagonistic muscles?

Fixed joints

Your skull is made of many bones and they join together by fixed joints. At birth, babies have a cartilage patch on top of their skull, so that the bones of the skull can be squeezed as the baby passes down the birth canal. When these joints in the skull are fused, the skull protects the brain well.

Synovial joints

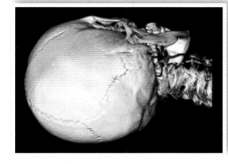

▲ Human skull showing the seams between the different bones

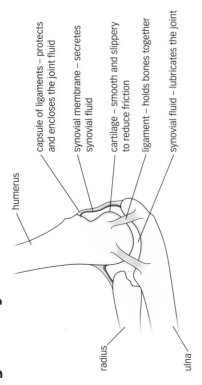

▲ A **synovial joint**

Joints that are freely movable are also called synovial joints. Synovial joints are well adapted to allow smooth, almost friction-free movement:

- The ends of the two articulating (moving) bones are covered in smooth, slippery cartilage.
- The whole joint is enclosed in a capsule.
- Lining the inside of the capsule is a synovial membrane.
- This membrane secretes (makes) synovial fluid.
- Synovial fluid lubricates the joint.

Ligaments join the two bones of a synovial joint together. They stretch and allow movement.

Examples of synovial joints are:

Hinge joints

At your elbow you have a hinge joint. It allows movement in one plane. This allows you to bend and straighten your arm and to also lift heavy weights. Your knee joint is also a hinge joint. You can bend and straighten your leg to walk, but it can also lock into place to bear your weight.

Ball and socket joints

Shoulder and hip joints are ball and socket joints. At these joints you can rotate the limb bones.

Labels on synovial joint diagram:
- humerus
- capsule of ligaments – protects and encloses the joint fluid
- synovial membrane – secretes synovial fluid
- cartilage – smooth and slippery to reduce friction
- ligament – holds bones together
- synovial fluid – lubricates the joint
- radius
- ulna

Questions

1 Where do you have fixed joints? → E

2 Name two places in your body where you have hinge joints.

3 Name two places in your body where you have ball and socket joints.

4 Explain why tendons are not stretchy. → C

5 What are synovial joints?

6 Describe the functions of the following structures in a joint: (a) synovial membrane (b) synovial fluid (c) cartilage (d) ligaments.

7 When you lift a heavy book, your biceps muscle exerts more force than the weight of the book. However, it enables you to lift the book through a large distance. Explain how it does this. → A*

Single-celled organisms

Small organisms such as amoebae do not need a circulatory system. They have a large surface area compared with their volume. They are surrounded by the water they live in. Dissolved oxygen diffuses from this water into the cell through the cell membrane. Waste material can diffuse out of the cell. There is no need for a special transport system.

Larger animals need a circulatory system because diffusion alone cannot efficiently transport substances to and from their cells. They need blood to do this.

Open systems: insects

Insects have an open circulatory system. They do not have arteries or veins, but their blood flows freely through their body cavity.

The blood makes direct contact with the organs and tissues. Blood travels in the aorta from the heart up to the head. It bathes the organs and muscles of the head and then trickles back through the body cavity. It passes over the gut and gets back into the heart through small holes.

Insect blood does not carry oxygen, because the insect's breathing tubes deliver oxygen directly to the tissues. Their watery, greenish yellow blood carries amino acids, sugars, and ions. There are some white cells to ingest pathogens.

Closed systems: vertebrates

Vertebrates have a closed circulatory system. The blood is contained in **blood vessels** – arteries, veins, and capillaries.

Fish

The blood circulates once around the body, from the **heart** to

- the gills, where it collects oxygen and unloads carbon dioxide
- the body organs and tissues.

The fish heart is a single pump consisting of two chambers.

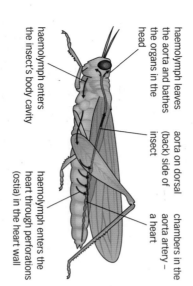

haemolymph leaves the aorta and bathes the organs in the head

aorta on dorsal (back) side of insect

chambers in the aorta artery – a heart

haemolymph enters the insect's body cavity

haemolymph enters the heart through perforations (ostia) in the heart wall

▶ An insect's circulatory system. It is an open system because the blood is not always in vessels.

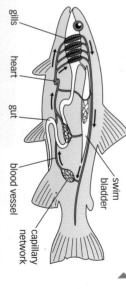

gills

heart

gut

swim bladder

blood vessel

capillary network

▲ The circulatory system in a fish. Because the blood passes through the heart only once on each circuit around the body, the heart needs only two chambers.

A Explain why single-celled organisms do not need a circulatory system.

B Why is an insect circulatory system described as an open system?

Humans

Humans and other mammals have a double circulatory system. There are two circuits from the heart.

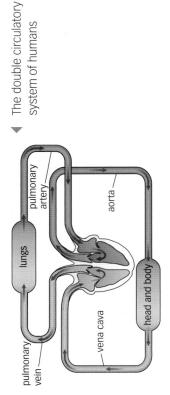

▲ The double circulatory system of humans

Blood passes

- from the heart to the body organs and tissues
- back to the heart
- to the lungs to remove carbon dioxide and collect oxygen
- back to the heart before being pumped out to the body again.

Because the blood makes two circuits from the heart; the heart needs four chambers. It is a double pump. Blood in a double circulatory system is under high pressure and so it transports materials more quickly around the body.

Galen and Harvey

In the second century AD, Galen, a Roman physician (doctor) of Greek origin, dissected monkeys and pigs. He noticed that blood in veins was darker than blood in arteries. He mistakenly thought that the liver made blood and pumped it in the veins to the organs, which consumed it. Galen's ideas influenced medicine for well over 1000 years. In the sixteenth century, Leonardo da Vinci studied anatomy and made drawings showing how blood passed through the heart chambers, and how the heart valves worked.

In the seventeenth century, William Harvey, a doctor at St Bartholomew's hospital in London, published a book showing how blood circulates in the body, from the heart and back again, and to and from the lungs. He realised that the pulse in arteries was linked to the contraction of the left ventricle of the heart. He discovered that veins have valves to prevent backflow. He postulated that there were capillaries, but did not see them as he did not have a microscope.

Exam tip OCR

✔ Remember the difference between a closed circulatory system, where the blood is always in vessels, and an open system, where the blood flows through the body cavity.

Questions

1 Fish and humans both have a closed circulatory system. What is a closed circulatory system? → E

2 Why do you think insects do not have red blood cells or haemoglobin in their blood? → C

3 Explain why fish need only a two-chambered heart.

4 Why do humans and other mammals need a four-chambered heart?

5 Find out more about the contribution William Harvey made to our understanding of the circulatory system. → A*

The human heart

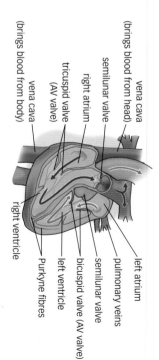

Section through a human heart showing the path of oxygenated and deoxygenated blood

vena cava
(brings blood from head)
semilunar valve
right atrium
tricuspid valve
(AV valve)
vena cava
(brings blood from body)

right ventricle

left atrium
pulmonary veins
semilunar valve
bicuspid valve (AV valve)
left ventricle
Purkyne fibres

Heart muscles contract to cause the blood to move. It contracts rhythmically to squeeze blood out of the **atria**, into the **ventricles** and then out into the arteries and around the body. The powerful heart muscle needs a continuous supply of glucose, fatty acids, and oxygen so that the muscle cells can respire aerobically and release energy for contraction. The strong contractions of the heart mean that blood leaving the heart in the arteries is at high pressure. As it passes along the circulatory system through increasingly branching arterioles to the capillaries, the blood pressure falls. In the wide tubes of the veins the blood pressure is very low; valves are needed to keep the blood flowing in one direction.

The left ventricle wall is thick muscle that produces enough pressure to push blood in the arteries all over the body. The right ventricle wall is thinner and the muscle is less powerful – it only has to send blood as far as the lungs. The lungs are delicate and too much pressure in the blood entering them could damage them.

The rate at which the heart contracts is controlled by a group of cells called the pacemakers. These produce a small electrical current that stimulates the cardiac muscle to contract.

The pulse: a measure of heart rate

As the ventricles contract and send blood into the arteries, the thick, muscular, and elastic walls of the arteries expand and recoil as a spurt of blood enters. This is the **pulse** that is transmitted all along the length of the arteries in the body. You can detect it where an artery passes over a bone or is near to your skin. Pulse rate is a measure of heart rate.

The cardiac cycle (heartbeat)

The series of events during one contraction is the cardiac cycle.

- The sinoatrial node (**SAN**) produces electrical impulses.
- These spread quickly across the two atria, which contract.
- This forces open the atrioventricular (AV) valves and pushes blood into the ventricles.
- A patch of muscle fibres called the atrioventricular node (**AVN**) conducts the impulses to special conducting muscle fibres, called Purkyne fibres, which carry the impulses to the tip of the ventricles.
- The two ventricles contract. This closes the AV valves and pushes blood out of the ventricles, through the open semilunar valves, into the arteries.
- The atria relax and fill with blood.

Then the cycle starts again. Each cycle is one heartbeat.

Changing the heart rate

When you exercise, your skeletal muscles respire more oxygen and glucose and make more carbon dioxide, which enters the blood. Part of the brain detects the extra carbon dioxide in the blood. It sends impulses to the heart's pacemaker to speed up the heart rate.

You also make more adrenaline when you exercise, and when you are frightened or excited. Adrenaline travels in your blood and affects many target tissues, including the heart's pacemaker, which speeds up the heart rate.

An increased heart rate also delivers more oxygen and glucose to the heart muscle itself, via the coronary arteries. The heart muscle needs to respire more if it is beating more times each minute.

Monitoring the heart

Doctors and cardiac technicians can measure the electrical activity in your heart. They get a trace called an **ECG** (electrocardiogram) and this tells them whether your heart is normal or not. A patient with an irregular heart rate or one that is too fast or too slow may need an artificial pacemaker fitted.

An echocardiogram uses ultrasound to make a scan and show any heart defects.

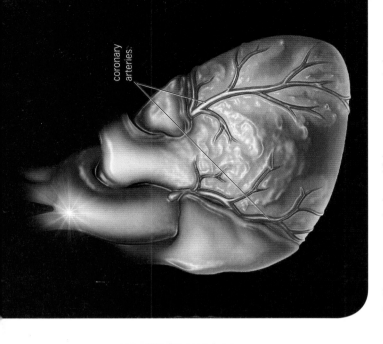

coronary arteries

▲ The coronary arteries, which carry oxygenated blood from the aorta to the heart muscle

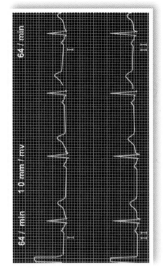

▲ A normal heartbeat shown on an ECG trace

Questions

1 Explain how heart muscle causes blood to move. **E**

2 Explain why your heart rate needs to increase when you exercise. **C**

3 Find out why some people need an artificial pacemaker.

4 A person exercising has a pulse rate of 120 beats per minute. How long does each cardiac cycle last? **A***

There are many heart diseases and conditions, including:

Artificial pacemakers

Some people have an irregular heartbeat. They can have an artificial pacemaker. This is usually implanted just under the skin in the chest. A wire passes from it into a vein and into the right atrium.

The pacemaker has a long-life battery. It sends impulses to the heart muscle, to make it contract at the correct rhythm. A pacemaker can detect when the person is more active, and sends impulses to the heart at an increased rate.

Some people have a damaged AVN. Its impulses do not travel to the ventricles. In this case the artificial pacemaker wire goes to the ventricle and makes it contract.

Pacemakers have to be replaced about every ten years.

Hole in the heart

Some people have a 'hole in the heart'. Blood can flow directly from one side of the heart to the other. There is less oxygen in the blood, causing fatigue and breathlessness. The hole may be repaired with surgery.

Why a hole in the heart means less oxygen

Fetuses have a small hole between the left and right atria. They obtain oxygen from the placenta. Oxygenated blood enters the right side of the heart and flows through the hole to the left atrium, and then to the head and body. There is a connecting vessel between the pulmonary artery and the aorta, so most blood bypasses the lungs.

At birth, the baby needs to oxygenate its blood via the lungs rather than the placenta. The hole closes and the blood follows the normal circulation. In some babies, the hole does not close, allowing oxygenated blood to flow from the left to the right atrium. This means that a smaller amount of oxygenated blood leaves the left ventricle, and the body tissues receive less oxygen. Patients suffer fatigue and breathlessness. The right side of the heart has to work harder to cope with the increased flow of blood through it. A hole in the heart can be repaired with surgery.

Damaged heart valves

As people age, their heart valves may become stiff. Valves may also be damaged, such as by bacterial infection (endocarditis). If the valves in the heart do not close properly, blood will flow backwards. This leads to heart failure, and not enough oxygenated blood can reach body tissues.

▶ An artificial heart valve. The wires are used to secure the valve in place in the patient's heart. Heart-assist devices may be used after surgery to take the strain off the heart.

Surgeons can replace faulty heart valves with artificial valves or valves from pigs or cows. Because the heart valves have no capillaries supplying them, there is no **rejection** of these transplanted valves.

Blocked coronary arteries

As you get older, and especially if you eat too much saturated fat and smoke tobacco, fatty deposits or plaques build up in your artery walls. These can become quite large and obstruct the flow of blood. If this happens in your coronary arteries, your heart muscle does not get enough oxygenated blood. Heart muscle cells cannot respire anaerobically, and without enough oxygen they cannot release enough energy to contract efficiently. You may develop angina, or have a heart attack.

Surgeons can correct this condition with **bypass surgery**. A piece of blood vessel, usually a vein, is taken from the patient's arm or leg and transplanted to bypass the blockage (or blockages) in the coronary artery.

When people have had a heart attack, surgeons can quickly insert a stent, a tube to open up the blocked coronary arteries. If this is done soon enough, the damage to the heart from the heart attack is slight.

Heart transplants

Since the first heart transplant in 1967, many of these operations have been carried out in the UK each year.

A heart transplant is a **traumatic** operation and the recipient must take drugs to suppress the immune system and prevent rejection. There is a shortage of donor hearts. Heart valve replacement and artificial pacemakers are less traumatic with no risk of rejection, but pacemakers have to be replaced. All operations carry the risk of infection.

Donor cards

Some people carry donor cards so that doctors can take their organs when they die, without expecting bereaved relatives to make a painful decision. Because there is a shortage of donors, another system could be used. Everyone would be a potential donor unless they carried a card to opt out. Some people would opt out for religious reasons; Jehovah's Witnesses regard blood as sacred.

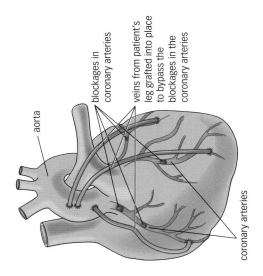

aorta

blockages in coronary arteries

veins from patient's leg grafted into place to bypass the blockages in the coronary arteries

coronary arteries

▲ How blocked coronary arteries are bypassed. The resulting ease of blood flow relieves angina and reduces the risk of a heart attack.

Key words

rejection, bypass surgery, traumatic

Questions

1 List four diseases or conditions of the heart. → E

2 What causes a heart attack?

3 Why are there no problems with rejection of transplanted heart valves? → C

4 Discuss the pros and cons of the opt-out rather than opt-in system for organ donation.

5 Discuss the relative advantages and disadvantages of heart transplant surgery compared with valve replacement or having an artificial pacemaker fitted. → A*

Learning objectives

After studying this topic, you should be able to:

* describe the reasons for and process of blood donation and transfusion

* explain the basis of the ABO blood grouping system

* describe the process of blood clotting

Key words

platelets, fibrin, agglutinins

Did you know...?

This is how the blood clots:

* The **platelets** in blood are exposed to air.

* This causes a series of chemical reactions.

* Eventually a soluble protein in your plasma changes to insoluble **fibrin**.

* Fibrin fibres form a clot.

▶ Donated blood is stored in plastic bags. A chemical to prevent clotting is added. The bags are carefully labelled and refrigerated.

Blood transfusions

* In 1818 Dr James Blundell performed the first successful transplant of human blood to a patient with a haemorrhage (bleeding).

* In 1840 a haemophiliac was treated by a blood transfusion at St George's Hospital, London. In haemophilia the blood does not clot, so sufferers who cut themselves keep on bleeding.

* In 1901 an Austrian doctor discovered human blood groups and transfusions became safer. In the next ten years, scientists found that if they added anticoagulant and refrigerated the blood, it would keep for some days.

* Blood banks were established during the First World War.

* In 1950 plastic bags replaced breakable glass bottles for storing the blood.

* People may voluntarily give blood three times a year. This keeps the blood banks full to supply hospitals. Blood is warmed before being transfused into a patient.

In a transfusion, blood groups are now carefully matched between the donor and recipient. There are four main blood groups called A, B, AB, and O. These are further subdivided into groups called Rhesus positive and negative.

Why are anticoagulants needed?

If you cut yourself, your blood should clot to heal the wound. This prevents bacteria from entering and stops blood loss.

Blood kept in a bag would clot in this way. Chemicals are added to block the chemical reactions and prevent clotting (coagulation).

We need vitamin K to help blood clot. Bacteria in our gut make vitamin K, but we can also get it from green vegetables and cranberries.

Abnormal clotting

People with haemophilia have blood that clots very slowly. People with fatty deposits in their arteries may develop clots in the arteries. These could cause heart attacks or strokes. Smoking tobacco and drinking alcohol increase the risk of blood clots forming. Warfarin, aspirin, and heparin reduce the ability of the blood to clot and can be used to reduce the risk of strokes in some people.

Who needs a transfusion?

Some examples are:

- people who have lost a lot of blood through injury or during surgery
- haemophiliacs
- some cancer patients.

A Why is it useful for your blood to clot when you cut yourself?

B Why are blood clots in blood vessels dangerous?

Why are some blood transfusions unsuccessful?

If the donor and recipient bloods are not matched properly, agglutination or clumping happens. The blood cannot circulate and the recipient dies.

Your red blood cells have proteins called **agglutinins** (a type of antigen) on their membranes. There are different shaped agglutinins. Your blood plasma has antibodies against the agglutinins. You don't have antibodies in your plasma that can react with the antigens on your own red blood cells.

When transfusing blood, doctors have to think about the antibodies clumping the red cells together. They need to consider how the antibodies of the recipient will react to the donor's red blood cells.

Blood group	Agglutinins (antigens) on surface of red blood cells	Antibodies in plasma
A	type A	anti B
B	type B	anti A
AB	type A and type B	none
O	none	anti A and anti B

Matching donors and recipients

- People of group O can donate blood to anyone as their red blood cells do not have any antigens, so the recipient's antibodies have nothing to react with.
- People of group AB can receive any type of blood as they do not have any antibodies in their plasma to react to donors' antigens.
- People of group A cannot receive group B blood because their anti B antibodies would coagulate it.
- People of group B cannot receive group A blood because their anti A antibodies would coagulate it.

People are also classified according to the rhesus factor. Your blood is rhesus positive if your plasma has a D protein, and rhesus negative if it does not. Rhesus-negative people cannot receive rhesus-positive blood as they would make antibodies against the D protein.

Questions

1	Who might need a blood transfusion?	→ E
2	How can the risk of blood clots be reduced?	→ C
3	Describe how blood clots when you cut yourself.	
4	Why do you think people of blood group O are called universal donors?	
5	Why do you think people of blood group AB are called universal recipients?	→ A*
6	Explain why people of blood group A cannot receive blood from donors of blood group B.	

Aerobic respiration

The first life forms on Earth, three and a half billion years ago, were ancient types of bacteria. These obtained energy from chemical reactions. Some used anaerobic respiration. There was no free oxygen in the Earth's atmosphere at that time. Then some bacteria developed the ability to photosynthesise. This released free oxygen into the atmosphere. Oxygen killed many of the anaerobic bacteria around at the time, but some survived. Some coped with oxygen, and most of the life forms that have since evolved use aerobic respiration. Some organisms can use both anaerobic and aerobic respiration, depending upon the conditions. You probably know that your muscle cells can respire anaerobically for a while.

Gaseous exchange

If an organism respires aerobically, it has to get oxygen to its cells (and then to the mitochondria in its cells). The waste carbon dioxide from aerobic respiration has to be removed from the organism as it is toxic; it would lower the pH and disrupt enzyme activity. The exchange of these two gases, into and out of the organism, is called gaseous exchange.

Single-celled organisms

Simple one-celled organisms such as aerobic bacteria and amoebae have a large surface area compared with their volume. There is enough cell surface membrane to allow sufficient oxygen to diffuse into the cell. The carbon dioxide produced can all diffuse out.

Earthworms

Earthworms have many cells, but they are long and thin. They have a large surface area compared to their volume. Oxygen diffuses through their thin, **permeable** skin and into their blood vessels. The blood carries oxygen from the skin to respiring cells. It also carries carbon dioxide from respiring cells to the skin. Earthworms, like all organisms, contain a lot of water. They do not have waterproof skin, as humans do, so they secrete mucus to stop themselves drying out. They also live in damp places.

Amphibians

Most of the gaseous exchange in a frog happens across its skin. Frogs also have simple lungs, and can obtain oxygen from the floor of their mouth.

▶ The leopard frog Rana pipiens lives in grasslands and woodlands throughout North America. It eats insects and sometimes small fish. It returns to water to breed.

Learning objectives

After studying this topic, you should be able to:

❧ know that many living things respire using oxygen

❧ understand that organisms need gaseous exchange surfaces

Key words

permeable

A Why did the first living organisms on Earth, early bacteria, respire anaerobically?

B How did photosynthesising bacteria alter the Earth's atmosphere?

Water loss

Because their skin is permeable to gases, frogs are susceptible to excessive water loss. To avoid drying out they need to live in damp places. Some survive in drier habitats by having a layer of slime over the skin.

Fish

Fish also have gills for gaseous exchange. Remember that fish have a single circulatory system.

- The blood flows from the heart to the gills.
- The gills have filaments which give a very large surface area.
- Each filament is well supplied with blood.
- As the fish swims, it gulps water into its mouth.
- Then with the mouth closed, it raises the floor of its mouth and forces the water out over the gills.
- Oxygen dissolved in the water diffuses into the fish's blood at the gills.
- Carbon dioxide diffuses from the blood in the gills into the water.
- The oxygenated blood then flows to the fish's body organs.

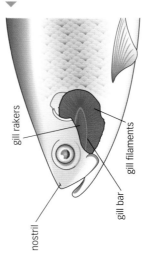

nostril

gill rakers

gill bar

gill filaments

▼ The position of the gills in a fish. The gill flap is cut away. The gill bar supports the filaments.

Did you know…?

Some fish breathe air. They are lung fish. They can survive for long periods in moist mud, if their watery habitat dries up. Some have fins that resemble paddle-like legs and they can 'walk' to a new habitat. Some can even climb trees. There were many lung fish around 350 million years ago, and they were probably the ancestors of land-dwelling vertebrates.

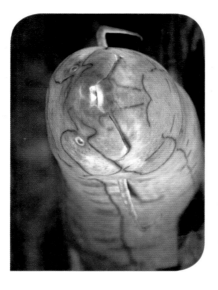

▲ The South American lung fish. It has a pair of lungs, one on either side of its throat.

Exam tip · OCR

- Do not confuse gaseous exchange with breathing. Breathing is the ventilation movement that brings air to the gaseous exchange surface. Fish are ventilating when they open their mouths, gulp water, then close their mouths and open the gill flaps to force water over the gills. Gaseous exchange is the diffusion of oxygen and carbon dioxide into and out of the blood at the gills or lungs.
- Do not confuse either breathing or gaseous exchange with respiration. Respiration happens in the cells.

Questions

1. Explain why all living organisms that respire aerobically need to have gaseous exchange. **E**

2. Explain why larger complex organisms need a special surface for gaseous exchange.

3. Make a table to compare gaseous exchange in: (a) an earthworm (b) an amoeba (c) a frog (d) a fish. **C**

4. Describe how fish force water over their gills.

5. Explain why frogs are at risk of drying out. **A***

The main parts of the human respiratory system

Learning objectives

After studying this topic, you should be able to:

- identify the main parts of the human respiratory system
- explain the terms breathing, inspiration, expiration, and respiration
- describe ventilation and gaseous exchange
- explain how the alveoli are adapted for efficient gaseous exchange

Did you know...?

If you could get all your alveoli and open them out and lay them flat side by side, they would cover an area about half the size of a football pitch. They tuck away neatly in your lungs inside your chest.

Exam tip OCR

- The human respiratory system is the system that enables you to breathe. Remember that **respiration** is what happens inside cells – the release of energy from glucose.

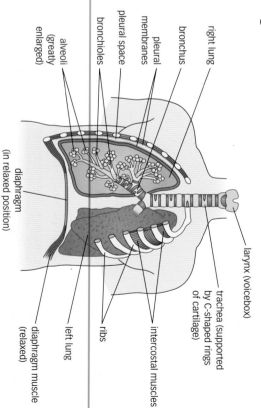

▶ This diagram shows a surface view of the left lung, and a section through the right lung showing the airways and air sacs inside. Pleural membranes cover the lung and the inside of the rib cage. The pleural space between them contains pleural fluid, which allows easy slippage of the moving lungs during breathing, and also helps prevent the lungs from collapsing.

larynx (voicebox)

trachea (supported by C-shaped rings of cartilage)

right lung

bronchus

pleural membranes

pleural space

bronchioles

alveoli (greatly enlarged)

diaphragm (in relaxed position)

intercostal muscles

ribs

left lung

diaphragm muscle (relaxed)

Breathing (ventilation)

Your lungs are your gaseous exchange surface. The many millions of air sacs (alveoli) in the lungs give a large surface area for oxygen to diffuse into your blood and for carbon dioxide to leave your blood and be breathed out. **Breathing**, or **ventilation**, is how you get the air in and out of your lungs.

Inspiration (breathing in)	Expiration (breathing out)
• Your intercostal muscles contract and raise your rib cage up and out.	• Your intercostal muscles relax and your rib cage lowers.
• Your diaphragm flattens.	• Your diaphragm domes upwards.
• These two things increase the volume inside your chest and lungs.	• These two things reduce the volume in your chest.
• The air pressure in your lungs is lower than outside.	• The air pressure in your lungs is greater than outside. Your elastic alveoli also recoil (snap back) to normal size.
• So air enters the lungs from outside. It passes along the trachea, bronchi, and bronchioles to the alveoli.	• So air is pushed out from your lungs to outside. However, some air stays – this is **residual air**. If it didn't stay, your alveoli would close up.

Using a spirometer

Doctors may measure a patient's lung function, using a spirometer. The patient breathes while attached to a machine. It can measure

- **tidal volume** – the volume of air you breathe in, in one breath
- **vital capacity** – the maximum volume of air you can breathe in, plus your tidal volume, plus the maximum volume of air you can breathe out after taking a big breath in
- **lung capacity** – your vital capacity plus your residual air.

The alveoli

The alveoli form your gaseous exchange surface. They link your blood to the air. At the alveoli:

- Oxygen diffuses from the alveoli into the bloodstream.
- Carbon dioxide that has entered your blood at your body tissues diffuses from your blood into the alveoli, to be breathed out.

Like all of your organs and tissues, the alveoli and the lungs are moist. Your cells are about 70% water, as all the chemical reactions inside them take place in solution. Oxygen actually diffuses quicker when not in solution, but your lungs are moist. Fortunately, oxygen will dissolve in the very thin film of moisture and will still diffuse in solution.

The alveoli are surrounded by blood capillaries. The walls of your alveoli are just one single layer of cells. The walls of your capillaries are also just one single layer of cells. So the oxygen and carbon dioxide do not have far to diffuse. Alveoli are adapted for efficient gaseous exchange because they

- are permeable
- have thin walls
- have a large surface area
- have a good blood supply.

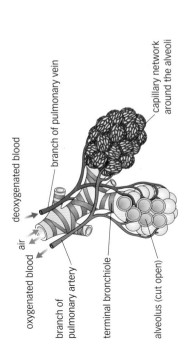

oxygenated blood
air
deoxygenated blood
branch of pulmonary artery
branch of pulmonary vein
terminal bronchiole
capillary network around the alveoli
alveolus (cut open)

▲ How the alveoli and capillaries in the lungs aid gaseous exchange

A Describe inspiration (how you breathe in).

B Describe expiration (how you breathe out).

Questions

→ E

1 Where does gaseous exchange happen in humans?

→ C

2 When you breathe out, the exhaled air contains much more carbon dioxide than inhaled air. Explain where the extra carbon dioxide has come from and how it got to the lungs.

3 Explain how your gaseous exchange surface is well adapted for efficient gaseous exchange.

4 Look at the diagram below. It is a spirometer trace on graph paper. For the person whose trace this is, find:
(a) their tidal volume
(b) their vital capacity.

→ A*

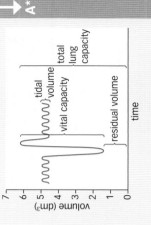

tidal volume
vital capacity
total lung capacity
residual volume
volume (dm³)
time

▲ A spirometer trace for a 15-year-old boy

5 Explain why your vital capacity is not the same as your lung capacity.

Learning objectives

After studying this topic, you should be able to:

- know about diseases of the respiratory system, including pneumonia, asthma, and lung cancer, and their causes
- explain what happens during an asthma attack

Key words

macrophage, constrict

Did you know...?

People often say that cancerous cells divide very quickly. This is not true. They do not divide any quicker than normal dividing cells; they just do not 'know' when to stop dividing. This is because something, such as the tar in tobacco smoke, has caused a mutation to the genes that control cell division. Lung cancer is slow growing. It takes up to 30 years for a lung cancer tumour to become large enough to detect. Smokers may think they are fine after 20 years of smoking, but the tumour may be growing slowly and not yet causing symptoms.

A How is the respiratory system protected from infection?

B Explain why damaged cilia can make you more prone to lung infection.

How the respiratory system protects itself

You have hairs in your nose which can trap large particles of dirt in the air you breathe in. However, small particles and pathogens may get past these hairs.

There is a layer of cells lining the trachea and bronchi. Some of these cells have cilia and some secrete mucus.

- The mucus traps small particles and pathogens such as bacteria, viruses, and fungal spores.
- The cilia beat and waft the mucus up to the back of the throat.
- Once there it can be swallowed, and the stomach acid kills the trapped pathogens. Or it can be removed by coughing or blowing your nose.

You also have special white blood cells, called **macrophages**, that squeeze out of capillaries and patrol the lung tissues. They ingest foreign particles and some pathogens.

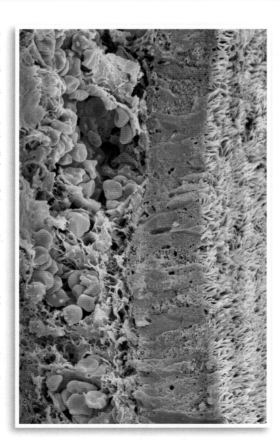

▶ Section through the lining of the trachea, seen with a scanning electron microscope (×600). False colour has been added.

What happens if this sweeping system is not working?

The airways end in the lungs and go no further – they are a dead end. Any pathogens entering the lungs will cause infection unless they are trapped and wafted back up the airways, out of the lungs. If the cilia are not working properly, small particles and pathogens remain in the lungs and can cause disease.

Some respiratory diseases

Disease	Cause	Symptoms
Bronchitis	Virus or bacteria, can also be triggered by breathing in smoke	Cough (often bringing up a yellow-grey mucus), sore throat, wheezing, blocked nose.
Asbestosis	Asbestos fibres trapped in the alveoli. This is an occupational disease. Some people have been exposed to the fibres during their work.	Inflammation and scarring of the alveoli, leading to difficulty breathing and reduced gaseous exchange. May lead to cancer.
Cystic fibrosis	Genetic and inherited	Cells lining the airways are affected. Thick mucus is secreted. Cilia are not hydrated enough and cannot waft. Mucus with trapped pathogens builds up, and this leads to chest infections and reduces gaseous exchange. Lungs eventually become damaged.
Lung cancer	Most commonly tar in tobacco smoke	Cells lining the bronchioles keep on dividing, forming a tumour. This reduces the surface area for gaseous exchange, and causes chest pain and a prolonged cough, with blood.
Asthma	Inhaling pollen or other allergens, infection, cold air, hard exercise, or stress	Difficulty breathing, wheezing, tight chest. Can be treated with bronchodilator drugs taken via an inhaler. Lining of the airways becomes inflamed, causing a build up of fluid. The muscles in the bronchi contract. This makes the bronchi constrict (become narrower), restricting the airways.

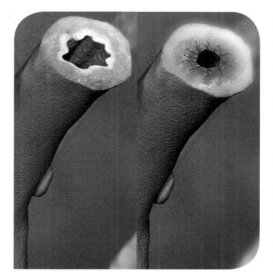

▶ Lung cancer. Coloured scanning electron micrograph of a small cancerous tumour filling an alveolus of the lung (×400). Some of the cancer cells have separated from the main tumour. If they enter the blood, they may be carried to other tissues and set up secondary tumours.

▶ A section through a normal bronchus (top) and an inflamed, **constricted** bronchus during an asthmatic attack (bottom)

Questions

1 Describe what happens during an asthma attack. **E →**

2 Describe how lung cancer may develop. **C →**

3 Explain how some people developed asbestosis after working for a long time where they were exposed to asbestos fibres.

Learning objectives

After studying this topic, you should be able to:

- explain why food has to be digested
- explain the role of enzymes in chemical digestion
- describe the functions of the parts of the human digestive system
- explain how digested food molecules are absorbed into the blood

▶ The human digestive system and its functions

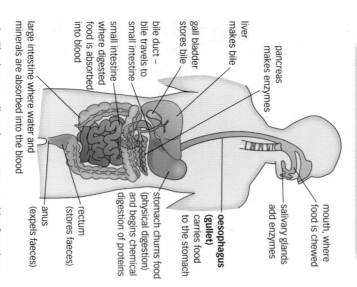

liver
makes bile

gall bladder
stores bile

bile duct –
bile travels to
small intestine

small intestine
where digested
food is absorbed
into blood

large intestine where water and
minerals are absorbed into the blood

pancreas
makes enzymes

mouth, where
food is chewed

salivary glands
add enzymes

**oesophagus
(gullet)**
carries food
to the stomach

stomach churns food
(physical digestion)
and begins chemical
digestion of proteins

rectum
(stores faeces)

anus
(expels faeces)

What happens to the food you eat?

While food is in your gut, it is still really outside your body. The large molecules in the food have to be broken down (digested) into smaller molecules so that they can pass across your gut wall and into your blood or lymph. Then your circulatory system takes the digested food to your cells and tissues. Here, you use the food for energy or growth and repair.

Physical digestion

Chewing food in your **mouth** and squeezing food in your **stomach** are both forms of physical digestion. The resulting smaller pieces of food can move more easily through the rest of the digestive system.

Chemical digestion

Carbohydrates, fats, and proteins are digested by specific enzymes in certain parts of the digestive system.

Food	Type of enzyme	Part of gut where enzyme works	Products of digestion
carbohydrates	**carbohydrases**	mouth and small intestine	starch, converted to maltose and then to glucose, a simple sugar
fats (lipids)	**lipases**	small intestine	fatty acids and glycerol
proteins	**proteases**	stomach and small intestine	amino acids

Enzymes have a specific optimum pH

You have hydrochloric acid in your stomach, giving it a very low pH of between 1 and 2. This is primarily to kill any pathogens in your food. The protease enzyme in your stomach is well adapted to this low pH and will not work at higher pH values. However, other enzymes in your mouth and small intestine work best at higher pH values of between 7 and 8.

Exam tip

- Always try to use technical terms. Talk about food being digested, rather than being broken down.

Bile

To help you digest fats in the small intestine, your liver makes bile. Bile is stored in your gall bladder and released into the small intestine. Bile emulsifies the fats (breaks the fats into smaller droplets). This gives the lipase enzymes more surface area to work on.

A Describe the functions of each of the following:
(a) oesophagus (b) stomach (c) small intestine (d) large intestine.

B Explain the difference between physical and chemical digestion.

Absorption of digested food in the small intestine

The products of digestion diffuse across the wall of the **small intestine** into the blood plasma or lymph.

Adaptations of the small intestine

The small intestine is well adapted to absorb digested food efficiently:

- It is very long.
- It has a large surface area because its lining is folded and has finger-like projections called villi.
- The cells covering each villus have microvilli, which increase the surface area even more.
- The lining is thin.
- There is a good blood supply.

▼ Coloured scanning electron micrograph of villi in the small intestine (× 100)

The large intestine

The **large intestine** absorbs water and some minerals into the blood. The semi-solid waste (faeces) that is left in the large intestine is then passed out of the anus. This is called egestion.

Questions

1 What is the function of the large intestine? **→ E**

2 Where in your digestive system are each of the following chemically digested? (a) carbohydrates (b) fats (c) proteins

3 Digested food enters your blood in your small intestine and leaves your blood at body tissues. Why does it leave your blood at your body tissues? **→ C**

4 What is the function of bile in digestion?

5 The pH in your stomach is around 1.2 and in your small intestine it is about 7.8. Proteins are digested in both places. Do you think the same protease enzyme works in both places? Explain your answer.

6 Explain how the small intestine is well adapted to efficiently absorb digested food. **→ A***

Waste disposal

During digestion, the semi-solid waste (faeces) that is left leaves your body via your anus. This is egestion, not excretion – this waste was not made in your body.

Some chemical reactions in your cells make toxic waste products. Respiration produces water and carbon dioxide. Your body has to remove toxins, otherwise you would be poisoned. Your body also has to regulate the amount of salts and water in it. It is important that the concentration of water molecules in your blood plasma is kept constant. Too much water, and blood cells would swell and burst. Too little water, or too much salt, and they would shrivel and not function. Your nerves would not work properly if there were too many or too few salts in your body.

The main organs of excretion

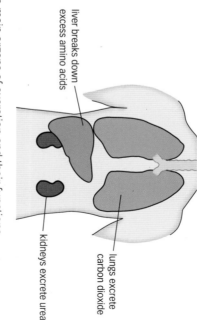

liver breaks down
excess amino acids

kidneys excrete urea

lungs excrete
carbon dioxide

▶ The main organs of excretion and their functions

The skin

Your skin makes sweat to cool you. The water in the sweat uses your body heat to evaporate. Sweating also gets rid of excess water and salts.

The lungs

Your respiring cells make carbon dioxide. It is carried in the blood to the lungs and then diffuses into the alveoli to be breathed out. So your lungs excrete carbon dioxide that was made in your cells. The carbon dioxide would otherwise poison you because it would lower your blood pH. Your enzymes would not work properly and you would die. As carbon dioxide levels in your blood increase they are detected by the brain. The brain then increases your breathing rate to remove the carbon dioxide more quickly.

Learning objectives

After studying this topic, you should be able to:

⌄ understand the difference between egestion and excretion

⌄ name and locate the main organs of excretion and name the substances they excrete

⌄ explain why substances have to be excreted

Key words

urea

A Explain the difference between egestion and excretion.

B Name four organs of excretion.

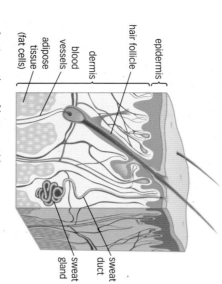

epidermis

hair follicle

dermis

blood
vessels

adipose
tissue
(fat cells)

sweat
duct

sweat
gland

▶ A section of human skin

Did you know…?

The skin is your largest organ. It weighs about 4–5 kg.

The liver

Your liver breaks down old red blood cells. The chemicals from them go into the bile and pass out with the faeces. Your liver also breaks down hormones and medicines or other drugs, such as alcohol.

If you have eaten more protein than your body needs, the liver breaks down excess amino acids into ammonia. Ammonia has a high pH and is very soluble, so if it got into your blood it would be very harmful. Enzymes would not be able to function. In your liver cells the ammonia reacts with carbon dioxide (another waste product) to make **urea**. Urea is toxic, but not as toxic as ammonia. Your blood carries the urea to your kidneys, which remove it.

The kidneys

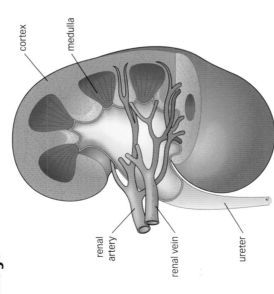

cortex
medulla

renal artery
renal vein
ureter

◀ The structure of the kidney. Blood flows in through the renal artery, is filtered and leaves the kidney in the renal vein. The waste urine, containing water, salts, and urea, passes down the ureter to the bladder.

Each of your kidneys has about one million filtering units. Blood enters your kidney in the renal artery. It is filtered under high pressure and lots of substances are filtered out:

- glucose
- salts
- water
- urea.

Then the useful substances:

- all the glucose
- some salts
- some water

are reabsorbed into the blood. The remaining liquid, called urine, passes down the ureter to the bladder. It is stored in the bladder and passed out when convenient.

As well as removing urea, your kidney also regulates the amount of salts and water in your body.

Exam tip

➤ Remember that it is the water in sweat that evaporates, not the sweat itself. The evaporation changes water from a liquid to a gas, and that takes heat energy from your skin, blood, and body. This is how sweating cools you.

OCR

Questions

→ E

1 For each organ you named in Question B, state its main excretory product.

→ C

2 Explain why carbon dioxide has to be removed from the body.

3 How do you think the amount of urea in your urine would change if you started eating a high protein diet? Explain your answer.

4 How do you think the water content of your urine would change if you drank a lot of tea and lemon squash? Explain your answer.

→ A*

5 How do you think the water content of your urine would change on a hot day if you ran around and did not drink any extra water? Explain your answer.

6 How do you think your urine would change after you ate a very salty meal?

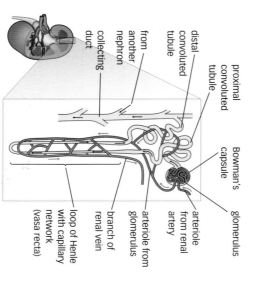

proximal convoluted tubule

distal convoluted tubule

from another nephron

collecting duct

Bowman's capsule

glomerulus

arteriole from renal artery

arteriole from glomerulus

branch of renal vein

loop of Henle with capillary network (vasa recta)

▶ The position of nephrons in the kidney, and the structure of a nephron

A Why is it important that salts and water in the blood are carefully regulated?

The nephron

You have learnt about the gross structure of a kidney. There are about a million filtering units, called nephrons, in each kidney. Each nephron consists of:

- a knot of capillaries, called a **glomerulus**, inside a capsule, where high pressure filtration occurs
- a region for **selective reabsorption**, where useful substances eg glucose pass into the blood
- a region for salt and water regulation.

▶ Detailed structure of a nephron showing the regions for high pressure filtration, selective reabsorption, and salt and water regulation. The tubule is surrounded by capillaries so that substances can easily pass back into the blood.

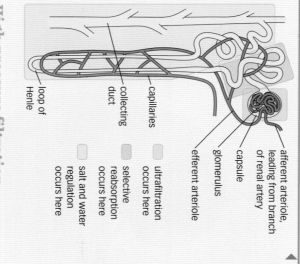

afferent arteriole, leading from branch of renal artery

capsule

glomerulus

efferent arteriole

capillaries

collecting duct

loop of Henle

ultrafiltration occurs here

selective reabsorption occurs here

salt and water regulation occurs here

High pressure filtration

Blood enters your kidney, in the renal artery, under high pressure. Many arterioles branch off from the renal artery and one arteriole goes to each glomerulus. Blood goes from the **afferent arteriole** into the glomerulus. It then leaves the glomerulus in another arteriole, called the **efferent arteriole**.

The efferent arteriole has a narrower diameter than the afferent arteriole. This produces a bottleneck effect. The blood cannot leave the glomerulus as fast as it is entering, so it is under high pressure, and the capillaries of the glomerulus are very leaky. The result is high pressure filtration. Substances with small molecules – water, salts, urea, glucose, amino acids, vitamins, and spent hormones – are filtered out of the blood. They pass along the tubules of the nephron dissolved in liquid that was squeezed out from the glomerulus.

From the first part of the nephron, all the useful substances – glucose, amino acids, vitamins, some salts, and some water – are reabsorbed by selective reabsorption. The loop of Henle, the rest of the tubule, and the collecting duct regulate the amount of salt and water in the body.

- If your blood is very watery, less water is reabsorbed from the kidney tubules and a lot of dilute urine is produced.

- If your blood is not very watery, more water is reabsorbed from the kidney tubules and a smaller volume of concentrated urine is produced.

Antidiuretic hormone (ADH)

The hormone ADH is released from a gland in the brain, your **pituitary gland**, directly into the blood. Your blood carries it to its target organs, the kidneys. This hormone makes the walls of the collecting duct more permeable to water, so more water can be reabsorbed into the blood.

A negative feedback mechanism is involved. As your blood passes through your brain, your hypothalamus detects how watery it is.

- If your blood is watery, less ADH is released. Less water is reabsorbed in the kidneys and more water is lost in urine. This adjusts the water content of your blood.

- If your blood is not very watery, more ADH is released. More water is reabsorbed in the kidneys and less water is lost in urine.

Renal dialysis

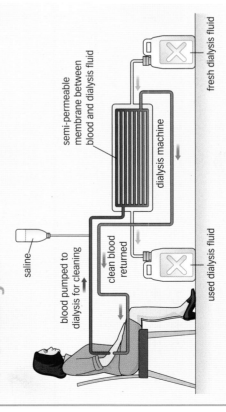

saline

blood pumped to dialysis for cleaning

clean blood returned

semi-permeable membrane between blood and dialysis fluid

dialysis machine

used dialysis fluid

fresh dialysis fluid

▲ Sometimes people's kidneys stop working properly. When this happens their blood can be filtered by a dialysis machine.

Exam tip **OCR**

- How can you remember when more ADH is released?
  Diuresis means *making urine*. *Anti-* means *against*. Antidiuretic hormone reduces the volume of urine. More ADH is released if your blood/body needs to conserve water – if you have been sweating and/or not drinking much. Less ADH is released if your blood is watery – if you have been drinking a lot.

- How can you remember which is the afferent and which is the efferent arteriole?
  Affere is Latin and means to carry *towards*; *effere* is Latin and means to carry *away from*.

Questions

1 What substances are reabsorbed into the blood during selective reabsorption?

2 Explain how high pressure filtration occurs in the glomerulus.

3 Describe how ADH release is controlled using negative feedback.

→ A*

Growth and development

At birth we can tell what sex the child is because of the external **genitals** – the primary sexual characteristics. At puberty, children's bodies begin to change into those of sexually mature adults. This stage of a person's life is called adolescence, and lasts several years. The first thing that happens is that the ovaries in females, and testes in males, develop and begin to produce the **sex hormones**.

The female sex hormones oestrogen and progesterone are made in the ovaries. They are involved in controlling the menstrual cycle.

▶ The female reproductive system and its functions

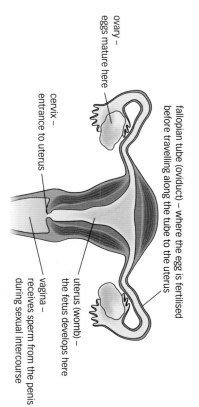

ovary – eggs mature here

fallopian tube (oviduct) – where the egg is fertilised before travelling along the tube to the uterus

cervix – entrance to uterus

uterus (womb) – the fetus develops here

vagina – receives sperm from the penis during sexual intercourse

Secondary sexual characteristics

At puberty, your sex hormones cause your secondary sexual characteristics to develop.

Male secondary sexual characteristics	Female secondary sexual characteristics
• The voice breaks (deepens).	• The breasts develop.
• Hair grows on the face and body.	• Pubic hair and hair under the arms grows.
• The body becomes more muscular.	• The hips widen.
• Genitals develop.	• Periods start (menstruation) and eggs mature.
• The testes start making sperm.	

A Name the female and male sex hormones.

B List four secondary sexual characteristics for males and four for females.

▶ The male reproductive system and its functions

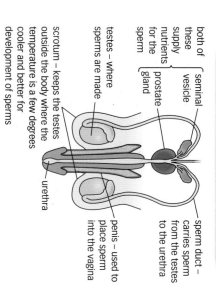

both of these supply nutrients for the sperm { seminal vesicle / prostate gland }

sperm duct – carries sperm from the testes to the urethra

penis – used to place sperm into the vagina

urethra

testes – where sperms are made

scrotum – keeps the testes outside the body where the temperature is a few degrees cooler and better for development of sperms

Did you know...?

At puberty males produce small amounts of oestrogen and progesterone and females produce small amounts of the male sex hormone, testosterone. In females testosterone causes pubic hair and hair under the arms to grow.

The menstrual cycle

At puberty, females begin to have a menstrual period each month. They have a monthly menstrual cycle.

Several hormones help coordinate the menstrual cycle.

- The pituitary gland in the brain releases a hormone called FSH.
- FSH causes an egg in one of the ovaries to mature.
- It also stimulates the ovaries to make the hormone oestrogen.
- Oestrogen stimulates the pituitary gland to release another hormone, LH.
- LH triggers the release of the egg (**ovulation**) from the ovary.
- Oestrogen also inhibits further production of FSH and it repairs the uterus lining (the endometrium, which is the innermost layer of the uterus wall).
- Progesterone maintains the uterus lining and inhibits LH.

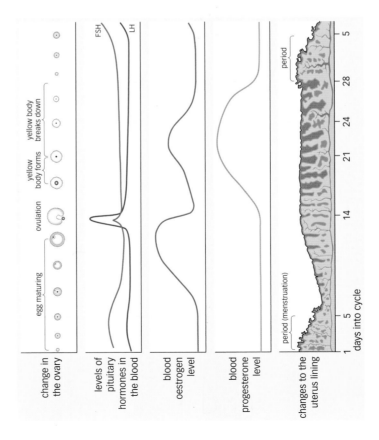

▲ Events in the menstrual cycle

Conception happens if a sperm meets the egg and fertilises it. If the egg is not fertilised, at the end of the cycle the uterus lining passes out of the body. This is the period. If the egg is fertilised then the uterus lining stays so that the fetus can develop.

Key words

genitals, sex hormones, ovulation, conception

Exam tip

✓ It may seem complicated, but you need to learn the names and functions of all the hormones involved.

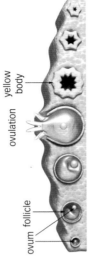

▲ Changes in the ovary during the menstrual cycle. The egg develops in a follicle. It then bursts out of the follicle. The empty follicle develops into a yellow body which makes progesterone; this stops menstruation.

Questions

1 Where is FSH made in the body?

2 What does FSH do?

3 What is the function of progesterone?

4 What is the role of oestrogen in the menstrual cycle?

5 During which part of the menstrual cycle is a woman most likely to conceive?

6 When during the menstrual cycle is the level of LH highest?

→ C

→ A*

Controlling fertility with female hormones

Humans can control fertility by using female sex hormones. These hormones can be used to reduce fertility or to promote fertility.

Reducing fertility

During pregnancy, both oestrogen and progesterone levels are high and they inhibit FSH and LH production from the pituitary gland. This prevents the development and release of any more eggs.

Scientists realised that if women took oestrogen and progesterone in a daily pill, the high levels in the body would mimic pregnancy and prevent ovulation. Without ovulation you cannot become pregnant. Preventing pregnancy is called **contraception**.

The first contraceptive (birth-control) pills contained high amounts of oestrogen. They prevented ovulation but many women suffered from side-effects. Contraceptive pills now contain a much lower dose of oestrogen and some progesterone, or just progesterone. These give fewer side-effects.

Increasing fertility

Some couples are infertile and therefore cannot conceive. Possible causes of infertility are:

* blocked fallopian tubes or sperm ducts
* eggs do not develop or are not released from ovaries
* the testes do not produce enough sperms.

Fertility treatment may help.

A procedure called in vitro fertilisation (**IVF**) may be used to treat women who cannot become pregnant naturally. *In vitro* means 'in glass'. In IVF:

* The woman is injected with FSH, which stimulates her ovaries to produce eggs.
* The eggs are then collected from the woman and mixed with the man's sperm in a glass dish.
* To make the procedure more likely to work, healthy sperms are selected and one is injected into each egg.
* The fertilised eggs begin to develop into embryos.
* When they are tiny balls of cells, two are chosen and inserted into the woman's uterus.

Learning objectives

After studying this topic, you should be able to:

* explain how female hormones can be used to reduce fertility
* explain how FSH can be used to treat infertility
* describe other treatments for infertility and discuss the arguments for and against fertility treatments
* discuss ethical issues raised by fetal screening

Key words

contraception, IVF, amniocentesis, miscarriage

Contraceptive pills in a blister pack. Each pack contains enough pills for one month. They are usually taken for 21 days of each month and then not taken for 7 days, so the woman has a period.

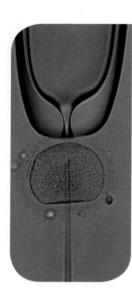

▶ A human sperm being injected into a human egg

Other treatments for infertility

Treatment	Description and reason for treatment
Artificial insemination	If the male's sperm count is low, sperm can be donated from another male and inserted into the woman's vagina. Also used for single women or lesbian couples who wish to become pregnant.
Egg donation	A woman may donate some of her eggs to another woman who cannot make eggs. Women undergoing IVF often donate 'spare eggs'.
Surrogacy	If a woman has had her uterus removed, another woman (the surrogate mother) may have the first woman's embryo (the result of IVF) implanted in her uterus. After the birth the surrogate mother gives the baby back to its biological mother.
Ovary transplants	So far only a few ovary transplants have been carried out, with the donor being the identical twin of the recipient. This could restore the fertility of women who undergo early menopause and are no longer fertile, or who have had radiation treatment for cancer. A woman could have her ovaries removed before being treated for cancer, have them frozen and have them transplanted back after the treatment.

Being childless can cause distress and sadness to people who want a family, and fertility treatments allow some people to have a child who could not do so otherwise. However, these treatments are very expensive and there is no guarantee they will work. All medical procedures carry some risk.

Checking fetal development

Ultrasound scans are used to check fetal development. However, some abnormalities cannot be seen on a scan. Down's syndrome is caused by the presence of an extra chromosome. To check for Down's syndrome, doctors can insert a needle into the uterus and take some amniotic fluid containing fetal cells. This procedure is called **amniocentesis**. The cells are grown in a lab so that they divide. Their chromosomes can be observed under a microscope and counted.

If the fetus has an extra chromosome, the couple have to decide whether to terminate the pregnancy. Some people think that screening out disabilities means that disabled people are undervalued in society. There is a 1% (1 in 100) chance that amniocentesis could cause a **miscarriage** and could abort a healthy fetus.

A What does IVF stand for?

B Explain how FSH can be used to increase fertility in women who cannot conceive (become pregnant).

Questions

E →

1 Name two female hormones produced in the ovaries.

C →

2 Discuss the advantages and disadvantages of: (a) IVF (b) egg donation (c) surrogacy (d) ovary transplants.

3 Some fertility drugs contain a chemical that inhibits oestrogen. How do you think this might increase fertility?

A* →

4 Some families have a history of a particular genetic disorder. In these cases, fertilisation can be in vitro and the embryos can be tested for genetic defects. Only healthy embryos will be implanted. Do you think this is a good idea? Give reasons for your answer.

Monitoring growth and development

Before you were born, doctors and midwives used ultrasound scans to monitor your development in the uterus. They monitored your rate of growth and increase in head size as well as your heart rate. This told them if you were growing and developing at a normal rate.

At birth and during the first six months, the midwife measures a baby's

• head circumference   • body length   • mass

and plots them on average growth charts. The baby's growth is compared with the range of average values. This regular monitoring can alert the midwife if you have any growth problems.

If a baby is growing too slowly, its pituitary gland may not be producing enough growth hormone. Growth hormone stimulates general growth, especially that of long bones and muscles. A deficiency can be treated with injections of human growth hormone.

Stages of human growth

We do not grow at a constant rate. The graph on the left shows the stages of human growth.

infancy	– First two years of life – Highest rate of growth, gaining around 15–24 cm in a year
childhood	– From 2–11 years of age, until puberty starts – Growth occurs at a slower rate than during infancy
adolescence	– From 11–15 years of age, when puberty begins – Growth spurt for girls aged 10–12 and boys aged 12–15 years
maturity	– Males may continue to grow until the age of 18–20 years – Most females reach their full adult height by 16 years of age
old age	– Above 60–65 years – Physical abilities start to deteriorate

Learning objectives

After studying this topic, you should be able to:

⌄ understand why a baby's length and mass are monitored

⌄ recall the factors that determine a person's final height

⌄ recall the main stages of growth and identify them on a human growth curve

⌄ discuss the implications of increased life expectancy

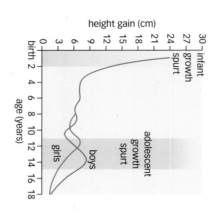

height gain (cm)

30 – infant growth spurt
27 –
24 –
21 –
18 –
15 –
12 –   adolescent growth spurt
9 –
6 –   girls
3 –   boys
0 –
birth 2 4 6 8 10 12 14 16 18
age (years)

▶ The growth rate, as height gain per year, from birth to 18 years

Charts like the one above are based on an average of the population. Not everyone's growth will follow this pattern.

A Name and describe the main stages of the human growth curve.

Your final height is determined by

- your genes – many genes determine your height potential
- your diet – you need good quality protein for growth and enough food for your energy needs
- the amount of exercise you do – exercise stimulates growth of bones and muscles
- your hormones – growth hormone, thyroxine, and insulin
- health and disease – if you are often ill or do not get enough sleep you may not grow properly.

Life expectancy

In the developed world, **life expectancy** has increased. We expect to live to between 75 and 80 years. This does not mean everyone will live this long. Many die earlier and some later. **Old age** is officially above 60–65 years but many older people carry on working and living full and active lives.

Life expectancy has increased in developed countries because we have

- less industrial disease such as asbestosis, and fewer accidents in the workplace
- healthier diets, with few cases of vitamin or mineral deficiencies
- better housing
- improved lifestyle so people can have a positive outlook on life
- vaccinations to prevent many infectious diseases
- better treatments for cancer and heart disease.

However, there may be problems with increased life expectancy:

- a large ageing population – there are more people aged over 65 than under 16 in the UK
- many of these will need medical treatment or care
- this could affect the job prospects for younger people as more older people need to keep working for economic reasons and/or because they want to
- the state pension system will need to be redesigned as it cannot afford to pay pensions for 30 or more years to people; the retirement age will also be raised.

▲ Increased life expectancy has led to a large ageing population

Questions

1 What factors determine your final height? **→ E**

2 Use the graph of growth rate on the previous page to answer the following questions. What is the average height gain per year: (a) aged 1 year (b) aged 2 years (c) aged 6 years (d) for boys aged 14 years? **→ C**

3 Why do you think more people are living longer in the UK today, compared with 50–100 years ago? What possible problems may arise as a result? **→ A***

Learning objectives

After studying this topic, you should be able to:

- recall that some body parts can be mechanically replaced
- recall that some organs can be transplanted
- discuss the ethical issues concerning organ donation

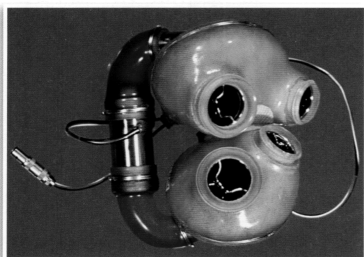

▶ The Jarvik-7 artificial heart was developed by Dr Robert Jarvik and a biomedical engineer, Dr Lyman. It is made from polyurethane and titanium. The inside is smooth and seamless so it does not cause blood clots that would lead to strokes. Many people have had this type of artificial heart while waiting for a heart transplant. However, the wires protrude through the skin.

Mechanical replacements

Many mechanical replacements for body parts are used outside the body, for example

- heart–lung machines, used during open heart surgery to divert blood from the heart
- kidney dialysis machines, used to filter the blood of people with renal (kidney) failure, removing urea, excess salts, and water
- mechanical ventilators, used to aid breathing in patients whose rib cage muscles are paralysed.

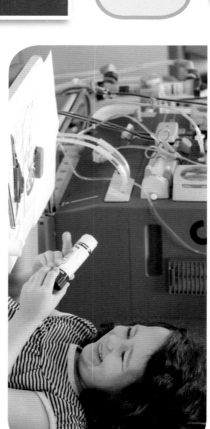

▶ A renal dialysis machine in action

Other mechanical devices can be implanted into the body. These include:

- heart pacemakers
- artificial hearts
- artificial knee and hip joints
- eye lenses.

When medical engineers are designing these implants they need to consider certain factors, such as:

- size – this is why there is no artificial kidney that can be implanted; dialysis machines are very large
- battery life (if powered) – pacemaker batteries last 7–10 years
- body reactions – inert materials that do not react with body fluids are used to construct implants; artificial hearts are made of titanium and plastic
- strength – titanium is used for artificial joints.

A   Describe two mechanical organ replacements that can be used (a) outside, and (b) inside the body. Explain why they are used.

Organ transplants

Many body parts can be replaced by transplanting donated organs.

Blood transfusions	Successfully carried out for over 100 years, using blood from live **donors** that is stored in blood banks. Blood types must be matched.
Cornea transplants	Also known as corneal grafts. A cornea removed from a recently dead donor is transplanted into the recipient's eye. No risk of rejection as the cornea has no blood vessels.
Heart transplants	First carried out in 1967 in South Africa. Donors are usually recently dead, but may be living – if someone has a heart–lung transplant to replace diseased lungs, the recipient's healthy heart can be donated to someone else.
Lung transplants	Lungs from a recently dead donor may be transplanted into a recipient suffering from cystic fibrosis, for example. Usually a heart–lung transplant is carried out.
Kidney transplants	Donor may be dead or living, as we can survive with only one kidney. A close relative may donate a kidney to a recipient.
Bone marrow transplants	Used to treat leukaemia. Living donors are tissue-typed and recorded on a register so that they can be matched to a recipient. They then give bone marrow.

All donors need to be a good tissue match and the right age and size for the recipients. Living donors have to be healthy and willing to donate. There is currently a shortage of organ donors.

Rejection

With most transplants there is a risk that the recipient's immune system will reject the transplant. **Tissue matching**, matching the donor and recipient's tissue type, and **immunosuppressant drugs** both reduce the risk of rejection. However, these drugs increase the risk of infections.

Exam tip

OCR

➤ When discussing ethical issues, be objective and give some pros and some cons.

Questions

1 Explain why tissue types for donor and recipients have to be matched for most organ/tissue transplants. → C

2 Explain how a living heart donor may be used.

3 Why is there no problem of rejection with cornea grafts? → A*

4 What problems are associated with taking immunosuppressant drugs?

5 Discuss the ethical issues concerning organ/tissue transplants.

Module summary

NOW USE THE B5 GRADE CHECKER ON PAGE 240

Revision checklist

- Some animals have no hard skeleton. Some have an external skeleton and some have an internal skeleton.

- Joints and muscles allow you to move. Muscles work in antagonistic pairs.

- Multicellular animals have a circulatory system to transport material to and from cells.

- Mammals have a double circulatory system consisting of heart and blood vessels (the cardiovascular system) and lymph.

- The cardiac cycle describes the events of each heartbeat.

- Artificial pacemakers, valve replacements, surgery, and heart transplants may treat disorders of the heart.

- Blood can be transfused. Blood groups have to be compatible.

- Organisms have special surfaces for gaseous exchange, such as skin, gills, and lungs, to obtain oxygen.

- Breathing moves air into and out of the lungs. Alveoli give a large surface area for gaseous exchange. Respiratory diseases include pneumonia, asthma, lung cancer, cystic fibrosis, and asbestosis.

- Food is digested to smaller molecules to be absorbed into the blood. Chewing is physical digestion; enzymes cause chemical digestion.

- Excretion is the removal of toxic waste made in the body. The skin excretes sweat; lungs excrete carbon dioxide; the kidney excretes urea, excess water, and excess salts. Urea is made in the liver from excess amino acids.

- Each kidney contains many filtering units called nephrons. Antidiuretic hormone controls how much water is reabsorbed. Renal dialysis can treat people with kidney failure.

- Secondary sexual characteristics and male and female reproductive organs develop at puberty. Hormones play an important part in growing up.

- Many treatments are available to treat infertility. Female hormones can also be used in contraceptives. Fetal development can be checked using ultrasound scans and amniocentesis.

- Humans pass through many stages of development: infancy, childhood, adolescence, and adulthood. Rate of growth depends on genes, diet, hormones, and health status.

- Some parts of the body can be replaced with mechanical devices or with organ or tissue transplants.

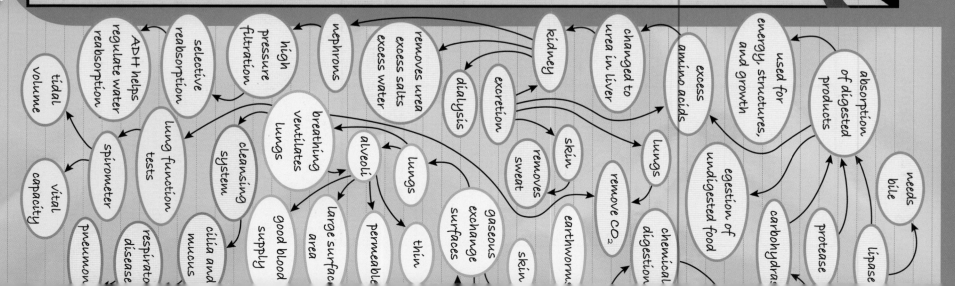

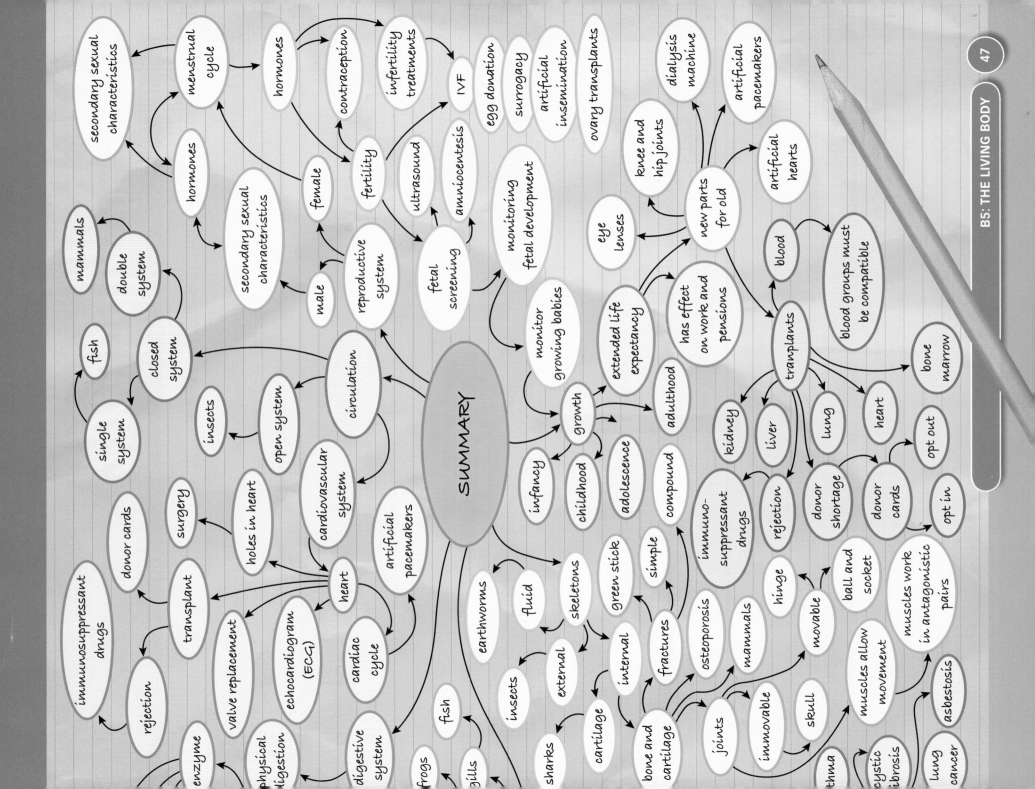

OCR gateway Upgrade

Answering Extended Writing questions

QUESTION

Describe the structure of a long bone. Explain how bones can be broken and why elderly people are particularly prone to fractures. What are the risks when someone has a suspected fracture?

The quality of written communication will be assessed in your answer to this question.

← E

Bones are hard because you need calcium for them. That's why you should drink lots of milk but I don't like it. Old people's bones break easily. You have to get the bone set in plaster.

Examiner: This response has not answered the question. It has stated that bones are hard, but has not described their structure. The answer does not explain why older people's bones may break more easily; it just repeats the question. The risks associated with a suspected fracture have not been given. The reference to plaster, although true, is not relevant. The spelling, punctuation, and grammar are good.

← C

There is marrow inside bones where red blood cells are made. At the ends there is cartilage. This is so joints work smoothly. Bone is living tissue. Bones break if you knock them sharply. Some people, specially old people have weak bones so they break more often. their bones don't have enough calcium. If you break your arm and the bone sticks out through the skin, it could get infected.

Examiner: This answer shows some knowledge of bone structure. There is an explanation of why older people suffer more fractures, and a risk from a fracture is described. However, if the bone is sticking out through the skin as the candidate describes, this is a definite fracture and not a suspected one. There are a few grammatical errors.

← A*

Long bones have a shaft and inside is marrow where blood cells are made. At each end there is cartilage which is smooth and slippery. It helps joints work.

Bones contain protein and calcium and they are strong. But if you knock them sharply or fall awkwardly they can break. Many old people have osteoporosis and their bones break easily. You shouldn't move someone who might have a broken bone as it could damage it more, especially the spine.

Examiner: A clear answer using lots of technical terms properly. Each part of the question has been answered correctly. The answer is easy to follow and the spelling, punctuation, and grammar are good.

Exam-style questions

1   Here is a list of body organs:

   muscle   heart   kidney   skin   bone

   A01 **a** Which organ contains hair follicles?

   A01 **b** Which organ receives blood from the coronary artery?

   A01 **c** Which two organs may be joined together by a tendon?

   A01 **d** Which organs carry out excretion?

2   Some women find it difficult to become pregnant. They may use IVF, which involves taking eggs from the woman just before ovulation.

   A01 **a** What does IVF stand for?

   A01 **b** Which organ in a woman's body makes eggs?

   A01 **c** What normally happens in a woman's body at ovulation?

   A01 **d** During IVF, what is added to an egg to fertilise it?

3   **A01** **a** Which gas is excreted by the lungs?

   A02 **b** What happens in the lungs to cause an asthma attack?

4   In 1901, Dr Landsteiner discovered blood groups. He said there were three. Scientists now know that there are four blood groups.

   A01 **a** Name the four blood groups.

   A02 **b** Which group is safe for anyone?

   A01 **c** Some people have an inherited condition that means their blood does not clot properly. What is the name of this condition?

   A01 **d** Explain the difference between a single and a double circulatory system.

→ **E**   → **C**

5   The graph gives information on organ transplants between 1996 and 2005.

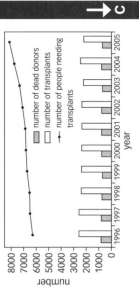

Legend:
- number of dead donors
- number of transplants
- number of people needing transplants

number / year

A03 **a** Describe the general trends over the 9 year period shown by the graph.

A02 **b** Describe the 'opt out' organ donation system that could be adopted to boost organ donation.

→ **C**

6   Bypass surgery can treat blocked coronary arteries using a piece of vein from a patient's arm or leg.

A02 **a** Explain why blocked coronary arteries have to be bypassed.

A01 **b** A blocked coronary artery can also be treated with a stent. Explain what a stent is.

→ **A***

Extended Writing

→ **E**

7   **A01** Describe how single-celled organisms, earthworms, frogs, fish, and humans carry out gaseous exchange.

→ **C**

8   **A01** Describe the causes and symptoms of lung cancer and asthma. How can an asthma attack be treated?

→ **A***

9   **A01** Explain how the small intestine is well adapted for digestion of food and absorption of the products of digestion.

A01   Recall the science

A02   Apply your knowledge

A03   Evaluate and analyse the evidence

B6

Beyond the microscope

Why study this module?

As soon as biologists had the microscope as a basic laboratory instrument, a whole new micro world opened up for us. As microscopes have become more precise, so has our understanding of a new branch of biology called microbiology. From this has come the new scientific field of biotechnology.

In this module you will study the amazing world of the microbe, learning about types of microbes – bacteria, viruses, and fungi. These microbes can be either harmful or helpful. Harmful microbes can cause disease. You will study the ways in which diseases can be transmitted, and consider the early work of some of the pioneers of microbiology. The uses of microbes in the brewing and biofuel industries will also be explored.

You will enter the microscopic worlds of soil and water, investigating some of the impacts of human pollution. Some of the more high-tech uses of microbes will be reviewed, such as the use of microbial enzymes in the food, medical, and detergent industries. Finally, you will examine the use of bacteria or their enzymes in the biotechnological techniques of genetic engineering and DNA fingerprinting.

You should remember

1 The structure of microbial cells.
2 Harmful and helpful microbes.
3 How enzymes work.
4 The action of genes.

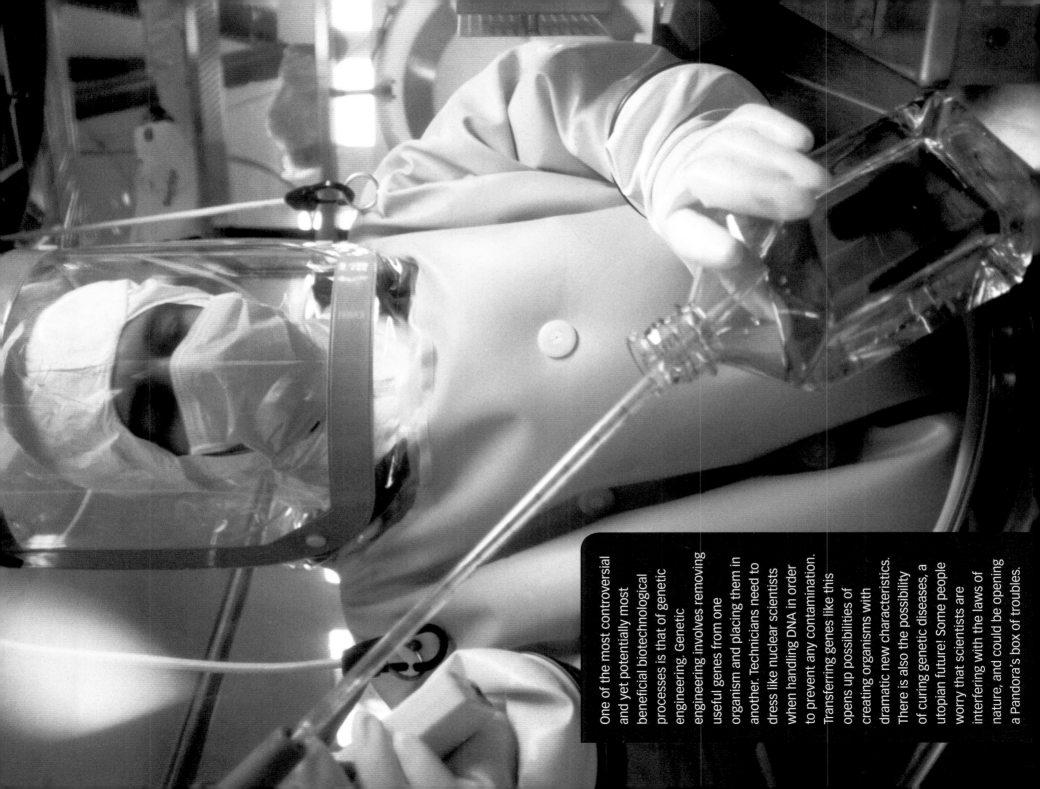

One of the most controversial and yet potentially most beneficial biotechnological processes is that of genetic engineering. Genetic engineering involves removing useful genes from one organism and placing them in another. Technicians need to dress like nuclear scientists when handling DNA in order to prevent any contamination. Transferring genes like this opens up possibilities of creating organisms with dramatic new characteristics. There is also the possibility of curing genetic diseases, a utopian future! Some people worry that scientists are interfering with the laws of nature, and could be opening a Pandora's box of troubles.

Learning objectives

After studying this topic, you should be able to:

- know the structure of bacterial cells
- recognise that bacteria occupy a wide range of habitats
- understand that bacteria reproduce using binary fission
- understand the safe handling of bacteria

Life under the microscope

There is a wide range of organisms that can only be seen using microscopes. Some of these microscopic organisms, or microbes, are helpful to humans; others are harmful. There are three main groups – bacteria, fungi, and viruses.

Bacteria

The microbes that make up the **bacteria** kingdom are single-celled organisms. They are extremely small – a typical bacterium is only a few **microns**, or a few thousandths of a millimetre, long. Bacteria are very important to us. There are many different bacteria, and we can tell them apart and classify them by their shape (see left).

Bacterial cells

At first sight bacterial cells look quite simple. However, they carry out all the functions of other cells.

Bacterial cells can only just be seen using a light microscope. To see fine detail, biologists use high powered microscopes called electron microscopes. These microscopes magnify thousands of times more than a light microscope.

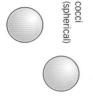

cocci
(spherical)

- Cocci bacteria (*Staphylococcus aureus*) which cause acne spots (×7000)

bacilli
(rod-shaped)

- Bacillus bacteria (*Escherichia coli*) which can cause food poisoning (×3000)

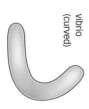

vibrio
(curved)

- Vibrio bacteria (*Vibrio cholerae*) which cause the disease cholera (×3500)

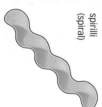

spirilli
(spiral)

- Spiral bacteria (*Helicobacter pylori*) which cause stomach ulcers (×12000)

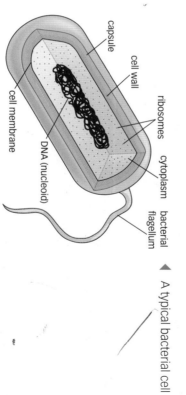

capsule

cell wall

ribosomes

cytoplasm

DNA (nucleoid)

cell membrane

bacterial
flagellum

▲ A typical bacterial cell

The electron microscope reveals the following features of bacterial cells:

- cell membrane, controlling the movement of molecules into and out of the cell
- cytoplasm, a jelly-like substance where most of the cell's reactions occur
- cell wall, having the same function as in a plant cell of maintaining the shape of the cell and preventing it from bursting, but made of a different chemical instead of cellulose
- loop of DNA, controlling the cell and its replication. Bacterial cells do not have a nucleus.

- capsule, a slimy protective capsule around the outside of the cell wall in some bacteria. It is this capsule that protects bacteria against antibiotics
- flagellum, whip-like flagella for movement in some bacteria.

Reproduction in bacteria

Bacteria can reproduce very fast. Most of the time they reproduce by dividing into two, and they can do this as quickly as once every two hours. This type of division is called binary fission.

An unfortunate consequence of this is that harmful bacteria, such as those that spoil food, can reproduce fast. So food such as milk left out in a warm room will go off very quickly. If you then eat this food, the bacteria may reproduce very quickly in your body. The rate of reproduction may be too fast for your immune system to handle, making you ill.

Bacterial habitats

Bacteria have such a wide range of adaptations that they are found living in almost all environments on Earth. They can live from the depths of the ocean up to the highest mountain peaks. They span cold arctic wastes to volcanic areas and hot springs.

Bacteria survive by obtaining energy from a wide range of sources – some from the Sun by photosynthesis, but others from dead bodies, and from chemical reactions in their cells.

Growing bacteria in the lab

To study bacteria in the lab, they are grown on a jelly called agar in a plate-like dish called a Petri dish. The plates are incubated to keep them warm, and the bacteria grow very fast.

Whenever you grow bacteria you need to take care not to contaminate the plates with other bacteria, and not to allow the bacteria to infect yourself. To do this you need to keep instruments and surfaces free of microbes, or **sterile**. Working in this way is called aseptic or sterile technique.

When bacteria are grown commercially to make a product, they are grown in huge numbers. This is done in a large tank called a fermenter. Again, sterile technique is important.

Key words

bacteria, micron, sterile

A Why do biologists need powerful electron microscopes to study bacterial cells?

B Which part of a bacterium performs the function of a nucleus?

Exam tip OCR

➤ When making a list of the parts of a bacterial cell, focus on the parts that are not found in a plant or animal cell.

Did you know…?

There are bacteria that can survive very high temperatures. They have been found living in environments at temperatures above 80°C.

Questions

→ E

→ C

→ A*

1 Describe the common shapes of bacteria.

2 What is the function of the flagellum?

3 How do bacteria reproduce?

4 Explain why sterile technique is important.

Fantastic fungi

Fungi are another important kingdom of organisms. They include mushrooms, moulds, and importantly yeasts. Yeasts are commercially useful to us in the making of bread and beers.

Yeasts are single celled, but larger than a bacterial cell. They can be clearly seen under a light microscope, but the internal detail can be seen better using an electron microscope.

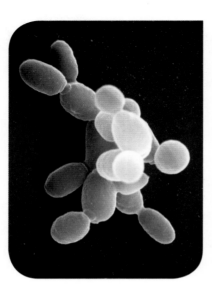

▶ Baker's yeast seen under a powerful light microscope (× 1000)

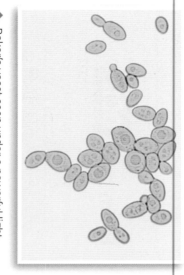

▶ A group of yeast cells all budding from one another

The features of a fungal cell

Fungal cells have many parts in common with other cells. The fungal cell has a membrane, cytoplasm, and nucleus which function as they do in plant cells. The cell wall is similar to a plant or bacterial cell. It has the same function, but is made of a different chemical called chitin.

cell wall

nucleus

cell membrane

cytoplasm

vacuole

mitochondria

▶ A typical fungal cell

Reproduction in yeast

Yeast cells reproduce mainly asexually by a process called budding. The nucleus divides first, then a bulge forms on the side of the parent cell, which will develop into a new cell. Often the cells remain joined.

Budding can be a fast process. Like binary fission in bacteria, it allows the population of cells to increase rapidly. The optimum growth rate is controlled by

* availability of food
* pH
* temperature
* amount of waste products.

Yeast growth rate

For every 10°C rise in temperature, the growth rate of yeast doubles. This is only true up to an optimum temperature, above which the yeast's enzymes begin to be damaged.

A Name three types of fungi.

B State one way in which a fungal cell and a bacterial cell are: (a) similar (b) different.

C Explain what budding is in yeast.

Viruses

One fascinating group of organisms is the **viruses**. Viruses are much smaller than bacteria or fungi. They are so small they were not seen until the electron microscope was invented. They are about one-hundredth the size of a bacterium.

Viruses do not have a cell structure, and they do not carry out many of the processes of living things. For these reasons, some biologists don't consider viruses to be living things.

The features of a virus

Viruses are made of a protein coat inside which is the genetic material. They cannot live independently – they can only live inside the cells of another organism, called the **host**. Each virus can only invade specific host cells; for example, animal viruses cannot invade plant cells. However, plant, animal, and bacterial cells all have viruses that can invade them. Once inside a host's cell, the virus takes over the cell.

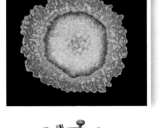

coat

genetic material

▲ Drawing of a flu virus

▲ A flu virus as revealed by an electron microscope (×300 000)

Reproduction in viruses

The virus takes over the host cell in order to reproduce itself. This reproduction occurs in four main steps.

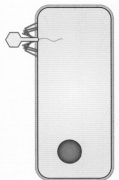

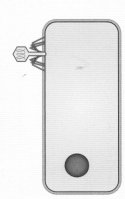

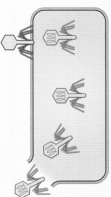

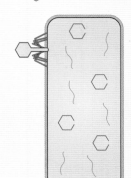

1 The virus attaches to a specific host cell.

2 The genetic material from the virus is injected into the host cell.

3 The viral genes cause the host cell to make new viruses.

4 The host cell splits open, releasing the new virus.

▲ The four main stages in viral reproduction

Keeping the microbes out

Some microbes, called **pathogens**, cause disease. The body has a number of ways of preventing microbes getting in and causing disease. These features are sometimes referred to as our first line of defence.

Feature	How it prevents entry of microbes	How microbes may overcome the barrier
Skin	Acts as a physical barrier to prevent microbes entering.	Cuts in the skin allow microbes in.
	Washing reduces numbers of microbes on skin.	Insect bites penetrate the skin.
		Infected needles carry microbes through the skin.
	Blood clots at a cut to form a scab and seal the skin.	
Digestive system (through mouth)	Acid in the stomach kills bacteria.	Eating undercooked food or drinking infected water containing large numbers of microbes.
Respiratory system (through nose)	Cells lining the airways produce a sticky mucus which traps microorganisms.	Some airborne microbes such as cold viruses can get past the cilia.
	Fine hair-like cilia move the mucus with trapped microbes up to the throat for swallowing.	Smoking stops the cilia working.
Reproductive system	Acidic urine kills many microbes.	Some microbes are resistant to acid.
		Microbes are passed from one person to another by sexual contact.

Learning objectives

After studying this topic, you should be able to:

- know about the body's defences against infection
- know how microbes are transmitted from one person to another
- understand that major disasters may impact upon the transmission of microbes

Key words

pathogen, contamination, transmission

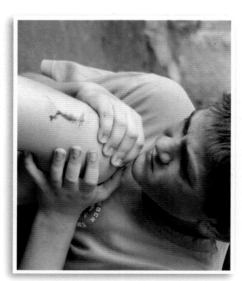

▶ A cut in the skin forms a potential site for the entry of microbes

Exam tip OCR

✓ Remember that all of the first-line mechanisms are to stop microbes getting into the body. It is the immune system that deals with microbes once inside the body.

A List three ways that microbes can enter the body through the skin.

B Describe two ways in which the entry of microbes is prevented in the lungs.

C Why does eating food which is starting to go off make you ill?

Breaking and entering

In order to survive, microbes need to find and enter a host. There are a number of ways that they can get past the host's defences. Here are just a few.

- **Contaminated** food: many bacteria such as *Salmonella* and *E. coli* are common on unwashed vegetables and meat. If the food is not washed or cooked correctly, the bacteria will grow and reproduce. They will then be ingested along with the food. High levels of the bacteria will lead to food poisoning. These bacteria can even spread from uncooked food to cooked food, if people are not careful about food hygiene.

- Contaminated water: cholera is a disease caused by drinking water contaminated with sewage. This water contains the bacterium *Vibrio cholerae*, which causes the disease.

- Contact: many microbes are spread or **transmitted** by direct contact with an infected person. The microbe can also be transferred by touching a surface that an infected person has touched. One common example of this is athlete's foot, which is caused by a fungus called *Trichophyton*.

- Airborne transmission: viruses like the influenza virus are spread in small water droplets in the air. When someone sneezes, the droplets are fired out into the air for someone else to breathe in.

Natural disasters can spread disease

Natural disasters such as volcanic eruptions and earthquakes can disrupt the systems that prevent the spread of diseases. Cholera and food poisoning may spread easily because

- sewage pipes may be broken, causing sewage to leak out
- water supply systems may be damaged, cutting off the supply of clean fresh water
- electricity may be cut off, so food cannot be refrigerated
- many people may lose their homes and live crowded together in camps, where disease can spread
- the health service may become over-stretched, and lacking in supplies.

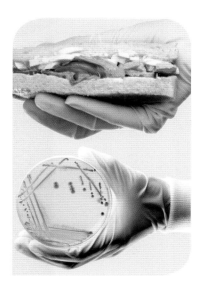

▲ Samples from food can be cultured on an agar plate to test for *E. coli* in the food

▲ Athlete's foot is a common fungal disease spread by direct contact

▲ Sneezing fills the air with cold or flu viruses

◄ An open well can easily become polluted, leading to cholera

Questions

1 Explain how the boy in the picture on the previous page can prevent his knee from becoming infected. → E

2 Explain why colds and flu may easily be transmitted on a crowded bus. → C

3 What do you think would be the main priorities to prevent disease after a major disaster? → A*

D Explain why it is important to wash your hands after sneezing.

Diseases and their microbes

Disease is a state in which the body is not healthy. There are many different diseases, with different causes and different symptoms. Some microbes can cause disease, and these disease-causing microbes are called a pathogen. If the pathogen spreads rapidly from one person to another, the disease is described as infectious. There are pathogens in all the groups of microbes – bacteria, viruses, and fungi.

Bacterial diseases

The table shows some examples of diseases caused by bacterial pathogens. The **symptoms** of a disease are the effects that a patient feels.

Disease	Pathogen and means of transmission
Cholera	Caused by a *Vibrio* bacterium transmitted in contaminated drinking water. The symptoms of the disease are severe diarrhoea and vomiting which lead to dehydration. Cholera is often fatal and develops particularly quickly in children.
Food poisoning	Bacteria are ingested in contaminated food. The symptoms include stomach pains, diarrhoea, and vomiting. It can be so severe that it can be fatal in children and elderly people.

Viral diseases

Here are some examples of viral diseases.

Disease	Pathogen and means of transmission
Influenza	The influenza virus is usually breathed in. Flu is one of the most common diseases. The symptoms include headaches, a running nose, coughs, and sneezes. The disease can occasionally be fatal in weak and elderly people.
Chickenpox	This disease spreads by direct contact, or by breathing in viruses transmitted by an infected person coughing. Symptoms include a rash on the skin that becomes very itchy. Headaches and fevers are also common. Chickenpox is not usually fatal.

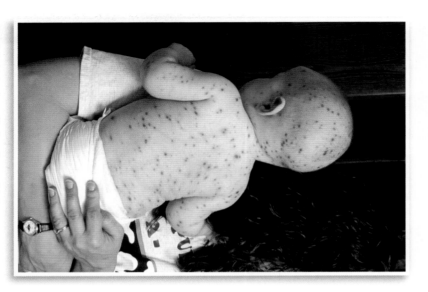

▶ This baby is suffering from chickenpox, a viral disease

Learning objectives

After studying this topic, you should be able to:

❯ know that microbes cause many diseases

❮ know the stages of an infectious disease

Key words

disease, symptom, toxin

Fungal diseases

Fungal diseases include:

Disease	Pathogen and means of transmission
Athlete's foot	The fungus infects the skin between the toes because it is often moist here. The symptoms include cracked flaking skin. It can be painful and in severe cases may bleed.

How an infectious disease develops

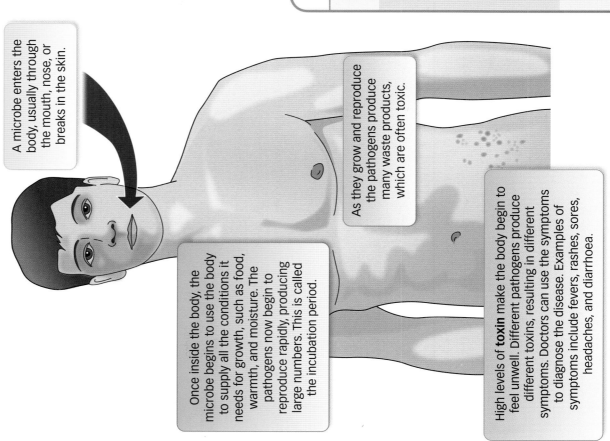

A microbe enters the body, usually through the mouth, nose, or breaks in the skin.

Once inside the body, the microbe begins to use the body to supply all the conditions it needs for growth, such as food, warmth, and moisture. The pathogens now begin to reproduce rapidly, producing large numbers. This is called the incubation period.

As they grow and reproduce the pathogens produce many waste products, which are often toxic.

High levels of **toxin** make the body begin to feel unwell. Different pathogens produce different toxins, resulting in different symptoms. Doctors can use the symptoms to diagnose the disease. Examples of symptoms include fevers, rashes, sores, headaches, and diarrhoea.

▲ Once inside your body, a pathogen reproduces and causes the symptoms of disease

A What is a pathogen?

B What are the symptoms of cholera?

C What makes cholera a particularly serious disease?

Questions

1 How do we get food poisoning? → E

2 Why is heart disease not termed an infectious disease? → C

3 Describe how a pathogen produces its symptoms.

4 Explain why you do not feel ill as soon as a microbe enters your body.

5 Explain how a doctor might use a person's symptoms to diagnose a disease. → A*

Learning objectives

After studying this topic, you should be able to:

✓ know about the work of Pasteur, Lister, and Fleming in treating infectious diseases

✓ understand the development of antibiotic resistance

It's a mystery

Until the 1800s, people did not know about microbes. They thought that food decayed because moulds would spontaneously generate on food. Diseases were explained as the effects of evil spirits, or caused by bad smells. There are three great microbiologists who revolutionised our understanding of infectious diseases.

Louis Pasteur

A French scientist called Louis Pasteur (1822–95) proved that decay was caused by microorganisms in the air. He went on to explain that microbes entering the body would cause disease. He proposed the idea that if we could stop microbes entering the body, we could prevent illness. These ideas are known as the germ theory.

▶ Louis Pasteur

▶ Joseph Lister

Joseph Lister

Armed with the knowledge that microbes entering the body caused illness, Joseph Lister (1827–1912) developed the idea of **antiseptics**. These are solutions that kill microbes. Lister was a surgeon, and he sprayed his instruments with a solution of carbolic acid. This killed microbes on the instruments, which greatly reduced the number of postoperative infections.

Today, many types of antiseptic are used. They are much safer than the acids used by Lister. We use them to kill bacteria on all types of surfaces and on our skin. This contains the spread of microbes, and greatly reduces the number of infections.

Did you know…?

One of the world's most famous microbiology institutes is named after Louis Pasteur. His body is buried underneath the Pasteur Institute in Paris.

▶ Sir Alexander Fleming

Alexander Fleming

More recently, Alexander Fleming (1881–1955) worked in St Mary's Hospital in London. He discovered that a mould called penicillin produced a chemical that would kill bacteria. The fungus grew on one of his agar plates of bacteria. It caused an area where the bacteria could not grow, as they were killed by the penicillin.

During the Second World War scientists were able to make sufficient penicillin to give to a patient, and the patient recovered from the illness. Penicillin was the drug that killed bacteria – the first **antibiotic**.

A Who proposed that microbes caused disease?

B Explain how Lister made surgical procedures safer.

C Explain why the discovery of penicillin was so important.

Resistance to antibiotics

Antibiotics were regarded as wonder drugs. However, they cannot cure all infectious diseases:

- Antibiotics do not kill viruses. This is because viruses do not feed, and do not have a cell structure to damage. These are the two main ways that antibiotics work on bacteria.

- Some bacteria can develop **resistance** to an antibiotic, and the drug no longer works on them.

How bacteria develop resistance

The development of antibiotic resistance by bacteria is one of the best examples of evolution by natural selection.

- A mutation occurs in some bacteria, which gives them resistance to the antibiotic.

- Treatment by the antibiotic kills the bacteria in the population that do not have this mutation, so are not resistant.

- The bacteria with the resistance survive.

- The surviving bacteria reproduce, passing the resistance gene on.

- Eventually, the whole population becomes resistant.

Modern doctors are very aware of the problems of antibiotic resistance. They have changed their use of antibiotics over the last 20 years. There are two main practices that they now follow:

1. Doctors only prescribe antibiotics when really necessary. They do not use them for viral conditions or minor illnesses. This reduces the chance of antibiotic-resistant bacteria becoming the most common strain.

2. Patients are encouraged to complete the course of any antibiotics that they are given. This way all the microbes should be killed before resistance can fully develop.

Exam tip OCR

- You need to remember the names of Pasteur, Lister, and Fleming, what they did, and how it improved our understanding of microbes and diseases.

Questions

→ E

1 Before Pasteur, what did people think caused infectious diseases?

→ C

2 Explain why it was important that Lister was aware of the work of other scientists like Pasteur, before he made his discoveries.

3 Why do you think the original penicillin discovered by Fleming is virtually useless today?

→ A*

4 Explain why modern biologists need to carry out large numbers of clinical trials on any new antibiotic, before it can be used by doctors.

Learning objectives

After studying this topic, you should be able to:

- know how some bacteria are useful to humans
- understand the role of bacteria in some biotechnology processes

Microbes in industry

Microbes are not all bad. Both bacteria and fungi can be used by humans to carry out useful tasks, such as to make a useful product on both a domestic and a commercial scale.

Products from bacteria

Bacteria have been used in a variety of ways for centuries. However, with our greater understanding of bacteria modern biologists have been able to make more efficient use of them. Today bacteria are used in the manufacture of:

- Yoghurt: this popular dairy product made for over 5000 years. It is made by adding the bacterium *Lactobacillus* to milk. Yoghurt is a very nutritious food which is rich in protein, calcium, and vitamins.

- Cheese: another common dairy product made for about 5000–8000 years. Cheese is made by causing milk to curdle, or separate into a solid curd and liquid whey. Curdling can be achieved using a mix of enzymes and bacteria such as *Lactobacillus*. The solid part of the milk is then turned into cheese. Like yoghurt, cheese is rich in protein, calcium, and vitamins.

- Vinegar: used for at least 5000 years, it was even recorded in Egyptian times. It is produced by the acidifying of wine, cider, or beer to produce wine, cider, and malt vinegars. The production of vinegar uses bacteria such as *Acetobacter*.

▶ These dairy products are made using processes that depend on bacteria

A Name three useful products made by bacteria.

B Explain why cheese and yoghurt are important in the diet.

▶ Vinegars are made by the action of *Acetobacter* on wine, cider, or beer

- Silage: a common winter fodder for cattle, which has been in use since the 1880s. Green cut vegetation is piled up in a large heap and covered in plastic, or placed in a silo. The vegetation is broken down by **fermentation**, or anaerobic respiration. The process will occur naturally, but it is speeded up by adding another *Lactobacillus* species.

- Composting: a natural process used for at least 2000 years. Since the 1920s it has become important in organic farming. The dead remains of plants and animals are digested by bacteria and fungi to form nutrient-rich soils. Often the remains are simply piled up at the end of the harvest and allowed to rot down until the next planting season.

C How is silage important to farmers?

A closer look at yoghurt-making

The yoghurt industry is worth millions of pounds a year. Making yoghurt involves adding bacteria to milk. Like all processes involving microbes, it is important that all equipment is sterile – clean and free from microbes – throughout the process.

▲ Silage bales in Wales

▲ Quality control sampling in a yoghurt-making factory

▲ Colours and flavours are added to make the final product

Exam tip **OCR**

- Remember the process of yoghurt-making as a sequence of steps.

Questions

1 Why are fruit and sugar added to many yoghurts? **→ E**

2 Explain why sterile technique is important when producing yoghurt. **→ C**

3 Explain why a sample from a previous batch is added at the start of the yoghurt-making process. **→ A***

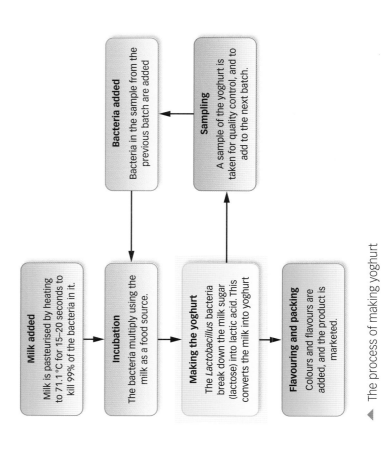

Bacteria added
Bacteria in the sample from the previous batch are added

Sampling
A sample of the yoghurt is taken for quality control, and to add to the next batch.

Milk added
Milk is pasteurised by heating to 71.1°C for 15–20 seconds to kill 99% of the bacteria in it.

Incubation
The bacteria multiply using the milk as a food source.

Making the yoghurt
The *Lactobacillus* bacteria break down the milk sugar (lactose) into lactic acid. This converts the milk into yoghurt

Flavouring and packing
Colours and flavours are added, and the product is marketed.

▲ The process of making yoghurt

Useful fungi

As well as bacteria, fungi are also used to make useful products commercially. Yeast is probably the most widely used fungus. Among other products, fungi are used to make alcoholic drinks and bread.

Brewing

Brewing is the production of alcoholic drinks by the process of fermentation. Yeast makes the alcohol by fermenting sugars found in plants, usually in the fruit or grain (seed).

- Wine is made from grapes.
- Beer and lager are made from malted barley.
- Cider is made from apples.

Step	Process	Explanation
1.	Malting	This happens in beer- and lager-making. The barley seeds start to germinate (grow), which converts the starch stored in the seeds into sugar.
2.	Extracting the sugar	The plant material is either crushed or soaked in water to get the sugar out.
3.	Flavouring	Wines get their flavour from the fruit juice used, while beers are flavoured with hops, the female flowers of the hop plant, *Humulus lupulus*.
4.	Adding yeast	The container is sealed to prevent air and other microbes entering. The yeast can respire aerobically for a very short time, until any oxygen in the container is used up. This allows the yeast to reproduce. The liquid is kept warm.
5.	Fermentation	The culture quickly becomes anaerobic and the yeast starts to produce alcohol. If there is too much oxygen in the container, anaerobic respiration does not occur and vinegar is produced. This process happens in large stainless steel vats called fermenters. The mixture is kept at a constant temperature of 25–30 °C, which gives the best rate of respiration to produce alcohol. This temperature also gives a better flavour.
6.	Extracting the wine and beer	After fermentation is over, the liquid is separated from the yeast cells. Usually the yeast is allowed to sink to the bottom to separate it out of the liquid. The liquid may need clarifying by a filtration process.
7.	Pasteurising and packaging/ bottling	The product is heated and quickly cooled to kill any remaining microbes. This gives the product a longer shelf life when stored in bottles.

The fermentation reaction

This is the anaerobic respiration reaction (without oxygen) that occurs in the yeast cells:

glucose (sugar) → ethanol (alcohol) + carbon dioxide

Symbol equation for the fermentation reaction

Here is the symbol equation for anaerobic respiration in yeast:

$$C_6H_{12}O_6 \rightarrow 2C_2H_5OH + 2CO_2$$

Making it stronger

There is a limit to the concentration of alcohol that can be produced by the brewing process. Alcohol is toxic and eventually kills the yeast in the fermenter when it reaches a certain concentration. Some yeasts can tolerate more alcohol than others. This results in drinks with different alcohol contents:

- Beers and lagers usually contain 3–5% alcohol.
- Wines usually contain 11–12% alcohol.

Spirits such as vodka and whiskey contain high levels of alcohol. To make spirits, the first step is fermenting plant material, similar to the production of beers and wines.

- Rum is made from sugar cane.
- Whiskey is made from malted barley.
- Vodka is made from potatoes.

Spirits typically contain 40% alcohol. To increase the concentration of alcohol from the fermentation process, the liquid is **distilled**. To do this the liquid is placed in a large container, or still, and heated. The alcohol boils at a temperature of about 80°C, which is lower than the boiling point of water. The alcohol rises up the column as a vapour, leaving the water behind. The vaporised alcohol passes along a collecting arm, and cools. This product contains a lot more alcohol than the fermentation liquid.

Stills at a whiskey distillery. Alcohol is distilled off the fermentation liquid to produce a spirit with a higher alcohol content. Distillation can only be carried out in premises licensed for the production of alcohol.

Key words

brewing, distillation

Did you know…?

Food processing factories produce waste water containing sugars. Yeast can be used to ferment the sugars and clean the waste water.

Exam tip **OCR**

✔ The fermentation process is a sequence of steps. Remember the differences between brewing and making yoghurt.

A Which microbe is involved in the making of alcohol?

B Name the two products of alcoholic fermentation.

C Why are hops added to beer?

Questions

1 Name two alcoholic drinks produced by fermentation. → E

2 Why do spirits keep longer than beers and wines? → C

3 Explain why fermentation alone does not produce spirits.

4 Explain why the temperature must be carefully regulated:
   (a) in the brewing process
   (b) in the distilling process. → A*

8: Biofuels

Learning objectives

After studying this topic, you should be able to:

- know that biological materials can be used as a fuel source
- give examples of biofuels
- understand the production, uses, and composition of biogas
- know that fuel can be made from alcohol

Key words

biofuel

A What is the source of energy for making biofuels?

B Name three types of biofuel.

Greener fuels

The burning of fossil fuels harms the environment as it produces waste gases including carbon dioxide, which leads to global warming. A variety of fuels from biological materials can be used as an alternative. These are called **biofuels**. They are better for the environment because the carbon dioxide produced when they burn is balanced by the carbon dioxide they use in photosynthesis while they are growing.

Common biofuels include wood, biogas, and alcohol.

What are biofuels?

As in fossil fuels, the energy in biofuels originates from sunlight used in photosynthesis. Photosynthesis produces the biomass in plants, and this biomass can be used directly or indirectly as biofuel. Wood can be burnt directly to release energy. Fast-growing trees can be used to fire power stations.

Advantages of using biofuels	Disadvantages of using biofuels	
Reduce fossil fuel consumption by providing an alternative fuel.	Cause habitat loss because large areas of land are needed to grow the plants.	
No overall increase in levels of greenhouse gases, as the plants take in carbon dioxide to grow, and release it when burnt.	Habitat loss can lead to extinction of species.	
Burning biogas and alcohol produces no particulates (smoke).	Data shows that some biofuels transfer less energy than other fuel types.	

Balancing the books

To burn fuels while maintaining no overall increase in greenhouse gases is a difficult balancing act. When we burn biofuels we have grown, the carbon dioxide taken in during photosynthesis is then released during the combustion.

However, land is needed to grow these crops. In some areas forests are cleared for the cash crop and this leads to a loss of plants to absorb carbon dioxide, and an increase in carbon dioxide released by decaying wood. It also causes a loss of habitat.

Biogas

Biogas is made by the fermentation of carbohydrates in plant material and sewage by bacteria. This fermentation occurs naturally, for example in marshes, septic tanks, and even inside animals' guts. Biogas is also produced at some landfill sites, where the gas can be burnt. Sometimes the biogas can explode, making the landfill site unusable for many years.

Biogas is a mixture of gases that will burn in oxygen, forming a useful fuel:

- methane (50–75%)
- carbon dioxide (25–50%)
- hydrogen, nitrogen, and hydrogen sulfide (less than 10%).

Small-scale biogas production

In remote areas of Nepal and India biogas is made for families and used for cooking. The fermentation happens in a large tank sunk into the ground, which keeps the temperature constant. The family place organic material like dead plants and animal waste in the tank. The bacteria digest this waste, releasing the gas.

Biogas production on a larger scale

The gas is generated commercially in large anaerobic tanks. Wet plant waste or animal manure is constantly added, and the gas produced is removed. Gas production is fastest at a temperature of 32–35°C, because the fermenting bacteria grow best at this temperature. The remaining solids need to be removed from the tanks and can be used as a fertiliser in some cases.

Biogas has a number of uses:

- as vehicle fuel
- to generate electricity
- for heating systems.

Bioethanol

Alcohol is produced from plant material by yeasts in brewing. On a larger scale this alcohol can be used as a fuel. Mixed with petrol it produces gasohol, which is a common fuel for cars. This is a particularly economic fuel in countries that produce large amounts of plant waste, such as Brazil. Brazil has no oil reserves and plenty of sugar cane waste to make the alcohol.

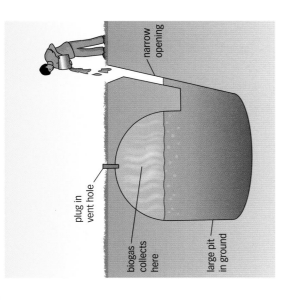

plug in vent hole

narrow opening

biogas collects here

large pit in ground

▲ Section through a biogas digester

Problems with biogas

There are a few technical issues with the production of biogas. First, since many different waste materials are used, a large range of bacteria are needed to digest the waste.

Biogas is a cleaner fuel than petrol or diesel, as fewer particulates are released. However, burning biogas releases 4.5–8.5 kWh/m^3 of energy compared with natural gas, which releases 9.8 kWh/m^3. This is because biogas contains less methane than natural gas.

A final difficulty is that if the biogas becomes mixed with air, so that there is more oxygen and the methane content drops to 5–20%, the mixture becomes explosive. This is not a problem when the gas is contained and not allowed to mix with the air.

Questions

1 Explain why biogas from landfill sites is particularly dangerous. → E

2 Give two reasons why gasohol is used in Brazil.

3 Why must a biogas digester be kept airtight? ▶ C

4 Explain why using biofuels should not contribute to any net increase in greenhouse gases, in contrast to using fossil fuels. → A*

Solid ground

The land surface is covered in either bare rock or soil. Rock is weathered to form the soil.

Key words

humus

Learning objectives

After studying this topic, you should be able to:

- know that the land surface is covered in rock or soil
- know the composition of soil
- describe organisms that live in the soil
- understand the importance of the earthworm

What is soil?

Soil contains a number of different components:

- Fragments of rock (minerals) – these are produced when rock is weathered. The size varies, and this determines the type of soil.

- Air spaces – gaps between the particles.

- Water – this fills some of the spaces between particles.

- Dead material – fragments of dead plants, animals, or organic waste.

- Living organisms – there is a huge variety of life in and on the soil. Plants rely on the soil for minerals, water, and to anchor them.

Soils have different structures depending on the size of their particles.

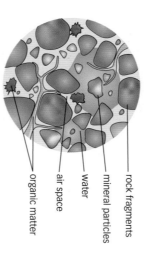

▶ The constituents of soil

organic matter
air space
water
mineral particles
rock fragments

Soil constituent	How to test a soil sample for it
moisture	Weigh, bake, and reweigh sample
humus	Weigh, burn, and reweigh sample
air	Weigh the sample and measure its volume

Soil type	Particle size	Air spaces	Permeability to water
clay — small clay particles, tiny air spaces	small (less than 0.002 mm)	few and small	low – water is retained in soil; soil can flood
loam — clay and sand particles, many air spaces of different sizes	mixture of small and large	many and variable in size	medium – water retention is good
sand — large sand particles, many large air spaces	large (0.05–2 mm)	many and large	poor – little water retained in soil

A Name three types of soil.

B Which type of soil retains water best?

Soil as a habitat

Most organisms in the soil need water and also oxygen for respiration. The amounts of water and oxygen in a soil depend on the soil particle size.

If the particles are small (clay soil) there will be few air spaces, and they will often be full of water, reducing oxygen levels.

- If the particles are big (sandy soil) there will be plenty of oxygen in the air spaces, but the water will drain away.

An ideal soil (loam) has a mixture of particle sizes, providing both air spaces and water retention. Gardeners improve their soil by digging to allow in air and to increase drainage.

Dead material decomposes in the soil to produce **humus**. This releases minerals into the soil which are needed by plants for growth. Humus adds a fibrous quality to soil – it tends to hold soil particles apart, improving aeration. It also helps retain water in the soil.

Soil pH also affects what can live there. Some plants such as heathers grow well in acidic soil. Many plants prefer relatively neutral soils. Alkaline soils are rare in the UK. Many farmers add lime to neutralise acidic soils so that they can grow more crops.

What lives in soil?

There is a whole community of organisms living in soil, linked together to form a food web.

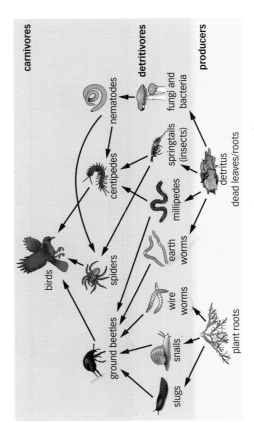

carnivores

detritivores

producers

birds
nematodes
centipedes
springtails (insects)
spiders
millipedes
earth worms
fungi and bacteria
detritus
wire worms
ground beetles
snails
plant roots
slugs
dead leaves/roots

▲ Soil food web

Did you know…?

The famous biologist Charles Darwin was one of the first to study the biology of the earthworm. He recognised how important earthworms are in improving the fertility and structure of the soil.

Worms pull dead leaves down into the soil, burying them. This organic material is then slowly decayed by bacteria and fungi, improving the nutrient content of the soil.

Earthworm burrows create gaps which aerate the soil. As the worms move through the burrows they push air through them. The cavities also allow water to drain more freely, reducing the chance of flooding.

The earthworm mixes the soil by eating soil and passing out waste elsewhere in the soil.

Earthworms release calcium carbonate into their gut to help the digestion of leaves. This then passes out in their waste, and has the added bonus of helping to neutralise acidic soils.

▲ Earthworms as soil improvers

Questions

1 List the main components of soil. → E

2 Using the food web, explain why soils with little detritus contain few organisms. → C

3 Detritivores eat detritus. Name three detritivores in the soil food web. → C

4 If a gardener used an insecticide that killed ground beetles, what might happen to the earthworm population? → A*

Living in water

There is a huge diversity of life in water, including microorganisms.

The wonders of water

There are several advantages of living in water:

- Buoyancy – water is more dense than air, so it gives more support to the organisms that live in it. The largest animal, the blue whale, can measure up to 30 m in length and weigh up to 170 tonnes. These animals could not support their weight on land.

- Removal of waste – animal waste is washed away and does not build up, as it is greatly diluted in the water and broken down.

- Steady temperature – surface waters vary in temperature, but not as much as the air does. Water requires a lot of energy to heat it up. The waters at the poles are at about 0 °C, while temperatures near the Equator can be up to 30 °C. Deeper water has a very stable temperature, about 4 °C. Aquatic organisms do not have to cope with extremes or rapid changes in temperature.

- Ready water supply – living in fresh water means that there is no risk of dehydration.

The woes of water

There are also disadvantages of aquatic habitats:

- Movement – water is more dense than air, making it harder to move through, so aquatic animals use more energy.

- Water balance – water is everywhere; the problem is balancing the amount of water in the body.

Learning objectives

After studying this topic, you should be able to:

- list some advantages and disadvantages of living in water

- know that phytoplankton are the producers in ocean food webs

- explain seasonal fluctuations in plankton numbers

Key words

plankton

Water regulation

In fresh water, too much water can enter the body by osmosis. This is not a problem for plants, as cell walls stop cells expanding and prevent excess water getting in. In animals, excess water must be removed from the body. Freshwater fish urinate frequently, removing the excess. Microscopic organisms such as amoebae have a cell structure called the contractile vacuole, into which the excess water goes. The vacuole then moves to the cell surface, fuses with it, and releases the water.

Sea water is salty, and this affects osmosis. Many invertebrates have bodies at the same salt concentration as the sea and so have no problem, but some larger fish do not. They actively get rid of the salt in the water they drink.

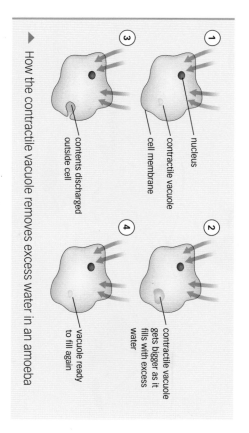

1 — nucleus, contractile vacuole, cell membrane

2 — contractile vacuole gets bigger as it fills with excess water

3 — contents discharged outside cell

4 — vacuole ready to fill again

▶ How the contractile vacuole removes excess water in an amoeba

Aquatic food webs

There are microscopic organisms living in water called **plankton**. There are two types:

- Phytoplankton are photosynthetic microorganisms – they are producers.
- Zooplankton are animal-like microorganisms – they are consumers.

Plankton float in the open waters, moving in currents. The numbers of the phytoplankton vary during the year. Three factors control their numbers:

Factor	Seasonal effect	Effect of depth
Light	As day length increases, the numbers of phytoplankton increase.	Light only penetrates surface waters, so phytoplankton are limited to the surface waters.
Temperature	As surface water temperatures rise in spring, the numbers of phytoplankton increase.	At depth the temperature is a constant 4°C, too cold for phytoplankton to grow.
Minerals	Minerals rise to the surface during the winter, so there is a ready supply for phytoplankton in the spring.	Mineral concentrations increase at depth, but phytoplankton are limited there by light and temperature.

Seasonal changes in phytoplankton numbers will influence the numbers of zooplankton.

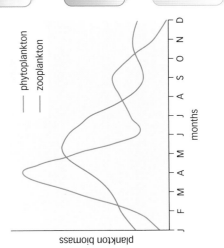

An algal bloom, or an increase in phytoplankton. The numbers increase because of increased light, temperature and minerals.

The increase in phytoplankton causes an increase in the zooplankton. This is because there is more food to eat.

Autumn light and temperature levels cause plankton numbers to decrease. Zooplankton numbers also fall due to less food being available.

— phytoplankton
— zooplankton

months

plankton biomass

J F M A M J J A S O N D

▲ Seasonal cycles in plankton populations in the North Atlantic

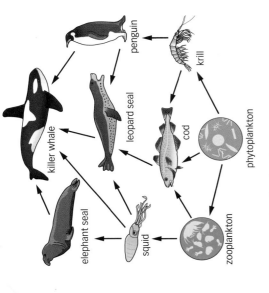

killer whale
penguin
krill
leopard seal
cod
phytoplankton
elephant seal
squid
zooplankton

▲ A marine food web

Aquatic grazing

Grazing food webs, based on photosynthetic producers, are common in the surface layers of the oceans.

In deep water food webs do not start with phytoplankton as there is no light. Food chains at these depths rely on dead food falling from above, called marine snow. These are detrital food chains.

Other food chains start with bacteria – producers that get their energy from chemical reactions in a process called chemosynthesis.

Questions

1	Explain why phytoplankton do not grow in the deep oceans.	→ E
2	Why is the phytoplankton population at its peak in April?	→ C
3	Explain why the phytoplankton population is low in June, when growing conditions are good.	→ A*

11: Water pollution

What a waste!

Unfortunately, humans generate a lot of waste. Many of these wastes pollute water, affecting the number and type of organisms (including microscopic ones) that live there.

▶ Scientists cleaning a pelican caught in the 2010 oil spill in the Gulf of Mexico. It was estimated that hundreds of thousands of gallons were spilling into the water each day.

▶ Sources of water pollution

Oil escapes from tankers and oil pipelines.

Treated sewage from sewage plants contains nitrates and bacteria.

Farms use fertilisers and pesticides which wash into rivers and lakes.

Detergents from our homes can reach the water via sewage plants.

PCBs are toxic waterproofing chemicals in paints used on boats.

Acid rain contains acids. This falls into the water, lowering the pH.

A Name two pollutants of water.

B Explain how fertilisers sprayed on crops get into water.

C In 2010 there was a rupture in an oil pipeline off the coast of New Orleans, which released vast quantities of oil into the sea. What is the effect of oil on wildlife?

Eutrophication: a case study

One major pollutant of water is nitrates. Nitrates enter the water in untreated sewage or directly from fertilisers. When this happens the process of **eutrophication** occurs.

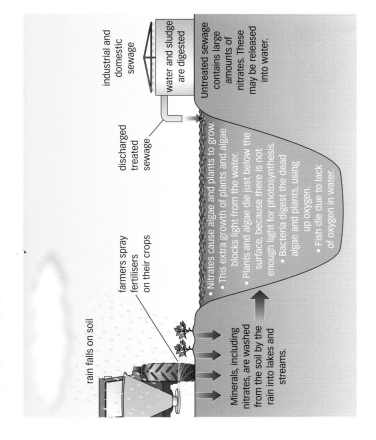

▲ River pollution causing severe algal bloom

rain falls on soil

farmers spray fertilisers on their crops

industrial and domestic sewage

discharged treated sewage

water and sludge are digested

Minerals, including nitrates, are washed from the soil by the rain into lakes and streams.

Untreated sewage contains large amounts of nitrates. These may be released into water.

- Nitrates cause algae and plants to grow.
  - This extra growth of plants and algae blocks light from the water.
  - Plants and algae die just below the surface, because there is not enough light for photosynthesis.
    - Bacteria digest the dead algae and plants, using up oxygen.
    - Fish die due to lack of oxygen in water.

Indicators of pollution

Biologists can get an idea of the level of water pollution by looking for the presence of **indicator species**. For example:

- pH changes in water can be indicated by a reduced number of amphibians in polluted streams and bogs.
- Reduced oxygen levels are indicated by rat-tailed maggots.

Poisoned whales

Certain chemicals do not break down in the environment quickly. Examples include commonly used industrial chemicals called PCBs, and the pesticide DDT. You may remember that chemicals like these can build up in food chains. They will eventually reach toxic levels in the top carnivores.

Both of these chemicals can build up in the bodies of whales over many years. The result is that some whales, such as killer whales, are among the most contaminated animals on Earth. PCBs are known to suppress the immune systems of these animals. This may contribute to the decrease in their numbers. Before the 1960s, whaling was common practice in many communities. Humans ate the whale meat. The whale meat was so contaminated that the levels of PCBs had a harmful effect on the people who ate it.

Questions

E →

1 What is the effect of pollution on the numbers of aquatic organisms?

C →

2 Draw a flow diagram to describe eutrophication.

3 Explain how indicator species might suggest reduced oxygen levels in water.

4 Environmentally friendly detergents do not contain as many nitrates and phosphates as mainstream detergents. Explain how this will reduce eutrophication.

A* →

5 Explain how PCBs build up in whale meat.

Making microbes work for us

Enzymes are catalysts, and in biotechnology scientists often use enzymes to speed up chemical reactions. This use of enzymes in industry is called **enzyme technology**. Bacteria are easy to grow in large quantities, so they are used to produce these enzymes on a large scale.

Industrial uses of enzymes

Industry	Enzyme	Use
dairy (eg cheese making)	protease (eg rennet)	Causes solids (curds) to separate from the liquid (whey) in milk.
food processing	proteases	Digest proteins in foods such as soy and citrus products, to remove bitter tastes.
fruit juice	cellulases	Break down cell walls in the fruit, releasing juice.
	amylases	Reduce cloudiness and increase sweetness by breaking down starch.
medical	glucose oxidase	Present in kits used by people with diabetes to test for glucose in urine or blood.
biological washing powder	proteases, lipases, and amylases	Remove organic stains such as food and grass stains from laundry.

Learning objectives

After studying this topic, you should be able to:

∨ understand how enzymes are used in the food industry to make food sweeter

∨ know that enzymes are used in biological washing powders

Key words

enzyme technology, biological washing powders

A Give one reason why enzymes are used in a variety of industries.

B Name two industries that use enzymes, and suggest why they are used.

C Why are different enzymes used in different industries?

Exam tip OCR

∨ Remember that, like all catalysts, enzymes speed up a reaction but don't get used up.

Sweet enough?

The food industry makes great use of enzymes. As a nation we have a very sweet tooth. Processed foods and soft drinks contain a lot of sugar to sweeten the product. The sugar extracted from plants like sugar cane is called sucrose. This is not as sweet to the taste as other sugars like fructose unless it is broken down by enzymes.

An enzyme called invertase (sucrase) digests sucrose into glucose and fructose. The food industry now has a much sweeter product. They can use fructose to sweeten food. This way less sugar is needed to produce a sweet product. This is common practice in producing low calorie foods and drinks.

Cleaning power

Biological washing powders contain soap powder, enzymes, and minerals. Why are the enzymes added?

* Enzymes digest stains.
* Enzymes digest fibres in the dirt, releasing bobbles.
* They allow stain removal to occur at a lower temperature, which saves energy and money.

These washing powders contain several different enzymes, each of which does a different job. The enzymes break down the stains into small soluble products that wash off the fabric. Unfortunately, the enzymes in biological washing powders don't work at high temperatures or extreme pH levels.

Disadvantages of biological washing powders

Biological washing powders allow us to use less energy and to machine wash delicate fabrics, because they do not need high temperatures. However, there are a few limitations to using enzymes in this way:

* The enzymes may be destroyed at high temperatures so do not work for a hot wash.
* The enzymes are pH sensitive, so they may not work so well in areas of the country with particularly acidic or alkaline water.
* They may cause allergies.

▲ Slimming products

> Amylases digest carbohydrate stains such as starch from foods like pasta and flour.

> Lipases digest fats and fatty stains like grease.

> Proteases digest protein stains such as blood.

▲ Biological washing powders contain a combination of enzymes

D Suggest why people might want to reduce their sugar intake. → E

E Explain why less fructose than sucrose is needed to sweeten food. → E

Questions

1. Why are enzymes used in cheese making? → E

2. Explain why biological washing powders are better at removing stains than non-biological powders. → C

3. Why is it not efficient to use biological washing powders in a hot wash? → A*

Learning objectives

After studying this topic, you should be able to:

- know that enzyme technology is used in medicine
- understand immobilised enzymes and their advantages
- be aware of the use of immobilised enzymes in coping with lactose intolerance

Key words

immobilised

Doctor, doctor!

The medical industry makes great use of enzymes. Two examples are:

- Testing for sugar – people with diabetes need to keep a watchful eye on the glucose levels in their urine or blood. The normal blood glucose level is from 4–8 mmol/l. Diabetics often experience higher levels. They monitor their blood glucose level to prevent it rising for too long, as persistent high levels can damage blood vessels in organs like the eyes. If their blood glucose level falls too low, they could become unconscious. Testing could be done using the food test called Benedict's test for glucose. This is not very practical in our modern lives. Now we use reagent sticks to test for glucose. These sticks make use of enzymes.

- Lactose intolerance – some people don't make the enzyme lactase, and so they cannot digest the sugar lactose in their gut. Bacteria in their digestive system digest it instead, leading to diarrhoea and wind. Enzymes are now used to produce lactose-free foods.

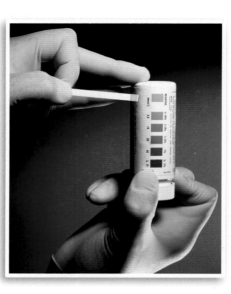

▶ Reagent sticks are used to test for glucose in urine. They contain a range of enzymes.

Immobilised enzymes

Enzymes are delicate molecules. They are highly temperature sensitive. This can make them difficult for scientists to use and store. Scientists have developed a method to help make enzymes more stable and easier to use.

The enzymes are **immobilised**, which means they are attached to a more inert substance. There are two common ways of doing this. The enzyme can be added to a fibre mesh, as on reagent sticks. Another method is to produce gel beads containing the enzymes. To do this:

- The enzymes are mixed with a solution of sodium alginate.
- The mixture is dropped into a calcium chloride solution.
- This causes small beads of alginate gel to form.
- Embedded in the gel are the enzymes.

The advantages of the use of immobilised enzymes are:

- The beads are easier to use than free enzymes.
- The beads support the structure of the enzyme, making it less sensitive to temperature and pH.

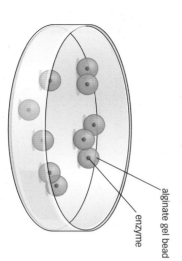

alginate gel bead

enzyme

▶ Alginate beads can be used to immobilise enzymes